THE
BANTU
LANGUAGES

Other works in the series

The Romance Languages
The Celtic Languages
The Slavonic Languages
The Germanic Languages
The Dravidian Languages
The Uralic Languages
The Semitic Languages
The Bantu Languages
The Austronesian Languages of Asia and Madagascar
The Oceanic Languages
The Mongolic Languages
The Indo-Aryan Languages
The Sino-Tibetan Languages
The Indo-European Languages
The Turkic Languages

Forthcoming works in the series

The Tai-Kadai Languages
The Iranian Languages

THE
BANTU
LANGUAGES

Edited by Derek Nurse and Gérard Philippson

Routledge
Taylor & Francis Group

LONDON AND NEW YORK

First published 2003
by Routledge
2 Park Square, Milton Park, Abingdon, Oxon, OX14 4RN
270 Madison Ave, New York,NY1006

Simultaneously published in the USA and Canada
by Routledge

Reprinted 2006

Routledge is an imprint of the Taylor & Francis Group

Typeset in Times New Roman by
Newgen Imaging Systems (P) Ltd, Chennai, India
Printed and bound in Great Britain by
The Cromwell Press, Trowbridge, Wiltshire

British Library Cataloguing in Publication Data
A catalogue record for this book is available from the British Library

Library of Congress Cataloging in Publication Data
  The Bantu languages/edited by Derek Nurse and Gérard Philippson.
      p. cm – (Routledge language family series; 4)
    Includes bibliographical references and indexes.
      1. Bantu languages. I. Nurse, Derek, II. Philippson, Gérard. III. Series.

  PL8025 .B35 2003
  496'.39–dc21   2002068231

  ISBN10: 0-415-41265-X
  ISBN13: 978-0-415-41265-0

CONTENTS

ILLUSTRATIONS

TABLES

CONTRIBUTORS

Yvonne Bastin, Royal Museum of Central Africa, Tervuren, Belgium
Thomas Bearth, University of Zurich, Switzerland
Robert Botne, Indiana University, Bloomington, USA
Katherine Demuth, Brown University, Providence, USA
Edward D. Elderkin, University of Namibia, Windhoek, Namibia
Derek Gowlett, University of Cape Town, South Africa
Claire Grégoire, Royal Museum of Central Africa, Tervuren, Belgium
Gladys Guarisma, Laboratoire de Langues et Civilisations à Tradition Orale, Villejuif, France
Tom Güldemann, University of Leipzig, Germany
Teresa Heath, SIL
Larry M. Hyman, University of California, Berkeley, USA
Francis Katamba, University of Lancaster, UK
Charles Kisseberth, Tel Aviv University, Israel
Myles Leitch, SIL
Constance Kutsch Lojenga, University of Leiden, The Netherlands
Ian Maddieson, University of California, Los Angeles, USA
Jouni Maho, Göteborg University, Sweden
Marie-Laure Montlahuc, INALCO, Paris, France
Maarten Mous, University of Leiden, The Netherlands
Salikoko S. Mufwene, University of Chicago, USA
Derek Nurse, Memorial University of Newfoundland, Canada
David Odden, Ohio State University, Columbus, USA
Gérard Philippson, INALCO, Paris, France
Thilo C. Schadeberg, University of Leiden, The Netherlands
Gabriele Sommer, University of Bayreuth, Germany
Lolke J. van der Veen, University of Lyon II, France
John R. Watters, SIL

ABBREVIATIONS

The Bantu area was divided by Guthrie into fifteen zones, lettered A, B, C, D, E, F, G, H, K, L, M, N, P, R, S. Tervuren scholars added a sixteenth, J, drawn from parts of D and E (leading to abbreviations such as DJ, EJ, or JD, JE). So one of these capital letters may refer to a zone. The zones are further broken down into groups, referred to by numbers, thus, A10, A11, A12, A13, etc. See, Ch. 31.

Many of the lower case abbreviations in this list may also occur as capitals.

#	word boundary	compl.	complement
.	syllable boundary	Con/con	connective
$	syllable boundary	Cond	conditional
ø	zero, null; toneless	CONN	consecutive
=	pre-(micro-)stem boundary	CONTR	contrastive focus
-	morpheme boundary	CS	comparative series (in Guthrie
1	first person; Class 1		1967–71)
2	second person; Class 2	DAT	dative (applicative)
3	third person; Class 3	DEF	definite
4	Class 4	Dem	demonstrative
5	Class 5, etc.	DIM	diminutive
1S	first person singular	Dist	distal
2S	second person singular	DP	dependent prefix
A	adjective; zone A	DRC	Democratic Republic of Congo
adj	adjective	dv	default vowel
Adnst	adnominal stem	E	(verbal) extension
Adv	adverbializer; adverb	EPx	enumerative prefix
ag	(nominal) augment	FAR	far (past, future)
ANT	anterior	F	final (vowel, suffix): zone F
Appl	applicative	fem	feminine
ASS	associative (reciprocal)	FUT	future
Ast	adjective stem	FV	final vowel
ATR	Advanced Tongue Root	GEN	general
B	verbal base; zone B	G	glide; zone G
Badv	bound adverbial	H	high tone; zone H
BEN	benefactive	HAB	habitual
C	consonant; zone C	HITH	hither
CAR	Central African Republic	HOD	hodiernal
CAUS	causative	Hum	human
cl./cl/Cl	(noun) class (cl.1/cl1/Cl1, cl2, etc.)	hv	harmonic vowel
coll.	collective	IMM	immediate
COP	copula	IMP	imperfect

xvi

IMPF	imperfective	PPX	pronominal prefix
INC	inceptive	pr	prefix
INDEF	indefinite	PREC	precessive
Indep	independent	prep	preposition
infin.	infinitive	pres	present
IP	independent prefix	pro	pronoun
Instr	instrumental	PROG	progressive
Intr	intransitive	Pron	pronoun; pronominal
IRR	irrealis	PROP N	proper noun
IV	initial vowel	PRX/prox	proximal
L	low tone; zone L	Q	question
LOC	locative	QUOT	quotative
masc	masculine	R	radical; zone R
mod	modifier	REC	reciprocal
N	noun; zone N	RED	reduplicated
NC	prenasalized consonant	ref	referential
NEG	negative	REL	relative (pronoun)
NP	noun phrase	S	subject: zone S
NPx	nominal prefix	sb	somebody
Nst	noun stem	SC/SCD	subject concord
num	numeral	SEP	separative
NW	northwest(ern) (languages)	sg/sg.	singular
O	object	SIM	simultaneous
obj	object (marker)	SM	subject marker
OCP	obligatory contour principle	SUB	subordinate
OM	object marker	subj	subject (marker); subjunctive
OP	object pronoun	SVO	subject verb object (order)
OPT	optative	T(A)	tense (aspect)
pass	passive	TAM	tense-aspect-mood
PB	Proto-Bantu	TBU	tone-bearing unit
perf	perfect	Temp	temporal
PERS	persistive; personal	TM	tense marker
PFV	perfective	v	verb: vowel
pfx	prefix	Vb	verb(al) base
PL/pl	plural; pluractional	VP	verb phrase
poss	possessive	Vst	verb stem
PP	prepositional phrase		

CHAPTER ONE

INTRODUCTION

Derek Nurse and Gérard Philippson

1 IDENTIFYING THE BANTU LANGUAGES

Bantu-speaking communities live in Africa south of a line from Nigeria across the Central African Republic (CAR), the Democratic Republic of Congo (DRC: formerly Zaire), Uganda, and Kenya, to southern Somalia in the east. Most language communities between that line and the Cape are Bantu. The exceptions are pockets: in the south, some small and fast dwindling Khoisan communities; in Tanzania one, maybe two, Khoisan outliers; in the northeast of the area, larger communities speaking Cushitic (part of Afro-Asiatic); and along and inside the northern border many communities speaking Nilo-Saharan languages and Adamawa-Ubangian (Niger-Congo but non-Bantu) languages. North of that line, in Africa, there is also a longstanding Swahili-speaking community on the island of Socotra, off the Somali coast but technically part of the Republic of South Yemen. Excluding this, then we find communities speaking Bantu languages indigenous to twenty-seven African countries: Angola, Botswana, Burundi, Cameroon, CAR, Comoros, Congo, DRC, Equatorial Guinea, Gabon, Kenya, Lesotho, Madagascar, Malawi, Mayotte, Mozambique, Namibia, Nigeria, Rwanda, Somalia, South Africa, Sudan, Swaziland, Tanzania, Uganda, Zambia, and Zimbabwe. The Bantu family is recognized as forming part of the Niger-Congo phylum. Non-Bantu Niger-Congo languages are spoken north and mainly west of Bantu. Starting in the north of the DRC, they stretch west across the CAR, Cameroon, Nigeria, and right across all west Africa as far as Senegal. Of some 750 million Africans (Times Atlas 1999) the most recent publication (Grimes 2000, also pc) estimates that around 400 million people speak Niger-Congo languages, of whom some 240 million are Bantu-speakers, roughly one African in three.

Many people in Africa are bi- or multilingual. Typically in sub-Saharan Africa that might mean acquiring a local language first, a language of wider communication or a national language second, and an international language last. Or it might mean being able to communicate in several local languages. In the past the second pattern was more common than the first, because people typically lived in and spoke the language of one area and had to be able to communicate with neighboring communities. Today people are more mobile and more inclined to use languages of wider communication or national or transnational languages, and less able or inclined to learn the languages of their neighbors. While it is likely that in the past multilingualism was more widespread than today there are still many millions of multilinguals in Africa.

Linked to this is a new phenomenon – urban speech forms. In the past it must have always been true that languages rose and fell, and were modified by contact with their neighbors. But the twentieth century saw the growth of big cities with mixed populations of people from different linguistic and ethnic backgrounds. This led to the appearance of new language varieties. While some might be dubbed as varieties of existing languages (see Ch. 12), others are not so easily pigeon-holed. Thus urban forms of South African Bantu languages (Finlayson and Slabbert 1997, 2000, Slabbert and Myers-Scotton 1997,

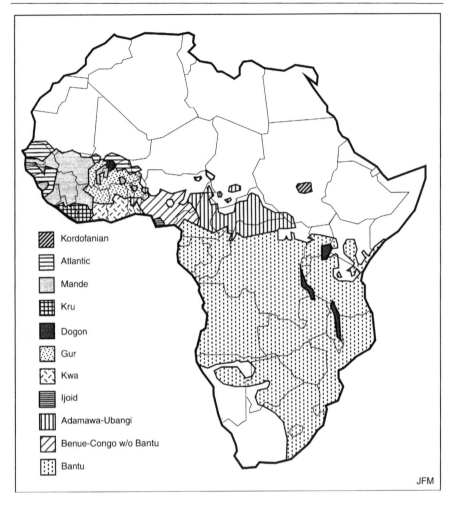

Kordofanian

Atlantic

Mande

Kru

Dogon

Gur

Kwa

Ijoid

Adamawa-Ubangi

Benue-Congo w/o Bantu

Bantu

JFM

MAP 1.1 NIGER-CONGO LANGUAGES

Wolff 2000), Bantu-English mixtures in Nairobi (Sheng/Engsh: Abdulaziz and Osinde 1997, Kiptoo 2000, Mazrui 1995, Moga and Fee 2000, Osinde 1986, Spyropoulos 1987, Sure 1992) and the attempt to cobble together a common form (Ru-nya-kitara) of related Bantu languages in western Uganda (Bernsten 1998).

The total number of Bantu languages is hard to state with certainty. Guthrie (1967–71) names some 440 Bantu 'varieties', Grimes (2000) has 501 (minus a few 'extinct' or 'almost extinct'), Bastin *et al.* (1999) have 542, Maho (this volume) has some 660, and Mann *et al.* (1987) have *c.*680. In the past it could rightly have been said that languages were still being 'discovered' so the number was increasing and the total unsure. Some recent works, for instance, Maho and Mann *et al.*, certainly mention more varieties than Guthrie. But the flow of new 'discoveries' has slowed to a trickle, while smaller language communities are now increasingly vanishing before the spread of languages of wider communication (for language death, see Sommer 1992). The main difficulty is rather: what is language and what is dialect, and where is the line between them? The conventional, largely sociolinguistically based, answer says that a language tends to be the standard variety, be written, have more speakers, have some form of official status, have prestige, and not be intelligible to speakers of other 'languages'. By contrast, dialects are not the standard, not written, have fewer speakers, have no official status, have little or no prestige, and are mutually intelligible. In sub-Saharan Africa these distinctions are only partly true and in any case any distinction between language and dialect is part linguistic, part political, part prestige-related. In fact there is a cline of structural difference between the linguistically very similar and the fairly dissimilar: where to cut a cline? All this can be exemplified by considering the nine Kenyan varieties labelled E72 and E73 (see Maho's Appendix to this book). All are mutually intelligible, some highly, some (e.g. E73) less so. Several are written, Giryama having the largest body of literature. Giryama also has by far the largest number of speakers and the most prestige. But speakers of at least some of the others would feel that for a community to have its own language is central to the community's self-identity and so they would hotly dispute that Giryama is the single standard form, and in any case it has no special official status. Outsiders might consider these all to be varieties but what would the language be called? Non-Giryama would not want to accord this status to Giryama, because that would reduce the status of the others, so today they are called ki-Miji Kenda, the language of the nine villages. Without being able to resolve the issue of which is language and which dialect, and what the language is called, these are certainly nine 'dialects' in most people's minds. If our purpose is to assess how many Bantu languages there are, then this is one language with nine dialects. If we applied this reduction procedure to all the varieties in the works named at the start of this paragraph, then the several hundred Bantu varieties would reduce to a smaller number of 'languages'. Our guesstimate would be perhaps 300, or less.

2 REFERRING TO THE BANTU LANGUAGES

There are so many Bantu languages that they are often referred to by a combination of letter and number. The whole Bantu-speaking area is conventionally divided into sixteen zones (A, B, C, D, E, F, G, H, J, K, L, M, N, P, R, S), which in turn divide into a number of decades. These total approximately eighty. So A10, A20, B10, etc. each refer to a group of languages, and A11, A12, A13, etc. each refer to a specific language within A10. This system is based on Guthrie (1967–71) and an updated version can be found in Chapter 31 of this book.

3 WHAT IS A BANTU LANGUAGE?

Readers may think that any language family or phylum ought to be definable in typological or historical/genetic terms, that it should be possible to find a set of (typological or genetic) features that define it and set it apart from other families or phyla. It ought to be possible to find a set of features, a bundle of isoglosses, that uniquely define the Bantu family within the Niger-Congo phylum. So far this has proved an elusive goal. For this there are three reasons.

One has to do with numbers. The more members a family/phylum has, the larger its geographical distribution, and thus the greater the number of variables, the greater the difficulty in defining it and the lesser the reliability of the results. That can be seen at the micro-level by considering the Bantu languages of the Great Lakes, called Zone J, dealt with in Chapter 25 of this volume. There has been tacit agreement among linguists over

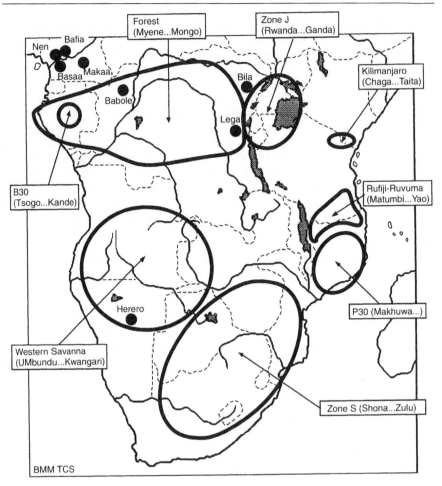

MAP 1.2 BANTU LANGUAGES

the last two or three decades that these languages likely form a genetic/historical unit, yet neither in Chapter 25 nor in any of the other works dealing with Zone J languages (Schoenbrun 1994, 1997, Muzale forthcoming) has any linguist yet been able to identify unambiguously a shared set of linguistic innovations that will satisfactorily and uniquely define these languages. Zone J has only a few dozen varieties, compared with the several hundred of the Bantu family, and the 1,489 'languages' attributed to the Niger-Congo phylum, the world's largest genetic grouping (Grimes 2000). Bantu is large and Niger-Congo is huge.

The second concerns data. Niger-Congo and Bantu languages are underdescribed. Few (10 percent?) have a reasonable grammar. For many we have only a word list, often of dubious quality, and often the items on one word list are not those on another, making comparison hard. For some we have no data. So far, most definitions of Bantu have depended heavily or exclusively on the use of vocabulary, in one application or other, with the addition of a few dubious phonological features or innovations. This is because in so many cases all we have is vocabulary. We need more basic descriptions. Linguists agree that ultimately a satisfactory definition has to go beyond vocabulary to the application of morphosyntactic features. What those features might be or assembling the data for them is some distance away (Ch. 10 proposes an initial set).

The third and major reason results from how languages develop over time and space. For Bantu that development started some five millennia ago, even longer for Niger-Congo. While there is some disagreement on details, the general historical picture of Bantu development and settlement is clear (Clist 1995, Vansina 1995, Diamond 1997, Ehret 1998). Some five millennia ago early Bantu peoples started out of their original homeland astride the Nigeria/Cameroon borderland. By 3000 BC they had spread east and south, occupying most of the rainforest in what is today the DRC. Over the next millennium they moved out of the rainforest into parts of eastern, followed by southern, Africa. The archaeological record tells us that these major initial movements were complete by the early centuries of our era. Over the next two millennia offshoots of the initial communities gradually spread across nearly the whole area. During much of the period most Bantu communities were small and adjacent to other communities, mostly Bantu, a few non-Bantu (Khoisan, Cushitic, Nilo-Saharan, Adamawa-Ubangian, also perhaps Pygmy, whose linguistic status remains doubtful (Blench 1998)). The original divergence was followed and overlaid by millennia of convergence, during which language communities interacted with their neighbors. Some communities waxed, some waned, some vanished, all changed. Looking at the whole area and the whole period is like looking into a kaleidoscope, with constantly changing patterns. Most vexed is the northwest of the Bantu area, among the languages of Guthrie's zones A and B especially, but to a lesser extent C, D, and H. Although they are geographically closest to what we think was the Bantu cradleland, they are not thereby linguistically most similar to what we assume were the shapes and features of early Bantu. In fact, the opposite is true and we think that languages in eastern and southern Africa are in general more conservative than those in the northwest (but see Ch. 11 for a contrary view). This is because the northwest languages form the eastern end of a geographical and typological area that embraces adjacent languages in West Africa, including many non-Bantu Niger-Congo languages. Immediately to the north and west of the northwestern Bantu languages, in Cameroon, are what are probably their nearest relatives, the Grassfields languages, some seventy in number (see Ch. 14). Just to their north and west, in Nigeria, are the other Bantoid languages, the next nearest relatives, over 100. That is, in an area consisting of Cameroon and eastern Nigeria, literally hundreds of related languages coexist. During the past five millennia, or longer, this area has been a Sprachbund, within which new common features have spread, obscuring or replacing older ones, while most Bantu languages, further east and south, were removed and immune.

The result is that the northwest languages form exceptions to many possible generalizations for Bantu. It has so far proved impossible to draw a clear line between Bantu, however defined, and non-Bantu Niger-Congo. The northwest Bantu languages show 'non-Bantu' features, while their relatives and neighbors show Bantu features. This problem besets typological (e.g. Guthrie 1948:11–12) and historical work (e.g. Bennett and Sterk 1977, Williamson 1989, Williamson and Blench 2000).

3.1 Towards an historical definition

Since the idea that Bantu communities split from other Niger-Congo and originated in a homeland between Nigeria and Cameroon was first advanced by Greenberg half a century ago, there has been a series of proposals about how Narrow Bantu emerged from the rest of Niger-Congo (e.g. Williamson 1971, Greenberg 1972, 1974, Meeussen 1974; for an overview, see Williamson and Blench 2000; for an early view, Johnston 1919–22). Most are represented by a series of tree diagrams. The latest (Williamson and Blench 2000:18, 31, 35) has Narrow Bantu as part of a grouping known as Southern Bantoid, together with other languages in Cameroon and Nigeria. Southern Bantoid forms part of Bantoid, which in turn is one of several lower twigs on the Benue-Congo branch of the Niger-Congo tree.

What is all this based on? What defines Bantu historically? There is as yet no convincing consensus on how to define Bantu historically. Recent attempts are based on several approaches:

- Lexicostatistical (e.g. Bastin and Piron 1999, Bastin *et al.* 1999, Piron 1996, 1997, and many earlier works). The difficulty with all of these lies with the languages at the geographical intersection of Bantu and non-Bantu Niger-Congo. In some surveys some northwest Bantu languages align with non-Bantu while in others the same languages align with Bantu, albeit with varying subsets of Bantu, because for millennia lexical waves have been lapping to and fro.
- Lexical innovations (Stewart 1973, Bennett and Sterk 1977, Watters and Leroy 1989).
- A series of stimulating although speculative proposals about phonological innovations in consonant and vowel systems (Stewart 1973, 1993, 1999, 2000a,b, 2001a,b). The main difficulty with the phonological innovations is in determining at which level they were innovated. Working upwards within Bantu it is possible to reconstruct probable consonant, vowel, and tone systems for Proto-Bantu (henceforth PB). Comparing these with those from other closely related coordinate or superordinate branches of Niger-Congo it is possible to reconstruct probable but somewhat different consonant, vowel, and tone systems for a proto-language several stages above PB. But it has so far proved tricky to link a specific set of innovations to a single precise node on the tree, particularly the 'Bantu node'.
- The proposal that in some classes Bantu, by contrast with Niger-Congo, innovated nasals in the nominal prefixes. For a contrary view, see Miehe (1991).
- A set of features in Williamson and Blench (2000) across all the major branches of Niger-Congo: presence or absence of noun class systems, presence or absence of verbal extensions, nature of pronoun systems, order of sentence constituents, and order of noun phrase constituents (noun and modifiers). They also mention another feature – lexical items shared across at least some of Niger-Congo. Of these, two features – a noun class system and verbal extensions – can be clearly assigned to Proto-Niger-Congo but do not constitute evidence for Bantu within Niger-Congo. For a third – the set of lexical items common to Niger-Congo – we cannot decide what is Niger-Congo and what is Bantu until the evidence is clearly set out. For the other three (pronoun systems, order of sentence constituents, order of noun phrase constituents) we have a good idea what can be assumed for PB, but as there is not yet a consensus for Niger-Congo, we cannot be sure which innovations occurred between Niger-Congo and PB. Readers should note that strictly speaking these suggestions, while implicitly historical, are in fact typological and the authors do not make specific historical suggestions or reconstructions.
- A very recent suggestion by Ehret (ms) that some pronoun shapes may be Bantu-specific.

What can we say of this? It has to be described as work in progress, still to be evaluated. The noun class system and the verbal extensions are likely to validate Proto-Niger-Congo, unless they can be shown to have been innovated locally and then transferred internally, which is improbable. In the near future a lexicon and a sound system may be tentatively established for Proto-Niger-Congo. The innovations defining PB within Niger-Congo are less clear because, while internal Bantu evidence suggests features defining PB innovations, we do not yet know whether they define PB or a higher node, i.e. whether Narrow Bantu is really valid. At the time of writing the suggestions above have not found universal approval. To possible lexical and phonological innovations we can suggest as further candidates for investigation the following, all of which occur widely across Bantu:

1 Two contrastive negatives, one in pre-initial position, associated with main/ independent clauses, the other in post-initial position, associated with dependent or minor structures such as relatives, subjunctives, and infinitives (Kamba Muzenga 1981, Güldemann 1999a).
2 Certain verb final aspectual suffixes (-ile, -i, -a(n)ga).
3 Two patterns of locative formation, the use of classes 16–18 vs. the use of prepositions. Locative classes occur in at least some non-Bantu languages (e.g. Beboid).
4 Multiple degrees of past and future reference (Nurse, Ch. 6, this volume).
5 Nasal harmony. We have a fairly although not totally complete picture of its distribution in Bantu (Greenberg 1951), but we are not yet sure of the early or pre-Bantu developments that led to it.

In all these cases we need to know more about the distribution of these features in Niger-Congo outside Bantu.

3.2 Typological characteristics

Three points should be made in any attempt to characterize Bantu typologically. One is that definitions of what is useful for typological characterization have changed and change (Johnston 1919–22, Guthrie 1948, Greenberg 1963a, 1966, 1978b, Meeussen 1967, Heine 1976, Heine and Vossen 1981, Comrie 1989, Nichols 1992). The second is that, as with the attempts to define Bantu historically, we can state with some confidence what characterizes Bantu but we are not sure what is specific to Bantu alone within Niger-Congo. The third is to repeat the caveat that the northwest Bantu languages are often exceptions to these generalizations, because they did not innovate or have lost some of the features.

What follows represents a summary of Chapters 2–9 and 11 of Part 1 of this volume, to which we have added a few other features. We divide it into six broad categories.

Phonology (see Chs 3 and 4, also Chs 2, 5, 7, and 9).

Vowels. PB is assigned 7 contrastive vowels, and most Bantu lgs today have 7 or 5 vowels (a few have more, a few have nasalized vowels). PB is credited with contrastive vowel length, which however does not appear to have distinguished many lexical pairs; some languages today keep the distinction, other have neutralized it. Synchronic vowel lengthening is widespread and occurs in certain typical contexts (after glides, before moraic nasal and consonant, in penultimate position). Certain processes affecting vowels are widespread: vowel height harmony (esp. from stems into extensions) and the gliding of *u/o* and *i/e* to *w* and *y*, respectively, before non-identical vowels.

Consonants. The PB consonant system was relatively simple, having 4 (or 3, depending on how *c* and *j* are interpreted) positions of articulation, and distinctive voicing. While there was a series of voiceless stops, it is not clear whether the voiced congeners were continuants or stops. Remarkable features were clusters of nasal and homorganic stop (*mp, mb, nt*, etc.) and a general lack of fricatives. Some languages, especially those with the original 7 vowels, retain this system fairly exactly, while others, usually those that have undergone spirantization/affrication before the two highest vowels and the subsequent 7 > 5 vowel shift, have expanded the system and developed fricatives. Processes such as aspiration, lenition in general, palatalization, (Bantu) Spirantization, postnasal voicing, and nasal harmony (Greenberg 1951) are widespread.

Syllables are open ((N)CV, NV, V) in most languages.

Tones. Most Bantu languages, maybe 97 percent, are tonal. That is, unlike Standard Swahili or English, tones are just as much a part of a syllable or a word as are consonants and vowels. All languages distinguish two surface tones (H, L), often analyzed as /H/ vs. ∅. Widespread tonal processes are: downstep; spreading/shifting, usually to the right; the disfavoring of successive H's (Obligatory Contour Principle); the avoidance of contour tones.

Nominal tonology is fairly simple. Disyllabic stems can in principle be HH, HL, LH, or LL. Noun prefixes are L, pre-prefixes (or augments) H, and derivational suffixes also have distinctive tones. Verbal tonology is more complicated, mainly because the verbal word is more complicated. Many languages have lexical tone associated with the verb stem and most grammatical morphemes carry a tone. Thus, e.g. first and second person object markers were usually L in PB (and still are in many languages), as were singular person subject markers, whereas all other subject and object markers are H. On top of this, there may also be grammatical tone in that a H is assigned to a particular mora in the stem or verbal word, depending on the particular (TMA) category. Some grammatical morphemes are typically toneless, e.g. the extensions. Tone in general also demarcates phrasal and syntactic constituents.

Morphology (Chs 5, 6, 7, 8, 9, and 11). Bantu languages are agglutinating. Verbs have an elaborate set of affixes. Most Bantu languages have non-derived and derived nouns, the latter having an inflectional prefix and a derivational suffix. For verbs and nouns, the conventional analysis (Ch. 5) starts with an (abstract) root/radical, most often of the shape -(i)CV(C)-. For nouns a stem is formed by the addition of a derivational suffix (mostly consisting of a single vowel). For verbs, an (abstract) base may be derived from the root, via the suffixation of an extension, and the addition of a final inflectional suffix then provides a stem, to which pre-stem inflection is added. The set of suffixes is limited, for nouns and verbs.

For nouns a class prefix is then added, and in some languages, a pre-prefix. All nouns are assigned to a class. Over twenty such classes are reconstructed for PB, although most of today's languages have between twelve and twenty (a few languages reduced or even eliminated classes, see e.g. Chs 15, 16, and especially 23). A class is characterized by: a distinct prefix, a specific (and characteristic) singular/plural pairing (a 'gender'), and agreement with other constituents. During most of the twentieth century the semantic arbitrariness of noun classes was emphasized but recent years have seen attempts to find semantic generalizations.

Bantu languages have been described as verby. The verb is pivotal in the sentence, it incorporates much information, and may stand alone as a sentence. Nearly all Bantu languages are prodrop. In many languages verbs have six possible pre-stem positions, and since some of these may be filled by more than one morpheme, it is often possible to get a string of a dozen or more morphemes in one verbal word. An extreme example, kindly supplied by Philip Mutaka, would be:

Kinande (DJ42): *tu-né-mu-ndi-syá-tá-sya-ya-ba* ≠ *king-ul-ir-an-is-i-á* = *kyô*
'We will make it possible one more time for them to open it for each other.'

Between them, the verbal prefixes and suffixes commonly express negation, relativization, tense, aspect, conditional, subject (person/noun class), object (person/noun class), focus/assertion, derivational extensions, mood, and links to syntactic and discourse features. Other categories may also be encoded, especially at the verb-initial and verb-final positions. Many Bantu languages have two negative formants, one occurring in main clauses, the other in dependent or minor structures. Many Bantu languages are characterized by a rich set of tense contrasts, and a core set of aspectual contrasts also occurs widely. Many also have compound verbs, where an inflected main verb can be preceded by one or more auxiliary verbs, also inflected.

Agreement, both anaphoric and grammatical, radiates out from the head noun across the noun phrase and into the verb. In some classes the concord prefix is identical for all constituents. In others there is one shape for nouns and adjectives, and a second shape for possessives, demonstratives, connective, verb subject markers, often object markers, and other minor categories. In yet others, noun and adjective are marked differently.

In demonstratives, many Bantu languages have a three-way contrast ('near speaker, near addressee/previously referred to, far from both').

Syntax (Ch. 8, also Chs 9 and 11). The default order of sentence constituents across Bantu is S (Aux) VO (Adjuncts). A very few languages, as their only or their dominant order, have OV (A44 (Ch. 16)) and few allow V + Aux (JE42–3, F33–4). For pragmatic purposes objects may be preposed and subjects postposed (wh-constituents are rarely preposed). Thus focus may be marked by word order or by intraverb morphemes. Information coded in the syntax may also be coded in the verb morphology (double representation: Ch. 8). Zero, one, two, or three arguments may be encoded intraverbally, depending on the language. The third will be the beneficiary of an extended verb, or alternatively, a locative adjunct. The order of the intraverb morphemes mirrors that of the external arguments, which themselves follow a certain hierarchy.

As expected from languages which are VO and largely prefixing, the N precedes its modifiers within the NP. The common order is N + Adj + Numeral + other constituents, but pragmatic considerations lead to much flexibility. Most Bantu languages have few real prepositions or adjectives. Nor do they have articles, although definiteness can be expressed via the nominal augment (subject), object markers in the verb (object), or ordering of the demonstrative in the NP.

T. Bearth (personal communication) suggested this overview:

Considered from what is often called its basic structure, Bantu syntax offers nothing very particular. Neither its word order – SVO being the commonest order in the world – nor its agreement system based on noun classification, are unusual. Even double representation of core constituents, by incorporating pronominal elements in the verb, so favoring the reduction of sentential structures to just the verb, is not unique to Bantu or Niger-Congo.

It seems to be the combination of these features with certain dynamic properties of Bantu sentential structures which accounts for the originality of Bantu syntax. The universal dichotomy between the inner and outer layers of the sentence – the former prototypically expressing entities participating in the state-of-affairs expressed by the sentence, the latter locating the state-of-affairs in external circumstances – is never watertight. But the extent to which Bantu syntax, through its apparatus of verbal extensions, pronominal incorporation, and controlled positional shift, supports crisscrossing and especially the promotion of outer core elements to the inner core, is possibly unmatched in the world's languages (excepting maybe Philippine and Kru languages, which however do not share the other typical Bantu features).

The originality of Bantu syntax is seen more clearly if one recognizes how this system – of which passivization, objectivization, and (locative) inversion are further extensions – interacts subtly with pronominal incorporation, which in turn reflects nominal classification. This interplay, with all its variation and co-varying properties, defines what might be called the Bantu syntactic economy as a specific and unique solution to the most general problem that syntax is supposed to solve: the projection onto a linear structure of potentially contradictory principles of hierarchical and sequential ordering imposed by the relation of sentence elements to thematic discourse structure on the one hand, and by the need for reducing semantic randomness of predicate organization to a restricted set of types of verb-argument structures on the other.

4 THE INTENDED AUDIENCE

This is a reference book, providing a set of descriptive, analytical, and typological statements about Bantu, up-to-date statements which are linguistically informed. It is intended to be useful to different populations of readers: students and others at all levels seeking an introduction to Bantu languages; general linguists looking for information (they will find much new data here); theoretical linguists and typologists interested in specific topics and kinds of data: Bantuists seeking to broaden their horizons; and non-linguists specializing in sub-Saharan Africa who will be interested in the presentation of certain linguistic data. We asked authors to write as clearly as possible and to provide extensive references for readers wishing to delve further. Readers should bear in mind that it is not always easy to write for such a diverse audience.

An obvious issue here is the role of theory. In North America students and others tend to come at African languages after they are exposed to some linguistic theory, while in Europe and Africa it tends to be the reverse. So students and others will approach this book with quite different backgrounds and we have to accommodate them. Our general position is that each chapter is theoretically informed but not theory-oriented.

5 THE CONTENTS

The book is divided into two parts. Part 1 covers core linguistic areas, such as phonology, morphology, syntax, and historical linguistics. It also includes: phonetics because Bantu includes a huge range of important phonetic variation; tonology because, most Bantu languages being tonal, it is an indispensable topic, and because the languages and the authors have been central to thinking about tonal theory over the last decades; 'genetic' classification because it is a central topic in Bantu work, with a host of unresolved issues; grammaticalization because African, and especially Bantu, languages have been much involved in the development of grammaticalization theory in the late twentieth century;

contact languages because in a crowded linguistic space such as sub-Saharan Africa contact phenomena are ubiquitous; and finally language acquisition because while this has been a growth area in general over the last three decades, little has been done in Africa and we hope this chapter will spur new work. We originally planned to have a single chapter on morphology but finally divided it in three, due to the richness of Bantu morphological systems. Nominal and especially verbal derivation, particularly verbal extensions, are there because they are so typical of Bantu. Equally, no book on Bantu would be complete without an overview of the noun class sytem. And, as Dahl (1985) noted, Bantu inflection for aspect and tense is among the most luxuriant in the world. Most of the authors in Part 1 will be familiar names to readers. They have been in the African field for a long time and several are well known internationally in general linguistics.

In Part 2 we were faced with the task of deciding how to cover several hundred languages. This is done in two ways. On the one hand, a number of chapters treat individual languages or clusters. These were chosen because the languages were inadequately known to the outside world, or of particular interest, or because the author had spent years working at them, or some combination of these factors. Thus languages such as A43, A44, A53, A83, the B40 varieties, C101, D25, D32, E60–74, the Rufiji-Ruvuma languages (N10, P10, P20), P30, and R30 were chosen. On the other hand, other chapters are overviews of whole areas or sets of languages. These are dealt with in this way when we felt the author had a commanding grasp of the whole range and/or there were several languages in an area, all equally interesting or little known. So Grassfields, the Forest languages, Western Savanna, and Zones J and S are dealt with.

6 GEOGRAPHICAL COVERAGE

Readers will see that the Bantu area is not evenly covered. We include four languages from Zone A, one each from B, C, E, and R, two each from D and P, plus the languages covered by the survey chapters, but there is no detailed description of any individual language from Zones F, G, H, K, L, M, N, or S. Some whole areas are hardly mentioned. For this there are several reasons. The most obvious is that the seventeen chapters of Part 2 forced choices on us, and the space simply does not allow the book to cover every language or language group. Our choice was also partly dictated by the availability of authors. Given that ideally we would have liked to cover certain areas or languages, we found that for some of these there was simply no living expert. (We also had the opposite problem – in some cases we had to make a choice among living authors and we apologize to any who might feel unjustly excluded.) We were also constrained by available data. That is, some parts of the Bantu-speaking area are relatively well analyzed, whereas in others little linguistic work has been done – this is especially, but not only, true for parts of Angola, the DRC, Congo, and the CAR. Finally, we sometimes had to make choices in areas where some or most languages have had at least a minimum of linguistic treatment. In this case, we opted for lesser, rather than better known languages. So Kilimanjaro Bantu (E60–74) is chosen rather than the better-known languages of Central Kenya, for which there are descriptions or analyses of E51 and E55. Zones J and S are merely surveyed because at least some of their larger languages have received book length treatment (EJ10, EJ30, DJ42, DJ53, DJ60, S10–50 but not S60). Zones F, G, H, and M are omitted because each contains at least one language that has been reasonably well described (F21, F22, G11, G20, G40, H10, H30, M40, M50, M60). That said, we are aware there remain gaping holes. We hope that our readers will be challenged to go forth and fill the gaps so that twenty years from now this would be a different Introduction.

We would like to extend our thanks to Laurel-Anne Hassler (for translating Ch. 25) and Lynn Kisembe (for preparing the Bibliography), and to Thomas Bearth, Roger Blench, Bruce Connell, Chris Ehret, Rosalie Finlayson, Tom Güldeman, Jean-Marie Hombert, Larry Hyman, Maarten Mous, Ngessimo Mutaka, Thilo Schadeberg, and Ekkehard Wolff, for help of various kinds.

REFERENCES

Abdulaziz and Osinde 1997; Bastin and Piron 1999; Bastin *et al.* 1999; Bendor-Samuel 1989; Bennett and Sterk 1977; Bernsten 1998; Blench 1998; Comrie 1989; Dahl 1985; Diamond 1997; Doke 1954; Ehret 1998, ms; Finlayson and Slabert 1997, 2000; Greenberg 1951, 1963a, 1966, 1972, 1974, 1978; Grimes 2000; Güldemann 1999c; Guthrie 1948, 1967–71; Heine 1976; Heine and Nurse 2000; Heine and Vossen 1981; Hombert and Hyman 1999; Johnston 1919–22; Kamba Muzenga 1981; Kiptoo 2000; Mann *et al.* 1987; Mazrui 1995; Meeussen 1967, 1974; Miehe 1991; Moga and Fee 2000; Muzale forthcoming; Nichols 1992; Osinde 1986; Piron 1996, 1997; Schoenbrun 1994, 1997; Slabbert and Myers-Scotton 1997; Sommer 1992; Spyropoulos 1987; Stewart 1973, 1993b, 1999, 2000a, 2000b, 2001a, 2001b; Sure 1992; Times Atlas 1999; Vansina 1995; Watters and Leroy 1989; Williamson 1977; Williamson and Blench 2000; Wolff 2000.

PART 1

CHAPTER TWO

THE SOUNDS OF THE BANTU LANGUAGES

Ian Maddieson

1 INTRODUCTION

This chapter will describe some of the major phonetic characteristics of the (Narrow) Bantu languages based on first-hand familiarity with some of them and a reading of available literature. Since the number of languages is so large, and relatively few of them have been the object of much serious phonetic study, it will necessarily be very selective. Among phoneticians, the Bantu languages have a reputation as not having many interesting features – with the exception of the clicks and other exotic consonants introduced in the southern area largely through contact with speakers of Khoisan languages. Although it's true that many languages within the Bantu group are phonetically quite similar to each other, there is considerably more diversity in their phonetic patterns than is often believed. Some of this diversity may be disguised by the widespread use of simplifying transcriptions and orthographies which normalize away variation within and between languages, or underrepresent distinctions. Part of the aim of the chapter is therefore to draw greater attention to this diversity. Since this group of languages has received very extensive historical analysis the Bantu languages also provide a fertile field for examining inferences about the nature of phonetic sound change. Some sections of this chapter will therefore consider phonetic properties from a comparative or historical perspective.

The chapter is organized into two major sections, on vowels and consonants, with a shorter section on prosody. There are many important interactions between these three aspects of phonetic structure and some of these will be taken up at the point where it seems appropriate to do so. For example, the Bantu languages provide very striking examples of vowels affecting consonant realizations, particularly considered diachronically, and the nature of particular segments also has significant impacts on prosodic quantity and on tonal patterns. It is hoped that the brief discussions of selected issues here will encourage more attention to be paid to phonetic aspects of these languages.

2 VOWELS

2.1 Vowel spacing and high vowels

The majority of Bantu languages (with some notable exceptions, particularly in the northwest) have simple-looking systems of five or seven vowels in which the expected relationships between the features of vowel height, backness and rounding hold. That is, the back non-low vowels are rounded, and the low and front vowels are unrounded. The vowels of the five-vowel systems are therefore usually transcribed as /i, e, a, o, u/ and the seven-vowel systems are most often transcribed as /i, e, ɛ, a, ɔ, o, u/ (as noted in Hyman

1999). However, these standardized transcriptions may disguise significant differences between languages, especially with respect to the nature of the vowels written /e/ and /o/.

In the five-vowel system of Xhosa (S41), e.g. /e, o/ are genuinely mid in character. The positions of vowels in an acoustic space are often shown by plotting values of the first two formants (readers unfamiliar with acoustic analysis might see Ladefoged (2000) for an introduction to the concept of a formant). The mean formant values for Xhosa vowels given by Roux and Holtzhausen (1989) are plotted in this way in figure 2.1. In this and following figures of the same type, the origin of the axes is in the upper right, with first formant (F1) values increasing down from the origin, and second formant (F2) values increasing to the left. The distances along the axes are scaled to reflect auditory/ perceptual intervals. This kind of display closely parallels the traditional auditorily based vowel space based on perceived 'height' and 'backness' values used, e.g. in the IPA Handbook (IPA 1999) but has the advantage of being based on verifiable measurement. In figure 2.1 it can be seen that in Xhosa /e, o/ are located almost equidistant from the high vowels /i, u/ and the low vowel /a/. (There is a raising process in Xhosa which results in higher variants of /e, o/ when /i, u/ occur in the next syllable: the means for /e, o/ plotted here do not include tokens of these raised variants.)

Compare the spacing of Xhosa vowels with those of Kalanga (S16), shown in figure 2.2 (the maxima are higher in this figure compared to figure 2.1, due to male/female differences in formant range). In this case, the 'mid' vowels /e, o/ are relatively close to the high vowels /i, u/ and far from /a/. As a rough rule of thumb, vowels with a first formant lower than 400 Hz may be considered high vowels in a female voice. On this basis these particular vowels would not quite justify being considered high, but they are clearly markedly higher than those of Xhosa.

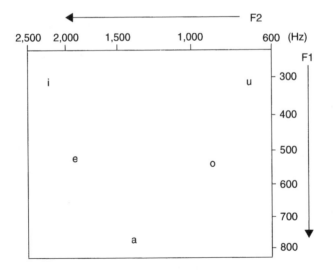

FIGURE 2.1 XHOSA VOWEL FORMANT MEANS

Source: After Roux and Holtzhausen 1989.

Note: Each point represents the average of measurements of at least thirty tokens of the vowel from one male speaker reading a text.

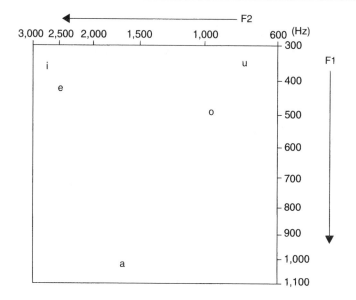

FIGURE 2.2 KALANGA VOWEL FORMANT MEANS

Source: Measurements by the author.

Note: Each point represents the average of at least twenty-eight tokens of the vowel in penultimate position in a word list spoken by a female speaker.

There have been relatively few acoustic studies of other Bantu five-vowel systems, but Swahili (Nchimbi 1997) has a pattern similar to Xhosa, while Ndebele (S44) and the Zezuru dialect of Shona (S12) (Manuel 1990) have a pattern similar to Kalanga. The distribution seen in Xhosa or Swahili is similar to that most typically found cross-linguistically in five-vowel systems transcribed /i, e, a, o, u/, such as Spanish, Hadza or Hawaiian. This is also the pattern predicted by computational models of vowel system structure from Liljencrants and Lindblom (1972) to Schwartz *et al.* (1997) based on the principle that vowels should be expected to be roughly equally dispersed in a space defined by the major formant resonances. In Kalanga on the other hand the vowels are crowded into the upper part of the vowel space, with the front pair in particular being very close together.

Parallel variations in the structure of seven-vowel systems are also found. A plot of vowel distribution in Nyamwezi (F22) is shown in figure 2.3. In this language the vowels are to a large degree placed where they might be expected, given a respect for dispersion principles. This is particularly apparent for the front vowels, which are equally spaced from each other. The word list available for measurement included a more balanced sample of front than of back vowels, and the back vowels are probably in reality more separated than this plot indicates. These data suggest that transcription of this vowel set as /i, e, ɛ, a, ɔ, o, u/ (as in the figure) is appropriate, rather than the /i, ɪ, e, a, o, ʊ, u/ preferred by Maganga and Schadeberg (1992). For Sukuma (F21), the more northerly dialect of the same language, Batibo (1985) also provides acoustic evidence for a relatively wide separation of the seven vowels, with /e, ɛ, ɔ, o/ all being clearly mid vowels.

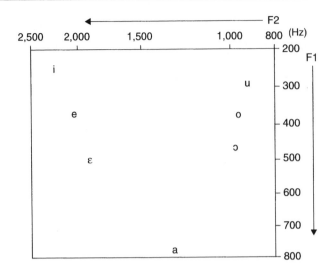

FIGURE 2.3 NYAMWEZI VOWEL FORMANT MEANS

Source: Measurements by the author.

Note: Each point represents the mean of between nine and twenty-three tokens of unreduced final or penultimate vowels in a word list spoken by a male speaker.

The relationship between the seven vowels of Vove (Pouvi) (B305) is notably different, as demonstrated in figure 2.4. Here a pair of vowels in the front and a pair of vowels in the back have such low values of F1 that they are all appropriately considered to be high vowels. The means are 248 Hz for /i/, 313 Hz for /ɪ/, 277 Hz for /u/ and 334 Hz for /ʊ/. The next lower vowels are markedly lower. In addition we may note that the front pair /i/ and /ɪ/, and the back pair /u/ and /ʊ/ have F2 values which are identical or nearly so, whereas Nyamwezi /e, o/ have F2 values intermediate between the higher and lower vowels in the system.

These data show that Bantu vowel inventories, both five- and seven-vowel systems, are split between those which are similar to global norms in their spacing and those in which the vowels are atypically crowded in the higher part of the vowel space. This fact bears directly on the issue of the appropriate reconstruction of the Proto-Bantu (PB) vowel system. According to the historical arguments of Meinhof (1899), followed by Meeussen (1969) among others, PB had a seven-vowel system with four high vowels, including two 'super-close' vowels usually notated /i̧, u̧/ in addition to 'normal' high /i, u/. Guthrie (1967–71), in his ahistorical compilation of 'Common Bantu' forms, adopts the same convention. Some recent interpretations of what the phonetic reality might have been have tended towards picturing the PB system as similar to modern West African vowel systems with harmony in which there are four high vowels, distinguished pairwise by tongue root position. This is unlikely to be correct. Under this scenario we would not expect to find reconstructed forms which mix the two high categories, such as *kúnį 'firewood' *kúpí 'be short'. We therefore prefer another hypothesis.

Among the significant facts which led Meinhof to posit two unusually high vowels are the striking diachronic effects on consonants preceding the reconstructed *i̧, u̧/. The

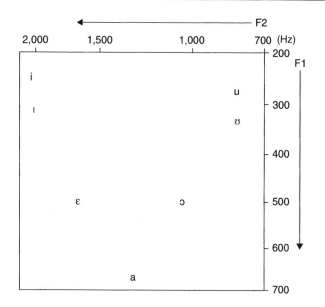

FIGURE 2.4 VOVE VOWEL FORMANT MEANS

Source: Measurements by the author on a recording made by J.-M. Hombert, made available by L. Van der Veen.

Note: Each point represents the mean of twenty or thirty measurements on minimal sets of words differing only in the penultimate vowel, spoken by a male speaker.

changes in question are often conveniently referred to as spirantization (Schadeberg 1994–5, Mpiranya 1997, Labroussi 1999, Hyman, Ch. 3, this volume), but are more complex than this label may suggest, involving not only manner but also place, and sometimes producing unusual and complex outcomes. The results are also quite varied across languages, suggesting repeated independent developments triggered by inherited characteristics of the vowels. The patterns of the major stem-initial reflexes of PB labial and alveolar stops in Fang (dialect of Cocobeach) (A75), Swahili, Yeyi (R41), and Kalanga before */i̧/, before */u̧/ and before other vowels (_V), including 'normal' high /i, u/, are given in table 2.1 (data from Medjo Mvé 1997, Nurse and Hinnebusch 1993, Baumbach 1997 supplemented by Gowlett 1997, and Mathangwane 1998, 1999, respectively).

Diachronic (or allophonic) spirantization preserving consonant place in sequences such as /ti/ or /pu/ is not uncommon cross-linguistically, as in Japanese [tsi] and [ɸu], but a labial consonant outcome from inputs /tu, du/ (i.e. */tu̧/, */du̧/) as in Swahili, or a lingual consonant outcome from input /pi, bi/ (i.e. */pi̧/, */bi̧/) as in Yeyi is much rarer. In these cases the character of the vowel has dominated over that of the preceding consonant. Particularly unusual are products such as the so-called 'whistling fricative' reflexes of */pi̧, bi̧/ in Kalanga and some Shona varieties, which reduce the original consonant to a secondary feature. ('Whistling fricatives', notated [s̨, z̨]), will be discussed later.) Also the 'superclose' vowels quite frequently preserve the stop character of PB *voiced stops, either as simple stops or as part of an affricate, when sonorant realizations are found before other proto-vowels. These facts combine to suggest that the distinctive

TABLE 2.1: SPIRANTIZATION IN FOUR LANGUAGES

Vowel context	Fang	Swahili	Yeyi	Kalanga
*p/_i̧	f, v	f	s	s ω
*b/_i̧	bz	v	z	z ω
*t/_i̧	tʃ	s	s	tsʰ ω
*d/_i̧	dz	z	z	dz
*p/_u̧	f, v	f	f	f
*b/_u̧	bv	v	v	v
*t/_u̧	ts	f	tsʰ	tʰ
*d/_u̧	dz	v	dz	d
*p/_V	f, v	p	p	p
*b/_V	b	w, Ø	β, w	β
*t/_V	t, l	t	t	t
*d/_V	y	l, Ø	r	l

characteristic of these original vowels was indeed an unusually narrow constriction, nearly consonantal in character. This notion is supported by a particularly rare phenomenon reported in Hendo (C73) and described in detail by Demolin *et al.* (1999). In this language the class 5 prefix, reconstructed in PB as *di̧-, is realized as an unreleased voiced palatal stop ([ɟ]) before a voiceless stop or affricate, e.g. in [ɟpaka] 'moth'. Magnetic resonance image (MRI) scans indicate that this segment is appropriately viewed as a hyperarticulation of the vowel /i/.

The reconstructed 'super-close' vowel pair may therefore have been similar to the 'fricative vowels' known to occur in certain modern Sino-Tibetan languages, such as Liangshang Yi (Ladefoged and Maddieson 1996) as discussed in Connell (2000). Some plausibility for this idea is provided by the comparisons provided by Connell between PB reconstructions and words in the Len variety of Mambila, a North Bantoid language which clearly has fricative vowels ([z̮i] and [v̮ɯ] in Connell's transcription).

2.2 Tongue root position?

Co-occurrence restrictions of a harmonic nature between vowels, very typical of sub-Saharan African languages, are quite commonly found in Bantu languages (though often limited in extent, e.g. only applying in certain morphological contexts such as between verb roots and extensions). Bantu vowel harmony constraints do not seem to be a survival of an older Benue-Congo, or even Niger-Congo, harmony (Stewart 2000a) but to be mostly more or less local innovations with diverse patterns of implementation (Hyman 1999). Vowel height, backness and rounding can all be factors in control of Bantu harmony. Vowel harmony in Africa often involves the independent use of pharyngeal cavity size, i.e. adjustments of pharynx volume which cannot be accounted for as a function of the height and frontness of the tongue body (see Ladefoged and Maddieson 1996 for discussion). This is usually discussed as a contrast between advanced and retracted (or neutral) tongue root position, ± ATR (advanced tongue root). An interesting issue is therefore whether the Bantu languages, particularly those with seven or more vowels, make use of the ATR feature in this phonetic sense. (Phonologists often use ATR as a diacritic feature, even to distinguish pairs of vowels such as i/ɪ in English 'beat'/'bit' where tongue root position is not the phonetic mechanism involved.) The question of

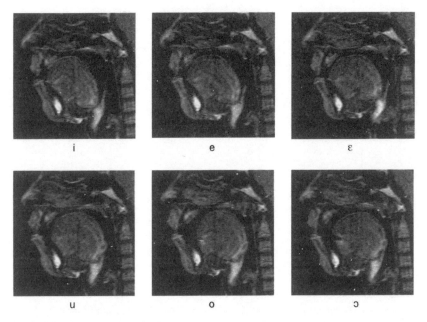

FIGURE 2.5 ARTICULATORY POSITIONS OF SIX OF THE VOWELS OF FANG (DIALECT OF BITAM)

Source: Mid-sagittal MRI scans of isolated vowels made available by Didier Demolin.

Note: Top row, front vowels; bottom row, back vowels.

the role of ATR interacts with the question of the nature of the high vowels, as the *super-high/*high contrast might have been an expression of an ATR contrast, or transformed into one in daughter languages.

It is difficult to be certain that ATR contrasts exist in a language unless direct articulatory data on the vocal tract configuration during vowel production are available. There are very few studies of this type available so far for Bantu languages, but one data set is shown in figure 2.5. These pictures are magnetic resonance images of sustained vowels produced by Pither Medjo Mvé, a speaker of the Bitam dialect of Fang (Demolin *et al.* 1992). Figure 2.5 show very clearly that independent tongue root adjustment does not contribute to the distinctions between any members of the front vowel set /i, e, ɛ/, nor the back vowel set /u, o, ɔ/. The pharynx width, measured as the distance from the tongue root surface to the back wall of the pharynx at the height of the top of the epiglottis, in /e/ is intermediate between that in /i/ and /ɛ/, and that in /o/ is intermediate between /u/ and /ɔ/. It can be predicted from tongue body position – front vowels have wider pharynx than back vowels, lower vowels have narrower pharynx than higher vowels. The three front vowels and the three back vowels can therefore be distinguished one from another solely by height.

Bitam Fang has eight vowels, seven peripheral vowels plus mid central /ə/ (Medjo Mvé 1997). An acoustic plot of these vowels is given in figure 2.6. Note particularly the slope of a line connecting the back vowels which points roughly to the position of the central

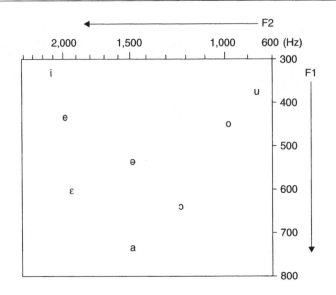

FIGURE 2.6 FANG VOWEL FORMANT MEANS

Source: Recording by Pither Medjo Mvé made available by Didier Demolin; measurements by the author.

Note: Each point represents the mean of six measurements, three of isolated vowel tokens, plus three tokens in final vowels in /alV/ nonsense words.

vowel /a/, similar to that seen in figures 2.1 and 2.2, and attributable to the fact that F1 and F2 frequencies co-vary in these vowels. This pattern is typical of that found in vowel systems where the back series is distinguished by degrees of height with no other factors being significantly involved. In this dialect lexical stems are marked by a strong tendency for V1 and V2 to be identical except if V2 is /a/, when /i, ǝ, a, o, u/ are all relatively common as V1 but /e, ɛ, ɔ/ are not (note that as many PB *CVCV items have become monosyllabic in Fang, the V2 in these cases is often not the *V2 of the reconstructed form). This pattern of co-occurrences is not one which suggests a phonological role for ATR.

On the other hand the harmonic behavior and acoustic characteristics of vowels in Nande (D42) considered together suggest that this is likely to be a genuine example of the use of ATR for phonetic distinctions. Mean formant values of the nine phonologically distinctive vowels, plus the allophonic variations of /a/ for one speaker are plotted in figure 2.7. Harmonically related pairs are noted by the use of the same symbol with and without a minus sign. In each case the putatively [-ATR] vowel has a substantially higher first formant (hence a lower position on the figure 2.7) than its harmonic counterpart. Most strikingly, the 'high' vowels /i-, u-/ are placed lower than the 'mid' vowels /e, o/. Narrowing the pharynx raises the first formant, other things being equal. The pair /u, u-/ where F2 is the same are thus quite likely (almost) solely different in pharynx width. The other back vowel pair /o, o-/ shows a smaller than expected F2 difference given the size of the difference between their first formants; a substantial pharynx width difference coupled with a degree of opening of the oral constriction may be inferred. Note that a sloping line can be fit to the vowel set /u, o, a/ and a second roughly parallel lower one

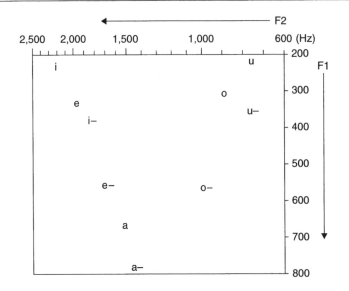

FIGURE 2.7 NANDE VOWEL FORMANT MEANS

Source: Data from Ngessimo Mutaka; measurements by the author.

Note: Each point represents the mean of between six and twenty-one tokens of phonetically long vowels in penultimate position in words spoken by a male speaker.

to the set /u-, o-, a-/, but a straight line cannot be fit to the set /u, o, o-/ as is possible for Fang /u, o, ɔ/. The pattern for the front vowels suggests a greater interaction of the major features of vowel height and backness with pharynx width (not surprising, as retracting the tongue root is more likely to pull the tongue back and down when the tongue body position is front).

We may now revisit the Kalanga and Vove high vowels in figures 2.2 and 2.4. The members of the high vowel pairs /i, ɪ/ and /u, ʊ/ in Vove have virtually the same second formant values as each other and differ only in F1. The Kalanga vowel pairs transcribed /i, e/ and /u, o/, which are acoustically equally as high as the Vove pairs, differ in both F1 and F2. Plausibly, the Vove vowel pairs differ phonetically in pharynx width, which is consistent with the auditory impression they create, while the Kalanga pairs differ in height (and to a lesser degree in backness), which is consistent with the auditory impression *they* create. Although these acoustic measurements are suggestive, it should be borne in mind that inferences from simple formant measures concerning vowel articulation must be made with caution.

2.3 Nasalized vowels

Distinctive nasalized vowels are not particularly common in the Bantu languages but are found in certain mostly western areas, e.g. in Ngungwel (B72a) in the Teke group (Paulian 1994), in UMbundu (R11, Schadeberg 1982), in Bajele (Renaud 1976), and in a few words in the Bitam dialect of Fang (Medjo Mvé 1997). As is generally the case cross-linguistically, there are fewer distinct nasalized vowels than oral ones, at least in

TABLE 2.2: NASALIZED VOWELS IN *ŋgùŋgwèl*

Vowel	Word	Gloss
ĩː (stem)	dzĩĩ	'tooth'
ẽ (prefix)	ẽbĕl	'kolanut trees'
ɛ̃ː (stem)	ntsíɛ̃ɛ̃	'horn'
ã (prefix)	ãpăb	'wing'
ãː (stem)	bã̂ã̂	'children'
ɔ̃ː (stem)	ekúɔ̃ɔ̃	'broom'
õ (prefix)	ṍkáa	'woman'
ũː (stem)	ŋkṹṹ	'name'

lexical stems. In Ngungwel (B72a), there are three oral and three nasalized vowels in pre-fixes [e, a, o; ẽ, ã, õ]. Lexical stems have a system of seven oral vowels but only five nasalized vowels. Nasalized vowels in the stem are reported to have the qualities [ĩ, ɛ̃, ã, ɔ̃, ũ] and to be invariably long (Paulian's article does include a few words with short nasalized vowels in stems; these may be misprints). There are thus seven *phonetic* qualities among the nasalized vowels, but no contrast between all seven in any environment. Examples are given in table 2.2.

A role for vowel nasalization in the transmission of nasal consonant harmony (Greenberg 1951, Hyman 1995b) across intervening vowels seems likely in the history of Bantu.

3 CONSONANTS

3.1 Consonant overview

Most Bantu languages are reported as having two series of plosives, voiced and voice-less, and this is the standard PB reconstruction (Meeussen 1969). Except in post-nasal environments and sometimes before the *super-high vowels, the reconstructed voiced plosives most commonly correspond to voiced continuants of one type or another, or to implosives, in the modern languages (an alternation of some kind is probably to be recon-structed to an early stage, possible even pre-Bantu). Bantu orthographies usually do not indicate these alternations, unless subsequent developments have created a contrast between, say, /b/ and /ɓ/, or /b/ and /β/. This illustrates one instance where the occurrence of cross-linguistically less common phonetic segments may be disguised by notational practices. Aspiration is a contrastive property of voiceless stops (and affricates) in some languages, principally in eastern and southern languages, where it is often a reflex of an earlier voiceless prenasalized stop. Engstrand and Lodhi (1985) provide one of the few phonetic discussions of aspiration in a Bantu language (Swahili).

Most Bantu languages have a full set of nasals at each place of articulation where a stop or affricate appears, but often intricate (morpho)phonological processes govern nasal/oral alternations and syllabification and other prosodic processes concerning nasals. Most of the languages have relatively limited sets of fricatives of the cross-linguistically common types, although lateral fricatives (and affricates) have developed in or been borrowed into a number of the southern languages, such as Sotho, Xhosa and Zulu. Particularly striking in this connection is the velar ejective lateral affricate [kꞎ'] of Zulu, which is auditorily reminiscent of a lateral click. There is often only one liquid: /l/,

/ɾ/ or /r/ (though Chaga E60 is among those with more, see Davey *et al.* 1982, Philippson and Montlahuc, Ch. 24, this volume). The two vocoid approximants /j, w/ occur in many languages, often alternating with high vowels /i, u/.

Although most Bantu languages use only one coronal (typically alveolar) and one dorsal (velar) place of articulation, contrasts between dental and alveolar places are found in Mijikenda and coastal dialects of Swahili (see Hayward *et al.* 1989) and between velars and uvulars in Qhalaxarzi (S31d, Dickens 1987). Consonant gemination has developed through internal processes in languages such as Ganda (E15), and by contact with Cushitic languages in Ilwana (E701).

In the rest of this section two of the particular issues of phonetic interest, the possible occurrence of articulatorily complex consonants, and the nature of the so-called 'whistling fricatives' mentioned in the section on vowels will be briefly discussed. Longer sections of the chapter will be devoted to aspects of laryngeal action in consonants, to the description of clicks and their distribution in Bantu, and to some of the interesting aspects of nasality which occur in these languages.

3.2 Complex or simple consonants?

Doubly articulated labial-velar stops (and nasals) are found almost exclusively in the languages of Africa, but they occur in only relatively few of the Bantu languages, including Londo (A11, Kuperus 1985), 'Sawabantu' (Mutaka and Ebobissé 1996–7), Fang (Medjo Mvé 1997) and Mijikenda (E70, Nurse and Hinnebusch 1993, Kutsch Lojenga 2001) among others. However, from the phonetic point of view, the Bantu languages have fewer articulatorily complex consonants than is sometimes suggested. An interesting process of intensification of secondary articulations into obstruents occurs, inter alia, in Nyarwanda (Jouannet 1983) and Shona. This process does not result in double articulations that are almost totally overlapped, as in labial-velars, but sequential articulations which are overlapped either not at all, or no more than is typical of sequences such as /tk/ or/ pk/ in English words like 'fruitcake' or 'hopkiln'. On the other hand it does produce rather unusual consonant sequences in onset positions.

Examples of the Nyarwanda strengthening of an underlying /u/ or /w/ into a velar stop after a non-homorganic nasal or stop are illustrated by the spectrograms in figures 2.8–2.10. As these show, the first segment is released before the closure for the second is formed. When the sequence is voiced, as in /mg, bg/, a quite marked central vocoid separates the two segments. When the sequence is voiceless, as in /tk/, there is a strong oral release of the first closure. There is no overlap in the closures for the two segments, except optionally in the case of the nasal sequence /mŋ/. Somewhat similar facts have been shown for the Zezuru dialect of Shona (Maddieson 1990); however, as was observed long ago by Doke (1931a,b), the phonetic patterns vary quite considerably across the different varieties of Shona.

A particularly interesting claim is made by Mathangwane (1999) concerning her pronunciation of parallel forms in Kalanga. She suggests that elements like the /pk/ which evolve from earlier or underlying /pw/ are pronounced with almost fully overlapped closures and their duration is similar to that of simple /k/ and /p/ segments, i.e. they are [p͡k, b͡g]. She reports that the labial closure is formed first – this would therefore be an important counterexample to the normal pattern found in labial-velar doubly articulated segments in other languages in which the labial closure is formed very slightly later (10–15 ms) than the velar one. The one spectrogram of a word containing /pk/ published in this study actually shows that the duration of the element is considerably longer than a simple stop,

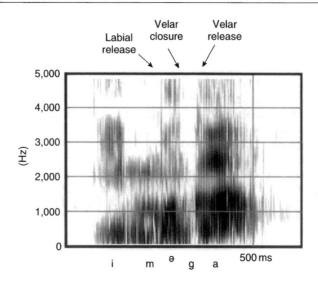

FIGURE 2.8 SPECTROGRAM OF NYARWANDA *imwa* /imga/ 'dog'
Note: Male speaker.

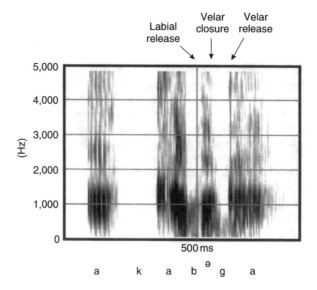

FIGURE 2.9 SPECTROGRAM OF NYARWANDA *akabwa* /akabga/ 'dog (diminutive)'
Note: Same speaker as figure 2.8.

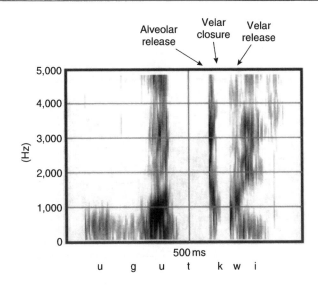

FIGURE 2.10   SPECTROGRAM OF NYARWANDA *ugutwi* /ugutkwi/ 'ear'

Note: Same speaker as figure 2.8.

suggesting it contains a sequence of articulations, although no burst is visible for the /p/. Recordings made by the author of two other speakers of Kalanga, one from Francistown in Botswana and one from Palmtree in Zimbabwe, did not replicate the pattern suggested by Mathangwane. For example, the word meaning 'armpit', transcribed by Mathangwane as [ɦapk̚ʰa], could receive three pronunciations – [hakʰwa] with no labial closure, [hapxa] with a labial stop followed by a fairly long velar fricative, or [hapkʰa] with a sequence of stops with clearly separate releases, as illustrated in figure 2.11. This third pronunciation was characterized by one of the speakers as being more typical of speakers of fifty or more years of age. Evidently more study of the phonetic and sociolinguistic variation in this area would be of great interest.

3.3 'Whistling' fricatives

Shona and Kalanga are also marked by the occurrence of a type of labialization co-produced with alveolar fricatives which has led to these segments being named 'whistling fricatives' (Doke 1931b, Bladon *et al.* 1987). Unlike 'ordinary' labialization, which involves rounding and protrusion of the lips accompanied by a raising of the tongue back, i.e. a [w]-like articulation, this labialization involves primarily a vertical narrowing of the lips with little or no protrusion and no accompanying tongue back rais-ing. The acoustic effect is to concentrate the frication noise in a relatively narrow fre-quency band which is indeed somewhat reminiscent of a whistle. The gesture is also timed differently from 'ordinary' labialization in that it covers the fricative duration rather than being primarily realized as an offglide; hence 'whistling fricatives' can them-selves be labialized in their release phase. Similar segments are very rare in the world's languages but do occur in the Dagestanian language Tabarasan.

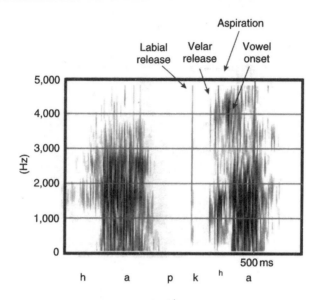

FIGURE 2.11 SPECTROGRAM OF KALANGA /hapkʰa/ 'armpit'

Note: Female speaker from Zimbabwe.

4 LARYNGEAL ACTION IN CONSONANTS

4.1 Implosives and ejectives

Languages of the northwest, the eastern coastal area and the southeast often have at least one implosive, most frequently a bilabial, but implosives are generally absent in the languages of the Congo basin and southwest. Ejective stops and affricates are more rarely found in the Bantu languages, although they occur as variants of the unaspirated voiceless stops in languages of the south, especially in post-nasal contexts. The ejection is generally weak compared to that found in languages of the Afro-Asiatic family, except for Ilwana where the ejectives are in borrowed Cushitic vocabulary, and the ejective lateral affricate of Zulu mentioned earlier.

The segments labeled as implosives are sometimes described as if a glottal constriction is characteristic of their production. In Bantu, this is typically not the case; the vocal folds are in the normal position for voicing. Rather, what is critical is that the larynx is lowering during their production, so that the size of the supralaryngeal cavity is being enlarged while the oral closure is maintained. This may have two principal effects – first, it allows the amplitude of vocal fold vibration to increase during the closure, giving a particularly strong percept of voicing at the time of the release, and second it may mean that the intra-oral pressure is relatively low at the time when the closure is released so that at the moment of release the initial airflow is ingressive (Hardcastle and Brasington 1978). The waveform of an intervocalic bilabial implosive in GiTonga (S62) is shown in figure 2.12. Dashed vertical lines mark the onset and offset of the bilabial closure. Voicing is continuous through the closure; upper and lower lines have been constructed on the figure linking respectively the positive and negative peaks in the waveform in order to dramatize the growing amplitude of the voicing during the closure.

4.2 Depressor consonants

Another special laryngeal action occurs in the 'depressor' consonants which are characteristic of certain Bantu languages of the eastern and southern regions. This term was originally applied to consonants which have a particularly salient lowering effect on the pitch of the voice in their neighborhood (Lanham 1958). It has since sometimes come to be used for any consonant which has any local lowering effect on pitch (or, more accurately, on the fundamental frequency of vocal fold vibration, abbreviated F_0), such as an ordinary voiced plosive, and has even been used for those which may simply block a raising or high-tone spreading process. However, the original notion of a depressor consonant is quite different from this expanded use. The most detailed study remains that of Traill *et al.* (1987) on depressor consonants in Zulu. This study shows that the F_0 associated with depressors is lower than a low tone, and the lowest pitch is centered on the depressor consonants themselves. At vowel onset the F_0 difference between High and Low tones after a set of non-depressor consonants is 22 Hz; but a High tone onset after depressor consonants is 44 Hz lower than after the non-depressors, and a Low after depressors is 23 Hz lower than after non-depressors (mean across three speakers, two male and one female). Thus a High after a depressor begins considerably lower than a Low elsewhere. Figure 2.13 compares the pitch contours of the Swati words /líhala/ 'aloe' and /líhálà/ 'harrow', where /.. / is a diacritic to mark the fact that the consonant is a depressor in the second word. Despite the fact that the lexical tone after the depressor is high (Rycroft 1981), the onset F_0 is about 30 Hz lower than the low tone onset after the non-depressor, and a rapid pitch fall begins during the vowel which precedes the depressor.

Figure 2.13 also illustrates the fact that depression is not necessarily associated with voicing as both /h/ and /h̲/ are voiceless. Equally, voiced segments such as nasals and approximants may contrast in depression (see also Traill and Jackson 1988, Wright and Shryock 1993, Mathangwane 1998). Since these segments make for easy tracking of Fo through the consonant, the centering of the depression on the consonant can be most easily visualized with them. Two examples from Giryama (E72a) are illustrated in figure 2.14. In these cases there is a substantial fall in F_0 from the onset to the middle of the nasal, and pitch begins to rise before the consonant is released; the pitch peak on the vowel is 40 Hz (left panel) or 50 Hz (right panel) higher than the lowest pitch in the nasal.

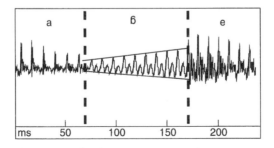

FIGURE 2.12 WAVEFORM OF THE MIDDLE PART OF THE GITONGA WORD /ɓàɓé/ 'father', ILLUSTRATING THE INCREASING AMPLITUDE OF VOICING DURING THE IMPLOSIVE

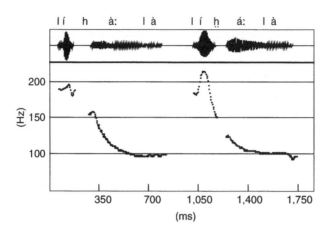

FIGURE 2.13 PITCH CONTOURS ILLUSTRATING EFFECTS OF NON-DEPRESSOR AND DEPRESSOR /h/ IN SWATI

Note: Male speaker.

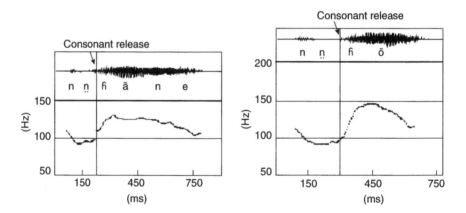

FIGURE 2.14 PITCH EFFECTS OF DEPRESSOR NASALS IN THE GIRYAMA WORDS /nhane/ 'eight' (LEFT PANEL) AND IDEOPHONE /nho/ (RIGHT PANEL)

Source: Recording courtesy of Constance Kutsch Lojenga.

In these words there is noticeably breathy phonation during part of the consonant and at the vowel onset (transcribed [ɦ]), but breathiness is not an invariable accompaniment of depression as had been proposed by Rycroft (1980). Following Traill *et al.* (1987), we understand true 'depression' to consist of a special laryngeal posture consistent with very low pitch co-produced with the consonant it is associated with. This gesture may become associated with any class of consonants and thus is capable of becoming itself an independent phonological entity deployed for grammatical effect as in the 'depression without depressors' described by Traill (1990).

5 CLICKS

Clicks are unique to Africa as speech sounds and as they are of unusually great phonetic interest they will be described in some detail. They have been incorporated into the consonant inventories of a number of languages in the southern part of the Bantu area, indisputably as a result of contact with Khoisan languages. The languages concerned are separated into two geographical clusters. In the southeast, the core is formed by the languages of the Nguni group (S40), especially Zulu which has twelve click consonants, and Xhosa which has fifteen, as also does Phuthi. More far-flung Nguni varieties, such as Zimbabwean Ndebele, Malawian Ngoni and Tanzanian Ngoni, have (or had) fewer clicks (Doke 1954, Ziervogel 1959). Clicks also are found in Southern Sotho (Guma 1971), in some speech varieties of the Tsonga group (S50) such as Nkuna, Dzonga and Ronga (Doke 1954, Baumbach 1974, Afido *et al.* 1989), and, more marginally, in the Ndau dialect of Shona in Mozambique (Afido *et al.* 1989). They do not occur in the Shona varieties of Zimbabwe, nor in Northern Sotho (Poulos and Lowrens 1994), Venda, Kalanga, Tswa, Chopi, GiTonga and other languages neighboring or closely related to those in which clicks are found.

In the southwest, the largest number of clicks is found in Yeyi (Gowlett 1997, Sommer and Vossen 1992), which has at least ten, and maybe as many as twenty (accounts are quite variable, only in part because of dialectal differences). Clicks are also found in Gciriku (including in the ethnonym itself), Shambiu, Kwangali, Mbukushu, Fwe and Mbalangwe (Möhlig 1997, Baumbach 1997). They are not found in languages of the Wambo cluster (R20) such as Kwanyama, Mbalanhu and Ndonga, nor in Herero, UMbundu, Totela, Subiya, Lozi, Kgalagadi, Tswana and other languages spoken near the area where the borders of Namibia, Angola, Botswana and Zambia meet.

This distribution in shown approximately by the map of Southern Africa in figure 2.15, prepared with the Bantu Mapmaker software (Lowe and Schadeberg 1997). Languages

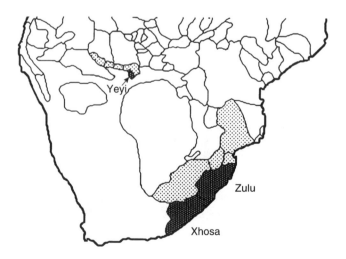

FIGURE 2.15 BANTU LANGUAGES WITH CLICKS

Note: See text for details.

with clicks are shown stippled – heavily for those with more elaborate click inventories, and lightly for those with small click inventories. Neither the dispersed Nguni languages (Ndebele and Ngoni) nor Ndau are included here. The separation of the areas as well as the distinct nature of the vocabularies involved (Louw 1975, Sommer and Vossen 1992) indicate that borrowing of clicks happened independently in these two areas. In the southeast it is reasonably certain that clicks spread from Nguni to the neighboring languages, and in this process the number of click distinctions was reduced (in fact, click spreading is an ongoing process with clicks penetrating into Ndau, urban varieties of Northern Sotho and beyond; like most linguistic maps, this map represents a somewhat fictitious ethnographic idealization not corresponding precisely with any exact time or population distribution). In the southwest it is less certain that clicks were borrowed first into one language (in this case it would be Yeyi) and spread from there, but this scenario seems quite possible in view of the reduced inventories of clicks found in the other languages. It is noteworthy that none of the Bantu languages of East Africa have acquired clicks from the surviving or former languages of this area with clicks (Maddieson *et al.* 1999).

The mechanism of producing clicks is now well understood. A closure in the vocal tract is formed by the back of the tongue contacting the roof of the mouth in the velar or uvular area. A second closure is then formed in front of the location of this closure by the tip or blade of the tongue or the lips. This entraps a small quantity of air between these two closures. The center portion of the tongue is then lowered while the two closures are maintained, enlarging the volume of the space between them. Consequently, the pressure in the air inside this space is reduced well below that of the air outside the mouth. Next, the closure at the front of the mouth is released and the abrupt equalization of air pressures inside and outside the mouth results in a sharp acoustic transient. Finally, the back closure is released, and this release may be separately audible. A pronunciation of a click where the velar release is clearly detectable is illustrated in figure 2.16.

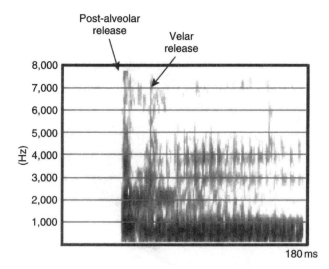

FIGURE 2.16 SPECTROGRAM OF THE FIRST PART OF THE NDEBELE WORD [!kò:βá] 'slice!'

Note: It shows an unaspirated post-alveolar click in onset position. The interval between the two releases is 20 ms.

The basic click mechanism does not determine what the larynx is doing while these movements are taking place in the oral cavity, nor whether the velum itself is raised or lowered to block or permit air from the lungs to flow out through the nose. Thus, a click can be accompanied by simple glottal closure, by modal or breathy voicing, by open vocal folds or by use of the ejective mechanism. Changes in larynx activity can be variously timed in relation to the action in the oral cavity, and to the timing of movements raising and lowering the velum. The possible variations are thus very numerous, and many different categories of individual clicks are found when all the languages which use them are considered (Ladefoged and Maddieson 1996).

In describing clicks it is customary to talk of the click type and the click accompaniment. The click type refers to the location of the front closure and the manner in which it is released, which may be abrupt or affricated, central or lateral. The accompaniment refers to all the other aspects of the click – laryngeal action and timing, nasal coupling and the location (uvular or velar) and manner of release (abrupt or affricated) of the back closure. In Bantu languages, no more than four click types are used and probably no more than seven accompaniments are found. Zulu and Xhosa have affricated dental, affricated alveolar lateral and non-affricated apical post-alveolar click types. The last of these was often described as 'palatal' in older literature. Yeyi has these three as well as a laminal post-alveolar type (variously called 'alveolar' or 'palatal' in different sources).

Thomas Vilakazi's analysis of Zulu click types (Thomas [Vilakazi] 1998, 2001), combining insights from acoustic, aerodynamic and electropalatographic techniques, is by far the most detailed study of click production in a Bantu language. Thomas Vilakazi confirms that the velar closure always precedes the front closure; this accounts for the fact that nasals preceding clicks assimilate in place to velar position, and corrects a misobservation by Doke (1926), who believed the front closure was formed first (the velar closure *must* be released after the front closure for the click mechanism to work, but it could in principle be formed later). Velar closures for all three click types in Thomas Vilakazi's data are held for about 175 ms, but the front closures show some significant timing differences. The front closure for dental clicks is formed earlier and held longer (about 105 ms) than that for post-alveolar or lateral clicks (about 80 ms). The relative timing and durations of velar and front closures deduced from acoustic and aerodynamic data are graphed in figure 2.17.

More details on the articulations of clicks are given by electropalatography (EPG). Speakers wear a thin custom-made acrylic insert moulded to the shape of their upper

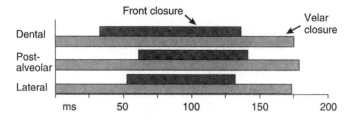

FIGURE 2.17 CLOSURE DURATIONS AND TIMING RELATIONS IN THE THREE CLICK TYPES OF ZULU

Source: From Thomas Vilakazi (1999).

Notes: Means for voiceless clicks in three vowel environments spoken by three speakers. Front closure durations are shown in the dark tint.

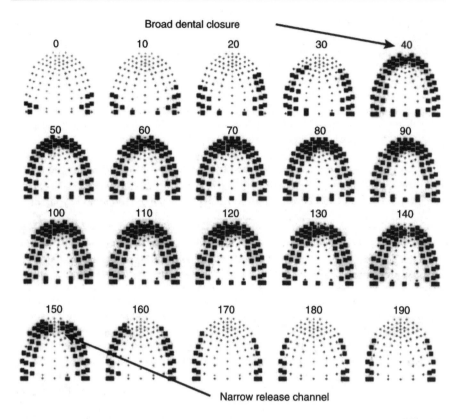

FIGURE 2.18 EPG FRAMES SHOWING A DENTAL CLICK SPOKEN BY A MALE ZULU SPEAKER

Source: From Thomas Vilakazi (1999).

teeth and hard palate in which a number of electrodes are embedded which sense contact between the tongue and the roof of the mouth. In Thomas Vilakazi's study, inserts with ninety-six electrodes were used, together with software allowing a sweep of the contact patterns to be made every 10 ms. The articulatory contacts can then be examined using stylized displays such as those in figures 2.18–2.20, which represents the arc of the teeth and the vault of the palate. Contacted electrodes are shown as black squares and uncontacted ones as grey dots. Figure 2.18 shows the production of a dental click. The first frame, numbered 0, is close to the time that velar closure is first made, as detected from the accompanying acoustic record. Because the insert does not cover the soft palate, this closure cannot be observed on the EPG record at this time. The seal around the inside of the teeth is made by 40 ms later, and as the contact area of the back of the tongue enlarges, the front edge of the velar contact is now visible as a line of contacted electrodes at the bottom of the arc. The closures overlap for 100 ms, until frame 140. During this time rarefaction is occurring. This figure makes clear that the expansion of the cavity is not due to moving the location of the back closure further back, as phoneticians have sometimes suggested. That dental clicks are produced with controlled affrication is also clear from the way the front release initially involves formation of a narrow channel, clearly visible in frame 150.

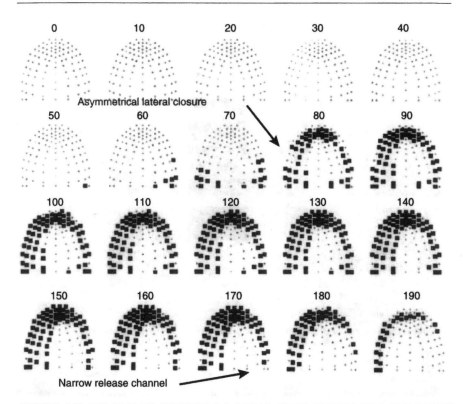

FIGURE 2.19 EPG FRAMES SHOWING A LATERAL CLICK SPOKEN BY A MALE ZULU SPEAKER

Source: From Thomas Vilakazi (1999).

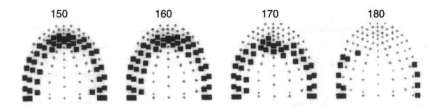

FIGURE 2.20 EPG FRAMES SHOWING THE RELEASING PHASE OF A POST-ALVEOLAR CLICK SPOKEN BY A MALE ZULU SPEAKER

Source: From Thomas Vilakazi (1999).

Production of a lateral click is illustrated in figure 2.19. In this particular token there is a long lag between the time the velar closure is made and when the front closure is sealed, about 80 ms later. The contact of the front of the tongue is asymmetrical, as the side of the tongue opposite to where the release will be made is braced contra-laterally against the palate. The release of a lateral click is also affricated, occurring initially through a narrow channel quite far back, as shown in frame 170 and continuing in

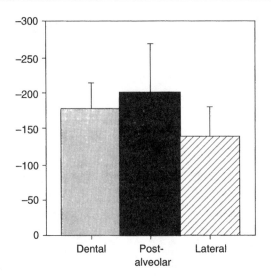

FIGURE 2.21 PEAK NEGATIVE PRESSURE IN THE THREE CLICK TYPES OF ZULU

Source: From Thomas Vilakazi (1999).

Note: Means for voiceless clicks in three vowel environments spoken by three speakers.

frame 180. In contrast to these two affricated click types, a post-alveolar click is released without affrication. As figure 2.20 shows, the shift from sealed to open occurs rapidly and completely, here between the two frames numbered 170 and 180. These frames also illustrate the retraction of the tongue tip which occurs just before release of this click type. From frame 150 through to frame 170 the contacted area moves back, so that the configuration at the moment of release is clearly post-alveolar.

During the time period in which the two closures of a click overlap, lowering of the center of the tongue creates a partial vacuum in the cavity between them. Thomas Vilakazi's work provides the first direct measures of how powerful the energy generated by this gesture is. Air pressure in the oral cavity is measured in relation to the ambient atmospheric pressure in hectoPascals (hPa, equivalent to the pressure required to support 1 cm of water). For an ordinary pulmonic stop, peak pressure behind the closure ranges between about 5 and 20 hPa, depending on the loudness of the voice. The peak negative pressures reached in clicks are typically -100 hPa or more and may reach over -200, as shown in figure 2.21. Post-alveolar clicks have the greatest rarefaction, lateral clicks the least – perhaps because the contra-lateral bracing of the tongue in the lateral clicks may constrain the amount of tongue-center lowering that is possible. Thomas Vilakazi's aerodynamic data also reflect the different dynamics of the affricated and abrupt clicks. The equalization of internal and external pressure at release occurs much more quickly in post-alveolar clicks than for dental and lateral clicks. This can be shown by calculating the average rate of pressure change over this phase of the click, which is 14.4 hPa/ms for post-alveolars, 7.9 for dentals and 4.2 hPa/ms for laterals. Only a small part of this difference can be accounted for by the difference in peak pressure between the click types.

Zulu has four different accompaniments to its three click types, voiceless unaspirated, voiceless aspirated, voiced and voiced nasalized. The IPA recommends that these be

TABLE 2.3: IPA SYMBOLS AND ZULU ORTHOGRAPHY FOR CLICKS

	IPA transcription			Orthography		
	Dental	Post-alveolar	Lateral	Dental	Post-alveolar	Lateral
Voiceless unaspirated	k|	k!	k‖	c	q	x
Voiceless aspirated	k|ʰ	k!ʰ	k‖ʰ	ch	qh	xh
Voiced	g|	g!	g‖	gc	gq	gx
Voiced nasalized	ŋ|	ŋ!	ŋ‖	nc	nq	nx

noted in each case by writing a symbol for a dorsal consonant (velar in this case) before the click type symbol, so that click consonants are always represented by at least a digraph, and may require additional symbols or diacritics. The correspondence between IPA transcription and Zulu orthographic symbols is given in table 2.3. Xhosa has five accompaniments, three of which are the same as in Zulu. The 'voiced' clicks are breathy-voiced, and there is a distinct breathy-voiced nasalized accompaniment; these two series are 'depressor consonants'. Yeyi has a click accompaniment described by Gowlett as 'ejective' but represented phonetically by digraphs with [ʔ]. This could indicate that there is glottal closure but no ejection.

One of the most striking things about clicks in Bantu is the lack of respect for place distinctions when few categorical contrasts exist. In Nkuna (Tsonga) Baumbach (1974) indicates that clicks are indifferently pronounced as dental or post-alveolar. In Mbukushu (K333) the one series of clicks is reported to be pronounced 'either as dental, palatal or [post-]alveolar sounds' (Fisch 1977). In Gciriku (K332), clicks are 'mostly dental, however, with a broad individual variation' (Möhlig 1997:219). Such context-free liberty to vary place of articulation is rarely encountered with other classes of consonants.

6 NASALS AND NASALITY

The special phonetic interest of consonantal nasality in the Bantu languages involves principally the prenasalized segments and the realization of 'voiceless' nasals. In both cases aspects of timing are particularly relevant. Detailed studies of timing in prenasalized stops are included in Maddieson (1993), Maddieson and Ladefoged (1993) and Hubbard (1994, 1995). Using data from these sources, figure 2.22 compares the durations of nasals and voiced prenasalized stops as well as of the vowels that precede them in two languages, Ganda and Sukuma. In both languages the oral stop duration in voiced prenasalized stops is very short, so the total segment duration is not so very different from that of a simple nasal. Both languages have contrasts of vowel quantity and compensatory lengthening of vowels before prenasalized stops. But there are interesting differences between the two. Lengthened vowels are much closer in duration to underlying long vowels in Ganda than they are in Sukuma. Sukuma lengthened vowels are almost exactly intermediate between underlying short and long vowels, and the nasal portion is quite long. Nyambo (E21) is similar to Sukuma in its pattern, and Hubbard suggests that the difference from Ganda is related to the fact that lengthened vowels count in a different way in tone assignment rules in these languages.

Hubbard also compared the durations of vowels in three further languages with different patterns. The mean results are given in table 2.4. Ndendeule has no long vowels and no lengthening. Yao (P21) has a long/short contrast and significant compensatory lengthening so that vowels before prenasalized stops are as long as underlying long vowels and

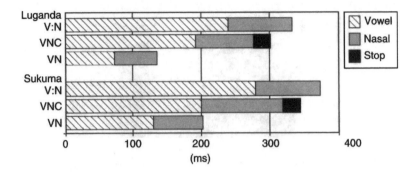

FIGURE 2.22 COMPARISON OF SELECTED VOWEL AND CONSONANTS LENGTHS IN GANDA AND SUKUMA

Note: See text for explanation.

TABLE 2.4: COMPARISON OF MEAN VOWEL DURATIONS IN THREE LANGUAGES, ONE SPEAKER PER LANGUAGE

Vowel duration in ...	Ndendeule	Yao	Tonga
... CVC	148	61	100
... CVNC	146	130	101
... CV:C	–	132	241

Source: After Hubbard (1995).

have more than double the duration of short vowels. Tonga (M64) has long vowels but does not show any compensatory lengthening before NC. This difference seems to be related to the different origin of long vowels; Yao maintains PB vowel length distinctions (and adds to them). Tonga does not preserve PB vowel length, but has developed long vowels from intervocalic consonant loss.

In several areas earlier voiceless prenasalized stops have developed into voiceless nasals or related types of segments, including in Sukuma (Maddieson 1991), Pokomo (E71) and Bondei (G24) (Huffman and Hinnebusch 1998), Kalanga (Mathangwane 1998), and Nyarwanda (Demolin and Delvaux 2001). Aspects of the original sequencing of nasal + oral and voiced + voiceless portions found in prenasalized stops are sometimes retained, and small variations in the timing and magnitude of the different component gestures create quite large variability in the acoustic pattern of these segments as critical alignments are made or missed.

This variation in the realization of 'voiceless nasals' is at least in part correlated with position in a word. Figure 2.23 shows a spectrogram of the Nyamwezi word /ŋapo/ 'basket' spoken in isolation. Dotted vertical lines separate the major phonetic components of the first syllable. The portion marked A, between the first two lines, is phonetically a voiceless velar nasal [ŋ]. The second line marks the time-point at which the velar closure is released. The fragment marked B has voiceless oral airflow, with resonances similar to those of the following /a/ vowel. Fragment C is the voiced portion of the vowel /a/. This type of segment might well be described as an 'aspirated voiceless nasal'. Figure 2.24

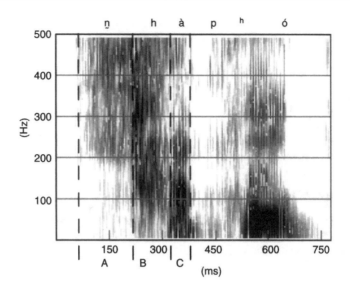

FIGURE 2.23 SPECTROGRAM OF THE NYAMWEZI WORD /ŋapo/ 'basket'

Note: See text for discussion of the phonetic segmentation.

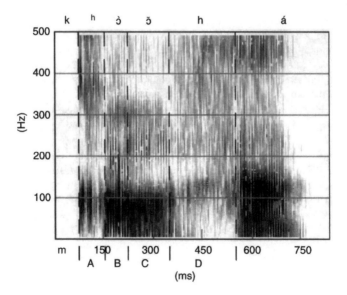

FIGURE 2.24 SPECTROGRAM OF THE NYAMWEZI WORD /koŋá/ 'to suck'

Note: See text for discussion of the phonetic segmentation.

shows a realization of a medial instance of the same segment in the word /kɔ̃ŋá/ 'to suck'. In this case there is no consonantal nasality; the nasal feature is realized as nasalization of the latter part of the vowel /ɔ/ in Fragment C, following an oral portion, B, and the aspiration of the initial stop, A. Fragment D, which is the consonantal part of the /ŋ/, is voiceless but oral, and as often in an [h]-sound, the transition of the formants of the flanking vowels can be traced through its duration.

In Sukuma, the nasal portion of the 'voiceless nasals' is often at least partly voiced or breathy voiced, as described in Maddieson (1991), whereas the parallel segments in Nyarwanda are fully-voiced (except after voiceless fricatives) but produced with a modified kind of voicing described by Demolin and Delvaux as whispery-voice.

7 PROSODIC CHARACTERISTICS

A discussion of Bantu phonetics would not be complete without reference to some of the studies of the major prosodic characteristics of the languages. As is well known, the great majority of the Bantu languages have a tonal distinction of High and Low tones, which often may combine into falling contours. The phonetic shapes of tone sequences of this type can usually be modeled on the basis of the position and height of local H targets, with the Low tones treated as automatically filled valleys between these points. Certain more complex patterns, such as those noted by Hombert (1990) in Fang and Roux (1995) in Xhosa, may require a more elaborate model, and provision would have to be made for the special effects of depression.

The most extensive body of work on the phonetics of tone in a single Bantu language concerns Chewa (Carleton 1996, Myers 1996, 1999a, 1999b, Myers and Carleton 1996). Detailed studies of this type not only illuminate the individual language studied but may provide insights into diachronic issues. For example, in Chewa, as is common cross-linguistically, the High pitch peak is realized at the end of the syllable to which it is associated (Myers 1999a). This pattern may form the basis for the frequent shifting of a High tone to a later syllable. These studies also address several issues in the relation between intonation and tone. For example, Myers (1999b) shows that syntactically unmarked yes/no questions are characterized by a slower rate of pitch declination than statements. Carleton (1996) demonstrated that units of paragraph length are organized by long-range patterns of tonal declination and resetting.

Some additional aspects of timing beyond those linked to prenasalization are discussed by Hubbard (1994, 1995). In both Nyambo and Ganda, she finds that the mean duration of a word is more accurately predicted from the number of moras it contains than from the number of syllables it contains. Hence these languages fit best into the typological category of mora-timed languages. We do not know how generally true this is of Bantu languages, or how this finding relates to the phrase-penultimate syllable lengthening which is a widespread feature of the family, or if different timing relations would be found in those Bantu languages with accent or stress (with or without tone).

Compared to the quantity of work on segmental phonetics, prosodic phonetics is relatively neglected. This in part is explicable by the fact that more appropriate conceptual frameworks for dealing with such aspects have only been developed in recent years. Prosodic phonetic analysis of Bantu languages is likely to provide some of the most exciting work in the next few years.

REFERENCES

Afido *et al.* 1989; Batibo 1985; Baumbach 1994, 1997; Bladon *et al.* 1987; Carleton 1996; Connell 2000; Creissels 1999c; Davey *et al.* 1982; Demolin and Delvaux 2001; Demolin *et al.* 1992, 1999; Dickens 1987; Doke 1926, 1931a, 1931b, 1954; Engstrand and Lodhi 1985; Fisch 1977 [1998]; Gowlett 1997; Greenberg 1951; Guma 1971; Guthrie 1967–71; Hardcastle and Brasington 1978; Hayward *et al.* 1989; Hombert 1990; Hubbard 1994, 1995; Huffman and Hinnebusch 1998; Hyman 1995b, 1999; IPA 1999; Jouannet 1983; Kuperus 1985; Kutsch Lojenga 2001; Labroussi 1999; Ladefoged 2000; Ladefoged and Maddieson 1996; Lanham 1958; Liljencrants and Lindblom 1972; Louw 1975; Lowe and Schadeberg 1997; Maddieson 1990, 1991, 1993; Maddieson and Ladefoged 1993; Maddieson *et al.* 1999; Maganga and Schadeberg 1992; Manuel 1990; Mathangwane 1998, 1999; Medjo Mvé 1997; Meeussen 1969 [1980]; Meinhof 1899; Möhlig 1997; Mpiranya 1997; Mutaka and Ebobissé 1996–7; Myers 1996, 1999a, 1999b; Myers and Carleton 1996; Nchimbi 1997; Nurse and Hinnebusch 1993; Paulian 1994; Pongweni 1990; Poulos and Louwrens 1994; Quilis *et al.* 1990; Renaud 1976; Roux 1995; Roux and Holtzhausen 1989; Rycroft 1980, 1981; Schadeberg 1982b, 1994–95; Schwartz *et al.* 1997; Sommer and Vossen 1992; Stewart 2000a; Thomas Vilakazi 1999; Thomas [Vilakazi] 2000; Traill 1990; Traill and Jackson 1988; Traill *et al.* 1987; Van der Veen 1986, 1987, 1991; Vossen 1997; Wright and Shryock 1993; Ziervogel 1959.

CHAPTER THREE

SEGMENTAL PHONOLOGY

Larry M. Hyman

1 INTRODUCTION

As in other parts of the grammar, Bantu segmental phonology can be characterized as a theme and variations: despite the large number of languages and great geographic expanse that they cover, the most noteworthy properties concerning Bantu syllable structure, consonant/vowel inventories, and phonological processes are robustly attested throughout the Bantu area. However, these shared features, although striking, mask a wide range of differences which are equally, if not more, important in understanding Bantu phonology in general. It is helpful in this regard to consider both the phonological system inherited from Proto-Bantu (PB), as well as the innovations, often areally diffused, which characterize present-day Bantu subgroups and individual languages.

2 PROTO-BANTU

According to most Bantuists, e.g. Meeussen (1967), PB had the relatively simple consonant and vowel systems in (1).

(1) (a) consonants   (b) vowels (long and short)

p	t	c	k	i̯	u̯
b	d	j	g	i	u
m	n	ɲ		e	o
				a	

Of the two series of oral consonants in (1a), all scholars agree that the voiceless series *p, *t, *k were pronounced as stops. There is, however, disagreement as to whether *b, *d, *g should be reconstructed as stops or as continuants, i.e. *β, *l, *ɣ, as they are pronounced in many daughter languages today. It also is not clear whether *c and *j should be viewed as palatal stops or affricates – or whether they were palatal at all. Many Bantu languages realize *c as /s/, and some realize *j as /z/. Realizations of the latter as /y/ or /j/ (i.e. [dʒ]) are, however, probably more common. Although various scholars have occasionally posited additional consonants and series of consonants (e.g. fortis vs. lenis stops) in the proto system, none of these have been demonstrated to the satisfaction of the Bantuist community. On the other hand, much more complex systems have been innovated in the daughter languages as seen in Chapter 2 and below.

There is, by comparison, more stability in the vowel system, which is reconstructed as in (1b). Most scholars agree that PB had seven distinct vowels (7V). As transcribed in (1b), there would have been an opposition in the high vowels between [+ATR] *i̯ [i] and *u̯ [u] and [−ATR] *i [ɪ] and *u [ʊ]. Such a system, exemplifed from Nande DJ42 in (2a), is widely attested, especially in eastern Bantu:

(2) (a) *lịm-*   'exterminate'   *lụm-*   'be animated'
       lim-   'cultivate'   *lúm-*   'bite'
       lem-   'fail to carry sth. heavy'   *tom-*   'put aside'
       lam-   'heal'
    (b) *ting-*   'hook'   *tung-*   'become thin'
       beng-   'chase'   *tóng-*   'construct'
       kéng-   'observe'   *tɔ́ng-*   'gather up'
       tang-   'flow'

Other Bantu languages such as Koyo C24 in (2b) have the 7V system /i, e, ɛ, u, o, ɔ, a/, where there is instead an advanced tongue root (ATR) opposition in the mid vowels. Such a system is particularly frequent in western Bantu. (See Stewart 1983 and Hyman 1999 for further discussion of the reconstructed PB vowel system.)

The syllable structures allowed in PB were limited to those in (3).

(3)   (a) CV, CVV   (b) V, N

Most syllables in PB had one of the two shapes in (3a): a single consonant followed by a vowel that was either short (V) or long (VV), e.g. **pád-* 'scrape', **páad-* 'quarrel'. The syllable shapes in (3b) were most likely limited to prefixes, e.g. **à-* 'class 1 subject prefix', **ǹ-* 'class 9 noun prefix'. PB roots with non-identical vowels in sequence have also been reconstructed, e.g. **bàịj-* 'carve', **bịad-* 'give birth', but may have involved 'weak' intervening consonants, e.g. glides, that dropped out in pre-PB. Many vowel sequences, including some identical ones, e.g. **-tú-ud-* 'rest, put down load', are analyzable as heteromorphemic, such that Meeussen (1979) questioned whether PB actually had long vowels at all. Others have subsequently arisen through the loss of PB consonants, e.g. **ŋ-gobị, *n-jidá, *n-jogu* > Kamba E55 *ŋ-goi* 'baby sling', *n-zɪa* 'hunger', *n-zou* 'elephant' (Hinnebusch 1974). In many languages this consonant loss is restricted and results in synchronic alternations between C and Ø. For example, while **did-* 'cry' is realized *li-a* (with FV -a) in Swahili G42, the final **d* is realized [l] before the applicative suffix *-i-*: *lil-i-a* 'cry to/for'. Since this form derives from **did-id-a*, Swahili appears to disallow /l/-deletion in two successive syllables (forbidding **li-i-a* in this case, even though words with three vowels in a row do appear in the language, e.g. *teu-a* 'appoint'). In contrast with PB **VV sequences, which are tautosyllabic, neo-VV sequences typically remain heterosyllabic. On the other hand, many Bantu languages have lost the inherited V/VV opposition, e.g. **dóot-* 'dream' > Tonga M64 *lót-*, Cewa N31b *lót-*, Tswana S31 *lór-*. Others have lost the vowel length contrast only in onsetless syllables, but have retained and even favor CVV, where possible. This is the case in roots such as *-(y)er-* 'sweep' in Ganda EJ15, where the initial 'unstable-*y*' is realized in all environments except when preceded by a CV- prefix with which the following vowel fuses, e.g. *tw-éer-a* 'we sweep' vs. *a-yér-à* 'he sweeps', *ɲ-jér-a* 'I sweep'.

The last syllable type, a low tone nasal, is reconstructible in classes 9 and 10 noun prefixes, while syllabic nasal reflexes of the first person singular subject- and object prefixes derive from earlier **ni-*. The nasal of morpheme-internal nasal complexes (NC) sequences appears never to be itself syllabic, although it frequently conditions length on a preceding vowel, e.g. **gènd-* [gè:nd-] 'walk'. If correctly analyzed as two segments, NC constitutes the only consonant cluster in PB. This includes heteromorphemic N+N sequences, although these are subsequently degeminated in many Bantu languages.

At the same time, new syllabic nasals often derive from the loss of the vowel of *mV-prefixes, especially *mu-CV > $m̩$-CV > $ɴ$-CV.

Some Bantu languages have developed additional syllable structures, typically by the loss of vowels or consonants – or through borrowings. Most word-final vowels have been lost in Ruwund L53, whose word-final syllables therefore usually end in a consonant, e.g. *m-$bụda$, *du-$kúnị$ > $ń$-$vùl$ 'rain', $rú$-$kùn$ 'firewood' (Nash 1992). Basaá A43, on the other hand, has not only lost final vowels, e.g. *mu-$dúme$ > n-$lóm$ 'male', but also creates non-final closed syllables by syncopating the medial vowel of CVCVCV stems, e.g. $tiŋil$ 'untie' + a 'passive suffix' → $tiŋla$ (Lemb and de Gastines 1973). Closed syllables may also be found in incompletely assimilated borrowings, e.g. Swahili G42 m-$kristo$ 'Christian'; Yaka H31, $mártóo$ 'hammer' (<French $marteau$).

Most Bantu languages maintain a close approximation of the PB situation as far as syllable structure is concerned. The open syllable structure is, in fact, reinforced by the well-known Bantu agglutinative morphology. The typical structures of nouns and verbs are schematized in (4).

(4) (a) Nouns

	AUGMENT-	PREFIX-	STEM
	CV	CV	CV(V)CV
	V	N	CV(V)
		V	VCV

e.g. Bukusu EJ31

$kú$-mu≠$xono$	'arm'	(class 3)
$ó$-mu-$xasi$	'woman'	(class 1)
$é$-n-$juxi$	'bee'	(class 9)
$cí$-n-$juxi$	'bees'	(class 10)
$lí$-i-$beele$	'breast'	(class 5)

(b) Verbs

PI-	SP-	NEG	TP-	AP-	OP-	STEM
CV	CV	CV	CV	CV	CV	CV(V)CV ...
V	V	V	N			
N						

e.g. Nande DJ42 $mó$-tu- $téta$- ya -$mú$≠$túm$-a

PI- SP- NEG- AP- OP- ROOT- FV

'we didn't go and send him'

(PI = preinitial morpheme, including augment; SP = subject prefix; NEG = negative; TP = tense prefix; AP = aspect prefix; OP = object prefix; FV = inflectional final vowel)

(c) Verb stems

ROOT-	EXTENSION(S)-	FV
CVC	VC	V
CV	V	

e.g. Cewa N31b lim-its-il-an-a

ROOT-CAUS-APPL-REC-FV

'cause to cultivate for each other'

(CAUS = causative; APPL = applicative; REC = reciprocal)

In the above schemas, V stands for any of the seven PB vowels, while C stands for any of the proto-consonants, including, potentially, NC. The most common shape of each morpheme is given in the first row. As seen in (4a,b), pre-stem morphemes (prefixes) are restricted to the shapes CV-, V-, and N-. In (4c), on the other hand, we see that post-root morphemes (suffixes) have the shapes -VC- and -V-. Since most roots begin and end with a C, morpheme concatenation provides almost no potential for consonant clusters, but rather a general alternation of consonant-vowel-consonant etc. The one exception to this occurs when Vs meet across a morpheme boundary. In this case specific rules modify the resulting V + V inputs (see §3.2). Other assimilatory and dissimilatory alternations occur when morphemes meet, some of which are restricted to specific domains, e.g. the stem (root + suffixes). Many of these alternations produce output segments beyond those in the above V and C inventories. The most widespread phenomena are treated in the following sections, first for vowels (§3), then for consonants (§4).

3 VOWEL PHONOLOGY

While PB had the 7V system in (1b), the majority of Bantu languages spoken in a large and contiguous area have merged the degree 1 and 2 vowels to achieve the five-vowel (5V) system in (5a).

(5)   Swahili G40   Budu D35   Bafia A53

	(a) i u	(b) i u	(c) i ɨ u
	ε ɔ	ɪ ʊ	e ə o
	a	e o	ε ʌ ɔ
		ε ɔ	a ɑ
		a	

A few languages have gone the other direction and developed the 9V system in (5b). While this system appears to be underlying in Budu D35 (Kutsch Lojenga 1994a), other languages such as Nande DJ42 in nearby Northeast République Démocratique du Congo and the Sotho-Tswana S30 group in South derive the eighth and ninth vowels [e] and [o] from the tensing/raising of the degree 3 vowels *ε and *ɔ, respectively. Finally, some of the languages in zone A, such as Bafia A53 in (5c), have developed 'rectangular' vowel systems with back unrounded vowels (see Guarisma, Ch. 17, this volume) and also nasalized vowels, e.g. in the Teke B70 group, both of which also appear in Grassfields Bantu (see Watters, Ch. 14, this volume).

3.1 Distributional constraints on underlying vowels

As indicated in §2, Bantu phonology is highly sensitive to morphological considerations. Underlying vowel distribution within specific morphological slots and morphological or prosodic domains is thus highly restricted in both 7V and 5V languages. Meeussen (1967), e.g. allows for the following vowels in each of the indicated positions:

(6) PB vowel reconstructions by position

	*i̯	*u̯	*i	*u	*e	*o	*a
first stem syllable	x	x	x	x	x	x	x
final stem vowel	x	x	x	x	x	x	x
elsewhere	x		x	x			x

As seen, the seven vowels of PB contrast in the first and last syllables of a stem, but not in prefixes, extensions or stem-internal position, where only four vowels contrast. In a few cases involving reduplication, the vowel *u appears in the first two syllables of a verb, e.g. *dudum- 'rumble, thunder', *pupum- 'boil up, boil over'. The root *tákun- 'chew', on the other hand, appears to be exceptional.

Some languages, particularly 5V ones, have further restricted this distribution by position within the stem or word. Thus, Punu B43, which has the underlying system /i, u, ε, ɔ, a/, restricts /ε/ and /ɔ/ to stem-initial syllables only (Kwenzi Mickala 80). In Bobangi C32 (7V), /u/ may not occur in prefixes, nor may any of the rounded vowels /u, o, ɔ/ appear later than the second syllable in stems.

3.2 Vowel alternations

In addition to underlying constraints on vowel distribution, most Bantu languages severely restrict the sequencing of vowels, particularly within stems. Thus, while Punu B43 allows only /i, u, a/ in post-stem position, /a/ is reduced to schwa in this position, and the expected post-stem sequences [əCi] and [əCu] surface instead as [iCi] and [uCu], e.g. the historical suffix sequences /-am-il-/ (positional-applicative) and /-am-ul-/ (positional-reversive tr.) are realized [-imin-] and [-umun-]. In addition, a post-stem /a/ ([ə]) assimilates to a FV -*i*, and both post-stem /a/ and /i/ assimilate to a FV -*u* (Fontaney 1980). The Punu case demonstrates two general properties of Bantu vowel systems: (i) there are typically more contrasting underlying vowels in the stem-initial syllable, and (ii) vowels in this position may be exempt from reduction and assimilation processes that post-stem vowels undergo. Ruwund L53 (5V) once had the same vowel distribution as Punu, disallowing mid vowel from post-stem position. However, it has since undergone considerable vowel reduction, e.g. by dropping most word-final vowels, e.g. *mu≠ána > mwáàn 'child', *mu≠kádị > mú≠kàj 'wife' (Nash 1992). While unusual in tolerating word-final closed syllables (analyzed with a phantom vowel by Nash), Ruwund is perhaps unique in its overall vowel system in (7a).

(7) (a) i   u   ii   uu
                    ee   oo
        a   aa
    (b) *e > i   e.g. *dèm- > lím   'be lame', *dèd- > -lìl   'raise (child)'
        *o > a   e.g. *bón- > -màn   'see',   *pót- > pwàt   'twist'

As seen in (7a), short /e, o/ are missing, since they have reduced, respectively, to the peripheral vowels [i] and [a], respectively, as illustrated in (7b). In this atypical case, vowels in the stem-initial syllable were successfully targeted.

By far the most widely attested assimilatory process is vowel harmony, particularly vowel height harmony (VHH). As indicated in (8) and (9):

(8) Front height harmony (FHH)
    (a) General: i → e / {e, o}   C ___
    (b) Extended: i → e / {e, o, a}   C ___

(9) Back height harmony (BHH)
    (a) General: u → o / {o}   C ___
    (b) Extended: u → o / {e, o}   C ___

the historical degree-2 vowels (*i, *u) harmonize in height with a preceding mid vowel. The process is frequently different with respect to the front vs. back vowel (Bleek 1862). In a wide range of central and eastern Bantu languages, degree-2 /i/ lowers after both /e/ and /o/, while degree-2 /u/ lowers only after /o/. Examples of such 'asymmetric' FHH vs. BHH are seen from Nyamwezi F22 in (10), based on

Maganga and Schadeberg (1992):

(10) Root + Applicative *-ıl-*   Root + Separative *-ʋl-*

    (a) *ßis-íl-*   'hide for/at'   *ßis-ʋ́l-*   'find out'

      gub-íl-   'put on lid for/at'   *gub-ʋ́l-*   'take off lid'

      pıınd-ıl-   'bend for/at'   *pıınd-ʋl-*   'overturn'

      shʋʋn-ıl-   'gnaw for/at'   *shʋʋn-ʋl-*   'show teeth'

      gaß-ıl-   'divide for/at'   *gaß-ʋl-*   'divide'

    (b) *ßon-íl-*   'see for/at'   *hong-ól-*   'break off'

    (c) *zeeng-el-* 'build for/at'   *zeeng-ʋl-*   'build'

There is no harmony in (10a), where the root vowel is either high or low. In (10b) VHH applies to both *-ıl-* and *-ʋl-* when the root vowel is /o/. However, in (10c), where the root vowel is /e/, *-ıl-* lowers to *-el-*, but *-ʋl-* remains unchanged. This contrasts with the situation in the E40 group, e.g. Gusii E42 (7V), as well as in many Northwest Bantu languages, e.g. Mongo C61 (7V), whose vowel systems are analyzed as /i, e, ɛ, u, o, ɔ, a/. In languages such as Mongo-Nkundo in (11), the back degree-2 vowel also harmonizes, and FHH and BHH are thus 'symmetric':

(11) Root + Applicative *-el-*   Root + Separative *-ol-*

    (a) *-iy-el-*   'steal for/at'   *-is-ol-*   'uncover'

      -lúk-el-   'paddle for/at'   *-kund-ol-* 'dig up'

      -ét-el-   'call for/at'   *-bét-ol-*   'wake up'

      -tóm-el-   'send for/at'   *-komb-ol-* 'open'

      -kamb-el- 'work for/at'   *-bák-ol-*   'untie'

    (b) *-kɔt-ɛl-*   'cut for/at'   *-mɔm-ɔl-* 'unglue'

      -kend-ɛl- 'go for/at'   *-téng-ɔl-* 'straighten out'

As indicated in (8b), harmony of /i/ to [e] after /a/ is also attested, particularly in languages towards the Southwest of the Bantu zone, e.g. Mbundu H21a, Kwangali K33a, Herero R31. While VHH is generally perseverative and limited to the stem domain minus the FV, some languages – particularly those with symmetric FHH/BHH – have extended harmony to the FV and to prefixes. It is important to note that in many 5V Bantu languages, only those /i/ vowels that derive from *i harmonize, while those that derive from *ɪ do not. Other languages have modified this original situation and harmonize the perfective ending *-ɪd-e as well (Bastin 1983b). In Yaka H31 and certain dialects of Kongo H10, VHH is anticipatory and is triggered primarily by the *-e of perfective *-ɪd-e. In addition, some of the same languages that have symmetric VHH have extended the process to prefixes, e.g. Mituku D13 (7V) /tú-mú-lok-é/ → tó-mó-lok-é 'we bewitch (subjunctive)'. For more discussion of variations in Bantu VHH, see Leitch (1996), Hyman (1999) and references cited therein.

    Besides height, other features may also participate in vowel harmony. Closely related Konzo DJ41 and Nande DJ42 have introduced an ATR harmony, whereby /ɪ, ʋ, ɛ, ɔ/ become [i, u, e, o] when followed by /ɪ̯/ or /ʋ̯/. They thus have an underlying 7V system (cf. (2)), but introduce two additional, non-contrasting vowels, [e] and [o], by ATR harmony. Clements (1991) provides an overarching framework to treat VHH and ATR harmony in related fashion. Other Bantu languages have innovated rounding harmonies, e.g. perseverative *i → u / u* ___ in Lengola D12 vs. anticipatory *i → u /* ___ *u* in Punu B43. In Maore G44D, regressive rounding harmony even reaches the root vowel: *u#finiki-a* 'cover', *u#funuku-a* 'uncover'. Finally, it should be noted that many Northwest Bantu 7V languages modify /a/ to [ɛ] after /ɛ/ and to [ɔ] after /ɔ/, e.g. Bakweri A22, Tiene B81, Lingala C36d or, in the case of Bembe H11 (5V), to [e] and [o], respectively.

The above shows the assimilation of one vowel to another across a consonant. When vowels occur in direct sequence, they typically undergo gliding or deletion. Thus, in Ganda EJ15, when followed by a non-identical vowel, e.g. the FV -a, the front vowels /i, e/ glide to [y], as in (12a), and the back vowels /u, o/ glide to [w], as in (12b):

(12) (a) /lí-a/   'eat'   [lyáà ...]   cf. a≠lî-dd-è   'he has eaten'
          /ké-a/   'dawn'   [kyáà ...]   lú≠kê-dd-è   'it has dawned'
      (b) /gu-a/   'fall'   [gwaa ...]   a≠gú-dd-è   'he has fallen'
          /mo-a/   'shave'   [mwaa ...]   a≠mwé-dd-è   'he has shaved'
      (c) /bá-a/   'be'   [báà ...]   a≠bâ-dd-è   'he has been'
          /tá-a/   'let go'   [tâa ...]   a≠tâ-dd-è   'he has let go'
                                             (SM + Root + Perf + FV)

As seen in the outputs, gliding of /i, e/ and /u, o/ is accompanied by compensatory lengthening of the following vowel. In Ganda, this length will be realized if word-internal (or if the above verb stems are followed by a clitic). Otherwise it, as well as the length obtained from concatenation of /a/ + /a/ in (13c) will undergo final vowel shortening (FVS), e.g. ku≠lyáa = kô 'to eat a little' vs. ku≠lyâ 'to eat'.

The details of vowel coalescence may depend on whether the vowels are tautomorphemic vs. heteromorphemic, and whether the vowel sequence is contained within a word or not. Thus, instead of gliding, the mid vowels /e, o/ join /a/ in undergoing deletion when followed by a non-identical vowel across a word boundary:

(13) (a) mu≠sibê + o≠mû   → [mu.si.bóò.mû]   'one prisoner'
          mu≠walâ + o≠mû   → [mu.wa.lóò.mû]   'one girl'
      (b) m≠bogô + e≠mû   → [m.bo.géè.mû]   'one buffalo'
          n≠diga + e≠mû   → [n.di.gee.mû]   'one sheep'
      (c) ba≠sibê + a≠ba-o → [ba.si.báà.bo]   'those prisoners'
          ba≠kô   + a≠ba-o → [ba.káà.bo]   'those in-laws'

As also seen, deletion, like gliding, is accompanied by compensatory lengthening.

In many cases, the expected glide may not be realized if preceded by a particular consonant or followed by a particular vowel. In Ganda, an expected [w] is not realized when preceded by /f, v/, e.g. /fu-a/ → fw-aa →[faa ...] 'die'. Similarly, an expected [y] is 'absorbed' into a preceding by /s/, /z/ or palatal consonant, e.g. /se-a/ → sy-aa → [saa ...] 'grind'. In Ruwund L53, [w] is usually absorbed when preceded by an /m/ or /k/ and followed by /o/, e.g. /ku≠ooš-a/ → [kwooš] ~ [kooš] 'to burn'.

In cases where /a/ is followed by /i/ or /u/ (typically from PB *į and *ų), a coalescence process can produce [ee] and [oo], respectively, e.g. Yao P21 /ma≠ísó/ → méésó 'eyes'. This coalescence also occurs in the process of 'imbrication' (§4.2), whereby the [i] of the perfective suffix is infixed and fuses with a base vowel, e.g. Bemba M42 ísal-il-e → ísail-e → íseel-e 'close (tr.) + perfective'.

With these observations, we now can summarize three of the five sources of vowel length in Bantu: (i) from underlying representations (lim- 'cultivate', liim- 'extinguish'); (ii) from vowel concatenation, e.g. /bá≠agal-a/ → [báàgala] 'they want'; (iii) from gliding + compensatory lengthening, e.g. /tú≠agal-a/ → [twáàgala] 'we want'. A fourth source is the rule of vowel lengthening that occurs before a moraic nasal + consonant, e.g. /ku-ń≠sib-a/ → [kúúnsìba] 'to tie me' (cf. §4.1.5). A fifth source is penultimate vowel lengthening, which occurs in most eastern and southern Bantu languages which have lost the lexical vowel length contrast, e.g. Cewa N31b, t-a≠meeny-a 'we have hit', t-a≠meny-eel-a 'we have hit for', t-a-meny-el-aan≠a 'we have hit for each other'.

Besides these lengthening processes, vowel shortening may also apply in one of three contexts. First, there may be FVS with languages varying as to whether this occurs at the end of a word or phrase (or 'clitic group', as in Ganda EJ15). Second, there are a number of languages which restrict long vowels to penultimate or antepenultimate position. Thus, any long vowel that precedes phrase-antepenultimate position will be shortened in Mwiini G412 (Kisseberth and Abasheikh 1974): *reeba* 'stop', *reeb-er-a* 'stop for', *reb-er-an-a* 'stop for each other'. Similar observations have been made about the Kongo H10 languages and nearby Yaka H31 (which also restricts long vowels to occurring within the stem-initial syllable): *zááy-á* 'know', *zááy-il-á* 'know + appl', *zááy-is-á* 'cause to know'; but: *záy-ákán-á* 'be known', with shortening. In Safwa M25, the shortening process appears to count the two moras of a CVV penultimate syllable: *a-gaa≠gúz-y-a* 'he can sell', *a-ga≠buúz-y-a* 'he can ask' vs. *a-ga≠buz-y-aág-a* 'he may ask'. Finally, a few languages have closed syllable shortening, e.g. before geminate consonants in Ganda EJ15: /tú-a-eé≠ 'tt-a/ → [twéttà] 'we killed ourselves'.

In addition to length, vowel height may be sensitive to boundaries. In a number of Interlacustrine languages, historical *i and *u lower to [e] and [o] at the beginning of a constituent. This is particularly noticeable in comparing the augment + prefix sequences across languages, e.g. class 3/4 *u-mu-/i-mi-* in Rwanda DJ61 vs. *o-mu-/e-mi-* in Haya EJ22. In Nyambo EJ21, lowering of /i/ and /u/ occurs only initially in a phrase. As a result, the lowered [o] of the phrase-initial form, *o-mu≠kázi* 'woman', alternates with [u] in *ku-bón ú-mu≠kázi* 'to see a woman', where the final -a of *ku≠bón-a* 'to see' has been deleted – in this case, without compensatory lengthening. Besides lowering, vowels are sometimes deleted initially, especially in roots, e.g. PB **jị̀b-a* > *ìb-a* > Cewa N31b [ba] 'steal'. Although restructured as a prefix, the original [i] appears in the imperative form *i-ba* 'steal!' (phrase-finally, [iiba]), where it is needed to fill out the bisyllabic minimality condition on Cewa words.

4 CONSONANT PHONOLOGY

As indicated in §2, PB is believed to have had a relatively simple consonant system. In addition, all syllables were open in PB, and syllable onsets mostly consisted of a single consonant. The two possible exceptions to this are nasal + consonant and consonant + glide.

4.1 Nasal + consonant

Besides the consonants in (1a), PB and most present-day languages also have NC, written *mp, mb, nt, nd, ŋk, ŋg,* etc., and analyzed either as clusters of homorganic nasal + consonant or single prenasalized consonants, e.g. **búmb-* 'mould', **gend-* 'go', **táŋg-* 'read' (Herbert 1986). The class 9/10 nasal prefix N- produces equivalent NCs across morphemes, e.g. Tuki A64 *m̀≠búā* 'dog', *ǹ≠dòànè* 'cow', *ŋ̀≠gì* 'fly'. The PB first person singular morpheme is also often realized as a homorganic nasal in present-day languages, e.g. Ganda EJ.15 *m̀≠bal-a* 'I count', *ǹ≠dúm-à* 'I bite', *ŋ̀≠gw-a* 'I fall'. While the prefix is an underspecified homorganic N- in 9/10, we know from such forms as Yao P21 *n-áá≠díp-il-é* 'I paid', where the nasal appears before a vocalic tense marker, that the 1sg prefix has an underlying /n/. In some languages where 9/10 is N-, the 1sg prefix has a CV shape, e.g. Swahili G42, Cewa N31b *ni-*, Shona S10 *ndi-*, Nande DJ42 *ɲi-* (alternating with *n-*).

The 9/10 prefix *N-*, on the other hand, rarely occurs directly before a vowel, since roots generally begin with a consonant.

In PB, noun and verb roots did not begin with NC. Root-initial NC has subsequently been introduced in Bantu languages which have lost root-initial *jį* or *ji*, e.g. Kalanga S16 *ngín-a* 'enter' (*jįngid-*), *mb-á* 'sing' (*jimb-*). This is true also of the root *-ntu* 'person, thing, entity', which derives from *jįntu*. In other cases where a stem appears to begin with NC, the nasal may have originally been a prefix, e.g. transferred from 9/10 with the *N-* to another class, which then imposes its own prefix. It is sometimes still possible to analyze such forms as double prefixes, e.g. Cewa N31b *chi-m≠bombó* 7/8 'glutton' (cf. *m≠bombó* 1/2 'greedy person').

While most Bantu languages preserve NC, many have restrictions either on which N+C combinations are possible, or in where within the word structure NC may occur. Thus, Tiene B81 allows NC across morpheme boundaries, e.g. class 9 *n≠tàbà* 'goat', but simplifies stem-internal NC, e.g. *mù≠òtò* 'person' (*-(jį)ntu*). In the same language, stem-internal *mb*, *nd* become [m, n] with compensatory lengthening or diphthongization of the preceding vowel, while *ŋg* is deleted with no trace, e.g. *tùùm-à* 'cook' (*tùmb-*), *kúón-a* 'desire' (*kúnd-*), *tú-a* 'build' (*túng-*). On the other hand, Yao P21 deletes a root-initial voiced consonant after the 1sg prefix *N-*, but not after the 9/10 prefix *N-*. Thus, /ku-n≠gaadil-a/ → *kuu≠ŋáádila* 'to stare at me' vs. *ỳ≠gùbò* 'cloth' (< PB *ŋ≠gùbò*).

Where a consonant C is realized differently (C′) after N, it is important to note that this may be due to either of two logical possibilities: C is modified to C′ after N; or C′ becomes C except after N. The latter situation is frequently found with respect to the weakening of *p* to [h] or [w], which is typically blocked after a homorganic nasal, e.g. Nyambo EJ21 *kú≠h-a* 'to give' vs. *m≠p-a* 'give me!'. Through subsequent changes, the relation between C and C′ can become quite distant. In Bukusu EJ31c, the [h] observed in Nyambo has dropped out, and the preserved labial stop becomes voiced after N, such that the alternation is now *úxu≠a* 'to give' vs. *ḿ≠b-a* 'give me!.' Depending on the nature of the post-nasal consonant, the various N+C inputs can undergo a variety of processes:

4.1.1 Nasal + voiceless stop

Perhaps the most widespread process affecting NC is post-nasal voicing, attested in Nande DJ42, Kikuyu E51, Bukusu EJ31c and Yao P21. Examples from Yao are illustrated in (14).

(14)   (a) *ku≠pélék-a*   'to send'   (b) *kuu-m≠bélek-a*   'to send me'
            ku≠túm-á   'to order'   *kuu-n≠dúm-a*   'to order me'
            ku≠cápíl-a   'to wash'   *kuu-ŋ≠jápil-a*   'to wash for me'
            ku≠kwéél-á   'to climb'   *kuu-ŋ≠gwéel-a*   'to climb on me'

Another process affecting voiceless stops is aspiration, e.g. in Cewa N31b, Kongo H10, Pokomo E71 and Swahili G42. The illustration in (15) is from Kongo:

(15)   (a) /ku-N≠pun-á/   →   *kú-m≠phun-á*   'to deceive me'
           (b) /ku-N≠tál-a/   →   *kú-n≠thal-a*   'to look at me'
           (c) /ku-N≠kiyíla/ →   *kú-ɲ≠khiyíl-a*   'to visit me'

The resulting NCh unit may then undergo nasal effacement (*nt* > *nth* > *th*), as in Swahili G42, or de-stopping (*nt* > *nth* > *nh*), as in Rwanda DJ61, Rundi DJ62, and Shona S10, where *umu≠(jį)ntu* 'person' is realized as *(u)mu≠nhu* (cf. Nyamwezi F22 *m≠nhʊ*).

The resulting *Nh* may then simplify to *N*. This is presumably the chain of events that have characterized the southern Tanzanian languages Hehe G62, Pangwa G64 and Kinga G65, which have *nt* > *n*, as seen from closely related Wanji G66, which has *nt* > *nh*.

4.1.2 Nasal + voiceless fricative

Three different strategies are also commonly seen when a nasal is followed by a voiceless fricative. First, the nasal may simply be effaced, even in languages such as Yao P21, which voice post-nasal voiceless stops, e.g. *ku-n≠sóosa* → *kuu≠sóosa* 'to look for me'. The second strategy is seen in Nande DJ42, which extends post-nasal voicing to include fricatives, e.g. *o-lu≠sáŋgá* 'pearl', pl. *e-n≠záŋgá*. A third strategy found in languages such as Kongo H10, Yaka H31 and Venda S21 is affrication. As seen in the Kongo forms in (16), post-nasal affrication can also affect voiced fricatives:

(16) Post-nasal affrication in Kongo (Carter 1984)

> (a) /ku-N≠fíl-a/ → *kú-m≠pfil-a* 'to lead me'
> /ku-N≠síb-a/ → *kú-n≠tsib-a* 'to curse me'
> (b) /ku-N≠vun-á/ → *kú-m≠bvun-á* 'to deceive me'
> /ku-N≠zól-a/ → *kú-n≠dzol-a* 'to love me'

In Tuki A64, which has nasal effacement before voiceless consonants, /n+s/ becomes [ts], as expected, but /n+f/ becomes [p], e.g. /a-n≠seya-ḿ/ → *a≠tseya-ḿ* 'he abuses me', /a-n≠fununa-ḿ/→*a≠pununa-ḿ* 'he wakes me up'. This is presumably because [f] comes from earlier *p*. Thus, besides conditioning changes which can be characterized as 'strengthening' or 'fortition', a nasal can block the opposite lenition processes (e.g. *p* > *f*).

4.1.3 Nasal + voiced consonant

As mentioned above and seen in (17a),

(17) (a) /ku-n≠búúcil-a/ → *kuu≠múúcil-a* 'to be angry with me'
> /ku-n≠láp-á/ → *kuu≠náp-a* 'to admire me'
> /ku-n≠jíím-a/ → *kuu≠ɲíím-a* 'to begrudge me'
> /ku-n≠gónék-a/ → *kuu≠ɲónek-a* 'to make me sleep'
> (b) /ku-n≠mál-a/ → *kuu≠mál-a* 'to finish me'
> /ku-n≠nósy-a/ → *kuu≠nósy-a* 'to take care of me'
> /ku-n≠ɲál-a/ → *kuu≠ɲál-a* 'to cut me in small pieces'
> /ku-n≠ŋáádil-a/ → *kuu≠ɲáádil-a* 'to play around with me'

Yao P21 deletes post-nasal voiced consonants – other than [d], e.g. *ku-n≠dípa* → *kuu-n≠dípa* 'to pay me'. This includes nasal consonants in (17b), since many Bantu languages do not tolerate NN sequences. On the other hand, voiced continuants may alternate with stops (or affricates) after a nasal, e.g. Ganda EJ15 /n≠láb-a/ → *n≠dáb-à* 'I see', Tuki A64 /a-n≠rama-ḿ/ → *a≠dama-ḿ* 'he pulls me'.

Post-nasal voiced consonants may also be nasalized, in which case a geminate nasal is produced. This is most readily observed in the case of Meinhof's Law. Known also as the Ganda Law, and illustrated from that language in (18):

(18) /n≠bomb-a/ → *m≠momb-a* 'I escape'
> /n≠limb-a/ → *n≠nimb-a* 'I lie'
> /n≠jung-a/ → *ɲ≠ɲung-a* 'I join'
> /n≠gend-a/ → *ŋ≠ŋend-a* 'I go'

a nasal + voiced consonant becomes a geminate nasal when the next syllable also begins with a nasal. The original motivation for this change is seen as the simplification of NCVNC sequences (cf. §4.5). However, many of the languages have extended the process to include forms where the second nasal is not an NC complex, e.g. Ganda EJ15 /n≠lim-a/ → n≠nim-a 'I cultivate'. Interestingly, Yao P21, which fails to delete [d] after a nasal in an oral context, will as a result of Meinhof's Law do so if the following syllable is an NC complex, e.g. /ku-n≠dííng-a/ → ku-n≠nííng-a → kuu≠nííng-a 'to try me'.

4.1.4 Other processes

The above seems to indicate that Bantu languages prefer that post-nasal consonants be [+voice] rather than [−voice] and [−continuant] rather than [+continuant]. Voiceless stops tend to become aspirated, and voiced stops tend to become nasalized. While these generalizations reflect the common processes affecting post-nasal consonants, it is important to note that opposing 'counter-processes', though less common, are also found. For example, voiced stops are devoiced and variably pronounced as ejectives in Tswana S31 and Sotho S33: bón-a 'see!', m≠pón-á 'see me!'; dís-á 'watch', n≠tís-á 'watch me!'. Aspirated stops are deaspirated in Nguni languages, e.g. Ndebele S45 ulu≠thi 'stick', pl. izin≠ti. Affricates become deaffricated in a number of languages, e.g. Shona S10 bvum-a 'agree, admit', vs. m≠vum-o 'permission, agreement'. Finally, and perhaps most unusual, nasal consonants are denasalized after another nasal in Punu B43, Lingala C36d, Bushong C83, Kongo H10, Yaka H31, e.g. Yaka m≠bák-íní 'I carved' (mak- 'carve'), n≠dúúk-íní 'I smelt' (nuuk-).

4.1.5 Moricity

In most Bantu languages there is no vowel length opposition before an NC complex. Rather, as seen in many of the cited examples, the preceding vowel is frequently lengthened. The standard interpretation is that this nasal is 'moraic', i.e. it contributes a unit of length or 'beat', which readily transfers to the preceding vowel. It also is potentially a tone-bearing unit. This is most transparently seen in languages which allow NN sequences, or when the nasal is syllabic and phrase initial, e.g. Haya E22 ḿ-bwa 'dog'. However, even when the nasal loses its syllabicity and compensatorily lengthens the preceding vowel, some languages still treat it as a tone-bearing unit, e.g. Ganda EJ15, while others do not, e.g. Haya EJ22, Bemba M42 (see Ch. 4).

4.1.6 New cases of NC

While the preceding subsections characterize the phonology of NC complexes inherited from PB, many Bantu languages have introduced new sequences of N+C. The most common source is the loss of [u] in mu- prefixes, e.g. Swahili G42 m≠thu 'person', m≠toto 'child'. The resulting syllabic [m] may then undergo homorganic nasal assimilation, as it does in most dialects of Yao P21, e.g. ŋ' ≠kúlú 'elder sibling' 1, ǹ'≠sééNgó 'horn of antelope' 3, ŋ'≠gólógolo 'in the weasel' 18 (N' = syllabic). The loss of the [u] of mu- prefixes also extends to the second person plural SP and the class 1 OP, but will frequently not take place if followed by a vowel or NC, e.g. Yao mu≠uso 'bow of boat' 3, muu≠ndu 'person' 1, mw-ii≠gaasa 'handful' 18 (cf. (d)i≠gaasa 'palm of hand' 5). Vowel-deletion can also be blocked if the stem is monosyllabic, e.g. mu≠si 'village' 3.

The resulting NC may contrast phonetically or phonologically with PB *NC in several ways. First, as the Yao examples illustrate, the nasal from *mu- is typically syllabic, while the nasal from *NC loses its syllabicity (Hyman and Ngunga 1997). Second, the nasal from *mu- does not condition the same alternations on the following consonant (e.g. voiceless stops do not become voiced after N'- in Yao). In Tswana S31, where m+b is normally realized [mp] (cf. §4.1.4), mu- loses its vowel when followed by stem-initial /b/, which in turn is realized [m], e.g. mu≠bús-i → m≠músí 'governor' (cf. bús-á 'to govern'). Contrast this last example with Matuumbi̧ P13 (Odden 1996), where class 9/10 N- does not condition changes on voiced stops (lu̧≠gói̧ 'braided rope', pl. ŋ≠gói̧), but N'- from *mu- does (e.g. mu≠gaála ~ ŋ≠ŋaála 'in the storage place' 18). A third difference is that N'- does not condition lengthening on the preceding vowel, cf. Haya EJ22 /a-ka-ń-biŋg-a/ → a-káá-m-biŋg-a 'he chased me' vs. /a-ka-mú≠biŋg-a/ → a-ka-ḿ≠biŋg-a 'he chased him'. Finally, there can be a tonal difference, even in cases where there is no difference in syllabicity. Thus, in Basaá A43, class 3 N- (<*mu-) is a tone-bearing unit, while class 9 N- is not. Thus, the rule of high tone spreading applies in the phrase púbá m≠bɔndɔ 'white lion' (<m≠bɔndɔ 'lion' 9), but not in púbá m≠ɓomga 'white hammer' (<m≠ɓomga 'hammer' 3), since, although non-syllabic, the m- in this case 'counts' as the tone-bearing unit to which the high tone spreads.

4.2 Consonant + high vowel

Besides the post-nasal environment, consonants are frequently realized differently before high vs. non-high vowels. First and foremost is the process of frication which affects consonants when they are followed by *i̧, and *u̧, producing changes such as those schematized in (19).

(19)   (a) $*pi̧ > p^H i̧ > pfi̧$ $> fi̧ > fi$
            $*bi̧ > b^H i̧ > bvi̧$ $> vi̧ > vi$
      (b) $> psi̧ > (tsi̧) > si̧ > si$
                  $> bzi̧ > (dzi̧) > zi̧ > zi$
      (c) $*ti̧ > t^H i̧ > tsi̧$ $> si̧ > si$
            $*di̧ > d^H i̧ > dzi̧$ $> zi̧ > zi$
      (d) $*ci̧ > c^H i̧$ $> si̧ > si$
            $*ji̧ > j^H i̧$ $> zi̧ > zi$
      (e) $*ki̧ > k^H i̧ > ksi̧ > (tsi̧) > si̧ > si$
            $*gi̧ > g^H i̧ > gzi̧ > (dzi̧) > zi̧ > zi$

As indicated, these changes are first triggered by the development of 'noise' in the release of a consonant before the tense high vowels *i̧ and *u̧. Indicated as 'ᴴ' in (19), the present-day reflex can, in fact, be aspiration, as in Makua P31 – cf. Kalanga S16 thúm-á 'sew' (*tu̧m-) vs. túm-á 'send' (*-túm-). Similarly, /t, d/ are aspirated before /i/ in Doko C31 (7V): /ká≠tísá/, /í-dínó/ → [ká≠tʰísá] 'traverse', [i≠dʰíno] 'tooth'. In most languages, however, Cᴴ is further modified either to an affricate or fricative, as indicated, e.g. Ngom B22b kfuɓa 'chicken' (*ku̧ɓa). Such modifications are found in all 5V languages except Lengola D12, as well as in many 7V systems (Schadeberg 1994–5).

As seen above in (6), *u̧ was almost entirely restricted to the first and last stem syllables in PB, although it also occurs in stem-internal position in the PB root *-táku̧n-, 'chew' which has reflexes such as Cewa N31b tafun-a, Pende L11/K52 táfun-a, Venda S21 ṭáfun-a, Yao P21 táwún-a, and (with metathesis), Nkore-Kiga EJ13/14 and Nyambo EJ21 *fútan-a.* Synchronic alternations are found in languages which use the *-u̯* suffix to derive adjectives or nouns from verbs, e.g. Ganda EJ15 *nyeet-* 'become fat' → *nyééf-ù* 'fat'; *lebel-* 'be loose' → *lebév-ù* 'loose'; *tamiir-* 'become drunk' → *mu≠tamíiv-ù* 'drunkard'.

*i̯ also most frequently occurred in the first and last stem syllables in PB, but also in noun class prefixes, e.g. class 8 **bi̯-* > Shona S10 class 8 *zvi-* (with a 'whistled' labioalveolar [ʐ]). In many Bantu languages, synchronic alternations are conditioned by one or more of the three suffixes reconstructed with **i̯*. The first of these is the causative suffix **-i̯-* (which must in turn be followed by a FV). As seen in the Bemba M42 forms in (20):

(20)   (a) *-leep-*   'be long'   → *-leef-i-*   'lengthen'   [leef-y-a]
           -lub-   'be lost'   → *-luf-i-*   'lose'   [luf-y-a]
       (b) *-fiit-*   'be dark'   → *-fiis-i-*   'darken'   [fiiš-a]
           -cind-   'dance'   → *-cins-i-*   'make dance'   [cinš-a]
           -lil-   'cry'   → *-lis-i-*   'make cry'   [liš-a]
           -buuk-   'get up (intr)' → *-buus-i-*   'get [s.o.] up' [buuš-a]
           -lúng-   'hunt'   → *-lúns-i-*   'make hunt'   [lúnš-á]

when followed by causative **-i̯-*, labial /p, b/ become [f] and lingual consonants become [s] (subsequently modified to [š] by palatalization, e.g. /sit-/ → [šit-] 'buy'). The second suffix is **-i̯*, which derives nouns, often agentives, from verbs, as in Ganda EJ15 *o-mú≠ddus-i* 'fugitive' (<-'dduk-* 'run (away)'), *o-mu≠lez-i* 'guardian' (<-ler-* 'raise (child)'). Finally, the bimorphemic 'perfective' suffix **-i̯d-e* also frequently conditions frication (Bastin 1983b), e.g. Nkore E13 *-réet-* 'bring', perfective *-réets-ir-e*; Rundi DJ62 *rir-* 'cry', perfective *riz-e* (<*rir-y-e* < **did-i̯d-e*).

While such frications occur frequently throughout the Bantu zone, there is considerable variation. Not only can the exact reflexes differ, but so can the environments in which they occur. In Bemba M42, for instance, only causative **-i̯-* regularly conditions frication. In Yao P21, frication before causative **-i̯-* is more widespread than before perfective **-i̯d-e*, but will almost always occur before the latter if the preceding consonant is either [l] or [k], i.e. the two consonants which occur most frequently in extensions (Ngunga 2000). What this indicates is that frication, although originally an across-the-board phonological process, has acquired morphological restrictions and, in some cases, has been leveled out completely. Thus, the [i] of Bemba M42 *-il-e* not only fails to condition frication, but has been restructured, on analogy with suffixes such as applicative *-il-/-el-*, to undergo, e.g. *fik-il-e* 'arrive + perfective' vs. *bep-el-e* 'lie + perfective'. The perfective suffix *-il-e* continues to differ from the applicative *-il-* in its ability to fuse or 'imbricate' with verb bases that end in a range of consonants, e.g. *kúngub-* 'gather' → perfective *kúngwiib-e* vs. applicative *kúngub-il-a* (Bastin 1983, Hyman 1995a).

The vowels **i̯* and **u̯* may have effects on preceding consonants other than frication. While nasals are usually exempt from the effects of degree 1 high vowels, Ganda EJ15, **i̯* palatalizes /n/, e.g. *o-mu-soɲ-i* 'tailor' (< *-son-* 'sew'). A much more frequent phenomenon concerns the realization of PB **d*, which may be preserved as [d] before [i], but realized as [l] or [r] before other vowels. This occurs both in 7V languages, e.g. Duala A24, Tiene B81, Bobangi C24, as well as in 5V languages, e.g. Kongo H16, Lwena K14, Kwezo K53, Dciriku K62, Kete L21 and certain dialects of Yao P21. In the 5V languages **di̯* is typically realized as [dzi] or [zi], and **di* is realized [di]. (Unless preceded by a nasal, **d* is realized as [l] or [r] before other vowels.) The synchronic situation is considerably obscured in Ruwund L53, where **di* is realized [di] and **de* is realized as [li] (cf. §3.2). In other languages the effect is extended to the high back vowel **u̯*, e.g. Tswana S31

(7V). In Kalanga S16 (5V), *dʉ* is realized [du], while *du* is realized [lu] (Mathangwane 1999). Finally, Cewa N31b exhibits the 'hardening' of /l/ to [d] only before glides, e.g. *dy-a* 'eat', *bad-w-a* 'be born' (cf. *bal-a* 'bear (child)'). Occurring in both eastern and western Bantu – indeed, throughout the zone – there is dialectal evidence in both the Kongo H10 and Sotho-Tswana S30 groups that the [d] was originally pronounced as retroflex [ʈ] before high vowels (cf. also much of Caga E60, where *d* is realized [r ~r] before *i*, *ʉ*, elsewhere as [l] or Ø - see also Ch. 24).

4.3 Consonant + glide

The post-consonant glides [y] and [w] are typically derived from underlying vowels. As a result, consonants often show the same alternations before the glides [y] and [w] as before the corresponding high vowel. Thus, [y, w] from *i*, *ʉ* produce frications, while [y, w] from *i, *u or *e, *o typically do not. An exception to this is found in the Mongo C60 group (7V). In some dialects of Mongo, /t/ is realized [ts] before the high tense vowels /i, u/, while /l/ (< *d) is realized as j [dʒ]. However, all dialects appear to produce the affricate realizations before [y, w] – even if they derive from /e, o/: *tó≠kamb-a* 'we work', *ló≠kamb-a* 'you pl. work' vs. *tsw-án-a* 'we see', *jw-án-a* 'you pl. see'.

In many Bantu languages, *ky/gy* develop into alveo-palatal affricates. This is seen especially in the different realizations of the class 7 *ki-* prefix before consonants vs. vowels, e.g. Nyamwezi F22 (7V) *ki≠jùkò* 'spoon' vs. *c≠èèyò* 'broom'; Swahili G42 (5V) *ki≠kapu* 'basket' vs. *c≠ama* 'society'; Ha DJ66 class 7 *íki* 'this' vs. *ic-o* 'that (near you).' Other languages front velars with a noticeable offglide, i.e. *kʸ, gʸ*, first before high front vowels, then before mid front vowels as well. Thus, Ganda EJ15 *èkʲì≠kópò* 'cup', ultimately *èci≠kópò*. While different patterns of velar palatalization are found throughout the Bantu zone (Hyman and Moxley 1992), some languages in the Congo basin show analogous developments with respect to alveolar consonants. While /li/ is realized [di] in both Luba Kasai L31a and Pende L11/K52, /ti/ is realized *ci* [tši]: Luba *mac-il-* 'plaster + appl' (*mat-*), Pende *šíc-il-* (~ *šít-il-*) 'close + appl' (*šít-*).

While a [y] glide (or offglide) can trigger palatalization, [w] is responsible for velarization, e.g. in the Rundi-Rwanda DJ60 and Shona S10 groups. Meeussen (1959) summarizes the reflexes of labial+glide and coronal+glide complexes in Rundi as in (21).

(21) (a)   (b)
    bw [bg]   *fy* [fˢy]
    fw [fk]   *vy* [vᶻy]
    mw [mŋ]   *my* [mŋ]
    tw [tkw]   *ty* [rtky, r̩ᵗky]
    rw [rgw (gw)]   *ry* [rgy]
    sw [skw, sᵏw]   *sy* [sᵏy]
    zw [ᵈzᵍw]   *nny* [ny, nⁱy]
    tsw [tskw, tsᵏw]
    cw [tʃkw, tʃᵏw]
    jw [ᵈʒᵍw]
    shw [ʃkw, ʃᵏw]

As seen in (21a), Cw hardens to Ck/Cg/CN, and the labial offglide is lost (absorbed) when the C is labial. (22a) shows that Cy undergoes a comparable hardening process.

When the C is velar, one obtains the expected Cw sequence. Similar processes occur in the Shona S10 complex. In Kalanga S16, /l/ becomes [g] before [w], e.g. *tól-a* 'take', *tóg-w-a* 'be taken'. Compare also Basaá A43, where the class 4 *mi-* and class 8 *bi-* prefixes are realized *ŋw-* and *gw-* when directly followed by a vowel, e.g. *bì≠tɔ́ŋ* 'horns' vs. *gw≠ɔ́m* 'things' (*y≠ɔ́m* 'thing' ?) – cf. the object pronouns *ŋw-ɔ́* (cl. 4) and *gw-ɔ́* (cl. 8). Finally, geminate w + w and y + y become, respectively, [ggw] and [ggy] in Ganda EJ15:

(22) (a) /pó-a/ → *wo-a* → *ww-aa* → *ggwaa* ...   'become exhausted'
     (b) /pí-a/ → *wi-a* → *yy-aa* → *ggyaa* ...   'get burnt'

As seen, both glides derive from *p – cf. *m≠pw-êdd-è* 'I have become exhausted' and *m≠pî-dd-è* 'I have gotten burnt' (~ *n≠jî-dd-è*).

4.4 *i + consonant

Consonants may harden not only after nasals or before glides, but also after PB *i, particularly when this vowel is either word-initial or preceded by a vowel. Thus, Tswana S31 devoices stops not only after N-, but also after reflexive i-: *i≠pón-é* 'see yourself!', *i≠tís-é* 'watch yourself!' (*bón-*, *dís-*). In Lega D25, PB *t normally becomes [r], but is preserved as [t] after the class 5 prefix *i,, e.g. *i-táma* 'cheek', pl. *ma-ráma*. Ganda EJ15, on the other hand, develops geminates from *i-C. Thus, compare *o-mu≠sâjjà* 'man' and *bajj-a* 'carve' with Haya EJ21 *o-mu≠šáija* and *baij-a*. This process also produces root-initial geminates, e.g. *´tt-à* 'kill' and *´bb-à* 'steal', and singular/plural alternations in classes 5/6 such as *e-g≠gulu* 'sky', pl. *a-ma≠gulu* (cf. Haya EJ21 *ít-a*, *íb-a*, *e-i≠gulu*). While class 5 *i- typically 'strengthens' following consonants, it is known also to condition voicing (and implosion), e.g. Zezuru S12 *ɓáŋgá* 'knife' (pl. *ma≠páŋgá*), *ɗaŋgá* 'cattle enclosure' (pl. *ma≠taŋgá*), *gáŋgá* 'large helmeted guinea-fowl' (pl. *ma≠káŋgá*).

4.5 Long-distance consonant phonology

In all of the processes discussed thus far, the trigger of the phonological process is adjacent to the targeted consonant. Bantu languages also are known for the ability of a consonant to affect another consonant across a vowel (and beyond). There are several such cases.

The first, Meinhof's Law, was seen already in §4.1.3, whereby a nasal+voiced stop is realized NN or N when followed by a second nasal complex (sometimes just N) in the next syllable. Another version of this simplification occurs in Kwanyama R21, where the second nasal+voiced stop loses its prenasalization (Schadeberg 1987): *N≠gombe > oŋ≠gobe* 'cattle', *ŋ-gandu > oŋ≠gadu* 'crocodile'. These dissimilatory changes have the effect of minimizing the number of NC complexes in a (prefix+) stem. Another well-known dissimilatory process is Dahl's Law, whereby a voiceless stop becomes voiced if the consonant in the next syllable is also voiceless. This accounts for the initial voiced reflexes in Nyamwezi F22 roots such as *-dakún-* 'chew' (*-tákụn-*), *-guhɪ* 'short' (*-kụpi*). Dahl's Law is also responsible for the /t/ or /k/ of prefixes to become voiced (and sometimes continuant), e.g. Kuria E43 /ko≠tɛma/ → [ɣo≠tɛm-a] 'to beat'. While there is considerable variation (Davy and Nurse 1982), multiple prefixes may be affected, e.g. Southern Kikuyu E51 /ke-ke-ko≠eta/ → [ɣe-ɣe-ɣw≠eet-a] 'he (cl. 7) called you'. Alternations are also sometimes found stem-internally, as in Rundi DJ62 *-bád-ik-* 'transplanter', *-bád-uk-* 'pousser bien' vs. *-bát-ur-* 'arracher (plantes) pour repiquer'.

Other long-distance consonant processes are assimilatory in nature. In Bukusu EJ31c, an /l/ will assimilate to a preceding [r] across a vowel, e.g. *-fúk-il-* 'stir + appl' vs. *-bir-ir-* 'pass + appl'. The process is optional when the trigger [r] is separated by an additional syllable, e.g. *-rám-* 'remain', *-rám-il-* ~ *-rám-ir-* 'remain + appl'. Several languages in the western Lacustrine area show a process of sibilant harmony which disallows or limits the co-occurrence of alveolar and alveo-palatal sibilants, e.g. [s] and [š]. In Rwanda DJ61 and Rundi DJ62, /s/ becomes alveo-palatal across a vowel, when the following consonant becomes (alveo-)palatal as the result of a *y*-initial suffix, e.g. *soonz-* 'be hungry' vs. *a-ra≠shoonj-e* 'he was hungry' (< *soonz-ye*). In Nkore-Kiga EJ13/14, the process produces alternations in the opposite (depalatalizing) direction, e.g. *shígish-* 'stir', *o-mu≠sígis-i* 'stirrer'. Finally, a third long-distance assimilation involves nasality. A wide range of Bantu languages nasalize [l] or [d] to [n] after an NV(V) syllable (Greenberg 1951), e.g. Bemba M42 *cít-il-* 'do + appl' vs. *lim-in-* 'cultivate + appl'. While Suku H32 optionally extends this process across additional syllables, creating extension variations such as *-am-ik-il-* ~ *-am-ik-in-*, such long-distance assimilation is obligatory in Kongo H10 – and in nearby Yaka H31, e.g. *ziik-il-* 'bury + appl' vs. *mak-in-* 'climb + appl', *miituk-in-* 'sulk + appl', *nutuk-in-* 'lean + appl'.

Other forms of apparent long-distance phonology are highly morpheme-specific. Thus, the passive suffix *-w-* (*-u-*) causes the palatalization of a preceding labial consonant in the Sotho-Tswana S30 and Nguni S40 groups, e.g. Ndebele S45 *dal-w-* 'be created' (*dal-*) vs. *bunj-w-* 'be moulded' (*-bumb-*). In Ndebele and other Nguni languages, this process can actually skip syllables, e.g. *funjath-w-* 'be clenched' (*-fumbath-*), *vunjulul-w-* 'be uncovered' (*-vumbulul-*). In a number of languages, where causative *-i-* conditions frication, the effect is sometimes seen on non-adjacent consonants. In Bemba M42, the roots *lub-* 'be lost' and *lil-* 'cry' form the causatives *luf-y-* and *lis-y-* (> *liš-*) and the applicatives *lub-il-* and *lil-il-*. However, their applicativized causative forms are *-luf-is-y-* and *-lis-is-y-*, with frication applying twice. As seen in (23), this is the result of a 'cyclic' application of the frication process (Hyman 1994):

(23)

	UR		MORPHOLOGY		PHONOLOGY		MORPHOLOGY		PHONOLOGY
(a)	*-lub-*	→	*-lub-i-*	→	*-luf-i-*	→	*-luf-il-i-*	→	*-luf-is-i-*
	'be lost'		'lose'				'lose for/at'		
(b)	*-lil-*	→	*-lil-i-*	→	*-lis-i-*	→	*-lis-il-i-*	→	*-lis-is-i-*
	'cry'		'make cry'				'make cry for/at'		

In the second morphology stage, applicative *-il-* is 'interfixed' between the fricated root and the causative suffix *-i-* (> *y* before a vowel). Bemba and certain other Bantu languages show the same multiple frications when the *-id-* of perfective *-id-e* is interfixed, e.g. *luf-is-i-e* [lufiše] 'lose + perfective'. In other languages, frication appears to apply non-cyclically, affecting only the applicative consonant, e.g. Mongo C61 /kál-/ 'dry', /kál-i-/ (→ [káj-a] with FV -a) 'make dry', /kál-el-i-/ → *kál-ej-i-* 'make dry + applicative' (→ [kál-ej-a] with FV -a). Still others show evidence of cyclicity by 'undoing' frication in a fixed (often non-etymological) manner. In Nyamwezi F22, the verb /gul-/ 'buy' is causativized to /gul-j-/ 'sell', which undergoes frication to become *guj-i-* (> surface [guj-a] by gliding of *j* to [y] and absorption of [y] into the preceding alveo-palatal affricate). However when *guj-i-* is applicativized, yielding intermediate *guj-el-i-*, the result is *gug-ej-i-* (→ [gug-ej-a]). The [j] is 'undone' as velar [g], on analogy with *-og-* 'bathe intr.', *-oj-i-* 'bathe (s.o.)', *-og-ej-i-* 'bathe + appl', not as the [l] one would expect if the process were non-cyclic. The most extreme version of this process is seen in languages such as Nyakyusa M31, which uses a 'replacive' [k] no matter what the input consonant of an applicativized causative. Thus, *-kees-j-* 'make go by' (the causative of *-keend-* 'go by') is applicativized first to *-kees-el-j-*, which then undergoes frication and de-frication of the s to k: *-keek-es-j-* 'make go by + appl' (→ [keek-es-y-a]).

5 CONCLUSION

The above gives a sketch of some of the phonological properties of syllables, consonants, and vowels in Bantu languages. It emphasizes languages which have preserved the basic morphological and phonological structure inherited from PB. In order to be complete, it is necessary to point out that quite a few languages in zones A and B have modified this structure significantly, e.g. by allowing closed syllables, developing back unrounded vowels, etc. The tendency to break down the inherited structure is even more pronounced in groups just outside 'Narrow Bantu', e.g. Grassfields Bantu.

REFERENCES

Bastin 1983b; Carter 1984; Clements 1991; Davy and Nurse 1982; Fontaney 1980; Greenberg 1951; Hinnebusch 1974; Hyman 1994, 1995a, 1995b, 1999; Hyman and Moxley 1992; Hyman and Ngunga 1997; Kisseberth and Abasheikh 1974; Kutsch Lojenga 1994a; Kwenzi Mikala 1980; Leitch 1997; Lembs and de Gastines 1973; Maddieson, this volume; Maganga and Schadeberg 1992; Mathangwane 1999; Meeussen 1959, 1967, 1979; Nash 1992; Ngunga 2000; Odden 1996; Schadeberg 1987, 1994–5; Stewart 1983; Watters, this volume.

CHAPTER FOUR

TONE

Charles Kisseberth and David Odden

1 INTRODUCTION

Sophisticated and revealing studies of Bantu tone have long existed, including overviews (van Spaandonck 1967, Stevick 1969a, Hyman 1976a); tone-marked descriptive studies arising from the Belgian involvement in the Congo (e.g. Burssens 1939, Coupez 1955, Stappers 1964, Meeussen 1954); analyses of tone in specific languages such as Tonga (Carter 1962, Meeussen 1963), Sukuma (Richardson 1959), Ganda (Meeussen 1966, Stevick 1969b, McCawley 1970), Kinga (Schadeberg 1973), Safwa (Voorhoeve 1973). The advent of autosegmental phonology (Goldsmith 1976) spurred an explosion of theoretically oriented, data-intensive research ranging across a variety of Bantu languages. Space precludes exhaustive listing, but the following may be mentioned: Kikuyu (Clements and Ford 1979), Makhuwa (Cheng and Kisseberth 1979, 1980, 1981), Tonga (Goldsmith 1981), Shona (Odden 1981), Ganda (Hyman 1982), Ruri (Massamba 1982), Venda (Cassimjee 1986), the Lacustrine subgroup (Goldsmith 1987), Jita (Downing 1990), Zigula (Kisseberth 1992), Matuumbi (Odden 1996), Kalanga (Mathangwane 1998), Xhosa (Cassimjee 1998). A wide range of languages are described and analyzed in various collections focusing on Bantu tone: Yukawa (1987a, 1989, 1992); Clements and Goldsmith (1984); Hyman and Kisseberth (1998); Blanchon and Creissels (1999).

Most Bantu languages are tonal, and many have complex tonal phonologies. There is considerable variation between languages, and dialects such as the Shona or Pare dialects may have very different tone systems. Still, there is considerable deep similarity, and much of the variation is due to surface principles that disfavor or favor certain tonal configurations. Divergences in surface pitch can be understood in terms of the distribution of 'primary' High tones (generally, though not always 'underlying' Hs), and their surface modifications.

A few languages (Swahili, Tumbuka, Pogolo and others) are non-tonal. The vast majority have two tones, H and L, and in many languages there are significant asymmetries between H and L suggesting privative analysis as H vs. toneless. Many languages have distinctive register-lowering between Hs (downstep) under conditions which are largely synchronically predictable. A very few languages (Kamba, Chaga) have four tone levels, with a robust contrast between H and L (or H and Ø) plus secondary superhigh and superlow tones. Consonantal effects have also contributed to a three-way contrast in Nguni languages whose phonological interpretation remains controversial. Some discussions of Bantu tone also make reference to 'accent'. Numerous languages have automatic prominence on the penultimate syllable, realized as vowel length or local pitch perturbation, which may be referred to as 'stress' or 'accent'. In addition, 'accent' is used in an abstract analytic sense to refer to (certain) H-toned syllables: see Odden (1999) for an overview.

The question of the 'tone bearing unit' (TBU) remains uncertain in the theoretical and Bantu literature, largely because many criteria are called on, often contradictorily.

In languages lacking length, it is impossible to distinguish syllable and mora as TBU. Languages with length can give conflicting evidence. Matuumbi seems to support the mora as TBU since certain generalizations are best stated in terms of the count of vowels (mora), such as the fact that H is assigned to the third vowel irrespective of syllable count (Odden 1995a). Or, rising and falling tones are usually subject to restrictions, generally appearing only on bimoraic syllables. However, in Matuumbi and Bantu in general, a contrast between rising and falling tone is almost never represented underlyingly. This makes sense if the syllable is the TBU, where syllable-internal positional contrasts would not be possible.

We organize this chapter as follows. The first two sections examine the distribution of primary Hs. Section 2 deals with nouns while §3 deals with verbs. This division is motivated by significant differences in tone distribution in these word classes. Section 4 catalogues phonological principles that lead to the diversity of tone patterns found in Bantu. Section 5 discusses the extent to which tonal phenomena in Bantu may be specific to morphological and syntactic structures.

2 NOMINAL TONOLOGY

Nominals in Bantu have the structure (pre-prefix+) class-prefix + stem. Class prefixes are typically toneless. The canonical stem is disyllabic, where four tone patterns are reconstructable to Proto-Bantu (PB): HH, HL, LL and LH. In some languages such as Venda a stem containing n moras displays 2^n possible tonal shapes, i.e. every imaginable configuration of either tone on any syllable. A monomoraic stem may be H or toneless: *mu#rí* 'tree', *mu#thu* 'person'. A bimoraic stem has four patterns: ØØ (*mu#tuka* 'youth'), ØH (*mu#rathú* 'brother'), HØ (*mu#sélwa* 'bride'), and HH (*mu#sádzí* 'woman'). A trimoraic stem has eight patterns: ØØØ (*mu#kalaha* 'old man'), ØØH (*mu#tukaná* 'boy'), ØHH (*mu#kegúlú* 'old woman'), HHØ (*mu#dúhúlu* 'grandchild'), etc.

There may be even more distinctions. Disyllabic stems in Makonde fall into eight tone patterns, cf. *shi#ndoolo* 'sp. bean', *lí#maanga* 'sp. pumpkin', *li#daáda* 'medal', *shi#ndiili* 'termite net', *li#doôdo* 'leg', *lí#njaáno* 'sp. condiment', *vá#máaka* 'cats', *shí#mbeêdi* 'shadow', which is twice the expected number given specification of H vs. Ø for each syllable. Hehe has similar problems: *mu#guúnda* 'field', *mu#véengi* 'fruit sp.', *lú#fwiíli* 'hair', *mú#teela* 'stirring stick', *ki#tóofú* 'potato'.

Languages may historically reduce the number of patterns. The most common reduction is neutralization of the HH vs. HL contrast. Commonly this reduction will have taken place long ago, and the contrast may be reintroduced through borrowing or sound changes, such as loss of vowel length. In Tsonga, historical HL stems became HH (*nyóká* 'snake') while historical HH stems remain unaltered (*m-béwú* 'seed'). However, HL stems do occur (*mu-fána* 'boy'). In some languages, reduction may be restricted to isolation pronunciation. In Bondei, original HL, LH and LL nouns all surface in isolation without H: *mbuzi*, *nyumba* and *nyama*. However, their patterning in phrases is distinct (albeit with a developing tendency to merge the original LH and LL contrast).

In some languages, nouns are restricted to at most one H, e.g. Matuumbi or Lacustrine languages like Kerewe and Ganda. Extreme reductions in contrast are found in Kuria and Makhuwa. In Kuria the only contrast is whether CVVCV stems have final H (*e#séésé* 'dog') or not (*iri#tɔɔ́kɛ* 'banana'). In some dialects of Makhuwa, H always appears on the second mora of the nominal word (*i#mátta* 'field', *nakhúwo* 'maize', *ni#váka* 'spear').

It is also important to consider prefixal tone. In PB, the pre-prefix was H-toned. In languages that have retained the pre-prefix, the pre-prefix may reveal the H directly, e.g. Gusii *ó-bo#bé* 'evil', *ó-mo#bere* 'body', *é#mbero* 'speed'. The pre-prefix H is often opacated by other processes, so in the Nguni languages which retain pre-prefixes, the H may undergo shift/spread, depending on the tone of the stem. In Zulu, nouns lack a pre-prefix as complements to a negative verb: *ba#ntu* 'people', *mi#nyango* 'doors', *si#hlalwana* 'small seat'. When the pre-prefix is added, H appears on the prefix in the first two examples and on the first stem syllable in the last: *a-bá#ntu, i-mí#nyango, i-si#hlálwana*. The 'extra' H of the citation form must be attributed to the pre-prefix, whose H moves rightward according to general principles in the language.

Sometimes H appears on the pre-prefix only in certain contexts. In Zinza, the pre-prefix does not have H in isolation: *a-ma#súnunu* 'fresh milk'. However, whenever the initial vowel coalesces with a preceding syllable, the coalesced syllable emerges with the H intact: *yáá#guliize* 'he has sold' plus *a-ma#súnunu* 'fresh milk' yields *yáaguliiz' áámasúnunu*.

3 VERBAL TONOLOGY

While nouns have a fairly simple tone system, tone in the verb is often very complex, matching the morphological complexity of the verb. The typical situation is the following. Stems usually reveal a lexical contrast between H and toneless; given that a verb has an H, one can predict the tonal shape of the stem whatever its structure. Prediction of the tone shape of an H stem is simplest if one assumes that the H is located on the first stem mora. For instance, Mbaga Pare has few general tone processes obscuring the realization of primary Hs, and all H verbs have H on the first syllable: *ku#chw-á* 'to cut', *ku#vón-a* 'to see', *ku#bánik-a* 'to dry', *ku#fínikir-a* 'to cover'. Bantu tonology is, for the most part, remarkably free of lexical exceptions. There are occasional synchronic lexical exceptions, so in Shambaa a general process spreading H from the penult to the final syllable where /ku#kóm-a/ becomes *ku#kóm-á* 'to kill' is exceptionally blocked in a handful of stems (*ku#lál-a* 'to sleep', *ku#vyál-a* 'to give birth'), many of which historically have penult long vowels. Similar exceptions are found in Qhalaxari (Dickens 1984) and some dialects of Nguni.

Some languages lack lexical contrasts in the verb stem. Instead, stem tone is determined by principles of tone assignment which may be specific to particular tenses or may hold for a variety of tenses. Such languages are often said to have 'predictable' tone systems (at least with respect to verbs). The languages of zone P are of this type (see Odden, Ch. 26 and Kisseberth, Ch. 27, this volume), as are many languages of SW Tanzania, and Saamia and Kuria near Lake Victoria: see Odden (1989) for a general survey. In Kuria, primary H can appear on any of the first four vowels of the macrostem (the subdomain of the verb beginning with object prefixes) – this H may then spread right – viz. V4 in the perfect (*n#tɛrɛkeéye* 'I have cooked for'), V3 in the subjunctive (*n#tɛrɛkɛr-ɛ* 'I should cook for'), V2 in the recent past (*naaga#tɛrékéeye* 'I just cooked for') and V1 in the completive past (*nnaa#térékɛr-a* 'I cooked'). In Makhuwa, the targeted positions are V1, V2, V3 and penult; Yao targets V1, V2 and final; Matuumbi targets V1, V2 and V3; Hehe targets V1 or penult. In Makonde, the tense-determined contrast is not in the location of the H, since stem Hs generally appear on the penult, but rather the kind of contour, ranging over LL (*atu#taleeka* 'we won't cook'), LH (*tu-ndi#táleék-a* 'we cooked'), HH (*a-tu-si#taléék-a* 'we weren't cooking') and LHL (*tu-ka#taleêk-a* 'if we cook').

Even in languages with a lexical contrast in the verb, there are tenses with what is usually referred to as 'grammatical tone', which involves assignment of H to a particular mora in the stem. The favored locations of grammatical H are the final mora or the second stem mora. In Yambasa (Yukawa 1992), the remote past tense is marked by an H spanning from the second to final syllables, so *gu#dóŋeno* 'to call' and *gu#nyongolonyo* 'to tickle' have the remote past tense forms *amba#dóŋénó* 'he called' and *amba#nyongólónyó* 'he tickled'. A similar pattern is found in Kamba *nétwáa#konéthésyê* 'we made hit' (/kon/), *nétwáa#táléthésyê* 'we make count' (/tál/). Namwanga has a grammatical H assigned to the final vowel in the potential tense, cf. the toneless stem *tungámú#sakuliil-á* 'we can comb for him/her' and the H stem *tungámú#'wándúliil-á* 'we can blacksmith for him/her' (there is also rightward spreading of H).

Commonly, languages specify different locations where grammatical H is assigned, determined by tense-aspect. Namwanga also assigns H to V2 in the future (*túli#sakúliíl-á* 'we will comb for', *túli#'wándúliíl-á* 'we will blacksmith for') and subjunctive (*túmú#sakúliíl-é* 'that we comb for him/her', *túmú#'wándúliíl-é* 'that we blacksmith for him/her'). While V-final and V2 are the most common positions for grammatical H, other positions may be targeted, so in Kerewe, the two patterns of melodic H assignment are final with prepausal leftward spread (*a#kalaang-ílé* 'he fried (hesternal past)') and the penult (*alaa#kalááng-a* 'he will fry (near future)').

The position of the grammatical tone may also depend on the lexical tone of the root; so in Shona, H roots realize the grammatical H on the final vowel (*havá#tóréséran-á* 'they didn't make take for e.o') and toneless roots put H on the second stem vowel of the stem (*havá#bikisíran-a* 'they didn't make cook for e.o'). Most Rutara languages have a similar pattern, with the complication that prepausal H shifts to the penult and the underlying lexical tone is deleted in the presence of the grammatical tone; so in Nyankore, the toneless stem of *oku#bariran-a* 'to count for e.o' has H on the second syllable in habitual *ba#baríran-a* 'they count for e.o', but the H-toned stem of *oku#bóneran-a* 'to see for e.o' has H on the surface penult (or word-final in phrase medial position) in *ba#bonerán-a* 'they see for e.o'.

Tone of prefixes can vary considerably, especially to mark differences in tense-aspect, as discussed in §5.

4 TONAL PHENOMENA IN BANTU

In the absence of principles to the contrary, one expects a direct relationship between location of primary Hs and their surface manifestation, so if the first and third TBUs have primary Hs, just those TBUs will have surface H. The term 'primary' refers, roughly, to H tones specified in the lexicon or by virtue of the morphology – i.e. they are not phonological in their origin. In many (perhaps most) Bantu languages, other tonal phenomena result in a very indirect relationship between primary H and surface tone. We mark primary Hs by underlining the TBU.

4.1 H-tone spreading/shifting

The most fundamental phenomenon in Bantu tonology is the mobility of H. Specifically, even though H may be initially associated with a given mora, very often that H will be realized (a) not just on that mora, but on one or more other moras to its right (less often, left), or (b) will not be realized on that mora, but rather on some other mora to its right (or left). The case in (a) is often referred to as 'tone spreading'; the situation in (b) is often referred to as 'tone shifting'. There does not appear to be a fundamental difference between spreading and shifting. Whenever we are not specifically referring to spreading as opposed to shifting, we use the term 'movement'.

In Ikorovere Makhuwa, H spreads one mora to the right. Wherever an H is specified in the word, it will be followed by another H on the following mora. In the negative infinitive, the only primary H is on the negative prefix *hi*, and whatever vowel follows *hi* is also H-toned: *u-hí#lím-a* 'to not cultivate', *u-hí#máal-a* 'to not be quiet', *u-hí-kí#thumel-a* 'to not buy for me'. In the negative past, there is a primary H on the first mora of the prefix *aa* as well as the second mora of the stem. Again, each of these moras is in turn followed by another H tone: *(k)a-k-áá#ttupúlále* 'I did not cut', *(k)a-k-áá#lokóttániŋhe* 'I did not pick up pl'.

Tsonga (cf. Kisseberth 1994) spreads its H tones rightward in an unbounded fashion. This can be seen by comparing 1sg., 1pl. present forms with 3pl. (the notation '*a*' indicates that present tense *-a-* is deleted on the surface), so, compare *ndz-a#xav-a* 'I am buying' vs. *vá-a#xáv-a* '[cl.2] are buying', *h-a#xaviselan-a* 'we are selling to e.o.' vs. *vá-a#xávísélán-a* '[cl.2] are selling to e.o.' (See below for the exclusion of the last syllable from receiving a H tone by spreading.)

Rightward binary shift is found in Nyamwezi (Maganga and Schadeberg 1992) so /kʊ#túm-a/ becomes *kʊtʊmá* 'to send', /kʊ#tʊmɪl-a/ becomes *kʊtʊmíla* 'to send for' and /kʊ-bá#túm-a/ becomes *kʊbatʊmá* 'to send them'. Unbounded rightward shift (albeit with the final syllable excluded) occurs in Zigula: /ku#hángany-a/ 'to lie' becomes *ku#hangány-a*, /ku#kíngiliz-a/ 'to catch with a container' becomes *ku#kingilíz-a*, and /ku#hángalasany-a/ becomes *ku#hangalasány-a*. Leftward movement, though much less common (except as a strategy for avoiding final H tones), is also found, so Luba (Yukawa *et al.* 1992) has unbounded leftward spread whereby /ku#loongesh-á/ becomes *kúlóóngéshá* 'to teach' and /ku-mu#táandish-á/ becomes *kú-mútaandíshá* 'to threaten him'; Zambian Tonga has binary leftward shift.

Less commonly attested is tone tripling, where H spreads to the following two TBUs, as found in the Kanye dialect of Tswana (Creissels 1998). The lexical H of a verb stem spreads three syllables to the right, as in the medial context form *go#símólólɛlan-a* 'to begin for one another'. The same pattern appears in other southern Bantu languages, including Shona, Venda, Kalanga and Tsonga. Double rightward shift of H is found in Sukuma (Richardson 1959), where H can be displaced two TBUs to the right, as in /bákʊkʊ#solel-a/ → *bakʊkúsolela* 'they will chose for you'.

Spreading and shifting do not appear to represent fundamentally different operations. They have in common the extension of H to the left or right, and the factors that block spreading (see later) may also block shifting. The difference between the two phenomena seems to be simply whether the H is realized just on the mora to which it has been extended (the 'endpoint') or also on the original TBU and intervening moras. This unity is demonstrated by the fact that in some languages such as Xhosa (cf. Cassimjee and Kisseberth 1998) a structure may surface as shifting or spreading dependent on context. We discuss the Xhosa case in §4.6.

Another argument for not making a crucial differentiation between spreading and shifting is that there are intermediate stages between the two. In Kerewe, there is phonological spread of H one syllable to the right (to a non-final syllable), cf. *ku#bóh-a* 'to tie', *ku#bóhán-a* 'to tie each other'. Phonetically, the pitch peak on these two H syllables is not reached until the second syllable, so the initial mora in the couplet is only a little higher in pitch than the preceding toneless syllable, and not as high as the second member of the couplet: phonetically this comes out as *ku#bōhán-a*. With sufficient lowering of the initial pitch, this results in categorical tone shift. Imitthupi Makhuwa exhibits exactly the same character as Kerewe, while Eerati Makhuwa has categorical shift.

Both spreading and shifting are found in Holoholo (Coupez 1955). H shifts from the root initial vowel to the following vowel in *ku#mon-à* 'to see' from /ku#món-a/, and if there is another syllable, H spreads as in *ku#monán-â* 'to see other' from /ku#mónan-a/ and *ku#tẹgélél-a* 'to listen' from /ku#tégelel-a/. Spreading in Holoholo is binary, not unbounded.

There is sometimes evidence that the extension of H by degrees intermediate between binary and unbounded movement may be due to separate phenomena. Taita moves H once rightward, cf. *ku#dẹkíaana* 'to cook for e.o.'. But compare now *na-dáa#gwa* 'I just fell', *na-dá#líima* 'I just cultivated', *na-da#búduuka* 'I just fell'. The H from *na* always extends onto the following prefix *da*, as expected by virtue of bounded movement. However, the H on *da* can now extend one more syllable to the right across the stem-prefix boundary (except where the stem is monosyllabic and nonfinality comes into play). Other cases of intermediate degrees of tone movement have often been analyzed as the result of combining separate movement phenomena: see Odden (1981) for Shona, Roberts (1992) for Sukuma, Hyman and Mathangwane (1998) for Kalanga.

4.2 Nonfinality

'Nonfinality' refers to a preference that the end of certain phonological structures not be realized on a H tone. The structure most commonly involved is the 'intonational phrase' (IP). Sometimes a smaller 'phonological phrase' may be involved, or even the word. The most common manifestation of nonfinality is the failure of H-tone movement to target a final mora. In Makhuwa tone doubling targets a phrase-medial final vowel but not a IP-final vowel: *u#thúmá nakhúwo* 'to buy maize', but *u#thúma*. Tsonga does not spread H onto the final vowel of a phrase: compare *ndzi#xavela xi#phukuphuku fole* 'I am buying tobacco for a fool' with *vá#xávélá xí#phúkúphúku fole* 'they are buying tobacco for a fool'. Although the complement nouns are in the same phase as the verb, spreading only affects the first complement. Makhuwa and Tsonga are representative of bounded and unbounded spreading respectively. Shifting languages may similarly be restricted by nonfinality.

A second nonfinality effect is failure of H to be realized on a final mora, as in Bondei. The verb stem in *ku#dya* 'to eat' and *n-a#dya* 'I am eating' has no surface H tone. There is evidence that the stem is H-toned, so in *ku#dyá* ʼn#khánde* 'to eat food' and *n-a#dyá* ʼn#khánde* 'I am eating food', the H surfaces. It is only in IP-final position that the H of /dyá/ does not surface. Although deletion of final H is usually in IP-final position, sometimes the end of the word exhibits similar behavior. In Zulu, nonfinality leads to the deletion of a word-final H when the word is phrase-medial but not phrase-final (e.g. *i-sí#dakwá* has a final H in phrase-final position, but not in phrase-medial position: Khumalo 1987).

A third manifestation of nonfinality is for H to shift leftward. In Nyankore (Poletto 1998), final H shifts to the penult prepausally, as in /omukamá/ → *omukáma* 'chief' (cf. *omukamá waanje* 'my chief'). In contrast, nouns with an underlying penult H retain the H on that syllable both prepausally and finally; e.g. *enkóko* 'chicken', *enkóko yaanje* 'my chicken'. A process at least historically connected to the strategy of shifting H from the final syllable is prepausal backspread. In a number of languages, such as Kerewe, pre-pausal H spreads to the preceding syllable, so *ku#lyá* becomes *kú#lyá* 'to eat'. This step is presumably the precursor to the situation in Zinza and Nyankore where prepausal Hs shift to the penult: see Odden 1994 for discussion of the progression of this process in Tanzanian Yao dialects.

A fourth manifestation of nonfinality is for H to become falling just in case that H-toned mora is final. This phenomenon is generally restricted to IP-final position. In Matuumbi, the V3 H assigned in the subjunctive is a surface short level H in *utelekẹ kịndoólọ* 'you should eat cassava', but prepausally it is a long falling tone (*utelekée*).

4.3 OCP

One of the most extensively discussed principles of Bantu tonology is disfavoring of successive Hs, known in the theoretical literature as the 'obligatory contour principle' (OCP). The manifestations of the OCP are varied. One is to block movement, so an H which should spread may fail to do so if the target is followed by an H TBU (independent of whether the TBU phonetically realizes the H). Tsonga provides an example: the H at the end of a verb can spread onto all toneless syllables in a following noun except for the last. Thus *xi#hlambetwana* 'cooking pot' when combined with *ndzi#vọná...* 'I see' results in *ndzi#vọná xí#hlámbétwána*. However, *ma#tandzá* 'eggs' only permits the H to extend onto its prefix: *ndzi#vọná má#tandzá*.

Other manifestations of the OCP involve repairing would-be violations: there are different repairs possible. One repair – often called 'Meeussen's Rule' after the Belgian linguist who first pointed out the phenomenon – is elimination of one of the primary Hs. In Nilamba (Yukawa 1989a), H deletes after another H, so compare *ku#d ͑ágila* 'to obstruct' where the root retains its underlying H vs. *kuku-kú#dạgila* 'to obstruct us', *naá#dạgila* 'they obstructed' where the root H is deleted after an H-toned tense marker or OP. Deletion of H may also target the H to the left. In Rimi (Yukawa 1989a), H tones shift one vowel to the right, so *u#tégheya* becomes *utẹghéya* 'to understand' and *u-vá#righitya* becomes *uvạríghitya* 'to speak to them'. When an H-toned object prefix precedes an H root, the H of the OP is deleted and /u-vá#tẹgheya/ becomes *uvạteghéya* 'to understand them'. There are also long-distance versions of H-dissimilation. One of the most common is found in the Rutara languages. In these languages, only a single H is possible within the (macro)-stem. When inflected with the grammatical H, preceding Hs are deleted, viz. Kerewe *ku#hịlíingita* 'to crawl', *a#hịliingisílẹ* 'he crawled'.

Karanga Shona has a special manifestation of the OCP, wherein H generally deletes only if it is between Hs. At the phrasal level, this two-sided OCP accounts for the alternation *murúmẹ* 'man', *murúmẹ ákạpá* 'the man gave', *murúmẹ mukúrú* 'big man'; cf. also *mukómaná ákạpá* 'the boy gave' showing that a preceding H is crucial. Within the word, the same dissimilation affects the object prefix *mú* in *handạ-mu#ọ́ná* 'I didn't see him', cf. *ku-mú#ọ́ná* 'to see him', *handạ-mú#bikíra* 'I didn't cook for him'.

Another repair is to introduce 'register lowering' (= downstep) between primary Hs. In Shambaa, whenever two Hs come together across morphemes, a downstep appears both within words (*atẹ́ˈ#kọ́má* 'he killed', *angẹ́ˈ#já* 'he should have cooked') and phrasally (*ázakọ́maˈ nyọ́ká* 'he killed a snake', *nịˈkúi* 'it's a dog').

A third repair is enveloping the H moras into one domain, also seen in Shambaa. Unexpectedly, there is no downstep at the junction of an H object prefix and an H root, cf. *ku-wạ́#kọ́má* 'to kill them', *ni-tẹ́ˈ-í#kạ́ángíya* 'I fried with it', nor between the melodic H and the lexical H, cf. *fụmbạ́tíshá* 'tie securely!', not *fụ́ˈmbạ́tíshá*. Lack of downstep can be explained by fusing adjacent Hs within the macrostem. Tone deletion further supports this analysis. Remote future tense verbs with an object prefix show that in subjunctive-based tenses, melodic H is selected, which fuses with the H of the root and OP (so no downstep appears): cf. *nẹze nịˈ-wạ́#kạ́ángíyé* 'I will fry for them'. Outside this tense, all other subjunctive verbs delete the last macrostem H. As a consequence of

H fusion, we find that in the near future, the melodic H, root H and OP H are all deleted in *ná ní-wa#kaangiye* 'I won't fry for them', as they are in negative remote *séze ní-wa#kaangiye* 'I won't fry for them'. We thus have two arguments that adjacent Hs fuse within the macrostem. Similar arguments have been advanced, based on downstep and patterns of across-the-board lowering, for Pare and Namwanga.

4.4 Avoiding contours

There is much cross-linguistic evidence of a trend restricting tone contours (rise, fall, rise-fall, fall-rise) to bimoraic syllables, and Bantu languages conform to this pattern. Short contour tones are rare and are usually predictably derived from level tones. For example, word-final syllables in Bantu generally do not have a vowel length contrast. An H on such a syllable is realized as falling in various languages (GiTonga, Matuumbi). Short contours not associated with end of phrases are largely phonetic in nature. For example, certain (breathy)-voiced consonants, called 'depressors' lower the initial portion of an H-toned syllable in Nguni languages, creating a phonetically rising syllable.

Some Bantu languages have contrastive vowel length; other languages have no contrastive length, but lengthen the phrasal penult in a phrase. When a language has bimoraic syllables of either type, two types of contours may occur: rising and falling. Languages such as Kuria with a robust length contrast and Makonde with only derived vowel length impose no significant restrictions on either (long) rising or falling tones. An example of a language with a vowel length contrast and no phonological contours is Kerewe. Phonetic contours arise in penultimate position when a primary H spreads to a long penult, cf. *ku#báága* 'to slaughter' vs. *ku#káláanga* 'to fry'. There is a particularly strong tendency to avoid rising tones in Bantu. In Kamba there are no rising tones though there are falling tones (*ko#kóolokà* 'to advance'). The infinitive prefix has an L but when combined with an H vowel-initial stem, the resulting syllable has level H, not a rise, as in *kw#éétekà* 'to answer' from /ko#étekà/. Unless a language has a mechanism for specifically assigning an H tone at the level of the mora within a syllable, H-toned syllables are typically level H or falling, not rising, so in Matuumbi nouns, H-toned syllables are realized with a falling tone, e.g. *mabáago* 'axes'. However, rising tones can be created by attraction of H to a preceding long vowel, as in *mboópo* 'machete' from /mboopó/.

Even phonetically induced rising tones may be eliminated. As mentioned above, in Nguni languages (e.g. Zulu), an H-toned syllable is rising if the syllable has a depressor onset. However, an H may occur on a depressed syllable only if that syllable is phrase-final (e.g. [isígo:dǐ] 'chair'), in penult position in the word (e.g. [úkuzǎ:la] 'to give birth'] or followed by a depressed syllable (e.g. [angǎda:kwa] 'he may get drunk'). In other situations, H shifts away from the depressed syllable (and thereby avoids a rising tone), e.g. [isílo:nda] 'wound', [izilô:nda] 'wounds'. The H in both words originates from the initial vowel; general principles predict that this H would appear on the antepenult. The expected antepenult rising tone of *[izǐlo:nda], however, shifts to the penult.

Although falling tones are generally preferable to rising tones, Nyamwezi, which shifts H once to the right, makes almost all falling tones become level H (*ku#kúmuucha → kukumúúcha* 'to make well known', *bá-lɪɪ#lola → balíílola* 'they are looking'), but does not modify rising tones (*ku#léeta → kuleéta* 'to bring').

Languages may also actively avoid falling tones, Yao being representative. In the infinitive H is assigned to the first stem vowel and spreads rightwards by one mora, cf. *ku#tátánika* 'to hesitate'. When spreading targets a long syllable, extra spreading is found to avoid creation of a fall as in *ku#sápáángula* 'to take apart'. Apart from Nyamwezi, active avoidance of falling tone seems to occur in languages which also avoid rising tones.

4.5 Penult-phenomena

The penultimate syllable also plays a key role in Bantu tone (see also Philippson 1998). In a number of languages H-tone movement is blocked from targeting the penult. Zigula exhibits unbounded spreading in some contexts and this spreading extends only to the antepenult syllable. For example, compare *n-a#guha ma#tunguja* 'I am taking tomatoes' with *a̱-a#gúhá má#túnguja* '[cl.1] is taking tomatoes'. In the latter example, the subject prefix H shifts to the penult of the verb and then spreads from there as far as the antepenult syllable.

In Nguni languages, unbounded movement is just to the antepenult. Compare *ndi-ya#khohlakalela* 'I am cruel for' with the toneless prefix *ndi*, and *ba̱-ya#khohlakálela* 'they are cruel for' with the H prefix /bá/ whose tone shifts to the antepenult. In the stem-initial melodic tone patterns, Hehe exhibits penult-avoidance. H is assigned to the first stem vowel in the future tense, cf. *situ#lóot-a* 'we will dream', *situ#fí_ungulaang-a* 'we will untie'. If the stem is bisyllabic, and thus the stem initial mora is also the penult, H appears instead on the pre-stem mora, as in *situ#lḭm-a* 'we will cultivate'.

Section 4.4 noted that contours are often avoided. At the same time, the penult is often required to have a falling tone before a toneless syllable. This phenomenon is found particularly in languages which have automatic lengthening of phrase-penult syllables. Thus in Kanye Tswana, a word like *mosá̱:di* 'woman' is pronounced as [mosâ:di]; no words have level H on a lengthened penult followed by a toneless syllable. Examples of penult fall in languages with a length contrast are found in Rutara, where H bimoraic syllables in pre-penult position are level H, but are falling-toned when in penult position and followed by a toneless syllable; thus compare Nyankore *okutée̱ra* 'to beat', *okutéérera* 'to beat for'.

4.6 Plateau

Working at cross-purposes to the OCP, there is also a strategy of avoiding HØH sequences, which we refer to as the Plateau principle: avoid a valley between two peaks. Two versions of the principle can be observed: (a) a single toneless mora between Hs is avoided, or (b) an unbounded number of toneless moras between Hs are avoided.

Plateau may trigger H-tone spreading where otherwise it does not occur. Esaaka Makhuwa (Cassimjee and Kisseberth 1999) illustrates bounded spread triggered by Plateau. In this dialect there is no general Tone Doubling, so we have *o-thókola n-thá̱le* 'to sharpen a bamboo stalk', where the H in the verb does not double onto the following vowel. There is doubling in Esaaka, however, when the post-H mora is immediately followed by an H (so HØH would occur), as in *woó̱ná mḭri* 'to see trees' from /o-ó̱na mḭri/. The infinitive provides many examples of Plateau since the morphology places H on the first and the third moras of the stem. In this context, the second stem mora is always raised: *o-rúkúnú̱sa* 'to turn s.t. over', *o-thú̱kúmé̱lihaca* 'to shake'.

Our earlier discussion of spreading and shifting cited Xhosa as a language with unbounded shifting in some contexts but unbounded spreading in others: Plateau motivates the unbounded spreading. As noted earlier, Nguni languages typically shift H to the antepenult, so *u̱-ku-qononóndiisa* 'to emphasize' has underlying H on the initial vowel.

If this infinitive is a complement to *ndi-fṵna* 'I want ...', the final vowel of the verb elides, placing H immediately in front of the infinitive. In response to this H, the tone-less syllables at the beginning of the infinitive are raised: *ndi-fṵn' ú-kú-qónónóndiisa*. Unbounded spreading occurs just in the context of an immediately preceding H tone.

Plateauing may, in some languages, be regarded as a matter of phonetic detail. For example, Zinza has monomoraic and bimoraic syllables, but there are no underlying contrasts with respect to whether H is located on the first or the second mora of a bimoraic syllable. Bimoraic syllables bearing an underlying H are pronounced as 'High' (*bakatḛ́ḛkelana* 'they cooked for e.o.') when located to the left of the penult. Such syllables are usually implemented with a slightly rising pitch, except when there is a preceding H-toned mora, in which case the pitch is level, as in *bḛ́ḛ́tḛ́ḛkelana* 'they cooked for each other (hodiernal)'.

5 NONPHONOLOGICAL FACTORS

A significant issue in Bantu tonology is the fact that tonal phenomena are often restricted to certain morphological or syntactic contexts. Such restrictions can assist in parsing morphosyntactic structures, resulting in characteristic tone properties for a given morphological or syntactic structure. See Odden (1995b) for an overview of phrasal phonology in Bantu.

Grammatical melodies discussed in §3 are a prime example of tone marking morphosyntactic properties. In Shona, melodic H is assigned to all negative and subordinate clause verb tenses (participials, relative clauses, subjunctives). Thus, *áká#bíka* 'he cooked' and *áká#biká* 'he having cooked' are distinguished solely by stem tone patterns. In Matuumbi, this same class of contexts defines where one finds assignment of tone to V2 or V3 instead of V1. More commonly, the set of tenses selecting a grammatical melody is fairly arbitrary, and must essentially be listed.

Tone on verbal prefixes is often determined by morphosyntactic structure. Commonly there is a tonal contrast between H-toned and toneless subject prefixes, especially first/second person vs. third person subject. In Shona, all subject prefixes are H toned in nonassertive tenses (*ha-ndí-chá#bikí* 'I won't cook', *ha-á-chá#bikí* 'he won't cook'), and toneless in certain conditional tenses (*kana ndi-ka#bika* 'if I had cooked', *kana a-ka#bika* 'if he had cooked'); but in assertive tenses, third person subject prefixes are H (*á-chá#bíka* 'he will cook', *vá-chá#bíka* 'they will cook') and 1, 2 person subjects are L (*ndi-chá#bíka* 'I will cook', *u-chá#bíka* 'you will cook', *ti-chá#bíka* 'we will cook'). Bondei is similar to Shona in having the three behavior patterns sketched above, but in the perfect has an additional pattern whereby 1/2 singular and class 1 subject prefixes are toneless, whereas 1/2 plural and subject prefixes for all other noun classes are H-toned.

Some languages show a special connection between the object prefix and the verb stem proper in that the object prefix *counts* for determining where the grammatical H is located. In Kuria, tone is assigned base on a count of vowels from the (left) edge of the macrostem, which includes the object prefix. Thus in the infinitive, H tones appear on the first and fourth vowels counting from the object prefixes, resulting in forms such as *oko#géséra-hó* 'to harvest for at a place', *oko-mó#gésérá-ho* 'to harvest for him at', *oko-gé-mó#gesérá-ho* 'to harvest them for him at'. Languages do not always treat OPs the same for all tone assignment principles, so in Matuumbi, OPs are usually included in the count of vowels (*ṵ#telekí* 'you should cook for', *ṵ-tṵ#telḛ́kí* 'you should cook for us'), but the reflexive prefix, which induces a second- and-final pattern of tone, is not part of the domain counted for tone assignment (cf. *w-ị̀-#telẹ̀kị̀* 'you should cook for yourself'). The H of an OP and a root-initial H often interact in ways not otherwise found in the language. A peculiar case is provided by OPs in Tsonga. In conjunction with an H-toned verb (*ku#vọ́ná* 'to see', *ku#lángútá* 'to look at', *ku#dyángátéla* 'to cheat', *ku#cạ́kányétéla* 'to crush'), the OP H simply disappears: *ku-vạ#vọ́ná, ku-vạ#lángútá, ku-vạ#dyángátéla* with cl.2 OPs. However, with a toneless stem (*ku#xava* 'to buy', *ku#xavisa* 'to sell', *ku#rivalela* 'to forgive', *ku#tsutsumela* 'to run to'), the OP induces H, sometimes on the next syllable and sometimes two syllables away, cf. *ku-xị#xává* 'to buy [cl.7]', *ku-yị#xavísa* 'to sell [cl.9]', *ku-vạ#riváléla* 'to forgive [cl.2]', *ku-n'wị#tsutsúméla* 'to run to [cl.1]'.

Patterns of tone deletion or spreading and shifting may commonly exhibit restrictions on morphosyntactic domains. Shona has both bounded and unbounded tone spreading, the choice being determined by morphosyntactic information. There is obligatory unbounded rightward spread of H from a prefix syllable e.g. *mu#chero* 'fruit tree', *sá-mú#chéro* 'owner of tree'; *mu-ma-zi-mi#chero* 'in the huge fruit trees', *mú-má-zi-mi#chéro* 'it's in the huge fruit trees'; *ku#bikira* 'to cook for', *ku-mú#bíkira* 'to cook for him'. In the domain of prefixes, spreading is unbounded, but between prefixes and stems, spreading only affects the root initial syllable, as shown in the last example. At the phrasal level, spreading only targets the first syllable of the next word, hence *akabika* 'and he cooked', *mukómaná ákabika* 'and the child cooked'. Within the stem (and only there), the root initial H is subject to a pattern of double spreading, so *ku#tóreseserana* becomes *ku#tóréséserana* 'to make take a lot for each other'.

Another major demarcative function of tone in Bantu is as an indicator of phrasal relations. Many languages have phrasal phonological processes whose domains of application are defined in terms of syntactic and semantic relations between words. The most typical situation is sandhi that applies only between phrasal heads and their complements. For instance, in Zinza, H is deleted from a verb that is followed by a complement, so compare *aka#zína* 'he sang' and *aka#zịna géeta* 'he sang in Geita'. If the following word is not a complement, there is no deletion, cf. *aka#zína Bulemo* 'Bulemo sang'. Application of this sandhi rule gives a clear indication of the functional relation between verbs and following words. The kinds of syntactic information which can be reflected in Bantu tone can be rather complicated.

In a number of languages, negative verbs behave differently from corresponding positive forms with respect to tone sandhi. In Tsonga, negative verbs spread their H unfettered by restrictions that operate in affirmative verbs. Thus the H-toned subject prefix in *vá#xává nyáma* 'they are buying meat' (cf. *ndzi#xava nyama* 'I am buying meat') cannot extend onto the final vowel of the nominal complement in this affirmative tense. However, in the case of the negative *a-ndzí#xáví* 'I am not buying', the H tone at the end of the verb can extend through to the end of the noun: *a-ndzí#xáví nyámá*.

H tones are commonly deleted in certain morphologically governed phrasal contexts. In Zinza, an H in certain verb tenses but not others deletes before words within the phrase. For example, the past tense form *a-ka#tẹ́eka* 'he cooked (remote)' has an H-toned stem. When a complement follows, the stem loses its H: *a-ka#teeka ma#lạ́aya* 'he cooked bananas'. There is no deletion of H in the present tense: *ni-ba#tẹ́eka malạ́aya* 'they are cooking bananas'. In Makhuwa, on the other hand, the initial H-tone of a nominal complement elides after a verb in some but not all tenses. Thus, *nakhụ́wo* 'maize' appears with its H tone intact in *ki-nọ́ó#límá nakhụ́wo* 'I am cultivating maize', but without its H tone in *ki-n#límá nakhuwo* 'it's maize that I am cultivating'.

6 CONCLUSION

Although a great deal is known about Bantu tone, we have detailed studies of only a fraction of the Bantu languages. Most of the languages for which we do have material seem to exhibit variations that range from subtle differences to what amounts to essentially different systems. We have identified in this chapter many principles and patterns that are pervasive. Doubtless there is still much more to be learned. The continued documentation of Bantu tone systems remains a critical need – not just for the student of African languages, but also for the general linguist.

The close examination of Bantu tonal systems reveals patterns of extraordinary complexity. The ultimate goal of the study of linguistic systems is to understand how a child learns such systems automatically by virtue of being a human being born into these linguistic communities. There are few other phonological phenomena as complex as Bantu tone, which at the same time are clearly the consequence of the speaker's knowledge of a system of principles rather than the memorization of specific forms. As a result, the importance of Bantu tone systems for the theoretical study of phonology cannot be overestimated.

ACKNOWLEDGMENTS

We would like to thank our numerous language consultants, and the many funding agencies who have supported our research on Bantu tonology over the years, especially the National Science Foundation, National Endowment for the Humanities and the Fulbright Foundation. Data with no reference to source derive from our own notes. We would also like to thank Lee Bickmore for providing supplementary data on Namwanga and Gusii. We follow the standard Bantuist convention of marking only H syllables, except that in Kamba which has four tone levels we mark superlow as $\grave{v}$. Underlining indicates location of a 'primary H' (see especially §4).

REFERENCES

Blanchon and Creissels 1999; Burssens 1939; Carter 1962; Cassimjee 1986, 1998; Cassimjee and Kisseberth 1998, 1999; Cheng and Kisseberth 1979, 1980, 1981; Clements and Ford 1979; Clements and Goldsmith 1984; Coupez 1955; Creissels 1998; Dickens 1984; Downing 1990; Goldsmith 1976, 1981, 1987; Hyman 1976a, 1982; Hyman and Kisseberth 1998; Hyman and Mathangwane 1998; Khumalo 1987; Kisseberth 1992, 1994; Maganga and Schadeberg 1992; Massamba 1982; Mathangwane 1999; McCawley 1970; Meeussen 1954, 1963, 1966; Odden 1981, 1989, 1994, 1995a, 1995b, 1996, 1999, 2000; Philippson 1998; Poletto 1998; Richardson 1959; Roberts 1992; Schadeberg 1973; Stappers 1964; Stevick 1969a, 1969b; Van Spaandonck 1967; Voorhoeve 1973; Yukawa 1987a, 1989a, 1992.

CHAPTER FIVE

DERIVATION

Thilo C. Schadeberg

Bantu languages are rich in morphology, inflectional as well as derivational. The line between the two kinds of morphological processes is usually easy to draw. The major derivational processes are surveyed in this chapter. General statements refer to "proto-typical" Bantu, which is Proto-Bantu (PB), usually directly reflected in Savannah Bantu but also in much of Forest Bantu.

This chapter draws heavily on work done at the Royal Museum of Central Africa, most importantly on "Bantu grammatical reconstructions" (Meeussen 1967) and "Bantu lexical reconstructions 2" (BLR2 = Coupez, Bastin and Mumba 1998). Other comparative sources (in chronological order: Meinhof 1899, 1906, Meinhof and Warmelo 1932, Doke 1935, Guthrie 1967–71) dictionaries and grammars from which isolated examples are drawn are not referenced. Cross references within this chapter are indicated by §§.

1 INTRODUCTION: STEM, BASE, RADICAL, EXTENSION

The typical nominal or verbal word-form consists of a *stem* preceded by one or more bound morphemes. A nominal stem is usually preceded by a *nominal prefix* (NPx), and preceding a verbal stem we may find prefixes specifying, amongst other things, the person or noun class of the subject as well as inflectional categories (such as time, aspect, negation, etc.). The stem-initial position often has special stress-related phonological properties (tone, length, vowel quality); we mark the stem-initial boundary with the equal sign (=); the simple hyphen or dash (−) represents other word-internal boundaries. Verb stems can further be divided into a verbal *base* (B) and a *final suffix* (F). The same analysis into B and F is possible for those nouns that are derived from verbs; most other nominal stems are not amenable to further morphological analysis. In finite verb forms, F is part of inflectional morphology; in deverbative nouns, F is a nominalizing suffix.

UMbundu (R11):

tw-à=lìm-á	'we cultivated'	SCd − TAM=[B − F]$_{stem}$
ókú=lím-à	'to cultivate'	NPx=[B − F]$_{stem}$
á=lím-ì	'cultivators'	NPx=[B − F]$_{stem}$
á=lím-à	'years'	NPx=[B − F]$_{stem}$
á=$^{\downarrow}$límá	'bats'	NPx=Stem

The first four words above all contain the verbal B °=*lìm*-; the last item contains the unanalyzable nominal stem °=*límá*.

The B is the domain of derivational (lexical) morphology of the verb. The B may be simple or extended. The simple B consists just of a root or *radical* (R). The extended B consists of a R followed by one or more *extensions* (E). An E may be analyzable as to form and meaning, in which case we may call it a suffix, or else segmentation may be purely formal, in which case the analysis yields a (formal) radical and an *expansion* (or: formal suffix). Such formal segmentation can be justified by the parallel phonological

71

behavior of expansions and extensions (tonally neutral, reduced vowel system). For example, the B *=ták-un- is analyzed as consisting of the R=tak- and the E -un-.

Bantu verbs have a very regular morphological and phonological structure. The R has the structure CVC, where C_2 may be prenasalized or empty. The set of CV-verbs is small but contains some very basic verbs (e.g. *=lì- 'eat', *=pá- 'give', *=kú- 'die'). Almost all verbs longer than CVC can be shown to result from derivational processes, at least from a comparative point of view.

- One or more E may be suffixed to the R (§§2.1–11).
- The initial CV of the R may be reduplicated (§§2.12).
- The verb may be derived from a nominal stem (§§5).

Compounded verbs are very rare (§§6.3); total reduplication of verbs applies to the stem rather than the base and is rarely lexicalized (§§6.4). There are some verbs of the shape *=(j)iCVC- where the initial *(j)í is suspect of being a petrified unidentified morpheme; e.g. *=(j)íbak- 'build', *=(j)íkut- 'be satiated', *=(j)ípul- 'ask'. Most verbs of the shape =CVVC- and =CGVC- can be derived from a R =CV- followed by an E -VC-. Whether or not the derivational process underlying those verbs with more than one vocalic segment is transparent, all longer verbs obey general structural restrictions in that only the first (R) vowel is tonally distinctive and exploits the full seven-vowel system.

2 VERB-TO-VERB DERIVATION

2.1 Summary of verb extensions

The following verb extensions have been reconstructed for PB; they occur in the body of PB reconstructions and their reflexes are found in languages from all zones.

*-i-/-ici-	causative
*-ıl-	dative (applicative)
*-ık-	impositive
*-ık-	neuter
*-am-	positional (stative)
*-an-	associative (reciprocal)
*-ag- ~ -ang-	repetitive
*-al-	extensive
*-at-	tentive (contactive)
*-ʋl-; -ʋk-	separative tr.; itr. (reversive)
*-ʋ-/-ibʋ-	passive

The canonical extension has the shape -VC-; the two E with the shape -V- have -VCV-allomorphs. Extensions have a reduced five-vowel system; the mid vowels (*e o) only occur as the result of vowel harmony with extensions having a second-degree vowel (*ı ʋ); the absence of *u may be coincidental since it occurs in expansions. Nasal harmony affects the consonants *l and *k. Verb extensions of the shape -VC- are tonally neutral (or, alternatively, Low); there is some slight evidence that the tone of the two extensions with the shape -V-, i.e. *-i- and *-ʋ-, may have been High (Meeussen 1961).

The element *-a(n)g- behaves tonally as an extension, but it often enters into the inflectional paradigm (with various imperfective meanings such as durative or habitual); it is not discussed further in this chapter (cf. Sebasoni 1967; Nurse, Ch.6, this volume).

Extensions differ widely along the productivity scale, from totally unproductive expansions occurring in just a few verbs to fully productive suffixes.

Several extensions may combine with one root. The last extension determines the syntactic profile of the B. The addition is cyclical in the sense that when the meaning of a B consisting of R + E₁ has developed a specific meaning, this meaning is retained in a further derivation R + E₁ + E₂. The causative E offers particularly interesting challenges to morphological analysis since it appears to change its position or has multiple representations. In general, more productive E follow less productive ones, and the last two positions are causative-passive.

Bantu verb extensions do not form a neat semantic or syntactic system. The idea that Bantu verb extensions originate from serial verb constructions may be true in some cases but not in others. The only two etymologies that have been suggested concern reciprocal *-an- (from the clitic preposition na- 'with, and') and extensive *-al- (from *=jal- 'to spread').

2.2 Causative

Two PB causative extensions have been reconstructed with an original complementary distribution (Bastin 1986): *-i- after C and *-ici- after V. Leaving aside some exceptional vowel-final verb stems, this means that the long causative extension was used after short roots of the shape =CV-, and the short causative extension was used after the longer stems of the shape =CVC(-VC)-. Later developments have generally extended the range of environments in favor of reflexes of *-ici- which more closely correspond to the canonical shape VC of other extensions.

The causative extension may be added to transitive as well as to intransitive verbs. In both cases a new argument is added to the syntactic frame of the simple verb. This new argument has the syntactic function of subject and the semantic function of agent-causer.

Mituku (D13):

kʊ=súm-ís-a	'to boil (tr.)'	< kʊ=súm-a	'to boil (itr.)'
kʊ=tút-ís-a	'to make s.o. beat'	< kʊ=tút-a	'to beat'

In the case of transitive verbs, it is usually the agent-subject of the simple verb that ends up as the object of the derived causative verb with the semantic function of causee. Most cases where the object of the simple verb also appears as the object of the derived causative verb involve lexicalization.

Shi (JD53)

=gul-iis-a	'to cause (s.o.) to buy'		
=guz-a	'to sell (sth.)'	< =gul-a	'to buy'

In some languages, particularly in the southeast, the causative extension expresses specialized meanings in addition to its general causative semantics. Two of these are the "adjutive" (< Latin adiutare "to help") and the "imitative" meanings.

Zulu (S42):

ba-yo =fika ba = vun-is-e ba = bhul-is-e	'they will come and help to harvest and thresh'
u = hamb-is-e okoonwabu	'he walks like a chameleon'

The adjutive meaning is typically associated with verbs denoting communal activities where helping makes the event possible. The shift from causative to imitative becomes transparent when we paraphrase our example as 'he made a chameleon walk (as an actor)'.

Another recurring meaning of the causative extension is "intensive", where the derived verb behaves syntactically the same as the simple verb. In some languages, formal distinctions between causative and intensive verbs have evolved, e.g. in Zulu and Shona the intensive meaning is expressed by the reduplicated causative extension. This shift of meaning is more difficult to understand.

2.3 Dative (applicative)

The dative extension *-ɪl- is best known in Bantu studies under the term "applicative"; other common labels are "prepositional" and "directive". Dative verbs are transitive, the object of the dative verb fulfills the semantic roles of (i) beneficiary, (ii) place and – by extension – time, cause and reason, and (iii) instrument. Of these, the beneficiary function is the most wide-spread and the most productive (cf. Dammann 1961, Kähler-Meyer 1966).

Ganda (JE15):

a=kol-er-a abaami babiri	'he works for two masters'
kol-er-a wano	'work here!'
a=yimb-ir-a nsimbi	'she sings for money'
a=tambul-ir-a ku-ppikipiki	'he travels by/on a motorcycle'

Dative verbs can be derived from about any other verb; when the basic verb is transitive, the object of the basic verb typically loses its object properties in the dative construction. Less commonly, the object of the basic verb may keep its object status (as seen by the presence of an OCd), in such constructions the dative extension marks the added argument as providing essential new information.

Ganda (JE15):

ente zino, zi=gob-e	'these cattle, drive them away'
ente zino, zi=gob-er-e mu-kiraalo	'these cattle, drive them into the kraal!'

Examples such as these, together with the body of reconstructed dative verbs, suggest that the primary function of the dative extension was to tie the non-patient complement closer to the verb. The first such non-patient complements may well have been locative ones, from which the other roles of the dative object have evolved.

2.4 Impositive

For more than a century, the impositive extension *-ɪk- has been understood as a kind of causative, expressing typically "direct causation" (i.e. adding 'cause to' to an intransitive verb), but some "locative" element of meaning has also been observed in several older descriptions (cf. Dammann 1958). Inspection of any list of verbs carrying this extension, either from a particular language or from the body of PB reconstructions, confirms that the more precise meaning is 'to put (sth.) into some position', hence the term "impositive" <Latin *(im)positus* 'put'. The impositive extension *-ɪk- does not appear to be very productive in any particular language. It typically commutes with positional *-am- and separative *-ʊl-/-ʊk-, but commutation with zero is less common. In most languages it is homophonous with the neuter extension; notable exceptions occur in the southeast (Kwanyama, Ndonga, Herero) where the "assimilating final vowel" suffix of certain tenses is -e after the impositive (as well as the dative) extension, but -a after all other extensions including the homophonous neuter one, and also in Chewa where the

homophonous neuter extension adds a High tone to certain verb forms but the impositive extension does not.

Nen (A44; *-ε < *-ɪk-*):

=án-è	'stretch out hand'	cf.=án (dto.)	< *=(j)án-ɪk-	'spread out'
=léŋ-è	'bend, incline'	cf.=léŋ-ém	'be bent'	
=kóŋ-è	'lean (sth. against sth.)'			

2.5 Neuter

The neuter extension **-ɪk-* is generally homophonous with the impositive extension (§§2.4). It is poorly represented in the body of PB reconstructions, but reflexes probably occur in all zones. Reconstructions as well as examples from languages where the neuter extension is least productive show that the extension is best represented with two semantic classes of verbs: verbs of destruction ('be breakable/be broken (itr.)' < 'break (tr.)', 'be splittable/be split (itr.)' < 'split (tr.)'), and experiencer verbs ('be visible' < 'see', 'be audible' < 'hear'). The label "neuter" has the disadvantage that it suggests a general syntactic function (closer to passive than to active voice). It does not express the specific link with the two semantic categories mentioned.

Ewondo (A72; *-i / -e < *-ɪk-*):

=búg-i	'break off (itr.)'	cf.=bûk	'break off (tr.)'
=sal-i	'split (itr.)'	cf.=sa(l)	'split (tr.)'
=yén-e	'become visible'	cf.=yên	'see'

In some languages, the neuter extension has gained a high productivity and can be combined with a wide range of transitive basic verbs. A more precise semantic–syntactic label for this extension would be "neutro-passive". Verbs with this extension indicate that the subject is potentially or factually affected by the action expressed by the verb; the difference between the potential and the process-or-state interpretations may be linked to the aspectual meaning of the particular inflectional category of the verbal form or else may have to be inferred from the context. No agent is implied, and it is typically impossible to express the agent.

Two other labels found in the literature are "stative" (cf. Mchombo 1993a) and "intransitive"; we avoid these labels because they are too general and could (and have) been applied equally well to other extensions.

2.6 Positional (stative)

The following PB reconstructions contain the positional extension **-am-* and are typical for the meaning and the commutational properties of this extension.

* = (j)ég-am-	'lean against (itr.)'	* = (j)ég-ek-	'lean against (tr.)'
* = (j)m-am-	'bend over (itr.)'	* = (j)m-ʊk-	'straighten up (itr.)'
* = co-am-	'hide (itr.)'	* = co-ek-	'hide (tr.)'
		* = co-	'set (of sun)'
* = kúk-am-	'kneel'		

The common element of meaning is 'assuming a position', or – when used in a perfective aspect form – 'to be in a position'. The positional extension is the intransitive counterpart of the impositive extension with which it often commutes. (For another pattern of commutation see the separative extensions below.) The label "positional" is preferred over the more widely used one "stative", which is generally used in a grammaticalized, syntactic sense that is not typically associated with this extension.

The positional extension has been generalized to form passive verbs in a group of contiguous languages in zone C (Lingala, Ngombe, Mongo). This change of function has been triggered by the loss of *k which led to a merger of the passive extension *-ʊ- with the intransitive separative extension *-ʊk- (see Meeussen 1954).

2.7 Associative (reciprocal)

The most productive use and meaning of the associative extension *-an- is reciprocal.

Chewa (N31b):

kodí ßantu ßámúná ßa-ka=kum-an-a sá=lónj-er-an-a
Q 2.people 2.man 2-TAM=meet-ASS-TAM NEG:TAM=greet-DAT-ASS-TAM
'When men meet do they not greet each other formally?'

Reciprocal verbs require more than one agent, and the agents are at the same time mutual patients of their action. Syntactically, a single plural subject may fulfill these roles, or there may be two noun phrases which then may be either a "conjoint subject", or one may be the subject and the other one a "prepositional phrase". The marker of conjunction or "preposition" generally is the associative preclitic na- 'with, and'. When the associative NP follows the verb, agreement may be either with the subject NP or the corresponding plural form – even when the subject is singular.

Zigula (G31): *mthu na-mbuyaye wa=pang-an-a dende dya-mphasi.*
           'A man and his friend share the leg of a grasshopper.' (proverb)
Zulu (S42):   *ingwe i=f-an-a n'eekati.*
           'The leopard resembles ('with') the cat.'
Mwera (P22): *tu-na=lek-an-a na-mbuya njangu.*
           'I (lit. 'we') am parting with my mate.'

In most languages of Angola (zones H, K, R), the reciprocal use of *-an- is more or less obsolete; its function has been taken over by the reflexive object concord. A similar tendency can be observed in Mongo (C61) and some other languages of zone C where *k has become zero and *-an- has taken over the function of neuter *-ik-. (Cf. also French *se quereller* and German *sich zanken*, both with reciprocal meaning.)

In addition to expressing reciprocity, examples of related but not exactly reciprocal uses are attested from all over Bantu. In Nen (A44; cf. Mous, Ch. 16, this volume), the reflex of *-an- is used to express joint actions by several agents (and also the plurality of the addressee of imperative forms). In Kela (C75), *-an- expresses repetitive or intensive actions, in Songye (L22) it expresses actions directed towards several other people, and in Shona (S12) it is "used of a single subject with reference to its parts and their relation to one another" (Fortune 1955:219; e.g. =gony-an-a 'curl' <=gony-a 'bend'). Similar examples could be cited from many other languages.

In view of such evidence I suggest that the reciprocal meaning derives from the wider associative meaning. The opposite view is held by Guthrie (1967–71:iii.218, §2.11); cf. also Dammann (1954) and Mchombo (1993b).

2.8 Extensive

The extensive extension *-al- comes closest to being productive in some southern languages. In Northern Sotho (S32) it expresses "the (active) entering of a passive state where the action expressed by the basic verb potentially or actually affects the subject"; e.g. *=bɔ́n-al-a* 'to let oneself be seen, to appear' *<=bɔ́n-a* 'to see', cf.*=bɔ́n-ɛx-a* 'to be visible' (Endemann 1876:65). The same extension (with loss of its consonant) is probably also contained in the complex extensions described for Lamba (M54) but also occurring elsewhere (e.g. in UMbundu R11):

> A derivative form of the verb which indicates that the action is extended in time or space or repeated extensively. The *extensive form* in Lamba is indicated in the intransitive by the suffix *-aaka, -auka* or *-aika*; in the transitive by *-aala, -aula* or *-aila*; in the causative by *-aasya, -ausya* or *-aisya*.
>
> (Doke 1931a:105)

Inspection of the sets of verbs containing the extension *-al-*, either in the body of PB reconstructions or in particular languages, point to a central element of meaning 'to be in a spread-out position'. Recurring derived meanings are various words for being ill and suffering. The label "extensive" seems to fit this meaning rather well (cf. Schadeberg 1994). Some of the best-attested PB reconstructions follow below; others are given in §4 on noun-to-verb derivation.

= (j)ik-al-	'sit, dwell, stay'		< *= (j)ik-*	'descend'
= tíg-al-	'remain'		< *= tíg-*	'leave (behind)'
= dú-al-	'wear (clothes)'		cf. *= dú-ɪk-*	'put on (clothes)'
= dʊ́-al-	'be ill'			

2.9 Tentive (contactive)

The tentive extension *-at-* is not known to be productive in any language. Some of the most widely spread verbs with this extension are represented by the following PB reconstructions.

= kʊ́-at-	'seize'		
= dɪ-at-	'tread on'	variants:	*= dɪb-at-*, *= nɪ-at-*
= kúmb-at-	'hold, embrace'	variant:	*= kʊ́mb-at-*
= dam-at-	'stick to'	variant:	*= nam-at-*

The meanings of these four verbs are typical and are taken to contain the common element of 'actively making firm contact'. The label "tentive" is preferred over "contactive" (cf. Dammann 1962) because it refers to the active element of the contact and is derived from the prototypical verb of this class in Latin: *tenere/tentus* 'to hold'.

2.10 Separative (reversive)

Most descriptions report two separative extensions: transitive *-ʊl-* and intransitive *-ʊk*. Further morphological segmentation seems to be indicated, but the consonants *l* and *k* do not recur as morphemes with the meanings 'transitive/intransitive'. The separative extensions occupy an intermediate position on the productivity scale: separative verbs are quite frequent but cannot freely be formed from other verbs.

Commutation between the two separative extensions is the norm but exceptions exist.

Swahili (G42d; *-u-/-o-* < *-ʊl-*):

=ond-o-a	'take away'	*=ond-ok-a*	'leave, go away'
=chag-u-a	'choose'	—	
—		*=am-k-a*	'wake up'

Other common patterns of commutation are:

Swahili (G42d):

with zero:	=zib-u-a	'unblock'	=zib-a	'block'
with impositive:	=fun-u-a	'uncover'	=fun-ik-a	'cover'
with positional:	=in-u-a	'lift up'	=in-am-a	'stoop'
with neuter:	=v-u-a	'take off (clothes)'	=v-a-a	'wear (clothes)'
none:	=pas-u-a	'split'		

The most common label for theses extensions is "reversive" or "inversive". In more detailed descriptions we read that only some of the verbs with these extensions have a "reversive" meaning. The two other most frequently recurring senses are "intensive" and "repetitive" (cf. Dammann 1959).

Mongo (C61):

reversive sense:	=bák-ol-	'detach'	=bák-	'fix'
iterative sense:	=nyɔm-ɔl-	'knead again'	=nyɔm-	'knead'
augmentative sense:	=miny-ol-	'smash'	=miny-	'shatter
causative sense:	=tsíl-ol-	'stretch out (limbs)'	=tsíl-	'agitate (limbs)'
multiple senses:	=band-ol-	'detach, fix again, fix solidly'	=band-	'fetter, gag'
other senses:	=bumb-ol-	'steal'	=bumb-	'find, visit'
	=lek-ol-	'surpass'	=lek-	'pass'
'no sense':	=bang-ol-	'begin'	=bang-	'begin'

The synchronic situation described above with respect to frequency, patterns of commutation and various senses is also found in the body of PB reconstructions.

The label 'reversive' is rejected because (i) it fits only a small portion of the data, (ii) it does not explain which member of a given pair, e.g. 'put down' / 'pick up', will have the extension; and (iii) because there are numerous verbs with these extensions for which no plausible non-reversive source can be imagined, e.g. 'choose', 'comb', 'jump'. The common element of meaning which best fits the total data and from which the various senses can be derived is 'movement out of some original position'. The reversive sense appears only in the specific case where the basic verb incorporates the semantic element 'join' (cf. Schadeberg 1982).

2.11 Passive

Two allomorphs of the passive extension have been reconstructed (cf. Stappers 1967): *-ʊ- occurring after C and *-ibʊ- occurring after V. The non-canonical shapes -V- and -VCV- and the conditioning of the allomorphs find their parallel with the causative extension (§§2.2). Since the passive extension occupies the last position in a sequence of several extensions, the long allomorph not only appears after short radicals of the shape =CV- but also after the causative extension *-i- / -ici-. Because of the great productivity coupled with syntactic and semantic regularity, few passive verbs have been reconstructed for PB. The one with the largest spread is *kól-ʊ- 'get drunk': the corresponding non-passive verb most commonly means 'to be strong'; other attested meanings are 'take', 'intoxicate' (back formation?), 'choke' and 'work'.

In most of zone A and B there are no clear reflexes of *-(ib)ʊ-; instead, there are suffixes of the general shape *-(a)b(e) (the vowels differ from language to language), with a meaning described as passive, neuter or middle voice. Since Basaá (A43) attests both passive *-ib(ʋ)- and reflexive *-ab(e)-, and some other languages of the area also attest *-ʋ- (Ngumba A81, Myene B11, Tsogo B31), we reject doubts expressed by Guthrie (1967–71) and Heine (1973) as to the presence of the passive extension(s) in PB.

There are several other areas where the passive extension is used sparingly or not at all. One of these areas covers parts of zones H, K and L, but generally a few synchronically underived verb stems attesting *-ʋ- have survived. In the greater part of zone C the passive extension has been lost due to a phonologically triggered merger with *-ʋk- (Meeussen 1954). Where the passive extension is not commonly used, other extensions (*-am-, -an-) have filled the gap, or other types of constructions are used. Luba (L31a) and Mbundu (H21) use a "passive participle"; more widespread is the use of an active verb with a class 2 SCd.

Luba-Ks. (L31a):

n=dí mw=ipíkílá nkundé léélo ku=di máámu
I-am being.cooked.for beans today there.where-is my.mother
'Beans are cooked for me today by my mother.'

ba=kwacilé mbují ku=di nkashaama
they-seized goat there.where-is leopard
'The goat was seized by the leopard.'

2.12 Partial reduplication

There are a good number of verbs of the shape =CVCVC- where the first two CV-sequences are identical and which contain 'repetitive motion' or 'oscillation' as a recurring element of meaning.

Swahili (G42d):

=babat-a	'tap (as in metal working)'
=gugun-a	'gnaw, nibble, nag'
=kokot-a	'pull by tugging'

Some of these verbs are derived by partial reduplication: =CV.CVC-. Where C_2 of the R is NC, the nasal may or may not be reduplicated.

Rundi (JD62):   Lamba (M54):

| =ríriimb-a | 'sing' | =sansant-a | 'be in pain' |
| =ruruumb-a | 'burn' | =fyomfyont-a | 'suck' |

In many cases, the actual path of derivation is difficult to trace. Other possible sources are =CVC-VC-, or derivation from a (reduplicated) noun (§§5.2) or ideophone (§§5.3). Compare the following set reconstructions, where the noun has the widest distribution (zones A B J L S), and BLR2 adds the comment "iconique dans certaines langues" about the reflexes of *p.

| *=papal- | 'flap wings, flutter' | *=papá | 'wing' |
| *=papam- | 'flap wings, flutter' | *=pap- | 'flap wings, flutter' |

3 VERB-TO-NOUN DERIVATION

The derivation of nouns from verbs involves several productive processes, some of which are so widespread that they have been reconstructed for PB. The process involves two parts: the derivation of a nominal stem from a verbal base B by the addition of a final suffix F, and the assignment of the derived nominal stem to a nominal class (or gender).

3.1 Infinitives

From a morphological point of view, infinitives are nouns by virtue of having a nominal prefix, but they also have verbal characteristics such as the possibility to include an OCd as well as a limited range of inflectional morphemes in pre-stem position (motional *-ka-*, negative markers).

The infinitive stem has the F *-a*, and is thus the same as the default stem used in verbal inflection. In some languages the infinitive has a conjoint form with F *-á* linking it syntactically to a following complement. The negative infinitive sometimes has a different F which it shares with certain negative tenses.

Infinitives are generally assigned to class 15, NPx *kʋ-*, less commonly also to class 5, NPx *i-*; some languages attest both (cf. Forges 1983, Hadermann 1999). Other noun classes (9, 14) are also sometimes employed. The use of the prefix *ka-* after verbs of motion may derive from the motional *-ka-* rather than from class 12. The homophony between the NPx of class 15 and the locative class 17 raises the question whether the infinitive with *ku-* derives from the locative. Whatever the answer may be, the infinitive has in many languages displaced the original small set of non-verbal nouns from class 15 (*kʋ=bóko* 'arm', *kʋ=gʋlʋ* 'leg', *kʋ=tʋ́i* 'ear', *kʋ=jápa* 'armpit').

3.2 Agent nouns

The primary kind of agent nouns are derived from verbs by adding the F *-i* to the B; stems are generally assigned to class 1/2 since typical agents are human, but other classes may also be used.

mʋ=jíb-i	(cl. 1/2)	'thief'	< *=jíb-* 'steal'
mʋ=kó-i	(cl. 1/2)	'in-law'	< *=kó-* 'pay bridewealth'
mʋ=jéd-i	(cl. 3/4, 15)	'moon, moonlight'	< *=jél-* 'shine, be clear'
mbón-i	(cl. 9/10)	'pupil (of eye)'	< *=bón-* 'see'

The F suffix is *-á* (rather than *-i*) when it follows a causative or passive extension.

Nyamwezi (F22):

m=βʋúj-á	'the one who asks'	<°=βʋʋj- 'ask' = caus.<°=βʋʋl- 'reveal'
m=toól-w-á	'bride'	<°=toól-w- = pass.<°=toól- 'marry'

(For complemented agent nouns, see §§6.3.)

3.3 Actions, results, instruments

Deverbative stems with a F *-o* are very common and appear in all classes except 1/2. Such nouns refer to the action itself, the result of the action, the place or the instrument (often with applicative *-il-*). Unlike the formation of infinitives and agent nouns, the derivation of nouns in *-o* is generally not fully productive and the meaning of such nouns is not entirely predictable.

mʋ=long-o	(cl. 3/4)	'line'	< *=long-* 'arrange, pack'
i=tém-o	(cl. 5/6)	'hoe'	< *=tém-* 'cut, cut down'
i=lí-il-o	(cl. 5)	'place or thing for eating'	< *=lí-il-* 'eat + APPL'
kɪ=lɪl-o	(cl. 7/8)	'mourning'	< *=lɪl-* 'cry, weep'
mpúk-o	(cl. 9/10)	'mole'	< *=púk-* 'dig, fling up (earth)'

| *lʊ=gend-o | (cl. 11) 'journey' | < *=gend- | 'walk, travel' |
| *bʊ=lɪmb-o | (cl. 14) 'birdlime' | < *=lɪmb- | 'stick to sth.' |

3.4 Adjectives

Stems derived from verbs of quality with F *-ú function as adjectives, i.e. they take a NPx in agreement with the syntactic head noun. Further derivation leads to nouns of quality (class 14; §§4.2) and sometimes to nouns denoting persons (class 1/2). This kind of formation is productive in some languages, e.g. Nyamwezi F22; isolated examples occur much more widely and a few such stems have been reconstructed.

Swahili (G42d):

=bovu	'rotten'	< *=bol- (class 5 with NPx *i-)
=ovu	'bad, evil'	< *=bol- (class 1, other classes)
=kavu	'dry'	< *=kal- (tone?)
=gumu	'hard'	< *=gʊm- (cf. * =júm- 'be dry')
=refu	'long'	< *=dai-p-
m=fumu	'chief [loanword?]'	< *mʊ=kúm-ú < *=kúm- 'be honoured'

3.5 Other final suffixes

Practically all vowels, with different tones, are attested as F in deverbative nouns, with a wide range of meanings. Nouns with F -a are particularly frequent; their exact path of derivation is not always traceable (§§5.2). The examples are too varied to allow firm reconstructions, but a good candidate is the F *-'.e (HL rather than "polar" tone) deriving nouns or participles often referring to a state (cf. Bastin 1989). The best such reconstruction, *=lúm-e 'male, husband' < *=lúm- 'bite', does not fit this meaning. (It rather appears to be an agent noun, a metaphoric reference to male sex.)

*kɪ=unt-í	(cl. 7)	'fist'	< *=kunt-	'knock'
*mʊ=dumb-í	(cl. 3)	'continuous rain'	< *=dumb-	'rain'
*=kál-ɪ	(adj.)	'bitter, sharp'	< *=kál-	'be bitter, be sharp'
*ngob-é	(cl. 9)	'hook'	< *=gob-	'bend, crook'
*mpét-é	(cl. 9)	'ring'	< *=pet-	'bend, curve (tone!?)'
*mʊ=kél-e	(cl. 3)	'salt'	< *=kél-	'filter'
*kɪ=pac-e	(cl. 7)	'splinter'	< *=pac-	'split'
*mbíl-á	(cl. 9)	'call'	< *=bíl-	'call'
*kɪ=lɪm-ɪl-a	(cl. 7)	'pleiades'	< *=lɪm-	'cultivate'
*lʊ=kómb-ó	(cl. 11)	'broom'	< *=kómb-	'sweep'
*=kúl-ʊ́	(adj.)	'old'	< *=kúl-	'grow'
*=jél-ʊ	(adj.)	'white'	< *=jél-	'shine, be clear'

Some languages have developed new productive derivational processes. For example, Nyamwezi (F22) has two kinds of manner nouns, and Luba-Ks. (L31a) has active and passive participles.

Nyamwezi (F22):

| =zeeng- | 'build' | >kɪ=zeeng-elé | class 7 | (type of construction) |
| | | >ka=zeeng-elé | class 12 | (manner of building) |

Luba-Ks. (L31a):

=súng-ul- 'choose'   > bá=súng-ul-é 'they having chosen'
                      > bá=súng-úl-á 'they having been chosen'

4 NOUN-TO-NOUN DERIVATION

Nouns are derived from nouns by shifting them from one class (gender) to another. Nouns are derived from adjectives by assigning them to a specific class. It is this derivational or "autonomous" use of noun class assignment which most clearly shows (some of) the semantic content of Bantu nominal classes. In addition to the widespread and productive processes listed in §§4.1–4.6, there are sporadic, non-recurring cases in the body of PB reconstructions:

*mʊ=ntʊ	(cl. 1/2)	'person, someone'	> *kɪ=ntʊ	(cl. 7/8)	'thing, something'
*mʊ=jʊ́ma	(cl. 1/2)	'person, someone'	< *kɪ=jʊ́ma	(cl. 7/8)	'thing, something'
*mʊ=tí	(cl. 3/4)	'tree'	> *kɪ=tí	(cl. 7/8)	'stool; stick'
*njíkɪ	(cl. 9/10)	'bee'	<> *bʊ=jíkɪ	(cl. 14)	'honey'

The direction of such sporadic noun-to-noun derivations is not always easy to determine. The following series of derivation by shifts of noun class has been analysed by Grégoire (1976).

*kɪ-bánjá	(cl. 7/8)	'clearing prepared for building'
*mbánjá	(cl. 9/10)	'chief's village'
*lʊ-bánjá	(cl. 11/10)	'dwelling-place, courtyard, family;' 'meeting, affair, lawcourt, guilt'
*i-bánjá	(cl. 5)	'debt'

4.1 Locatives

Locative nouns are formed by adding one of the locative NPx to a whole noun (NPx=stem). Three locative classes have a general geographical distribution; they indicate spaces which are described relative to the entity referred to by the basic noun. A fourth locative NPx, *ɪ=, has a more sporadic spread and limited use (cf. Grégoire 1975).

Cewa (N31):

class 16: *pa=	'space adjacent to X'	pa=phiri	'on the mountain'
class 17: *kʊ=	'space anywhere in' 'the area of X'	ku=mudzi	'at the village'
class 18: *mʊ=	'space inside X'	mu=mphika	'in the cooking pot'

In *pa=ntʊ 16, *kʊ=ntʊ́ 17, *mʊ=ntʊ 18 'place' (and in parallel forms with *=jʊ́ma) the locative NPx directly precedes the stem which is the rule for adjectival stems but atypical for nouns.

A locative suffix *-inɪ is used, often together with the locative NPx, in languages of the extreme east (zones E, G, P, S).

Locative NPx are not directly prefixed to nouns referring to people. Locative nouns behave syntactically much like ordinary nouns, not as prepositional phrases. They control agreement within the nominal phrase as well as on the verb, and a phrase such as 'the fish in the lake' or 'lake fish' has to be rendered as 'fish of in-lake', e.g. Nyakyusa (M31): ɪɪ=swi ɪsya mu=nyaanja.

4.2 Diminutives and augmentatives

Diminutives are widely formed by assigning nouns to classes 12/13 (NPx *ka-/tʊ-*), in the NW also to classes 19/13 (NPx *pi-/tʊ-*). Classes 12 and 13 have very few nouns inherently assigned to them, and these have no obvious semantic feature of 'smallness' (e.g. **ka=nʊa* 'mouth', **ka=já* 'home', **tʊ=bíi* 'excrements', **tʊ=ló* 'sleep').

Augmentatives are widely formed by assigning nouns to classes 5/6 (NPx *i-/ma-*) or 7/8 (NPx *kɪ-/bi-*). In some eastern languages, there is also an augmentative class *gʊ-*. In Nyamwezi (F22), animals shifted to the "augmentative" gender 5/6 are individualized. Augmentative and diminutive classes often have affective values; common pairings are "small is beautiful" and "big is ugly and dangerous", but the inverse relationship also occurs. Such secondary meanings may explain the occurrence of shifts between augmentative and diminutive meanings.

In the formation of diminutives and augmentatives, the derived NPx is sometimes placed before the inherent NPx (rather than substituted for it), especially with classes 9/10 where the (historical, underlying) identity of the stem-initial C may be obscured by the sound changes of prenasalization (NPx **N-*).

4.3 Qualities

Nouns of quality are freely derived from adjectives and from nouns denoting kinds of people (generally classes 1/2) by placing the stem into class 14 (NPx **bʊ-*). Underived nouns belonging to this class have no obvious semantic feature of "quality" or "abstractness" (e.g. **bʊ=játo*, 'boat', **bʊ=táa* 'bow', **bʊ=joga* 'mushroom', **bʊ=tíkʊ* 'night'). Some reconstructible lexicalizations attest the ancientness of this derivation.

*bʊ=log-i	'witchcraft'	< **mʊ=log-i* (cl. 1/2) 'witch'	< **=log-* 'bewitch'
*bʊ=ti	'medicine, witchcraft'	< **mʊ=ti* (cl. 3/4) 'tree'	

4.4 Peoples, countries, languages

Many languages freely assign ethnonymic stems to different classes (genders), deriving words for the specific people, the country, and the language or manner. People are generally in classes 1/2, the country in class 14, and the language in class 11 or 7 (also referring to manner). Some languages may also assign some ethnonyms to other classes.

Gogo (G11):

va=gogo (cl. 1/2)   *ci=gogo* (cl. 7)   *u=gogo* (cl. 14)

Ganda (JE15):

(a)ba=ganda (cl. 1/2)   *(o)lu=ganda* (cl. 11)   *(o)bu=ganda* (cl. 14)

UMbundu (R11):

óvi=mbúndu (cl. 7/8)   *ú=mbúndu* (cl. 14 = 3)

4.5 Trees and fruits

Trees and their fruits are often referred to by words of the same root in different classes. Trees are in classes 3/4, their fruits in classes 5/6, sometimes also in class 9 or 14.

Economically highly relevant plants and their fruits may be referred to by unrelated words.

Koti (P30):

n=ráraṅca	(cl. 3/4)	'orange tree'	> *n=ráraṅca*	(cl. 5/6)	'orange'
n=khunazi	(cl. 3/4)	'ziziphus sp.'	> *khunazi*	(cl. 9/10)	'(its fruit)'
n=lapa	(cl. 3/4)	'baobab tree'	> *o=lapa*	(cl. 14)	'(its fruit)'
m=oopo	(cl. 3/4)	'banana plant'	cf. *laazu*	(cl. 5/6)	'banana'
n=nazi	(cl. 3/4)	'coconut palm'	> *naazi*	(cl. 9/10)	'coconut (fully ripe)'
			cf. *n=xala*	(cl. 5/6)	'half-ripe, for drinking'

4.6 Number

If shift of noun class is the formal characteristic of noun-to-noun derivation, the formation of plurals (or singulars) may also be considered as a derivational process in Bantu. Many languages also form collectives and plurals of non-count nouns with the meaning 'kinds of X'; the most common class for this kind of derivation is class 6 (NPx **ma-*).

Swahili (G42d):

simba/simba	(cl. 9/10)	'lion/lions'	*ma=simba*	'a pride of lions'
u=gonjwa	(cl. 11~14)	'illness; disease'	*ma=gonjwa*	'(kinds of) diseases'

Number ('singular' and 'plural') is at best a marginal category in Bantu grammar to which reference is hardly ever needed; "3rd person singular" and "3rd person plural" have no common exponents due to the presence of specific noun *class* agreement markers.

5 NOUN-TO-VERB DERIVATION

5.1 Verbs from adjectives

Noun-to-verb derivation is not a productive process in Bantu languages. The only clearly attested regular process involves the suffix **-p-*, which is added to adjectival stems to derive inchoative verbs of quality: 'to become (be) X'. When added to monosyllabic roots the vowel always appears as long; the reconstructed inherent length of such adjectival roots should be considered as doubtful.

*=kée-p-	< **=kée*	'small'		**=néne-p-*	< **=néne*	'big'
*=lai-p-	< **=lai*	'long'		**=jípí-p-*	< **=jípí*	'short'
*=bíı-p-	< **=bíı*	'bad'		**=jangʋ-p-*	< **=jangʋ*	'quick'
*=kálı-p-	< **=kálı*	'bitter, sharp'				

5.2 Verbs from nouns or ambivalent derivation

There are pairs of obviously related nouns and verbs where the derivational path is difficult to trace. Most of these pairs consist of a nominal stem =CVCV and a verbal stem =CVCVC-*a*. In some cases, both stems may be derived from a no longer existing root =CVC-, but often a derivation of a verb by adding a C to the nominal stem seems more likely.

Swahili (G42d):

ki=pofu 'blind person' < **=póku* (various classes, attested in all zones)
=pofua,=pofuka,=pofusha 'to blind, be blind, make blind'

The noun is attested from all zones (A to S), the verbs are probably independent innovations in Swahili and a few other eastern languages. The verbs cannot be analyzed as =CVC-VC- since there are no extensions of the shape *-ul-/-uk-* (first degree vowel, no vowel harmony). The noun semantically fits the derived adjectives in **-ú* (§§3.4), but the noun has a final Low tone, and there is no trace of a (verbal) root *-pók-*. BLR2 contains many comparable sets.

*=kókó 'crust'   **=kókot-* 'scrape, crunch'   **=kókol-* 'remove crust'

Again, the final High tone of the noun and the unattested expansion *-ot-* point to a denominal derivation. (The form with **-ul- ~ -ol-* semantically and formally fits the separative extension.) The consonantal suffix is problematic in that most PB consonants are attested (*p t k b l m n*). In some cases, it seems that the final vowel of the nominal stem is replaced or deleted, often resulting in a form with the appearance of containing a semantically fitting extension. In view of this, a verb such as **=jót-* 'warm oneself' could be a back formation from **mu=jóto* 'fire'.

*bu=jóga	'fear'	> **=jógop-*	'fear'
*lu=jigı	'door'	> **=jigal-*	'shut'; **=jigul-* open
*mu=túe	'head'	> **=tú-al-*	'carry on the head'; also: ** = tú-ık-*, **=tú-ul-*, **=tú-uk-*
*tu=ló	'sleep'	> **=lóot-*	'dream' > **=lóótó*,
		*=lóóto,	** =lóóta, *=lóóti* 'dream'

5.3 Ideophones and derivation

Basic ideophones have the shape CV and verbs are occasionally derived from them in the same way as from adjectives and nouns (§§5.1, 5.2). Derivation of nouns and adjectives is also possible, by assigning the ideophonic stem to a noun class. (The ideophonic origins given in parentheses are assumed rather than attested; note that the chicken was introduced long after the PB period.)

(ko-ko)		> **nkókó, *nkúkú* 'chicken'; > **=kókol-* 'cackle'
(di)		> **=didi* 'cold'; > **=didim-, *=didil-* 'be cold, shiver'
*tú	'blunt'	> ** = túup-, *=túun-, *=túump-*
*pi	'black'	> **=piip-, *=piit-; *=pínd-* (tone?); **=pınd-* (V?)
		> **=pi* (adj.); **=piipí* 'darkness', **mu=piiti* 'very dark person'
*pe	'white'	> **=pémb-; *=pémbé, *=pémbá* 'white clay'

The derivations from **pi* and **pe* with voiced prenasalized C_2 are doubtful. As an alternative one could assume the inverse derivational path: the first syllable of a verb stem – or the first two in the case of trisyllabic stems – may be used as an "ideophone", which then has to be redefined as an adverbial part of speech giving a vivid description of the event without necessarily involving sound symbolism. This procedure is extremely common in Zulu and well attested other southern languages.

Zulu (S42):

=*mony-ul-a,* =*mony-uk-a*	'pull out'	> *mónyu*
=*volokohlel-a*	'trample down'	> *volokohlo*
but: = *ngqongqoz-a*	'knock'	< *ngqo*

Grammars written in the school of Doke analyze *all* such verbs as derived from the ideo-phone (Doke 1931: "radical"), which is unlikely in view of the fact that some of these forms include VC-sequences that are analyzable as extensions, and the corresponding verbs but not the ideophones exist elsewhere in Bantu (e.g. *=*móny-ul-,*=*móny-uk-* 'break off'). Doke, like other early Bantuists, may have believed that ideophones represent the earliest form of words from which other categories have evolved.

6 COMPOUNDING

Compound nouns of the structure A + B generally refer to a "B-like kind of A", i.e. the first part is the head of the compound. This is also true of the more petrified types of compounds (§§6.1 and 6.2). Most types of compounds are restricted to fully lexicalized forms; regional productive processes are the formation of names (§§6.1) and diminutives (§§6.2), compounds with *mw=ana* and *mw=ene* as well as agent nouns with comple-ments (§§6.3). Compound verbs are extremely rare (§§6.3), but reduplication is much more common with verbs than with nouns (§§6.4).

6.1 Pre-stem elements

The elements *na-* or *nya-* and *ca-* or *ci-* are often prefixed to a noun or a nominal stem. These forms are derived from the words for 'mother' (**nyangú,* **nyokó,* **nina ~ jina* 'my, your, his/her m.') and 'father' (**cángú,* **có,* **cé ~ jicé* 'my, your, his/her f.'). The result-ing nouns have no NPx and are generally assigned to class 1a. They refer to more com-plex kinship relations, but are also used as personal names and ethnonyms, and as name-like common nouns often referring to small animals and plants. The formation of personal names is productive in some languages such that one element is used to form proper names of women and the other proper names of men.

UMbundu (R11):

ná-ngómbe   (n. pr. fem.)   sá-ngómbe   (n. pr. masc.)   < *óngómbe* 'cattle'

The interpretation of such nouns is not necessarily 'mother/father of X'; the relationship may be the inverse one: 's.o. whose mother/father is X', e.g. someone born during a famine may be called *Nya-nzala* (< *njala 'hunger'), and the *Nya-mwezi* are 'people from the west' (*mwezi* 'moon = west').

The element *ka-* is usually synchronically analyzable as a class 12 NPx; historically it seems to have a second origin, i.e. the Niger-Congo "person marker" (Greenberg 1966:152) which also survives in Bantu as class 1 verbal prefix. This origin is manifest in its use to form names and name-like common nouns which have no semantic link with the mainly diminutive class 12, and formally by the frequent absence of the augment and/or assignment of such nouns to class 1a, which is another typical feature of names.

Kwanyama (R21):

ka=lunga	'God'	
ka=dina	'namesake'	< **i=jína* 'name'

6.2 Post-stem elements

Five nominal stems (rather than full nouns) often occur as quasi-suffixes: *=ntʊ 'person', *=lúme 'husband, male', *=kádí 'wife, woman, female', *=jána 'child', *=kúlú 'adult, old, big'. The form *=kádí also appears as kái > ké, which may make it difficult to distinguish it from reflexes of *ké 'small'. Some of these stems may even combine with each other.

*mʊ=kái-ntʊ	'woman'	*mʊ=kái-kúlú	'old woman'
*mʊ=kádí-jána	'girl, daughter-in-law'	*mʊ=jána-kádí	'woman'

The stem for 'child' has become a diminutive suffix, most productively used in the south.

Zulu (S42):

intatshana	'a small mountain'	< intaba	'mountain'
izinsukwana	'a few days'	< izinsuku	'days'

6.3 Syntactic compounds

N+N is not a common syntactic phrase (except with names and titles), but most languages have compounds consisting of two nouns. The second noun may sometimes shed its NPx. In some but not all cases such nouns may originate from a genitival (connexive) construction.

*mbúlú-kʊtúi	'ear'	< *mbúlú (an animal ?) + *kʊ=túi 'ear'
*nkólo-tíma	'breastbone'	< *nkólo 'heart, breastbone' + *mʊ=tíma 'heart'

Two kinds of N+N compounds have gained complete productivity in some languages. In Swahili (G42d), =enye + X (< *mʊ=jéné 'owner, chief'), with a NPx of class 1 or a PPx of any other class, refers to someone or something that owns or has X; mw=ana + X (< *mʊ=jána 'child' – the relational term) refers to a person who is characterized by X.

miti yenye-matunda	'trees with fruits'		
mwana-siasa	'politician'	< siasa	'politics'

N+A compounds may look like phrases; their status as compound words manifests itself by their meaning and by (external) agreement, which is class 1/2 in the Swahili example below.

kalamu-mbili	'secretary bird'	< kalamu 10 'pens' + =wili 'two'

Swahili also attests two A + Ideophone compounds ("paradigm levelling" accounts for the initial mid vowel in 'black'):

=eupe 'white'	< *=elu < *=jél-ʊ 'white' + *pe 'white'
=eusi 'black'	< *=elu < *=jíl-ʊ 'black' + *pi 'black'

Connective phrases (N + PPx-a-N) may become lexicalized as nouns. The generic head nouns *mʊ=ntʊ 'someone' and *kɪ=ntʊ 'something' are often omitted.

Koti (P30):

etthú y'oóca	'food'	< e=tthú ya o=c-a 'sth. of to eat'
(ntthú) w'oohóóni	'blind (person)'	< (n=tthú) wa o-hí=on-i '(s.o.) of not to see'

A productive type of compound has the form [NPx=B-**a**] + N, as in *mʋ=lɪnd-a +mi
=nʋe 'ring finger' (lit. 'watcher + fingers'). Such nouns are basically agent nouns with
complements (though not necessarily objects in the traditional syntactic sense).

Swahili (G42d):

mwenda	kimya	mla	nyama	'the one (lion) who walks silently will eat the
walker	silence	eater	meat	meat'

In some examples, the noun seems to be the subject of the preceding verb:

Ganda (JE15):

e-bugwa-njuba 'west'   < =gʋ- 'fall' + i=júba 'sun'

UMbundu (R11):

úkúɲá-mbámbi 'tree sp.'   < =kʋɲ- 'gnaw' + o-mbambi 'gazelle'

Note that these compounds as a whole refer neither directly nor metaphorically or
metonymically to the apparent agent, in our examples the falling sun and the gnawing
gazelle. A more consistent analysis therefore is to regard the syntactic source or correlate
of such compounds as sentences with locative subjects (e.g. "there-falls the sun").

Derivation of verbs by incorporation of nouns is extremely rare; a widespread exceptional case is the verb 'to sit down' < *=jikal-a + ncɪ 'sit + ground' (cf. Botne 1993).

Makhuwa (P30):

o=khala-thi, o=kilathi   > *o=kilathiha* (caus.), *o=kilathihiwa* (caus.-pass.)

6.4 Reduplication

Reduplication occurs with all kinds of words. Reduplicated nouns and adjectives are usually lexicalized, and generally only the stem is reduplicated. Pronouns and confirmative
demonstratives are frequently reduplicated. In all kinds of non-verbal words, reduplication is particularly frequent with monosyllabic stems, which indicates a rhythmic preference for polysyllabic stems. Semantically, reduplication often appears to indicate
smallness and/or repetition or iteration.

*maamá	'mother'		
*=kéeké	'small'	< * =ké	'small'
*=nainai	'eight'	< * =nai	'four'
*mʋ=didi	'root'	< *mʋ=di	'root'
*kɪ=díʋngʋdí(úngʋ)	'vertigo'	< *=díʋngʋ	'vertigo'
			(<> *=díʋngʋl- 'turn around')

Reduplication of verbs is a productive process, indicating repetition often coupled with
low intensity. Reduplication affects the verb stem, languages differ as to how they treat
the reduplicand. In the most complete case, the whole stem with its F suffix and tonal
profile is reduplicated. More commonly the first part (the reduplicand) carries the lexical tone on its first mora and has the unmarked F **-a;** the second part carries the inflectional F, and the tonal profile is spread over the whole reduplicated stem. Sometimes, the
reduplicand is limited to two syllables, in which way it approaches the process of partial

reduplication (§§2.12). Reduplication of monosyllabic stems requires multiple application or the intercalation of the infinitive NPx or some other "stabilizing" element.

Nyamwezi (F22):

ku=lyaá-lyaa-lya   <*°ku=lí-a*   'to eat'

Swahili (G42d):

ku=la-ku-la   <*ku=l-a*   'to eat'

Zulu (S42):

uku=dla-yi-dla   <*uku=dl-a*   'to eat'

REFERENCES

Bastin 1986, 1989a; Botne 1993; Büttner 1881; Coupez *et al*. 1998; Dammann 1954, 1958, 1959, 1961, 1962; Doke 1931, 1935; Endemann 1876 [1964]; Forges 1983; Fortune 1955; Greenberg 1963a; Grégoire 1975, 1976; Guthrie 1967–71; Hadermann 1999; Heine 1973; Kähler-Meyer 1966; Mchombo 1993a, 1993b; Meeussen 1954, 1961, 1967; Meinhof 1899 [1910], 1906 [1948]; Meinhof and Van Warmelo 1932; Schadeberg 1982, 1994; Sebasoni 1967; Stappers 1967.

CHAPTER SIX

ASPECT AND TENSE IN BANTU LANGUAGES

Derek Nurse

1 PURPOSE, DATA BASE

Authors have been writing about verbs in Bantu languages for well over a century. Literally thousands of works deal in one way or other with the topic. The authors have had a range of purposes and backgrounds, and what they wrote varies in length from a few lines to a huge volume. At the risk of overgeneralization, most of this work has been concerned with the structures, and, more recently, with the tones, of aspects, tenses, and moods. It has dealt much less well with the semantics of these verbal categories, and with how they fit together in a coherent morphosemantic system for each language. The emphasis in what follows is to start to deal with the semantics, drawing on contemporary general linguistic theory (Bybee *et al.* 1994, Comrie 1976, 1985, Dahl 1985), and the systems involved. Once the structures (including tones), the categories, their semantics, and the overall system have been established for each language, a later step will be to establish the pragmatics, how the categories are used in practice.

As a basis for what follows I have examined approximately 120 languages. I have looked at analyses of at least one language from each of Guthrie's zones and groups except A30, all B, C20, C50, F10, H20, H30, L40, M50, N20, N40, S50, and S60. However, I have looked vicariously at some of the holes via the work of others. How much detail was examined depended on the source. The description of any language involves three main variables: the author's knowledge of how the language (esp. tense and aspect) works, how much data is presented, and the theoretical approach. The data presented tend to support the approach. Readers coming to any description with a different theoretical stance and looking for different data will not find all they seek. Many general grammars and even some specialized analyses use quite disparate terminology for the same phenomena, and the quantity of good and relevant data presented for tense and especially aspect is often limited. Although it is hard to draw a firm line between 'good' and 'less good' data, I would say there was 'good' data for 20–5 languages, and 'less good' for the rest.

2 VERB STRUCTURES

The verbal word has a similar structure in most Bantu languages (cf. Meeussen 1967, who has a slightly more elaborate schema, summarized by Bastin in Ch. 25):

(1) Initial – Subject – Negative – T(A) – Object ≠ root – Extension(s) – Final – Suffix

All the slots to the left and right of root – Extension in (1) involve verbal inflection. The Initial expresses only two categories common to many Bantu languages, negative and relative, but individual languages express a range of other categories at Initial because this is a slot where new material often becomes grammaticalized. The Extension involves a closed and small set of valency-changing categories, of which causative, applicative, stative, reciprocal, reversive, and passive are the most common. The Final also includes a small, closed set originally having to do with mood and aspect, but now including negation and tense in some languages. Across Bantu, Suffix includes only a marker of imperative plural, although, as the Initial, newly grammaticalized material can become attached here. The other labels are self-explanatory. This chapter deals with the three slots which are important to the expression of tense and aspect: Initial, T(A), and Final.

Many Bantu languages also have compound verbs, treated by some analysts as biclausal. In such structures, the first word is usually an inflected auxiliary, and is followed by the second or lexical word, which can be inflected or infinitival in shape. Thus:

(2) Kimbu F24   *Xʋ-xa≠lı ##*   *xʋ-xʋ≠gʋla*   'We are still buying'
              we-still-be   we-ing-buy   (two inflected verbs)

      Chewa N31   *Ti(≠li-)##ku ≠ gúla*   'We are buying'
              we-(be)INFIN-buy (buying, to buy)

              Ti-na≠lí##kú≠gúla   'We were buying'
              we-past-be INFIN-buy

      Ngindo P14   *Tu-Ø≠tenda ## ku≠hemera*   'We are buying'
              we-do   INFIN-buy

Some languages even have compounds with three words, as in:

(3) Hehe G62   *Saa*   *tu-Ø≠va*   *tu-Ø≠gus-ile*   'We will have bought'
              come=FUT   we-be   we-buy-
                                  retrospective
      Sukuma F21   *D-àà≠lí*   *dú-tààlı*   *dù-líí≠gúlà*   'We were still buying'
              we-past-be   we-still-be (?)   we-ing-buy

Structures of the three types just set out are common across the Bantu area. In the far northwestern area, in some Cameroonian languages, there may be a structural spectrum, from languages having the one word structure just described, through languages where this structure is loosening, to languages where some or all of the pre-stem material is not phonologically bound at all (Beavon 1991, Ernst 1991, Hedinger pc). One corollary of this is that grammaticalized material forms into what are known as serial verbs. Because of this typological discrepancy between a few northwestern languages and all the rest, they are sometimes exceptions to the generalizations that follow. I deal with the typical rather than the atypical.

3 CATEGORIES EXPRESSED IN THE VERB

Tense and aspect are not the only categories expressed at Initial, T(A), and Final in the verb. Lack of space prevents proper discussion of these other inflectional categories. Instead, I just list them, and mention surveys or works giving an overview, where I am aware of them.

The categories are: negation, occurring at the Initial and/or Negative slots above, or less commonly via a separate word (Kamba Muzenga 1981, Güldemann 1996); mood, typically indicative vs. subjunctive, always marked at Suffix; relatives, marked at Initial,

Suffix, tonally, or via a separate word (Nsuka Nkutsi 1982); focus and assertion, indicated at Initial, T(A), or tonally (Dalgish 1979, Hyman and Watters 1984, Wald 1997); degrees of certainty in affirmation, marked variously; and conditionals (Saloné 1979, Parker 1991a).

4 HOW TENSE AND ASPECT ARE ENCODED

Most tense and aspect encoding in Bantu languages involves a combination of three main components: inflection of the verb, as outlined in (1), tone, and the use of verbs additional to, and preceding, the main verb. These additional verbs occur as auxiliaries in most Bantu languages, or as serial verbs in a few northwestern languages.

The simplest way of encoding tense and aspect is via a single marker, segmental or tonal, in a single word. Standard Swahili (StSw) exemplifies the segmental approach:

(4) StSw   *Tu-ta≠nunu-a*   we-FUT-stem-Suffix   'We will buy'
     G42   *Tu-li≠nunu-a*   we-PAST-stem-Suffix   'We bought'

While each form here is one word with four morphemes, only the pre-stem morpheme is significant: *ta* marks future, and *li* marks past. Prosodic features play no distinctive role here, as all StSw words automatically carry penultimate stress, regardless of their syntactic status. Contrary to most other eastern Bantu languages, the fourth morpheme above in Swahili, the Final, also plays no role in the marking of tense and aspect. StSw has three possible Final vowels, one being associated with general negation, one with subjunctive, leaving -*a* as the default case, associated with any and all tenses and aspects and thus semantically neutral for tense and aspect. In StSw all tense and aspect marking has to be carried at the pre-stem position. It thus stands at one end of a typological continuum today because historically it shed the use of tone and contrastive finals.

Since Bantu languages are typically tone or pitch accent languages, most use tone in a major way in indicating verbal categories. First, lexical stems typically fall into one of a small number of underlying tone classes. Then, on the left of the stem the (tense) marker may carry its own tone, and on the right, the (aspect) Final likewise. Additionally, total verb forms may carry an imposed tonal melody for individual tenses and aspects. There may also be floating, and other kinds of tones, which tend to fuse with the kinds of tones described. Finally, a number of phonetic processes link these underlying tones to each other and to surface realizations, so that underlying and surface tones are rarely the same. Surface tones normally therefore carry grammatical information. We exemplify only three of the myriad tonal possibilities that result from all these variables. The three are Lingala (Dzokanga 1992), Haya (Muzale 1998), and Koozime (Beavon 1991).

(5) Lingala   *To≠sal-aka*   we-work-HAB   'We work regularly'
     C36   *To≠sal-áká*   we-work-Far Past   'We worked'
               Tó≠sal-aka   we-work-HAB   'Let's work regularly' (subjunctive)

Lingala has a quite simple tonal system: the surface tones are also the underlying tones. So the differences between the three forms are the tone differences at Subject and Final.

(6) Haya E22   [tu-Ø≠gúr-a]/tu-Ø≠gur-á/   we-zero-buy-a   'We buy' (IPFV)
                [ti-tu-Ø≠gúr-a]   NEG-we-zero-buy-a   'We don't buy'
                [ni-tu-Ø≠gúr-a]   PROG-we-zero-buy-a   'We are buying'

Haya is a pitch accent language with limited tonal function. The subject *tu*, stem *gur*, NEG *ti*, and progressive (PROG) *ni* are underlyingly L, while final -*á* is H. There are several possible explanations for the H on -*á* but the tone of any verb final cannot be predicted on general grounds (so other final -*a* in Haya are low). None of the three words has a tense morpheme at T(A), because none is marked for time reference. There is a regular process whereby final H is thrown back to the penultimate before pause. (For a much more complete analysis of the role of tone in such paradigms in Haya, see Hyman and Byarushengo 1984.)

By contrast, Koozime is more complicated tonally. It has two past tenses, in which the nearer of the two (P₁) is only marked tonally and in four places:

(7)   Koozime   *Be*   -   *si*   ≠ *fumo*   *mi-*   *mbɛr*   'They built houses'
      A84   H   L   H   L   L   H   L   LH
                they   P₁   PFV   P₁   build   P₁   P₁   cl. 4   house

In this sequence, as analyzed by Beavon, *be* 'they', *fumo* 'build', and *mi-mbɛr* '4-house', have tones as indicated (the LH on 'house' is realized as rising). PFV *si* is inherently toneless. P₁ is indicated by the four underlying tones, which surface in different ways. The first (L) fuses with the preceding H, giving an H. The second (H) surfaces on the preceding toneless PFV. The third (L) appears on the second syllable of the verb 'build', while the fourth replaces the following L.

A common pattern is where prefixes and finals combine to show tense-aspect. Typically, the pre-stem morpheme(s) mark tense while the finals indicate aspect. So Gikuyu (Johnson 1980):

(8)   Gikuyu E51   *Tw-a≠hanyok-irɛ*   'We ran (before yesterday)'
                                        (we-past-run-PFV)
                   Tw-a≠hanyok-etɛ   'We had run (before yesterday)'
                                        (we-past-run-ANT)
                   Tw-a≠hanyok-aga   'We were running (before yesterday)'
                                        (we-past-run-IPFV)

There is some evidence to suggest that this type of pattern, as found in Gikuyu, is older and that the structurally and categorially reduced system of StSw is newer.

A major source of innovation is the constant emergence of forms based on auxiliaries or modals and a main verb which is either in the infinitive or in an inflected form. Consider Mwera:

(9)   Mwera P22   *Ci-tu-ji-e≠uma*   'We will buy (Far Future)'
      (Harries 1950)   FUT-we-come-FUT-buy

This is the remotest of the three (?) degrees of futurity in Mwera. A Mwera speaker would have little trouble analyzing the form as deriving from *Ci-tu-Ø-≠ji-e ku≠uma* 'We-will-come to-buy', by simple deletion of infinitival *ku*. One could easily imagine the next stage to be simplification of the vowel sequence [ieu]. The previous two stages are also pretty transparent. All future formation in Mwera involves the subjunctive -*e*: (non-factual) subjunctive was semantically extended to (non-factual) future. The initial *ci*- points to an even earlier stage as it is a grammaticalized form of 'say', used in all future tenses in Mwera, and common in the languages of the area (Botne 1998).

Another transparent case is the Haya Present Progressive Negative:

(10)   Haya   Stage 1 (historical)   *Ti-tú≠ri ku≠gura*   'NEG-we-be to-buy'
              Stage 2 (today)   *Ti-tú-ri-ku≠gur-a*   'NEG-we-ing-buy/
                                                            We aren't buying'
       Stages 3–6 (today, personal or dialectal)
       [titwìíkugura, titúùkugura, titúúkugura, titwííkugura]

Here Stage 1 represents an assumed past stage, in which auxiliary and main verb were separate. At Stage 2, auxiliary and lexical verb have fused in a form commonly heard today. Stages 3–6, dialectal or personal forms also heard today, derive from 2 by r-deletion, not otherwise a regular Haya feature, and by other tonal and segmental adjustments. The forms with falling tone are still to be analyzed as compounds, while those with level H are one word.

This kind of grammaticalization is a constant process. All the languages examined in detail show signs of recent or ongoing grammaticalization.

A possible stage, intermediate between the eastern/southern and northwestern patterns, is where successive operations of grammaticalization result in a complex string of pre-stem morphemes, up to four in number, unlike the more usual single morpheme. This occurs in two geographically limited areas: one centred on north-east Tanzania, the other in a few languages on the eastern side of Lake Victoria (Guthrie's E40):

(11) Chaga E60, Vunjo dialect   *À-lé-màà-èndà≠írzérzâ*
      (Moshi 1994)   s/he-past-asp-asp-speak   'S/he had already
                                                              spoken'

      Shambala G23 (Besha 1989) *Ní-tà-zà-nà-hè-mù≠ítángà*   'I might call her'

      Gusii E42   *Ba-tá-á-kó-raa-ná-gó≠*
      (Whiteley 1960:37)   sang-er-er-ek-an-a   (-sang- 'meet')
                                                              'They should meet
                                                              together first
                                                              perhaps'

This section has outlined five strategies for encoding tense-aspect: purely segmentally, purely tonally, a combination of segments and tones, the use of two word structures with auxiliaries, and a string of morphemes at T(A). Although for purposes of exposition they have been presented discretely, more often some combination of these carries the grammatical message.

5 ASPECT AND TENSE CATEGORIES

The terms tense and aspect have been used hitherto without definition. Tenses are representations of the time that contains the event. They locate events in universe time. Aspects are different representations of the time within the event.

In many Bantu languages, aspects can be identified by considering the two word structures mentioned in (1) above, and illustrated in the first example in (2). The first, auxiliary verb of such structures may be inflected for several categories, of which the most prominent is tense. The auxiliary itself carries limited semantic material, its main function being as a place holder to carry the categories which set the temporal scene. Aspect is marked in the second verb. Since encoded aspects are few, only a few morphemes can typically occur in the T(A) position in the second verb. Thus a good method of identifying aspect is to examine the morphology of the second verb. In daily discourse, since the time framework is usually known to the participants, the first verb is often omitted, leaving only aspect marked on the verb.

This chapter makes certain assumptions about tense and aspect. One is that the best place to find clues to these categories in Bantu is in the morphology. Affirmative, negative, and relative forms are three interlocking dimensions of the same system but they are not necessarily mapped directly on to one another. Affirmatives tend to show the largest set of tense-aspect contrasts. Negatives and relatives usually have a reduced set of contrasts.

It is also assumed that any discrete verbal tense-aspect form has a specific and unique range of meanings, which will be different from that of other forms in the language. All such forms fit into a single coherent system. While there are some notable exceptions, many treatments of Bantu languages have tended to treat individual tense-aspect forms as self-standing, which are listed, have labels attached and meanings given, with little or no reference to the other members of the system. As a result it is often claimed that it is hard to distinguish tense from aspect. I hope to show that it is in fact not so hard to distinguish one from the other.

A form derives its basic meaning by contrast with other forms within the verbal paradigm, although that meaning is flexible and can be modified in use and discourse. Since each form and meaning is so derived, while there can be some overlap between forms, there is never total overlap, because that would make a form redundant. Some speakers of StSw would claim that:

(12)   StSw   *Tu-na≠sema* and *Tw-a≠sema*

are always or often semantically identical ('we talk, we are talking'), as are

(13)   StSw   *Tulikuwa tu-ki≠zungumza* and *Tulikuwa tu-na≠zungumza* ('we were chatting')

There are two possibilities here. Either the many speakers are wrong, because they have overlooked certain subtle semantic differences which they have trouble articulating, or they are right, in which case one member of each pair above can probably look forward to a short life, as language does not usually tolerate absolute redundancy for long.

A further assumption is that tense and aspect form an interlocking system, in which most tenses co-occur with most aspects (Hewson and Nurse 2001, Hewson *et al.* 2000).

Regardless of their morphological exponence, tenses and especially aspects have certain common semantic features in most languages. While these may not be quite universal, they are certainly widespread. This is an assumption shared by, *inter alia*, Bybee *et al.* (1994), Comrie (1976, 1985), and Dahl (1985). Their conclusions drew on the languages of the world and their reliance on Bantu languages was thin (Bybee *et al.*, one Bantu language, Comrie half a dozen, Dahl three shown, more discussed). I hope to be able to expand on their conclusions about Bantu.

Finally I assume, unlike Reichenbach (1947), that the various verbal categories do not directly reflect the events or objects of this world, but that they rather reflect human organization, human categorization of these objects and events. There is a strong cognitive component to these categories. That is why the categories themselves tend to be relatively stable over time, and they tend to reoccur across languages.

There are two practical assumptions. One is that tense reference occurs first, aspect second. This is independent of the structure. The structure may be a single word with pre-stem tense, and Suffixal aspect, or it may be a string of pre-stem morphemes (see (11)), or it may be a tense-marked auxiliary, possibly a second aspect-marked auxiliary, and an aspect-marked lexical verb. The northwestern languages mentioned above are apparent exceptions to this generalization.

The second assumption is that a single verbal word can have tense and aspect(s), or several aspect(s), but only a single tense, as an event cannot normally take place at two different times. Multiple aspects are possible because an event can be viewed and represented in more than one way simultaneously. However, verb compounds can encode two tenses, one representing the relationship between speech time and first event time, the second that between first event time and a second event. Views differ on whether such structures should be considered biclausal.

5.1 Aspect

Aspect appears to be more basic than tense across Bantu. That is, the same few aspect-categories occur constantly, with relatively little variation, while tenses vary more. Even when their morphological exponents are destroyed or recycled, aspects are often maintained in a new guise.

This claim may seem strange to some readers, given the prevailing welter of nomenclature. Latinate terms such as continuous, progressive, habitual, iterative, imperfect, imperfective, generic, performative, persistive/perstitive, perfect, perfective, completive, conclusive, anterior, retrospective, resultative, aorist, etc., are confusing and less transparent than simple terms such as past, present, or future. Our analytic tradition has inured us to 'tenses', not aspects. We associate aspect with Slavic languages. But much of this confusion comes from the terminology, the muddled thinking that goes with it, and the desire of linguists to devise new terminology that is distinct from the old, with the result that the number of labels keeps increasing.

A survey of the literature on languages worldwide suggests three widespread aspectual categories: imperfective, contrasting with perfective, and anterior. Also widespread worldwide, but less so, are progressive and habitual. These five categories also occur widely across Bantu. A sixth, persistive, seems to be a specific characteristic of Bantu. There are other, less widespread, categories, not treated here. The advantage of reducing aspects to a few major categories (and labels!) is that they become more transparent. The disadvantage is that the picture may become oversimplified; it may ignore other subtleties and less common aspectual categories.

The classic definition of anterior (abbreviated ANT: also called perfect or retrospective) is that it refers to an earlier action which produced a state which either lives on, or whose consequences or relevance live on. All languages examined seem to have an ANT, or a past which doubles as an ANT. It is primarily expressed by reflexes of the Proto-Bantu final *-ɪde ([-ile, -ele, -ire, -ie], etc.), which suggests this is a category with a long Bantu history. From the definition and the facts it becomes clear that ANT easily shades over into past, or into stative. It becomes past by loosening and then losing the requirement that it have present relevance. Our analysis suggests that since the kinds of past event that have present relevance are often recent events, ANT first becomes near or middle past, and then perhaps is associated with far past, or all pasts. Many languages have reflexes of *-ɪde associated with some form of past. On the other hand it can become purely stative by losing the requirement that some past event have led to the present state. There are many fewer examples of languages which have gone or are going in this direction and there is then a possibility that it will become completely associated with a small set of stative verbs ('lie, sleep, sit, be, stand, know') and will be no longer productive (e.g. in Shona S10, Yeyi R40, some dialects of Chaga E60).

Our data suggest that where *-ɪde has been replaced as a marker of ANT, it is most often replaced by grammaticalized forms of verbs meaning 'finish'.

A perfective (PFV) presents an event as an undifferentiated and time-bounded whole, without regard to the internal constituency of the event. It takes an exterior view of the event as a whole. It typically answers questions such as 'When did you X?', to which the answer could be 'We X-ed this morning (yesterday, last week)'. The X could take a longer or a shorter time. Thus 'wrote' as in 'wrote the number 2' or 'wrote a long letter' or 'wrote a book' refers to time periods of different lengths but presents the past writing as a single act, and in Bantu languages would typically be represented by the same form. Dahl (1985) has a list of questions which typically produce PFV responses (also other kinds of responses). Although perfectives can occur in the future, they more often co-occur with past, because past events are better known and more easily defined than future ones. All languages examined had PFV forms, often restricted to past. They are typically expressed by one word forms, inflected at T(A).

By contrast, imperfectives (IPFV) have to do with the internal constituency of events. They usually represent events that characterize a longer period, so are not punctual. They often represent backgrounded events for events foregrounded by the use of a PFV.

Analysts have viewed IPFV in two ways. For Comrie (1976) IPFV contrasts with PFV, and is a cover term for habitual, progressive, and continuous. While later scholars endorse the basic IPFV:PFV contrast, they see IPFV, habitual, continuous, generic, and other similar categories as rather being coordinate. This is an interesting issue, as are others on which Comrie and e.g. Bybee *et al.* (1994) differ, such as whether continuous is a discrete category. I tend to side with Bybee *et al.*, because the Bantu facts suggest the frequent coexistence of IPFV, PROG, and HAB forms. In this scenario, IPFV represents an event as occurring over a longer or undefined period. However, the available data sometimes get in the way of a clear decision for individual languages. Often I have had to rely on data which are not exemplified but merely translated (inadequately) into English or other languages. For instance, in several cases a single form might be translated as 'We were buying', which could be progressive or imperfective, and also as habitual 'We used to buy': is it progressive, imperfective, habitual, or do the terms need revising? Similarly, some writers have several 'present tenses', which all translate as English 'We buy, we are buying', and none of which is really a present. While most languages have some overlapping forms, three or four semantically identical 'presents' are implausible.

Given this situation, it is currently impossible to state IPFV categories common to all Bantu languages with certainty. The best that is possible is to describe common situations. All the languages examined have a contrast between a PFV and at least one IPFV category (in Comrie's sense). The PFV is unmarked, or morphologically simpler than the IPFV. Thus:

(14)		PFV		IPFV
	Kakɔ A93 (Ernst 1991)	*À tă≠kwą́*	'She'll leave'	*À tă≠bé ké ≠kwà* 'she will be leaving = she is about to leave'
	Punu B43 (data from J. Blanchon)	*Á-tsí≠lá:mb-ə*	'She cooked'	*Ù≠lá:mbà à-tsì≠lá:mba: ng-ə* 'she was cooking'
	Leke C14 (Vanhoudt 1987)	*Bá≠támbuz-í*	'They walked'	*Bá≠bé-ak-í mô≠támbud-é* 'they were walking'
	Lega D25 (Meeussen 1971)	*Tu-ka≠buluta*	'We will pull'	*Tu-ka≠bulut-aga* 'we will be pulling, pull regularly'
	Langi F33	*Tw-a:≠sék-iré*	'We laughed'	*Kʋ≠séka tw-á:≠rɪ* 'we were laughing' (or *tw-á:≠rí t-á≠séka?*)

Pogoro G51	*Tu-Ø≠sek-iti*	'We laughed'	*Tu≠wer-iti tw-a-n-ku≠seka*
			'we were laughing'
Nyakyusa M30	*A-tʊ-kʊ≠ʊla*	'We will buy'	*A-tʊ-kʊ≠j-a pa-ku≠ʊla*
			'we will be buying'

As these data suggest, IPFVS may be expressed by inflection, usually at Final, or by the use of auxiliaries (tones not marked in most cases because not reliably known). The Final *-a(n)ga* is often associated with IPFV. A zero form (see (6)), unmarked for aspect or tense, and suggesting that an action characterizes a huge, unspecified, period, occurs in many languages. It is used when the distinction to IPFV, PROG, or HAB is not important, relevant, or known.

The fourth category is PROG, which represents an action ongoing at the point that some second event occurs, and for a short preceding period, thus contrasting with IPFV. As noted above, PROGS are often hard to distinguish in the available data from similar categories (e.g. continuous). Whereas in English 'We were fishing' is both PROG ('... when you saw us') and continuous ('... all week'), many Bantu languages may contrast these two, so when the data source simply gives a single translation into English, without context, it is not possible to know which category is intended. So, although we cannot state with certainty that all Bantu languages have this category, it appears to be common.

Progressive seems to be a category so often and widely renewed that it is hard to say whether older Bantu might have expressed it by a single inflected form. Across Bantu it is mainly expressed by grammaticalized forms that visibly derive from 'be' or 'have', plus locative and verbal noun ('be in, be at, be with, have, etc.' Bastin 1989b, 1989c; Heine *et al.* 1993). Bantu has several verbs that translate 'be' and the one that figures most often in PROG is the one that indicates temporary being (*-li, -ri*): 'be in/at a particular place' becomes 'be at a particular time'. 'Have' across Bantu often derives from 'be + with'. So present PROGS that involve *-li/-ri* 'be' plus *-ku-/-i-* 'verbal noun', often with an overt locative, are common. Non-presents often add an auxiliary to indicate time.

(15)	Luvale K14	*Ngu-Ø≠li (na) ku≠tángisa*	'I am (with) teaching'
	(Yukawa 1987b)	I-Ø-be (with) INFIN-teach	
		Ngu-ná≠p-ú ##(na##) ku≠tángisa	'I was teaching'
		I-past-be-past (with) INFIN-teach	
	Luba L33	*Ngi-Ø≠di ## mu-ku≠dima*	'I am (in) cultivating'
	(Beckett 1951)	I-be LOC-INFIN-cultivate	
	Umbundu R11	*Ha-vi≠Ø-lí ## l(a)## óku≠kolà*	'They are not growing'
	(Schadeberg 1990)	I-be index INFIN-be ill	
		Ó-Ø-≠kasí ## l(a) ## óku≠ywá	'She is bathing'
		she – be index INFIN-bath	
		Nd-a≠kála ## l(a) ## óku≠túnga	'I was building'
		I-past-be index INFIN-build	

Habitual (HAB), denoting an activity that characterizes a period, also occurs widely. It is very often associated with reflexes of *-a(n)ga* at final.

(16)	Mbala H41	*Ga≠loomb-aanga*	'Which she used to request'
		Ga-gu≠loomb-aanga	'Which she used to request (recently)'

If limited in time reference, it is mostly to past or timeless situations, for pragmatic reasons. HAB can merge semantically with other IPFVS, apparently the common cause for its disappearance.

Persistive (PERS, also called perstitive) denotes an activity that started in the past and is ongoing at the time of reference, hence the common label 'be still ...'.

(17)   Sotho S30   *Re-sá≠rék-a*   'We still buy, are still buying'
       (Ziervogel *et al.* 1979)

Since many investigators tend to speak, or be influenced by, European languages in which this is expressed lexically, not grammatically, they did not always ask about this category and it is less well represented in the data. Despite this, it seems widely enough represented to support the assumption of its cross-Bantu status. The data suggest it is often marked by a fusion of two elements, either at T(A), or of two verbal words. In both cases, one element encodes verbally the '... ing IPFV' notion, while the other suggests the past starting point or ongoingness since the past. This needs more examination.

5.2 Tense

Tenses also reflect not the world but our categorization of the world, and different languages divide the time line up differently, resulting in a different number of tenses. In principle, the time line can be cut at many points. Many Bantu languages – but notably not some of the widely used ones such as Swahili or Shona – are known for their multiple time divisions, leading analysts to comment that Bantu had the richest set of contrasts in their sample. This richness is a second characteristic of Bantu verbal inflection.

Before looking at the various past and future categories, we should look at some practical problems. As stated already, I rely to some extent on languages with which I have personally had experience but to a larger extent on descriptions by others. In such descriptions, statements about past tenses are clearer than statements about 'present' and futures. Past time and past tenses are generally easier to characterize than non-pasts.

I start from the position that present is the moment of time between past and future and in many discourse situations that moment is fleeting. When grammars claim that a language has several presents, i.e. several identical ways of referring to the same fleeting moment, we have to be sceptical. In my experience, these 'presents' are usually aspects rather than tenses, i.e. they are different representations of the time within the event. Often forms referring to 'present' are not marked, or are minimally marked, for time: why mark for time what is obvious to the participants? Present is the default case after past and future.

Future is problematic in a different way. Because it hasn't happened yet and especially if it is only a short distance away, it can be an extension of the 'present' and thus often represented by progressive or habitual. This is a natural semantic extension of 'present' and such forms have not been counted as discrete futures in what follows. Such extensions of the present are often coeval with formally discrete near futures, differing only by factors such as degree of certainty or firmness of intent, or not at all. Firmness of intent or degree of certainty appear often in characterizations of all futures, and some languages are even described as having, for instance, a near future, a far future, and an uncertain future. Just because future is not only concerned with stating firm facts, it relies quite heavily on the use of modal or volitional verbs, on auxiliary verbs (in our sample the commonest are 'come' and 'go'), and on the subjunctive. Future reference is more often renewed than past, and the morphemes involved range along the grammaticalization path from full auxiliary to post-subject inflectional morpheme with classic CV shape. Younger and older speakers of the same language sometimes differ in their choice of future alternatives.

With these caveats in mind, certain generalizations are possible about the data. With few exceptions, all Bantu languages we have examined have either one, two, three, or four past tenses (Hyman 1980b mentions a Grassfields language with five pasts and five futures, and western Gogo seems also to have five). Those with two (49) and three (47) are the most numerous, followed by those with one (23) and finally with four (16). In those with three, near past normally refers to the events of today, starting this morning (most Bantu days start at sunrise); middle past refers either just to the events of yesterday, or yesterday and some few days before; and far past to events prior to those of the middle past. In languages with four pasts, the fourth most often refers to events that occurred immediately before the time of speaking/present. In those with two pasts, the near past refers either to the events of today, or today and yesterday, with the further past referring to prior events. In languages with one past, reference to recent events can also often be made via the ANT.

For examples of languages with two, three, and four pasts, see the sketches of Rundi, Haya, and Bemba, respectively, in Hyman and Watters (1984). For one past, see (4) above.

With very few exceptions, all languages examined had one, two, or three discrete future tenses. Those with one (50) and two (48) are the largest groups, followed by those with three (20). With a doubtful exception (Mwera) the number of futures never exceeded the number of pasts. Most languages have more pasts than futures. General temporal divisions mirror those of the past, except that the semantic extension of the 'present' often overlaps with the nearest future.

Swahili (see (4) above), Aghem (Hyman and Watters 1984), Hehe (Nurse 1979a), and Logooli exemplify languages with one, two, three, and four futures, respectively:

(18)   Logooli E41   *Ku-ra≠gur-a*   'We will buy, Near Future'
                     Na-ku≠gur-ı   'We will buy, Middle Future' (subjunctive suffix)
                     Ku-rika≠gur-a   'We will buy, Far Future'
                     Ku-ri≠gur-a   'We will buy, uncertain future'

The exceptions to the statement that all languages have between one and four discrete pasts are Mwiini (Somali coast), Ilwana (northeast Kenya), Comorian, and some Zone S (southern Africa) languages. The first three have collapsed ANT and Past and use the former ANT final to encode the combined single category. In the first two this seems to have come about under heavy influence from neighboring Cushitic communities. It would be interesting to see other such cases from other parts of the Bantu area. The exceptions to the claim about the number of futures are some G30 (Tanzania) languages, plus R40 (Yeyi), which have a single non-past category.

Widespread inherited markers of past outnumber those of future, although whether this reflects the original situation or results from the frequent renewal of future markers is unclear. Most languages surveyed had reflexes of *-ka-*, *-a(a)-*, and *-ile* in past reference. *-a(a)-* is so written because both long and short forms occur, often tonally contrastive, semantically different, and sometimes in languages which have otherwise neutralized the inherited vowel length distinction. This merits further examination. The Final *-ile* probably originally represented ANT but has become a past, or the past, marker in a significant number of languages.

It may surprise some readers that so many Bantu languages have multiple past reference, yet apparently involve so few morphemes. Any overview of Bantu tense and aspect encoding is bound to conclude that there is in fact no contradiction. With two or three pre-stem morphemes, two Finals (*-ile*, and neutral *-a*), two contrastive tones, occasional new grammaticalized morphemes, a large number of tense contrasts can be achieved, and the overall data strongly suggests constant flux, and constant systemic and semantic permutation.

Although -*laa*- and -*ka*- seem to be inherited markers of futurity, both – especially -*laa*-, which occurs only in eastern Africa (although a morpheme with similar meaning and shape occurs in some Grassfields) – appear to be geographically limited. The constant renewal of future reference via grammaticalization should be kept in mind here. Reflexes of the former subjunctive -*e* occur in a majority of contemporary languages associated in some way with future reference. A zero pre-stem marker is the commonest indicator of 'present'/non-past/IPFV.

A matter not much discussed in the literature is whether time reference is flexible or fixed. Since neither my own data nor that in the source grammars is complete on this issue, I rely on impression rather than hard figures. The impression is based on detailed examination of a few languages, on discussions with speakers of some of those languages, and on a visible discrepancy between analytical statements and actual textual use in some descriptions. While some representations of time are quite concrete ('We saw him on 23 January at 2pm'), many are not. Some variability is factual. Thus, if your language has three pasts and you refer to something you do several times a day, every day, the three pasts will be as described above (today; yesterday and maybe a few days earlier; prior to that). But if you are referring to planting, which in large parts of Africa occurs annually, then the near past can refer to the most recent planting, which could be several months earlier, the middle past to last year's planting, the far past to planting seasons before that. If you are referring to acts of God, or the origins of your ethnic group, far past would have a different referent again. Some variability can also be subjective, in how the speaker sees or represents the facts. Events can be moved nearer or further using appropriate tenses (cf. Besha 1989:288–300). It is my impression that this flexibility of reference occurs widely across Bantu.

5.3 Other categories

It must be admitted there are categories that do not fit easily under the rubric tense/aspect, categories expressed in the same slots and in the same ways as tense/aspect, categories other than those mentioned in §3. While some are local innovations, others are not. Of the latter the most obvious is what is here called consecutive (CONS) (for a discussion of CONS, subsecutive, narrative, and similar categories, see Hyman and Watters 1984). In narratives, many Bantu languages establish the time framework in the first verb and subsequent verbs use another form to indicate subsequent events. In fact, use of the CONS often does not need an initial verb, if the time framework is already clear to the participants. This sequencing can be done in different ways but a common way is to mark all the subsequent verbs with -*ka*- (other languages use a null form). This is a third Bantu feature. All the languages for which there is adequate data have a form which is used after a time framework has been established. A number of features characterize the CONS. First, the subject of the verbs concerned do not have to be co-referential. That is, as long as the narrated events occur in linear and connected sequence, each verb will be marked by the CONS, regardless of its subject. Second, CONS occurs mainly as a dependent form. Third, past (or presumably future, for which we have no real data) tense distinctions are neutralized in the CONS. Languages with multiple pasts, as far as we can see, will have only one CONS, since it does not need to contrast with other pasts. If a change of timeframe is needed, a different past marker is inserted. Fourth, while the CONS occurs most typically in the past, because narratives – hence the alternative label – most often involve sequences of events, it need not necessarily so occur. The limited data suggest that some languages more or less restrict it to past reference, while in others it is freer. A clear case of non-past occurrence is in imperatives of the type: 'Go and X', which do not involve any kind of past, only of the temporal (and locative) sequence 'First go (there), then X'. In many languages, the CONS marker (often -*ka*-) will appear in such constructions as well as in past narratives. Imperative uses can be seen in:

(19) StSw *Nenda u-ka≠nunu-e*   'Go and = in order to buy'
             go you-CONS-buy-subj
      Punu *Wê:ndɔ̀! ù-kɔ̀≠díbìyɔ̀ ndáyù*   'Go, and then close the door' (subject not H)
             Wê:ndɔ̀ ú-kɔ̀ ≠ díbìyɔ̀ ndáyù   'Go, in order to close the door' (subject H)

where Swahili marks a sequence of events with *ka* and the non-factual status of the second verb with -*e*, and Punu makes similar distinctions using a combination of morpheme and tone. For a detailed discussion of various -*ka*- across Bantu, see Botne 1999.

How would this CONS category be labeled? It is not an aspect because its main function is not to represent the internal constituency of an event. Although it is not a (primary or independent) tense in the conventional sense as its primary function is not to locate an event in universe time, it is probably best regarded as a secondary or dependent tense, whose function is to locate it relative to another time already established.

6 SUMMARY, AGENDA

This chapter has set out a general analysis of aspect and tense systems across Bantu. Its main thrust is to view aspect and tense categories in general linguistic terms, and concludes that aspect is more fundamental than tense. This synchronic overview inevitably involves discussion of structures and of what might be assumed for an earlier stage of Bantu. Although space has not permitted a full exposé, this approach is informed by the belief that aspect and tense are interlocking members of a system, that the system is intended for use, and is thus modified by use.

I would suggest that useful future investigation on aspect and tense would focus on three issues: what categories are involved, how they fit together into systems, and then on how the categories are used in practice. The basic components of Lego systems can be labeled and fitted together in conventional ways, but are also used in many less obvious ways.

Thanks go to Robert Botne and Gérard Philippson for comments on earlier versions of this chapter, to John Hewson for some of the ideas underlying it, and to Jean Blanchon and Sam Mchombo for the Punu and Chewa data, respectively.

REFERENCES

Anderson and Comrie 1991; Bastin 1989b, 1989c; Beavon 1991; Beckett 1951; Besha 1989; Botne 1998; Bybee *et al.* 1994; Clements and Goldsmith 1984; Comrie 1976, 1985; Dahl 1985; Dalgish 1979; Dimmendaal 1986; Dzokanga 1992; Ernst 1991; Goldsmith 1976; Güldemann 1996; Harries 1950; Hedinger pc; Heine *et al.* 1993; Hewson *et al.* 2000; Hewson and Nurse 2001; Hombert and Hyman 1999; Hyman 1980b; Hyman and Byarushengo 1984; Hyman and Watters 1984; Johnson 1980; Kamba Muzenga 1981; Meeussen 1967, 1971; Moshi 1994; Muzale 1998; Nsuka Nkutsi 1982; Nurse 1979a; Nurse and Hinnebusch 1993; Nurse and Muzale 1999; Parker 1991a; Reichenbach 1947; Saloné 1979; Schadeberg 1980, 1990; Vanhoudt 1987; Wald 1997; Whiteley 1960; Yukawa 1987b; Ziervogel *et al.* 1979.

CHAPTER SEVEN

BANTU NOMINAL MORPHOLOGY

Francis Katamba

1 INTRODUCTION

Noun class systems are a strong areal feature in Africa. Heine (1982) reports that two thirds of the approximately 600 African languages he surveyed have noun classes. In all branches of Niger-Congo, except Mande, the simple noun can usually be analyzed as consisting of a stem and an affix, normally a prefix (Welmers 1973:159). This is especially true for Bantu where nouns are categorized into numerous 'noun classes' on the basis of the prefixes that they take.

Note that as well as prefixation, suffixation also occurs in Bantu nouns. Many languages have derived nouns that are formed by suffixation, e.g.:

(1)   Rundi JD62 (Meeussen 1959)

Agentive nominalizing	*-rimyi*	'cultivator'	(*-rim-* 'cultivate')
suffix *-yi*	*-vunyi*	'protector, helper'	(*-vun-* 'protect, defend')
Locative/instrumental	*-báago*	'abattoir'	(*-báag-* 'slaughter')
nominalizing suffix *-o*	*-sékuro*	'mortar'	(*-sékur-* 'pound')
	-sékuzo	'pestle'	

However, it is prefixation, and in particular the system of noun class prefixes, that is the hallmark of Bantu nominal morphology and it is to this that the rest of this chapter is devoted. Consider the Nyankore sample pairings of noun stems with the prefixes *mu-/ba-*, *ki-/bi-* and N/N to mark number (tone marking is not included, where the original source omitted it):

(2)   Nyankore JE13 noun classes

	Singular		Plural
Class a	*mu-ntu*	'person'	*ba-ntu*
Class b	*ki-rabyo*	'flower'	*bi-rabyo*
Class c	*m-bwa*	'dog'	*m-bwa*

Each set of classes i.e. thus paired is often referred to as a 'gender'.

2 HISTORY OF NOUN CLASSIFICATION

Noun classification has always occupied a central place in Bantu linguistics. The earliest study of noun classes was by Brusciotto (1659) who, in his grammar of Kongo H16, classified nouns on the basis of their concords – especially those appearing in possessive constructions (cf. Doke 1960). The next landmark studies were by Bleek. In the first volume of *A Comparative Grammar of South African Languages* published in 1862 Bleek proposed, on the basis of a comparative study of the phonology of southern African languages, that these languages shared a common ancestry. The second volume, which appeared in 1869, focused on morphology, in particular the structure of the noun, pronoun and adjective. Bleek's most significant legacy was the reconstruction of eighteen noun classes of 'Ancient Bantu' and their prefixes which he numbered 1–18. Bleek's reconstruction and numbering of the noun classes of Proto-Bantu (PB) facilitated comparative studies. It turned out to be robust and has required only minor revisions. See Table 7.1.

The first revision was made by Bleek himself, who later reversed the order of 13 and 14 – *ka- became 13 and *bu- became 14. A further slight revision was proposed by Jacottet (1896) resulting in the ordering that has since become standard: *ka- 12, *tu- 13 and *bu- 14.

The next significant changes were introduced by Meinhof in his reconstructions of 'Ur-Bantu'. While keeping Bleek's numbering unaltered, Meinhof (1899/1932, 1906)

TABLE 7.1: FOUR OFTEN-CITED LISTS OF RECONSTRUCTED PB NOUN PREFIXES

	Bleek's Ancient Bantu (Bleek 1869: 282ff.)	Meinhof's Ur-Bantu (Meinhof and Van Warmelo 1932:39ff.)	Meeussen's PB (Meeussen 1967:97)	Guthrie's PB (Guthrie 1971:9)	Welmers's PB (Welmers 1973)
1	*mŭ-	*mu-	*mu-	*mo-	*mo-; 1a ∅
2	*ba-	*υa-	*ba-	*ba-	*va-; 2a *va-
3	*mŭ-	*mu-	*mu-	*mo-	*mo-
4	*mi-	*mi-	*mi-	*me-	*me-
5	*di- ~ *li-	*li-	*i̧	*yi-	*le-
6	*ma-	*ma-	*ma-	*ma-	*ma-; *ma-
7	*ki-	*ki-	*ki-	*kȩ-	*ke-
8	*pi-	*υî-	*bi̧-	*bi-	*vi-; 8x *li-
9	*n	*ni-	*n-	*ny-	*ne-
10	*thin-	*li̧-ni-	*n-	*ny-	*li-ne-
11	*lu-	*lu-	*du-	*do-	*lo-
12	*ka- (13)	*ka- (13)	*ka-	*ka-	*ka-
13	*tu- (12)	*tu- (12)	*tu	*to̧-	*to
14	*bu-	*υu-	*bu-	*bo-	*vo-
15	*ku-	*ku-	*ku-	*ko̧-	*ko-
16	*pa-	*pa-	*pa-	*pa-	*pa-
17	–	*ku-	*ku-	*ko̧-	*ko
18	–	*mu-	*mu-	*mo̧-	*mo-
19	–	*pí-	*pi-	*pi-	*pi-
20	–	*yu-	–	–	*yo-
21	–	*yî-	–	–	*yi-
(22)	–	–	–	–	*ya
23	–	–	i- (24)	–	*ye-

Source: Based on Maho (1999:247).

Notes: Original Bleek–Meinhof numbering appears in parentheses where it differs from current numbering; subclasses are also included; [υ] corresponds to IPA [β].

TABLE 7.2: SUMMARY OF RECONSTRUCTIONS OF LIKELY PB NOUN CLASSES

	Probable	Less
Probable system type	1/2; 1A/2X; 3/4; 5/6; 7/8; 9/10; 11/6; 11/10; 12/13; 14/6; 15/6; 16; 17; 18; 19	(3/10); (9/4); (14/4); 20; 23
Infinitive	15	
Diminutive	12; 19	(5) (11)
Augmentative	7	(20)
Locative	16; 17; 18	(23?)
Language class	7 (kintu)	

Source: From Maho (1999:270).

reconstructed five additional classes for Ur-Bantu: class 17 **ku-*, class 18 **mu-*, class 19 **pî-*, class 20 **γu-* and class 21 **γî-*. Bleek's system, as revised by Meinhof, is generally accepted and is normally referred to as the Bleek-Meinhof system.

Subsequently, a few minor alterations to the Bleek-Meinhof system have been proposed. Doke (1927b) added sub-classes 1a and 2a; Cole (1967) added sub-classes 2b and 8x and Meeussen (1967) reconstructed a new class 23 class **i-*.

While the question of the noun classes that have to be reconstructed has been largely resolved, the related question of the phonological shape of the class prefixes of PB has remained much more controversial. Space constraints do not permit a detailed exploration of the issues but I have listed competing reconstructions in table 7.1.

Less contentious has been the reconstruction of the tones of the prefixes. The reconstructions by Meeussen (1954, 1967:97) shown in (3) are generally accepted.

(3)   Tones of the prefixes

- nominal prefix is low
- numeral and pronominal prefix is high (except in cl. 1 and 9)
- verbal prefix is low for first person singular and second person singular (cl. 1) and high for all other forms
- infix is low for all persons in cl. 1 for all forms (first person singular, second person singular, etc.) but high for all other forms (first person plural, second person plural in cl. 2, cl. 3, cl. 4, etc.)

All the classes that can be reconstructed for PB did not sprout at the same time. Which classes were present in PB and which ones were later innovations? Two excellent comparative studies by Kadima (1969) and Maho (1999) have provided historical overviews of Bantu noun classification. I will draw on both, and especially on the latter, as it subsumes many of Kadima's findings and incorporates recent advances in Bantu linguistics.

Maho's reconstructions seem to be essentially right and only need minor tweaking. At the intersection of Less and Infinitive, there should be class 5. Hadermann (1994a, 1999) shows that PB had classes 15 and 5 as possible verbal noun classes, maybe with different meanings. In eastern Africa, class 5 infinitives occur in Chaga E60 and Sonjo E46; some languages in Zone F mark infinitives with *kwi-* (< *ku* (15) + *i-* (5)). Furthermore, in Zones A, B and C, numerous languages have class 5 *i-* or *li-* as the infinitive prefix.

3   BANTU AND NIGER-CONGO NOUN CLASSES

Although the genesis and purpose of gender marking have received a considerable amount of attention, as yet a satisfactory account of this phenomenon remains elusive

(Corbett 1991:30). Gender systems at best mark superfluously distinctions that are patently obvious (e.g. '... that a noun meaning "woman" is "feminine", that a noun meaning "dog" is "animate", or that a noun meaning "grapefruit" belongs to a class of nouns referring to fruits' (Claudi 1997:63) and at worst, introduce distinctions that are semantically arbitrary and difficult to learn (e.g. in Lingala C36d *ma-wa* 'pity' is in class 6 but *bo-lingo* 'love' is in class 14).

Functionalists argue that gender is not pointless: it helps to keep tabs on elements of a sentence that are in construction with each other by 'referential tracking' showing anaphoric and endophoric reference (cf. Foley and van Valin 1984:327 cited in Claudi 1997:64). Whether this is a cost worth paying is debatable. After all, genderless languages track anaphoric and endophoric reference without the aid of such devices. With the advantages of having a gender system far from clear, why and how did Bantu develop a gender system historically?

The 'why' question cannot be properly answered but it might be possible to answer the 'how' question. Claudi hypothesizes that gender marking on nouns might have arisen from nouns whose original function was to render an abstract idea more 'concrete'. This could have been done by taking one of three routes, namely the 'demonstrative channel', the 'derivational channel' and the 'numeral classifier channel'. We will focus on the second which is the most relevant for Bantu.

According to Claudi, in the 'derivational channel' the head noun of a compound may have been a noun referring to a generic category but in due course it may have become re-analyzed as a derivational affix, and eventually as a gender marker. Earlier, Mufwene (1980) had claimed that derivation is the primary role of noun class prefixes in Bantu. When a prefix is combined with a root, the outcome may be a new lexical item with an unpredictable meaning, a situation also often found in compounding.

(4)   Lingala (Mufwene 1980:249)

ø-mpángi	'relative'	:	*ki-mpángi*	'kinship'
mu-kóngo	'Kongo person'	:	*ki-kóngo*	'Kongo language'

Earlier still, Bleek (1862) hypothesized that noun class prefixes in Bantu originally were nouns in their own right which could appear in compounds 'person-x', 'tree-x', etc. As a result of grammaticalization and semantic bleaching those nouns lost the ability to appear independently and always had to be appended to another noun. Bleek proposed that the head nouns (prefixes) of the compounds may have acquired a pronominal role.

Whatever their genesis, it is generally agreed that PB had noun class affixes traceable to its ancestor, Proto-Niger-Congo. The puzzle is to determine whether those affixes were prefixes or suffixes, or both. This is a puzzle because it is also often claimed that Proto-Niger-Congo had SOV word order (cf. Givón 1975b, 1979b, Hyman 1975, Williamson 1986). But, as Heine (1976) has shown, synchronically no African language with SOV basic word order has noun class prefixes. Yet the norm in Bantu and Niger-Congo today is prefixes. So, Givón's (1979b:221) claim that Proto-Niger-Congo must have had noun class suffixes is questionable. Waters are muddied by the existence of both prefixes and suffixes in some Bantu languages, e.g. Adere, a Mbam-Nkam language of Cameroon, where in various grammatical contexts, noun classes are marked by prefixes alternating with suffixes (e.g. class 5 *dì-* and *-de*, class 6 *mù:-* and *-mə*, etc.) (Voorhoeve 1980c).

Despite this, Heine (1980) argues that the evidence in favor of noun class prefixes is much stronger. The Kordofanian branch has a preponderance of prefixes as do the majority of the sub-branches of Niger-Congo. Mukarovsky (1976–7), the most substantial reconstruction of Niger-Congo, also observes that 'according to all evidence, the

Proto-Nigritic language must be assumed to have been a real noun class language with prefixes and full concord'. This makes the reconstruction of SOV as the basic word order of Proto-Niger-Congo implausible since SOV syntax is incompatible with noun class prefixes (see Welmers 1958, 1973:184, Greenberg 1963a:150–3, 1977, 1978b and Gregersen 1977).

4 THE AUGMENT

In many Bantu languages, the noun class prefix may be preceded by another formative which is variously referred to as the augment (or the pre-prefix or the initial vowel – because often, though not always, it is just a vowel) (see table 7.3).

The augment is not found in all Bantu languages. For instance, it is absent from Tuki A601, Lingala and Swahili – however, the augment is found in many of Swahili's close relatives (see Nurse and Hinnebusch 1993:338–45). Where it is present, as de Blois (1970) shows, the augment varies considerably both in its shape and function. Some of the variation in shape is captured in table 7.3.

As for function, rarely, if ever, can the augment be reduced to a single function. Many early scholars incorrectly equated it with the article in European languages. For instance, Bleek (1869:150) claimed that though the initial vowel in Xhosa S41 was originally a pronoun, it had evolved into an article. Other writers on Xhosa continued the tradition (cf. Torrend 1891:64) as did many scholars elsewhere. For example, Brown (1972) refers to the Masaaba pre-prefix as the determiner.

As Hyman and Katamba (1991, 1993) show, in Ganda the augment may serve a range of functions. It cannot simply be equated with a determiner. It can play the pragmatic role of indicating definiteness, specificity or focus. But just as important, the presence or absence of the augment may be syntactically driven. For instance, it may depend on whether a noun is in a main or dependent clause, appears after an affirmative or negative verb and so on. The augment is normally present on the noun and on the adjectives and

TABLE 7.3: THE AUGMENT IN SELECTED LANGUAGES

| Noun class | Masaaba JE31 | | Ganda JE15 | | Zulu S42 | |
	Augment	Class prefix	Augment	Class prefix	Augment	Class prefix
1	*u-*	*mu-*	*o-*	*mu-*	*u-*	*mu-*
2	*ba-*	*ba-*	*a-*	*ba-*	*a-*	*ba-*
3	*gu-*	*mu-*	*o-*	*mu-*	*u-*	*mu-*
4	*gi-*	*mi-*	*e-*	*mi-*	*i-*	*mi-*
5	*li-*	*si-*	*e-*	*li-*	*i-*	*(li-)*
6	*ga-*	*ma-*	*a-*	*ma-*	*a-*	*ma-*
7	*ki-*	*ki-*	*e-*	*ki-*	*i-*	*si-*
8	*bi-*	*bi-*	*e-*	*bi-*	*i-*	*zi-*
9	*i-*	*N-*	*e-*	*N-*	*i-*	*N-*
10	*zi-*	*N-*	*e-*	*N-*	*i-*	*zi-N-*
11	*lu-*	*lu-*	*o-*	*lu-*	*u-*	*lu-*
12	*ka-*	*ka-*	*a-*	*ka-*	–	–
13	–	–	*o-*	*tu-*	–	–
14	*bu-*	*bu-*	*o-*	*bu-*	*u-*	*bu-*
15	*ku-*	*ku-*	*o-*	*ku-*	*u-*	*ku*

numeral in construction with it in affirmative, main clause subject nominal prefixes (NPs) as seen in (5):

(5)   Ganda augment

    (a) *ò -mú- límí   ó- mú- néné   ó- mú-kâddé   ó- mû   à- Ø-gênda*
        ag-1-farmer   ag-1-fat   ag-1-old   ag. one   he-pres.-go
        (**mù- límí   mùnéné   mù-kâddé   ó- mû   à- Ø-gênda!*)
        'One fat, old farmer is going.'
    (b) *è- nkóbé   é- n- néné é- n-kâddé é- mû   è- Ø-gênda!*
        ag-9-baboon   ag-9- fat   ag-9-old   ag.-one   it-pres.-go
        (* *`n-kóbé      `n- néné   `n-kâddé   é- mû   è- Ø-gênda!*)
        'One fat, old baboon is going.'
        (ag = augment; 1 = class 1; 9 = class 9; pres. = present)

But the augment is absent in certain syntactic contexts, e.g. after a negative verb:

(6)   *tè-   tú- Ø- làbà   mú- límí mú- néné*   'We don't see a fat farmer.'
      neg.   we-pres.-see 1-farmer 1-fat

5 CANONICAL VS. REDUCED NOUN CLASS SYSTEMS

In no single language are all the approximately twenty-four noun classes reconstructed for PB attested (cf. table 7.1). The number of noun classes has suffered attrition to varying degrees in the daughters of PB. The highest number of classes retained by a single language seems to be twenty-one, as is the case in Ganda (see table 7.4). Languages with numerous noun classes are said to exhibit the canonical Bantu noun class system, while others with 'reduced' noun class systems have only retained a rump of the original set.

Languages with a canonical noun class system have about six classes paired for singular and plural, plus about the same number of classes that are not paired (e.g. infinitive and locative classes). That is true of languages in table 7.4 as well as languages like Duala A24, UMbundu R11 and Lingala, as seen in table 7.5. Table 7.4 lists nouns with augments, where these are present.

At the other extreme from the languages with a canonical noun class system stands Komo D23, a language whose noun class system has been reduced to zero and Kakɔ A93 which has only three classes (cf. Guthrie 1971:42). But such reduction is the exception rather than the rule. Canonical noun class systems are more widespread than reduced ones (cf. Kadima 1969, Maho 1999). Maho reports that in his sample of 333 languages, the majority have at least seven noun classes (not including the locative classes). He suggests that if a language has only three genders or less, it is appropriate to refer to it as having a reduced system (Maho 1999:54). He refers to languages with seven or more genders as having a 'traditional' (our canonical) class system. However, he hastens to point out that the exact size of a class system may not have any serious typological consequences. If the number of noun classes in a particular language is whittled down say, from fifteen to two, the principles underlying the classification system may remain essentially unchanged. Citing Guthrie (1971:42), Maho observes that in Kakɔ, e.g. animacy remains the driving force behind noun classification. There are two genders marked in the plural, one animate and the other inanimate; singular nouns are not marked for gender.

Because canonical systems are so typical of Bantu languages, their presence has been used sometimes as a litmus test for membership of the Bantu family (cf. Guthrie 1948). This is unfortunate since having a gender system of any kind is a typological feature that

TABLE 7.4: COMPARATIVE TABLE OF NOUN CLASSES

Cl.	Ganda JE15	Chewa N31	Ndonga R22	Venda S21	Sotho S33	Xhosa S41	Lingala C36d	Tuki A601
1	o-mu-	mu-	o-m-	mu-	mo-	u-m-	mo-	mo-
1a	Ø-		Ø-	Ø-	Ø-	u-		
2	a-ba-	a-	a-a	vha-	ba-	a-ba-	ba-	ba-
2b			o-o-	vho-	bô-	o-o-		
3	o-mu-	mu-	o-m-	mu-	mo-	u-m-	mo-	o-
4	e-mi-	mi-	o-mi-	mi-	me-	i-mi-	mi-	i-/iN-
5	e-ri-/CC-	Ø-	e-	ḽi-	le-	i-li-	li-	i-/ni-
6	a-ma-	ma-	o-ma-	ma-	ma-	a-ma-	ma-	aN-/a-
7	e-ki-	chi-	o-shi-	tshi-	se-	i-si-	e-	i-
8	e-bi-	zi-	i-i-	zwi-	di-	i-zi-	bi-	bi-
9	e-N-	Ø-	o-N-	N-	N-	N-	N-	Ø-/N-
10	e-N-/zi-	Ø-	o-N-	dzi-	diN-	i-ziN-	N-	Ø-/N-
11	o-lu-		o-lu-	lu-		u-lu-	lo-	no-/nu-
12	a-ka-	ka-	o-ka-					
13	o-tu-	ti-						to-/tu-
14	o-bu-	u-	u-u-	vhu-	bo-	u-bu-	bo-	wu-
15	o-ku-	ku-	o-ku-	u-	ho-	u-ku-	ko-	
16	wa-	pa-	pa-	fha-		pha-		
17	ku-	ku-	ku-	ku-	ho-	ku-		
18	mu-	mu-	mu-	mu-		u-m-		mu-/mo-
19								i-
20	ogu-			ku-				
21				ḓi-				
22	a-ga-							
23	e-					e-		

Source: Based on Hendrikse and Poulos (1992), Guthrie and Carrington (1988) and Hyman (1980b).

can be acquired (or lost); it is not a trait that proves genetic relationship. So, a language like Komo that has lost all noun classes is no less Bantu than languages such as Sotho and Lingala with a canonical noun class system.

6 DISTRIBUTION AND PAIRING OF NOUN CLASSES

Next we consider the pairings and areal distribution of noun classes. As seen in table 7.5, certain pairings are more common than others (cf. Kadima 1969, Maho 1999).

Skewing is common. For instance, Hedinger (1980) reports that in a sample of 1,166 nouns in Akɔɔsɛ́ A15C of which 80 percent of the nouns are countable, genders 1/2, 3/4, 5/6, 7/8 and 9/10 are the most typical and account for the pairings of 72 percent of the sample. The situation in other languages does not differ very substantially in most cases. The pairings 1/2, 3/4, 5/6, 7/8, 9/10, 11/10, 12/13 and 14/6 are very widespread. By contrast, the pairings 3/6, 7/10 and 19/13 are less common. Hedinger also shows that in Akɔɔsɛ class 6 is the most widely used plural class. Apart from class 1, at least some nouns in any other class may form their plural using the class 6 prefix /me-/.

Maho (1999:226) confirms the general preference for certain pairings (see table 7.6). Probably the most uniform pairing is of class 1/2. So widespread is it that Guthrie (1967–71:347) believed it to be universal. In fact, he was wrong. The pairings class 1/4

TABLE 7.5: BANTU PAIRED NOUN CLASSES

Duala A24		UMbundu R11		Lingala C36d		Sotho S33		Akɔ́ɔ̀sɛ̀ A15C	
Singular	Plural	Singular	Plural	Singular	Plural	Singular	Plural	Singular	Plural
1 ——— 2		1 ——— 2		1 ——— 2		1 ——— 2		1 ——— 2	
3	4	3	4	3 ——— 4		3 ——— 4		3	4
5	6	5	6	5 ——— 6		5 ——— 6		5	6
7	8	7		7	8	7	8	7	8
9	10	9	10	9	10	9 ——— 10		9	10
14		11		11		14		14	
		12 ——— 13						19 ——— 13	
		15							

Sources: Dugast (1967) for Duala; Guthrie and Carrington (1988) for Lingala; Hedinger (1980) for Akɔ́ɔ̀sɛ̀; Schadeberg (1990) for UMbundu.

TABLE 7.6: THE MOST WIDELY OCCURRING NOUN CLASS PAIRINGS

Maximally wide and very dense	Very wide and fairly dense
Type 1a noun class systems	3 = 14, 9/6, 15/6, 16, 17 and 18
1/2, 1a, 3/4, 5/6, 7/8, 9/10 and 14/6	augmentative use of class 7
Infinitives in class 15	*ki*-names

and 1/6 are also fairly widely attested in various areas. In several zone B and C languages, a class 1 noun may have as its plural class 4 (cf. Buja C37 cited in Kadima 1969:88). This is also the case in the Zone S languages Zulu and Venda. A possible explanation for this is analogical levelling resulting in all nouns with the singular form *mu-*, be they class 1 or 3, having *mi-* (class 4) as their plural prefix.

As already noted, the most typical pairing of class 3 is with class 4. But the pairing 3/6 is also quite common in languages scattered across Bantu though it is concentrated in the northwest region. Some of the less usual pairings might be the result of mergers. In Mbete B61 the pairings 3 = 13 = 15/2 = 6 are found; in Lombo C54 the mergers 3 = 14 and 2 = 6 are attested and in UMbundu the pairing 3 = 14/2 = 6. However, mergers do not account for all cases of 3/6 pairings given the case of a language like Tswana S31 that shows no evidence of merger (Maho 1999).

Despite the variation, distributional characteristics of noun classes show a high degree of coherence. Particular pairings of singular and plural markers, as well as the typical semantics of noun classes, tend to show strong areal bias even though some traits are not restricted to particular areas. For instance, typically the merger of classes 4 and 8, the pairing of 11 with 3 and the use of class 11 as a diminutive are western areal features though they sporadically turn up elsewhere. As well, the classes 4 = 8 mergers occur in the south and east in Makhuwa P31, Venda and Shambala G23. By contrast, in eastern languages there is a bias towards mergers or near mergers of classes 8 = 10. Also restricted to the east is locative class 23, the merger of classes 15 and 17 and the use of class 20 for diminutives or augmentatives. But again some of these properties turn up outside the region. Herero R31, spoken in the southwest, shares comparable use of class 20.

Given the often spotty distribution of mergers and near-mergers, any claim that there is a genetic split – the so-called East–West Divide (cf. Guthrie 1971) – seems to be unjustified.

7 CONCORD

Noun class prefixes are at the heart of an extensive system of concord (i.e. agreement) in Bantu, as seen in the Swahili data in (7):

(7) *M-toto*   *m-dogo*   *a-mefika*   'The little child arrived.'
     cl. 1 child   cl. 1 little   cl. 1 arrived
     Ki-kapu   *ki-dogo*   *ki-mefika*   'The little basket arrived.'
     cl. 7 basket cl. 7 little   cl. 7 arrived

The head noun takes a prefix marking its class and other words in construction with it take an appropriate matching prefix. Thus in (7) the noun *mtoto* belongs to class 1, which is marked by the prefix *m-*, and so the adjective as well as the subject pronoun (*a-*) agreeing with it in the verb take matching prefixes. Likewise, the noun *kikapu* belongs to class 7 which is marked by the prefix *ki-* and so the adjective as well as the subject pronoun agreeing with it in the verb also take the class 7 prefixes. The fact that in some cases it is an identical shape that is prefixed, as in the case of class 7 *ki- ki- ki-*, prompted linguists to speak of 'alliterative concord'. But as the first example with the prefixes *m- m- a-* shows, concord need not be alliterative.

Normally, each class prefix has a form that appears with words belonging to the following classes:

(8) Concord patterns (Meeussen 1967:96–7)

    nominal prefix (NP) in nouns, locatives and adjectives;
    numeral prefix (EP) in words for ≪ 1–5 and ≪how many;
    pronominal prefix (PP) in substitutives, connectives, possessives, demonstratives, determinatives, (≪other, ≪which, etc.) and relative verb forms; verbal initial prefix (VP) in absolute verb forms;
    verbal pre-radical prefix (infix) in verb forms; the infix has, besides persons and classes, a reflexive form.

The array of concords for Ganda noun classes in table 7.7 illustrates the richness of the concordial system.

As table 7.7 and the data in (9) show, different adnominal concords are normally required to go with the noun.

(9) Some Ganda class 3 concord patterns

    (a) Noun + Adjective
         mutí munene   'big tree'
         tree big
    (b) Noun + Demonstrative
         mutí guno   'this tree'
         tree this
    (c) Noun + Numeral
         mutí gùmû   'one tree'
         tree one
    (d) Noun + Associative construction
         mutí gwá (< *gu* + *á*) *múkázi*   'woman's tree'
         tree of woman
    (e) Noun + Relative
         (*o*+)*mutí o-gw-agwa*   'tree that fell' (< *o* + *gu* + *a*)
         tree   Ag.-rel + fell   (Ag. = Augment)

TABLE 7.7: BANTU CONCORDS: A GANDA EXAMPLE

Classes	NP	EP	PP	VP			Infix		
				I	II	III	I	II	III
1	mu-	o-	u-	N-	o-	a-	N-	ku-	mu-
2	ba-	ba-	ba-	tu-	mu-	ba-	tu-	mu-	ba-
3	mu-	gu-	gu-			gu-			gu-
4	mi-	e-	gi-			gi-			gi-
5	li-/Ø	li-	li-			li-			li-
6	ma-	a-	ga-			ga-			ga-
7	ki-	ki-	ki-			ki-			ki-
8	bi-	bi-	bi-			bi-			bi-
9	N-	e-	e-			e-			gi-
10	N-	C-	zi-			zi-			zi-
11	lu-	lu-	lu-			lu-			lu-
12	ka-	ka-	ka-			ka-			ka-
13	tu-	tu-	tu-			tu-			tu-
14	bu-	bu-	bu-			bu-			bu-
15	ku-	ku-	ku-			ku-			ku-
16	wa-	wa-	wa-			wa-			wa-
17	ku-	ku-	ku-			ku-			ku-
18	mu-	mu-	mu-			mu-			mu-
20	gu-	gu-	gu-			gu-			gu-
22	ga-	a-	ga-			ga-			ga-
23	e-	–	e-			e-			–

Note: C- indicates gemination of the initial consonant, e.g. *mbuzi C-táano* > *mbuzi ttáano* 'five goats'. Meeussen reconstructs this as *j-*.

(f) Subject
  (*o+*) *muti gu- lí- gwa*   'the tree will fall'
  tree   subj-fut-fall
(g) Object
  (*o+*) *muti tu- lí-gu -tema*   'we will chop the tree'
  tree   we-fut.obj.chop

Observe that an adjective used as a noun will take the appropriate nominal prefix in the absence of an explicit head noun.

(10) Swahili
   Lete vi-dogo   'Bring little ones'
   bring cl. 7-little

Concord plays an important role in separating noun classes. Seemingly identical classes are separable if their singular/plural pairings and their concords differ. For instance, classes 1 and 3, both marked by *mu-* are distinguished on that basis. Consider Masaaba:

(11)
   (a) *mu-* cl. 1
      u- mu- seeza   *a-*   *gw-iile*   'the man has fallen'
      ag-cl. 1-man   SM-cl. 1- fall-perf.
      a- ba- seeza   *ba-*   *gw- iile*   'the men have fallen'
      ag-cl. 2–man   SM cl. 2- fall-perf.

(b) *mu-* cl. 3

u- mu- ti	*gu-*	*gw-iile*	'the tree has fallen'
ag-cl. 3–tree	sm cl.1-	fall-perf.	
gi-mi- ti	*gi-*	*gw-iile*	'the trees have fallen'
ag-cl. 4–tree	sm cl. 2-	fall-perf.	

(ag = augment (see §4); sm = Subject marker; perf. = perfect aspect)

8 GENDER CONFLICT RESOLUTION

Heine (1982:194–5) observes that there appear to be two basic principles used in allocating nouns to particular genders and assigning agreement markers to them. Gender may be assigned on the basis of semantic criteria like sex: masculine nouns refer to males and feminine nouns to females. Alternatively, nouns may be allocated to genders in a mechanical, semantically arbitrary fashion.

Nyankore agreement as in *mushaija muhango* 'large man' vs. *kitabo kihango* 'large book' is a case of semantic agreement. The noun *mushaija* is in class 1 and has the prefix *mu-* since it denotes a human and the adjective modifying it takes the prefix *mu-*, the agreement marker of class 1, since it qualifies a human noun. Conversely, the noun *kitabo* which refers to an inanimate object is assigned to class 7, a typical class for inanimates, and takes the prefix *ki-*. The adjective modifying it takes the agreement marker *ki-* for inanimates.

By contrast, German *das Mädchen* 'the girl' is an instance of mechanical gender assignment. Though the noun refers to a female and ought to be feminine, it is arbitrarily allocated to the neuter gender. Furthermore, the agreeing definite article *das* is also neuter as it follows the grammatical categorization of the noun as neuter.

Bantu languages show both semantically motivated and mechanical agreement. The Swahili situation is typical. In the case of animate nouns, animacy considerations are paramount and hence an animate noun takes gender 1/2 agreements regardless of the class membership of the noun itself as in (12a, 12b) but with non-animates the gender of the noun determines its agreements as in (12c) (cf. Wald 1975).

(12) Swahili agreement

(a) *ki-boko*	*m-kubwa*	'large hippo'
cl. 7-hippo	cl.1-large	
(b) *ki-durango*	*m-bingwa*	'clever dwarf'
cl. 7-dwarf	cl.1-clever	
(c) *ki-tabu*	*ki-kubwa*	'large book'
cl. 7-book	cl. 7-large	

Heine (1982) points out that Swahili speakers have a choice between semantic and mechanical agreement with animate nouns of the augmentative (5/6) and diminutive (7/8) classes. In this instance, semantic agreement is the norm and mechanical agreement is marked:

(a) *zee*	*yu-le*	'that old man'
cl. 5 old man	cl.1 -that	
(b) *zee*	*li-le*	'that funny/extraordinary/extremely old man'
cl. 5 old man	cl. 5 -that	

If a coordinate noun phrase contains nouns belonging to the same class, the corresponding plural prefix is used. Consider the Haya JE22 data in (13) taken from Kageyama (1977) where two class 1 nouns are coordinated and a class 2 plural concord appears on the verb:

(13)   *omusháija n'ómwáana bá- á- genda*   'the man and child went' (cl. 2 SM)
       man   and child   they-past-go

       (SM = Subject marker)

Coordination raises problems for gender agreement when nouns belonging to different classes are involved. The gender conflict that arises may be resolved in a variety of ways in Bantu (see Givón 1970a). In Haya, if one of the nouns refers to a human and the other to an animal, a class 2 human concord is required in the plural:

(14)   (a) *omusháija n'émbwá bá- á- genda*   'the man and dog went'
            man   and dog they-past-go (cl. 2 SM)
       (b) **omusháija n'émbwá zá-á-genda* (cl. 10 SM)

Where gender conflict involving human and non-human nouns would arise, a favorite solution is avoidance of coordination and opting for the comitative construction:

(15)   *omusháija y- áá- genda n'émbwá*   'the man went with the dog'
       man   he-past-go   with dog

Where nouns referring to inanimates are conjoined a class 8 plural concord is required as in (16) where class 3 *omutí* 'tree' is coordinated with class 7 *ekyaalo* 'village':

(16)   (a) *omutí n'ékyaalo ni-bí-hya*   'the tree and the village are burning'
            tree and village pres.-they-burn
       (b) **omuti n'ékyaalo n-éé-hya* (cl. 4 SM)

As the ungrammaticality of (16b) shows, the agreement is not determined by proximity to the verb in Haya.

However, the Haya gender resolution rules are by no means universal in Bantu. In similar circumstances, Bokamba (1985:45) points out that Swahili has the verb agreeing with the nearest NP. Both sentences in (17) are grammatical.

(17)   (a) *ki-ti   na   m-guu wa meza u-mevunjika*
            7-chair and 3-leg of table 3-be.broken
            'The chair and the leg of the table are broken.'
       (b) *m-guu wa meza na ki-ti ki-mevunjika*
            3-chair of table and 3-leg 3-be.broken
            'The leg of the table and the chair are broken.'

9 SEMANTICS OF NOUN CLASSES

Next we consider the semantic basis of noun classification. Often nouns belonging to the same gender have some degree of semantic coherence. However, the extent to which this holds varies, with noun classes, and with languages. Table 7.8 summarizes the traditional consensus on the broad semantic characteristics of various noun classes.

As seen, the traditional meanings encompassed by many of the genders form what looks like a ragbag. Apart from the diminutive and augmentative use of certain classes (7, 8, 11, 12, 13, 20, 21), noteworthy cases of semantic coherence are class 1/2 which

TABLE 7.8: SEMANTIC CONTENT OF NOUN CLASSES

Class	Semantic content
1	Human beings
1a	Proper names
	Kinship terms
	Personifications
2	Regular plural of class 1
2b	Regular plural of class 1a
3	Natural phenomena
	Body parts
	Plants
	Animals
4	Regular plural of class 3
5	Natural phenomena
	Animals
	Body parts,
	Collective nouns
	Undesirable people
	Augmentatives
	Derogatives
6	Regular plural of classes 5 and 14;
	Mass terms and liquids
	Time references,
	Mannerisms
	Modes of action
7	Body parts
	Tools, instruments and utensils
	Animals and insects
	Languages
	Diseases
	Outstanding people
	Amelioratives
	Derogatives
	Augmentatives
	Curtatives (shortness and stoutness)
	Mannerisms
8	Regular plural of class 7
9	Animals
	People
	Body parts
	Tools, instruments and household effects
10	Regular plural of class 9
11	Long, thin entities
	Languages
	Body parts
	Natural phenomena
	Implements, utensils and other artefacts
12	Augmentatives
	Derogatives
	Diminutives
	Amelioratives
	Derogatives
13	Regular plural of class 12
14	Abstracts
	Collectives

(CONTINUED)

TABLE 7.8: (CONTINUED)

Class	Semantic content
15	Infinitives, a few body parts e.g. arm, leg
16	Location terms
17	Location terms
18	Location terms
19	Diminutives
20	Derogatives
	Augmentatives
	Diminutives
	Amelioratives
	Mannerisms
21	Augmentatives
	Derogatives
22	Plural of class 20
23	Location terms

Source: From Hendrikse and Poulos (1992:199–201).

hold human nouns; class 15 which contains infinitives and some body parts that come in pairs (e.g. 'arm', 'leg', 'ear'); and classes 16–18 which contain locatives. Semantic incoherence prevails elsewhere. For instance, gender 9/10 contains most names of animals but also has other assorted nouns – e.g. loanwords referring to non-humans are entered here; gender 3/4 typically contains most nouns referring to trees and plants, and to that extent is coherent. But it also holds a disparate set of other nouns, e.g. words meaning 'river', 'hill', 'moon', 'ghosts' as well as some body parts (e.g. the heart, arms). According to Richardson (1967:378), the lack of a clear semantic basis for noun classification in contemporary Bantu reflects the situation in PB.

This pessimism has been taken as a challenge by scholars who have attempted to provide a sound methodology for establishing some underlying coherence behind the apparent chaos of the semantics of noun classes. According to Creider (1975) and Denny and Creider (1986), the majority of PB noun prefixes were associated with a particular configurational or shape meaning. They divide the classes into two basic sets, with partly overlapping morphology. One set includes classes 1/2, 7/8 as well as 9/10 which contain nouns that indicate 'kinds of entities' (i.e. people, tools and animals, respectively). The other set contains nouns that indicate spatial and shape configurations such as roundness, length and size. They claim that 'configurational classes are distinguished according to whether solid shape (3/4, 5/6) or outline shape (9/10, 11/10) is being utilized as the basis of the classification' (Denny and Creider 1986:220). In their scheme, great significance is attached to the opposition between 'outline' and 'solid' shape which distinguishes between, on the one hand, objects with clear profiles, edges or boundaries such that there is a clear difference between an outside and an inside and, on the other hand, objects that do not have this property. In the mass noun categories, a distinction was drawn between 'cohesive' and 'dispersive' entities.

More recently, the analysis of the semantics of noun classes along the lines proposed by Denny and Creider has been undertaken by Contini-Morava (1997) and Moxley (1998) using the framework of cognitive linguistics provided by Cognitive Grammar (Langacker 1987) and by Lakoff (1987). Cognitive Grammar rejects the traditional Aristotelian view that linguistic categorization is only valid if a set of necessary and sufficient conditions for membership of a class can be found. Cognitivists argue that

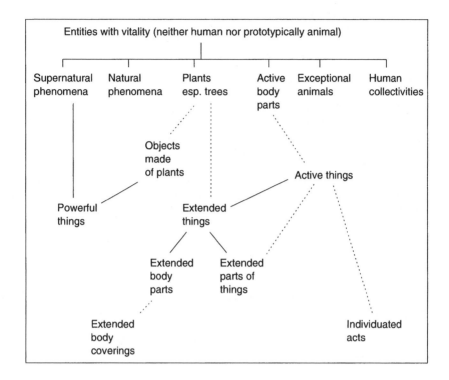

FIGURE 7.1 A SEMANTIC NETWORK FOR CLASS 3

class membership can be justified on the basis of multiple criteria, including 'family resemblances', metaphor, metonymy, etc.

Contini-Morava (1997) reports on a large-scale computerized study of all the 4,650 nouns in the *Standard Swahili-English Dictionary* (Johnson 1939), put in a database according to over seventy-five morphological and semantic criteria. She focuses on classes 3, 7, 5, 9 and 11. She provides a diagram of the cognitive semantic networks of each class showing the relations of instantiation, metaphoric and metonymic extension within the class as seen in figure 7.1 dealing with class 3. The schema moves from the more general to the more specific. The most typical members of the class are entities with vitality which are neither human nor prototypical animals. This is exemplified in (18):

(18) Subtype   Example

    Supernatural phenomena   *mzimu* 'spirit of a dead person or ancestor'
    Natural phenomena   *mto* 'river'
    Plants   *mkindu* 'palm-tree'
    Active body parts   *moyo* 'heart'
    Exceptional animals   *mchumbururu* 'sword fish'
    Human collectivities   *mji* 'town'
    Objects made from plants   *mkeka* 'mat'
    Powerful thing   *mkuyati* 'aphrodisiac'
    Active things   *mshale* 'arrow'

Extended body parts	*mguu* 'leg'
Extended things	*mkanda* 'strap'
Extended parts of things	*mwamba* 'ridge pole of roof'
Extended body coverings	*mfuria* 'loose coat'

Although this analysis suggests that there is more order in the system than is at first apparent, sceptics might feel uncomfortable at the sheer number of parameters put forward as distinguishers for members of this class, and the vagueness of some of the distinguishers (e.g. 'exceptional animal'). Moreover, this very rich system still leaves the presence of many abstract nouns in this gender unaccounted for, e.g. *mbisho* 'strife, argumentativeness', *mkano* 'denial', etc. (see also (22) below).

Moxley (1998), also focussing on Swahili, proposes to establish the reality of semantically motivated noun classification. Her analysis is modelled on the treatment of Dyirbal by Dixon (1982) and the reinterpretation of Dyirbal noun classification in the cognitive approach by Lakoff (1987). She claims that Lakoff's cognitive approach enables the linguist 'to show the validity of semantic networks structured by motivated extensions, through the establishment of conceptual devices that structure cultural realities reflected in this aspect of language' (Moxley 1998:229).

Some of Moxley's claims are uncontroversial. Where class membership has a fairly clear semantic basis Cognitive Grammar seems to offer a useful way of looking at the semantics of noun classes. For instance, she points out that gender 1/2 is the gender of animate nouns and is largely restricted to humans. A more challenging task is presented by genders such as 3/4 that appear to have a degree of semantic cohesion coexisting with considerable incoherence. Moxley, like previous analysts, observes that this gender contains the majority of nouns referring to trees and other plants:

(19)   Plants, plant parts, made from plants

Class 3	Class 4	
(a) plants		
mti	*miti*	'tree'
mkindu	*mikindu*	'palm-tree'
mpingo	*mipingo*	'ebony tree'
(b) plant parts		
mzizi	*mizizi*	'root'
mbegu	*mibegu*	'seed'
(c) made from plants		
mkeka	*mikeka*	'mat (normally made from palm leaves)'
mkate	*mikate*	'bread'

Moxley proposes that there are a few other strands of meaning that run through this gender. One strand consists of objects that are long, thin or extended in shape:

(20)   Shape: long, thin or extended

Class 3	Class 4	
mguu	*miguu*	'leg'
mkia	*mikia*	'tail'
mto	*mito*	'river'
mshale	*mishale*	'arrow'
mpini	*mipini*	'pestle'

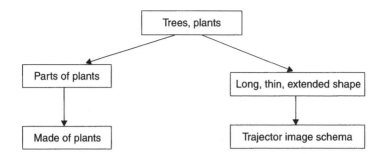

FIGURE 7.2 SWAHILI CLASS 3/4 STRUCTURE

Drawing on the role of the journey metaphor in semantic extension, she classifies together the nouns in (21):

(21) Journey/travel/time trajectory

Class 3	Class 4	
mwaka	*myaka*	'year'
mwendo	*myendo*	'journey'
mwisho	*miisho*	'end'

She claims there is a progression by semantic extension from the most basic core meanings relating to plants to other meanings as depicted in figure 7.2.

Unfortunately, there is a very substantial number of nouns in class 3 which seem to be a random collection of concrete nouns, abstract nouns, various nominalisations, etc. which cannot be accounted for thus. They include the following:

(22)

mbwoji	'spring (of water)'	*mgota*	'beating, blow'
mchanganyiko	'mixture'	*mguno*	'grumbling, murmuring, grunting'
mcheche	'a spark, small drop'	*mgumio*	'bark (of a dog)'
mchinjo	'act (place, manner, etc.) of slaying'	*mwaka*	'year'
		mwangwi	'echo'
mchuzi	'gravy'	*mwezi*	'month'
mdaawa	'legal process'	*mwanya*	'gap, hole'
mdahalo	'debate, discussion'	*mwongo*	'number, account'
mgango	'time (method, means, etc.) of curing'	*mjengo*	'act (process, style method) of building; architecture'
mgorogoro	'obstacle, difficulty, nuisance'		
mgono	'kind of fish trap'		

These attempts to make sense of the semantic principles behind the allocation of nouns to the various noun classes are to be welcomed. They have clarified some of the issues though real problems still remain unresolved.

10 CONCLUSION

The pervasiveness of concord, which spreads from nominals to other elements of the sentence is a key characteristic of Bantu languages. Classifying nouns into genders on the basis of the noun class affixes and concords based on those semantico-syntactic morphemes has often been seen as the hallmark of this sub-family.

While the broad picture is simple, in close-up the situation is complex. Noun classes are neither unique to this sub-group in Niger-Congo nor always present in force in all its members. Reconstructing the noun classes of PB and explaining the attrition or expansion of the noun class system in the daughter languages is a challenge that Bantuists have tried to meet. Other tasks that they have tackled, with a good degree of success, include throwing light on the semantic basis of the gender system, and establishing the range and distribution of genders attested across the Bantu field, the pairing of noun classes and the operation of the concord system.

ACKNOWLEDGMENT

I wish to acknowledge the extensive helpful comments that I have received from the editors.

REFERENCES

Bleek 1862, 1869; Bokamba 1985; Brown 1972; Brusciotto 1659; Claudi 1997; Cole 1967; Contini-Morava 1997; Corbett 1991; Creider 1975; de Blois 1970; Denny and Creider 1986; Dixon 1982; Doke 1927b, 1960; Dugast 1967; Foley and van Valin 1984; Givón 1970a, 1975b, 1979b; Greenberg 1963a, 1977, 1978b; Gregersen 1977; Guthrie 1948, 1967–71; Guthrie and Carrington 1988; Hadermann 1994a, 1999; Hedinger 1980; Heine 1976, 1980, 1982; Hendrikse and Poulos 1992; Hyman 1975, 1980; Hyman and Katamba 1991, 1993; Jacottet 1896; Johnson 1939; Kadima 1969; Kageyama 1977; Lakoff 1987; Langacker 1987; Maho 1999; Meeussen 1954a, 1959, 1967; Meinhof 1899, 1906; Meinhof and Van Varmelo 1932; Moxley 1998; Mufwene 1980; Mukarovsky 1976–7; Nurse and Hinnebusch 1993; Richardson 1967; Schadeberg 1990; Torrend 1891; Voorhoeve 1980c; Wald 1975; Welmers 1958, 1973; Williamson 1986.

CHAPTER EIGHT

SYNTAX

Thomas Bearth

1 INTRODUCTION AND PREVIEW

Our main concern in this chapter is to understand ways in which Bantu languages organize meaningful elements, i.e. words and phrases, to form minimal units for self-contained communication, i.e. sentences. How are constituents arranged in the sentence? Which sequences of words and phrases are most characteristic of Bantu? Are Bantu languages rather homogeneous in respect to word order, as is usually assumed, or does closer inspection reveal typologically significant divergence between them? If there is a basic word order, is it rigidly fixed, or is it permitted to vary for specific communicative purposes? And if the latter is the case, how does word order relate to the context in which verbal interaction takes place, or more generally, to meaning? How do Bantu languages make sense of syntax?

But syntax is not simply a matter of arranging words and phrases in linear sequence. In relating participants and entities to events, processes or states, it crucially interacts with the semantics of its organizational center, the verb (§2). It also interacts with the morphology of the verb (§§2–4), more rarely of the noun (§5.3.1). In addition, syntax plays a major role in relating sentences or their constituent parts to the larger textual or interactional context within which they are being used (§5). In short, syntax, and its specific contribution to verbal communication, can only be understood in synopsis with relevant aspects of morphology, semantics and pragmatics. Also, the diagnostic signifi-cance of grammatical processes such as passivization, topicalization and relativization for identifying syntactic functions in the sentence call for a dynamic rather than a merely structural approach to Bantu syntax (§§6–7).

Most published descriptions of Bantu languages concentrate on lexical and morpho-logical structure (Hinnebusch 1989:468). Studies explicitly dealing with syntactic phenomena are rare and are unevenly distributed over the area. For instance, studies high-lighting word order variation are limited to just a few languages, among them Swahili, Makua, Xhosa and some Grassfields Bantu languages. Work within the theoretical frameworks of Lexical-Functional Grammar (Bresnan and Kanerva 1989, Bresnan and Moshi 1990) and Relational Grammar (Blake 1990, Palmer 1994) dealing with the interrelation between sentence structure and grammatical processes has concentrated primarily on languages of the interlacustrine area and Swahili.

Scarcity of published data on the one hand and limitations of space on the other make it difficult to offer a balanced account covering syntactic essentials in a way representative of the Bantu area as a whole in its unity and diversity. In spite of these limitations, adopting both a synoptic and a dynamic perspective will enable us to sketch a typology of what might be termed the core syntax of Bantu languages, and meaningfully to address such fundamental issues as the relationship between semantic roles and sentence structure, word order variation, the status of objects in double object constructions, locative inversion and subject vs. topic-prominence.

2 VERB VALENCY – A KEY TO ELEMENTARY SENTENCE STRUCTURE

The structural and semantic subclassification of verbs is a principal key to understanding elementary syntactic structure. From a primarily structural view, the first criterion to consider is the number of nominal phrases (called 'arguments') which are required or allowed to occur in combination with a given verb or class of verbs by virtue of the latter's inherent lexico-semantic properties, i.e. their valencies. These in turn reflect a language-specific way of conceptualizing the class of state-of-affairs or processes denoted by a given verb.

2.1 Argument structure: simple verb stems

Simple, non-derived verbs in Bantu, suggest a three-way classification based on the number of arguments. Thus, the following examples from Swahili illustrate typical one-place (1–2), two-place (3) and three-place (4) verbs. Arguments may be realized (a) as lexically specified nouns or nominal phrases (1); (b) as pronominal elements incorporated into the verb, often called clitics, concords, prefixes or subject/object markers (2); (c) as independent pronouns; and (d) as zero (10). For present purposes, we may neglect (c).

2.1.1 One-place verbs and subject agreement

The following one-place verb construction from Swahili shows grammatical agreement between the lexical subject and the initial class-marking prefix of the verb, i.e. the subject marker (SM):

(1)   *Ki≠tabu   ki-me≠anguka*   'The book has fallen down.'
      cl7≠book cl7-ANT≠fall

Subject agreement is pervasive throughout Bantu. It is generally obligatory; deletion of the subject marker *ki-* at the beginning of the verb would make sentence (1) ungrammatical.

On the other hand, the lexical subject may be omitted without the sentence becoming ungrammatical. In this case, the subject is represented by the subject marker alone:

(2)   *Ki-me≠anguka*   'It (the book) has fallen down.'
      cl7-ANT≠fall

The subject prefix still shows agreement with its lexical counterpart *kitabu* 'book'. The latter, though no longer an explicit lexical argument of the verb, is assumed to be recoverable from the context. This type of agreement – by contrast with 'grammatical agreement' where the prefix refers to an explicit argument – is called 'anaphoric agreement' (Bresnan and Mchombo 1987:741).

2.1.2 Two-place predicates and object underspecification

Two-place verbs take a complement in addition to the subject.

(3)   *M≠toto   a-na≠soma   ki≠tabu*   'The child is reading the book.'
      cl1≠child cl1-PROG≠read cl7≠book

The vast majority of verbs, on account of the maximum number of core arguments capable of associating with them, belong to the class of two-place verbs: e.g. *kula* 'to eat', *kuleta* 'to bring', *kuoa* 'to marry', *kuona* 'to see', *kupika* 'to cook'.

The syntactic relation involving a single complement such as *kitabu* 'book' in (3) will be called 'object'. While subject–verb agreement is obligatory, the verb–object phrase does not normally show grammatical agreement unless:

- the object denotes a specific human referent. In this case an object marker (OM) precedes the verb stem:

(4) *Mama   a-na-m≠penda   m≠toto*   'The mother loves the child.'
    mother cl1-PROG-cl1 ≠ love   cl1 ≠ child

- the referent of the object is already established as a discourse topic:

(5) *M≠toto   a-na-ki-≠soma   ki≠tabu*   'The child is reading that book.'
    cl1 ≠ child cl1-PROG-cl7 ≠ read   cl7 ≠ book

If the lexical object remains unexpressed, the object marker, showing anaphoric agreement, will normally substitute for it:

(6) *M≠toto   a-na-ki≠soma*   'The child is reading it.'
    cl1 ≠ child cl1-PROG-cl7 ≠ read

In addition to full lexical specification and anaphora, Bantu syntax generally admits a third option: object underspecification. Depending on the particular verb, the object may be expressed or left unspecified:

(7) *Na≠taka   ku≠oa*   'I want to marry.'
    (1s-)PROG ≠ want   INF ≠ marry

Contrary to what has been suggested (Vitale 1981:33), the grammatically optional object marker is not omitted because the speaker assumes that the hearer will be able to retrieve the identity of its referent from contextual information. Rather, as (7) well illustrates, it is a means of limiting what is being said to the main point – here the desire of the speaker to change his marital status – in compliance with the conversational maxim of quantity (Grice 1975), according to which a contribution must not be more informative than the situation requires it to be. If referent retrieval was the speaker's intention, the complement would obligatorily be represented by an object prefix:

(8) *Na≠taka   ku-mw≠oa*   'I want to marry her.'
    (1s-)PROG ≠ want   INF-cl1 ≠ marry

The function of object underspecification – or 'argument reduction' as it is also called – is to expand the range of options for the selective presentation of states of affairs.

2.1.3 Three-place predicates – double object constructions

Underived three-place – or ditransitive – verbs are few in number. In terms of their semantics, they usually serve to denote transactions involving a giver, a goal or beneficiary, and a 'patient' undergoing the transaction – as in the prototypical case of the verb 'to give':

(9)   *Mama   a-li-m≠pa*   *m≠toto   ki≠tabu*   'Mother gave the child a book.'
      mother cl1-PAST-cl1≠give   cl1≠child cl7≠book

In accordance with the semantic template, the two co-occurring objects are commonly distinguished on the basis of their semantic roles. The goal, typically a human or animate entity, preferentially occupies the position immediately after the verb. It is also, in Swahili, obligatorily represented verb-internally by object agreement.

The patient preferentially occupies the second position following the verb. Contrary to the object of a two-place verb (cf. (4)–(5)), the patient of a double object construction cannot take agreement:

(10) *Mama   a-li-m≠pa*   *m≠toto*   'Mother gave it (the book) to the child.'
      mother cl1-PAST-cl1≠give   cl1≠child

In terms of its meaning, (10) is to (9) what (6) is to (4). Note that the absence of the object marker in (10), in contrast to its pragmatically motivated absence in (7), is grammatically conditioned, i.e. obligatory. It implies reference to a contextually retrievable object and may therefore be described as 'zero anaphora'.

Some Bantu languages, among them Swahili, allow the goal to be moved to second object position as a marked alternative to the generally dominant goal-patient ordering:

(11) *Mama   a-li-m≠pa*   *ki≠tabu   m≠toto*
      mother cl1-PAST-cl1≠give   cl7≠book   cl1≠child
      'Mother gave the book to a/the child.'

As the English translation of (11) suggests, the postposed goal is the sentence focus (Krifka 1983:95), or at least is less topical than its counterpart in (9) and than the patient in (11). What distinguishes this type of object movement in Swahili from the well known phenomenon of 'dative shift' in English – as illustrated in the English translation of (11) as against (10) – are its agreement properties: object agreement stays with the goal whatever the latter's position.

2.1.4 Object agreement constraints and syntactic typology

Constraints on object agreement, due to their variation among Bantu languages, are a key to their typological differentiation. We may distinguish between OM-1, OM-2 and OM-0 languages. OM-1 languages – e.g. Swahili, Chewa and Xhosa – allow maximally one object marker inside the verb. In OM-2 languages, such as Chaga, Haya, Rwanda and Tswana, 'any or all multiple objects may be expressed by object markers' (Bresnan and Moshi 1990:150). These languages allow strings of up to three or even four object markers preceding the verb stem (cf. (20)). At the other end of the spectrum, OM-0 languages (e.g. Lingala) do not allow any trace of an object in their verb morphology.

Cutting across the OM-based classification of languages, two other criteria having to do with the representation of objects are relevant to syntactic typology:

(i)   Within OM-1 and OM-2 languages, some languages permit only anaphoric agreement but disallow grammatical agreement (e.g. Chaga, Rwanda and Shona), while others allow or, in some cases, require both (e.g. Swahili, cf. (4)–(5); Xhosa, cf. (22)).

(ii) So-called 'symmetrical' languages (e.g. Chaga, Rwanda) assign object markers without discrimination to different types of objects, whereas 'asymmetrical languages' (e.g. Swahili), restrict object marking with respect to semantic role, a restriction usually paralleled by constraints on grammatical processes such as passivization (see Bresnan and Moshi (1990) and §6.1).

However, this diversity must not be allowed to obscure the fundamental principle of double representation which is common to most Bantu languages, albeit to greatly varying degrees: information coded in the syntax of the sentence may be cumulatively or alternatively coded in the verb morphology. Any sentence can be reduced to its verb without ceasing to function as a sentence – the finite verb is the minimal form of the sentence.

This has important consequences for the overall structure of natural text, since it allows fully specified states of affairs to be expressed very economically by a single verb whenever the participants are retrievable from context:

(12)   *A-li-m≠pa*   'She (mother) gave (it, the book) to him (the child).'
       cl1-PAST-cl1≠give

2.1.5 Adjuncts vs. arguments

Any of the sentences used for illustration above may be further expanded by adding adjuncts whose purpose it is to locate the process or state of affairs in space or time, or to describe some circumstance applying to it. Adjuncts representing new information generally follow the postverbal core arguments:

(13)   *Mama a-li-m≠pa   mtoto kitabu kwa upesi nyumba-ni leo*
       Mother she-PAST-him≠give child book with speed house-LOC today
       'Mother gave the child quickly the book at home today.'

(13) exemplifies the basic or canonical word order assumed to prevail in Bantu languages:

S V O1 O2 (X_1, X_2, X_3)

Adjuncts, subsumed under 'X', are clearly distinguishable from arguments (S and O) in the following respects:

(i)   Their occurrence is not constrained by the valency of the verb.
(ii)   In contrast to core arguments, they are not represented in the verb morphology.
(iii) Their internal order tends to be variable.
(iv)   Nominal expressions functioning as adjuncts of manner or place are marked by prepositions (*kwa upesi* 'with speed') or specialized suffixes (*nyumba-ni* 'house-in').

Circumstantial expressions, in particular locatives, tend to be ambivalent with regard to the adjunct/argument dichotomy. The following example (Abdulaziz 1996:82) shows that, in Swahili, locatives may be co-expressed by locative agreement in the verb, just as objects may be co-represented by an object marker (5):

(14)   *Hamisi a-li-ku≠ingia   ndani ya nyumba*   'Hamisi went inside the house.'
       Hamisi cl1-PAST-cl16≠enter   inside of house

For a fuller treatment of locative arguments in a Bantu language, see du Plessis and Visser (1992:Ch. 2) on Xhosa.

2.2 Argument structure: derived verb stems

Bantu languages typically have a rich array of derivative morphemes – so-called 'verb extensions' – that may be suffixed to the verb stem. For our purpose, we may ignore morphological and semantic details of these extensions (cf. Ch. 6). What is of interest here is the way in which adding one or more extensions to the verb stem modifies the syntactic frame associated with the verb. Thus the applicative extension, if added to the two-place simplex verb *-let-a* 'to bring (something)', changes the latter into a three-place verb *-let-e-a* 'to bring (something to somebody).' In terms of the semantics of the state-of-affairs expressed by the verb, the suffixation of the derivative morpheme alternant *-e-* correlates with the addition of a beneficiary participant role. Compare:

(15) *M≠toto   a-me≠let-a   ki≠tabu*   'The child brought the book.'
cl1 ≠child cl1-ANT≠bring-FV cl7≠book

(16) *M≠toto   a-me≠m-let-e-a   baba yake   ki≠tabu*
cl1 ≠child cl1-ANT≠bring-FV father his   cl7≠book
'The child brought his father a/the book.'

The agreement conventions for (16) are the same as those described for double object constructions in §2.1.2.

Similarly, one-place verbs extend their valency so as to accommodate a second argument:

(17) *Wa≠geni   wa-me-ku≠j-a*   'Strangers have come.'
cl2≠foreign cl2-ANT-EXPL≠come-FV

(18) *Wa-geni   wa-me-m-j-i-a   baba*
cl2≠foreign cl2-ANT-cl1 ≠come-FV   father
'Strangers have come to (visit) father.'

However, as (18) shows, the 'extended case' (Wald 1994) does not, in terms of agreement, behave like an inherent object of a two-place verb (§2.1.2), but like the inherent goal of a three-place verb (§2.1.3).

3 WORD ORDER, AFFIX ORDER AND THE TOPICALITY METRIC

As shown above for Swahili postverbal objects, the order of constituents in Bantu follows clearly defined rules. OM-2 languages, with their multiple object representation in the verb, are particularly revealing in this respect. The following pair of sentences from Rwanda (Kimenyi, quoted in Dryer 1983:137) juxtaposes a fully specified (19) and a pronominalized version (20) of an otherwise identical four-place predication:

(19) *Umugóre a-ra≠hé-er-a   umugabo imbwa ibíryo*
                          1   2   3
woman she-PRES≠give-BEN-FV man (BEN) dog (IO) food (DO)
'The woman is giving food to the dog for the man.'

(20) *Umugóre a-ra-bi-yi-mu≠he-er-a*
                  3 2 1
woman she-PRES-it(DO)-it(IO)-him(BEN)≠give-BEN-FV
'The woman is giving it to it for him.'

In (19), the derived benefactive verb 'to give on behalf of someone' takes three postverbal complements which occur in the following order: (1) Beneficiary (BEN: *umugabo* 'man'); (2) Goal or Indirect Object (IO: *imbwa* 'dog') (3) Patient or Direct Object (DO: *ibíryo* 'food').

In (20), the same arguments are represented verb-internally by a series of prefixes sandwiched between the present marker -*ra*- and the benefactive verb stem (Kimenyi 1980:15). The prefixes show class agreement with the heads of the nominal phrases in (19) which they substitute. As can be seen by comparing the numbers underneath the argument positions of the two constructions, the order of the internal arguments is the mirror-image of the order of the external complements. The constituent following immediately after the verb correlates with the prefix immediately preceding the verb, the constituent in second postverbal position is represented by the prefix in the second preverbal position, etc.

Similar evidence from other languages, e.g. Tswana (Creissels 1992:263, n. 15) and Haya (Krifka 1995:1407) suggests that the mirror-image arrangement of external and verb-internal constituents is not a matter of chance.

As already noted for Swahili (2.1.3), lexical animate entities tend to occur immediately after the verb, before inanimate ones. Correspondingly, verb-internal ordering of object markers places animate referents after inanimate ones, i.e. as closely as possible to the verb stem. In the case of two co-occurring animate arguments, the ranking of argument roles determines their ordering relative to the verb: the beneficiary generally takes precedence over the patient, as in Xhosa (du Plessis and Visser 1992:23):

(21)   *Ndì≠n ìkà   úmfâzì   úmntwáná*   'I am giving a child to the woman.'
        I-am-giving woman   child   *'I am giving a woman to the child.'

The widespread tendency in Bantu languages is to assign preferentially the positions next to the verb on account of a hierarchy of parameters variably defined, according to Duranti (1979:32), in terms of (i) animacy of the nominal referent (human > animate > inanimate), (ii) semantic role relationship to the process expressed by the verb (Beneficiary > Goal > Patient > Locative), (iii) participant category (first > second > third person) and (iv) number (Plural > Singular). The cross-linguistic and cross-categorial regularity of this pattern suggests an underlying common motivation. What unites human/animate, benefactive, egocentric and plural referents is, according to a broadly supported view (Duranti 1979, Hyman and Duranti 1982, Wald 1994), their high status on the scale of 'inherent topicality', or 'cognitive accessibility' (Rapold 1997:45).

Duranti (1979:31) shows that in Shambala and Haya, nominal phrases with higher inherent topicality status 'govern OM's closer to the verb stem than those lower in the hierarchies'. As will be seen in §6.1, the topicality metric plays a major role not only in determining basic order, at the level of both the sentence and verb morphology, but also in the licensing of syntactic processes such as passivization.

Since the various categories defining the competing topicality hierarchies are themselves independent variables, it is natural to expect that conflicts will arise in assigning their respective positions to multiple complements, or in allowing them to undergo passivization or other processes. For instance, in the case of co-occurrence of a third person human beneficiary and a first person human patient, the latter is lower than the former on the topicality scale defined by semantic role, but is higher on the topicality scale defined by the dimension of person.

Space limitations do not allow us to list various principles and strategies for resolving such conflicts that have been described for a number of languages. We refer the reader to

Duranti (1979), Wald (1994) and others. From a historical-comparative perspective, 'topicality conflicts' seem to have played a major role in shaping competing contemporary rule systems of syntax in sub-areas of Bantu. If we assume for Proto-Bantu full intraverbal representation of multiple objects, we may see the reduction of this freedom of occurrence to a single occurrence, or its total abolition as in Lingala, as strategies for resolving or, in the latter case, avoiding conflicts of topicality (Wald 1994:245–8).

4 WORD ORDER VARIATION AND CANONICAL WORD ORDER

Variability of verb-external constituent order is a widespread although insufficiently studied phenomenon of Bantu syntax.

A construction such as the following from Xhosa, which comprises a verb and two arguments, i.e. three sentential constituents, permits all six theoretically possible permutations (adjusted from du Plessis and Visser 1992:13), without any difference in sentence meaning between them:

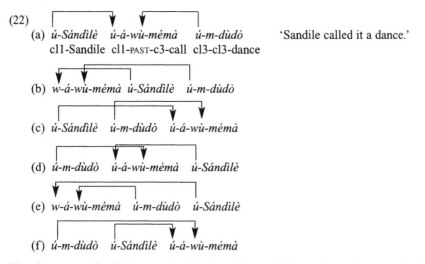

(22)

    (a) *ú-Sándìlè   ú-á-wù-mémà   ú-m-dùdò*   'Sandile called it a dance.'
          cl1-Sandile cl1-PAST-c3-call cl3-cl3-dance

    (b) *w-á-wù-mémà ú-Sándìlè   ú-m-dùdò*

    (c) *ú-Sándìlè   ú-m-dùdò   ú-á-wù-mémà*

    (d) *ú-m-dùdò   ú-á-wù-mémà   ú-Sándìlè*

    (e) *w-á-wù-mémà   ú-m-dùdò   ú-Sándìlè*

    (f) *ú-m-dùdò   ú-Sándìlè   ú-á-wù-mémà*

The class concords which occur in fixed positions relative to the verb stem and which invariably refer to the lexical constituents *ú-Sándìlè* 'Sandile' and *ú-m-dùdò* 'dance', allow for the latter to be unambiguously identified in spite of their changing position: *ú-Sándìlè* is identified as subject via its cross-referencing relationship to class 1 concord *ú-* (realized *w-* before the remote past marker *-á-* in (22a/d)), which invariably occurs in the verb-initial subject prefix position. On the other hand, *ú-m-dùdò*, whichever position it occupies in the sentence, it is unambiguously identified as the object due to its being cross-referenced to class 3 concord *wu-*, which invariably occupies the object prefix position between the tense marker and the verb stem.

Extrapolating from du Plessis and Visser's (1992:13) remark on Xhosa that 'the different alternations in (22) are only possible because the subject and object have different class features', one might suspect that freedom of word order in Bantu (and perhaps beyond) is contingent on the availability of grammatical agreement as a compensating mechanism for resolving syntactic ambiguities resulting from word order variation. However, evidence from other Bantu languages does not support the idea of a necessary correlation between the two phenomena. In Rwanda for instance, where – apart from subject agreement – grammatical agreement is virtually absent from verb morphology, 'there is a free word order of objects except that it is the new information which always comes last' (Kimenyi 1988:356). And although Rwanda has no distinct subject and object markers allowing to retrieve the syntactic functions of shifted-around constituents, even subject and object may be inverted: see (65)–(66) below.

On the other hand, the question might be asked: how does identical class membership of invertible constituents affect freedom of word order? For in this case discrimination of syntactic functions through class agreement becomes inoperative as a criterion for assigning syntactic function. Presumably, this sort of syntactic ambiguity occurs most often with human or animate referents, as in the following Xhosa example (du Plessis and Visser 1992:13):

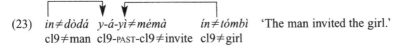

(23) *in≠dòdá   y-á-yì≠mémà   ín≠tómbì*   'The man invited the girl.'
      cl9≠man cl9-PAST-cl9≠invite cl9≠girl

There seems to be considerable cross-linguistic support for the idea that in the case of unresolved ambiguity, speakers of Bantu languages fall back on canonical word order for disambiguating the meaning of the sentence. Applying the postulated default order SVO to (23), it follows that the preverbal constituent is the subject of the sentence, making mandatory the reading which attributes the active role to the male participant.

From this it would follow that even if some Bantu languages, such as Xhosa, tolerate all theoretically possible permutations of sentence constituents, word order is never free in an absolute sense. Its variation is subject to the condition that syntactic functions and semantic roles can be identified independently of word order. Canonical word order functions as a 'safety-net' that guarantees disambiguation in cases of otherwise unresolved syntactico-semantic ambiguity.

However, the credibility of the disambiguating role of canonical word order is challenged by Stucky (1985) in her study of Makua word order. Her example (Stucky 1985:61):

(24) *Hín-Sepété á≠hóón-á   Aráárima*   'Sepete saw Araarima.'
      Sepete   SM ≠see-FV Araarima

resembles Xhosa (22) in that both arguments are class-identical. The difference is that there is no overt object agreement. Word order in Makua, according to Stucky, is quite unrestricted – the three constituents may follow each other in any of the six possible orders. At the same time, spontaneous informant reaction to (24) seems to favor the reading by which Sepete is the one who sees and Araarima the one who is being seen – thus apparently confirming the claim made for the subsidiary role of canonical word order in the Xhosa parallel case. However, Stucky observes that, given an appropriate discourse context, the inverse OVS reading of (24), attributing to Araarima the role of the one who sees and identifying Sepete as the one being seen, is also acceptable. Moreover, the spontaneous preference for the SVO reading of (24) as against the apparently dispreferred OVS reading can be explained by factors having nothing to do with syntax.

Thus doubt is being cast not only on the methods used for establishing claims of canonical word order, but on the validity of the concept itself. The conclusion would be, at least for Makua, that, (i) given appropriate discourse conditions, any order of constituents is possible, (ii) this freedom of order is merely constrained by discourse pragmatic conditions and not by syntax and (iii) claims according to which grammatical agreement is the major factor licensing word order variation need to be carefully double-checked against a large body of textual evidence for various languages.

5 PRAGMATIC FUNCTIONS OF WORD ORDER IN CORE BANTU AND IN PERIPHERAL BANTU

One reason why word order variation is often, if at all, dealt with in a rather cavalier manner is its apparent indifference to meaning. Yet, in many Bantu languages, word order contributes crucially to define the intended purpose of the sentence as part of the communicative event. Thus, so-called information structure reflects the speaker's assumptions about the interlocutor's current state of mind (Dik 1989:Ch. 13) in regard to the relative (un)predictability or (un)disputedness of an element referred to or implicated by the sentence. Less predictable or disputed elements of the sentence tend to be marked as 'focus', while specific elements relating the sentence to the preceding discourse tend to be marked as 'topic' (cf. Bearth 1995 for Swahili). Word order change *per se*, as well as grammatical processes affecting word order (§6–7), besides or in conjunction with morphological, inflectional and prosodic marking strategies (Bearth 1999; Geitlinger in press), are important means predominantly used in Bantu languages for expressing information structure of the sentence and ensuring textual cohesion.

5.1 Subject postposing in Swahili and Xhosa

A suitable environment in which the expression of 'focus' may be tested are wh-questions. Thus in Swahili, a perfectly correct sentence in canonical order (SVX):

(25)   *Ali   a-li≠fika   jana*   'Ali came yesterday.'
       Ali   cl1-PAST≠arrive yesterday

is not acceptable as an answer to the question:

(26)   *Jana   a-li≠fika   nani?*   'Who came yesterday?'
       yesterday c1-PAST-arrive who

As demonstrated in Krifka (1983:155–6), this sentence, in order to be interpreted as an acceptable answer to (26), requires the subject to be placed after the verb:

(27)   *Jana   a-li≠fika   Ali*   'Ali came yesterday.'
       yesterday cl1-PAST≠arrive Ali

The inversion marks the subject as completive focus – as the missing piece of information which the utterance purports to supply and which, in the particular case of a wh-question, is the object of a preceding explicit request by the hearer (Dik 1989:282).

The following example from Xhosa (du Plessis and Visser 1992:131) illustrates the use of subject inversion as a means of identifying an element of a state-of-affairs against a controversial background:

(28)   *Kù≠sèbénzà ámá≠dódà, háyì ábá≠fázi*
       cl17≠work   cl6≠men   not cl2a≠women
       'The MEN work, not the women.'

The postposed subject *ámá≠dódà* 'men' correlates with contrastive focus (Dik 1989:282). The inverted word order does two things: (a) it asserts the predication as being true for the focused item (the men) and (b) it implies the rejection of a competing claim according to which the predication would have been true for some other element belonging to the same presupposition set (the women).

In Xhosa, according to du Plessis and Visser (1992:132), the inverted subject moves to the position immediately after the verb (IAV) and necessarily precedes other complements (VSX). By contrast, in Chewa (Bresnan and Kanerva 1989:3f.), the postposed subject obligatorily follows other postverbal complements (VXS), i.e. it occurs in sentence-final position. (It is not clear, though, from Bresnan and Kanerva, if, in terms of its discourse-function, the sentence-final subject in Chewa is in fact equivalent to the Xhosa postverbal subject.)

5.2 Verb-final strategy

An analogous reordering principle results in focus being assigned to the verb: constituents which follow it in the canonical order move to preverbal position. The following excerpt from a Swahili play (Yahya and Mulwa 1988:35) illustrates inversion from OV to VO:

(29) *Ku-na mapenzi na chuki.*   'There-is love and hatred ...'
Watu wengine u-ta-wa≠penda,   *na wengine u-ta-wa≠chukia*
People some   you-will-them≠love, and others   you-will-them≠hate
'... Some people you will love, others you will hate.'

Evidently, the thrust of the passage is not to identify and contrast two groups of people but two types of behavior. The focus is on the referents of the verbs, not of the objects. The net result of the 'castling' strategy illsutrated in (29) is to make the verb appear to have been moved rightwards into a position which naturally attracts focus.

5.3 Aghem – when pragmatics overrides semantics

In Aghem, basic word order is as follows (Watters 1979:143):

S Aux V (O$_1$) (â O$_2$) (Loc) (Temp)

(30) *fíl   á mɔ́ fúo kí-bé â bvʉ́-tɔ́* 'The friends gave fufu to the dogs.'
friends sm P$_2$ give cl-fufu to dogs-cl

While resembling the dominant Bantu word order in terms of the overall post-modifying structure which places the object(s) after the verb, the Aghem pattern differs from it in several respects:

(i) The only strictly invariable position is the Auxiliary (Aux), usually represented by a tense-aspect operator (P$_1$ 'today past', P$_2$ 'before today past', etc.). Contrary to the tense-aspect markers in core-Bantu languages, Aux may be separated from the verb by one or more objects (see (34)–(35)). Aux is preceded by the subject which, if nominal, contains a subject marker (sm).

(ii) The beneficiary or goal follows rather than precedes the direct object in the unmarked sequence.

(iii) Double objects are not inherent in the valency of the verb, but require the presence of the case marker *â*. Glossing *â* as a preposition with the meaning 'for, to' may help understand its semantics, but its role in Aghem syntax, as will appear later, is better described as that of a verb particle.

5.3.1 Pragmatics of word order in single object sentences

Following Watters (1979:144ff.), let us look at word order variation in sentences with a single object:

(31)   fíl   á mɔ̂ zì̠ <u>kì-bé</u> án'sóm   'The friends ate fufu in the farm.'
        friends SM P₁ ate cl≠fufu in the farm

(31) may be used to state an all-new fact, or to answer a question such as 'What did the friends do?', or 'What did the friends eat (on the farm)?.' The scope of focus (underlined) extends maximally from the verb to the end of the sentence, but minimally includes the object.

The following sentences illustrate narrow focus assignment to non-objects: the location *án'sóm* 'in the farm' in (32), and the subject *áf̠ín* 'friends' in (33).

(32)   fíl   á mɔ̂ zì̠ <u>án'sóm</u>   bé-kɔ́   'The friends ate fufu *in the farm*.'
        friends SM P₁ ate in the farm fufu-cl

(33)   à mɔ́   zì̠   <u>áì̠f̠ín</u>   bé-kɔ́ án'sóm   'The *friends* ate fufu in the farm.'
        It   P₁   ate   SM friends   fufu-cl in the farm

In both cases, the focused elements are moved to IAV position. The IAV position corresponds to the position of the syntactic object in the basic order. As said in commenting (31), if the object occupies this position, it must be part of the focus. That the IAV position is the natural focus position in Aghem is confirmed by the observation that (a) question words obligatorily occur in this position and (b) that constituents other than objects, in order to become the focus of the sentence, must be shifted to IAV position, as in (32)–(3). (32) answers the question 'Where did the friends eat fufu?', (33) the question 'Who ate fufu in the farm?'

In addition, however, Aghem uses word order as an indirect means of marking counter-assertive focus: postverbal elements which are not in its scope are shifted to the position immediately before the verb (IBV), as is the case with *án'sóm* 'the farm' in (34), where the object *kì-bé* 'fufu' *is* counter-asserted (as compared to (31) where it carries 'normal' focus):

(34)   fíl   á mɔ̂ án'sóm   zì̠ <u>kì-bé</u>
        friends SM P₁   in the farm ate cl-fufu
        'Friends ate *fufu* (not yams) in the farm.'

Similarly, if the place where the eating took place is controversial, the object is moved to IBV position:

(35)   fíl   á mɔ̂ bé-kì̠ zì̠ <u>án'sóm</u>
        friends SM P₁   fufu-cl ate   in the farm
        'Friends ate fufu in the *farm* (not the house).'

The Aghem verb lacks the typical Bantu morphological complexity. By way of compensation, its nominal arguments show remarkable morphological alternation co-varying with their information status:

(i)   The position of the nominal class marker relative to the nominal stem co-varies with the nominal argument's position relative to the verb in a way reminiscent of the mirror-image arrangement of incorporated affixes in the verb morphology of core-Bantu (cf. (19)–(20)): the IAV order 'verb + class-*prefix* + nominal-stem' ((31): *zi̧ ki̧-bé* 'eat fufu') is replaced in IBV position by the reverse order 'nominal-stem + class-*suffix* + verb' ((35): *bé-ki̧ zi̧* 'fufu eat'). Since the prefix noun may only occur in the IAV position, it correlates with the preferred focus position, as in (31) and (34). Similarly, the suffix noun correlates with out-of-focus use, or, as Watters (1979:149) terms it, a 'marked presupposition' status of the nominal, illustrated in (35).

(ii) A modified form of the class suffix (*bé-ki* 'fufu') is used in focus-neutral positions before or after the focus-relevant IBV and IAV positions (cf. (32)–(33)); it is moreover mandatory in IAV position if the normal focus effect associated with IAV is cancelled due to some operator focus (negation, polar assertive or counter-assertive focus, etc.) having scope over the sentence as a whole (Watters 1979:150).

5.3.2 Pragmatics of word order in double object sentences

Returning to the three-place construction of (30), we notice that it involves the verb 'to give', an agent ('friends'), a patient ('fufu') and a goal ('to dogs'). In its canonical order, it serves to establish the fact that 'friends gave fufu to dogs' (Watters 1979:152).

Compare now the variants carrying focus respectively on the patient (36) and on the goal (37):

(36) *fi̧l   á mɔ́ fúo ti̧-bvú â   <u>bé-kɔ́</u>*   'The friends gave the dogs *fufu.*'
      friends SM P$_2$ give cl-dogs to fufu-cl

(37) *fi̧l   á mɔ́ fúo â <u>bvú-tɔ́</u> bé-kɔ́*   'The friends gave fufu to the *dogs.*'
      friends SM P$_2$ give to dogs-cl   fufu-cl

The assignment of focus to 'fufu' in (36) and to 'dogs' in (37) flies in the face of all we have seen above about focus marking in Aghem. As to (36), one should expect, on the basis of (31) and the principles of focus assignment discussed above, that *ti̧-bvú* 'dogs', which (a) occupies IAV position and (b) is realized in its 'in-focus' prefix form, ought to be the focus. Contrary to this expectation, it turns out that the focus of this sentence is *bé-kɔ́* 'fufu' which conforms to neither of the two focus-marking criteria.

Comparing (36) and (37) to (30), one notes that the order of the arguments with respect to the particle *â* may vary. Word order variation revolving around the particle *â* is called 'transposition' by Watters (1979:152). Narrow focus on 'dogs' is obtained in (37) by moving the whole phrase introduced by *â* to IAV position. This appears to conform to the positional rule according to which focus is assigned to constituents other than direct objects by moving them to the IAV position. On the morphological level, however, the focused noun takes the 'out-of-focus' suffix form *bvú-tɔ́* in (37), whereas in (36), where it occurs in the 'in-focus' prefix form *ti̧-bvú*, it is not the focus.

Can syntacticians make sense out of such inconsistencies? They can. Notice first that from (37), a counter-assertive sentence stating that dogs, not some other kind of being, received the fufu, can be derived by shifting the patient to IBV position:

(38) *fi̧l   á mɔ́ bé-ki̧ fúo â <u>bvú-tɔ́</u>*
      friends SM P$_2$ fufu-cl give to dogs-cl
      'The friends gave fufu to the *dogs* (not the cats).'

Similarly, from (36), the counter-assertive focus on the patient 'fufu' is derived by shifting the goal expression to IBV position:

(39) fíl   á mɔ́ bvú-tí   fúo â bɛ́-kɔ́
      friends SM P$_2$ dogs-cl give to fufu-cl
      'The friends gave the dogs *fufu* (not yams).'

In neither case, the particle *â* is moved to IBV position together with the out-of-focus nominal. By retaining its postverbal position, the particle stands in the characteristic position of the 'focus assigner'. The apparently contradictory focus assignments in (36) and (37) fall into line if we assume that the position immediately following the particle *á* plays an analogous role for focus assignment in double object constructions as the position immediately following the verb in single object constructions. The shift of the 'pivotal' function from the verb itself to the particle becomes perfectly natural if the latter is considered as an extension of the former, rather than as a preposition. As a result, a single positional principle is applicable to both types of constructions: the focus, whether assertive or counter-assertive, occurs in the position immediately after the pivot, i.e. after the particle *â* if it is there, in IAV position otherwise. On the other hand, as (36) shows, the verb, not the particle, maintains control over the alternation between prefix and suffix nominals, which explains the apparent inconsistencies between the specific form of the nominals and their function in the focusing system in (36) and (37).

One tends to agree with Hyman (1979a:56) that the complex interplay of positional variation and noun-morphology in expressing focus categories in Aghem is 'quite unusual in Cameroonian Bantu and in Bantu in general'. However, the individual mechanisms contributing to making Aghem syntax look so different from, say, Swahili or Xhosa are all found elsewhere in Bantu, from the mirroring arrangement of pre- and postverbal elements to subject postposing, verb-finalization (Watters 1979:150), and object preposing. It is the degree of their grammaticalization and their pragmatic specialization which accounts for the typological difference.

5.4 Tunen – a case of SOV basic word order

Mous (1997) shows that basic word order in Tunen, another Cameroonian Bantu language, is SOV rather than SVO, as found elsewhere in Bantu. SVO sentences do occur, but the postverbal object then carries obligatory contrastive focus, whereas assertive object focus – which is normally associated with unmarked focus constructions – requires the object to occur before the verb:

(40) Mè-ná mwɔ̀lúkú tál   'I put wine (on the table).'
      I-PAST wine   put

(41) Bò mè-ná tálá á   mwɔ̀lùk 'No, I put WINE (on the table).'
      No I-PAST put PART wine

(40), with the object in preverbal position, could be used for completive focus in response to the inquiry 'What did you put on the table?' (41), with the object in postverbal position, requires that in addition to identifying the object which was put on the table, the sentence has the exclusion of another object in its scope. (41) would be used to express constrative focus after the lead question 'Did you put the book on the table?', thereby correcting the assumption expressed in the question.

While there is little evidence from Bantu at large in support of the widespread use of SOV even as a marked option, much less as a possible alternative basic word order, some other cases of canonical SOV word order have been reported from western Bantu, e.g. Manyanga, a dialect of Kongo (K. Mukash, pc). The Aghem facts presented above suggest a possible explanation for SOV isolates in terms of a 'markedness shift' (Dik 1989:41–3), bringing them in harmony with general Bantu developments: if on the one hand, the IAV position becomes exclusively associated with contrastive focus – remember that this is but one of its functions in Aghem – the IBV position then becomes a likely candidate for 'hosting' all other occurrences, including those associated with non-contrastive focus – exactly the state of affairs we observe in Tunen.

6 PASSIVIZATION

For convenience, we reintroduce here the already familiar Swahili example (15):

(42) *M≠toto*   *a-me≠let-a*   *ki≠tabu*   'The child brought the book.'
      cl1≠child cl1-ANT≠bring-FV cl7≠book

To express the same state-of-affairs we may use the passive construction:

(43) *Ki-tabu*   *ki-me≠let-w-a*   *na*   *m-toto*
      book   cl5-ANT≠bring-PASS-FV with cl1-child
      'The book was brought by the child.'

An obvious way to describe the difference between (42) and (43) would be to say that, in (43), the object of (42) is encoded as the subject, and the subject of (42) as a 'displaced' agent. However, not only is this a rather clumsy way of describing the difference – it disregards the fact that the semantic roles assigned to the referents remain unaffected by the changes in the syntax of the sentence and in the morphology of the verb (*let-a* → *let-w-a*). The term *kitabu* 'book', promoted to subject position, still denotes the referent which undergoes the action. The term *mtoto* 'child', while being demoted from subject position to a peripheral position and introduced by associative *na*, is still recognizable as the performer of the action. Moreover, the interrelatedness of corresponding active and passive sentences is by no means a construct invented by linguists, but is part of the reproducible knowledge available to native speakers, a fact which can easily be tested by asking for a paraphrase, e.g. of a passive utterance.

Promotion and demotion, prototypically illustrated in this example, are asymmetrical syntactic processes: the object of the active sentence – here *kitabu* 'book' – may be promoted to subject, but the active subject – here *mtoto* 'child' – never becomes the object in a passive sentence. Apart from lower textual frequency and greater morphological complexity, it is this syntactic asymmetry which justifies the derivation of the passive from the active sentence, rather than vice versa.

6.1 Subjectivization of core arguments

In order to see how passivization works in the case of three-place verbs, let us again start from a partially familiar example (cf. (9)):

(44) *Mama*   *a-li-m≠pa*   *m≠toto*   *pesa*
      mother   cl1-PAST-cl1≠give cl1≠child money
      'Mother gave the child money.'

The first object, representing the goal, is easily subjectivized:

(45)   *M≠toto   a-li≠p-ew-a   pesa   (na mama)*
       cl1≠child cl1-PAST≠give-PASS-FV money (with mother)
       'The child was given money (by mother).'

The initial prefix of the verb agrees with 'mother' in (44), but with 'child' in (45). By contrast, the subjectivization of the second object, representing the patient, is widely rejected as ungrammatical:

*(46)   *Pesa   zi-li≠p-ew-a   m≠toto*
        money   cl10-PAST≠give-PASS-FV cl1≠child
        'The money was given to the child.'

Similarly, if, due to the subjectivization of the goal, the patient becomes the only post-verbal complement, its representation by an OM tends to be unacceptable:

*(47)   *Mtoto a-li-zi≠p≠ew-a   pesa*   'The child was given money.'
        child cl1-PAST-cl10-give-PASS-FV money

Discounting dialectal or even individual variation, which could make (46) acceptable to some speakers, (47) to others, and to some both (Shepardson 1982:117f.; Kamwangamalu 1985:124), we conclude that at least some major varieties of Swahili allow the goal, but not the patient, to become subject of the passive. This reflects the topicality metric as spelled out above (§3) and parallels the restrictions on object marking observed in the active construction (10). The systematic co-variation of restrictions on agreement and on subjectivization in terms of the syntactic entities to which these processes may apply characterizes the 'asymmetric' type of language (§2.1.4) to which Swahili belongs. This co-variation typically extends to other processes such as limitations on unspecified object deletion, and reciprocalization. For details, we refer the reader to the rich literature on this subject: cf. Bresnan and Moshi (1990:147ff.). By contrast, in a 'symmetric' language, both types of objects are, in the event of their co-occurrence, equally capable of being represented as pronominal objects inside the verb, and also have equal access to subjectivization. In Chaga, for instance, the subject marker in (48) agrees with *m̀-kà* 'wife', i.e. with the beneficiary, whereas in (49) it agrees with *k-èlyá* 'food' (Bresnan and Moshi 1990:150):

(48)   *m̀≠kà   n-ă-í≠lyì-í-ò   k≠èlyâ*
       cl1≠wife FOC-cl1-PRES≠eat-APPL-PASS cl7≠food
       'The wife is being benefited/adversely affected by someone eating the food.'

(49)   *k≠èlyá   k-í≠lyì-í-ò   m̀≠kà*
       cl7≠food cl7S-PRES≠eat-APPL-PASS cl1≠wife
       'The food is being eaten for/on the wife.'

(49), which is perfectly acceptable in Chaga, corresponds to the ungrammatical Swahili (46), thus pinpointing the difference between symmetrical and asymmetrical syntax.

   The assumption that in asymmetric Bantu languages, it is always the goal or beneficiary that takes precedence over the patient in being admitted for promotion to subject and related processes, has been challenged for at least some western Bantu languages, e.g. UMbundu (Wald 1994:240) and Lingala (Rapold 1997:37). Lingala, contrasting in this respect with Swahili, allows passivization of the patient but not of the beneficiary (like German, French, etc.), while prohibiting passivization of either in applicative constructions. This latter restriction may point to a general regression of passivization supported by verbal extension in western central Bantu and its replacement by a passive derived by reanalysis from second person plural active constructions (cf. Givón 1990:606 for Kimbundu).

The inversion of the promotion hierarchy between the two types of object asymmetry is illustrated in the following Lingala series (Rapold 1997:37):

(50) *Kengo a≠pes-í mwána mbongo* 'Kengo gave the child money.'
Kengo 3s≠give-ANT child money

(51) *Mbongo e≠pes-ám-í na mwána* 'Money was given to the child.'
money 3≠give-PASS-ANT PREP child

*(52) *Mwána a≠pes-ám-í mbongo* 'The child was given money.'
child 3s≠give-PASS-ANT money

The acceptable Lingala sentence (51) corresponds to the unacceptable Swahili sentence (46), and the unacceptable Lingala sentence (52) to the acceptable Swahili sentence (45).

6.2 Subjectivization of adjuncts

Rwanda is particularly suited for demonstrating the extent to which almost any complement, including locatives, instrumentals and expressions of manner, may be passivized in at least some Bantu languages. In presenting the relevant facts, we are following Kimenyi (1980, 1988); see also Givón (1990:585–8).

As noted in §2.1.5. iv above, adjuncts, contrary to core arguments (patients, goals and beneficiaries), tend to be encoded as prepositional phrases:

(53) *Umwáalimu a-ra-andik-a amasómo ku kíbáaho n'íngwa*
teacher he-PRES-write-FV lessons on blackboard with chalk
'The teacher is writing lessons on the blackboard with chalk.'

Two different strategies are available for subjectizing locatives:

1 Shifting the locative expression as a whole to subject position:

(54) *Ku kíbáaho ha-ra-andik-w-a amasómo n'umwáalimu*
on blackboard LOC-PRES-write-PASS-FV lessons by teacher
'The blackboard is being written lessons on by the teacher.'

The subject marker *ha-* agrees with the locative class feature of the prepositional phrase introduced by *ku* 'on.'

2 A two-step process involving first objectivization, then subjectivization of the locative expression:

(a) advancement to object:

(55) *Umwáalímu a-ra-andik-á-ho ikíbáaho amasómo*
teacher he-PRES-write-FV-LOC blackboard lessons
'The teacher is writing lessons on the blackboard.'

The locative complement is cross-referenced by the locative clitic *-ho* and moves to immediate postverbal position, thus preceding the original direct object.

(b) advancement to subject:

(56) *Ikíbáaho*   *cyi-ra-andik-w-á-ho*   *amasómo n'umwáalimu*
      blackboard   it-PRES-write-PASS-FV-LOC lessons   by teacher
      'The blackboard is being written lessons on by the teacher.'

The subject marker in (56) agrees with the inherent class of the subjectivized noun rather than with the nominal class of the original locative expression as in (54).

Subjectivization of the object *amasómo* 'lessons' from (55) is no longer possible: the original object is 'demoted' and becomes a 'chômeur' (Blake 1990). This means that it can no longer do any of the things a 'normal' object would do: it cannot passivize/ subjectivize, it cannot pronominalize, it cannot relativize, whereas the locative which has been promoted to the postverbal position originally occupied by the object can do all these things. This shows, as far as argument structure is concerned, that the advanced locative has taken the place of the object. But contrary to the object, the goal and/or beneficiary may co-occur with the advanced locative and may still be passivized or pronominalized (Dryer 1983).

Returning to (53) above, let us look at the instrumental. Contrary to the locative, it cannot be passivized by simply shifting it to subject position. The indispensable prerequisite to instrumental subjectivization is the suffixation of an instrumental extension *-iish-* to the verb stem and the accompanying objectivization of the instrumental:

(57) *Umwáalimu a-ra-andik-iish-a   íngwa amasómo ku kíbáaho*
      teacher   he-PRES-write-INSTR-FV chalk lessons   on blackboard
      'The teacher is using chalk to write lessons on the blackboard.'

As the locative in (55), the instrumental moves to the position immediately following the verb, from where it can then be subjectivized:

(58) *Íngwa i-ra-andik-iish-w-á   amasómo ku kíbáaho   n'umwáalimu*
      chalk it-PRES-write-INSTR-PASS-FV lessons   on blackboard by teacher
      'The chalk is being used by the teacher to write lessons on the blackboard.'

Thus Rwanda allows both locatives and instrumentals to be passivized via the intermediate step of objectivization.

However, this is not the whole story. In (55) and (57) only one of the two adjuncts was objectivized while the other remained in its original prepositional form. But nothing prevents the simultaneous objectivization of both adjuncts:

(59) *Umwáalimu a-ra-andik-iish-a-ho   íkíbáaho   íngwa amasómo*
      teacher   he-PRES-write-INSTR-FV-LOC blackboard chalk lessons
      'The teacher is writing lessons on the blackboard using chalk.'

The verb contains both the instrumental extension and the locative clitic. However, the objectivized locative obligatorily precedes the objectivized instrumental. Moreover, the doubly objectivized construction (59) allows only the locative to subjectivize:

(60) *Íkíbáaho cyí-ra-andik-iish-w-a-ho   amasómo íngwa n'umwáalimu*
      blackboard it-PRES-write-INSTR-PASS-FV-LOC lessons   chalk by teacher
      'The blackboard is written lessons on with chalk by the teacher.'

Hence, while the locative can be subjectivized if an objectivized instrument is present in the same sentence, the instrument cannot be subjectivized in the presence of an objectivized locative. In Rwanda, the asymmetry in terms of access to promotion to subject in the presence of objectivized adjuncts provides a formal syntactic criterion for establishing the hierarchy of semantic argument roles:

> Beneficiary > Goal (indirect object) > Patient (direct object) > Locative > Instrument

While all of these elements can undergo passivization under certain conditions, those at the upper end of the scale are the least restricted, and those on the lower end the most restricted in terms of the conditions of access to passivization.

Rwanda is a model case, exploiting to its outer limits as it were the potential for variation and differentiation inherent in a set of principles and mechanisms present to a greater or lesser extent in all Bantu languages.

7 INVERSION

A widely acknowledged alternative strategy of locative promotion is known as 'locative inversion.' The locative expression appears to have been moved from its original postverbal to preverbal position, displacing the original subject to postverbal position. As with passivized locatives, the initial class-sensitive prefix agrees with the front-shifted locative. Superficially, the only systematic difference with the passivized locative as illustrated in (54) above is the lack of passive morphology. The verb morphology of the inverted construction is the same as that of the uninverted construction. (61) illustrates the latter, (62) the former in Chewa (Bresnan and Kanerva 1989:2):

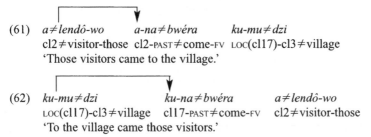

(61) a≠lendô-wo   a-na≠bwéra   ku-mu≠dzi
      cl2≠visitor-those cl2-PAST≠come-FV LOC(cl17)-cl3≠village
      'Those visitors came to the village.'

(62) ku-mu≠dzi   ku-na≠bwéra   a≠lendô-wo
      LOC(cl17)-cl3≠village cl17-PAST≠come-FV cl2≠visitor-those
      'To the village came those visitors.'

While the semantic roles of the arguments remain unchanged, the locative subject of (62) shows locative class agreement (class 17) with the subject marker.

Agreement of the 'container-contained' type (class 18) is seen in the following inversion:

(63) M-mi≠têngo   mw-a≠khal-a   a≠nyáni
      cl18-cl4≠tree cl18-ANT≠sit-FV cl2≠baboon
      'In the trees are sitting the baboons.'

But if the verb 'to sit (down)' – used here in its present perfect form with stative meaning (ANT) – is replaced by an active verb, the sentence becomes ungrammatical:

*(64) M-mi≠têngo   mu-ku≠imb-á   a≠nyáni
       cl18-cl4≠tree cl18-PROG≠sing-FV cl2≠baboon
       'In the trees are singing the baboons.'

In Chewa (Bresnan and Kanerva 1989:15–17), Comorian (Picabia 1994), and probably most other languages where locative inversion is attested, it is restricted to a semantically well defined subgroup of intransitive verbs, comprising motional and postural verbs, as well as verbs expressing a container-contained relation between arguments. By contrast, in Luba, as Kamwangamalu (1985) shows, locatives can not only be passivized in exactly the same way as any other argument, but can also be subjects of active transitive and ditransitive sentences.

The most controversial question pertaining to locative inversion concerns the syntactic status of the rear-shifted original subject. In (63), for instance, what is the syntactic role of *a-nyáni* 'baboons'? From the assumption that the constituent controlling the agreement with the verb-initial class-marking prefix is the subject (cf. §2.1), it would follow that the inverted locative must be the subject. But it seems to go against the grain of linguistic intuition to deny this very same status to the postposed subject.

Various solutions have been proposed to this dilemma. It is therefore essential to realize that inversion and corresponding realignment of the agreement feature is not limited to locatives. As has been shown for a number of languages, other types of arguments may undergo a similar kind of process of inversion and be assigned, in the course of it, control over agreement. Rwanda, for instance, allows object inversion (Kimenyi 1980:146):

(65) *Umuhuûngu a-ra≠som-a igitabo* 'The boy is reading the book.'
boy he-PRES≠read-FV book

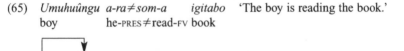

(66) *Igitabo cyi-ra≠som-a umuhuûngu* 'The book is being read by the boy.'
book it-PRES≠read-FV boy

Here, the inverted object controls subject agreement. The postposed agent, on the other hand, does not trigger agreement nor is it introduced by the preposition which a passivized agent would require, as seen in (54) above.

Examples such as (66) are by no means accidents nor are they due to sloppy oral performance. They are widely attested and have been systematically observed e.g. by Bokamba (1979) for Dzamba (also Givón 1990:607), Lingala and Likila. They are also attested in Swahili (Maw 1994:309–10; Krifka 1995:1408) and Comorian (Picabia 1994). Krifka (1983:164–7) gives an overview of earlier literature on this phenomenon which had been noticed, among others, by Meeussen (1967).

For Swahili, Abdulaziz (1996:39) gives the following examples:

(67) *M≠lima u-li≠panda m≠tu* 'The man climbed the mountain.'
cl3≠mountain cl3S-PAST≠climb cl1-person

(68) *Ch≠akula ki-li-ku≠la m≠toto* 'The child ate the food.'
cl7≠food cl7S-PAST≠eat cl1≠child

Examples such as these defy the logic of a syntax that maintains that the constituent which agrees with the initial class-marking prefix must be the subject. Rather than saying that 'the structural subject is semantically understood to be the object' (Abdulaziz 1996:39), we prefer to conclude that inversion creates, for Bantu languages, a generally favorable environment for topic agreement in replacement of the generally prevailing strategy of subject agreement. The following (partial) derivation, proposed by

Shephardson (1982:114), is helpful for imagining how the shift from the latter to the former could take place in the particular case of locative inversion:

(69)

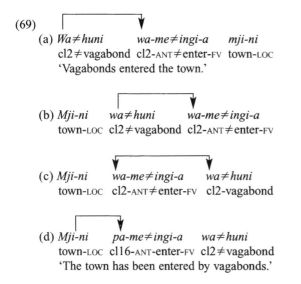

    (a) *Wa≠huni*   *wa-me≠ingi-a*   *mji-ni*
       cl2≠vagabond cl2-ANT≠enter-FV town-LOC
       'Vagabonds entered the town.'

    (b) *Mji-ni*   *wa≠huni*   *wa-me≠ingi-a*
       town-LOC cl2≠vagabond cl2-ANT≠enter-FV

    (c) *Mji-ni*   *wa-me≠ingi-a*   *wa≠huni*
       town-LOC cl2-ANT≠enter-FV cl2-vagabond

    (d) *Mji-ni*   *pa-me≠ingi-a*   *wa≠huni*
       town-LOC cl16-ANT-enter-FV cl2≠vagabond
       'The town has been entered by vagabonds.'

(69a) illustrates basic word order, (69b) preposing of a postverbal complement, (69c) subject postposing. Up to this point, the original subject maintains control over the agreement, while the preposing of the locative in (69b) and (69c) justifies the latter's interpretation as sentence topic. The switch from subject agreement to topic agreement takes place in passing from (69c) to (69d) and is explained quite naturally as a transfer of the prevailing pattern of subject agreement to a non-subject topic that occupies the same sentence-initial position as the subject normally would.

If we accept the premise that verb-initial agreement, while being primarily oriented towards the subject, may under given well-defined circumstances become topic-oriented, all instances of seemingly aberrant case assignment fall into place, and the strangeness of some of the inverted constructions in Bantu languages disappears.

This should not be taken to mean that all subject agreement is topic agreement, as suggested by Krifka (1995:1408). The following instance of a Swahili proverb used in conversation shows that even if subject and topic are inverted, subject agreement is still an option (Othman *et al.* 1991:5):

(70)   *Ny≠imbo m≠baya h-a≠bembelez≠e-w-i*   *m≠toto*
     cl9≠song cl9≠bad NEG-cl1s≠soothe-APPL-PASS-NEG cl1≠child
     'A bad song will not soothe a child.'

The proverb serves to disqualify a remark which had just been made. As signalled by the applicative verb form, *nyimbo mbaya* 'bad song' is, syntactically speaking, an instrumental object. Its discourse-related role as sentence topic is indicated by its sentence-initial position in which it constitutes a natural link to the preceding context and thereby suggests co-reference with the incriminated remark. Nevertheless, the inverted subject *mtoto* 'child' retains control over the agreement. as evidenced by the class identity of the verb prefix.

ACKNOWLEDGMENTS

Research on this chapter was supported by grant nr. 1213-054020.98 of the Swiss National Science Foundation entitled 'Topic, focus and countervalue – a discourse typological study'. Thanks to K. Geitlinger and O. Mwarape for helpful comments on the Swahili examples.

REFERENCES

Abdulaziz 1996; Baker 1988; Bearth 1995, 1999; Blake 1990; Bokamba 1979; Bresnan and Kanerva 1989; Bresnan and Mchombo 1987; Bresnan and Moshi 1990; Creissels 1992; Dik 1989; Dryer 1983; du Plessis and Visser 1992; Duranti 1979; Geitlinger (in press); Givón 1990; Grice 1975; Hinnebusch 1989; Hyman 1979a; Hyman and Duranti 1982; Kamwangamalu 1985; Kimenyi 1980, 1988; Krifka 1983, 1995; Maw 1969, 1994; Meeussen 1967; Mous 1997; Othman *et al.* 1991; Palmer 1994; Picabia 1994; Rapold 1997; Shepardson 1982; Stucky 1985; Vitale 1981; Wald 1994; Watters 1979; Yahya and Mulwa 1988.

CHAPTER NINE

HISTORICAL LINGUISTICS

Thilo C. Schadeberg

1 INTRODUCTION

1.1 Overview

Comparative Bantu studies are leading the field of historical linguistics in Africa. Bantu historical linguistics mainly proceeds from the comparison of living languages. Written sources from the past – not older than a few centuries – may teach us interesting facets of regional developments but add little to our knowledge of Bantu history as a whole. Fortunately, historical linguistics does not depend on old documents, and the full comparative method has been and is being applied to Bantu languages.

There are about 500 Bantu languages; no exact number can be given because of the unresolvable problem of defining the notion *dialect* in a purely linguistic way. Bantu languages are a close-knit linguistic unit, even if geographically distant languages can be quite different. Owing to the large number of languages, Bantu offers a unique laboratory of linguistic change where any particular lexical or grammatical or phonological theme usually exists in many variations.

The linguist trying to understand the theme is well advised to look at the variation. This is why in the study of Bantu, descriptive and comparative-historical linguistics are intimately linked. There are an estimated 10,000 publications and theses dealing with the grammar and lexicon of Bantu languages. Although languages and language areas are unevenly documented and there are still white spots, we now have at least word lists and grammar sketches from a large number of Bantu languages.

Comparative Bantu studies have produced impressive results in some areas, especially in phonology (tone!), morphology and lexicon, but have been less successful in providing a genetic subclassification and a detailed account of historical developments leading to the present situation.

In §2, we present an overview of reconstructed Proto-Bantu (PB) phonology, grammar and lexicon, pointing out some areas where future research appears to be promising. This is done briefly since many details and subsequent developments are dealt with elsewhere in this book.

Reconstructed PB closely resembles Eastern Bantu languages (e.g. Nyamwezi F22), lexically as well as in its rich morphology. In the absence of a well-argumented genetic subclassification, the validity of our view of PB may well be questioned. This topic is further developed in §3, where we also try to explore the links between history of languages and history of peoples.

We start, however, with a look at the growth of Bantu linguistics, especially historical-comparative linguistics (§1.2), and we point the reader to the leading reference tools, bibliographical resources and maps (§1.3).

1.2 The growth of Bantu linguistics

The early history of Bantu linguistics has been described by Doke and Cole (1961). The first books about and in Bantu languages were catechisms, grammars and dictionaries, written in the seventeenth century by Catholic missionaries in the Portuguese sphere of influence near the lower Congo.

The name *Bantu* was first used by W. H. I. Bleek (1827–1875) who may be considered the founder of comparative Bantu studies. Following up the work of others, notably H. Lichtenstein, Bleek (1856) recognized not only the unity of the Bantu language family but also its relation to Niger-Congo and Kordofanian; he names as speakers of related languages "the Otsi, or Ashantee" (Akan), "the Bullom, and the Timneh of Sierra Leone", "the wide-spread Fulah" (Fulfulde), "the Accra" (Ga), "the Wolof", "the Ukuafi" (Maasai, some of whom speak Bantu languages) and "the Tumale of Darfur" (speaking a Kordofanian language). His major work is his *Comparative grammar of South African languages* (1862–69), which includes a typological comparison between "Bâ-ntu" and "Hottentot" (Khoesan). Bleek's system of numbering Bantu noun classes is the one still used today.

It was Carl Meinhof (1857–1944) who brought to Bantu studies the comparative method as it had been developed in the nineteenth century for the study of Indo-European languages. He published his *Comparative phonology* in 1899; an English version was co-authored with Van Warmelo in 1932; the companion volume *Comparative grammar* appeared in 1906. When Meinhof started, the outlines of the Bantu language family were roughly known as we know them today. Meinhof relied heavily on a small set of better-known sample languages, but included other material as he saw fit. His reconstructed sound system has stood the test of time rather well; the main correction has been the merger of his two palatal series $*t$ l and $*k$ y into $*c$ j; tone and vowel length have since been added. His reconstruction of Bantu morphology is also still valid in its general outline. Meinhof also pioneered Bantu lexical reconstructions, an effort that was taken up by his students and colleagues, notably Dempwolff and Bourquin.

Meinhof's two major books on comparative Bantu are designed to be used by those who are working 'in the field' trying to record, analyse and describe Bantu languages. Numerous grammars of Bantu languages have been written, mostly by missionaries, who followed Meinhof's guidelines – and did a better job for it than they could have done otherwise. Meinhof dominated Bantu studies during the first half of the twentieth century. In South Africa, his approach was developed by C. M. Doke and his students.

Two names stand out in the history of Bantu linguistics during the second half of the twentieth century: Malcolm Guthrie and Achille E. Meeussen.

Malcolm Guthrie (1903–1972) was Professor of Bantu languages at the School of Oriental and African Studies in London. As a linguist he was a self-made man, and developed his own rigorous but idiosyncratic methods for comparing Bantu languages. His grand project started with *The classification of the Bantu languages* (1948), in which he tried to "define" the set of languages that would occupy him for the rest of his life without presupposing their historical relatedness. The book also contains the first version of the famous coding of Bantu languages by geographical "zones" (cf. map 9.1, §1.3).

Guthrie's *Comparative Bantu* appeared during 1967–71. The first volume is a detailed account of his methods and conventions; volumes 3 and 4 are a beautiful compilation of his data arranged in *c.* 2,500 "comparative series", each representing a set of words or bound morphemes from different languages connected by regular sound correspondences and identical meaning. The second volume – which appeared last – contains mainly

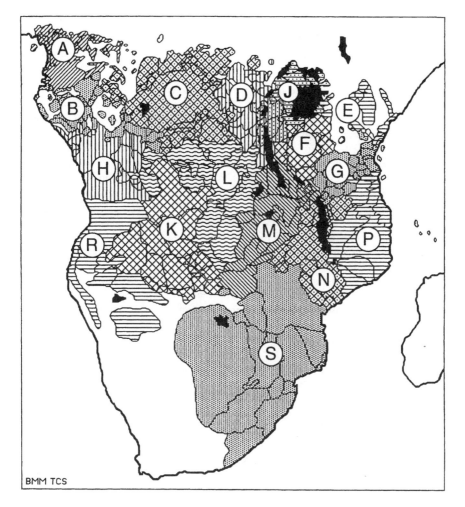

BMM TCS

MAP 9.1 GUTHRIE'S ZONES

indices for the data in volumes 3 and 4, including a set of statements about the sound correspondences. It also contains summary historical inferences based on statistical analyses of the spread of his comparative series, a rudimentary sketch of a genetic sub-classification, and a list of 670 lexical reconstructions – as distinct from "starred forms" (see §2.4 for some critical remarks).

A. E. Meeussen (1912–1978) was the founding head of the linguistic section of the Africa Museum at Tervuren (Brussels) and also professor of Bantu languages at Leuven and at Leiden. His comparative work on Bantu is dispersed over a large number of brief but succinct articles; his two most comprehensive publications are "Bantu grammatical reconstructions" (BGR 1967) and *Bantu lexical reconstructions* (BLR 1969). Meeussen initiated the research programme "Lolemi" (**lʊ=límí* 'tongue, language'), a collective enterprise resulting in a large number of publications on comparative Bantu, many of which were published at Tervuren in the series *Africana linguistica*. The present writer considers himself as one of Meeussen's many students, as is apparent in §2 which relies heavily on Meeussen's BGR and BLR, and on subsequent work by the Lolemi school.

1.3 Reference tools

The most widely used reference tool is Guthrie's referential classification (1948), the definitive version of which can be found at the beginning of volume 3 of his *Comparative Bantu* (1970), where Bantu languages are divided into "zones" (represented by letters), and zones into "groups" (represented by decimal digits); e.g. Sukuma F21 is the first language of the second group of zone F. Groups and zones are set up with an eye on overall similarity, but it must be stressed that this coding system is referential and not genetic, it can neither be "false" nor can it be "improved"; it is useful (in the same way as postal codes) precisely because it is independent of differing opinions about genetic classification. The occasional practice to shift languages from one group to another is based on the misplaced hope that the coding system could evolve into a genetic classification; such efforts are confusing and gradually render the whole coding system useless. Maho (in this volume) uses a method for expanding this coding system to include languages not figuring in the original list used by Guthrie.

The most complete list of Bantu languages is contained in the *Ethnologue* (Grimes 2000). Also still useful is Bryan (1959). A specialized bibliography is Bastin (1975), complemented by Bastin (1978). Most sources mentioned in this section contain partial or total maps of Bantu languages. The best total (loose, folding) map comes with Bastin (1978). Lowe and Schadeberg (1997) provide a tool for drawing maps that show the areal spread of user-definable linguistic (or any other) features of Bantu languages.

The Comparative Bantu OnLine Dictionary web site (www.linguistics.berkeley.edu/ CBOLD), directed by L. M. Hyman at Berkeley University, offers a variety of searchable and downloadable resources: dictionaries, a bibliography, *Bantu lexical reconstructions 2* (Coupez, Bastin and Mumba 1998), *Bantu map maker* (Lowe and Schadeberg 1997), and more.

2 PROTO-BANTU RECONSTRUCTIONS

2.1 Phonology

The reconstructed sound system of PB is, at first sight, rather simple.

Consonants:	*p*	*t*	*c*	*k*
	b	*l/d*	*y/j*	*g*
	m	*n*	*ny*	
	mp	*nt*	*nc*	*nk*
	mb	*nd*	*nj*	*ng*
Vowels:	*i*	*ɪ*	*e*	*a*	*o*	*ʋ*	*u*
Tones:	*H*(igh)	*L*(ow)		

The allophonic variation *[d] /_{i u} vs. *[l]/elsewhere has been reconstructed by Stewart (1993; more precisely, Stewart posits [d']/[l]). Guthrie (1967–71) distinguishes stem-initial *j from *y, but BLR2 recognizes only *j to the exclusion of vowel-initial stems; I regard the two as allophonic but the question needs re-evaluation. The reconstruction of the phonetic values of the palatal consonants is problematic; [s] and [z] are also likely candidates. Earlier (Bantoid, Benue-Congo) *η has been lost in Bantu; e.g. PBC *ku-$tu\eta i$ > PB *ku=$t\acute{u}i$ 'ear', but its nasality has sporadically been retained as in Nyokon (A45) u=$t\acute{o}\eta$ and UMbundu (R11) $\acute{e}$=$^{\downarrow}tw\tilde{i}$.

Prenasalized consonants (NC) occur word-initially where prenasalization represents the NPx of classes 9 and 10. In stems, NC occurs as C_2 but not as C_1 – with the famous exception of *mu=ntu 'person'. Voiceless NC are rare in stems even in position C_2.

The seven-vowel system of PB has been represented in several equivalent ways:

degree of aperture:	1st	2nd	3rd	4th	3rd	2nd	1st
Meinhof:	$\hat{\imath}$	i	e	a	o	u	$\hat{u}$
Guthrie, Meeussen:	$i̧$	i	e	a	o	u	$u̧$
Greenberg:	i	e	ε	a	$\mathfrak{o}$	o	u
BLR2:	i	ι	e	a	o	υ	u
phonetic:	i	I	ε	a	$\mathfrak{o}$	υ	u

Meinhof's term for the "first degree" vowels [i u] was "schweres i/u", where "heavy" is supposed to express the spirantizing influence of these vowels on the preceding consonant. Meinhof's phonetically meaningless circumflex was replaced by the equally meaningless cedilla to make space for tone marks. Greenberg's system is graphically convenient but misses the essential phonetic point, i.e. the marked nature of the second degree vowels. The system of BLR2 (which I follow) is superior since it allows the most direct visualization of corresponding seven- and five-vowel systems.

7 V i ι e a o υ υ
5 V i e a o u

In all five-vowel systems, it is the second degree vowels that are lost by merging with the first degree vowels, which are retained. The term "super-close" vowels should be avoided since it wrongly suggests untenable hypotheses about the phonetic nature of first ("heavy") and second degree vowels as well as about the common process of the 7V > 5V merger.

Vowel sequences are reconstructed mainly for the first (or only) syllable of roots. They also arise from juxtaposition of morphemes, e.g. in passive stems such as *=$t\acute{u}m$-u-a 'be sent'. When V_1 of such sequences is non-low and different from V_2 the most common reflex is a (C)GV sequence. Vowel sequences, especially sequences of identical vowels, may also result in phonetically long vowels. A relatively small set of roots has been reconstructed with such long vowels, cf. 'breast' and 'lie, sleep' in the Appendix. Most such roots are recognizable as morphologically complex at the level of PB (Meeussen 1979). No contrastive vowel length is reconstructable preceding prenasalized consonants (*contra* Guthrie 1967:45).

The dominant syllable structure is *(N)CV. However, most PB reconstructions are morphemes (roots and affixes), and morphemes often do not fit syllable structure. In the following word from Kwanyama (R21), syllable and morpheme boundaries never coincide: om=bel-el-a [ombele$la] 'relish'.

Noun class markers (NPx, PPx) and verbal extensions have a reduced vowel system lacking the third degree vowels *e and *o. However, verbal extensions with one of the vowels *ι or *υ are subject to a kind of vowel harmony: *ι appears as *e after *e and *o, and *υ appears as *o after *o. (For a different analysis, see Hyman 1999.)

We have already mentioned the widespread 7V > 5V merger, by which the second degree vowels *ι and *υ are raised to *i* and *u*. This change is practically always preceded by another set of changes which turn obstruents followed by *i and *u into strident fricatives or affricates. This set of changes is referred to as Spirantization (Schadeberg 1994–5).

An interesting rule of consonant dissimilation occurs in a range of northeastern languages (cf. Davy and Nurse 1982). It applies to CVCV sequences where both C are voiceless and turns the first C into its voiced counterpart, e.g. Gikuyu from Kikuyu. The rule was first described by Meinhof (1903) and named "Dahl's Law"; Meinhof exaggerated its likeness to Grassmann's Law in Indoeuropean by claiming that it affected sequences of aspirated consonants although aspiration is not distinctive in the languages concerned. The true cousin of Grassmann's Law is Katupha's Law as it occurs in Makhuwa (Schadeberg 1999).

A series of rules and/or changes having to do with nasality are in urgent need of further investigation from a historical point of view. First, a large number of western languages have "nasal harmony" affecting mainly verbal extensions of the shape -*Vl*- which are represented as -*Vn*- when preceded by a nasal consonant (Greenberg 1951). Second, stem-initial prenasalized consonants (where prenasalization is a nominal or verbal prefix) are widely represented as pure nasals (sometimes long) when followed by a nasal onset in the following syllable. Meinhof's Rule is the name given to this alternation of prenasalized consonants: **N**CVN(C)V vs. **NN**VN(C)V. There are several variants of this rule, one of which, the Kwanyama Rule, removes prenasalization from the second consonant (cf. Herbert 1977, Schadeberg 1987).

PB root 'cattle'   Mongo C61   Ganda E15 'horn'   Kwanyama R21
*=*gombe*   *ŋgombe*   *eŋŋombe*   *oŋgobe*

There are other cases of unexpected nasality (or its unexpected absence). For example, the verb root *=*bón*- 'see' (zones BCEFGJMNPS) appears widely as *=*món*- (zones BDHKLMR), but with *=*bín*- 'to sing and dance' (zones ACDEFGJKMNPRS) the variant *=*mín*- is much more restricted (zones CD). The verb 'to swallow' appears in four variants: *=*mil*- (FGJPS), *=*min*- (ABCDHKLMRS), *=*mel*- (ABCEGJNS), *=*men*- (ABCDR). Stewart (1993b, 1995, 1999, 2000a and elsewhere) has connected these and other facts about nasality, prenasalization and vowel height, and reconstructs nasalized vowels and nasalized consonants for PB even though UMbundu R11 appears to be the only language having retained such sounds. Stewart's ongoing research, relating Bantu to its Niger-Congo relatives, may profoundly alter our view of PB phonology.

Verbal extensions not only have a reduced vowel system, they also lack tonal distinctiveness. In the verbal word, they generally adopt the (first) tone of the final suffix ("tonal extension assimilation" by anticipation). More generally, tonal profiles have often been drastically changed by complex rules of High tone spreading. In the extreme west, on the Atlantic coast from Gabon to Namibia, High tone spreading from the augment has produced distinct tonal profiles for nouns tied to specific syntactic and pragmatic functions (Blanchon 1998).

2.2 Morphology

Bantu words fall into a number of categories according to their morphological paradigm: nouns, adjectives, numerals, pronominal forms, invariables and verbs. The basic distinctive feature of word categories is their behaviour with respect to noun classes (agreement) and their selection of specific class markers (concords) (table 9.1).

TABLE 9.1: MORPHOLOGICALLY DEFINED WORD CATEGORIES; EXAMPLES FROM NYAMWEZI (F22)

Noun	Adjective	Numeral	Pronominal	Invariable	Verb
(A-)NPx	(A-)NPx	EPx	PPx	–	SCd, OCd
(ɪ)ŋ.gano	(ɪ)n.sogá	i=dátʊ́	zi=ngí	pyé	tw.aá-zí=málaá
'stories'	'beautiful'	'three'	'other'	'all'	'we finished them'

TABLE 9.2: PB NOMINAL AND PRONOMINAL PREFIXES

Class	NPx	PPx	Class	NPx	PPx
1	mʊ-	jʊ-	11	lʊ-	lʊ́-
2	ba-	bá-	12	ka-	ká-
3	mʊ-	gʊ́-	13	tʊ-	tʊ́-
4	mɪ-	gɪ́-	14	bʊ-	bʊ́-
5	i-	lɪ-	15	kʊ-	kʊ́-
6	ma-	gá-	16 (loc.)	pa-	pá-
7	kɪ-	kɪ́-	17 (loc.)	kʊ-	kʊ́-
8	bi-	bí-	18 (loc.)	mʊ-	mʊ́-
9	N-	jɪ-	19	pi-	pí-
10	N-	jí-	(24 loc.)	(ɪ-)	(í-)

Note: All NPx have Low tone; PPx of classes 1 and 9 have Low tone, other PPx have High tone. The NPx of class 5 is often replaced by a more canonical CV-prefix lɪ- or di- which has its origin in the contraction of the augment (= PPx) *lɪ- and the NPx i-.

Nouns are lexically specified for class and gender, and morphologically marked by a NPx (nominal prefix) as belonging to a specific class. Kinship terms often lack a NPx. The NPx may be preceded by the *augment* which has its origin in the PPx but is generally reduced to a single vowel with High tone (table 9.2). The expression of number (singular, plural, collective …) is built into the noun class system: specific classes are paired and used to derive plural meanings from singular meanings, or vice versa. Such class pairings are referred to as genders. Common genders are: 1/2, 3/4, 5/6, 7/8, 9/10, 11/10, 12/13, 15/6, 19/13. All classes except 1/2 as one-class genders; the largest sets are found in class 6 (liquids), 14 (various), 15 (infinitives), as well as the locative classes 16–18 (and 24). For more detailed descriptions of noun classes, nominal morphology and the derivation of nouns see Katamba and Schadeberg (both in this volume).

Adjectives take a NPx in agreement with the head noun. There may be interference from forms with a PPx. Sometimes, nouns have a larger set of NPx than adjectives; this is a sign of noun class merger in progress. The number of underived reconstructable adjectives is small, some adjectives derived from verbs and ideophones can also be reconstructed.

*=jijá	'good'	*=bíɪ	'bad'
*=jípi >=kʊ́.pi	'short'	*=dai	'long'
*=bícɪ	'unripe'	*=díto	'heavy'
*=gima	'whole, healthy'	*=jíngɪ	'many'

derived from ideophones:

*= (kée)ké	'small'	*= (toó)toó	'small'
*= (né)ne	'big'	*= (nii)ní	'small'
*= pi, = piipí	'black'	*= pe (tone?)	'white'

derived from verbs:

*= jíl-ʋ	'black'	*= jél-ʋ	'white'
*= kʋ́l-ʋ	'big'	*= pí-ʋ	'red'
*= jʋ́m-u	'dry'	*= bod-ú	'rotten'

Numerals (as a morphologically defined word category; cf. Stappers 1965) take the EPx (enumerative prefix), although interference with PPx and NPx is frequent. The reconstruction of the EPx is still somewhat shaky: it is *í- in class 10. Less certain are class 1 and 3 *ʋ́-, class 4 and 9 *í-, class 6 *á-; forms of other classes are identical with the PPx.

*= moi	'one'	*= nai	'four'
*= balí, = bɪlí	'two'	*= táano	'five'
*= tátʋ	'three'	*= ngá	'how many'

Many languages distinguish referential forms (for counting things: N Num) from forms for absolute calculations; the reconstructed absolute number 'one' is *mʋ=otí (cf. Vanhoudt 1994). Bantu speakers also employ gestures for numbers, again distinguishing counting gestures from absolute ones. Words for the numbers 'six' through 'nine' may be derived from names of such gestures or formed by addition, e.g. *ncambʋ (also *ncambʋadɪ) 'seven' < *=camb- 'leap over' (followed by *=badí ?), *mʋ=nainai 'eight'. Numbers higher than 'five' are nouns; *i=kʋ́mi 'ten' is attested in all zones. Ordinals are expressed as "numeral possessives", as in *mʋ=ána jʋ-a ntátʋ 'the third child'.

Pronominal forms are defined by taking a PPx in agreement with the head noun. Pronominal forms are a mixed set in semantic and syntactic terms. They include substitutives (PPx-o, which translate as pronouns, but also as 'here' and 'there' and 'thus' in the case of locative and other classes with an inherent or autonomous meaning), demonstratives, as well as some quantifiers, specifiers and question words. Syntactically complex pronominal forms include connexives and relative verb forms.

"Connexives" are genitival constructions. They consist of a PPx, followed by -á- (tone?) followed by either a noun (nominal possessive) or a pronominal stem (pronominal posssessive) referring to the possessor. There are pronominal stems for participants and for class 1 for which no firm reconstructions exist. Possessors of classes 2ff. are represented by the substitutive (PPx-o).

Nyamwezi (F22):

βa=geni βaá-m̀=kɪ́ima	'the guests of the woman'	βa=geni βaá-kwé	'her guests'
mi=zi yaa-m=tɪ́í	'the roots of the tree'	mi=zi yaá-goó	'its roots'

Invariables are a remnant category of words which have but one form and neither impose nor undergo class agreement. Invariables include ideophones and a few other words such as participant pronouns and interrogatives. Synchronically, the category is often swelled by nouns, pronominal and inflected verbal forms functioning as adverbs, conjunctions and exclamations. (Prepositions and conjunctions are not reconstructable word categories in Bantu.)

TABLE 9.3: VERBAL PREFIXES FOR PARTICIPANTS AND CLASS 1

	1sɢ	1ᴘʟ	2sɢ	2ᴘʟ	Class 1	Reflexive
SCd	*N-*	*tʊ-*	*ʊ-*	*mʊ-*	*ʊ́- a-*	
OCd	*-N-*	*-tʊ́-*	*-kʊ-*	*-mʊ́-*	*-mʊ-*	*-i-*

Verbs have the richest morphological paradigm. The verbal base is the domain of derivation (see Schadeberg, this volume), from which various verb stems are formed by the addition of a final inflectional suffix. Morphemes in pre-stem position include obligatory subject agreement markers and "optional" object markers. The morpheme categories SCd and OCd have forms for all classes which are identical with the PPx except in class 1 (and have a High tone in class 9). Verbal prefixes also include forms for the first and second person singular and plural, also called "(dialogue) participants"; a reflexive marker occurs in the same slot as the OCd (table 9.3).

The class 1 SCd *ʊ́-* resembles the PPx; the SCd *a-* is used in the Optative and related tenses. This allomorphy evades homophony between forms of 2sɢ and class 1 since tonal distinctions between different SCds and verb roots are neutralized in the Optative.

In addition to argument markers (SCd, OCd), inflected verb forms contain combinations of morphological markers including tone. Bantu languages may have several dozen distinct "tenses", specifying a whole range of semantic parameters in addition to the well-known triad time, aspect and mood (ᴛᴀᴍ): polarity (affirmative vs. negative), deixis (ventive and itive), syntactic linkage and/or focus (disjoint vs. conjoint), embedding in discourse and/or syntactic structures (background, consequential, consecutive, independent vs. dependent, absolute vs. relative), expectation or presupposition (counter-expectational, persistive, tardative). Voice distinctions, on the other hand, are expressed mainly by (lexical) derivation, not by inflection or syntax.

The general morphological structure of tenses follows a recurring pattern and some of the particular morphemes involved are spread over large areas. However, there is much variation due to constant rebuilding of the inflectional system. In the scheme below, TM1 represents the main "tense marker", and TM2 additional ones such as the itive marker. (For more details on verbal inflection, see Nurse, chap 6 and Güldemann, chap 11 both in this volume.)

clitic + [Neg − SCd − Neg − TM1 − TM2 [− OCd [= VB − Fi]]] + clitic

The reconstruction of particular inflectional morphemes is still incomplete. Kamba Muzenga (1981) reconstructs the negative markers *nkà-* (preinitial) and *ti-/*-i-* (postinitial, optative). Reconstructed tense markers include *-à-, *-á-* (TM1, different references to past time) and *-ka-* (TM2, itive). Reconstructed Finals include *-a* (default), *-e* (optative, see below) and *-ide* (perfective) which often fuses with preceding extensions ("imbrication", cf. Bastin 1983b).

Some complete tenses, including the Optative and the Imperative, can be reconstructed for PB. In the Imperative (without OCd), the root has its own lexical tone, the Final *-á* is High preceded by a "polar" tone (i.e. High after a Low radical and Low after a High radical). In the Optative (without OCd), the SCd and the Final *-e* are High and all syllables in between are Low (i.e. the inherent tones of the SCd and the verb root are neutralized).

Imperative: [R   E]   *a*   Optative: SCd [R   E]   *e*
          H   [L   H]   H   L   [L   H]
          L   [H   H]

Clitics are phonologically bound morphemes that attach to whole words. Associative **na-* 'with, and' and comparative **nga-* 'as' attach mainly to nominal forms, as do affirmative and negative predicative (Shambala *ní* and *só*) as well as presentative clitics (Luba L31a *ké+bá=lúmé ábó* '*those* are men'). The enclitic **-ini* marks the addressee as plural and attaches mainly to verbal forms. The locative substitutives (PPx-o) **-po* (16), **-ko* (17) and **-mo* (18) attach to verb forms. Question words may also occur as enclitics. The locative NPx may in some languages be considered a clitic, but is better analysed as a prefix when it controls or expresses agreement.

2.3 Syntax

While Bantu comparative historical studies are dominated by phonology, morphology and lexicon, BGR (Meeussen 1967) does include six rich pages on syntax. Subsequent studies on Bantu syntax have been concerned more with typological than with historical comparison (see Bearth, chap 8 this volume).

Verbal morphology plays an important role in marking relationships which other languages often indicate by syntactic means. The whole array of voice and case-related distinctions (passive, stative, causative, dative) is expressed by derivational verbal morphology. Likewise, negation and syntactic subordination is frequently expressed through verbal inflection: negative and relative verb forms, conditional, concessive and conjunctive tenses. Even discourse-related meanings often find their expression through verbal inflection: consequential and subsecutive tenses, situative tenses marking co-occurrence or backgrounding, specific forms to mark syntactic linkage and focusing.

The semantic main verb of the predicate may be preceded by one (or even more) inflected "auxiliary" verbs adding modal, aspectual, temporal and deictic distinctions. One typical constellation consists of the verb 'to be' followed by the semantic main verb, where both verbs are fully inflected and have the same SCd. In such constellations the verb 'to be' itself adds little or nothing to the meaning of the sentence; its main purpose is to accommodate extra inflectional markers. Complex verbal constructions are a constant source for grammaticalization processes, creating more and more complex tense markers within the existing system.

The basic word order is SVO; within the nominal phrase the dominant word order is Noun–Modifier. The order of noun phrases relative to each other and to the verb is relatively "free"; preposing and postposing of NPs serves to mark pragmatic functions, notably topic and focus.

At first sight, Bantu syntax appears to be dominated by formal noun class agreement. The superimposition of semantic features, such as [human] and/or [animate], is probably due to later developments. Agreement operates with the noun phrase, but also between the NP and the verb. SCd and OCd are the primary means to identify the arguments that function as subject and object. This line of reasoning often leads to semantically unusual syntactic configurations.

Swahili (G42d):

ku-m=sema mtu   'to speak badly about someone'
NPx.15-OCd.1=speak someone

njia-ni ku-na=pita watu   'people are passing along the road'
9.road-LOC SCd.17-PRO=pass 2.people

    njia hii i-na=pita watu   'people (can/may/do) pass along this road'
    9.road 9.this SCd.9-PRO=pass people

Such cases suggest that discourse considerations interact with and influence purely syntactic relations.

2.4 Lexicon

Meinhof, together with students and colleagues, reconstructed 5–700 Bantu lexical items; for the largest list see Bourquin (1923). Greenberg (1948) marks an important step in being the first to reconstruct tone. From about 1950 onwards, Meeussen and Guthrie both worked on lexical reconstruction, independently of each other. Meeussen's *Bantu lexical reconstructions* (BLR), which contains *c.* 2000 items, includes the work of his predecessors, some of which is rejected and much of it is improved. Meeussen shared his BLR in manuscript form (1969) with whoever wanted a copy; it was published posthumously (1980). Guthrie's *Comparative Bantu* contains *c.* 2500 "starred forms" (including *c.* 100 bound morphemes) based on "comparative series" (CS) from which 670 reconstructions are derived.

In Guthrie's "two-stage method", CS are non-historical constructs ("stage one") combining words from different languages with identical meaning and regular sound correspondences. Reconstructions are seen as historical speculations ("stage two") based on CS and may allow for unexplained sound change, analogical change (reanalysis, paradigm levelling) and non-systematic semantic change. Since Guthrie demands a certain minimum spread of corresponding words to set them up as a CS, any morphologically derived or semantically shifted form that does not itself have the required distribution is filtered out at "stage one" and thereby no longer available for reconstruction at "stage two". (For an illustration see Grégoire 1976.) On the other hand, Guthrie's "Common Bantu", the body of all "starred forms", contains many sets of items representing a single PB reconstruction.

ps 44	*-bʋlʋkʋtʋ (cl. 9/10)	'ear'
CS 1243	*-kʋtú, *-kʋtʋí (cl. 5/6)	'ear'
CS 1801	*-tú, *-túʋ (cl. 5/6, 15/6)	'ear'
CS 1809	*-túé (cl. 5/6)	'ear'
CS 1813	*-túí (cl. 5/6)	'ear'
CS 1950	*-yatú (cl. 5/6)	'ear'

Guthrie infers from this a PB item *-tú (in his spelling: *-TÓ); the superior reconstruction is *kʋ=túí (classes 15/6), from which the other forms are derivable by regular sound change and by morphological reanalysis. (For a critical review of Guthrie's method of reconstruction, see Meeussen 1973.)

Although Guthrie made it quite clear that his CS are not reconstructions, most scholars regard them as such. It has been a common but deplorable and in the end unhelpful practice amongst comparativists, working either within Bantu or in a wider Niger-Congo context, to claim that a particular item is cognate with or derived from the CS that appears to be closest to it.

Bantu lexical reconstructions 2 (Coupez, Bastin and Mumba 1998 = BLR2) is the latest major advance in the field, although it is still more like a tool than a definitive statement. It is a computerized data base with almost 10,000 records, including all of Guthrie's CS. It allows quick detailed and complex searches impossible in a linear book-like publication, particularly since each entry is represented as a sequence of phonological segments (including tone) and includes a statement about its attested distribution (in terms of zones) and about its reliability as a reconstruction. BLR2 contains about 800 sets of related items ("roots") which have reflexes spread over more or less the whole Bantu-speaking area, including at least one of the northwestern zones (A B C). In the Appendix at the end of this chapter I cite some reconstructions from BLR2.

3 BANTU HISTORICAL LINGUISTICS AND HISTORY

3.1 External and internal classification

Bantu languages are part of the largest African language family: Niger-Congo. Although this genetic unity had been recognized since the middle of the nineteenth century, the division of labour between the two leading Africanists in the first half of the twentieth century, Meinhof – Bantu vs. Westermann – "Sudanic", together with the large number of Bantu languages and the vast territory which they occupy, may have created the impression, or "working assumption", that Bantu was a more or less self-contained linguistic unit. This view has been forcefully attacked by Greenberg since *c.* 1950 (final publication 1963). Greenberg's subclassification of Niger-Congo languages is constantly being revised and modified, most recently by Williamson and Blench (2000); a compiled and adapted version of their tree diagrams appears here as figure 9.1. While many details of this genetic tree are still debated and will certainly need modification once subjected to the rigorous test of the comparative method, it is safe to say that the closest relatives of Bantu are located at the northwestern apex of the Bantu-speaking area in the region of central Cameroon and southeastern Nigeria.

Some linguists regard the Niger-Congo family as a speculative hypothesis. Dixon (1997:32–4) gives a rather unfair account of its linguistic base; Campbell (1998:312–13) lists Niger-Congo (together with Afroasiatic, Nilo-Saharan and Khoesan) on a par with Nostratic and Proto-World, as "unconfirmed proposals of distant genetic relationship". Nevertheless, Bantu's inclusion in a wider Niger-Congo family has been demonstrated, e.g. by Stewart's reconstructions for Proto-Volta-Congo (from 1973 onwards); for a comparison between Kordofanian and Volta-Congo (incl. Bantu) noun classes, see Schadeberg (1981:123).

The precise innovations defining Bantu within Bantoid are still a matter of debate. Most proposals have turned out to be unconvincing; e.g. Miehe (1991) is a book-length refutal of Greenberg's original hypothesis (1963:35): "Bantu has the prefixes *mu-* and *mi-* as against Semi-Bantu and West Sudanic *u-* and *i-*. This is certainly a Bantu innovation". The latest proposal comes from Nurse and Philippson (Introduction, this volume) who suggest that good candidates for specific Bantu innovations may be found in the system of verbal inflection. They mention the two negative markers, one preceding and the other following the SCd, and also certain stem-forming "Final" suffixes.

It has been possible to reconstruct large parts of PB phonology, grammar and lexicon; it has been much more difficult to ascertain that the reconstructed entities do not recur in any of the related groups, and if they don't, whether this might not be due to loss. The problem of finding specific Bantu innovations is aggravated by the fact that Bantu's nearest neighbors (in the geographical as well as in the genetic sense) are part of a larger linguistic area where phonological attrition has led to a general reduction of morphology, and this linguistic area extends into the northwestern part of Bantu itself.

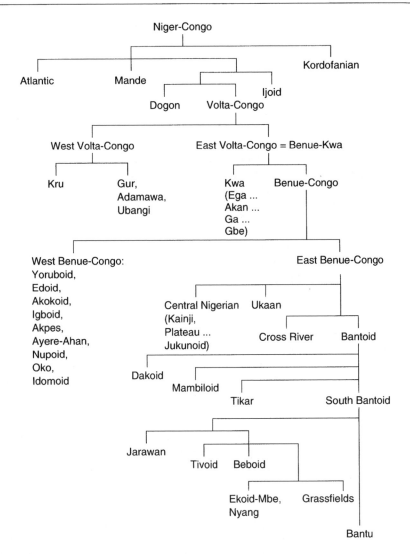

FIGURE 9.1 THE POSITION OF BANTU WITHIN NIGER-CONGO

Source: Adapted from Williamson and Blench (2000).

The lowly position of Bantu in the Niger-Congo tree diagram contrasts sharply with its model role for our understanding of the whole language family. Many morphological features of Bantu, notably its noun-class system with extensive agreement as well as its rich system of verbal derivation, recur, in modified form, in several distant branches of Niger-Congo (e.g. Kordofanian, Atlantic, Gur).

The *internal classification* (subgrouping) of Bantu has been a major concern of Bantu historical linguistics since the 1960s (see Nurse 1994/5 for a succinct overview; see also Nurse 1999). While some undeniable advances have been made, no satisfactory complete subclassification has been achieved – or it must be Nurse and Philippson in this volume.

In view of the general historical importance such a subclassification would have, we may well ask what the great obstacles have been.

Two commonly assumed reasons are the sheer magnitude of the problem and insufficient documentation. I don't believe that these are valid explanations. True, there are still many poorly documented languages, and true, applying the comparative method to vast amounts of lexical and morphological data from the remainder of the *c.* 500 Bantu languages is far beyond the available means. Nevertheless, if the primary genetic subgroupings of Bantu were as clearly distinguishable as, e.g. Germanic, Romance, Celtic and Slavic languages are distinguishable from each other, the number of languages involved and the lacunae in our knowledge would not prevent us from seeing these divisions.

The comparative method, when applied to a group of related languages, leads to the reconstruction of (parts of) the common ancestral language. Unfortunately however, there is no comparable step-by-step procedure that is guaranteed to lead to the true and only subclassification. There is just one kind of argument for any subgroup: shared innovations. There is no shortage of suitable innovations, such as typologically uncommon sound changes, morphological creations and semantic shifts. The problem is that as soon as one such innovation is interpreted as being "shared" and hence diagnostic for membership in a certain subgroup, all other innovations cutting across the hypothesized classification (i.e. affecting languages inside *and* outside the proposed subgroup or "branch") must be considered as being "parallel" historical coincidences, or as having spread "laterally", i.e. by contact. This then immediately raises doubts about the validity of the initial assumption: could it not be that the assumed "shared" innovation is itself one that has spread by contact?

Not having a subclassification in which at least the primary branches are clearly defined, together with the recognition of seemingly unbridled areal diffusion, poses a problem for the reconstruction of PB. Given that any reconstruction may only be assigned to the latest common ancestor, how can we be sure whether the languages lacking a reflex of our reconstruction do not form a primary branch of Bantu, thus relegating our reconstruction to some later, intermediate proto-language? The cleanest solution is reliance on external (non-Bantu) cognates, but this eliminates specific PB innovations – a clearly undesirable consequence. The common strategy to counter this problem is to assume a broad picture of the internal subclassification of Bantu, without sharply defining its details.

This broad picture minimally assumes that northwestern languages (roughly zones A B C) represent one primary branch, or more probably several ones, and that the remaining languages may well be more closely related to each other. Alternative terms for this division are "Forest Bantu" and "Savannah Bantu". A valid PB reconstruction should therefore be supported by reflexes in Savannah Bantu *and* Forest Bantu. A further division of Savannah Bantu into Western (roughly zones H K R) vs. Eastern (the rest) is less obvious.

Many older reconstructions have correctly been criticized for leaning too heavily on Savannah Bantu. Some linguists have argued that the NW languages, being descendants of the earliest split-offs from the Bantu tree, would have preserved essential facets of PB that have been lost or reshaped in Savannah Bantu. This expectation has not been borne out. In fact, NW Bantu is in many ways less conservative than Savannah Bantu. This is particularly visible with morphological elements (e.g. locative classes, verbal extensions), which in Forest Bantu are frequently reduced by phonological attrition but whose traces can – with some effort – be identified once the model has been provided by Savannah Bantu. The same is true for several Bantu-border languages in the northeast of the Democratic Republic of Congo (D30, part of D20); they owe their apparent grave differences from mainstream Bantu to intensive contact with non-Bantu languages rather than to their being one or more primary branches of Bantu.

3.2 Trees, waves and history

A good general introduction to the subject of this section is Nurse 1997b. But let us start with an example. Map 9.2 shows the spread of the locative suffix *-ini*. According to widely shared assumptions about language change and historical linguistics, the distribution of this morpheme should be an excellent indicator of genetic subgrouping.

The morpheme *-ini* is certainly an innovation and not a retention from PB, as evidenced by its absence from all central and western languages including the northwestern ones (zones A B C). As a morphological innovation it is less likely to be borrowed than words

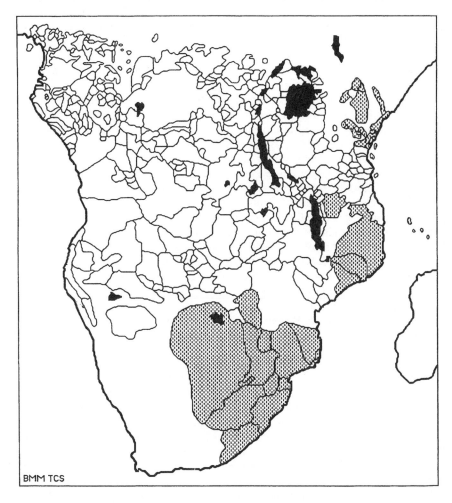

BMM TCS

MAP 9.2 THE DISTRIBUTION OF THE LOCATIVE SUFFIX *-ini*

or syntactic constructions. Moreover, it does not appear in a ready-made grammatical slot since suffixation to (or compounding of) nominal stems is not a productive process, and its etymological origin is a bit of a mystery (Samsom and Schadeberg 1994); these properties make several parallel creations highly unlikely. Its appearance interacts and interferes with the noun class system – a basic and very stable part of Bantu morphology; for this reason one might assume that it is not easily lost once acquired, at least not without leaving traces.

The suffix *-ini* occurs in the following language groups: Sabaki (E70 and Swahili G40, but not in Mwani), Thagicu (E50, with the possible exception of Embu E52), Kilimanjaro (E60), Shambala group (G20), Makhuwa group (P30, but not in Koti), Southern (zone S plus Ngoni N12, but not in Shona S10). I don't know of any proposal that would group these languages together, to the exclusion of other eastern Bantu languages, and I am not suggesting this now. If we were to choose other features that could qualify as shared innovations, they would certainly cut across this putative subgroup, excluding some of its members and combining the remaining ones with languages outside. For example, Dahl's Law (§2.1) would exclude Sabaki, Makhuwa and southern Bantu, but group Thagicu and Kilimanjaro together with Lacustrine (e.g. Rwanda D61 and Rundi D62), Southern Tanzania Highland (G60), parts of Western Tanzania (e.g. Sukuma F21 and Nyamwezi F22), as well as some other language groups in East Africa.

The conclusion has to be that Bantu languages have the remarkable ability to act much more like a dialect continuum than as discrete and impermeable languages. Such progressive differentiation and convergence across dialects or languages is commonly referred to as the wave model (as opposed to the tree model). Unfortunately, its graphic representations lack the simple beauty of tree diagrams.

In sociolinguistic terms, this means that Bantu speakers have long lived in a multilingual continuum, where many speakers master not just their own variety of speech but also those of their neighbours. Linguistic differentiation and convergence are actively pursued, one serving to establish distinct group identities, the other one to forge alliances and to foster good neighborship. The almost wilful selective adoption of new features is facilitated by structural similarities between Bantu languages. The comparativist can easily be misled by the apparent historical accuracy with which foreign words are adopted. For example, the word *i=tára* 'lamp' in Ha D66 is not a true cognate with but a borrowing from Swahili G42d *taa*, but we know this only because the Swahili word is itself a loan (from an unidentified source, possibly Indian). The "sound correspondences" as such are unexceptionable, cf. Ha *umu=kára* : Swahili *ma=kaa* 'charcoal', where Swahili has lost the *r* (< *l*) by regular sound change, whereas Ha has ingeniously inserted it in *i=tára*.

It is sometimes said that rapid expansion and separation lead to differentiation, whereas contact leads to convergence. Dixon (1997) feels that these two states, which he calls "punctuation" and "equilibrium", shape a given linguistic area during different periods. The dichotomy may not be quite as simple. The Bantu language family appears to have been formed by both kinds of processes at the same time. Contact may lead to differentiation by inspiring speakers to create new identities, manifested by new speech forms. Bantu offers some convincing cases: the Ngoni in Tanzania, the Koti in Mozambique, the Lozi in Zambia. They are easily recognizable because they are relatively recent and because they involve migrations (by small groups) over great distances bringing together rather distinct languages. In these respects these cases may be special, but frequent contact situations between peoples living in more remote times and often speaking less distinct languages would explain the bewildering mosaic of isoglosses and linguistic networks we encounter today.

Language contact is most easily detectable between unrelated languages. In the case of Bantu, such external contacts are visible at the northern and at the southern edge, but its effects have not generally spread very far. Southern Bantu languages have borrowed words from Khoesan languages, and their adoption of clicks is highly conspicuous. Still, these contacts have had little influence on the overall morphological and syntactic structure of southern Bantu languages. In the north, Bantu borders on many different language families, e.g. Cushitic, Nilotic, Central Sudanic, Ubangian; there is one district in north-western Tanzania where speakers of all four primary African language families talk to each other in one market. Again, as far as we can tell, structural influences have been restricted to relatively few marginal languages though some words of non-Bantu origin have been more widely adopted. This is, by the way, perfectly in line with the impact from non-African languages from overseas on the eastern coast.

I leave it open whether the view here sketched conflicts and competes with the tree model or is an amendment to be superimposed. Either way, it is suggested that contact has been a vital motor for the differentiation of Bantu and accounts for a very large part of Bantu history. I owe this view in part to Vansina's narrative on the history of Forest Bantu (1990). More recently (1995), he expanded it, more sketchily, to all of Bantu, rejecting a single huge migration to account for the "Bantu expansion". He also warns against accounting for the successful spread of Bantu by a small set of technological superiorities such as iron working and food production: "The prestige of the Bantu language flowed more from their sedentarity and the size of their social organization than from their technology" (Vansina 1995:192).

The reconstructed non-universal vocabulary tells us something about the culture and the environment of the original speakers. We assume that the speakers of PB played the drum (*ηgoma), kept goats (*mbúdi), made pottery (*=búmb-), built boats (*bu=játo), and caught fish with line and hook (*=lób-) as well as with some other technique, probably using a net (*=dub-), because all these words have reflexes throughout the Bantu-speaking area. On the other hand, we reject the idea that the speakers of PB were producing and using iron tools because the terms referring to iron working represent post-PB semantic shifts, e.g. 'to pound' > 'to forge', 'stone' > 'iron ore', 'thing' > 'made thing' > 'thing of value' > 'iron' (cf. De Maret and Nsuka 1977, Nsuka and De Maret 1980). Just as the quest for (genetic) subgrouping leads to the study of language contact, so does the comparative search for lexical meanings turn out to be inseparable from the study of loan words and involves disentangling complex webs of diffusion.

The method of inferring history from reconstructed words, called *Wörter und Sachen*, has not yet been exploited to its full extent. Ehret (2000) briefly sets out his version of the words-and-things method and its achievements in Africa; Ehret (1998) is a brave book-length application to eastern and southern Africa. While Ehret pays attention primarily (but not exclusively) to food production, Vansina (1990) is more (but again not exclusively) concerned with social structures and institutions in Forest Bantu.

Smaller regional studies have sometimes been hailed as the appropriate stepping stones towards the reconstruction of PB. In this respect, they are often disappointing since the reconstructed intermediate proto-language all too often very closely resembles PB – which should not surprise us if we think of Bantu diversification as occurring largely *in situ*. In other ways, however, regional studies are of the utmost importance: they alone provide the proper scale to investigate local contacts, movements and interactions. The most detailed such study of a small language group is about Swahili and Sabaki

(Nurse and Hinnebusch 1993); Labroussi (1998) tackles the complex history of the 'corridor' between Lake Nyasa and Lake Tanganyika.

Finally, let us turn to dates. Historical linguistics is strong in relative chronology but has no creditable means to provide absolute datings. For these, links have to be made to other history-oriented disciplines. In the case of Bantu, we usually turn to archaeology. I can do no better than cite Vansina (1995:188f.):

> With regard to absolute chronology, one can use indications from Proto-Bantu vocabulary and later from proto-West and East Bantu vocabularies and relate them to archaeological data. Because Proto-Bantu attests to the making of pottery and the cultivation of rootcrops in fields, the first Bantu dispersal must have occurred after pottery and farming had been introduced. Archaeological evidence suggests that this situation first occurs near the Bantu cradle area from the fourth millennium onwards, and specifically around 3000 BC, for the Bamenda highlands [Cameroon]. The expansion of Bantu therefore began after 3000 BC. But Proto-Bantu speakers neither smelted nor used metals, and neither did proto-Western Bantu or proto-Eastern speakers. The first sign of metallurgy in the Great Lakes region, now an East Bantu-speaking area, has been dated to *c.* 800 BC. It follows that by then the original North Bantu expansion was over and that the West and East Bantu dispersals had begun.

APPENDIX: LEXICAL RECONSTRUCTIONS

One of the largest ever lexicostatistic projects (Bastin, Coupez and Mann 1999) may not have yielded the definitive genetic subclassification of Bantu, but it did assemble comparative wordlists of 92 items from *c.* 550 Bantu languages. The list below contains reconstructions for these words as they are found in BLR2 (lower case zones = unexplained phonological or morphological deviations).

Gloss	PB	Gram	Distribution
'all'	*=nce	(PPx-o-)	ABCDEFGHJKLM n pRS
'arm'	*ku=bóko	N 15/6	ABCDEFGHJKLMN–RS
'ashes'	*mu=tó (=tói ?)	N 3 (14)	ABcD–––H–KLMnpr s
dust, soil, ashes	*i=bú	N 5 (3, 6)	A–CDEFG–JKLM–PRS
'bark (skin)'	*i=gula	N 5	– – c – –F– HjKL – – – – –
	*ki=kúkú	N 7	– –CD– – – – j–LM– – – –
	*lu=pú	N 11	– –CD– – – – J–LM– – – –
'belly'	*i=bumo	N 5	AB– – – – – H–KLM– –R–
	*i=tumbo	N 5	– – – –E–G– – – – – NP–S
'big'	*=néne	Adj.	ABCDE–GHJKLM– –R–
	*=néne-p-a	V	– – – –E–GHJ– – – NP– –
	*=nén-a	V	ABC– – – – – – – – – – –
'bird'	*ka=juni	N 12/13 (9/10)	ABc DeFGHJK1MNP–S
'bite'	*=lúm-a	V	ABC– EFG– J– –MNPRS
'black'	*=jíl-a	V	ABCDEF g HJKLMNp r s
	*=jíl-u	Adj.	ABCDEFGHJK– – N– – –
	*pi	Ideo., Adj.	– –C– –FG– – – – – – –S
	*i=piipí	N 5	–B– – –F– – JKLMn P–S
'blood'	*ma=gilá	N 6	ABCD– – –H–KL – – – – –
< avoid	*=gil-a	V	A–C –EFGHJKLMN–RS
	*ma=gadí	N 6	– – –d e F– – – – –MNP– S

Gloss	PB	Gram	Distribution
< oil palm, palm oil	*=gadí	N 9, 6	-BC----HJKLM--R-
	*mʊ=lopa	N 3	---D--G--KLMN--S
	*ma=ɲínga	N 6	-b--EF-HJKL-----
'bone'	*i=kúpa	N 5/6	ABCDEFGHJKLMNPRS
'breasts'	*ma=béele	N 5/6	ABCDEFGHJKLMNPRS
'burn, be hot'	*=lʊng-ʊl-a	V	--C-EFGHJKLMNpRS
	*=pí-a	V	ABCDEFGHJKLMNPRS
'cloud'	*i=lʊnde	N 5/6	-----FG-----NPR-
'cold'	*mʊ=didi	N 3	-BC----H---N---
	*=didim-a	V	--C-EFGH---MN-RS
cool	*=pól-a	V	ABcDEFGHJKLMNPRS
'come'	*=jij-a	V	ABC-EFGHJKLMNPRS
'die'	*=kú-ɛ	V	ABCDEFGHJKLMNPRS
'dog'	*mbúa	N 9/10	ABCDEFGHJKLMNPRS
'drink'	*=nyó-a	V	ABCDEFGHJKLMNPRS
'dry'	*=jʊ́m-a	V	ABCDEFGHJKLMNP-S
	*=jʊ́m-u	Adj.	-B---F--JKL-NP--
'ear'	*kʊ=túi	N 15/6	ABCDEFGHJKLMNPR-
'eat'	*=lí-a	V	ABCDEFGHJKLMNPRS
'egg'	*i=gí	N 5/6	ABCDEFGhJKLMnPRS
'eye'	*i=jíco	N 5/6	ABCDEFGHJKLMNPRS
'fat'	*ma=kúta	N 6	ABCDEFGHJKLMNP-S
'feather'	*lʊ=cála	N 11 (5/6)	ABCD---HJKL---R-
'fire'	*mʊ=jóto	N 3/4	-BC-EFGHJKLMNPRS
< warm oneself	*=jót-a	V	ABCdEFGHJKLMNPRS
(< burn; v.s.)	*tʊ=pí-a	N 13	A-CDE---JKLMnprS
	*tʊ=jíja	N 13	A-CD---H-KL-----
	*mʊ=lɪlo	N 3/4	----E---J-LMN-RS
'fish'	*ncúɪ	N 9/10	ABCDE-GHjKLM--R-
'flea'	*ndá	N 9/10	ab-DEF--J--MN-rS
'fly'	*=gʊl-ʊk-a	V	A--DE-G-J-LMNP--
'full'	*=jíjal-a	V	ABCDEfGHjKLmNPRS
'give'	*=pá-a	V	ABCDEFGHJKLMNPRS
'go'	*=gɪ-a	V	ABCDEF-HJKLMNPRS
'good'	*=jijá	Adj.	----EF-HJ-L-----
'ground; (below)'	*(pa-)ncí	N (16+) 9	ABCDEFGHJKLMNPRS
'hair'	*=cíti(LL?)	N (class?)	A-------J-LMN-RS
	*lʊ=cʊkí	N 11/10	ABC----HjKL---R-
	*lʊ=jʊílí (ɪ ~ e)	N 11/10	---DEFG-J-1M----
'head'	*mʊ=túe	N 3/4	ABCDEFGHJKLMNPR-
'hear'	*=jígu-a	V	--c--FGHjKLMNPRS
'heart' *(> liver)*	*mʊ=tíma	N 3/4	ABCDEFGHJKLMNPR-
'horn'	*lʊ=pémbé	N 9/10	--CDEFG-J--MN---
(object made from horn)	*mʊ=céngo	N 3/4	---D---HJKLMNP--
'kill'	*=búl(-ag)-a	V	ABCDEFGH-KL--PRS
	*=jíp(-ag)-a	V	a-cDeF-h-KLMNPrS
'knee'	*i=dúí (HL?)	N 5/6	A-CDEFG-JK1M---S
	*i=bóngó	N 5/6	ABCDE--H--L-----
'know'	*=jíjɪ(b-a)	V	ABCDEFGHJKLMN-RS
	*=many-a	V	AbCDEFG-J-LMNP--
'leaf'	*i=jáni (tone?)	N 5/6	ABCDE-G-JKLMN--S
'leg'	*kʊ=gulʊ	N 15/6	ABCDEFGHJKLMN-R-
'lie, sleep'	*=lá-al-a	V	ABCDEFGHJKLMNpRS
'liver' *(see also 'heart')*	*=balɪ	N (class ?)	ABC-----K------

Gloss	PB	Gram	Distribution
'long, far, long ago'	*=lai	Adj.	- BCDEFGHJKLMNPRS
	*=lai-p-a	V	A - - - EFGHJKLM - pRS
'man, husband'	*mʋ=lúme	N 1/2; Adj.	ABCDE-GHJKLMNPRS
(< 'bite', v.s.)			
'many'	*=jíngí	Adj.	a B c DEFGHJKLMNPRS
'meat, animal'	*ɲama	N 9/10	ABCDEFGHJKLMNPRS
'moon' (< 'white', v.i.)	*kʋ=jédi	N 15/6, 3/4	ABCDEFGHJKLMNPRS
'mountain, hill'	*lʋ=gʋlʋ	N 11/10	- B - D - F - - J - L - - - R -
< top, sky	*i=gʋlʋ (~ LH)	N 5	ABC - EFGHJKLMNPRS
'mouth'	*ka=nʋa	N 12	a BCDE- g HJKLMn pRS
lip, mouth	*mʋ=lomo	N 3/4	- - CDEFG - JKLMN - - S
'nail'	*lʋ=jála	N 11/10	ABCDE f GHJKLMn pRS
'name'	*i=jína	N 5/6	ABCDEFGHJKLMNPRS
'neck'	*nkíngó	N 9/10	ABCDEFGHJKLMNPRS
nape	*nkoti	N 9/10	ABCDE- GHJKLMNPRS
'new' (< 'burn', v.s.)	*=pí-a (HH?)	Adj.	- - - DEFG - JKLMN - - S
'night, 24 hour period'	*bʋ=tíkʋ (i ~ ú)	N 14	A b CDEFGh JK l MN pRS
'nose'	*i=júlʋ	N 5/6	ABCDEF - HJKL - - - R -
'one'	*=moi	Num.	ABCDEFGh JKLM n pRS
'path'	*njɩla (LH?)	N 9/10	ABCDEFGHJKLMNPRS
'person'	*mʋ=ntʋ	N 1/2	ABCDEFGHJKLMNPRS
'rain'	*mbúlá	N 9/10	ABCDEFGHJKLMNPRS
'red' (substance)	*nkúla	N 9	ABC d - - - HJKLM - - - -
red soil	*nkúndú	N 9	a - C - E - G - - K - - pR -
	*=tɩl-a (tone?)	V	- BCD - - - H–KL - - - R -
'root, fibre'	*mʋ=di	N 3/4	ABCDEFGHJKLMN - RS
'round' (be, make)	*=búlʋng-a	V	- - C - - - Gh J - LMN - r S
make round and smooth	*=kúlʋng-a	V	- - C - - - G - J - - MN - RS
'sand'	*mʋ=céké	N 3	A b CD - - - HJKLMN - RS
	*i=cenga (e ~ a)	N 3	a BCDe F g HJKLMN p r s
'say, quote'	*=tɩ	V	- - C - E -GHJ - - MNPRS
do, say	*=gɩl-a	V	ABCD - - - - JK - M - P - S
speak, answer	*=gamb-a	V	ABCDEFGHJKLMNP - S
'see'	*=bón-á (b ~ m)	V	- BCDEFGHJKLMNPRS
'seed'	*mbút-o	N 10	- BCD - - - HJKLMN - R -
'sit'	*=jikal-a	V	ABCDEFGHJKLMNPRS
'skin, strap, cloth'	*=kánda	N 3/4, ...	AB c - EFGHJKLMNP r S
skin, strap, bark	*mʋ=kóbá	N 3/4, ...	ABCDEFG - JKLM n pRs
skin, cloth	*ngúbo	N 9/10	A - - d E f GH–k LMNP - S
'sleep'	*tʋ=ló	N 13	ABCDEFGHJKLMN pRs
'small'	*=(kée)kée	Adj.	- BCD - - GHJ - LM - P - -
	*=kée-p-a	V	- - - D - FG–JKLMN - - S
'smoke'	*mʋ=jíki (i ~ ó)	N 3/4	ABCDEFGHJKLMNPRS
'stand'	*=jím(-al)-a	V	A b CDeFG - JKLMN p - S
'star'	*nyénye(di)	N 9/10	- B - - E - g HJ - LMN - - S
'stone'	*i=bʋe	N 5/6	- - CDEFG - JKLMNPRS
stone, iron ore	*i=tále	N 5/6	ABCD - F - HJKLMNPRS
'sun'	*i=júba	N 5	AB c DEFGHJKLMNPRS
'swim, bathe'	*=jóg-a	V	ABCDEFGHJKLMNPR -
'tail'	*mʋ=kíla	N 3/4	ABCDEFGHJKLMNPRS
'tongue'	*lu=lími	N 11/10	AB c DEf GHJKLMNPRS
'tooth'	*i=jíno	N 5/6	ABCDEFGHJKLMNP - S
molar	*i=gego	N 5/6	ABC - EFG - jKL - - PRS
'tree'	*mʋ=tí	N 3/4	ABCDEFGHJKLMNPRS
'two'	*=balí (a ~ ɩ)	Num.	ABCDEFGHJKLMNPRS

Gloss	PB	Gram	Distribution
'walk'	*=gend-a	V	ABC- EFGh JKLMNP r S
'warm, hot' (< 'burn', v.s.)	*=pí-ʊ	Adj.	- - - - EFG- j - LMNPR-
'water'	*ma=jíjɪ	N 6	A bCDEFGHJKLMN p r S
water, pool	*i=diba (HH?)	N 5/6	ABCDEFGHJKLMNPRS
'what'	*kɪ=í	N 7	- -CDEFGHJ - LMN - - -
where, which	*pa=i	N 16	A - - - - - - - - JKL - - -RS
'white, bright'	* =jél-a	V	- BCD-FG - J - L - N- RS
	* =jél-ʊ	Adj.	- -CDEFGHJ - -M - - - -
	*pe (tone?)	Ideo.	- -C - - -GH- - LM - - R-
'who'	*n(d)ai (tone?)	Inv.	- -C - - -G - J - - - - - - -
'woman, wife'	*mʊ=kádí	N 1/2	ABCD e f g HJKLMNp r S

REFERENCES

Bastin 1975, 1978, 1983b; Bastin, Coupez and Mann 1999; Blanchon 1998; Bleek 1856, 1862–9; Bourquin 1923; Bryan 1959; Campbell 1998; CBOLD; Coupez, Bastin and Mumba 1998 (BLR2); Davy and Nurse 1982; De Maret and Nsuka 1977; Dixon 1997; Doke and Cole 1961; Ehret 1998, 2000; Greenberg 1948, 1951, 1963a; Grégoire 1976; Grimes 2000; Guthrie 1948, 1967–71; Herbert 1977; Hyman 1999; Kamba Muzenga 1981; Labroussi 1998; Lowe and Schadeberg 1997; Meeussen 1967 (BGR), 1969 (1980; BLR), 1973, 1979; Meinhof 1899 (1910), 1903, 1906 (1948); Meinhof and Van Warmelo 1932; Miehe 1991; Nsuka and De Maret 1980; Nurse 1994–5, 1997b, 1999; Nurse and Hinnebusch 1993; Samsom and Schadeberg 1994; Schadeberg 1981, 1987, 1994–5, 1999; Stappers 1965; Stewart 1993b, 1995, 1999, 2000a; Vanhoudt 1994; Vansina 1990, 1995; Williamson and Blench 2000.

CHAPTER TEN

TOWARDS A HISTORICAL CLASSIFICATION OF THE BANTU LANGUAGES

Derek Nurse and Gérard Philippson

> A complete comparative study requires full descriptions for all the languages involved .... With some 600 Bantu languages, this is a tall order. It will take generations before the raw data are assembled, if ever. To cope with this sort of situation Morris Swadesh developed a shortcut ... lexicostatistics.
>
> (Vansina 1995:179)

1 AIM

We would have liked to present here the first comprehensive non-lexically based historical classification of the Bantu languages. For us that would be a statement that reflected, not so much the origins and whole evolution of the languages spoken by Bantu communities over the 5,000 or so years that have elapsed since late Proto-Bantu (PB), but rather the development of their early ancestors out of PB during the first two or three millennia of that period. We have been unable to do this satisfactorily in the time available due to the huge mass of data it would be necessary to collect, examine and interpret: this is discussed further in §4. Instead, in §4 we set out our original intended methodology and our perforce modified method, and in §5, we present an initial set of proposals for a non-lexically based historical classification. These should be treated as a base for future work. We hope that even if parts of this attempt are judged unsuccessful, that will be progress, since it should then be possible to state the progress achieved and the reason(s) for failure.

2 MODELS

Any language has three components: what it inherited from its ancestors, what it innovated during its evolution, and what it absorbed from other languages along the way. We think that contemporary languages which are related derive from a common ancestor, so we do believe in a PB, we do think that many features found in modern languages can be traced back to PB, and we do think of PB as a real language, and thus probably dialectally divergent. We are centrally concerned with just which features can be derived from PB. This is divergence, from a mother to a small number of offspring, ultimately to a larger number of offspring. This is also the predominant older paradigm – that most innovation found in the offspring can be attributed to the mother. However, in recent decades a new view has risen to prominence: almost any linguistic feature can be transferred from language to language to language, leading to mixed languages. Not just vocabulary but sounds, sound patterns, morphemes, morphological patterns, and syntactic patterns can all diffuse across languages. Our analysis here incorporates both mechanisms.

We share the common current view that the PB community, and early Bantu communities, had their home in eastern Nigeria, and spread thence, starting some five millennia or a little longer ago (Vansina 1990:49–54, Kliemann 1997). We see this spread, not as a vast wave or a series of large waves, but as a slow, gradual and steady movement, characterized by fits and starts, conditioned by environmental, demographic, economic and social factors. We think it true that for many areas of Bantu settlement an initial period of immigration was followed by a later period of local expansion(s). We think it important to emphasize that most of the initial periods were probably short and the later periods long. This has the practical consequence that most language communities have had many centuries or millennia of local innovation, and of interaction with each other or with pre-existing communities. Since these periods of convergence have been more recent and longer than the initial period of divergence, it follows that many, maybe all, Bantu languages share areal features with their neighbors, features assumed to have diffused regionally. Because these areal features have had so long to diffuse, they often outnumber features inherited from earlier proto-languages, whether PB or one of its offspring. In writing this historical classification, it is our job to try to distinguish the early inherited from the later innovated and diffused, although this is not always easy. These general notions can be illustrated by three brief examples.

Early Bantu communities emerged east out of the rain forest between 2,500 and 3,000 years ago (Ehret 1998). Some moved east, others south, and their expansion gradually filled all eastern and southern Africa, finally reaching far south Africa by the middle of the first millennium AD. Linguists and historians are still not agreed on all the details of the early movement. In any particular area, there would have been a fairly short initial period of migration, followed by between 1,500 and 2,500 years of local expansion, merger and overlap. In recent centuries, in eastern and southern Africa, the larger communities have been spreading rapidly and steadily outwards, colliding with and over-running their neighbors, and the most recent stage for this is the city, where new language forms are emerging.

The same can be seen in more intense form in what we will call the Forest languages, those spoken in the northwest of the Bantu area, in the area today occupied by Cameroon, Gabon, Congo, and parts of the Democratic Republic of Congo (DRC). These are the languages labelled A, B, C, and small adjacent groups of D and H. This area has been much longer settled, following initial movement out of Cameroon, and linguists agree that the languages in this area are quite different from those in east and south Africa, and often from each other, just because they have had so long to develop. It also becomes clear that for the same reason these languages are also characterized by shared features, and although linguists are not fully agreed on how far these are inherited vs. innovated and diffused, our analysis in §5 suggests sets of innovated or diffused features.

Third, a glance at the map suggests that parts of D30, D20, D10, H (esp. H40), L, K (esp. K40), and M60 sit squarely between geographically western and eastern blocks of languages. So over the last two millennia or more, they have absorbed influences from both sides. The result is that they have proved contentious for classifiers – comparisons of various classifications shows that they have now formed part of eastern Bantu, now of western, which has sometimes been reconciled by positing a central (Savanna) Bantu.

Examination of all the lexically based classifications to date reveals other language groups which have caused their authors problems, just because they are lexically mixed.

All this gives our work a different bias from that of much other previous work. We have tried to sort current linguistic features into those inherited from PB and those which emerged and diffused later. We did this on the twin bases of the current geographical distribution of the features, and the relative plausibility of the possible directions of linguistic change involved.

We reject the use of lexically or lexicostatistically based approaches as the sole or the principal basis for subgrouping, although we have considered the distribution of some lexical items and we are aware of the many classifications using these approaches. We reject such approaches for several reasons. One is that the raw data is frequently missing in claims of shared innovations, as are the bases of similarity in lexicostatistical work: this makes it almost impossible to verify many of the claims made. Another is that, while there is today widespread agreement that almost any linguistic feature or system can be transferred, vocabulary is the component of language that is most readily and quickly transferred, and over millennia it is possible for the vocabulary of any language to be so overwhelmed that its original core is hard to discern. Third, lexical loans are often hard or impossible to detect, having been phonetically manipulated by the recipient community (Hinnebusch 1999). Finally, the construction of linguistic trees forces their builders to posit binary splits and a percentage difference of a point or two often makes a big difference in how a linguistic tree is structured, and thus in how linguistically based history is made.

We cite two examples in support of our position vis-a-vis the use of vocabulary. One is Ilwana, spoken on the Tana River in northeast Kenya. Nurse (2000) shows that of the approximately 2,000 words of Ilwana currently available, only just over 20 percent are inherited. In other words, nearly 80 percent of that total has been absorbed from one external source or other over the past two millennia. In case it might be objected that the Ilwana community would always have been too small to protect itself against a flood of foreign words, we use English as a second example. When England was first exposed to direct French influence in AD 1066, its population exceeded a million and the size of the Norman army is estimated at 5,000. During the following centuries, as the population of England grew steadily, French vocabulary poured into English. The results can be seen in e.g. Williams (1975:67), who shows that of the 2,000 most often used English words, 66 percent are of foreign, mainly French, origin, and of the first 10,000, 75 percent. That is, a similar-sized majority of English vocabulary at these levels is also not inherited. So we feel that all lexically based classifications need non-lexical corroboration. Where lexical and non-lexical indices differ widely, the former usually reflect recent transfer while the latter result from shared inheritance.

Our work differs also from the two previous approaches (Bastin 1978, Möhlig 1979, 1981) not based on the use of vocabulary. Möhlig relies on stratificational 'theory', i.e. he does not accept the notion of a single proto-community dividing and subdividing, which is part of our approach. Bastin does accept the concept of PB but her approach is rather to count the features shared by her target languages, assigning a plus or minus value, without clear reference to whether each feature can be assumed to have a PB origin or not. We assume a proto-language and try to state – rightly or wrongly – which shared features are due to divergence from a shared ancestor and which to convergence or innovation.

3 PREVIOUS STUDIES

Most previous studies have been referential or historical (for an overview, see Nurse 1994/5). Of the former (Guthrie 1967–71, Mann *et al.* 1987, Grimes 2000), the most widely used is a now slightly modifed version of Guthrie. All of the historical studies except the two mentioned above are based on the use of vocabulary (Heine 1973, Henrici 1973, Bastin *et al.* 1983, Ehret 1998, 1999, Bastin *et al.* 1999 (henceforth BCM)). Möhlig uses a set of widespread phonological changes, Bastin a set of fifty-four features, part phonological, part morphological. Nearly all rely on an incomplete sample of languages, from a few dozen to over 200. The exceptions are Mann *et al.* and especially BCM.

Most of these historical classifications share the general view that the initial split in Bantu was between the north-west languages and the others, the latter then divided into a Western and an Eastern Bantu, although they differ on the details of the latter.

4 METHODOLOGY

4.1 Step 1: the ideal methodology

The primary reason for the incomplete sampling just mentioned is the sad shape of the data base. Bantu languages total between 300 and 600, depending on where the line is drawn between language and dialect. For most the quality and quantity of the data available – lexical or non-lexical – are variable but in general poor. We tried partly to remedy this by a geographical balance. Guthrie divides the Bantu area into 15 zones (to which the Tervuren group added J, ignored in this paragraph), each in turn divided into a number of groups, these being 84 in all. Our approach has been to try and take at least one sample language from each of Guthrie's groups, so we used some 80+ languages. While there were lacunae, because data for some languages was just not available or because some groups were quite diverse, this gave a reasonable geographical coverage. The main languages used are: A15, A22, A44/6, A53, A62, A74, A83/84, A93, B30, C14, C32/36, C40, C54, D10 several, D25/27/28, D43, D53, several of each of D60, E10, E20, E25, E30, E40, E50, E60, and E70, F21/2/5, F31/2/3, G11, several G20/G30/G40, G51, several G60 and H11/4, H41/2, (K20 = S30), several K10/30/40 languages, L10, L21/3, L31, L50, L62, several M10/20, M30, M42, M54, M62/3, several N10, N20, N31, N44, P13/4, P21/3, P30 Makua, R11, R22, R30, R40, S10, S20, several S30 plus K20, S40. Besides the languages named we had incomplete data for many others. As can be seen, the principal holes are in B, parts of C, D30, H20/30, L40, and S50/60.

We then constructed an initial list of some thirty phonological and morphological features, which we thought might be historically diagnostic. These were: the verb suffix -*i* 'past/anterior'; the verb suffix consisting of a vowel which copied the root vowel 'past/anterior'; the verb suffix -*ile* 'anterior/past': the coexistence in one language of any combination of the first three; the verb suffix -*a(n)g-a* 'imperfective'; the shape of the verb person subject markers (esp.1/2/3 sg. and 1pl.); the use of -*li* as auxiliary or as part of the verbal tense marker; use and shape of primary vs. secondary negative formatives; relative formation; use of extra-locative suffixes (-*po*, -*mo*, -*ko*); locative formation; class and shape of infinitive; common noun pairings; number of noun classes; homophony of dependent and independent prefix; class 5 shape; number of contrastive vowels; contrastive lexical vowel length; contrastive vowel length in tense/aspect markers and in extensions; Dahl's Law; Meinhof's Law; /l/ becoming [n] in extensions; (in)variable vowel in extensions; tonal distinction in dependent prefixes; participants tonally distinct in verb prefixes; Bantu Spirantization (BS); lenition of **p*; lenition of **p*, *t*, and *k*; **li-* > *i-* > 0- in class 5; homophoneity of the prefixes for classes 9 and 10.

Besides these, we kept our eyes on the features in Bastin (1979), Guthrie (1948), Hinnebusch (1981), Möhlig (1979, 1981), Nurse (1988, 1999), and especially on those of theirs which did not overlap with ours.

4.2 Step 2: the difficulties

The difficulties are of two broad types. One has to do with the data. In examining over a hundred languages, we soon found that the poor quality and quantity of the data available for some features did not allow us to draw reliable maps covering the whole Bantu area adequately (e.g. tonal information, relative formation, use of extra-locative suffixes, contrastive vowel length in suffixes, negative markers, Meinhof's Law). For other features, our information suggested they were not useful on a broad scale, either because they were too general (*-li* as auxiliary, presence of *-a(n)g-a*) or too local (shape of 2/3sg. prefixes, shape of class 5).

The other problem is how to distinguish the results of divergence from those of convergence. Several hundred languages, two or three millennia of development, and several dozen significant variables make for an often opaque crisscrossing of isoglosses. Some of the problems and some of the results are illustrated in §5.3.

4.3 Step 3: the modified approach

We had, thus reluctantly, to replace this multi-layered approach by a simpler one consisting of two parts. The first was to use some of the features listed in §4.1, because the underlying data were good and could be reasonably interpreted, and their geographical distribution made sense and often overlapped with the distribution of other features. The second was to draw on existing classifications and on the accumulated knowledge and intuition of several linguists. Since the appearance of Guthrie's *Comparative Bantu* (1967–71), many linguists have emphasized the shortcomings of the book as a historical statement, which is rather unfair to Guthrie as he makes clear that he intended it as a work of reference, not a statement of history (Guthrie 1948). They know that many of his zones make little historical sense, although they are often used for historical purposes. They know which Bantu zones and groups are relatively coherent and which coherence probably derives from shared origins in a common ancestor. Few of their intuitions have been voiced in print or if they have, they have mostly been local. We have tried to pull these together in §5. There is an obvious danger here, in that these judgments are of different levels of reliability, and rely on different bases, often lexical ('these languages share certain words uniquely'), sometimes intuitive ('I feel this is a solid Zone C language'), sometimes based on other reasoning. We try, as far as possible, to make the bases for our judgments explicit. Use of the question mark means we have some doubts about the historical validity of the configuration.

5 PRELIMINARY RESULTS

5.1 Local groupings

It has often been said that whereas Guthrie's zones are flawed, his eighty-four groups are genetically coherent. As can be seen by examining the material below, this is no longer true. Many groups are now recognized as deficient, in a major or a minor way, or simply because new languages not known to Guthrie have been added meanwhile.

We need to say something here on the numbering system we are using. We took Guthrie (1967–71) as our baseline and have not changed his numbering system. However, we have added new languages not known to Guthrie, following a system suggested by Schadeberg. We consulted the inventory of languages in the Bantu Mapmaker

(Lowe and Schadeberg 1997) and that proposed by SIL (Grimes 2000). The resulting inventory and numbering system can be found in the Appendix by Maho, at the end of this book. During the 1960s and 1970s Tervuren scholars modified Guthrie's numbering system (as in e.g. Bastin 1978, BCM). We have found these numbering modifications to be confusing and we have the impression that others do too. We therefore retain Guthrie's system as a referential device. For historical purposes below, we have of course modified his groups while keeping his numbers, plus our additions.

The local (historical) groupings below are based on synthesizing a variety of sources and are largely non-controversial. It will be seen that we have adopted one of Tervuren's numbering modifications, 'Zone J' (plus a small addition of our own), because we feel it stands a chance of having historical validity. We cite J languages with double letters, i.e. by using newer J first, then either older D or E. Immediately below, and especially in §§5.2 and 5.3, we propose other modifications, not of numbering but of group membership and allegiance. Most of these modifications are from Tervuren or Ehret, who are thus the two main sources and we do not cite them in individual groupings below. For East Africa, some modifications are based on our own work, also not cited. For Zone J, Schoenbrun (1994) is the main source. We use Tervuren as an abbreviation for any of the (lexico)statistical work from Tervuren, their most complete statement being BCM. Ehret's work, which depends on shared lexical innovation, also covers a period of time, but his most complete statement is Ehret (1999). Ehret deals with Zones E, F, G, J, K, L, M, N, P, R, S, D20 and H20, i.e. he excludes the Forest. BCM covers the whole area including the Forest. These local groupings are thus mostly lexically based.

We would like it to be clear to readers that, while we use Guthrie's numbering system, what follows is an attempt at a historical statement, and thus not that of Guthrie. To make that as clear as possible we have not separated the zones, i.e. we do not think of them as having historical validity. Items preceded by a question mark are of uncertain status. It is impossible to deal with every little detail here, so readers should consult the sources for the minutiae involved here and in §5.2.

A15 ('Manenguba': Hedinger 1984)
?other A10 (poorly known), A20–30 less A31
A44–5–6, A60, ?A31 (Janssens 1992–3)
A41–2–3
A50
A70
A80–90
B10–30
B20 (?B21)
B40, some H12 and H13
B50, B73
B60
B70 less B73, B81, B83–4
B80 less B81, B83–4, some B85
C10, C31
C20 less C27
C27, C31–6, C61, C75
C37, C41, C46
C43–4–5, ?D30
C50–60 less C61

C70, C81, C89
C80 less C81, C89
D10 (?D12), ?D33
D21–2–3, D31–32
D24–5–6
D43, D55
E50, E46
E60, E74a
E71–2–3, probably plus G44 and ?E74b
F10
F20 less F23–4–5, maybe plus D28
?F25
F24, ?M11, F30 less F33–4
F33–4
G10
G21–2 (Nurse and Hinnebusch 1993)
G23–4, G31, G34
G32–3, G35–9

G40, probably less G44
   (Nurse and Hinnebusch 1993)
G50, P15 (Nurse 1988)
G60, N11 (Nurse 1988)
H10 less part of H12 and H13
H20 (?all)
H30, H42, B85
?H41 (see L10)
JD40 less D43
JD50 plus JD63, less D55
JD60 less JD63
JE11–14, JE21–3, others (islands)
   (Ladefoged et al. 1971)
JE15–18
JE25
JE30, JE41
JE40 less JE41, plus E46 and others
K10 (for K20, see S30)
K30 less K31
K31
K40
L10, part of H13, H41
L20–30–40, D27
L50
L60

M12–3–4–5, M21–2, M26
   (Nurse 1988)
M23–4–5–6, Lambya (Nurse 1988)
M30
M40–50, N21d = Senga
   (Guthrie 1948)
M60
N10 less N11, plus P14
   (Nurse 1988)
N20–30–40 less N21d
P10, less P14–5 (Nurse 1988)
P20
P30 (incl. Koti: Schadeberg and
   Mucanheia 2000)
R10
R20
R30
R40
S10
S20
S30, incl. K20 (Gowlett 1989)
S40
?S50
?S60

5.2 Intermediate groupings

The line between local and intermediate groups is not hard and fast. All intermediate
groups are larger than a single group in Guthrie's sense and in some cases as large as or
larger than his zones. We have incorporated the local groups into these larger sets. All are
proposals and need to be validated. The only one to have been validated by more than one
approach so far is NEC, although S, as defined below, seems to us largely validated by
Janson (1991/2). Otherwise, the basis for most of these groups is lexical. For many, this
lexical similarity can be buttressed by considering the phonological material in e.g.
Guthrie (1971) where it can be seen that sets of groups have identical or similar reflexes
of PB consonants and vowels.

   It can be seen that of Guthrie's fifteen zones, not a single one has survived as a self-
standing historical unit, although some still have a substantial core: A (less A44–5–6, A60
and maybe A50); B (less B10, B30, B80 and maybe B20); C with additions; F (less F10,
F23, F25, F33–4); G (less G50 and G60, plus E71–3 and additions); Tervuren's J; K (less
K20 plus additions); N (less N10); P (plus N10, less P30); R; S (plus K20 and P30, less
S10).

?A11–4, A20–30 less A31 ('Sawabantu': Richardson 1956, Jacquot and Kuperus 1985,
Ebobisse 1989)
?A31, A44–5–6, A60 ('Buneya': Dieu and Renaud 1983, Mous and Breedveld 1986)
A80–90

B10–30
B50–60–70–part of B80–H24
C10–20–part of C30–C41 and a few other C40
C50–60–70–80–part of C30–part of B80 (Motingea 1996)
C43–4–5, parts of D30 ('Boan')
?D12–part of D30 ('Lebonya')
D13–14, D21–2–3, D31–2 (Kutsch Lojenga various), plus the following?
D24–5–6 (member of the preceding, or of the following, or of J?)
D43, D55
E50–E46 ('Central Kenya')
E60–E74a ('Kilimanjaro-Taita')
F21–2 maybe +D28, maybe F24–31–2, maybe M11 (Labroussi 1999:346)
F33–4
G10–40 plus E71–3, possibly plus E74b ('North East Coast')
H10, H30, H42, B40–parts of B85 (Tervuren, and there is some phonological evidence)
J: JE10–40, most JD40–60, plus extras e.g. F23 ('Lacustrine') (Tervuren: Schoenbrun
    1994)
K10–30 less K31, L10–50–60, H21, R (perhaps L21–2, part of H13b, H41) ('Southwest')
L20–30–40, probably D27, maybe L60, maybe less L21–2
M10–M20 ('Corridor'), less M11 (Nurse 1988), maybe plus M30
M40–50, maybe N21d, M60, K40
N20 (N21d?)–30–40 (N43–44?)
N10, P10–20 ('Rufiji–Ruvuma') (Nurse and Philippson 1980)
R: see K10
Zone S: S20–30–40–?S50–?S60, plus P30 ('Southeast') (Janson 1991/2)
S10

At this level there are doubts about the internal consistency and/or external allegiance of
parts or all of A11–14, A50, B20, C10, D10, D20, D30, F10, F33–4, G50, G60, H20,
H30, H40, K40, L60, M11, M30, M60, small parts of N, S50, S60.

Although the evidence for most of these intermediate groupings is primarily lexical,
we think it would not be hard to buttress many of them with non-lexical data. For
instance, much of the phonological material in Guthrie (1971), where sets of groups have
identical or similar reflexes of PB consonants and vowels, supports some of the groups.
Similarly, some of the typological and geographically based evidence cited by Guthrie
(1967:29–73) in support of his zones has also a certain historical validity. Two illustratory
examples can be offered. One is the phonological innovations that characterize S (also
P30 but not S10), whereby the inherited voiceless stops (*p, t, k) became continuants.
This is likely to have happened just once and thus to have characterized their proto
(Janson 1991/2). The other is a varied set of features characterizing N (i.e. N20–30–40,
not N10): all have undergone Bantu Spirantization (BS), have five short vowels, have no
or restricted tonal distinctions, have lost *-a(n)ga and *-ile, have reduced their tense distinctions (e.g. have only a single past tense), and have 1sg. ti-: some of these are shared
with various combinations of their neighbors.

5.3 Large groups

Before setting out our proposals we sketch two other recent major proposals.

5.3.1 Tervuren

Over the last four and a half decades of the twentieth century, a group based in Tervuren, of varying membership, has used lexicostatistics to classify Bantu. Their data base has expanded steadily, culminating in their centennary work, BCM 1999, covering 542 varieties. The authors admit its coverage is not complete, having no language from F10, G50, JE40, K40, M20, P10, R40, or S60, and underrepresenting others: in all fairness we should say that Ehret's coverage (below) is not complete either. Based on the use of several different kinds of statistical approach, they (BCM: 125–9) see three main divisions of Narrow Bantu: North (B10, B30, Zone A less A31/A43–4–5/A60), East (Zones E, F, G, J, M, N, P, S, K31, and most of D and L), and West (C, H, R, most of B and K, bits of L20). Within this framework, some languages and groups show wavering allegiance: A50, B20, the 'Southwest' (K, R, parts of H10, H40, L20, and D). They also have a peripheral category but it has little genetic significance, being a ragbag of languages of constantly wavering allegiance (D10-30, A31–43–4–5–60, C43–4–5).

A historical interpretation of this is found in two works by Vansina. For communities speaking Forest languages he (1990:46–54) has an initial split of 'western' and 'eastern' Bantu some five millennia ago, movement of early 'western' communities out of Nigeria into Cameroon ('Zone A' languages) during the third millennium BC, across Cameroon during the second millennium BC, and into the rest of the Forest area during the remaining centuries BC. Dating here is based partly on correlations with archaeology.

Vansina (1995) has a careful and cautious scenario, mainly for 'eastern' languages. He distances himself somewhat from BCM's lexicostatistical picture; he juxtaposes migration of people with wave-like spread of language; he slightly modifies his earlier Forest interpretation; and archaeological dating is little used. His scenario for languages outside the Forest sees a single ancestral 'East Bantu language spread from the rainforests of Zaire somewhere east of the Ubangi/Zaire confluence towards the middle Zambezi' (Vansina 1995:188), then 'cover much of the large area where its daughter languages are now spoken. That suggests that the spreading took several centuries, during which the original language remained unified' (Vansina 1995:178). This spread southeast across Zaire out of the rainforest was followed by dispersal northeast, east and south across the Savanna. Major language differentiation is portrayed as occurring subsequently, starting at the periphery.

5.3.2 Ehret

Over the last three decades of this century Ehret has also steadily expanded his scope, which now embraces all four African language families. His most recent classificatory work deals in detail with the Bantu communities of eastern and southern Africa and has Savanna Bantu as a deep branch of Narrow Bantu (1999:47–53). Savanna divides into two, Western (R, H20, parts of Guthrie's L and K) and Eastern. Eastern Savanna divides into a coordinate set of smaller groups (D25, K40, L20-40, M40–50–60, N21) and one large group, which we might term Eastern Bantu. This in turn divides into northern (E, F, G, J, M10–20–30, N10, P10–20) and southern Eastern Bantu (K21, N20–30–40, P30, S). This is based on lexical innovation, i.e. the shared occurrence across a set of languages of words which are either borrowings from outside the system, or are phonological or semantic modifications of older inherited items. The model is the classic family tree: innovations starting at a node language is inherited by its offspring.

Ehret provides his own historical interpretation (Ehret 1998). The ancestors of the Eastern Bantu moved out of the rainforest to the west of the Great Lakes by just after 1000 BC. During the following millennium they moved slowly east and south, splintering into smaller groups on the way. Starting in the last centuries BC and finishing during the first centuries AD, the northern groups had moved into East Africa as far as the coast, the southern groups had passed west of Lake Tanganyika and diffused south into what is now Malawi, Zambia, Zimbabwe, Mozambique, and South Africa by AD 400. Dates (based on archaeological correlations) places, and specific movements are more explicit than Vansina's.

5.3.3 Our reaction to these two proposals

Our comment on BCM and Ehret is predictable, and BCM make essentially the same point themselves in their Introduction. Any lexically based model certainly reflects inheritance but it also reflects geographical and social conditions. Geographically, the longer communities are adjacent, the more vocabulary will seep across language boundaries. Socially dominant communities spread their lexical influence out as long as they are dominant, only to be replaced later as their fall is parallelled by the rise of other centers. As we have just seen, Forest groups have had four or five thousand years of these geo-graphical and social conditions, non-Forest groups a little less. The net effect is that of a kaleidoscope, with over 500 particles constantly separating and joining. We should not expect today's lexical groupings, today's tree diagrams, to reflect accurately the events of the last three millennia BC any more than we would be able to see the bottom of a pond through choppy, muddy water. We might expect the smaller and intermediate groups set out above to reflect recent events reasonably accurately, but we treat lexically based mega-groups with caution.

We now propose groupings we regard as having a good chance of reflecting older his-tory, because they are based on innovatory features we think of old standing. Following what we said about diffused features in §2, we do not regard the boundaries of some of the proposed groupings below as absolute – groups have cores while features diffuse across peripheries, making firm boundaries hard to determine at a distance of several millennia.

5.3.4 No unambiguous single '(Eastern) Savanna' group

The languages in the east, center, south, and southwest of the Bantu area are often called Savanna languages, and a Savanna group, variously labelled, has emerged in most recent classifications, including Ehret's (1999:53). Savanna is usually analyzed as comprising an eastern group and a western group, or an eastern, central and western group. 'Savanna' languages are generally more homogeneous than those in the Forest. This can be seen by considering levels of similarity provided by lexicostatistics. Thus Bastin *et al.*'s (1983) figures for inter-language comparisons for languages in the east and south fall mainly in the 50–60 (and 40) percent range of similarity, while those for the Forest languages fall predominantly in the 30–40 percent range, with some figures in the 20s, reflecting the longer period over which they have lost vocabulary. Bastin *et al.*

(1983:175) cite Swadesh's glottochronology:

% of shared vocabulary	Years of separation
86	500
74	1,000
64	1,500
55	2,000
40	3,000
30	4,000
22	5,000
16	6,000

While we doubt the accuracy of glottochronology for gauging time in individual cases, the general time scale suggested here fits well with the broad historical picture as suggested by historians, outlined above. The picture suggests that, since Savanna languages are of more recent formation, it ought to be easier to find some pan-Savanna non-lexical features, because there has been less time for older features inherited from a common ancestor to be overlaid by local, areal, recent, convergent features.

We have not found this to be true. Having examined the geographical distribution of our thirty or so features we found nothing non-lexical supporting the notion of a Savanna branch of Bantu. So we examined features which others in the past have suggested as being pan-Savanna:

- One such is BS, a process whereby earlier (non-nasal) consonants became (strident) fricatives, via a number of intermediate stages, when followed by the two highest vowels *i, u in the seven-vowel system. A majority of Bantu languages have undergone this process. The distribution of those that have not is revealing. The great majority of Forest languages show no signs of BS, although the data in Guthrie (1971:33–83) indicate possible BS in A81 and some B40, B70, B80 languages. This seems at first to support a split of Forest vs. Savanna, but then we see that BS has also not occurred in E50 (Kenya), most of Zone F (Tanzania), some J languages (JD 40–50, JE40, southern JE30), M11, a few other languages in East Africa (Labroussi 1999, Nurse 1999) and perhaps not in Tswana in South Africa (Creissels 1999). Since most of these standouts are geographically peripheral to the Bantu area, the current distribution of BS could be interpreted as resulting from either of two processes. One is inheritance: out of some intermediate proto-language(s) with BS emerged others that bore it also. The other would be diffusion across sets of languages in the post-PB era. Either way, it did not reach the languages of isolated, marginal, or 'resistant' communities. It apparently happened after PB; it does not support the division of East and West, and while its absence characterizes most Forest languages, they are not thereby unique. It should be noted that BS or BS-like phenomena are also found in non-Bantu Niger-Congo languages, such as Beboid and Noni. Whether these are related or independent phenomena remains to be established.
- Another such feature is the Ganda/Meinhof's Rule, a process which deletes the first C in sequences of NCVNC. The usefulness of this as a historical tool is discussed in Nurse (1999). As an active process it is limited to E50 and parts of J, but traces occur in a small set of lexical items across eastern and southern Bantu. Ehret (1999:55) suggests that it characterizes Eastern Savanna languages, which is at odds with facts suggested by Herbert (1977), who suggests it is also found in some Forest (C) languages, and Hyman (pc), who finds it in A62. Its exact domain is hard to determine

because the number of eligible words and of reliable dictionaries, especially for Forest languages, is small. We tend to agree with Meeussen (1967) and Herbert in seeing the considerable extent of this as probably best explained as inherited from PB but until the data base improves, we will not use this further.

- A third feature recently proposed as a Savanna feature (Ehret 1999:56) is the presence of asymmetric vowel height harmony in verb extensions. This is based on Hyman (1999, same volume), who shows that this characterizes many (not all) Savanna languages and does not occur in Forest. Hyman expresses himself carefully on the value of this feature. In one place (1999:236) he says: 'My tentative suggestion will be that this asymmetry was introduced into proto-Savanna Bantu after this split [from Forest: editors] was effected', while later (p. 256) he says it 'could be viewed either as the result of areal spread *or* as a one-time innovation affecting the relatively coherent subbranch of Bantu in which it occurs'. The second part of this latter claim does not propose asymmetric vowel height harmony as establishing a Savanna branch by itself but as supporting such a branch already established by other means.

Our point is that it has not yet been so established. The only evidence so far adduced is lexical. If one forces lexicostatistical methods on to a group of related languages they are bound to result in some grouping, but in our view this particular grouping has no a priori historical validity. There is at present no convincing evidence for a historical Savanna Bantu and therefore also not for any large subsets of it, such as Eastern (or Central) or Western Savanna.

However, there is some evidence for a grouping which we might call Northeast Savanna (Ehret's Northern subset of the Eastern Bantu subset of Eastern Savanna), partly based on lexical evidence to be sure, but mainly based on the geographical distribution of the process known as Dahl's Law (Davy and Nurse 1982). Although Ehret (1999:54) and Nurse (1999:20–1) do not entirely agree on its southern limit, they agree that it characterizes at least E50, E60–74a, F21–2, J, NEC, and G60 (Ehret adds G50, Rufiji-Ruvuma, M10–20–30). Unusual dissimilation such as involved in Dahl's Law is unlikely to have arisen independently at different times and places. The process is also unlikely to have diffused, because at least some of the groups attesting it (E60–74a, E50, Zone J, NEC) are not adjacent, and probably have not been so for the last 1,500 years. This would not prevent individual lexical items with the process from diffusing, which probably explains the disagreement over its presence in G50, Rufiji-Ruvuma, and M10–20–30. If the distribution of *p*-lenition, which has affected E50, E60, and J, is added, we can imagine a single ancestor for this whole group, either a single language or a dialect chain in which E50, E60–74a, and J were necessarily adjacent, spoken by a community probably living somewhere in the Great Lakes area.

South of the large Northeastern Savanna just outlined we see a set of smaller groups, outlined in §5.2: M10–M20 and maybe M30 ('Corridor'), M40–50, N20–30–40, Rufiji-Ruvuma, S10, and Southeast (S20–60, P30). We see no clear non-lexical reason to view these as a coherent single group. A possible shared non-lexical feature is tonological. In such of these languages as have retained tone and have been described, there are shared apparent irregularities in the reflexes of *HH and *HL tone patterns (Philippson 1999). To the southwest there is yet another set of languages, traditionally also 'Savanna', those in Zones, K, L, and R (see §§5.3.5–5.3.7), which we see as primarily connected to the north and northwestern languages.

At present we see no unambiguous link other than lexical between any of these three that would justify our seeing them as forming a single genetic Savanna group. Despite this, there are tantalizing possibilities. Why is the innovated -(V)ni 'locative' only found in parts of the Northeast Savanna (E50, E60, part of NEC), P30, and Zone S: is this independent innovation, retention of an archaic feature, or the result of Zone S communities trekking south with it from East Africa? What is the significance and origin of Hyman's asymmetrical VHH in verbal extensions, which occurs in all three groups of Savanna languages, mentioned above? What is the status of BS, which again occurs in many but not all Savanna languages? Wald (1994) has a set of other areal features, which he sees as having diffused along the eastern side of the continent.

5.3.5 Western Bantu

The largest grouping to stand out on the basis of what can reasonably be regarded as post-PB innovation is a grouping we might call Western Bantu (this is not necessarily coterminous with groups called 'Western Bantu' by others). It shares two features, with a slightly different geographical distribution, but the common distributional core consists of A, B, C, H40, K40, L10, L30, L40, and parts of D20 and M60. This area might be larger (e.g. it might include D10–30 and more H and K) and might be amended with a better data base.

The two defining features are nasal assimilation (Greenberg 1951), and suffixal -i 'affirmative anterior, near past' combined with the total or near total absence of forms of -ile. The first of these is fairly clear: the languages affected do not allow voiced non-nasal coronals when preceded by a nasal consonant in the preceding syllable (see Ch. 3). It also occurs in H10, other K languages, R, and M40. By contrast, the second occurs in some D10 and in D30, D50, H30 (and G22?).

The second is less clear, because it depends on how -i is interpreted. Within Bantu, there are three verbal morphemes, -ile, -i, and a third involving a copy of the stem vowel. All are suffixes, all typically refer to anterior and/or (near) past, all consist of or involve a high front vowel. In our view, these are too many similarities to be explained by mere coincidence. -ile appears almost universally and clearly across Bantu outside Zones A, B, C, the evidence for it in these northwestern zones being unclear or absent. As far as we know it is not attested in Niger-Congo outside Bantu (perhaps Igbo?) so can be assumed to have PB status and to have been innovated within PB. The second, -i, occurs in Zones A, B, C, L, and in ambiguous form or in parts of the zone in D, E (G22?), H, and K. That is, it occurs in the northwest languages, and to a limited extent outside. However, there are other -i, one being associated with negatives, a second with stative reference. If, as seems likely, these can be associated with the first -i, then its distribution expands somewhat. The third suffix consists of a single vowel which copies directly that of the verb stem vowel (with certain restrictions). This range of vowels obviously includes /i/. It has a more limited geographical distribution: K, L, R, and parts of D, H, and M. These are mostly languages which are adjacent or not far apart. That this current distribution might once have been wider is suggested by the presence of this suffix in southern Swahili and Comorian, geographically far removed from the other languages.

Traditionally, -ile is treated separately, the most widely accepted explanation to date being that of Voeltz (1980), deriving it from a reconstructed PB stem *-gil- 'do' via grammaticalization and suffixation at a time when the auxiliary followed the lexical verb. However, another explanation offers itself, which would link all three suffixes, as follows. As far as we know, two of the three occur outside Bantu and are thus wider in distribution than mere Narrow Bantu. Thus -i occurs in at least Akan (J. Stewart, pc) and Zande, a Ubangian language of Zaire, and -ile with allomorphs occurs in at least southern Igbo (V. Manfredi, pc). Let us assume -*i* to be of Niger-Congo origin and the oldest of the three suffixes. It was inherited by pre- or early Bantu and underwent two kinds of change. On the one hand, it underwent an extension whereby the single final vowel developed alloforms which reflected the stem vowel. This is based on a scenario suggested by Grégoire (1979). These vowel harmony forms are considered below, under Westcentral Bantu. The other development would have involved -*i* developing two allomorphs, [ile] after short stem (C(V)) verbs, and [i] after other verbs. A similar allomorphy still occurs in some Zone A languages. These allomorphs evolved into two separate morphemes, which became distributed geographically differently. Almost no Bantu language has reflexes of both today. In this scenario, both -*ile* and the vowel harmony suffix are innovations, while -*i* is a retention. (We recognize that some details need to be examined here: the geographical distribution of -*i* and -*ile*, the height of the two /i/, and the allomorphy in Zone A and perhaps elsewhere.)

Innovation is acknowledged to be more useful diagnostically than retention. In this scenario, the distribution of -*ile*, as later innovation, would be more useful than that of -*i*. However, at present we take a middle position here, by simply regarding affirmative -*i* and -*ile* as being in geographically complementary distribution, and regarding this distribution as significant.

5.3.6 Forest Bantu

The next largest group comprises A, B, C, large parts of H, and most (how much?) of D10–20–30, i.e. a subset of the previous group. The three innovations defining Forest are: (1) $*g > k$, and maybe the loss of $*k$, although this is not so widespread. (2) the independent prefix being extended to the dependent prefix, typically in classes 4 and 6, although occasionally extending to other classes (e.g. *mi-ti mi-gwa* 'trees fall', and not **miti i-gwa*), and (3) locatives being expressed by prepositions rather than nominal affixes. Bantu has three patterns for expressing locatives (Grégoire 1975): the use of the prefixes of classes 16–18, the use of suffixal -*(V)ni*, and the use of prepositions. The first is so widespread as to make safe its assumption for PB, and Watters (Ch. 14) says that Grassfields Bantu languages have 'residual or foreshadowing forms' of classes 16, 17 (and 18?), although not as prefixes. Note also Noni (Bantoid) *fo-* (Hyman, pc). The second seems to be local innovation, limited to the northeast and south. The last, while occurring sporadically across Bantu, is more solidly attested in the Forest.

Of the three innovations we are claiming for Forest, we think (1) the most solid, as (2) and (3) might be explained by diffusion, which is less likely for (1). Details of (3) need verifying: while the general pattern is widespread in Forest, the details vary somewhat, leading to the possibility that this might be a diffused calque.

This raises the status and origin of diffused features in Forest. To the west of the Forest languages lies the whole gamut of related Niger-Congo languages, characterized typologically by a set of features. These include, with their rough extent in Forest indicated in brackets: the phonetic reduction of strings so that often only one syllable of the word remains (much A, some B); the subsequent reduction of inflectional and derivational morphology (much A, at least some B20); the emergence of serial verbs (A70–80–90); replacement of the verbal subject marker by the use of independent pronouns (A40–80, B20, B70, C20 …). The last two presumably happened as devices to indicate morphosemantic categories threatened by morphological reduction, itself brought about by phonetic reduction. All this appears to be local and later areal innovation affecting Bantu and non-Bantu Niger-Congo languages.

5.3.7 Westcentral Bantu

A final group to emerge has a core of K (K10, K30–40), L (L20, 60), R (R20–30–40: R10?), parts of D10–20–30, and parts of H, and therefore might also well be a subset or extension of Western Bantu. It is defined by three features, of which the first is clearly innovation: (1) the vowel copy suffix 'anterior' and/or '(near) past', just mentioned, which is also found embarrassingly in two adjacent places on the East Coast, as mentioned; (2) negatives being wholly or partly expressed by a set of clitics of CV shape (*ki*, *ke*, *ka*); and (3) the neutralization of the inherited negative contrast. PB was characterized by a morphosyntactic contrast between two negatives, one prefixal and occurring in independent clauses, the other post-subject and occurring in dependent clauses. Westcentral languages have mostly neutralized this.

This set needs further examination, (1) because of its occurrence in southern Swahili and Comorian, and (2, 3) because the details are diverse and the origin not well understood.

As we saw in §5.3.4 above, this Westcentral group is mixed in that it also shares some features with groups to the south, east and northeast, features however whose status is unclear.

5.3.8 How to interpret Western, Forest, and Westcentral Bantu?

As constituted, these three overlap geographically. Western and Forest share A, B, C, and parts of H, Westcentral shares groups outside A, B, and C with Forest and Western. That is, northwestern, central, and western languages are better defined by apparent shared, although crisscrossing, innovations than are eastern/southern Bantu languages. Eastern/southern ('Savanna') languages are conservative and typologically more like PB, whereas Western, Forest, and Westcentral are innovative.

The distribution of these overlapping patterns might be explained in one of three ways. Either at one time there was ancestral to all three groupings a protolanguage, in which the innovations arose: in this scenario the innovations were initially coterminous but later lost severally in different parts of the area. Or they started at different points on a continuous area and were carried along by small-scale migrations of communities as their languages emerged and differentiated. Or the people were relatively stable but the innovations diffused wave-like across contiguous language communities. Our inclination at present is to favor one of the latter scenarios. The general distribution favors that, as does the fact that if they were all once part of a very early ancestral forest language, traces would be expected also in eastern and southern Savanna languages, which also once came out of the forest.

Before these models and scenarios can be accepted, the facts and distributions have to be better checked.

5.4 Summary

Guthrie's general classification (1967–71) is referential and, in an expanded version, worth keeping for that reason. It, and especially its zones, have little historical reality – as defined in §1 above – and we set out to present a tentative alternative proposal. We wanted this to be based on the use, not of vocabulary, but of phonological and morphological innovations shared by subsets of Bantu. We started with a slightly modified version of Guthrie's groups (§5.1) because most are essentially correct. We arranged them into larger sets (§5.2), using the work of others and our own judgment. What we present in (§§5.1, 5.2) is hardly controversial. We then applied a template of thirty phonological and morphological features across Bantu: some were useful, some not. We then drew up a few large groupings on the basis of our interpretation of the few features we found significant (§5.3).

Four large groups emerged. We have called them Western Bantu (the languages of Zones A, B, C, H40, K40, L10, L30–40, parts of M60, possibly some or all of D10–30 and other H and K), Forest Bantu (a subset of Western: A, B, C, parts of parts of H and D10–30), Westcentral Bantu (another subset of Western, comprising K10–30–40, L20, L60, R20–30–40: R10?, and parts of H and D10–30), and Northeastern Savanna (E50, E60/E74a, (northern) F21–2, F33–4, J, NEC, G60 (and maybe G50, Rufiji-Ruvuma, M10–20–30)). Not all Bantu languages are included in these four megagroups, there being two sets of exceptions: on the one hand several viable small sets of languages in the southeast of the area, on the other hand various peripheral languages whose group allegiance is not clear because for many centuries, even millennia, they have absorbed linguistic material from various sides. The Westcentral group has features from the north and east. In general we can say that geographically western and northwestern languages share more features than do eastern and southern languages, and that these shared features appear to result from innovation (or possibly areal diffusion?) rather than retention.

6 HISTORICAL IMPLICATIONS, FUTURE DIRECTIONS

6.1 Historical implications

The classification sketched above is not radically different from those currently on display (BCM 1999, Ehret 1999) and their interpretations (Vansina 1990, 1995, Ehret 1998). The main differences are three.

Our analysis underlines the relative strength of the historical connections between what we have called Forest, Western, and Westcentral (Zones A, B, C, western parts of D, H, L, K, R). This suggests to us an original community or continuum, located somewhere in the northwest of the current area, with a gradual spread of people, mainly south, partly east. For some time, language differentiation would have been relatively small, developing into a chain of communities, with innovations passing along. So far, our interpretation resembles that suggested by BCM.

Independently, a community ancestral to what in §5.3.4 we have called Northeast Savanna emerged to the east of the Forest and diffused across what we call today East Africa. Where this and the previous group came in contact, to the west of the Great Lakes, it left a mixed set of languages (D10–20–30), a picture further sullied by many centuries of contact with Ubangian and Sudanic languages.

To the southeast, we see the groups of languages in Zones S, P, N, and most of M. We see a relatively weak internal connection between the groups involved and between them and other groups. This weak connection is not so significant historically – all Bantu languages were carried out of Cameroon and across Zaire, at dates largely established by archaeology. What is less clear is whether their ancestral community or communities moved first into East Africa and then turned south, or whether they moved more directly southeast. The fact that they share no obvious innovations with the western groups we outline in §§5.3.5–5.3.7 rather suggests a loose affinity with the Northeast Savanna group.

The communities ancestral to those of today were mostly *in situ* by some two millennia ago in the east and south, earlier in the west and north. Prior to that, and certainly after that, the lines between the larger groups, and particularly those between our western group and those to the east, started to blur. Linguistic features, particularly vocabulary, started to cross group lines, and older links were dimmed. Some communities were fairly stationary and interacted at the periphery they shared with neighbors. In other situations, communities must have given up their language but carried bits of it over with them into their new adopted language. This becomes clear when looking at the results provided by the different lexicostatistical approaches in BCM: some of the groups in D, L, and M have different affiliations using different statistical models. It is equally clear when Ehret discusses tectonic effects and language shift for most of the same groups. It is most striking in zones L, K, and R (§5.3.7). We see these as originally western languages, whose umbilical cord was with the languages to their north. Yet Ehret finds a considerable body of lexical innovation, over sixty items shared with other Savanna Bantu languages, spoken by all the communities to the east and north of them. (It is striking that he finds a very much smaller body of lexical innovation uniquely defining his Western Savanna languages – R, K, L.) Not just vocabulary: non-lexical features, for instance, some of those mentioned at the end of §5.3.4, are shared by all Savanna languages and not by any or most Forest languages. Our current explanation for these is that they diffused across the Savanna communities, once they had formed a more or less continuous chain from southwest to northeast.

6.2 Future directions

The proposals offered above are tentative, meant to stimulate debate, and offer several possibilities for future work.

For several of the features on which our proposals are based we are sadly short of basic data of certain kinds for several areas (A, B, C, D10–30, H). The verbal suffixes, prepositional locatives, and negative clitics certainly need more attention. New data might amend the proposals.

The groups set out in §§5.2 and 5.3 need to be fleshed out and solid supporting innovations proposed. So, e.g. Zone J has been much heralded but so far no proper non-lexical historical innovations have been offered to justify it, and even the validity of the lexical innovations proposed by Schoenbrun are doubted by Muzale (1998). For §5.3 it can be seen that the shared innovations for each megagroup are few – is this because the proto-period for each was short and far distant, or is it because there is more to be found?

Can better groupings be worked out? Are there ways of better integrating the peripheral languages and groups? This will depend on several variables. One is that we have hitherto relied heavily on the use of vocabulary – it is time to move on to the use of phonological, morphological, and morphosynatic features. In our opinion, at present phonological patterns offer more hope than morphosyntactic ones, because shared phonological changes are not only systematic and irreversible, but are also currently better understood than morphosyntactic changes. Another need is for additional models. The models we have used during the twentieth century – binary trees, migrations, divergence – have taken us a long way but we need to supplement them now with more detailed analyses of contact and convergence situations. Finally, we should also make the data and methods more open to inspection, perhaps electronically. Judgments about lexical innovation and lexical relatedness depend crucially on the raw data and the phonological judgments being available for inspection. BCM (1999:8) say that 'in making cognation judgments, they ... took into account the systematic sound changes known to affect each language, but faced with minor variation they preferred to be inclusive'. That is, the rules could be bent. Without access to the lexical and phonological data, readers are not able to refute or support the hypotheses. We would not believe a biochemist who advanced hypotheses without showing her data.

REFERENCES

Bastin 1978, 1979, 1983a; Bastin *et al.* 1983, 1999; Davy and Nurse 1982; Dieu and Renaud 1983; Ebobisse 1989; Ehret 1998, 1999; Gowlett 1989; Grégoire 1975, 1979; Grimes 2000; Guthrie 1948, 1967–71; Hedinger 1984; Heine 1973; Henrici 1973; Herbert 1977; Hinnebusch 1981, 1999; Hombert and Hyman 1999; Hyman 1999; Jacquot and Richardson 1956; Janson 1991/2; Janssens 1992–3; Kliemann 1997; Kuperus 1985; Kutsch Lojenga 1994a, 1994b, 1995, 1999; Labroussi 1999; Ladefoged *et al.* 1971; Lowe and Schadeberg 1997; Mann *et al.* 1987; Meeussen 1967; Möhlig 1979, 1981; Motingea 1996; Mous and Breedveld 1987; Muzale 1998; Nurse 1988, 1994/5, 1999; Nurse and Hinnebusch 1993; Nurse and Philippson 1980; Philippson 1998; Polak-Bynon 1980a; Schadeberg and Mucanheia 2000; Schoenbrun 1994; Vansina 1990, 1995; Voeltz 1980; Wald 1994; Williams 1975.

CHAPTER ELEVEN

GRAMMATICALIZATION

Tom Güldemann

1 INTRODUCTION

The still central topic of grammaticalization research to explain how grammatical mark-ers (henceforth *grams*) emerge from lexical items or different grams has been, though not under this term, an important concern of Bantuistics since the earliest studies. One finds reliable etymological reconstructions of individual grams and observations on how cer-tain gram types evolve (see, e.g. Meinhof 1906/1948:113–14, 125–6, 176, 190) as well as rather fancy speculations (ibid.:63–4 on the origin of individual noun class prefixes). Yet, grammaticalization today no longer deals only with so-called *gram class-formation* (see Himmelmann 1992:16–18). It can be and often is conceived of as language change leading in general to *grammatical structure*. The problem of how to conceptualize and conclusively define the notion of grammar has also led to the concept of grammatical-ization becoming very diversified. While grammar traditionally comprises the two pur-portedly static and discrete domains of morphology and syntax, it is viewed in a very different and broader sense as the ever changing 'collectively possessed inventory of forms available for the construction of discourse' (Hopper in Bright 1992, I:366f., see also Hopper 1987). It is impossible here to tackle such theoretical issues or to discuss other general problems in grammaticalization. The reader should consult instead major works in this thriving research discipline like Givón (1979a), Lehmann (1995 [1982]), Heine and Reh (1984), Traugott and Heine (1991), Heine *et al.* (1991), Himmelmann (1992), Hopper and Traugott (1993), Bybee *et al.* (1994), Pagliuca (1994), or Giacalone Ramat and Hopper (1998). What most scholars agree on is that a grammaticalization change is the result of a complex composite of factors. Even when disregarding the important sociolinguistic parameters that determine the actuation of a given linguistic pattern leading eventually to its establishment within a speech community, there still remain several factors which directly relate to its function as a complex expression conveying meaning: for example, the semantic components of the individual linguistic signs involved, their relation to other signs on the paradigmatic dimension, and – most importantly – the larger communicative setting wherein an expression is used (including all its accompanying discourse-pragmatic implicatures).

An instructive example is the functional divergence of subordinate markers triggered by the variable position of the dependent clause: Swahili *kwamba* – a complementizer 'that' with a *postposed* subordinate clause – acquires a conditional reading when the dependent clause comes first.

(1) *kuamba yuwa~fáni-a   haya   a-ta~fung-o-a*
     SUB   CL1:TA~do-Ø   this   CL1-ꜰᴜᴛ~arrest-PASS-Ø
     'If he does this, he shall be imprisoned'
     (Krapf 1850:128, cited in Miehe 1979:232)

Similar effects with other subordination markers like the conjunction *kuti* in Shona (Güldemann 2002:267) or verb affixes encoding simultaneous taxis (compare (21) and (22) below, see Güldemann 1998 for more discussion) show that this is not an idiosyncratic case. There are no inherent semantic features of the individual grams explaining this change completely. It is first of all the coincidence of extending a dependent clause to a context where it is treated as given information and the general topicality of conditionals (Haiman 1978) that activates a novel reading of the entire preposed proposition.

Thus grammaticalization should not be described merely as a chain *lexeme > gram₁ > gram₂* ordering different meanings of one linguistic sign, but in terms of the expansion of an entire structure into new contexts of uses (see *inter alia* Himmelmann 1997 for such an approach). These contexts form a continuum linked to each other via relationships of family resemblance. The more fine-grained an analysis, the more apparent the formal and functional similarity between individual contexts will be. This is due to grammaticalization being a gradual process. Consequently, linguists make somewhat arbitrary decisions on when some pattern is incipient or fully developed as a *grammatical* construction or which function is clearly distinct from another related one. Regarding the latter aspect, linguists do have intuitions which class of uses in the continuum they should focus on in their categorization due to their experience that languages cross-linguistically tend to code similar linguistic functions. Nevertheless, one should keep in mind that a discrete functional category is a methodological abstraction: a *dative* in one language need not have the same extension of uses as in another one. Grammaticalization is comparable across different languages and different linguistic items; at the same time every process has its own specific history.

Despite the previous remarks, the following discussion cannot treat individual cases of grammaticalization in any great depth. Due to limitations in space, it will be biased towards the morphological makeup of Bantu languages and will focus on how the results of grammaticalization research can be utilized for their historical study.

2 BANTU WORD FORMS, MORPHOLOGY AND THEIR GRAMMATICALIZATION HISTORY

Morphologically complex word forms of the same functional domain often have a fairly strict order of slots filled by elements of a definable class. This synchronic ordering in a given language, called here morphotaxis, frequently correlates with the order of syntactic constituents in an earlier reconstructed stage. This can be explained by the attested process of univerbation of a loose syntactic structure into a morphologically complex word whereby constituent order becomes petrified in morphotactic regularity. Givón (1971) expressed this as *today's morphology is yesterday's syntax*. This historical approach to morphology can be applied fruitfully to most parts of speech in Bantu languages. The following remarks can only be an eclectic collection of the enormous variety of grammaticalization phenomena.

2.1 Verbal morphology

The verbal word encoding the state of affairs in a clause is the structurally most complex part of speech in Bantu. The importance of suprasegmentals which are extensively employed for marking clause linkage, certain focus types, or TAM-features has hardly been the subject of comparative work and cannot be considered. Its segmental structure, however, is described across Bantu in terms of a fixed order of individual element classes. The traditional schema as laid out in Meeussen (1967:108–11) will be simplified here in that some distinctions are combined into abstract positions defined more rigidly by order while disregarding certain other distinctions.

SLOT	(preinitial)	initial	(postinitial)^n	(preradical)^n	radical	(prefinal)^n	final	(postfinal)
FUNC-	TAM^{li}/	subject	TAM/	object	verb root	TAM/	TAM	participant/
TIONS	negation/		negation			valence		negation^{li}/
	clause type^{li}		clause type^{li}			change		clause type^{li}

FIGURE 11.1 THE MORPHOLOGICAL STRUCTURE OF FINITE VERB FORMS IN BANTU

Notes: (…) possibly empty; ^{n}possibly multiple occurrence; ^{li}presumably local innovations.

On account of comparative and internal reconstruction and processes still observable in Bantu today the core of this morpheme sequence can be shown to originate historically in a more isolating syntactic structure. A comparison of Bantu with its closest relatives within Bantoid such as Tikar is especially fruitful. There one finds two types of constituent order depending on the presence or absence of certain auxiliaries. The contrastive examples use deliberately pronominal participants:

(2) (a) *wù   sh-ê   mùn*
        2S.PRO   say-IRR   1S.PRO
        'Si tu me l'avais dit, …'
        (Stanley 1991:71)

     (b) *à   yɛn-nâ   mùn*
         CL1.S   see-PFV   1S.PRO
         'Il m'a vu.'
         (ibid.:247)

(3) (a) *mùn   kèn-mɛ   wù   nun   twɛ-li*
        1S.PRO go-PFV   2S.PRO   CL1.O   bring-Ø
        'Je m'en vais te l'amener.'
        (ibid.:136)

     (b) *à   tă   nun   fyɔ̀-a*
         CL1.S   IPFV   CL1.O   make.fun.of-Ø
         'Il plaisante sur lui.'
         (ibid.:105)

The examples (2a,b) with irrealis mood and perfective aspect show a clause order S-V-O, while (3a,b) with an auxiliary verb and imperfective aspect have an order S-AUX-O-V. Both orders are paralleled by what we find morphologically within the verbal word of modern Bantu. Given that Tikar verb stems are also subject to final changes triggered by the respective TAM-category and can be extended by derivational suffixes (Stanley 1991:355–84) we conclude that a language of this type has all the structural ingredients to develop an agglutinative verb form of the Bantu type via a process of univerbation of its more loose predicate structure. Consider the Swahili word:

(4)   *a-me-ni~on-a*
      CL1-PERF-1S~see-Ø
      'He has seen me.'

The *initial* slot is the result of grammaticalization of subject cross-reference (Givón 1976). As obligatory subject agreement is the ultimate criterion in Bantu of a stem's *verbiness* (see 'defective' verbs like **-di* or **-ti* sometimes taking only this inflection), this is tied to so-called *host class-formation* (see Himmelmann 1992:17–18, 21–2 under *carrier class-formation*), i.e. the emergence of a fixed co-occurrence pattern of grammaticalizing signs and full lexical signs whereby the latter become a formally well-defined lexical category.

The *postinitial* slot of Bantu results from the grammaticalization of the syntactic main verb in a complex two-verb predicate and can be identified with the AUX-position in Tikar. To this date this process has remained the most productive cradle of new verb morphology in Bantu which is evidenced by the immense amount of literature referring to it (for some recent contributions see Nsuka Nkutsi 1986, Botne 1989, 1990, Emanatian 1992, Nurse and Hinnebusch 1993: Ch. 4, Güldemann 1996). It is important that the content verb following the grammaticalizing auxiliary can be instantiated in variable morphological forms: (a) a plain stem (especially Rainforest Bantu), (b) a verbal noun (especially Savannah Bantu) and (c) a finite dependent verb form. The possibly substantial linguistic material between the auxiliary's subject marker and the content verb stem is often affected by truncation whereby every particular case has its own dynamics as to what of the original phonetic substance will survive this process. Meeussen's distinction in this position between *limitatives, formatives,* and (his negative) *postinitials* is already dimly discernible in Tikar and may be explained by differences in semantic scope and historical layering in grammaticalization (Hopper and Traugott 1993:124–6).

The *preradical* position of object cross-reference almost universal in Savannah Bantu can be assumed to be a remnant of object preposing in a Tikar-type AUX-construction as in (3). Given that most conjugation forms in Bantu do have a morpheme in the postfinal, earlier AUX-position, it is conceivable that the pre-stem position became generalized for pronouns. This was presumably enhanced by a particular focus configuration frequently found across Bantu. The postverbal position is associated with the pragmatic function to present new, asserted information. An object concord, however, most often refers to something given and extrafocal which would disfavor its place after the verb.

The three Bantu slots *radical, prefinal* and *final* show profound interaction and a high degree of phonetic fusion (see Hyman 1993, 1999). This again finds a parallel in Tikar's fairly grammaticalized verb suffixes encoding, as in Bantu, valence changes and some TAM-features. Thus, they seem to constitute the oldest stratum of verbal morphology in Bantoid in general. Yet, parallel to postinitials, some Bantu prefinals go back to younger grammaticalization layers. For example, Schadeberg (1994) proposes a verbal origin for the extension **-ad-* and Schladt (1998) explains the emergence of the reciprocal extension **-an-* via a process of gradual infiltration of the comitative marker *na* into the verb stem.

Bantu *postfinals* are mostly derived from pronominal enclitics. The placing of object markers after the verb instead of using the preradical slot in a number of Rainforest Bantu languages can be related to the alternative S-V-O clause order available in Bantoid and shown in (2) for Tikar. The functional dynamics of how postfinal pronominals came to encode – depending on the context – also such different functions as subject cross-reference, relative clause status, or negation still remain largely unexplored. This is probably due to Bantu-internal processes. Yet, at least the postfinal *-ni marking plurality of the addressee (see Schadeberg 1977) seems to go back to the pre-Bantoid era because reflexes appear already in Igboid, another branch of Benue-Congo (see also below for Tikar).

That the derivation of Bantu morpheme slots from loose predicate constituents in genetically close languages has some historical reality is supported by the observation that Tikar and Bantu elements in related positions are often similar in form and meaning: compare as potential cognates the class-1 subject marker in (2b) and (4), the Tikar auxiliary kɛ 'être encore' (Stanley 1991:148–50) with the persistive marker *-kí- reconstructed as a Bantu postinitial, the Tikar derivational suffixes encoding verbal pluractionality -a', -ka', ... ga' (ibid.:360–3) with the Bantu prefinal *-a(n)g- and final *-a, the Tikar irrealis suffixes -i and -è (ibid.:70–6) with the Bantu finals *-i and *-e, or the Tikar suffix -è-ni marking plural addressees in imperatives (ibid.:57–61) with the functionally identical Bantu postfinal *-ni. A careful comparative study will reveal whether these items are indeed etymologically related.

Morphemes at the margins of a Bantu verb form are often the result of innovative developments in this family due to its extreme tendency to predicate-centered coding of grammatical functions. A remark regarding the *postfinal* slot was made above. For *preinitial* morphemes one can say that they are mostly the result of concatenation and truncation of a binary predicate structure. The first part is a finite auxiliary or a nonfinite predicator while the second part is a dependent finite form comprising the content verb. In the first case with two finite constituents, the auxiliary is subject to phonetic truncation and the *initial* of the content verb continues to encode the subject. Compare in this regard Tumbuka:

(5) ni~ti   ni~timb-e   >   ti-ni~timb-e
     1S~QUOT   1S~strike-SUBJ   INT-1S~strike-Ø
     'I say I will strike.'   'I shall strike.'
     (Young 1932:37)

In the second case, non-finite predicator and initial subject concord simply merge. Güldemann (1996, 1999a) proposes this scenario to be the source of preinitial negatives and various markers of other functions. A typical case is the employment of the copula ni conveying 'it is ...' to mark assertive predication focus in several Kenyan languages. See an example from Masaaba:

(6) wa~tsy-a [wa < *u-a]   vs.   na~tsy-a [na < *ni-a-a]
     CL1:PAST~go-Ø   PF:CL1:PAST~go-Ø
     'He has gone.'   'He *has* gone.'
     (Purvis 1907:55)

It is especially the latter development that helps to identify the typical locus of innovation for Bantu verb morphology. Güldemann (1996) argues that elements expressing 'there is (not) ...', 'it is (not) ...' becoming proclitics to dependent verb forms condense the illocutionary act and the predicative force of an utterance. Thus, these markers of metalinguistic negation, affirmation, or assertion of truth are originally restricted to main clauses, while the highly reduced illocutive force of relative or adverbial clauses motivates their exemption from developing these pragmatically relevant functions. In general, this and other observations regarding the distribution of grams of varying age across different clause types strongly support Givón's (1979:89) statement:

> To the extent that syntactic innovation arises from reinterpretation of marked, topic-focus variants as the neutral pattern, it is expected that the clause-type which exhibits the greatest freedom of distribution of such variants – the main-declarative-affirmative-active clause – will be syntactically less conservative.

The synchronic morphotaxis of Bantu verb forms played an important role in the discussion on the earlier constituent order of this family and higher-order units like Benue-Congo or Niger-Congo as well as in general grammaticalization research dealing with the reconstruction of syntax from morphology. Givón repeatedly claimed, largely on theoretical grounds, a S-O-V clause order for pre-Bantu giving as evidence *inter alia* a general origin of verb suffixes in earlier auxiliaries and preradical object cross-reference. The above data and related discussions (Heine 1980, Williamson 1989:28–31, Claudi 1993) show that his approach is too simplistic. Considering Gensler's (1997) research one can even argue that the simultaneous existence of S-V-O and S-AUX-O-V clauses is a likely reconstruction for pre-Bantu and even older stages of the larger family. Such variability of order patterns in older chronolects must limit the capacity of syntax reconstruction which is exclusively based on synchronic morphotaxis.

It would also be a mistake to derive every gram from an older syntactic pattern within a given language. First, grams can expand within a language into word forms where they were not grammaticalized (see for some discussion Kingston 1983). Furthermore, morphemes can be borrowed. For example, the perfect marker -*me*- in Kae, a southern Swahili language of rural Zanzibar, cannot have grammaticalized there because the cline *-*mala* 'finish' > -*mele ku*- > -*me*(*ku*)- is tied to a stem-formation type found only in Northern Swahili (Miehe 1979:225–30). Thus, Kae -*me*- has its most probable origin in the language contact with urban Unguja – a variety which is grammatically close to Northern Swahili.

2.2 Nominal morphology

Much of Bantu's nominal morphology related mostly to the noun categorization system is old and its etymological reconstruction, if at all possible, will rest on a careful comparative analysis at least across the core of Niger-Congo. In principle, nominal affixes often derive from nouns that were the syntactic head of a compound or associative construction (see Haspelmath 1992). The head-*initial* noun phrase organization presumably has not changed since the pre-Bantu or even Benue-Congo stage and one can thus expect the creation of nominal *prefixes* in grammaticalization. Regarding new noun classes, this seems to have been the case with the prefix **pj*- of the Bantu diminutive class-19 which is said to be related to a stem 'small' ~ 'child' found across Niger-Congo (Kähler-Meyer 1971). Head-initial compound patterns are also responsible within Bantu for the creation of noun prefixes. Meinhof (1948:136–7) already noticed that terms for 'mother' and 'father' (C.S.1393 and 2027 in Guthrie 1967–71) have developed into prefixes of derived human nouns. The incipient stage of such a process can be observed today with the use of *mwana* 'child' in Swahili (see, e.g. Johnson 1939:150). A comparative study of such derivational devices which are widespread across the family is still lacking in Bantu philology.

Again, one must beware of always identifying morphotaxis with older syntactic configuration. Languages can acquire linguistic structures partly alien to their inherited design. For example, various noun suffixes in eastern and southern Bantu do not reflect earlier productive syntax, but could instead be accounted for by calquing from head-final non-Bantu languages (Güldemann 1999b).

Pronominal markers can also have a complex morphological history in that they can be augmented in pragmatically reinforcing structures by predicator particles. Such short clauses can be reanalyzed as non-predicative pronominal words. Givón (1974) showed that fronted content-question words preceded by a copula formed, in conjunction with a following relative clause, a clefted interrogative (for theoretical background see Schachter 1973). These can replace the older *in situ* construction and thus the original form of the question word without a copula. Compare *nani* 'who' in Swahili which presumably goes back to *ni-ani* COP-'who'. Dammann (1971) has proposed a sentential origin for various types of pronouns and demonstratives. Although some of his scenarios appear to be fairly speculative, the idea that modern demonstratives can have their origin in presentative sentences based on simple deictics is supported by general grammaticalization research (Himmelmann 1997). Following this line of reasoning, the Swahili demonstrative series with initial *h-* should be compared in structure with presentative demonstratives in other Bantu languages which have incorporated positive or negative copulas. Compare Umbundu with a predicator *ha-* 'there is':

(7)   *onjó*   *y-á-ngè*   *háyí*
      9.house   9-ASS-1S.POSS   PRS.COP:9.PROX.DEM
      'Look here, this is my house.'
      (Schadeberg 1990:20)

2.3 Function words

Not all words are morphologically complex from a synchronic viewpoint. Function words like predicators, sentence-type markers, clause and term relators, or discourse particles usually do not show paradigmatically changing elements, but are formally invariable. Historically, however, they have been recruited from other parts of speech. Their sound shape and the frozen morphology they possibly contain can give clues regarding their grammaticalization history.

Relational grams irrespective of whether they mark nominal phrases or sentence-like constituents can have a similar or even identical shape. This is due to the fact that their partly parallel functions are bound to be expressed by parallel sources. These are mostly nouns, nominalized verbs or finite dependent verb forms. A relational noun recruited for introducing both a nominal participant and an adverbial clause is exemplified by a case from Ewondo: the body part term *asú* 'face, forehead' when preceded by the preposition *á* is used as a benefactive (note the associative construction) and a reason clause marker:

(8)   (a) *a-ŋgá~lad*   *mkpámáɲ*   *íyé*   *ású*   *díé*
         CL1-REM.PAST~sew   new   cloth   LOC:5.'face'   5.AGR:CL1.POSS
         'He made the new dress for her.'
         (Redden 1979:158)

      (b) *yám*   *bĭdí*   *ású*   *é ósə*   *a~wóg*   *zie*
         cook:IMP   food   LOC:'face'   everyone   CL1:PRES~feel   hunger
         'Fix some food because everyone is hungry.'
         (ibid.:162)

Verbal nouns are also a frequent source for prepositions and conjunctions. The nominalizing element (usually the noun class prefix *ku*) can be lost in the course of grammaticalization. Compare Swahili *toka* 'from, since' which is derived from a verb meaning 'go~come out':

(9) (a) *toka   shule-ni*
         from   school-LOC
         'from the school'

     (b) *toka   tu-li-po~anz-a   ku~imb-a   katika kwaya*
         since   1P-PAST-TEMP~begin-Ø   INF~sing-Ø   in   choir
         'since the time we started singing in the choir'

The development from a quotative marker to a complement clause conjunction and possibly other subordinate functions is well known cross-linguistically. In Bantu this is also attested with the infinitives of the quotative verbs *-ti* (see Güldemann 2002 for a treatment of the entire grammaticalization complex involving this versatile stem) and *-gamba*.

The general process where a short predication undergoes concatenation toward a word with grammatical import was already observed in connection with pronominal elements. Semantically unspecific verbs like *-ba* 'be, become', *-di* 'be', *-na* 'be with' when conjugated as dependent forms are frequently employed to establish the relation between a nominal or sentential constituent and a matrix clause. For example, headless relative predicates referring notionally to a locative antecedent mark peripheral participant relations such as locatives, datives, standards in comparatives, agents in passives, or privatives (i.e. 'without'). Dammann (1971:43–4) has discussed the oblique markers *pasipo* 'without' and *kuliko* 'than' in Swahili; these are segmentally marked relatives. Many other languages encode a relative clause exclusively by suprasegmental patterns in verb forms. Compare Lwena introducing in this manner the agent in passives (the latter originates in an impersonal construction with the class-2 subject concord *va-*):

(10) *va-ci~teng-ele   ku~li   mwata wami*
      PASS-CL7~make-PAST   CL17:REL~be   elder   my
      'It was made by [lit.: where is] my elder.'
      (Horton 1949:147)

This strategy is often triggered when the involved participant is expressed by a noun of class 1a/2a (mostly proper names and kinship terms) or a pronominal element (demonstratives, independent pronouns, etc.). See a Shona example:

(11) *a-ka~taur-a   ku~na   amai*
      CL1:PAST-REM~speak-Ø   CL17:REL~be.with   1a.mother
      'He spoke to [lit.: where is with] mother.'
      (Dale 1972:316)

The same development can yield elements linking clauses. Thus Miehe (1979:121–3, 230–3) discusses cases in early Northern Swahili where relative and simultaneous taxis predicates became conventionalized as conjunctions. As a result, we find in modern Swahili items like *ijapokuwa* 'even if, although', *isipokuwa* 'except, unless', *ikiwa* 'if', or *kis(h)a* 'finally, then'.

It was shown that binary predicate structures develop into one-word verb forms. Yet this need not always be so. A case in point are inflected negative auxiliaries that can change via loss of their paradigmatic variability into preposed negative particles (see a case discussed in Güldemann 1996:296–7). These few examples should suffice to show how grammaticalization research can be applied fruitfully to the study of function words.

3 GRAMMATICALIZATION AND PHONETIC-PHONOLOGICAL PROPERTIES

Grammaticalization has a tremendous impact on the phonetic-phonological structure of a language. We have referred above to the process of univerbation creating morphologically complex words signifying the change from isolating to agglutinative and inflexional structures. 'Word' is intended here as a phonological entity and must not be confounded with the *orthographic* word of a language: e.g. there is no formal distinction between a disjunctively or conjunctively written predicate in different southern Bantu languages (see Creissels 2000 for the same problem in West Africa).

Within words, assimilation at morpheme boundaries, contraction and truncation lead to further changes in the phonetic substance of linguistic signs. In the final stages, the earlier lexical form will no longer be recognizable. At best, one can try to recover it theoretically with the help of a sophisticated method of reconstruction. The following example is the development proposed by Botne (1989:173–4) of the postinitial future marker *-ɔndɔ-* in UMbundu from a modal auxiliary *-andala* 'want' ultimately going back to a verb *-bida* 'want':

(12)   *-bida > -binda > -banda > -anda-la > -anda ku- > -anda u- > -andɔ- > -ɔndɔ-*

Phonetic truncation can go so far that a gram leaves only a suprasegmental trace on its host, as can be the case with the copulative predicator *ni* (see Spaandonck 1973). Thus, the difference in Holoholo between a nominal in citation and in an identificational clause is only tonal:

(13)   *baanĭ* [< *baáni*]   vs.   *baánĭ* [< *ní baáni*]
       'who?'   'who are they?'
       (Spaandonck 1973:98)

Which part in grammaticalizing structures undergoes truncation and loss depends on various factors. One will be the semantic relevance of a subsegment. For example, it is conceivable that the subject concord in a taxis-marking dependent verb form can be skipped when there is regular coreference with the subject of the matrix predicate. This scenario might be relevant for the emergence of a non-finite converb marking simultaneity in Chewa:

(14)   *m̥~pít-a*   *ká~mw-ɛ́r-a* [? < *initial-ka~stem]   *madzí*   *m̥*   *ⁿdji·ra*
       1S~go-PRES   SIM~drink-APPL-Ø   water   INE   path
       'I drink water from (them) while going along the path.'
       [lit.: I go along the path drinking water from (them).]
       (Watkins 1937:99)

The suprasegmental properties of words also play an important role: unaccented syllables are more prone to loss than accented ones. This factor might explain the emergence of morphologically awkward or irregular paradigms. See the following Zulu forms

with doubled subject concords (15) and a formal dissociation between different person
categories (16):

(15)   *nga~be*   *ngi~thand-a*   >   *nga:-ngi~thand-a*
       1S:REM~be:PAST   1S:SIM~love-Ø   REM.PAST.IPFV-1S~love-Ø
       'I was loving.'
       (Doke 1927a: §425)

(16)   *bengi-nga~thand-i* [*bengi* < *ngi~be ngi*]   vs.   *ubu-nga~thand-i* [*ubu* < *u~be u*]
       IMM.PAST.IPFV:1S-NEG~love-Ø   IMM.PAST.IPFV:2S-NEG~love-Ø
       'I was not loving.'   'You were not loving.'
       (ibid.: §424)

A gram can eventually lose its functionality and become petrified within another
linguistic sign. This 'process whereby new syntagmatic phonological segments are
created out of old morphemes' was called by Hopper (1994:31) *phonogenesis* – another
aspect in which grammaticalization affects the phonetic makeup of a language. In Bantu,
e.g. individual verb stems can be shown to have increased their phonetic substance via
the incorporation of earlier infinitive, reflexive, or derivational grams. This general
process can be relevant for the sound shape of grammatical items, too. For example,
a preinitial gram *ka-* which is fully productive in some languages has in various eastern
Bantu languages only remnant reflexes: most often one finds 2nd-person singular
ku < **ka-u* and class-1 *ka* < **ka-a* – significantly only from 'weak' vowel-initial subject
concords (see Güldemann 1996:237–44). The strengthening of the possessive pronouns
in the same person categories via prefixing a locative affix *ku* seems to be a similar
phenomenon (see Stappers 1986:68–9, 97–8). Another interesting observation in this
respect is the fact that innovative forms of the 1st-person singular subject concord
such as *ndi-*, *ngu-*, *ngi-*, *nga-* correlate highly with very common postinitials of Bantu
-li-, *-ku-*, *-ki-*, *-ka-*.

4   GRAMMATICALIZATION RESEARCH AND
HISTORICAL BANTU LINGUISTICS

Given that Bantu is a subgroup of Bantoid (and the latter a branch of Benue-Congo) it is
clear that successfully reconstructing the language type of the pre- or proto-Bantu era
and determining the origin of numerous grams depends on a thorough comparative
examination of related languages in Cameroon and Nigeria. Some promising fields of
investigation have been mentioned above with regard to the general properties of earlier
phrase and clause structure. As far as morphology is concerned, it is necessary to
compare the older layers of Bantu grams with bound or unbound functional items that
meet the requirement of resemblance in form, function and syntagmatic position in
Bantu's closest relatives. Since morphology can become sedimented in the phonetic
substance of lexemes it will also be useful to look at frequently occurring segments in
Bantu stems, e.g. final syllables in verbs, as far as one can plausibly hypothesize that they
formed a functional class in earlier chronolects.

Grammaticalization research is also relevant for Bantu-internal classification. Today
there exists a discrepancy between a high sophistication in *phonological* and *lexical*
comparisons and the enormous problems in implementing their results for establishing
and historically explaining an internal structure of the family. Although this is a frequent
problem of the traditional comparative method in general (see Durie and Ross 1996), the

somewhat neglected historical study of *morphology* and *syntax* in Bantuistics has contributed to this situation. While the linguistic tools in the past were limited in this field, research in diachronic typology and grammaticalization indicate that this is no longer the case.

Consider the reconstruction of morphology: a notorious problem in previous studies was to ascertain whether the existence of one form with different meanings within and across languages is an instance of *homonymy* or *polysemy* (see Hopper and Traugott 1993:69–72). Results from typologically informed grammaticalization research regarding morphotaxis, attested or plausible meaning changes, etc., improve today our ability to reach firmer conclusions – and this even when an item has changed semantically. For example, the verbal marker *-ki-* in early Bantu most probably encoded a *persistive* state of affairs, either realis as in (17) from Shona or irrealis as in (18) from Masaaba:

(17) *u-chi~ri*   *ku~ziv-a*   *nzira*   *here*
      2S-PERS~COP   INF~know-Ø   way   PQ
      'Do you still know the way?'
      (Dale 1972:274)

(18) *ba-ki~ri*   *ku~tek-a*
      2-PERS~COP   INF~cook-Ø
      'They are still (about) to cook, and so they have not yet cooked.'
      (Purvis 1907:71)

From this function other readings like *negative inceptive* and *precedence* are derived via contextual inferences. See Bemba and Lwena respectively:

(19) *ba-cilíí~bomb-a*
      2-NEG.INC~work-Ø
      'They're not yet working.' [<] 'They're [still] about to work.'
      (Givón 1969:175)

(20) *iman-a*   *ngu-ci~tal-e*   *mu-zuvo*
      wait-IMP   1S-PREC~look-SUBJ   INE-house
      'Wait, let me look in the house yet; i.e. before anything else is done.'
      (Horton 1949:126)

In a number of languages, it has become a marker of *simultaneous* or generally *imperfective subordinate clauses* and, when the latter are preposed to irrealis main clauses, *protases of open conditionals*. See Swahili:

(21) *ni-li-mw~on-a*   *a-ki~j-a*   *nyumba-ni*
      1S-PAST-CL1~see-Ø   CL1-SIM~come-Ø   house-LOC
      'I saw him coming home.'

(22) *u-ki-m~tembele-a*   *u-m~salimi-e*
      2S-COND-CL1~visit-Ø   2S-CL1~greet-SUBJ
      'If you pay him a visit, greet him!'

This list of related functions – though presumably incomplete – suffices to illustrate how one could eventually come up with a semantic map of a marker across the entire family. If we find other linguistic forms largely sharing a pattern of semantic changes – as is the case with *-ki-* (Güldemann 1996:126–49; 1998) – we possess a set of data that can be subjected to theoretical evaluation familiar from canonical historical reconstruction: languages will differ with respect to which element of such comparable items they possess and in what stage of grammaticalization; recurrent distributional configurations over a wide variety of grams may yield sets of isoglosses; there may exist quirky grammaticalization developments which have higher diagnostic value, etc. Such an element-oriented approach does not initially require the consideration of whole systems of morpheme classes and their oppositions. Family-wide surveys of individual grams with a fine-grained formal and functional evaluation as, e.g. Botne (1999) are desperately needed for such kinds of analyses. The foreseeable results, however, promise to make it worth the effort.

There is not only great potential benefit from grammaticalization research for Bantu studies. The reverse is also relevant especially owing to one factor: as a subgroup of Benue-Congo within the Niger-Congo stock, Bantu is in terms of its number of member languages the largest closely-knit family in the world (rivalled only by Oceanic in the Austronesian stock). It is the unparalleled wealth of empirical material for comparative and internal reconstruction that offers an advantage *vis-à-vis* smaller genetic units. The richness of data to work on increases the probability of identifying regular patterns of functional changes in grams and construction types. Beside changes already mentioned, many other common developments are attested in Bantu such as from impersonal to passive constructions (Givón 1976:179–80, compare (10) above), from demonstratives to relative markers (see *inter alia* Poulos 1986:291–3, Güldemann 1996:86, 91, 97, 101–3, 106, 109–10), from locative to attributive possessive expressions (Güldemann 1999c), from locative to infinitive markers (Meinhof 1948:108–9, for theoretical background see Haspelmath 1989), or from comitative to existential predicates (Heine 1997:206). Unsurprisingly, Bantu languages figure prominently in the cross-linguistic collection of grammaticalization paths by Heine *et al.* (1993). And this is only the tip of the iceberg.

More importantly, there are changes which are not (yet) attested and may even appear at first glance functionally unexpected. In a smaller family, the synchronic reflexes of such processes will usually be less solid and the interpretation of an isomorphism between different items in terms of grammaticalization must remain fairly speculative. On the basis of more empirical data in a larger family, however, the linguist might be able to state an assumed development more firmly. A telling example is the clear relation in Bantu between markers of predication focus and present progessives (Güldemann 1996:231–5, Hadermann 1996). Thus, compare the Masaaba gram for predication focus in (6) with the Haya progressive marker:

(23) *ba-mu~kóm-a*   > *ni-ba-mu~kóm-a*
      CL2-CL1~tie-PRES   PROG-CL2-CL1~tie-PRES
      'They tie him up.'   'They are tying him up.'
      (Hyman and Watters 1984:260)

In a more comprehensive study, Güldemann (forth.) argues that this phenomenon has a functional motivation the recognition of which can even lead to a modified theoretical conceptualization of the category progressive.

The examination of a large data base as provided by Bantu is even more important for the evaluation of linguistic functions that are heretofore rarely described cross-linguistically. Here, Bantu can be crucial for general insights into these phenomena and – important for grammaticalization research – for answering how they emerge and develop subsequently. For example, it is particularly interesting that such a wide variety of functions is morphologized in the finite predicate. Some of these, like the verbal marking of *theticity* or *predication focus* as discussed in Güldemann (1996:159–229), have hardly been the subject of any theoretical treatment, even more so, when restricting the analysis to coding via bound grams. The latter category is widespread in Bantu so that its presence can be assumed for pre-Bantu. Its recurrent regrammaticalization has taken different paths. A still transparent development of a preinitial marker was exemplified in (6) for Masaaba. Another marking device, a postinitial -*la*-, -*ra*- (possibly also southern Bantu -(*y*)*a*-), is historically older. Here is an example from Rwanda:

(24)   (a) *mu-gitoondo*   *Yohani*   *a-rá~kor-a*   vs.
          INE-morning   PROP   CL1-PF~work-PRES
          'In the morning John *works*.'

       (b) *Yohani*   *a~kor-a*   *mu-gitoondo*
          PROP   CL1~work-PRES   INE-morning
          'John works *in the morning*.'
          (Givón 1975a:197)

This gram may go back to an auxiliary which is cognate with the Benue-Congo verb *la* 'take', which is suggested by the fact that Hyman and Watters (1984:247) show its suppletive plural counterpart in Nupe to mark the same function of predication focus. Future research in genetically unrelated languages will show whether and to what extent one can profit from the possible progress in grammaticalization studies made in a single language family like Bantu.

ACKNOWLEDGMENT

Thanks go to Bernd Heine, Nikolaus Himmelmann and the editors of this volume for valuable comments on earlier drafts. Helen Galloway and Kim Blasco helped in improving my English.

REFERENCES

Botne 1989, 1990, 1999; Bright 1992; Bybee *et al.* 1994; Claudi 1993; Creissels 2000; Dale 1972; Dammann 1971; Doke 1927; Durie and Ross 1996; Emanatian 1992; Gensler 1997; Giacalone Ramat and Hopper 1998; Givón 1969, 1971, 1974, 1975a, 1976, 1979; Güldemann 1996, 1998, 1999a, 1999b, 1999c, 2002, forth.; Guthrie 1967–71; Hadermann 1996; Haiman 1978; Haspelmath 1989, 1992; Heine 1980, 1997; Heine and Reh 1984; Heine *et al.* 1991, 1993; Himmelmann 1992, 1997; Hopper 1987, 1994; Hopper and Traugott 1993; Horton 1949; Hyman 1993, 1999; Hyman and Watters 1984; Johnson 1939; Kähler-Meyer 1971; Kingston 1983; Krapf 1850; Lehmann 1995; Meeussen 1967; Meinhof 1948; Miehe 1979; Nsuka Nkutsi 1986; Nurse and Hinnebusch 1993; Pagliuca 1994; Poulos 1986; Purvis 1907; Redden 1979; Schachter 1973; Schadeberg 1977, 1990, 1994; Schladt 1998; Spaandonck 1973; Stanley 1991; Stappers 1986; Traugott and Heine 1991; Watkins 1937; Williamson 1989; Young 1932.

CHAPTER TWELVE

CONTACT LANGUAGES IN THE BANTU AREA

Salikoko S. Mufwene

1 INTRODUCTION

It is possible to interpret the phrase 'contact language' synonymously with 'lingua franca', viz. as that variety that enables two or more (groups of) individuals speaking different vernaculars to communicate when they come in contact with each other. The fact that, consistent with its title, *Status and use of African lingua francas*, Heine (1970) includes several traditional African languages whose morphosyntax is not significantly restructured may encourage this interpretation. However, this essay is only on a subset of that long list, focusing on varieties that have been identified misguidedly as pidgins or creoles (see below). This essay is primarily on *(Kikongo-)Kituba* and on *Lingala*, both spoken in the two Congo Republics, as well as on *Fanakalo* (also spelled *Fanagalo*), spoken primarily in South Africa today but formerly also in the mining belt stretching all the way north to the Shaba province of the Democratic Republic of the Congo, and on *Pidgin Ewondo*, spoken in Cameroon (see map 12.1). These are the most commonly cited contact languages in the literature in relation to the Bantu area. The reason for this practice may be

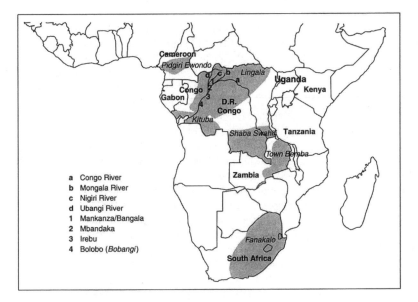

MAP 12.1 CONTACT LANGUAGES IN THE BANTU AREA

195

their highly simplified morphosyntaxes relative to their lexifiers (those languages from which they have inherited most of their vocabularies). Below, I refer to them as a group with the acronym KILIFAPE.

I also discuss *Shaba Swahili* (as a representative of inland varieties of Swahili) and *Town Bemba* (spoken in Zambia). They represent forms of traditional Bantu languages which, having been brought as exogenous varieties to colonial contact settings, have been influenced by the local and other languages they came in contact with, as well as conceptually by urban colonial and post-colonial, cosmopolitan life. Another reason is to clarify that they need not be lumped in the same category as KILIFAPE, although from the point of view of their developments under contact conditions, they represent outcomes of basically the same processes of language restructuring. That is, under specific conditions of language, dialect, or idiolect contact, some structural principles are lost, innovated, or modified, amounting to a new system for the language at the communal level. Sometimes the new, restructured system is identified as a new language or dialect, as in the case of KILIFAPE.

As fuzzy as the boundary proposed between the two subsets of language varieties is, the distinction appears useful to understanding the varying ecologies and consequences of language evolution in the Bantu area. I use the term 'ecology' as short for both the ethnographic conditions of language contact and – by analogy to 'gene pool' in biology – the feature pool constituted by the languages in contact and from which new structural principles are selected into the restructured variety. I focus on how these Bantu contact varieties evolved and, from a genetic linguistics point of view, on how they bear on our understanding of the speciation of Bantu into its many subgroups and languages. I assume the languages evolve and diversify on more or less the same pattern as parasitic species in biology, as explained in Mufwene (2001).

2 THE VARIABLE ROLE OF CONTACT: EXOGENOUS VS. ENDOGENOUS LEXIFIERS

The tradition which in genetic linguistics has invoked internally motivated change as the primary, more ordinary, more regular, or more natural reason for language change and speciation has led linguists to marginalize some languages as exceptional in having their origins in population movements and contacts. As they have been applied to KILIFAPE and to some extent to Shaba Swahili and Town Bemba, the terms 'pidgin' and 'creole' reflect this particular approach to language evolution, on which I raise issues in Mufwene (1997a, 1998, 2001). I refrain from using these labels in this essay for the following reasons among others:

1 The term 'creole' is not structurally motivated, as creoles vary among themselves regarding almost any structural feature that is claimed to be typical of them.
2 Creoles of the New World and the Indian Ocean developed in specific conditions of settlement colonization that have not been replicated where KILIFAPE emerged. The fact that the new African language varieties are outcomes of restructuring under contact conditions is not a sufficient justification, because it can be easily shown that all cases of language speciation have involved contact and restructuring to some extent. For instance, the Romance languages developed under contact conditions, and there is no evolutionary stage of English that can be dissociated from language contact. It is not obvious that in the case of Bantu languages the proto-language itself was structurally any more homogeneous than, say, the Kongo cluster of languages when

Kituba developed. Nor is it evident that it would have speciated into so many subgroups and languages if the dispersing Bantu populations had not come in contact with other ethnolinguistic groups, such as the Sudanic, Pygmy, and Khoisan populations, and/or among themselves after earlier splits. Based on archaeological and, ironically also linguistic, evidence, Vansina's (1990) and Newman's (1995) studies of the Bantu dispersal suggests that contact must have been a central factor in the speciation of the relevant languages.

3 The common position that creoles have developed from erstwhile pidgins is not supported by the socioeconomic histories of the territories where these vernaculars developed, as pointed out by Chaudenson (1992).

In any case, aside from the fact that they have typically been identified as contact languages, KILIFAPE, Shaba Swahili, and Town Bemba have been singled out of Heine's list for the following reasons which make it interesting to discuss them as a group:

1 They are recent developments from the nineteenth century in the case of Kituba, Lingala, and Fanakalo, or later in the twentieth century in the case of Shaba Swahili, Pidgin Ewondo, and Town Bemba.

2 They are associated with the European political and economic colonization of Africa and with the mobilization of labor from and to different parts of Africa (see map 12.2).

3 While the immigrant laborers typically adopted a traditional local Bantu language, viz., Kongo-Kimanyanga in the case of Kituba (Fehderau 1966), Bobangi in the case of Lingala (Heine 1970, Samarin 1982), Zulu (with some Xhosa vocabulary) in the case of Fanakalo (Heine 1970, Mesthrie 1989), and Ewondo in the case of Pidgin Ewondo, they also restructured it to the extent that the ensuing system is so different from its lexifier that it is considered a separate language. To be sure, there are varieties of Swahili in, for instance, Kenya, which are identified as *Kisetla* 'settlers' variety' and *Sheng* – blend of primarily Swahili and English – which will not be discussed here. My reasons are that Kisetla varieties are second-language approximations of the local Swahili spoken by the more indigenous African populations, and Sheng represents code-mixing, which, as discussed below, is understood as a process that may produce an autonomous variety but has not yet done so.

4 The varieties function as regional lingua francas, reflecting to some extent the linguistic regions where the colonial economic infrastructure provided the contact ecologies for their developments.

5 Their developments are partly reminiscent of those other cases also involving colonization in which European languages were adopted and restructured under contact conditions into varieties called 'pidgins' (e.g. Cameroon Pidgin English, Nigerian Pidgin English) and 'creoles' (e.g. Cape Verdian Crioulo/Kriolu, São Tomense, Angolar, and Mauritian Creole on some of the offshore islands).

It is nonetheless useful to remember that while KILIFAPE's lexifiers were local vernaculars, such was not the case for Shaba Swahili and Town Bemba. Swahili was brought to the Congo from Tanzania. Fabian (1986:136) argues that it was imported into Shaba by a deliberate decision of the Belgian colonial administration in part in order to counter British colonial influence in the mining belt and to put an end to the use of Fanakalo. In addition, Kapanga (1991) observes that, unlike second-language varieties of Swahili discussed by Polomé (1968, 1971), regular Shaba Swahili did not develop by downright simplification of East Coast Swahili's morphosyntax. Instead, this was adapted to patterns of the local Bantu languages. For instance, tense prefixes have been replaced by tense

MAP 12.2 LABOR MIGRATIONS

Source: Adapted from Cardine Wright (1997) 'Labor migration', in *Encyclopedia of Africa South of the Sahara*.

suffixes while aspect and mood are expressed periphrastically rather than affixally. The semantic distinctions have remained basically the same where they have not increased.

Town Bemba was likewise imported from northern Zambia to its mining towns of the Copperbelt where speakers of ethnic Bemba dominated numerically and where it developed from contacts with other Bantu languages. It differs from the more traditional, rural varieties of its lexifier less by an impoverished morphosyntax than by more structural variation and by marks of influence from English especially in domains of popular culture and modernity (Spitulnik 1999).

It is the difference in the geographical origins of the lexifiers that justifies the distinction proposed above between endogenous and exogenous contact languages. The former had local lexifiers, whereas the latter had external ones. I argue below that this difference is correlated with variation in how the immigrant laborers were integrated among speakers of the lexifier and this difference in socialization bore on how the lexifier evolved structurally.

2.1 What's in a name?

The motivation for grouping all the above contact varieties together may also lie in the popular names some of them bear. Town Bemba is known by other names too, such as

Chikopabelti 'language of the Copperbelt', *Citundu cukukalale* 'town language', *Ichibemba ca bushimaini* 'miners' language', and *ChiLambwaza* 'the Lambas' way of speaking' (Spitulnik 1999:39; translations modified by SSM). All these names refer indirectly to the role of contact and the appropriation of Bemba by non-native speakers as relevant factors in the development of its current peculiarities.

Kituba is also known under several names (see Heine 1970, Mufwene 1997b), including the following: *Kibula-matadi* 'the rock-breaker's way of speaking' in reference to the railroad construction between the Atlantic coast and Kinshasa, and *Kileta* 'the administration's way of speaking' in reference to the language variety heard from colonial administrators, especially their African auxiliaries. These too refer to the contact conditions of its development.

As made clear by Hulstaert (1974) and corroborated by Samarin (1989), the term 'Bangala', from which 'Lingala' was derived, has been used rather elusively since Morton Stanley's exploration of the Congo River in the nineteenth century. It designates not one single ethnic group but a cluster of populations speaking typologically similar languages in a geographic area along the Congo River bend, stretching from Irebu (south of Mbandaka), at the mouth of the Ubangi River, all the way to the Mongala River (*May Mongala*), past the town of Mankanza, also identified as Bangala. From west to east, the swampy area stretches from the Ubangi to the Congo Rivers (see map 12.1). The Bangala played a key role in the riverine trade, apparently using the Bobangi language, then the most prestigious language downstream from the Congo River bend. Other populations who traded with them must have taken it to be theirs. Incidentally, Hulstaert (1989) reports an incident during a fire at a convent, when a nun overheard a helper speak to her co-workers in what turned out to be the local vernacular. Having until then mistaken Lingala to be the local vernacular, the nun asks the helper whose language the lingua franca was. The latter replied that the local population assumed it was the missionaries' language. In fact, the missionaries, who named the new language variety 'Lingala', also misapplied a Bantu class prefixation rule, using *li-* rather than *ki-* for 'language of the Bangala' or 'riverine language'. Otherwise, Lingala's lexifier is primarily Bobangi (Alexandre 1967, Samarin 1982, Hulstaert 1989).

Pidgin Ewondo is also known as *Bulu bediliva* 'motorists' Bulu', in association with its function as a lingua franca in trade centers and along trade routes in southern and central Cameroon, where it developed during the construction of the railway between Yaoundé and Douala after World War I (Heine 1970) – a genetic history which is reminiscent of that of Kituba. (It has spread also to northern Gabon and to Rio Muni.)

Fanakalo has long been associated with Indian South Africans and identified as *Isikula* 'coolie language' (based on a pejorative colonial designation of Indian labor). It is also known by the names *Silunguboi* 'European-servant language', *Kitchen Kafir* (in more or less the same sense as the preceding name, with more explicit and derogative reference to Black domestics), and *Basic Bantu*, in reference to its oversimplified structure, marked especially by lack of agglutination on the verb and of prefixes on the noun (Mesthrie 1992:306).

It is such awareness of the role of interethnic and therefore interlinguistic contact in the development of these new varieties that led linguists to extend the terms 'pidgin' and 'creole' as technical labels to them (e.g. Polomé 1968, 1971, Samarin 1982, 1990, Ngalasso 1984, 1993, Mufwene 1988, 1989, Mesthrie 1989). However, Mufwene (1997a) argues that these names actually prevent us from realizing that the mechanisms by which KILIFAPE and the like developed are the same as those which account for the more traditional cases of language speciation in the first place. Nicolaï (1990:183f) may be right in arguing that Songhay must have developed pidginization and creolization, from the contact of Tuareg with Mande languages (see below).

2.2 The significance of a simplified morphosyntax

KILIFAPE have been associated with an impoverished morphosyntax compared to the Bantu canon, and with absence of tones in the case of Kituba, Fanakalo, and Shaba Swahili. Such restructuring is another reason why all the above varieties have been singled out as contact languages. As a matter of fact, Mufwene (1988) misguidedly used structural arguments alone to conclude that Kituba is a creole. He then disregarded the fact that Lingala, which preserves a reflexive prefix and both the lexical and grammatical tone systems, has not been restructured to the same extent under similar contact conditions (Mufwene 1989).

The apparent morphosyntactic impoverishment of KILIFAPE has been associated with loss of Subject-Verb and Head-Modifier agreement systems (as in Kituba and Fanakalo), or its reduction (as in Lingala). Thus Kituba has *bána méne dia* 'the children have eaten', *dínu lénda bukána* 'the tooth may break', in which the verb stem carries no agreement prefix, and *bána na móno* 'my children' and *dínu na móno* 'my tooth', in which possession is expressed by word order and the invariant connective *na*. However, while Urban Lingala exhibits much of the same Head Noun + Modifier behavior attested in Kituba, it has preserved a variable subject prefix on the verb and has also innovated a Subject-Verb agreement based in part on animacy, as is *moto a-kwéí* 'a man has fallen' and *elókó e-kwéí* 'something has fallen', with *a-* and *e-* as the alternating singular agreement prefixes of the third person. It is still not clear what accounts for the varying ways morphosyntactic simplification has affected the development of KILIFAPE.

Arguments invoking loss of tones, or perhaps their replacement by a pitch–accent contrast, have likewise ignored the fact that East Coast Swahili and related languages of the area are not tonal. Besides, as observed by Ngalasso (1991) and corroborated by Mufwene (1997b), the pitch–accent system, with the high pitch borne predictably by the penultimate syllable, is only partial in Kituba, which shares some lexical tone patterns with Lingala. The latter has preserved both lexical and grammatical tones, such as between *mɔtó* 'head' and *mɔ́to* 'fire' and between *ámɔ́na* (SUBJUNCTIVE) 'let him/her see' and *amɔ́ná* (REMOTE PERFECT) 'he/she saw [A LONG TIME AGO]'. To be sure, Kituba resembles Lingala only in not always having the high pitch on the penultimate syllable. It also has polysyllabic words with low tones only, as in *munɔkɔ* 'mouth, opening', or with more than one high tone (pitch?), as in *malálá* 'oranges', and other combinations. Together such examples call into question the position that there is a pitch-accent in the more common pattern attested in words such as *dísu* 'eye' and *kutúba* 'speak'. The latter word counts among the evidence that the apparent heterogeneity of the tonal/pitch–accent system in Kituba is not necessarily due to Lingala influence, in which the word is *kɔlɔba*, with low tones only. The above structural evidence questions the significance of impoverished morphosyntax as justification for identifying a restructured variety as a pidgin or creole, unless one could demonstrate that such structural complexity is a later development.

Structure-based arguments for identifying particular languages as pidgins or creoles would work if there were any combination of structural features that singled such languages out developmentally apart from others. McWhorter's (1998) effort to define a creole prototype have proved unrewarding, chiefly because of exceptions within the small set of the proposed prototypes. The very attempt to identify a handful of creoles as prototypical of the category is an implicit recognition of the fact that the vast majority of them diverge from this idealization and have features that reveal how similar they are to other languages. Mufwene (1998) also shows that the specific sociohistorical, exogenous colonial conditions of their emergence set aside, creoles have evolved by the same kinds of contacts that have influenced the development of, for instance, the Romance languages. These involved populations shifting from a particular language to the lexifier in naturalistic second-language acquisition settings, except that the contact ecology for every language restructuring was different. It is not helpful to treat every other case as one involving creolization when there is no specific combination of diachronic structural processes that ineluctably produce creoles. We will learn more by comparing more systematically cases of language speciation accepted in genetic linguistics with those of the development of creoles, paying attention to the ecologies of their evolutions (Mufwene 1998, 2001).

2.3 The conspicuous absence of KILIFAPE-like varieties in precolonial Africa

The trend to treat KILIFAPE, and to some extent Shaba Swahili and Town Bemba, as so special from a genetic linguistics perspective has been encouraged also by something pointed out by Samarin (1986), viz. no precolonial KILIFAPE-like varieties have been reported in the early colonial literature to have been in usage even in the continent's largest precolonial kingdoms. Apparently only those who knew the neighboring languages, or were accompanied by such speakers, would venture outside their homelands, communicating with the people they visited in their own local languages or in a lingua franca that was not significantly restructured. Lack of evidence to the contrary suggests that precolonial African kingdoms must have been regionally multilingual, in ways that must have enhanced the political status of interpreters in African royal courts, as well as during colonial expeditions. The current state of affairs in which lingua francas are associated with particular administrative regions are a legacy of the European colonial administration, which has been interpreted since the early post-colonial days as a means of fostering national or regional unity.

The long list of African lingua francas presented by Heine (1970) which do not seem to have evolved in the same way as KILIFAPE suggests that perhaps throughout African history several languages must have experienced evolutions similar to those that have produced Shaba Swahili and Town Bemba. Perhaps because their speakers had more prestige, some ethnic languages were adopted as trade languages. In some instances, they also became vernaculars of their later speakers. Missionaries used such lingua francas (for instance Bobangi, which they identified as Lingala) for the purposes of evangelization and formal education. European colonization appears to have depended on them in building its lower-level economic and administrative infrastructures. Nicolaï's (1990) hypothesis on the development of Songhay may not be so far-fetched if it is true that while it functioned as a lingua franca in trans-Saharan trade routes, Tuareg was eventually adopted as a vernacular among the people with whom its native speakers traded and was restructured in the process. As a matter of fact, it may be informative to re-examine the spread and speciation of, for instance, Bantu on the model of such a scenario, interpreting the dispersal of its speakers eastwards and southwards in sub-Saharan Africa as a form of colonization. During this sequence of migrations and dominations, they gradually assimilated the more indigenous populations, viz. the Pygmy and the Khoisan people, linguistically, but in turn the latter must have influenced the languages that they adopted.

2.4 The contrary fates of endogenous and exogenous models

There is something that distinguishes the emergence of KILIFAPE from the minor restructuring that has affected the other lingua francas. They are endogenous in the sense that they developed from a local language which was appropriated by outsiders who were brought from other parts of Africa as colonial auxiliaries and laborers but were apparently not absorbed by the indigenous populations. According to colonial history, these outsiders lived in special labor camps built by the companies that recruited them. As some of the names cited above suggest, the outsiders' varieties of the indigenous languages became associated with the new world order instituted by the colonial administration and accommodations to its exogenous speakers nurtured the development of these new varieties, especially after they were exported outside their birthplaces. In a way, the emergence of these varieties is also reminiscent of the development of foreign workers' varieties of European languages in Germany and France especially, except that speakers of the latter varieties carry no prestige. Nonetheless, in both cases an indigenous language was adopted by exogenous populations who were kept on the margins and precluded by the circumstances of their immigration from participating in the regular lives of the natives.

The developments of Shaba Swahili and Town Bemba represent the more traditional African trend, according to which an exogenous population succeeds in having their language prevail in the host territory. Its adoption by the local population and other immigrants causes it to be restructured but apparently not under the same conditions of linguistic heterogeneity that is typical of the contact ecologies in which KILIFAPE developed, nor to the same extent of divergence from the base language. An interesting ecological peculiarity of the varieties of Swahili discussed by Polomé (1968, 1971) is that they more or less reproduce the scenario of the development of KILIFAPE, because that allegedly pidgin variety of Swahili is spoken by people who have just migrated to the Swahili-speaking area and do not use it as a vernacular. In Lubumbashi and similar African cities, such speakers live with people who speak their ethnic languages and resort to the urban vernaculars (Swahili in this case) only to communicate with city-born children who often do not speak those ancestral languages or with people from other ethnic groups. The incipient pidgin-like varieties are considered transitional interlanguages and are often derided by native or more fluent speakers of the targeted varieties. Kapanga (1991) shows that the established position of Shaba Swahili as a vernacular and the continuous absorption of the newcomers into the local urban population prevents the Polomé varieties from gelling into a separate variety. Similar interlanguage varieties must obtain in all urban centers where rural populations have been migrating in search of jobs, trying to communicate in the local vernacular. Differences between mother-tongue and second-language varieties are to be expected under such contact conditions. Second-language varieties reflect the extent to which the speaker has become proficient in the variety.

2.5 The impact of European official languages

Spitulnik's (1999) discussion of the situation of Town Bemba reveals yet another aspect of the fate of African languages that function as lingua francas and/or as vernaculars in especially the urban settings in which they are ethnographically ranked second to the official languages, typically those of former colonizers. These lingua francas have constantly been challenged to adapt to communicative demands of non-traditional aspects of the new, cosmopolitan African culture. Many of their speakers are educated and experience the normal challenges of language contact in diglossic situations in which it is tolerated to mix the lower language with elements from the higher language, viz. English, French, or another European language, depending on the country. Although the literature has discussed discourse in mixed codes as if it were a deviation from putatively normal, monolingual discourse, its recognition as typical of some varieties of Town Bemba and other lingua francas suggests that the coexistence of European official languages and African lingua francas may be leading to new forms of African languages that admit contributions from European languages not only in the lexicon but perhaps also in grammar and discourse strategies.

In this vein, Knappert (1979:162) observes that 'present day Lingala in Kinshasa displays a complex spectrum of lexical and phonemic variation' with new sounds introduced from French. He concludes that 'Lingala is changing from a simple Bantu language of the middle Congo banks, and becoming a mixed language with a considerably extended vocabulary and phonemic inventory, a development that is comparable to that of Swahili, and in many ways to that of English' (ibid.:163). The future will tell what the structures of these lingua francas will be like and how many of the present Bantu structural features they will change or preserve. What is treated today as code-mixing or code-switching may very well contain micro-evolutionary processes that will shape up the evolutions of Lingala and other urban vernaculars into varieties more different from their lexifiers, the more traditional Bantu languages, than they are now. We must, however, note that not all speakers of these new Bantu vernaculars and lingua francas code-mix (as freely), although the phenomena are so common as to have stimulated the production of a large body of scholarship on code-switching (see Myers-Scotton 1993).

2.6 The impact of standardization

Observing that these new Bantu languages, especially Kituba and Lingala, were too impoverished for the purposes of evangelization and formal education, missionaries zealously developed standard varieties that would correspond to an idealized Bantu canon in which the Bible was translated and other literary texts were produced. The standard for Kituba was Kikongo-Kisantu. Ironically the modifier *Kisantu* means 'of saints', while it stands for the name of the mission-town in the Lower Congo region where Catholic missionaries developed this variety, in a senior seminary. To native speakers of Kituba like myself, it was as incomprehensible as any foreign language and few individuals learned to speak it, although the most successful of us who went on to earn a degree and proceeded with our formal education later in French passed our examinations on the texts we read. The missionaries themselves did not speak it either in preaching to, or in communicating with, the indigenous populations.

More successful in this respect was the development of Mankanza Lingala, developed at the Congo River bend, which continues to be used in the education system and in much of the media (Dzokanga 1979, Meeuwis 1998). It will probably not replace the regular urban Lingala that has developed naturally without conscious engineering, nor the 'mixed' variety described by Knappert (1979). The evidence suggests that these languages may be speciating in quite interesting ways that reflect both colonial and post-colonial trends.

Interestingly, attempts to standardize Swahili and Bemba have not been so extreme nor artificial. In the case of Bemba, Spitulnik (1999:34) observes that 'While Town Bemba does exhibit *minor* morphological simplification in comparison to rural Bemba, there is no evidence that it was ever a minimal communication code. Town Bemba is very complex linguistically, even if there is some morphological reduction'. It 'is better understood as a variety of Bemba or a hybrid language based on Bemba'. She also observes that 'the notion of standard Bemba derives from rural Bemba, and in particular the Bemba language from the villages at the center of the Bemba royal and ritual life, Chitimukulu and Chinsali, and from the neighboring town of Kasanta'. In the case of Swahili the standard is an approximation of coastal Tanzanian Swahili.

In any case, one learns from the above observation that these exogenous languages adopted by the local and other populations as lingua francas and/or vernaculars in the contact settings were influenced by these other languages. Kapanga (1991) suggests that the fact that a large proportion of the labor population was Luba and Lulua from Kasai, thus presenting a certain amount of substrate homogeneity, must have prevented extensive restructuring or simplification of the kind observed elsewhere. I personally suspect that integration with the native-speaking population in the industry's residential areas must have favored appropriations of the target with the least restructuring, past the interlanguage stage discussed by Polomé (1968, 1971). All the immigrant laborers were housed in the same labor camps, in specific quarters of the mining towns; and the new language varieties spread from there.

2.7 Examining things genetically

From a genetic linguistics point of view, one cannot dodge a question that arises from Nicolaï's (1990) conclusion that Songhay must have developed from Tuareg by pidginizing and creolizing from its contact with Mande (and presumably other West African languages), viz. is it possible that, as surmised above, several languages that are not identified as pidgins or creoles developed through contact-induced restructuring?

Although, given the history of population movements and contacts in Africa, it is difficult not to answer this question affirmatively, I do not subscribe to the view that there are restructuring processes specific to pidgins and creoles (Mufwene 1998). Nor should it be necessary to account for the development of Bantu contact languages by assuming the same conditions that obtained on plantations of the Atlantic and Indian Oceans, where creoles lexified by European languages developed. Nor is it even necessary to assume the same sporadic contact conditions that obtained in settings where pidgins lexified by the same languages developed before the political colonization of Africa (Fabian 1986:93, 100, 108), after the Berlin Treaty in 1885. Differences in the kinds and extent of restructuring that occurred reflect variation in the specific ecologies in which the relevant lexifiers came in contact with other languages (Mufwene 1998). It is this correlation which suggests that the speciation of Bantu languages, due to the dispersal of Bantu populations southwards and eastwards, must have been on the model of the development of Shaba Swahili and Town Bemba. According to this, an exogenous language was appropriated by the local populations and others as a lingua franca and/or a vernacular and was restructured in the process. Contact is certainly a factor that need not be ruled out by fiat, because internally motivated language change does not answer the actuation question, even if one admits that Proto-Bantu was internally variable already before the dispersal.

To understand more of the issues involved, it should help to provide a genetic synopsis of the development of Swahili on the East African coast before it penetrated its hinterland. Nurse and Spear (1985) show that it did not start as a pidgin or creole out of the contact of Arabic with Bantu languages spoken on the coast of East Africa. Although it has been penetrated lexically by Arabic in much the same way as English has by French (Nurse and Hinnebusch 1993), its essential morphosyntactic structures are very similar to those of related Bantu languages of the east coast. Nurse (1997a) groups it with languages of the Sabaki group and observes that even its use of pitch-accent, instead of the more common Bantu tone system, is a peculiarity it shares with some 'other languages in East Africa (e.g. Tumbuka and Nyakyusa), spoken far from the coast and not known to have been lingua francas, [which] have also replaced tone by stress' (ibid.:279). Among his conclusions about the genetic status of coastal Swahili are the following:

> Although some of the diachronic processes we can show to have taken place in Swahili are elsewhere documented for pidgins and creoles, especially in morphology, we cannot show conclusively that these occurred over a short period, as we would expect if they resulted from pidginization, nor can we show that they did not result from processes also known to operate widely in nonpidgins and noncreoles.
>
> (ibid.:291)

However, East Coast Swahili has served as a trade language on the coast and offshore islands since the ninth century. It was also used extensively by the Arabs who settled there, developed plantations, and traded in those coastal and insular communities, though they continued to practise their religion in Arabic (Brumfit 1980). As they engaged in trade for ivory, slaves, minerals, and other commodities with the African interior in the nineteenth century, they used the same language on their trade routes for communication with the local populations, all the way to the Congo. Citing Meyer (1944) and Lukas (1942), Heine (1970:84) observes that: 'The spread of SWAHILI was allegedly made the easier because it took place in an area in which *Bantu* languages were almost exclusively spoken, and common characteristics with SWAHILI in structure and vocabulary could be observed [and preserved].'

Little by little, Swahili was adopted as the lingua franca of East Africa, all the way to the eastern part of the Democratic Republic of the Congo, except in Uganda and in the monolingual Rwanda and Burundi. Its spread gained momentum when European missionaries, colonial administrators, and industrialists also adopted it to serve their missions of evangelization, formal education, colonization of the natives, and the development of colonial industry. In the urban centers which developed subsequently, Swahili soon became the vernacular, especially for the locally born children. Such a spread and contact with the local Bantu languages led to its speciation into several varieties distinct from the coastal varieties.

However, second-language and xenolectal varieties set aside, none of these new dialects has features that can be characterized as non-Bantu, unlike the extensive loss or reduction of Bantu morphosyntactic characteristics observed in, for instance, Kituba (Mufwene 1989) and Fanakalo (Mesthrie 1989, 1992). Kapanga (1991) interprets the restructuring that produced this speciation of Swahili in the eastern part of Central Africa as adaptation to the morphosyntax of the local Bantu languages, in fact in some cases as a complexification, instead of simplification. Thus he confirms the conclusion by Nurse and Spear (1985), Nurse (1997a), and Fabian (1986) that Swahili has not developed by a process comparable to what is called pidginization or creolization. The commitment of missionaries and colonial administrators to teach Standard Swahili must have also prevented more extensive divergence from East Coast Swahili, although one wonders why such an effort was not successful in the development of Kituba. Nor did a similar effort prevent the entrenchment of a simplified urban Lingala alongside Mankanza Lingala used in literature and the media.

The development of morphosyntactically impoverished varieties called Pidgin Swahili, Kisetla, and Kihindi in Kenya, or the Lubumbashi non-native subvariety discussed in Polomé (1968, 1971) correspond to the kinds and extents of the contacts in which the speakers are involved with those who speak Swahili as a vernacular. It reflects transitional stages in the way Swahili became the most important language of East Africa. More regular interactions with fluent speakers led to fewer and fewer deviations from the base language, despite influence from the local languages.

Town Bemba seems to have evolved according to a similar process as Shaba Swahili, as noted above, by importation and dominance of an exogenous language of northern Zambia to the mining towns of its Copperbelt and by its appropriation as a lingua franca and/or vernacular by the indigenous populations and speakers of other languages in these contact settings. However, it has remained essentially Bantu in its structures, according to Spitulnik (1999). This Bantu-preserving development of exogenous lingua francas is so different from what happened in the development of KILIFAPE, which has led linguists to associate them misguidedly with contact languages lexified by European languages and identified earlier as pidgins and creoles.

2.8 Back to KILIFAPE

Although everything seems to have to do with the importation of exogenous labor to the contact settings in which these lingua francas have developed since the nineteenth century, the social ecologies of interaction that influenced language evolution must have varied. In the cases of both Shaba Swahili and Town Bemba, on the one hand, and KILIFAPE, on the other, there were indeed workers' camps in the emerging factory or industrial towns. However, the fact that KILIFAPE turned out to be significantly restructured and simplified morphosyntactically in comparison with their lexifiers suggests that in this case the exogenous laborers who targeted the indigenous vernaculars were not absorbed or integrated by the indigenous populations.

In fact, the natives did not always want to participate in the colonial administration's work projects and were only forcefully drafted to them. Samarin (1989) observes that the Bakongo people did not participate much in building the railroad which crosses their territory from the Atlantic Ocean to Kinshasa. Neither did they volunteer to accompany colonial administrators outside their homeland, fearing to be enslaved. Thus Kimanyanga speakers played a limited role as model speakers to the exogenous laborers. They participated even less in the spread of the emerging Kituba outside its birthplace and we may surmise that this new language variety was appropriated in the Bakongo area as a colonial language perhaps remotely related to languages other than Kimanyanga in the Kongo cluster.

Perhaps such ethnographic factors explain why it wound up so simplified, although the majority of the exogenous laborers who appropriated Kimanyanga as their lingua franca were Bantu-speakers. Samarin (1982, 1990) may have been correct in emphasizing the role of West African colonial auxiliaries as the originators of Kituba. They identified Kongo-Kimanyanga as the lingua franca of precolonial trade in the region, targeted it and shared it with the exogenous Bantu laborers. Lack of documentation makes it difficult for us to answer myriads of relevant questions conclusively. The scenario is thus partly reminiscent both of those plantation settings where creoles lexified by European languages developed and of European settings where foreign workers' varieties have developed recently. I still maintain Mufwene's (1994) position that the appropriation of Kituba or Kongo-Kimanyanga by speakers of other Bantu languages prevented it from diverging much further from its lexifier, for instance in maintaining time reference distinctions which are almost the same in number as in the lexifier (Mufwene 1990), although the morphosyntactic system is now largely periphrastic. One must also bear in mind Owens's (1998) observation that the extent of restructuring toward an isolating morphosyntax is relative to the starting point. *Ceteris paribus*, lexifiers that have a very rich agglutinating morphosyntax have typically not been simplified to the same extent as those with a poor one, the case of western European lexifiers of classic pidgins and creoles.

We are led to more or less the same kind of conclusion with the development of Lingala, as with the emergence of Kituba. Samarin (1982) and Hulstaert (1989) agree that Bobangi was the riverine trade language between Stanley Pool and Irebu, south of the Congo River bend, before the late nineteenth century. Samarin (1989) observes that, like the Bakongo, the Babangi did not want to go upstream with the colonists and missionaries, but the latter took their language in the Bangala area as identified above. That is, the model which was presented in the new contact settings was non-native and it was restructured during its appropriation under exogenous conditions. We may also surmise that the predominance of the local populations speaking languages typologically close to Bobangi (among those who accommodated the colonists and missionaries in what they assumed to be the latter's language) kept Lingala close to the Bantu canon. Lingala has a somewhat simplified Subject-Agreement system, a reflexive pronominal prefix, and a normal Bantu tonal system (Mufwene 1989), unlike Kituba, which has no Subject-Agreement system, no reflexive prefix, and only a partial tonal system in coexistence with a pitch-accent system (Ngalasso 1991, Mufwene 1997a). Perhaps, the large involvement of populations speaking languages structurally close to Bobangi in the development of Lingala just prevented it from diverging from its lexifier as extensively as Kituba did. As a matter of fact, Owens (1998) argues that if creoles were defined by their structural features, a count of the morphosyntactic features that distinguish Kituba from Kimanyanga would make it one of the creole prototypes *par excellence*.

Pidgin Ewondo developed in yet a different way, on a trade route and apparently without a stable population of speakers who would develop it into a vernacular. Details of the ecology of the development of Fanakalo still remain unknown (Mesthrie 1992). It appears to be one of the two contact language varieties in the Bantu area to which the term 'pidgin' could be extended, because it does not function as a vernacular. It is also the only one to the development of which European settlers seem to have actively contributed. Colonial administrators and European missionaries typically provided the contact settings in the development of the other contact languages, except when they engaged themselves zealously in the production of varieties more consistent with the Bantu canon, viz. Kikongo-Kisantu and Lingala-Mankanza, which, ironically, were developed at extreme geographical opposites of where Bobangi is spoken. Apparently close to 30 percent of Fanakalo's vocabulary is Germanic, from English and Afrikaans; 70 percent of it is from the Nguni languages, especially Zulu and to some extent Xhosa. It developed in the heart of the Afrikaner territory and the patterns of the handbooks designed to teach it (see Further Reading) reflect many of the hierarchical contexts in which it was developed, in interactions between the white rulers and the non-European workers (including the Indian indentured laborers) on the plantations, in the mines, and in the Europeans' kitchens. Thus variation in the social and linguistic ecologies alone can account for differences in the kinds and extents of restructuring in the developments of KILIFAPE.

3 CONCLUSIONS

Overall, African contact languages are colonial phenomena. They do not seem to have developed in identical ways and fall in two or three categories from the point of view of their restructuring. Shaba Swahili, Town Bemba, and the like have preserved their traditional Bantu canon, despite marks of contact with other Bantu languages, whereas KILIFAPE reveal simplified morphosyntax compared to their lexifiers. On the other hand, Lingala seems less simplified than Kituba, and Kituba apparently less so than Fanakalo, and it appears that the specific ecologies of their developments, having to do with the exogenous identities of their developers, should shed light on the extent of restructuring. There is no strong argument against assuming that contact must have played a role in the speciation of Bantu languages over time and the model seems to be that of the development of Shaba Swahili and Town Bemba as exogenous varieties appropriated also by indigenous populations in the contact settings.

REFERENCES

Alexandre 1967; Brumfit 1980; Chaudenson 1992; Dzokanga 1979; Fabian 1986; Fehderau 1966; Heine 1970; Hulstaert 1974b, 1989; Kapanga 1991; Knappert 1979; Lukas 1942; McWhorter 1998; Meeuwis 1998; Mesthrie 1989, 1992; Meyer 1944; Mufwene 1988, 1989, 1990, 1994, 1997a, 1997b, 1998, 2001; Myers-Scotton 1993; Newman 1995; Ngalasso 1984, 1991, 1993; Nicolaï 1990; Nurse 1997a; Nurse and Spear 1985; Nurse and Hinnebusch 1993; Owens 1998; Polomé 1968, 1971; Samarin 1982, 1986, 1989, 1990; Spitulnik 1999; Vansina 1990.

FURTHER READING

Bold 1977; Erasmus and Baucom 1976.

CHAPTER THIRTEEN

THE ACQUISITION OF BANTU LANGUAGES

Katherine Demuth

1 INTRODUCTION

The systematic study of Bantu language acquisition began with Lwandle Kunene's (1979) dissertation on the acquisition of Swati. Subsequent studies of other languages (Nguni languages Zulu and Xhosa, Sotho languages Sesotho (henceforth Sotho) and Tswana, Malawian Chewa and the Gabonese language Sangu), have examined various aspects of children's language acquisition. While there are typological characteristics common to these and other Bantu languages, there are also different linguistic details that influence the course of acquisition in important ways. Thus, a comparison of the acquisition of Bantu languages offers an extremely rich area for research, providing insights not only into how language is learned, but also into the possible impact that language learning may exert on processes of historical change.

A brief summary of the Bantu acquisition literature by language is provided below. Children's ages are represented as follows: 2;11 = 2 years 11 months.

1.1 Swati

Kunene (1979) studied the acquisition of Swati nominal morphology, focusing on noun class prefixes and nominal agreement (possessives and demonstratives). Data are drawn from spontaneous speech samples and informal elicitation sessions with two children aged 2;2–3 and 2;11–3;6, and an experimental study with three children aged 4;6–6 years.

1.2 Zulu

Many of the Zulu acquisition data are drawn from a longitudinal spontaneous interaction study of three children aged between 1;10 and 3;5, plus data from other children collected for shorter periods of time (Suzman 1991). Studies investigate the acquisition of the noun class system (Suzman 1980, 1996), agreement (Suzman 1982), and passives (Suzman 1985, 1987). These topics, as well as the acquisition of relative clauses and tone (including an elicited production experiment with nine Natal children 2;6–4 years old), are discussed in Suzman (1991).

1.3 Xhosa

Most of the Xhosa research has examined the acquisition of consonants. Mowrer and Burger (1991) examine the acquisition of consonants with 2;6–6-year-olds, including clicks. Lewis (1994) and Lewis and Roux (1996) investigate the acquisition of clicks in an experimental study of 41 Xhosa-speaking children aged between 1;6 and 5;5 from near Cape Town.

1.4 Tswana

Tsonope (1987) conducted a longitudinal study of two Tswana-speaking children in Botswana aged 1;11–2;6 years and 2;5–3 years, focusing on the noun class system and nominal agreement with possessives and demonstratives, with some discussion of tone and disyllabic word 'templates'.

1.5 Sotho

Connelly's (1984) semi-longitudinal study of noun class prefixes examined two urban and two rural children in Lesotho aged 1;6–4;2 years. There is also a brief discussion of the acquisition of clicks. Demuth's (1984) longitudinal spontaneous production study of four rural children in Lesotho (aged 2;1–3;0, 2;1–3;2, 2;4–3;3 and 3;8–4;7 years) provides the data base for much of her subsequent work. Research has focused on question and prompting routines (Demuth 1984, 1987a), as well as the acquisition of word order (Demuth 1987b), the noun class and agreement system (Demuth 1988, 2000; Ziesler and Demuth 1995), passives (Demuth 1989, 1990), morphophonology (Demuth 1992a, 1994), the tonal system (Demuth 1992b, 1993, 1995a), relative clauses (Demuth 1984, 1995b), and applicative constructions (Demuth 1998, Demuth et al. 2000), including experimental data from 3–8-year-olds and adults. See Demuth (1992b) for a review of earlier work.

1.6 Chewa

Chimombo (1981) focuses on the acquisition of negation in English/Chewa bilingual children and monolingual Chewa-speaking children in Malawi between 1 and 2;6 years. Using data from spontaneous speech interactions with three Malawian children between 1;0 and 2;6, Chimombo and Mtenje (1989) examine the role of tone, syntax, and semantics in the acquisition of the Chewa negation system.

1.7 Sangu

The only acquisition study of a Bantu language outside southern and eastern Africa is that of the Gabonese language Sangu (B42) (Idiata 1998). Data were collected in a series of comprehension and elicited production experiments and narrative storytelling tasks with 2–13-year-olds and adults. The study examines morphosyntactic phenomena including noun class prefixes, nominal and verbal agreement, locatives, and verbal extensions such as the causative, applicative, imperfect, reversive, stative, durative, and passive. A CD-ROM containing the images used in the experiments and one of the first grammatical sketches of the language are also included.

The rest of this chapter is organized as follows: section 2 presents findings on the acquisition of the nominal system, including both noun class prefixes and agreement. Section 3 considers the acquisition of the verbal system, including inflectional and derivational morphology as well as various syntactic constructions. Section 4 addresses the acquisition of tone and clicks: Observations regarding other segmental and prosodic phenomena are included throughout the text. Section 5 concludes with a discussion of the theoretical import of acquisition research for the study of Bantu languages, and identifies areas for further research.

As many of the above issues have been investigated in Sotho, examples from Sotho will be used when appropriate. Speech directed towards children will be referred to as 'child-directed speech', 'caregiver speech' or 'the input', to be distinguished from 'adult-directed speech'. Both the child's utterance and the adult target (the intended/attempted utterance) are provided – either along side or underneath the child's utterance in parentheses. Children's utterances have tone marked when available (high = ', mid = +, low = unmarked). Examples are provided in phonemic form.

2 THE ACQUISITION OF BANTU NOUN CLASS AND AGREEMENT SYSTEMS

Much of the Bantu language acquisition research has focused on the morphological system, especially on nominal morphology. Of particular interest is the question of what happens in a language where both plurals and singulars are morphologically marked. Is the singular taken as 'unmarked', and/or treated as an unanalyzed whole with the plural added to it (Peters 1983)? What about the acquisition of morphological paradigms with 'holes' (e.g. ø marking for class 9 in many Bantu languages)? Are such gaps in the paradigm filled (Slobin 1985)? Given the residual semantics of the Bantu noun class system, do children use meaning to learn the noun class system (Demuth 2000)? How might the learning of Bantu noun class systems effect processes of historical change (Demuth *et al.* 1986)?

2.1 Noun class prefixes

Acquisition studies of Bantu nominal morphology report very similar findings. First, it appears that both singular and plural noun class prefixes are segmented as separate morphemes early on: there are no cases of plural morphemes being added to singular stems, nor of noun class prefixes being incorrectly added to nouns that have no prefix (Kunene 1979, Suzman 1980, 1982, 1991, 1996, Connelly 1984, Tsonope 1987, Demuth 1988, Idiata 1998). Monosyllabic stems provide the only evidence that children might be acquiring prefix and stem as a unit (Kunene 1979, Tsonope 1987, Idiata 1998), a phenomena for which there are prosodic explanations (Tsonope 1987, Demuth 1996). Furthermore, although singulars are more frequent than plurals in everyday discourse, there is no evidence that the acquisition of plural noun class prefixes is delayed.

All studies of the acquisition of Bantu noun class prefixes report the following three partially overlapping stages of development during ages 2–3:

(1)   Development of noun class prefixes

    (a) No prefixes (full or partial noun stems)
    (b) 'Shadow' vowel and nasal prefixes
    (c) Full and phonologically appropriate noun class prefixes

The first two of these are illustrated in the following Sotho examples, both spoken on the same day (cf. Demuth 1988:309):

(2)   (2;1 years)   *Child*   *Adult target*
               (a) *pônko*   < *li ≠ phɔqɔ*
               (b) *apóko*   'green corn stalk'

Noun class prefixes were generally used in their correct form by 2;6–2;8 years in Swati and Sotho (Kunene 1979, Connelly 1984:80, Demuth 1988:310). Suzman (1980) reports the appearance of noun class prefixes somewhat earlier in Zulu, suggesting that the pre-prefix may facilitate earlier emergence of noun class prefixes. Tsonope (1987) and Suzman (1980) suggest that the phonological shape of the shadow vowel might actually be the overgeneralization of noun class 9 e- for Sotho and Tswana (though note a- in (2b) above), and 'human class' 1a u- and 'default/loan word' class 5 i- in Zulu. More research is needed to determine if children's use of shadow vowels indicates an attempt to lump all nouns into one 'class', or is merely a morphological place holder, the phonological shape of which is yet to be determined (Peters 1997).

Once full noun class prefixes begin to be produced there is no evidence of semantic overgeneralizations, 'paradigm regularization' or 'plural overgeneralization'. The only 'error' comes from a child at 1;9 years selecting the more common class 10 prefix for a class 9/6 noun. By 1;11 years the correct class 6 plural was used (Connelly 1984:81).

It is remarkable that the acquisition of noun class prefixes should be so similar across Bantu languages. Kunene (1979:76–81) suggests that children have morphologized nouns, producing the more semantically contentful stem early on, ruling out the possibility that either penultimate lengthening or the high tone on Swati noun class prefixes contributes to the production of bare nominal stems at initial stages of acquisition. She also reports that Swati-speaking adults never omit noun class prefixes (though it is not clear if this includes child-directed speech), and children are therefore never provided with input that includes prefix-less nouns (though see Ziesler and Demuth 1995). In contrast, Tsonope (1987) argues that child-directed prefixless nominal input provides Tswana-speaking children with a Low–High toned disyllabic template, and that this is the source of children's early prefixless nouns. However, if Kunene is correct in claiming that Swati-speaking adults never omit noun class prefixes, the input explanation for Tswana will not be able to account for the cross-linguistic use of prefixless stems.

There is an alternative explanation for the occurrence of children's early CVCV nominal forms, which Kunene (1979) also notes. Many Bantu languages exhibit penultimate lengthening, a feature which has sometimes been called penultimate 'stress'. Allen and Hawkins (1980) suggest that children have a universal tendency to omit pre-stressed syllables and to produce trochaic feet. While the cross-linguistic relevance of this proposal has been controversial, it would appear that young children learning Bantu languages do tend to produce early disyllabic trochaic feet (Demuth 1992a, 1994, 1996).

The lack of noun class overgeneralization in spontaneous speech contrasts with Kunene's (1979) experimental results from Swati-speaking 4;6–6 year olds where there is difficulty with singular/plural pairs. When asked to form the plural of a novel (new) noun, children marked most plurals appropriately, but nouns from class 11 lu- were rendered as class 5 li-, and class 9 in- plurals were given as class 6 ema- rather than class 10 tin-. Class 2a bo- was added to class 1 nouns – umu-ntfu 'person' > bo-mu-tfu (class 1a has ø prefix), as well as to nouns from classes 14 and 15 that normally do not take plurals – bu-so 'face' > bo-bu-so, ku-dla 'food' > bo-ku-dla. Furthermore, class 7 si- and 8 ti- were given with only the vowel i-. Some class 9 nouns take class 6 plurals in Swati; thus children's over-production of class 6 ema- is the type of 'error' one might expect. The other noun class overgeneralizations are systematically phonological and morphological rather than semantic. Interestingly, these same children never made such errors in spontaneous speech.

2.2 Nominal agreement

The acquisition of Bantu nominal agreement again shows remarkable cross-linguistic uniformity, sharing the following partially overlapping 'stages' of development (Demuth 1988).

(3)   Development of nominal agreement markers
    (a) Shadow vowel
    (b) Well-formed morphemes

Appropriate marking of possessive and demonstrative agreement is in place by 2;4–2; 6 years, well before nouns are consistently marked with prefixes (Connelly 1984:102).

(4)   *Child*   *Adult target*
    (1;9 years)   *kwına a-ka!*   *ma≠kwınya a-ka*
                                            6-fat-cakes 6POSS-my
                                            'my fat-cakes'
    (2;3 years)   *ekausi tsa-ka* < *di≠kausi tsa-ka*
                                            10-socks 10POSS-my
                                            'my socks'

Kunene (1979:99–103) does report a Swati-speaking child at 2;2 years using the class 7 possessive agreement form *sa-* instead of class 8 *ta-* to refer to *ti-cathulo* 'shoes', and there are occasional examples of other possible 'errors', where a class 1 possessive agreement marker *wa-* was used instead of class 9 *ya-* (note, however, that both involve glides). The spontaneous speech findings contrast once again with experimental Swati findings that indicated a tendency to collapse class 11 *lwe-* agreement with class 5 *le-*. It would appear there is no class 11 for young Swati speakers.

2.3 Summary

In sum, the acquisition of the Bantu noun class system is in place by the age of 3, showing no systematic semantic or other overgeneralizations. Development follows three overlapping 'stages', indicating that children have some knowledge about the shape of specific noun class prefixes from an early age. This is supported by the fact that possessive and demonstrative agreement is in place several months before nouns are consistently marked with fully formed prefixes.

Performance factors, perhaps involving word formation constraints, may be responsible for early variable production. This would be expected if children's early word shapes consist of disyllabic feet; both possessives and demonstratives are disyllabic, being composed of the CV- agreement prefix plus the monosyllabic possessive or demonstrative stem. Further work on prosodic constraints on early word formation, especially with monosyllabic and multisyllabic nominal stems, will hopefully provide a better understanding of how Bantu noun class and agreement systems are acquired.

The relatively early and 'error free' acquisition of Bantu noun class and agreement systems suggests that learning complex morphological paradigms is easy when they are phonologically transparent. Further support for this hypothesis comes from the acquisition of languages where errors consist of phonological overgeneralizations like the Swati class 11 > 5 mentioned above (Demuth 1988). This type of phonological leveling apparently took place in languages like Sotho that have no class 11 today. Thus, phonological similarity, combined with frequency effects, may induce various aspects of morphophonological historical change (Demuth *et al.* 1986, Demuth 2000).

3 THE ACQUISITION OF BANTU VERBAL MORPHOLOGY AND SYNTACTIC STRUCTURES

Bantu languages also possess rich systems of verbal inflectional and derivational morphology. The acquisition of subject–verb agreement and tense/aspect marking has played a major role in the recent acquisition literature, the early lack of such morphemes being taken by some as a sign of impoverished syntactic representations (cf. Demuth 1992a, 1994). Given the complexities of the tense/aspect system of many Bantu languages (Ch. 7), information about how these systems are acquired might provide some insight into how cross-linguistic differences in this area arose. Finally, the rich set of verbal extensions provides an extremely interesting area for examining the acquisition of various grammatical phenomena.

3.1 Subject and object markers

The morphological development of subject markers in Bantu languages is similar to that reported for noun class prefixes above:

No marking > shadow vowel > well-formed morphemes

Again, these three developmental phases are not discrete, but overlap to some degree. Kunene (1979:85–91, 244) reports the use of bare verb stems in Swati at 2;2 years, with shadow vowels *a* or *i* around 2;3 years. The shadow vowel is generally *a* or *e* for Sotho (5) (Demuth 1988:312). Sotho and Zulu caregivers, when using 'baby-talk' with children, also tend to use the shadow vowel *a* in place of the subject marker.

(5)   (2;1 years)
    a lahlíle
    (*kɪ-di ≠ láhl-íl-e +*)
    1ssm-10obj-throw away-ant-fv
    'I threw them away.'

Around 2;4–2;5 years the first phonologically appropriately subject markers begin to appear. Idiata (1998) notes that these are in complementary distribution with tense/aspect markers, raising the possibility of morphophonological constraints on children's output forms. Consistent use of phonologically well-formed subject markers in all these languages appears somewhat before 3 years, about the same time as the marking of noun class agreement, though some collapsing/coalescence of subject marker and tense/aspect marker may persist, being more consistently differentiated by 3 years. Both Kunene (1979) and Idiata (1998) find overgeneralization of subject markers in storytelling tasks where human/animate referents that do not belong to class 1/2 are subsequently referred to with class 1/2 agreement. However, this is the norm in adult speech as well.

Like the rest of the agreement system, the development of object markers (and reflexives) exhibits the familiar pattern below, with the first object markers appearing between 2;6–3 years in Sotho, many being 1st person singular nasals, especially in imperatives (Demuth 1992b).

No marking > shadow vowel > well-formed morphemes

In Kunene's (1979) experimental study of Swati-speaking 4;6–5;11-year-olds, children used the class 1 object marker *m-* instead of class 3 *wu-* (the prefixes on the corresponding nouns are both *umu-*) and class 5 *li-* instead of class 11 *lu-*. Once again, Swati-speaking children make phonologically based generalizations about the noun class and agreement system in experimental conditions, collapsing classes 11 and 3 with phonologically similar classes 5 and 1 respectively.

Once object markers and reflexives are recognizable there is no evidence in Sotho of both being used in the same construction, nor are there attempts to use two object markers with ditransitive verbs. Both are ungrammatical for Sotho, but acceptable for closely related Tswana. It is not clear how and when children learn these language-specific differences.

3.2 Tense, aspect, mood, and negation

Bantu languages are known for their highly complex tense/aspect and negation systems (Ch. 7), yet there has been no systematic study of the acquisition of the tense/aspect system or negation in any Bantu language. Demuth (1992b) reports on one child's acquisition of Sotho tense/aspect and mood, where high-frequency tense/aspect forms such as present, anterior, and various futures are used at 2;1 years, though sometimes phonologically ill-formed. Around 2;5 years continuous, past continuous, recent past, potential, and hortative all appear. A month later the copula verb and the narrative past marker on subject markers appear, followed by the persistive at 2;9. Finally, the past and conclusive are used. Less is known about the acquisition of mood, though subjective/permissive questions are also used by 2–3-year-olds.

Chimombo and Mtenje (1989) report that three Chewa-speaking children all use several different semantic forms of negation by the age of 2 (negative permission, non-existence, non-occurrence, denial, rejection, not-knowing). These forms are used with a general High–Low tone 'melody', even when such constructions do not appear with an initial High tone. They suggest that negation is represented early in children's speech with a specific, autosegmental tonal melody that is overgeneralized to various syntactic and semantic forms of negation. Thus, by the age of 2, children learning Bantu languages may have some knowledge of negation and some of the grammatical means by which it is encoded. It is possible that these become increasingly more specified as the tense/aspect system and the concomitant marking of grammatical tone begin to be acquired over the next year.

3.3 Extraposition and topicalization

Bantu languages are notable for their flexibility in word order. Most children learning Bantu languages use basic (S)V(O) word order prior to 2;6 years, even when a switch to a different word order might facilitate communication (Demuth 1987b:98).

Subject postposing in Sotho comes in strongly around 2;6 years. This may be about the time that children realize their language is a null-subject language, that lexical subjects are optional, and that these can be extraposed.

(6)   (2;6 years)
   í-á-tsamay-a koloi yá:ka
   (*í-á≠tsamay-a kolóí yáka*)
   9SM-PRES-go-FV 9car 9POSS-my
   'It's going, my car.'

The use of postposed lexical objects increases around 3 years, once object markers are more consistently realized, and preposed, or topicalized objects become increasingly common around 4;6–5 years (Demuth 1987b).

In sum, it appears that children learning Bantu languages begin to use some of the word order possibilities of these languages in appropriate discourse contexts by 2;6 years, but that some flexibility with word order may await the more consistent realization of subject and object markers.

3.4 Applicatives and other verbal extensions

Relatively little is known about the acquisition of Bantu verbal derivational morphology (though see Demuth 1992b, Idiata 1998). However, children's early use of applicatives seems to be productive both in frequency and in the different verbs used, with Sotho-speaking 2–3-year-olds using applicatives with both intransitive (unaccusative and unergative) and transitive verbs (Demuth 1998, Demuth *et al.* 2000). Evidence of early 'productivity' comes not only from the wide range of verbs used in the applicative, but also from occasional morphophonological 'errors' (e.g. *tselela* < *tsella* 'pour for'), and from the lack of ability to handle multiple derivational morphemes (Demuth 1998, Idiata 1998).

Bantu languages differ in the order of objects permitted in ditransitive applicatives, some allowing either order of objects after the verb (symmetrical languages), and others being more restrictive (asymmetrical languages) (Chs 6, 9). In Sotho either order of objects is permitted when both have equal animacy. However, when the animacy of the objects differs, the animate object must be placed next to the verb. Most Sotho-speaking 2–3-year-olds' ditransitive applicative constructions include an animate and inanimate argument, as does adult speech. However, there were few cases of ditransitive applicatives where both objects are lexical. Rather, the animate/benefactive argument is generally pronominalized, the inanimate/theme argument often being realized as a null argument (Demuth 1998:793).

Thus, despite the extensive literature on applicative constructions in comparative Bantu, double object applicatives appear to be rare in everyday discourse, raising questions about how these constructions are learned. Experimental evidence shows that even 8-year-olds are not yet adult-like in their placement of animate applicative objects immediately after the verb (Demuth *et al.* 2000). Perhaps the low frequency of these constructions, and the subsequent protracted learning curve, give rise to some of the double object word order variation seen in Bantu languages.

3.5 Passives

The grammatical structure of passives in most Bantu languages closely resembles passive formation in languages like English (this volume, Chs 6, 9; Demuth 1989). It is therefore interesting to compare the acquisition of passives in Bantu languages with that of English, where the reported lack of passives in children's early productions fostered the claim that passives were linguistically/cognitively difficult to acquire (Pinker *et al.* 1987).

It has been surprising, then, to find that children learning Bantu languages such as Sotho, Zulu, and Sangu start using passive constructions productively around the age of 2;8 (Demuth 1989, 1990, Suzman 1991, Idiata 1998). At this time there is an increase in both the total number and percentage of passives produced, as well as an increase in the creative (non-rote) use of passives, many of which employ by-phrases, some of these with non-animate agents.

(7)   (2;8 years)
      ɔ-tla-hlaj-uw-a kɪ tshɛhlɔ
      (ɔ-tla ≠ hlaj-w-a kɪ tshɛhlɔ)
      2SSM-FUT-stab-PASS-FV by 9thorn
      'You'll be stabbed by a thorn.'

It appears that children learning Bantu languages have access to the formation of syntactic passives several months prior to that reported for English (Pinker *et al.* 1987). Demuth (1989) suggests that this may be due to the high frequency with which passives are used in the input children hear: approximately 6 percent of adult verbal utterances spoken to young children in Sotho contain a passive, contrasting with almost none in child-directed English (Brown 1973).

There are two explanations for why Bantu passives are so frequent. First, many Bantu languages can passivize both accusative and dative arguments, as well as many stative verbs. Many Bantu languages must also use a passive or cleft to question subjects, and much child-directed speech consists of subject questions. While only a few of children's early passives are questions, the high frequency of question-passive input provides early and ample practice with comprehension of passives, thereby facilitating early production.

3.6 Relative clauses and cleft constructions

The acquisition of relative clauses and cleft constructions also become productive quite early, around 2;5 years (Demuth 1984, 1995b, Suzman 1991). Subject relative markers are generally present, while object relative markers are frequently absent, or a demonstrative pronoun is used instead.

In the majority of Sotho-speaking 2–3-year-olds' relative clauses the subject of the embedded clause is the object of the main clause. However, some relative clauses were headless, the head noun having been used in the previous discourse. As in many Bantu languages, Sotho cleft constructions incorporate a relative clause. We might then expect cleft constructions to be acquired at about the same time as relative clauses, and this is the case: there is a burst in the use of cleft constructions at 2;5 years, many of them questions (RL = verbal relative suffix).

(8)   (2;5 years)
      kí: nthéɔ ka moɔ kí fuwáng?
      (kí íŋ nthɔ́ éɔ ká móɔ yéɔ ki-ɪ≠fúdú-á-ŋ́?)
      COP what 9thing 9DEM PREP here 9REL 1SSM-9OBJ-stir-FV-RL
      'What is this thing in here that I'm stirring?'

Like passives, relative/cleft constructions seem to be much more frequent in early Sotho and Zulu than in English. This is probably again due to the high frequency of cleft and relative constructions in Bantu languages. Part of this frequency may be due to the frequent use of cleft questions in the input – an alternative to passives when questioning subjects.

3.7 Locatives, impersonal, and existential constructions

Bantu languages vary greatly in the retention or loss of the locative noun class prefixes (classes 16, 17, and 18) (this volume, Ch. 8), yet there has been little study of how children use these prefixes in languages that have preserved them. Idiata (1998) finds that even young children use the class 17 noun class prefix early on, whereas the systematic use of classes 16 and 18 in experimental contexts is better with 7-year-olds, but not perfect with adults. Remnants of class 17 survive in languages like Sotho, where the rest of the locative noun class system has been lost. It would be interesting to know if class 17 in Sangu and other Bantu languages has higher frequency of overall use and/or special semantic characteristics that might contribute to its earlier acquisition and preservation over time. Most of the other research on the acquisition of Bantu locatives has been couched in terms of the acquisition of suffixes as opposed to prefixes (Kunene 1979:92–6, Connelly 1984:92), where the invariant locative suffix is acquired as early as 1;7 months and with little apparent difficulty.

In Bantu languages like Sotho which no longer have productive locative prefixes the class 17 noun class prefix *hò-* functions as a expletive/existential (Demuth and Mmusi 1997). Sotho-speaking children's first uses of class 17 are in existential constructions, weather constructions, and idioms. The first uses of class 17 with verbs occurs around 2;8 years, where the verbs have been passivized (Demuth 1989).

(9)   (2;8 years)
hò-tla≠shap-uw-a Dineo enwa
17SM-FUT-lash-PASS-FV D. 1DEM
'That Dineo, she will be lashed.'
Lit: 'There will be lashed Dineo, this one.'

Given the variation in such constructions across Bantu languages, further research in this area, and the potential implications for acquisition pressures on language change, would be most interesting.

3.8 Summary

In sum, studies of the acquisition of Bantu language syntax indicate that applicatives, high-frequency tense-aspect markers, passives, clefts, relative clauses, locatives, expletives, and extraposition of subjects and objects are all productive in Bantu languages before the age of 3. This is not to say that knowledge of any of these constructions is adult-like, but rather that children have some working knowledge of appropriate grammatical use. To the extent that the morphological and syntactic structure of Bantu languages is similar, we would predict similar patterns of development across other Bantu languages, as found in the case of noun class prefixes and agreement. Interestingly, it appears that the high frequency of both passives and clefts/relative clauses in the input probably contributes to the earlier acquisition of these constructions relative to other languages.

Even so, there is much we do not know about the acquisition of Bantu syntactic structures. Little is known about the acquisition of transitivity relations or argument structure, and even less is known about the acquisition of the tense/aspect system. In addition, there has been no research on the acquisition of binding and anaphora, anaphoric reference, complementation, conditionals, and other complex sentence structures. Much more research on these topics, as well as research on more children in a broader range of Bantu languages, is needed to develop a firmer understanding of the course of Bantu syntax acquisition.

4   THE ACQUISITION OF PHONOLOGY

There has been little formal study on the acquisition of Bantu phonological systems. Most has centered on the acquisition of clicks in Xhosa and Sotho, and the acquisition of the tonal system in Sotho.

4.1   Clicks

Mowrer and Burger (1991:157) report that clicks are acquired relatively late in Xhosa, noting the 'substitution' of clicks by alveolar or velar plosives which generally preserve the voicing and place of articulation of the click. Lewis (1994) and Lewis and Roux (1996) argue that these are really 'simplification processes', where only one of the places of articulation is preserved. In a series of experiments they examine the acquisition of 15 word-medial click phonemes by 41 Xhosa-speaking children between the ages of 1;6 and 5;5. They find that simplification processes are common, as are reduction processes (click omitted but accompaniment maintained, or visa versa). Although less thoroughly studied, these findings are consistent with reports from the longitudinal Sotho data where the palatal alveolar click is first used in isolation around 2 years, and is replaced in words by /k/ until around 3 years (Connelly 1984:132–5, Demuth 1992b).

4.2   Tone

Given the extensive phonological literature on Bantu tonal systems (this volume, Ch. 5), it is disappointing that there has been little acquisition research in this area. Although research on Asian languages indicates early acquisition of lexical tone, sometimes prior to that of segments, there has been relatively little discussion of the acquisition of tonal sandhi phenomena or grammatical tone like that found in most Bantu languages.

Demuth (1993, 1995a) examined the acquisition of lexical and grammatical tone on verbs in the spontaneous speech of one child at 2;1, 2;6, and 3;0 years, finding good control over the tone of subject markers at 2;1 years, but overgeneralization of High tone onto Low-toned verbs.

(10)   (2;1 years)
  a itíme+
  (*ka≠jithim-il-e*)
  1sSM-jump down-AND-FV
  'I am jumping down.'

By 2;6 there is significant expansion in the types of tense/aspect/mood constructions used, and the beginnings of tonal melody differentiation are discernible, especially in the imperative. At the same time High- and Low-toned verb stems become increasingly differentiated in the lexicon.

By 3 years, the tone on verbs was usually correctly marked as High or Low, and tonal sandhi, including High-tone doubling and OCP (Obligatory Contour Principle) effects have also been acquired, at least in some tonal melodies. This resulted in Low-tone surfacing on High-toned subject markers when subject markers and tense/aspect markers were collapsed into one syllable/tone-bearing unit.

Some have suggested that children's early preference for High tone on verbs is consistent with Clements and Goldsmith's (1984) proposal that children learning Bantu languages might initially adopt an accentual (rather than tonal) analysis, like that found in Bantu languages like Tonga. However, the early preference for High tone on verbs is also consistent with an initial 'default High hypothesis'. That is, when in doubt of a verb's tone, assign it a High tone. This would also appear to be the strategy used in assigning tone to Sotho loan verbs (e.g. *púʃa* 'push').

The Sotho findings are consistent with those reported for Zulu and Tswana. In addition, both Suzman (1991) and Tsonope (1987) report earlier acquisition of tone on nouns than verbs. This may be due to the fact that nominal tones are more 'lexical', with less tonal sandhi. Tsonope (1987) also notes cases of tonal 'preservation', where tones are preserved even where segments (or tone-bearing units) are not, giving rise to contour tones. This reinforces the Sotho and Chewa findings regarding the independence of tonal and segmental tiers, providing additional evidence of young children's early autosegmental representations.

4.3 Summary of phonological development

The phonological issues receiving the most attention in Bantu acquisition, clicks and tone, have been understudied in the field of phonological acquisition in general. The findings indicate that 2-year-olds can generally produce click consonants in isolation, but that producing clicks with a following vowel as part of a word is more difficult, being acquired only around the age of 3. This is probably due to the fact that clicks do not exhibit coarticulation effects, requiring more sophisticated articulatory expertise.

Findings on the acquisition of tone are also intriguing. The acquisition of tone on nouns and subject agreement markers has taken place by the age of 2, much in the way that lexical tone is acquired in languages like Mandarin and Thai. In contrast, grammatical tone melodies on verbs, where there is much more tone sandhi, is beginning to be acquired around the age of 2;6–3 as more of the tense/aspect/mood morphology is also acquired. Prior to this time children exhibit certain fixed melody forms, some of these being used for generic negation, others (such as iterative High tones) being used for verbal constructions in general.

Clicks are not the only consonants to be acquired, yet except for Mowrer and Burger (1991), there has been no systematic study of acquisition of Bantu segments or phonological processes. Demuth (1992b) notes the simplification of Sotho affricates to stops and processes of consonant harmony, both commonly found in the acquisition of other languages. Other morphophonological processes, such as the palatalization with passives and strengthening of verb-initial consonants before reflexives and nasal object markers, take a while to learn. Finally, processes of prosodic phonology, such as phrase-penultimate lengthening, also take some time to learn, though this will need to be investigated instrumentally. Certainly, it appears that children's early productions are prosodically constrained, typically including the final disyllabic foot, but often missing syllables or onsets of syllables that fall at the left edge of the prosodic word. This raises the question of the role of penultimate lengthening in the prosodic organization of children's early phonology.

5 DISCUSSION

The acquisition of Bantu languages is a rich and interesting area of research which is still only beginning to be systematically investigated. Most of the studies to date have focused on the acquisition of nominal morphology and agreement, with some attention paid to verbal morphology, syntactic constructions, and the acquisition of tone and clicks. Much more research, especially on the acquisition of syntax and phonology, is still to be done. Experimental methods may be especially effective at exploring some of these issues.

Yet, even with the limited number of Bantu languages investigated, the similarity in findings across languages is striking. This may be partly due to the fact that several of these languages are closely related southern Bantu languages, or it may be because most of these studies have examined the nominal system. Thus, we might expect to find more language-specific acquisition differences in areas where Bantu languages exhibit more variation, perhaps in the semantic and syntactic consequences of preservation/loss of locative noun classes 16, 17, and 18, in the tense/aspect system, or in the encoding of pronominal objects, where some languages permit one and others two. The phonological system is another area that has been little studied and where language variation abounds, in tonal systems, as well as in consonantal and vowel inventories, vowel harmony, and morphophonological processes.

Despite the need for further research, the findings from Bantu language acquisition have already had serious implications for the field of language acquisition as a whole. When compared with children learning languages like English, children learning Bantu languages seem precocious. Connelly (1984:113) suggests that children learning Sotho are 6–10 months in advance of their English-speaking peers in terms of using morphologically complex utterances, and Demuth (1989, 1990, 1995b) finds that they are several years more advanced in their use of grammatical constructions such as passives and relative clauses. Studies of other morphologically rich languages show relatively early acquisition of morphology and syntactic constructions such as passives as well (cf. Allen 1996). It appears that children tune in very early to the phonological, morphological, and syntactic constructions that are high frequency in the language(s) they are learning. This is not surprising given results from infant speech perception studies showing that even preverbal infants are extremely sensitive to statistically prominent aspects of the language to which they are exposed (cf. Jusczyk 1997 for review). More interesting, then, are aspects of the grammar that have high frequency but which are mastered later than might be expected, such as the gradual acquisition of noun class prefixes and subject markers (around 2;6–3 years). We must look elsewhere to explain the lag in acquisition of these constructions, perhaps to constraints on prosodic morphology (Demuth 1994, 1996). Also of interest are low frequency constructions such as double object applicatives, which occur extremely rarely in discourse directed to children (e.g. Demuth 1998, Demuth *et al.* 2000). In this case we expect a protracted course of development, with some individual difference found from child to child. Given the limited number of children examined in any of these studies, the issue of individual variation has hardly been addressed.

The implicit assumption throughout this chapter has been that processes of first language acquisition might influence language change. However, multilingualism is the norm in many parts of Africa. Some children learn more than one language from birth, yet there have been no systematic studies of children learning two or more Bantu languages simultaneously. It may be that large groups of adults learning a new language will influence the course of language change to a greater degree. Thus, language change may be especially noticeable when a language becomes a lingua franca, setting the scene for the loss of the tonal system in Swahili or loss of some of the plural noun class prefixes in Lingala. On the other hand, other types of language contact have given rise to the addition of grammatical complexity, as in the incorporation of clicks into southern Bantu languages (this volume, Ch. 11). We know relatively little about the sociolinguistics of these contact situations, and the role that young language learners may play in solidifying these developments.

Finally, the study of how children learn Bantu languages forces us to consider seriously how these languages are used in everyday discourse. Much theoretical linguistic research is concerned with grammaticality judgments – i.e. what types of constructions are permitted, and how these vary from one language to the next. The study of how children learn language forces us to examine the input language they hear, and to understand more about how these languages are actually used. Interestingly, some of the Bantu linguistic structures which have generated the most theoretical linguistic discussion turn out to be very low frequency constructions in actual discourse, being learned very late (e.g. double object applicatives). Data from acquisition studies therefore provide an invaluable resource regarding how Bantu languages are used in everyday discourse. The frequency effects embedded in this discourse provide key insights into the rate of acquisition for certain Bantu linguistic structures, and may prove critical for understanding aspects of Bantu historical change as well.

REFERENCES

Brown 1973; Chimombo and Mtenje 1989; Clements and Goldsmith 1984; Connelly 1984; Demuth 1988, 1989, 1990, 1992a, 1992b, 1993, 1994, 1995a, 1995b, 1998; Demuth *et al.* 2000; Idiata 1998; Juscyck 1997; Kunene 1979; Lewis 1994; Lewis and Roux 1996; Mowrer and Burger 1991; Pinker *et al.* 1987; Suzman 1980, 1982, 1985, 1987, 1991, 1996; Tsonope 1987.

FURTHER READING

Allen 1996; Chimombo 1981; Deen 2002; Demuth 1984, 1987a, 1987b, 1996; Demuth *et al.* 1986; Demuth *et al.* in press; Demuth and Mmusi 1997; Peters 1983, 1987; Slobin 1985; Ziesler and Demuth 1995.

PART 2

CHAPTER FOURTEEN

GRASSFIELDS BANTU

John R. Watters

1 INTRODUCTION

1.1 Context, history, scripts

Grassfields Bantu (GB) consists of more than fifty languages spoken in the mountainous region of the West and North West Provinces of Cameroon. Two of the languages are found in the contiguous, mountainous, northeast portion of the SouthWest Province. Much of the landscape is covered with tall elephant or napier grass (*Pennisetum purpureum*). As Richardson (1957:61) noted, these languages are 'often referred to by Europeans and Africans alike as "Grassfield" (or *grafil* in Pidgin) because of the nature of the terrain over which they are spoken'.

Besides the grass, mountains also serve as important natural features for the communities that speak these languages. Stallcup (1980a) points out that the mountain ridges serve as language boundaries. GB may be the most linguistically fragmented of any region in Africa. Stallcup calculates that on average each language occupies only 20 square kilometers or less. Breton and Fohtung (1991:18–19, 106–21, 129–41) provide excellent maps of the region and its languages. Greenberg (1980:40) suggests that the GB languages are spoken near the probable region of the origin of Bantu.

Despite this concentration of languages, the region had been among the more neglected in Africa for linguistic research. Stallcup (1980a:48–9) provides some of the geographic, demographic, political, and sociological reasons for this fact. Perhaps the earliest linguistic studies of Grassfields languages are Ward (1938) on Bamoun phonetics and Bruens (1942–5) on Nkom. Richardson (1957) included the GB languages in his survey of the northern Bantu borderland. The 1960s saw Dunstan (1963, 1964, 1966a, 1966b) produce articles on Ngwe, and Voorhoeve (1963, 1965, 1967, 1968) on the Bamileke languages. The most productive period began in the 1970s with Voorhoeve (1971, 1974), Hyman (1971, 1972), and Hyman *et al.* (1970), and the formation of the Grassfields Bantu Working Group. The results of this Group are reported in Hyman and Voorhoeve (1980, cf. Watters 1982). Work has continued through the 1980s and 1990s, including comparative, descriptive, and theoretical studies.

Until recently most of these languages had no recognized written form. The exceptions have been Bamoun (Shʉ pamǝm), Megaka (Bagam), Mǝdʉmba (Bangangte-Bamileke), Fe'fe'-Bamileke, Yemba (Dschang-Bamileke), and Mungaka. Bamoun, found in the West Province, has a syllabary that the Sultan of Foumban, from about 1903, devised and reduced from an original 510 characters to 80 (Dalby 1970:112). Bagam, a neighboring language, received a syllabary before 1917, possibly based on the Bamoun script. Both of these scripts are non-Roman. A written form of Mǝdʉmba was formalized in the 1960s with the translation of portions of the Bible. Written forms of Fe'fe'-Bamileke and

Yemba, both in the West Province, were developed primarily after Second World War and serve as examples of community initiative to develop a written form of their language (see Sadembouo and Chumbow 1990). Mungaka, around Bali in the North West Province, received a written form in the first half of the twentieth century from the efforts of the Basel Mission. A revised, translated edition of Tischhauser's Mungaka dictionary has recently been published (Stöckle 1992).

French and English are the official languages of Cameroon. For historical reasons French is predominant in the West Province and English in the North West and South West Provinces. Pidgin English serves as an important trade language throughout GB.

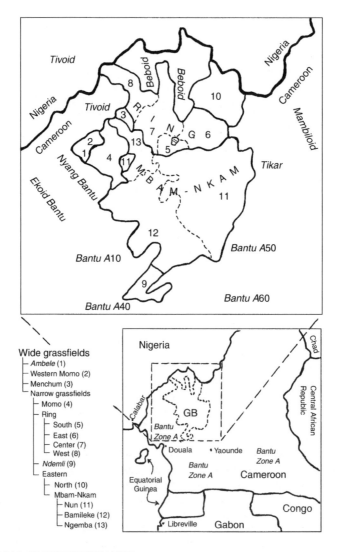

MAP 14.1 GRASSFIELDS BANTU

1.2 Classifications

1.2.1 External

The major question about external classification during the twentieth century has concerned the relationship of GB languages to Narrow Bantu. A more recent and yet equally important question has concerned their relationship to the other language clusters found in the immediate region of Cameroon and Nigeria. On the first question, most linguists today accept the GB languages, along with other language clusters in the Cameroon–Nigeria region, as the nearest cousins of Guthrie's Bantu.

On the second question, the GB languages are often listed as one language cluster among multiple parallel branches (e.g. Greenberg 1955, 1963a, Williamson 1971, Dieu and Renaud 1983, Watters and Leroy 1989). However, Bennett and Sterk (1977) and Piron (1995) provide more nuanced hypotheses, both based on lexicostatistical research. Bennett and Sterk suggest that at the lowest level the GB languages, represented by the Mbam-Nkam languages (a subset of GB), groups with the Ekoid cluster and the northwest Bantu languages. Piron suggests that at the lowest level GB groups with the Ekoid and Nyang clusters. These three then form a parallel branch with the Beboid and Tivoid clusters. Bennett and Sterk are reminiscent of Heine (1972–3) and Henrici (1973) in that a clear boundary does not appear between traditional Bantu and GB. In contrast, Piron suggests that a clearer boundary may exist, with GB closer to the Ekoid and Nyang than Narrow Bantu. Yet Piron (1995:15, 16) notes that GB does seem to have a close lexical similarity with at least Bantu A50.

In addition, when noun class features are included in the evaluation (see §1.2.2 and Stallcup 1980a:55, Voorhoeve 1980a), at least Eastern Grassfields languages group with Narrow Bantu. The western portion of GB – the Peripheral, Momo, and Ring languages – do not share these features and so remain more distant from Narrow Bantu.

1.2.2 Internal

The internal unity of GB is clear. Stallcup (1980a:54) claims these languages share a 60 percent lexical similarity, while Piron (1995:16) suggests 41 percent. The two major questions about the internal classification of GB languages concern the number of subdivisions and the criteria for making these divisions. Proposals have varied from two to twelve subdivisions. Richardson (1957:56–72) recognized a two-way division between the Nkom group and the Bamileke group. Later Williamson (1971:266) rejected Richardson's two-way division, suggesting twelve parallel groups (Williamson 1971:270–80).

More recent classifications return to fewer divisions. Stallcup (1980a:54–5) focuses on the major two-way split between eastern and western GB. He uses seven noun class criteria and two lexical criteria. Dieu and Renaud (1983), following Hombert's (1979) presentation at Leiden, recognize a four-way split. Hombert, like Hyman (1980c), excluded Menchum from GB, but Dieu and Renaud retained it, giving Menchum, Momo, Ring, and Eastern Grassfields. Watters and Leroy (1989) suggested a more graded division. Menchum was included on the basis of Boum's (1980) study. Menchum, Western Momo, and Grassfields thus formed three parallel branches. Grassfields then subdivided into Momo, Ring, and Mbam-Nkam. Piron's (1995) lexicostatistical study, comparing 169 items and using the branch average method, arrived at similar results to those of Watters and Leroy. The only exceptions involved single languages: Ambele was probably separate from Western Momo, and Ndemli probably was within the narrow GB. Piron noted that the higher division could be seen as a two-way split between the narrow

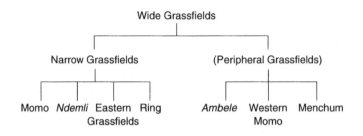

FIGURE 14.1 PIRON'S INTERNAL CLASSIFICATION OF WIDE GRASSFIELDS (BRANCH AVERAGE METHOD)

Note: Individual languages in italics.

Grassfields and the remaining languages as periphery. Piron's figure 7 (1995:16) is provided in figure 14.1, with the label 'Peripheral Grassfields' provided by me.

The major problem presented in these studies concerns the Mbam-Nkam languages vs. the rest. The Mbam-Nkam languages share certain noun class features with the Narrow Bantu languages that are completely missing in the remainder of GB. For example, the Mbam-Nkam languages have nasal consonants in the prefixes of classes 1 and 3, all nouns in classes 9 and 10 have a nasal consonant in the prefix, classes 6 and 6a are not distinguished, and all noun prefixes have a low tone (see Stallcup 1980a:55). None of the other GB languages share these morphological features. For a group of languages like GB that are so tightly linked lexically, the puzzle is to understand how this morphological difference emerged. Voorhoeve's (1980a) preferred explanation is that borrowing of vocabulary took place between these languages due to intensive economic contact. He cites Warnier (1976) to support this thesis. The scenario would involve the ancestor language of Mbam-Nkam coming into contact with the ancestors of the other GB languages through trade. The pre-Mbam-Nkam language already had the Bantu nasal innovations, and then over time took on significant vocabulary from their western neighbors. Hyman (1980c), however, suggests the thesis of possible multiple centers of innovation of the nasal classes coupled with spreading outward from these centers of innovation. For a third hypothesis, namely that the innovation is the *loss* of nasals, see Miehe (1991, cf. Hedinger 1993).

1.3 Language names and populations

The fifty-plus languages of GB are listed and classified below. The classification includes the language name, variants of the name, and an estimated population number. The subgroup classificatory names are given in bold and the individual language names in italics. Most of the names and alternative names come from Dieu and Renaud (1983) while the population estimates come from Grimes (2000). The classification follows Watters and Leroy (1989) but with more detailed modifications from Piron (1995). These modifications include: (1) the possible peripheral nature of Ambele, (2) the inclusion of Ndemli within Grassfields, and (3) the making of the North branch a parallel branch of Mbam-Nkam within Eastern Grassfields. Instead of using the binary split suggested by Piron in figure 14.1 above, the classification below lists the first three branches of GB, namely, Ambele, Western Momo, and Menchum, as parallel branches of the Narrow GB branch. The Narrow GB branch includes the majority of GB languages and three major branches: Momo, Ring, and Eastern Grassfields. Finally, within Eastern Grassfields, the North branch has been separated out based on Elias *et al.* (1984:71–4) and following Piron (1995:19), and made a parallel branch to Mbam-Nkam. Note that the GB languages do *not* include Tikar or the following groups: Beboid, Nyang, or Ekoid.

In the classification below, the primary name is in most cases the term used by speakers of the language. However, in some cases it is the name used in the linguistic literature. The following abbreviations are used:

a: administrative name (see Dieu and Renaud 1983)
s: speaker's name for the language
n: neighbors (see Dieu and Renaud 1983)
d: dialects (d+) additional dialects (see Dieu and Renaud 1983)
+:   other names (see Dieu and Renaud 1983)

Note that the population numbers from 1982 may today be 50–80 percent higher than those given, depending on population growth over the last two decades. Most population numbers are taken from Grimes (2000). Some questions that remain within each subgroup are listed at the end of each subgroup. These may serve as future research questions. The underlined names are those used in this chapter in place of the first and main name listed.

GRASSFIELDS BANTU   **Population**

(1) *Ambele* (see Piron 1995:15–16)   no estimate
    Question: Should Ambele be separate or included within Western Momo?

(2) **Western Momo**

    (a) *Manta* (+Menta, Amasi, Amassi, Anta, Banta,   13,600 (1982)
       Bantakpa)
    (b) *Busam*   no estimate
    (c) *Atoŋ*   no estimate

    Question: What is the relationship of Ngwo to these languages? A recent survey of
        Manta indicates that the region of the village of Amassi may be better classified
        as a dialect of Ngwo (Ed Brye pc).

(3) **Menchum**

    (a) *Modele-Befang* (d:usheida(a:Modelle)(n:mɔdɛlɛ,   no estimate
       idələ, ambabiko))
       (d:ushaku(a:Mukuru)(n:beɛkuru, iku, aku))(d:gə(a:Befang, Beba-Befang)(n:Bifaŋ))
       (d:Obang)(d:Bangwe (a:Bangwi, Bangui))(d:Okomanjaŋ (a:Okoromandjang))

    Question: Is Modele one language or are Modele and Befang different languages?

(4) **Narrow Grassfields**

    (a) **Momo**

       (i)   *Ngwɔ* (d:Ngwɔ(a:<u>Ngwo</u>, Ngwaw)(n:Nguni,   31,000 (1982)
           Mighuni))
          (d+:Konda, Basa/Bassa,
           Ikweri/Ekperi, Banya, Bako, Okorobi)
       (ii) *Ngɪshe* (a:Oshie; n:Mise)   5,000 (1984)
       (iii) *Ngie* (n:uŋgiə, ŋgi)   26,000–31,000 (1982)

(iv) *Menka*	12,500 (1982)
(v) *Moghamo-Menemo cluster (Widikum-Tadkon)*	120,000 (2000)
(d:*Meta* '(a:Metta, Menemo)(n: Uta?, Bameta) (+Muta,Mitaa))	50,000 (2000)
(d:*Moghamo*(n:Muywi)(d:Iyirikum(a:Widekum, Twirikum?))	70,000 (2000)
(d:Batibo, Besi, Kugwe))	
(d:*Ngamambo*(n:Mbu, Mungyen) (+Bafuchu, Banja, Nja, Ngembo))	no estimate
(vi) *Mundani*	34,000 (1987)

Note: Meta', Moghamo, and Ngamambo are treated as dialects of Moghamo-Menemo on Klaus and Janice Spreda's evaluation reported by Ed Brye.

Question: Should 'Njen' of Stallcup (1980a) be included with Mundani?

(b) **Ring**

(i) **South**

(a) *Wushi* (a:Babessi)(n:Vəsi, Pɛsii, Sii)	12,000 (1982)
(b) *Bamunka* (n:Mbɨka)	15,200 (1982)
(c) *Kənswei nsei* (a:Bamessing)(n:Vətəŋ, Vətwəŋ, Bəfi,Məsɪŋ)	12,500 (1982)
(d) *Vəŋo* (a:Babungo)(n:ŋgwa, ŋgə, Vəŋgɪ, Pəŋgə, ŋguu)	14,000 (1985)

Note: Watters and Leroy (1989) mistakenly referred to this group as 'North' (Piron 1995:17).

(ii) **East**

(a) *Lamnsɔ'* (s:nsɔ')(a:Nso, Nsaw, Banso, Bansaw) (n:Nshɔ', Banso')	125,000 (1987)

(iii) **Center**

(a) *Babanki* (n:Kəjəŋ)	22,500 (2000)
(b) *Kom* (n:Koŋ, Bikom, Nkom)(+Mbizenaku)	127,000 (1982)
(c) *Kuɔ* (a:<u>Oku</u>)(n:Bvukoo, Uku)	40,000 (1991)
(d) *Bum* (n:Bom)	20,000 (2000)
(e) *Mmɛn* (n:Bafmen)(a:Bafumen, Bafmeng, Bafoumeng)	no estimate

(iv) **West**

(a) *Aghem Cluster* (d:Aghem, Wi-isu(Wi(a:Weh)), Isu (+Esu, Umusu Zoa, Kumfutu, Kung, Kuk, Cha', Nyos, Fungom))

(i) *Aghem*	20,000–25,000 (1993)
(ii) *Weh* (+Wi)	7,000 (1994)
(iii) *Isu* (+Esu, Umusu)	10,400 (1994)
(iv) *Fungom*	1,000 (1994)
(v) *Oso* (+Osso, Southern Fungom, Ndum)	31,000 (1982)
(vi) *Laimbue* (+Cha', Nyos)	5,000 (1994)

(b) *Mundabli* (aka *Bum*) (+Mundabli, Mufu, Bu) (= Piron's 'Bu'?)	575 (2000)

Question: Are Aghem, Weh, and Isu separate languages? What of Laimbue (Cha' + Nyos), Oso, and Fungom? How do these three relate to Mundabli and Mmen of Center Ring? Piron's (1995:17) numbers suggest one Aghem language. What of mutual intelligibility?

(c) *Ndemli* (see Piron 1995:16)   no estimate

Question: Is Ndemli really an isolate? To what subgrouping could it belong?

(d) **Eastern Grassfields**

(i) **North**

    (a) *Limbum* (a:Wimbum) (n:Nsungli, Bɔjiin)   73,000 (1982)
      (+Nde yulana)
    (b) *Dzodinka* (a:Adere)   2,500 (1994)
    (c) *Mfumte* (+Nde Wuli, De wungtse)   25,000 (1982)
      (+1/2 Kwája, Ndaktup, Ncha, Bitui/Bitwi)
    (d) *Yamba* (a:Kaka yamba) (+1/2 Kwája)   30,000–40,000
                                           (1993)

Reference dialect is Mbem. Each of seventeen villages with a chief has its own dialect, forming a continuum of inter-intelligibility (Ginny Bradley pc)

    (e) *Mbə'* (a:Mbaw, Mbo)(+Mbɔ (= Piron's   no estimate
      'Nde bukwok'?))

Refers to area known as Mbɔ Plain, on northern border of Yamba. Each of thirteen villages has its own language, some more closely related to Tikar. Same as Mbe' in Grimes (2000:44) (Ginny Bradley pc).

(ii) **Mbam-Nkam**

    (a) **Nun**

        (i) *Mungaka* (d:Bali nyɔŋa(a:Bali))   50,000 (1982)
            (d:Bapakum(a:Baba I,Bapa))
            (d:Ti (a:Bati))(d:Ndɛ(a:Bandeng))
        (ii) *Bamoun cluster*

            [a] *Shʉpaməm* (a:<u>Bamoun</u>, Bamun)(n:pə   215,000(1982)
               shyɔ, tsə, mɛto')(+Bapi)
            [b] *Bafanji* (s:Nchufi)   8,500 (1982)
            [c] *Bamali*   5,300 (1982)
            [d] *Bambalang* (s:Mboyakum)   14,500 (1982)
            [e] *Bangolan*   6,000–15,000 (1994)

        (iii) *Mamənyam* (+Pamənyan)(a:Bamenyam)   4,000 (1994)

Question: Does the Bamoun cluster form five or fewer languages? [a] is in the West Province, [b] through [e] in the North West Province.

Question: Do the Nun and Bamileke languages actually comprise three parallel subgroups to Ngemba, giving (1) Western Bamileke (i.e. Western Mbam-Nkam), (2) Eastern Bamileke with Mədʉmba (i.e. Southern Mbam-Nkam), (3) Nun (i.e. Eastern Mbam-Nkam), (4) Ngemba (i.e. Northern Mbam-Nkam)?

(b) **Ngemba**

(Speakers of each language below refer to their language as 'Ngemba.')

(i) *Mundum* (d:Mberewi(a:Mundum I,   see Mankon
Bamundum I))
(d:Anyang(a:Mundum II, Bamundum II))

(ii) *Bafut* (d:Bufe = Afughe, Bafut)(d:Beba'
(a:Mubadji(nBaba'zhi)))   50,000 (1987)
(+Batadji, Shishong, Babadji, Bebadji,
Bazhi, Biba)

(iii) *Mankon* (d:Maŋkunə(a:Ngemba, Bandeng,
Bande, Mankon))   70,000 (1982)
(n:Bandə', Nkunə, Mukohn)
(d:Shomba(+Bamechom, Alamatson))
(d:Songwa(+Bangwa, Ngwa))(d:Mbutu
(+Bambutu, Alamatu))
(d:Njong(+Banjong))(d:Bagangu(a:Akum))

(iv) *Bambili* (d:Mbili(a:Bambili)(n:Mbələ,   10,000 (1984)
Mbøgoe))
(d:Mbui(a:Bambui))

(v) *Nkwen* (d:Nkwen(+Bafreng))
(d:Mendankwe/Mandankwe(+Munda,   10,000 (1994)
Bamenda))

(vi) *Pinyin* (d:Pinyin(n:Pəlimpo))(d:alatining)   16,000 (1982)

(vii) *Awing* (d:Mbwə'wi(a:Awing)(n:Awi,   7,000 (1989)
Bambuluwe))
(d:Bamunkumbit(+Bamunkum))

Question: On the basis of comparing vocabularies, Williamson (1971) suggested four subgroups: (1) Pinyin-Mankon-Awing, (2) Bafut, (3) Bambili-
Nkwen, and (4) Mundum. Leroy (1977:16) suggests seven units based
on intercomprehension. Piron (1995:19) suggests that Bafut-Bambili
might be considered one language as well as Mankon-Awing. Piron
further suggests that Pinyin subgroups with Bafut and Bambili. Recent
surveys suggest Bamunkumbit is separate from Awing. What would
further research on inter-comprehension, lexicostatistics, and reconstruction suggest?

(c) **Bamileke**

(i) *Ngombale* (d:Babadjou(Basso, Nchobela))   45,000 (1993)
(d:Bamessingue(Bassing))(d:Penyu)

(ii) *Məgaka* (s:gham(a:Bagam))   20,000 (1993)
(+Mengaka, Bamendjin, Galim, Ghap,
Benzing)

(iii) *Ngomba* (+Ndaa, Nda'a)   10,000–20,000
(d:Bamete(Babete), Bamenjinda, Bamesso,   (1994)
Bamenkumbo, Bamendjo)

(iv) *Ngyɛmbɔɔŋ* (<u>Ngiemboon</u>, previously   100,000 (1987)
Ngyemboon)
(d:Bangang, Batcham, Balatchi,
Bamoungong, Balessing)

(v)	*Yɛmba* (*Yemba*) (s:Atsaŋ)(a:Dschang) (d:East, West, Central, South, Southwest) (see Dieu and Renaud 1983 for details)	300,000 (1992)
(vi)	*Nweh* (*Ngwe*) (+ŋwe, bangwa) (d:Fossimobing, Fontem, Bamok)	50,000 (1992)
(vii)	*Ghɔmala'* (*Banjoun*) (d:South, Central, North, Ngɔmba) (see Dieu and Renaud 1983 for further details)	260,000 (1982)
(viii)	*Fe'fe'* (d:Central, North) (see Dieu and Renaud 1983 for further details)	124,000 (1982)
(ix)	*Kwa'* (d:Kwa(+Bɛkwa, Mipa)(a:Bakoua, Babwa))(d:Mbyam)	1,000 (2000)
(x)	*Nda'nda'* (d:East(Undimeha), West (Ungameha), South) (see Dieu and Renaud 1983 for further details)	10,000 (1984)
(xi)	*Mɔdumba* (+Bangangté, Bandounga, Tonga, Bangoulap)	210,000 (1991)

Question: What might be the possible subgroupings of the eleven Bamileke languages? Do they form one coherent unit? Hyman's (1972:7–9) comments based on noun class and phonological differences suggest that (*i*)–(*vi*) form a Western Bamileke, and (*vii*)–(*xi*) an Eastern Bamileke, with the western Ngɔmba dialect of Ghɔmala? serving as a transition dialect between the two. Would this be valid?

Question: Languages (*iv*)–(*vi*) form a continuum of dialects that might be considered one language as to mutual comprehension. We could refer to them as the 'Bamboutos Cluster' for the nearby mountains. Are the boundaries between these three and languages (*i*)–(*iii*) distinct?

2 PHONOLOGY

The phonologies referred to below represent differing levels of depth in their analyses. Re-analysis of those with larger phonemic inventories may reduce their inventories in significant ways.

2.1 Syllable and morpheme structure

The primary syllable structures for noun and verb roots include CV, CVC, CSV, CSVC and V, where S represents semi-vowels. In some cases CVV is interpreted as a single syllable, with VV being either a long vowel or a diphthong. Affixes and particles typically consist of CV, V, VC, N, and CVN. These features are true whether they be Momo languages such as Ngie (Hombert 1977) and Mundani (Parker 1981); Ring languages such as Babungo (Schaub 1985), Oku (Davis 1992), Aghem (Hyman 1979b); North languages of Eastern Grassfields such as Limbum (Fiore 1987) or Yamba (Scruggs 1980); or Mbam-Nkam languages such as Fanchi (Koopman 1994), Ngemba (Leroy 1977), Bafut (Mfonyam 1982), Fe'fe' (Hyman 1972), Ngiemboon (Anderson 1983), Ngwe

(Dunstan 1964), or Banjoun (Nissim 1981). In Limbum (Fiore 1987:15) some dialects simplify CV- prefixes to C-, so that *vi-* becomes *p-* or *b-*, and *li-* becomes *r-* or *l-*, as in [p-tʃê] 'trees' and [rbu:] 'egg'. In Ring languages, the prefix for classes 3 and 8 may include the labialization of the initial stem consonant: *àtám* 'trap' but *ətwám* 'traps' in Kom (Hyman 1980a:254–5).

Lexical stems are commonly monosyllabic. Nissim (1981:78) reports that for Banjoun (Bamileke) 46 percent are open (CV) and 54 percent are closed (CVC). Thus, for nouns, the canonical Bantu disyllabic stems have been reduced to monosyllabic stems.

Syllabic nasals are commonly used as prefixes and grammatical markers. In some cases, nasal noun prefixes have been reinterpreted as part of the stem, producing NCV(C) and similar stems. Typical Bantu verbal prefixes for person and tense-aspect behave more like monosyllabic verbal clitics, separate from the verbal word, than affixes. Therefore, verb stems are also often monosyllabic. Disyllabic stems that do occur are usually composed of two morphemes.

2.2 Vowels

Elias *et al.* (1984:41) reconstruct seven vowels for Proto-Mbam-Nkam, which is the probable proto-system for GB as a whole. Systems of seven vowels are reported for Oku (Ring) /i ɪ ɛ ə a u ɔ/ (Davis 1992:31), Limbum (North) /i e ɛ ɨ a o ɔ/ (Fiore 1987:60), Yamba (North) /i e ɪ ə a u o/ (Scruggs 1980:24), and Ngiemboon (Bamileke) /i e ɛ a u o ɔ/ (Anderson 1983:4). For these languages, the relevant distinctions are degrees of rounding and height.

Most GB languages, however, appear to have eight to ten vowels, whether they be found in the Momo, Ring, or Eastern Grassfields branches. These languages add the degree of backness to that of rounding and height. Examples include Mundani (Momo) (Parker 1981:22) with eight /i ə ɯ u e ɑ o ɔ/, Ngie (Momo) (Hombert 1976) with ten vowels /i e ɛ ɨ œ ə a u o ɔ/ (or seven to eight in Hombert 1977:3), Babungo (Ring) (Schaub 1985:259) with nine /i e ɛ ɪ ə a u o ɔ/, Aghem (Ring) (Hyman 1979b:1) with nine /i ɪ e ɛ a u ʊ o ɔ/, Mankon (Ngemba) (Leroy 1977:50) and Bafut (Ngemba) (Mfonyam 1982:17) having nine, and Banjoun (Bamileke) (Nissim 1981:176) having ten. Restricted environments within the word commonly accompany these larger vowel inventories, but one rarely finds more than seven vowels contrasting in any given environment. In some environments the contrasts are reduced to as few as two or three. Further research on these larger inventories might reveal only seven underlying vowels, with the additional phonetic variants resulting from the fusion of a semi-vowel with one of the seven vowels (Anderson pc).

Long vowels are common throughout GB, and so are diphthongs. One can expect that at least seven of the short vowel variants will also have long forms. In Limbum (Fiore 1987:58) 'one-third of all [CV] stems end in long vowels'.

Various processes of vowel assimilation, lengthening, deletion, nasalization, velarization and gliding are reported in environments where two vowels coalesce. Of interest is the vowel glide formation reported for Aghem (Hyman 1979b;11) where e → z, o → w, and a → gh when followed by /ɨ/ in demonstratives. Vowel harmony is not a significant issue given the monosyllabic nature of most stems in GB languages. However, vowel assimilation is found throughout GB in the form of 'echo vowels' – as suffixes on verbs and as final root vowels in nouns.

2.3 Consonants

Stops commonly include the opposition between the voiceless set /p t k/ and the voiced set /b d g/ (see Mundani (Momo) (Parker 1981:9)). However, the opposition between voiceless and voiced bilabials /p/ and /b/ may be weak, as in Ngie (Momo) (Hombert 1977:1), or be absent, as in Mbam-Nkam, so that [p] and [b] are allophones and analyses vary as to which is chosen as the phonemic form: /b/ for Fe'fe' (Bamileke) (Hyman 1972:30) and Ngiemboon (Anderson 1983:4), but /p/ for Yemba (Bird 1996) and Ngomba (Satre 1997). In Fanchi (Nun) (Koopman 1994:3) a distinction in aspiration substitutes for the more common voicing distinction, giving the aspirated set /pʰ tʰ kʰ/ and the unaspirated set /p t/. Elias *et al.* (1984:39, 41) reconstruct the full voiceless and voiced set for Proto-Mbam-Nkam. In Mundani (Momo) (Parker 1981:9), Aghem (Ring) (Hyman 1979b:3), Yamba (North) (Scruggs 1980), and Nweh (Bamileke) (Dunstan 1964), a set of double-stops /kp gb/ are reported. In other languages such as Oku (Ring), Limbum (North), and Fanchi (Nun) the set is simply labialized /kʷ gʷ/. Otherwise double-stops are absent in many GB languages. The glottal stop /ʔ/ is widely reported.

Fricatives include at least /f s/. However, various languages additionally include one or more of the following: /v z ɣ/. The Ring languages such as Babungo and Aghem use one or more of the alveo-palatal fricatives /ʃ ʒ/. Nweh (Dunstan 1966a) has the richest array of fricatives: labials /β f v/, alveolars /s z/, palatals /ʃ ʒ/, velars /ɣ/, and glottal /h/. The fricative glottal /h/ seems to be limited to only Eastern Grassfields languages, such as Limbum, Nweh, Fe'fe', and Banjoun. However, /h/ in many of the GB languages is found primarily in loan words (Steve Anderson pc).

The sets of affricates /tʃ dʒ/ or /ts dz/ are common, with GB languages using one set or the other. However, in Yamba the full set of four affricates is systematic: /ts dz ch dʒ/ (Scruggs 1980:11–15). Bamileke languages often have an additional set of affricates: /pf bv/. Banjoun (Nissim 1981:171–4) possesses both /pf/ and /bv/, while Ngiemboon (Anderson 1983:4) and Nweh (Dunstan 1966a) have only /pf/. The Ring language Aghem (Hyman 1979b:3) has /bv/.

The semi-vowels, or glides, /y w/ are nearly universal. In some cases, they occur as allophones, such as [y] as the realization of /j/ when not preceded by a nasal in Fe'fe' (Hyman 1972). A third semi-vowel /ẅ/ is reported in Ngiemboon (Anderson 1983:4).

Laterals /l/ but not trills /r/ are found in Momo and Ring languages. Among the Mbam-Nkam languages, Limbum, Yamba and Nweh have both /r/ and /l/. But in various Bamileke languages, such as Nyemboon, Fe'fe', Banjoun, [l] and [r] are often in allophonic relation with [d]. The Bamileke language Nweh (Dunstan 1966a), on the other hand, phonetically has both a voiced and voiceless bilabial trill [P] and [B]. These trills are releases of prenasalized bilabial stops (Ladefoged and Maddieson 1996:130–1).

The nasal set may include /m n ɲ ŋ/. The palatal nasal /ɲ/ occurs less frequently and its phonological status is often uncertain, but it is found in Momo languages such as Ngie and Mundani, and Ring languages such as Babungo and Aghem. In addition, Mundani and Aghem have the double-nasal [ŋm] before double-stops.

The consonants mentioned above all occur in the initial consonant position of the syllable (and stem). In contrast, the final consonant position of syllables, and stems, limits the consonants. Rather than fifteen to twenty-five consonants, only one to eight occur in the final position. The common sets involve three stops /p t k/ or /b d g/, and three nasals /m n ŋ/. Numerous languages include the glottal stop /ʔ/. Other reported final consonants include /r/, /l/, /s/, and /h/. The more limited sets are reported for Babungo (Schaub 1985:268), using only /ŋ ʔ/, and villages speaking Mfumte, namely Lus and Kofa (Elias *et al.* 1984:41), using only /ʔ/. If final consonants in ideophones were included in the inventory, the set might include a few more consonants.

Consonant harmony does not exist synchronically in GB languages. Consonant clusters are not common. Some noun forms initially have a homorganic nasal followed by stop or fricative. At times the nasal is syllabic, in other cases non-syllabic. Otherwise, consonant clusters derive from palatalization or labialization, or from clusters across morpheme boundaries.

Various consonant processes are reported. Those that have phonological significance account for most of the morphophonemic processes in GB languages. The most common processes include aspiration, palatalization, and labialization.

Aspiration-type phenomena are widely attested in GB. They vary phonetically from language to language, from aspiration to fricativization. In Fanchi (Koopman 1994:3) the aspiration of stops is contrastive. Some Bamileke languages have homorganic voiceless fricative consonant offglides that may combine with palatalization and labialization. In some cases they lead to long consonants (Anderson 1982). Nweh (Dunstan 1966a) has affricates /kx gɣ/ that may derive from an aspiration process. In Kom (Ring) (Hyman 1980a, Ladefoged and Maddieson 1996:366), a secondary articulation type occurs consisting of transitional labiodental fricatives (or 'aspiration'). Thus, in the word iku 'death' the transition from k to u is a voiceless bilabial fricative Φ, giving [ikΦu], and in the word iʒu 'sky' the transition is a voiced bilabial fricative v, giving [iʒvu]. This labiodental constriction is coarticulated with the velar and coronal closure. These varying realizations of aspiration may function quite differently in closely related languages: they are predictable in Ngiemboon and not predictable in neighboring Yemba. The historical source of these phenomena remains an open question.

In the Bamileke languages, palatalization and labialization represent a complex set of forms. For example, Ngiemboon (Anderson pc) has four phonetic offglide variants: front rounded and front unrounded, as well as back rounded and back unrounded. However, these converge to form only three phonological variants, with the front rounded and back unrounded as allophones (see also Haynes 1989 for Yemba). In Banjoun (Nissim 1981:175–6) four forms are reported: palatal, pre-dorsal, labio-velar, labio-palatal: /y ɥ w ẅ/. These may serve as 'S' modifications of the initial consonant in CSV(C) syllables (Nissim 1981:106–7), or as initial consonants in CV(C) syllables. As an initial consonant, the /ẅ/ is best reinterpreted as /yw/, a labialized palatal glide. In Aghem, labialization may produce double-stops, so that /k + w, b + w, g + w, ŋ + w/ produce /kp, gb, ŋm/. For example, the singular /kɨ-báʔ/ 'rope' takes an /ó-/ prefix in the plural which would labialize the initial root consonant, giving us /bʷ/. However, instead of the expected */ó-bʷáʔ/ we find the plural /ó-gbáʔ/ 'ropes'. Other examples include spirantization in Yamba, where /k/ becomes /x/ word final (Scruggs 1980:23), and affrication in Oku (Davis 1992), where /b k g/ become /bv kf gv/ before /ə/.

Another process is the assimilation of nasal prefixes to the point of articulation of the initial root consonant. In the process, the initial root consonant may also assimilate, such as voiceless stops becoming voiced and so neutralizing the voicing distinction following nasal prefixes. Neutralization also occurs with stops in the final consonant position before pause, where they generally devoice or are unreleased.

2.4 Tones

Grassfields Bantu languages have some of the most complex tone systems of any group of languages in Africa. It is generally assumed that historically they had a tone system of two tone levels, H(igh) and L(ow), as reconstructed for Proto-Bantu (Greenberg 1948 and Meeussen 1967:84). Verbs divided into two classes: those with H tone and those with L. Nouns divided into four classes, all with L tone prefixes: L-LL, L-LH, L-HL, L-HH.

Disyllabic noun roots then lost final vowels or entire final syllables. Only a few Ngemba languages have maintained a second vowel, and syllable, a schwa /ə/. The result was multiple monosyllabic noun roots. In the process, however, the tone of the lost vowel or syllable remained a feature of the root – an exception is the present-day deletion of certain L tones in Aghem in specific contexts (Hyman 1987). In some cases this extra word-final tone joined with the preceding root tone to form a tonal contour, whether falling tone (i.e. H-L) or rising tone (i.e. L-H). In other cases it became a floating tone – i.e. a tone not associated with a specific syllable. In still other cases it led to the elaboration of additional pitch levels, including downstep terracing.

Furthermore, some languages also lost the segmental substance of the noun prefix in some classes, but again did not lose the prefix tone. This meant that some roots today have a prefix tone and a final root tone, neither of which is associated with a syllable at an underlying level of representation. Similar processes applied to verb roots and grammatical markers, so that verbs and grammatical markers often have floating tones as a feature of the morpheme. In many cases the grammatical markers are only marked by a floating tone, particularly verbal affixes.

To account for the varied tonal phenomena found in GB languages, Voorhoeve (1971), in his study of Bangangte nouns, proposed an underlying sequence of three tones for every noun, each tone being either high or low. Since most current noun forms are monosyllabic or disyllabic, some of the tones were 'floating tones'. The tri-tonal nature of all nouns became the basis for most analyses of nominal tone in GB languages. More fundamentally, the assumption was that the best way to account for the complex tonal phenomena was to start with the historical antecedents and derive the modern-day surface forms from those antecedents. The evidence for this assumption was indirect, but lay in the impact of the floating tones on neighboring tones, and the otherwise inexplicable tonal behavior of nouns in various contexts. The assumption that tones can and do persist even when the segmental substance of entire syllables is lost became foundational to nearly all tone analyses of GB languages during the past thirty years. See Hombert (1976:11–15), Asongwed and Hyman (1976:32–43) and Hyman and Tadadjeu (1976) for examples. However, Chumbow and Nguendjio (1991) provide a synchronic analysis that does not use lexical floating tones for Bangwa (or Nda?nda? East, a Bamileke language). So what are some of the tonal phenomena that these analytical perspectives were created to address? If tone in GB languages is no longer a sequence of H and L tones, what was found? (See in particular Hyman 1976b, 1979c,d, 1987 for elaboration of the following comments.) All GB languages have at least four levels: high (H), mid (M), low (L^n), and low that falls (L). The mid tone in most languages is a downstepped high ($^{\downarrow}$H), with each new $^{\downarrow}$H establishing a new ceiling for all following H tones. So most GB languages contrast a HH sequence from a H$^{\downarrow}$H sequence. In some cases an additional pitch level is identified. For example, Meta' (Spreda 1986) has a 'raised low' that derives from the simplification of a HL sequence on a root with an L tone prefix. The $^{\downarrow}$H is commonly explained by the presence of a preceding floating L tone that lowers the H. However, Hyman (1979d:15–16) suggests that $^{\downarrow}$H ultimately derives from a preceding H-L contour tone so that H $^{\downarrow}$H derives from H-LH rather than HLH. Most languages also have two different L tones, one that falls before pause, and the other that remains level. The first is understood as simple L with phrase final intonation, while the second is considered to be L followed by a floating H. The H blocks the normal fall of the L. We symbolize this L as L^n. However, within Mbam-Nkam, for various languages in the Ngemba group, and for Bafanji in the Nun group the level low tone is not present. Instead of having a floating H following an L, the LH sequence is realized as a rising tone on the surface (Elias et al. 1984:62–70).

Besides these level tones, various contour tones are attested in all languages. Returning to the issue of M tones, some languages actually have M tone instead of $^{\downarrow}$H. These include most of the Center Ring and East Ring languages (Grebe and Grebe 1975,

Hyman 1979c, Grebe 1982). An example is Babanki, a Center Ring language, with both an M tone, that may only occur before an H tone and never following pause, and $^{\downarrow}$H. Other languages with M tone include Bafut (Ngemba) (Mfonyam 1982), that has H, M, L, L^n, and Modele, a Peripheral GB language, that has a $^{\downarrow}$H that could just as well be interpreted as an M tone (Hyman 1979d:20–1). So common tonal antecedents can lead to different tone systems.

This variation from common antecedents is well exemplified by the southern Bamileke languages in contrast to the other Bamileke languages. Bamileke languages generally have the sequence H$^{\downarrow}$H, but not the southern Bamileke ones. They have M tone. The M derives from what was previously the H tone, and the current day H tone derives from what was the H tone that preceded $^{\downarrow}$H. The historic H before $^{\downarrow}$H first became a super-H tone, then became simply H when the $^{\downarrow}$H became M (Hyman 1976b:128ff.). So these languages have taken a further step in tonal reinterpretation, moving from a language with H, $^{\downarrow}$H, L, L^n to one with H, M, L, L^n. The phenomenon of making a super-H out of the H that used to precede a $^{\downarrow}$H is also attested in Ngemba with its tonal upstep (Leroy 1977). Tonal upstep in Ngemba not only derives from raising H tone in anticipation of a $^{\downarrow}$H, but also from an underlying L-HL-H sequence which becomes L-H-super-H.

A feature of West Ring languages and Babanki from Center Ring (Hyman 1979c:176–7) is automatic downdrift. Accompanied by downstepped H, these languages demonstrate a standard 'terraced' tone system, in which every H following a L is a little lower than any H preceding that L. Thus, the range of the pitches changes over the time of the utterance. In contrast, most other GB languages do not have automatic downdrift. This includes Momo, various Ring, and Eastern Grassfields languages.

Many of the tonal complexities of GB languages show themselves when nouns and verbs occur in phrases. With nouns, e.g. they may appear to have identical tone patterns in isolation, but then in another context, such as following a locative preposition, they may diverge. Thus, ultimately they need to be separated into two or more distinct tone classes. In Mankon (Ngemba), e.g. which is part of Mbam-Nkam and so only has L tone noun prefixes, the underlying tone patterns L-LH and L-HH are neutralized in certain contexts. They both produce a surface sequence L-LH through the spreading of L tone prefix in the case of L-HH nouns (Leroy 1979). In Babanki (Center Ring), with noun prefixes that usually have H tone, nouns with H-LH and H-HH patterns neutralize when they occur in the genitive or locative position, or have a nasal consonant depressing the tone (Hyman 1979c:164–6).

One of the less complex tone systems in the GB region is found in Aghem (West Ring). Aghem (Hyman 1979b:1, 12) has H, L, and downstepped high $^{\downarrow}$H, plus automatic downdrift. Aghem has four kinds of tone rules: (1) 'tone grounding' for the floating tones; (2) 'tone spreading', particularly from noun prefix to noun root; (3) 'tone lowering' which lowers a noun prefix tone from H to L when it follows a verb with a final L; and (4) 'tone simplification', which simplifies sequences like LH-H to L-H and L-HL to L-L. Significantly, these rules are common in GB languages.

Moving away from the West Ring languages to other Ring, Momo, and Eastern Grassfield languages, the tone systems become more complex. Though they do not have downdrift, they do have multiple phonetic pitch levels. Ngamambo (Momo) as presented by Asongwed and Hyman (1976) has five phonetic pitch levels and at least ten tone patterns on bisyllabic nouns. (This analysis is superseded by Hyman 1986 based on different data.) Ngie (Momo) (Hombert 1976) similarly has ten contrastive patterns on bisyllabic nouns, bisyllabic being noun prefix plus the monosyllabic noun root.

Perhaps the most complex system in the GB region is that of Yemba (or Dschang-Bamileke) and its closest neighbors, Ngiemboon (Anderson 1983) and Nweh. Research on the tone system of Yemba has contributed significantly to the development of tone theory over the past thirty years. Following Voorhoeve (1971), Tadadjeu (1974) presented Yemba with its surprising combination of downstep without automatic downdrift, including both downstepped high and downstepped low tones. Downstepped low tones were something new. Yemba also allows for downstepped tones immediately after pause, another new twist. In addition, seven contrasts occur after H and eight after L, further confirming its complexities. These include discrete levels, downstepped levels, and double-downstepped levels (Hyman 1979c:13). Aghem, by contrast, would only have three contrasts after H and two after L.

Hyman and Tadadjeu (1976) provided a more comprehensive analysis of tone in the Mbam-Nkam languages, including a more detailed analysis of the unusual tone system of Yemba (Dschang-Bamileke). Additional studies of these complex systems are found in Anderson (1981, 1983), Stewart (1981), and Pulleyblank (1986). Pulleyblank notes that none of the other studies carefully distinguished between phonological and phonetic rules, which he concluded led to a certain confusion in their analyses. He himself argued for the application of a set of post-lexical rules: high tone spreading, lowering of high tone, and deletion of low and high tones. The unusual rule, however, involves metathesis of a HL tone sequence. The reversal of this order to LH accounts for surface-level downstepped-high tones as well as downstepped-low tones. Pulleyblank's metathesis rule for Dschang is reminiscent of a similar rule in Anderson (1983) for Ngyembɔɔŋ. Nissim (1981) reports a suffix in deverbal nouns with metathesis of H plus floating L to produce a rising LH tone. Articles that have contributed more recently to the theoretical discussion of Yemba tone include Hyman (1985), Clark (1993), Stewart (1993), and Snider (1999). Snider provides a different analysis of downstepped low tone.

3 MORPHOLOGY

3.1 Nouns

3.1.1 Noun classes

Some of the more significant studies of the noun classes in GB languages include Hyman and Voorhoeve (1980), Hyman (1980b), Leroy (1977), and Nissim (1981). Noun classes form a set of isoglosses that divide GB languages into two major subgroupings. One group consists of the Eastern Grassfields languages. The other consists of the Peripheral, Momo, and Ring languages. The following seven isoglosses distinguish these two subgroups (Stallcup 1980a:55). In table 14.1, 'Eastern Grassfields' is Stallcup's 'Mbam-Nkam' and 'Peripheral, Momo, and Ring' are his 'Western Grassfields'.

Contrary to table 14.1, Anderson (1980) claims that Ngiemboon (Eastern Grassfields) still has a class 4 based on its distinctive noun prefix *meN-*. Apart from the homorganic nasal *N* in the prefix, the *me* portion of the prefix and the concord is identical to class 6.

Hyman (1980c:182) provides a full set of reconstructed noun class formatives, specifically noun prefixes and concord affixes, for Proto-Eastern Grassfields as well as for the combination of Proto-Momo and Proto-Ring (i.e. 'Western Grassfields'). These reconstructions demonstrate the criteria listed above.

Both the 'n' and 'N' prefixes represent homorganic nasals. In table 14.2, noun classes consist of a noun prefix and concord element. However, in some specific languages

TABLE 14.1: SEVEN ISOGLOSSES DISTINGUISH EASTERN GRASSFIELDS FROM MOMO AND RING

Eastern Grassfields	Peripheral, Momo, and Ring
1 Presence of a nasal consonant in the prefix of classes 1 and 3	Absence of a nasal consonant in the prefix of classes 1 and 3
2 No distinction between classes 6 and 6a: a nasal consonant occurs in the prefix and concord of classes 6 and 6a	Distinction between classes 6 and 6a, with a nasal consonant only in class 6a
3 Presence of a nasal consonant in the prefix of all nouns in the gender 9/10	Absence of a nasal consonant in the prefix of some nouns (not all) in gender 9/10
4 Absence of classes 4, 13, and 19, though 19 is present in Ngemba group	Presence of classes 13 and 19, with 4 present in some of the subgroups
5 All noun prefixes have a low tone	Some noun prefixes have a high tone
6 No noun suffixes	Suffixes -*ti* or -*si* in class 10
7 Classes 6, 6a, or 2 are used as the general plural class	Classes 13 or 10 are used as the general plural class

TABLE 14.2: RECONSTRUCTED NOUN CLASS FORMATIVES FOR PROTO-EASTERN GRASSFIELDS AND PROTO-MOMO AND RING

	Proto-Eastern Grassfields		Proto-Momo and Ring	
	Noun prefix	Concord	Noun prefix	Concord
1	ǹ-	ù-	ù(n)-	ù-
1a	–	(=1)	–	–
2	bə̀-	bə̀-	bə̀-	bə̀-
3	ǹ-	ú-	ú-	ú-
3a	ì-	(=3)	–	–
4	–	–	í-	í-
5	lì-	lí-	í-	í-
6	(=6a)	(=6a)	á-	gá-
6a	mə̀-	mə̀-	mə̀-*	mə̀-
7	à-	í-	kí-	kí-
8	bì-	bí-	bi-	bí-
9	ǹ-	ì-	ì(N)-	ì-
10	ǹ-	í-	i(N)-	Cí-
13	–	–	tí-	tí-
19	fə̀-	fə̀-	fí-	fí-

Note:
* For class 6a in Proto-Momo and Ring, Hyman (1980c) does not give a tone on p. 182, but comments on p. 183 suggest this tone is low as indicated above.

a given class may use a noun suffix rather than a noun prefix, and in other cases the noun prefix may be null.

The reconstructions above make the explicit claim that the GB noun classes correspond to the Proto-Bantu noun classes 1, 2, 3, 4, 5, 6, 7, 8, 9, 10, 13, and 19. In addition, some GB languages distinguish noun class 6 from 6a, which is a pre-Proto-Bantu distinction. Class 6a is used for liquids and is phonologically similar to Proto-Bantu noun class 6. Class 4 is present in only a few Peripheral-Momo-Ring languages. No GB language attests to Proto-Bantu classes 11, 12, 14, or 15, though Schaub (1985:172) claims 15 for Babungo as distinct from 7.

As for the locative classes 16, 17, and 18, residual or foreshadowing forms of these Proto-Bantu classes are present in various languages. See §3.1.2 for more discussion.

Various articles on noun classes in GB support the reconstructions above. These include articles on Menchum (Boum 1980), a Peripheral GB language, as well as the Momo languages in general (Stallcup 1980b), and on Mundani (Parker 1989). Other articles include those on Babanki and the Ring languages in general (Hyman 1980a). Within Eastern Grassfields, they concern the North subgroup of languages such as Limbum (Voorhoeve 1980b) and Adere or Dzodinka (Voorhoeve 1980c). Mbam-Nkam is represented by Nun (Hombert 1980), Ngemba (Leroy 1977, 1980), and Bamileke, both eastern Bamileke (Nissim 1980) and western Bamileke (Tadadjeu 1980 and Anderson 1980).

3.1.1.1 Peripheral, Momo, Ring

The Menchum (Boum 1980), Momo (Stallcup 1980b), and Ring (Hyman 1980a) languages have maintained a larger set of noun classes than Eastern Grassfields and Mbam-Nkam. Thirteen are reconstructed in table 14.2. Not only do they have classes corresponding to 1 through 10, including class 4, but also 13, and 19, and the pre-Proto-Bantu 6a. Low tone is used for concord elements with classes 1, 9, and 6a, where the other classes use high tone.

In Menchum, and Modele in particular (Boum 1980), we find thirteen noun classes. Classes 1, 7, 9, and 6a all have what could be interpreted as double prefixes. The pre-prefix is lost, however, when the noun is the object of a preposition, whether locative or genitive ('associative marker'): e.g. *ùmbù* 'head (Cl.1)' > *áyé mbù* 'on the head', and *kùdə̀ŋ* 'chief' (Cl.7) > *ùmbù ɔ̀də̀ŋ* 'head of the chief'. Instead of having class 13 like other western GB languages, Modele has a class '18'. Class 18 uses a homorganic nasal in the prefix but *m* in the concord elements. Some concord elements in Modele take a concord prefix, while others simultaneously take a concord prefix and suffix. The genders in Modele include 1/2 (humans and borrowings), 3/4, 5/6, 7/8, 9/10 (many animals), 19/18, 6a, 5/4, 7/6, 3/10, and 9/2 (?).

In Momo, within Narrow GB, Moghamo (Stallcup 1980b:195) has eleven noun classes and Mundani (Parker 1989) has thirteen. Moghamo does not have classes 4 or 5, while formally classes 6 and 7 are fully merged in Mundani. Class 6 is plural, however, and class 7 singular. The merging of classes 6 and 7 is a feature of Momo languages in general, as well as Kom and Bum, both Center Ring languages, with class 7 using the formatives of class 6 (Stallcup 1980b:222–3). Class 10 commonly uses the noun suffix *-ti* rather than a prefix. In class 19 of Mundani (Parker 1989), *k* is present in both the prefix and concord elements. The expected *f* is present only in the concord elements along with *k*. This mixture is unusual and looks like an incomplete merger of the earlier 7 and 19. Also in Mundani, Gender 1b/2b may serve as a diminutive for a set of nouns such as *ø-nyà, ø-nyà-tsə̄* 'animal, animals' (gender 9/10) but *á-nyà, bá-nyà* 'small animal/ insect, small animals/insects' (gender 1b/2b). The genders for Mundani include 1/2 (1a/2a, 1b/2b), 3/4 (3/6a?), 5/13, 7/8, 9/10, 19/13, 5/6, 6a. Gender 1/2 includes most nouns referring to humans, but also nouns referring to non-human categories. The gender 1a/2a includes kinship terms and titles within the social hierarchy, including professions. The gender 1b/2b refers to small people or young people.

In Ring, Babungo (South Ring) has fourteen classes (Schaub 1985:172), Babanki (Center Ring) has twelve (Hyman 1980a:226), and Aghem (West Ring) has twelve. Formally, Aghem only has nine distinct classes since 2 and 6, 3 and 8, and 4 and 5 are fully merged. Aghem genders include 1/2 (only nouns designating human beings), 3/4, 3/6a, 5/6, 5/13, 7/8, 9/13, 19/6a, 1/13, 3/6, 3/13, 7/4, 7/6, 7/6a, 7/13, 19/13. The single class genders are 3(=8), 4(=5), 9, 13, and 6a (designating masses or liquids).

In Ring, concords are complex and vary according to the syntactic construction. Prefixes, pre-prefixes, and suffixes are common. For example, for most nouns in Aghem, when the prefixed noun is followed by a modifying possessive, adjective, demonstrative, or genitive noun phrase, the noun prefix is deleted. Only with numerals is the prefix maintained. Thus, *fí-nwín* 'bird' becomes *nwín* [↓]*fáŋá* 'my bird', *nwín fìdú*[↓]*úfɔ́* 'big bird', *nwín* [↓]*fín* 'this bird', *nwín* [↓]*fí* [↓]*wé* 'bird of child', but *fí-nwín fì-mɔ̀ʔ* 'one bird'. In addition, nouns in Aghem vary between a prefixed and suffixed form depending on the syntactic construction type. So a given noun may have as many as three forms:

> *kí-bé* 'fufu' (Object, 'in-focus', A-Form)
> *bé-*[↓]*kɔ́* 'fufu' (Object, 'out-of-focus', B-Form)
> *bé* [↓]*kí* 'fufu' (preceding verb, where *kí* is an agreement marker)

Considerable variation exists from language to language within Ring, and they indicate that morphological changes can be subject to areal diffusion in the same way that sound changes are (Hyman 1980a:256). Classes 10 and 13 are both found in Center Ring, but only 13 in West Ring, and only 10 in East Ring. In class 7, the Ring languages have the expected *k* both in the prefix and concord elements, with the exception of Kom and Bum. In class 9 nouns demonstrate an interesting variation, with some nouns having a nasal prefix and others no prefix. This difference in prefix corresponds to a difference in tonal behavior as well. The suffix *-sí* in class 10 is common in Ring except for West Ring. Aghem (West Ring), e.g. uses class 13 as the plural of class 9 in place of 10, which is absent. In Ring class 4 is commonly absent, with gender 4/6a being replaced by 13/6a. Class 6a also serves as the plural of class 19. In Aghem, apart from a few exceptional nouns, all noun prefixes take a high tone. Many nouns in class 13 take a suffix *-a*. The subject concord in classes 1 and 9 has been reduced to a floating low tone only.

3.1.1.2 Eastern Grassfields

Eastern Grassfields has up to ten noun classes. Classes 4, 6a, and 19 are absent, though the Ngemba group has 19. Eastern Grassfields languages may have merged class 4 with 6 at a pre-Eastern Grassfields stage, as Tadadjeu (1980) has noted for Yemba (Dschang-Bamileke). Low tone is used throughout for concord in classes 1 and 9, and high tone for other classes. Nasal prefixes are present in classes 1, 3, 6, 9, and 10.

The eastern languages of Eastern Grassfields, whether from the North or Mbam-Nkam subgroups, have significantly reduced their noun class systems, while the western languages have been more conservative. Thus the North, the eastern Bamileke, and the Nun languages have reduced their systems to six, and even five, formal noun classes. In Banjoun (Ghomala?) the system no longer even marks agreement between the subject noun and the verb, though other agreement marking is in force.

Among the various noun class mergers in Eastern Grassfields, it is common to find that all eastern languages have merged 1 and 9, while the merging of 2 and 8 is often in process, if not yet completely achieved. For the eastern Bamileke and Nun languages in particular, 3 has merged with 7, and 8 with 10.

In the North subgroup, Limbum (Voorhoeve 1980b) has a complex system. It has many singular/plural genders with a small number of nouns in each due apparently to the incomplete merger of classes 2 and 8. Curiously, the system uses singular concords for the plural of human beings. The system could be said to have seven classes, three singular and four plural (Voorhoeve 1980b, Fiore 1987).

In Nun languages such as Bamoun and Bali the system has simplified to the point that the pronominal subject markers for third person distinguish only animate vs. inanimate referents rather than the full set of noun classes (Hombert 1980:163). The subject pronouns have been reduced to four forms:

TABLE 14.3: THIRD PERSON SUBJECT MARKERS IN BAMOUN

	Animate	Inanimate
3rd person singular	yí	á
3rd person plural	pá	á

Most nouns in Bamoun distinguish their plural form from their singular form by the change in noun prefix. However, nouns with identical forms in the singular and plural, namely those without noun prefixes, mark number in various ways: (1) some use the quantifier *rén* 'many' for plural, as in *ɲū* 'bee' and *rén ɲū* '(many) bees'; (2) some use concord elements, as in *pàm á* 'my bag' and *pàm šá* 'my bags'; (3) some use tone, as in *š ìrə̀* 'trap' and *š ìrə́* 'traps'; still others use reduplication: *lǐʔ* 'place'/*lǐʔlǐʔ* 'places', and *mfɔ̀n* 'chief'/*fɔ̀nfɔ̀n* 'chiefs.'

By contrast, the western Bamileke languages such as Yemba (Dschang-Bamileke) (Tadadjeu 1980) distinguish eight classes and the Ngemba languages distinguish eight to ten. Those with fewer than ten have lost 19, or 19 and 10. Yemba has merged class 10 with 6. In contrast, Mankon (Leroy 1977, 1980) includes the full set of Eastern Grassfields classes, as well as class 19. Mankon also has nasals in the noun prefixes of classes 1, 3, 6, 9, and 10. These western and more conservative Eastern Grassfield languages have the following genders, using Mankon and Yemba as examples: 1/2, 3/6, 5/6, and 7/8. Mankon (Leroy 1980) has 19/6 and 9/10 where Yemba (Tadadjeu 1980:167–9) has 7/6 and 9/6. Both 7/6 and 9/6 along with 3/10 are secondary genders (i.e. genders with only a few members) in Mankon.

For the eastern and more change-prone languages, the genders are difficult to summarize because a given class corresponds often to two or more Proto-Bantu noun classes. Therefore, the noun class numbering system is less helpful. In any case, Limbum (Voorhoeve 1980b) has five major double class genders, Bamoun (Hombert 1980) has seven, and Banjoun (Nissim 1981:197–8) has three, and three secondary ones.

3.1.2 Locative noun classes

In 3.1.1 above, the Proto-Bantu locative noun classes 16, 17, and 18 did not surface. However, Chia (1983), Leroy (1983a, 1983b), and Annett (1983) demonstrate that residual or foreshadowing forms of Proto-Bantu locative classes are present in GB. Claims for forms reminiscent of classes 16 and 17 are fairly solid, but claims for class 18 are not firmly established (Grégoire 1983:140).

What distinguishes these classes from the other GB noun classes is that they do not have a noun prefix as the exponent of the class. Instead, what appears as a general locative preposition or pre-nominal locative clitic, *ā*, serves as the head of the noun phrase. This locative *ā* behaves like a noun prefix in that it controls agreement of various nominal modifiers.

The locative forms appear in Kom, a Ring language, as adverbial locatives (Chia 1983:75–8), anaphoric pronouns with a locative function (Chia 1983:80–2), as demonstratives, relative pronouns, and genitive markers (Chia 1983:82–7), and finally a locative interrogative. Examples of locative concord are given in (1) and (2).

(1) Chia (1983:82, Cl.9   demonstrative from table 2 p. 78)

mà lù   *ā* ndō   *yàyn/*yèn*
I PRESENT:come LOC Cl.9-house Cl.17-this/*Cl.9-this
'I am from this house.'

(2) Chia (1983:83)
   (a) ... ndō   **yèā/zia*   *mà   tí   yūin*
       Cl.9-house   **Cl.17-that/Cl.9-that* I   PAST:3 buy
       '... the house that I bought.'
   (b) ... *ā* ndō   *yèā/*zia*   *mà   tí   yūin*
       LOC Cl.9-house Cl.17-this/*Cl.9-this I   PAST:3 buy
       '... in the house that I bought.'

In (1) and (2b), the noun 'house' is in class 9 when it is singular, so we would expect class 9 concord like we find in (2a) /ndō zia/ 'this house'. Instead, since 'house' follows the locative preposition /ā/, we find class 17 concord /yàyn, yèā/, not class 9 /yèn, zia/.

In addition, Kom attests to a locative form with the concord consonant **t-** (Chia 1983:78–82). In some cases it parallels Proto-Bantu class 18 semantically, but in form it is reminiscent of class 13. However, class 13 in Kom has its own set of concords different from this additional locative class.

In Mundani, a Momo language, locative agreement appears in demonstratives and genitive markers (Annett 1983:123, 126). Consider the following examples of demonstrative agreement:

(3) *lób*   **yáā**   'this house'
    á lób **ŋáā**   'in this house'

The associative locative agreement shows up as a floating high tone on the prefix of the second noun in the genitive construction:

(4) *ŋgēl*   *ēwet* [L-L-H L L-H-L]   'the side of the fire'
    á ŋgél *éwēt* [**H** L-L-H **H** L-H-L] 'at the side of the fire'

The high tone locative marker, **á**, requires a high tone genitive marker between the nouns.

In Mankon (Leroy 1983a), a Ngemba language, locative agreement occurs with demonstratives, relative markers, and genitive markers. However, in the case of demonstratives and relatives, the noun they modify must be in the singular. Otherwise the normal plural class agreement is used.

In Yamba (Leroy 1983b), a North language, traces of a locative class show up in the locative interrogative and the adverbial locatives. They resemble class 16.

3.2 Pronouns

Independent pronoun systems in GB generally distinguish singular from plural, and first, second, and third persons. They also distinguish inclusive from exclusive. An additional 'dual inclusive' category opposed to 'plural inclusive' in the first person is reported for various Eastern Grassfields languages, including Bamileke languages, Mankon /tĭ/ (Leroy 1977:3) or Limbum /sò'/ (Fransen 1995:179). Case is distinguished, with nominative, accusative, and genitive forms.

Logophoric pronoun systems are found in Momo languages such as Ngie (Watters 1980) and Ngwo (Voorhoeve 1980d), and in Ring languages such as Kom (Voorhoeve

1980d), Babungo (Schaub 1985:111–13), and Aghem (Hyman 1979b:50–1). They are reported also in Mbam-Nkam languages such as Yemba (Dschang-Bamileke) (Hyman pc) and Ngiemboon (Anderson pc).

Pronoun systems indicating same subject vs. different subject across two coordinated clauses are also present. While logophoric pronouns occur in *embedded* clauses of reported speech to indicate the same referent as one in the main clause, same and different subject pronouns occur in the second clause of *coordinate* clauses. In these cases the different-subject marker is identical to the normal subject marker, while the same-subject marker has its own form. Some times the same subject marker is analyzed as a conjunction. See §4.7.1 on the Consecutive Clause for examples.

Demonstratives consistently distinguish three degrees of deixis: near speaker, near hearer, and distant. The 'near hearer' form is also often referred to as the anaphoric demonstrative (see Hyman 1980a for Ring, and Parker 1989 for Mundani). The relative marker or pronoun often consists of the demonstrative plus the vowel -*a*. Anaphoric demonstratives are used in ways reminiscent of definite articles. In Babungo (Ring) (Schaub 1985:192) their form varies according to noun class, but in Ngiemboon (Mbam-Nkam) (Anderson pc) it has an invariant form.

Pronoun conjunction is a common feature of GB languages. In Aghem, e.g. it includes both a 'cumulative bond' and an 'incorporative bond' (Hyman 1979b:53). In the cumulative pattern a plural pronoun takes the first position in the conjunction only if the second pronoun is higher on the pronominal hierarchy, where first person is higher than second, and second higher than third. So we can have *ghé à mùɔ* 'them and me'. In the incorporative pattern, the first position can only have a plural form, even if the meaning is singular (SG), as in *ghàʔà wò* 'we exclusive and you (SG)' = 'me and you (SG)'. So we can have *ghàʔà ghé* 'us including them; them including us; us including him/her; them including me', contrasting with the cumulative pattern in *ghé à mùɔ* 'them and me'.

According to Hyman (1980a:250), the Ring languages are the only GB languages that have introduced new third person pronoun forms using the root 'body'.

3.3 Verbs

The canonical form of verb stems in GB languages is generally -CV or -CVC. No final theme vowels operate. Verb stems of the form -CVV and -CVCV are also found. Most -CV and -CVV roots have gained this structure through the loss of a final, or second, consonant. GB languages have two verb classes, one class with high tone and the other with low tone.

GB languages have a limited set of verbal suffixes, or extensions. These do not include passive or applicative forms. They are generally productive with a limited set of verb roots, and their semantics are often complex. Primarily four suffixes are attested: -*sV* 'causative', -*tV* 'pluralizer, distributive, attenuative', -*nV* 'reciprocal, valence change', and -*kV* 'iterative'. Anderson (1979:80–1) and Schaub (1985:210ff.) report for Aghem and Babungo (Ring) the -*sV* and -*nV* suffixes. Mfonyam (1982:199ff.) and Leroy (1982) report for Bafut and Mankon (Ngemba) the -*sV*, -*tV*, -*nV*, and -*kV* suffixes. Nissim (1981:91–2), Harro (1989), and Mba (1996–7) give evidence from Banjoun (Ghomala) and Yemba (Dschang-Bamileke) for the -*tV* and -*nV* suffixes. Ngomba (Satre 1998) has a -*lV* extension in addition to -*tV* and -*nV*, but its meaning is not clear. Note, however, that Fransen (1995:198–208) reports seven extensions for Limbum.

The use of the Bantu pre-final -*a(n)g* (Meeussen 1967:110) is widely attested throughout Bantoid outside Narrow Bantu, the GB languages being no exception. In GB it serves as an imperfective suffix -*a*.

Denominative verbal bases (Meeussen 1967:90) are not productive, though it might be possible to find residual forms in GB.

The tense-aspect-mood (TAM) systems of GB are usually complex, involving a full set of past and future tenses. The Bamileke languages have among the most complex of these TAM systems within GB. For example, Ngiemboon (Anderson 1983:52–7) divides the TAM system between realis and irrealis forms as follows. Realis subdivides into past and present tense forms. Both of these further subdivide into perfective and imperfective categories, with imperfective distinguishing non-progressive (i.e. general imperfective) and progressive. Irrealis subdivides into present and future. Present is always imperfective in form, either non-progressive or progressive. Future is either perfective or imperfective, with imperfective again distinguishing non-progressive and progressive.

The internal structure of the Ngiemboon verb (Anderson 1983:58–9) is:

(5)   V → (Prefix-1) Prefix-2 Verb-Stem (Suffix-2) (Suffix-3)
       Verb-Stem → Verb-Root (Suffix-1)
       Where: Prefix-1 = realis imperfective prefix (*N-*)
                Prefix-2 = realis or irrealis polar tones
                Suffix 1 = toneless /-*te*/ syllable (see above for -*tV*)
                Suffix-2 = irrealis polar tone
                Suffix-3 = imperfective suffix (-*a*)

Note that the verb in GB languages consists primarily of the verb root and a set of TAM affixes. In GB, no language has object prefixes. Consider these examples of the tense distinctions in the realis and irrealis moods and their formal markers in Ngiemboon (Anderson 1983:246ff.). It distinguishes four degrees of past and four degrees of future, but only a few illustrative examples are given here. All are given in the perfective aspect. 'P' refers to PAST and 'F' to FUTURE, with the attached numbers referring to degrees of past and future.

(6)   (a)   P3 Perfective
             à **là** nz↓á mb↓áb   'he cut the meat (some time ago)'
             3s P3 cut   meat

       (b)   P2 Perfective
             à **kà** zàʔ mbàb   'he cut the meat (yesterday)'
             3s P2 cut meat

       (c)   F2 Perfective
             à **t↓ó** z↓áʔ mb↓àb   'he will cut the meat (tomorrow)'
             3s F2 cut   meat

       (d)   F3 Perfective
             à **l↓ù** z↓áʔ mb↓àb   'he will cut the meat (some time from now)'
             3s F3 cut   meat

These tenses are relative tenses in the sense that they do not necessarily refer to absolute points of time. Instead, the time reference is relative to the context provided by other tense markers and the larger context. In addition, as Hyman (1980d) demonstrated for Yemba (Dschang-Bamileke), closely related to Ngiemboon, some tense markers may co-occur with other tense markers to form additional, subtly different readings.

When comparing Bamileke languages, most mark four degrees of Past and four degrees of Future, along with a Present tense that also may serve as a Perfect. See

Nkemnji (1995:10ff.) for Nweh, Hyman (1980d) for Yemba (Dschang), and Nguendjio (1992) for Bangwa, a dialect of Nda'nda'. The future markers in Dschang and Bangwa clearly involve verb roots. For example, in Bangwa, *zi* in F3 means 'sleep' and *cɔ́* in F4 means 'stay'. In all of these languages, the past tense markers occur before the negative marker and the verb stem, while the future tense markers usually occur after the negative marker but before the verb stem. The future markers come from earlier consecutive constructions, or even relate to current consecutive constructions.

These forms can be compared to those found in Bafut (Mfonyam 1982:176ff.), a Ngemba, Mbam-Nkam language; Babungo (Schaub 1985:212ff.) and Aghem (Anderson 1979:86ff.), both Ring languages; and Ngie (Watters 1980), a Momo language. A general observation is that Mbam-Nkam (and perhaps Eastern Grassfields Bantu in general), exemplified by the Bamileke languages and Bafut, have the largest number of formal tense distinctions. As one moves to the Ring languages we see that in Babungo F1 and F2 form a single category, as do F3 and F4. In Aghem, P3 and P4 form a single category, as do F3 and F4. However, in Aghem, the P4-P3 category for distant past has the form *fí* and is found only in the first sentence of a narrative. It indicates the time setting for the story as the distant narrative past. Preliminary data in Ngie, a Momo language, indicate that P1 and P2 form one category as do P3 and P4. Both past tenses are indicated only by tone, although the presence of the tone motivates the presence of an additional vocalic element. In the future tenses only one form is used to mark a general future. So the Ring and Momo languages have less complex TAM systems than Mbam-Nkam.

Turning to imperfective forms, the non-progressive imperfective in Ngiemboon includes an imperfective vocalic suffix *-a*, while the progressive imperfective involves the progressive marker *nê* 'PROG' and the imperfective vocalic verbal suffix. The realis progressive may also be marked by *ssé↓*, or both *ssé↓* and *nê* together. Similarly Nweh uses *asé* or *nā*, or both together.

As for other GB languages, Bafut (Ngemba, Mbam-Nkam), Babungo (Ring, South), Aghem (Ring, West), and Ngie (Momo) display the following characteristics in the imperfective. Bafut (Mfonyam 1982:203ff.) has the following three imperfective markers: a replacive HL tone sequence in present tense and P1, while P2 and P3 have /sí/ immediately after the past tense marker, and future tenses use /kí/ following the future tense marker. Babungo (Schaub 1985:215ff.) uses tone to distinguish perfective from imperfective aspect, with perfective taking a floating low tone before the verb, and imperfective taking a floating high tone. In some cases this distinction is neutralized. The progressive aspect uses a CV-reduplication of the initial consonant of the verb root plus a central vowel. In Aghem (Anderson 1979:94ff.) and Ngie (Momo) (Watters 1980) the imperfective aspect is simply indicated by a verbal suffix /-a/ on to the verb with various realizations depending on the shape of the root and its root vowel.

Finally, it is not uncommon to find verbal categories with one form for main clauses and another for relative clauses. These relative forms may also be used with interrogative word questions and answers to those questions (see Hyman and Watters 1984).

4 SYNTAX

All of the syntax studies to date concern Narrow Grassfields languages rather than any Peripheral ones (see §1.2.2 and 1.3 for 'Narrow' vs. 'Peripheral'). Nkemnji's (1995) study of Nweh provides one of the more current syntactic studies – an insightful study within the Principles and Parameters theoretical model. It interestingly treats number and class within noun phrases as phrasal projections, i.e. as syntactic properties spelled out on the noun prefix rather than lexical properties of the noun. Within the same theory, Magba (1995) considers the INFL category in Mundani. Other syntactic studies include a descriptive one of Limbum by Fransen (1995), of Babungo by Schaub (1985), and a functional one of focus constructions in Aghem by Watters (1977). Otherwise most syntactic studies of these languages consist of articles on particular topics, including Parker (1989, 1991a,b) on the nominal phrase, conditional clauses, and complex sentences and subordination in Mundani.

4.1 Basic word order

The basic word order of GB is SVO, with some interesting variation in certain construction types. Head-complement order thus dominates. Possessive and demonstrative adjectives as well as genitive phrases and relative clauses all follow their head noun. Adpositions are universally prepositions. Objects and other adjuncts follow their head verb. As with other Bantu languages, agreement of noun complements with the head noun is pervasive.

Within the noun phrase, the Momo languages such as Modele (Boum 1980) and Mundani (Parker 1989:160ff.), as well as Ring languages such as Aghem (Hyman 1979b:27), have strict head initial noun phrases. Exceptions to this order include the following. First, in Ngie (Watters 1980), the possessive adjective for first and second person, whether singular or plural, precedes the head noun. Third person follows.

Second, for contrastive purposes, it is not uncommon for the order to be reversed to form phrases such as 'MY dog' or 'my OWN dog'. In the case of Nweh (Nkemnji 1995:28–9), when the order is reversed for contrastive purposes, the possessive form is prefixed with the verb agreement marker for the noun class of the head noun, thus serving as a type of predicate nominal form 'it is mine the bird'. Compare (7a) and (7b). ('SM' refers to the verb subject marker):

(7) (a) *séŋ   gè*   'my bird'
        1:bird 1:my

     (b) *à-   gè   séŋ*   **'my** (contrastive) bird'
        1:SM- 1:my 1:bird

Both *à-* and *gè* in (7b) agree with the noun class of 'bird' (Cl.1).

These types of variant word orders in noun phrases are found in various languages, particularly in the Mbam-Nkam region.

4.2 Agreement: subject, object, and VP

Verb phrases (VP) generally agree with their subjects. For most noun classes in most GB languages, the agreement marker is a (C)V- syllable or a homorganic nasal. In Aghem (Hyman 1979b:48), however, an exceptional form is used in which a low tone alone marks subject agreement on the verb for classes 1 and 9 when the subject is a noun. Also it is common for personal subject pronouns to be obligatorily present, including third person personal subject pronouns, in the absence of a subject noun. In Nweh (Nkemnji 1995:9–10), however, personal subject pronouns may be absent in third person singular, but a third person singular agreement marker is still present. In third person plural the norm holds with the personal subject pronoun required in the absence of a noun. In some languages, like Babungo (Schaub 1985), verb agreement seems to be absent, with only independent pronouns used to indicate subject number and person.

Grassfields Bantu languages do not have object agreement in the form of prefixes so common in Bantu. However, many GB languages use an object marker following the verb. Like so much else in GB languages, these are often minimal forms, sometimes a verb final vowel or simply a tone. In Ngiemboon (Anderson 1983:208ff.) e.g. the object marker varies according to the noun class membership of the object noun. If the object noun belongs to class 2, 4, 5, or 6, all classes with CV(N)- nominal prefixes, the object marker is a high tone / ´-/. For other noun classes (1, 3, 7, 8, 9, 10) the object marker is null. In Ngomba these object markers are identical to the possessive pronouns (Satre 1997).

4.3 Questions

4.3.1 Yes–no and leading questions

Grassfields Bantu languages form yes–no questions with a sentence final question marker. This marker varies from language to language, and may also vary according to phonological and syntactic conditions of a specific language, as in Nweh (Nkemnji 1995:151–6).

(8) (Nkemnji 1995:149, 152)
  (a) *Njikèm à   kè?   npfét akendɔ̀ŋ   ŋ̄*
       Njikem 3s PAST:1 eat   plantains QUESTION MARKER
       'Did Njikem eat plantains?'

  (b) *Njikèm à   kè?   njúɔ mbāb éē*
       Njikem 3s PAST:1 buy   meat QUESTION MARKER
       'Did Njikem buy meat?'

Leading ('evidential') questions also use special sentence final particles such as *kɔ́ɔ́* in Nweh (Nkemnji 1995:157) and *mē* in Babungo.

4.3.2 Interrogative word questions

Considerable variation exists in how interrogative word questions are formed. In Ngie (Momo) (Watters 1980) the interrogative word is used in a cleft-like construction such as 'It was WHO that bought the plantains?' More commonly GB languages simply substitute the interrogative word in the syntactic position of the noun phrase it questions. For example, in Nweh (Bamileke) (Nkemnji 1995:153), this strategy is used.

(9) Nweh (Nkemnji 1995:153)
  (a) ***awɔ́*** *à   kè?   npfét akendɔ̀ŋ   ŋ̄*
       who 3s PAST:1 eat   plantains QUESTION MARKER
       'Who ate plantains?'

  (b) *Njikèm à   kɔ̀   pfét **akɔ́** ɔjúa   ā*
       Njikem 3s PAST:2 eat   **what** yesterday QUESTION MARKER
       'What did Njikem eat yesterday?'

Babungo (Ring) (Schaub 1985:10) uses a similar strategy to that of Nweh, except that when the subject noun phrase is questioned, the interrogative word occurs following the verb and a reduplicated form of the verb follows. In this way, an SV order becomes VSV.

(10) *kɔ̀   **ndɔ́** kɔ̀   ká   tí Ndùlá*
      give:PFV **who** give:PFV money to Ndula
      'Who gave money to Ndula?'

Aghem (Ring) (Watters 1979) demonstrates a further development and generalization of the word order in Babungo. The general principle is that any questioned constituent occurs in the position immediately following the verb. The noun phrase that answers the question also occurs in the position immediately following the verb. This suggests the word order sv(foc)ox (foc = 'focus' position, x = adjuncts). Consider these examples that question the subject, object, and various adverbial adjuncts.

(11)　(a) *à   mɔ̀   zí   ndúghɔ́ bé-↓kɔ́*
　　　　 D:SM PAST:2 eat **who**　fufu
　　　　 'Who ate the fufu?'

　　　(b) *fíl   á   mɔ̀   zí   kwɔ̀*
　　　　 friends cl.2:SM PAST:2 eat **what**
　　　　 'What did the friends eat?'

　　　(c) *fíl   á   mɔ̀   zí   ghɛ́   bé-↓kɔ́*
　　　　 friends cl.2:SM PAST:2 eat **where** fufu
　　　　 'Where did the friends eat fufu?'

4.4 Negation

4.4.1 Sentence

The simplest way to negate a sentence is to modify the verbal word or phrase with a negative morpheme. Consider the following example from Aghem:

(12)　Aghem (Anderson 1979:86, 118)

　　　(a) *ò   bò   fí-ghâm*　'he has hit the mat'
　　　　 3SG hit c7-mat

　　　(b) *ò   kà   bó   ghâm-fɔ́*　'he has not hit the mat'
　　　　 3SG *NEG* hit mat-c7 (demphasized noun form required with negatives)

In fact, Aghem (Anderson 1979:118ff.) has a basic perfective, negative /kà/ which has four variant forms, and an imperfective, negative /yɔ́/. The perfective negative occurs between the subject and the verb, while the imperfective negative occurs following the verb and before any object.

More common in GB, however, is the use of a discontinuous form. The first morpheme occurs within the verbal word while the second morpheme occurs at the end of the clause or sentence. The negative forms in Ngiemboon (Anderson 1983), e.g. involve a discontinuous form, with *tè* positioned before the verb root and *wɔ́* at the end of the clause.

(13)　(a) P3 Negative Perfective

　　　　 à   là   tè   záʔ   mbàb   wɔ́　'he did not cut the meat (some time ago)'
　　　　 3s P3 NEG cut   meat   NEG

　　　(b) P3 Negative Non-progressive Imperfective

　　　　 à   làa   tè   nzʼàʔ   mbàb   wɔ́　'he did not use to cut meat (some time ago)'
　　　　 3s P3 NEG cut   meat   NEG

The discontinuous morpheme /tè … wɔ́/ is used for negation in all tenses but the present. In the present tense, it is /kà … wɔ́/. Note that the *tè* and *kà* occur after the past tense markers but before the future markers, and *wɔ́* is always a clause or sentence final clitic.

In Bangwa (Nguendjio 1992:95), the negative marker is also a discontinuous /kə̀ ... wɔ́/, used with past and future tenses. In Nweh (Nkemnji 1995:112ff.) one finds either /te ... bɔ́/, with bɔ́ occurring clause (or sentence) final, or bɔ́ is absent and the verb occurs in the clause final position, as follows.

(14) (a) *Njikə̀m à kə̀ **te** flá nkāp anbó Atem əjúa* **bɔ́**
Njikem 3s P2 NEG give money to Atem yesterday NEG
'Njikem did not give money to Atem yesterday.'

   (b) *Njikə̀m à kə̀ **te** nkāp anbó Atem əjúa* **flá**
Njikem 3s P2 NEG money to Atem yesterday give
'Njikem did not give money to Atem yesterday.'

The two ways of marking sentence negation in Nweh likely reflect two different scopes of negation: the entire verb phrase in (14a) and a specific constituent in (14b).

Turning to negative forms in other languages, Bafut (Ngemba, Mbam-Nkam), Babungo (Ring, South), Aghem (Ring, West), and Ngie (Momo) display the following characteristics. In Bafut (Mfonyam 1982:223ff.) negative constructions have these general properties: the verb is clause final, and the negative marker is a discontinous morpheme with the first morpheme kāā occurring clause initial and the second morpheme following the subject and tense marker. The second morpheme is either sī̀ or sí̀, in the present tense, and /wá'ā́/ in all past and future tenses.

Babungo (Schaub 1985:91ff.) also has a discontinous marking of sentence negation. The first negative morpheme kèe occurs after the past tense marker and before the verb, as well as before the future tense marker and verb, as in Ngiemboon. The second morpheme, mē, occurs at the end of the clause. In complex sentences, the second morpheme follows noun clauses or relative clauses, but precedes a following adverbial clause.

Ngie (Watters 1980) appears to have the commonly attested discontinous marker also, the first morpheme being kī with past tenses, kīrì with the future tense, and kə̄rə̀ with all imperfective forms. However, in the second position the morpheme is apparently the repetition of the subject after the verb in the form of the possessive pronoun. This pronoun agrees in person and number with the subject. In addition, rather than occurring at the end of the clause it occurs immediately after the verb and before the object.

(15) *wə̄-ə̀ **kī** kɔ̄m-ɔ́ **má** bə̀u* 'he did not hit the dog'
3s-P2 NEG hit-IMPFV 3s:POSS dog

Repetition of the subject after the verb by using a (possessive) pronominal form is also found in Momo (e.g. Ngamambo) and Mbam-Nkam (e.g. Ngemba in one tense).

4.4.2 Constituent negation

Most GB languages may use a cleft-like construction for negation of specific constituents. However, a combination of normal negation along with normal focus morphemes or focus constructions may also allow for negation of specific constituents. Consider the example from Nweh (Nkemnji 1995:140) where the verb, repeated, is focused and thus becomes the negated constituent.

(16) *Atem a kə̀ʔ **te** čúū akendɔ̀ŋ čúū **bɔ́***
Atem 3s PAST:1 NEG boil plantains boil NEG
'Atem did not BOIL plantains.'

4.5 Topics, passives, voice, valency

Grassfields Bantu languages do not have passive morphology or syntax. There is no presence of the Bantu -wa extension. Instead GB languages use an indefinite personal form, usually a third person plural pronoun, instead of passives. Thus, locatives and instrumentals do not have access to the subject position via promotion to object position and passivization. Other common extensions are absent or limited in use (see §3.3). Applicative notions such as benefactive and dative are generally expressed by prepositional phrases. However, they may also occur preceding the direct object to form SVOO constructions. Though some verbs take causative affixes, causative is also often expressed periphrastically using the verb 'to do'.

Topics commonly are sentence initial. In some cases a morpheme may set the topic off from the rest of the sentence; in other cases no special marking may be used; in others the subject may occur after the verb, producing a V-S order, as in Babungo (Schaub 1985:131).

Reflexive equivalents may use the noun 'body' and the possessive pronoun that is coreferential with the subject in person and number. Reciprocals in Babungo use the reduplication of the third person plural pronoun along with 'bodies' as in:

(17)   Babungo (South Ring) (Schaub 1985:199)

    vɔ̌ŋ gàŋtɔ̀   yìŋwáa vɔ̌ŋ, vɔ̌ŋ vɔ̌ŋ
    3PL help:PFV bodies   3PL,   3PL   3PL
    'They helped each other.'

4.6 Focus (or 'emphasis')

The more common way to mark emphasis or focus is to use morphological and syntactic marking. These mechanisms are used to indicate assertive focus (e.g. answers to interrogative word questions) and counter-assertive (or 'contrastive') focus (see Watters 1979). The simplest system might be that in Ngie (Momo), which uses cleft-like constructions to ask interrogative word questions, to answer them, and to mark counter-assertive focus.

Other languages, such as Nweh (Nkemnji 1995:136), use a focus marker for counter-assertive focus. In Nweh the focused constituent is the one that the focus marker *mɔ̂* separates from the verb: the subject in (18a) and object in (18b).

(18)   Nweh (Nkemnji 1995:136)
    (a) *Njikem **mɔ̂** a   kɛ̀ʔ   nčúū akendɔŋ*
        Njikem FOC 3s PAST:1 boil   plantains
        'NJIKEM boiled plantains.'
    (b) *Njikem a   kɛ̀ʔ   nčúū **mɔ̂** akendɔŋ*
        Njikem 3s PAST:1 boil FOC   plantains
        'Njikem boiled PLANTAINS.'

If the focus is the verb rather than the subject, object or adjunct, the verb root is simply reduplicated (Nkemnji 1995:138).

(19)   *Atem a   kɛ̀ʔ   **nčúū** akendɔŋ   **čúū***
    Atem 3s PAST:1 boil   plantains   boil
    'Atem BOILED plantains.'

Babungo uses a number of morphemes to mark assertive and counter-assertive focus (see Schaub 1985:120). In addition, Babungo has a movement strategy. However, it is used only with subjects. They are placed in a position immediately following the verb. If the sentence contains an object, the verb must be repeated (20b).

(20)   Babungo (Schaub 1985:122)

(a) *Làmbí gɔ̀   táa yìwìŋ*   → *gɔ̀   **Làmbí** táa yìwìŋ*
    Lambi go:PFV to   market   go:PFV Lambi to   market
    'Lambi has gone to the market.'   'LAMBI has gone to market.'

(b) *Làmbí nɔ̀ fìanɔ̀   ŋ̀ïi   nyɔ̀* → *nɔ̀ fìanɔ̀   **Làmbí fìanɔ̀** ŋ̀ïi   nyɔ̀*
    Lambi P4 build:PFV house this   P4 build:PFV Lambi build house this
    'Lambi built this house.'   'LAMBI built this house.'

A more elaborate system is found in Aghem (Watters 1979). In some cases it uses a focus particle *nô* 'focus (FOC)' to indicate counter-assertive focus. This morpheme may only mark one constituent per sentence, and must be postverbal.

(21)   Aghem (Watters 1979:167)

(a) *fú kí mɔ̂ **nyìŋ nô** á kí'-bé*
    rat it PAST run FOC in compound
    'The rat **ran** (did not walk) in the compound.'

(b) *fú kí mɔ̂ nyìŋ á kí'-bé   nô*
    rat it PAST run   in Compound FOC
    'The rat ran **inside the compound** (not inside the house).'

Aghem also uses word order. The *immediately postverbal* position is used for focus, whether interrogative word questions or answers to them. Consider the interrogative word questions in (11) in §4.3.4. Consider question (11c), repeated here as (22a), and its answers in (22b, c). The use of an *immediately preverbal* position for presupposed information that usually follows the verb is shown in (11c).

(22)   (a) QUESTION:

*fíl   á   mɔ̂   zí **ghé**   bé-$^{\downarrow}$kɔ́*
friends Cl.2:SM PAST:2 eat **where** fufu
'Where did the friends eat fufu?'

(b) ANSWER (assertive or counter-assertive)

*(fíl   á   mɔ̂ zí) **án $^{\downarrow}$sóm** (bé-$^{\downarrow}$kɔ́)*
(friends Cl.2:SM P2 eat) **in farm** (fufu)
'(The friends ate fufu) in the farm.'

(c) ANSWER (counter-assertive only)

(fíl   á   mɔ̂ bé-$^{\downarrow}$kí zí) án $^{\downarrow}$sóm
(friends Cl.2:SM P2 fufu   eat) **in farm**
'(The friends ate fufu) IN THE FARM.'

Finally, Aghem may mark counter-assertive focus on the truth-value of the utterance. This is marked through the use of a different set of tense-aspect markers (see Watters

1979:164 for details). A minimal contrast to show the distinction is:

(23)   (a) *énáʔ mɔ̀ fúo kí-bé â fín-ghɔ́*
          Inah p2 give fufu to friends
          'Inah gave fufu to (his) friends.'

       (b) *énáʔ máˆá fúo bé-kɔ́ â fín-ghɔ́*
          Inah p2 + FOC give fufu to friends
          'Inah *did* give fufu to (his) friends.' (=That Inah gave fufu to (his) friends
          is true.)

An affirmative and negative set of tense-aspect markers are available for p0,
p1, and p2.

4.7 Compound and complex sentences

Among the various compound and complex sentences, in this section only consecutive
constructions, serial constructions, and relative clauses are presented. Studies on other
topics involving sentences with multiple clauses include one on relative time reference
(Hyman 1980d), a couple on conditionals in Mundani (Parker 1991a) and complex
sentences and subordination in Mundani (Parker 1991b), markers of parallelism in Meta'
(Spreda 1991), and prominence in Bafut (Mfonyam 1991).

4.7.1 Consecutive constructions

Consecutive constructions are common in GB languages. In such constructions, the two
coordinated clauses agree in tense and aspect. In the examples below from Bafut
(Wiesemann *et al.* 1984:89) the nasal on the verb 'catch' in (26a) marks the sequencing
of the clauses and serves as a same-subject (SS) marker. The normal '3s' subject marker
á- in (26b) marks a different subject.

(24)   Bafut

       (a) *á-ghéè ̀ ñdá   ŋ́-kwérɔ̀ fórɔ̀*
          3s-go   house ss-catch rat
          'then he went to the house and caught a rat'

       (b) *á-ghéè ̀ ñdá   ŋgwà   á-kwérɔ̀ fōrē̄*
          3s-go   house of-Ngwa 3s-catch rat
          'then he went to Ngwa's house and he (Ngwa) caught a rat'

Identical same-subject markers are found in Fe'fe' (Mbam-Nkam) (Hyman 1971) and
Mundani (Momo). Mundani has a different form for the same-subject marker when it
occurs in the irrealis mood (Wiesemann *et al.* 1984:89–90).

4.7.2 Serial constructions

Sometimes what is linked by coordination are two verb phrases rather than two clauses.
In these cases we can talk of 'serial verb constructions' or 'serialization'. Consider this
example from Babungo.

(25)   *mɔ̀ gɔ̀   túŋ   nyàà*
         I   go-IMFV shoot-NEUTR animal
         'I went to shoot an animal.'

These sequences of verbs share the same subject noun phrase and may have an intervening object between the verbs. The second verb is not marked for tense-aspect. Often one of the verbs serves more as an auxiliary verb with a meaning different from its core meaning. In this case, 'go' means 'go with a purpose'.

4.7.3 Relative (adjectival) clauses

Generally, a distinction between restrictive and non-restrictive relative clauses has not been reported, except in the case of Babungo. If the subject of the relative clause is relativized, a gap is commonly left in the subject position, with the class subject marker still present. If the object is relativized, a gap is also generally left, though a resumptive pronoun may be used, either for emphasis or to disambiguate pronoun reference. If an oblique noun phrase is relativized, a resumptive pronoun is generally obligatory.

In Banjoun (Ghomala) (Nissim 1981:242) the relative is formed with a discontinuous morpheme that marks the beginning and end of the relative clause.

(26) *mo yə*   —   *e   jɔ́   sáŋ á'á*
      man REL   \<gap\>   3ps   see:PAST bird REL
      '… the man who saw the bird'

In Nweh (Nkemnji 1995:51ff.) the relative marker is identical to the 'distant' demonstrative pronoun. No discontinuous morpheme is used. In Babungo (Schaub 1985:32, 208) the relative clause is marked by a subordinating marker *fáŋ* 'which' (some people use the form *yúu*), different from any demonstrative form. This form is non-restrictive. To make it restrictive, the interrogative pronoun relevant to the noun class of the head noun must immediately precede the subordinating pronoun.

5 CONCLUSION

Enormous progress has been made during the past thirty years in our understanding of the GB languages. We have a clearer picture of the classificatory and historical issues, as well as the descriptive issues in the phonology and grammar of these languages. This understanding has contributed in particular to broadening the discussion on historical issues within Bantoid and Bantu, and also to what is possible phonologically – particularly with tone. However, as our understanding has grown we have also been left with a growing list of questions. Much remains to be researched and learned about these languages, whether through more in-depth studies of specific languages, or through comparative and historical studies.

ACKNOWLEDGMENTS

I want to thank those who commented on an earlier version of this chapter: in particular, Stephen Anderson, Robert Hedinger, Larry Hyman, Jacqueline Leroy, Derek Nurse, Gerard Philippson, Keith Snider, and Rhonda Thwing. Their comments were invaluable in making the chapter better, both in correcting my earlier errors and also in providing additional information and insights. Ed Brye provided valuable information and corrections on §1.3 from recent surveys of GB languages, along with comments he passed along from Ginny Bradley, Joseph Mfonyam, Janice Sprede, and Klaus Spreda. In the end, however, I have to take full responsibility for the choices made and any errors or shortcomings present in the chapter.

REFERENCES

Anderson 1979, 1980, 1981, 1982, 1983; Annett 1983; Asongwed and Hyman 1976; Bennett and Sterk 1977; Bird 1996; Boum 1980; Breton and Fohtung 1991; Bruens 1942–5; Chia 1983; Chumbow and Nguendjio 1991; Clark 1993; Dalby 1970; Davis 1992; Dieu and Renaud 1983; Dunstan 1963, 1964, 1966a, 1966b; Elias *et al.* 1984; Fiore 1987; Fransen 1995; Grebe 1982; Grebe and Grebe 1975; Greenberg 1948, 1955, 1963, 1980; Grégoire 1983; Grimes 2000; Harro 1989; Haynes 1989; Hedinger 1993; Heine 1972–3; Henrici 1973; Hombert 1976, 1977, 1979, 1980; Hyman 1971, 1972, 1976b, 1979a, 1979b, 1979c, 1979d, 1980a, 1980b, 1980c, 1980d, 1985, 1986, 1987; Hyman and Tadadjeu 1976; Hyman and Voorhoeve 1980; Hyman and Watters 1984; Hyman *et al.* 1970; Koopman 1994; Ladefoged and Maddieson 1996; Leroy 1977, 1979, 1980, 1982, 1983a, 1983b; Magba 1995; Mba 1996–7; Meeussen 1967; Mfonyam 1982, 1991; Miehe 1991; Nguendjio 1992; Nkemnji 1995; Nissim 1980, 1981; Parker 1981, 1989, 1991a, 1991b; Piron 1995; Pulleyblank 1986; Richardson 1957; Sadembouo and Chumbow 1990; Satre 1997, 1998; Schaub 1985; Scruggs 1980; Snider 1999; Spreda 1986, 1991; Stallcup 1980a, 1980b; Stewart 1981, 1993; Stöckler 1992; Tadadjeu 1974, 1980; Voorhoeve 1963, 1965, 1967, 1968, 1971, 1974, 1980a, 1980b, 1980c, 1980d; Ward 1938; Warnier 1976; Watters 1979, 1980, 1982, 1989; Watters and Leroy 1989; Wiesemann *et al.* 1984; Williamson 1971.

CHAPTER FIFTEEN

BASAÁ (A43)

Larry M. Hyman

1 INTRODUCTION

The Basaá [ɓasaá] language is spoken by an estimated 282,000 people (SIL 1982, cited in Grimes 2000), with relatively minor dialect variation, in Province du Centre and Province du Littoral in southern Cameroon. Guthrie (1967–71) separates Basaá into two groups: Mbénê A43a, spoken in the departments of Nkam, Wouri, Sanaga-Maritime, Nyong et Kellé and Kribi, and Bakóko A43b, spoken in the departments of Nkam and Sanaga-Maritime. The *Ethnologue* lists the following dialects: Bakem, Bon, Bibeng, Diboum, Log, Mpo, Mbang, Ndokama, Basso, Ndokbele, Ndokpenda, Nyamtam. The standard dialect, a form of Mbénê, is said to be spoken in the area around Pouma in Sanaga-Maritime, but has a widespread distribution in the Basaá-speaking region. In addition, Basaá is spoken as a vehicular language in the Bakóko and Tunen areas (Breton and Fohtung 1991:21). Although quite evolved, Basaá is easily identifiable as Bantu by its lexicon as well as by its morphology, e.g. its noun class marking and verb extensions. The language is particularly noteworthy for the phonological changes it has undergone, which have in turn had a major effect on the verb stem morphology.

Among the earliest grammatical works on Basaá are Rosenhuber (1908), Scholaster (1914) and Schürle (1912). More recent extensive works dealing with Basaá phonology, grammar, and lexicon which I have consulted are Bot Ba Njock (1970), Lemb and de Gastines (1973), Janssens (1982, 1986), Dimmendaal (1988), and Bitjaa Kody (1990). A wide-ranging Basaá bibliography of over fifty items is indexed by Barreteau *et al.* (1993:226).

The sections which follow are devoted to phonology (§2), noun and noun phrase (§3), verb derivation (§4), and basic clause structure and verb inflection (§5).

2 PHONOLOGY

It is in its phonology that Basaá seems so non-Bantu-like. Diverging from 'canonical' Bantu languages, Basaá allows both open and closed syllables and does not require surface syllable onsets, as exemplified in the following monosyllabic noun and verb forms:

CV:	sú	'face'	V:	ú	'night'
	pa	'machete'			
	jé	'eat'		é	'clear brush'
	lɔ	'come, arrive'		ɔ	'grow (plant)'
CVC:	kóp	'chicken'	VC:	ɔ́mb	'caterpillar'
	put	'forest, bush'		on	'island'
	lém	'become extinguished'		áŋ	'count, read'
	ɓɔl	'rot'		ɔk	'curse'

257

CVV:	péé	'viper'	VV:	ɛ́ɛ́	'tree'
	kɔɔ	'skin'		óó	'ear'
	hɛ́ɛ́	'cost'		óó	'make (sth.)'
	lɔɔ	'pass, surpass'		ɛɛ	'cry'

Also unexpected from a Bantu perspective, nouns need not have an overt prefix, nor are verbs required to end in a final vowel (FV) morpheme. As will be seen below, many noun class prefixes do still exist in Basaá (§3), as do verb extensions and FV morphemes (§4). We shall also see that surface onsetless syllables in lexical morphemes (e.g. noun and verb stems) always involve an abstract 'ghost' consonant, corresponding to a historical consonant that has been dropped, e.g. PB *-ti > ɛ́ɛ́ 'tree', *-did- > ɛɛ 'cry' (Janssens 1982, 1986).

2.1 Vowels

Basaá distinguishes the seven vowels /i, e, ɛ, u, o, ɔ, a/, which occur long and short, and which contrast in open and closed syllables:

/i/ : tí	'give'	sìì	'rub with force'	lim	'be silent'
/e/ : ye	'be' (pres.)	séé	'rejoice'	ɓép	'beat'
/ɛ/ : nɛ́	'grind'	sɛɛ	'sow'	kép	'tattoo'
/u/ : tú	'evaporate'	suu	'tease'	kun	'choose'
/o/ : jo	'bury'	soo	'savour'	hól	'sharpen'
/ɔ/ : lɔ	'come'	sɔɔ	'be permeable'	hɔk	'swim'
/a/ : lá	'lick'	sáá	'spread (sth.)'	pát	'pick'

However, as Janssens (1986:189–90) shows, the relation of these seven vowels to the seven-vowel system of Proto-Bantu (PB) is not always direct. For instance, the vowel of noun and verb stems which have lost a final *a are one degree lower than in PB:

*dĭbá	'water'	> ma≠lép	6 'water' (cf. lép 5 'rivière, ruisseau')
*kŭba	'hen'	> kóp	9 'hen, rooster'
*bíngá	'pigeon'	> hi≠bɛŋ	19 'pigeon'
*gumba	'sterile female'	> kɔm	9 'sterility'
*dĭm-a	'extinguish'	> lém	'extinguish'
*dŭt-a	'pull'	> ot	'pull, draw, smoke'
*bíd-(u)-a	'be cooked'	> ɓél	'be cooked'
*túm-a	'send'	> ɔ́m	'send'

The vowel alternations that occur in derived verb forms, e.g. applicative límîl, udul, ɓélêl, ómôl, are discussed in §4.2.

2.2 Consonants

The Basaá consonant system is considerably more complex and requires that one distinguish stem-initial vs. other positions in the word. For this purpose we recognize the 'prosodic stem' (root + suffixes) for which the following shapes are attested:

1 syllable

CV	lá	'lick'	nɔ	'rain'
CVC	hól	'sharpen'	ɓaŋ	'make (sth.)'

2 syllables (ŏ-σ)

CV.CV	*ɓá.lê*	'lend'	*he.ya*	'remove'
CV.CVC	*hɔ́.ŋɔ̂l*	'remember'	*no.mos*	'prolong'

2 syllables (ŏ-σ)

CVC.CV	*ɓám.da*	'press, squeeze'	*hɔh.lɛ*	'detach'
CVC.CVC	*mág.lak*	'opening'	*naŋ.lak*	'lying (down)'

3 syllables

CVC.CV.CV	*háŋ.lɛ.nɛ*	'fry for/with/at'	*ɓum.la.ha*	'make to knock'

As illustrated, the prosodic stem contains a maximum of three syllables, four consonants (C1, C2, C3, C4) and three vowels (V1, V2, V3). In addition, the initial syllable of bisyllabic stems may either be light or heavy, while the initial syllable of trisyllabic stems must be heavy.

Within the prosodic stem, the number of underlying consonant oppositions is progressively smaller as one passes from C1 to C2 to C3 to C4:

C1 = 22					C2 = 12			C3 = 6			C4 = 3
p	t	c	k	kw	p	t	k	p	t	k	k
	s		h			s			s		s
ɓ	l	j		gw		l			l		
	y		w				y				
m	n	ny	ŋ	ŋw	m	n	ŋ		n		n
mb	nd	nj	ŋg		mb	nd	ŋg				

The full range of 22 consonants contrast in C1 position vs. 12, 6 and 3 in each successive position. In addition, while /k, s, n/ all occur as C4 in CVCCVCV stems, only /k/ appears in CVCCVC stems, e.g. *máglak* 'en ouvrant'. The palatal affricates /c, j/ can be analyzed as /ty, ly/ and the voiced labiovelars /gw, ŋw/ as /ɓy, my/. In present day Basaá the only surface C + y sequence is [hy], which some speakers simplify to [h], e.g. *hyembí* ~ *hembí* 'song'.

Besides the gradual decrease in consonant oppositions, /p, t, k, s/ are realized differently according to their position within the template: in C1 position, /p, t, k, s/ are realized [p, t, k, s], independent of whether there is a preceding prefix or not, e.g. class 5 *li-*: *li≠pan* 'forest', *li≠tám* 'fruit', *li≠kuŋ* 'owl', *li≠saŋ* 'time, occasion'. /s/ contrasts with /h/ in this position; cf. *lì≠háŋ* 'animal track'. On the other hand, /p, t, k/ are realized voiced when not in C1 position, and when not occurring before pause. Written 'b, d, g', the voiced variants are often also spirantized to [β, r, ɣ], especially when occurring postvocalically. Thus, compare the following underlying, orthographic and phonetic representations of the following words (cf. Hyman 1990, 2000):

Underlying	Orthographic	Phonetic	
/títíkí/	*tídgi*	*tírgí*	'small'
/ɓomta/	*ɓomda*	*ɓòmdà*	'trip (v.)'
/pítip/	*pídîp*	*pírîp*	'scorn'
/li≠mapka/	*li≠mabga*	*lì≠maβga*	'taking form'
/kɔkna/	*kɔgna*	*kɔɣna*	'crush each other'

This voicing (and spirantization), which is predictable once the stem-boundary (≠) is recognized, also occurs in prefixes and other grammatical morphemes, e.g. *bi-* (class 8), *bí* (general past tense), *di-* (class 13), *di* (first person plural), *gá* (general future tense).

Exceptions which occur fall into two categories. The first consists of borrowings, e.g. *dɔ́kta* 'doctor', *dɔ́lâ* 'five francs' (< 'dollar'), *pásto* 'paster', *síta* 'sister', *sitâmp* 'stamp, seal', *hɔ́sì* 'horse', *pɔpɔ́* 'papaya', *kakáo* 'cacao'. The second category of exceptions consists of words whose two CV sequences are identical, e.g. *papáy* 'wing', *tatâ* 'my father', *kékét* 'edible caterpillar', *sísigâ* 'hiccup'. As we shall see in §3.1, nouns may undergo a diminutization process involving reduplication, which not only results in C2 [p, t, k, s], e.g. *sú* 'face' → *hi≠súsú* 'small face', but also permits underlying consonants that would not normally appear in C2 position, e.g. *ŋgwɔ́* 'dog' → *hi≠ŋgwɔ́ŋgwɔ* 'small dog'. It should be noted that non-stem-initial /p, t, k/ are written as *p, t, k* when word-final, otherwise as *b, d, g*, e.g. *níp* 'steal', *níb-â* 'be stolen' (passive).

When stem-final, the stops /p, t, k/ are typically realized voiced and continuant in connected speech (e.g. *corók + dínân* [coróɣ rínân] 'your (pl.) stars'), but as voiceless before pause. As a consequence, they are generally transcribed as voiceless whenever word-final, e.g. *li≠yép* 'poverty', *li≠yɔ́t* 'anger', *li≠lɔ́k* 'dancing'. However, there is variation, e.g. /mut/ 'person' can be heard as [mut°], [mutʰ], [mud] or even [mur]. /s/ is realized [s] as C1 and before pause, e.g. *li≠sún* 'red fly (sp.)', *li≠kás* 'corner, angle'. Elsewhere, /s/ is realized as [h], thereby neutralizing with /h/. The differential realization of /s/ as [s] vs. [h] is often seen in the derivational verb morphology, e.g. *tís* 'touch', *tíhâ* 'be touched' (passive), *tíhîl* 'touch for/at' (applicative), *tíhɓa* 'touch' (reflexive). Since only /k/ occurs finally as C4, C4 /s/ is always prevocalic and appears as [h], e.g. *pinglaha* 'make move', indirect causative of *pingil* 'move (sth.).' Finally, researchers concur that the prenasalized consonants /mb, nd, ŋg/ are voiced, even before pause, e.g. *li≠umb* 'alcohol', *li≠pend* 'barrier', *li≠séŋg* 'parasol-holder'.

2.3 Tone

As seen in the above examples, Basaá contrasts H(igh) and L(ow) tone (Bot Ba Njock 1964, Dimmendaal 1988). H is marked by an acute accent, while L is unmarked. A syllable may be either all H or L, or may involve a fall from H to L to a rise from L to H. The resulting four-way tonal opposition is found on CVC and CVV roots:

kón	'rice'	*ɓéέ*	'hole'
sɛl	'basket'	*lee*	'feather'
kɔ̂l	'charcoal'	*túu*	'shoulder'
nɔ̂p	'rain'	*nyɔɔ́*	'snake'

As Janssens (1986:184–6) demonstrates, these H and L tones generally correspond to PB, as seen in the following cases where PB *CVCV > CVV through the loss of the second stem consonant:

-gudu	'leg'	>	*koo*	'leg'
-bigá	'pot'	>	*hi-ɓɛέ*	'pot'
-tátu	'three'	>	*áà [áâ]*	'three'
-pídí	'viper'	>	*péé*	'viper'

Where the final vowel is lost, the one remaining tone is identical to the first tone of the PB reconstruction:

≠bùmo	'belly'	>	*li≠ɓum*	'belly'
≠dugú	'brother'	>	*lok*	'family, lineage, of the same tribe'
≠jánà	'child'	>	*m≠ăn*	'child' (/m`≠án/)
≠támbí	'sole of foot'	>	*támb*	'shoe'

The major tone rule in present-day Basaá is High Tone Spreading (HTS), by which a /H–L/ sequence becomes [H–HL] (high-falling) on the surface. The rule applies extensively to both nouns and verbs (Dimmendaal 1988:29):

/kémbɛ/	→	kémbê	'goat'
/li≠péhɛl/	→	li≠péhêl	'comb'
/hólol/	→	hólôl	'ripen'
/kéŋgɛp/	→	kéŋgêp	'get fat'

The rule also applies across a word boundary. Thus *njéé* 'which' + *mut* 'person' → *njéé mût* 'which person?'. Compare also *njɔk yɛm* 'my elephant' vs. *ŋgók yêm* 'my pride'.

In certain situations HTS provides a window into the underlying syllable structure of a form. This is seen particularly clearly in derived verb forms:

		passive	applicative
ɓép	'beat'	ɓíbâ	ɓíbîl
két	'pick'	kédâ	kédêl
kóbôl	'peel'	kóbla	kóblenɛ
ságâl	'unhook'	ságla	ságlenɛ

As seen in the first pair of examples, when the L tone passive suffix *-a* or applicative suffix *-Vl* is added to a H tone CVC verb, the H spreads to create a HL falling tone on the suffix. As also seen, root vowels sometimes undergo a vowel raising or umlaut process (cf. §4.2). In the second pair of examples involving CVCVC verbs, the passive is again marked by *-a*, while in this case the applicative suffix has the shape *-ɛnɛ*. In neither case does the root H create a falling tone on the next vowel. (Vowel raising also does not apply.) We can account for this most straightforwardly if we assume a derivation such as the following:

		HTS	syncope
/kóbol-a/	'be peeled'	→ kóbôla →	kóbla
/ságal-a/	'be unhooked'	→ ságâla →	ságla

First HTS spreading applies onto the medial vowel, as shown, and then this vowel is deleted by the following syncope rule:

$$V \rightarrow \emptyset \: / \: V \: C \: \_\_ \: C \: V$$

Besides its interaction with this syncope process, HTS can provide evidence for whether a long vowel should be analyzed as tauto- vs. heterosyllabic. Thus, consider the following minimal pair, whose derived forms should be compared to those seen above:

			passive		applicative	
sáá	/sáC/	'spread'	seâ	/séCa/	sêê	/séCeC/
sáâ	/sáCaC/	'pay'	sééa	/séCCa/	sááne	/sáCnE/

When the passive suffix -a is added to a H tone CVV verb, the latter undergoes vowel shortening (and vowel raising). As seen, such verbs are analyzed with a final ghost /C/, which can provide length only if it is in coda position. In addition, rather than adding /-Vl/, H tone CVV verbs typically form their applicative by changing their vowel and acquiring a HL tone. On the other hand, a CVV verb which has a HHL tonal contour keeps its length in the passive and uses the *-(ɛ)ne* allomorph of the applicative. As seen, such verbs are underlying bisyllabic with two ghost /C/s.

Note finally that contour tones often simplify when not in pre-pause position. Although there is variation, when followed by a H tone, a rising tone typically becomes L, e.g. *jŏy* 'name', *joy jɔ́ŋ* 'your name'. Similarly, a HL falling tone may simplify to H in connected speech, e.g. *tatâ* 'father', *tatá wĕs* 'our father'. When followed by a H, a falling tone will also be simplified to H. In this case, the delinked L tone causes a downstep on the following H, e.g. *n≠cêp* 'branch', *n≠cép ′wɔ́ŋ* 'your branch'. There are many other contexts in which downstepped Hs are produced. These all have in common that an unlinked or floating L tone is wedged between two H tones. There are two such downsteps in the following sentence:

```
a    bí    ′tí   ɓɔ́   ′kón        'he gave them beans'
|    |     |    |    |
L    H  L  H    HL  H
```

The first unlinked L follows the general past marker *bí*, while the second is a floating L prefix on class 9 *kón* 'beans, rice'. This latter L shows that all nouns have a L prefix, whether it is realized segmentally or not.

3 THE NOUN AND NOUN PHRASE

As in other Bantu languages, Basaá nouns consist of a prefix + stem and condition noun class concord on agreeing elements (cf. Bot Ba Njock 1970, Dimmendaal 1988). Table 15.1 provides an overview of noun class marking in Basaá. As seen, noun and concord prefixes may be either segmental or non-segmental and may have different realizations before consonant- vs. vowel-initial roots. Before a consonant, two kinds of homorganic nasal prefix must be distinguished: class 1,3 N≠, which is moraic and tone-bearing vs. class 9/10 N-, which is non-moraic and non-tone-bearing.

3.1 Nouns

In all cases, the basic tone of noun prefixes is L (which will float if the prefix is non-segmental or non-moraic, e.g. in classes 1a, 3a, 7, 9, and 10). Examples are provided in table 15.2.

TABLE 15.1: NOUN CLASS MARKING IN BASAÁ

Class	Noun prefix /__C	/__V	Concord prefix /__C	/__V
1(a)	N≠, Ø-	m-, ŋw-	u-, a-	w-
2	ɓa≠	ɓ-	ɓá-	ɓ-′
3	N≠	ŋ-	ú-	w-′
3a	Ø-	w-	ú-	w-′
4	miN≠	miŋ-	mí-	ŋw-′
5	li≠	j-	lí-	j-′
6	ma≠	m-	má-	m-′
7	Ø-	y-	í-	y-′
8	bi≠	gw-	bí-	gw-′
9	Ø-/N-	ny-	í-	y-
10	Ø-/N-	ny-	í-	y-′
13	di≠	c-	dí-	c-′
19	hi≠	hy-	hí-	hy-′

TABLE 15.2: NOUN CLASS MARKING ON NOUNS

Class	Singular	Plural	
1/2	*n≠lóm*	*ɓa≠lóm*	'husband, male'
	ŋ≠ɔɔ	*ɓa≠ɔɔ*	'enemy'
	m-ut	*ɓ-ot*	'person'
	m-udaá	*ɓ-odaá*	'woman'
	m-aaŋgé	*ɓ-ɔɔŋgé*	'child'
	ŋw-aá	*ɓ-aá*	'wife'
	nyámbê	*ɓa≠nyámbê*	'God'
3/4	*m≠pék*	*mi-m≠pék*	'bag'
	n≠tómbá	*mi-ntómbá*	'sheep'
	ŋ≠kɔl	*mi-ŋ≠kɔl*	'slave'
	n≠sém	*mi-n≠sém*	'flower'
	ŋ≠ɔ́	*mi-ŋ≠ɔ́*	'head'
	ŋ≠ém	*mi-ŋ≠ém*	'heart'
3a/6	*nyɔ́*	*ma≠nyɔ́*	'mouth'
	koo	*ma≠koo*	'leg'
	sú	*ma≠sú*	'face'
	óó	*ma≠óó*	'ear'
	w-ɔɔ́	*m-ɔɔ́*	'hand'
	w-ĕm	*m-ĕm*	'mushroom' (sp.)
5/6	*li≠pa*	*ma≠pa*	'forest'
	li≠ɓum	*ma≠ɓum*	'belly'
	li≠én	*ma≠én*	'oil palm'
	li≠áá	*ma≠áá*	'rock'
	j-ŏl	*m-ŏl*	'nose'
	j-ĭs	*m-ĭs*	'eye'
	j-alá	*m-alá*	'crab'
7/8	*tɔ́ŋ*	*bi≠tɔ́ŋ*	'horn'
	hes	*bi≠hes*	'bone'
	éé	*bi≠éé*	'tree'
	ɔ́mb	*bi≠ɔ́mb*	'caterpillar'
	y-ŏm	*gw-ŏm*	'thing'
	y-oó	*gw-oó*	'yam'
9/10	*pén*	*pén*	'arrow'
	tók	*tók*	'spoon'
	kúl	*kúl*	'tortoise'
	m-bɔm	*m-bɔm*	'python'
	n-dék	*n-dék*	'calabash'
	ŋ-gwɔ́	*ŋ-gwɔ́*	'dog'
	sóŋ	*sóŋ*	'moon, month'
	nyoy	*nyoy*	'bee'
9/6	*pɔ́ɔ́*	*ma≠pɔ́ɔ́*	'wound'
	kíŋ	*ma≠kíŋ*	'neck, voice'
	m-bɔ́t	*ma≠m-bɔ́t*	'cloth, clothing'
	n-dáp	*ma≠n-dáp*	'house'
	ŋ-gand	*ma≠ŋ-gand*	'feast'
	nyuú	*ma≠nyuú*	'body'
19/13	*hi≠tám*	*di≠tám*	'kidney'
	hi≠keŋ	*di≠keŋ*	'knife'
	hi≠sí	*di≠sí*	'earth, ground'
	hi≠nuní	*di≠nuní*	'bird'
	hi≠ee	*di≠ee*	'scorpion'
	hi≠ɔŋ	*di≠ɔŋ*	'flute, trumpet'
	hy-ăy	*c-ăy*	'leaf'
	hy-oŋ	*c-oŋ*	'hair'

As in other Bantu languages, most nouns occur in singular/plural pairs or 'genders', as illustrated in the table. The following points can be noted about the noun class pairings in table 15.2.

Class 1/2 nouns show a wide array of prefixal irregularity, usually involving a nasal in the singular and an implosive labial in the plural. While many members of 1/2 designate humans, many others do not. Most of these lack a nasal prefix in the singular and can be identified as class 1a: *tolo* 'mouse' (pl. *ɓa≠tolo*), *ɓɔɲá* 'brain' (pl. *ɓa≠ɓɔɲá*), *sap* 'type of trap' (pl. *ɓa≠sap*).

Class 3 nouns are marked by a homorganic moraic nasal prefix (N≠), realized as velar before a vowel, which is distinct in two ways from the non-moraic prefix (N-) found in 9/10. First, it can appear before the consonants [p, t, c, k, ɓ, s, h], while 9/10 N- appears only before [b, d, j, g]. Second, it counts as a tone-bearing unit for the purpose of HTS. Thus compare: *li≠wándá lí ŋ̀≠kɔl* 'friend of a slave (class 3)' vs. *li≠wándá lí m-bɔ̂m* 'friend of a python (class 9)' (*m-bɔm*). The plural in class 4 is constructed by adding *mi-* to the singular nasal prefix.

Class 3a conditions the same agreements as class 3. It differs from class 3 in its plural (class 6 vs. class 4) and its prefix. Rather than a nasal, the class 3a prefix is realized Ø before a consonant and *w-* before a vowel (< /u-/), which derives from PB *du-* (11), *bu-* (14) or *ku-* (15), which are not distinguished in Basaá.

Genders 3a/6, 5/6, 7/8, and 19/13 all show important prefix variants depending on whether the stem begins with a consonant or a vowel. These alternations, which are attested also in the concord system, are an important part of the phonetic history of the language and are duplicated within morphemes as well. Thus, the same *li-/j-* and *bi-/gw-* alternations seen in classes 5 and 8 are observed in verb roots such as *jé* 'eat' (< PB *≠dí-a*) and *gwâl* 'give birth' (< PB *≠bɟad-*). While vowel prefixes fuse before root vowels in several of the cited nouns, other nouns in the above table show the preconsonantal prefix forms Ø- or CV- before apparent vowel-initial roots. Thus compare class 3a *w-ɔɔ́* 'hand' vs. *óó* 'ear', class 5 *j-alá* 'crab' vs. *li≠áá* 'rock', class 7 *y-ɔ̌m* 'thing' vs. *éé* 'tree', and class 19 *hy-oŋ* 'hair' vs. *hi≠ɔŋ* 'flute'. The answer proposed by Schmidt (1994), Buckley (1997), and others is that non-fused root-initial vowels are preceded by a synchronic ghost consonant similar to the h-aspiré phenomenon in French, e.g. /li≠Cén/ 'oil palm' (vs. /li-ís/ 'eye'). In general, roots which fuse with their prefix are those which reconstruct with *ɟ and are vowel-initial in much of the Bantu area, while those which do not fuse have lost their historical initial consonant more recently, e.g. *j-ǐs* 'eye' vs. *li≠én* 'oil palm', from earlier *di≠jɟco* and *di≠téndé*, respectively. Note, finally, that when a prefix fuses with an H root, the result is a LH rising tone, e.g. *wǐp* (3a) 'theft' (< /u-íp/). This suggests that the class 9 nouns *nyɛ̌mb* 'death', *nyɔ̌y* 'bee', and *nyɛ̌t* 'buffalo' might be analyzed as vowel-initial with a *nỳ-* prefix. All vowel-initial verbs behave as if there is a ghost consonant, and the nasal prefix found in inflection takes a velar shape (as in noun class 3), e.g. *li≠kɔndɔ ŋ̀≠ɔ̂* 'the banana tree has grown' (*ɔ* 'grow').

Classes 9 and 10 provide an additional analytical dilemma: should the non-moraic nasal that is found in *mb, nd, nj,* and *ŋg* combinations be segmented off as a prefix, as in PB, or should it be considered part of the stem? Besides the historical argument, the major reason for considering the nasality to be a prefix is sheer numbers: class 9 initial *mb, nd, nj, ŋg* vastly outnumber all other initial consonants combined. However, other arguments suggest that the nasal is not a prefix, synchronically. First, Basaá has prenasalized consonants in other positions, including C2, e.g. *pend* 'fence in', *hɔŋg* 'snore', and C1 in verbs, where there is no question of prefixation, e.g. *ndéŋg* 'swing', *njáhâ* 'beg cleverly'. In addition, there are quite a few noun stems in classes other than 9 and 10 which begin with NC, e.g. *li≠ndu* 'palm fiber' (5/6), *hi≠ŋgɔŋ* 'Adam's apple'. Even if it could be shown that such nouns were shifted from class 9, there is no synchronic evidence for double prefixation, i.e. *li≠n-du, hi≠ŋ-goŋ*. The fact is that the nasal is not replaced by prefix substitution here, nor when class 6 *ma-* is added to the singular in 9/6 nouns, e.g. *ma≠n-dáp* 'houses'.

The same inseparability of 9/10 initial nasality is observed in the productive process of diminutivization. A noun may be diminutivized by reduplicating its stem and shifting it into 19/13. In addition, although there is considerable variation, a suffix -a is frequently added as is an H tone suffix. This produces variants such as the following in the singular (the corresponding plurals have the class 13 prefix *di-*):

yɛp	'buttock'	→	*hi≠yɛyép*	*hi≠yɛyêp*	*hi≠yɛ̌yɛba*
	(class 7)		*hi≠yɛyébá*	*hi≠yɛyéba*	*hi≠yɛyé'bá*
li≠ɓum	'belly'	→	*hi≠ɓuɓúm*		
	(class 5)		*hi≠ɓuɓúmá*	*hi≠ɓuɓúmà*	*hi≠ɓuɓú'má*
n-jeé	'leopard'	→	*hi≠njenjéé*	*hi≠njenjé'é*	*hi≠njěnjee*
	(class 9)		*hi≠njenjéá*	*hi≠njenjé'á*	*hi≠njěnjea*

As seen, the prefix *hi-* will replace the class 5 prefix *li-*, but not the nasal of class 9, consistent with the position that the nasal is no longer a prefix in that class. However, there is one problem with this argumentation, which can be seen from the following additional reduplications:

j-am/m-am	'thing, matter'	→	*hi≠jajámá*	*hi≠jǎjama*
	(class 5/6)		*di≠jajámá*	*di≠jǎjama*
			di≠mamama	*di≠mǎmama*
m-ut/ɓ-ot	'person'	→	*hi≠mumúdá*	*hi≠mumúda*
	(class 1/2)		*di≠mumúdá*	*di≠mumúda*
			di≠ɓoɓódá	*di≠ɓoɓóda*

Besides the tonal variants which are represented, we see a choice in the plural: the class 13 prefix can be added to either the reduplicated singular stem (*jam, mut*) or to the reduplicated plural stem (*mam, ɓot*). Although there is no difference in meaning, one can propose that *di≠jajámá* and *di≠mumúdá* are pluralized diminutives, while *di≠mamámá* and *di≠ɓoɓódá* are diminutivized plurals. The difference between Noun → Diminutive → Plural vs. Noun → Plural → Diminutive is only visible in cases where there is different fused prefix in singular and plural. What one does not obtain, however, is derivations like *jam* → *hyam* → *hyahyama, where class 19 *hi-* replaces the fused prefix. The observed inseparability of *j-, m-*, etc. does not argue that they are not prefixes, only that they are more tightly bound prefixes (e.g. spelled out at stratum 1 in a lexical phonology framework). The same can therefore be said about the preconsonantal nasal in classes 9 and 10: it is a prefix spelled out at an earlier stratum than non-fused prefixes.

Basaá does not have Bantu diminutive class 12 **ka-*, and has only relics of the locative classes, e.g. PB class 16 *pa > h-: *hɔmá* 'place' (1a/2), *héé* 'where', *háá* 'that place'; PB class 18 *mu > *mû* 'in it' (Grégoire 1975; cf. Boum 1983 for a treatment of Basaá locative expressions in general).

3.2 Possessive pronouns

Table 15.3 presents the possessive pronouns in all twelve of the formally distinct noun classes in Basaá. As can be extracted from this table, the six pronominal stems are

TABLE 15.3: POSSESSIVE PRONOUNS

Class	'mine'	'yours sg.'	'his/hers'	'ours'	'yours pl.'	'theirs'
1	wɛm	wɔŋ	weé	wɛs	nan	wǎp
2	ɓêm	ɓɔ́ŋ	ɓéé	ɓɛ́s	nân	ɓáp
3	wêm	wɔ́ŋ	wéé	wɛ́s	nân	wáp
4	ŋwêm	ŋwɔ́ŋ	ŋwéé	ŋwɛ́s	mínân	ŋwáp
5	jêm	jɔ́ŋ	jéé	jɛ́s	línân	jáp
6	mêm	mɔ́ŋ	méé	mɛ́s	mánân	máp
7	yêm	yɔ́ŋ	yéé	yɛ́s	nân	yáp
8	gwêm	gwɔ́ŋ	gwéé	gwɛ́s	bínân	gwáp
9	yɛm	yɔŋ	yeé	yɛ́s	nan	yǎp
10	yêm	yɔ́ŋ	yéé	yɛ́s	nân	yáp
19	hyêm	hyɔ́ŋ	hyéé	hyɛ́s	hínân	hyáp
13	cêm	cɔ́ŋ	céé	cɛ́s	dinân	cáp

-ɛm, -ɔŋ, -é, -ɛ́s, -nan and -áp. The concord prefixes are those found before a vowel, except before the second person plural root -nan, which begins with a consonant. Classes 1 and 9 have a L tone concord which creates an LH rising tone when combining with a H pronominal root. This tonal difference is seen in such 9/10 nouns as njɔk yɛm 'my elephant' (class 9), vs. njɔk yêm 'my elephants' (class 10). The tonal distinction on possessive pronouns is neutralized, however, when a preceding noun ends in a H and HTS applies: ŋgwɔ́ yêm 'my dog/dogs' (class 9/10). Note that when occurring in isolation or initially within the noun phrase, these possessive forms take an i- prefix, which general-ly assimilates to [u] before rounded consonants and to the nasal of classes 4 and 6. Thus, the respective forms for 'mine' are: u-wɛm, i-ɓêm, u-wêm, ŋ-ŋwêm, i-jêm, m-mêm, i-yêm, u-gwêm, i-yɛm, i-yêm, i-hyêm, and i-cêm.

3.3 Connective and demonstratives

Because of their formal similarity, the connective 'of', which is used when the possessor is a noun, and demonstratives are considered together in table 15.4. As in other Bantu languages, the connective is required between nouns within a genitive construction, e.g. liwándá lí kíŋê 'the friend of the chief'. Although only class 9 has a L tone marker, i, both it and class 1 nú may be deleted, particularly in the case of class 1a nouns, e.g. hɔmá ˈkón 'place of the rice', njɔk (i) li≠wándá 'elephant of the friend'. Whereas a possessive pronoun may either precede or follow the possessed noun, a genitive noun must follow it. In addition, if the genitive noun begins with an overt L prefix, this L will be raised to H without conditioning a downstep on a following H: liwándá lí míntómbá 'friend of sheep (pl.).' On the other hand, if the genitive noun is prefixless and L–H, e.g. nugá 'animal', a downstep will be obtained: liwándá lí núˈgá. The analysis is that the connective causes a prefix to be raised to H, which also applies between a verb and the following object (§5.3). This process is distinct from HTS, which may apply subsequently:

```
li     nuga  →  li     nuga  →  li     nuga
|      |  |      |      |  |      |     /   |
H L    L H      H H     L H      H     H  LH
```

The three demonstratives show considerable resemblance to the connective, especially as concerns class 1 nú (núnú, nû, núú) and the L of class 9 i (iní, i, ií). The demonstrative

TABLE 15.4: CONNECTIVE AND DEMONSTRATIVES

Class	Connective	'this' (n.s.)	'that' (n.h.)	'that' (far)
1	nú	núnú	nû	núú
2	6á	6áná	6â	6áá
3	ú	únú	û	úú
4	mí	míní	mî	míí
5	lí	líní	lî	líí
6	má	máná	mâ	máá
7	í	íní	î	íí
8	bí	bíní	bî	bíí
9	í	íní	i	íí
10	í	íní	î	íí
19	hí	híní	hî	híí
13	dí	tíní	dî	díí

TABLE 15.5: H TONE PREFIX ON NOUN + DEMONSTRATIVE 'THIS'

1	maaŋgé	ḿ≠maaŋgé núnú	'this child'
2	6ɔɔŋgé	í≠6ɔɔŋgé 6áná	'these children'
3	ŋ≠kɔl	ŋ́≠kɔl únú	'this slave'
4	mi-ŋ≠kɔl	mi-ŋ≠kɔl míní	'these slaves'
5	li≠wándá	lí≠'wándá líní	'this friend'
6	ma≠wándá	má≠'wándá máná	'these friends'
7	sɛl	í≠sɛl íní	'this basket'
8	bi≠sɛl	bí≠sɛl bíní	'these baskets'
9	n-jɔk	ń-jɔk íní	'this elephant'
10	n-jɔk	ń-jɔk íní	'these elephants'
19	hi≠nuni	hí≠nuni híní	'this bird'
13	di≠nuní	dí≠nuni tíní	'these birds'

'this' (near speaker) is best analyzed as $(C)V_i n V_i$, where the first (C)V is from the noun class and both vowels have the same quality. It is not clear whether to analyze the first (C)V as a prefix, since class 13 *tíní* (etc.) is realized with apparent stem-initial devoicing. The variant *díní* does exist, but since class 8 *bíní* (etc.) never devoices, a totally consistent morphological interpretation is probably not possible. The other two demonstratives mark 'that' (near hearer) and 'that' (far from both speaker and hearer'). The near-hearer form may also be used as a general referential 'the one in question'.

Demonstratives may either precede or follow the noun they modify, e.g. *tíní dinuni = dinuní tíní* 'these birds', *líí liwándá = li²wándá líí* 'that friend'. These examples show two interesting facts. First, there is no HTS between preposed demonstrative + noun. Second, whenever there is a postposed demonstrative, the noun class prefix acquires an H tone. Dimmendaal (1988:58) analyzes this as an underlying /í-/ which surfaces on nouns which are either prefixless or whose prefix has fused with its vowel-initial stem (see table 15.5). As seen, this H may also cause a downstep on the noun stem. If it is left out, the result is a presentative construction: *li≠wándá líní* 'here's a friend', *di≠nuni tíní* 'here are the birds'. This determiner H tone, which we can interpret as a trace of the PB augment, is also required when a noun is relativized:

di≠nuní dí bí kwɔ　　　　'the birds fell'
dí≠nuní dí bí kwɔ　　　　'the birds which fell'
di≠nuní li≠wándá lí bí 'téhê　'the birds (that) the friend saw'

3.4 Numerals

In isolation, e.g. when counting, the numbers 'one' to 'ten' are as follows:

pɔ́k	'one'	isámal	'six'
ɓaa	'two'	isâmbɔ́k	'seven'
áâ	'three'	jwɛm	'eight'
n.na	'four' (~ ina?)	ɓoó	'nine'
itan	'five'	jŏm	'ten'

Of these, only the numerals 'one' to 'seven' take noun class agreements, as seen in table 15.6. Here we also observe that the root for 'one' is -ádá rather than pɔ́k. These numerals follow the noun they modify, e.g. mut wadá 'one person', di≠nuní dínâ 'four birds'. The numeral jŏm 'ten' is a noun that belongs to class 5. It may be used either after the noun (as in the case of other numerals), e.g. ma≠wándá jŏm 'ten friends', or may be preposed, in which case the connective lí is required, e.g. jom lí máwándá. Both jŏm and its class 6 plural mŏm are used in combination with '1' through '9' to form compound numerals, e.g. jŏm ni ɓoó '19'. If the numeral following ni 'and, with' is '1' through '7', it will agree with the noun, e.g. ɓot jŏm ni wadá '11 people'. Decades are formed by multiples of mŏm 'tens', e.g. mom máà (~ moomáa) 'twenty' (lit. tens + two). Higher basic numbers include mbógôl '100' and hi≠kóó '1000' (pl. di≠kóo).

3.5 Adjectives

As in most Bantu languages (and many other African languages), adjectives are characterized by nominal morphology in Basaá and will be referred to as 'adjectival nouns'. As

TABLE 15.6: NOUN CLASS CONCORD ON NUMERALS '1'–'7'

	1/2	3/4	5/6	7/8	9/10	19/13
'1'	wàdá	wádá	jádá	yádá	yadá	hyádá
'2'	ɓáa	m̀máa	máa	bíɓáa	íɓáa	díɓáa
'3'	ɓáâ	máâ	máâ	bíáâ	íáâ	díáâ
'4'	ɓánâ	mínâ	mánâ	bínâ	ínâ	dínâ
'5'	ɓátân	míntân	mátân	bitân	ítân	dítân
'6'	ɓásámal	mísámal	másámal	bisámal	ísámal	dísámal
'7'	ɓásâmbɔ́k	mísâmbɔ́k	másâmbɔ́k	bisâmbɔ́k	isâmbɔ́k	dísâmbɔ́k

TABLE 15.7: ADJECTIVAL NOUNS

1	n≠lám	'beautiful'	n≠lám mut	'beautiful person'
2	ɓa≠lám		ɓa≠lám ɓá ɓot	'beautiful people'
3	m≠ɓóŋgó	'long, tall'	m≠ɓóŋgó mût	'tall person'
4	mi-m≠ɓóŋgó		mi-m≠ɓóŋgó mí ɓot	'tall people'
5	li≠kéŋgé	'clever'	li≠kéŋgé lí mût	'clever person'
6	ma≠kéŋgé		ma≠kéŋgé má ɓot	'clever people'
7	lɔ́ŋgê	'good'	lɔ́ŋgé ˈmût	'good person'
8	bi≠lɔ́ŋgê		bi≠lɔ́ŋgé ˈbí ɓot	'good people'
9	m-búk	'mute'	m-búk mut	'mute person'
10	m-búk		m-búk ɓot	'mute people'
19	hi≠yébâ	'poor'	hi≠yébá ˈhí mût	'poor person'
13	di≠yébâ		di≠yébá ˈdi ɓot	'poor people'

such, they themselves have inherent gender and belong to one of six noun class pairings. Illustrations of the six adjectival noun genders are seen in table 15.7. As we have seen, the noun class of the adjectival noun conditions the appropriate connective morpheme. Unlike the genitive construction, an adjective + noun must agree in number, hence *hi≠yébá ˈhí ɓôt, *di≠yébá ˈdí mût. Class 1/2 adjectival nouns show an interesting peculiarity (with some variation). While they participate in the above connective construction, they may also follow the noun, in which case they acquire a L tone prefix agreeing with the preceding noun: n≠tídgí hi≠nuní = hi≠nuní hi≠tídgí 'small bird', ɓa≠tídgí ɓá dí≠nuní = di≠nuní di≠tídgi 'small birds'. These postposed forms can be identified as 'adjectives' even though almost all of them are either derived from or related to adjectival nouns in class 1/2. When the adjectival noun precedes, a remarkable fact is that other modifiers that are present must agree with it, rather than the modified noun: mí≠n-langá mí dí≠nuní míní (*tíní) 'these black birds', mi≠n-langá mí dí≠nuní ŋwêm 'my black birds' (*cêm). The same is true when such modifiers precede the adjectival noun: míní mi≠n-langá mí dí≠nuní, ŋwêm mi≠n-langá mí dí≠nuni (cf. §3.7).

Adjectival nouns are numerous in Basaá. In some cases the adjectival noun may independently exist as a noun of quality, e.g. li≠kéngê 'intelligence', lóŋgê 'goodness'. The corresponding phrases in table 15.7 may thus have once meant '(an) intelligence of person', '(a) goodness of person', etc. There are also a few cases where the modifying noun appears as the second member of the connective construction. In this case it is invariable: mud wĭm 'greedy person', pl. ɓot ɓá wím (lit. people of greed), nugá má≠hóŋ 'fat(ty) animal', pl. bi≠nugá bí má≠hóŋ (lit. animals of fats; cf. sg. li≠hóŋ 'animal fat').

3.6 The pronominal system

Table 15.8 presents the major different forms of pronouns in Basaá (cf. Bot Ba Njock 1970:255). Subject pronouns precede the verb, while the independent pronouns are used for all other argument positions, including object (§5). As we have seen, the independent pronouns of classes other than class 1 end in -ó. Emphatic pronouns are formed by

TABLE 15.8: SIMPLEX PRONOUNS

	Subject	Independent	Emphatic	'... too'
1st pers. sg.	mɛ	mɛ	mɛn	mɛk
1st pers. pl.	di	ɓĕs	ɓes ɓón	ɓes ɓók
2nd pers. sg.	u	wɛ	wĕn	wek
2nd pers. pl.	ni	ɓee	ɓee ɓón	ɓee ɓók
Class 1	a	nyé	nyén	nyêk
Class 2	ɓá	ɓó	ɓón	ɓók
Class 3	ú	wó	wón	wók
Class 4	mí	ŋwó	ŋwón	ŋwók
Class 5	lí	jó	jón	jók
Class 6	má	mó	món	mók
Class 7	í	yó	yón	yók
Class 8	bí	gwó	gwón	gwók
Class 9	i	yɔ	yɔn	yɔk
Class 10	i	yó	yón	yók
Class 19	hí	hyó	hyón	hyók
Class 13	dí	có	cón	cók

TABLE 15.9: COMPLEX PRONOUNS

	me	you sg.	him/her	we	you pl.	them
		mɛ ni wɛ	mɛ ni nyɛ́		mɛ ni beé	mɛ ni bɔ́
me	mɛ ni mɛ	bɛ̌s na wɛ	bɛ̌s na nyɛ́	bɛ̌s ni bɛ̌s	bɛ̌s na beé	bɛ̌s na bɔ́
you sg.	mɛ ni wɛ		wɛ ni nyɛ́			wɛ ni bɔ́
	bɛ̌s na wɛ	wɛ ni wɛ	beé na nyɛ́	bɛ̌s ni wɛ	beé ni beé	beé na bɔ́
him/her	mɛ ni nyɛ́	wɛ ni nyɛ́		bɛ̌s ni nyɛ́		
	bɛ̌s na nyɛ́	beé na nyɛ́	bɔ́ na nyɛ́	bɛ̌s na nyɛ́	beé ni nyɛ́	nyɛ́ ni bɔ́
					bɛ̌s ni beé	bɛ̌s ni bɔ́
we	bɛ̌s ni bɛ̌s	bɛ̌s ni wɛ	bɛ̌s ni nyɛ́	bɛ̌s ni bɛ̌s	bɛ̌s na beé	bɛ̌s na bɔ́
	mɛ ni beé			bɛ̌s ni beé		beé ni bɔ́
you pl.	bɛ̌s na beé	beé ni beé	beé ni nyɛ́	bɛ̌s na beé	beé ni beé	beé na bɔ́
	mɛ ni bɔ́	wɛ ni bɔ́			beé ni bɔ́	bɔ́ ni bɔ́
them	bɛ̌s na bɔ́	opb;eé na bɔ́	bɔ́ ni nyɛ́	bɛ̌s ni bɔ́	beé na bɔ́	bɔ́ na bɔ́

suffixing -n to the independent pronouns, e.g. mɛ̌n 'it's me', gwɔ́n 'it's them' (cl.4). The last column shows the recent development of a set of pronouns having the meaning 'too'. Bot Ba Njock (1970:252) shows that these derive from a fuller form involving the independent pronoun + ki 'also', e.g. mɛ ki ~ mɛk 'me too', bɔ́k ~ bɔ́ kî 'them too'. In addition to the forms in table 15.8, a reflexive form is possible by adding mɛdɛ́ to the independent pronoun, nyɛ́ mɛdɛ́ 'himself', mɔ́ mɛdɛ́ 'themselves' (cl.6). The first and second person singular independent pronouns acquire a H tone: mɛ́ mɛdɛ́ 'myself', wɛ́ mɛdɛ́ 'yourself'. As in the independent and 'too' forms, the third person plural pronoun follows the first and second person plural pronouns: bes bɔ́ mɛdɛ́ 'ourselves', bee bɔ́ mɛdɛ́ 'yourselves'.

In addition, conjoined and compound pronouns are exemplified in table 15.9. There are potentially two ways to combine pronouns. The first is to conjoin them with the conjunction ni 'with, and', which is also used with nouns: mɛ ni nyɛ́ 'me and him', ŋgwɔ́ ni nyɔɔ́ 'a dog and a snake'. In this case, both conjuncts are interpreted independently. The second process derives what we might define as compound pronouns. In this case a plural pronoun is followed by the marker na, which indicates that the second conjunct is included in the first: bɛ̌s na nyɛ́ 'me and him' (literally, 'we including him'). Whereas the first conjunct marks person, the second conjunct is interpreted independently. The major constraint that determines the order of the two conjuncts in both conjoined and compound pronouns has to do with person: 1st ⊃ 2nd ⊃ 3rd.

3.7 Noun phrase structure

Noun phrase structure in Basaá is highly complex and subtle. Ignoring the various uses of the connective for the moment, the remaining noun modifiers show considerable variation in their ordering. Possessives and demonstratives may either follow or precede the noun: dinuni cêm/i ≠ cêm dinuní 'my birds', dínuní tíni/tíní dinuni 'these birds'. When a possessive pronoun precedes, it takes an i- prefix. When a demonstrative follows, the prefix of the first word of the noun phrase receives a H tone. When used together, one may precede and the other follow, both may precede, or both may follow. The following variants all mean 'these birds of mine':

í cêm dinúni tíni   tíní dinuni cêm
tíní cêm dinuni   í cêm tíní dinuni
dínuní cêm tíni   *dínuní tíní cêm

As seen, the only combination which is ruled out is when a demonstrative is followed by a possessive. Other modifiers such as adjectives and numerals, which must occur post-nominally, are freely ordered with respect to possessives, but also precede a demonstrative, which generally occurs last among postposed modifiers. The following variants all mean 'these five black birds of mine':

dínuní cêm dihíndí dítân tíní	cf.	*dínuní tíní cêm dihíndí dítân
dínuní cêm dítân dihíndí tíní		*dínuní tíní dihíndí cêm dítân
dínuní dihíndí cêm dítân tíní		*dínuní cêm tíní dihíndí dítân
dínuní dihíndí dítân cêm tíní		*dínuní cêm tíní dítân dihíndí
dínuní dítân cêm dihíndí tíní		etc.
dínuní dítân dihíndí cêm tíní		

The starred forms on the right are all ungrammatical because of the non-final placement of *tíní* 'these'.

In general, genitive nouns show the same flexibility as possessives, except that they cannot be preposed to the noun:

dinuní dí máwándá dihíndí	'the friends' black birds'
dinuní dihíndí dí máwándá	
dínuní dí máwándá dítân	'the friends' five birds'
dinuní dítân dí máwándá	
dínuní dí máwándá tíní	'these birds of the friends'
*dínuní tíní dí máwándá	
tíní dinuní dí máwándá	

As seen in the last set, a genitive noun may not follow a demonstrative, which must occur last or be preposed to the noun.

In addition to the above, the adjective, numeral or demonstrative may modify the genitive noun:

dinuní dí máwándá mêm	'the birds of my children'
dinuni dî mêm mawándá	
dínuni dí má'wándá máná	'the birds of these friends'
dínuni dí máná mawándá	
dinuní dí máwándá matídgí	'the small friends' birds'
dinuní dí máwándá mátân	'the children's five birds'

Circumstances permitting, each noun may be modified simultaneously:

tíní dinuní dí máwándá mêm	'these birds of my friends'
tíní dinuní dî mêm mawándá	
dínuní dí máwándá mêm tíni	
dínuní dî mêm mawándá tíni	
bifóto gwéé bí máwándá mêm	'his photographs of my friends'
bifóto gwéé bî mêm mawándá	
ugwéé bifóto bí máwándá mêm	
ugwéé bifótó bí mêm mawándá	

In addition, as in most other languages, Basaá allows genitive recursion involving both bracketings shown below:

dinuní dí máwándá má ɓɔ́ɔŋgɛ   *bifóto bí dínuní bi máwándá*
'the birds of the friends of the children'   'the friends' photographs of birds'

These clearly provide for even greater complexity when further modification of any or all of the nouns is involved.

Similar – but not quite identical – variations are found when the connective involves one or more adjectival noun. Except with a postposed adjective, where there is variation, agreement is with the adjectival noun rather than with the internal noun:

> *minlaŋgá mí dínuní ŋwêm*   'my black birds'   (*cêm)
> *ŋŋwêm minlaŋgá mí dínuní*
> *minlaŋgá ŋwêm mí dínuní*
>
> *minlaŋgá mí dínuní míni*   'these black birds'   (*tíní)
> *míni minlaŋgá mí dínuní*
> *minlaŋgá mí dínuní mitân*   'five black birds'   (*dítân)
>
> BUT:
> *minlaŋgá mí dínuní ditídgi* 'black little birds' (~ mitídgí)

Curiously, unless occurring adjacent to it, when there is more than one adjectival noun, agreement is preferentially with the closest rather than topmost one:

> *bilɔ́ŋgé bí minlaŋgá mí dínuní míni*   'these good black birds' (?bíní, *tíní)
> *bilɔ́ŋgé bí minlaŋgá mí dínuní ŋwêm*   'my good black birds'   (*gwêm, *cêm)
> *bilɔ́ŋgé gwêm bí minlaŋgá mí dínuní*
> *gwêm bilɔ́ŋgé bí minlaŋgá mí dínuní*

Attempts to place modifiers in other positions, e.g. preposed possessives, result in other interpretations:

> *bilɔ́ŋgé bî ŋwêm mínlaŋgá mí dínuní*   'the good ones of my black birds'
> *bilɔ́ŋgé bí minlaŋgá mî cêm dínuní*   'the good black ones of my birds'

What this shows is that adjectival nouns, like all other modifiers, can appear with a null head, e.g. *icêm* 'mine', *tíní* 'these', *dîtídgí* 'the small ones', *dítân* 'five (of them)'.

Finally, care should be taken to distinguish noun phrases from the presentative construction, which is formed with a (null head) demonstrative, but without the H prefix required in a noun phrase: *li≠wándá jêm líni* 'here's my friend' (cf. *li≠'wándá jêm líni* 'this friend of mine'), *di≠nuni di≠hindi di≠tân tíni* 'here are the five black birds' (cf. *di≠nuni di≠hindi di≠tân tini* 'these five black birds').

4 VERB DERIVATION

As illustrated in §2.2, the Basaá verb stem consists of a maximum of three syllables (Bitjaa Kody 1990:162) and exhibits the following shapes (where C can be null): CV, CVC, CVCV, CVCVC, CVCCV, CVCCVC, CVCCVCV. Also Basaá has a surface opposition between long and short vowels (§2.1). These do not correspond to the distinction in PB. Rather, there is clear evidence that long vowels more recently derive from

*VC sequences. The following vowel length alternations show that they still function as /VC/ within the synchronic phonology:

εε	'cry, weep for'	→	ea	'be wept for'	(< PB *-did-)
ɓuu	'chase (away)'	→	ɓua	'be chased'	(? < PB *-bɥim-)
sáá	'scatter'	→	séâ	'be scattered'	(? < PB *-cán-)

Monosyllabic CVV verbs lose their length when a vowel suffix follows, here passive -a. Since Basaá has been argued to have ghost consonants (Schmidt 1994, Buckley 1997), we can informally represent these roots as /CεC/, /ɓuC/, and /sáC/, and their passives as CεCa, ɓuCa, and séCâ. What we see then is that the ghost C contributes vowel length only if it is in the coda of the syllable, not if it is syllabified as an onset. We also explain why verbs such as sáá 'scatter' are single tone-bearing units, realized H rather than with a fall to L.

4.1 Verb stems

The morphological structure of the Basaá verb stem is as follows:

Verb root + (extensions) + (final vowel)

A verb stem may be monomorphemic or may include one or two derivational suffixes (extensions). Unlike most other Bantu languages, it need not end in a final vowel (FV) morpheme. There are at most three V positions. While all seven vowels occur as V1, the following generalizations characterize vowel shapes in V2 and V3 positions:

First, only the three vowels -i, -ε, -a occur as the FV of bi- and trisyllabic stems, and -i occurs only in CVC-i stems:

ɓúgî	'break (intr.)'	–		–	
jélê	'surpass'	ɓóblε	'touch'	sεglεnε	'sort for'
ɓɔma	'meet'	nɔlna	'kill e.o.'	cimbaha	'make sneeze'

CV verbs do not take a FV synchronically.

Second, V1 and V2 must be identical in CVCVC stems:

/i/ :	tiɲil	'detach'	limik	'being quiet'
/e/ :	sebel	'call'	ɓébek	'beating'
/ε/ :	lεgεl	'transmit'	kébêk	'tattooing'
/u/ :	núhûl	'stay up/awake'	kunuk	'choosing'
/o/ :	lóhôl	'skin'	hólôk	'sharpening'
/ɔ/ :	bɔgɔl	'dislodge'	hɔgɔk	'swimming'
/a/ :	bágâl	'separate'	pádâk	'picking'

Third, V2 and V3 must be identical in CVCCVCV stems, as in the following applicative and reciprocal forms of the above CVCV1 verbs:

/i/ :	tiɲlεnε	'detach for/at'	tiɲlana	'detach each other'
/e/ :	seblεnε	'call for/at'	seblana	'call each other'
/ε/ :	lεglεnε	'transmit for/at'	lεglana	'transmit to each other'
/u/ :	núhlεnε	'stay up for/at'	núhlana	'stay up at each other's'
/o/ :	lóhlεnε	'skin for/at'	lóhlana	'skin each other'
/ɔ/ :	bɔglεnε	'dislodge for/at'	bɔglana	'dislodge each other'
/a/ :	báglεnε	'separate for/at'	báglana	'separate each other'

Finally, the only CVCCVC verbs end in *-ak*, the allomorph of the imperfective suffix used with CVCVC verb bases:

/i/ : *tiŋlak*   'detaching'
/e/ : *seblak*   'calling'
/ɛ/ : *lɛglak*   'transmitting'
/u/ : *núhlak*   'staying up/awake'
/o/ : *lóhlak*   'skinning'
/ɔ/ : *bɔglak*   'dislodging'
/a/ : *báglak*   'separating'

As discussed in §2.2, there are fewer consonants possible in each successive C slot within Basaá verb stems. The attested C3 consonants are /p, t, k, s, l, n/, while the C4 consonants consist solely of /k, s, n/. Only /k/ occurs as stem-final C4.

4.2 Extensions

The above and other distributional properties of consonants and vowels can best be examined by means of the derivational suffixes or verb extensions found in Basaá and summarized in table 15.10. As seen, some suffixes appear only after monosyllabic CV or CVC verb roots, while others have special allomorphs when the verb base is longer. The symbol ¨ indicates a height umlaut that occurs with certain suffixes. In its most general form, the vowels /e, o/ raise to [i, u], /ɛ, a/ raise to [e] and /ɔ/ raises to [o] (Voorhoeve 1980c, Schmidt 1994, Mutaka and Bitjaa Kody, in press). The causative and applicative suffixes show this raising in table 15.11.

TABLE 15.10: VERB EXTENSIONS AND THEIR ALLOMORPHS

	After CV(C) radical	Later in verb stem
reversive	*¨-l, -l*	–
reflexive	*-b* [p], *-b-a, -b-a*	–
causative	*¨-s*	–
indirect causative	*¨-h-a /¨-s-a/*	*¨-h-a /¨-s-a/*
applicative	*¨-l*	*-n-ɛ*
reciprocal	*-n-a*	*-n-a*
passive	*¨-a, ¨-b-a*	*-a, -n-a*
habitual	*-a*	–
stative	*¨-i*	–
imperfective	*-g* [k]	*-ag* [ak]

TABLE 15.11: VOWEL RAISING WITH CAUSATIVE ¨-s AND APPLICATIVE ¨-l

		Causative ('make ...')	Applicative ('... for/with/at')
lim	'be silent'	*limis*	*limil*
bép	'beat'	*bíbîs*	*bibîl*
kép	'tattoo'	*kébês*	*kébêl*
kun	'choose'	*kúnûs*	*kúnûl*
hól	'sharpen'	*húlûs*	*húlûl*
bɔl	'rot'	*bólôs*	*bólôl*
pát	'pick off'	*pédês*	*pédêl*

Among the suffixes in table 15.10, the least productive is the reversive, which is responsible for verb pairs such as the following: *ték* 'lay (sth.) flat', *tégêl* 'remove (sth.) lying flat'; *lóŋ* 'cork, block', *lóŋɔ̂l* 'uncork, unblock'; *ɓamb* 'spread (in sun) to dry', *ɓambal* 'remove from heat'. In contradistinction with applicative ¨-*l*, only the mid vowels /e, o/ undergo raising with the reversive (Janssens 1986), e.g. *kwes* 'lock', *kwihil* 'unlock'; *teŋ* 'attach', *tiŋil* 'detach'.

The reflexive suffix has three allomorphs which can attach only to monosyllabic verb bases. CV verbs take the allomorph -*ba*, e.g. *hó* 'cover', *hóbâ* 'cover oneself'; *sɔ* 'purify', *sɔba* 'purify oneself'. A small number of CVC verbs, a number with 'adjectival meaning' use the allomorph -*b* (cf. Proto-Bantu *-*p*-), which devoices to [p] before pause, e.g. *teŋ* 'attach', *teŋep* 'attach oneself'; *hót* 'bend', *hódôp* 'bend oneself'. As seen, a V2 identical to V1 is required for syllabification. Most CVC verbs, however, take the reflexive suffix -*ɓ-a*, e.g. *nun* 'look at', *nunɓa* 'look at oneself'; *pék* 'fan', *pégɓa* 'fan oneself'. In addition four CVCɛ verbs have also been found to allow a -*ɓ-a* reversive suffix: *anɛ* 'to order', *anɓa* 'to order oneself'; *kwiyɛ* 'light (fire)', *kwiyɓa* 'light itself'; *pudɛ* 'fall on', *pudɓa* 'get oneself mixed up in something stupid'; *núyê* 'heat up', *núyɓa* 'be heated up'. The postconsonantal allomorph -*ɓ-a* provides additional evidence that CVV verbs are underlyingly CVC: *hɔɔ* 'smear, coat', *hɔɔɓa* 'smear oneself'; *kwɛɛ* 'circumcize', *kwɛɛɓa* 'get oneself circumcised'.

The (direct) causative suffix ¨-*s*, which was illustrated with CVC verb roots in table 15.11, can be added directly to CV verbs, e.g. *jé* 'eat', *jês* 'make eat, feed'; *lá* 'lick', *lês* 'make lick', *nɔ́* 'rain', *nôs* 'make rain'. CVV verbs also take ¨-*s*, e.g. *wáá* 'be tired', *wéês* 'make tired', where the latter's tones indicate a wéCês structure. The indirect causative suffix ¨-*h-a* may also be added to monosyllabic verb bases, e.g. *cé* 'destroy', *cíhâ* 'make destroy'; *han* 'be proud', *henha* 'make proud'; *lɔɔ* 'surpass', *looha* 'exaggerate, overflow'. In case the verb base is bisyllabic, only the indirect causative may be used: *cáŋgâp* 'be dishonest', *céŋgɓaha* 'make dishonest'; *jóŋôp* 'be silly', *júŋɓaha* 'make silly'; *nɔ́mɔ̂l* 'quarrel', *nómlaha* 'make quarrel'. As seen, the umlaut effect of ¨-*ha* goes right through the epenthetic [a] of -*aha* onto the root vowel. The following sentences illustrate the semantic difference between the two causative forms, both based on the verb *ɓét* 'go up, climb':

> *mɛ m≠ɓédés m-bégɛ hi≠koá* 'I carried the baggages up the hill'
> *mɛ m≠ɓédhá ɓɔ́ŋgé hi≠koá* 'I made the children go up the hill'

In the first sentence, direct causation requires that I physically carry the baggages, which is not the case with indirect causation in the second sentence, where it is not possible to substitute *mbegɛ* 'baggages' for *ɓɔ́ŋgé* 'children'. Note, finally, that the same formal suffix ¨-*h-a* may instead provide an aspectual connotation of simultaneity, e.g. *mɛmlɛ* 'contemplate', *memlaha* 'contemplate at the same time'; *gwâl* 'give birth', *gwélha* 'give birth at the same time'.

As in other Bantu languages, the applicative is used to mark dative objects, manner, location and time (Lemb and de Gastines 1973:37). The ¨-*l* allomorph, which was illustrated on CVC verbs in table 15.11 also occurs on CV verb bases: *jé* 'eat', *jêl* 'eat for/with/at'; *jo* 'bury', *jul* 'bury for/with/at'. CVV verbs, on the other hand, typically undergo vowel raising without the final -*l*: *hɔ́ɔ* 'smear', *hôô* 'smear for/with/at'; *káá* 'plead', *kéê* 'plead for/with/at'. This suggests the derived structure kéCêC, where the -*l* has "assimilated" to the ghost consonant of the root. A similar assimilation is found when the verb base has the shape CVy: *nɔy* 'rest', *noyoy* 'rest for/at'; *ɓáy* 'be sour', *ɓéyêy* 'be sour for/at'. Bisyllabic bases show one of the realizations of the (non-umlauting) -*n-ɛ* allomorph: *anɛ* 'order', *annɛ* 'order for', *ɓégês* 'praise', *ɓéghɛnɛ* 'praise for/at'; *hóyâ* 'forget', *hóyna* 'forget for/at'.

When added to verbs of the shapes CVlVl and CVCVV, the resulting outputs are CVVlnɛ and CVVCnɛ: *hólôl* 'ripen', *hóólnɛ* 'ripen for/at'; *ɓɛgɛɛ* 'carry', *ɓɛɛgnɛ* 'carry for/at'. In the case of CVCVl verbs, where the applicative form is expected to be CVClɛnɛ, a shortened CVClɛ form is also attested, e.g. *luhul* 'chase away' → *luhlɛnɛ* ~ *luhlɛ*.

The reciprocal suffix -*n-a* may be added to mono- or bisyllabic verbs: *cé* 'destroy', *cénâ* 'destroy each other'; *kɛk* 'hurt', *kɛgna* 'hurt each other'; *pɔhɔl* 'choose', *pɔhlana* 'choose each other'; *témbéɛ* 'lie', *téémbana* 'lie to each other'. It may also have an associative or comitative meaning, e.g. *hɔk* 'swim', *hɔgna* 'swim with'; *jop* 'enter', *jobna* 'enter with'.

The passive suffix has four allomorphs. The umlauting allomorphs ¨-*b-a* and ¨-*a* are used after CV and CVC/CVV verb bases, respectively: *cé* 'destroy', *cíbâ* 'be destroyed'; *ɓɔŋ* 'do', *ɓoŋa* 'be done', -*sɛɛ* 'plant', -*sea* 'be planted'. The non-umlauting allomorph -*a* is used on longer verb bases, e.g. *sagal* 'undo', *sagla* 'be undone'; *hɛŋɛl* 'change', *hɛŋla* 'be changed'; *kóbôl* 'peel', *kóbla* 'be peeled'. Finally, the allomorph -*n-a* seems to be used with (direct or indirect) causative bases: *jês* 'feed' (<*jé* 'eat'), *jésna* 'be fed'; *ɓédha* 'cause to go up' (< *ɓét* 'go up'), *ɓédhana* 'be caused to go up'. It is possible that this -*n*- is related to the applicative or comitative extension.

The habitual extension is -*a*: *nɔl* 'kill', *nɔlâ* 'kill habitually'; *nógôl* 'obey', *nógla* 'obey habitually'; *yagal* 'beg', *yagla* 'beg habitually'. It appears that the -*n-a* suffix also can be used with habitual meaning (e.g. with vowel-final verb bases): *jo* 'bury', *jona* 'bury habitually'; *léégɛ* 'receive', *léégana* 'receive habitually'.

The stative suffix ¨-*i* is restricted to CVC-í verb stems: *kwes* 'lock', *kwihí* 'be locked'; *pak* 'occupy', *pegí* 'be occupied'. When the base already ends in -*i*, one sometimes observes only a tonal change in the stative: *héndî* 'place crookedly', *héndí* 'be crooked'; *niŋí* 'lay', *niŋí* 'be lying'. Other bisyllabic bases replace their V2(C) by *i* in the stative, e.g. *núŋgê* 'set (trap)', *núŋgí* 'be set (trap)'; *koyop* 'become red', *kuyí* 'be red'.

The last suffix to be discussed is the imperfective, which has the allomorph -*g* ([-k] before pause), when added to monosyllabic bases: *cé* 'destroy', *cêk* 'destroying'; *ɔɔ* 'hate', *ɔɔk* 'hating', *ɓép* 'beat', *ɓébêk* 'beating'. Longer bases take the allomorph -*ak*: *tiŋil* 'detach', *tiŋlak* 'detaching'; *ɓégês* 'praise', *ɓéghak* 'praising'; *ɓíní* 'bend back', *ɓínâk* 'bending back'. In different tenses this suffix acquires imperfective meanings such as durative, progressive, iterative, and habitual (Bitjaa Kody 1990:414–15). It is also frequently used in deverbal nominals, e.g. *ɓép* 'beat', *li≠ɓébêk* 'way of beating'; *lok* 'deceive', *li≠logok* 'way of deceiving'.

While the above represents the general situation, there are small numbers of exceptions for many of the suffixes. Thus, the applicative and causative forms of *kɛ* 'go' are *kil* and *kis*, not the expected **kel* and **kes*. In addition, not every extension can be used on every verb root, nor is the meaning always compositional. Finally, there are possibilities for combining two suffixes, as long as one does not exceed the three-syllable maximum for prosodic stems. The extension sequences in table 15.12 are reported by Lemb and de Gastines for the verb *teŋ* 'attach' (*teŋ-ɓ-ah-a* is expected to be *tiŋ-ɓ-ah-a*).

TABLE 15.12: EXTENSION COMBINATIONS REPORTS BY LEMB AND DE GASTINES (1973:35)

	Basic	Applicative	Causative	Ind. caus.	Reciprocal	Passive
Root	*teŋ*	*tiŋ-il*	*tiŋ-is*	*tiŋ-h-a*	*teŋ-n-a*	*tiŋ-a*
Reversive	*tiŋ-il*	*tiŋ-l-ɛn-ɛ*	–	*tiŋ-l-ah-a*	*tiŋ-l-an-a*	*tiŋ-l-a*
Reflexive	*teŋ-eb*	*teŋ-ɓ-ɛn-ɛ*	–	*teŋ-ɓ-ah-a*	*teŋ-ɓ-an-a*	*teŋ-ɓ-a*
Stative	*tiŋ-í*	*tiŋ-n-ɛ́*	–	–	–	–
Habitual	*teŋ-a*	–	–	–	–	–

In addition, three other combinations have also been found on forms within the dictionary itself:

	input	causative	applicative	reciprocal
causative	*tomb-os*	–	*tomb-h-ɛn-ɛ*	*tomb-h-an-a*
applicative	*bemb-el*	–	–	*bemb-l-an-a*

tɔmb	'be soft, tired'	*bamb*	'spread (sth.) out'	
tombos	'soften, make tired'	*bembel*	'spread for/at'	
tombhɛnɛ	'soften for/with'	*bemblana*	'spread for each other'	

A small number of verb stems involve two instances of the same suffix, where one changes the meaning in unpredictable ways, e.g. *kap* 'share, distribute' → *kebel* 'feed' → *keblɛnɛ* 'feed for/with/at' (root + appl + appl); *teŋ* 'attach' → *tiŋha* 'make attach' → *tiŋhaha* 'hold/delay someone'.

The following schema accounts for the linear ordering of consonants observed in Basaá verb stems: Root C's ⊃ {b, l} ⊃ s [h] ⊃ n ⊃ g. In addition, examples cited above show that the FV -*a* overrides -*ɛ*, which in turn overrides -*i*, e.g. *bɛŋgɛ* 'look at', *bɛŋgna* 'look at each other'; *niɲí* 'be lying (e.g. in bed)', *niɲnɛ́* 'be lying at/on'.

The same generalizations cover deverbal nominals which are discussed by Bot Ba Njock (1970) and Lemb and de Gastines (1973). These can be based on simple verb bases or extended ones. Thus, from the verb *bɔŋ* 'do', one can derive *m≠bɔŋ/ba≠bɔŋ* 'doer(s)', and from its applicative *bɔŋol* 'do for/with/at', one derives *m≠bɔŋol/ba≠bɔŋol* 'servant(s)'. While deverbal nouns in class 1 express agentives, those in class 3 mark the state or situation of an action, e.g. *kap* 'share' → *ŋ≠kabak* 'that which has just been shared'; *keba* 'be shared' (passive) → *ŋ≠kĕbak* 'that which was shared some time ago'; *kabna* 'share with' (associative) → *ŋ≠kăbnaga* 'that which has been shared with/among'. Besides the temporal nuances indicated by Lemb and de Gastines (1973:46), the imperfective suffix -*g* is also present as it is in class 5 deverbal nouns which describe the manner of action: *gwɛl* 'catch, hold' → *li≠gwɛlɛk* 'manner of catching, holding'; *gwɛlba* 'cling' (reflexive) → *li≠gwɛlbaga* 'manner of clinging'. Verbs can also be nominalized as instruments in (prefixless) class 9, e.g. *gwɛl* 'catch, hold' → *gwelél* 'handle by which one grabs an object', *bomol* 'knock against, nail' → *bomlénɛ́* 'object used to nail with'. As seen, instrumental nouns require an applicative extension and an H suffixal tone.

Finally, although Basaá has no overtly marked infinitive, Dimmendaal (1988:65) hypothesizes that the class 3 verbal agreement that verbal nouns condition derives from PB class 15 *ku, e.g. *bat ú≠yé ꞌlɔ́ŋgê* 'to question is good'.

5 BASIC CLAUSE STRUCTURE

Although Basaá has maintained much of the original Bantu morphology, its clause structure shows a drift towards analytic marking of grammatical relations and inflection.

5.1 Word order

The basic word order in Basaá is Subject – Aux – Verb – Object – Adjunct:

li≠wándá	*jêm*	*lí*	*m̀≠*	*ꞌbéná*	*jé*	*bí≠jék*	*í*	*ꞌndáp*
friend	my	SP	PRES	do-often	eat	food	in	house

'my friend often eats food in the house'

As also seen in this example, the subject pronouns in table 15.8 are required for subject agreement, as in Bantu generally, although there is no evidence that such markers are prefixed to the auxiliary or verb that follows. In fact, although the nasal marking present tense in this example is typically written as a prefix, it too could be analyzed as a proclitic and written as a separate syntactic element. In short, Basaá lacks the Bantu prefixal system on verbs.

The independent pronouns in table 15.8 are used to express non-subject arguments, including object. They follow the verb in all cases: *a bí nuŋúl lí≠tám* 'he sold a fruit'; *a bí nuŋúl jɔ́* 'he sold it'. The direct object precedes any overtly marked prepositional phrase or other adjunct, e.g. *a m≠púhlé mê í ¹mbús* 'he surprised me from behind'; *malêt a m̀≠¹ɓíbíl ɓá≠údú ni ŋ≠ɔ́ŋ* 'the teacher is beating the students with a rattan stick'.

5.2 Grammatical relations

As in other Bantu languages, the major issue concerning grammatical relations is the analysis of object properties. Only a few unextended verbs can take two objects, e.g. *tí* 'give': *mɛ n≠tí ɓɔ́ŋgé bijék* 'I gave the children food'. The reverse word order, *?mɛ n≠tí bíjék ɓɔŋgé*, is dispreferred and gives the impression of meaning 'I gave the children to the food'. Either or both of the two objects can be pronominalized. When both are pronominalized, the recipient must precede the patient: *mɛ n≠tí ɓɔ́ gwɔ́* 'I gave them it' (**mɛ n≠tí gwɔ́ ɓɔ́*). Again, only one order is possible when only the recipient is pronominalized: *mɛ n≠tí ɓɔ́ bijék* 'I gave them food' (**mɛ n≠tí bíjék ɓɔ́*). On the other hand, the patient can be pronominalized *in situ: mɛ n≠tí ɓɔ́ŋgé gwɔ́* 'I gave the children it', in which case 'the children' is old information; or it can be pronominalized right after the verb: *mɛ n≠tí gwɔ́ ɓɔŋgé* 'I gave it to the children', in which case 'the children' is new information.

A natural interpretation of these facts is that the recipient is the 'primary' object, and that proximity to the verb is one criterion for such status. As seen, the tendency for a pronoun to precede a noun, motivated by discourse considerations, may cause a minor conflict, thereby producing both orders just seen.

Besides word order, the second criterion is that the primary object can become the subject of the corresponding passive, whereas the secondary object cannot: *ɓɔŋgé ɓá ń≠tíbá bíjék* 'the children were given food'; **bíjék bi ń≠tíbá ɓɔ́ŋgé* 'the food was given (to) the children'. Sentences involving the applicative form of the verb *lámb* 'cook' show the same word order facts as with the verb *tí* 'give' (Hyman and Duranti 1982:236):

mɛ n≠lémbél ɓɔ́ŋgé bijék	'I cooked the children food'
?mɛ n≠lémbél bíjék ɓɔŋgé	
mɛ n≠lémbél ɓɔ́ gwɔ́	'I cooked them it'
*mɛ n≠lémbél gwɔ́ ɓɔ́	
mɛ n≠lémbél ɓɔ́ bijék	'I cooked them food'
*mɛ n≠lémbél bijékɓɔ́	
mɛ n≠lémbél ɓɔ́ŋgé gwɔ́	'I cooked the children it'
mɛ n≠lémbél gwɔ́ ɓɔ́ŋgé	'I cooked it (for) the children'

It would thus seem that the benefactive is the primary object. However, unlike *tí* 'give', only the patient can become the subject of the corresponding passive in an applicative construction:

bijék bi ń≠lémbná ɓɔ́ŋgé	'the food was cooked for the children'
*ɓɔŋgé ɓá ń≠lémbná bijék	

(The agent of the passive may be introduced by *ni*.) However, given the shape of the applicative suffix in these examples, namely *-n-*, it would seem that they have the underlying structure of an applicativized passive, where this allomorph is chosen because the input base to applicativization is bisyllabic (*lémb-â* 'be cooked'). The expected form, *lembla*, is not accepted by all speakers, although when it is accepted, the syntax appears to be reversed:

bɔŋgé 6á ń≠lémblá bíjék   'the children were cooked food'
**bijék bí ń≠lémblá 6ɔŋgé*

It may be, therefore, that the two verbs have the following two different morphosyntactic structures and hence different syntactic properties as per the 'mirror principle' (Baker 1988b).

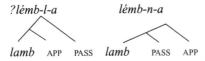

?lémb-l-a   *lémb-n-a*

lamb APP PASS   *lamb*   PASS   APP

In the case of the second structure, one can think of first deriving the passive *lemb-a* and then 'interfixing' the applicative *-n-* between *lemb-* and *-a*.

A similar complication is found when we applicativize the verb *ti* 'give', to create the following sequence of three unmarked objects:

mɛ   n≠tíné   múdaá   6ɔŋgé   bijék
I   gave/app woman   children food
'I gave the food to the children for the woman'

Recall that only the recipient could be the subject of simple passive of 'give' (*tíbâ*). In this more complex case, either the patient or the recipient can become the subject of the corresponding passive, but not the benefactive introduced by the applicative:

6ɔŋgé 6á ń≠tíbná múdaá bijék   'the children were given food for the woman'
bijék bí ń≠tíbná múdaá 6ɔŋgé   'food was given the children for the woman'
**mudaá a n≠tíbná 6ɔŋgé bijék*   'for the woman were the children given food'
(OK if it means 'the woman was given food for the children')

In this case note that the *-n-* of the applicative occurs between the two parts of the passive extension *-b-a*. Again, the analysis is that *tíbna* is an applicativized passive, not the more widespread Bantu passivized applicative.

In terms of Bresnan and Moshi's (1990) dichotomy, Basaá appears to be an 'asymmetric' object language in that one argument claims primary object status as judged by the word order and passive tests. However, some of its properties are still unexpected. As seen in the following, Basaá has widespread optional possessor raising which carries the nuance that the possessor is affected by the action:

mɛ   n≠jé   nú'gá   (i)   maŋgé   'I ate the child's meat'   child = [−affected]
I   ate   meat   (of)   child
mɛ   n≠jé   máŋgé nugá   'I ate the child's meat'   child = [+affected]

The first sentence is passivized as expected, with the full possessive noun phrase as subject:

nugá (i) maŋgé í ń≠jébá   'the child's meat was eaten'

With possessor raising, Basaá quite differently from other Bantu languages, allows only the possessed object to become the subject of the corresponding passive:

> nugá í n≠jébá maŋgé   'the child's meat was eaten' (lit. meat was eaten child)
> *maŋgé a n≠jébá nú'gá   (*child was eaten meat)

On the other hand, either or both nouns can be prominalized *in situ*:

> mɛ n≠jé nyé nugá   'I ate his meat' (lit. 'I ate him meat')
> mɛ n≠jé maŋgé yɔ́   'I ate the child's [meat]' (lit. 'I ate the child it') (*yɔ́ maŋgé)
> mɛ n≠jé nyé yɔ́   'I ate his' (lit. 'I ate him it')

Possessor raising potentially allows for multiple unmarked noun phrases in sequence:

> mɛ m≠bók [múdaá [man [wɔɔ́   'I broke the arm of child of the woman'
>   (lit. 'I broke the woman the child the arm')

Given the discourse-dependence of the different options, it is not surprising that whether one does possessor raising or not depends to a large extent on the context and the nature of the participants, e.g. whether first, second or third person.

Finally, a brief note that certain oblique objects may be introduced by *ni* 'with, and', sometimes as an option to the verb extension *-n-a*, e.g. *lɔná maŋgé* 'bring the child' (<*lɔ* 'come'), *lɔɔ́ ni maŋgé* 'come with/bring the child'. Locatives are typically introduced by *í*, e.g. *í 'ndáp* 'in the house' (Boum 1983).

5.3 Verb inflection

As mentioned, Basaá lacks the Bantu system of verb prefixation and most tense, aspect, mood, and polarity distinctions are expressed by means of clitics and particles, as well as newly grammaticalized auxiliaries.

The basic tense system is identified and exemplified in table 15.13 (vowel length automatically resulting from a rising tone). As seen, Basaá distinguishes three degrees of past and two degrees of future tense. The different verb tenses, subjunctive and imperative in table 15.13 are presented in the perfective, whose formation (including tones) is exemplified by the verbs *jé* 'eat' and *lɔ* 'come'. As seen, the verb stem may acquire a prefixal or suffixal tone, which may form a contour with the verb tone or condition downstep. The segmental marking of these forms precede the verb as particles or proclitics, except for the negative particle, which immediately follows the verb and precedes any object, e.g. *a gá 'jé 'bé bijék* 'he will not eat food'. The plural imperative is formed by a suffix *-ná*, which, however, is optional in the negative: *ni jé(ná) bá'ŋ* 'don't (pl.) eat!.' The corresponding imperfective can be formed by suffixing *-g/-ag* to the verb base in any tense. This suffix is also found in what Bitjaa Kody (1990:451) identifies as the persistive: *a ngí jêk* 'he is still eating', *a ngí lɔ́k* 'he is still coming'. He also reports a perfect/linger construction marked by /'ma/ (?<mal 'finish'): *a má 'jé* 'he has already eaten', *a má lɔ* 'he has already come'.

In addition to the tones which are involved in forming the tenses in table 15.13, there is a dichotomy with respect to the tone on a noun object that immediately follows the verb. In most tenses, an H appears between the two that will be realized on the V2 and V3 of the verb, if available, as well as on the noun prefix, e.g. *a bí nuŋul* 'he sold', *a bí nuŋúl bí≠sɛl* 'he sold baskets' (<*bi≠sɛl*). In the P3, future perfect, subjunctive and

TABLE 15.13: VERB TENSES + SUBJUNCTIVE AND IMPERATIVE

Tense/marking	Affirmative	Negative	Main uses
P1	*a n≠jé*	*a n≠jé 'ɓé*	today past tense
/N≠ H-/	*a n≠lɔ*	*a n≠lɔ 'ɓé*	
P2	*a bí 'jé*	*a bí 'jé 'ɓé*	general past tense, e.g.
/pí L-/	*a bí lɔ*	*a bí lɔ ɓé*	yesterday or earlier
P3	*a jé*	*a jé 'ɓé*	pluperfect; distant past
/-H/	*a lɔɔ́*	*a lɔɔ́ 'ɓé*	
Narrative	*a jé*	*a jé 'ɓé*	consecutive or
/H-/	*a lɔ́*	*a lɔ́ 'ɓé*	unspecified past
Present	*a ń≠'jé*	*a ń≠'jé 'ɓé*	present; habitual; near
/Ń≠L-/	*a ń≠lɔ*	*a ń≠lɔ ɓé*	'about to' future
F1	*a gá 'jé*	*a gá 'jé 'ɓé*	general future, e.g.
/(k)á L- ... -H/	*a gá lɔɔ́*	*a gá lɔɔ́ 'ɓé*	tomorrow, some days
F2	*aa jé*	*aa jé 'ɓé*	distant or unspecified
/a/	*aa lɔ*	*aa lɔ ɓé*	future
Future perfect	*á 'jé*	*á 'jé 'ɓé*	future perfect or consecutive;
/H≠L- ... -H/	*á lɔɔ́*	*á lɔɔ́ 'ɓé*	conditional 'if'
Subjunctive	*á jé*	*a jé ɓá'ŋ́*	subjunctive/hortative;
/H≠ ... -H/	*á lɔ́ɔ́*	*a lɔ ɓá'ŋ́*	future consecutive
Imperative	*jé* (pl. *jéná*)	*u/ni jé ɓá'ŋ́*	commands
/-H/; pl. /-ná/	*lɔɔ́* (pl. *lɔná*)	*u/ni lɔ ɓá'ŋ́*	

TABLE 15.14: PROGRESSIVE ASPECT

	Affirmative	Negative	
Present prog	*a yé 'jé*	*a ye ɓé 'jé*	'he is (not) eating/
/H-ye/	*a yé lɔ*	*a ye ɓé lɔ*	coming'
P2 prog	*a ɓé jé*	*a ɓé ɓé jé*	'he was (not) eating'
/ɓé/	*a ɓé lɔ́*	*a ɓé ɓé lɔ́*	(e.g. yesterday)
P3 prog	*a ɓá jé*	*a ɓá ɓé jé*	'he was (not) eating/
/ɓá/	*a ɓá lɔ́*	*a ɓá ɓé lɔ́*	coming' (long time ago)

imperative, the L prefix of such a noun is not affected, e.g. *nuŋúl bi≠sel* 'sell baskets!' These latter tenses are exactly those which have a floating H that causes an L CV verb to lengthen, e.g. *á lɔɔ́* 'he will have come'. Perhaps these acquire an HL rather than H floating tone.

As illustrated in table 15.14, three different forms of the copula are used to form the progressive aspect. The copula /ye/ may be replaced by /ta/ in the negative forms: *a ta ɓé 'jé* 'he is not eating', *a ta ɓé lɔ* 'he is not coming'. The forms /ɓé, ɓá/ are derived from *ɓá* 'be'. The negative marker *ɓé* always follows *ye* or *ta*. Although it follows the progressive markers, *ɓé, ɓá* in table 15.14, *ɓé* may alternatively follow the main verb: *a ɓé jé 'ɓé, a ɓé lɔ́ 'ɓé, a ɓá jé 'ɓé, a ɓá lɔ́ 'ɓé*. This may show the changing status of copular *ɓé* and *ɓá* from main verb to auxiliary. In other periphrastic constructions, the negative must follow the auxiliary verb, as in table 15.15.

Other auxiliary verbs are treated in Bitjaa Kody (1990).

TABLE 15.15: OTHER PERIPHRASTIC FORMS

	Affirmative	Negative	
Pres perfect = P1 +	*a n≠tip 'jé*	*a n≠tip 'ɓé jé*	'he has (not) just eaten/
tip 'finish'	*a n≠tip lɔ*	*a n≠tip 'ɓé lɔ*	come'
Pres hab = Pres +	*a ḿ≠'ɓéná jé*	*a ḿ≠'ɓéná ɓé jé*	'he (doesn't) often eats/
ɓena 'do often'	*a ḿ≠'ɓéná lɔ*	*a ḿ≠'ɓéná ɓé lɔ*	comes'
Past hab = P3 +	*a ɓé ɓéna jé*	*a ɓé ɓena ɓéé jé*	'he (didn't) used to eat/
ɓena 'do often'	*a ɓé ɓéna lɔ*	*a ɓé ɓena ɓéé lɔ*	come'

ACKNOWLEDGMENTS

My personal familiarity with Basaá stems mostly from a field methods course which I taught at the University of Southern California in 1983–4, followed up by additional informant work with Victor and Anne Bikai-Nyounai and Jean-Pierre Nyounai. I have benefitted from the contributions of Jose Hualdé, Mohammad I. Mohammad and Deborah (Schlindwein) Schmidt, as well as from consultations with Marie Anne Ndongo Séméngué and Zachée Denis Bitjaa Kody. I am also grateful to Gisèle Teil-Dautrey of the Laboratoire Dynamique du Langage (Université de Lyon2/CNRS) and my undergraduate student, Peter Wong, whose electronic lexicons of Basaá were particularly helpful to me in preparing this chapter.

REFERENCES

Baker 1988b; Barreteau *et al.* 1993; Bitjaa Kody 1990; Bot Ba Njock 1964, 1970; Boum 1983; Bresnan and Moshi 1990; Breton and Fohtung 1991; Buckley 1997; Dimmendaal 1988; Grégoire 1975; Grimes 2000; Guthrie 1967–71; Hyman 1990, 2000; Hyman and Duranti 1982; Janssens 1982, 1986; Lemb and de Gastines 1973; Mutaka and Bitjaa Kody in press; Rosenhuber 1908; Schmidt 1994; Scholaster 1914; Schürle 1912; Voorhoeve 1980.

NEN (A44)

Maarten Mous

ABBREVIATIONS

BJ	Baudouin Janssens
DC	Dugast (1975)
DG	Dugast (1971)
DL	Dugast (1967)
EB	Emanuel Bakoui
HB	Honoré Boyoleba Balehen

1 INTRODUCTION

Nen (Tunen, Tunɛn, Tunən) is spoken by over 35,000 speakers (Grimes 2000, based on figures from 1982) in and around the town of Ndikinimeki in Cameroon where the forest becomes savannah. The people are known as Ba-nen, which is an adaptation of *mùnə̀nì* 'man in power and rich'. The language has the code A44 in Guthrie's system but, together with its closest relatives Nyokon or Nyo'o (A45), Maande (A46) and Bonek, it is closer to the A60 languages, such as Gunu and Yambasa, than it is to its neighbor Basaá A43 (Mous and Breedveld 1986). In a number of lexicostatistic classifications, Nen and its relatives often appear as a group separate from the other zone A languages and separate from central Bantu languages (Bastin and Piron 1999:153–5). Among the many influences that Nen underwent, one possible influence can be attributed to the influx of slaves (Abwa 1995). Ndiki, Aliŋa or Eling, Ndogbiakat are names for dialects. A large community of speakers reside in Duala, which can be reached by a path through the forest. Education by the Protestants here used to be in Duala, which explains the Duala loans. Other loans come from Pidgin English, which at one time was actively used in Ndikinimeki and is still remembered by older men. Nen has an official orthography. Some of the older publications in Duala deviate from this orthography. The development of a written tradition is still incipient.

Present-day studies including this article draw heavily on the monumental work by the French ethnographer Idelette Dugast. She published a two-volume ethnography (1955, 1960), a lexicon (1967), here referred to as DL, a descriptive grammar (1971), DG, and a collection of stories (1975), DC. All these works show a high quality of precision. They are also characterized by the lack of linguistic abstraction and generalization. Both qualities are evident in the very detailed tone notation in the texts where all downstepped levels are indicated, without recognizing the concept of downstep, while in the lexicon the isolation form of the words is given. Unfortunately, in isolation many of the lexical tonal distinctions are neutralized and the final vowel is not realized. Subsequent synchronic linguistic analyses were done by Wilkinson (1975), Stewart and Van Leynseele (1979), Mous (1986, 1997), Janssens (1988), and Bancel (1991).

From a Bantu point of view Nen has a number of interesting features:

- The object precedes the verb; and this is not limited to certain moods or tenses as is the case for related languages such as Tikar.
- There is a full vowel harmony system with the word (and beyond) as domain and with alternations not only in affixes but also in roots.
- One of the verbal derivations, expressing middle voice, is a prefix and not a suffix.

The consonant harmony for the feature fortis/lenis as proposed by Van Leynseele and Stewart (1980) for a previous stage is not synchronically valid. The three remarkable features mentioned above are innovations.

2 PHONETICS AND PHONOLOGY

2.1 Consonants

The consonant inventory is given in table 16.1.

The bilabial stop varies between [b] and [p]; the variation is both lexically and individually determined and typically one of a sound change in progress. Nen has no voice opposition; the variation *b/p* is not phonemic. The velar fricative *x* does not occur word-initially; it is realized as [h] between vowels and has a palatalized realization after front vowels. The labial stops are rounded before *ə*.

The coalescence of a nasal and an obstruent results in a prenasalized voiced stop; thus fricatives become stops and voiceless becomes voiced; nasal + *h* becomes *mb*. When the second consonant is a nasal or liquid the coalescence results in simple nasal with no oral stop component.

There is sporadic consonant metathesis, e.g. *ndés* or *sínd* 'limp', *èmbéndá* 'hero' from *ndámb* 'be warlike'.

2.2 Vowels

Length is not distinguished in vowels. Vowel reduction to whispered vowels or deletion occurs word-finally depending on the final tone sequence (see 2.3). The most pervasive quality of the vowel system is the vowel harmony system (see table 16.2). There are two sets of vowels that are mutually exclusive within the word.

TABLE 16.1: CONSONANT PHONEMES

b [p]	t	.	k	
f	s	.	x	h
m	n	ny [ɲ]	ŋ	
mb	nd	nj [ɲj]	ŋg	
w		y		
	l			

In accordance with common usage for the cross-height vowel harmony systems of Africa, I use (+)ATR as the feature distinguishing the dominant from the recessive set, without making claims about the articulatory realization of the phonological distinction. Recessive −ATR vowels change to their dominant +ATR counterpart under the influence of dominant +ATR vowels in the same word. Affixes with recessive vowels alternate with their dominant +ATR counterpart when combined with a dominant root. The vowel alternation pairs are *u–o, o–ɔ, ə–a,* and *i–ɛ* (or *i–e*). Alternation in affixes occurs predominantly in noun prefixes (1) and verb suffixes (table 16.3). The alternation of the mid-vowels *o–ɔ* occurs only in roots, not in affixes. Root vowels of verbs alternate under the influence of the dominant causative suffix *-i* (table 16.3).

(1)   ò-ndɔ̀mb (class 3), pl: è-ndɔ̀mb (class 4), coll: mà-ndɔ̀mb (class 6) 'sheep'
      (ò→)ù-mbu (3), pl: (è→)ì-mbù (4), coll: (mà→)mʷə̀-mbù (6) 'grass'

Dominant prefixes occur in the pronominal prefixes of classes 3, and 13 containing *u,* 4 (= 10) and 19 containing *i*. Dominant prefixes are rare in vowel harmony systems and in Nen they are restricted to closed sets of pronominals. Optional harmony across word boundaries is strictly leftwards (3).

There is some dialectal variation in the pronunciation of the vowel that acts as the recessive counterpart of the high round vowel. In some dialects, notably in Ndokbassabem and the dialect of Bancel's informants, this vowel is realized as different from the dominant mid-round vowel *o*; in the dialect described by Dugast and on which I have most data, there is no such distinction and there is complete neutralization between the recessive high round vowel and the dominant mid round vowel (2). A comparison of Bancel's and my own recordings showed dialect differences in this respect. Booklets in Tunen printed in Duala make a distinction.

TABLE 16.2: VOWEL PHONEMES AND HARMONY SETS

Dominant (+ATR): i	ə	o	u
Recessive (−ATR): ɛ	a	ɔ	o

TABLE 16.3: EXAMPLES WITH RECESSIVE AND DOMINANT VERB SUFFIX

Root	Dom/rec	Meaning	-ɛn APPL rec	-ì CAUS dom
fàlàb	rec	build	*fàlàbèn*	*fʷə̀lə̀bì*
fəŋ	dom	exchange	*fəŋìn*	*fəŋì*
fɔl	rec	borrow	*fɔ̀lèn*	*fòlì*
kòl	rec	go and buy protective medicine	*kòlèn*	*kùlì*
kòl	dom	create	*kòlìn*	*kòlì*
húk	dom	blow	*húkín*	*húkì*

(2)   Dugast and Mous: *ù-kòl* 'create',   *ò-kòl* 'go and buy medicine'
     Bancel and Ndokbassabem: *ù-kùl* 'create',   *o-kòl* 'go and buy medicine'

The alternation *i–e* occurs in noun class prefixes only; elsewhere, in roots and in suffixes, the alternation in the front vowels is *i–ɛ*. In the noun class prefixes too there is variation in the phonetic realization of the recessive front vowel, *e* or *ɛ*, but for some classes, such as class 19 *hɛ-*, *ɛ* is obligatory; otherwise prefixes tend to be realized as *ɛ* when the first root vowel is *ɛ*, or, to a lesser extent, when it is *ɔ*. A similar assimilation, though less frequent, can be observed in the prefixes containing *o* which assimilate to *ɔ* before roots with a mid-vowel as their first vowel. The vowel *e* does not occur in roots; hence synchronically, I consider these instances of [e] as a phonetic variant of *ɛ*. Dugast has [e] in some roots; I have [ɛ] in those cases. The dominant *ə* is sometimes realized as [e] before *n* and *y*. Phonetically [e] is parallel to [o] in that it can co-occur with vowels of either set; phonemically it does not exist.

The domain of the vowel harmony is the word. In fast speech, however, the final syllable of the preceding word can also be affected (3). This rule may operate iteratively across monosyllabic words or clitics (Bancel 1991). As a kind of playful language usage whole sentences can be uttered with dominant vowels (Janssens pc).

(3)   *nèhɔká né mòndǫ*   *nèhɔkɔ ní mw*↓*ɔ́ndų*
     'axe of man'   'axe of woman'

In addition to vowel harmony, there are other non-adjacent vowel sequences that do not occur in roots; in particular only low or identical vowels precede round vowels, and a mid round vowel may not be preceded by a low vowel. Thus, excluded sequences are: *i–o, i–u, ɛ–o, ɛ–ɔ, o–ɔ, o–u, ɔ–o, u–o; ə–o, a–ɔ*. In addition *o–ɛ* is excluded.

Vowel coalescence: if two vowels coalesce in morphological derivation, then the first vowel drops if it is low; it fuses with the second vowel if the two are identical or otherwise it becomes a glide, often written as a high vowel; when the first vowel is round the realization need not be a glide; it can also be realized as [o]. The tones remain; although some people simplify rising tones to Low as a late realization rule. There are a few exceptions to the coalescence rule such as *nǐs*, pl: *mʷɔ̌s* (not *mǐs*) 'eye'.

2.3 Tone

Phonemically there are two units of tone, High and Low. Highs after Lows are realized lower (automatic downstep). Downstepped Highs also occur as the manifestations of unrealized Lows before Highs. The High immediately preceding a downstepped High is realized slightly higher, thus producing an allophonic phonetic effect aiding the perceptual distinction but without phonemic consequences. In several respects tone rules and rules affecting syllable structure are interdependent.

One of the most drastic tone rules is that of sentence final lowering. This process is intricately related to that of sentence final vowel reduction. A final vowel is only fully realized if the underlying tone sequence of the last two syllables is rising, LH. The tonal realization of such a sequence is LL, however; it is as if an underlying rise induces more power or breath and thus a full realization of the vowel. The formulation of the tone and vowel reduction rule is cumbersome in any phonological framework that separates tones from vowels and that does not allow vowels and tones to be treated in one statement, as pointed out by Janssens (1988). Evidence for these underlying tones comes from drum language in which the underlying tone pattern is drummed, e.g. *òndɔmb* 'sheep' is drummed LHH, *màsɔ̀ŋ* 'palm oil' LLL, and *mùtèkà* LLH (Dugast 1959:575, 579, 600). Sentence final sequences of High vowels on noun roots are realized as low. In fact, unless the preceding consonant is a nasal, the reduction of the final vowel is not necessarily deletion, but rather devoicing. The realization of disyllabic noun roots before a pause is given in table 16.4 (see Janssens (1988) for lexical exceptions).

The same rules apply to trisyllabic noun roots: HHH > LL, HHL > HH, HLL > HL, LLL > LL, LHL > LH, LHH > LL, LLH > LLL, HLH > HLL.

The same rule of vowel elision also applies optionally to final vowels that are followed by a vowel initial word, that is, final vowels are elided unless the root has a final LH sequence, which in this context is still realized as LH. The High tone of such an elided vowel is realized on the next vowel. The Low tone of an elided vowel disappears; it is not realized on the next syllable and it does not induce downstep.

Syllable structure plays a role in these reduction rules in that monosyllabic roots do not undergo final vowel reduction. In non-final position before a consonant initial word these nouns with monosyllabic roots are even 'expanded' by an epenthetic vowel *a/ə*, but the vowel sequence is immediately reduced again by the rule of vowel coalescence. Nouns with monosyllabic roots ending in dominant *o* are excluded and do not receive an epenthetic vowel in this environment. The High tone lowering before a pause does occur with words containing monosyllabic roots; here there is a group of exceptions that can be characterized as historically containing HL roots and this Low is still realized on the epenthetic vowel when present.

H tone perseveration: a High tone spreads and replaces the Low of the next syllable. The process applies only once; a High tone that has arisen from this process cannot spread again to the next Low, as in (4). The High tone does not spread to a 'double' Low tone, i.e. a vowel that resulted from coalescence of two Low-toned vowels (5).

(4) *bá-ná nùíyì sàk-ak-´* → *báná ꜜnúíyí sàkák* 'They made a bridge of lianas across the river' (DL 166)

(5) *hì-nòni hè-ès* → *hìnòni hès* 'a nice bird', but *mù-ílí mù-ɔ́s* → *mùílí múɔ̀s* 'a new moon' (DG 154–5)

The process applies in certain environments and is blocked by stronger syntactic boundaries. Within the noun, H perseveration is a feature of fast speech. Within verb stems the High tone of the Middle prefix *bé* spreads, as do the High tones of verb roots onto derivational suffixes (6).

(6) *bé-fàlàb* → *béfálàb* 'MIDDLE-build' (DG 239), *lɔ́ŋ-ɛn* → *lɔ́ŋɛ́n* 'whistle-APPL' (DG 232)

TABLE 16.4: TONE AND FINAL VOWEL REDUCTION IN DISYLLABIC NOUN ROOTS

CV̀CV̀	→	CV̀C
CV̀CV́	→	CV̀C
CV́CV̀	→	CV́C
CV̀CV́	→	CV̀CV̀

Within the noun phrase the High spreads to the following adjective (7), with the exception of numeral adjectives and the quantifier *kìm* 'all'. The High of the connective spreads to the next noun (8), but not the High of the head noun to the connective (9).

(7)   *mòkòló mò-tàtán* 3.foot 3-big   → *mòkòló mótàtán* 'big foot'

(8)   *mòkàŋá wá bòlè* 3.root 3.of tree   → *mòkàŋá wá bólè* 'root of tree' (DG 104)

(9)   *mìɔkɔ́ yè mùənd* 9.chicken 9.of woman 'chicken of a woman' (DG 133)

The final High of modifiers that precede the noun spread to the noun (10), in particular the contrastive particle *á* which is often added to the possessive modifier (11), but not the proximal demonstrative that consists solely of the pronominal prefix, nor the quantifier *èŋàná* 'without'.

(10)   *máyé mà-hɔk* 6:those 6-hoe → *máyé máhɔk* 'those hoes' (DG 95)

(11)   *yɔmì á mèsɔ́* 4:my calabash → *yɔmià mésɔ́* (→) *yɔ* ⁱ*myɔ mésɔ́* 'my calabash'

Within the verb phrase the High tone of the object spreads to the verb (13) and from the verb to a following noun only if it is an object, but not from the tense marker to the object; exceptions are the rising tones of the future markers *nǎ* and *sǎ* whose High does spread. In imperative sentences the High tone of the first object spreads to the second object noun (14).

(13)   *mè-ná bèlèmá lèmánák* → *mèná bèlèmá lémánák* 'I dreamt (dreams)' (DL 103)

A rising tone is realized as a downstepped High after a High (5, 11). A Low tone after a High and before a High on a monosyllabic root is realized as a downstepped High (14).

(14)   *ósókínə mòná bóŋàn* → *ósókínə* ⁱ*móná bóŋàn*
       sing   child   song
       'Sing the child a song!'

3 VERBS

The verb root is most often CVC, sometimes CV. The initial consonant may be absent; the final consonant may be a voiced nasal stop cluster. Examples of CV stems are *sì* 'look for', *bè* 'pull out', *wə* 'die', *sò* 'wash', *bò* 'like each other', *yò* 'feel ashamed', *nyò* 'work', *hɔ́* 'talk; finish', *bɔ́* 'get medicine, undergo divination', *nyá* 'drink', *là* 'say', etc.

The verb does not have the common Bantu inflectional final vowel. Under certain circumstances which include a Low toned verb root and a tense that changes the tonal shape of the verb, final vowels do show up. These circumstances suggest that the original inflectional final vowel eroded due to reduction processes similar to those in noun roots. While monosyllabic verb roots contain a final vowel that is not necessarily the usual inflectional final vowel *a*, nor a derivational vowel, but part of the root itself, polysyllabic verb roots that end in a vowel are instances of a frozen derivational suffix that consists of a vowel only. Both the form of the final vowel and the meaning of these verbs are in line with such an interpretation. Roots that are polysyllabic contain a frozen extension, e.g. *òmbòk* 'throw', *búŋúl* 'mix', *bílən* 'be joyful, triumph', *tèŋèn* 'damage' (DG 255-7). In addition, there are a number of polysyllabic roots that do not contain a frozen extension or they contain one that is synchronically no longer recognizable as a former extension, e.g. *tíáb̠* 'cut', *fàláb̠* 'build', *fìàbàn* 'be missing, fail', *mìɔ̠t* 'wring'. Finally, there are a number of polysyllabic roots that begin in *i* and that have a final vowel; not all of these can be analysed as a frozen extension, rather the initial *i* is a candidate for a frozen formative: *ìtì* 'hold', *índì* or *èndɔ̀* 'give'.

3.1 Verbal derivation

There are a number of verbal derivational suffixes, some of them not so common in Bantu, such as a Diminutive and an Intensive. There is no passive extension. Also remarkable is the Middle *prefix be-*. Apart from the Middle prefix *be-*, the verbal extensions are the following: Applicative *ɛn/in*, Diminutive *ɛl/il* and *al/əl*, Positional *ɛm/im*, Intensive *ɛn/in*, Separative *on/un*, Reciprocal *an/ən*, Short Causative *i*, Long Causative *əsi*, Neuter *ɛ̀/i* and a non-productive Impositive *ɛ/i*, and the Pluractional suffix *ak/ək*, which has an inflectional function in the tense system as well. Fixed combinations of extensions are Double Intensive *ɛnɛn*, Strong Repetitive *olon* and *alien*; a recurrent combination is Applicative-Reciprocal *ɛnan*.

The extensions that end in (consist of) a vowel, that is the Causative, the Impositive and the Neuter, only occur at the very end. The Pluractional suffix always occurs immediately after the root as can be seen in the behavior of the lexeme *sìn* 'see', which contains a frozen Applicative and has *sìèkìn* as its Pluractional form. The Diminutive is also close to the root; the Diminutive form of 'see' is *sìèlìn*. This is also reflected in the fact that the Diminutive is the first formative in fixed combinations of extensions such as *olon* and *alien*.

All suffixes containing low vowels show height harmony after *o*. The neuter *ɛ* undergoes complete assimilation to the preceding round vowel if the intervening consonant is an alveolar consonant, *l*, *n*, and *nd* (no examples of *d*).

All derivational final vowels have a Low tone. As a rule, the derivational suffixes are Low but a High tone of a verb root spreads one syllable onto the first extension. High tone verbs with frozen extensions do not spread their High tone (again), thus *tábón-àn*, *sábón-àn*, *búŋúl-ìn*, *bílə̀n-ìn*, but also *tíáb-èn*. High tone verbs that have a final (Low) vowel in their base form (i.e. a frozen neuter, impositive or causative extension) have a Low tone on the following extension, thus *bák-èm* from *bákè*, *lúŋ-ìm* from *lúŋì*, *él-òn* from *élè*, *leŋ-òn* from *léŋè*, *bésákòn* from *bésákè*, *èkèn* from *ékè*. These lexemes may also have other derivations with a regular High tone spread; such regular forms are taken to be derived from the original CVC root, e.g. *lúŋ-ún* from **lúŋ* as opposed to *lúŋ-ìm* from *lúŋì*, *ék-ón* from **ék* as opposed to *ékèn* from *ékè*.

Pluractional *-ak* indicates that the action is plural because it is repetitive or durative or due to a plurality of objects, or, only for intransitive verbs, due to a plurality of subjects. Verbs with an Intensive derivation take the Pluractional if the action is plural. The Pluractional is (obligatory) part of the hodiernal future tense and is excluded from certain other tenses, notably in negative verb forms. Thus functionally the Pluractional is inflectional rather than derivational.

Diminutive extensions *-al* and *-el* indicate that the action is shorter than usual, less intensively, to a lesser extent, only once, with less attention, in a careful way. Both extensions have the same meaning and undergo the usual harmony processes, but the choice between them is lexically determined.

(15) *tàn*   'cut'   *tànèl*   'injure lightly'
      sèm   'sell'   *sèmàl*   'sell in small amounts'
      ìtì   'hold'   *ìtìəl*   'touch'

Positional *-ɛm* indicates a position reached through the activity of the verb. A number of these have a transitive counterpart with a frozen impositive extension *ɛ*; these are *léŋè* 'bend', *èlè* 'hang', *fàŋè* 'put behind a rod', and *bákè* 'move apart'.

(16) tén   'plant'   ténέm   'be upright'
      bít   'hide'   bítím   'be hidden, hiding oneself'
      kònd   'add'   kòndèm   'climb to the top'

Applicative extension *-ɛn* indicates that the action is directed to or from, that is, benefactive to a person or directed against a person, using a certain instrument, at or from a certain place, caused by a certain fact. The extension thus always has an effect on the semantic scheme of the argument(s) of the verb: a new person, object or place to or from which the action is directed is always introduced.

(17) kànj   'lie'   kànjèn   'lie to, about, because of'
      lún   'forge'   lúnín   'forge for somebody, at a certain place'

Separative *-on* indicates that the action separates two entities. In a number of cases the underived verb brings the two objects together and the separative reverses that action.

(18) há   'put'   hún   'lift the excess'
      sùm   'put a pot on the fire' sùmùn   'take off the fire'
      bák   'twist a rope'   bákón   'unravel a rope'

Reciprocal *-an* indicates that the subject (or the addressee) is plural and that the patient is included in the subject, while the action is singular. It can be followed by the fixed combination *-mɔté na -în* 'each other', lit. one and that one. The reciprocal is also used to indicate the plural addressee of imperatives. Verbs with the reciprocal extensions always have patients and therefore reciprocal derivations of some intransitive roots require an extra Applicative extension, *-ɛnan*. The fixed combination *ənì* REC:CAUS expresses simultaneous action by a plural subject.

(19) sàl   'cut'   sàlàn   'divide between two people'
      sábón   'pay'   sábónàn   'pay each other'
      hɔ́   'talk'   hɔ́énàn   'talk to each other'
      kùn   'open'   kùnənì   'open together'

Intensive *-ɛn* and its reduplicated form *-ɛnɛn* indicate that the action is intensive, repetitive, for a long time, often, or executed to the extreme. A greater degree of intensity is expressed by the fixed combinations *-olon* DIM-SEP or *-elian*. Frequency or intensity can also be expressed by reduplication.

(20) kènd   'walk'   kèndèn   'walk many times'
      lèl   'cry'   lèlèn   'cry a lot'
      kànj   'lie'   kànjènèn   'lie all the time'
      ɔ̀ng   'follow'   ɔ̀ngɔ̀lòn 'follow all the time'
      kònd   'add'   kòndèlìàn 'continue to add a lot'

Neuter *-ɛ* indicates that the subject, which is also the agent, has no control. The vowel completely assimilates to round vowels if the intervening consonant is an alveolar consonant *n, l* or *nd*.

(21) nɔk   'break tr' nɔkè   'break intr'
      fát   'close hands' fátè   'clench spontaneously'

Causative *-i, -əsi* introduces an external causer of the action which is expressed as subject of the verb. The long form is used with CV roots. Some lexemes have two causative derivations, a short one and a long one, or, for CV roots, a long one and double long one, *-əsəsi*. The second causative indicates a causative of a causative i.e. an indirect causative.

(22) *fín*   'enter'   *fínì*   'introduce'
      nàŋ 'be white'   *nàŋì*   'whiten'
      yɔ̀   'be ashamed' *yòsì*   'shame tr'
      ním   'extinguish' *ním^wə̀sì*   'let disappear'
      sò   'wash'   *sùə̀si, sùə̀sə̀sì* 'let sb wash'

The middle is expressed by a prefix *bé-*. The High tone spreads to the first syllable of the verb stem. It is indeed part of the verb word because vowel harmony applies obligatorily and the vowel coalescence rule applies with vowel-initial verb roots. The prefix is derivational, however, because some derived verbs have specialized meaning, e.g. *bílúŋì* 'put the head down' from *lóŋ* 'hang from'; and the derived form with *be-* is used as basis for nominalization, e.g. *hèbésákènè* 'carrying instrument', or *nèbésákè* 'carrying' from *bésákè* from *sákè*. Dugast calls it 'passive' but the derivation is not restricted to transitive verb roots, e.g. *bisəkəl* 'complain about' is derived from *sək* 'be bitter'; and the result need not be intransitive, e.g. *biɔ́ndɔ́n* 'cost' from *ɔ́nd* 'buy'. The basic meaning is middle. It can also be used with a fixed pronoun combination 'each other' that is usually combined with the reciprocal extension (23).

(23) *bí-ə̀sù bíólí ná-bé-lát-áká bó-mɔ̀té nà bú-ìn* (DG 338)
     8-our 8:work HOD.PAST-MIDDLE-mix-PL 14-one and 14-that.one
     'Our activities are mixed with each other.'

3.2 Verbal inflection

The tenses are expressed by a combination of inflectional elements and tone on the verb. These inflectional elements are separate words and not prefixes to the verb since they are separated from the verb by the object. The verb itself has no inflectional affixes, apart from the Pluractional *-ak* and a final High tone inducing tonal changes. The inflectional element may contain several TAM markers and can be followed by the deixis markers *ka* thither or *nda* hither. The inflectional element is preceded by the subject pronoun. The subject pronominals immediately precede these inflectional elements but the vowel harmony rule cannot give us a clue whether the subject pronominals and the inflectional elements form one phonological word or not since all the relevant morphemes are recessive; the same applies to the deixis elements that follow the inflectional element. For nominal subjects there is no additional subject pronominal unless the subject is a topic and followed by a pause. Nen is a 'pro-drop' language which is uncommon among Bantu languages. The tone of pronominal subjects is part of the inflectional complex and may be influenced by a preceding floating High in certain tenses. The following TAM markers occur: ´, *lé, 'ndò, nó, ná, 'sà, 'sá, să, nă, ŋò, só*. The order of inflectional elements are summarized in (24), where # symbolizes a word boundary.

(24) (Subj) $(\text{TAM})_0^2$(DEIXIS) # (Obj) # Verb(-T)

Verb roots are lexically High or Low and these types again have two tonal shapes across the various tenses: the basic shape and the High tone shape which originates in an inflectional final High tone. The High tone shape of Low tone verbs can be derived from the base verb by assuming a final High tone that grounds on the last vowel and on any additional preceding syllable i.e. not part of the root and toneless underlyingly, i.e. an extension. Since the object precedes the verb, the verb is usually sentence final; but if it is not, it receives an epenthetic vowel. In the basic form this epenthetic vowel has the same tone as the preceding vowel. In the High tone shape the final High tone grounds on the epenthetic vowel. The epenthetic vowel coalesces with a following vowel, which is often the locative preposition *o*; it does show up, however, before consonant initial words, which is often the general preposition *na*. Another approach would be to consider these epenthetic vowels part of the verb and use the sentence final reduction rules introduced for the nouns to derive the verb shape in sentence final position. I opt for an epenthetic vowel solution because the vowel quality is predictable, the tone in the basic shape is copied, and because there are other final vowels that appear in the tense system that have to be distinguished from the 'epenthetic' vowels. These other final vowels show up in the High tone shape of certain Low-toned roots, and these are present even in sentence final positions, see DG 229–32 for an incomplete list of such verbs. The fact that these roots are limited to Low tone roots and that the final vowel only appears in the High tone shape suggests that this final vowel resisted a general reduction of final vowels in sentence final position as a consequence of the LH tone sequence, parallel to the resistance to vowel reduction in sentence final nouns. For the verbs I consider this vowel reduction to be a historical process. I tentatively assume an extra final floating High tone for these verbs as a way of marking them lexically. Although most verb tokens end in a consonant, there are four sources of vowel final verbs:

1 CV roots
2 Verbs with a (frozen) derivational suffix (causative *i*, neuter or impositive *è*)
3 Verbs (marked by ´) with a Low tone root and a final vowel in the H shape form
4 Verbs that are not in sentence final position.

The H tone shape occurs in most negative tenses, in the hodiernal past, and in the optative (see table 16.7 for details), and this distribution suggests an origin in a High tone final vowel inflection. Table 16.5 gives an overview of the High tone shapes for the

TABLE 16.5: THE FINAL H SHAPE

	Underlying (U)	Basic shape (B)	H shape with epenthetic vowel (H-ep)	H shape sentence finally (H-fi)
A1	Cv̀	Cv̀		Cv̀
A2	Cv́	Cv̀		Cv̀à
A3	Cv́	Cv́		Cv̀
B1	Cv̀C	Cv̀C	Cv̀Cá	↓Cv̀C
B2	Cv̀C′	Cv̀C		Cv̀Cà
B3	Cv́C	Cv́C	Cv́Cá	Cv́C
C1	Cv̀Cv̀	Cv̀Cv̀		Cv̀Cv́
C2	Cv́Cv̀	Cv́Cv̀		Cv́Cv́
D1	Cv̀CvC	Cv̀Cv̀C	Cv̀Cv́Cá	Cv̀Cv́C
D2	Cv́CvC	Cv́Cv́C	Cv́Cv́Cá	Cv́Cv́C
D3	Cv́Cv́C	Cv́Cv́C		Cv́Cv́C
E1	Cv̀CvCv̀	Cv̀Cv́Cv̀		Cv̀Cv́Cv́
E2	Cv́CvCv̀	Cv́Cv́Cv̀		Cv́Cv́Cv́
F1	Cv̀CvCvC	Cv̀Cv̀Cv́C		Cv̀Cv́Cv́C
F2	Cv́CvCvC	Cv́Cv́Cv́C		Cv́Cv́Cv́C

various classes of verb roots. I have only a few examples for the non sentence-final position, but I assume that those forms with a High final lexical vowel in sentence final position are identical to their equivalent in non-final position, i.e. C1-2, E1-2. Examples for these shapes are given separately in table 16.6.

The High tone shapes in non-final position can be derived from the underlying form by adding the epenthetic vowel *a* and grounding the final floating High tone onto it while any preceding tonally unspecified vowel (extensions) takes a High tone from the final tone. The same is true for verbs ending in a derivational vowel (C1, C2, E1, E2) regardless of the position, sentence-final or not. The verbs that are marked lexically with a floating High tone show a realization of the final vowel and a lowering of the tone to Low in sentence final position (A2, B2), LḤH → LL. The most common verb shapes, B1 and B3, A1 and A3 show a tone in sentence final position for the High tone shape i.e. opposite to the one in the basic tone shape; this is why Dugast calls the High tone shape, *ton contraire*. However, comparison with the form with the epenthetic vowel shows that this is not an instance of polar tone but rather the effect of sentence final tone lowering. The lowering does not occur on stems of three (or more) syllables (F1–2). This lowering is reminiscent of the sentence-final tone lowering in nouns. Assuming a final floating High tone for the High tone shape, the lowering rule for the verbal system is $H_{lex}(H)Ḥ \rightarrow L(L)$, which accounts for the sentence final lowering in A3, B3, D2. For B1, Low tone CVC roots, the final High tone moves on to the root vowel and displaces the Low tone of the root to the left, which shows itself in the form of a downstep, provided that the preceding syllable is High. Examples can be found in objectless hodiernal past sentences with a High tone *ná* TAM marker.

The first syllable of the verb optionally becomes High under High spread from the preceding object noun. The High tone of the tense markers does not spread, not onto the verb radical, nor onto a following object, with the exception of *sǎ* NEG.FUT and *nǎ* INDEF.FUT.

TABLE 16.6: EXAMPLES OF HIGH TONE SHAPES

	Basic	Meaning	H-ep	H-fi	Source
A1	*mɔ̀*	launch prohibition		*mɔ́*	DL 118
A2	*kɔ̀*	fall		*kɔ̀à*	DL 96
A3	*né*	eat		*nè*	DG 173
B1	*twɔ̀n*	sit		*ꜜtwɔ̀n*	DG 173, 178
B1	*sɔ̀m*	lie in wait for	*sɔ̀mɔ́*		DL 175
B2	*mèn*	harm sb, swallow		*mènà*	DL 113, BJ 142
B3	*fám*	leave		*fàm*	BJ 260
B3	*tíŋ*	hang on	*tíŋɔ̀*		DL 185
C1	*nɔ̀kè*	break intr		*nɔ̀ké*	BJ 157, 173
C2	*sámbè*	put down	*sámbé*	*sámbé*	DG 178–9
C2	*sɔ́mbè*	cut intr	*sɔ́mbè*		BJ 479
D1	*lìŋìn*	angry		*lìŋín*	DG 233
D1	*sèkàk*	saw	*sèkáká*		DL 170
D2	*tábón*	repair		*tàbòn*	DG 179
D2	*sábón*	pay	*sábóná*		BJ 482
D3	*pélèn*	put down, marry		*pélén*	DL 233
E1	*bàyònò*	open intr		*bàyónó*	DG 236
E2	*bítìmì*	hide sb		*bítimʷɔ̀kí*	DG 237
F1	*kòndèmèn*	arrive at		*kòndémén*	DG 237
F2	*béfálábén*	MIDDLE:build:APPL		*fálábén*	DL 50

3.2.1 The imperative

The imperative verb form consists of the stem (25), and for durative verbs of the stem with the Pluractional extension (26). Imperative verb forms also have a final High tone, which does not always show up in isolation (45) but as soon as any material follows the imperative verb, e.g. an object, the High tone appears on the epenthetic vowel after the verb stem (27); a resultant rising tone is simplified to a Low (97). Any extension, including the Pluractional of durative verbs, assimilates in tone to this final High tone.

(25) kònd   'add!'

(26) kèndák   'walk!'   from kènd 'walk' (DG 191)

(27) kòndá tùɔ̀fɔ̀ 'add fish' (DG 108)

The final High tone does not spread to the following object (28). However if the imperative final High tone is realized on an epenthetic vowel following a Low toned root syllable, it may optionally spread to the next syllable (29); it appears also on the initial vowel of the next word when that vowel prevents the addition of an epenthetic vowel and when the preceding vowel is a Low tone root vowel (30).

(28) tòmɛ́ná yɔ̀kɔ́ ó nìbún   'Place the chair to touch the gable' from tòmɛ̀n 'touch' (DL 186)

(29) kòndá bélòŋòt   'add seeds!' (DG 106)
      bàtá mútèkà   'ask the slave!' from bàt (DG 106),
                        bátá hìsìn 'Pick up the pot!' from bát (DG 96)

(30) kònd'ɛ́fɛ̃ny   'add maize porridge!' (DG 102)

Imperatives are marked for plural addressee by the addition of a reciprocal extension with a High tone assimilated to the final High tone (31). Orders are also expressed by optative and negative optative verb forms (§3.2.2).

(31) nòkólón èmbánj   'break (pl) the sticks!' from nɔ̀k 'to break' (DL 148)

3.2.2 The simple tenses

The tenses can now be listed as combinations of inflectional elements and presence or absence of final High tone. In the table of the basic tenses the label is from DG; the glossing follows the proposals by the editors of this book. The gloss is not meant as characterization of the tense but used for glossing the TAM marker only. The third column tells whether there is a High tone that makes the subject pronoun High. The fourth column gives the polarity marker and the fifth column gives the TAM marker. The subject pronoun, if there is one, precedes the (polarity marker and) TAM marker. The sixth column indicates whether the Pluractional suffix -ak is impossible (−), obligatory (+) or permitted (±) for the tense in question. The last column indicates whether the tense has a final High tone (H) or not.

Some negative tenses are in form based on an affirmative equivalent and derived by adding a negative element lè before the TAM marker; other tenses with a negative meaning are formally on a par with the affirmative tenses and replace the TAM marker with a negative TAM marker containing sa; the negative future adds a negative element só in the polarity slot. The various negation markers with sa as segmental material are taken to be different TAM markers synchronically because nothing can be gained in terms of

TABLE 16.7: THE SIMPLE TENSES

Label	Gloss	Pre subj pro	Polarity	TAM	ak	F
aoriste		–	–	–	±	–
aoriste nég	NEG	–	lè	–	–	H
présent ponctuel	PROG	–	–	'ndò	–	–
présent ponctuel nég	NEG-PROG	–	lέ	ndò	–	–
passé immédiat	IMM.PAST	–	–	nó	±	–
passé proche	HOD.PAST	–	–	ná	±	H
passé proche nég	NEG.PAST	H	–	sá	–	–
passé ancien	PAST	–	–	kà	±	–
passé ancien nég	NEG.PAST.TIME	H	–	sà	–	–
passé très ancien	FAR.PAST	–	–	lè	±	–
passé très ancien nég	NEG.FAR.PAST	–	lè	lè	–	H
futur proche	HOD.FUT	–	–	'ndò	+	–
futur indét	INDEF.FUT	–	–	nǎ	–	–
futur proche nég	NEG.FUT	–	–	sǎ	–	–
futur dét.	FUT	H	–	ŋò	±	–
futur dét. nég	NEG-FUT	–	só	ŋò	–	–
optative	OPT	H	–	–	±	H
optative nég	NEG.OPT	–	lè	–	–	H

economy of description by extracting a common negative element *sá* and several floating tones and tone rules. Negative tenses exclude the use of Pluractional *-ak*. Most but not all negative tenses have a final H tone.

The floating High tone in the position preceding the subject pronoun is assumed in order to allow for the generalization that the downstep on High TAM markers is induced by a displaced Low tone from the subject pronoun due to the grounding of High on the following subject marker. However, in the case of the progressive marker *ndò* it is attractive to assume a floating High before the TAM marker because the negative equivalent of the progressive has a High tone on the negative element *lɛ* which occurs immediately before the TAM marker and after the subject prefix.

3.2.3 Complex tenses

In addition to the basic tenses, there is a more complex tense that consists of a High subject pronoun with a TAM marker *sè* which in its turn is followed by a second subject pronoun, which is High again. And there are two tenses that consist of a fixed element of verbal origin followed by a basic tense. In one of these, *étàsè*, the element *sè* appears again. These three additional tenses with Dugast's labels are:

(32)   *étàsè* + optative   futur immédiat   IMM.FUT
       àbákà 'it is' + SUB.PRO-V   présent habituel
       ´ + SUB.PRO + *sè* + ´ + SUB.PRO-V   imminence   IMM

The imminent tense expresses that the action starts at the moment or just after the moment of speech, or the point of reference, 'is about to', 'être sur le point de' (33).

(33)   *èmólá yé sè yé kɔ* (DG 175)
       9.rain 9 IMM 9 fall
       'It is about to rain.'

3.2.4 Compound tenses

Compound tenses exist as well. A regular pattern is that of an inflected verb 'to be' followed by the verb in the progressive to indicate iterativity. For the indeterminate iterative future the verb is in its basic form (aorist) rather than in the progressive and the High tone of *bá* 'to be' spreads onto the subject marker. A double progressive indicates a durative immediate past.

(34)   PROG *bá* + VPROG   passé immédiat duratif
       HOD.PAST *bá* + VPROG   passé proche itératif
       PAST *bá* + VPROG   passé ancien itératif
       FUT *bá* + VPROG   futur déterminé itératif
       INDEF.FUT *bá* + V   futur indéterminé itératif

Other fixed combinations with 'to be' are:

(35)   ?-*bák* + V-*ak*   imminence
       SUBJ.PRO-*bák* + *òbán* + infinitive présent ponctuel
       lè COP + locative   présent ponctuel
       lè COP + *hóy* 'near' + V-*ak*   imminence

Dugast uses the term *présent ponctuel* for several tenses (see also table 16.7); the differences in meaning and function, if any, remain unclear. A very common auxiliary which takes the infinitive as its complement, is the verb *bàl* 'to start, begin', very often in the hodiernal past (37).

3.2.5 The function of the tenses

Note that the term 'tense' is used here in its common meaning of a conjugation of the verb; it is not meant to be opposed to aspect. Semantically the tenses can be schematized as in table 16.8.

3.2.5.1 Aorist or default tense

The tense consisting of just the verb (DG, *aoriste*) indicates a general fact, situation, habit or character (36); or is used in continuation of the tense of the previous verb within one sentence (37).

(36)   *mèsè lè bèlábénìà bé bèndò nè* (DG 173)
       chimps NEG 8.food 8:of 2.people eat:H
       'Chimpanzees don't eat food that humans eat.'

(37)   *à ná-bàl óŋgwáy ùsì à kèndàk à hìàmàk* (DG 172)
       1 HOD.PAST-start friend 15:look.for 1 walk:PL 1 look.about.for.sb:PL
       'He started to look for his friend, he walked and he looked for him'

3.2.5.2 Progressive

The progressive tense (DG: présent ponctuel) indicates that the action is taking place at this moment, or at the moment of reference. It is always implied that the action takes

TABLE 16.8: SEMANTIC SCHEME OF TENSES

(GEN)PAST	GEN	(GEN)FUT/INDEF.FUT
FAR.PAST HOD.PAST IMM.PAST	IMM	IMM.FUT HOD.FUT
	PROG	
	OPT	

some time. The marker may combine with active verbs, as well as with (non-permanent) stative verbs (38). The Pluractional extension -*ak* which normally expresses multiplicity of the action, including duration, is not needed with the progressive marker '*ndò* to indicate duration. In fact, if one adds the Pluractional marker, the meaning becomes 'near future', which is treated as a separate tense.

(38)   *mè ndò wó mòndò kólóm* (DG 176)
        1SG PROG 1:DEM.PROX 1.person afraid
        'I am afraid of that person.'

3.2.5.3 Optative

The optative indicates a wish, an imperative, a hortative, an intention. These senses of the central optative meaning can be differentiated according to the exponent of the category of person of the subject: with a second person subject a strong imperative is expressed, with a first person plural the function is hortative, with the first person singular an intention is expressed, and with a third person subject a wish of the speaker is expressed. The optative is also used for an action linked to a preceding imperative, (39).

(39)   *ètà mb ó ↓sɔ́n* (DG 189)
        take and OPT:2SG come:H
        'Take and come!'

3.2.5.4 Past tenses

The *ka* tense, PAST (40), is a general or default past tense which is often used with time expressions. In addition there are specific past tenses for actions that have just happened, IMM.PAST (41,42), happened today, HOD.PAST (43), or happened long time ago, FAR.PAST (44). The imminence in the immediate past can be highlighted by reduplicating the verb root (42). The hodiernal past (an inappropriate term for Nen) is the most common one in stories which are situated in an unspecified far past where it serves to indicate a succession of events. The far past also functions as a pluperfect (45).

(40)   *ò kà mùnɔ̀nì sìèkìn òmbélà* (DG 180)
        2SG PAST chief see home
        'Did you see the chief at his home?'

(41)   *mè nó mòkòló nɔ̀k* (DG 176)
        1SG IMM.PAST 3.foot break
        'I just broke my foot.'

(42)   *à nó ↓tómbótómb òbàn* (DG 177)
        1 IMM.PAST pass(red) really
        'He really just passed this minute.'

(43)   *mè ná nìfú sámbé ó bùàná númwɔ̀* (DG 178)
        1SG HOD.PAST parcel put:H LOC bed under
        'I have put the parcel under the bed.'

(44)   *mèkɔ̀ lè wàmíá món ɔ́n* (DG 182)
        leopard FAR.PAST my child kill
        'The leopard killed my child.'

(45)   *mèkɔ̀ lè fèkàk à sèʔ ìkítí bákà mènyàmà y'ìŋgìn* (DG 182)
        leopard FAR.PAST think:PL 1 that ram be 9.animal 9:of strength
        'The leopard thought that the ram was strong.'

The so-called *passé indéterminé* is used in temporal conditions ('when'). It consists of the hodiernal past marker *ná* and the verb is in the basic tone pattern, not in the deviant one with a final High tone.

(46)   *nɔ́yé mè ꜜná bòlíá bɔ̀ŋɔ̀ mè ná mènyàmà mìkìm élìàkèn* (DG 178)
       thus 1SG COND.PAST tree see 1SG COND.PAST 4.animals 4:all call:PL
       'When I saw the tree, I called all the animals.'

DG (181) reports on a special non-specified past tense *ká* (High tone instead of Low tone), *passé ancien indéfini*, but the single example that she gives does not reveal whether it is really different from the *kà passé ancien* because in the example the High tone on *ká* could have been spread from the preceding High tone syllable.

3.2.5.5 Negative past tenses

The far past tense has its own negation in form, but it negates the verb for the whole past period until now (47). In addition there are two past negative tenses, differing only in the tone on the TAM marker *sa*. The High tone *sá* is the default negative past (48). The Low tone *sà* is used to negate an indicated period of time in the past rather than the action as such, e.g. 'A year was not finished when the pangolin died' and 'The antelope didn't sleep hungry (not even) one day' (DG 181).

(47)   *wàmíá món àtà mɔ̀tè à lè lè nà* (DG 182)
       1:my 1.child even one 1 NEG FAR.PAST ill
       'None of my children has ever been ill.'

(48)   *ó sá mìàŋó sìn* (DG 179)
       H:2SG PAST.NEG me see
       'You didn't see me.'

3.2.5.6 The future tenses

The most common future marker is the general future marker *ŋo* FUT for something that will happen at a point in time that is known either from context or from a time expression in the sentence (49). Other future tenses are: an immediate future (50), a hodiernal future (51), and an indefinite future, INDEF. FUT (DG: *futur indeterminé*). The last one is used when the exact point in the future is not known and not relevant, as in (52) 'at that moment in the future when we die, whenever that is'.

(49)   *mé ŋò ndá-sá búlílɔ* (DG 187)
       H:1SG FUT HITH-come tomorrow
       'I'll come tomorrow.'

(50)   *èkì ó sá là bɔ̀k ò b ó ná ꜜnɔ́k-én,*
       if H:2SG PAST.NEG say 8.thing LOC 8:rel 2SG HOD.PAST laugh-APPL:H,
       étàsè nèbélènà né bʷɔ̀sú hɔ̀ (DG 183)
       IMM.FUT 5.marriage 5 1PL finish
       'If you don't say why you laugh, our marriage is finished.'

(51)   *mé ndò búá bùhínɔ́ sábón-àk* (DG 184)
       1SG PROG 14:your 14.debt pay-PL
       'I'll pay your debt.' ('today' is implied)

(52)   *mbà bá nǎ bwə̀sú nyə̀ mùny ómòtì* (DG 185)
        and 2 INDEF.FUT 1PL bury 3.grave 3:one
        'And they will bury us in one grave.'

3.2.5.7 The negative future tenses

The future marker *ŋò* has its own negative form (53) and it negates an action in the future, without referring to any particular point of time in the future. The only other negative future tense has the TAM marker *sǎ* (54), which negates the action for the whole period of the future. The latter is often reinforced by the addition of the hither marker.

(53)   *à só ŋò fám ó ꜜmímə̀* (DG 188)
        1 NEG FUT leave LOC house
        'He won't leave the house.'

(54)   *mé sǎ nd áꜜŋó ból ìndì* (DG 186)
        1SG NEG.FUT HITH 2SG 14.thing give
        'I will never give you anything.'

The markers *na* and *sa* appear with different tonal patterns in several tenses which are taken to be distinct tense markers. Presenting them together suggests that the tonally distinct *na* and *sa* developed from markers that indicated time *distance* or focus rather than (relative) time:

(55)   *ná*   HOD.PAST   *sá*   NEG.(HOD.)PAST
        ꜛ*ná*   when-PAST   *sà*   NEG.PAST
        nǎ   INDEF.FUT   *sǎ*   NEG.INDEF.FUT

4 NOUNS AND NOMINALS

On the basis of agreement of the pronominal prefix, twelve noun classes can be distinguished. The noun class prefixes and the agreement prefixes are given in table 16.8. The numbering follows the usual Bantu reference system. Nouns occur in the following singular/plural pairs: 1/2, 3/4, 5/6, 7/8, 9/4, 19/13, 14/6. Minor pairs are: 7/13 (two words), 9/8 (21 words), 14/8 (12 words), 9a/6 and 3a/6. The noun classes with an initial *m*, 1, 3, 4, 6 and 9, have subclasses 1a, 3a, 4a, 6a and 9a, for which the prefix lacks the initial nasal. The nouns in these subclasses are the only ones that can have collectives. This difference manifests itself only in noun prefixes and not in any of the agreement prefixes. That is why I consider these groups of nouns *sub*classes, see 4.3. The nominal derivation is summarized in 4.4 where I also mention an adverbalizing clitic.

The class pair 1, 1a/2 contains mainly humans but it does also contain some words that are not humans, or animates. The first and second person pronouns also take class 1 (sg)/2 (pl) agreement in the expression -*mə̀té na* -*în* NUM.PFX-one and PRO.PFX-that:one 'each other', but such semantic agreement with the feature human does not extend to human nouns in other classes.

There is a minor pair 3/6 which has its origin in an earlier pair 15/6, containing words such as 'ear', 'foot', 'arm'. The class pair 5/6 contains two nouns that have a prefix *nù*- from a former class 11, *nùiy, mʷə̀iy* (5/6) 'river' and *nùàt, mǎt* (5/6) 'coconut pestle'.

Nouns in class 6 derived from verbs of collecting and harvesting denote a large quantity or the totality of collection: *nìhú* (5) 'harvesting yams', *mʷə̀hú* (6) 'a large quantity of harvested yams' from *hú* 'harvest'. The same semantic effect is achieved by deriving a class 6 plurals of abstract class 14 words, e.g. *màhὲk* (6) 'extreme beauty, all kinds of beauty' from *bòhὲk* (14) 'beauty', ultimately from *hὲk* 'be beautiful'.

Placing nouns from other classes into 19/13 renders them diminutive. This derivation is often coupled with reduplication of the root and for those nouns that are ultimately derived from verbs, a Diminutive verbal extension is sometimes added.

4.1 Agreeing modifiers and pronominals

The basis of the noun class system is the agreement with the head noun of words that depend on it. The various agreement prefixes are presented in table 16.9. The noun prefix is given in the second column for comparison. The last column gives the subject pronouns. The remaining columns give the three sets of agreement prefixes for modifiers of the head noun and pronominals that refer to a noun: the independent pronominal prefix, the numeral prefix and the pronominal prefix. The numeral prefix is used with the numerals 'one, some', 'two' and the question word 'how many'; the pronominal prefix is used with the connective, the possessive modifiers and the possessive pronominals, the demonstrative modifiers and the demonstrative pronominals, the question modifers 'which?', 'whose?', and 'where?', and with the emphatic complement pronouns; the independent pronominal prefixes are used with the emphatic demonstrative modifiers and pronominals and with the complement pronouns (see tables 16.10–16.13). On adjectives the noun prefix is used.

The nominal and independent pronominal prefixes differ from the numeral and the pronominal prefixes in that they have an initial *m-* in classes 1, 3, 4 and 9. Nominal prefixes all have a Low tone; independent pronominal prefixes are all High; the pronominal prefixes and the subject pronouns are Low in classes 1 and 9 only; the numeral prefix in class 1 only. The agreement prefixes, as opposed to the noun prefixes, have high dominant vowels in classes 3, 4, 19, and 13, but not in classes 1, 5, 7, 8, 14, which have recessive mid vowels. Such a distinction is not present in the value of the vowels of the Proto-Bantu agreement prefixes. The pronominal prefixes and subject pronouns have an initial homorganic glide where the corresponding numeral prefix only consists of a vowel. The noun prefixes that only consist of a vowel are realized as glides before vowel-initial roots.

TABLE 16.9: NOMINAL AND PRONOMINAL PREFIXES

Class	Noun. pfx	Indep.pron. pfx	Num. pfx	Pron. pfx	Subj. pro
1	*mò, ò*	*mó*	*ò*	*wò*	*à*
2	*bà*	*bá*	*bá*	*bá*	*bá*
3	*mò, ò*	*mú*	*ó*	*wú*	*wó*
4	*mὲ, ὲ*	*mí*	*í*	*yí*	*yé*
5	*nὲ*	*né*	*né*	*né*	*nέ*
6	*mà, a*	*má*	*má*	*má*	*má*
7	*ὲ*	*yé*	*έ*	*yé*	*yé*
8	*bὲ*	*bé*	*bé*	*bé*	*bé*
9	*mὲ, ὲ*	*mé*	*έ*	*yὲ*	*yὲ*
19	*hὲ*	*hí*	*hí*	*hí*	*hέ*
13	*tò*	*tú*	*tó*	*tú*	*tú*
14	*bò*	*bó*	*bó*	*bó*	*bó*

TABLE 16.10: MODIFIERS WITH A NUMERAL PREFIX

Root	Gloss	Examples
mɔ̀té	one (sg), some (pl)	mòlyáf ómòtí 'one branch' (cl. 3), bǎná bámɔ̀té 'some children' (cl. 2)
fàndè	two	bǎná báfàndè 'two children' (cl. 2), mèlyáf ífɘ̀ndì 'two branches' (cl. 4)
nè̀	how many?	bǎná bánè̀ 'how many children' (cl. 2), mèlyáf íni 'how many branches' (cl. 4)

TABLE 16.11: PRONOMINALS WITH INDEPENDENT PRONOMINAL PREFIXES

Root	Gloss	Examples
↓táná	emph.dem.prox	mú↓tɘ́nɘ̀ mòlyáf 'this very branch' (cl. 3)
↓téní ~ ↓tɘ̀ni	emph.dem.dist	má↓téní 'those (cl. 6) very ones'
↓táyé	emph.dem.ref	mó↓táyé 'this very one (cl. 1) mentioned'
		mú↓téyé 'this very one (cl. 3) mentioned'
ét	compl.pro	mí-ét → míít → mít 'it' (cl. 4) and bé-ét → bé-ét → bét 'it' (cl. 8)

Note: The human classes have deviant forms for the complement pronominals: wéy cl. 1, báb or bʷɘ́bú cl. 2.

TABLE 16.12: THE MODIFIERS AND PRONOMINALS WITH PRONOMINAL PREFIXES

Root	Gloss	Example
á	con	mòkàŋá wɘ̀ bólè 'the root of the tree' (DG 133)
ámè	poss.mod	wàmè̀ mòn 'my child' (cl. 1), níá↓míá néhɔ̀ká 'my hoe' (cl. 5) (DG 135)
ámɛ́	poss.pro	yɘ̀m émɔ́ ↓bákà mèbɛ́, tɘ́tɘ́níɘ̀ yɘ̀ù mùès 'My dogs (cl. 4) are bad, watch yours (cl. 4).' (DG 136)
–	prox.dem.mod	né nèhɔ̀k 'this hoe' (cl. 5) (DG 136)
íni	dist.dem.mod	níní néhɔ̀k 'that hoe' (DG 136)
éyé	ref.dem.mod	néyé néhɔ̀k 'this hoe (mentioned)' (DG 136)
ˆCᵢ	prox.dem.pro	ó wàmè wów 'this one (cl. 1) is mine'
în	dist.dem.pro	wɘ̂n 'that one' (cl. 1), bʷɘ̂n 'those ones' (cl. 2)
íní	ref.dem.pro	
áyé	emph.compl.pro	ò níáyé 'it' (cl. 5)
ɘ̀nì	which?	ó níɘ́níɘ̀ nèhɔ̀ká nɘ̀ nìmìn 'which hoe disappeared?' (DG 147)
ánɛ́	whose?	níánɛ̀ néhɔ̀k 'whose hoe is it?' (DG 147)
íní	where?	níní nèhɔ̀k 'where is the hoe?' (DG 148)

Note: The proximal demonstrative modifier consists of just the pronominal prefix; the proximal demonstrative pronoun copies the consonant of pronominal prefix to the pronominal prefix with a falling tone imposed on it.

The possessives are made up of the pronominal prefix plus the connective and the person roots which are given in table 16.13 together with the personal pronouns (subject and oblique). For emphasis one can use the possessive pronominals as oblique personal pronouns (last column).

TABLE 16.13: PERSONAL PRONOUNS

Person	Possessive stem	Subject pronoun	Oblique	Emphatic oblique
1sg	*mè*	*mè*	*mìàŋó*	*mìámè*
2sg	–	*ò*	*àŋó*	*wǎŋà*
3sg.hum = cl. 1	*y(è)*	subj.pro.1	*wéy*	*ǎyé*
1pl	*sú*	*tú*	*bʷə̀sú*	*tùə̀sú*
2pl	*nú*	*nú*	*bʷə̀nú*	*nùə̀sú*
3pl.hum = cl. 2	*bu*	subj.pro.2	*bʷə́bú*	=

4.2 Adjectives

Adjectives follow the head noun and agree in noun class with the noun prefix as agreement marker; first and second person take class 1 and 2 agreement (57). The adjectival
agreement with nouns in the subclasses is the nasal initial *mV-* noun prefix (56). For predicative usage the copula *lè* or the verb *bak* 'be' can but need not be used (56,57). DG 153
gives the following list of adjectives: *kìm* 'complete (sg), all (pl)', *té↓té* 'small', *éŋéŋ* 'big',
tàtán 'long' *kítíkìt* 'short', *ós* 'fresh, raw', *tótó* 'new, weak, soft', *ómóm* 'new', *nàŋànàŋ*
'white, clean', *inó-inó* 'other, different', *əŋ* 'many', *bé* 'bad', *ès* 'good, nice', *mbány*
'nice'. Half of the adjectival roots contain segmental reduplication.

(56)   *òmbàlá mó-té↓té* 3a.bag 3-small   'a small bag, the bag is small'

(57)   *mè lè mù-ès* 1sg cop 1-good   'I am fine'

4.3 Nouns with vowel prefixes

The nasal-initial noun prefixes have a variant that could be analysed as *VN-*. Although
historically the shape of these variants is *VN-*, synchronically I analyse them as consisting of a vowel only. As a consequence, those roots that show traces of nasals in the root-
initial consonant after these vowel prefixes are root variants. The distinction of the
subclasses of nouns with such a *V-* prefix instead of an *mV-* prefix is lexical: no semantic characterization has been found with the exception of class 6a which is the collective
variant of class 6; class 6, *ma-*, can be used for collectives of the vowel-initial subclasses
3a/4a and 9a/4a (58). Due to a reinterpretation of the collective as regular plural, the
minor class pairings 9/6 (68 words) and 3a/6 arose. The collectives refer to 'all sorts' of
the referent implying that the individual entities differ from each other (59). There may
be some individual variation in the productivity of collectives, or the fact that collectives
involve root alternation (DG 68, 72) may be a reason that they are under threat because
my informant in Ndikinimeki (Emmanuel Bakoui) did not accept them.

(58)   *òndɔ̀mb* (3a), pl.: *èndɔ̀mb* (4a), coll.: *màndɔ̀mb* (6)   'sheep'
        nìbíl (5), pl.: *mʷə̀bíl* (6), coll.: *əmíl* (6a)   'palm oil'
        nèfè (5), *màfè* (6), coll.: *àmbè* (6a)   'melon'
        nèkɔ̀kɔ̀l (5), pl.: *màkɔ̀kɔ̀l* (6), coll.: *àmbɔ̀kɔ̀l* (6a)   'cola nut'

(59)   *indìnò mìŋ* 'many tree trunks', *mʷə̀ndìnò mʷə̀ŋ*   'many tree trunks of various
        sizes and sorts'

The subclasses show in most but not all cases a trace of a nasal preceding the noun root.
The presence of a nasal element in the prefix can be deduced from the alternations in
1a/2, 3a/6 and in the collectives of 3a/4a and of 9a/4a (60), as well as in 3a or 9a nouns

derived from verbs. Note that the prenasalized counterpart of *h* and *k* is *mb*. Some roots in the subclasses show no sign of nasals (61). There are also alternations between plain consonants and nasals or nasal compounds in other parts of the grammar where there is less reason to assume a nasal element in an affix (62).

(60) *òmbòm/bàhòm* (1a/2) 'older man'
      èmbɔ́m 'forest' (9a/4a), coll.: *màhɔ́m ~ màmbɔ́m* (6)
      nèkɔ̀kɔ̀l 'cola nut' (5), coll.: *àmbɔ̀kɔ̀l* (6a)

(61) *òsànó* (3a/6) 'rising sun'
      òbàŋó (3a/6) 'elephant tusk', coll.: *àmàŋó* (6a)
      ùkùl (3a/6) 'sort, type'

(62) *èmbékét* (7/8) 'complaint' from *békét* 'be dissatisfied'
      mànjɔ́lɔ̀l (6) 'duck's cry' from *síɔ́lɔ̀l* 'cry like a duck'

4.4 Nominal derivation

A number of nouns are derived from other nouns by transferring them into another noun class. There are also nouns derived from verbs by placement into a noun class which may or may not be accompanied by a vowel suffix. These derivations are not productive and given the final vowel reduction, the derivational suffix cannot always be traced. Clear examples of a derivational suffix are the agentive nouns ending in -*i*. Some nouns derived from verbs contain the Pluractional -*ak* (DG 361). Many nominalized verbs contain a reduplicated root. The only fully productive nominalization is the infinitive in class 3a.

The only productive deverbal suffix is -*ato*. The suffix is invariable; it does not undergo vowel harmony. It is often preceded by the Pluractional extension -*ak*. The meaning is to indicate resultant state (64), quality or capacity (63). The *ato*-derived forms are used as the complement of a copula (DG 362). The word class of the *ato*-derived form is neither a noun nor an adjective since it lacks a noun class prefix, nor is it a verb since it requires a copula; thus it is an adverb.

(63) *mǒná lè kènd-ák-átò*
      child COP walk-PL-ADV
      'The child is capable of walking.'

(64) *bòté bákà tìt-ə̀k-átò*
      savannah be burn-PL-ADV
      'The savannah is burnt.'

5 SYNTAX

This section is based on Mous (1997). The order within the noun phrase is generally Modified–Modifier. Adjectives, connectives, relative clauses follow the head noun (65).

(65) *mòndò mò-tàtán* 1.man 1.tall 'a tall person'
      mòndò wà bòkólóm 1.man 1.CON 14.fear 'a man who is afraid'
      wó mònd [òwá áná mòné pàt á jéan nánèkól] *àná mìàŋó pàt nìə̀fɛ̀n*
      that man REL 1:HOD.PAST money ask to Jean yesterday 1:HOD.PAST me ask today
      'The man who asked Jean money yesterday asked me today.'

However selectional modifiers precede the head noun with the appropriate noun class concord. Such selectional modifiers are demonstratives, possessives, the question words 'whose?', 'which?', 'where?', and 'how many?' as well as the numeral 'one' when it means 'another' or 'some'. All these modifiers select from a given set. Possessives follow the noun in lexicalized contractions involving words for relatives or friends which shows that the possessive followed the noun at an earlier stage of the language (66).

(66)   *mùkìnâm*   'my in-law'   from   *mùkìnə̀ wàmìà* (DG 137–8)
        òŋwâm   'my friend'   from   *òŋwáyè wàm*

5.1 The position of the object

In imperative sentences, the object follows the verb. If there are two objects, the recipient obligatorily precedes the goal object, and the two objects form one phrase since H spread does apply. Syntactic phrases can be deduced from the boundaries over which H spread does not apply.

(67)   *ìndìə̀ mìàŋó mìɔf* (EB)
        give me hoe
        'Give me the hoe!'

Otherwise, objects precede the verb. If there are two objects, the recipient object (mostly human or animate) precedes the goal object. H spread may apply between the two objects and between the object and the verb, all of them forming one phrase; it cannot apply between the TAM marker and what follows. We have to assume a stronger syntactic boundary after the tense marker even if it is prefixed to a following verb radical adapting to it in vowel harmony; such cliticization never happens to the object noun (phrase).

(68)   *mé-ŋò àŋó mímé fʷə́lə̀bì* (EB)
        H:1SG-FUT you house build:CAUS
        'I'll build a house for you.'

Placing the object after the verb is comparable in function to placing the modifier before the noun; it selects the object in question against all other possible objects expressing contrastive emphasis, with a contrastive preposition *á* (69), in particular after particles for 'only', 'just', or 'even'. A bare noun object (which is not a locative) after the verb forms one phrase with it, as H-spread shows, reminiscent of the conjoint verb forms in Southern Bantu (70).

(69)   *mé-ndò ní á bónìàk* (EB)
        1SG-PROG eat CONTR yams
        'What I eat is yams.'

(70)   *à-ná kèmáká mʷə́lùk* (DG 58)
        1-HOD.PAST tap:H palm wine
        'He tapped palm wine!'

5.2 Discontinuous complement noun phrases

Modifiers can occur after the verb while their head noun precedes the verb to indicate contrastive focus on the modifier (71). Only post-nominal modifiers and only modifiers of the last preverbal noun phrase can follow the verb. Numeral modifiers are mostly postverbal due to their selectional property (72). The postverbal modifier still agrees in noun class with the preverbal head noun, but semantically it seems to be somewhat loose from the noun it refers to and syntactically it is a separate phrase; H spread does not apply.

(71)   *mè-ná ìmìtà yè m^wə̀nífí índí mè-ŋéŋ ò hèlɔ́bátɔ̀* (EB)
     1SG-HOD.PAST 9:calabash 9:of 6:water give:H 9-big LOC 19:child
     'I gave the BIG water calabash to the child.'

(72)   *èbàkó ná émɔ̀à nèbɔ̀à lúmwɔ̀ nétɔ̀tè* (DC 63)
     lizard HOD.PAST dog medicine hit:H one
     'The lizard hit the dog by magic.'

5.3 Locative and infinitival complements

Locative complements always follow the verb even if they are objects in the sense of an obligatory complement of the verb (73), in which case they are part of the VP since H spread applies. Locative phrases tend to have a preposition *ò* LOC; nouns that are inherently locative can occur without the initial *ò* (74).

(73)   *à-ná hísíní tálà ò nèkɔ́* (EB)
     1-HOD.PAST pot put:H LOC fire
     'She put the pot on the fire.'

(74)   *à-ná-[↓]ndá-híán ésèl* (DC 65)
     1-HOD.PAST-HITH-arrive:H riverside
     'He arrived at the riverside.'

Infinitival complements behave like locatives; they are placed after the verb and the infinitive is a class 3a noun with the nominal prefix *ò*, homophonous with the locative preposition *ò* (75). An infinitival phrase with a patient noun preceding the infinitive begins in this locative preposition *ò*, which may precede any other noun in the infinitival phrase (76).

(75)   *á ná-bàl ólèl* (DC 63)
     1 HOD.PAST-begin 3a:rain
     'It starts to rain.'

(76)   *à-ná húánánà ò wâw ò m^wə̀lúk òwíndì* (EB)
     1-HOD.PAST must:H LOC you LOC wine 3a:give
     'She/He must give you wine.'

ACKNOWLEDGMENTS

I thank Eithne Carlin, Baudouin Janssens and Thilo Schadeberg for their comments on an earlier version of this paper, Baudouin Janssens for sharing his data with me (BJ), Honoré Boyoleba Balehen (HB) and Emanuel Bakoui (EB) for sharing their insight into their language with me.

REFERENCES

Abwa 1995; Bancel 1991; Bastin and Piron 1999; Dugast 1955, 1959, 1967, 1971, 1975; Grimes 2000; Janssens 1988; Mous 1986, 1997; Mous and Breedveld 1986; Stewart and Van Leynseele 1979; Van Leynseele and Stewart 1980; Wilkinson 1975.

CHAPTER SEVENTEEN

Kpāʔ (A53)

Gladys Guarisma

SYMBOLS AND ABBREVIATIONS

+	Coalescence	INCEP	Inceptive
*	Reconstruction	INJ	Injunctive
/	Clause limit in complex	INTR	Intransitive
	utterances	IPFV	Imperfective
[ ]	Phonetic realization	ITER	Iterative
| |	Structural form	MET	Metatony
H	Accented High Tone	MID	Middle
v	Accented Vowel	PER	Persistive
ANAPH	Anaphoric	POY	Potential
C	Clause	RAD	Radical
CONC	Conclusive	REF	Reflexive
CONT	Continuous	RET	Retrospective
DIR	Directional	VM1	Pre-Stem Marker 1
FOC	Focus	VM2	Post-Stem Marker 1
HYPO	Hypothetical	VM3	Post-Stem Marker 2

1 INTRODUCTION

The *kpāʔ* language is spoken in the northern Bantu border area in Cameroon, where languages belonging to three linguistic families (Niger-Congo, Nilo-Saharan and Afro-Asiatic) are to be found side by side with the two official languages: English and French.

kpāʔ is usually known as 'Bafia', a name more widely applied to Guthrie's A50 group. There are about 25,000 speakers occupying an area on the right bank of the Mbam, Bafia Prefecture, Mbam Department.

The members of Guthrie's A50 are: A51 *faʔ* (*là-fàʔ* or Balom), A52 *kaaloŋ* (*rì-péʔ* or Mbom), A53 *kpa* (*rì-kpāʔ* or Bafia), A54 *ngayaba* (*tì-ɓèà* or Djanti).

This classification is broadly confirmed by a dialectometric study (Guarisma and Paulian 1986) which also shows that *rì-kpāʔ* and *là-fāʔ* form a close cluster (similarity index above 800), whereas *tì-ɓèà* is more distant (indices around 300, barely above those with neighboring A70 dialects).

Apart from my own contributions, *kpāʔ* is little documented: two books and a few articles. G. Tessmann (1934) is a reference work on Bafia society and culture, including an overview on noun classes and a copious glossary. L. K. Anderson (1935), focuses more on the language: phonology (although tones are only indicated in the Bafia–English glossary), noun classes and noun qualifiers, an inventory of verb forms (tense, aspect, extensions), prepositions, adverbial forms, order of meaningful elements in utterances.

The articles include an instrumental phonetic study of vowels and tones (Aroga Bessong and Marchal n.d.), an attempt at translation of Bafia verb forms (Aroga Bessong 1982), and a study of Bafia conjugation according to the linguistic model 'Meaning ⇔ Text' (MTS) (Aroga Bessong and Mel'čuk 1983).

My own data base includes a large amount of lexical material with sentences collected by myself in the field from about twenty speakers, as well as oral literature texts, proverbs and spontaneous narratives.

The theoretical approach followed here is that of the French functionalist school, with an attempt at adapting the terminology to an Anglo-Saxon audience. The transcription is based on the principles of the IPA, with the exception of IPA [j] rendered here as [y] and IPA [dʒ], here [j].

2 PHONOLOGY

Stem-initially, there are twenty-five consonants in *kpāʔ*:

2.1 Consonants

	Anterior		Central			Posterior	
ORAL	Bilabial	Labio-dental	Apical	Post-apical	Palatal	Velar	Labio-velar
Implosives	ɓ		ɗ				
−voice +voice	p b	f v	t d	s z	c j	k g	kp gb
Continuants	w		l	r	y	ɣ	
NASAL	m		n		ɲ	ŋ	

Oral consonants are basically arranged in pairs on the basis of the [voice] feature (p/b, f/v, t/d, s/z, c/j, k/g, kp/gb). Voiced obstruents are generally found initially in nouns belonging to cl. 9/10 (as a result of coalescence with the nasal prefix). *v* is found in a handful of items (ideophones or loans): *ɓì-vyáà* 'squint', *váà* 'guard' (cf. German *Wacht*), *vàp* 'heavily', *véèmzèn* 'breathing' (cf. *-féèmzèn* 'breathe'), *vìlìmvìlìm* 'impulsive', *kì-vììŋ* 'sling', *vùráŋ* 'gaping', etc. *ʃ* and *ʒ* (not included in the table) are variants of *sy* and *zy* respectively.

Word-final consonants include only *p, s, ʔ, l* and *m, n, ŋ*:

		Anterior	Central	Posterior
ORAL	−voice	p	s	ʔ
	−voice		l=y	
NASAL		m	n	ŋ

p alternates with *b* before vowel (cf. suffixation, noun and verb phrases).

rì-kàp	'sell'	*ǹ-kàbì*	'seller'
rì-túp	'pierce'	*à-túbì*	'he pierced'
		cl. 1 −pierce + PFV	

Final *?* is always preceded by a short [+high] vocalic transition with the same point of articulation as the syllable center (except when the latter is itself [+high]):

-i, with front vowels (e, ɛ, a):

tì-bí?	[tì-bí?]	'excrement'
ì-tē?	[ī-tēⁱ?]	'strength'
rì-wè?	[rì-wèⁱ?]	'laughing'
ǹ-tā?	[ñ-tāⁱ?]	'basket sp.'

-u, with back [+round] vowels (o, ɔ):

kì-tù?	[kì-tù?]	'old man'
kì-bō?	[kī-bōᵘ?]	'mortar for pounding (maize or beans)'
kì-fɔ́?	[kì-fɔ́ᵘ?]	'shed'

-ɨ with back [-round] vowels (ə, ʌ, ɑ):

d̂-ī?	[d̂-ī?]	'egg'
rì-bə́?	[rì-bə́ⁱ?]	'premeditate'
ǹ-tʌ́?	[ñ-tʌⁱ?]	'load'
fì-bā?	[fì-bāⁱ?]	'obstacle'

Items of the type /CwV[-back]?/ can be compared with items of the type /CV[+back]l(= y)/ frequently encountered in *rì-kpā?*:

rì-fwé?	[kìfwéⁱ?]	'sniff'	*ból*	[bwéy/é:]	'rain'
rì-fwè?	[kìfwéⁱ?]	'fill'	*rì-fɔ́l*	[rìfwéy/é:]	'get tired'
kì-kwì?	[kìkwì?]	'cloud'	*kúl*	[kwí:]	'turtle, leprosy'

Under the influence of the final alveolar consonant the [+back] feature is removed from the vowel and associates to the initial consonant.

Following a vowel, *?* generally alternates with *r* after [−back] and *y* after [+back]:

? > r

rì-wè?	'laugh, criticize'	*mà-wèrì*	'laughter, criticism'
rì-té?	'take'	*à-térì*	'he took'
		cl. 1-take+PFV	

? > y

rì-pì?	'throw'	*à-pìyì*	'he threw'
rì-fə̀?	'think'	*à-fə̀yì*	'he thought'
rì-bó?	'beat'	*à-bóyì*	'he beat'
rì-bɔ́?	'climb'	*à-bɔ́yì*	'he climbed on the tree'

In *fà?* (A51) *?* corresponds to *t* (after [±back]) and to *k* (after [+back] only). *?* in *kpā?* thus represents the neutralization of the *t/k* opposition stem-finally; this consonant neutralization is compensated by the creation of a new vocalic series: the [+back] [−round] vowels (Guarisma 1980):

	rì-kpā?	là-fà? tìŋgɔ̀ŋ
	C(C)V [−back] ?	CV [−back] t
'excrement'	tì-ɓí? |tì-ɓít|	tì-ɓít
'caterpillar *sp.*'	zyè? |ǹ-syèt|	nsyèt
'ten'	ǹ-tè? |mù-tèt|	ǹ-tèt
'leave (tr)'	rì-cà? |ɗì-càt|	tì-càt
	(C)wV [−back] ?	(C)wV [+back] t
'cloud'	kì-kwì? |kì-kùt|	kì-kùt
'sniff'	rì-fwé? |ɗì-fót|	tì-fwót
'criticize'	rì-wè? |ɗì-wɔ̀t|	tì-wɔ̀t
	CV [+back] [−round] ?	CV [+back] [±round] k
'throw'	rì-pì? |ɗì-pìk|	tì-pìk
'yoke'	kì-ɓə̀? |kì-ɓèk|	kì-ɓə̀k
'plait'	rì-nɨ́? |ɗì-nèk|	tì-nɨ́k
'feel, smell, hear'	rì-wó? |ɗì-wók|	tì-wók
'crush'	rì-kɔ̀? |ɗì-kɔ̀k|	tì-kɔ̀k
'buy'	rì-là? |ɗì-làk|	tì-làk

2.2 Vowels

[−back]	[+back]	
i	ɨ	u
e	ə	o
ɛ	ʌ	ɔ
a	ɑ	
[−round]	[+round]	

Vowels can be short or long. [+back] [−round] vowels are generally short (except in the case of coalescence with a vowel-initial morpheme) and are mostly to be found in contact with a [+back] consonant or else in affixes (always non-accented); this confirms their being innovations with respect to the original system. There is however a tendency for these vowels to spread even to alveolar or palatal contexts: zɨ 'earth', ɲɨ 'he, him (cl. 1)', rì-yɨ 'know'.

2.3 Tones

Bafia is essentially a two-tone language. Phonetically, however, three registers are to be found: v́ (High, realized as slightly rising after a [+voice] non-implosive consonant b, d, z, ʒ, j, g), v̄ Mid and v̀ (Low, slightly falling). Low and Mid registers are only distinct before pause (especially with older, non-urban, speakers):

bép	'cane rat'	[̄ ̇]
bēn	'termite(s) *sp.*'	[̇]
bèn	'rib(s)'	[̇ ̇]
kì-kə́?	'calabash tree'	[̇ ̄ ̇]
kì-kɔ̄m	'liver'	[̇ ̇ ̇]
kì-kòp	'box'	[̇ ̇ ̇]

Elsewhere only H and L are found:

bép	*yɨ*	'these cane rats'	[̄ ̄]
bēn	*yɨ*	'these termites *sp.*'	[̇ ̄]
bèn	*yɨ*	'these ribs'	[̇ ̄]
kì-kə́?	*kɨ*	'this calabash tree'	[̇ ̄ ̄]
kì-kɔ̄m	*kɨ*	'this liver'	[̇ ̇ ̄]
kì-kòp	*kɨ*	'this box'	[̇ ̇ ̄]

The two complex tones (rising v̌v́ and falling v́v̀), always associated with long vowels (*mɔ̌ɔ́* 'oil', *táàn* 'five'), can be analysed as combinations of LH and HL respectively.

Apart from stems derived by suffixation or reduplication, lexemes are generally mono-syllabic. Their behaviour in the spoken chain, however, suggests that these lexemes must formerly have been disyllabic, of the type (C)VCV(C) (V=accented vowel), and that the deletion of the final non-accented vowel has led to the restructuring of the tone system: creation of the M tone from **BH**, and collapsing of **HB** and **HH**, thus: | **B B** |>**B**, | **B H** |>**M**, | **H B** | and | **H H** |>**H**. This analysis is corroborated by tone correspondences between kpā? and Common Bantu, as well as by the percentages for single tones: L 27 percent, M 15, 47 percent, H 54, 26 percent (i.e. more than L and M combined) (Guarisma 1983, 1992, 2000).

2.4 Downstep and upstep

These two phenomena clearly reveal the underlying tonal structure. Their realization depends conjointly on two factors: tonal structure and the accentual status of morphemes. These facts can be subsumed under two rules (Guarisma 1992, 1994, 2000):

- Any floating tone will be represented on the following item: an L lowers a following H and an H raises a following L (replacing a non-accented and combining with an accented L).

bép	*yɨ*		| *ǹ-bép´*	*ɨ*|	'these cane-rats'
bén	*'yɨ*		| *ǹ-bén`*	*ɨ*|	'these handles'
bēn	*yɨ*		| *ǹ-bèn´*	*ɨ*|	'these termites *sp.*'
bèn	*yɨ*		| *ǹ-bèn´*	*ɨ*|	'these ribs'
bép	*ɨ-nə́*		| *ǹ-bép´*	*ɨ-nə́*|	'this cane-rat'
bén	*i-nə́*		| *ǹ-bén`*	*ɨ-nə́*|	'this handle'
bēn	*i-nə́*		| *ǹ-bèn´*	*ɨ-nə́*|	'this termite *sp.*'
bèn	*ɨ-nə́*		| *ǹ-bèn´*	*ɨ-nə́*|	'this rib'
bép	*yə́ɛ̀m*		| *ǹ-bép´*	*ɨ-ɛ̀m*|	'my cane-rats'
bén	*'yə́ɛ̀m*	[yɛ̀m]	| *ǹ-bén`*	*ɨ-ɛ̀m*|	'my handles'

bēn	*yéèm*		|*ǹ-bèn´*	*ì-êm*|	'my termites *sp.*'
bèn	*'yéèm*	[*yèm*]	|*ǹ-bèn`*	*ì-êm*|	'my ribs'

- When two accented Hs follow each other, the second is downstepped:

(1) *mà-rɔ́ʔ*   *mʌ́-'gwéy* | B-BB H-H | → BB H- 'H   'much wine'
    cl. 6-wine cl. 6-much

(2) *ǹ-yíí-'ɓì* | B-H-H | → B-H-'H   'I don't know'
    I- know+PFV- NEG

(3) *à-ɓóʔ*   *'ɲí* | B-H H | → B-H 'H   'he beats him'
    cl. 1 - beat   him

Downstep is thus to be seen as a manifestation of accent, with an essentially demarcative function: it separates items making up a phrase or utterance.

2.5 Downdrift

Downdrift is systematic in every succession HBH: the second H is realized lower than the first:

bóòɓó	'medicine'		[¯ . -]
ɓàáràá	'tree *sp.*'		[. ¯ . -]

(4) *m-úm*   *à-nɔ́*   'this man'   [¯ . -]
    cl. 1-man cl. 1-this

(5) *à-wél-à*   *gɔ̀n*   *ì*   *gíp*   [. ¯ . . . -]
    cl. 1-marry-RET cl. 9+girl cl. 9 cl. 1+woman
    'he married a girl'

(6) *à-kpáŋ*   *jàŋ*   *bóʔ*   *rì*   *m-ɛ́ɛ́*   [. ¯ . - .]
    cl. 1 - arrive cl. 9+place cl. 9+one with cl. 6-house
    'he came near the house'

It is possible for a H to be realized L, sometimes slightly falling, before pause, similar to a L (cf. following examples).

The limit of downdrift is the utterance, or the clause in complex utterances.

(7) *m-úm*   *à-sà-yà*   *mín*   *ɓy-āʔ* *ɓì ń-'*   *tó*

\|*mʌ̀-úm`*   *à-sà-yà*   *mín* *ɓì-àk´*   *ɓì* *mù-tó´*\|
cl. 1-person cl. 1-put-RET then cl. 8-hands on cl. 3-head

'The person then put his hands on his head'

(8) *nɔ́* *'m-úm*   *à-yù-yà,*   *à-kpáŋ*   *'fʌ́lɛ́* *'ɓì* *'sú* *ú* *m-ɛ́ɛ́*

\| *ńǹ-nɔ́ mʌ̀-úm`* *à-yù-yà,*   *à-kpáŋ* *fʌ́lɛ́* *ɓì*   *ì-sú´* *ú´*   *mʌ̀-ɛ́ɛ́*\|
then cl. 1 -person cl. 1-come-RET / cl. 1-come out thus to cl. 3a-face cl. 3 cl. 6-hut

'Then the person came and came out in front of the house.'

3 NOUN CLASSES

Classes	Table of prefixes			
	NP	Dependent Prefixes		
	Nominal	I	II	III
1	*m*-V | mʌ- | ǹ-C	ǹ-C | mʌ- | ø-C [+voice]	w-V | v̀- | à-C	| à- |
1a	| ø̀-C |			
2	6-V | 6ʌ- | 6ʌ-C	| 6ʌ- | 6ʌ-C	6-V | 6ʌ́- | 6ʌ́-C	| 6ʌ́ - |
3	ŋw-, w-V | mù- | ǹ-C	| ù- | ù-C	w-V | ú- | ú-C	| ú- |
3a	| ì- | ì-			
4	my-V m-i | mì- | mʌ-C	| mʌ- | mʌ-C	m-V m-i | mʌ́- | mʌ́-C	| mʌ́ - |
5	ɗ-i, ɨ, u ɗy-V | ɗì- | ri-C	| ɗì- | ɗɨ-C	ɗy-V | ɗí- | ɗɨ́-C	| ɗí- |
6	m-V | mʌ- | mʌ-C	| mʌ- | mʌ-C	m-V | mʌ́- | mʌ́-C	| mʌ́ - |
7	c-V | kì- | kɨ-, ì-C	| kì- | kɨ-C	k-V | kí- | kɨ́-C	|kí - |
8	6y-V | 6ì- | 6ɨ-C	| 6ì- | 6ɨ-C	6y-V | 6í- | 6ɨ́-C	|6í -|
9	| ǹ- | ø-C [+voice]	| ǹ- | ø-C [+voice]	y-V | ì- | ɨ-C	| ì- |
10	| ǹ- | ø-C [+voice]	| ì- | ì-C	y-V | í- | í-, yɨ-C	| í- |
19	fy-V | fì- | fɨ-C	| fì- | fɨ-C	fy-V | fí- | fɨ́-C	| fí- |
13	ty-V | tì- | tɨ-C	| tì- | tɨ-C	ty-V | tí | tɨ́-C	| tí- |

kpá? has twelve noun classes (genders : 1/2, 3/4, 5/6, 7/8, 9/10, 19/13). Each class is indicated by a nominal prefix (NP) and dependent prefixes (DP) varying according to the category of the item in question: DP I | (C)v̀- |: adjectives (colors, deverbatives), stem for 'all' and numeral 'one'; DP II | v̀- | (cl. 1 and 9), | (C)v́ | (other cl.) : demonstrative, anaphoric, possessives, stem for 'other, some', dependent interrogatives, nominal substitute, adjective (cf. determinative phrase); DP III | v̀- | (cl. 1 and 9), | (C)v́'- | (other cl.): connective, numeral and verbal prefixes. The distinction between DP II and III is based on the tonal behaviour of determiners:

- with DP II of classes other than 1 and 9, L determiners remain L, whereas H determiners are downstepped:

(9) *ɓ-úm*   *ʼɓʎ́-ɓàŋ* | *ɓʎ̀-úmˋ ɓʎ́-ɓàŋ* | 'brown people'
     cl. 2-people cl. 2-red, brown
(10) *ɓ-úm*   *ʼɓʎ́-fín* | *ɓʎ̀-úmˋ ɓʎ́-fín* | 'black people'
     cl. 2-people cl. 2-black

- with DP III for the same classes, L determiners are raised to H, whereas H determiners remain H:

(11) *ɓ-úm*   *ʼɓʎ́-ɓéè* | *ɓʎ̀-úmˋ ɓʎ́ʼ-ɓèèʼ* | 'two people'
     cl. 2-people cl. 2-two
(12) *ɓ-úm*   *ʼɓʎ́-ráá* | *ɓʎ̀-úmˋ ɓʎ́ʼ-ráá* | 'three people'
     cl. 2-people cl. 2-three

Classes 1 and 3 are differentiated by their concords and by the NP of vowel-initial stems (m- / ŋw-). Classes 4 and 6 are differentiated by the NP of vowel-initial stems (*my-* / *m-*) and their singular-plural pairings (3/4 vs. 5/6) (cf. Kadima 1969).

3.1 Nominal prefixes

All are L-toned |(C)v̀-|. A small number of cl. 1/2 stems take a nasal prefix in the sg. which is retained in the pl. They mostly refer to plants and animals and can be considered as being originally cl. 9/10 items transferred to 1/2:

ǹ-bènè/ɓʎ̀-ǹ-bènè   'thick porridge made of cassava'
ǹ-dàmbàl/ɓʎ̀-ǹ-dàmbàl   'rubber'
ǹ-lóŋ/ɓʎ̀-ǹ-lóŋ   'larva of *Rhynchophorus phoenicis*'
ǹ-gón/ɓʎ̀-ǹ-gón   'leopard'

A few 7/8 nouns, also referring to plants or animals have a [+voice] stem-initial consonant (probably also due originally to the 9/10 nasal prefix):

kì-zén / ɓì-zén | *kì-ǹ-sén / ɓì-ǹ-sén* | 'fish'
kì-gòm / ɓì-gòm | *kì-ǹ-kòmˋ / ɓì-ǹ-kòmˋ* | 'adder *sp.*'

Two 3/4 nouns have an alternation of sg. *w* and pl. *m*: *wēl/mēl* 'war'<CB **bịtá*, *wén/mén* 'dance'<**bịnà*. The *w-*b* correspondence shows, however, that *w* (stem-initial consonant) has been reanalyzed as a class prefix. This is confirmed by the comparison with the normal shape of cl. 4 prefix before vowel-initial stem (*my-*, not *m-*).

3.2 Dependent prefixes I

These are prefixed to color adjectives and deverbatives when in attributive function (see below DP II-Adj in N+Adj. phrases), to the numeral -fó? 'one' and the stem -cèm 'all'. They are distinct from NP in cl. 3 and 10 only:

(13) kì-làà   kí-rí   kì-púp   'the cloth is white'
     cl. 7-cloth cl. 7-be   cl. 7-white

(14) bú   'í-rí   ì-fín   'the dogs are black'
     cl. 10+dog   cl. 10-be   cl. 10-black

(15) ŋw-óm   ù-fó?   'one mouth'
     cl. 3-mouth cl. 3-one

(16) ɓ-úm   ɓʌ-cèm   'all the people, everybody'
     cl. 2-people cl. 2-all

(17) ty-ɔ́l   tì-cèm | tì-ɔ́l' tì-cèm | 'all the stars'
     cl. 13-star cl. 13-all

3.3 Dependent prefixes II (pronominal)

These are L in cl. 1 and 9 and H (accented) in other classes. They mark agreement on a large number of determiners.

3.3.1 Anaphoric -v̀n

The anaphoric stem-vowel assimilates to the vowel of the prefix, with the following results: ɛ after [+back] v, i after [>high] v. In classes 1 and 9, the anaphoric stem is preceded by -nɔ́:

cl. 1   à-néèn | à-nɔ̀-èn | 2   ɓéèn | ɓʌ́-èn |
     5   dḯin | dí-in | 6   méèn | mʌ́-èn |
     9   ì-néèn | ì-nɔ̀-èn | 10 yíin | í-ìn |
     19 fíin | fí-ìn | 13 tíin | tí-ìn |

The tones remain the same whenever the DP is H (i.e. in all classes but 1 and 9) and the tone pattern of the previous noun stem is BB, BH or HH, or whenever the DP is L (cl. 1 and 9) and the noun stem LL:

(18) d-ùm   d-íin | dì-ùm` dí-in | 'the stomach in question'
(19) mʌ̀-fōm   m-éèn | mʌ̀-fòm' mʌ́-èn | 'the chiefs in question'
(20) béé   y-íin | ǹ-béé'   í-èn | 'the path in question'
(21) ŋàm   ì-néèn | ǹ-ŋàm`   ì-nɔ̀-èn | 'the animal in question'

In all other cases, the anaphoric is realized L:

(22) ŋás ì-néèn   [ì-nèn] | ǹ-ŋás`   ì-nɔ̀-èn | 'the sesame in question'
(23) mʌ̀-ní?'m-éèn   [m-èn] | mʌ̀-ní?` mʌ́-èn | 'the water in question'
(24) gíp á-ˈnéèn   [á-nèn] | ǹ-yíp'   à-nɔ̀-èn | 'the woman in question'
(25) béé ì-ˈnéèn   [í-nèn] | ǹ-béé'   ì-nɔ̀-èn | 'the path in question'

3.3.2 Indefinite -dʌ́ʌ́ŋ 'other, some'

(26) m-úm   à-dʌ́ʌ́ŋ | mʌ̀-úm` à-dèéŋ | 'another/some person'
     cl. 1-person cl. 1-other

(27) *βì-té*   *βí-dλλη* | *βì-té' βí-dèéη* | 'other/some trees'
      cl. 8-tree   cl. 8-other

3.3.3 Possessives

		Singular	Plural
	1st	*-èm*	*-ís*
Persons	2nd	*-ɔ́ɔ́*	*-ín*
	3rd	*-íí*	*-áá*

The forms resulting from the coalescence of the DP with these stems, are under the influence of the previous noun stem:

(28) *m-án*   *w-èm* | *mλ-án` ù-èm* | 'my child'
      cl. 1-child   cl. 1-my

(29) *gíp*   *w-éèm* | *n-yíp' ù-èm* | 'my wife'
      cl. 1+woman   cl. 1-my

(30) *béé*   *y-íìs* | *ǹ-béé` ì-ís| 'his path'
      cl. 9+path   cl. 1-his

(31) *c-éé*   *'k-ɔ́ɔ́* | *c-éé` kí-ɔ́ɔ́* | 'your palm bunch'
      cl. 7-bunch (palm) cl. 7-ton

(32) *fì-fín*   *f-íí* | *fì-fín' fí-íí* | 'his dirt'
      cl. 19-dirt   cl. 19-his

3.3.4 Dependent interrogatives *-áη* 'how many/much?' et *-bé* 'which?'

(33) *béé*   *y-áη* | *ǹ-béé' i-áη* | 'how many paths?'
      cl. 10+path   cl. 10-how many?

(34) *m-án*   *à-bé* | *mλ-án` à-bé* | 'which child?'
      cl. 1-child   cl. 1-which?

(35) *β-úm*   *'βλ- 'bé* | *βλ-úm` βλ-bé* | 'which people?'
      cl. 2-person   cl. 2-which?

3.3.5 Adjective

Within the phrase (NP-N+PII-Adj.) except in cl. 1 and 9:

(36) *β-úm*   *'βλ-'púp* | *βλ-úm` βλ-púp* | 'white persons'
      cl. 2-person   cl. 2-white

(37) *c-ó?*   *kí- 'fín* | *kì-ók' ki-fín* | 'a black forest'
      cl. 7-forest   cl. 7-black

(38) *β-úm*   *'βλ-βàη* | *βλ-úm` βλ-βàη* | 'brown people'
      cl. 2-person   cl. 2-red, brown

In cl. 1 et 9, the 'adjective' behaves as a cl. 1 nominal:

(39) *m-án*   *à*   *ǹ-fín* | *mλ-án` à ǹ-fín* | 'a black child'
      cl. 1-child cl. 1   cl. 1-(the) black

(40) záʔ   ì   ǹ-púp | ǹ-sák´ i ǹ-púp | 'a white chicken'
      cl. 9+chicken   cl. 9   cl. 1-(the) white

3.3.5.1 Nominal substitutive

Apart from cl. 1 (ɲí or ɲí) (which is an unanalyzable morpheme, like the person markers), nominal substitutives are based on a stem -ɔ́:

Person markers					
	Singular			**Plural**	
1st	| mà |	mà	lère	| mìnì |	mìnì
2nd	| wɔ̀ |	wɔ̀, wà	2ème	| ɓìsì |	ɓìsì
Nominal substitutives					
	Singular			**Plural**	
cl. 1	| ɲí |	ɲí	cl. 2	| ɓʌ́-ɔ́ |	ɓ-ɔ́
3	| ú-ɔ́ |	w-ɔ́	4	| mʌ́-ɔ́ |	m-ɔ́
5	| dî-ɔ́ |	dy-ɔ́	6	| mʌ́-ɔ́ |	m-ɔ́
7	| kî-ɔ́ |	k-ɔ́	8	| ɓî-ɔ́ |	ɓy-ɔ́
9	| ì-ɔ́ |	y-ɔ̀	10	| í-ɔ́ |	y-ɔ́
19	|| fî-ɔ́ |	fy-ɔ́	19	| tî-ɔ́ |	ty-ɔ́

(41) à-fá   ɲí   ɓy-ɛ́n   'She gives him (cl. 1) meat'
      cl. 1-give him (cl. 1) cl. 8-meat

(42) à-fá   y-ɔ̀ ɓy-ɛ́n | ì-ɔ́ | 'She gives it (cl. 9) meat'
      cl. 1-give cl. 9-it cl. 8-meat

(43) ɓʌ̀-ɓóʔ   'ɓ-ɔ́ | ɓʌ̀-ɔ́ | 'They beat them (cl. 2)'
      cl. 2-beat cl. 2-they

DP II serve also as demonstratives (with an element -nɔ́ in cl. 1 et 9):

(44) ɗ-ùm   ɗì | ɗì-ùm` ɗì | 'this stomach'
      cl. 5-stomach   cl. 5

(45) ì-sík   `kì     | kì-sík` kì | 'this lid'
      cl. 7-lid   cl. 7

(46) gíp   á- `nɔ́ | ǹ-yíp´ à-nɔ́ | 'this woman'
      cl. 1+woman   cl. 1-this

(47) ɲàm   ì-nɔ́ | ǹ-ɲàm` ì-nɔ́ | 'this animal'
      cl. 9+animal   cl. 9-this

3.4 Dependent prefixes III

Due to their formal identity we designate thus the connective, or genitive marker, the prefixe of numeral stems (2 to 5) and the verbal subject prefix. For the distinction DP II/DP III, see above:

(48) ɲàm   ì   c-óʔ | ǹ-ɲàm` ì kì-óʔ` |
      cl. 9+animal cl. 9   cl. 7-forest
      'animal of the forest'

(49) ty-òŋ   tí   ɓʌ́-'yíp | tì-òŋ` tí' ɓʌ̀-yíp' |
      cl. 13-hair   cl. 13   cl. 2-woman
      'women's hair'

(50) ɓì-té   ɓí-ráá | ɓì-té' ɓí'-ráá | 'three trees'
      cl. 8-tree   cl. 8-three

(51) m-íʔ   mʌ́-nîin | mʌ̀-ìk' mʌ́'-nìn | 'four eggs'
      cl. 6-egg   cl.6 -four

(52) kì-té   kí-kpíì | kì-té' kí' -kpì | 'the tree falls'
      cl. 7-tree   cl. 7-fall

4 DIMINUTIVE AND AUGMENTATIVE

These are originally nouns (*m-án/ɓ-ɔ́n* 'child/children' and *c-óm/ɓy-óm* 'thing(s)'). They still keep the tonal trace of the corresponding connective (L in cl. 1, H in 2, 7 and 8). In principle, nominal qualifiers take the class concords of the diminutive (1/2) or augmentative (7/8).

(53) <u>m-áà</u>   záʔ   <u>á</u>   ṅ-púp | mʌ̀-áá` ṅ-sák' à ṅ-púp |
      <u>cl. 1</u>-small cl. 9+chicken <u>cl. 1</u> cl. 1-the white
      'the small white chicken'

(54) <u>c-óó</u>   ṅ- 'tó   `<u>kí</u>   'zyón      | <u>kì</u>-óó' mù-tó` kí' ṅ-syón` |
      <u>cl. 7</u>-big   cl. 3-head   <u>cl. 7</u> cl. 9+antelope sp.
      'big head of the antelope'

However, if the genitive reference is that of container to content, the head nominal can determine the concord (especially with the augmentative):

(55) c-óó   <u>bós</u>   <u>ì</u>   m-élì | kì-óó' ṅ-bós` ì mʌ̀-élì` |
      cl. 7-big   <u>cl. 9</u>+calabash <u>cl. 9</u> cl. 6-milk
      'a big calabash of milk'

5 VERB MORPHOLOGY

The maximal verb structure is: Prefix-VM1-**RAD** (-extensions) -VM2 -VM3 -VM3' -VM3".
The markers generally coalesce with surface results often quite different from their underlying shape.

5.1 Extensions

-sì (-zì) CAUSative, *-àʔ* HABitual, *-ì* INTRransitive, *-tì (-dʼì)* PERsistive (Intensive), *-kì (=-gì (?))* ITERative, *-(C)èn* REFlexive=RECiprocal. Two extensions in succession can be seen in the following example:

(56) à-pwágìtì   ɓʌ̀-kām   'He gnaws the lianas'
      cl. 1-gnaw (ITER, PER)   cl. 2-liana

Extensions of the type -(C)èn, glossed as REFlexive, take a reciprocal meaning with a plural subject marker:

(57)   *m-úm*   *à-kwíí*   *m-án* | *à-kúl-ɨ* |
       cl. 1-person cl. 1-beat+PFV cl. 1-child
       'The person beat the child.'

(58)   *m-úm*   *á-kúlènkúlèn* | *à-ǿ-kúlénkúlèn* |
       cl. 1-person cl. 1+PROG- beat oneself (REF, CONT)
       'The person is beating himself.'

(59)   *ɓ-ɔ́n*   *ɓéè-kúlènkúlèn* | *ɓʌ́' -ê-kúlénkúlèn* |
       cl. 2-child   cl. 2+PROG-fight (REF, CONT)
       'Children fight (with one another).'

These same extensions when preceded by certain consonants indicate, besides reflexive, strong involvement of the agent, sometimes combined with passive (-*mèn*), associative, causative (-*sèn, -zèn*), intensive (haphazard) (-*tèn, -dèn*), applicative or autobenefactive (-*rèn*).

-sì?	'catch unawares'	*-sìkmèn*	'be caught unawares'
-yé?, -yérì	'acquiesce'	*-yéésèn*	'salute'
-sàà	'spill'	*-sààtèn*	'disperse (intr.)'
-fɔ̀?	'think, measure'	*-fɔ̀ɔ̀rèn*	'attempt, try'

5.2 Indicative verb forms

They always include a person marker or DP III and often other prefixes and/or suffixes.

Person markers					
Singular			Plural		
1st	| mʌ̀- |	ǹ-C, m-	1st	| tì- |	tì-C, ty-V
2nd	| wʌ̀- |	ù-C, w-V	2nd	| ɓì- |	ɓì-C, ɓy-V
Class prefixes					
Singular			Plural		
1	| à- |	à-	2	| ɓʌ́- |	ɓʌ́-C, ɓ-V
3	| ú'- |	ú-C, w-V	4	| mʌ́- |	mʌ́-C, m-V
5	|dɨ̃'- |	dɨ-C, dy-V	6	| mʌ́- |	mʌ́-C, m-V
7	| kɨ́'- |	kɨ-C, k-V	8	| ɓí'- |	ɓì-C, ɓy-V
9	| ì- |	ì-C, y-V	10	| í'- |	í-C, y-V
19	| fĩ'- |	fɨ-C, fy-V	13	| tí'- |	tɨ-C, ty-V

5.3 Prefixes (VM1)

These generally refer more to aspect than tense. Two sub-categories can be distinguished (VM1 and VM1') according to their combinatory possibilities.

VM1	-á- -ń- -ê- -rí-	IMMediate MIDdlle PROGressive HYPOthetical	Same day Previous days In progress Possible but not certain
VM1'	-mʌ̀- -ká- -kí-	INCEPtive ANTerior CONClusive	Intended or initiated action Action previous to another Action taking place eventually (unexpectedly)

5.4 Suffixes

5.4.1 VM2

They mostly have modal value (view of the speaker on the process): Perfective (PFV - realis), Imperfective (IPFV - virtual), RETrospective.

-i̧-	PFV	Realis: Action viewed as certain
-MET-	IPFV	Virtual: Action viewed as non-certain
-yà-	RET	Action viewed as prerequisite to another

The verbal radical (± ext.) with or without VM2 suffixes (-ø-=no VM2). VM1 and VM1' necessarily combine with VM2: VM1+PFV, VM1'+IPFV ou RET. Imperfective is manifested by METatony: a H associates to the post-radical syllables (extensions or reduplicated part) as well as to a following non-accented L syllable, if and only if the verb is not phrase-final (see examples below).

			-ø-	-í- PFV	-MET- IPFV	-yà- RET
					VM2	
VM1	-ø- -á- -ń-	 IMM MID	+ 	+ + +		+
VM1'	-ê- -rí- -mʌ́- -ká- -kí-	PROG HYPO INCEP ANT CONC	 (+) (+)	+ + + + +	+ + +

5.4.1.1 -ø- R -ø-

This form is neutral as to aspect or mood:

(60) ń-yù   'I come'
       I come

(61) m-án   à-ɓʌ́ʔ   'ŋw-áp | -ɓék | 'The child breaks the branch'
       cl. 1-child cl. 1-break cl. 3-branch

(62) kì-té   kí-kpîi | kí' -kpì | 'The tree falls'
       cl. 7-tree   cl. 7-fall

It is found in clauses referring to actions consecutive to a previous (main) clause:

(63)   *m-án*   *à-kèn*   *á*   *fy-èè,*   *à-là?*   *bì-zén*
      cl. 1-child cl. 1-go   to   cl. 19-market   /   cl. 1-buy   cl. 7-fish
      'The child goes to the market and buys fish.'

(64)   *zyón*   *i-rén*   *ǹ-kpás,*   *i-bó?*   *ǹ-gón*
      cl. 9+Antelope sp.   cl. 9-cut   cl. 3-whip   /   cl. 9-beat   cl. 1-Panther
      'Antelope sp. cuts a whip and beats Panther.'

5.4.1.2 -ø- R -VM2

-ø- R -ɨ

-CVC (p, ?)+-ɨ>+-consonant alternation (see above).
-CV- et -CVn+-ɨ>lengthening of radical V.

(65)   *ǹ-yùú* | *-yù-ɨ* | 'I came'
      I-come+PFV

(66)   *ù-kpìí* | *-kpì-ɨ* | 'You fell'
      you -fall+PFV

(67)   *à-bóó*   *'róó 'róp* | *-bóó-ɨ* | 'He treated the sick person'
      cl. 1-treat+PFV   cl. 1a+sick person

(68)   *bʌ̀-yéé*   *zò?* | *-yén-ɨ* | 'They saw an elephant'
      cl. 2-see+PFV   cl. 9+elephant

-ø- R -ɣà

-ɣà (nasal C-ɣà>-gà, CVk-ɣà>kà, CVl-ɣà>là) is most frequent in oral literature texts, especially in main clauses of complex sentences where it defines the background to the process:

(69)   *bèl*   *i-bá-ɣà*   *rì*   *b-ɔ́n*   *b-íí*   *bʌ̀- 'ráá*
      cl. 9+Ancestor   cl. 9-be-RET   with   cl. 2-child   cl. 2-his   cl. 2-three
      'God had three children ...'

(70)   *ń 'nɔ̀ ɨ*   *à-bɔ́k-à*   *mʌ́-tén,*   *à-té?*   *mʌ̀-rɔ̀?*
      then   if   cl. 1-climb-RET   cl. 6-palm-tree   /   cl. 1-take   cl. 6-wine
      'Then, if he climbed the palm-trees, he tapped wine.'

(71)   *yèé*   *gém*   *i-kpì-ɣà,*   *i-búnbùn*   *c-ā?*
      when   cl. 9+monkey   cl. 9-fall-RET   /   cl. 9-break (CONT)   cl. 7-arm
      'When the monkey fell, he broke his arm.'

5.4.1.3 -VM1- R- VM2

- á- R -ɨ

(72)   *à-á-'yál-ɨ*   *rì-fǎs* | *à-á-yál-ɨ* |
      cl. 1-IMM-give birth-PFV   cl. 5-twins
      'She gave birth to twins (today).'

- ń- R -ɨ

(73) βì-ń-kèé   á   fy-èè | βì-ń-kèn-ɨ|
      you-MID-go+PFV   to   cl. 13-market
      'You went to the market.'

5.4.1.4 -VM1'- R- VM2

This form includes a VM1' (PROG, HYP, INCEP, ANT, CONC) which, apart from PROG, is generally found in dependent clauses of complex sentences.

- ê- R - MET

-ê- is in fact likely to be the same morpheme (FOCUS) found in the presentative nominal form, as well as in focalization (see below):

(74) rì-fòm   dy-éè   dɨ | dɨ' -ê dɨ | 'Here is the chief.'
      cl. 5-chief   cl.5 -FOC   cl. 5

(75) zɨ   y-éè-nə | ì-ê ì-nə | 'Here is the land.'
      cl. 9-land   cl. 1-FOC-cl. 9+this

(76) c-óʔ   k-éè   k-ìn | kɨ' -ê kɨ-ìn | 'Here is the forest in question.'
      cl. 7-forest cl. 7-FOC   cl. 7-ANAPH

The use of -ê- in verb forms is accompanied by reduplication of the stem (CONTINUOUS). The following examples show the identity of the PROG form with those involving focalization of the subject.

(77) ǹ-dém   w-éè-fáfá   'bwáp | ú' -ê-fáfá-MET |
      cl. 3-heart   cl. 3-PROG-give (CONT)+IPFV   cl. 9+blood
      '(It is) the heart (which) gives blood.'

(78) kì-púŋ   k-éè-bóʔbóʔ   kì-'té | kɨ' -ê-bókbòk-MET|
      'cl. 7-albino   cl. 7-PROG-hit (CONT)+IPFV   cl.7-tree'
      '(It is) the albino (which) is hitting the tree.'

With subject markers for persons and cl. 1 and 9, PROG adds a H to their basic L tone.

(79) tí-kènkèn   'We are going' | tì-ǿ-kènkèn-(MET)|
      we+PROG-go (CONT)+(IPFV)

(80) á- 'dídɨ   ì- 'pén   ' He is eating fufu' | à-ǿ-dídɨ-MET |
      cl. 1+PROG-eat+IPFV   cl.7-stiff porridge

- rɨ- R -MET

(81) à-rì- 'kpáŋ   rì   'dúrì | à-rì-kpáŋ-MET |
      cl. 1-HPYO-leave+PFV   with   cl. 9+dawn
      'He would go tomorrow.'

- m à- R -MET

(82) d-ùm   dì-mǎ- 'tórèn   ɲì   fʌlʌ | dɨ' -mʌ-tórèn-MET |
      cl. 5-stomach cl. 5-INCEP-swell+IPFV   him   thus
      'His stomach starts swelling.'

(83) *ń̀ nɔ́ sɔ́m <u>à-mʌ́-pèèsí</u> tí- 'wón* | *à-mʌ́-pèèsì-MET* |
then cl. 1a+giant rat cl. 1-INCEP-lift+IPFV 13-firewood
'Then Giant Rat attempts to lift the firewood'

(84) *'kúl*   <u>*à-mʌ́- 'kpáŋ-yì*</u>, | *à-mʌ́-kpáŋ-MET-yì* |
cl. 1a+tortoise cl. 1-INCEP-come out+IPFV-DIR /
'As soon as Tortoise comes out, …'

- ká- R -MET

(85) *ɓʌ́-ká- 'káá*   *kí- 'ʃɔ́?*   *kí   fí- 'róp* | *ɓʌ́' -ká-káá-MET kì-syék|*
cl. 2-ANT-search+IPFV cl. 7-disease cl. 7 cl. 19-illness
'They first of all look for the disease (which is at the base) of this illness.'

(86) <u>*à-kà-lɔ̀ksí-ɓí*</u>   *kì-fáà   m-ɔ̀nі́   mʌ́   mʌ́- 'yín*
cl. 1-ANT-finish+IPFV-NEG cl. 7-give cl. 6-money cl. 7 cl. 6-
                                                                  bridewealth
'He hasn't finished yet to pay the bridewealth.'

- kí- R -MET

(87) *à-kí- 'té?*   *kí-làà* | *à-kí-tét-MET kì-làà`* |
cl. 1-CONC-take+IPFV cl. 7-clothes
'He eventually takes the clothes.'

(88) *d-ùm*   *dí-mіkì*,   <u>*dí-kí-tètè?*</u> | *dі́' -kí-tètèt-(MET)* |
cl. 5-stomach cl. 5-swell / cl. 5-CONC-harden (CONT)+(IPFV)
'…, the stomach swells and eventually hardens'

(89) *…<u>à-kí- 'túm</u>*   *rí-tʌ̀?*   *dі̀ ɓʌ́- 'yíp* | *à-kí-túm-MET* |
cl. 1-CONC-begin+IPFV cl. 5-abduction cl. 5 cl. 2-woman
'…, he eventually abducts women.'

- kí- R - í

(90) <u>*ú-kí-yùú*</u>   *á   (ì-)lɔ̀ŋ   k-íí,* | *í ù-kí-yù-í·|*
if+you-CONC-come+PFV in   (cl. 7-)home cl. 7-sa
ù-kɔ̀rì   *fɔ̀   ɓí*   *'dɛ́m*
you-stay   here at   cl. 9+field
'If you eventually come to his place, you stay here in the field.'

-MV1'- R -γà

(91) *à-mʌ́- 'wélà*   *ɲí* | *à-mʌ́-wél-γà* | 'He had tried to kill him.'
cl. 1-INCEP-kill+RET him (cl. 1)

(92) *à-ká-kèn-gà* | *à-ká-kèn-yà* | 'He had gone at first.'
cl. 1-ANT-go-RET

(93) *à-kí- 'rén-gà* | *à-kí-rén-yà* | 'He had eventually cut.'
cl. 1-CONC- cut-RET

		DIR -yì	POT -gá	NEG -6í´
-í-	PFV	+	+	+
-MET-	IPFV	−	−	+
-yà-	RET	+	−	+

5.4.2 VM3

Three markers are suffixes to the verb stem (with or without VM2). They can combine, which justifies their being distinguished as VM3 (DIRectional (centrifugal)), VM3' (POTential), VM3" (NEGative).

(94) 6á-yéèn-yì   fì-rāp   'They see from afar.'
      cl. 2-see-DIR   cl. 19-(the) remote

-gá generally combines with PFV, even when the VM1 is rí- (only possibility), in spite of the fact that this marker is normally accompanied by MET.

(95) à-kpáŋ-í- 'gá
      cl. 1-leave-PFV-POT
      'He may/might leave.'

(96) à-rí- 'kpáŋ   rì   'dúrí | à-rí-kpáŋ-MET |
      cl. 1-HYPO-leave+IPFV   with cl. 9-tomorrow
      'He'd leave tomorrow.'

(97) à-rí- 'kpáŋ-í- 'gá
      cl. 1-HYPO-leave-PFV-POT
      'He'll doubtless leave.'

Use of gá as a noun in the following proverb, plus its initial [+voice] consonant (cl. 9?) suggest a nominal origin.

(98) ìsóŋ   à   ǹ-búsì   à-rɔ̀kà   gá | à-rék-yà ǹ-gá |
      cl 1a+Isong cl. 1 cl. 1-Mbusi cl. 1-prohibit+RET cl. 9+future
      'A man called Isong (son) of Mbusi had prohibited the future.' (i.e. never put
      off until tomorrow...)

6í |-6í´ | is used in simple sentences, in combination with PFV or RET.

(99) à-kpáŋ-í- '6í   'He hasn't left.'
      cl. 1-leave-PFV-NEG

(100) à-kpágà-6í | à-kpáŋ-gà-6í´ | 'He hadn't left.'
      cl. 1-leave+RET-NEG

In complex sentences, it only appears in the main clause or in a conditional or causal dependent clause.

(101) mà   ǹ-tánéé- '6í   c-óm,   c-óm   kí-yín   6í rì-6éé
      I   I-meet+PFV-NEG   cl. 7-thing / cl. 7-thing cl. 7-not be in cl. 5-pit
      'I didn't find anything, there is nothing in the pit.'

(102) ì   6á-kà-kìì- '6í   kì- 'ʃɔ́ʔ   k-ìn ...
      if cl. 2-ANT-do+PFV-NEG   cl. 7-cure sp. cl. 7-ANAPH
      'If you don't first do the kì-ʃɔ́ʔ, ...'

(103) à-kpáŋ-í   'lá   ù-yùú-6í
      cl. 1-leave-PFV   because you-come+PFV-NEG
      'He left because you hadn't come.'

Apart from the above contexts, negation is rendered by a morpheme *kèè* 'without' plus the injunctive (cf. negative injunctive).

-ɓí appears also in a verb form found in sayings expressing a prohibition and having a marker *-â-* (?), always in combination with IPFV.

(104)   <u>*ɓ-áà-fyàrì-ɓí*</u>   *ń-kēn* | *ɓʌ́' -â-fyàrì-*MET-*ɓí'* |
       cl. 2-?-disappoint+IPFV-NEG   cl. 1-stranger
       'One does not disappoint a stranger.'

(105)   *gépsèn*   <u>*y-áà-ɓá-ɓí*</u>   *kì-* '*ɓʌ́?*   *kì-fó?* | *ì-â-ɓá-*MET-*ɓí'* |
       cl. 9+help   cl. 9-?-be+IPFV-NEG   cl. 7-side   cl. 7-one
       'Aid should not always be one-sided.'

If the subject is in cl. 1, the shape of the marker is *-mâ-* instead of *-â-*, thus | *à-ø-mâ-R-*MET-*ɓí* | :

(106)   *ǹ-kēn*   <u>*á-máà-sì?-ɓí*</u>   *zì*
       cl. 1-stranger   cl. 1+PROG-?-have an exclusive privilege+IPFV-NEG   cl. 9-land
       'A stranger cannot have exclusive usage of the land.' | *à-mâ-sìk-*MET-*ɓí'* |

Another example also illustrates how *-â-* combines with a VM1' (ANT):

(107)   <u>*w-áà-ká-dî-ɓí*</u>   *ì-* '*dyán*   *lʌ́cé* | *ù-â-ká-dî-*MET-*ɓí'* |
       you -?-ANT-eat+IPFV-NEG   cl. 7-cassava   why?
       'Why don't you eat cassava leaves instead?'

5.5 Imperative

Affirmative imperative is formed with a suffix *-á* (plural *-ì ná*), without person marker:

(108)   (a) *yén-á*   (b) *yén-ì 'ná*
         look-IMP   look-IMP pl.
         'Look (sg.)!'   'Look (pl.)!'

If the verb stem ends with an extension, this associates to a H tone:

(109)   (a) *pèèsén*   (b) *pèèsén-ì 'ná*
         go away+IMP   go away+IMP pl.
         'Go away (sg.)!'   'Go away (pl.)!'

The shape of the negative imperative is identical to the negative INJunctive (see below).

5.6 Affirmative injunctive

The INJunctive has the following characteristics: H tone for all subject markers (in the case of the basically L-toned person and cl. 1 subject markers, this H superimposes itself on the L) followed by HB(H) for the verb stem; if both the subject marker and the verb radical are H, there is no change:

(110)   *tí-kéèn* | *tì-----kèn* | 'Let's go!'
         we+INJ-go   ⌒

(111)   *á-dîì*   *kì-pén* | *à-----dî* | 'Let him eat fufu!'
         cl. 1+INJ-eat   cl. 7-fufu

(112)   *ɓá-kéèn* | *ɓá'-∽-kèn* | 'Let them go!'
        cl. 2+INJ-go

(113)   *ɓá-pésì*   *tì-wón* | *ɓá'-∽-pèsì* | 'Let them lift the logs!'
        cl. 2-+INJ-lift   cl. 13- log

(114)   *ɓá-yéésì*   *ɓλ-génì* | *ɓá'-∽-yéésì* | 'Let them pester the
        cl. 2+INJ-annoy   cl. 2-brother   brothers'!

(115)   *á-yèèsí*   *ɓá-génì* | *à-∽-yéésì* | 'Let him pester the brothers'!
        cl. 1+INJ-annoy   cl. 2-brother

(116)   (a) *ɓá-dì*   *kì-pén* | *ɓá'-∽-dì* | 'Let them eat fufu'!
        cl. 2+INJ-eat   cl. 7-fufu

5.7 Negative imperative/injunctive

These are formed from the Injunctive combined with the morpheme *kèè*, marking negative noun coordination (*kèè m-ɔní* 'without money'). *kèè* follows the lexical subject, the independent personal pronoun, the subject marker for persons and cl. other than 1 and 9; with cl. 1 and 9 it precedes the subject marker. In the cases where it follows the subject marker, it seems to coalesce with FOC (see PROG). The general scheme is:

IPP	*kèè*	IP	
(NP)	*kèè*	I cl. (+FOC)	+ INJ-RAD + IPFV
(NP)	I cl.+FOC	*kèè*	

(116)   (b) *kɔɔ-'dì*   *í-'pén* |*kèè-ù _∠ ∠ ∠ _ dí-*MET|
        without+you+ INJ-eat+ IPFV   cl. 7-fufu
        'Don't eat fufu!'

(117)   *kèè-'kpáŋ*   'Don't go (pl.)'! |*kèè-à _∠ ∠ ∠ _ kpáŋ-*MET|
        without-you+ INJ-leave(+ IPFV)

Negative Injunctive appears in negative main clauses preceded by a dependent condition clause and in certain negative dependent clauses.

(118)   *í   ù-tɔɔ-'ɓì*   *bóòbó,*   *kɔɔ-wɔn* |*kèè-ù _∠ ∠ ∠ _wɔn-*MET|
        if   you-take+PFV-NEG   cl. 9+medicine/ without+you + INJ-recover+ IPFV
        'If you don't take the medicine, you won't recover.'

(119)   *ù-rì-'tɔʔ*   *m-éé*   *m-íí,*   *kèé-'kálì*   *wɔ̀*
        you-HYP-ask+IPFV   cl. 6-house   cl. 6-his/   without+cl. 1+INJ-tell+IPFV   you
        |*kèè-à_∠ ∠ ∠ _kálì-*MET| 'If you asked him where his house is, he wouldn't tell
        you'

(120)   *rì-fōm*   *dý-áá-'kpáŋ-i*   *kèè-dý-éè-yén*   *'m-án*
        cl. 5-chief   cl. 5-IMM-leave-PFV/without-cl. 5-FOC+INJ-see+IPFV   cl. 1-child
        'The chief left without seeing the child.' | *kèè dí'-ê_∠ ∠ ∠ _ yén-*MET |

(121) à-á-kàŋ-ɨ   bú   lɨ́   <u>yè-kéè-ɗɨ</u>   6y-én
      cl. 1-IMM-tie-PFV cl. 9+dog   so that cl. 9+FOC+without   cl. 8-meat
                                             +INJ+eat+IPFV
      'He tied the dog so that it should not eat the meat.' | i-ê-kèè--⌁-ɗɨ-MET |

5.8 Other verb forms

Other verb forms include a 'verboid' stem (without any marker) or a motion verb followed by another verb. Verboids are: *-rɨ* 'be', *-tɨ* 'be (PFV)' and *-yín* 'be (NEG)'

(122) à-rɨ   á   'm-ɛ́ɛ́   'He is at home.'
      cl. 1-be   at   cl. 6-house

(123) à-rɨ   ǹ-fɔ́lén   'He is tired.'
      cl. 1-be   cl. 1-tired

(124) à-rɨ   rɨ   ty-óŋ   tɨ-fín   'He has black hair.'
      cl. 1-be   with   cl. 13-hair   cl. 13-nlack

(125) à-tɨ   á   ǹ-syòm   'He already was at
      cl. 1-be (PFV) at   cl. 3-river   the river.'

(126) à-yín   á   'm-ɛ́ɛ́   'He is not at home.'
      cl. 1-be (NEG) at   cl. 6-house

In all verb forms including a 'verboid', this can be considered as a modal auxiliary.

5.8.1 *cl.-*t̲ɨ̲*+cl.-Verb* (CONT, HAB, PER, ITER)

These utterances refer to actions performed either habitually or exclusively:

(127) wɔ̀-tɨ   wɔ̀-fyə̀gà?-yɨ   fə̀   yɔ́   'Which way do
                                                                 you usually pass?'
      you -be (PFV) you-pass (HAB)-DIR   where?   INTERR

(128) à-tɨ   à-kwéngɨ   réès   'He only likes rice'
      cl. 1-be (PFV) cl. 1-take (ITER)   cl. 1a+rice

5.8.2 *cl. -*r̲ɨ̲, *-*t̲ɨ̲ *or -*y̲í̲n̲*+*l̲ɨ̲́*+cl.-Verb*

In their various combinations (±INJ), these forms refer to the possibility, impossibility or
intention to carry out an action:

(129) à-rɨ   lɨ́   à-kèn   'He could go.'
      cl. 1-be   in order to cl. 1- go

(130) à-tɨ   lɨ́   à-kèn   'He can go.'
      cl. 1-be (PFV) in order to cl. 1- go

(131) à-yín   lɨ́   à-kèn   'He cannot go.'
      cl. 1-not be in order to cl. 1- go

(132) à-tɨ   lɨ́   á-kéèn   'He is ready to go.'
      cl. 1-be (PFV) in order to cl. 1+INJ-go

(133) à-yín   lɨ́   á-kéèn   'It is impossible for him to go.'
      cl. 1-not be in order to cl. 1+INJ-go

5.8.3 cl.-Motion verb+cl.-Verb

These utterances appear as juxtaposed clauses (same subject in both, with the second a consequence of the first), but the first verb behaves as an auxiliary (i.e. no VM, nor complement) only the second is semantically defined, the whole being indissociable.

(134)　*m-úm*　　　　*à-kèn*　　　*à-ɲáàmzèn*　'The person goes into hiding.'
　　　　cl. 1-person　cl. 1-go　　cl. 1-hider

(135)　*ǹ-yù*　　　　*ǹ-téʔ*　　　*wɔ̀*　　　'I've come to fetch you.'
　　　　I-come　　　I-take　　　you

(136)　*tì-wón*　　　　*tí-yúù*　　　*tí-káàŋ*　*rì*　*kì-té*
　　　　cl. 13-firewood　cl. 13-come　cl. 13-tie　with　cl. 7-tree
　　　　'The firewood had come and tied itself to the tree.'

6 SENTENCE STRUCTURE

Word order is Subject Predicate Complement. Complements can be either direct or indirect. If only one direct (non-circumstantial) complement appears, it generally refers to the object (patient):

(137)　*màá-làà*　　　　　　　*ɲás*　　　'I bought sesame.'
　　　　I+PRO-buy+PFV　　　cl. 9+sesame

(138)　*bá-túm*　　*dì-rén*　　　'They start crying.'
　　　　cl. 2-begin　cl. 5-tear

(139)　*c-ɔɔzèn*　　*kí-kí*　　*ˈm-úm*　　'Heat overwhelms the person.'
　　　　cl. 7-heat　cl. 7-make　cl. 1-person

(140)　*à-ɣáɣì*　　*ì-sénì*　　　'He rushes coming down.'
　　　　cl. 1-rush　cl. 7-coming down

In some such cases, the verb has a more or less fossilized extension -(C)èn ('wash', 'be mistaken', 'forget', 'meet', 'resemble', 'hate') and an object which can be a part of the body, a faculty, a person, etc.:

(141)　*à-sòktènsòktèn*　　　　*by-āʔ*　　　'He washes hands.'
　　　　cl. 1-wash (REF, CONT)　cl. 8-arm, hand

(142)　*à-nànèn*　　　　　　*bì-tòkì*　　　'He talks nonsense.'
　　　　cl. 1-be mistaken　　cl. 8-words, speech

(143)　*gíp*　　　*á-ˈtánèn*　*m-án*　　'The woman meets the child.'
　　　　cl. 1a-woman　cl. 1-meet　cl. 1-child

(144)　*à-dˈìimzèn*　　　　*zēm*　　　'He forgets the machete.'
　　　　cl. 1-forget ('make　cl. 9+machete
　　　　oneself disappear'?)

(145)　*à-pìsèn*　　*génì*　　　*w-íì*　　'He looks like his brother.'
　　　　cl. 1-resemble　cl. 1a+brother　cl. 1-his

A number of examples illustrate the use of a verb with a direct complement which cannot be considered an object:

- V (motion)+Complement (traditional activity). These examples imply that the agent is directly affected. They contrast with examples where the same complement is preceded by a preposition:

(146) (a) à-á-kèé   rì-wéy   (b) à-á-kèé   á   rì-wéy
       cl. 1-IMM-go+PFV cl. 5-wedding   cl. 1-IMM-go+PFV   at   cl. 5-wedding
       'He went and got married.'   'He attended (someone else's) wedding).'

- V (state, change of state, physiology, feeling)+Obligatory Complement (state, attribute of agent, result or cause of process, means by which the agent fulfils or undergoes action):

(147) à-rɔ́p   ì-sékèrì   'He remains a cripple.'
       cl. 1-stay   cl. 7-cripple

(148) à-yáy   ǹ-gɔ́n   'He becomes a panther.'
       cl. 1-become   cl. 1-panther

(149) à-lɔ̀ɔ̀rɛ̀n   ɲàm   'He turns into an animal.'
       cl. 1- turn (int.) cl. 9+animal

(150) ǹ-'dóróp   kí-'tám   'I suffer from an abcess.'
       I+PROG-be sick (CONT)+IPFV   cl. 7-abcess

(151) à-á-'ŋwáŋ-ɨ́   mʌ́-rɔ̀?   mʌ́   bàdzì
       cl. 1-IMM-get drunk -PFV   cl. 6-wine cl. 6 9+maize
       'He got drunk on maize beer.'

(152) à-sɨ̀kmèn   rì-yù   dɨ́   'génì   w-îì
       cl. 1-be surprised cl. 5-coming cl. 5 cl. 1a+brother cl. 1-his
       'He is surprised at his brother's coming.'

In the case of several non-circumstantial direct complements, the order is generally: beneficiary (goal)+object (patient) (+other).

(153) à-fá   'gíp   m-ɔ̀nì   'He gives the woman money.'
       cl. 1-give   cl. 1+woman   cl. 6-money

(154) ból   ì-yóksíí   mʌ̀   gòò
       cl.9+rain   cl. 9-spoil+PFV me   cl. 10+shoe
       'The rain ruined my shoes.'

(155) à-yásì   m-án   ì-yɔ̀?   'He makes the child crazy.'
       cl. 1-make become   cl. 1-child   cl. 7-crazy

With state or motion verbs, the direct complement is generally an adjunct:

	Locative	Temporal	Manner
Interrogative	fɔ̀ 'where ?'	fín 'when?'	lá 'how?'
Affirmative	fʌ́ 'here' wɔ́ 'there' fó 'yonder'	c-èénkò 'evening' géènɔ̀ 'now'	fɔ́lɔ́ 'thus'

(156) wàá-kpìí   'fɔ̀   'Where did you fall?'
       you+IMM-fall+PFV   where?

(157) màá-kpìí   wɔ́   'I fell there.'
       I+IMM-fall+PFV   there

Complements can be indirect (governed by a preposition):

Explaining	ńsóò 'even' lí 'that, such as'
Comparing	yèé 'as'
Associating + —	rì 'with' ɓéè 'together with' kèè 'without' á 'at, to'
Localizing	ɓí 'at, to, on, in, by, towards, from, on account of' yèé 'at (someone's place)'

(158) à-ń-kàŋ-í   bàm   rì   m-áá   ǹ-dʼíʔ
cl. 1-MID-tie-PFV   cl. 1a+bag   with   cl. 1-small   cl. 3-rope
'He tied the bag with a string.'

(159) à-ń-dʼùú   ɓéè   rìŋkàŋ   w-íí
cl. 1-MID-fight-PFV   with   cl. 1a+friend   cl. 1-his
'He fought with his friend.'

(160) à-réli-yà   ɓí   i-té
cl. 1-stand-RET   on   cl. 7-tree
'He was standing on the tree.'

(161) ɓí-fɔ̀ʔ   ɓí-ɓɔ́ʔ   ɓí   ǹ-tó   ɓí   mí-cèp
cl. 2-thought   cl. 1-rise   in   cl. 3-head   through   cl. 6-vein, nerve
'Thoughts ascend to the head through conduits.'

(162) à-pèèséé-yì   ɓí   náá.à.ʒày
cl. 1-leave+PFV-DIR   from   prison (hunger room)
'He came out of jail.'

(163) à-á-kèè   rì-wéy   yèé   rí-fōm
cl. 1-IMM- go+PFV   cl. 5-wedding   at   cl. 5-chief
'He went and got married at the chief's.'

To specify location, á and ɓí combine with a few nouns (zí 'earth, ground', dy-óó 'sky, top', i-sú 'face', jèm 'behind', dy-ɔ̀m 'outside', d-ùm 'stomach, inside', etc.); concords are always determined by the class of the nominal:

(164) á   ˈzí   ì   kì-té   'under the tree'
at   cl. 9+ground   cl. 9   cl. 7-tree

(165) á   ˈsú   ú   gíp   'before the woman'
at   (cl. 3a-)face   cl. 3   cl. 1+woman

(166) ɓí   d-ùm   dí   fì-ˈyɔ́ŋ   'inside the pot'
in   cl. 9-stomach   cl. 5   cl. 19-pot

(167) ɓí   ˈsú   ú   gíp   'in front of the woman'
in   (cl. 3a-)face   cl. 3   cl. 1+woman

These locative phrases can be postposed to the nominal; this implies greater involvement of the agent:

(168) à-kʌ̀ʌ̀kʌ̀ʌ̀   gíp   á   'sú
       cl 1-walk (CONT)   cl. 1+woman   at   (cl. 3a) before
       'He is walking before the woman.'

Direct non-circumstantial complements precede circumstantials (±direct):

(169) à-róòm-yì   ɓʌ̀-géní   6-ìi   'fʌ́
       cl. 1-send-DIR   cl. 2-brother   cl. 2-his   here
       'He sends his brothers here.'

(170) à-tìrì   m-úm   c-āʔ   6ì   6y-ās
       cl. 1-pass   cl. 1-person   cl. 7-hand   on   cl. 8-back
       'He passes his hand on the person's back.'

Several (direct and/or indirect) circumstantial complements can combine:

(171) à-yùú   'fʌ́   'tóróòp
       cl. 1-come+PFV   here   noon
       'He came here at noon.'

(172) à-kɔ̀rì   fó   rì   6-ɔ́
       cl. 1-stay   yonder   with   cl. 2-them
       'He stays there with them.'

(173) à-kpì   rì   ɲí   6ì   mʌ̀-nìʔ
       cl. 1-fall   with   him (cl. 1)   in   cl. 6-water
       'He falls with him into the water.'

When two circumstantial complements (direct+indirect) follow each other, the second refers to the first:

(174) à-nɔ̀ŋì   fʌ́   6ì   'zì
       cl. 1- lie down   here   on   cl. 9+ground
       'He lies down here on the ground.'

6.1 Complex sentences

They are made up of two or more clauses (C) in juxtaposition or linked by a subordinating element (pre- or postposition).

6.1.1 Clauses in juxtaposition

Generally, C2 (subordinate)=explanation or consequence of C1. Formal characteristics: a) no VM in C2; b) if the complement of the verb in C1 is also that of the verb in C2, it is not repeated in the latter; c) a subordinating element (mʌ̀ʔ) can optionnally be inserted in C2.

(175) gíp   á-kèé   á   fy-ēē,   à-làʔ   6ì-zén
       cl. 1+woman   cl. 1-go+PFV   to   cl. 19-market/   cl. 1-buy   cl. 7-fish
       'The woman went to the market and bought fish.'

(176) à-ɓán   'gám,   à-pìʔ   á   'zí
       cl. 1-catch cl. 9+spider/ cl. 1-throw to cl. 9+ground
       'He catches the spider and throws it on the ground.'

(177) à-ɣéé   bùù,   à-dìŋì   mìiʔ
       cl. 1-see+PFV cl. 9+hole/ cl. 1-enter within
       'He sees a hole and enters it.'

6.1.2 Clauses introduced by a subordinating element

There are six subordinating prepositions (P), of which four are also nominal prepositions:

P1	*i* 'if'
	yèé 'as, when'
	ńsóò 'even if'
P2	*lɑ́* 'that, so that, because'
	dì 'while, until, when'
	kèè 'without'

(178) i   ù-kpáŋ-i,   mʌ̀   ǹ-kèn   ìriʔ
       if   you-go-PFV/ I   I-go   too
       'If you go, I go too.'

yèé can introduce C1 or C2.

(179) yèé gém   i-kpì-yà,   i-ɓúnɓùn   c-āʔ
       as   cl. 9+monkey   cl. 9-fall-RET   / cl. 9-break (CONT)   cl. 7-arm
       'As Monkey fell, he broke his arm.'

(180) gɔ̀rɔ̀   yí-súùrèn   ɓí rì-ɓày   lɑ́   rúʔ,
       cl. 10+bird sp cl. 10-return (REF) in cl. 5-river that   in flock /
       yèé yí-ɓá-yày
       as   cl. 10-be-RET+DIR
       'The gɔ̀rɔ̀ birds returned to the river, as they were (before coming).'

ńsóò introduces concessives. It can combine with *yèé* 'as' et avec *lɑ́* 'that':

(181) ńsóò yèé ù-màá   mʌ̀,   ǹ ɓí i-ɓàà
       even as   you-throw+PFV   me   / I on cl. 7-answering
       'Even if you were to reject me, I would answer.'

(182) ńsóò lɑ́   à-yí   mɑ́-yēē,
       even that cl. 1-know   cl. 6-witchcraft/
       wɔ̀   bèy   wè-éè-nɔ̀ɔ́tí   'ɲí
       you cl. 9+God   you-FOC-chase   him (cl. 1)
       'Even if he knows witchcraft, it is you, God, who chase him.'

lɑ́ introduces:

• completives of main clauses whose verb is *-kálì* 'say', *-yén* 'see', *-kɔ̀n* 'want', *-yérèn* 'accept', *-rési* 'show', *-yí* 'know':

(183) à-*káli*   <u>*ki*</u>   *wɔ̀-rì*   *ì-yɔ́?*   'He says that you are mad.'
       cl. 1-say   that   you-be   cl. 7-mad

• purpose or goal clauses:

(184) à-*rì*   *rì*   *kì-ɲáá*   <u>'*ki*</u>   *gíp*   *w-ii*   *à-á-'yál-ì*
       cl. 1-be   with   cl. 7-joy   because   cl. 1+   cl. 1-his   cl. 1-IMM-give
                                  woman   birth-PFV
       'He is happy because his wife gave birth (to a boy).'

dì (cf. *rì* 'with'?) introduces a clause simultaneous with the main clause:

(185) á-*'káákáá*   <u>*dì*</u>   *á-d̀undùn*   'She sings as she is pounding.'
       cl. 1+PROG-sing   while   cl. 1+PROG-pound
       (CONT)+IPFV   (CONT)+IPFV

kèè is a negative coordinating element:

(186) *ù-rì-'tɔ́?*   *m-ɛ́ɛ́*   *m-íí,*   <u>*kèé-kàlì*</u>   *wɔ̀*
       you-HYPO-   cl. 6-house   cl. 6-his/   without+cl. 1+   you
       ask+IPFV   INJ-tell+IPFV
       'If you were to ask him where his house his, he wouldn't tell you.'

6.1.3 Relative clauses

They determine nominals and are always introduced by a demonstrative:

(187) *m-úm*   <u>*à-nɔ̀*</u>   *à-ń-yùú*   *rì*   *ǹ-kòò,*   *à-rì*   *rì-fõm*
       cl. 1-person   cl. 1-this   cl. 1-MID-   with   cl.1(?)-   cl. 1-be   cl. 5-chief
                         come+PFV   yesterday
       'The man who came yesterday is the chief.'

(188) *à-á -'téri*   *kì-làà*   <u>*kí*</u>   *màá-fáá*   *'ɲì*
       cl. 1-IMM-   cl. 7-clothes   cl. 7   1+IMM- give-PFV   him (cl. 1)
       take+PFV
       'He took the clothes I gave him.'

(189) *kpáŋ-á*   *jáŋ*   *ì-nɔ̀*   *wɔ̀-yíí*
       go out-IMP   cl. 9+place   cl. 9 -this   you-know
       'Go out through the place you know.'

6.2 Focalization

Subject focalization is formed with FOCUS *-ê-* and *-rì* 'be' (same tone pattern in all classes, save 1 and 9):

(190) *ɲàm*   *y-ɛ́'ɛ́-rì* | *ǹ-ɲàm` í' -ê-rì* | 'They are animals.'
       cl. 10+animal   cl. 10-FOC-be

(191) *c-ó?*   *k-ɛ́'ɛ́-rì* | *kì-ó?' kí' -ê-rì* | 'It is a forest.'
       cl. 7-forest   cl. 7-FOC-be

(192) *ɲàm*   *y-ɛ̀ɛ́-rì* | *ǹ-ɲàm` ì-ê-rì* | 'It is an animal.'
       cl. 9+animal   cl. 9-FOC-be

In cl. 1, the independent pronoun is used instead of the subject prefix:

(193)   *m-án*   *ńɲéé-rì* | *mà-án`ɲí-ê-rì* | 'He is a child.'
        cl. 1-child   him (cl. 1)-FOC-be

Complement focalization is marked by a presentative construction (with FOC) and preposing of the noun:

(194)   *kì-pén*   *k-èè*   *kì,*   *à-á-ɗíí*   'It is fufu that he ate.'
        cl. 7-fufu   cl. 7-FOC   cl. 7| cl. 1-IMM-eat+PFV

6.3 Thematization

This is indicated by preposing of the complement:

(195)   *bàʔ,*   *bʌ́-báày*   *bí*   *wɔ̀*   'Years, they are counted thanks to you.'
        cl. 10+year   cl. 2-count   on   you (Moon)

This can combine with determination of the complement by a relative clause:

(196)   *b-úm*   *`bʌ́*   *ù-sèèɗì-yà*   *fʌ́ní,*   *ǹ-tòòtóó*   *rì*   *b-ɔ́*
        cl. 2-person   cl. 2   you-take   yonder /   I-speak   with   cl. 2-them
                                  down-RET   (CONT)
        'The people that you had taken down there, I had talked with them.'

Word order change also serves to enhance salience:

(197)   *mʌ́*   *ǹ-yéréè-ʹbí,*   *m-án*   *w-èm,*   *ʹlʌ́*   *á-kéèn*
        I   I-accept+PFV-NEG |cl. 1-child   cl. 1-my /   that   cl. 1+INJ-go
        'I don't accept for my daughter that she should go away.'

REFERENCES

Anderson 1935; Aroga Bessong 1982; Aroga Bessong and Marchal n.d.; Aroga Bessong and Mel'čuk 1983; Guarisma 1980, 1983, 1992, 1994, 2000; Guarisma and Paulian 1986; Kadima 1969; Tessmann 1934;

MAKAA (A83)

Teresa Heath

1 INTRODUCTION

Makaa is spoken in the Upper Nyong department of the Eastern province of the Republic of Cameroon. The Makaa people are a predominantly agricultural society; an estimated 15 percent of the 80,000 speakers live in cities throughout Cameroon.

The Makaa people refer to both themselves and the language as Məkaa. Guthrie (1971) identifies Maka as (A83), part of the Maka-Njem group. Grimes (2000) lists it as Makaa (or Mekaa, South Makaa, South Mekaa). Dieu and Renaud (1983) classify it in Zone 4 under the Equatorial branch of the Bantu languages and refer to it as *maka*. They also indicate that the administration uses the names *maka* and *makya*, whereas neighboring people groups use the names *məkyɛ*, *məkaɛ*, *məkay*, *məkɛy*, *mɔka*, or *mika*. In linguistic write-ups, we use the name Makaa when writing in English, and *mekaa* when writing in French.

Makaa is still heavily used in oral communication, even among highly educated speakers. French has long been used for written communication and education. Churches have been using other Cameroonian languages, Ewondo and Bulu, and French. The Makaa people are beginning to show an interest in written Makaa in the schools and churches.

Makaa has many sub-dialects, due to the mixing of family groups by colonials at the beginning of the twentieth century. We have identified four major dialects (Mbwaanz, Bəbɛnd, Shikunda, and Besəp), which are ethnic subgroups as much as linguistic dialects. The differences are mostly phonological and lexical, but also syntactic. Dialects of neighboring languages usually understand each other, so that the situation is actually a language chain, where boundaries of languages are difficult to determine. This is especially true of Bikele, the language to the south and intelligible to the Bəbɛnd dialect; similarly, Byep or Northern Makaa, the language to the north, is intelligible to the Besəp dialect. Other neighboring languages in the Maka-Njem group are Koonzime and So to the south.

2 PHONOLOGY

2.1 Segmental phonemes

Makaa has eleven vowels, twenty-two consonants, and two phonemic tone levels (table 18.1).

The vowel system is very unusual for Bantu languages, in that it is not symmetrical (Welmers 1973). It has four front vowels, *i*, *ɪ*, *e*, and *ɛ*, and only two back vowels, *u* and *o*. The vowel *o* has two allophones, *o* and *ɔ*, which occur in free variation in many environments. Instead of one central vowel, there are three, *i*, *ə*, and *a*. Only two of the vowels, *ɛ* and *o*, have phonemic nasal counterparts, *ɛ̧*, and *o̧*, even though all the vowels are nasalized before *z* and *zh*.

TABLE 18.1: VOWELS (UNDERLYING)

		Front	Central	Back
High	close	*i*	*i̠*	*u*
Mid-high	close	*ɪ*		
Mid	close	*e*	*ə*	*o* & *ǫ*
	open	*ɛ* & *ɛ̧*	*a*	

TABLE 18.2: CONSONANTS

	Labial	Alveolar	Palatal	Velar	Labio-velar
Stops		*t*	*c*	*k*	*kp*
	b	*d*	*j*	*g*	
Prenasalized	*mp*	*nt*	*nc*	*ŋk*	
stops	*mb*	*nd*	*nj*	*ŋg*	
Nasals	*m*	*n*	*ny*	*ŋ*	
Fricatives	*f*	*s*	*sh*	*h*	
	v	*z*	*zh*		
Lateral		*l*			
Semi-vowels	*w*		*y*		

All the vowels can occur long and short, making a total of twenty-two, e.g. *jì* 'to stay' and *jìì* 'to cry'. We have interpreted long vowels as single phonemes, because native speakers react to these as one vowel, not two. The same tone patterns found on short vowels are also found on long vowels.

Makaa has twenty-two simple consonants, plus eight prenasalized stops, as shown in table 18.2. Like many languages in the area, it has the doubly articulated stop *kp*, though it is very rare, occurring only syllable-initially, and never prenasalized. The voiceless stop *p* occurs only with prenasalization (*mp*) or in the doubly articulated stop (*kp*). This is also common of many Bantu languages of southern Cameroon, especially A70 languages.

The stops lose their voicing contrast word-finally, where they are realized as unreleased and devoiced, e.g. the final consonant in *cúd* 'empty'. When a suffix is added, they are realized as the voiced stop, e.g. *cúdïgə̂* 'really empty'. Therefore, we write them with the symbols for voiced stops.

Stops can be prenasalized. The fricatives are not prenasalized as in neighboring languages such as Ewondo (A70). However, when *z* and *zh* occur medially or finally, they always occur following phonetically nasalized vowels. It may be that *z* and *zh* were prenasalized historically, but now the prenasalization is reflected in nasalization of the preceding vowels. The voiceless fricative *h* is rare.

Labialization and palatalization are syllable-level prosodies, realized on the consonant in the onset, and sometimes on the vowel. The vowel *ə* becomes ɪ (high front open allophone) following palatal or palatalized consonants, e.g. *yə̀* [*yɪ̀*] 'give'.

2.2 Syllable types

Makaa has three types of syllables, CV, CVC, and V. The most common are CV and CVC, e.g. *L-ká* 'leaf' (C7) and *Ø-kâm* 'monkey' (C1). (Note that *L* stands for a floating low tone, Ø stands for a zero prefix, and later, *H* stands for a floating high tone. These tones are morphophonological.)

The onset of these syllables can be labialized or palatalized, e.g. *Ø-kwâm* 'bag' (C9) and *myèèg* 'to spread'. The V syllable occurs word-initially, usually as a prefix, or word-finally, after a CV syllable, e.g. *ì-fî-î* 'ashes' (C8). This complex tone pattern, a low followed by a high–low, suggests that a consonant has been dropped. This complex tone pattern occurs only rarely, and only word-finally. Native speakers recognize it as a complex pattern. Interpreting this as a sequence of vowels does not add another syllable pattern, since there is already a V syllable. Interpreting other long vowels as two phonemes would add the VC syllable pattern, as in *Ø-wààg* 'chimpanzee' (C1).

Closed syllables always occur word-finally, because Makaa does not allow consecutive consonants. When two consonants do occur consecutively at morpheme boundaries, the epenthetic vowel *i* is inserted to avoid having to pronounce consecutive consonants. Prenasalized consonants are considered single consonants, because there is no intervening *i* and in reduplication both are reduplicated, e.g. *L-njinjów* 'small house' (C7). Prenasalized stops can occur in the onset or final position, e.g. *cénd* 'to change'. Nasals can be syllabic when carrying grammatical tone, e.g. *ŋgòw* 'where' with locative high tone on *ŋ*.

2.3 Morphophonemic processes

Morphophonological processes include elision and assimilation. Vowel elision occurs where the subject marker is followed by a vowel-initial tense marker, such as *mà à kà* 'I went' becoming [*mà kà*], where the *à* is slightly lengthened.

Vowel assimilation occurs in reduplication. In order to derive a participle from a verb or a diminutive from another noun, the onset and tone of the first syllable are duplicated, and the epenthetic *i* is inserted, e.g. *kíkágá* 'small child'. Following a labial or labialized consonant, the *i* becomes *u*, as in the gerund *fùfùmâ* 'whiteness'. Following a palatal or palatalized consonant, the *i* becomes *i*, as in *yíyínd* 'blackness'.

In the attributive noun phrase, the associative marker *í* or *ó* becomes a semi-vowel *y* or *w* when followed by the marker *á*. Thus, *ì-sá í à lèl* 'third thing' becomes [ì-sá yâ lèl]. Similarly, the class 2 noun prefix *ò* becomes *w`* when preceding a noun beginning with *a-*, as in *w-ălàndá* 'hot pepper'.

Consonant assimilation occurs during prefixation, as part of the process of deriving nouns from verbs. When a nasal prefix is added to a verb stem, it assimilates to the place of articulation of the stop to which it is prefixed, as in *Ø-ŋgwáágílá* 'anointed one' (C3) from *gwáágìlà* 'to anoint'.

2.4 Tones

Məkaá is a tonal language, with contrastive high and low, e.g. *Ø-kà* 'wicker' (C5) and *L-ká* 'leaf' (C7). The tones may occur singly or in sequences, resulting in high-low and low–high tone sequences, e.g. *kâ* 'down there' and *dělà* 'eating'. A high tone may be lowered in certain environments, which results in downstep, e.g. *mà mà↓ díg* 'I have seen', or in downdrift.

Some morphemes have polar tone, e.g. *àlâm* 'beloved one' where the tone of the nominalizing prefix *a-* is opposite to the following tone. Some syllables are analysed as being toneless, e.g. *kə* 'to go'; if they do not receive a grammatical tone, they receive a default low tone. We discuss the tonal processes more in the relevant sections of the chapter.

3 NOUNS AND NOUN PHRASES

3.1 Nouns

3.1.1 Noun class system

Every Makaa noun belongs to a class, and the ten noun classes and their prefixes are as listed in table 18.3. (Note that N stands for a nasal consonant.)

There remain a few vestiges of other classes, e.g. the locative *wú* 'place' takes an unusual relative marker, *wá*, which is usually a plural, C2, and also, the head noun *ndà* 'manner' is the only word to take the relative marker *nɔ́*. The ten noun classes form the following genders: 1/2, 1a/2a, 3/4, 3/6, 5/6, 7/8, 7/10, and 9/6. The single class genders are 4, 6, 8, and 10.

The 1/2 gender includes most nouns referring to humans and many animals. Nouns denoting paired body parts often are in 5/6. Derived diminutives and nouns denoting objects or tools are often in 7/8. C6 includes most mass nouns (liquids and uncountables) and abstract derived nouns. C4 or 8 include abstract nouns for qualities or habits. C10 is made up of collective nouns and takes the same concord as C9, including tone.

Class membership is changing somewhat. Some nouns, e.g. *Ø-sás* (C5) 'young woman' may now take C1 concord because people are usually in C1. Nouns may change class membership between dialects, e.g. 'tree' is *Ø-lí í* (C5) or *L- lí í* (C7).

3.1.2 Reduplicated nominals

A diminutive noun is formed by reduplicating the tone and the onset consonant of the first syllable of the noun stem, including any segmental class prefix, and assigning it to gender 7/8. The vowel in the reduplicant is usually an epenthetic *i*, e.g. *L-kíkágɔ́* 'small child' (7/8) from *L-kágɔ́* 'child' (7/8). The vowel may be assimilated to become a *u* or *i* as described in §2.

3.1.3 Nominal derivation

Nouns may be derived either from action verbs or from other nouns by adding various derivational affixes (table 18.4). The type of affix added to the verb stem indicates the

TABLE 18.3: MAKAA NOUN CLASS PREFIXES

Class	Prefix	Example	Class	Prefix	Example
1	m-	m-ùùd 'person'	2	b-	b-ùùd 'people'
	N-	n-jôŋ 'stranger'			ò-jôŋ 'strangers'
1a	Ø-	Ø-kâm 'monkey'	2a	ò-	ò-kâm 'monkeys'
		Ø-àcéncéní 'stars'		w`-	w-àcéncéní 'stars'
3	L-	L-lâm 'heart'	4	mì-	mì-lâm 'hearts'
5	Ø-	Ø-lùùn 'hole'	6	mɔ̀-	mɔ̀-lùùn 'holes'
	d-	d-ɔ́nd 'home village'		m-	m-ɔ́nd 'home villages'
	j-	j-wôw 'day'		m-	m-wôw 'days'
7	L-	L-ká 'leaf'	8	ì-	i-ká 'leaves'
		L-bùmɔ́ '(one) seed'			ì-bùmɔ́ 'seeds'
9	Ø-	Ø-fà 'machete'	10	N-	m-pùmɔ́ 'seed'

TABLE 18.4: SUMMARY OF NOUN DERIVATION IN MAKAA

Noun type	Verb +	Affixation	→ Noun	Noun class
Agent	*wéésh* 'reveal'	*-è*	*Ø-wéésh-è* 'revealer'	C1/2
Instrument	*fàfìlà* 'to blow on'	*-à*	*L-fàfìlà* 'fan'	C7/8
Result or	*cèèl* 'to love'	*-V́*	*L-cèèlí* 'love' (C7)	Not
Object	*jíígìli* 'to teach'		*L-njíígílá* 'teaching' (C3)	predictable
Result	*làl* 'to be/become hard'	Ø	*mà-làl* 'hardness'	C6
	ncwôŋ 'to be sweet'		*mà-ncwôŋ* 'sweets'	
Action	*bâ* 'to marry'	spreading high tone	*Ø-bá* 'marriage' (5/6)	Not predictable
Action	*júwò* 'to steel'	Ø	*L-júwò* 'theft' (7)	C3/4; 5/6; or
	jàànd 'to walk'	vowel change	*L-njòònd* 'journey' (3)	7/8

TABLE 18.5: MAKAA NOUN COMPOUNDING PROCESSES

N + N	*mpàgì* 'vaccine' (C9) + *Ø-bàg* 'shoulder'(C5) → *Ø-ámpàŋìbàg* 'vaccination' (C1/2)
V + N	*kòlà* 'to transmit' + *mì-lòsú* 'discussions'(C4) → *Ø-kòlàmìlòsú* 'interpreter'(C1/2)
V + V	*gwàà* 'to be distant' + *zhù* 'to come from' → *Ø-ágwààzhù* 'foreigner'(C1/2) *féèl* 'to explain' + *féèl* 'to explain' → *Ø-féèlìféèlî* 'explanation'(C1/2)
N + V	*Ø-mpwòòmbú* 'forehead'(C9) + *tî* 'to be red' → *Ø-mpwòòmbàtî* 'white man'(1/2)
N + Conj + N	*Ø-yôŋ* 'the cold'(C5) + *nò* 'and' + *Ø-yôŋ* 'the cold'(C5) → *Ø-ayôŋìnòyóŋ* 'malaria'(C1)
V + Adv.	*tôw* 'to stand' + *shwóg* 'in front' → *Ø-tówèshwóg* 'leader'(C1/2)

semantic type of the derived noun. After the derivational affix is added, the noun is assigned to a noun class. If assigned to 3/4, 9/6, or 10, it is prenasalized. This prenasalization is relexicalized as part of the noun stem. Finally, the noun class prefix is added as an inflectional prefix.

3.1.4 Compound nominals

Compound nouns may be a combination of nouns, verbs, adverbs, or conjunctions in Makaa, as shown in table 18.5. A high tone is often added at the juncture of the two lexemes.

Many compounds take the nominalizing prefix *a-* with polar tone. This prefix also occurs on many gender 1/2 nouns, where this prefix seems to have been added and then relexicalized, before the noun class prefix is added, e.g. *Ø-ákpàg*, *w-ăkpàg* 'bark clothing'.

3.2 Noun modifiers

Noun modifiers include 'real' adjectives, possessives, demonstratives, numerals, quantifiers, interrogatives, and determiners. Except for adjectives, each modifier takes concord to agree with the noun it modifies and a *H* occurs between the noun and modifier. This *H* coalesces with any following high tone.

Noun modifiers normally occur post-nominally. Possessives, demonstratives, and interrogatives may be fronted to precede the noun, in order to signal focus. When fronted, the concord on noun modifiers remains the same, except for demonstratives (see table 18.7:I). However, adjectives that emphasize size and determiners that pragmatically add emphasis to the noun always occur pre-nominally.

With possessives, demonstratives, quantifiers, interrogatives, and numerals, the head noun may be implied, as in *À jì-sɔ̀ (mwán) wâm* 'He is mine (my child)'. Such a modifier appears to be a pronoun, replacing a noun, but it has the same form as the modifier occurring with the noun. Therefore, we still consider them modifiers. The different forms and some examples of the *possessives* are listed in table 18.6.

'Real' adjectives are few in number, including *zhwòg* 'many' (e.g. *zhwòg b-ùùd* 'many people'(C2)), *ncúlyá* 'many', *bíbíyá* 'little', *ŋkán* 'someone else's', and *shús* 'different'.

Demonstratives make a three-way spatial distinction: near to speaker -*gà*, further from speaker (still in sight of speaker) -*nì*, and out of sight of speaker -*mí* (see table 18.7:I). Each has two forms, e.g. *L-tòw ʹgaʹ* 'this goat' (C7) [tòw í gà], and fronted, *jí-gà L-tòw* 'this goat'.

Quantifiers include -*êsh*, which means 'every' or 'each' in the singular and 'all' in the plural (table 18.7:II), and -*né* 'how many?' (table 18.7:IV). The *interrogative* is -*éyé* 'which?' (table 18.7:III). *Numerals* 'two' through 'six' take low tone concord, e.g. *b-wán*

TABLE 18.6: POSSESSIVE CONCORD

Noun class	1SG	2SG	3SG	1PL (excl)	1PL (incl)	2PL	3PL
	-ám	-óó	-é	-sú	-shé	-ín	-áŋ
1	w-ám	w-óó	y-é	wú-sú	í-shé	w-ún	w-áŋ
2	b-ám	bw-óó	b-ɛ́	bí-sú	ó-shé	b-ín	b-áŋ
3	w-ám	w-óó	y-é	wú-sú	í-she	w-ún	w-áŋ
4	my-ám	my-óó	my-ɛ́	mí-sú	mí-shé	m-ín	my-áŋ
5	d-ám	dw-óó	d-é	dí-sú	í-shé	d-ín	d-áŋ
6	m-ám	mw-óó	m-ɛ́	mí-sú	mɔ́-shé	m-ín	m-áŋ
7	j-ám	gw-óó	j-é	jí-sú	í-shé	j-ín	j-áŋ
8	by-ám	by-óó	by-é	bí-sú	í-shé	b-ín	by-áŋ
9/10	ny-ám	nyw-óó	ny-ɛ́	nyí-sú	í-shé	ny-in	ny-áŋ

Note: Examples: *b-wán bw-óó* 'your (SG) children' (C2); *j-ám L-bòòg* 'my hoe' (C7).

TABLE 18.7: NOUN MODIFIER AND COPULA CONCORD

Noun class	I (normal)	I (fronted)	II	III	IV	V	VI	VII	VIII
	-gà /-nì / -mí		-êsh	-éyɛ́?	-né?	-lígá	-òŋgú	-áŋ	-sɔ̀
1	ɛ́-	nyí-	y-	ny-		ŋgwó-	w-	ny-	jì-
2	ó-	bí-	b-	b-	ó-	bóó-	b-	b-	bɔ̀-
3	H-	wú-	w-	w-		wú-	w-	w-	wú-
4	mí-	mí-	my-	my-	mi-	mí-	my-	my-	mí-
5	H-	dí-	d-	d-		dú-	d-	d-	dɔ̀-
6	mɔ̀-	mɔ̀-	m-	m-	mɔ̀-	móó-	m-	m-	mɔ̀-
7	H-	jí-	j-	j-		gú-	j-	j-	jí-
8	í-	bí-	by-	by-	í-	bí-	by-	by-	bí-
9/10	H-	nyí-	ny-	ny-		nyú-	ny-	ny-	nyí-

Note: Column VIII shows the concord on the copula, which agrees with its subject.

wúúm nə̀ ò-bá 'twelve (ten and two) children (C2)'. The *H* that occurs between noun and numeral is realized on the concord, e.g. *b-wân ó-bá* 'two children' (C2). Except for this low tone, numerals take the same concord as *-né* 'how many?' (table 18.7:IV).

Determiners are here defined as modifiers that indicate the type of reference. They include the non-anaphoric *-lígá* 'a' or 'another' (e.g. *dú-lígá j-wów* 'one day' (C5)) (table 18.7:V), the anaphoric *-òŋgú* 'that' (e.g. *Ø-njów w-òŋgú* 'that house'(C3)) (table 18.7:VI), and the contrastive *-âŋ* 'this, that' (e.g. *ny-âŋ Ø-mpàwó ... ny-âŋ Ø-mpàwó* 'this animal ... that animal' (C9)) (table 18.7:VII).

3.3 Associative noun phrases

An associative noun phrase usually consists of a head noun and its modifying noun plus the associative marker (or connective) between the two nouns (see table 18.8). The associative marker agrees in class with the first or head noun, e.g. *mì-njów* (C4) 'houses' + *mí + b-ùùd* (C2) 'people' → *minjów mí bùùd* 'families'. Sometimes a gerund, an adverb, an ordinal numeral, or even a prepositional phrase replaces the second noun, e.g. *mì-káándə́ my-â fùfùmə̀* 'white clothes' (C4) where *fùfùmə̀* is derived from *fùmə̀* 'to be white'.

Complex rules govern the realization of the *H*, similar to the rules for the realization of the *H* in the verbal unit (§4.2). When the first tone on the second noun stem is high or high–low, and there is no syllabic prefix, the *H* coalesces with that high or high-low tone, e.g. *L-shìshà* (C7) 'big' + *H* + *Ø-cúdú* (C1) 'animal' + *j-òŋgú* (C7) 'that' → *shìshà cúdú jòŋgú* 'that big animal'.

When the second noun has a low tone syllabic prefix, the *H* replaces the low tone, and the low tone is deleted (as in example 1 below). When the second noun has a low tone noun stem and no syllabic prefix, the *H* is realized to the left, on an epenthetic vowel (as in 2) or on the preceding vowel if the first noun ends in an open syllable (as in 3). For more rules, including one where the segmental associative marker takes a low tone after a low tone noun and before a high tone noun of class 1, 5, or 9/10 (as in 4), see Heath (1991a).

(1) *L-mə̀mà* (C7) 'big' + H + *mì-kwàs* (C4) 'pencils' → *mə̀mà mí-kwàs* 'big pencils'
(2) làl 'to be hard' + *L-njòònd* (C3) 'trip' → *làl í njòònd* 'hard trip' (walked fast)
(3) *L-mbèè* (C7) 'inferior' + H + *L-kwàs* (C3) 'pencil' → *mbèé kwàs* 'inferior pencil'
(4) *mì-fìidyè* (C4) 'sticks' + *mí* + *Ø-cúdú* (C1) 'animal' → *mifìidyè mì cúdú* 'sticks of animal'

When one noun possesses the other in an associative phrase, the possessive marker *mə̀* is used instead of the associative marker when the first noun is singular, e.g. *L-njów* (C3) 'house' + *mə̀* + *L-kúkùmà* (C7) 'chief' → *njów mə̀ kúkùmà* 'house of the chief'.

When the second noun expresses an attribute or characteristic of the first noun, the attributive marker *á* is inserted after the associative marker, e.g. *Ø-kwáádə̀* (C9) *á Bə́l* 'village named Bə́l' and *L-kándə̀* (C3) *á mə̀-bwàm* (C6) 'dirty cloth' or 'cloth that has dirt'.

TABLE 18.8: ASSOCIATIVE NOUN PHRASE CONCORD

Noun class	1	2	3	4	5	6	7	8	9/10
Associative marker	Ø	ó	H	mí	lí	mə̀	H	í	Ø

TABLE 18.9: OBJECT PRONOUNS AND SUBJECT AND OBJECT MARKERS

Noun class	Person	Subject marker	Object pronoun	Object marker	Noun class	Subject marker	Object pronoun
1	1	m-ə̀	m-ə̀	m-ə̀	3	í	w-ə̀
	2	wò	wò	wò	4	mí	my-ə̀
	3	ny-ə̀ / à*	ny-ə̀	ɛ̀	5	í	dw-ə̀
2	1(excl)	s-ə̀	s-ə̀		6	mía	mw-ə̀
	(incl)	sh-é	sh-é		7	í	gw-ə̀
	(DU)	shw-ə́	shw-ə̀		8	í	by-ə̀
	2	bí	bí		9/10	í	nyw-ə̀
	3	bwó	bw-ə̀				

Note:

* *nyə̀* indicates a change in action or subject; *à* indicates continuing action and same subject as previous clause. But *nyə̀* occurs before vowels and introduces reported speech.

3.4 Pronouns

All personal pronouns are marked for person, number and noun class of the referent, but not sex. In addition to the singular and plural distinction in the second and third person pronouns, first person pronouns also distinguish between dual and plural, inclusive and exclusive. Table 18.9 shows how similar the object pronoun is to the subject and object markers (verbal prefixes) in classes 1/2, described in sections 4.2.1 and 4.2.6.

Object pronouns can take suffixes to form restrictive or contrastive pronouns, which may be used along with the noun or another pronoun, to focus on the referent. The *restrictive pronoun*, indicating that the person referred to is acting alone, is formed by suffixing *-méfwó* (or *-mɛ́*) onto the object pronoun, e.g. *nyə̀méfwó* 'himself' or 'by himself'.

The *contrastive pronoun* indicates that the speaker refers to a specific referent and not to others. For singular pronouns, the suffix *-ɛ̀* is added, e.g. *nyə̀-ɛ̀* 'he (not others).' For plural pronouns, the determiner *-áŋ* with concord is suffixed, e.g. *sə̀-báŋ* 'we (not they).'

Coordinate pronouns indicate that two parties (A and B) are involved in an action, or that the party in focus, A, is accompanied by B. A coordinate pronoun consists of a plural pronoun and a suffix. The pronoun is in the same person as party A and the suffix is either the dual *-ná* or the plural *-nóŋ*, e.g. *bíná Zhàŋ* 'you and John' or *sə̀-nóŋ* 'we (I and they).' The suffixes were formed by fusing the preposition *nə̀* 'with' with the class 1 prefix *a-* or the class 2 prefix *ó-*. A noun or pronoun identifying party B may follow the coordinate.

The pronoun *-àŋg* functions as the *head of a relative clause*, e.g. *b-àŋg bwó ŋgə́ sêy wá* 'those who are working', taking the same concord as *-òŋgú* 'that' (table 18.7:VI).

4 VERB

Makaa verbs consist of a radical, usually monosyllabic, preceded by free morphemes marking tense, aspect and mood, and sometimes followed by derivational extensions.

4.1 Verbal radicals and extensions

Makaa verbal radicals are monosyllabic, CV or CVC. Verbal radicals that appear to be polysyllabic are a radical with one or two extensions.

Certain verbal extensions change the valency of the verb, e.g. passive *-òw* (*-yòw* after vowels), reciprocal/reflexive *-là* or *-yà*, causative *-àl* or vowel change *a→e*, and resultative *-yà* plus vowel change. The passive may follow another extension, e.g. *bwáád* 'to clothe oneself' + causative + passive *→ bwééd-òw* 'to be worn'. The limiting extension is unique, consisting of full reduplication plus the suffix *-g*; it indicates that the agent is doing only the action indicated and not any action that logically follows, e.g. *à ŋgò lás lás-ɨg* 'he is only talking (but will not follow through on anything said).'

Other extensions add new nuances to the meaning of the radical in different, unpredictable ways, e.g. *wáámb* 'to chase' *→ wáámb-ɨ̀-là* 'to sweep'. Sometimes the radical no longer occurs without the extension, e.g. for *bàg-ɨ̀-wò* 'to be clear or open' with no corresponding radical *bàg*.

4.2 Verbal unit

The Makaa verbal unit has two parts, the Inflection (subject and tense markers) and Macrostem (rest of the verbal unit), as shown in the table 18.10.

The verbal unit is divided into the Inflection and the Macrostem for two reasons. First, an inflectional clitic (indicating imperative, hortative, or negative) may be attached to the first morpheme of the Macrostem, but it is never attached to a morpheme of the Inflection.

Second, a floating high tone, labeled Macrostem High (MacH) occurs in certain TAM constructions. This tone occurs after every morpheme in the Macrostem, but not in the Inflection. A similar tone occurs in Koonzime, but marks different TAM construcions.

The morphemes in the Macrostem include pre-root and post-root morphemes. The preroot morphemes (clause marker, aspect marker, adverbs, and auxiliaries) are more loosely linked to the verb radical, because they can have both a MacH and an inflectional clitic (negative, hortative, imperative) separating them from the verb. Neither the MacH nor a clitic can separate the post-root verbal extensions from the verb radical. Some pre-root morphemes can also occur in other contexts as verb roots. Therefore, the pre-root morphemes are free forms, having the same syllable structures as other words, while post-root verbal extensions are bound forms, usually a suffix consisting of a continuant (*l, y, w, sh*, or *s*) and a vowel.

The MacH is sensitive to the tone on its right. When the following associated tone is high, the MacH coalesces with it. When the following associated tone is low, the MacH associates with the preceding word. However, a MacH that occurs following the verb root and preceding a noun of class 1, 2, 4, 5, 6, 8, or 9, spreads right. It disassociates the low tone in the plural prefix (class 2, 4, 6, or 8) or the first tone in the stem after the Ø prefix (class 1, 5, or 9), as in 5 below. When the MacH occurs following the verb and

TABLE 18.10: MAKAA VERBAL UNIT

Inflection		Macrostem				
Subject *mkr*	Tense *mkr*	Clause *mkr**	Aspect *mkr**	Adverb and/or auxiliary*	Object *mkr*	ROOT* Radical + extension(s)

Note: * An inflectional clitic (imperative, hortative, or negative) may be added to whatever morpheme occurs first in the Macrostem (except object marker).

preceding a noun of class 3 or 7, or a preposition or pronoun, the MacH associates leftward, with the preceding word, as in 6.

(5) mə̀   ámə̀   díg   ´   Ø-kùùs   →   Mə̀ ámə̀ díg kùùs.
     I   P1   see   MacH   C1-parrot   'I saw the parrot.'

(6) mə̀   ámə̀   nyìŋgə̀ ´   gù   ´   L-gwòó
     I   P1   again   MacH   pick   MacH C7-mushroom
     Mə̀ ámə̀ nyìŋgə̌ gǔ gwòó.   'I again picked a mushroom.'

4.2.1 Subject markers

The different subject markers are listed in table 18.9. Third person subject markers in class 1/2 may be deleted when a noun is the subject.

4.2.2 Tense

Tense markers in Makaa, listed in table 18.11, all occur in the Inflection, except the distant future marker bá. Bá occurs in the Macrostem as a clause marker and can take the negative clitic, e.g. àbɨ́lɛ́ 'will not'. In addition to tense markers, the distant past is distinguished by being the only tense that does not include the MacH in the Macrostem.

When the morpheme following the H carries a high tone, the H coalesces with it, and the tone of the morpheme preceding the toneless segment a or e spreads onto it. When the following morpheme carries a low, the H spreads left, onto the toneless segment if present.

(7) Mə̀   e´   càl   ´   mə̀-ləndú   → Mə̀ é càl mə̀ləndú.
     I   F1   cut down   MacH   C6-palm tree   'I will cut down the palm trees
                                                   (today).'

4.2.3 Clause markers

Clause markers are morphemes within the verbal unit that function more on the clause level than on the phrase level, e.g. shí, a counter-assertive marker, and bá, the distant future or certainty marker. Some morphemes in this position never allow the attachment of an inflectional clitic, and thus they do not function as part of the verbal unit as much as on the paragraph level, e.g. kà 'therefore', mú 'then' and músə̀ 'finally'.

4.2.4 Aspect

A three-way aspectual distinction exists in Makaa, perfective (zero-marked), progressive (ŋgə̀), and habitual or iterative (dɨ); it is indicated in the second position of the

TABLE 18.11: TENSE IN THE INDICATIVE

Tense	Time frame	In inflection	In Macrostem
Distant past (P2)	Earlier than yesterday morning	a + H	
Recent past (P1)	Earlier today or yesterday	ámə̀	MacH
Present (PRES)	Now or in the immediate future	H	MacH
Near future (F1)	After present but during same day	e + H	MacH
Distant future (F2)	After today		bá + MacH

Macrostem. The habitual and progressive markers may occur together. The anterior, also in the second position of the Macrostem, is marked by *mə̀* followed by a floating L, which causes downstep of a following associated high tone. The progressive marker seems to block the MacH from occurring on any part of the Macrostem that follows it, as shown below.

(8)   *mə̀ kú`*   ′   *nyìŋgə̀*   ′   *ŋgə̀*   *wáámbɨ̀lə̀*   *ì-fàmbə̀*
      I   NEG HORT MacH again   MacH PROG clear   C8-field
      Mə̀ kú nyìŋgə̀ ŋgə̀ wáámbɨ̀lə̀ ìfàmbə̀. 'I am not again clearing the fields.'

4.2.5 Adverbs and auxiliaries

Adverbs that occur within the Macrostem include *ná* 'still, not yet', *ŋwá* 'almost', and *lèèl* 'quickly'. Auxiliaries can occur in other verbal units as the verb root, e.g. *zə̀* (inceptive) from *zə̀* 'to come', *kə̀* (terminative) from *kə̀* 'to go', and *bwèy* 'long ago' from *bwèy* 'to take a long time'.

4.2.6 Object markers

The object markers are listed in table 18.9. In some dialects of Makaa, an object marker may occur within the Macrostem, but only if the object is a C1 noun. Otherwise, the object occurs as a noun or pronoun following the verb. The object marker is considered a prefix on the verb radical because an inflectional clitic may not separate it from the verb root. When there are no other morphemes preceding the verb root in the Macrostem, the inflectional morpheme is attached to the verb root and the object occurs following the verb, as a pronoun or noun.

(9)   *Mə̀* *a* ′ *shigé* *ɛ̀*   *díg* → *Mə̀ à shigé ɛ̀ díg.*
      I   P2 NEG him(C1) See   'I didn't see him.'

4.2.7 Mood

Makaa distinguishes three moods: indicative, hortative, and imperative; these are marked by an inflectional clitic on the first morpheme in the Macrostem. The indicative is the unmarked or default construction, used to express realis situations, or irrealis situations with auxiliaries, adverbs, or clause markers (e.g. *jé* 'might' or *é bá* 'certainly') to indicate different degrees of necessity or possibility.

The hortative and imperative are both marked by the inflectional clitic *-g* and a high tone. In the hortative, the high tone replaces the first tone of the Macrostem, e.g. *wò cá-lɨ̀g* 'you should cut down' from *càl*. In the imperative the high tone occurs on the final vowel of the first word of the Macrostem, e.g. *càl-ìg!* 'cut down!' The MacH does not occur in present plural imperatives. In a plural imperative, the clitic *-g* takes the plural marker *-a* as suffix, e.g. *càl-ùg-á mə̀-lə̀ndú!* 'cut down (pl) the palm trees!' compared to *càl-ìgí mə̀-lə̀ndú* 'cut down (sg) the palm trees!' with the MacH.

4.2.8 Negation

Negation in the indicative is expressed by a discontinuous clitic on the first word of the Macrostem. The clitic (toneless *a* prefix + H + suffix *è* or *é*) varies somewhat from tense to tense. In past tenses, the clitic has no prefix and attaches on the counter-assertive morpheme *shi*, resulting in *shigé* as in example (9) above. In the present, the negative clitic also has L as well as *a-* in the prefix. The toneless *a-* takes the same tone as the preceding subject marker or pronoun. If the *a-* is associated to a low tone, the L coalesces with it. If the *a-* is associated to a high tone, the L remains a L and causes downstep of a high tone that immediately follows it.

(10) | *Mə* | *a-* | *cal* | *-ɛ* | | | *mə-ləndu* |
      |------|------|-------|------|---|---|-----------|
      | L | L | L H | H | H | | L H H |
      | 1 | NEG | cut + NEG | NEG | MacH | | C6-palm tree |

   Mə̀ àcálé mə́lə́ndú 'I do not cut down palm trees.'

(11) | *Sə* | *a-* | *cal* | *-ɛ* | | | *mə-ləndu* |
      |------|------|-------|------|---|---|-----------|
      | H | L | L H | H | H | | L H H |
      | We | NEG | cut + NEG | NEG | MacH | | C6-palm tree |

   Sə́ á↓ *cálé mə́lə́ndú* 'We do not cut down palm trees.'

Negation is expressed by the clause marker *kú + L* in the hortative and imperative, where the L causes downstep of a following high.

(12) | *ku* | | *wiiŋg* | | *o-mpyə* |
      |------|---|---------|---|---------|
      | H | L | HH | H | L-HL |
      | NEG | | chase | MacH | C2-dog |

   Kú↓ *wííŋg ómpyə̀!* 'Do not chase the dogs!'

5 SYNTAX

5.1 Word order and variability

Makaa is an SVO language with most word order patterns following a head-initial syntax. Any argument of the verb may be left-dislocated for topicalization. A fronted personal pronoun takes a contrastive suffix, described in §3.4. Often the fronted noun or pronoun begins a cleft construction; see §5.2 below.

5.2 Main clause types

Verbal clauses have action or process verbs in the predicate. The subject of process verbs is the semantic patient, e.g. *L-nywáág í mə̀ tî* 'the mango has ripened (is ripe).' This construction can also carry a resultative sense, e.g. *Ø-fəb í mə̀ jíg* 'the paper was burned', with focus on the state of the subject. Such process verbs become transitive by adding the causative extension *-àl*, which in effect adds an argument (the agent, as subject), e.g. *mə̀ mə̀ jígàl Ø-fəb* 'I burned the paper'.

In the passive voice, the agent is usually left unexpressed, e.g. *L-kàándə̀ mə̀ nyèyòw* 'the cloth was torn'. The passive often carries a negative implication, that the agent was at fault, whereas the resultative construction carries no negative implications.

An instrument or location cannot be subject of a passive verb, but a benefactive NP can serve as subject of a passive verb, if it is in the indirect object position in the active clause. This construction is also pejorative, implying negative feelings towards the passive subject.

(13) | *mù-ùd* | *nyə̀* | *à* | *yə́* | *-yòw* | *L-kúwò* |
      |---------|--------|-----|-------|--------|----------|
      | C1-person | he | P2 | Give | PASS | chicken(C7) |

   Mùùd nyə̀ á yə́yòw kúwò.

   'The person was given a chicken.' (implying he forced the gift)

Non-verbal clauses include both those with the copula -sə̀ and those with the focus marker ó. Clauses with the copula as the predicate express attribution, equation, location, or possession. In the present perfective indicative, the copula takes a concord prefix (see table 18.7). Often the -sə̀ is deleted, leaving only the concord. In other TAM constructions, the copula becomes bə̀ without concord prefix, and takes limited TAM inflections.

In locational clauses, a locative follows the copula, as in b-wán bí-sə̀ tóón 'the children (C2) are outside'. Locative nouns are usually marked either by a high tone prefix, e.g. í-fàmbə́ 'to the fields' (C8), or by the suffix, -'d in Ø-kúdə̀-d 'in the basket' (C5), or -dí in L-tíwùlì-dí 'on/at/near the table' (C7). Location may be further specified by an adverb, e.g. L-njów-dí (C3) with cúu 'in'. Locational clauses can also be formed with stative verbs that are limited in TAM forms, e.g. À mbùg shì 'He's lying down'.

Attribution clauses have a noun modifier, formed by prefixing ŋkí to a verb root, following the copula, e.g. L-njów wí-sə̀ ŋkí-fùmə̀. 'The house (C3) is white'. In possession clauses, a prepositional phrase beginning with nə̀ 'with' follows the copula, as in b-wán bí nə̀ ò-kálàd 'the children are with (have) books'.

Non-verbal clauses that use the focus marker ó instead of the copula -sə̀ are cleft constructions, e.g. j-ínə̀ d-ám ó Mpa 'it is my name (C5) that is Mpa', or nyə̀ ó Ø-yígìlì 'it is he who is the teacher (C1)', or mə̀ ó 'gà 'it's me here'. The cleft construction often includes what seems to be a relative clause (RC) though lacking a relative marker.

(14) Mə̀ dí   mə̀ jáámb   →   Mə̀ dí mə̀ jáámb.
      me   NEG FOC I   cook   'It's not me who cooks.'

5.3 Subordinate clauses

All subordinate clauses, whether RCs, adverbial clauses, or complement clauses, are marked with a high tone on the conjunction or in the verb.

Relative clauses are postnominal in Makaa. The head of the RC can be a noun or the pronoun -àŋg with concord. Tonally, a high tone that replaces the first tone of the subject NP, and another high tone that replaces the tones on the first morpheme of the verb mark the RC. Finally, a relative marker/relativizer agreeing with the head occurs at the end of the RC: yé (C1), wá (C2), yí (C3, 5, 7, 8, 9/10), myá (C4), or má (C6).

(15) mə̀ cèèl b-àŋg   bwó   dí   ' bùl ' sêy   wá
      I   want C2-those C2:they HAB   MacH   lot MacH work   C2:REL MKR
      Mə́ cèèl bàŋg bwó dí bùl sêy wá. 'I like those who work hard.'

When the head noun of the RC (NP$_{REL}$) is the subject or direct object of the RC, there is gapping, with the NP$_{REL}$ unexpressed within the RC, although the subject marker remains on the verb. When the NP$_{REL}$ is the indirect object or the object of a preposition, it is marked by a pronoun trace: an object pronoun or the uninflected pronoun ndí. When the NP$_{REL}$ is locative, the locative -d is suffixed to the relative marker, or a locative word is used, e.g. kíl 'place' (C7) as head noun and gapping as if the locative is direct object.

(16) mì-njów   L- kíl   bwó   ŋgə̀   wúl   ø-cúdú   yí
      C4-houses C7-place   they   PROG   boil   C1-meat   C7:REL MKR
      Mìnjów, kíl bwó ŋgə̀ wúl cúdú yí
      'The houses, (the place) where they are boiling meat'

When the NP$_{REL}$ is a possessor in the RC, there is a possessive adjective, which agrees in person and number with the head noun and in class with the genitive noun.

Subordinate clauses that express time, location, or manner, are not adverbial clauses, but RCs, in which the head noun signals the type of clause, e.g. L-*jà* 'C7-time', *L-kíl* 'C7-place', or L-*mbíí* 'C3-way', and gapping as if the head is direct object.

Adverbial clauses in Makaa are marked by a conjunction or a morpheme in the verb, always carrying a high tone, e.g. the conjunction *shú nə́* or *nə́* 'in order that' for purpose clauses, *nəcé* 'because' for reason clauses, and the adverb *tèèm ΄* 'even if' for concessive clauses. Simultaneous clauses are marked only by the progressive marker carrying a high tone, *ŋgə́*, in the second clause, following the main clause.

(17) ò-jôŋ   ó   mə́   wóós   sə́-mə́   ŋgə́   də̀
      C2-visitor C2:they ANT   arrive   we   PROG + II   eat
      Ojôŋ ó mə́ wóós, sə́ mə́ ŋgə́ də̀.   'The visitors arrived while we were eating.'

'Real' conditional clauses (Thompson and Longacre 1994) are marked either by *ŋkí* 'if' clause initially or by *ká* 'if-non past', *bág* 'if-past', or *bə̀ kú* 'be not' (negative) following the subject. Imaginary conditionals include counterfactual conditionals, marked by the auxiliary *ŋwá* 'would have', and hypothetical conditionals, marked by *mbə́* 'if' following the subject in both the main and conditional clauses.

Complement clauses include sentence-like clauses (in the indicative or hortative) and gerundive clauses. Sentence-like clauses begin with the complementizer *nə́* 'that'. The indicative mood is used after verbs of cognition, utterance, and perception, e.g. *gwág* 'hear'. The hortative mood occurs after verbs of feeling, manipulation, and comment, e.g. *i jìì* 'it is necessary (literally, it wants).'

A gerundive clause consists of a gerund (formed by suffixing *'lə̀* onto the first morpheme of the Macrostem) that may have its own subject and/or object. This clause functions as the object of complement-taking verbs such as *tèèd* 'begin' and *cèèl* 'like', as the subject or complement of non-verbal clauses, or as the object of prepositions.

(18) mə̀   ŋgə   - 'lə̀   wóós   ó   gà
      I   PROG   -GERUND SUFFIX   arrive FOC   this
      Mə̀ ŋgə́lə̀ wóós ó gà.   'This is my arrival.'

6 CONCLUSION

Makaa is an SVO language, with a verb phrase that differs strongly from more typical Bantu languages. Makaa still has an elaborate noun class system and complex tone rules. The tone rules in the Makaa noun phrase and the verbal unit are strikingly similar, both containing a floating high tone. The phonology is interesting, with its assymetrical vowel system and its prenasalized stops in syllable-final position.

ACKNOWLEDGMENT

I would like to thank Rhonda Thwing for her help in writing, Bekolo Emini for language data and insights into usage, and Daniel Heath for his insights into the language.

REFERENCES

Dieu and Renaud 1983; Grimes 2000; Guthrie 1971; Heath 1991a; Thompson and Longacre 1994; Welmers 1973.

FURTHER READING

Heath 1984, 1991b; Heath and Heath 1982, 1984.

CHAPTER NINETEEN

THE BANTU LANGUAGES OF THE FOREST

Claire Grégoire

1 INTRODUCTION

1.1

One conclusion immediately imposes itself when one considers the totality of the languages spoken in the vast region covered by the equatorial forest. The forest is not an area of linguistic homogeneity: quite the contrary, it is an area of contacts and borders. Although it is imaginable that all the peoples of the forest have a rather analogous way of life, the study of the linguistic divisions rather points to the fact that the forest is an environment that is difficult to access, where communication is essentially established via the waterways and where the absence of regular contacts maintains the existing borders between different linguistic groups. Thus, the forest is the place where the Bantu languages border on the Ubangian languages to the west and on the Central Sudanic languages to the east. It is also the place where one finds the dividing lines which the classification shows between, on the one hand, the Bantu languages of the eastern and the western block; and, on the other hand, between the Bantu languages of the northwest (zone A + B10, B20, B30) and the rest of the western languages. All types of borders can thus be found in this biotope: borders between different genetic families, borders between different groups of the same family and borders between the major subgroups that are distinguished within the group of Bantu languages itself.

1.2

The languages of zone A and of the B40–50 groups will not be discussed here. But, dealing with the other Bantu languages of the forest (B10–70, C10–70 and D10–40 in Guthrie's classification) in about twenty pages remains a bold venture. The diversity of the languages that should be presented is considerable and is directly reflected in all classifications, above all in the lexicostatistical ones. Moreover, the particularly delicate question raised by the presence of Pygmy populations throughout the forest zone at least has to be dealt with. Finally, the documentary gaps are still very numerous and hamper our knowledge of the languages of the forest to the extent that any synthesis is still problematic.

1.3

Obviously, the reading of the following pages presupposes a basic knowledge of the Bantu languages in general, be it of their major phonological and phonetic characteristics or of the general make-up of their morphology. Only the specific characteristics of the groups under discussion will be described here; characteristics which, sometimes, are proper to the languages of the forest in general, but which, most of the time, individualize certain

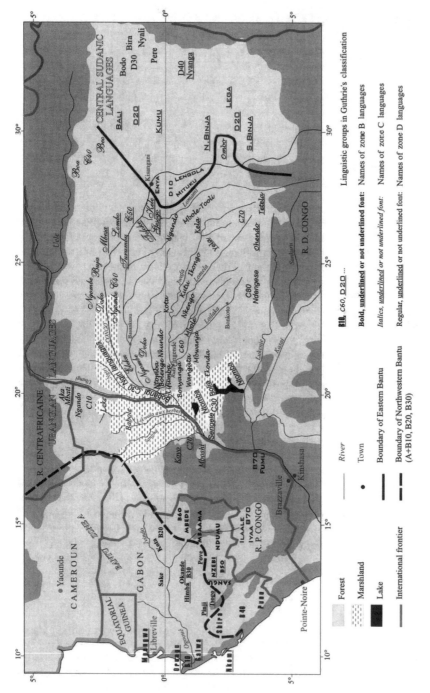

MAP 19.1 THE MAIN BANTU LANGUAGES OF THE FOREST (ZONES B, C AND D)

Forest

Marshland

Lake

International frontier

——— River

• Town

—— Boundary of Eastern Bantu

▪▪▪ Boundary of Northwestern Bantu (A+B10, B20, B30)

B10, *C60*, <u>D20</u> ... Linguistic groups in Guthrie's classification

Bold, <u>underlined</u> or not underlined font: Names of zone B languages

Italics, <u>underlined</u> or not underlined font: Names of zone C languages

Regular, <u>underlined</u> or not underlined font: Names of zone D languages regional, more or less extensive language groups with variable internal coherence. Although the models inspired by the reconstruction of Proto-Bantu cannot be entirely absent from such a description, an effort will be made to present the facts from a synchronic perspective. Surely, to speak of the Bantu languages from the eastern block when discussing languages such as Nyanga (D43), Lega (D25), Binja North and Binja South (D26) or Mituku (D13) could already be seen as a concession to comparative classifications. It will be shown, however, that this grouping is equally justified by purely descriptive criteria.

The reader should keep in mind that very few of the currently available descriptions give direct and unambiguous access to detailed phonetic data. Finally, phonology and morphology will be treated successively, except in those cases where both aspects are so intricately related and intertwined that a separate presentation would render the treatment of the facts completely artificial.

2 PHONOLOGY

2.1 Vowel systems

The majority of the Bantu languages of the forest have a vowel system with seven oppositions [i e ɛ a ɔ o u]. One could say that this is a major property these languages have in common, as if they had been spared the innovation that reduced the number of vowels to five [i e a o u]. Yet, some languages are exceptional. Two examples of the rare languages with a system reduced to five distinctive vowels are Lengola (D12) and Nyali (D33). Others, conversely, have more than seven vowel phonemes, like Boa (C44) and Bali (D21) which have eight [i e ə ɛ a ɔ o u], or Bodo (D35) which, according to Asangama (1983) and Kutsch Lojenga (1994a), counts nine vowel phonemes [i ɪ e ɛ a ɔ o ʊ u] and applies a process of vowel assimilation based on an opposition of the type [± ATR]. All these languages are located in the northeast of the forest zone and show several properties that might originate from an enduring contact with the Central Sudanic languages. This, however, is a hypothesis that demands further scrutiny.

Eventually, a number of forest languages present nasalized vowels, the status of which is often phonetic. But they can be on the way of becoming phonological like in Bali (D21) or in Boa (C44). This is not the place to give a survey of the languages which possess nasalized vowels, but it is important to note that in certain idioms such as the Myene-languages (B10), Fumu (B77b) or Binza (C30 Ngiri), these vowels appear either between a nasal consonant and an NC-sequence or between two nasal consonants (cf. Myene-Nkomi: òng̱nzì 'professor'; inḁ̀ŋgò 'smells'), whereas in Ndumu (B63), Boa (C44) and Bali (D21), they appear word-initially before a sequence NC or NS (cf. Bali: ṵnzì 'village'; ɔ̰:mvá 'dog'; ṵŋkwɔ́ 'salt'; ɔ̰ntíñìgà 'he has cut'). In Bali, the nasal consonant is hardly perceptible when followed by a voiced consonant. For Boa, free allophony has been reported between realizations of the type [ɔ̰nyèká] and [ɔ̰yèká] 'you (sg.) leave him', which clearly testifies of a tendency towards phonologization of the nasalized realizations. In Leke (C14), the disappearance of the consonant m in prefixes causes the next vowel to be nasalized. The latter then assimilates the previous vowel with which it enters into direct contact, either with or without the feature of nasalization. The following are examples of this: |bá–`–bá-mà-n + kúbá| → /báa̰nkúbá/ or /báa̰nkúbá/ 'small fields'; |≠dòdè ≠ mò + sándá≠| → /dòdɔ̰ ɔ̰sándá/ or /dòdò ɔ̰sándá/ 'a great man'; |≠mí + `zí≠mì + kúzì≠| → /mízì ḭkúzì/ or /mízɪ̰ ḭkúzì/ 'it is painful'. Clearly, in these languages the nasalized vowels ḭ, a̰, ṵ, and ɔ̰ are distinctive, which is rather exceptional among the forest languages described at present.

Another characteristic that seems to be fairly widespread among these languages is the extreme tolerance they show for vowel sequences, a tolerance that often coincides with a rather unsystematic application of either vocalic elision or semi-vocalization wherever morphemes come into contact. In certain languages, vowel sequences can equally appear due to the elision of certain consonants placed in specific environments. This elision can be obligatory or optional, or be linked to the speed of speech. Except in the groups B10, B60 and B70, the languages of the forest generally display numerous vowel sequences within nominal stems as well as at the contact between morphemes, especially between prefixes and stems, within the derived verb or in the sequences of morphemes placed before the verb stem. Several authors insist on the fact that the different successive vowels belong to different syllables, even if they do not analyze the syllable structures along the lines of contemporary theories. Certain languages, like Aka (C10), exclude sequences of two front or two back mid-vowels which only differ in aperture, but other languages tolerate them (cf. Bodo D35: *àpèè* 'before'; Tsogo B31: *gèèdù* 'beard'; Babole C14: *èèlɔ* 'thigh'). Several languages, finally, attest sequences of three or four vowels. For example:

(1) Aka (C10)   *mògúìà*   'depth'   (vs. *èpùyà* 'ant')
                    ngùìà   'river hog'   (vs. *èngùyà* 'kind of dance')
                    mòèì   'belly'

     Tofoke (C53)   *béáísò*   'our (class 2)'

     Lombo (C54)   *lìóì*   'speech'
                    bàúè   'cries'

     Mongo (C61)   *lòúá*   'water on the plants'
                    lɔèù   'lip'
                    ǎòátà   'he has acquired'
                    ěòékà   'he has sung'

     Kela (C75)   *âóísà*   'he hides'
                    bâóàisà   'they hide them'

     Enya (D14)   *mòìàbà*   'in the river'

Detailed phonetic studies together with a profound analysis of the possible syllable structures would be extremely interesting in these languages. They would allow us to solve the problems that a conventional notation often leaves undecided. A notation like *ɛi*, for instance, can cover the realizations [*ɛi*] or [*ɛy*], and the sources do not always provide a choice between them. Likewise, notations of the type VxVx can refer to successions of two identical vowels (what certain authors explicitly state), but equally well to long vowels. In certain cases, like in Mongo (C61), the author himself hesitates between these distinct realizations (Hulstaert 1938). Thus, although it appears to be rather clear that vowel length is phonological in the B60, B70 and B80 languages, as well as in Bobangi (C32), Ngombe (C41), Boa (C44), Tofoke (C53), Tetela (C71), Lengola (D12), Enya (D14) and Bali (D21), the exact geographical distribution of this feature is difficult to establish at present. But note that various authors point out that, although vowel length is relevant, minimal pairs that oppose a short vowel to a long vowel of the same quality are rare.

Two peculiarities deserve some more attention. The first concerns Lega (D25), a forest language from the eastern Bantu block. This language accepts vowel sequences such as *ɛi* or *iɔ* (cf. *bɛíbì* 'thieves'; *bòsíɔ* 'face'), yet it features a succession of the type *Vzi* in a series of words where the forest languages of zone C most often have vowel sequences. Examples are:

(2) 'ear'   Lega *kòtózì* Aka *dìlúè* Nkundo *lìtóì* Lengola *òtóì*
     'four' Lega *-nàzì* Aka *-náì* Nkundo *'-nèì*

'long'   Lega   -làzì   Aka   -làí   Bomboma   -léí
'leopard'   Lega   ngɔ̀zì   Aka   ngòè   Nkundo   nkɔ̀ì

The second peculiarity is that in Zamba (C30 Ngiri) and in Leke (C14) final vowels tend to be devocalized, whereas in Nkundo and Eleku (C60), final *i* and *u* are elided if preceded by the consonant *m*, which is then realized as syllabic if the elided vowel carried a high tone (cf. Nkundo C61: *nkúmú* → *nkúm̀* 'dignitary', *bɔ̀nkɔ̀mú* → *bɔ̀nkɔ̀m̀* 'tree (species)', *lòlémì* or *lòlémù* → *lòlém* 'language', *jóm* 'ten'; Eleku C60: +*lám* 'good', *bòlám* 'goodness'). Meeussen (1952) signals the same fact for Ombo (C76), where one has: *jŏm*, pl. *bàóm* 'ten', *lòlém*, pl. *ndém* 'language(s)', while it hasn't been recorded for the C50 languages nor for Tetela (C71), Yela-Kela (C74–75) and Mbole-Tooli (C60), in other words, for the languages which separate Ombo from the so-called Mongo languages. Note that the forest languages, especially those of zone C, border on languages more to the south in which the syllables with a consonantal coda are regular word-finally. This could be a case of accidental correspondence, but these facts could equally well follow from a similar tendency.

2.2 Consonant systems

The consonant systems of the languages of the forest are marked by a rather large number of particularities. It is impossible to envisage them all in this limited synthesis. Only the most salient ones will be treated here in a succinct manner.

Although the labiovelar consonants *kp*, *gb*, *ŋkp*, *ŋgb* or the implosives *ɓ*, *ɗ* are not limited to this area, they are much more frequent here than elsewhere in the Bantu domain. A possible influence from adjacent non-Bantu languages cannot be excluded, but as far as I know this has never been proven.

The different labiovelar consonants are not equally well represented: the voiceless *kp* is more frequent than the voiced *gb*, which is also less frequent than pre-nasal *ŋgb*. Certain languages display a free alternation between *kw* and *kp*, (*ŋ*)*gw* and (*ŋ*)*gb* and, at least from a comparative perspective, it seems clear that sequences of the type *kw*, *gw* and *bw*, preceded or not by a nasal, are most often at the origin of the reported labiovelar consonants. Further note that *gb* is the representation of the nominal prefix of class 14 before stems with an initial vowel in Doko (C40), whereas in Beo (C45), a nominal prefix *kp-*, which could be the one from class 15, alternates with the nominal prefix of class 6 *m-* before stems of this type (cf. *kpálà*, pl. *málà* 'nail(s)', *kpìnyò*, pl. *mìnyò* 'tooth/teeth'). This is characteristic of the languages of the C30 Ngiri[1] or of the C50 languages such as Lombo, Gesogo and Tofoke, however. The languages spoken in the northwest of zone D have labiovelar consonants the origin of which is definitely different. Thus, Bali (D21), for instance, has the consonants *kp*, *gb* and *ŋgb*, while having *kwá* 'die!' and *gwá* 'fall!'

The languages of zone A excluded, labio-velar consonants can only be found in the C-River languages, in the Aka-Mbati-Ngando group (C10), in the C50 languages, and in the northern languages of zone D (Lengola D12, Mituku D13, Enya D14, Bali D21, Bira D32, Bodo D35, etc.). This is equally the zone where one finds the implosive consonants *ɓ* and *ɗ*, which are either optional vs. contextually determined realizations of *b* and *d*; or phonologically opposed to these consonants like in Boa (C44) and Lengola (D12); or else have phonological status in a language in which *b* and *d* do not occur, such as Aka and Ngando (C10) or the Myene-idioms of group B10. It should be noted that in at least one C30 Ngiri language, Motembo, *ɓ* and *ɗ* are the only voiced labial or dental plosives, and that, curiously, *ɓ* is often dropped in word or phrase internal position. The latter is a typical behavior of the non-implosive *b* in very many languages of the centre of zone C.

The languages of B30, B60, B70, C60 and C70 groups generally have no implosive consonants, nor labio-velar phonemes (except sometimes in the ideophones).

Another strange phenomenon that marks the use of consonants in a particular region is the absence of labial nasals in the prefixed forms. This phenomenon is both of a phonological and a morphological nature, because the *m*-consonants of the other languages correspond to *b* in the prefixes of the type CV-, but correspond to *m* elsewhere. This can be observed in the area which is covered by the C60 languages of the so-called Mongo-group and which extends to Ngando (C63), Yela-Kela (C74–75) and Ndengese (C81) as well as to Ombo (C76). Tetela (C71) exhibits this feature as well in the concord prefixes, but not in the nominal prefixes, which in this language are vocalic in the relevant classes. The same applies to Mbole-Tooli (C60). In the C50 group, Kele and Gesogo display this characteristic, whereas in other languages it only shows up in certain classes. Thus, Tofoke (C53), for instance, has a locative preposition *mò* which corresponds to the prefix of class 18; and Mbesa (C51) has a class 6 with prefix *ba-*, but prefixes of the type *mV-* in all other classes where one expects to find them. This is clearly bound to a rather compact region. Nevertheless, it is interesting to note that it is equally found in the northern variant of Bubi of Bioko (A31), where it is extended to all nasal consonants in most of the contexts in which they should appear, except in final position.

Several languages of zone C show a marked tendency to drop certain consonants in rapid speech, at least in some specific contexts. The most vulnerable consonants are *b* and *l*, but in several languages it can also apply to *m*, *t*, *k* and *z*. These optional elisions can only be observed for consonants in intervocalic position inside the clause or phrase, and essentially for prefix-consonants. The same consonant in clause-initial position is never elided. The speaker applies the elision of consonants in normal speech but is always able to re-establish the dropped consonants, without any difficulty or hesitation.

The optional elision of *b* is rather typical of the so-called Mongo languages (C60) but can also be observed in several nearby languages such as Ngando (C63), Mbesa (C51), certain variants of Tofoke (C53) or Kela (C75). Thus, one can find in Kela: *bònt'ònd'ômbé* for *bòntò bòndá bòmbé* 'an ugly man'. The optional omission of a *t* in prefixes or of a nasal consonant *n* in the initial position of pronominal stems can also be observed in certain languages known as Mongo but it is much rarer and restricted to particular phrases. Leke (C14) jointly applies the optional but regular elision of *b* and *m* in prefixes, and the elision of *z* and *k* in some specific contexts. Non-nasal labial plosives are only omitted in prefixes if situated between two identical vowels, one of which is in word-final or morpheme-final position (cf. *à*à*mbó bòkònzì bòdò ~ àà*mbó òkònzì bòdò* 'accept the title of chief'; *tàbáyèngyé ~ tàáyèngyé* 'you (pl.) search them (cl.2)'). Nasal labials are elided in the same contexts, except that the two surrounding vowels do not have to be identical. If they are different, the first assimilates to the second and both can be nasalized (cf. *béèdé màkámbá ~ béèd*ạ̀ *ạ̀kámbá* 'they cut up the branches'; *bómòkàngyí ~ b*ọ̀ọ̀*kàngyí* 'they have joined it'). Finally, *z*, *k* and *b* are omitted in initial position of the pronominal forms which participate in the expression of the possessive (cf. *isángwá zi zábàngá ~ isángwá zá ábàngá* 'our maize'; *ìnkàsò zí z'éí ~ ìnkàsw' îi z'éí* 'his wrist').

In conclusion, the languages C60 and 70, spoken in a continuous area going from the confluence of the Ruki and the Congo river to the border of the Tetela-region between the Jwafa and the Loilaka, apply elision of the *l* of the prefix of class 11 and of the prefix of class 5 (singular of class 6 and plural of class 7) when these prefixes are in phrase-initial position. In Mbole, Kutu and Mbwanja (C60), *l* is elided in any case (cf. Mbwanja: *là lìtóò lìné ~ là ìtóò ìné* 'with these cloths'). In Eleku (C60), Yela (C74) and Kela (C75), the elision of *l* brings about the appearance of a vowel *a*, possibly epenthetic because its tone is identical to the tone of the preceding vowel (cf. Eleku: *línò lìnámì ~ lín' àìnámì* 'my tooth';

lɔ̀ɔ̀kɔ̀ lònámì lòlè lòtálé ~ *lɔ̀ɔ̀k' àònámì lòl' àòtálé* 'my arm is long'), while in Ntomba-Bolenge, Losikongo, Bonyanga, Wangata and Lifumba, a vowel *e* replaces the nominal prefix of class 11 and the verbal prefix of the second person plural in the very same conditions (cf. *ínyó lósàngákì* ~ *íny' ésàngákì* 'you (pl.) have said', *là lòkámò* ~ *l' èkámò* 'hastily').

This kind of phenomenon certainly deserves to be studied in much more detail, because it is interesting in more than one respect, notably concerning the appearance of prefixes of the vocalic type and with respect to the existence of particular realizations of the prefixes of class 5 and 11 in the languages of the northwest, the origin of which is still not understood. But it is also interesting with regard to the determination of the syntagmatic units within the clause or the occurrence of syllable schemes and successions that are not frequent in the Bantu languages. An example like:

(3)   Kela (C75)   *lìpèlɔ́ lìndá bèsàlì*
      lìpèlw' áìnd' êsàlì
      'slim thighs'

combines the aphaeresis of the consonant *b* and the representation of the prefix-consonant *l* as a vowel *a*. It shows the very important effect these two phenomena have on the representation of utterances.

In the same geographical area, and more specifically in the western part of it, the glottal stop *ʔ* systematically replaces the prefixes of the type *bi-* (cl. 8) and *ji-* (cl. 5) if they are not followed by a sequence *mC* and if they are not in clause-initial position. Some languages introduce a vowel *a* in the same case, which precedes the glottal stop. For example: *m̀pà là ʔkàmbò jĭmɔ́* 'I have no other concern any more' (cf. *jìkàmbò* 'concern'); *bìmbèngá ʔtsátò* 'three doves'; *áfòkìsì à ʔpàngà* 'he doesn't live in Jipanga'; *ăòòmà ʔnkéj' ằʔtsátò* 'he has killed three ants' (cf. *bìnkéjì* 'ants'). In Nkengo, the glottal stop *ʔ* is the obligatory representation of the prefix *li-* of class 5 (singular of class 6 and plural of class 7) in every context. Its presence brings about the presence of a stop or an affricate in the initial position of stems whose plural of class 2/6 or singular of class 7 have an initial fricative or glide (cf. *ʔbá*, pl. *bavá* 'palm tree', *ʔpàfú*, pl. *bàfàfú* 'wing', *ʔtsókò*, pl. *bàsókò* 'shoulder', *èwá*, pl. *ʔbwá* 'domesticated animal'). This is all the more interesting because there are some Hendo idioms (C70) adjacent to Tetela, in which the class 5 prefix is represented by *ʔ*, while in others this prefix is marked by a lengthening of the stem-initial consonant, which is also strengthened in case it is not a stop (cf. *bbóngɔ́*, pl. *àbóngɔ́* 'knee'; *kkɔ̀cì*, pl. *àkɔ̀cì* 'tooth'; *nnù*, pl. *ànù* 'frog'; *ddémbà*, pl. *àlémbà* 'body'; *ccɔ́kɔ̀*, pl. *àsɔ́kɔ̀* 'buttock'; *èkfútú*, pl. *kkfútú* 'calabash'; *èsénjè*, pl. *ccénjè* 'squirrel'; *èsàmbè*, pl. *ccàmbè* 'house'; *èpèkò*, pl. *ppèkò* 'iron object' etc …). In Tetela (C71), the same type of phenomenon is much more systematic, not only in class 5 singular and plural, but also in class 19 and inside stems. Being better known, these facts are analyzed in many sources and will not be discussed in detail here. But note that consonant lengthening equally exists in Lega (D25) where every consonant is long if preceded by a vowel *i* in word- or morpheme-initial position. In this environment, the representations of *l* and *y* are [d:] and [dʸ:] respectively.

The sequences of a nasal and an oral consonant which can be found in the languages of the forest also exhibit some interesting characteristics, be it of their own, or by their geographical distribution. The first point that merits some discussion is the presence or absence of sequences of a nasal and a voiceless consonant. These sequences are absent in numerous languages of zone B (Pove B22c, Kota B25, Tsogo B31, Pinji B30, Nzebi B52, Fumu B77b, etc.), as well as in Koyo (C24) and Mboshi (C25), in Aka (C10), in the northern languages of the Ngiri (C30), in the languages of group C50, and also in certain languages in the north of zone D (Lengola D12, Mituku D13, Bira D32, Nyali D33, Bodo D35, etc.). Generally speaking, this absence is predominantly found in the north. The southern languages (Teke B70, Bobangi C32, the so-called Mongo group C60, Tetela C71, Ombo C75, Lega D25, Nyanga D43) have both the sequences N + voiceless consonant and N + voiced consonant. Certain more specific facts should also be mentioned. First of all, it is clear that the situation as observed in the languages of group C50 or in Lengola (D12) is particular in more than one respect. Lengola has only one N + voiceless C sequence in which the nasal is not syllabic: viz. *nt*, attested in class 9. In class 3, where the nasal consonant carries a tone, this language admits all sequences of N + voiceless C. In the languages of group C50 and in adjacent languages, some sequences are admitted, such as *mp* in Mbole-Tooli (C60), for instance (cf. *lòsò*, pl. *mpòsò* 'shell'). However, the most interesting characteristic is, that in Mbesa (C51) and Gesogo (C52), the sequence *ŋk* found in other languages tends to appear as *ŋg*, at least in word-initial position (cf. Gesogo: *ŋgíŋgó* 'neck'; Mbesa: *ngímà* 'ape'), while certain N + voiced C sequences are represented by the corresponding voiceless consonant (Gesogo: *kàngà* 'healer'; Mbesa: *kòì* 'leopard', *sòkù* 'elephant'). Mbole-Tooli evolves towards a confusion of *ŋg* and *ŋk*, which tend to merge into a single representation, viz. *k*, in word-initial position (cf. *kòì* 'leopard', *kàngà* 'healer', *kíngó* 'neck', *kòkò* 'chicken') but the language has also *ngémà* 'ape' and *ngùfú* 'hippopotamus').

Finally, in some languages more to the south, NC sequences can undergo other types of reduction. In one rather compact area (Tetela C71, Kela C75, Ombo C76, and Mituku D13), Meinhof's Rule reduces the successions of a nasal and a voiced oral consonant to a homorganic nasal (which is sometimes long) if the onset of the next syllable is a nasal or a sequence of N + voiced C. The same phenomenon also applies to the representations *mb-* and *nd-* of the prefixes of the type (-)N- which appear before stems with an initial vowel. We thus find in Kela (C75): *ŋòndé* 'crocodile', *ŋòmò* 'drum', *lìsòŋŋànà* 'to marry'; and in Mituku (D13): *òlàŋgà*, pl. *màŋgà* 'spear'; *kònàmbà* 'to criticize me' but *kòndétà* 'to call me' with a first person singular object prefix which is *nd* before verb stems beginning in a vowel but *n* if the verb stem is of the type + VNC-; in Ombo (C76): *lòángá*, pl. *mmáŋgá* 'chin'; *ménà* 'to see' (verb stem: +*én*-) but *mbìyà* 'to arrive' (verb stem: +*ìy*-).

Nkengo and Ngando (C60) systematically reduce N + voiced C sequences to a homorganic nasal consonant in all contexts, in word initial as well as in interior position. Thus, Ngando has: *múlà* 'rain', *mwá* 'dog', *èsénà* 'cloth' (cf. Nkundo: *èséndà*); Nkengo has: *ʔŋkònò*, pl. *bàŋkònò* 'banana'; *músà* 'back'; *bòŋíní* 'marshy land' (cf. Nkundo: *bòŋgíní*). Finally, Hulstaert (1978), Picavet (1947) and Motingea (1993) signal that the Pygmy languages of the Ingende and Bonkoto regions systematically reduce the NC sequences (apart from *mb*, sometimes) to the non-nasal consonant or at least to a corresponding non-nasal consonant. Examples are:

(4)	Tswa-Lonkundo	*tàgé*	'bed'	Nkundo	*ntàngé*
		kígó	'neck'	Nkundo	*nkíngó*
		òfòfò	'wind'	Nkundo	*bòmpòmpò*
		lìtídí	'heel'	Nkundo	*lìtsíndí*
	Tswa-Bonkoto	*bokoofi*	'chief'	Nkundo	*bò(n)kònjì*
		likòodò	'banana'	Nkundo	*lìnkòndò*
		taba	'goat'	Nkundo	*ntàà*
		eggabi	'firstborn'	Ntomba	*èŋgàmbí*
		boa	'dog'	Nkundo	*mbwá*
		baloggo	'blood'	Nkundo	*bàlóngó*

Note that a long consonant alternates with the lengthening of the preceding vowel in the notations. These are certainly compensatory mechanisms that may differ depending on the dialect group, but the notations are not sufficiently precise and phonetically too unreliable to be integrated into a more elaborated reflection.

None of the facts signalled here is restricted to the forest languages. A more complete study of them would be useful for a better understanding of similar processes which can be observed in other languages of the northwest, or even in certain southern Bantu languages.

2.3 Tonality

The tonal systems of the forest languages don't show any uniformity either. They are of quite variable types, so that it is difficult to give an overall description of them in a relatively succinct way, the more so because many are not completely described.

The central and southern forest languages (like Bobangi C32, the so-called Mongo group C60, Tetela C71, Lega D25, Nyanga D43) can be considered as having a rather classical tone system, which does not normally pose major problems to the descriptive linguist. While certain languages of zone D such as Lega (D25) have two register tones and downstep of high tones, most languages of the south and centre of zone C attest high tones, low tones and contour tones which manifest great stability and are hardly modified within the clause, if one excludes the rules which apply at the contact between morphemes or words. However, these contacts have an important impact on the tonality because of the numerous elisions of vowels and consonants (optional or obligatory) which have been discussed in the preceding paragraphs. Most often the tones are combined and they may form the contour tones HLH or LHL, which are exceedingly abundant in these languages. Also note that Tetela (C71) has a process of high tone spread, which is rather frequent in the Bantu family as a whole, but appears to be rare in this part of zone C, although it equally exists in some languages of the C30 Ngiri group.

Probably under the influence of the Central Sudanic languages on the one hand and the Ubangian languages on the other hand, some northernmost languages of zone D and C have three tones: high, mid and low. This is the case in Bira (D21) and in Nyali (D33), and also in Mbati (C10), where an extra-high tone level appears in addition. However, the tone systems of these languages are not sufficiently known yet.

The most complex tone systems delimit two particular areas: these are on the one hand the area occupied by the languages of the C30 Ngiri group and on the other hand the western forest region where the languages are classified in zone B. We do not yet know the tone systems of all C30 Ngiri languages very well, but we can affirm that they belong to two types. Languages like Bobangi, Binza, Loi, Mbonji and Balobo, which are all situated between the Congo and the Ngiri, have tone systems of the Lingala type, the analysis of which is rather uncomplicated. The languages situated either more upstream alongside the Congo River (Mabale, Poto, Motembo, Doko) or between the Ngiri and the Ubangi (Zamba, Lobala, Bomboma, Lingonda, Ebuku), on the other hand, have a very complicated tonality. According to Twilingiyimana (1984) and Kamanda (1991), Doko and Zamba have downstep. Moreover, the tone contours of nominal forms are highly dependent on the influence of initial high tones, which are present due to the persistence of the augment. In Bomboma, nominal forms show tonal modifications that depend on their function and place in the clause. This reminds us of similar phenomena in various languages of zone B and in the languages of the Kongo type. Conversely, the C10 and C20 languages do not display these particularities, as far as their tone systems are known. Aka (C10), Koyo (C24) and Mboshi (C25), for instance, have a tone system of the classical type. The same goes for Leke (C14), although this language exhibits downstep, as in Zamba or Doko, and applies numerous contact tone rules due to the marked tendency of many of its consonants not to be represented in more rapid speech.

The languages of zone B, which occupy the western part of the forest, often have complex tone systems as well, but these are rather well known at present. These systems can have 'tonal cases' and thus are of the Kongo type. The reader is referred to the works of Blanchon for the B40 and B50 languages, and to Marchal-Nasse (1989) for Nzebi (B52). The B30 languages do not belong to this type, but the tonality of their nouns could be influenced by the more or less residual augment, which is the case in Himba e.g. Tsogo (B31) exhibits a mechanism of high tone shift, rather frequent in the Bantu languages. The situation is more complex in the idioms of group B10 where the opposition definite vs. indefinite is expressed by means of the tones on the nominal forms, which is rather rare and which determines realizations for which no complete explanation has yet been proposed, although Philippson and Puech (n.d) represents a significant progress towards an acceptable solution.

2.4 Syllable structures

The forest languages exhibit some peculiarities with respect to the syllable structures they admit or privilege. Apart from the forest languages of zone A, which will not be discussed here, they generally have almost no syllables with a consonantal coda. This type of syllable appears more systematically in the B80 and C80 languages that are spoken immediately south of the forest. Yet, it has been noted above that several so-called Mongo languages (C60) as well as Ombo (C76) exhibit a syllable scheme with coda *m*, where the adjacent languages display a final syllable *mi*, and sometimes *mu*.

The most notable peculiarity with respect to the syllabic types in the forest languages of the groups B30, C10, C50, C60, C70 and D10 seems to be the abundance of syllables reduced to the nucleus. This is provoked by several of the phonological facts described above and, particularly, the unstable character of certain consonants in onset position. It would be interesting systematically to study the strategies of resyllabification used by the languages that attest this type of consonantal instability, but it has been noted in §2.1 that many forest languages admit the realization of more than two successive vowels. An accurate study of syllable types and of their combinations within words would then be all the more interesting since to these problems are added, in several languages, other problems posed by the emergence of long consonants in onset position, the reduction of NC sequences to either the oral consonant or the nasal consonant even outside the context of application of Meinhof's rule; and the often peculiar treatment of *ŋg* and *mb*, which, e.g. in the reduplicated infinitives or nominal forms of Tetela (C71), can function in a manner which differentiates them from the other NC groups.

3 MORPHOLOGY

3.1 Class systems and nominal forms

3.1.1

Certain features of the class system deserve some attention, although only a very small number of properties specific to the forest languages can be determined. Most characteristics that will be discussed are only attested in parts of the geographical area dealt with and thus only concern certain more closely related languages.

3.1.2

If one excludes the forest languages of the south of zone D, which mostly have a full class system, resembling very much those of the central Bantu languages, the languages of the forest have, at least, one particularity in common: location is not expressed by means of nominal classes whose pre-prefixed morphemes regularly determine agreement within the noun phrase as well as on the verbs that have the locative as their subject.

Exceptions to this situation are rare and very divergent anyway when compared to what can be observed in the centre of the Bantu domain. Thus, Tsogo (B31) has two locative nouns *gòmá* and *vòmá* 'place', the second determines concord that is proper to it and that belongs to a remaining class 16 (cf. *vòmá vé évà vándé tè vávò gó mbóká nè édùé* 'this place is unique in the village'). Beo (C45) has four nominal prefixes which mark location (*hu-* 'in', *na-* 'towards', *ka-* and *ta-* 'near'), which is rather curious if one considers its very northern position. Formally, these prefixes do not directly correspond to those of class 16, 17 and 18. Nevertheless, they determine concord within the phrase, notably on the adjective and on the connective. In general, however, the languages of the forest do not have locative classes. The locative morphemes are of the type *gó-* in the languages of zone B, of type *ò* or *ó* in the C10 languages and the languages of the C30 Ngiri group, as well as in Bolia and in Ntomba (C35), of the type *ndá* or *ǎ* in the C60 languages, and of the type *lá* in the Tetela group (C71–3). Ngando (C63) has a preposition *má* (cf. *má lìhòkù* 'in the ditch'). A morpheme *ka* has been found in Boa (C44), Bira (D32) and Nyali (D33), where it coexists with *da* 'at'. The same morpheme possibly also occurs in the locative noun *kǎmà* in Ombo (C76) which determines agreements in *ka-* within the noun phrase, but verbal agreement of class 15/17. The locative morphemes of Tofoke (C53) and Gesogo (C52) are more classic, of the type *gò* and *mò*. Lombo-Turumbu (C54) has *ko*, but also *ta*, which can equally be found in Beo (C45) and Ngombe (C41). All these morphemes function synchronically as prepositions and have to be analyzed as such. The most ambiguous situations are the ones that can be found in zone B where the disappearance of class 17 and, at times, class 16 has not yet been accomplished.

3.1.3

The number of non-locative classes is by and large reduced because of the generalized absence of class 12, which hardly exists in the forest zone, except in Tetela (C71) and in the southwestern languages of zone D (Mituku D13, Enya D14, Lega D25, Nyanga D43, etc …). Class 15 as well is not frequent in the central forest languages, but exists in the southern languages of zone D and in certain languages of zone B. In Bali (D21) there are a class 15 singular of class 6 and a class 15 plural of class 3, the origin of which is not very clear. But note that in zone B a class with nominal prefix *o-* often results from the fusion of class 15, 11 and/or 14. Some remnants of noun class 15 have been observed in Ndumu (B63), where *kulu* (pl. *mili*) 'leg' and *kwogo* (pl. *mogo*) 'arm' have their agreements in class 7, but also in Aka (C10), where *òbó* 'arm' takes its concords in class 3, as well as in Lengola (D12) where the same can be stated of *òtói* (pl. *màtói*) 'ear' or of *òbó* 'arm'. In zone C, infinitives are not generally of class 15. However, traces of this class can sometimes be identified in composed conjugation, and some isolated languages do have infinitives of class 15, such as Likata, Ebuku, or Loi among the C30 Ngiri languages. On the other hand, class 13 and 19, which form the class pair of the diminutive, are very well represented. But class 19 is absent in the southern languages of zone D and the pair 13/19 exists neither in the B60–70 languages (Mbaama-Lempiini B62, Ndumu B63, Laale B73b, Yaa B73c, Fumu B77b), nor in Bobangi (C32), in the C30 Ngiri group, in Leke (C14), in certain languages of the northeast like Boa (C44), Beo (C45) and Bali (D21).

Finally, the reduction of the number of nominal classes is particularly drastic in the central forest languages (C60 and C70) where the prefixes of type *mV-* do not exist and where, consequently, the classes 1, 3 and 14 and also the classes 2 and 6 tend to merge or to be confused. Class 4 and 8 usually remain distinct, due to the degree of aperture of their prefix vowel (cl. 4 *be-*, but cl. 8 *bi-*). This process is typical for the so-called Mongo languages (C60) as well as for languages like Kela (C75), Ndengese (C81) and even Tetela (C71) where it can only be recognized in the form of the concord prefixes, because the nominal prefixes are vocalic in the relevant classes. In the languages of group C50 this phenomenon is much less systematic. Thus, Mbesa (C51) only mixes up class 2 and 6 (PN *ba-*); Tofoke (C53), which has a locative preposition *mò*, has concords of class 1/14 that are different from those of class 3, which is also the case in Ombo (C76).

It might be interesting to draw attention to the fact that, according to Picavet (1947), the Pygmies of Bombwanja and Wangata employ a nominal prefix of class 1 *mo-* in some nouns (cf. *mòtò* 'person', *mĕnà* 'child') and that, according to Hulstaert (1978), the Pygmies of Basankusu alternately use *bo-, vo-* and *mo-* forms in class 1, *ba-* and *ma-* in class 6, and *mo-* and *vo-* in class 3. Hence, these Pygmy variants to a certain extent seem to maintain nominal prefixes of the *mV-* type, which the adjacent Mongo languages do not exhibit at all. It should be stressed that, apart from a dialectal variant of Bubi of Bioko (A31), this type of reduction of the class system is found nowhere else, and particularly that it is absent in zone B, in the C10 languages, in Bobangi (C32), in the C30 Ngiri group and in zone D.

3.1.4

Several other characteristics of the class system deserve some discussion. One of these is the existence of a class 1 with nominal prefix *a-* in a series of languages generally situated in the northeast of the forest. This subclass groups a small number of nouns designating animals and plants, and, more rarely, members of the family. It has been attested notably in Buja (C37), Doko (C40), Boa (C44), Lombo-Turumbu (C54), Kele (C55), Mbole-Tooli (C60), Lengola (D12), Mituku (D13) and Nyali (D33). In a region where the consonant *k* rarely occurs in prefixes, one could wonder whether this is not a residual class 12, the more so because Lengola (D12) has a word *ànùà* 'mouth', which is usually of class 12 in Bantu. This hypothesis, however, is not very satisfactory, since Mituku (D13), for instance, has at the same time: cl.1 *àgbálá* 'pepper', *àtóngú* 'cock', *àsèlà* 'cucumber' and a diminutive class 12 of which the nominal prefix is *kà-*. As far as Enya is concerned, it simultaneously has a pair 12/13 of which the prefixes are *kà-* and *tò-*, and some nouns of class 1, the nominal prefix of which is *àmò-* or *à-* followed by a syllable *mò* which is integrated in the noun stem (cf. *àmǒ:mè*, pl. *báómè* 'man', *àmòkálí*, pl. *bámòkálí* 'woman'). The latter examples rather point to a unified augment *a-*, which exists in Nyanga (D43) for instance. Additional research could be done in order to determine the origin (or origins?) of this class 1 with prefix *à-*. The matter is not without importance, even though it is geographically restricted.

The following facts should also be mentioned:

- The existence of a class with nominal prefix *mò-, mɔ-* or *mà-* which forms the plural of one of the classes 15 *kù-* in Bali (D21) and of class 11 *lù-* in Nyali (D33). This class might also exist in Boa (C44) in the alternation of the forms *mò-* and *mà-* of the so-called class 6 prefix. This might be interesting with respect to the frequent occurrence of a plural class with prefix *mù-* in the northwestern Bantu languages.
- The rather widespread occurrence of a plural class with a nominal prefix *li-* or *di-* which can be identical to the one of class 5, but doesn't necessarily have to. Two separate forest regions exhibit this plural class and it is consequently difficult to say whether the two are linked in one way or another. The first of these regions is the one covered by the B10–B30 languages, where the phenomenon is known as class 10b. This name is justified by the fact that the plural class with nominal prefix *di-*, and with

a singular generally in class 11/15 (/14) has the same agreement morphemes as class 10 with prefix N-. In this area, the nominal prefix of the plural class under discussion is different from the prefix of class 5. A lot has been written on this subject. Therefore, more attention will be given to the second relevant area, covered by a series of C60 languages, going from the confluence of the Congo river and the Ruki, between the Jwafa, the Lomela and the Loilaka to the area occupied by the C70 languages (Yela C74, Kela C75 and Tetela C71). In this zone, there is a class which forms a pair with class 7 and is generally described as a plural class 5, because the forms of its prefixes are identical to those of class 5, the most particular representations of them included. This remark concerns the C60 and 70 languages, in which the prefixes of type *li-* sg. and pl. are represented by *ai-* in intervocalic position and in rapid speech (cf. Yela C74: *lìtóò líkɔ́ ~ lìtóò àikɔ́* 'these fabrics'). It is equally valid for the languages of the region where the same nominal prefix is represented either by the glottal stop *ʔ* followed by a strengthened consonant (cf. Nkengo C60: cl. 7, 5 *èyɔ̀ŋɔ̀*, pl. *ʔjɔ̀ŋɔ̀* 'china clay'), or by the lengthening of this strong consonant without any other segmental representation (cf. Tetela C71: cl. 7, 5 *ètèndò*, pl. *ttèndò* 'bed'; *èlèmbà*, pl. *ddèmbà* 'thigh of an animal'; *èlòngálóngà*, pl. *ddòngálóngà* 'bird of the poultry yard'). There is also a plural class with a nominal prefix of the type *jù-, jò-, ɟ-* which exists in Mbole-Tooli (C60) and Lengola (D12) where it forms the plural of class 11 without being mixed up with class 10, which has N- as its prefix (cf. Lengola D12: *lùmbó*, pl. *jùmbó* 'song'; *lògùɓò*, pl. *jògùɓò* 'wall'; *lòɓíkò*, pl. *jòɓíkò* 'dispute'; Mbole-Tooli C60: *lwǎlà*, pl. *zálà* 'nail'; *lókà*, pl. *zókà* 'day'). The situation in Nyali (D33) is difficult to assess, but certain nouns with prefix *i-* in the singular form their plural with the prefixes *li-* or *di-* (cf. *ìságà*, pl. *lìságà* 'branch'; *ìkóndó*, pl. *dìkóndó* 'arm').

- The indubitable existence of augments which sometimes fulfil a grammatical role, sometimes have become frozen, although they can still contribute to the expression of definiteness in certain cases, and finally sometimes are simply present in the structure of the nominal prefixes. The clearest augments are found in the C30 Ngiri languages like Zamba, in Doko (C40), and in the languages of the group B10–30 such as Myene and Himba. Nevertheless, although Zamba, for instance, expresses the opposition definite vs. indefinite by means of the presence or absence of the augment (Kamanda 1991), it is rather the alternation of different types of nominal prefix which permits to affirm that there are traces of the augment in most of the languages cited. As a matter of fact, the nominal prefixes in the forest languages are most often of the type CV-, except in class 7 and 19 where their vocalic structure results from the absence of the consonants *k* and *p* in prefixes. These classes only have a CV- prefix in the southern languages of zone D (Mituku D13, Enya D14, Lega D25, Binja D20), in Tetela (C71) and in part of zone B (Tsogo B31, Pove B22c, Nzebi B52, Ndumu B63). For the other classes, however, there are many languages where the prefixes are either of the type V- vs. VC-, depending on the class (e.g. Tetela C71; Mbole-Tooli C60), or of the type (C)V- vs. (V)C(V)-, depending on the syllable structure of the noun stem. Thus, in Doko (C40) for instance, the nominal prefixes take a (C)V-form before stems with an initial consonant and a VC(V)-form before stems which begin in a vowel (cf. *ósálí*, pl. *básálí* 'worker' but *ómáná*, pl. *ábáná* 'child'). The same is true for certain languages of group B60 and for languages outside the forest of group C20, such as Koyo (C24) and Mboshi (C25) where the nominal prefixes are of the type V- or C(V)-depending on the structure of the stem. In the B10 languages, the alternating prefixes are of the type *Vm-* in class 1, 3, 4 and 6 when the stem begins in a labial consonant, of the V-type in all classes before stems with any other consonant in initial position, and of the VC(V)-type when the stem begins in a vowel. It seems that this situation, as well as the existence of prefix sequences of the type CVC(V)- in some languages like Himba (B30) or Zamba (C30 Ngiri), can be attributed to the existence of augments, more or less incorporated in prefix sequences, which makes it difficult to decide on their synchronic analyzability or complete petrification. It is interesting to note that in the far east of the forest zone, Nyanga (D43) has a perfectly functional augment of which the segmental manifestation is a vowel *á-* pre-prefixed to all classes, whereas Nande (DJ42) has augments which are similar to those of the interlacustrine languages.

- With respect to the structure of the nominal prefixes it can be mentioned that in many languages of zone B, in part of zone C (Bolia and Ntomba C35, Konda C60, certain C30 Ngiri languages) and in zone D, the nominal prefix of class 5 is of the type *i-* or *e-* before stems with an initial consonant, but of the type CV- or C- before stems which begin in a vowel, the consonant in this latter type being *d, l* and, less frequently, a fricative *z, ʒ* or an affricate *dʒ*. Certain languages like Lengola (D12) and some so-called Mongo idioms (C60) have an *l-* when the stem begins with +*i* or with a vowel of the first degree, whereas before other vowels a consonant *dʒ-* or *ʔj-* is used (cf. Lengola D12: *ìkómì* 'ten', *líɲɔ* 'tooth', *lidʒɔ* 'eye' but *ʔjói* 'voice, speech'). Conversely, in a more central region, the noun prefix of class 5 is always of the type CV- (or even VCV- or CVCV), independent of the syllable structure of the stem. This latter situation can be found in some B60–70 languages (Ndumu B63, Fumu B77b), in most of the known languages of group C10 (Aka, Ngando and Babole), in the majority of the C30 Ngiri languages, in Bobangi (C32), in some of the so-called Mongo languages (C60), in Yela (C74), Kela (C75) and Ombo (C76), as well as in the C50 group. The consonant of the nominal prefix in these languages is mostly *l* or *d*, but it is *z* or *dʒ* before stems with an initial vowel. However, a number of languages (Aka C10, Babole-Dzeke C14, Nkengo C60, Ombo C76, etc.) maintain the consonant *l* when the initial vowel of the stem is *i* (cf. Ombo C76: *lìbélè* 'breast', *jŏm* 'ten' but *línɔ*, pl. *bàínɔ* 'tooth'). Also note the existence of prefix sequences like *izi-, lizi-* in Zamba or *lij-* in Lilenge (cf. *lìjói*, pl. *màmói* 'business'), which appear in the Ngiri region where the augment is prominently present. Finally, in certain languages the nominal prefix of class 5 is Ø, without any modification of the initial consonant of the stem (cf. Laale B73b: *bá*, pl. *màbá* 'palm tree') or with an initial voiced consonant opposed to the voiceless consonant which is used in the plural (cf. Aka of Bayanga C10: *bàpá*, pl. *màpàpá* 'wing'; *dòngà*, pl. *màtòngà* 'double oyster'). It has already been mentioned that the nominal prefix of class 5 can also manifest itself by the appearance of a sequence *ʔ* + strong consonant (cf. Nkengo C60: *ʔbá*, pl. *bàvá* 'palm tree'; *ʔtsókò*, pl. *bàsókò* 'shoulder'; *èyɔ̀ŋɔ̀*, pl. *ʔjɔŋɔ* 'china clay') or by the appearance of a long strengthened consonant (cf. Tetela C71: *ddèmbà*, pl. *àlèmbà* 'body').

3.1.5

Although considerable progress has recently been made in this domain, our knowledge of the Bantu languages that are isolated between the Ubangian or Sudanic languages remains fragmentary. The same is true of certain Bantu languages situated on the border of the Bantu domain. Their detailed description, however, would lead to a better comprehension of the history of the linguistic fragmentation in the region and to a refinement of the theories concerning the creation of 'mixed' languages arising from the contact between languages of different groups or families. Some particular facts can briefly be cited. For example, Boa (C44) features class suffixes which can be used together with nominal prefixes: this is sufficiently exceptional to deserve mention. Languages like Mbati (C10),

Pere (D31) or Bira (D32) show a strong breakdown of the class system, which is not present in certain adjacent languages such as Aka and Ngando (C10), or Nyali and Bodo (D30). Thus, Mbati (C10) opposes a singular *mò-* or *ò-* to a generalized and often additive plural *ɓà-* (cf. *mòté*, pl. *ɓàmòté* 'tree'). There is no agreement, except with adjectives, and the choice between the only two singular verbal prefixes *à-* and *è-* depends on whether the subject is animate or not, while the verbal prefix of the plural is always *ɓà-*. The opposition [± animate] is also basic in Pere (D31) and in Bira (D32). Indeed, in the first of these languages, the nouns of which the stem designates an animate entity generally have a prefix of the type *mò-*, *mù-*, *n-* in the singular and a prefix *bà-* in the plural (cf. *mùkù:ŋgá*, pl. *bàkù:ŋgá* 'weaver'), while nouns with a stem designating inanimate entities do not have a commutable prefix and form their plural by the attachment of *-áti* 'many, a lot' or by reduplication (cf. *mɔ̌:*, pl. *mɔ̌:áti* 'head'; *mbátá*, pl. *mbátámbátá* 'chair'). In Bira (D32), [+ animate] nouns have a singular with prefix *m(V)-* and a plural with prefix *ɓa-*; they only determine agreement on the adjective in the singular (cf. *micá mòlúkù*, pl. *ɓàicà lúkù* 'small boy'), whereas [−animate] nouns do not have a morphological plural but trigger the appearance of a morpheme *á-* which is prefixed to the verb.

It is not possible here to digress on systems of this type, on which the reader is invited to consult the available descriptions. They are all the more interesting since they coexist, in the same region, with sometimes less classic, though extremely productive class systems, which definitely implies that contacts between languages from different phyla have been established following different processes.

3.2 Verbs and verbal morphemes

3.2.1 The verbal prefixes

In the classes, the verbal prefixes do not exhibit any marked particularities in the languages of the forest. The verbal prefix of class 1 is generally *à-* (*á-* in Tofoke C53 and Lega D25), but *ò-* in Mituku (D13) and *ó-* in Enya (D14). Some C30 Ngiri languages have alternating forms *ka-* (Libobi, Lobala, Kunda, Motembo) or *ta-* (Babale) which are used in certain tenses. These forms could stem from the agglutination of a pre-initial element, but this still has to be proved.

For the persons, the languages of the forest have less classic verbal prefixes. Most often they have *nà-* for the first person singular. This prefix can be found in Tsogo (B31), Aka (C10), Ntomba-Tumba (C35), Doko (C40), Mpunza, Lifonga, Loi, Mbonji, Litoka, Balobo, Ndobo (C30 Ngiri), Beo (C45) and Bodo (D35). Alternating forms *nè-* or *ni-* figure in some C30 Ngiri languages (cf. Likata: *nè ~ nà*; Libobi: *ne-*, *na-*, *ni-*), in Boa (C44) and in Mituku (D13) where a form *nè-* is attested. Lega (D25) and Bira (D32) only have one form *ni-*, while Lombo (C54) and Tetela (C71) respectively display a form *lè-* and a form *là-* alternating with *ǹ-*. In B10, B30 or Pove (B22c) the verbal prefix of the first person singular is *me-*, which certainly originates from the substitutive. This form seems to agglutinate to the verbal prefix of class 1a- in Ndumu (B63), where the authors note *m'a-* or (*me*) *a-*. A verbal prefix *i-* exists in Mbudza (C30 Ngiri) as well as in Tofoke (C53), Kele (C55) and Mbole-Tooli (C60). The other C60–70 idioms (Nkundo, Nkengo and Kela) as well as Babale (C30 Ngiri), Bolia (C35) and Enya (D14) have a verbal prefix N- which also occurs in Fumu (B77b) where it alternates, according to the tense, with a prefix *e-*.

The verbal prefix of the second person singular is *ò-* in almost all languages. Nevertheless, Ndumu (B63) and Fumu (B77b) use the substitutive pronoun with the verbal prefix *a-* of class 1. Lega (D25) has *ò-* ~ *gò-*. Kele (C55) and Tofoke (C53) respectively have (*b*)*o-* and *bò-*. Some languages of the C30 Ngiri group alternately have *o-* ~ *ko-* (Libobi, Lobala, Kunda and Motembo). The most remarkable fact is definitely that a rather high number of C10 (Leke), C30 Ngiri (Lifonga, Likata, Libobi, Lobala, Kunda, Motembo, Babale), C40 (Doko), C50 (Kele, Tofoke) and C60 (Mbole-Tooli) languages have the same verbal prefix in the second person singular and in the second person plural (except if, by any chance, there exists a tonal difference which is not marked in the sources). The strategy employed by these languages to neutralize the ambiguity is not always known, but it is interesting to note that some of them have generalized, in the set of ambiguous verb forms, the usage of the morpheme of the type (*-*)*áni*, which often marks the plural of the imperative in Bantu. Thus, Mbole-Tooli (C60) has: *òsôkàmbà* 'you (sg.) work' and *òsôkàmbááyì* 'you (pl.) work'. Lifonga and Likata (C30 Ngiri) have a morpheme *ni* in clause-final position (cf. Lifonga: *oikɛ obokila gbala ni* 'you (pl.) are not going to hunt'; Likata: *óikà ò bà bòkìlà gbàlà nì*, same meaning).

In those cases where it is not identical to the one of the second person singular, the verbal prefix of the second person plural is *nò-* (Tsogo B31 and Pove B22c), *bò-*, *wò-* (Tofoke C53, Lombo C54, Kele C55, Enya D14, Bira D32, Ntomba C35 and C30 Ngiri: Mpunza, Loi, Litoka, Balobo). It is *lì-* or *lè-* in Ndumu (B63) and Fumu (B77b), *lò-* in Bolia (C35), Mongo-Nkundo (C61), Kela (C75), Zamba and Mbonji (C30 Ngiri), *mò-* in Boa (C44), Beo (C45), Mituku (D13) and Lega (D25). In Tetela (C71) it is *nyó-*.

The verbal prefix of the first person plural is most often *tò-* (*tè-* in Boa C44), although Ndumu (B63) has *lì-*, Loi and Ndobo (C30 Ngiri) have *lò-*, and Bira (D32) *ki-*.

In most of the Bantu languages of the forest, the verbal prefixes have a low tone for the persons and in class 1 and a high tone in the other classes.

3.2.2 The object prefixes

Virtually all the forest languages examined have a full range of object prefixes, for the persons as well as for the classes or the reflexive. Mbole-Tooli (C60), Enya (D14) and the C50 languages (Lombo, Tofoke, Kele), however, are exceptional: they do not feature these morphemes, although, curiously, object prefixes can be found in Mituku D13, Bira D32, and Bodo D35 where they can be obligatory in case there is an object noun, e.g. in Mituku. Also note the absence of object prefixes in the B10 group, in Pove (B22c), as well as in Ndumu (B63) and Fumu (B77b). Leke (C14) alternatively exhibits utterances like *àdèzéí ngá* 'he made me cry' and *àmómbédé* 'he makes me come' where the postposed substitutive pronoun alternates with the first person singular object prefix *-ǹ-*. This object prefix is the only one that exists for the persons in Leke, whereas all object prefixes of the classes as well as the reflexive object prefix are attested. The situation is the other way round in Boa (C44), where the object prefixes only exist in the persons, in class 1 and 2 and for the reflexive. Moreover, in this language the object prefixes of the first and second person singular are *-è-* or *-ò-*, those of the first and second person plural are *-é-* or *-ó-*; and the reflexive prefix is *-é-*. This points to a tendency towards a formal confusion of different object prefixes, a tendency which is very clear in the C30 Ngiri languages, as well as in Mbole-Tooli (C60). The general tendency is to mix up the prefixes of the second person singular and plural. Thus, Mbole-Tooli (C60) has *-ò-* and *-ò-*; Mpundza, Mbonji and Balobo (C30 Ngiri) have *-bo-* and *-bo-*; Lifonga, Likata, Libobi and Lobala (C30 Ngiri) have *-e-* and *-e-*. The formal confusion can even go further in C30 Ngiri because, according to Motingea (1996), Kunda has the same object prefix *-mo-* for the first person plural, the second person singular and plural; and for class 1, whereas in Babale, -mo- is used in class 1 and in the second person singular and plural.

The object prefix of the first person singular is generally a nasal consonant; the one of the first person plural is normally -to-, but Zamba, Loi and Mbonji have -lo-, which is the object prefix of the second person plural in Bolia (C35), in Nkengo and Nkundo (C60) or in Kela (C75). It is by far the reflexive object prefix that has the most particular forms. The two dominant forms in the forest languages are -yá-, which is to be found in Leke (C14), Ntomba (C35), the so-called Mongo languages (C60), Kela (C75) or Tetela (C71), and -mí- which figures in the C30 Ngiri languages. Doko (C40) has alternately -mí- or -má-; and -ma- is the only form cited in the sources for Motembo (C30 Ngiri). Several more isolated forms can also be mentioned, like -ka- in Bolia (C35), -kǐ- in Bira (D32) or forms of the vocalic type like -á- in Mbudza (C30 Ngiri) or -é- in Boa (C44) and Beo (C45).

According to the authors, the object prefixes are either low for the persons and class 1, but high for the other classes, or low for the singular persons and for class 1, but high for the plural persons and for the other classes.

3.2.3 The derivation

Although there are few particularities concerning the verb stems, some things can be noted about the verbal derivation. Generally speaking, this procedure functions rather well in the Bantu languages of the forest, even though the number of derivational suffixes is lower here than in the central Bantu languages. The following are found in almost all forest languages: the applicative suffix (-ee-, -e-), the reciprocal suffix -an-, the stative suffix -am-, -em-, sometimes -Vm-, the pair of reversive suffixes: transitive -ol- and intransitive -o-, and less frequently a neuter suffix -eg-, -ik- or -i-. The long causative suffix of the type -is-, -ih-, -es- is attested in quite a lot of languages, notably in Ndumu (B63), Leke (C14), Balobo, Lilenge, Kunda, Mbonji, Zamba, Lobala, Libobi, Lifonga (C30 Ngiri), Doko (C40), Boa (C44), Beo (C45), Tofoke (C53), Lombo (C54), Kele (C55), Mbole-Tooli (C60), Mituku (D13), Bira (D32) and Bodo (D35). But the short form -i-, -y- isn't rare either. It coexists with the long form in Beo (C45) or Leke (C14), and seems to be dominant in the central languages of the south, like Ntomba and Bolia (C35), the so-called Mongo languages (C60), Kela (C75) and some C30 Ngiri languages such as Litoka, Loi or Motembo. Pove (B22c) has -i- and a -id-i sequence, while Tsogo (B31) has a causative suffix -éd- and an applicative suffix -é- (cf. èkàdàmédì 'he has made cicatrize'; màbòkámèì 'I raised my eyes towards...').

The forest languages often convey the passive by means of a verb form derived with the suffix -am-. The passive suffix of the type -u-, -ibu- is very rare among these languages, although it has been found in zone B (Pove B22c, Tsogo B31), in C30 Ngiri (Mpunza: -ubu-, -iubu-), in C40 (Beo C44: -u-) and in C50 (Kele C55: -o-).

Sequences of derivational suffixes have been attested in all languages and certain descriptions give numerous examples showing the productivity of the derivational microsystem.

3.2.4 The conjugation

It is impossible to give an overview here of the conjugation or of the verbal morphemes used in it. The forest languages are too numerous and too diverse for this to be possible, the more so because in this region, as in the entirety of the Bantu domain, the conjugation is the microsystem in which the distinctions are the strongest. We will therefore limit ourselves to note a number of interesting particularities.

- Without being unique to the forest languages, the existence of conjugated forms which clearly result from the agglutination in one single form of sequences containing an auxiliary verb and an infinitive form is massively attested in the central forest languages, and notably in the C60 and southern C30 (Ntomba, Bolia) languages. The reader is referred to Hadermann (1994b), especially for the conjugated forms that include formatives of the type -yo- or -to-, which have an evident relation with the auxiliaries meaning 'to come' or 'to go'. In order to stay within a purely synchronic perspective, this analysis will not be further pursued. The generalized presence of a past tense with a final morpheme -i in the forest languages and the almost complete absence of the final element -ile are more directly accessible to a synchronic approach. The latter final as such is only present in Bolia (C35) in the affirmative perfect past forms, as well as in Ntomba (C35), Beo (C45) and Lombo (C54) in the negative perfect past, to the exception, of course, of the southern languages of zone D, such as Lega (D25), which belong to the eastern block. Next to the past tense with finale -i, many forest languages also have a past tense with final -ak-i or -ik-i. This tense is often described as a remote imperfect past (cf. Babale C30 Ngiri: bàbâtò bàsúsù bámòyèndákìnì 'all men looked at you (pl.)'; Mbole-Tooli C60: òlámbíkí 'you cooked before, yesterday' vs. òlámbí 'you cooked today').
- Another striking characteristic of the conjugation in the forest languages seems to be the use of temporal/aspectual morphemes which have the status of either postfinal elements or adverbs which come after the verb, the two of which are not always clearly distinguished in the sources. These morphemes are numerous and their presence has been attested in zone B as well as in zone C and D, but there is very little formal correspondence between them. Their meanings, by contrast, are fairly recurrent. These are notably either the affirmative and negative inceptive (cf. Pove B22c: -tĕ in the affirmative inceptive and -dó in the negative; Mbudza C30 Ngiri: -yŏ in the negative inceptive), or specifications meaning 'near' or 'remote' with respect to the past or future tense (cf. Babale C30 Ngiri: -é(ò)bí or -énò for the remote future and -kâbí for recent past; Doko C40: -bî in the remote past and -dê in the remote future; Motembo C30 Ngiri: -bí in the past tense which refers to yesterday), or else they refer to perfect or imperfect aspect (cf. Litoka C30 Ngiri: -ko in the perfect; Motembo C30 Ngiri: -ti in the imperfect). Tofoke (C53) uses a postfinal element -ndé the signification of which is difficult to assess, as well in the future tense (cf. bŏlògàndé 'you will braid') as in the near and remote past (cf. bélògêndé 'they have braided today'; élògándé 'he has braided a long time ago'). Finally, in zone D, Enya (D14) expresses remoteness (in the past and in the future) by placing an adverbial mɔ̀nɔ̀ ~ mɔ̂ after the verb; and temporal proximity by postponing sénɔ̀ ~ sê, whereas òbĭ expresses the fact that the past or future action is situated in the preceding or following day. Mituku (D13), a language that is close to Enya, also uses the adverbial mɔ̀nɔ̀ to express temporal remoteness and a postfinal element -bí for the recent past perfect.
- Most of the forest languages have a postfinal morpheme of the type -(v́)nì. One of its functions is to express the second person plural of the imperative (opposed to the second person singular). This morpheme has been found in zone B (Myene B10, Tsogo B31, Pove B22c), zone C (C30 Ngiri: Mbudza, Kunda, Babale, Motembo; Doko C40, Boa C44, Beo C45, Tofoke C53, Lombo C54, Kele C55) and zone D (Mituku D13, Lega D25, Bira D32, Bodo D35). It is interesting to note that in Bodo (D35) the same morpheme is used for the second person plural in the conditional and in the subjunctive,

while in Mbole-Tooli (C60) it is used with the same function in all tenses where the final morpheme is -*e* or -*a*, which can possibly be explained by the fact that, in this language, the verbal prefixes of the second person singular and plural have an identical form *ò*- (cf. *òsôkàmbà* 'you work (sg.)' vs. *òsôkàmbááyì* 'you work (pl.)'), as has been said above. Some other noteworthy facts can be mentioned. Babale (C30 Ngiri) uses the morpheme -*nì* to counterbalance the ambiguity that rests on the object prefix -*mò*- of the second person singular and plural (cf. *bámòyèndákínì* 'they looked at you (pl.)'). Doko (C40) forms its negative imperative by postponing an infinitive of class 5 to a form *kàkè* (cf. *kàkè ísálá* 'do not work (sg.)'). In the second person plural, the postfinal -*ní* is attached to the infinitive, which gives *kàk'ìdúáni* 'do not come (pl.)', for instance. Finally, Lifonga (C30 Ngiri) in its turn expresses the imperative plural with a morpheme *ni*, which is placed in clause-final position and is thus not a postfinal morpheme. For example: *gyá tómá tòtò nì* 'eat (pl.) these things'.

In general, the morpheme of the type -(*v̀*)*nì* is present in zone B and D, in the C40 and C50 groups, and in part of the C30 Ngiri group. On the other hand, it does not exist in several languages, such as the so-called Mongo idioms and in the C70 group. It has not been attested in the C10 languages either, but these are not well known yet.

• Some comments can be added concerning the morphemes that are proper to the negative verb forms, even though the languages of the forest are not radically distinct from the other Bantu languages in this respect. The most common final morphemes in the negative conjugation are -*i* and -*e*. Negation markers as a rule are either preinitial morphemes (fairly often of the type (*n*)*tà*- or (*n*)*tá*-), or postinitial morphemes that can be of the type -*sí*-, -*sá*-, -*tí*-, -*tà*-, but also -*i*- (Mbole-Tooli C60, Lombo C54 and C30 Ngiri: Likata, Libobi). Ntomba (C35), Nkengo, Nkundo (C60), Tetela (C71) and Kela (C75) have postinitial morphemes -*pa*-, -*po*-, -*fa*-, -*fo*-, -*há*-, etc. in which a form of the negative copula can be recognized. Another means of expressing negation is certainly more typical of the northern forest languages: it consists of using an independent negative morpheme that modifies the entire clause. It is usually placed in sentence final position and most often supposes the use of a negative verb form or, in certain languages, of another negative morpheme, which is placed before the verb and which is described as a separate word in the sources. Examples are: Loi (C30 Ngiri): *tò̰ lòbétémíkí ò tòkó ká* 'we have not laid on the mat'; Mbudza (C30 Ngiri): *tót̰ítómé tɛ̰́* 'we have not sent'. Other examples of phrasal negatives of this type are: *wo* or *we* in Fumu (B77b), *kpá* in Kunda (C30 Ngiri), *ka* in Ndobo (C30 Ngiri), *kòmó* or *tĩ* in Bodo (D35), *wé* in Bira (D32). These languages belong to the groups B70, C30 and D30, but the list is not necessarily exhaustive.

3.2.5 The infinitive

The forest languages exhibit a complex situation with respect to what is traditionally called the infinitive. This is not so much the case for the languages of zone B, although the nature of the nominal prefix used to form the infinitive is rather diverse here: class 5 *è*- in Tsogo (B31), class 15 in Mbaama (B62), Laale (B73b), Yaa (B73c) and Fumu (B77b), but class 7 in Ndumu (B63) and in certain Teke languages (B70), class 3 in Himba (B30), class 5 with zero nominal prefix in Pove (B22c). Even if the situation is rather heterogeneous in the languages of this zone, it is much more so in the forest languages of zone C and D (except, of course, in the south of zone D, where the infinitive is of class 15 and can co-occur with a deverbal nominal form of class 5). In zone C, most authors list an impressive number of nomino-verbal forms the uses of which certainly differ, but in a way that the actual descriptions do not allow us to understand exactly.

Thus, for instance, the term 'gerund' is often used by the authors without being defined, and the least one can say is that its meaning is not very clear. Moreover, the languages of zone C frequently compose verb forms, as well as structures in which auxiliaries (or pseudo-auxiliaries) are followed by a deverbal nominal form the structure of which differs according to the circumstances and should be systematically analyzed. We will limit ourselves to establishing a non-exhaustive typology of the nomino-verbal forms most frequently attested in the languages of zone C and the north of zone D. While the different types are listed, an overview of their distribution will be given. The name of the same language can appear for different types, due to the very frequent co-occurrence of several 'infinitive' forms in the described languages. The 'classic' type NPcl.15 + stem *-a, -á* exists in C30 Ngiri (Lifonga, Likata, Libobi, Loi, Balobo), C50 (Kele, Tofoke), C60 (Nkundo, Mbole-Tooli) and D10–20 (Mituku, Enya, Lega), whereas the equally classic type NPcl.5 + stem *-a, -á* can be found in C30 (Bolia, Lifonga, Likata, Litoka, Ndobo), C60 (Nkengo) and C70 (Kela). Also well represented are: the forms of the type PNcl.14 + stem *-é, -a, -i* which can be found in Leke (C14) and in C30 Ngiri (Mbudza, Lifonga, Likata, Mbonji, Babale, Motembo, Litoka, Balobo); the forms of the type Ø + stem *-a, -á, -e, -ɛ́* which one encounters in Aka (C10), C30 Ngiri (Libobi, Lobala, Zamba, Mbonji, Balobo), Boa (C44), Bodo (D35) and Bira (D32); then also forms of the type *na, ne* + stem *-a, -á* which are restricted to C30 Ngiri group (Zamba, Loi, Mbonji, Balobo, Ndobo) and Sengele (C33), as well as the forms of the type NPcl.9 + stem *-á, -a, -i* to be found in Ntomba and Bolia (C35), Boa (C44), Nkengo and Nkundo (C60), Tetela (C71) and Ombo (C76). Some languages equally have a form NPcl.11 + stem *-i* (C30 Ngiri: Zamba, Kundo and Lombo C54), a form of the type *ka* + stem *-á, -a* (Ndobo C30 Ngiri and Beo C45) or a form of the type *ya* + stem *-a, -á* (C30 Ngiri: Lobala, Loi and Mbonji).

It is often impossible to specify the concords of the forms with a zero nominal prefix or of those with a prefix *na-, ne-, ya-* that does not correspond to an easily recognizable noun class. Furthermore, the concords of the infinitival forms are at times surprising. In Ombo (C76), for instance, the infinitives with a nasal consonant as prefix have their concords in a class 15/17 with prefixes of the type *ko-*. A systematic study of the set of nomino-verbal forms found in the forest languages would be useful, also of the negative infinitives, which are fairly frequent (cf. Tofoke C53: *ngòlèmà* 'not to cultivate', *ngɔ̀gɔ́gà* 'not to collect') or of the infinitives that include displacement markers (cf. Bolia C35: *ikèlà* 'to make', *iyókèlà* 'to come and make' and *itókèlà* 'to go and make').

Other points of interest also merit some attention, like the manifestations of the rule of metatony which is applied, for example in the infinitive and in certain tenses in Mituku (D13) and Lega (D25), in the infinitive in Mbole-Tooli (C60) (cf. *òlámbà̀* 'to cook, to prepare' vs. *òlámbá̲ yèkà* 'to cook food') and in the present affirmative in Pove (B22c) (cf. *mèkàpùndà̀* 'I dig' vs. *mèkàpùndá̲ èbèmb'ɛ́* 'I dig the hole'), or like the manifestations of the nominal prefix of class 9 in the infinitives of Tetela (C71) and Ombo (C76) (N- before +C; *mb-* before +V if the second consonant of the verbal stem is an non-nasal consonant; application of Meinhof's rule when the verb stem is of the type +(C)VNC- or +(C)VN-). Note also the application of assimilation rules to the final vowel of nomino-verbal or the unusual appearance of infinitives with a final vowel *-o* (cf. Himba B30: *mótŏnágò* 'to deny', *móbĭkágò* 'to live'). This small list is far from complete.

4 CONCLUSION

Very numerous, very diverse, sometimes marked by their adjacence to languages that belong to other families or to other Niger-Congo groups, the Bantu languages of the forest still form an open domain of research, very interesting if only for the study of substrate and adstrate phenomena, or for the study of the typical features of the language use of Pygmy groups and of Bantu isolates, fairly numerous in this part of Central Africa. In spite of the progress that has been made in the past decades, a lot of work is still to be done in order to arrive at a sufficiently profound knowledge for the reconstruction of the ancient linguistic history of the region.

The reading of the preceding pages, even though it only provides a very superficial view on the facts, should show to what extent the forest is an area of linguistic diversity, where very different languages meet and border each other. If one excludes the languages of zone A (without forgetting them), one can surely identify four major typological groups within the Bantu languages of the forest: a western group including the languages of zone B, a central group which contains the languages of zone C, a northeastern group with the northern languages of zone D and a southeastern group covering the zone D languages of the south, which belong to the eastern Bantu block.

More particular sets can be identified, at least as a working hypothesis. Thus, it is rather obvious that, within zone C, the C30 languages of the Ngiri and the adjacent C40 languages exhibit features that neatly set them apart (presence or traces of augments, presence of *m*V- prefixes, tone systems with tonal reduplication and/or tonal shift, lexical peculiarities, etc. ...). The southern C30 languages (Ntomba and Bolia C35), in contrast, share some characteristics with the C60 languages of the so-called Mongo group. The latter is certainly far less homogeneous than has been maintained by Hulstaert. Note, on the one hand, the very specific traits that can be found in the languages of the zone covered by the river complex Jwafa–Lomela–Loilaka. These traits represent a transition towards Yela (C74), Kela (C75) and Hendo (C70), which already display some features that are shared by Tetela (C71), notably the existence of a class 5 singular of class 6 and plural of class 7, with all the special representations of its prefixes. The C50 languages (Mbesa C51, Tofoke C53, Lombo C54, Kele C55, etc.) equally have some very marked characteristics and form a zone of transition where certain innovations of the central C60 languages, such as the mixing up of the prefixes *b*V- and *m*V-, are irregularly applied. With Mbole-Tooli (C60) or Ombo (C76) situated more southward, these languages are spoken on the fringe of the northeastern group and sometimes exhibit features similar to those of the adjacent D languages. One could suggest that the same holds, in the west, for the C10–20 languages, which seem to have characteristics that principally belong to zone C, but also some peculiarities typical of the languages of the neighbouring zone B. The C10–20 cluster is not sufficiently known yet to give anything more about them than some superficial impressions. Nevertheless, it is interesting to note, for instance, that the word for 'person(s)' has a final vowel -*u* in singular, but -*i* or -*e* in the plural, not only in C20 languages (Mboshi C25: *mòrò*, pl. *bàrè*), but also in certain B60 and B70 languages (Ndumu C63: *mutu*, pl. *bati*; Mbaama-Lempiini B62: *mvuuru*, pl. *baari*; Teke of Gabon B70: *mvùrù*, pl. *bàrè*). Moreover, certain C10 languages have words that are very frequent in zone B, like *mbóándé* 'dog' in Aka (C10), or like +*hese* 'bone' and +*pei*, +*pondi* 'path' in certain Babole idioms (C14), whereas other C10 languages express the same meanings with words that are more common in zone C. So we have: *mbóá* 'dog' in Ngando (C10), *mbúá* 'dog' in Mbati (C10), +*kua* 'bone' and *ndzela* 'path' in other Babole idioms (C14). It would be interesting to see, on the basis of more complete lexical surveys, whether the C10 group isn't crossed by a significant number of isoglosses of this type.

By way of conclusion, a word on the language uses of the Pygmy groups scattered throughout the forest zone. Significant progress has been made in recent years with respect to their description. Yet, the language or dialectal peculiarities of too many of these Pygmy groups remain unknown, so that it is impossible to formulate anything more than some hypotheses about a linguistic history that could only be understood by means of more and better descriptions. These descriptions should not only take into consideration the languages or variants used by the Pygmies, but also those of the non-Pygmy groups living in the same regions. Would it otherwise be possible to affirm that certain words are exclusively Pygmy; that some Pygmy group has its proper language or speaks a certain language with some special characteristics that are not observed elsewhere? Would it above all be possible to emit anything else than suppositions about the older linguistic history of the Pygmy groups? To continue the descriptive efforts already started, would certainly be more successful, in the hope that one of the most interesting problems posed by the ancient history of Africa could be solved progressively.

ACKNOWLEDGMENTS

I am much indebted to Mark Van de Velde for translating this paper into English. Many thanks are also due to J. Renard for drawing the map.

NOTE

1 For a map of C30 Ngiri languages, see Motingea Mangulu, 1996.

REFERENCES

1 Introduction Bastin *et al.* 1999; Blanchon 1987, 1988a, 1988b, 1989, 1990; Blanchon and Alihanga 1992; Blanchon and Mouguiama 1997; Cloarec-Heiss and Thomas 1978; Jacquot 1983; Picavet 1947.

2 Phonology 2.1 Asangama Natisa 1983; Bolingola Mwarabu 1995; Harries 1959; Hulstaert 1938; Kutsch Lojenga 1994a; Leitch 1997; Meeussen 1952; Nkabuwakabili 1986; Spa 1973; Stappers 1976; Tassa 1994. **2.2** De Rop 1958; Forges 1977; Gérard 1924; Grégoire 1994; Hulstaert 1938, 1948, 1961, 1970, 1987; Jacobs 1964; Motingea Mangulu 1993; Picavet 1947; Twilingiyimana 1984. **2.3** Blanchon 1987b, 1988a, 1988b, 1989, 1990; Blanchon and Creissels 1999; De Boeck 1951b; Kamanda Kola 1993; Marchal-Nasse 1979, 1989; Philippson and Puech (n.d.); Toronzoni 1985; Van der Veen 1991a. **2.4** Forges 1977; Hulstaert 1961; Meeussen 1952; Ngulinzira 1977.

3 Morphology 3.1: 3.1.1 Cloarec-Heiss and Thomas 1978; Gérard 1924; Marchal-Nasse 1979; Meeussen 1952. **3.1.2** Biton 1907; Motingea Mangulu 1993, 1996; Picavet 1947; Stappers 1971. **3.1.3** Amboulou 1998; Fontaney 1988, 1989; Forges 1977; Gazania 1972; Grégoire and Janssens 1999; Grégoire and Rekanga 1994; Harries 1959; Hulstaert 1961; Jacquot 1983; Kamanda Kola 1991, 1993; Leitch 1991; Nkabuwakabili 1986; Puech 1988; Spa 1973; Stappers 1971, 1973; Van der Veen 1986. **3.1.4** Bokula 1966, 1970; Bouquiaux and Thomas 1994; Dz'Ba Dheli 1972; Kabuyaya (n.d.); Nkabuwakabili 1986. **3.2: 3.2.1** De Rop 1958; Forges 1977; Marchal-Nasse 1979; Motingea Mangulu 1993, 1996; Stappers 1973. **3.2.2** De Rop 1958; Mamet 1960; Mickala-Manfoumbi 1994; Motingea Mangulu 1993, 1996; Vanhoudt 1987. **3.2.3** Mamet 1955, 1960; Marchal-Nasse 1970; Mickala Manfoumbi 1994; Motingea Mangulu 1993, 1996; Vanhoudt 1987. **3.2.4** Asangama Natisa 1983; Forges 1977; Hadermann 1994b; Hulstaert 1961, 1970; Mamet 1955, 1960; Motingea Mangulu 1993, 1996; Mickala-Manfoumbi 1994; Tassa 1994; Twilingiyimana 1984; Spa 1973; Stappers 1973. **3.2.5** Kamanda Kola 1991; Marchal-Nasse 1970; Motingea Mangulu 1993, 1996; Meeussen 1971; Stappers 1973; Tassa 1994.

4 Conclusion Bouquiaux and Thomas 1994; Cloarec-Heiss and Thomas 1978; Thomas 1976; Thomas and Bahuchet 1983.

CHAPTER TWENTY

THE B30 LANGUAGE GROUP

Lolke J. van der Veen

1 INTRODUCTION

For a long time B30 has been one of the least studied and documented language groups of Gabon. Although Guthrie (1953 and 1967–71) provided scholars with a first approximation of its main characteristics, his account was necessarily incomplete. As a matter of fact his research was based on rather limited personal field notes and on data taken from Raponda-Walker (RW) (1950) concerning only two out of seven languages (see below).

More recent investigation has allowed us to elaborate a much more accurate picture of the group as a whole and of its individual languages. In order to describe the present state of affairs, this chapter will present a summary of the main results of linguistic research on this barely known but nonetheless very interesting language group. These results not only concern sociolinguistic aspects such as the internal composition of the group and its relationships with other language groups, but most obviously also descriptive linguistics. The (predominantly) sociolinguistic aspects will be set out hereafter, whereas the main phonological and morphological features of the individual varieties as well as the common structural features will be discussed in some detail in the sections following this introduction. Syntax, for which only limited data are available, will be discussed as a subsidiary (see Conclusion).

1.1 The inventory

The B30 group comprises seven language varieties, all of which are spoken in the central, rainforest, part of Gabon. The group as a whole doesn't have one distinct and generally accepted (ethnic) name. According to some of its members it ought to be called *Okani* (meaning 'Let's go!' in most of the B30 languages); others prefer *Mbembe* or do not name it at all. The generally accepted names of the individual varieties are Tsogo, Vove, Viya, Pinzi(pinzi), Kande, Himba(ka) and Bongwe. Each of these varieties will be presented briefly. (See also Map 20.1, for their approximate location.)

Tsogo

(*γe-tsɔyɔ*; T hereafter; speakers: Mitsogo)
Classification: B31 (Guthrie 1953).
Location: a rather elongated area situated to the northeast of Mouila on the right bank of the River Ngounié, having as upper limit the village of Sindara, north of Fougamou.
Estimated number of speakers: 9000.
Neighboring languages: B30, B40 and B50 languages.
Main publications: RW (1950). Guthrie (1967–71) (T's reflexes). Marchal-Nasse (1979) (outline of T's phonology and morphology). Jacquot (1983), focusing mainly on noun

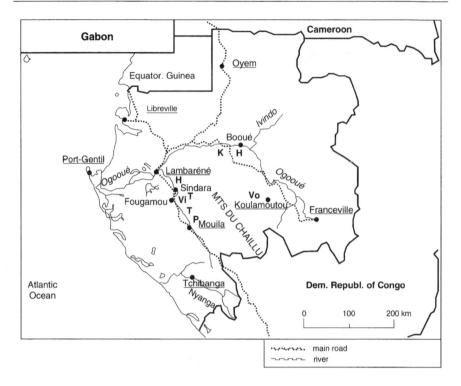

MAP 20.1   MAP OF GABON SHOWING THE APPROXIMATE LOCATION OF EACH OF THE B30 LANGUAGES (EXCEPT FOR BONGWE)

Key: T = Tsogo, Vo = Vove, Vi = Viya, P = Pinzi(pinzi), K = Kande and H = Himba(ka).

class morphology. Van der Veen (VdV) (1991b). A non-published dictionary (about 6000 entries) elaborated by RW.

Other: being the privileged means of communication of the local Bwiti cult which has initiates all over the country, T has considerable social and cultural prestige.

Vove (Pove)

(*γè-βòβè*; Vo hereafter; speakers: Bavove)

Classification: not mentioned as a B30 language by Guthrie. B22c according to Bryan (1959). However, Jacquot (1978, 1983) has shown Vo to be a typical B30 language from a morphological perspective. VdV's work (1986, 1987, 1991a) on the phonology, the morphology, the lexicon and the syntax of one of the southern varieties of Vo has corroborated this conclusion.

Location: area to the south-west of Koulamoutou defined by the town of Koulamoutou (east side), a village called Mouila (west side) and the village of Bagnati (north side; bordering an uninhabited region).

Estimated number of speakers: 4000.

Neighboring languages: Sangu (B40) and Nzebi (B50) (southern region).

Main publications: Jacquot (1978, 1983), VdV (1986, 1987, 1991), Mickala-Manfoumbi (1994).

Other: Vo is a cluster of language varieties. Their exact number is unknown. The southern dialects seem to have been considerably influenced by the neighboring languages. The more conservative Pove varieties are situated in the northern region.

Viya

(*yè-βíyà*; Vi hereafter; speakers: Eviya (also Evia or Avias))

Classification: not mentioned by Guthrie (1953), Bastin (1978) or Jacquot (1978, 1983). RW (1967) considers Vi to be a mixture of T and Sira (B41). As VdV has shown, Vi fundamentally is a B30 language variety but its lexicon has indeed been rather strongly influenced by the Sira language. This conclusion corroborates and refines Blanchon's (1988c) earlier findings.

Location: the village of Mavono, on the right bank of River Ngounié, facing the town of Fougamou.

Estimated number of speakers: 300–400. Real fluency for 50 speakers at the most.

Neighboring languages: T (same village), Sira (Fougamou) and other B40 languages.

Main publications: Blanchon (1988), VdV (1991a, 1999a/b), Bodinga-bwa-Bodinga and VdV (1995), VdV and Bodinga-bwa-Bodinga (2002) (i.e. a dictionary containing more than 6300 entries).

Other: due to epidemics, rural depopulation, bilingualism, etc., Vi is nearly extinct.

Pinzi(pinzi)

(*ye-pinzi(pinzi)* or *ye-pipinzi*; P hereafter; speakers: Apindji/Gapindji)

Classification: mere dialectal form of T according to Guthrie (1953:64). Jacquot (1983) and VdV (1991a), both based on more or less extensive field work, have shown P to be clearly distinct from T. The Gapindjii themselves consider their language to be very closely related to the B30 varieties Kande (below) and Himba(ka) (below).

Location: seven villages situated on the right bank River Ngounié, between Mouila and River Waka.

Estimated number of speakers: 200–300 (?).

Neighboring languages: Punu (B43) and Sira (B41) (opposite side of River Ngounié).

Main publications: Jacquot (1978, 1983), VdV (1991a).

Other: nearly extinct minority group. Dialectal differences exist. The data examined by VdV correspond to a somewhat different variety from the one described by Jacquot (1983). The latter is slightly closer to T and this may explain why Guthrie assumed it to be a dialect of T.

Kande

(*o-kande*; K hereafter; speakers: Okande)

Classification: B32 (Guthrie 1953). Confirmed by more recent investigation.

Location: three villages situated on the left bank of River (Moyen-)Ogooué, between the confluence of River Boleko and River Aschouka.

Estimated number of speakers: a few dozen at the most.

Neighboring languages: B10, B20, A70 (Fang).

Main publications: Guthrie (1953, 1969–71), VdV (1991a) (basic outline based on some 300 lexical items).

Other: the Okande were once a culturally significant and rather well-known ethnic group. Reliable historical documents refer to intensive trading with the Nenga of Lambaréné (B10), the Galoa (B10), the Sake and the Kota (B20). At present, they are near to extinction.

Himba(ka)

(*ye-himba(ka)*; H hereafter; speakers: Simba or Himba)

Classification: H's main phonological and morphological characteristics (see VdV 1991a:233–41) unambiguously show that it is to be reckoned among the B30 languages. According to the Simba themselves, H is closely related to P and K, and only slightly less to Vo and T.

Location: a limited number of villages of which three are situated in the Booué area and one in the area situated to the north of Mimongo in the Ngounié district, i.e. Massima Camp.

Estimated number of speakers: a few hundred. Complete fluency is rare.

Neighboring languages: B10, B20, A70 (Fang).

Main publication: VdV (1991a) (basic outline of phonology and morphology).

Other: nearly extinct group. Very poorly documented B30 variety.

Bongwe

(*((y)e-bɔŋgwɛ*; B hereafter; speakers: Babongo)

Classification: variety considered to be a mere amalgam of various Gabonese idioms by RW (1937). VdV (1991a) has shown it to be very closely related to T.

Location: (Ngounié) districts of Sindara-Fougamou and Mimongo-Gendjambwe, south to the Apindji.

Estimated number of speakers: unknown.

Neighboring languages: unknown.

Main publications: RW (1937), VdV (1991a:410–11).

Other: dialectal B30 variety spoken by the Babongo pygmies (*-bɔŋgɔ* 1/2). Although diachronically very interesting as it corresponds in many ways to an earlier stage of T, B is the least known variety of B30. As no recent and reliable data are available for the time being, B will only incidentally be taken into account below.

1.2 B30's internal structure

A rather accurate picture of B30's internal organization has been obtained from VdV's dialectometrical and lexicostatistical study (VdV 1991a:353–68). The main conclusions of this study clearly corroborate the results of the study of the phonology and the morphology of the B30 languages (see below). Fundamentally, two subgroups need to be distinguished: one being the closely united P/K/H cluster, the other being the considerably less solidly knitted 'agglomerate' T/Vo/Vi. The former will henceforth be referred to as *Northern B30* (N-B30) and the latter as *Southern B30* (S-B30). P, K and H can be regarded as three dialectal varieties of one language (cluster) but the varieties of S-B30 cannot. As shown on Map 20.1, the N-B30 varieties are not geographically close nowadays. One must therefore conclude that this group has come to split up only quite recently. Within the group as a whole T holds a rather central position.

1.3 The group's lexical identity

The outcome of another detailed comparative study bearing on B30's lexical stock (VdV 1991a:368–402) allows us to define common lexical forms on different levels: group level, subgroup level, etc. Taking into account both Guthrie's CS (Comparative Series) and data from the highest possible number of Gabonese languages, this study has also pointed out potential lexical innovations, on various levels. An adequate picture of B30's lexical identity is now available. For reasons of conciseness, only the main results will be presented here.

One of the most important findings has turned out to be the difficulty or even the impossibility in quite a number of cases to reconstruct just one lexeme for the group as a whole. Divergences between N-B30 and S-B30 are rather numerous. Nevertheless, it has proved to be possible to set up a list of diachronically interesting lexical items.

The following lexemes are possible candidates for common-B30 lexical innovations. Not all of these items can be put forward with the same degree of certainty. Further research, taking also into account non-Gabonese languages, will allow us to restrict their number.

Item	Gloss	Gender	Distribution
*-bɛnd-	'(to) say', '(to) tell'	–	
*-bolongo	'egg'	5/6	(borrowed from B40?)
*-bumba	'liver'	5/6	
*-buni	'belly'	5/6	
*-dɛkɔ	'chin'	7/8	
*-dyale	'seed'	3/4	
*-dyɔ	'hair', 'fur'	3/4	
*-eko	'bark'	11/10	
*-ɣunz-	'(to) hit', '(to) strike'	–	
*-its-	'(to) give'	–	
*-kondo	'buttock'	9/10	(?)
*-mboma	'chest'	9/10	
*-mɛnɔ	'neck'	7/8	(elsewhere only B44)
*-ngina	'louse'	9/10	
*-nzima	'ten'	9/10	
*-saɣo	'iron'	3/4	
*-sakɔ	'firewood'	7/8	
*-tanda	'leg'	3/4	
*-tseba	'horn'	9/10	
*-tsuma	'knife'	9/10	
*-βɛl-	'(to) fly'	–	(elsewhere only B42)
*-βumbe-	'(to) blow'	–	(S-B30/H/(P))

Other potential candidates, common on some inferior level, are:

Item	Gloss	Gender	Level
-buka	'nine'	–	N-B30
-bwan-	'(to) sit down'	–	N-B30

-dyɔ-	'(to) go away', '(to) leave'	–	Vi/Vo
-ɣab-	'(to) grow (vegetables)'	–	S-B30
-ɣam-	'(to) want'	–	P/H
-ikedy-	'(to) show'	–	N-B30
-kaka	'tortoise'	7/8	N-B30
-kɔkɔ	'bed'	9/10	T/Vi
-kɔβɛ	'hair', 'fur'	11/10a	P/H
-meneto	'male'	1/2	N-B30
-naŋga	'star'	3/4	T/Vi
-nenele	'tongue'	11/10a	N-B30
-nɔŋgɔn-	'(to) know'	–	P/H
-odi	'river'	3/4, 11/10	Vi/Vo
-sanzedy-	'(to) swell'	–	N-B30
-tol-	'(to) sing'	–	T/Vi/K
-tomb-	'(to) push'	–	T/Vo
-tsidi	'louse'	9/10	Vi/Vo
-tsind-	'(to) grow (vegetables)'	–	N-B30
-βinz-	'(to) push'	–	N-B30

For other potential innovations and also for outstanding features (as formal properties, content or exclusive use in Gabon) concerning common-B30 words which have a corresponding reconstructed CB form, see VdV (1991a:399–400).

1.4 Relationship with other language groups

VdV (1991a) has pointed out that substantial and probably rather ancient morphological and lexical affinities exist between B30 as a whole and B10 (Myene), as well as some quite ancient but less obvious lexical affinities between B30 and certain B20 languages. (Cf. Bastin and Piron 1999.)

Lexical ties are strongest between N-B30 and B10. These links are reinforced by some morphological affinities (see Noun morphology, pp. 382–387 below). Since syntax doesn't seem to be affected, the most probable scenario for their origin is that B30 acquired these features by borrowing during a period of intensive (trade) contact (see below).

At S-B30 level, lexical affinities are less easy to define. Altogether, this subgroup predominantly presents lexical similarities with the neighboring B40 and B50 languages. It is not always easy to determine whether the latter influenced S-B30 or vice versa. For historical and sociolinguistic reasons (e.g. B30's fragility), it is reasonable to think that the neighboring languages have been exerting considerable pressure on this subgroup for quite a long time. (For a more detailed specification, see VdV (1991b, 1999a).)

1.5 The historical and geographical origin of the group

The available (oral) literature almost unanimously refers to the Ivindo District (situated in the northeastern part of the country) as the geographical origin of the B30-speaking ethnic groups. This may be correct, but in that case the region referred to is more probably to be regarded as a place of transit. Furthermore, most of the oral texts mention a subsequent migration into the coastal region as well as a rather long stay in this area, intensive trade contacts with members of the Myene group (B10) during that period, a return to the inner parts of the country (most probably due to the slave-trade), and finally, social and cultural interaction with several other ethnic groups (especially B40, B50) after settling down in this central area.

Although information of this type should be treated with caution, the presently available linguistic evidence tends to confirm the oral documents. It furthermore suggests that Guthrie's (1953) claim about lexical similarities between T and zone C are erroneous (cf. VdV 1991a:407). Instead, more or less important lexical resemblances have shown up with languages that have come from the North or the North East (zone A). According to VdV (1991a:444–51), B30 possesses a vast majority of lexical items reconstructed (by Guthrie) for the following zones: N., W., N. & C. West., NW. and CW.

1.6 Chances for survival

Most B30 languages are doomed to disappear in the near future. The splitting up of the group is nowadays being accelerated by several extralinguistic and (socio)linguistic factors, such as the uneven multilingualism, the growing pressure exerted by the surrounding groups, the loss of prestige, the gradual loss of linguistic competence, the very low birthrate, diseases, exogamy and rural depopulation.

The most seriously threatened varieties are K and Vi. T, because of its special cultural and religious prestige (see above), appears to be more resistant.

This disastrous state of affairs, however, raises important theoretical questions, especially concerning language death and the linguistic processes that accompany this worldwide phenomenon. B30 languages offer the extraordinary opportunity to observe changes while working in the field and explore simultaneously different hypotheses about the presumed relationship between language change, language acquisition and language death.

2 PHONOLOGY

This section will highlight the main phonological features encountered in B30. Both segmental and suprasegmental characteristics will be briefly discussed. Emphasis will be placed on common features, but specific diverging features will also be pointed out. The B variety will only occasionally be taken into account.

2.1 Segmental phonology

2.1.1 Phoneme inventories

2.1.1.1 Vowel systems

All B30 languages have a seven-vowel system in which length and nasalization do not play a distinctive role:

	Anterior	Back
High	*i*	*u*
Mid-high	*e*	*o*
Mid-low	*ε*	*ɔ*
Low	*a*	

It should be noted that the mid-high vowels of Vo are realized as particularly close ([ẹ] and [ọ] respectively). Vowels in root position are significantly longer than in any other position. See VdV (1987, 1991a) for these features.

In this language, especially in rapid speech, vowels in word-final position undergo several phonological processes:

(a) Final non-high vowels will be realized with a centralized quality in isolation (V_2##). The low vowel will also be centralized preceding consonant-initial words (a_2#C). For example, /mùŋgòŋgà/ 'neck' gives [mùŋgòŋgə] in isolation or in front of a consonant, and /tsèɣέ/ 'mandrill' is realized [tsèɣɔ] in isolation.
(b) Final non-low vowels become phonetic glides (i, e, ɛ → y and u, o, ɔ → w) when they precede vowel-initial words (V_2#V). For example, /póyò ɛ́/ 'the (specific) rat' gives [póɣwέ].
(c) The final low vowel drops when it precedes vowel-initial words (a_2#V). For example, /mùŋgòŋgà ɛ́/ 'the (specific) neck' is realized [mùŋgòŋgέ].
(d) The intermediate degree vowels (mid-high and mid-low) become phonetically high when followed by a consonant (V_2#C). For example, /nzèɣɔ́ díné/ 'these panthers over there' is very frequently realized as [nzèɣúdíné].

Moreover:

(a) All final vowels tend to become devoiced. This regressive devoicing process may also affect the preceding voiced consonants, as is shown in [èbèɣọ̀] 'word'.
(b) In prefixal position the anterior mid-high vowel is always realized as a central vowel ([ə]). For example, [ɣə̀βòβè] for /ɣèβòβè/ 'Gevove (language)'.

These processes considerably reduce the phonetic word-final vowel inventory. Instead of seven distinct vowel qualities, often only three qualities are found, i.e. [i], [u] and [ə]. This change is presently taking place at the phonetic level in Vo, whereas in non-B30 languages like B52 a very similar process has already brought about important structural changes (cf. Blanchon 1987:33, VdV 1991b:68). See VdV (1987, 1991b) for a more detailed account.

2.1.1.2 Consonant systems

The B30 consonant systems have in common the following structural features and characteristics:

- a high degree of resemblance;
- very regular synchronic correspondences;
- the presence of two prenasalized series (plosives and fricatives);
- the very marginal status of the phonemes /w/, /r/ (Vi only) /f/ (Vi and N-B30) and /mf/ (Vi and K) or the absence of these segments of which /r, f, mf/ cannot be reconstructed at the proto-B30 level;
- the absence of a velar nasal phoneme and a velar plosive phoneme.

It should be noticed that in all languages the /ⁿz/ phoneme is realized as a prenasalized affricate [ⁿdz]. The voiced plosives are all realized as implosives. T has the least complex system (18 segments), and Vi the most complex one (23 segments). For that reason, the latter will be given here for reference. The other systems will be succinctly compared to it.

	Labial	Coronal	Dorsal
Affricate		ts	
Palatalized		d^y	
Vless plosives	p	t	k
Vd plosives	b	d	
Vless fricatives	f	s	
Vd fricatives	β	γ	
Prenasal. plosives	^mb	nd	$^{\eta}g$
Prenasal. fricatives	(^mf)	^nz	
Nasals	m	n	$\textipa{J}$
Lateral liquid		l	
Non lateral liquid		r	
Approximants	w	y	

In Vi the /w/ phoneme is realized [ɥ] in front of high front vowels. The coronal nasal has a strong tendency to palatalize before /i/. Vi is the only language that has a /r/ phoneme, most probably obtained by borrowing from neighboring B40 languages.

T doesn't have the following phonemes: /dy/ (having merged with /y/; earlier varieties of T however possessed this phoneme, cf. RW 1950), /f/, /^{m}f/, /l/ and /r/. B has /l/ and /dy/ where T has Ø and /y/ respectively. Furthermore, it has Ø where all the other varieties have /ɣ/.

Vo doesn't have /f/, /^{m}f/, /l/ and /r/. In this language, the /w/ phoneme is realized [ɥ] in front of high front vowels, as in Vi and in H (*infra*).

P, K and H (N-B30) have very similar systems. All of them have a marginal /f/ phoneme. None of them have a /r/ phoneme. The only difference between P and H is that H has /h/ instead of /s/. In both varieties the coronal nasal is not found in the C_2 and C_3 positions before /i/. K is the only variety of these three that has a (very marginal) /^{m}f/ phoneme. Its /ts/ phoneme is realized as a post-aveolar affricate [tʃ] and its /w/ phoneme as [ɥ] before high front vowels.

A detailed study of regular sound correspondances (VdV 1991a:259–85) leads to positing the following common-B30 vowel and consonant systems:

Vowels   : *i, *e, *ε, *u, *o, *ɔ, *a.
Consonants: *ts, *d^y; *p, *t, *k; *b, *d, *g ??; *^{m}b, *^{n}d, *$^{\eta}$g; *^{n}z; *m, *n, *ɲ; *β, *s, *ɣ; *l, *w and *y.

The *g is highly hypothetical. Its existence has been assumed in order to account for certain specific sound correspondances (see VdV 1991b:284–5). Evidence from Janssens (1991) has nevertheless pointed out that these correspondences can best be interpreted as the result of morphological alternations of which the conditioning environments have become opaque (see also p. 381).

2.1.2 Syllable types

No closed syllables are found. Prenasalized consonants having been interpreted as units, it can be stated that the only possible syllable types, occurring in all seven languages, are (C)V and (C)AV (where A = approximant).

2.2 Suprasegmental phonology

2.2.1 Vowel harmony in B30

All languages examined in VdV (1991a) possess a (progressive) vowel harmony system (within the noun stem or the verb stem) which has as its main feature the mutual exclusiveness of the second and third degree of vowel height. This can be shown from the following data:

	P	T	Vi	Vo
'skin'	/moɣɔbɔ/	/mòɣɔ́bɔ̀/	/mòɣɔ́bɔ̀/	/mùɣɔ́bɔ̀/
'woman'	–	/mòɣɛ́tɔ̀/	/mòɣɛ́tɔ̀/	/mùɣɛ́tɔ̀/
'husband'	/monome/	/mómè/	/mómè/	/mómè/
'buttock'	/kondo/	/kóndó/	/kóndó/	–

Some differences exist, however. T and N-B30 (at least P and H) share an important feature: they are less restrictive than Vo and Vi, which possess additional constraints. These constraints may schematically be described as the incompatibility between high or low vowels (in root position) and mid-low vowels (in non-root position). The following items exemplify these differences.

	P	T	Vi	Vo
'eye'	/itsɔ/	/ísɔ̀/	/ísò/	/ísò/
'tooth'	/inɔ/	/ínɔ̀/	/ínò/	/ínò/
'sand'	/mosiɣɛ/	/mòsíɣè/	–	/mùsíɣè/

2.2.2 Tone systems

T, Vo and Vi have in common a tone system with four underlying melodies for the nouns (i.e. H, L, HL and LH) and two for the verbs (i.e. H and L). Tonal correspondences are about regular. No reliable tonal data are available for N-B30 so far.

	T/Vi/Vo	Gloss		T/Vi/Vo	Gloss
H	/tsósó/	'chicken'	H	/-bénd-/	'say'
L	/tàbà/	'goat'	L	/-dùt-/	'draw'
HL	/mò-témà/	'heart'			
LH	/mò-bòngɔ́/	'pygmy'			

Within S-B30, two basic types of tone systems can be distinguished: one characterized by the absence of tone spreading and the other by the presence of such a parameter.

Tones don't spread in Vo. Some simple (mostly vertical) assimilation rules suffice to account for its system. For example, /ɣwátà dyá wàbɔ̀ŋgɔ́ é/ 'fingernails of the Pygmies' will be realized [ɣwátádyáwàɓɔ̀ŋgwè] in rapid speech. These processes are the result of the particular weakness of the final syllable (above).

The absence of the LH pattern in monosyllabic stems should be noticed. The noun prefixes are all underlyingly L. Word games have shown that the stem is the domain of tone, not the syllable. Downdrift occurs in HLH sequences: the second H is phonetically lower than the first. It also appears in a series of L-tones.

One other interesting feature is neutralization that results in lowering in utterance-final position. The only tone that can occur in this position is a low (falling) tone. See example above.

Rightward Tone Spreading occurs in T and Vi. In T they spread freely within a certain number of well-defined domains. For a detailed but tentative description, see Marchal-Nasse (1979).

As far as Vi is concerned, it is not the syllable but the phonological word that has proved to be the domain of tone. Tones associate in a one-to-one fashion, from left to right, after which spreading may occur. This process is entirely conditioned by the nature of the underlying tone situated immediately to the right. If the following structural tone is low or if the subsequent morpheme is tonally unspecified, spreading takes place. If an H-tone follows, the tone(s) remain linked to their initial skeletal position.

Moving tones undergo automatic delinking if a major pause, a tonally unspecified segment or a structural L-tone precedes them. Only the final reassociation link will be maintained. This results in tone lowering on the surface. No delinking will occur if an H-tone precedes. In the latter case, a plateau of H-tones will appear, as shown in the following example.

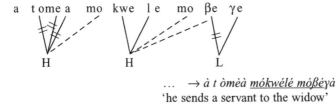

... → à t òmèà <u>mókwélé móββéyà</u>
'he sends a servant to the widow'

Spreading ceases when the moving tone reaches an H-tone (cf. the preceding example: spreading of first H-tone). Besides, a tone on the move will never go beyond the root vowel of the following lexeme (cf. preceding example: spreading of second H-tone) or cross a second word boundary. For example, *tòmà yó pìndì á Pùyàmù* 'send him into the forest of Fougamou' where the underlying H-tone of the verb (*e-toma* H 'to send') spreads to the clitic on its right without going beyond.

Vi avoids contour tones and downstep. Only one tone at a time can be associated with a skeletal position. If for some reason this Well-formedness Condition is violated, a repair strategy will apply. It won't, however, apply in utterance-penultimate position, which is the only (prosodically marked) position where a falling HL-tone may appear. For example, *nà ŋgámòpêkà* 'I'll send him' (*e-pɛka* L 'to seize'; H-tone originating from the Object Marker).

In order to explain a certain number of Vi's tonal phenomena, the existence of floating tones has been claimed. Their behavior is governed by specific constraints which will not be be commented on here, owing to limitations of space.

For more detailed descriptions concerning T, Vo and Vi, see VdV (1991a, 1992 and 1999a/b).

2.3 Some diachronic aspects

Only a few remarks on reflexes and sound changes can be made here. For a detailed discussion of especially the main hypotheses proposed to account for the 'multiple reflexes dilemma', i.e. the fortis/lenis hypothesis and the derivation hypothesis, see VdV (1991a), Stewart (1989), Van Leynseele and Stewart (1980) and Janssens (1991). The group as a whole has double or sometimes even triple (apparently) non-conditioned reflexes for *p, *c, *k, *d, and *g.

B30 vowel reflexes are extremely conservative. In the large majority of cases the B30 vowels match perfectly with the ones found in the CB reconstructed forms. The two subgroups can also be distinguished by means of the following diachronic features:

N-B30

- double reflexes for *g in C_2 position and triple reflexes for *d (in particular the n reflex).
- the sound 'change' *$d > d/$ ___ *i.
- the change *$c > ts/no-$ ___ (noun class 11 marker).
- isolated cases of consonant alternations, stem-initially, for the 5/6 pairing, with, in parallel, a tendency towards reanalysis by analogy.

S-B30

- the absence of double reflexes for *g in C_2 position.
- triple reflexes for *d (the most interesting features being the non-segmental reflex Ø and the absence of the n reflex).

The T/B/P/H cluster shares the conditioned sound change *$n > \emptyset/$ ___ *i

3 NOUN MORPHOLOGY

This second main section will sketch a brief outline of the most important facts the study of B30 noun morphology has revealed so far.

Noun stems in B30 are predominantly bisyllabic. Although less common, plurisyllabic stems are well represented too. Most of them have either three or four syllables, e.g. (Vi) *ye-sɛta + miso* B + HB 'dizziness'. Monosyllabic stems are rare, e.g. (Vo) *mu-ɲa* L 'mouth', (P) *e-fa* 'dog'.

A considerable set of reduplicated stems exists in S-B30, most of which are reduplicated bisyllabic stems, e.g. (Vi) *pɛdi + vɛdi* HB + HB 'lightning'. Semantically, reduplication often denotes intensiveness, large size or repetition, e.g. (Vi) *ye-yɛtɔ + yɛtɔ* HB + HB 'a real woman' (from *mo-yɛtɔ* HB 'woman').

Other frequent morphologically complex nouns are either compounds (having generally a V + N or $N_1 + N_2$ structure) or associative structures (N_1 + Associative Marker + N_2). Cf. *ye-sɛta + miso* (above), which has a V + N structure.

An important number of noun stems have been derived from verbs. They often bear a derivational suffix. Some of these suffixes are still highly productive (cf. the very common agentive suffix /-i/).

3.1 Noun class markers

The following table (table 20.1) presents the B30 noun class markers (*NCM*). In most cases, two allomorphs exist for each marker, one occurring before consonant-initial stems and the other before vowel-initial stems. A few cases of (apparently) free variation have been recorded. All markers are underlyingly L, at least in S-B30.

Some of the NCM have played or still play a role in derivation. (For more details, see VdV 1999a:20–7 on Vi's noun morphology.)

TABLE 20.1: B30 NOUN CLASS MARKERS

cl.	T	Vo	Vi	P	K	H
1	*mo-/*	*mu-/*	*mo-/*	*mo-/*	*mo-/*	*mo-/*
	mw-/m-	*mw-/m-*	*mw-/m-*	*om-*	*omw-*	*omw-/om-*
2	*a-*	*wa-/*	*wa-/*	*a-*	*a-*	*a-*
		w-	*w-*			
3	*mo-/*	*mu-/*	*mo-/*	*mo-/*	*mo-/*	*mo-/*
	mw-/m-	*mw-/m-*	*mw-/m-*	*omw-/ow-*	*omw-*	*omw-/om-*
3a				*o-*	*o-/om-/ow-*	*o-*
4	*mi-/*	*mi-/*	*mi-/*	*mi-/*	*mi-/*	*mi-/*
	my-	*my-*	*my-*	*my-/mim-*	*mim-*	*mim-*
5	*e-/*	*e-/*	*e-/*	*ø-*	*n̩-*	*i-*
	ø-, (e-)	*ø-, (e-)*	*ø- e-*			
5a		*di-/*	*di-/*			
		dy-	*dy-*			
6	*ma-/*	*ma-/*	*ma-/*	*ma-/*	*ma-/*	*ma-/*
	m-	*m-*	*m-*	*mam-/m-*	*mam-*	*mam-*
7	*γe-/s-*		*γe-/s-*			
7a	*γe-/*	*γə-/*	*γe-/*	*γe-/*	*γe-/*	*γe-/*
	γy-	*γy-/γ-*	*γy-*	*γes-*	*γes-?*	*γeh-*
8	*e-*	*bi-*	*e-*	*e-/*	*e-*	*e-*
				ey-		
9	*(N)-, ø-*	*(N)-, ø-*	*(N)-,*	*((N)-, ø-)*		*((N)-, ø-)*
			ø-/			
			ny-			
9a				*e(N)-/*	*e(N)-/*	*e(N)-/*
				e-	*e-*	*e-*
10	*(N)-, ø-*	*(N)-, ø-*	*(N)-, ø-*	*((N)-, ø-)*	*((N)-, ø-)*	*((N)-, ø-)*
10a	*di-/*	*di-/*	*i-/*	*di(N)-/*	*di(N)-/*	*di(N)-/*
	dy-	*dy-*	*dy-*	*din-*	*din-*	*din-*
11	*o-/*	*o-/*	*o-/*	*no(N)-/*	*no(N)-/*	*no(N)-/*
	w-, ø-	*w-, ø-*	*w-*	*non-*	*non-*	*n-*
13	*to-/*	*tu-?*	*to-/*	*to-/*	*to-/*	*to-/*
	tw-		*tw-*	*tot-*	*tot-*	*tot-*
14	*bo-/*	*bu-/*	*bo-/*	*??*	*??*	*??*
	bw-	*bw-*	*bw-*			
16	*βa-/*		*βa-/*	*?*	*?*	*?*
	β-		*β-*			
17	*γo-/*	*γu-/*	*γo-/*	*?*	*?*	*?*
	γw-	*γw-*	*γw-*			
19	*βi-/*	*βi-/*	*βi-/*	*βi-/*	*βi-/*	*βi-/*
	βy-	*βy-*	*βy-*	*βiβ-*	*βiβ-*	*βiβ-*

Note: Distribution of allomorphs (separated by a slash): the first form appears before consonant-initial stems, the other(s) before vowel-initial stems. The nasal consonant of classes 9, 10 and 10a (as well as perhaps the P/K/H cluster's class 11), put in brackets, doesn't synchronically belong to the prefix but to the stem. All markers are underlyingly L.

The following features deserve special attention:

(a) The group as a whole shares some specific features:

- the absence of noun class (<u>NC</u>) 15, rather frequent in surrounding languages. All B30 varieties however, preserve one or two traces of this NC: eg. T/Vi/Vo *o-ɣɔyɔ/m-ɔyɔ* (11/6+), P *o-ɣɔyɔ/mi-yɔyɔ* (3a/4), K *n-gɔyɔ/mam-ɔyɔ* (5/6) and H *o-yɔyɔ/m-ɔyɔ* (3a/6+) 'arm'; T/Vi/Vo *o-yodo/m-odo* (11/6+) 'foot'. The plural forms (except the one of P) show that both items have a vowel-initial stem, i.e. respectively *-ɔyɔ* and *-odo*. These lexemes have undergone one or more class changes.

- the existence of a NC 10a (plural) (except for Vo), also found in B10.
- the *e-* shape of NCM 8 (opposed to *∅-* or *y-* in B10, *bi-* or *be-* in B20 and *bi-* in B40 and B50).

(b) The northern subgroup differs from S-B30 by the following features:

- the existence of a distinct NC 3a and of some (isolated) cases of consonant alternations (stem-initially).
- the absence of the traditional NCs 9 and 10 (replaced by classes 9a and 10a), well represented in S-B30.
- the shape of NCM 9a and 11: *e*(N)- and *no*(N)- respectively.
- the ((C)VC(G)-) shape NCM take when they precede vowel-initial stems. Having a more elaborated structure than the more traditional NCM found in S-B30, this shape most probably results from the addition of an *augment* to the NCM. In this respect, VdV (1991a:344) demonstrates that B10 shares this particular structural feature and has argued that N-B30 may even reflect an anterior stage of what is found in the languages of this group where the augment still seems to be partly functional.
- the absence (or extreme rarity) of NC 14. This NC may have undergone morphological reanalysis. It may also be that this NC initially did not occur in B30 at all and that S-B30 has acquired it by borrowing from surrounding languages where it appears to be rather common.

(c) As far as NC 5 is concerned, some kind of free variation exists in T, Vo and Vi (*e-* ~ *∅-*). The zero prefix seems to be the generally preferred allomorph, especially before vowel-initial stems. Only Vo and Vi have a (rare) NC 5a (plural: 6), borrowed from surrounding B40 or B50 languages.

3.2 Noun class pairings

Table 20.2 shows the main B30 noun class pairings (NCP) as well as their occurrence in the individual languages.

TABLE 20.2: B30 NOUN CLASS PAIRINGS

Class	T	Vo	Vi	P	K	H
1/2	✓	✓	✓	✓	✓	✓
3/4	✓	✓	✓	✓	✓	✓
3a/4	–	–	–	✓	✓	✓
5/6	✓	✓	✓	✓	✓	✓
5a/6(a)	–	✓	✓	–	–	–
7/8	✓	–	✓	–	–	–
7a/8	✓	✓	✓	✓	✓	✓
9/10	✓	✓	✓	✓	✓	✓
11/10	✓	✓	✓	–	–	–
11/10a	✓	?	✓	✓	✓	✓
11/6	✓	✓	✓	–	–	✓?
19/13	✓	✓	✓	✓	✓	✓

Note: A tick indicates that the pairing in question exists. A dash indicates its absence.

The following important features can be isolated:

(a) For the group as a whole (B included), the NCP 19/13 and 11/10a (except for Vo!). The former still functions as a diminutive marker in most B30 languages, but its productivity is rather low and not always semantically transparent. In Gabon, this gender is only found in some of the B20 languages (Seki, Kele, Ngom and perhaps also Sake).

The astonishing 11/10a gender, which has almost completely replaced the more traditional 11/10 pairing, could possibly be a B30 innovation, but as VdV (1991a:341-2) has shown, it also exists in B10 where it has erroneously been interpreted as a (highly unusual) 11/19 pairing (cf. Guthrie 1953 and Jacquot 1983). Its origin, however, remains obscure.

(b) N-B30 differs from S-B30 by a 3a/4 pairing, the absence of genders 11/10 and 11/6 (still sporadically found in S-B30).

The items belonging to the (not very frequent) NCP 3a/4 correspond in S-B30 to items that predominantly occur as part of 11/10a (or 11/10, see below). NCM 3a (N-B30) and 11 (S-B30) are homophones. Considering its rather uncommon nature, the preceding statements and the strong lexical links with B10, borrowing from this group is the most plausible hypothesis concerning its origin (VdV 1991a:342–3).

The gender 11/10a is found instead of 11/10. The latter occasionally occurs in S-B30 (T, Vi), but the lexical items that belong to it are increasingly used with the 11/10a pairing. (Cf. (Vi) 'hair' can be *isôyè* or *tsôyè* (the latter form being judged to be more archaic).)

3.3 Noun modifiers

The noun modifiers presented here mainly concern S-B30. In some cases, however, data are available for P and allow a broader comparison. It should be noticed that whereas in S-B30 all modifiers generally follow the head of the NP, P makes some of them precede it (see below).

Although not shown here, some qualifiers have been found in T and Vi. Their number, however, does not exceed three or four. The same is true for P.

3.3.1 Demonstrative markers

Two types of demonstratives occur in S-B30: a close demonstrative and a distant one. In Vi, and probably also elsewhere, prosodic features add a third degree (i.e. extremely distant). The close demonstrative systematically has the rather curious structure: concord marker$_i$ + / − V − / + concord marker$_i$, e.g. (Vo) *yèbótò yééyé* 'this old man over here'. (In T, its central part corresponds to the weak demonstrative (see below).) The distant demonstrative is /-né/ (/-né`/ for Vi), e.g. (Vo) *wàyétò dyótsò wáné* 'all these women over there'. The latter also exists in P.

In N-B30 the structure of the near demonstrative, however, is far less complex than in S-B30 and corresponds often to nothing else than the (appropriate) concord marker, as mostly is the case in the surrounding B10 and B20 languages.

3.3.2 Referential marker (or weak demonstrative)

S-B30 has the rather common marker /-é/ (see the Vo example in §2.1.1 Vowels systems). A different form has been found for P, which is the only language that places this marker before the head it determines, e.g. *àŋgátómídyá àsé ó̱ mwánà* 'he'll make us send the child'.

3.3.3 Associative marker (AM)

All S-B30 languages (including B!) as well as P, have the (for Gabon) more conservative form /-à/. Many surrounding languages have /-∅/. The concord markers, which precede the AM, are underlyingly H, except for classes 1 and 9 (S-B30).

3.3.4 Possessive determiners

Table 20.3 presents the Possessive Determiners found in S-B30 and in P. No clear tendencies emerge from these data. T shares features with Vo and Vi on the one hand, but on the other also with P. T's forms (and to a lesser extent the ones that occur in P) look very similar to those described for B11a (i.e. *-ami, -ɔ, -ɛ, -azo, -ani, -ao*).

3.3.5 Indefinite determiners (ID)

S-B30 Indefinite determiners (table 20.4) all follow the head of the NP. In case the noun is followed by the Referential or by a Demonstrative, the ID follow this modifier. Examples: for 'all', see the example given in §3.3.1 above. 'Only'/'self': (Vi) *nà dyɔ́ mé mwéné gó mbòkà* 'I go to the village myself'. 'Other': (Vo) *yèmɔ́nì yéèŋé yíŋgé* 'this other lemon'.

TABLE 20.3: POSSESSIVE DETERMINERS

		T	Vo	Vi	P
sg.	1	*-àmí*	*-àmɛ́*	*-àmɛ́*	*-ayi*
	2	*-ɔ́*	*-ɔ́ɔ́*	*-ɔ́ɔ́*	?
	3	*-èdí*	*-èdí*	*`-èndí*	*-aŋgo*
pl	1	*-àsó*	*-àtó*	*`-àtó*	*-aso*
	2	*-à̱ɲó*	*-ànó*	*`-ènú*	*-aɲo*
	3	*-àó*	*-àá*	*`-àó*	*-aŋgo*

TABLE 20.4: INDEFINITE DETERMINERS

	T	Vo	Vi
'all'	*-étsɔ̀*	*-ɔ́tsɔ̀*	*-étsɔ̀*
'only'	*-ènɛ́*	*-ɛ́nɛ́*	*-ɛ́nɛ́*
'self'			
'other'	*-βɔ́*	*-íŋgé*	*-mɔ̀sí*

3.3.6 Some interrogative markers (table 20.5)

TABLE 20.5: SOME INTERROGATIVE MARKERS

	T	Vo	Vi	P
'who'	*ndá*	*(í)nzá*	*(ní) nzá*	*ndêndè*
		náà		
'what'	*ndé*	*7/8-áà*	*ndé*	*yé*
'where'	*yòní*	*yóó*	*yó yé*	?
	βàní	*βáá*	*βá yé*	
'why'	*yòndé*	*náà*	*yé ndè*	?
'how many'	*-ké*	*-ké*	*-ké*	?

3.3.7 (Cardinal) numeral determiners (table 20.6)

TABLE 20.6: NUMERAL DETERMINERS

	T	Vo	Vi	P
'one'	-βɔ́/-pɔ́	-mwétá	-mwàtátá	-pɔkɔ
				-mɔtsi
'two'	-bàé	-bà	-báè	-bale
'three'	-tátó	-tátò	-tátò	-tatu
'four'	-nàé	-nàì	-nà	-nai
	-nai (RW, J)			
'five'	-tàé	-tánè	-tànì	-tane
	-tai (RW, J)			
'six'	mòtòbá	mùtóbá	motóbá	motoba
'seven'	tsàmbwé	nátátò	-nà na -tátò	napɔ
'eight'	γénàná	nánàì	γenáàná	γenana
'nine'	-tàé nà -nàé	tánánàì	kámbú mwàtátá	buka
'ten'	nzímá	nzímá	eγómì	nzima
'hundred'	kàmá (MN)	mùkámá	mokámá	kama
	mokama (RW, J)			

4 VERB MORPHOLOGY

Only the main lines of B30 verb morphology have been studied so far. This section will present in a systematic way the most important facts that have emerged.

The syllable structure of the verb stem and more generally of the verbal constituent obviously depends on the morphological complexity. The verb has the following overall morphological structure in (S-?)B30:

> Subject Marker (Negation M.) Tense/Aspect M. (Object M. if any) Verb Stem.

(E.g. (Vi) _tò sà + ŋgá + mó + tómá_ yó pìndì 'we will not send him into the forest'. For more examples, see §4.3 below.) The verb stem is typically composed of a root, one or more extensions, and a final vowel. With rarely more than four syllables, it is the domain of Vowel Harmony processes that have been extensively described in VdV (1991a:Part I). (See §2 on Phonology.) One specific constraint concerns the final -_a_ suffix: immediately following a mid-low back vowel in root position, this suffix fully harmonizes, e.g. (Vi) /e-sòmb-á/ 'borrow' becomes [èsòmbɔ́]. This constraint also applies to some extensions.

The canonical morphological structure of the root is -C(A)VC-. It may also be less complex: -VC-, -C(A)V- or even -V-, -(C)A-. For the extensions, the most common shapes are -VC- and -V-.

Infinitives bear the NC 5 marker in S-B30 (though Ø- in Vo) and the NC 3 marker in N-B30. Examples: /è-tùmbà/ 'burn (tr.)' (Vi) (cf /tùmbàkà/ (Vo)) vs. /mo-γendaγa/ 'go' (P).

4.1 Subject marking

All examined languages have both Subject Markers (SM) and Subject Pronouns (SP). The latter function as strong forms in independent clauses. Only the SM are part of the verb's morphology.

4.1.1 Subject markers

SM are attached to the verb as prefixes. For Vi however, VdV (1999b) has seriously questioned this prefixal status. Vi's SM tonally behave as proclitics!

Table 20.7 only presents the SM that formally differ from the corresponding NCM. Tone is underlyingly high except for classes 1 and 9 and for first and second person markers.

P's forms have been taken from Jacquot (1983), but match my data. Should also be noticed the class 5 SM: *ɲi-*. No data are available for classes 3, 3a, 4, 7, 8 and 10a.

A homogeneous picture arises here. The *nà-* marker (1st p. sing.) certainly is the most interesting form, for it doesn't occur anywhere else in Gabon. Vo has *mè-*, a form most probably borrowed from B52 which has *mè-*, just as many other neighboring languages. Altogether, the SM present similarities with markers found in at least some of the B40 languages.

4.1.2 Subject pronouns

In independent clauses, the SP generally precede the SM, e.g. (Vi) *mè(nì), tsáßàndàkà* 'me, I never practice witchcraft'. In relative clauses, they immediately follow the verb, e.g. (Vi) *à bàŋgí móyètɔ́ à síŋgìkì mênì* 'he has killed the woman I loved'. T and P share the highest number of forms. Vo and Vi also have several forms in common. Of these two, Vo diverges most from T and P (table 20.8).

4.1.3 Reflexive marker

T and Vi have /-á-/ (tone uncertain for T), not found in Vo so far, e.g. (Vi) *à máɑ̱̀bàŋgà* 'he has killed himself (recently)'.

TABLE 20.7: SUBJECT MARKERS THAT FORMALLY DIFFER FROM THE CORRESPONDING NOUN CLASS MARKERS

	T	Vo	Vi	P
1 p.sing.	nà-	mè-	nà	na-
1 p.plur.	tò-	tù-	tò	to-
2 p.sing.	ò-	ò-	ò	o-
2 p.plur.	nò-	nù-	nò	no-
3 p./cl.1	à-	à-	à	a-
3 p./cl.2	á-	wá-	wá	wa-
-/cl.9	è-	è-	è	e-
-/cl.10	dí-	dí-	dí	–

TABLE 20.8: SUBJECT PRONOUNS

		T	Vo	Vi	P
sg.	1	mɛ́	mè(ní)	mè(ní)	ímè
	2	èwè	wè(ní)	èwè	ɛ́wè
	3	àŋgó	ɛ́dì	èndì	àŋgò
pl.	1	wé	ìtú	ìtó	àsé
	2	àɲɛ́	ìnú	ìnó	àɲɛ́
	3	àŋgó	wâ	(è)àò	àŋgó

4.2 Object marking

At least two out of the four languages examined so far have two formally distinct series: (infixed) Object Markers (OM) and (independent) Object Pronouns (OP). They are found in T, Vi, and also in some dialects of P (cf. Jacquot 1983). Only the OM are part of the verb's morphology. Vo and other dialects of P possess only one series.

4.2.1 Object markers

The (infixed) OM are placed between the predicative marker (below) and the verb stem, e.g. (Vi) *nà màmótòmà* 'I've just sent him'. Table 20.9 only presents the OM that are not identical to the corresponding NCM. T and Vi have many identical forms.

4.2.2 Object pronouns

(Independent) OP either precede or follow the verb, e.g. (Vo) *mèkàdyànzá mè̱ mwéné* 'I alone am working', *mè̱ní, mèkàtɔ́ndɔ́ yínáká* 'Me, I like dancing'. They are formally identical with the SP presented above (table 20.8), e.g. (P (no-OM varieties)) *àŋgátómídyá à̱sé ó mwánà* 'he'll make us send the child'. Specific markers have been found for classes 3 to 19, i.e. *-àŋgó* (T), *-è-*(Concord Marker)-*óó* (Vo) and *-ɔ̀ɔ́* (Vi), e.g. (T) *nènà yésàmbí, nàbɔ̀ŋgɔ̀ sá̱ŋgó yó píndí* 'I see a basket. I take it into the forest'.

OP adopt the same order as noun phrases in complement position (dative-accusative), e.g. (Vo) *àkàbíkí mè̱ní è̱yyóó* 'he gave it (the lemon) to me'.

4.3 Predicative markers (PM)

Table 20.10 shows the main Tense/Aspect Markers and also some Negation Markers. A blank square points out that no particular PM has been encountered. All the examples that follow except one have been taken from Vi: (*e-pɛka* L 'to seize', *e-puma* H 'to go out') *nà mà̱mópèkà* 'I've just seized him', *nà mòpêkị̀* 'I sent him (recently)', *nà mà̱mòpêkà* 'I've sent him (a long time ago)', *nà ŋgá̱mòpêkà* 'I'll send him', *tò kị̀pékànà* 'we'll seize each other (once, in the future)', *nà kó̱púmá yó òbwà* 'I'm going out into the courtyard', *nà yè̱mópèkà* 'I seize him once more', *tsà̱mópèkà* 'I don't seize him' (NB *t* 1st p sg is an allomorph of *na*), *tsị̱mópèkà* 'I didn't seize him (recently)'. (Vo) *mè̱míbòmá wè* 'I'm going to beat you (now)'.

In spite of several differences and uncertainties, a common stock emerges. The latter comprises among others the future tense marker *´-ŋgà-* and the negation markers *-sá-* and *-sí-*. The FTM has not been found in any other Gabonese languages. T and Vi share the

TABLE 20.9: OBJECT MARKERS THAT FORMALLY DIFFER FROM THE CORRESPONDING NOUN CLASS MARKERS

Person	T	Vi
1 p. sing.	*-má-*	*-ní-*
1 p. plur.	*-tó-*	*-tó-*
2 p. sing.	*-yó-*	*-yó-*
2 p. plur.	*-nó-*	*-nó-*
-/cl.3	*-ó-*	*-ó-*
-/cl.9	*-mí-*	*-é-*
-/cl.10	*-dí-*	*-dí-*

TABLE 20.10: PREDICATIVE MARKERS

Value	T	Vo	Vi	P
IMM PAST	-má-		-má-	-fate-
HOD PAST	-ì	-ì	-ì	?
Distant PAST	-mà-	-mà-	-mà-	-ma-
IMM FUT		-mí-		?
FUT (MID ?)	'-ŋgà-	'-ŋgà-	'-ŋgà-	-ŋga-
FAR FUT	-ké-?		-ki-	?
PROG		-ka-	-kó-	?
Repetitious	-yé-		-yé-	-e
NEG	-sá-	-sá-	-sá-	-sa-mbé-
NEG (HOD PAST)	-sí-	-sí-	-sí-	-si-

largest number of forms. Vo often uses periphrastic constructions to express the tense/aspect values examined here.

A broad comparison, taking into account the PM found in neighboring languages, has revealed some similarities between S-B30 and B40/B50. It should be kept in mind, though, that these domains are still to be studied much more extensively. Very few resemblances with B10's PM have come up so far.

4.4 Verbal extensions

Compared to the verbal extensions found in the other neighbouring languages, the following suffixes have shown to be the most productive in T, Vi and Vo. (Insufficient data available for N-B30.)

-ed(y)-	CAUS	(P: -idy-)
-e-	APPLIC	(less clear for Vo)
-an-	RECIPR	(also in K)
-am-	STAT	
-ak-	HAB	
-oy-\-uy-	INTRANS	
-o-\-u-	TRANS	

The extensions can be exemplified by data from Vi: nà mótòmèdyà 'I make him send' (e-toma H 'to send'), nà mótòmèà 'I send on his behalf', wà pékànà 'they seize each other' (e-pɛka L 'to seize'), e-bebama H 'to be closed in' (e-beba H 'to close in'), nà mòpékàkà 'I seize him habitually' (e-pɛka L 'to seize'), nà kùndùyà 'I rise', nà kùndùà 'I raise'.

From a comparative perspective, the shape of the Causative Marker is the most intriguing. It has not been found as such in any of the surrounding languages and is probably a specific B30 feature, at least within the Gabonese context.

The Passive Marker is -u in S-B30. Example: (Vi) e-pɛku L 'to be seized'. In Vi one encounters the suffix /-eo/ too. Other interesting facts emerge from the study of copulas and subjunctive structure(s). Because of lack of space, these aspects cannot be commented on.

5 CONCLUSION

Recent linguistic research on B30 has furnished a much more accurate picture of a typologically interesting group. Several structural features define its identity. T's central position within this group stands out clearly. Although the available syntactic data show a somewhat less homogeneous picture, the same subdivisions appear.

The homogeneous northern subgroup presents noteworthy lexical and morphological similarities with B10. From a syntactic perspective, however, similarities appear to be much rarer.

Within S-B30, T and Vi are closest. Vo stands out as the most innovative of all three in its syntax (e.g. subordinating conjunctions, /-na-/ morpheme following the concord marker in relatives (cf. *tsóßà dinàkàéná mèní* 'the calebashes I see') and in some parts of its (verb) morphology (periphrastic constructions)). From a tonal perspective, though, it is more conservative than T/Vi. It should furthermore be kept in mind that more conservative varieties of Vo exist.

Unfortunately B30 is in the process of splitting up and is not far from total disintegration. Scientific investigation should therefore speed up in order to refine our knowledge of this group. The recently published Viya-French dictionary is one important contribution to this cause.

REFERENCES

Bastin 1978; Bastin and Piron 1999; Blanchon 1987a, 1988c; Bryan 1959; Guthrie 1948, 1953, 1969–71; Jacquot 1978, 1983; Janssens 1991; Marchal-Nasse 1979; Mickala-Manfoumbi 1994; Raponda-Walker 1937, 1950, 1967, n.d.; Stewart 1989; Van der Veen 1986, 1987, 1991a, 1991b, 1992, 1999a, 1999b; Van der Veen and Bodinga in press; Van Leynseele and Stewart 1980.

FURTHER READING

Bodinga-bwa-Bodinga and Van der Veen 1995; Van der Veen 1991a, 1999b; Van der Veen and Bodinga-bwa-Bodinga 2002.

CHAPTER TWENTY-ONE

BABOLE (C101)

Myles Leitch

In this chapter, I provide an overview of the phonology, morphology and syntax of Babole, a representative Bantu C language. I will look first at phonological issues of segmental contrasts in consonants and vowels, vowel harmony and tone in nominal forms. Next I will survey aspects of nominal and verbal morphology, including the noun class system, de-verbal nominalization, and tense/mood/aspect (TMA) morphology in verbs. Finally I will sketch selected elements of the syntax of Babole, including the demonstrative system, the associative system, pronouns, and various aspects of noun phrase modification. I conclude with a description of Babole relative clauses.

1 SPEECH COMMUNITY, CLASSIFICATION, AND DIALECTS

The Babole language is spoken by about 4000 people living in 14 villages (between one and two degrees of latitude North) along the Likouala-Aux-Herbes river system in the District of Epena, Likouala Region, of the Republic of Congo (Brazzaville). The Babole

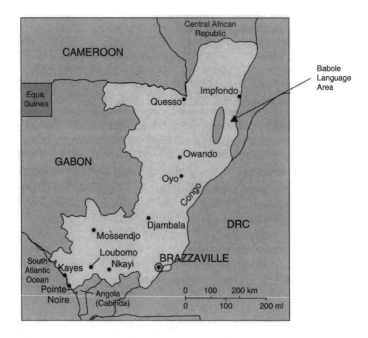

MAP 21.1 CONGO (BRAZZAVILLE) AND BABOLE LANGUAGE AREA

area is only accessible by going south on the river from the town of Epena, the district capital. Adults who have had access to secondary education normally speak some French, the official language of Congo. Everyone except small children speaks and understands Lingala, the regional national language, to some degree. However Babole people in their own villages rarely speak anything but the Babole language. French and Lingala are considered appropriate only for communicating with non-Babole, according to the situation, French being more 'official' and of higher status. The Babole area is almost 100 percent linguistically homogeneous, mainly because of the extreme isolation of the language area. The author lived for three years in the Babole village of Dzeke and was able to observe these language use patterns and attitudes directly.

Although each village has a characteristic speech form, Babole divides into three main dialect areas, North, Central, and South (Leitch 1989). The dialects are distinguished by lexical differences and by phonological 'accent' effects such as whether initial '*p*' is as [p] (Northern and Southern Dialect) or as [ɸ] (Central Dialect). The variety described in this chapter is that spoken in the villages of Impongui and Dzeke in the Northern dialect area. Babole was undescribed and unclassified before the author conducted an intensive period of fieldwork from 1988 to 1992. Summarizing the linguistic surveys conducted in the region by the author and colleagues (Leitch 1989, Gardner 1990), it is clear that Babole is somewhat distantly related to the other language spoken in the district of Epena, Bomitaba (see Vanhoudt 1987 on the Leke variety of Bomitaba). On the basis on this fieldwork I propose that Babole be classified tentatively as C10 in the Guthrie 1967 system. Detailed comparative work would be needed to clarify the complex relationships between C10 (Bongili type), C20 (Mbosi type) and C30 (Bobangi type) languages.

2 PHONOLOGY

2.1 Vowels and vowel harmony

Babole shares with most Bantu C languages the seven-vowel inventory in (1).

(1)   Bantu C seven-vowel inventory

Front	Central	Back	
i		*u*	high
e		*o*	'closed' mid
ɛ		*ɔ*	'open' mid [rtr]
	a		low

Babole vowels participate in a vowel 'harmony' system where only certain vowels are found together in particular morphological domains. This harmony system involves only the low and mid-vowels and may be characterized in the following way. The 'open' and 'closed' mid-vowels are never found 'mixed' in the morphological stem domain in either verbal or nominal forms. Similarly, the low vowel [a] is never found together with [ɛ] or [ɔ]. Otherwise any vowels may co-occur freely. This system may be analyzed as involving assimilation (or 'spreading') of a phonological 'retracted tongue root' feature [rtr], which is a basic lexical property of root morphemes (Archangeli and Pulleyblank 1995 and references therein). A root morpheme is hypothesized to either have or not have the harmonic feature. This results in nouns as in (2), where stems with mid-vowels are either uniformly 'open' if the harmonic feature is present, or 'closed', if the harmonic feature is absent. Nothing in this description depends on the choice of [rtr] as the crucial harmonic feature.

(2)   Babole Nouns and Tongue Retraction Feature

with [rtr]		without [rtr]	
mo≠sékɔ̀	'joke 3/4'	mo≠kèngò	'trimming of wine palm 3'
mo≠lèkè̀	'alouette 3/4'	bo≠hèlè	'man 14'
di≠pɔ̀té	'labyrinth 5/6'	mo≠kóté	'house 3/4'
di≠ɔ̀ngɔ̀	'art of pottery 5'	bo≠lòlò	'bitterness (taste) 14'

Note that mid-vowel prefixes are not affected by the vowel harmony process affecting the stem. This is a peculiarity of Babole that is shared by several other of Bantu C languages. Lomongo (Hulstaert 1961), on the other hand, does show mid-vowel prefixes harmonizing with [rtr] in the stem. See *Vowel Harmonies of the Congo Basin* (Leitch 1997), for a thorough treatment of vowel harmony variation over the whole Bantu C zone.

In the verbal system there are interesting vowel harmony alternations that are not observable in static noun morphology. In particular note in (3) when there is an open mid-vowel in the verb root that any low vowel suffixes become a copy of the preceding vowel. So both underlying [e] and [a] become [ɛ] following [ɛ], and both [o] and [a] become [ɔ] following [ɔ]. To see this clearly, compare the Applicative and Passive paradigms in (3), in particular the forms indicated by a bolded arrow, which have a open mid-vowel in the root.

(3)   Suffixal low assimilation in Babole verbal morphology under harmony

	Imperative	Gloss	Applicative	Passive	Subjunctive passive
	sìl-á	'sharpen!'	sìl-él-á	sìl-ám-á	sìl-àm-è
	kèl-á	'make!'	kèl-él-á	kèl-ám-á	kèl-àm-è
→	hék-ɛ́	**'cut!'**	hék-ɛ́l-ɛ́	hék-ɛ́m-ɛ́	hék-ɛ́m-ɛ́
	sál-á	'do!'	sál-él-á	sál-ám-á	sál-àm-è
→	kɔ́s-ɔ́	**'gather!'**	kɔ́s-ɛ́l-ɛ́	kɔ́s-ɔ́m-ɔ́	kɔ́s-ɔ́m-ɛ́
	kòh-á	'take!'	kòh-él-á	kòh-ám-á	kòh-àm-è
	tsùm-á	'dip!'	tsùm-él-á	tsùm-ám-á	tsùm-àm-è

2.2 Consonant inventory and consonant processes

Babole has the consonant inventory shown in (4). The consonant segments shown in brackets do not have a robust positional distribution in Babole and so do not fully participate in the system of contrasts normally associated with 'phonemes'. They are either 'derived' in the morphophonology from vowels (the case of [w], [y] and [dz], [ts]) or they have a very skewed distribution.

(4)   Babole consonants

p ~ h	t		k	
(b ~ φ)	(d ~ l)			
	s			h
		(ts)		
		(dz)		
(mp)	(nt)	(nts)	(nk)	
mb	nd	(ndz)	ng	
	(ns)			
	l			
m	n			
(w)		(y)		

2.2.1 Voiced occlusives

A striking feature of the Babole consonant system is the marginality of the voiced occlusive series (line 2 in the chart in (4)). The voiced velar occlusive [g] simply is not found at all while both [d] and [b] have a highly restricted distribution. The phone [d] is best analyzed as an allophone of the phoneme [l]. Basically we find [l] before each of the vowels except [i], and we find [d] only before [i].

[d] / ____[i]
[l] / ____[a, ɛ, e, ɔ, o, u]

Similarly, the phone [b] is only robustly attested in two environments, (i) before the high vowels [i] and [u] and (ii) phrase initially. Where the local trade language Lingala has root-initial [b], Babole has a 'silent' or 'ghost' consonant which has no articulatory manifestation but acts like a consonant in terms of syllabic structure. The [b] has 'dropped out' in the stem initial position before non-high vowels.

(5)   Loss of [b] in Babole

Babole	à≠òm-í	'he killed'
	3s≠kill-FV	
Lingala	à≠b̠òm-í	'he killed'

With vowel-initial verbs like -òm-, as in (6), the 'ghost' [b] is not perceived directly but it shows up explicitly in class 9 nominalizations and in the maintenance of vowel-hiatus in class 3/4 forms. In a form like /mo-òmì/, e.g. one would normally expect vowel elision to yield [mòmì] but in fact we get [moòmì]. There is a systematic failure of vowel elision where historically there was a [b].

(6)   'Ghost' [b]-initial roots

Root	Gloss	Class 9	Gloss	Other	Gloss
-òm-	'kill'	mb̠òmi	'slaughter'	moòmì	'killer 3'
				miòmì	'killers 4'
-és-	'complain'	mb̠ésá	'complaint'	moésá	'complainer 3'
				mwésá*	
				miésá	'complainers 4'
				myésa*	
-ót-	'give birth'			diótà	'family likeness 5'
				dzótà*	
-èd-	'blame'	mb̠èdí	'blaming'	moèdì	'blamer 3'
				mièdì	'blamers 4'

In contrast to (6), there is a class of true vowel-initial roots, exemplified in (7), which show a different pattern of class 9 nominalization and exhibit the normal hiatus avoidance processes of vowel elision, gliding, and affrication across the prefix-stem boundary in classes 3, 4, 5, and 14. In particular, contrast the class 3 forms for 'bailing tool', [mò.hò] from underlying /mo≠òh-ò/ in (7) with the word for 'killer', [mo.ò.mì] from underlying /mo≠òm-ì/ in (6).

(7)   Real vowel-initial roots

Root	Gloss	Class 9	Gloss	Other	Gloss
-òh-	'bail out'	ndzòhà	'jungle pond'	mòhò	'bailing tool 3'

	('a boat	mbòhà*		moòhò*	
	or pond')			myòhò	'bailing tools 4'
				miòhò*	
-àne-	'dry out'	N/A		bwánò	'sun-drying 14'
				boánò*	
-òmb-	'peel'	ndzòmbí	'act of peeling'		
		mbòmbí*			
-èp-	'search for'	N/A		dzèpɔ̀	'research 5'
				dièpɔ*	

Because of the difference between true-vowel initial roots (7) and 'ghost b' roots (6), there are pairs like the following in the lexicon:

bo.á.tò	'femininity 14'	bwá.tò	'canoe 14'
di.à.lè	'liver 5'	dzá.lé	'open space in floating vegetation 5'

These contrasts confirm the presence of a 'silent' consonant which is blocking gliding or affrication processes in the Babole forms for 'femininity' and 'liver' but not in the forms for 'canoe' and 'open space in floating vegetation', where gliding and affrication transform the underlying prefix shapes bo- and di- to bw- and dz- respectively.

2.2.2 Prenasalized consonants

The distribution of the voiced and voiceless prenasalized segments is worthy of a close look since there are interesting asymmetries that exist. The first fact to note is that the whole range of prenasals is found freely in the stem-initial position (following a noun-class prefix). This is illustrated in (8).

(8) Stem-initial prenasalized obstruents following noun class prefixes

Singular	Plural	NC	Gloss
mu≠mpɔ́mbɔ̀	mimpɔ́mbɔ̀	3/4	'message drum'
mu≠mbàká	mimbàká	3/4	'succulent wild fruit'
di≠ntùmù	mantùmù	5/6	'aggressive arboreal ant'
di≠ndúndù	mandúndù	5/6	'air bubble in water'
di≠ntsòtsá	mantsòtsá	5/6	'a punch with the fist'
di≠ndzókà	mandzókà	5/6	'traditional hat'
di≠nkɔ̀tì	mankɔ̀tì	5/6	'horn of an animal'
di≠ngàsé	mangàsé	5/6	'little cola nut'
di≠nsòì	mansòì	5/6	'domestic duck'
e≠nsùè	binsùè	7/8	'finger/toe nails'

Second, the full range of prenasals is found word-initially in class 9 nominal forms, as illustrated in (9). Even though the class 9 prefix is ex hypothesi a syllabic nasal [N-], identifying a prefix-stem boundary is not always straightforward. This is most dramatic in forms like [ŋgɔ́ndɔ̀], 'chimpanzee' where the morpheme analysis should be /N-gɔ́ndɔ̀/, but the phone [g] does not otherwise exist on its own and so /gɔ́ndɔ̀/ is not a possible theme morpheme. Contrast this with nsáèlò 'downstream', which is clearly derived by prefixation of the verb root -sá- 'float downstream', with the class 9 prefix N- and the suffix -elo.

(9)   Initial prenasals in class 9 nouns

Class 9	Pronunciation	Gloss
mpàkó	[ĩ.pà.kó]	'stubbornness'
mbésé	[ɪ.ᵐbé.sé]	'turtle (species)'
ntéhì	[ĩ.té.hì]	'saliva'
ndèngà	[ɪ.ⁿdè.ⁿgà]	'unmarried person'
ntsètsí	[ĩ.tsè.tsí]	'the ripping apart of something'
ndzɔmbɔ	[ɪ.ⁿdzɔ.ᵐbɔ]	'species of large eel'
nkétì	[ĩ.ké.tì]	'anger'
ngɔ́ndɔ̀	[ɪ.ᵑgɔ́.ⁿdɔ̀]	'chimpanzee'
nsáèlò	[ĩ.sá.è.lò]	'downstream'

'Ordinary' prenasalization is expressed with the voiced prenasal set in (9) as a super-scripted preceding nasal in the pronunciation column. In contrast there is only slight nasalization of the epenthetic initial high vowel in the case of voiced obstruents (I have thus shown the initial vowel without nasalization in the voiced obstruent case). When the obstruent is voiceless, on the other hand, the nasalization is very heavy on the initial vowel, but the stem initial obstruent carries almost no nasalization. The disfavoring of nasality on voiceless obstruents is expressed positionally as well in the language. Although we find many verb roots like the ones in (10), a parallel verb root such as -_hámp_- would be completely impossible in Babole, only the voiced prenasal series occurs in the root-internal C_2 position.

(10)   Verb roots with C_2 prenasalized

Verb root	Gloss
≠_hámb_-	'to curse'
≠_hànd_-	'to start again'
≠_hàng_-	'become mean'

Schematically in Babole stems, we see that C_1, the stem initial consonant position, may be filled by any prenasal or other consonant, while the C_2 position cannot be [mp, nt, ns, nts, nk]. This recalls the prosodically motivated distributional asymmetries pointed out in Hyman (1989).

Consider finally verb roots with initial prenasalized consonants. In the Babole lexicon there are a good number of verb roots beginning with either voiced and voiceless pre-nasalized obstruents. In the completive paradigm (11), nasalization is clearly manifested in both the voiced and voiceless cases, with the phonetic provisos sketched above.

(11)   Prenasal-initial verb roots in completive paradigm

   (i)   /à-ndùm-í/   [à.ⁿdù.mí]   'he stuffed his mouth'
          3s-stuff_mouth-CMPL
   (ii) /à-ntèng-í/   [ã̀.tè.ngí]   'he writhed'
          3s-writhe-CMPL

Now the imperative of a root like ≠_ndùm_-, 'to stuff the mouth', is morphologically /ndùm-á/. This is pronounced simply [ⁿdù.má], with two syllables. However the imperative of a root such as ≠_ntèng_-, 'to writhe', while morphologically represented as /ntèng-á/, is pronounced as [tè.ngá], completely dropping the root-initial nasalization. Since no prefix vowel can license the nasality in the case of the imperative, the nasalization is just lost when the initial consonant is voiceless. The prohibition on [mp, nt, nts, ns, nk] in the root-internal C_2 position requires a different explanation. See Leitch (1994b) for an explanation of the overall Babole prenasalized distribution pattern within Optimality Theory (Prince and Smolensky 1995). All of these considerations lead us to consider the voiceless prenasalized series [mp, nt, nts, ns, nk] as *not* participating robustly in the systematic phonological oppositions of the language.

2.3 Tone in nominal forms

Babole displays the classic Bantu pattern of four basic tone patterns on disyllabic noun stems; IIL, IIII, LL, LII. These four patterns are more or less equally represented in the nominal lexicon with no pattern being dominant and no gaps occurring. Nominal prefixes are always low-toned and so I do not represent tone on noun prefixes in this chapter.

(12)   Minimal tone pairs in disyllabic noun stems

Pattern	Word	Gloss	Pattern	Word	Gloss
LH	e-lòngó	'caterpillar'	LH	mu-ntɔ̀tɔ́	'sweet banana'
HL	e-lóngò	'stable'	HH	mu-ntɔ́tɔ́	'young leaf'
HL	mu-mpúlù	'fever treatment'	LH	mu-nsèsé	'date palm leaf'
HH	mu-mpúlú	'mushroom'	LL	mu-nsèsè	'louse egg'
LL	mu-ngòlò	'tabacco'	LL	dɪ-kàsà	'palm of hand'
HH	mu-ngóló	'water shortcut'	HH	dɪ-kásá	'writing paper'

Tone patterns on nominals derived from verbs are more complex and reflect the tonal properties of verbal stems where, as we will see, the tone of the initial (left-most) syllable is lexically determined, and the following span of syllables are all characterized by a single tone depending on the type of nominalization. Good examples of this come from nominalizations of verb roots where one can note that the tone on the non-initial stem syllable is determined by the kind of nominalization, as in (13).

(13)   Suffixal Tone Patterns on Deverbal Nouns

Root	Gloss	Nominalization	Gloss
≠sá-	'go downstream'	e≠sá-él-á	'descent of a river 7'
≠sá-	'go downstream'	n≠sá-èlò	'downstream 9'
≠dínd-	'fall (tree)'	n≠dínd-àk-à	'felling of trees 9'
≠dìnd-	'sink, flood'	n≠dìnd-àk-à	'flooding of ground 9'
≠hɔ́-	'speak'	e≠hw-és-ák-á	'which causes talk 7'
≠òngo-	'complement'	di≠òngó	'cooperative work 5'
≠òngo-	'complement'	mo≠òng-òd-ì	'cooperative worker 3'
≠pómb-	'arrive'	mo≠pómb-ì	'person arriving 3'
≠tɔ́ng-	'to visit'	mo≠tɔ́ng-í	'visit 3'

2.4 Tone and prosodic structure of verb roots/stems

The structure of Babole verbs is such that a lexical tone (High or Low) is always associated with the initial verb root syllable. The tone-bearing unit (TBU) is the syllable in Babole and there is no contrastive vowel length. Depending on the tense/mode/aspect involved, the subsequent syllables of the stem will have particular tonal properties as sketched in the section on verbal stem morphology. The basic stem tone situation can be abstractly schematized in the autosegmental representation in (14).

(14)   Basic stem tonal schema

The initial verb root syllable has a fixed lexical tone, either H(igh) or L(ow), which may be thought of as underlyingly associated with the stem-initial vowel. The non-initial stem syllables take a tonal specification provided by suffixal inflection tone melodies. Additional suffixal tones add complexities which will be treated later in this chapter (see §3.2.2 for details). Except for the final vowel, all non-initial syllables in the verb stem can be analyzed as underlyingly toneless. Verb roots come in many different prosodic shapes. The examples provided below in (15) show the attested range. Although the basic root shape is -CVC-, historical consonant loss on the one hand and incorporation of suffixal material on the other has resulted in a rather large variety of possible root shapes. I have provided examples with near past and hortative forms to illustrate the pattern schematized in (14). Completives involve a plateau of final high tones while hortatives show a plateau of final low tones.

(15)   Prosodic shape of verb roots

Shape	Root	Gloss	3s completive	3s hortative
-V-	-ú-	'be cancelled'	àúí	áúè
-VC-	-àk-	'hit your foot on a stone'	àùkí	áùkè
-VCV-	-àke-	'become caught on something'	àùkéí	áùkèè
-VCVC-	ékod-	'study, learn'	àékódí	áékòlè
-CV-	-há-	'become'	àhái	áháè
-CVV-	-sáo-	'become faded or insipid'	àsáóí	ásáòè
-CVC-	-sát-	'help'	àsátí	ásátè
-CVVC-	-sáan-	'complain'	àsáání	ásáànè
-CVCV-	-sènɛ-	'press or push'	àsènéí	ásènèì
-CVCVC-	-sìsod-	'frighten'	àsìsódí	ásìsòlè
-CVCVCV-	-kɔ̀ngɔmɔ-	'roll'	àkɔ̀ngɔ́mɔ́í	ákɔ̀ngɔ̀mɔ̀è
-CVCVCVC-	-kɔ̀tumbod-	'cough'	àkɔ̀túmbódí	ákɔ̀tùmbòlè

While forms like -kɔ̀ngɔmɔ-, 'roll', might be attributed a morphological analysis /kɔ̀ng-ɔm-ɔ/ involving the passive derivational suffix -ɔm- (a vowel harmony variant of -am), no root -kɔ̀ng- with a related meaning exists in the current language.

3 MORPHOLOGY

This section covers first nominal morphology and then verb morphology. The section on verb morphology contains much detail that could equally have been treated in the section on syntax.

3.1.1 Noun class system

Babole shows the range of noun classes in (16). A distinct class is considered to exist when either the prefix has a distinct phonological form or different concord/agreement markers are generated. See Leitch (to appear) for an exhaustive analysis of the Babole noun class system. I also show the corresponding verbal agreement markers corresponding to each noun class. While the noun prefixes are always low toned the verbal prefixes corresponding to nouns are high-toned.

(16)   Babole noun classes and verbal agreements

Class	Noun prefixes	Examples	Glosses	Verb agreement prefix
1	mo-	molómì	'husband'	à-
1a	φ	kàlé	'field'	à-
2	baa-	baalómì	'husbands'	bá-
		baakàlé	'fields'	
3	mo-	mokóté	'house'	ó-
	mu-	mungàté	'shrimp (fresh water)'	
	mw-	mwàngò	'beak of bird'	
	m-	mɔ́kɔ̀	'palm tree climber's belt'	
4	mi-	mikóté	'houses'	mí-
		mingàté	'shrimp (pl)'	
	my-	myàngò	'beaks'	
		myɔ́kɔ̀	'palm tree climber's belts'	
5	di-	dibitɔ́	'python'	dí-
	dz-	dzúmbá	'thing'	
6	ma-	mabítɔ́	'pythons'	
	m-	múmbá	'things'	má-
7	e-	ehɔ̀sɔ́	'hunting net (traditional)'	é-
8	bi-	bihɔ̀sɔ́	'hunting nets (traditional)'	bí-
	by-	byúmbá	'things (specific counted number)'	
9	n-	mbɔ̀mɔ̀	'boa constrictor'	à-
10	n-	mbɔ̀mɔ̀	'boa constrictors'	í-
11	lo-	lɔ̀nɔ̀	'cleanliness'	bó-
14	bo-	bodítò	'weight'	bó-
	bw-	bwátò	'canoe'	
	b-	bɔ́dì	'adultery'	
16	ha	húkà	'place (general area)'	há
17	lo	lúkà	'place (specific)'	ló
18	mu	múkà	'places'	mú
19	mwá		'diminutive (singular)'	hi-
20	báná		'diminutive (plural)'	tó-

The singular–plural pairings of noun classes are traditionally referred to as 'genders'. So there is a 1/2 gender, a 3/4 gender, etc. Babole has the unusual characteristic of allowing many nouns to form a concrete 'counting' plural in the regular gender pair, and also an abstract non-counting plural in class 10. A class 5 noun that allows both a regular class 6 counting plural and a class 10 non-counting plural would be designated by the gender 5/6,10, etc. The diminutives determine the agreements generated by the NP to which they attach. They attach to fully formed words and so are different from the other noun prefixes which attach to stems.

The singular–plural pairing possibilities are quite complex. These are summed up graphically in (17).

(17)   Singular/plural pairings (genders)

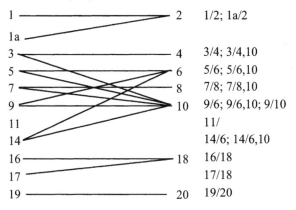

1 —— 2	1/2; 1a/2	
1a		
3 —— 4	3/4; 3/4,10	
5 —— 6	5/6; 5/6,10	
7 —— 8	7/8; 7/8,10	
9 —— 10	9/6; 9/6,10; 9/10	
11	11/	
14	14/6; 14/6,10	
16 —— 18	16/18	
17	17/18	
19 —— 20	19/20	

3.1.2 Deverbal noun suffixes

In (18) I provide examples of various deverbal single-vowel suffixed forms. There are two interesting gaps that occur. One is the complete absence of forms with a low-toned -e suffix. Parallel to this there is only one true example of a form with a high-toned -o suffix. These gaps are unexplained.

(18)   Single vowel nominal suffixes

Suffix	Example	Gloss	Root	Gloss
-ì	mo≠là-ì	'person who spreads out' cl. 1.	-là-	'spread out'
	mo≠pòd-ì	'person who arrives'	-pòd-	'arrive'
-í	bo≠pòd-í	'arrival' cl. 14	-pòd-	'arrive'
-è				
-é	e≠là-é	'manner of spreading'	-là-	'spread out'
	e≠sè-é	'place where manioc is left underwater'	-sè-	'put X under water'
	e≠kùnd-é	'place where someone is buried (cemetary)'	-kùnd-	'bury X'
	e≠kúm-é	'temporal or physical ending (result)'	-kúm-	'come to an end'
	n≠sák-é	'an extra portion (gift)'	-sák-	'be joyful'
-à	bo≠hàng-à	'meaness/toughness'	-hàng-	'become mean'
	bo≠hìnd-à	'rightness (judicial)'	-hìnd-	'be right'
	bo≠lèmb-à	'sorcery/knowing'	-lèmb-	'know'
	n≠túk-à	'state of well-being'	-túk-	'become rich, get fat'

-á	e≠túk-á	'place of importance'	-túk-	'become rich, get fat'
	di≠tén-á	'dam'	-tén-	'cut'
	bo≠tínd-á	'parcel'	-tínd-	'send'
	e≠hál-á	'pursuit'	-hál-	'pursue'
	e≠làk-á	'promise (N)'	-làk-	'promise'
-ò	bo≠hínd-ò	'darkness'	-hínd-	'become dark'
	bo≠dìt-ò	'heaviness'	-dìt-	'become heavy'
	dzás-ò	'research'	-ás-	'search'
	mo≠hámb-ò	'curse'	-hámb-	'curse'
-ó	ma-n≠sés-ó	'praise names'	-sés-	'praise, admire'
	di≠bútó	'return (N)'	-búto-	'return'
	n-dzùpó	'clean-up of a palm'	-ùpo-	'clean a palm'
	di≠kipó	'jealousy'	-kípo-	'be jealous'
-ù	bo≠ás-ù	'theft'	-ás-	'steal'
	e≠ém-ù	'sigh, groan'	-ém-	'sigh, groan'
	mo≠kùnd-ù	'garbage dump'	-kùnd-	'bury'
-ú	bo≠ònd-ú	'slimming-down'	-ònd-	'become small'
	bo≠tèh-ú	'refusal, disobedience'	-tèh-	'refuse, disobey'

Note that a form like *mansésó*, 'praise names', is based on the root *-sés-*, 'praise', but undergoes a double prefixation process, first with class 9 *N-* and then with class 6 *ma-*. The other forms such as *di≠bútó* and *di≠kípó* shown as examples of high-toned final *-o* are in fact false examples since the final *o* is part of the verb root in each case and not a suffix.

3.1.3 *-elo/-ɛlɔ* nominalizations

As can be seen in (19) below, most *-elo* nominals have a base meaning of 'the place where action X takes place', or 'the place where you end up after doing X'. A few forms have *manner* type meanings. Note also the obligatory passive morpheme *-am-* in *enwámèlò*, 'spring'; *ekósàmèlò*, 'exit'; and *ekwèlàmèlò*, 'entrance'. The tonal melody associated with the *-elo* derivation is a plateau of lows following the lexical verb root tone. This suffixal process is most productive in classes 5 and 7 as can be seen in (19), an exhaustive list of derived *-elo* nominals from my lexicon.

(19)   *-elo/-ɛlɔ* Derived nominals

-elo form	Meaning	Root	Meaning
Class 3 forms			
mo≠dzéèlò	'way of eating'	-dzé-	'eat'
mo≠kèlɔ̀	'way of walking (or a walk)'	-kè-	'go, walk, leave'
mo≠sènàkèlò	'greeting'	-sèned-	'greet'
Class 5 forms			
di≠nkɔ́mbɔ̀tèlɔ̀	'circular ring of iron wire for scraping'	-kɔ́mbɔt-	'scrape the bottom of X'
di≠tàlèlò	'place of cutting up meat'	-tàl-	'cut up meat'
di≠yèlɔ̀	'place of sharing'	-yè-	'share'
dzáhwèlò	'entrance to a secondary path'	-áho-	?

di≠kwélò	'nightfall'	*-kwé-*	'fall'

Class 7 forms

e≠kwélò	'place where animals bathe'	*-kwé-*	'fall'
e≠ándèlò	'reason for a refusal'	*-ánd-*	'refuse'
e≠àndèlò	'beginning'	*-ànd-*	'begin'
e≠búmbàmèlò	'place sthg is hidden'	*-búmb-*	'hide sth.'
e≠hólèlɔ̀	'resting place'	*-hól-*	'rest'
e≠kèlɔ̀	'trip, voyage'	*-kè-*	'go'
e≠kósàmèlò	'place where X is exited'	*-kóse-*	'exit'
e≠kwèlàmèlò	'place where X is entered'	*-kwèl-*	'enter'
e≠kyèlò	'act, action'	*-kèl-*	'do, make'
e≠nwámèlò	'place where water is drunk'	*-nwé-*	'drink'
e≠ókwèlò	'indifference, lack of consistency'	*-óko-*	'get up, wake up'
e≠swéèlò	'place you are coming from'	*-swé-*	'come from X'

Class 9 forms

n≠sáèlò	'downstream'	*-sá-*	'float downstream'

Class 14

bo≠kúmbùtèlò	'water canal that has been dug'	*-kúmbut-*	'drag X across the earth'

3.2 Verbal morphology

As in many Bantu languages much of the morphosyntactic complexity of the language shows up in the verb morphology where both inflectional and derivational morphology are realized. I go into quite a bit of detail on the preverbal inflectional morphology but give less attention to the suffixal derivational morphology and final vowels.

3.2.1 Inflectional morphology

In Babole the verbal prefixes mark tense, mood, aspect, negation, and subject agreement. There is an additional optional morpheme which marks reflexivity and functions as a direct object pronoun anaphorically bound by the agreement features of the syntactic subject.

(20) Verbal morphology schema

AGR-(NEG)-({TNS/COND})-({FUT/PROG})-(RFLX)-[VERB ROOT]-EXT$_1$-EXT$_2$-EXT-PRE-FV

Such a 'slot-and-filler' schematic, while helpful expositionally, can only ever tell a small part of the real story since many of the syntactic constraints and complexities of the languages syntax are reflected in the verb morphology. I provide an example of a conditional verb form below to give the reader a feel for the complexity of the verbal morphology.

(21) Example of complex verb morphology

dihásà	*díkáꞌsóꞌáꞌbímbèdzá nà mohúmà*		
di-hásà	*dí-káꞌ-só ꞌ-áꞌ-bímb-èdz-á*	*nà*	*mo-húmà*
5-twin	AGR5-NEG-COND-RFLX-hit-INTNS-FV	in	3-morning

'The twin would not hit himself very hard in the morning.'

3.2.2   Survey of tense/mode/aspect forms

In this section, I will describe the range of tense/mode/aspects (TMA) forms in Babole. For the description of each TMA form I will provide an illustrative sample sentence and show how the form would be negated. Examples are built using personal pronoun subject agreement rather than full NP subjects, but I provide one example of agreement morpheme corresponding to a full NP in each case. The 'personal' pronoun agreement prefix set is shown in (22a). These 'bound' morphemes are all low-toned, except for the third person plural which is high-toned. The verb agreement prefixes corresponding to each noun class are high-toned except for class 1 (humans) and class 9 (animals), which are low-toned (see (16)). I include the independent object pronouns in (22b) for comparison's sake. Note that the plural object pronouns all have a tonal downstep built into them.

(22)   (a)   **Bound** 'personal' prefixes   (b)   **Free** object pronouns

1s	*nì-, ĩ-, n-*	'I'	*àmé*	'me'
2s	*ò-*	'you'	*àwé*	'you'
3s	*à-*	'he, she, it'	*èí*	'him, her'
1p	*tò-*	'we'	*bí'sé*	'us'
2p	*bò-*	'you (plural)'	*bí'né*	'you (plural)'
3p	*bá-*	'they'	*bá'ngó*	'them'

I will look first at the 'epistemic' forms, past and future tenses, aspectualized forms, etc., and then turn to the 'deontic' forms: imperatives and subjunctives (see Palmer 1986 for the epistemic/deontic distinction).

3.2.2.1 Near past tense/completive aspect

This form is the morphologically simplest form in the language and is statistically the most commonly used TMA in conversational discourse. With psychological or experiencer predicates such as *-én-*, 'see', *-lèmb-*, 'know' and *-dìng-*, 'want', the meaning is 'present'. With all other verbs, the meaning is of Recent past (earlier today) as in (23). This form has an aspectual sense of completion (hence the gloss 'completive' for the final vowel suffix *-i*). Nonetheless this form is unmarked for aspect and differs formally from constructions like the progressive where aspect is formally marked.

(23)   Recent past
       báásí byèkà
       bá-ás-í   byèkà
       3p-steal-CMPL   8:food
       'They stole the food.' / 'They have stolen the food.'

There is no overt tense prefix, but other facts indicate that this form participates in the formal tense system of the language, as the unmarked member of that family. The agreement or personal prefix is attached directly to the verb root in the affirmative voice, but I assume a null present tense prefix in this case. Phonetically there is no tone lowering (downstepping) between the three high tones in an example like (23), but just a plateau of 3 high-toned syllables pronounced with the same pitch. The negation is shown in (24). The morphological negation morpheme *-ká-* is always followed by a tonal downstep (an small audible drop in pitch), indicated by a superscripted exclamation mark. In (24) there is a single pitch lowering following *-ká-* and the next two syllables are pronounced on the same lowered high pitch.

(24)   Negative recent past

> *báká'ásí byèkà*
> bá-**ká**-às-í   byèkà
> 3p-NEG-steal-CMPL   C8:food
> 'They have not stolen the food.'

The use of the pre-final morpheme *-ak-* with the recent past as in (25) gives a meaning of anteriority that distances the action from the present (while maintaining the 'today' requirement). Someone recounting at dusk an incident that had happened in the morning might use this construction.

(25)   Anteriorized recent past

> *báásákí byèkà nà mohúmà*
> bá-ás-ak-í   byèkà   nà   mo-húmà
> 3p-steal-ANT-CMPL   8:food   of   C3-morning
> 'They stole the food this morning.' / 'They had stolen the food that morning.'

French-bilingual native speakers of Babole frequently translate these anteriorized expressions by a French *plus-que-parfait*, rendered by English *past perfect* in the free-translation line of (25) above. Note that (25) could be negated just by adding in the negation morpheme as in the previous sentence. Note that with a vowel initial verb root there is neither gliding nor vowel elision lexically across the agreement/verb root boundary in (26).

(26)   Recent past paradigm (vowel-initial verb)

1s	nìásí	'I stole'	/nì≠ás-í/	
2s	òásí	'you stole'	/ò≠ás-í/	
3s	àásí	'he stole'	/à≠ás-í/	
1p	tòásí	'we stole'	/tò≠ás-í/	
2p	bòásí	'you stole'	/bò≠ás-í/	
3p	báásí	'they stole'	/bá≠ás-í/	*básí no vowel elision
cl. 5	díásí	'it worked'	/dí≠ás-í/	NP = dingóndélé 'child'

Post-lexically (in casual speech) one can find /bò-ás-í/ pronounced as [bwà.á.sí] which although relieving the vowel-hiatus, nonetheless preserves the prosodic structure of 3 syllables and corresponding tones.

3.2.2.2 Present statives

Formally the present forms of the stative (27 and 28) are not part of the near past paradigm. There is no evidence of the presence of suffixal *-i*. Possessives and existentials are both based on the stative verb and are followed by the genitive preposition *nà* whose function is presumably to assign (genitive) case to the post verbal NP (Chomsky 1982).

(27)   Present stative

1s	nè	'I am'	/n-è/	
2s	wè	'you are'	/ò-è/	
3s	è	'he is'	/à-è/	
1p	twè	'we are'	/tò-è/	
2p	bwè	'you are'	/bò-è/	
3p	bé	'they are'	/bá-è/	
cl. 5	dzé	'the child is'	/dí-è/	NP = *dingóndélé*, 'child'
cl. 16	hé nà múmgwà	'there is salt ...'	/há-è/	existential
	nè nà múngwà	'I have salt ...'	/n-è/	possessive

(28)   Negative present stative

1s	nètí	'I am not'	/n-ètí/	
2s	wètí	'you are not'	/ò-ètí/	
3s	ètí	'he is not'	/à-ètí/	
1p	twètí	'we are not'	/tò-ètí/	
2p	bwètí	'you are not'	/bò-ètí/	
3p	bé'tí	'they are not'	/bá-ètí/	
cl. 5	dzé'tí	'the child is not'	/dí-ètí/	NP = dingɔ́ndélɛ́ 'child'
cl. 16	hé'tí nà	'there is not …'	/há-ètí/	existential

In (27) and (28) when the subject agreement prefix is high-toned, vowel elision (together with constraints that preserve High tones rather than Low tones) produces a downstep in the middle of the word. The low tone that produces the downstep is underlyingly associated with the initial syllable of -ètí. In addition to these present stative forms, there is a stative verb root -ék- which does conjugate regularly in the near past and true past.

3.2.2.3 True past

For events that happened yesterday or farther back, the true past is used. This construction shares some formal characteristics with the recent past (negation with -ká-, e.g.) that set it apart from other constructions but it crucially differs from the recent past it in the tonal properties displayed under relativization. We will see this in detail in the section on syntax later in the chapter. The true past is marked by both a prefix -á'- and a final vowel morpheme -á (or vowel harmony variants -é /-ɔ́)

(29)   True past paradigm

1s	ná'sálá	'I worked'	/n-á'-sál-á/	
2s	wá'sálá	'you worked'	/ò-á'-sál -á	
3s	á'sálá	'he worked'	/à-á'-sál -á/	
1p	twá'sálá	'we worked'	/tò-á'-sál-á/	
2p	bwá'sálá	'you worked'	/bò-á'-sál-á/	
3p	bá'sálá	'they worked'	/bá-á'-sál-ắ/	
cl. 5	dzá'sálá	'it worked'	/dí-á'-sál-á/	NP = dzòkò 'otter'

In the true past, a high-toned morpheme -á'- follows the negation morpheme when it is present: the order is AGR-(NEG)-TNS. Note that there is both gliding and vowel elision to relieve vowel hiatus across the agreement/tense morpheme boundary, consistently at the expense of the subject agreement low tones, which are simply lost in (29). As with the negation morpheme, the true past morpheme is always followed by a downstep (the downstep is of course only audible when a high tone follows). The meaning of the true past is that the event happened yesterday or farther back, diminishing the relevance of the event from the pragmatic context of the speaker. If we added the anteriority morpheme -ak- to the affirmative true past form, as in (30) we get an even 'more remote' past reading. The reader will recall that all postinitial stem syllables, including all extensions and the prefinal -ak-, are underlyingly toneless. Descriptively all non-initial verb stem syllables 'receive' a tonal specification from the final vowel. This is a fairly common pattern in the Bantu C zone and is found in Lingala (Dzokanga 1979) as well. See (14) in §2.4 for an informal autosegmental representation of this pattern.

(30) Remoter past paradigm

1s	ná'sáláká	'I worked'	/n-á'-sál-ak-á/	
2s	wá'sáláká	'you worked'	/ò-á'-sál-ak-á/	
3s	á'sáláká	'he worked'	/à-á'-sál-ak-á/	
1p	twá'sáláká	'we worked'	/tò-á'-sál-ak-á/	
2p	bwá'sáláká	'you worked'	/bò-á'-sál-ak-á/	
3p	bá'sáláká	'they worked'	/bá-á'-sál-ak-á/	
cl. 5	dzá'sáláká	'it worked'	/dí-á'-sál-ak-á/	NP = dzòkò 'otter'

In the negation of the true past, (31), I posit elision between the vowels of the negation and past tense morphemes, which reduces underlying /ká'-á'-/ to surface [-ká'-]. Of interest here is that the prefinal morpheme -ak- is obligatory under negation in the true past. I have no explanation for this.

(31) True past negative paradigm

1s	nìká'sáláká	'I didn't work'	/nì-ká'-á'-sál-ak-á/	*nìká'sálá
.				
.				
.				
3p	báká'sáláká	'they didn't work'	/bá-ká'-á'-sál-ak-á/	
cl. 5	díká'sáláká	'it didn't work'	/dí-ká'-á'-sál-ak-á/	NP = dzòkò 'otter'

I consider the recent past (which has a zero tense prefix) and true past (-á'-) paradigms to pattern together as true tensed forms in Babole. They share the formal features of -ká- negation and optional use of -ak- with an anteriorizing meaning in the affirmative. They also differ in crucial ways, such as the true past requirement for -ak- under negation and in the suffixal tone pattern under relativization. The true past stative is built from the same verb root -ék- as the near past stative. The final vowel -é is the vowel harmony variant of the true past final vowel morpheme -á. The true past stative is negated parallel to regular true past negation in (31).

(32) True past stative

1s	ná'éké	'I was'	/n-á'-ék-á/	
.				
.				
.				
3p	bá'éké	'they were'	/bá-á'-ék-á/	
cl. 5	dzá'éké	'the child was'	/dí-á'-ék-á/	NP = dingóndélé 'child'
cl. 17	há'éké nà	'there was ...'	/há-á'-ék-á/	existential

3.2.2.4 Future and conditional forms

There are three prefixal morphemes which relate to future or conditional time:

F¹	-pá'-	future possible prefix
F²	-tá'-	future possible (same meaning as F¹) prefix
F³	-só'-	conditional prefix

In all of these forms the final vowel is -á or a vowel harmony variant. But the suffixal tone pattern is different from the near and distant past forms we have seen so far. The suffixal tone melody associated with the future and conditional forms is a low–high melody, but the high only manifests under certain conditions. I will explain this below, in the context of a concrete example. These morphemes appear to occupy the same '*slot*' as the past tense morpheme, but otherwise have very different formal properties in the verbal system. For example the pre-final morpheme -*ak*- is not permitted with these forms and -*ká*- negation is available only with F^3 (although this is subject to dialectal variation). In addition to the formal criteria for grouping these forms, the semantics of futurity and conditionality have a lot in common. All treat the realm of possibility, rather than certainty. Using the now familiar root -*ás*-, 'steal', I provide examples of this form in (33).

(33) Future tonal melody with 'short' verb stem

(a)	bápá'ásà	(b)	bápá'á'sá	byèkà
	bá-pá'-ás-á		bá-pá'-ás-á	bi-èkà
	3p-steal-CMPL		3p-steal-CMPL	C8-food
	'They will steal.'		'They will steal the food.'	

The suffixal high tone in all the future time forms is manifested on the final vowel -*a* only if there is some postverbal material. It may be a argument of the verb (as in (33b)) or any kind of postverbal adjunct or adverbial. Any postverbal material causes the high tone to manifest on the final vowel. However if the final vowel is pre-pausal, (33a), the high tone is simply lost and the final vowel becomes low-toned. Note that this is independent of the phrase-final-lowering of High tones that occurs across the board. With CVC or VC roots like -*ás*- there is a downstep between the High of the stem-initial syllable and the high of the future suffix. The suffixal melody for the future group of forms appears to be a low tone followed by a High tone. The mysterious second downstep in (33b) becomes less so when we consider verbs with longer stems. Consider the reduplicated verb root -*béndɛndɛd*-, 'to become very fat', as an example. What we see in (34a) is that the two syllables following the stem-initial high-toned syllable are low-toned and then the final syllable of the verb stem is high when followed by some postverbal material.

(34) Future tonal melody with longer verb stem

(a) bápá'béndèndèlɛ́ bwá.
bá-pá-béndɛndɛl-á   bwá
3p-FUT-become_fat-FV   thus
'They will become very fat in that way.'

(b) bápá'béndèndèlɛ̀.
bá-pá-béndɛndɛl-á
3p-FUT-become_fat-FV
'They will become very fat.'

The same low tone that is causing the downstep in (33b) is manifesting as a trough of pre-final Lows in (34a). The suffixal 'boundary' high tone associated with these tenses is forced to manifest on the FV by any material following the verb. If there is a syntactic pause (phrase boundary) instead, the High is lost. This stem tone pattern will be seen with other TMA configurations as well.

To negate the -*pá*- future, a periphrastic strategy using the negative of the copula followed by a complementizer is used. Syntactically this is very interesting since it preserves the future morphology within a negated matrix complementizer phrase.

(35)   Periphrastic complement structure negation of future

twèti tĕ tòpá'ás'á byèkà

tò-èti	tĕ	ò-pá'-ás-á	by-èkà
1p-be:NEG	that	1p-FUT-steal-FV	C8-food

'We will not steal the food.' (Literally: 'We are not that we will steal the food.')

The future morpheme -tá- has the same meaning and morphosyntactic properties as -pá-future.

The conditional is used to convey *contrary-to-fact* meaning as in (36).

(36)   Contrary to fact conditional

Dzĕngà bísé nà muntèkú, tòsólàá l'éàlè.

Dzĕngà	bísé	nà	mu-ntèkú	tò-só-là-á	lá e-àlè
C5:be	us	with	C3-fish_net,	1p-COND-lay_out-FV	at C7-river

'If we had a fish net, we would put (it) in the river.'

In contrast to the future forms, the conditional in Dzeke Babole may be negated morphologically with -ká- as in (38).

(37)   Contrary to fact *Negative* Conditional

Dzĕngà bísé nà muntèkú, tòká'sólàá l'éàlè.

Dzĕngà	bísé	nà	mu-ntèkú	tò-ká'-só-là-á	lá e-àlè
C5:be	us	with	C3-fish_net,	1p-NEG-COND-lay_out-FV	at C7-river

'If we had a fish net, would **not** put (it) in the river.'

The facts above hold for the Dzeke dialect of Babole. The Mongouma-Bailly variety, in contrast, allows all three of -pá'-, -tá'-, and -só'-, to be negated with -ká'-. I have chosen to group these in Babole on the basis of the segmental and tonal properties of the FV suffix and the shared prohibition on -ak-.

An interesting fact is that both the conditional and future prefixes can show up in nominal or infinitive forms while tense and negation never do. From my lexicon and texts I have these examples.

(38)   Nominals/infinitives with incorporated prefixes

(a) [nsóhói]	/n-só'-hó-í/	'sth. dangerous that can be predicted'
	C9-COND-say-FV	(literally: 'thing one would say')
(b) [téé l'ó'pá'pó'mb'éì]	/téé lá (b)o-pá'-pómb-à' èì/	'until his
	until at C14-FUT-come-FV he	(future) coming.'

The lack of vowel harmony in (38a) is a clue that -só- is outside of the stem vowel harmony domain. Recall that infinitives in Babole are simply class 14 nominals. (38b) is a futurized infinitive nominal following the case-assigning preposition lá, 'at'. The point here is that neither negation or tense morphemes ever appear in these kind of deverbal nominals so the grouping of future and conditional together is justified by independent morphosyntactic evidence.

3.2.2.5 Imperatives and hortatives

These 'deontic' forms share enough formal characteristics to be treated together in a descriptive essay, although the syntactic structures involved vary. In particular, the prefinal morpheme -ak- is permitted in the affirmative of both 'deontic' forms but with the aspectual meaning of *habitual* or *repetitive* action. The anteriority/pragmatic-distance meaning for -ak- is restricted to 'epistemic' or 'tensed' forms, in a kind of complementary distribution of meaning by formal environment. In addition, there is neutralization of negative form possibilities with the deontic forms; a single set of negative forms is used with both imperatives and hortatives. I provide the basic imperative and hortative paradigms below. There is no prefix in the singular imperative.

(39)   Imperatives: (a) singular (b) plural

    (a)   *làá muntèkú l'éàlè*

        là-á   *mu-ntèkú*   *lá*   *e-àlè*

        lay_out-FV:IMP   C3-fish_net   at   C7-river

        'Put the fish-net in the water!'

    (b)   *bòlàá muntèkú l'éàlè*

        bò-là-á   *mu-ntèkú*   *lá*   *e-àlè*

        2p-lay_out-FV:IMP   C3-fish_net   at   C7-river

        'You all put the fish-net in the river!'

(40)   Habitual/repetitive imperatives

    làáká muntèkú l'éàlè

    là-ak-á   *mu-ntèkú*   *lá*   *e-àlè*

    lay_out-HAB-FV:IMP   C3-fish_net   at   C7-river

    'Continue to (repeatedly or habitually) put the fish-net in the water!'

The negative imperatives are simply the second person forms of the negative hortative forms from (45) below.

(41)   Negative imperatives: (a) singular (b) plural

    (a)   *kólàáká muntèkú l'éàlè*

        kà-ó-là-ak-á   *mu-ntèkú*   *lá*   *e-àlè*

        NEG-2s:HORT-lay_out-PRE-FV   C3-fish_net   at   C7-river

        'Do not put the fish-net in the river!'

    (b)   *kàólàáká muntèkú l'éàlè*

        kà-(b)ó-là-ak-á   *mu-ntèkú*   *lá*   *e-àlè*

        NEG-2p:HORT-lay_out-PRE-FV   C3-fish_net   at   C7-river

        'You all do not put the fish-net in the river!'

(42)   Hortative affirmative

    ínlàè   *ín-là-è*   'I should lay out'

    ólàè   *ó-là-è*   'you should lay out'

    álàè   *á-là-è*   'he should lay out'

    tólàè   *tó-là-è*   'we should lay out'

    bólàè   *bó-là-è*   'you (pl) should lay out'

    bálàè   *bá-là-è*   'they should lay out'

(43)   Hortative affirmative habitual

Low-toned verb

ínlààkè	*ín-là-ak-è*	'I should habitually lay out'
ólààkè	*ó-là-ak-è*	'you should habitually ...'
álààkè	*á-là-ak-è*	'he should habitually'
tólààkè	*tó-là-ak-è*	'we should habitually'
bólààkè	*bó-là-ak-è*	'you (pl) should habitually ...'
bálààkè	*bá-là-ak-è*	'they should habitually ...'

In case there is a full NP subject for a hortative, the appropriate verbal concord prefix with a high tone would be used in place of the 'personal' prefixes. A few comments are in order for the hortative affirmative forms in (42) and (43). The Hortative is marked by high tones on the 'personal' prefix set (normally they are low-toned except for 3p) *and* by a low-toned suffix *-è*. The habitual aspect suffix *-ak-* is low-toned because the FV is low-toned. In the case of a high-toned verb root in the hortative, there is a raising of the pitch that occurs between the hortative prefix high and the initial verb root syllable high as in (44). Whether this audible pitch rise is because the prefix high is lowered or because the second high is raised is unclear at present. An acoustic study of the fundamental frequency values for various classes of Babole high tone, downstepped high tone and raised high tone would be very revealing in this regard. Snider (1998) is an excellent example of such a study.

(44)   Hortative tonal upstep

/á-ás-è/   [á↑ásè] [‾‾ —]
3s-steal-FV:HORT

The negative hortatives, (45), use the familiar negation morpheme *-ká'-*, but this time the morpheme is initial and is low-toned. The personal agreement markers are high-toned as in the affirmative hortative and there is an anomalous third person singular form *-mó-*, instead of *á-* as in the affirmative. Finally, this form requires the presence of *-ak-* in the negative just as the True Past negative did. The requirement for *-ak-* under deontic negation is unexplained.

(45)   Negative hortative with high root

Affirmative	Negative	Underlying	Gloss
ní↑ásè	*kàní'ásáká*	*kà-ní'-ás-ak-á*	'I shouldn't steal ...'
ó↑ásè	*kó'ásáká*	*kà-ó'-ás-ak-á*	'you (sg) shouldn't steal/don't steal!'
á↑ásè	*kàmó'ásáká*	*kà-mó'-ás-ak-á*	'he shouldn't steal/let him not steal'
tó↑ásè	*kàtó'ásáká*	*kà-tó'-ás-ak-á*	'we shouldn't steal/let's not steal!'
bó↑ásè	*kàó'ásáká*	*kà-(b)ó'-ás-ak-á*	'you shouldn't steal/don't you (pl) steal!'
bá↑-ásè	*kàá'ásáká*	*kà-(b)á'-ás-ak-á*	'they shound't steal/let them not steal'

Note that the regular process of 'b-drop' is at work in the second and third person plural forms in (45), but that vowel elision does not *follow* 'b-drop' within 'words' but rather hiatus is maintained in [kà.ó ...] and [kà.á ...] just as with the 'ghost' [b] forms in (6). In contrast, the prepositional phrase /lá ḅosálò/, *in the yard*, is simply [ló'sálò] in normal connected speech. The underlined word-initial [b] drops out creating vowel hiatus which is resolved by eliding the vowel [a], V₁. The generalization is that you can have vowel elision in derived environments (those created by [b]-drop) post-lexically, but not lexically.

3.2.2.6 Progressive aspect

This form has an inherent meaning of progression, *being in the process of* doing an action. The prefinal aspectual morpheme -*ak*- is obligatory in the progressive aspect construction. The prefixal morpheme -*ó'*- occasions a downstep which can be heard when the verb root tone is high. The stem suffixal tone pattern is the same low–high melody described for the future and conditional forms. I do not attempt to represent the low–high tonal melody in the underlying representations below.

(46)   Present progressive with low verb -*lèl*- 'cry'

Affirmative	Underlying	Gloss
nólèlàkà	*n-ó'≠lèl-ak-a LH*	'I am crying'
ólèlàkà	*ò-ó'≠lèl-ak-a*	'you are crying'
ólèlàka	*à-ó'≠lèl-ak-a*	'he is crying'
tólèlàka	*tò-ó'≠lèl-ak-a*	'we are crying'
bólèlàka	*bò-ó'≠lèl-ak-a*	'you (pl) are crying'
bólèlàka	*bá-ó'≠lèl-ak-a*	'they are crying'

(47)   Final high tone in progressive

(i)   ólèlàká ndé?
    ó≠lèl-ak-á
    2s-PROG-cry-HAB-FV
    'What are you crying (about)?'

(ii)   ólèlàkà
    ndé?   ó≠lèl-ak-á
    what   2s-PROG-cry-HAB-FV
    'You are crying'

(48)   Present progressive with high verb -*sál*- 'do' (Dzeke dialect)

Affirmative	Morpheme analysis	Gloss
nó'sálàkà	*n-ó'≠sál-ak-a*	'I am doing'
ó'sálàkà	*ò-ó'≠sál-ak-a*	'you are doing'
ó'sálàkà	*à-ó'≠sál-ak-a*	'he is doing'
tó'sálàkà	*tò-ó'≠sál-ak-a*	'we are doing'
bó'sálàkà	*bò-ó'≠sál-ak-a*	'you (pl) are doing'
bó'sálàkà	*bá-ó'≠sál-ak-a*	'they are doing'

Note that there is homophony between the second and third person forms (both singular and plural) in the Dzeke dialect in (46) and (48) because of regular vocalic elision processes operating in the language. The Mongouma Bailly dialect, however, shown in (49), has a rule that produces a labial glide [w] rather than V$_1$ vowel-elision in the environment [... o-o ...].

(49)   Present progressive affirmative with high verb -*sál*- 'do' (Mongouma Bailly dialect)

Affirmative	Underlying	Gloss
nó'sálàkà	*n-ó'≠sál-ak-a*	'I am doing'
wó'sálàkà	*ò-ó'≠sál-ak-a*	'you are doing'
ó'sálàkà	*à-ó'≠sál-ak-a*	'he is doing'
twó'sálàkà	*tò-ó'≠sál-ak-a*	'we are doing'
bwó'sálàkà	*bò-ó'≠sál-ak-a*	'you (pl) are doing'
bó'sálàkà	*bá-ó'≠sál-ak-a*	'they are doing'

(50) Present progressive negative of high verb -sál- 'do' (Dzeke dialect)

Rapid speech	Careful speech	Underlying	Gloss
nètsó'sálàkà	nètíòsálàkà	n-èti-ó'≠sál-ak-a	'I am **not** doing'
wètsó'sálàkà	wètíòsálàkà	ò-èti-ó'≠sál-ak-a	'you are **not** doing'
ètsó'sálàkà	ètíòsálàkà	à-èti-ó'≠sál-ak-a	'he is **not** doing'
twètsó'sálàkà	twètíòsálàkà	tò-èti-ó'≠sál-ak-a	'we are **not** doing'
bwètsó'sálàkà	bwètíòsálàkà	bò-èti-ó'≠sál-ak-a	'you (pl) are **not** doing'
bé'tsó'sálàkà	bé'tíòsálàkà	bá-èti-ó'≠sál-ak-a	'they are **not** doing'

The careful speech negative forms in (50) show the progressive morpheme with a low tone. The progressive morpheme displays tonal polarity in that it is high-toned when preceded by a low tone (49), but low-toned when preceded by a high tone (50). This only emerges clearly in the careful speech paradigm and is hidden by the normal speech affrication of [t] to [ts] before a high vowel and the by now familiar phonological processes that produce a downstep. Recall that ètí is simply the negative of the present stative (see (28)).

Note the similarity to the future forms which could not be negated simply with -ká-. In essence only 'tensed' forms can be negated with -ká-. For the forms marked for futurity or aspect, a negative form of the copula is 'inserted' in the morphosyntactic structure to host the semantic feature of negation. In fact the progressive reveals a lot about how this system works because the progressive can be construed with past tense as well. Parallel to the negation case above, an aspectualized verb cannot be further inflected for tense directly. The past form of the progressive involves the idiosyncratic past tense forms of the stative verb that we have already seen (see (32)).

(51) Past progressive of high verb -sál- 'do'

	Underlying	Gloss
ná'ékèòsálàkà	n-á'-éké-o'≠sál-ak-a LH	'I was doing'
wá'ékèòsálàkà	ò-á'-éké-o'≠sál-ak-a	'you was doing'
á'ékèòsálàkà	à-á'-éké-o'≠sál-ak-a	'he was doing'
twá'ékèòsálàkà	tò-á'-éké-o'≠sál-ak-a	'we were doing'
bwá'ékèòsálàkà	bò-á'-éké-o'≠sál-ak-a	'you (pl) were doing'
bá'ékèòsálàkà	bá-á'-éké-o'≠sál-ak-a	'they were doing'

(52) Past progressive negative of high verb -sál- 'do'

	Underlying	Gloss
nìká'ékèòsálàkà	nì-ká'-éké-o'≠sál-ak-a LH	'I was not doing'
òká'ékèòsálàkà	ò-ká'-éké-o'≠sál-ak-a	'you were not doing'
àká'ékèòsálàkà	à-ká'-éké-o'≠sál-ak-a	'he was not doing'
tòká'ékèòsálàkà	tò-ká'-éké-o'≠sál-ak-a	'we were not doing'
bòká'ékèòsálàkà	bò-ká'-éké-o'≠sál-ak-	'you (pl) were not doing'
báká'ékèòsálàkà	bá-ká'-éké-o'≠sál-ak-a	'they were not doing'

3.2.2.7 Hortative Motional Verb Forms

This form builds on the hortative form as a base and has the meaning of 'come over here and do X'. It is the softest and most gentle form of request possible in the language and is frequently used with small children.

(53)   Hortative motional with high verb

kó'sá'lé mosálà   *kó'sálè*
kà-[ó-sál-è]-(H   *mo-sálà ##*   *kà*-[ó-sál-è]-(H ##
MOT-[2s:HORT-do-FV]-(H   C3-work   MOT-[2s:HORT-make-FV]-(H
'Come here (child) and do this work!'   'Come here (child) and do (this)!'

With a high-toned verb (53), it becomes clear that the motional morpheme imposes a suffixal high tone on an already composed hortative verb-word. The low tone of the subjunctive final vowel is retained as a downstep when the motional suffixal high tone is added. In autosegmental terms, the high docks on the final vowel, floating the hortative low and producing a downstep. If the habitual prefinal morpheme *-ak-* is added to one of the forms in (53), the low tone manifests on the available penultimate vowel as in (54). This is the same stem tone alternation that we saw in the future and progressive forms earlier.

(54)   Hortative motional habitual

kàó'sálàké mosálà
kà-[bó-sál-**ak**-è]-(H   *mo-sálà ##*
MOT- [2p:HORT-do-**HAB**-FV]-(H   C3-work
|_____↑

'Come here children and do this work **continuously**.'

The internal structure of these motional subjunctive forms is better understood when one considers the overall paradigm of complements of motional verbs. Intransitive motional verbs may take a special 'motional purposive' complement.

(55)   Motional purposive complements

nìkèí kàtòká mái
nì-kè-í   *kà-tòk-à*-(H   *mái ##*
1s-go-CMPL   MOT-fetch-FV-(H   6:water
'I am going to fetch water.'

The class of motional verbs that may take *-kà-* complements includes *-swé-*, 'come from', *-kè-*, 'go', and a few others. The motional complement prefix *kà-* is a kind of special locative complementizer. The *kà-* complement imposes the same stem tone pattern as future, progressive and hortative motional forms: low plateau if phrase final, otherwise a single final high. The parallel stem tone melody suggests that all the verbal paradigms having this tone pattern evolved from verb-verb or auxiliary-verb complementation structures like (55).

3.2.3 Reflexive

The Babole reflexive morpheme appears directly preceding the verb root. It has the particularity of being both preceded and followed by a tonal downstep. The crucial contrast for this case is seen by looking at (56) and (57) introduces downsteps before and after the morpheme showing that the downsteps must be included in the underlying form of the reflexive morpheme. Other preverbal morphemes have downsteps following but never preceding.

(56)   Simple completive

bábimbí Jean
bá-bimb-í   *Jean*
3p-hit-CMPL   Jean
'They hit John.'

In (57) one can see the reflexive morpheme with its double downstep structure.

(57)   Completive Reflexive

bá˩á˩bímbí
bá-˩á˩-bímb-í
3p-RFLX-hit-CMPL
'They hit themselves.'

3.2.4 Derivational suffixes (extensions) and final vowels

Babole has the set of derivational suffixes (extensions) in (58). Except for *-edz-* (intensive) the extensions change the verbs argument structure in various ways. The combinations and sequences of extensions that are allowed and disallowed are complex and depend on subtle issues in the argument structure of particular verb classes. Extensions are toneless and receive a tonal specification from suffixal inflections.

(58)   Extensions

-am-	'passive'	*bá≠bímb-**ám**-í* (*nà Serge*)	'They were hit (by Serge).'
-el-	'applicative'	*à≠bímb-**éd**-í àmé Serge*	'He hit Serge for me.'
-edz-	'intensive'	*à≠bímb-**édz**-á Serge*	'He really hit Serge.'
-y-	'causitive'	**à≠bík-**y**-á Serge*	'He caused Serge to become well (healed him).'
-ol-	'reversive'	*%tó≠kánd-**òl**-è èí*	'Let's remove him from dominating (us).'
-an-	'reciprocal'	*Bísé na Serge to≠ bímb-**án**-i*	'Serge and us guys hit each other.'
* *-bík-*	'be healed, be well (intransitive)'		
% *-kánd-*	'dominate'		

Babole has three final vowels (not counting vowel harmony variants). The morphological default final vowel is used in all tense/mode/aspect forms other than completive and hortative and is high or low depending on the TMA involved.

(59)   Final vowels

-í	'completive'	'completive (high tone)'
-e, -ɛ	'non-completive'	'hortative (low tone)'
-a, -ɛ, -ɔ	'default'	'past, progressive, future, conditional (high or low)'

4 SYNTAX

4.1 Demonstrative/deictic system

The Babole demonstrative deictic system can be described as a simple matrix generated by the noun class system and five deictic categories giving a total of $5 \times 17 = 85$ forms.

(60)   Babole deictic forms

		Proximate 1 -ò	Proximate 2 -nì	Distant 1 -wà	Distant 2 -nà	Interrogative -sò
Class	Prefix.	-ò	-nì	-wà	-nà	-sò
1	ø, mo-	óò	óní	ówà	óná	ósò
2	baa-	báò	bání	báwà	báná	básò
3	mo-	óò	óní	ówà	óná	ósò
4	mi-	míò	míní	míwà	miná	mísò
5	di-	díò	díní	díwà	díná	dísò
6	ma-	máò	mání	máwà	máná	másò
7	e-	éò	éní	éwà	éná	ésò
8	bi-	bíò	bíní	bíwà	bíná	bísò
9	N-	óò	óní	ówà	óná	ósò
10	N-	íì	ìní	íwà	íná	ìsò
11	lo-	bóò	bóní	bówà	bóná	bósò
14	bo-	bóò	bóní	bówà	bóná	bósò
16	há	háò	hání	háwà	háná	hásò
17	ló	lóò	lónò	lówà	lóná	lósò
18	mú	múò	múní	múwà	múná	músò
19	mwá	híò	híní	híwà	híná	hísò
20	báná	tóò	tóní	tówà	tóná	tósò

Four of the deictic categories have a clear spatial interpretation:

(i)   close to the speaker   -nì   dzúmbá díní   'this thing close to me'
(ii) close to the hearer   -ò   múmbá máò   'those things close to you'
(iii) far but within sight   -wà   nyámà íwà   'those animals over there'
(iv) far and out of sight   -nà   lúkà lónà   'that place out of sight'

The fifth deictic category has interrogative meaning:

(v)   which thing   -sò   dzúmbá dísò   'which thing?'

The interrogative deictics above, where one is questioning the correct choice among a range of identified entities, are different from the invariable WH-interrogative particles *ndzá* and *ndé*.

(61)   Interrogative wh-words

ndzá	'who?' 'what?'
bwéndó ndzá?	'what day?' 'when?'
ndzá àpòdí?	'who came?'
ndé	'what?'
mbándó ndé?	'what reason?' 'why?'
òdìhí ndé ?	'what did you get?'

These two are used where the identity of the questioned person or thing is not established, that is to say, they are not referential. The invariable interrogative particles do not require an antecedent in the pragmatic or discourse context. I note in passing that these wh-words occur *in situ* and are not fronted in Babole.

The deictics can either be used modificationally as in (62a) or as stand-alone pro-forms (62b).

(62)   Modifier and pronominal uses of deictics

(a)   Demonstrative modifier

dzúmbà	dínì	(dzé)	dibé.
5:thing	5:this (close to me)	5:be	5:bad
'This thing is bad.'			
múmbá	máò	(mé)	mabé.
6:things	6:those (close to you)	be:6	6:bad
'Those things are bad.'			

(b)   Demonstrative pronoun

dínì	(dzé)	dibé.
5:this (thing close to me)	5:be	5:bad
'This (one) is bad.'		
máò	(mé)	mabé.
6:those (things close to you)	6:be	6:bad
'Those (ones) are bad.'		

The -wà demonstratives also serves the crucial function of discourse reference as illustrated in the example below.

dzúmbá	díwà	(dzé)	dilámù.
5:thing	5:that	5:be	5:good
'That thing (just mentioned) is good.'			

4.2 Pronouns, quantifiers, adjectives, cardinals

Just as the demonstrative system shows a fully developed concord set, pronouns, quantifiers, cardinal numbers, and adjectives all show concording behavior. There are some tonal subtleties to be noted in the summarizing table (63). Classes 1 and 9 show low toned prefixes in pronouns, quantifiers, and modifying adjectives, while the other classes have a high-downstepped high melody.

(63)   Babole concording pronouns, modifiers, and quantifiers

Class	'it, them'	'all'	Nominal adjectives	Modifier adjectives	Cardinals	Gloss
1	wàngó	wèsù	molámù	ómòlámù	mòhɔ́kɔ́	'one'
2	bá'ngó	bésù	balámù	bá'lámù	bá'éngé	'two'
3	wá'ngó	wèsù	molámù	mó'lámù	mòhɔ́kɔ́	'one'
4	myá'ngó	mésù	milámù	mî'lámù	mî'éngé	'two'
5	dzá'ngó	dzésù	dilámù	dí'lámù	dìhɔ́kɔ́	'one'
6	má'ngó	mésù	malámù	má'lámù	má'éngé	'two'
7	yá'ngó	yésù	elámù	é'lámù	éhɔ́kɔ́	'one'
8	byá'ngó	byésù	bilámù	bí'lámù	bí'éngé	'two'
9	yàngó	yèsù	ndámù	ǹdámù	m̀pɔ́kɔ́	'one'
10	yá'ngó	yésù	ndámù	í'lámù	í'éngé	'two'

11	bwá'ngó	bwésù	bolámù	bó'lámù	bòhɔkɔ	'one'
14	bwá'ngó	bwésù	bolámù	bó'lámù	bòhɔkɔ	'one'
16	há'ngó	hésù	halámù	há'lámù	hàhɔkɔ	'one'
17	lwá'ngó	lwésù	lolámù	lo'lámù	lòhɔkɔ	'one'
18	mwá'ngoá	mwésù	mulámù	mú'lámù	mú'éngé	'two'
19	hyá'ngó	hyésù	hilámù	hí'lámù	hìhɔkɔ	'one'
20	twá'ngó	twésù	tolámù	tó'lámù	tó'éngé	'two'

There is a small class of 'adjective' roots in Babole including:

-bé	'bad'
-lámù	'good'
-sɔní	'small'
-ngàtà	'big'

These have the property of being able to appear with any nominal prefix. In stative and 'presentative' constructions the adjectives look and act like ordinary nouns with a low-toned prefix ('nominal' adjectives in fact). The 'nominal' adjective constructions in (64) have propositional meaning whether the stative verb is present or not.

(64)   'Nominal' adjectives

Stative with 'be'   without 'be'

dihɔ dzé dilámù   =   dihɔ dilámù   =   'The affair is good.'
mahɔ mé malámù   =   mahɔ malámù   =   'The affairs are good.'
byèkà byé bilámù   =   byèkà bilámù   =   'The food is good.'

In the modificational use of adjectives, a high tone is imposed on the noun class prefix, creating a high-downstepped high sequence if the initial stem tone is high as in (66).

(65)   Modificational use of adjective
dihɔ dí'lámù dísídi.

di-hɔ   H-dí-lámù   dí-síd-í
C5-affair   C5-good   AGR5-finish-CMPL
'The good affair is finished.'

In (66) I propose a sample derivation for the modificational adjective. An initial high tone is added to the 'nominal' adjective. This high tone obligatorily links to the vowel of the prefix and causes the prefix low to 'float', creating the downstep configuration.

(66)   Derivation of modificational adjective

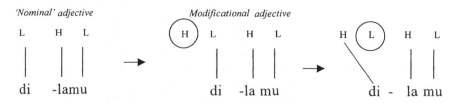

There are significant parallels between the structure of modificational adjectives and relative clauses (see §4.4).

4.3 Associative noun phrases

Associative markers are used to link nouns that are in a semantic relationship of possession or association of some kind. The associative marker 'agrees' with the head noun in
the associative construction (normally the first NP in an NP-ASSOC-NP sequence). The
'short' associatives lack the initial 'determiner' vowel which is obligatory with possessives. The short associatives are the only ones allowed in a variety of non-possessive
associatives. See examples (d), (e), and (f) in (68).

(67)   Babole associative markers

Class	Full form	Short
1	óà	wà
2	íˈbáˈ	ˈbáˈ
3	óˈáˈ	ˈwáˈ
4	íˈmyáˈ	ˈmyáˈ
5	íˈdzáˈ	ˈdzáˈ
6	íˈmáˈ	ˈmáˈ
7	éˈáˈ	ˈyáˈ
8	íˈbyáˈ	ˈbyáˈ
9	éà	yà
10	íˈáˈ	ˈyáˈ
11	óˈbwáˈ	ˈbwáˈ
14	óˈbwáˈ	ˈbwáˈ
16	íˈháˈ	ˈháˈ
17	óˈlwáˈ	ˈlwáˈ
18	íˈmwáˈ	ˈmwáˈ
19	íˈhyáˈ	ˈhyáˈ
20	óˈtwáˈ	ˈtwáˈ

(68)   Examples of associative construction

(a)   byèkà   byá   bàà-bútì
      8:food   8:ASS   2:visitors
      'food (set apart) for the visitors'

(b)   byèkà   [íˈbyá   àmé]
      8:food   8:ASS   me
      'my food'

(c)   [íˈbyá   àmé]   byèkà
      8:ASS   me   food
      'my food'

(d)   milɔ̀ngó   ˈmyáˈ   nsósò
      4:rows   4:ASS   10:chickens
      'rows of chickens'

(e)   bokìlà   bwáˈ   ngámbá
      14:hunt   14:ASS   10:elephants
      'elephant hunt'

(f)   molómì   wáˈ   nsósò
      3:male   4:ASS   9:chickens
      'male chicken'

(g)   *eámbá* ' *yá*'   *bwátò*
      7:wreck 7:ASS   14:canoe
      'an old wreck of a canoe'

The basic distinction in associatives is between those requiring the determiner-like initial
vowel and those prohibiting it. Although this topic requires more research, it appears that
it is the semantic feature of definiteness i.e. carried by the initial vowel in Babole associatives. Thus it is only in true genitive possessives like (68b). that the definiteness feature is inherent and so required. The semantic feature of definiteness is inappropriate on
the other hand in the non-possessive associatives and so the initial vowel is disallowed
there. Associative 'inversion' is only allowed in the special sub case of a pronominal possessor, (68c). The associative inversion phenomena can be explained by cliticization of
the pronominal 'head' to the associative followed by optional 'raising' of the clitic-host
to a pre-nominal determiner position.

4.4 Syntax of relativized verbs

4.4.1 *Relativized completives*

In this final section, I will present the basic structure of relativized verbal constructions
in Babole. I will present both subject and object relatives for the completive verb form.
In a straightforward affirmative sentence like (69), we see the underlying
Subject–Verb–Object (SVO) word order with the verb 'agreeing' with the preverbal class
5 subject NP.

(69)   Simple affirmative with SVO order

       dingúngù dídzéí byèkà
       di-ngúngù   *dí-dzé-i*   *bi-èkà*
       C5-mosquito AGR:C5-eat-CMPL   C8-food
       'The mosquito has eaten the food.'

In (69) note that there are no tonal downsteps in the inflected verb, neither between the
high-toned subject agreement marker and the high-toned verb root, or between the verb
root and the high-toned completive final vowel. Now compare this with (70), a subject
relative based on (69). The relativization consists of two tonal downsteps which separate
the three high tones in the verb phrase. In non-relative contexts the subject agreement
markers are never followed by a downstep. In a relative clause the subject agreement
marker is followed by a downstep. An additional downstep appears following the verb's
high tone. I interpret these tonal pitch drops as due to the presence of floating low-tone
relative markers in the morphological verb phrase. This is shown in the morpheme
analysis line in (70).

(70)   Subject relative with full NP subject

       [*dingúngù dí*'*dzé*'*í byèkà*] *dzé dilámù*
       di-ngúngù   *dí-* ` *-dzé-* ` *-í*   *bi-èkà*   *dí-è*   *di-lámù*
       C5-mosquito AGR:C5-REL-eat-REL-CMPL   C8-food AGR:C5-be good
       'The mosquito **who** has eaten the food is good.'

The object relative version of the same sentence is shown in (71). The relativized object
is now in the sentence initial subject position (has become the syntactic subject of the
relative clause) and the relativized verb agrees with it. The 'underlying' subject now

appears immediately following the relativized verb. The matrix clause verb *byé* agrees with the relative head *byèkà*.

(71) Corresponding object relative

[byèkà bí'dzé'í dingúngù] *byé bilámù*
bi-èkà   bí- ` -dzé- ` -í   di-ngúngù   bí-è   bi-lámù
C8-food AGR:C8-REL-eat-REL-CMPL C8-food AGR: C8-be C8-good
'The food **that** the mosquito has eaten is good.'

A different relativization pattern occurs when the subject is a 'personal' pronoun rather than a full NP. In (72) we find a class 8 associative marker *ibyá* agreeing with the class 8 relative head NP *byèkà*. This associative marker is drawn from the 'full form' column of associative markers in (67). The preference of a 'definite' interpretation of relative clause head nouns explains why the 'short' form associatives are not acceptable as relative pronouns in such clauses.

(72) Object relative with personal pronoun subject

[byèkà í'byá nidzé'í] *byé bilámù*
bi-èkà íbyá   ni-dzé- ` -í   bí-è   bi-lámù
C8-food ASS:8 1s-eat-REL-CMPL AGR:C8-be C8-good
'The food **that** I ate is good.'

The presence of the subject pronoun clitic/prefix prevents the verb from agreeing directly with the relative head noun and so the associative is inserted to host the complementizer, agreement and definiteness features. I point out in closing that the suffixal tone pattern on a true past relative is different. The crucial difference is seen in (73) where I use an anteriorized true past to show that the expected suffixal low tone is missing and we find only a plateau of highs just as in the non-relativized verb.

(73) Object relative in true past with personal pronoun subject

[byèkà í'byá ná'dzáká] *byá'éké bilámù*
bi-èkà íbyá   n-á'-dzé-ak-á   bi-á'-ék-é   bi-lámù
C8-food ASS:8 1s-PST-eat-PRE-FV AGR:C8-PST-be:PST-FV C8-good
'The food **that** I had eaten was good.'

This difference between the suffixal tone pattern on near past and true past relatives suggests that the near past suffix is relatively 'shallow', being added 'after' relativization (perhaps originally an adverb). With the true past relative, there is no inserted low tone to cause a downstep, suggesting that relativization in some sense 'follows' true past morphology formation in the word building process. The derivational order would be (i) true past formation, (ii) relativization, (iii) addition of recent past suffix.

ACKNOWLEDGMENTS

The author is grateful to the Babole language communities in Dzeke and Brazzaville for all their help and advice. Special thanks to the language consultants: MAKOSSO, Charly, BIEMBEDI, Celestin, ESSATOLE, Seraphin, MOSSANGAMI, Lucien.

REFERENCES

Archangeli and Pulleyblank 1995; Chomsky 1982; Dzokanga 1979; Gardner 1990; Guthrie 1967; Hulstaert 1961; Hyman 1990; Leitch, to appear, 1989, 1994a, 1994b, 1997, 2000; Palmer 1986; Snider 1998; VanHoudt 1987.

CHAPTER TWENTY-TWO

LEGA (BEYA DIALECT) (D25)

Robert Botne

1 INTRODUCTION

Lega, or Kilega, is spoken in the eastern region of the Democratic Republic of Congo by an estimated 440,000 people (Grimes 2000), situated primarily in the southern area of Kivu Region, an area that is primarily equatorial rainforest.

Lega can be subdivided into two major varieties: Isile (also Kisile or Ishile), also referred to as Lega-Ntara, and Lega-Malinga, having about 67 percent lexical similarity (Grimes 2000). Isile is spoken in the eastern part of Lega territory, primarily in the north and east of the district of Mwenga (Lungumbu 1988). Lega-Malinga, which comprises the remainder of the Lega-speaking community, includes a number of major sub-varieties: Kikanu in the north (southern Walikale District); Kigala, Kiyoma, Kiliga, Kisede, and Gonzabale in the central area (Shabunda District); Beya (also called Kinyamunsange) in the west (Pangi District). There appears to be no clear consensus on names and not always an indication of location (cf. Grimes 2000, Kadima *et al.* 1983, and Lungumbu 1988). This chapter outlines the Beya variety of Pangi District, which may be compared with the Gonzabale variety of Mwenga District (Lungumbu 1988) and with what Meeussen calls the Banagabo (= Kiliga?) variety of Shabunda District (Meeussen 1971).

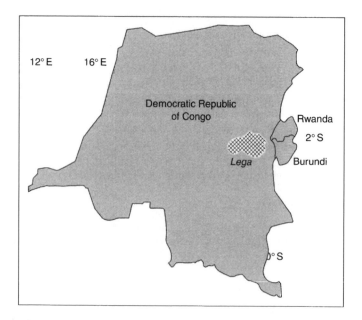

MAP 22.1 LOCATION OF LEGA IN THE DRC

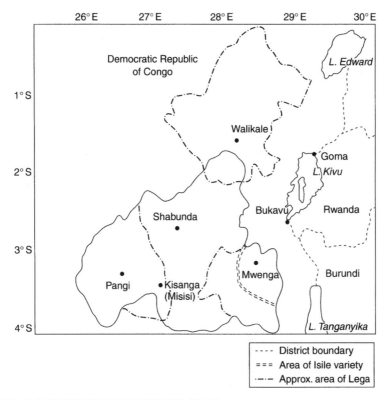

MAP 22.2 APPROXIMATE LEGA DIALECT AREAS

Lega has been introduced as a language of instruction in schools. However, it is not known what materials, if any, have been published in the language. No standard orthography exists.

2 PHONOLOGY

2.1 The vowel system

Lega has a system of seven vowel phonemes: /ị, i, e, a, o, u, ụ/. The vowels /ị, i,/ and /u, ụ/ are all high vowels. Advanced Tongue Root (ATR) is, perhaps, the differentiating feature.

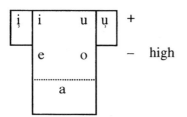

2.2 Vowel assimilation

There are two types of vowel assimilation, both involving /i/ and /u/. First, in verbal suffixes these vowels remain unchanged following +ATR vowels or low /a/, but assimilate in height to a mid-vowel in the preceding stem. Second, /i/ and /u/ of noun class prefixes become [j] and [ɰ], respectively, i.e. assimilate in ATR value to high vowels in the stem.

2.2.1 Assimilation in verb suffixes

Vowel assimilation occurs in verbal suffixes that have the vowel /i/ or /u/. There are four suffixes with /i/ (see §4.2 for discussion of labels): applicative /-il-/, efficerative and ostensive /-ik-/, and persistive /-ilil-/. In each case, the vowel [i] alternates with the vowel [e], the latter occurring following a mid vowel in the verb stem, either [e] or [o].

Applicative -il- ~ -el- [-in- ~ -en- following a nasal]
-básila	'go/come via a place'	<	-bása	'go out'
-búmina	'bark at'	<	-búma	'bark'
-réndela	'speak on behalf of'	<	-rénda	'speak'

Efficerative -ik- ~ -ek-
-gyika	'cook'	<	-gyá [−gi+a]	'burn vi'
-sendeka	'put into a leaning position'	<	-sendama	'be leaning'

Ostensive -ik- ~ -ek-
-ínika	'be soft'	<	-ína	'soften by soaking'
-béleka	'be broken'	<	-béla	'break'
-móneka	'be in sight, visible'	<	-móna	'see'

Persistive -ilil- ~ -elel-
-úngwilila	'listen (to)'	<	-úngwa	'hear'
-ógelela	'swim'	<	-óga	'bathe vi'

With suffixes having the comparable back vowel [u], i.e. the suffixes -ul- and -uk-, whether iterative, reversive, or valency changing, assimilation only occurs when the preceding stem vowel is round.

-bangula	'peck at repeatedly'	<	-banga	'strike with a pointed obj'
-remuka	'drip'	<	-rema	'drop intentionally'
-gelula	'turn sth'. vt		-bobola	'soften by soaking' vt
-geluka	'change position' vi		-boboka	'become soft' vi

2.2.2 Assimilation in nouns

The vowels /i/ and /u/ in noun class prefixes assimilate in ATR value to following high vowels appearing in the noun stem. Thus, /i/ → [j] and /u/ → [ɰ] when the vowel of the root is either /i̠/ or /u̠/, but remain /i/ and /u/ elsewhere.

mi̠.ki̠lá	'blood'	mi.kíla	'tails'
ki̠.guma	'fruit'	ki.bukúsa	'viper (sp.)'
bu̠.kúba	'chest'	bu.gema	'breast milk'
lu̠.ki̠ndo	'sound of a footstep'	lu.kumbí	'talking drum'

This assimilation also occurs in two other contexts. The prefix vowel /i/ is usually realized as [j] if the stem has a non-high vowel followed by a high vowel.
Hence, /i/ → j / __ + C V C V
$$[-\text{hi}]\ [+\text{hi}]$$

kị.belụ	'thigh'	ki.lega	'Lega language'
kị.gonụ	'fish weir'	ki.rógo	'vegetable'
kị.kasị	'palm nut' but	ki.kámbị	'mouthful'

The prefix vowel /u/ is realized as [ụ] in a similar environment, but the second vowel must be [ụ] (and cannot be [j]).

/u/ → ụ / __ + C V C V
$$[-\text{hi}]\ [+\text{hi}]$$
$$[+\text{bk}]$$

mụ.lesụ́	'fly'	mu.lezị	'nursemaid'
mụ.zóngụ́	'cassava loaf'	mu.búlị	'louse'
lụ.págụ́	'small wooden spoon'	bu.zámbị	'poverty'

2.3 Glide formation

The high vowels /ị, i/ and /ụ, u/ become glides /y/ and /w/, respectively, when they occur before another vowel that is not of the same set, as for example in /-gj-ik-/'cook' > ku-gyik-a 'to cook'. Before vowels of the same set, they delete.

2.4 Vowel length

Underlying long vowels occur most commonly in ideophones (as below), although a few other words have them as well, e.g. kináaná 'eight', -kéeké 'small', and Zuúla 'a woman's name'.

mwaamwaa	'of being scattered willy-nilly'
kwoókwoó	'of gulping food'
pịị	'of becoming very dark'
zuu	'of looking fixedly'

Vowels are lengthened in the penultimate syllable of a word in phrase-final position, as in [nákārịlē ŋkuːsu] 'I trapped a grey parrot'. However, if there is a high tone on the final vowel, lengthening does not occur, as, e.g. in [nákārịlē kapusú] 'I trapped a fisherman'.

2.5 Consonant inventory

Lega has a relatively small inventory of eighteen consonant phonemes. Of these eighteen, four – /f, v, č, ǰ/ – only occur in words borrowed from other languages, primarily from Swahili. The fricative sh [š] is extremely rare, appearing in only a few words. The approximant [w] is normally derived from an underlying round, back vowel. However, there are several instances where it appears to be phonemic.

	Labial	Alveolar	Palato-alveolar	Velar
Stops				
−vox	p	t		k
+vox	b		ɟ(?)	g
Affricates				
−vox			(č)	
+vox			(ǰ)	
Fricatives				
−vox	(f)	s	[š]	
+vox	(v)	z		
Approximants	(w)	l		
Nasals	m	n	ɲ	

/t/ is realized intervocalically as [r], except following the class 5 noun prefix *i-*. /l/ is realized as [d] following a nasal or the class 5 noun prefix *i-*. /g/ is often realized as the fricative [ɣ] intervocalically. In some instances – particularly when it appears in the last syllable of a word – it is even deleted altogether, producing a long final vowel.

The phonemic status of /ɟ / is uncertain. Cases of palatalized [gʸ] arising from the shift of a front vowel to a glide before another vowel are very similar, if not identical, in pronunciation. Both [ɟ] and [gʸ] are written here as *gy*.

2.6 Nasals and nasal sequences

The palatal nasal /ɲ/ is clearly distinct from the phonetically similar palatalized nasal [nʸ], which is pronounced as a sequence of nasal and glide. In careful speech, [nʸ] is apt to occur as [ni]. There are nine prenasalized obstruents that occur. In all cases the nasal onset is homorganic with the obstruent.

> mp nt ŋk
> mb nd ɲgy ŋg
>   ns
>   nz

Each nasal may occur as geminate. Usually this arises from the addition of a nasal noun class prefix to a nasal initial root, as in *ɲ̩ɲoko* 'your mother'. Only one instance of a geminate nasal in a root was found: *-inna* 'squeeze or press'.

The glides [w] and [y] occur following a consonant and preceding a vowel. The only exceptions to this generalization are the verb *-waza* 'think' (borrowed from Swahili) and the adverbs *wálubí* 'yesterday; tomorrow'; and *wándélé* 'day before yesterday'.

All consonants, with the exception of palatals, can co-occur with the glides.

2.7 Syllable structure

The canonical syllable structure is CV; other types are V, NCV, CGV, and NCGV.

2.8 Tone

Lega is a tone language, having the following tones: H(igh), M(id) or downstepped H(igh), R(ising), F(alling) and L(ow). H and L are phonemically distinctive, as, apparently, is F in a few words. R and downstepped H tones are always derived, R from a combination of underlying L plus H. R and F may occur on short vowels. Mid tones pose a problem in that it is not clear whether they should be considered downstepped Hs. The environments for M and downstepped Hs are inadequately understood at this time, as it has not been possible to analyze tonal phenomena fully. Examples of the five phonetic realizations of tone are illustrated below.

High (′)	*masángá*	'bead'
Mid (‾)	*bábānō*	'this very one'
Downstepped (high) (ꞌ)	*bịswịꞌnéné*	'ourselves'
Rising (ˇ)	*gŏzo*	'that'
Falling (ˆ)	*mubûlá*	'nine'
Low (unmarked)	*kisogo*	'mud'

3 NOUN MORPHOLOGY

3.1 The noun class system

Lega has a system of 19 noun classes, most of which have an overt class prefix (NPfx), as e.g. in *mụ.lịmu* 'ghost, spirit' and *ki.kúko* 'broom' (see table 22.1). A few nouns consist only of a root, as in *gyegya* 'older sibling or cousin', and consequently, are treated as having a null (∅) class prefix. Unlike many Bantu languages, Lega does not have augments (pre-prefixes). In several cases subclasses have been added to the traditional class numbers where Lega has innovated new forms. Prefixes are, with one exception, low-toned.

The form of the noun class prefix varies according to phonological features of the noun stem. For underlying /Ci/ and /Cu/ prefixes, the form of the vowel depends on three factors. First, if the stem is consonant-initial and the first stem vowel is close /ị/ or /ụ/, the prefix is realized as *Cị-* or *Cụ-*; otherwise it is realized as *Ci-* or *Cu-*. Second, if the stem is vowel-initial, *Ci-* and *Cu-* are realized as *Cy-* and *Cw-*, respectively, with two exceptions. *Ci-* becomes *C-* before high front vowels; *Cu-* becomes *C-* before round vowels. Underlying /Ca/ prefixes are realized as *C-* before vowel-initial stems. The class 5 prefix is realized as *ịz-* before *ị*-initial stems, as *ịgy-* before other vowel-initial stems, and

TABLE 22.1: NOUN CLASS PREFIXES

Class	Lega NPfx	Class	Lega NPfx
1	*mu-, mụ-, mw-, m-,*	8	*bi-, bị-, by-, b-*
1a	∅	9	*n-, m-, ɲ-, ŋ-*
1a′	*n-, m-, ɲ-*	9a	∅
1b	*wa-*	10	*n-, m-, ɲ-, ŋ-*
1c	*mú-*	10a	∅
2	*ba-, b-*	11	*lu-, lụ-, lw-, l-*
2a	*bá-*	12	*ka-, k-*
3	*mu-, mụ-, mw-, m-*	13	*tu-, tụ-, tw-, t-*
4	*mi-, mị-, my-, m-*	14	*bu-, bụ-, bw-*
5	*ị-, ịgy-, iz-*	15	*ku-, kw-*
5a	*lị-, ly-, l-*	16	*ga-*
5b	∅	17	*ku-*
6	*ma-, m-*	18	*mu-*
7	*ki-, kị-, ky-, k-*	19	*sị-, sy-, s-*

as *i-* before consonant-initial stems. Nasal class prefixes are homorganic with consonant-initial stems, [ɲ] before vowel-initial stems.

Noun classes are usually linked in singular/plural pairs, called genders, of which there are 18 in Lega. Sub-classes, when the agreement patterns and the paired plural are identical, are subsumed under the main class, hence, 1a under 1. Most genders subsume at least one coherent semantic concept that links a large set of the nouns occurring in that gender. This underlying semantic nexus is listed in table 22.2 following the prefix forms. *N-*, in table 22.2, indicates that the prefix consists solely of a homorganic nasal. Although most nouns occur in gender pairings of two noun classes, some occur only in a single noun class. Non-paired nouns usually occur with what would be a singular class prefix in the gender pairings, although a few do occur with a plural class prefix. These single-class genders are listed in table 22.3, following the same classificatory schema used for the

TABLE 22.2: NOUN GENDERS: PAIRED SINGULAR/PLURAL CLASSES

Class	Singular prefix	Plural prefix	Semantic nexus
1/2	*mu-*	*ba-*	humans
1a/2	*Ø*		kin terms (older than ego)
1a'/2	*N-*		terms for 'mother (in-law)'
1b/2	*wa-*		[only 2 words]
1c/2	*mú-*	*bá-*	'close friend of POSS'
3/4	*mu-*	*mi-*	extension in space
5/6	*i-*		natural sets (esp. paired or doublets);
5a/6	*li-*	*ma-*	borrowed words
5b/6	*Ø*		
7/8	*ki-*	*bi-*	small, diminished, defective items; super-augmentative
9/10	*N-*	*N-*	repository; outline shape; animals
9a/10a	*Ø*	*Ø*	borrowed words
9a/6	*Ø*	*ma-*	borrowed words
11/10	*lu-*	*N-*	curved contour; augmentative
12/13	*ka-*	*tu-*	diminutive
14/6	*bu-*	*ma-*	body parts
15/6	*ku-*	*ma-*	paired extremities
19/13	*si-*	*tu-*	super-diminutive (derived only)

TABLE 22.3: NOUN GENDERS: NON-PAIRED NOUN CLASSES

Class	Lega NPfx	Semantic nexus
3	*mu-*	aggregates
4	*mi-*	borrowings from French
5	*i-*	non-countable mass
6	*ma-*	liquids; granular items
7	*ki-*	languages; manner; spirits
8	*bi-*	unsafe/tainted item or mass
9	*N-*	sensations; physical/emotional traits
9a	*Ø*	borrowed words
11	*lu-*	pain and illness; bitter things
12	*ka-*	illness
14	*bu-*	gelatinous substances; abstract nouns
15	*ku-*	infinitives

paired genders above. As with the paired noun classes above, nouns in the non-paired noun classes often exhibit some semantic links. Any apparent semantic nexus, if there is one, is indicated following the form of the prefix.

3.2 Nominal derivation

Nouns may be derived from verbs by adding an appropriate class prefix and, in most cases, replacing the stem final vowel -*a* with another vowel, most commonly -*į* or -*o*.

-*į* (agentive)	*mu.régį*	'hunter'	< *ku.réga* 'to hunt'
	mu.sámbį	'sick person'	< *ku.sámba* 'to become sick'
-*į* (non-agent)	*m.bogįbogį*	'happiness'	< *ku.bogaboga* 'to become happy'
	ki.kósozį	'cough'	< *ku.kósola* 'to cough'
-*e* [rare]	*m.pyĕné*	'heir'	< *ku.pyéna* 'to inherit'
	n.sáse	'spark'	< *ku.sásuka* 'to fly off, as sparks'
-*o*	*įgy.ŭgo*	'odor'	< *k.ŭga* 'to smell'
	ma.lebo	'courtship'	< *ku.lebela* 'to seek a spouse'
-*a*	*kį.bįmba*	'boil, abcess'	< *kų.bįmba* 'to swell'
	į.búra	'birth'	< *ku.búra* 'to give birth'

3.3 Compound nominals

Compound nominals appear to be rare. The few that exist are formed in one of three ways: (1) noun + connective + noun, (2) noun + noun, or (3) verb + noun.

Noun + connective + noun
m.balezįzų   'kneecap'   *m.bale* 'lg. oval seed' + *za* 'of' + *įzų* 'knee'

Noun + noun
mwĩgyakyumo   'village chief'   *mwĩgya* 'owner' + *kyumo* 'village'

Verb + noun
ka.nkųmbamazų 'great, great grandchild'   -*kųmba* 'bend' + *mazų* 'knees'

3.4 Reduplicated nominals

Reduplicated nominals, though more common than compounds, are infrequent. Examples below illustrate reduplication of both mono- and disyllabic stems, and of the entire word.

Monosyllabic stems		Disyllabic stems	
ma.ruru	'navel'	*ki.ségésége*	'baldness'
kį.kųkų	'cave'	*lu.kenįkenį*	'star; firefly'

Word	
n.sekųnsékų	'hiccup'
į.kįlaįkįla	'spider'

3.5 Diminutives

Semantically, there are two diminutives, one for 'small', the other for 'very small, tiny'. This distinction is made only in the singular – class 12 *ka*- for a small entity, class 19 *sį*- for a tiny one. The plural for both is the class 13 prefix *tu*-.

Diminutives are formed in two ways. In pattern 1, the inherent nominal class prefix is replaced with the appropriate diminutive prefix. In pattern 2, the class prefix attaches to associative -á preceding the normal noun.

Pattern 1:	DIM + root			
Singular	Plural	Source		
kantu	*tuntu*	(<*muntu*)	'small person'	
sịntu			'tiny or sickly person'	
kapéné	*tupéné*	(<*mpéné*)	'small goat'	
sịpéné			'tiny goat'	
Pattern 2:	DIM + á + CL + root			
Singular	Plural	Source		
kákyina	*twăbyina*	(<*kyĭná*)	'small fish'	
syăkyina			'tiny fish'	
káɲama	*twăɲama*	(<*ɲɲama*)	'some meat'	
syăɲama			'tiny bit of meat'	

The distribution of these two patterns of construction is not clearcut. Classes 1/2 (humans) are always formed on the basis of diminutive pattern 1. Nouns from genders 7/8, 11/10, 12/13, and 14/6 are formed on the basis of pattern 2, with occasional exceptions, such as *kịzịmu* 'insect', which may have either form: *kazịmu* or *kákịzịmu* 'small insect'. Nouns from genders 3/4 and 9/10 appear in both forms or in pattern 2 alone.

3.6 Augmentatives

Augmentatives, like diminutives, pattern in two ways: Class 11 *lu-* indicates a large entity, class 7 *ki-* a huge one; the plural in both cases is the class 8 prefix *bi-*. Like the diminutive, the augmentative can be constructed in two ways: (1) by simply replacing the inherent class prefix with the augmentative prefix, or (2) by attaching the class prefix to the associative -*a* preceding the normal noun.

Pattern 1:	AUG + root			
Singular	Plural	Source		
luntu	*bintu*	(<*muntu*)	'large person'	
sịntu			'huge person'	
lụzụmbá	*tụzụmbá*	(<*ɲụmbá*)	'big house'	
kịzụmbá			'huge house'	
Pattern 2:	AUG + á + Cl + root			
Singular	Plural	Source		
lwăkimena	*byăbimena*	(<*kimena*)	'large crocodile'	
kyăkimena			'huge crocodile'	
lwăɲama	*byăɲama*	(<*ɲɲama*)	'large animal'	
kyăɲama			'huge beast'	

It appears from the limited data available that the simple replacement pattern most frequently occurs with gender 1/2 nouns (human). Others usually take pattern 2, even in cases where the diminutive may have alternate forms.

3.7 Pronouns

3.7.1 Subject pronouns

Independent subject pronouns, typically used emphatically, occur in singular, dual, and plural forms.

	Singular	Dual	Plural
1	nne	ịswé	bịswé
2	ugwe	ịɲwé	bịɲwé
3	gwě	bo	bábo

ịɲwé bábíli mukwenda kwịswá   'you two, you are going to the field'
bịɲwé básáru mwâmukáryé   'you three will help her'

3.7.2 Object pronouns

Object pronouns are similar to their subject counterparts, but no dual distinction is made. They are typically used when a second object pronoun is necessary, since only one object prefix can be marked on the verb (see §5.2 for discussion of object marking).

		Singular		Plural
1		ịnne		(b)ịswé
2		ugwe		(b)ịɲwé
3	1	gé	2	(bá)bo
3		gó	4	zǒ
5		lyó	6	mó
7		kyó	8	byó
9		zǒ	10	zó
11		ló	see 10	
12		kó	13	ró
14		bó	see 16	
15		kó	see 16	

nịgyubakịnde zó   'I built it [house] (by) myself'
/n-ịgy-ubak-ịn.de/
1S-REFL-build-BEN.CMP

ímba n'ịnne   'sing with me'
mịna nagé   'dance with her'

3.7.3 Reflexive pronouns

Reflexive pronouns, like the object pronouns, occur only in singular and plural.

	Singular	Plural
1	nnịnéné	bịswị'nēnē
2	ugwịnéné	bịɲwị'nénē
3	(g)wị'néné	-bị'néné

twákágwịnde ịswǎ bịswíb'néné   'we cleared the fields ourselves'
árūrịle mumpunge wị'néné   'she pounded the rice by herself'

3.7.4 Possessive (agreement prefix + POSS)

Possessive pronouns are formed by combining the agreement marker (see table 22.4 and §3.8) of the appropriate noun class with the possessive root.

1s	-áné	1p	-ítú
2s	-óbé	2p	-íɲú
3s	-ágé	3p	-ábó
líɟyo li lyăné		'that's mine (field)'	
tázi zăgé		'it's not his'	

3.8 Agreement

All modifiers and verbs exhibit agreement with the head noun through affixation of an agreement prefix. The form of the agreement prefix attached to the modifier or verb differs for each noun class. There are two general patterns, as shown in table 22.4.

3.9 Connective -á

Connective -á is used to join two nouns in a genitive construction, requiring agreement with the head noun.

bunga bwá mɨzóngú	'cassava flour' [lit. flour of cassava]
bantu bá lubanda	'people of the forest'

TABLE 22.4: AGREEMENT PREFIXES

Pattern		1	2a		2b	
Class	N pfx	Adjs & -ké 'which/what'	Nᵒs & -ngá 'how many'	Dems	Conn. -a & Colors	Verbs
1	mu-	mu-	(g)o-	(g)o-[1]	w-	á-/é-
2	ba-	ba-	ba-	bá-	b-	bá-/bé-
3	mu-	mu-	(g)o-	(g)ó-	w-	(g)u-
4	mi-	n-	i-	zé-	z-	zi-
5	i-/li-	i-/li-	li-	lí-	ly-	li-
6	ma-	ma-	ma-	má-	m-	ma-/mi-
7	ki-	ki-	ki-	kí-	ky-	ki-
8	bi-	bi-	bi-	bí-	by-	bi-
9	n-	n-	i-	(z)é-[2]	z-	zi-
10	n-	n-	i-	zé-	z'-	zi-
11	lu-	lu-	lu-	lú-	lw-	lɨu
12	ka-	ka-	ka-	ká-	k-	ka-/ki-
13	tu-	tu-	tu-	tú-	tw-	tu-
14	bu-	bu-	bu-	bú-	bw-	bu-
15	ku-	ku-	ku-	kú-	kw-	ku-
16	ga-					ga-/ge-
17	ku-					ku-
18	mu-					mu-
19	sɨ-	sɨ-	sɨ-	sɨ-	sy-	sɨ-

Notes:

1 (g)o- appears with a high tone with the quantifier 'all'.

2 é- is an optional form for the quantifier 'all'.

3.10   Demonstratives

There are six demonstrative roots in Beya Lega. Five are used spatially, two are used specifically in discourse. In table 22.5, templates of the pre-stem pattern for the various demonstratives are given for the non-nasal class prefixes, followed by examples from class 2. The appropriate prefix forms for other non-nasal classes are given in table 22.6.

Demonstratives formed from class prefixes containing a nasal require a different pre-stem template from the non-nasal prefixes. These are given in table 22.7; examples of class 1 and pre-stem forms for the other classes are shown in table 22.8.

Demonstratives precede the noun they modify.

kíno kįgųma kyábolá	'this fruit is rotten'
lílyo ibakúlį lyáné	'that bowl of mine'
mámo masúpa	'those bottles'
zelyá mpéné	'that goat yonder'

3.11   Adjectives

There exist only about twenty true adjectives in Lega, listed in table 22.9. These adjectives follow the noun and require agreement with the noun that they modify. Certain English

TABLE 22.5:   TEMPLATES FOR NON-NASAL PREFIXES

		Cl. 2 demonstratives
cv́cv̄-nō	'this' (very one)	*bábā-nō*
cv́-no	'this'	*bá-no*
cv́c(G)-o	'that'	*báb-o*
cv́cv̄-lyā	'that yonder'	*bábā-lyā*
c-óngo	'that' (just mentioned)	*b-óngo*
cv́-lyá	'that' (discussed previously)	*bá-lyá*

TABLE 22.6:   DEMONSTRATIVE PREFIXES BASED ON TEMPLATE FORMS FOR EACH NON-NASAL CLASS

Class	5	6	7	8	11	12	13	14	15
	lílī-	*mámā-*	*kíkī-*	*bíbī-*	*lúlū-*	*kákā-*	*rúrū-*	*búbū-*	*kúkū-*
	li-	*má-*	*kí-*	*bí-*	*lú-*	*ká-*	*rú-*	*bú-*	*kú-*
	lílly-	*mám-*	*kíky-*	*bíby-*	*lúl-*	*kák-*	*rúr-*	*búb-*	*kúk-*
	lílį̄-	*mámā-*	*kíkį̄-*	*bíbī-*	*lų́lū-*	*kákā-*	*rúrū-*	*búbū-*	*kų́kū-*
	ly-	*m-*	*ky-*	*by-*	*l-*	*k-*	*r-*	*b-*	*k-*
	lį-	*má-*	*kį-*	*bį-*	*lų́-*	*ká-*	*rų́-*	*bų́-*	*kų́-*

TABLE 22.7:   TEMPLATES FOR NASAL CLASSES

N class	10	3	1, 4, 9	
	cv́v-no	*cv́v-no*	*cv́v̄-nō*	'this' (very one)
	cv́-no	*cv́-no*	*cv-nó*	'this'
	cv̌-zo	*cv̌-zo*	*cv̌-zo*	'that'
	cv́-lyá	*cv́-lya*	*cv-lyá*	'that yonder'
	c-óngo	*c-oóngo*	*c-oóngo*	'that' (just mentioned)
	cv́-lyá	*cv́-lya*	*cv-lyá*	'that' (discussed previously)

TABLE 22.8: DEMONSTRATIVE FORMS BASED ON NASAL CLASS PREFIXES

Class	1	3	4, 9	10
	góo-nó	góo-	zée-	zée-
	go-nó	gó-	ze-	zé-
	gŏ-zo	gŏ-	zĕ-	zé-
	go-lyá	gó-	ze-	zé-
	g-oóngo	g-	z-	z-
	gu̧-lyá	gú̧-	zi̧-	zi̧-

TABLE 22.9: ADJECTIVE ROOTS

-bí	'bad, ugly'	-kéeké	'small, a few'	-nse	'sweet'
-bísi	'unripe, raw, fresh'	-kúlú	'old, mature'	-úgu	'light (not heavy)'
-bi̧bu	'strong'	-kúngú	'old (animates)'	-ró	'young'
-énge	'intelligent, wise'	-lazi̧	'tall, long, far'	-sóga	'good, beautiful'
-gu̧mi̧	'rich'	-mulúme	'male'	-zi̧ndu	'deep'
-i̧gi̧	'short'	-néné	'big, main'	-zi̧ru	'heavy'
-káli	'fierce, intense, nasty'				

adjectives are expressed through intransitive verbs in Lega, e.g. 'be red' -kísimina vi, 'become thin' -ónda vi, and 'be fatty' -nona vi. In such cases, the adjectival phrase consists of the head noun followed by a conjugated form of the verb.

nsu̧lú̧ zakísímáná	'red cloth' [lit. 'cloth which is red']
i̧dyá lyáku̧ká	'stale food' [lit. 'food which has become stale']
mu̧sáké mwénge	'intelligent/wise doctor'
i̧gyĕmbé i̧kéeké	'small hoe'
kikángá kinéne	'large family'

Most English adjectives are rendered by phrasal constructions employing a noun as modifier. The head noun may precede its modifier, conjoined by the connective -á, or follow the modifier, conjoined by low-toned connective -a.

bintu byá kizungu	'modern things' [lit. 'things of European']
i̧kúzi̧ lyá mu̧rú̧lá	'cooking stone' [lit. 'stone of hearth']
nzi̧ zá i̧gyiligyili	'new baskets' [lit. 'baskets of newness']
mbángílwá za mukíngá	'beautiful woman' [lit. 'beauty of a woman']
kikongolo kya mwăna	'stupid child' [lit. 'idiot of a child']
mulúmi wa mpéné	'male goat' [lit. 'male of a goat']

Other modifiers include various quantifiers.

-i̧ngi̧	'many'	-nsé, -nsenyá, -nséngwá	'all, whole'
-ngó	'(an)other'		
bíngó birógo	'other vegetables'		
mbogó zinsé	'all the buffaloes'		

3.12 Numbers

3.12.1 Cardinal numbers

1	-mozį	emozį	6	murúbá
2	-bílí	įbílí	7	murúbakámu
3	-sáru	įsáru	8	kináaná
4	-nazį	įnazį	9	mubúlá
5	-ráno	įtáno	10	įkúmį
11	įkúmį nú -mozį		100	mmyá
12	įkúmį nú -bílí		200	mmyá įbílí
	...			...
20	makúmį mábílí		1000	kakoka
30	makúmį másáru			
	...			

muntu umozį	'one person'
bimena biráno	'five crocodiles'
masángá mmyá įbílí	'two hundred beads'

3.12.2 Ordinal numbers

Pattern: N_{sg} AGR' + a PL + root N_{sg} AGR' + a ENUM
        [*exception:* one only takes AGR]

1st	-á kwanza, -sókį	6th	-a murúbá
2nd	-bílí	7th	-a murúbakámu
3rd	-sáru	8th	-a kináaná
4th	-nazį	9th	-a mubúla
5th	-ráno	10th	-a įkúmį

mbúla nsókį	'the first rains'
kįndį kyá kwanza	'the first day'
mwăna wá básáru	'the third child'

3.13 Interrogatives

-ki, kikí, kįkįzį, kįzį	'what, which'	bunį bu	'how'
nází, ni	'who'	kúnį ku	'how far'
-a názį	'whose'	gání ga, kúnį ku, múnį mu	'where'
ka.bamba	'why'	nkungú nki	'when'
-ngá	'how many, how much'		

4 VERB MORPHOLOGY

The simple infinitive in Lega consists of the class 15 prefix *ku-*, the verb root, and final vowel *-a*. Verb roots are inherently either high- or low-toned, hence, *ku-téndek-a* 'to tie up with string' and *ku.kangul-a* 'to clear a field after burning'. The verb root may be inflected for person and number, tense, aspect, and mood, and negation among other

TABLE 22.10: -C(G)V STEMS

-bá	'be(come)'	*-lyá*	'eat'
-bwa	'come'	*-nwá*	'drink'
-gwa	'fall'	*-tá*	'throw (away)'
-gwá	'be well-cooked'	*-twá*	'bite'
-gyá	'burn, be burned'	*-sa*	'miss a target'
-kwá	'die'		

TABLE 22.11: SOME -CVCVC(VC)- ROOTS

-bų́lųga	'rub'	*-kélįma*	'flash (as lightning)'
-gilįmįna	'shiver'	*-kųkųmena*	'rumble'
-gyágyila	'sweep'	*-pįlįnga*	'twist'
-kísimana	'become red'	*-rálanina*	'look good on'
-kéleruka	'turn one's head'	*-sólongola*	'strain/filter liquids'

categories. Types of verb roots and the various inflectional categories are listed and discussed below.

4.1 Verb roots

The canonical form of the verb root in Lega is -CVC-. Table 22.10 provides an inventory of -CV- roots, table 22.11 of some -CVCVC(VC)- roots (i.e. complex roots not obviously derived by the addition of verbal extensions).

There are several 'defective' verb roots that do not have an infinitival form in *ku-* and do not permit any verbal suffixes: *-li* 'be', *-ízį* 'know (how)', *-íbíze* 'sleep'.

4.2 Verb extensions

Verbs may change valence or voice by the addition of verb extensions, of which there are thirteen in Lega: *-am-* stative, *-an-* attributive, *-an-* reciprocal, *-ik-* efficeretive, *-ik-* ostensive, *-il-* benefactive, directional, and locational, *-ilil-* persistive, *-uk-* iterative, *-uk-* neuter, *-ul-* iterative, *-ul-* reversive, *-w-* passive, and *-y-* causative. Reduplication of the verb stem indicates continuation of an action, and is termed the perseverative. The role and forms of each are provided below.

- *-am-*

   STATIVE: indicates an existing state or the inception of a state. It differs from the passive in not permitting an expressed agent, from the ostensive – which indicates a potential for an event to occur – in indicating a resulting state.

k.ombama	'to be dug out'	<	*k.omba*	'to dig'
ku.kígama	'to lie across'	<	*ku.kíga*	'to dam, block'

- *-an-*₁

   ATTRIBUTIVE: the action denoted by the verb reflects a characteristic of the subject.

ku.káranya	'to be helpful' *vi*	<	*ku.kárya*	'to help' *vt*
ku.gambana	'to gossip' *vi*	<	*ku.gamba*	'to slander' *vt*

- *-an-₂*

RECIPROCAL: the action denoted by the verb is done simultaneously one to another.

| *ku.káranya* | 'to help one another' | < | *ku.kárya* | 'to help' |
| *ku.gambanana* | 'to gossip about one another' | < | *ku.gambana* | 'to slander' |

- *-ik-₁ ~ -ek-₁*

OSTENSIVE: indicates that an object is clearly apparent or conspicuous, that the potential inherent in the verb is realizable. It reduces the valency of the verb, changing a transitive verb to an intransitive; it differs from the passive in that no agent may be expressed.

| *ku.gulika* | 'to be sold' | < | *ku.gula* | 'to sell' |
| *ku.móneka* | 'to be visible' | < | *ku.móna* | 'to see' |

- *-ik-₂ ~ -ek-₂*

EFFICERETIVE (from Latin *efficere* 'effected'): indicates that an agent has brought about a new state for some object. It increases the valency of the verb by one.

| *ku.sendeka* | 'to put into a leaning position' | < | *ku.sendama* | 'to be leaning' |
| *ku.gyika* | 'to cook' | < | *kṵ.gyá* | 'to burn' *vi* |

- *-il- ~ -el- ~ -in- ~ -en-*

Traditionally termed the applicative extension, the vowel in this suffix alternates according to the preceding vowel: [e] following /e/ or /o/, [i] elsewhere. The consonant is realized as [n] following a final nasal in the stem.

BENEFACTIVE: indicates that the action is carried out on behalf of someone.

| *ku.réndela* | 'to speak on behalf of' | < | *ku.rénda* | 'to speak' |
| *ku.kambila* | 'to labor for' | < | *ku.kamba* | 'to labor' |

DIRECTIONAL: indicates that the action is carried out away from the subject.

| *k.ŏgelelela* | 'to swim off' | < | *k.ŏgelela* | 'to swim' |
| ku.búmina | 'to bark at' | < | *ku.búma* | 'to bark' |

LOCATIONAL: indicates that the action is carried out at a certain place.

| *ku.básila* | 'to go/come via a place' | < | *ku.bása* | 'to go out' |
| *ku.bwila* | 'to bring [come with]' | < | *ku.bwa* | 'to come' |

- *-ilil- ~ -elel- ~ -inin- ~ -enen-*

PERSISTIVE: indicates that the action denoted by the verb persists over a longer duration than the simple action. Often, the new lexical item has a slightly idiosyncratic meaning. The vowel alternates according to the preceding vowel: [e] following [e] or [o], [i] elsewhere. The consonant is realized as [n] when the suffix follows a stem-final nasal.

| *k.ṵngwilila* | 'to listen (to)' | < | *k.ṵngwa* | 'to hear' |
| *ku.meɲenena* | 'to know deeply' | < | *ku.meɲa* | 'to know' |

- *-uk-₁ ~ -ok-₁*

NEUTER: non-passive state of being. This extension reduces the valency of the verb.

| *ku.panguka* | 'flap' | < | *ku.pangula* | 'shake out sth.' |
| *ku.gondoka* | 'be untied' | < | *ku.gondola* | 'untie' |

- -*uk-*₂ ~ -*ok-*₂

  ITERATIVE: indicates that a semelfactive action (i.e. one that happens only once) is reiterated. It reduces the valency of the verb, the patient of the transitive verb becoming the grammatical subject of the intransitive verb.

     ku.temuka 'to drip' < *ku.tema* 'to drop intentionally'

- -*ul-*₁

  ITERATIVE: indicates that a semelfactive action of a transitive verb is reiterated. Valency remains unchanged.

     ku.bangula 'peck at repeatedly' < *ku.banga* 'to strike with a pointed object'

- -*ul-*₂

  SEPARATIVE: indicates movement out of, or reversal of the original state of an item.

     kw.anzula mụgụ 'to undo a bed' < *kw.anza mụgụ* 'to make a bed'
     ku.lịmbula 'to uncover' (pot) < *kụ.lịmba* 'to cover' (pot)

- -*w-* ~ -*bw-*

  PASSIVE: requires that the recipient or goal of the action be the grammatical subject. It differs from the ostensive in that the agent may be (optionally) expressed. The form -*bw-* occurs following causative /j̧/.

     ku.lungwa 'to be well-seasoned' < *ku.lunga* 'to season (food)'
     ku.bábazịbwa 'to be hurt' < *ku.bábazya* 'to hurt' *vt*

- -*y-* [< /j̧/] ~ -*sy-*

  CAUSATIVE: increases the number of arguments of the verb by one; hence, intransitive verbs become transitive, transitive become ditransitive. The form -*sy-* occurs with vowel-final stems.

     ku.gyúkya 'to wake s.o. up' < *ku.gyúka* 'to wake up'
     kụ.zịmya 'to extinguish' < *kụ.zịma* 'to go out (of a fire)'
     kụ.lịsya 'to feed' < *kụ.lyá* 'to eat'

- reduplication of verb stem

  PERSEVERATIVE: indicates a continuous or persevering interpretation of the action denoted by the verb.

     ku.lalukwalalukwa 'to shout continuously' < *ku.lalukwa* 'to shout'
     ku.réndarenda 'to speak on and on' < *ku.rénda* 'to speak'

4.3 Order of extensions

Extensions may co-occur. The following sequences have been noted:

   -il$_{\text{BEN}}$-an₁-; -an₁-an₂-; -an₂-j̧-; -ilil-il$_{\text{LOC}}$-; -il-j̧-; -ul-am-

The causative extension -j̧- occurs between the -*il*- and -*e* of the tense/aspect markers: -il$_{\text{ASP}}$-j̧-e. The passive extension -*u*- always precedes the final vowel of the verb stem. The variant -*bw*- is split with the imperfective marker, hence, -j̧-b-ag-w-a.

4.4 Verb categories

The verb in Lega comprises eight grammatical categories ordered in the following manner: (SUB) + (NEG₁) + SP + (NEG₂) + T/A/M + (OBJ) + ROOT + (EXT) + T/A.

4.4.1 Subordinators (SUB)

There are three primary subordinating prefixes in Beya Lega: *ga-* is used for affirmative temporal clauses with the sense of 'if' or 'when' (see also §5.8) *bu-* is used for negative temporal clauses; relative clauses take an appropriate agreement marker determined by the noun (see also §5.3). (See §4.5 for discussion of abbreviations of tense forms.)

ga- clauses

*ga-*SP-*na*-CVCVC-*á*	*garúnákangulá įswá*	'if we clear the field'
*ga-*SP-*á*-CVCv́C-*é*	*garwákangúlé įswá*	'when we clear the field' (T_x Fut)
*ga-*SP-*á*-CVCv́C-*á*	*garwákangúlá įswá*	'when we cleared the field' (T_c CMP)
*ga-*SP-*á*-ROOT-*įlé*	*garwákangulįlé įswá*	'when we cleared the field' (T_x Pst)
ga-SP-*á*-CVCv́C-*įlé*	*garwákangúlįlé įswá*	'when we cleared the field' (T_r Pst)

bu- clauses

*bu-*SṔ-NEG-CVCVC-*įlé*	*burútákangulįlé įswá*	'when we didn't clear the field' (T_x Pst)
*bu-*SṔ-NEG-CVCv́C-*įlé*	*burŭtákangúlįlé įswá*	'when we didn't clear the field' (T_r Pst)

4.4.1.1 Relative prefixes

In object relative clauses, the relative prefix occurs in the SUB slot. In subject relative clauses, the prefix occurs in the SP slot (see §5.3 for examples).

Class:	1/2	3/4	5/6	7/8	9/10	11/10	12/13	14/6	15/6	19/13
Sg.	*u-*	*(g)u-*	*li-*	*ki-*	*zi-*	*lu-*	*ka-*	*bu-*	*ku-*	*sį-*
Pl.	*ba-/be-*	*zi-*	*ma-*	*bi-*	*zi-*	*zi-*	*tu-*	*ma-*	*ma-*	*tu-*

4.4.2 Negative markers (NEG₁)

Two negative markers occur in this position for non-subordinate clauses: *nt-* is used for second and third person singular, *ta-* for all plural forms.

nt-á-kangúl-á įswá	's/he is not (yet) clearing the field'
ta-tú-ku-kangúlágá įswá'léngó	'we are no longer clearing the field'

4.4.3 Subject prefixes (SP)

The following subject prefixes are used for the respective participants and noun classes. See table 22.4 (§3.8) for prefixes for appropriate noun class agreement.

Person:	1	2	3
Sg.	*n(i)-*	*u-*	*á-/é-*
Pl.	*tu-*	*mu-*	*bá-/bé-*

4.4.4 Negative (NEG₂)

The NEG₂ position is used for first person singular negation, *-si-*, and for marking negation in infinitives and in relative clauses, *-ta-*.

n-sy-á-kangula įswá	'I did not clear the field (T_x Pst)'
įswá lį-bá-tá-ka-kangulá	'the field that they won't clear (T_r Fut)'

4.4.5 Tense, aspect, and mood markers

Tense, aspect, and mood markers occur in two positions, one preceding the verb root and one at the end of the verbal complex. The affixes occurring in the prefix position are the following:

Mood:	*na*	potential marker [POT]
Tense:	*ka*	remote future [T_r Fut] (= later time unit, e.g. 'in two weeks')
	ă	near past [T_x Pst]/near future [T_x Fut] (= approximal time unit)
	a	remote past [T_r Pst] (= earlier time unit, e.g. 'two months ago')
	nŭ	sequential marker ('and then')
Aspect:	*a*	completive [CMP T_c] (= completed within current time unit)
	ku	continuous
	să	inceptive

4.4.6 Object markers and reflexive (OBJ)

The following object markers are used for the respective participants and noun classes. Only one object marker at a time may be prefixed to the verbal unit.

Person:	1	2	3									
Class:			1/2	3/4	5/6	7/8	9/10	11/10	12/13	14/6	15/6	19/13
Sg.	*n-*	*ku-*	*mu-*	*(g)ú-*	*lí-*	*kí-*	*zí-*	*lú-*	*ká-*	*bú-*	*kú-*	*sí-*
Pl.	*tú-*	*mú-*	*bá-*	*zí-*	*má-*	*bi-*	*zí-*	*zí-*	*tú-*	*má-*	*má-*	*tú-*

Reflexive -*í*-
          -*így*- [before V-initial stems]

4.4.7 Tense, aspect

In verb final position occur the second set of tense/aspect markers. The imperfective co-occurs with all the other markers in this category except the remote past -*ílé*, which it replaces. Following the applicative extension -*il*-, the near and remote past markers – -*ile* and -*ílé*, respectively – coalesce with it to form -*inde/-índé*. For monosyllabic verb roots, the suffixes -*ile/-ílé* vary in form, e.g. [-*bule*] with the root -*bu*- 'come', [-*nune*] with the root -*nų́* 'drink'.

-*ílé* ~ -*íné*	T_r past (remote)
-*ile* ~ -*ine*	T_x past (approximal)
-*é*	T_x future (approximal)
-*á*	completive/continuous
-*a*	inceptive/future
-*ag*-	imperfective

4.5 Simple TAM constructions

Simple verb constructions comprise a main verb alone, which is marked for tense/aspect. The list below provides the basic templatic patterns for a low-tone -CVCVC- verb root. A major division is that between imperfective -*ag*- forms and their counterparts. Tense markers loosely divide time into 'metric' units, pivoting on the speech event (S), which is included in the non-past. At S, aspects typically fall within the current time unit (T_c), e.g. -*ku*- could be used for 'today' or 'this month', -*a*- 'earlier today' or 'this past week'.

Moving away from S, tenses typically mark an approximal time unit (T_x) and a more remote time unit (T_r), respectively. Although seemingly based on a 'metric' division of time, the different tenses often appear to be used subjectively.

```
                              S
                              /
  ┌─────────────────────────────────────────────────────────→
  (    T_r   )(   T_x   )(   T_c   )(   T_c   )(   T_x   )(      T_r      )
  └────────────────────────────────────
  Remote Next unit  Current time unit
```

Non-imperfective patterns   *Imperfective patterns*

SP-*ku*-CVCV́C-*á*	SP-ku-CVCV́C-*ág-á*	V-ing/V; will V/be V-ing (T_c)
SP-*a*-CVCV́C-*á*	SP-*ǎ*-CVCVC-*ag-a*	(have) V-ed/was V-ing (T_c)
SP-*ǎ*-CVCVC-*ịl-e*	SP-*ǎ*-CVCVC-*ag-ịl-e*	V-ed/was V-ing (T_x past)
SP-*a*-CVCVC-*ịl-é*	SP-*a*-CVCVC-*ág-á*	V-ed/was V-ing (T_r past)
SP-*ǎ*-CVCV́C-*é*	SP-*ǎ*-CVCV́C-*ág-é*	will V/be V-ing (T_x future)
SP-*ka*-CVCVC-*a*	SP-*ka*-CVCVC-*ag-a*	will V/be V-ing (T_r future)
SP-*ná*-CVCVC-*a*		can V
SP-*ná*-CVCVC-*ịl-e*	SP-*ná*-CVCVC-*ag-a*	could/would (have) V(-ed)
SP-*sǎ*-CVCVC-*a*		have started to-V/V-ing
SP-*nǔ*-CVCV́C-*á*		and then V-ed
SP-*a-nú*-CVCVC-*a*		V nevertheless

mpéné zikunóná nabusinabusí	'the goats are getting fatter every day (T_c)'
tukukangúlá ịswá mugúno mwězi	'we will clear the field this month (T_c)'
barégi búmbúlá kumangeni	'the hunters have camped at their camp (T_c)'
nǎnụne kabwa mumukélo	'I drank coffee in the morning (T_x)'
bá'líkangúlágá	'they were clearing it (the field) (T_r)'
á'rórábangịnde gatwá'básịlé	's/he visited us (T_r) when we arrived'
nǎ'réndéké kịkụmá	'I will tie up the bundle (T_x)'
nkasábokaga mwịgolo	'I will fish in the evening [hab.] (T_r)'
túnábwa	'we can come'
bénágyanịne songó bábezaga	'they could/would play if they had a ball'
na lwenze	
ánǔgunwa	'and then s/he drank it (water)'
nanúkangola iswá	'I am clearing the field (nevertheless)'

4.6 Periphrastic constructions

Lega has many periphrastic constructions which comprise one or more auxiliary verbs plus a main verb, either conjugated or infinitival in form. Patterns and examples of these constructions with low-tone -*kangula* 'clear (a field)' are provided in the following sections.

4.6.1 Auxiliary -li 'be'

The defective verb -*li*, a suppletive form of -*ba* 'be', occurs as an auxiliary in three forms: unmarked (progressive), with -*ki*- (persistive), and with -*se*- (permansive 'already' or inceptive). It is optional in the latter two.

(a) SP-*li* SP-*ku*-CVCV́C-*á*   *tuli tukukangúlá ịswá*
                              'we are clearing the field (now)'

(b)   SP-*kí*(-*li*) SP-*a*-CVCVC-*a*   *tukí(li) twakangula ịswá*
                                             'we are still clearing the field'
        SP-*kí*(-*li*) SP-*na*-CVCVC-*a*   *tukí(li) túnákangula ịswá*
                                             'we are still able to clear the field'
(c)   SP-*sĕ*(-*li*) SP-*a*-CVCV́C-*á*   *tusĕ(li) twakangúlá ịswá*
                                             'we have already cleared the field'
        SP-*sĕ*(-*li*) SP-*a*-CVCVC-*a*   *tusĕ(li) twakangula ịswá*
                                             'we have started clearing the field'

4.6.2 Auxiliary -ba 'be'

-*ba* 'be' (-*bez*- before -*ag*-) occurs as an auxiliary verb in a large number of constructions.
It may be marked in five ways, corresponding to T_c, T_x, T_r past and non-past tenses. Each
of these forms may occur with any of three different aspectual forms of the main verb:
inceptive, continuous, or completive. The potential patterns for the auxiliary and the main
verb for a low-tone -CVCVC- verb root are listed below, followed by several illustrative
examples.

Auxiliary   Main verb
SP-*ă-bez-aga*   (T_c past)   SP-*să*-CVCVC-*a*   inceptive ('start V-ing')
SP-*ă-bez-ag-ịle*   (T_x past)   SP-*ku*-CVCV́C-*á*   continuous ('be V-ing')
SP-*a-béz-ágá*   (T_r past)   SP-*a*-CVCV́C-*á*   completive ('V-ed')
SP-*â-b-é*   (T_x future)
SP-*ka-b-á*   (T_r future)

twăbezaga tusăkangula ịswá   'we had started clearing the field (today)'
twăbezagịle tukukangúlá ịswá   'we had been clearing the field (yesterday)'
twabézágá twakangúlá ịswá   'we had cleared the field (before yesterday)'
twâbé tusăkangula ịswá   'we will have started clearing the field (tomorrow)'
tukabá twákangula ịswá   'we will have cleared the field (after tomorrow)'
twăbezaga tusĕ twakangúlá   'we had already cleared the field'
  ịswá
twăbezaga tusĕ twakangula   'we had already started clearing the field'
  ịswá

-*ba* may also occur with the potential marker -*na*-, and may be followed by the main
verb in either the affirmative or negative with -*ku*- or -*a*-.

Auxiliary   Main verb
SP-na-bá   (Pot)   SP-*ku*-ROOT-*a*   'must V'
                   SP-*á*-ROOT-*ịle*   'must have V-ed'
SP-na-bá   (Pot)   NEG-SP-*ku*-ROOT-*a*   'not V-ing'
                   NEG-SP-*á*-ROOT-*a*   'didn't V'

Moké énabá ákorwa   'Moke must be tired'
bánabá bánune maku   'they must have drunk (some) beer'
túnabá tatúkukangula ịswá   'even if we aren't clearing the field'
túnabá tatwákangula ịswá   'even if we didn't clear the field'

4.6.3 *Auxiliary verb + infinitive*

Several verbs occur in constructions in which the main verb is infinitival in form. These include *-londa* 'look for', *-sa* (from ??), *-anza* 'start', *-túka* 'come from', *-ima* (from ??), and *-síla* 'finish'. *-londa* and *-sa* differ from the others in that they always occur with the formative *-să-* and may occur with auxiliary *-bez-* 'be'.

sp-*ă-bez-aga*	(T$_c$ past)	SP-*să-londa* INF	'about to V'
sp-*ă-bez-ag-įle*	(T$_x$ past)	SP-*să-sa* INF	'about to V'
sp-*ă-béz-ágá*	(T$_r$ past)		

tusălonda kukangúlá įswá	'we are about to clear the field'
twăbezagįle tusălonda kukangúlá įswá	'we were about to clear the field (yester.)'
tusăsa kukangula įswá	'we are about to clear the field'
twăbezaga tusăsa kukangúlá įswá	'we were about to clear the field (today)'

-anza 'start'

sp-(*a*)-*ănz-įle* INF	*twănzįle kukangúlá įswá*	'we started clearing the field' (T$_x$ Pst)
sp-(*a*)-*ănz-ílé* INF	*twănzílé kukangúlá įswá*	'we started clearing the field' (T$_r$ Pst)
sp-*s*(*ă*)-*anza* INF	*tusánza kukangúlá įswá*	'we had started clearing the field'
[contracted form of sp-se (-li) sp-anza INF]		

-túka 'come from'

sp-*a-rúká* INF

twarúká kukangúlá įswá	'we just cleared the field (a few minutes ago)'
bá¹túká kuténdéká kįkųmá	'they just tied up the bundle (a few minutes ago)'

-ima

sp-*îm-é* INF	*twîmé kukangúlá įswá*	'we are able to clear the field'
sp-*n*(*a*)-*ím-a* INF	*túníma kukangúlá įswá*	'we are able to clear the field'
sp-*n*(*a*)-*im-įne* INF	*túnímįne kukangúlá įswá*	'we could have cleared the field'
sp-*k*(*a*)-*im-a* INF	*tukima kukangúlá įswá*	'we are willing to clear the field'

-síla 'finish'

sp-*a-síl-a* INF	*twasílá kukangúlá įswá*	'we finished clearing the field'

4.7 Optative

The optative expresses a wish or desire on the part of the speaker.

sp-*á-nŭ*-ROOT-*a*	*mbúla zánŭlóka é*	'if only it would rain'
sp-*a-nŭ*-ROOT-*aga*	*twanŭkangulaga įswá*	'if only we had/could have cleared the field'

4.8 Imperative

The imperative occurs only in second person, formed from the bare verb root in the singular, with suffix *-zį* in the plural. In the negative, the singular takes prefix *nt-*, the plural *ta-*. Tone patterns change according to verb structure. Examples illustrate the low-tone verbs *-bwa* 'come', *-gyanga* 'follow', and *-kangula* 'clear (a field)', and the high-tone verbs -*nwá* 'drink', -*kátya* 'help', and -*ụ́ngwilila* 'listen'. There is no negative form; rather, the negative subjunctive form is used.

Low-tone root		Sg. w/OM	Pl. w/OM
Monosyllabic: cv̌	*bwǎ(zị)* 'come (pl.)'	–	–
Disyllabic: cvcv́	*gyangá(zị)* 'follow (pl.)'	*mugyangé* 'follow him'	*mugyangázị* 'follow (pl.) him'
Multisyllabic: cvcvcv́	*kangúlá(zị) ịswá* 'clear (pl.) the field'	*líkangúlé* 'clear it'	*líkangúlázị* 'clear (pl.) it'
High-tone root			
Monosyllabic: cv́	*nwá(zị)* 'drink (pl.)'	*gúnwé* 'drink it'	*gúnwázị* 'drink (pl.) it'
Disyllabic: cv́cv	*kárya(zị) mwǎna* 'help (pl.) the child'	*mokátyé* 'help her'	*mokátyázị* 'help (pl.) her'
Multisyllabic: cv́cvcv	*ụ́ngwilila(zị)* 'listen (pl.)'		

4.9 Hortative

The hortative indicates a request, but is more polite than the imperative, more urgent in intent than the subjunctive. All persons may occur as subject. The only tone on the verb complex is that of the verb root. There is no negative form; rather, the negative subjunctive form is used.

SP-*a*-ROOT-*a*	*twakangula ịswá*	'we should clear the field'
	twaréndeka kịkụmá	'we should tie up the bundle'

4.10 Subjunctive

The subjunctive occurs with all persons as subject. It takes final -*e* with high tones on the initial and final vowels of the verb complex, both low-tone and high-tone verbs.

SṔ-ROOT-*é*	*níbwe*	'let me/I should/that I come'
	túkangulé ịswá	'let's/we should/that we clear the field'
	nínwé more	'let me/I should/that I drink the medicine'
	múkaryé bana	'you (pl.) should/that you (pl.) help the children'

4.11 Negative subjunctive

The negative subjunctive requires a negative prefix, *nt-* for singular, *ta-* for plural, except first person singular, which requires -*si-* following the subject prefix. This form is used not only as the negative of the subjunctive, but also as the corresponding negative for the imperative and hortative.

	L-tone root	H-tone root
	ntúbwe	*ntúnwé murí*
Singular (2nd)	'(that) you should not come'	'(that) you should not drink the medicine'
	ntúkangule ịswá	*ntúkárye bǎna*
	'(that) you should not clear the field'	'(that) you should not help the children'

	tatúbwe	tatúnwé murí
Plural (1st)	'(that) we should not come'	'(that) we should not drink the medicine'
	tatúkangule iswá '(that) we should not clear the field'	tatúkáryé băna '(that) we should not help the children'

5 SYNTAX

5.1 Basic word order: S-V-IO-DO-OO

The basic word order of Lega is SVO, with indirect objects preceding direct objects. Oblique objects follow IO and DO.

năsínginde	Zuúla musagú	'I sent Zuula a message'
1S-Hest-send-APP-Hest	Zuula message	
násíngile	musagú kwa Zuúla	'I sent a message to Zuula'
1S-Hest-send-Hest	message 17-of Zuula	
násínginde Zuúla musagú kwa Kikuni		'I sent a message for Zuula to Kikuni'
Kisanga álisizye Lukulu byámá		'Kisanga fed Lukulu yams'

5.2 Object marking

Lega permits only one object marker prefixed to the verb itself (see §3.7.2). If more than one pronominal object is referred to, the second is realized in an independent pronominal form following the verb.

á^{1}lígikinde bíswé	'she cooked it [verb OM] for us [free pro]'
á^{1}rúgikinde lyó	'she cooked it [meat] for us'

5.3 Relative clauses

Relative clauses follow the noun they modify. In some tenses, there are differences in tone between the relative verb form and the simple indicative (see §4.4.1 for a brief discussion of relatives).

5.3.1 Subject relatives

Subject relatives have no overt relative pronoun, marking of the relative status being indicated by the form of the subject prefix and/or tone of the verb construction.

kimena ky-á-l-ilé mbwá kitílwe	[cf. kimena kyálíle mbwá]
7.crocodile 7REL-T$_x$PST-eat- CMP 9.dog 7.kill.CMP.PASS.FV	'the crocodile ate the dog'
'the crocodile that ate the dog was killed'	
muntu w-ă-kangol-ilé iswá	[cf. ákangulíle iswá]
1.person 1REL-T$_x$PST-clear-CMP 5.field	's/he cleared the field'
'the person who cleared the field'	

mukįkulu u-tá-kamb-á   *ásųngwįndwe*
1.woman 1REL-NEG-work-FV 1.talk.CMP.PASS.FV
'the woman who didn't work (earlier today) was talked to (yesterday)'
ampú twîzį bazungú bekųlyágá mirende
'indeed, we know white people who eat frogs'

5.3.2 Object relatives

Object relative constructions require two agreement prefixes, a relative prefix determined by the object noun, followed by a subject prefix determined by the agentive subject. If a subject noun occurs (following the verb), no subject agreement prefix appears.

kyumo ki-n-á-rabang-įle mųkyó kí kisúga
7.town 7-1S-T$_x$PST-visit-CMP 18.7.PRO 7.COP 7.beautiful
'the town that I visited is beautiful'

nnyama zi-bá-tá-gik-é zábolé
9.meat 9-3P-NEG-cook-FV 9.T$_x$FUT.rot.FV
'the meat that they don't cook will spoil'

įdégá lí'kútágílágá Syába mănzi mųlyó lyábųgįle
'the pot that Syaba draws water in is broken'

tuságyika įswá lįtwákangwíndé
'we are planting the field that we cleared (remote)'

luzį lwábįsįndemu falánga lukųmbúsa kwá mųgu
'the basket that she hid the money in is beside the bed'

mųzįnga mwákolokįndé ɲɲama gú munéné
'the pit into which the animal fell is large'

5.4 Direct objects as subjects

Direct objects may be promoted to subject from either ostensive or passive constructions.

- from ostensives

ndįmu tazíkugulíká língó kwįsoku   'oranges are not sold anymore at the market'
/ta-zi-ku≠gul-ik-a/
mųzígį wásesekįle   'the string was cut'
/u-a≠ses-ik-įle/

- from passives

mukoko wágulįlwe (na Muke)   'the sheep was sold (by Muke)'
/u-a≠gul-įl-w-e/
mųsílí wálungwá busóga   'the sauce was well-spiced'
/u-a≠lung-w-a/

5.5 Coordinate and comitative constructions

Linking of multiple nouns as subjects may be achieved through the use of different coordinate or comitative constructions (for fuller discussion, see Tak and Botne 1998).

- comitative construction

Lukulu álįndįnde Muké na Zuúla   'Lukulu waited for Muke with Zuula'
Nkusu éndįle kumusúmbá na mukází 'Nkusu went to town with his wife'
  wăgé

- asymmetric coordination

Amísị bíbịbe falánga na Kibúngé	'Amisi and Kibunge stole some money'
Nkusu béndịle kumusúmbá	'Nkusu and his wife went to town'
na mukází wăgé.	
Garúsambá na mubitu wăné,	'between me and my brother, it is I who am
nne ú mulazị	taller'
	[lit. between 1P and my brother ...]
bábụ̄ndwe bŏno bíkalé	'they and the leader were told that they be
kịma na kikundí	quiet'
	[lit. they were told that they stay
	quiet and the leader]

- symmetric coordination

Lukulu nu Zuúla bálịndịnde Muké	'Lukulu and Zuula waited for Muke'
Nkusu nu mukázị wăgé béndịle	'Nkusu and his wife went to town'
kumusúmbá	

5.6 Presentative constructions

In presentative constructions, the logical subject of the verb follows the verb, which itself is marked by a preposed *g(á)-* (probably the class 16 prefix), but shows no agreement with the subject noun. This construction appears to be used to introduce new information in discourse.

gârịngé myăka kinâná na ganábwile kwAmelịka
'there will pass eight years before I come to America'
mụnda mwaluzị găbịsịndé falánga gíli nzóka
'under the basket where she hid the money there is a snake'

5.7 Focus: ú-

One type of focus construction places a proclitic *ú-* before the relevant verbal unit.

ú wabá	's/he's the one who survived'
gŏzo ú wamusákịndé	'he it is who cured her'
Amísị ú wálị̄ngịzyé nsaké	'Amisi is the one who began (initiated) the
	dispute'
ampú gáno ú gabwábêndé	'indeed, right here is where it happened'
ú băna bíbịlé nságo zăné	'they are the children who stole my purse'
nne ú ukukálá mabelá	'it is I who harvests the rice'
mwịdégá ú mubékutágílá măzi	'it is the pot into which they draw water'

5.8 Dependent clauses

- *ga*-clauses of time

The verb prefix *ga-* introduces subordinate clauses of time, typically with the sense of 'when' or 'whenever'.

> *twǎbēzaga tusé twalyá gǎbásįlé*   'we had already eaten when she arrived'
> *na gǎbwagá nabézágá nįbíze*   'whenever he came, I was sleeping'

- hypothetical and counterfactual *ga-/gi*-clauses

When *ga-* co-occurs with the potential prefix *-na-* it marks hypothetical or counterfactual clauses. The form *gi-* occurs primarily in 3S constructions.

> *ganinénda kuZai, nínábogaboga*
> 'if I ever happen to go to Zaire, I will be happy'
> *gínábųlé, mmǎge énábogįlebogįle*
> 'had she come (expected to, but didn't), my mother would have been happy'

- *andí*-clauses

The particle *andí* indicates that the proposition expressed should be assumed to be true before any evidence is provided.

> *andí ábwa, mmáge ábogébógé*
> 'if (assuming) she comes, my mother will be happy'
> *andí mbųla zálōka, ntábwe*
> 'if (assuming) it rains, she won't come'
> *andí nzóka!*
> 'watch it (= presumably), [it's] a snake! (hence, behave accordingly)'

- *kųngwá*-clauses

These clauses indicate that the proposition expressed is a hypothesis and no evidence supporting it need be expressed.

> *kųngwá ánwa gúno murí, ôné*
> 'if he drinks this medicine, he will be cured'
> *kųngwá mbųla záloka, ntábwe*
> 'if (supposing) it rains, he won't come'

- *songó*-clauses

The particle *songó* typically occurs in the apodosis of a conditional construction and indicates the consequence of an action. It may also occur in the protasis, in which case it indicates uncertainty or counterfactivity.

> *Amísi ánǔbwaga, songó túnéndįle kumusúmbá*
> 'if only Amisi had come, (so that) then we could have gone to town'
> *songó êndá ku Pangi, songó ámóná múnganga*
> 'if she would go to Pangi [but she doesn't want to], then she would see a doctor'

5.9 Evidentials

Unlike most Bantu languages, Beya Lega has two sentence level adverbial elements that indicate the speaker's evidence for and extent of confidence in the proposition asserted in an utterance. These words are employed when the speaker feels compelled to indicate either the factuality of the assertion or doubt in the assertion (see Botne 1997).

- *ampú*: indicates that the speaker has cogent and compelling evidence supporting the assertion; hence, it expresses certainty on the speaker's part. It may also function to emphasize or reaffirm a proposition.

ampú Zuúla nú Muké ú bekįlé įsaga lyá Pįla
'(I know that) it was Zuula and Muke who took Pila's ax'
ampú Masụ́dí ézį nzilá
'[without a doubt] Masudi knows the way'

- *ámbu*: indicates that the speaker has only indirect evidence for the proposition asserted, evidence based on report, hearsay, or inference from sources other than vision.

  ámbu Zuúla nú Muké ú bekįlé įsaga lyá Pįla
  '(it appears that) it was Zuula and Muke who took Pila's ax'
  nkụngwágá (búno) ámbu bazungú békụlyágá mirende
  'I hear (that) Westerners eat frogs [though I find that unlikely]'

ACKNOWLEDGMENT

Data for this chapter were obtained through work with Kisanga Salama-Gray and Jeanine Maluguza, whom I thank for their time, energy, and effort.

REFERENCES

Botne 1995, 1997; Grimes 2000; Kadima *et al.* 1983; Lungumbu 1988; Meeussen 1971; Tak and Botne 1998; Wamenka 1992.

FURTHER READING

Botne 1994; Burke 1940, 1956; Delhaise 1900; Malasi 1988; Meeussen 1962b; Struck 1910.

BILA (D32)

Constance Kutsch Lojenga

1 INTRODUCTION

Bila is one of the languages of the northern Bantu borderland spoken in the NE of the Democratic Republic of Congo, in the BaKwanza and the BaBombi *Collectivités* of the *Territoire* of Mambasa in the *Province Orientale* in and around Mambasa and Lolwa on the road between Bunia and Kisangani.

Guthrie (1970) has only one entry Bira, D32, with two dialects: 'Plains Bira', in the east, and 'Forest Bira', further to the west. However, the two appear to have only about 60 percent core vocabulary in common on a list of about 200 words (Kutsch Lojenga and Raymond 1985) and should on that basis alone be considered separate, but still related languages. A more elaborate survey done several years later comes to the same conclusion, and shows 59 percent cognates (Wit 1994:12–13).

The names of these two languages have caused some confusion. At first sight, they may give the impression of being the same; however, there is not only an *r/l* difference in the second consonant, but also a clear vowel difference in the first syllable: [ɓera] for 'Plains Bira', and [ɓila] for 'Forest Bira'. This chapter concentrates on the latter.

It is not clear how many native Bila speakers there are. The Ethnologue lists 5,000 in 1987 (Boone 1993:9). If that figure was realistic at the time, the total population would not exceed 20,000 at present. However, census figures from the Mambasa Zone indicate that there were 60,000 Bila people around 1995. It is not impossible that this figure includes the entire population of Mambasa town, which means also many non-native Bila speakers (Boone 1993:16).

The results of the linguistic and sociolinguistic Bila survey (Boone 1993:13–14) show that three major speech varieties can be distinguished: Bombi, the Mambasa dialect, Nyaku, the dialect spoken in and around Lolwa, and Kaiku, to the southwest of Mambasa. A specific sound difference between Bombi and Nyaku is explained in the section on consonants. Although the people belonging to the Bombi and Nyaku dialects consider Kaiku yet another dialect, they constantly indicate that there is very little mutual intelligibility with Kaiku. The Mambasa dialect is central, with the other two varieties contiguous on either side: the Lolwa dialect to the east, and Kaiku to the southwest. The latter two are not contiguous.

Some of the differences relate to the vowel system: in Kaiku, verbs never end in the vowel *-o*, but always in the vowel *-a*, which could well indicate that Kaiku has only seven vowels. Lexically, it seems that quite a few *k*s have dropped out, e.g. Nyaku and Bombi: *njoka* 'snake'; Kaiku: *njoa*; Nyaku and Bombi: *mbuko* 'seed, fruit'; Kaiku: *mbua*. With Kaiku apparently so difficult to understand and the fact that there seems to be only around 80 percent lexical similarity, it may therefore be justified to consider Kaiku a separate language. It is therefore cited as such in the list later. I will then consider the other two, Bombi and Nyaku, as the two main Bila speech varieties, also referred to as the Mambasa and Lolwa dialects respectively.

Bantu languages of the northern Bantu borderland in northeastern Congo are (listed in alphabetical order): Amba[1] (also called Humu), Beeke, Bali, Bira, Bhele, Bila, Budu (with two quite distinct dialects, called Koya and Neta), Kaiku, Kango,[2] Komo, Lika, Mbo, Ndaka, Nyali, Vanuma. Most of them are represented on the map. Those which are mentioned in Guthrie's classification are found in D20 and D30. However, D20 contains also several languages which are spoken much further south and which are more closely related to the languages of D40, D50, and D60, which have full noun-class systems with up to nineteen classes.

After some basic studies of several of these languages, and considering the result of linguistic and sociolinguistic surveys done in the area, two main groups of related languages can be distinguished, based on lexical similarities (Wit 1994:12–13). The grouping based on lexical similarities happens to coincide with a number of structural similarities relating among others to the vowel inventory, noun-class system, which strengthens the internal coherence of each of these two groups. Bila is special in that it seems to have borrowed some phonological features from the neighboring group, possibly from Ndaka which is spoken immediately to the west of Bila.

The first group contains those languages which have a somewhat reduced noun-class sytem which is still functioning in that there is agreement between the noun and the other elements of the noun phrase, and also between the noun and the inflected verb. These

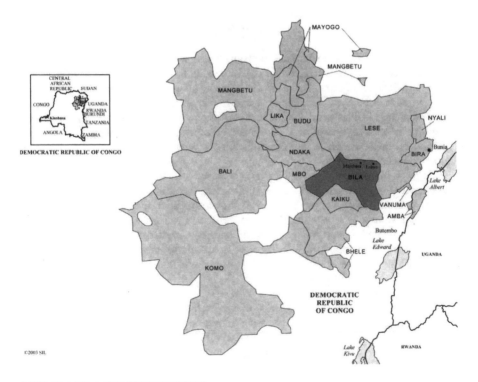

MAP 23.1 BILA AND ITS NEIGHBORS

languages are: Budu, Ndaka, Mbo, Nyali, Vanuma.[3] Most if not all of these languages have a nine-vowel system with ATR-harmony, something also found in several Central-Sudanic languages, and, in a slightly modified form, also in Mayogo. The five languages of this group show a high degree of lexical, phonological, and morphological similarity. The lowest percentages of lexical similarities between these languages is 73% (Wit 1994:13).

The second group consists of the languages Amba, Bira, Bhele, Bila, Kaiku, Kango, and Komo. These languages no longer have a functioning noun-class system, though the nouns are often preceded by recognizable but petrified noun-class prefixes. Nouns are divided into a system of animate and inanimate, and only in the former is a distinction made between singular and plural. There is no agreement between the elements of the noun phrase or between the noun and the verb phrase other than that based on animacy, and number within the set of animate nouns. Most of these languages have a system of seven vowels, with Bila having acquired a nine-vowel system. Four of these languages, geographically contiguous, seem to form a continuum: Bila–Kaiku 81% cognates, Kaiku–Bhele 82%, Bhele–Komo 80%, and Komo–Bila, non-contiguous, only 70%. All four have only 60% lexical similarity with Bira and Amba. For Kango, lexical data were collected, but have not been fully analysed. It is closest to Komo, with 78% lexical similarity, and is therefore considered to belong to this subgroup. The percentage of lexical similarities between this subgroup of Border-Bantu languages and the previous one is between 20 and 30% only (Wit 1994:12–13).

These two main groups cover most but not all of the Bantu languages spoken in the area. The genetic affiliation of the others, particularly Bali and Lika, is not yet completely clear. They may appear to be closer to some C-languages spoken further to the west, possibly the Bua group.

Since these languages are situated in the northern Bantu borderland, there are several non-Bantu languages bordering on some of these Bantu languages: Lese and Mangbetu (both Nilo-Saharan, Central-Sudanic) and Mayogo (Niger-Congo, Ubangi). From work done on both Bantu and non-Bantu languages in the area, it is clear that there has been interaction and influence on the lexicon (borrowing), in the phonology (e.g. vowel inventory, depressor consonants), and in the grammar (verbal derivational categories). This mutual influence makes the Bantu languages in this area interesting but also quite complex in certain domains.

Bila has a number of most unusual and unexpected features for a Bantu language. In this chapter, I will particularly focus on these interesting features, namely: its nine-vowel system with Advanced Tongue Root (ATR) harmony, the lack of a set of voiced stops, three contrastive tone levels and downstep, no functional noun-class system, but only petrified remnants of the prefixes, and an unusual verbal derivational category, with prefixes marking the obligatory presence of animate singular or animate plural object. These are some topics of initial study, but much remains to be studied of this Bantu language of the northern Bantu borderland.

The oldest article relating to Bila was written by Vorbichler (1966). He focused on the tonal structure of verbal infinitives and of subject prefixes in the various tense/aspect forms. In his article, the language has been transcribed with five vowels and two tones.

Kutsch Lojenga and Raymond did an initial rapid survey by short comparative word lists of a number of the Bantu languages of the northern Bantu borderland in 1985. A more in-depth linguistic and sociolinguistic survey on Bila was conducted by Boone (1993). Comparative results with other related languages are provided in Wit (1994), and word lists containing 250 words of twelve Bantu languages in the area are found in Wit and Hasselaar (1995).

This chapter contains the first results of a period of field work on the language which took place in Mambasa in 1993, where I worked with a group of Bila speakers on phonological, morphological, and syntactic structures.[4] Day after day, the results of our linguistic research showed that Bila does not conform to the expectations when comparing it with the closely related languages Bhele and Komo, but that this Bantu language of the northern Bantu borderland has developed a number of interesting and unusual features. I first reported on the vowel system and the tone system in two conference papers (1994b and 1995). Information from these papers has been reworked for the section on the phonology of Bila, below. Some of the data in the sections on nominal morphology and verbal morphology below were briefly cited in the above-mentioned articles, but only for the purpose of exemplifying phonological or tonological features. In this chapter, a lot of new data are provided focusing on nominal and verbal morphology.

2 PHONOLOGY

2.1 Vowels

Bila has a nine-vowel system with ATR-based vowel harmony, not like Komo, Bhele, and the others in its group, but like Budu, Nyali, Ndaka, and others in the neighboring subgroup.

[+ATR]	i		u
[−ATR]	ɪ		ʊ
[+ATR]	e		o
[−ATR]	ɛ	a	ɔ

The verbal system shows these nine vowels most clearly. Disyllabic noun roots, however, present some interesting co-occurrence restrictions between V_1 and V_2, which are a clear reminder of a seven-vowel system, like the other languages in the subgroup to which Bila belongs. It seems, therefore, that Bila is in the process of exchanging its original seven-vowel system for a nine-vowel system.

In the following subsections, we will first look at the vowels in the verbal system, and subsequently treat different aspects of the vowels in the nominal system.

2.1.1 Vowels in the verbal system

The verbal system shows a clear contrast between nine vowels, with ATR-based vowel harmony. Identical systems are found in the languages of the other subgroup of Bantu languages: Budu, Nyali, Vanuma, and probably Ndaka, spoken immediately to the west of Bila.

[−ATR]		[+ATR]	
ɪ	ʊ	i	u
ɛ	ɔ	e	o
	a		

Nine-vowel qualities contrast in monosyllabic verb roots. There is no infinitive prefix, and the verb-final vowel is underlyingly -á, with -ó as its [+ATR] counterpart in this position only.

mɪd-á	'to swallow'	pìk-ó	'to come'
chéch-á	'to run'	més-ó	'to put upright'
támb-á	'to walk'		

hɔ́t-á	'to insult'	*njók-ó*	'to play, dance'
ɓʊl-á	'to pull'	*kúmb-ó*	'to carry'

Two verbs have been found which do not fit the vowel-harmony pattern in that their root-vowel is /a/, [−ATR], whereas they take the suffix *-ó*, as if they were [+ATR]. In both, C_2 is a palatal(ized) consonant, which is probably causing the final vowel to be [+ATR].

pachó	'to close'
lalyó	'to wipe'

2.1.2 Vowels in the nominal system

Noun roots (with or without a prefix) containing two identical vowels show a contrast between seven vowels only.

The following are examples of CVCV nouns without prefix.

hĩhi	'bird, sp.'
héle	'snake, sp.'
ɓéɓέ	'sheath for knife'
ɓáɓá	'quiver for arrows'
ɓɔ́mbɔ	'arm'
dodó	'earth'
ɓúlu	'leaf, sp.'

The following are examples of CVCV nouns with the prefix *e-/ε-*. Nouns with two identical [+ATR] vowels /i/, /e/, /o/, or /u/ take the prefix *e-*, and nouns with two identical vowels /ε/, /a/, or /ɔ/ take the [−ATR] prefix *ε-*. There are no words with two identical vowels */ɪ/ or */ʊ/. So, once again, these noun roots display contrast between seven-vowel qualities only.

ekingí	'mortar'
esélé	'crown'
εɓéle	'breast'
εdăka	'tongue'
εɓɔ́kɔ	'throat'
eɓókò	'banana'
ekúpù	'navel'

When looking at noun roots containing two different vowels, the following observations can be made:

1 The vowels /e/ and /o/ are mutually exclusive with /ε/ and /ɔ/, a restriction also found in the other seven-vowel languages.

mbɔ́tè	'okapi'	*sóngé*	'moon'
ngbεkɔ́	'big brother'	*sembó*	'flour'

2 The vowels /ɪ/ and /ʊ/ only occur in V_1-position when V_2 is occupied by /ε/, /ɔ/, or /a/. If /ɪ/ and /ʊ/ only occurred in V_1-position before /ε/ and /ɔ/, like in the following examples, they could be considered allophones of /i/ and /u/.

kɪpὲ	'leg'	*ɓʊtε*	'cow'
lɪnyɔ́	'dew'	*súɓɔ́*	'stomach'

However, since /ɪ/ and /ʊ/ also occur in V₁-position before /a/, a nine-vowel contrast is found in that particular environment. When V₂ is /a/, it appears that, in fact, there is contrast between /i/ and /ɪ/ on the one hand, and /u/ and /ʊ/ on the other hand in V₁-position, and consequently between nine vowel qualities.

ngìmá	'snake, sp.'
njíkà	'hand'
èpà	'father'
kpèká	'tortoise'
ɓáɓá	'quiver for arrows'
njɔ́ka	'snake'
ngoyá	'pig'
pʊnga	'rice'
kúha	'small antelope'

Some examples of near-minimal contrast between the two [+high] vowels in V₁-position of CVCV and CVV roots are:

[+ATR]	*ngìmá*	'snake, sp.'	*kúha*	'small antelope'
[−ATR]	*ngíná*	'tree, sp.'	*kʊ́ma*	'place'
[+ATR]	*kipà*	'snake, sp.'	*súa*	'day'
[−ATR]	*kíma*	'thing'	*sʊ́à*	'arrow'

It is not clear whether there is contrast between /i/ and /ɪ/ on the one hand, and /u/ and /ʊ/ on the other hand when they appear in V₂-position. When the vowel /a/ is found in V₁-position, only the [+ATR] high vowels /i/ and /u/ have been found to occur as V₂ so far.

káli	'woman'	*kàtù*	'bird, sp.'
pasi	'peel, shell, bark'	*njáku*	'ant, sp.'
tápì	'branch'	*pàngú*	'squirrel, sp.'

The petrified noun-class prefix alternates between *e-* and *ɛ-*, as in Komo and Bhele, which each have a seven-vowel system. However, since Bila has a nine-vowel system, the environment causing the alternation is not exactly identical. In Komo and Bhele, the prefix *ɛ-* is only found when the root contains the vowels /ɛ/ and/or /ɔ/; in all other cases, preceding the vowels /i/, /u/, and /a/, the *e-*prefix is used. However, in Bila, the alternation now corresponds to the ATR-value of the root or stem, as exemplified below.

[+ATR] roots/stems:

elíhé	'day'	*énjèkù*	'tree, sp.'
etita	'tribe'	*ehelí*	'advice'
elóli	'clothes'	*esúmbí*	'price'
ekómbu	'armpit'	*ekumó*	'work'

[−ATR] roots/stems:

ɛndíka	'horn of animal'	*ɛkʊ́ndɔ*	'love'
ɛpìnjé	'squirrel, sp.'	*ɛlʊ́ká*	'hoe'
étɛkɔ̀	'evening'	*ɛkɔ́lɛ*	'nail'
ɛtɛla	'tree, sp.'		

Roots in which V₁ is occupied by /a/ are treated as [+ATR] when V₂ is the [+ATR] vowel /e/ (and probably also /o/; no examples available).

etálè   'stone'
éɓalé   'two'

Roots in which V₁ is /a/ are treated as [−ATR] when V₂ is the [−ATR] vowel /ɔ/ (and probably also /ɛ/; no examples available), but also when V₂ is /i/ or /u/, which can be considered a neutralization of the contrast of [+ATR] and [−ATR] high vowels, since /ɪ/ and /ʊ/ never occur in this position.

ɛkákɔ   'palm of hand'
ɛɓámbu   'tree, sp.'
èkàní   'folktale'

2.2 Consonants

Bila does not have a very large consonant inventory.

	Bilabial	Alveolar	Palatal	Velar	Labial-Velar	Glottal
Implosives	ɓ	ɗ				
Vl. stops	p	t	ch [tʃ]	k	kp	
Vd. stops	−	−	−	−	−	
Prenas. stops	mb [ᵐb]	nd [ⁿd]	nj [ndʒ]	ng [ŋg]	ngb [ŋᵐgb]	
Vl. fricatives	Φ	s				h
Nasals	m	n	ny [ɲ]			
Approximants		l	y		w	

The following observations can be made:

1 Whenever the Bombi dialect (spoken around Mambasa) has /h/, the Nyaku dialect (spoken around Lolwa, further to the east) has /Φ/: e.g. ahé ~ aΦé 'path', and kího ~ kíΦo 'night'. I have inserted both /Φ/ and /h/ in the chart to cover both dialects.
2 The chart shows one other peculiar thing, namely an empty row: there are no voiced egressive stops. There is a series of voiceless stops and a series of prenasalized voiced stops. In addition, there are implosives, but only at the bilabial and alveolar points of articulation.

A comparative study with Komo and Bhele words which contain voiced egressive stops has shown that in Bila, a sound shift must have taken place in which all voiced stops have become voiceless: the bilabial, alveolar, velar, and labial-velar voiced stops have become voiceless stops: p, t, k, kp; the voiced palatal affricate has become a voiceless sibilant: s.

The following set may serve as example, and could easily be extended to cover more data.[5]

Komo	Bhele	Bila	
b	b	p	
tébá	tébá	tépà	'to laugh'
ntábe	ntábi	tápì	'branch'
d	d	t	
demá	demá	tìmá	'to deceive'
didá	didá	tìtò	'to descend'

j	j	s	
jɔ́	jɔ́	sɔ̀	'basket'
jóngá	jóngá	sùngá	'to boil (intr.)'

g	g	k	
ágɔ́	ágɔ́	ákɔ̀	'bat'
gabá	gabá	kàpà	'to divide'

gb	gb	kp	
gbómá	gbómá	kpùmá	'to bark'
gbútu	gbútu	kpǔtu	'stick, stool'

This sound shift in Bila has repercussions for the tonal system as will be seen in §2.3.

2.3 Tone

Bila being a Bantu language, one would expect to find a two-tone system with or without downstep. However, when making a first attempt at analysing nouns and verbs in isolation, it appears that a two-tone analysis, even with downstep, does not yield a satisfactory result in that it cannot account for the various surface tonal melodies found. Minimal pairs and sets like the following rule out an analysis into two tones underlyingly.

súà	'arrow without poison'	mmbé	'tree'
súa	'day'	mmbe	'back'
súà	'fish, sp.'	m̀mbè	'fish, sp.'
ɛkaní	'thoughts'	apúlá	'baboon'
èkàní	'folktale'	àpùlá	'tree, sp.'
etítí	'bird, sp.'	éka	'to hear'
ètìtì	'banana, sp.'	ékà	'to wash'

My conclusion is therefore that Bila has three underlying tones synchronically, High, Mid, and Low, which I call High (H, acute accent), Low (L, zero marking), and extra-Low (xL, grave accent) respectively, for the sake of comparison with the neighboring languages Komo and Bhele.

In addition to the three level tones, there are two rising tones: one from L to H, / ˘ /, and one from xL to H, /ˇ/. These rising contours may occur on any non-final syllable in nouns, though are also found on final syllables in the verbal system. An LH rising tone can never be preceded by an xL tone, nor can an xL tone be preceded by an L tone.

LH	hǐhi	LH.L	'bird, sp.'
	elǔlu	L.LH.L	'waste'
	mǎ	LH	'to destroy'
xLH	ngbĕngbɛ	xLH.L	'bird, sp.'
	èkǎla	xL.xLH.L	'grief'
	ápŏlo	H.xLH.L	'earthen cooking pot'
	átĕtè	H.xLH.xL	'leaf, sp.'
	sǎ	xLH	'to do'

In addition, Bila also has downstep of H tone, though not as a result of H-spreading and subsequent delinking of L tones, but in certain grammatical environments, the most significant of which is the boundary between Verb and Object. I suggest a floating L tone at this syntactic boundary, which lowers the register in such a way that a following H tone is lowered one step, namely to the level of L, as exemplified with the words *míkí* 'child' *kíma* 'thing', and *ɓáꜜwá* 'who(m)?'.

mimoní ꜜ *míkí*			'I have seen the child.'
I-see	child		
omoní ꜜ *míkí*	*kó?*		'Where have you seen the child?'
you-see	child	where	
osúmbí ꜜ *kíma*	*sínó?*		'What have you bought?'
you-buy	thing	what	
wěꜜɓóní ꜜ *ɓáꜜwá*			'Whom (pl.) have you seen?'
you.pl-see	who		

Downstep is also frequently found within noun phrases between the head noun and certain modifiers. It seems that a number of H-toned grammatical morphemes are preceded or followed by a floating L tone, causing downstep, and that there are (derived) lexical items, nouns and verb infinitives with a tonal melody containing a downstep.

It seems plausible that Bila once had a two-tone system with downstep, like its genetically most closely related neighbors Komo and Bhele. Synchronically, Bila must be analyzed as having a three-tone system, with still 'symptoms' of a two-tone system present.

We also need to assume a link between the sound shift from voiced obstruents to voiceless obstruents and the development of the third tone, extra-Low, since this xL tone is very frequently attested in words with a voiceless obstruent which corresponds to a voiced obstruent in the neighboring languages. Voiced obstruents are well-known for their tone-lowering effect. However, this is not evident in Komo and Bhele, but rather in some languages spoken to the north and possibly west of Bila: Mayogo (Ubangi), a three-tone language with LM and LH rising tones as a result of depressor consonants, and both Budu and Lika, Bantu languages of different subgroups, which exhibit LH rising tones in syllables with an initial depressor consonant.

I therefore believe that the xL tone is new in the system, and has emerged as a result of a process in which depressor consonants once caused tonal depression, presumably lowered L tones, and apparently also H tones, to an xL level. Subsequently, a sound shift must have taken place, in which voiced egressive stops, the depressor consonants, became voiceless, and thus caused the xL level to become contrastive, which has resulted in the present-day three-tone system.

3 NOMINAL MORPHOLOGY

3.1 Nouns

Bila does not have a typical noun-class system as found in many other Bantu languages, with regular singular and plural class prefixes to the nouns; it only has petrified remnants of such a system. Instead, the language has a system which differentiates between animate and inanimate nouns and in which animate nouns have separate singular and plural forms, whereas inanimate nouns only have one form used for both singular and plural.[6]

A few [+human] nouns have a syllabic nasal as singular prefix, alternating with 6a- in the plural (or m-/6- before a vowel); most other [+animate] nouns have a *zero*/ 6a- alternation.

N-kpá	6a-kpá	'man, person'[7]
N-6ila	6a-6ila	'Bila person'
N-kíngí	6a-kíngí	'deaf and dumb person'
mĕkálí	6ĕkálí	'sister'
mĕlókó	6ĕlókó	'brother'
emá	6emá	'mother'
èpà	6èpà	'father'
mbúté	6a-mbúté	'pygmy'
mwamé	6a-mwamé	'king'
ngèndɔ	6à-ngèndɔ	'visitor'
míkí	6a-míkí	'child'
léú	6a-léú	'twins'
kɔtá	6a-kɔtá	'young person'
sàlà	6à-sàlà	'boy'
kálí	6a-kálí	'woman'
sɪka	6a-sɪka	'girl'
mémé	6a-mémé	'goat'
njɔ́ka	6a-njɔ́ka	'snake'
sú	6a-sú	'fish'
mbongó	6a-mbongó	'elephant'

The following are examples of recognizable but petrified remnants of noun-class prefixes, whereby all prefixes with a vowel other than /a/ have two forms, the basic one used for roots with [−ATR] and the other one for roots with [+ATR] vowels.

a-, amá- (with variants *amé-* or *amé-* after coalescence with the initial [+ATR] or [−ATR] high vowel of a V-initial stem), and *àpà-* (with variants *àpá-, àpĕ-* or *àpĕ-* after coalescence with the initial vowel of a V-initial stem): used predominantly for trees, plants, and small animals like birds, fishes, insects. The prefixes *amá-* and *àpà-* are obviously related to the words *emá/6emá* 'mother' and *èpà/6èpà* 'father'. Especially the prefix *amá-* occurs very frequently.

a6ɛnjé	'banana, sp.'
akélé	'antelope, sp.'
alomo	'fish, sp.'
akálé	'vine, sp.'
amáhɔhɔ	'small brown snake'
amákisálápè	'scorpion'
amákókó	'big black ant'
amátòngòlòlò	'tree, sp.'
amékʋá	'flea'
améuli	'chameleon'
àpàlélé	'tree, sp.'
àpăkùmó	'banana, sp.'
àpĕmukù	'bird, sp.'

Other recognizable but petrified prefixes are *ma-*, *kɪ-/ki-*, *ɓʊ-/ɓu-*, and *lɪ-/li-*.

ma- (several uncountables and liquids)

maká	'soot'
màkɔ̀kɔ́	'riddle'
màkyò	'blood'
malɔnga	'words'
manyɛ́	'urine'
mayá	'flowers'

kɪ-/ki-

kɪká	'crab'
kiɗelu	'chin'
kisámo	'hair'
kitói	'ear'
kitúkpu	'hat'

ɓʊ-/ɓu-, / *ɓw-* or *ɓ-* before V (among others some abstract nouns)

ɓʊlambɔ	'earth, world'
ɓùsĕɗe	'anger'
ɓuséki	'desire'
ɓùtùó	'family'
ɓwamɛ́	'kingdom' (cf. *mwamé* 'king')
ɓóki	'honey' (cf. *njóki* 'bee')

lɪ-/li-

lɪmyɔ́	'dew'
lìɓàtà	'duck'

In addition, many words have a recognizable but non-functional nasal prefix, resulting in prenasalization of voiced stops; words with other consonants have no prefix. These probably represent former class 9/10 words, with a variety of meanings, including animals. There are also a number of nouns derived from verbs with no prefix which fall in this category (see §3.2).

ɓɔ́mbɔ	'arm'	*mbongó*	'elephant'
ɓutɛ	'cow'	*mbɪká*	'cooking pot'
chɔ̀ɗɔ̀	'mud'	*mbuko*	'seed'
kásá	'leaf'	*mbúò*	'rain'
kondó	'tail'	*ǹnjì*	'village'
kɔ́kɔ́	'chicken'	*nnja*	'hunger'
kɔ̀sɔ̀	'skin'	*ngákà*	'jaw'
kúò	'bone'	*ngòpò*	'body'
mɛ́mɛ́	'goat'	*ngoyá*	'pig'
nyama	'animal'	*ngɔ́mbɛ́*	'clothes'
nyɔkɔ	'mouth'	*njíkà*	'hand'
sóngé	'moon, month'	*njóki*	'bee'
tápì	'branch'	*njɔ́ka*	'snake'

The prefix *ɛ-/e-* is the most frequent, and is used for things, but also for plants, trees, insects, fishes, birds, and also, in conjunction with a [+ATR] suffix *-i* to derive nouns from verbs (see §3.2).

ebókò	'banana'	*εbέlε*	'breast'
ebundu	'clouds'	*εbele*	'liver'
ekingi	'mortar'	*εbɔ́kɔ*	'throat'
ekómbu	'armpit'	*èkànì*	'folktale'
ekundú	'intestines'	*εkɔ́lε*	'nail'

There are no infinitive prefixes.

The only two nouns which might have a remote possibility of incorporation of a former class 17 prefix *ku-* would be:

kúma 'place'
kúpà 'heaven'

Then, there are the following two locative adverbs, possibly derived from classes 16 and 17 respectively.

-wá	'where?'
-kó	'where?'
òkě ! kó/òkě ! wá	'where did you go?'
endú kó/endú wá	'where is the house?'
omoní ! míki kó/wá	'where did you see the child?'

3.2 Verb – noun derivation

The following are examples of a quite productive system of verb–noun derivation by means of the prefix *ε-/e-* and a nominalizing suffix *-i*. This [+ATR] suffix *-i* changes the vowels of a [−ATR] verb stem to [+ATR], and the prefix is therefore at all times the [+ATR] variant *e-*.

Noun derived from a [+ATR] verb root:

ebelí	'anger'	<	*beló*	'to be angry'

Nouns derived from [−ATR] verb roots/stems:

ehelí	'advice'	<	*hεlá*	'to advise, teach'
ehóti	'insult'	<	*hɔ́tá*	'to insult'
elehí	'payment'	<	*lεhá*	'to pay'
elókí	'vomit'	<	*lɔ́ká*	'to vomit'
elótí	'dream'	<	*lɔ́tá*	'to dream'
ememí	'prayer, request'	<	*mεmá*	'to pray, request'
esúmbi	'price'	<	*súmbá*	'to buy'

Some nouns derived from verbs using the *e*-prefix, but without the *-i* suffix:

elúhú	'words'	<	*lúhúó*	'to speak'
ekŭbo	'theft'	<	*kubó*	'to steal'

There are also examples of zero derivation, or of derivation by tonal changes only:

é!kaná	'agreement'	<	*é!kaná*	'to agree'
njókó	'game'	<	*njókó*	'to play'
susó	'wind'	<	*susó*	'to blow (of the wind)'

támbá	'walk, trip'	<	*támbá*	'to walk, travel'
kúmbó	'load'	<	*kúmbó*	'to carry'
ɓíno	'dance'	<	*ɓínó*	'to dance'
ɓókúlo	'question'	<	*ɓókúló*	'to ask'

3.3 Agreement

Bila shows agreement between a noun and a following adjective, numeral, or demonstrative. It is a system differentiating, once again, between inanimate, animate singular, and animate plural nouns. Modifiers to inanimate nouns may take the following prefixes *á-, ɛ́-/é-, Ń-*. For animate nouns in the singular, *ma-* or *mú-/mú-* are used; animate plural forms take *ɓá-* or *ɓú-/ɓú-*.

	Adjectives	Num.: 2, 3, 5	Demonstratives
[−animate]	*á-*	*ɛ́-/é-*	*Ń-*
[+animate, sg.]	*ma-*		*mú-/mú-*
[+animate, pl.]	*ɓá-*	*ɓú/ɓú*	*ɓú-/ɓú-*

In a noun-plus-noun associative construction, the various connectives with agreement marking which are used are *á, ma, ɓá*, as well as a lexically determined *sá/só*. In the pronominal possessive construction, a distinction must be made between alienable and inalienable possessive constructions according to the set of pronoun roots used. The prefixes used with the pronoun roots for the alienable possessive construction are *á-, ma-*, and *ɓá-*. In the inalienable possessive construction, the prefixes used with the pronoun roots are: *á-, ó-/ɔ-, má-, ɓá-*, and *sá-, só-/sɔ-*.

A special marker *lí* may be found between the noun and the modifier in some of the constructions obligatorily, in others optionally, and in yet other constructions, it is obligatorily absent. The function of this marker is not entirely clear at present.

3.3.1 Adjectives

The following are some adjectives in their citation forms, with the [−animate] agreement marker *á-*:

á-hí	'black'	*á-ngbó*	'big'	*á-tɔ*	'new'
á-pù	'white'	*á-si*	'big'	*á-njá*	'good'
á-njɛ	'red'	*á-ngbí*	'short'	*á-kpɛ́*	'old'

They take the concord markers *á-* (others take *ɛ́-/é-*, lexically determined by the adjective, it seems), *ma-* and *ɓá-*, as shown above, and follow the noun they modify. With the inanimate nouns, the marker *lí* obligatorily precedes the adjective. Its vowel /í/ is deleted when the following word begins with a vowel. It is always downstepped from a preceding H tone. In most cases, the adjective root is reduplicated when the noun is in the plural.

[−animate]	[+animate, sg.]	[+animate, pl.]
endú 'house'	*míkí* 'child'	*ɓamíkí* 'children'
endú (ꜜl)*-áhí*	*míkí mangbí*	*ɓamíkí ɓángbíꜜngbí*
endú (ꜜl)*-átɔ*	*míkí manjá*	*ɓamíkí ɓánjáꜜnjá*

3.3.2 Numerals

The numeral roots from 1–10 are presented below. Only the numerals 2, 3, and 5 have a high-toned prefix *é-/é-*.

kǎɗi	'one'	*mʊtúɓá*	'six'
éɓalé	'two'	*soɓé-lalɔ*	'seven'
ésálɔ	'three'	*lalɔ*	'eight'
sìnà	'four'	*soɓé-kómi*	'nine'
étánɔ	'five'	*mɔkɔ́*	'ten'

These are their default forms, used with inanimate nouns. When used with animate nouns, they take the high-toned prefix *ɓú-/ɓú-*. As an idiosyncratic exception, the initial *ɓ-* in *ɓúɓalé* has been lost.

endú	'house(s)'	*ɓakpá*	'people'
endú éɓalé	'two houses'	*ɓakpá úɓalé*	'two people'
endú ésálɔ	'three houses'	*ɓakpá ɓúsálɔ*	'three people'
endú étánɔ	'five houses'	*ɓakpá ɓútánɔ*	'five people'

The question word *éngá* 'how many' should be included in the set of numerals, since it also takes the same prefix when used with [+human] nouns:

endú éngá   'how many houses?'   *ɓakpá ɓúngá*   'how many people?'

3.3.3 Demonstratives

The following demonstrative roots have been found:

-ndé	'this/these, close to speaker'
-ndɔ́	'that/those, close to hearer'
-ndohú	'that/those, away from speaker and hearer'

The demonstratives used for animate nouns take the prefixes as shown in the table above. The prefix agreeing with inanimate nouns is a syllabic nasal, in this case preceding a prenasalized consonant.

In addition, a downstep is found at the boundary between noun and demonstrative, as is shown in the following examples:

mbátá ! *ńndé*	'this chair'
míki ! *múndɔ́*	'that child'
ɓamíki ! *ɓúndohú*	'those children'

3.3.4 Associative construction

The following are examples of noun-plus-noun associative constructions with the connectives *á* (inanimate), *ma* (animate sg.), and *ɓá* (animate pl.). The marker *lí* is optional.

ngómbé (¹*l*)-*á míki*		'the clothes of the child'
clothes	child	
kɔndɔ́ (¹*l*)-*á*	(*ɓa*)*nyama*	'the tail(s) of the animal(s)'
tail	animal(s)	

míkí (¹*lí*) *ma kálí*		'the child of the woman'	
child	woman		
kálí (¹*lí*) *ma mwamɛ́*		'the wife of the king'	
woman	king		
ɓakálí (¹*lí*)	*ɓá mwamɛ́*	'the wives of the king'	
women	king		

3.3.5 Pronominal possession

Pronominal possession is quite complex in Bila. First of all, a distinction must be made between alienable and inalienable possessive constructions on the basis of two different possessive pronoun roots in the first person singular only. In addition to that, the connectives used as prefixes for the alienable possession are the same as those used in the associative construction; however, the ones used in the inalienable possessive construction are not the same, as is shown in the examples below.

Possessive pronoun roots

	alienable possession	inalienable possession	
1sg.	*-mɔ*	*-mi*	'my'
2sg.	*-kɔ*	*-kɔ*	'your'
3sg.	*-kɛ́*	*-kɛ́*	'his/her'
1pl.	*-sú*	*-sú*	'our'
2pl.	*-nú*	*-nú*	'your'
3pl.	*-ɓɔ́*	*-ɓɔ́*	'their'

There are three paradigms for the alienable possessive construction, differentiating between inanimate, animate singular, and animate plural nouns. Their respective prefixes are: *á-*, *ma-*, and *ɓá-*.

In addition, the marker *lí* is obligatorily used following [−animate] nouns, and is optionally found following [+animate] nouns. The vowel of the marker *lí* is elided when followed by the [−animate] prefix *á-*. Following a noun ending in H tone, *lí* is downstepped. When the marker *lí* is not present, there is no downstep between the noun and the possessive pronoun.

Paradigm for inanimate nouns:

endú ¹*l-ámɔ*	'my house(s)'
endú ¹*l-ákɔ*	'your house(s)'
endú ¹*l-ákɛ́*	'his/her house(s)'
endú ¹*l-ású*	'our house(s)'
endú ¹*l-ánú*	'your house(s)'
endú ¹*l-áɓɔ́*	'their house(s)'

Paradigms for animate nouns:

míkí (¹*lí*) *mamɔ*	'my child'	*ɓamíkí* (¹*lí*) *ɓámɔ*	'my children'
míkí (¹*lí*) *makɔ*	'your child'	*ɓamíkí* (¹*lí*) *ɓákɔ*	'your children'
míkí (¹*lí*) *makɛ́*	'his/her child'	*ɓamíkí* (¹*lí*) *ɓákɛ́*	'his/her children'
míkí (¹*lí*) *masú*	'our child'	*ɓamíkí* (¹*lí*) *ɓású*	'our children'
míkí (¹*lí*) *manú*	'your child'	*ɓamíkí* (¹*lí*) *ɓánú*	'your children'
míkí (¹*lí*) *maɓɔ́*	'their child'	*ɓamíkí* (¹*lí*) *ɓáɓɔ́*	'their children'

3.3.6 Inalienable possession

In the inalienable pronominal possessive construction, the possessive pronoun immediately follows the noun; the marker *lí* is not used. The series of possessive pronoun roots differs from those used in the alienable possessive construction only in the 1st person singular: *-mi*. However, several series of prefixes are used for agreement. The choice of series seems unpredictable and must therefore be lexically determined.[8] Could it be that we find remnants of a class system here? The forms with *bá-* are used for plural forms (mainly with the kinship terms).

The following series of possessive pronoun roots preceded by a prefix with connective are found in the language:

ámi/ómi	sámi/sómi	mámi	bámi
ákɔ/ɔ́kɔ	sákɔ/sɔ́kɔ	mákɔ	bákɔ
áké/ɔ́ké	sáké/sɔ́ké	máké	báké
ású/ósú	sású/sósú	mású	bású
ánú/ónú	sánú/sónú	mánú	bánú
ábɔ́/ɔ́bɔ́	sábɔ́/sɔ́bɔ́	mábɔ́	bábɔ́

The series with *má-* follows in several instances a noun with a petrified *ma-* prefix.

màkyò mámi	'my blood'
măku mámi	'my knee(s)'

The series with the *-ɔ-/-o-* connective vowel follow nearly exclusively [+ATR] nouns, though it must be noted that the connective takes the ATR-value of the possessive pronoun root. The series with the connective vowel *-a-* follow in the majority of cases [−ATR] nouns, though not exclusively. An exceptional case is e.g.:

sisó mámi	'my vein(s)'
sisó máké	'his vein(s)'

The semantic subset of nouns which take the forms for the inalienable possessive construction contains the traditional categories: kinship terms, body parts, and some other nouns which normally have an inherent relationship to a possessor.

njíkà sámi	'my hand(s)'		kitói sómi	'my ear(s)'
njíkà sáké	'his hand(s)'		kitói sɔ́kɛ	'his ear(s)'
mʊyá sámi	'my sister-in-law'		amái sómi	'my sister-in-law'
mʊyá sáké	'his sister-in-law'		amái sɔ́ké	'her sister-in-law'
mmɔ ámi	'my head'		endelu ómi	'my beard'
mmɔ áké	'his head'		endelu ɔ́ké	'his beard'
kʊlá ámi	'my paternal aunt'		kió ómi	'my brother-in-law'
kʊlá áké	'his paternal aunt'		kió ɔ́ké	'his brother-in-law'
bakʊlá bámi	'my paternal aunts'			
bakʊlá báké	'his paternal aunts'			

4 VERBAL MORPHOLOGY

The first subsection presents infinitives, the basis for the following subsections on inflection and derivation. Only a limited number of different verb paradigms are available for the present study. More paradigms will undoubtedly come to light with further study.

Interpretations of the structure and meaning of these paradigms are provided, but may need to be adapted when further data are available.

4.1 Infinitives

Infinitives are formed by the verb stem followed by a verb-final suffix -*á* or -*ó* following a [−ATR] or a [+ATR] stem respectively.

hɔlá	'to rot'	hikó	'to build'
ɓulá	'to pull'	pìkó	'to come'
ɓétíkáná	'to be beaten'	ɓongísó	'to repair'

There is a three-way lexical tone contrast between H, L, and xL, realized on the first stem vowel.

H	ɓíkó	'to be many'
L	hikó	'to build'
xL	pìkó	'to come'

Examples of lexical minimal pairs:

ɓúlá	'to lack'	kɔ́ɓá	'to be silent'
ɓulá	'to pull'	kɔ̀ɓá	'to finish'

Originally, there must have been a two-way lexical tone contrast in the verbal system. The three-way lexical tone contrast is due to an historical process, namely the development of the xL tone through tonal depression of voiced obstruents in C_1 position and the subsequent sound shift from voiced to voiceless obstruents. Syllables with voiceless obstruents which are not historically derived from voiced obstruents may, of course, carry H and L tones.

All verbs with an initial xL tone followed by the verb-final H-toned suffix -*á* or -*ó* have an initial voiceless obstruent.

pèɗá	'to take'
tèmá	'to cultivate'
sùngá	'to be boiling, hot'
kɔ̀ɓá	'to finish'
kpèɗó	'to be deep'

When C_2 was an original depressor consonant, now a voiceless obstruent, the H tone of the verb-final suffix has become xL. If it concerns an underlyingly H-tone verb, the result-ant tonal pattern of the verb is H.xL; if it concerns an underlyingly L-tone verb, the L has assimilated to the xL of the second syllable, and the result is an xL.xL tone pattern.

H-tone verbs: H.xL		L-tone verbs: xL.xL	
ɓúkà	'to smoke'	lɔ̀kà	'to bewitch'
tépà	'to laugh'	mèkà	'to shine'
ɗĕpà	'to tarry'	tìkpò	'to shake'

Some verbs have a CV-radical, followed by the verb-final -*á* or -*ó*. All three lexical tone classes are represented. The following are some tonal minimal pairs.

kúó	'to die'	túá	'to pierce'	ɓúá	'to tie loosely'
kùó	'to fall'	tùá	'to pound'	ɓuá	'to take (from the hand)'

There are several monosyllabic verbs, also with a three-way lexical tone contrast. Each of these verbs has its inherent lexical tone, followed by the H tone of the verb-final suffix (which has merged with the vowel of the verb root), resulting in H, LH, and xLH melodies on the monosyllabic verbs. All verbs with xLH have an initial voiceless obstruent, which, once again, shows the historical process of tone lowering through a voiced obstruent and subsequent sound shift from voiced to voiceless.

H		L		xL	
ɓá	'to be'	mǎ	'to destroy'	kǎ	'to go'
pá	'to give'			sǎ	'to do'
má	'to get up'			kpǎ	'to carry away'

A number of infinitives have an initial prefix é-/é-, in many cases followed by downstep. The semantics of such verbs show that this morpheme represents an incorporated reflexive pronoun, or in other cases the incorporation of an inanimate object pronoun to mark transitivity with an inanimate object.

kpesyó	'to scratch'	mikpesí ! míkí	'I scratch the children'
ékpesyó	'to scratch oneself'	měkpesí	'I scratch myself'
múá	'to kill' (+animate O, sg.)		
é'múá	'to commit suicide, kill oneself'		

é-/é- as reflexive pronoun or marking an obligatory object:

ékà	'to wash'
é'ká	'to hear'
épò	'to know'
ékó	'to be seated'
é'kúó	'to open'
é'kpá	'to catch'
é'mbá	'to cook'

4.2 Inflection

4.2.1 Pronouns and subject prefixes

The following table shows both the independent pronouns as well as the subject prefixes.

	Pronouns	Subject prefixes
1sg.	imɛ	m(i)-
2sg.	uwɛ	ɔ-/o- ~ ɛ-/e-
3sg.	éyé	a-
1pl.	ɓésú	ɓɪ-/ɓi-
2pl.	ɓénú	ɓɔ-/ɓo- ~ ɓɛ-/ɓe-
3pl.	éɓɔ	ɓá-

In 2sg. and 2pl., there is individual variation between the back vowels ɔ-/o- and ɓɔ-/ɓo- on the one hand, and the front vowels ɛ-/e- and ɓɛ-/ɓe- on the other hand. In the paradigms below, the forms with the back vowels are used.

The choice between the [−ATR] and the [+ATR] variants is determined by the ATR-value of the following vowel.

pìkó	'to come'	*támbá*	'to walk'
ò-pìkí	'you.sg. have come'	*ɔ-támbí*	'you. sg. have walked'
ɓò-pìkí	'you.pl. have come'	*ɓɔ-támbí*	'you. pl. have walked'

All subject prefixes except 3pl. have inherently an L tone. However, when any of the L-tone prefixes is found preceding a verb stem beginning with an xL tone, the prefix assimilates and surfaces as xL. The 3pl. prefix *ɓá-* has an H tone.

The following are some examples of verb forms with the 3sg. L-tone pronoun *a-* and the 3pl. H-tone pronoun *ɓá-* used with the H-tone verb *chéchá* 'to run', the L-tone verb *ɓulá* 'to pull' and the xL-tone verb *pìkó* 'to come'.

a-chéchí	'he has run'
ɓá-chéchí	'they have run'
a-ɓulí	'he has pulled'
ɓá-ɓulí	'they have pulled'
à-pìkí	'he has come'
ɓá-pìkí	'they have come'

4.2.2 Perfect

The Perfect is marked by a [+ATR] suffix *-í*. Since [+ATR] is dominant, it changes the vowels of [−ATR] roots as well as any [−ATR] vowels of the subject prefixes into [+ATR]. The vowel /a/ in the root does not change, and the subject prefix preceding such verbs remains [−ATR].

With verbs of action, this paradigm marks a completed action in the recent past, with emphasis on the present relevance. The most common translation for verbs of action is: 'he has …': *a-támb-í* 'he has walked'. With verbs of state, the Perfect marks the result of a process getting to the present state: *ě⌐ní* 'he sees' (< *é⌐ná* 'to see').

	Infinitive		Perfect, 3sg.	
[−ATR]	*mɪɗ-á*	'to swallow'	*a-mɪɗ-í*	'he has swallowed'
	chéch-á	'to run'	*a-chéch-i*	'he has run'
	támb-á	'to walk'	*a-támb-í*	'he has walked'
	hɔt-á	'to insult'	*a-hót-í*	'he has insulted'
	ɓul-á	'to pull'	*a-ɓul-i*	'he has pulled'
[+ATR]	*pìk-ó*	'to come'	*à-pìk-í*	'he has come'
	més-ó	'to put upright'	*a-més-í*	'he has put upright'
	pach-ó	'to close'	*a-pach-í*	'he has closed'
	njók-ó	'to dance, play'	*a-njók-í*	'he has danced'
	kúmb-ó	'to carry'	*a-kúmb-í*	'he has carried'

In the case of verbs which have an xL tone on the final syllable, the final H tone of the *-í* suffix causes an xLH contour tone.

ɓúkà	'to smoke'	*a-ɓúkï*	'he has smoked'
kàpà	'to bring'	*à-kàpï*	'he has brought'

With the monosyllabic verbs, the -*i* coalesces with the vowel /a/ of the verb, and is always realised as [+ATR] /e/, carrying the respective H, LH, or xLH tone patterns.

yá	'to hate'	*a-yé*	'he has hated'
mǎ	'to destroy'	*a-mě*	'he has destroyed'
sǎ	'to do'	*à-sě*	'he has done'
kǎ	'to go'	*à-kě*	'he has gone'

The particle *do* may be added to this paradigm as an affirmative marker.

Perfect	3sg.	*a-chéchí (do)*	'he has run'
	3sg.	*a-midí (do)*	'he has swallowed'

To express the Remote Past, the suffix vowel -*i* is lengthened to -*ii*, then obligatorily followed by the particle *do*.

Remote Past	3sg.	*a-chéchíi do*	'he has run (a long time ago)'
	3sg.	*a-midíi do*	'he has swallowed (a long time ago)'

4.2.3 Negation

The negative marker consists of a prefix *ká-*, which precedes the subject prefix. The vowel /a/ of this negative prefix assimilates to the vowel of the subject prefixes singular, and may freely vary with the vowel of the subject prefixes plural. The underlying tone of the subject prefixes 1–3sg. and 1 and 2pl. assimilates to the H tone of the negative prefix.

ká + mi	→	*kám- ~ kim-*
ká + ɔ/o	→	*kɔ́-/kó-*
ká + a	→	*ká-*
ká + 6i	→	*ká6í- ~ kí6í-*
ká + 6ɔ/6o	→	*ká6ɔ́-/ká6ó- ~ kɔ́6ɔ́-/kó6ó-*
ká + 6á	→	*ká6á-*

Negative paradigms corresponding to the Perfect cited above take the negative prefix *ká-* and retain the final [+ATR] -*i* suffix. In the Remote Past, the final vowel -*i* is lengthened, as in the affirmative paradigm. The particle *do* is no longer present.

Perfect		Remote past	
6étá	'to hit'		
kim-6étí	'I have not hit'	*kim-6étíi*	'I did not hit (long ago)'
kó-6étí	'you have not hit'	*kó-6étíi*	'you did not hit'
ká-6étí	'he has not hit'	*ká-6étíi*	'he did not hit'
kí6í-6étí	'we have not hit'	*kí6í-6étíi*	'we did not hit'
kó6ó-6étí	'you have not hit'	*kó6ó-6étíi*	'you did not hit'
ká6á-6étí	'they have not hit'	*ká6á-6étíi*	'they did not hit'
támbá	'to walk'		
kim-támbí	'I have not walked'	*kim-támbíi*	'I did not walk (long ago)'
kɔ́-támbi	'you have not walked'	*kɔ́-támbíi*	'you did not walk'
ká-támbi	'he has not walked'	*ká-támbíi*	'he did not walk'
kí6í-támbí	'we have not walked'	*kí6í-támbíi*	'we did not walk'
kɔ́6ɔ́-támbí	'you have not walked'	*kɔ́6ɔ́-támbíi*	'you did not walk'
ká6á-támbí	'they have not walked'	*ká6á-támbíi*	'they did not walk'

pìkó	'to come'		
kím-pìkí	'I have not come'	*kím-pìkíí*	'I did not come (long ago)'
kó-pìkí	'you have not come'	*kó-pìkíí*	'you did not come'
ká-pìkí	'he has not come'	*ká-pìkíí*	'he did not come'
kíбí-pìkí	'we have not come'	*kíбí-pìkíí*	'we did not come'
kóбó-pìkí	'you have not come'	*kóбó-pìkíí*	'you did not come'
káбá-pìkí	'they have not come'	*káбá-pìkíí*	'they did not come'

4.2.4 Present Continuous

The Present Continuous is formed by the verbal prefix *-á-* followed by the infinitive form of the verb. The vowel of the subject prefix does not merge with this verbal prefix, but each vowel retains its vowel quality and its tone. A downstep is inserted between the H-tone *-á-* and H-tone verbs.

ma-á-ꜜchéchá	'I am running'
ɔ-á-ꜜchéchá	'you are running'
a-á-ꜜchéchá	'he is running'
бɪ-á-ꜜchéchá	'we are running'
бɔ-á-ꜜchéchá	'you are running'
бá-á-ꜜchéchá	'they are running'

ma-á-mɪdǎ	'I am swallowing'
ɔ-á-mɪdǎ	'you are swallowing'
a-á-mɪdǎ	'he is swallowing'
бɪ-á-mɪdǎ	'we are swallowing'
бɔ-á-mɪdǎ	'you are swallowing'
бá-á-mɪdǎ	'they are swallowing'

ma-á-pìkó	'I am coming'
ɔ-á-pìkó	'you are coming'
a-á-pìkó	'he is coming'
бɪ-á-pìkó	'we are coming'
бɔ-á-pìkó	'you are coming'
бá-á-pìkó	'they are coming'

4.2.5 Future

The Future is formed by a verbal suffix *-anɔ́* or *-onɔ́*, following [−ATR] and [+ATR] verb stems respectively. In fact, it is only the first vowel of this suffix which changes according to the regular vowel-harmony rules. The syllable *-nɔ́* is invariable. The L tone of the first syllable of the suffix is realized as xL following an xL tone in the verb stem.

mésó 'to put upright'	*mɪdǎ* 'to swallow'	*pìkó* 'to come'
m-més-onɔ́	*m-mɪd-anɔ́*	*m̀-pìk-ònɔ́*
o-més-onɔ́	*ɔ-mɪd-anɔ́*	*ò-pìk-ònɔ́*
a-més-onɔ́	*a-mɪd-anɔ́*	*à-pìk-ònɔ́*
бi-més-onɔ́	*бɪ-mɪd-anɔ́*	*бì-pìk-ònɔ́*
бo-més-onɔ́	*бɔ-mɪd-anɔ́*	*бò-pìk-ònɔ́*
бá-més-onɔ́	*бá-mɪd-anɔ́*	*бá-pìk-ònɔ́*

The corresponding negative paradigms are formed with the negative prefix *ká-* preceding the affirmative paradigms, including the morphophonological changes as presented earlier. The verbal suffix is *-ɛnɔ́*, for both [−ATR] and [+ATR] verbs.

		mɪdǎ 'to swallow' [−ATR]	*pikó* 'to come' [+ATR]
Fut. aff.	3sg.	*a-mɪd-anɔ́*	*à-pìk-ònɔ́*
Fut. neg.	3sg.	*ká-mɪd-ɛnɔ́*	*ká-pìk-ènɔ́*

4.3 Derivation

Bila has several more or less productive derivational categories which are recognizably Bantu. The causative derivation is very productive. Next is a reciprocal extension, though often without a base verb. There are some examples of what may have been an applicative extension. No passive extension as such has been attested. However, there are a few examples of passive meaning expressed by a non-productive combination of an *-ɪk-* + *-an-* extension.

Quite unusual is the formation of infinitives which take a prefix marking singular or plural animate object. It is obvious that the prefixes relate to the 3sg. and 3pl. concord prefixes seen elsewhere; however, here they are incorporated in the verb stem. Object prefixes are used in addition to these verbal prefixes creating new infinitives.

4.3.1 Causative derivation

The most productive derivation is a causative, marked by the verbal extension *-ís-* [+ATR], which changes any [−ATR] vowels of the verb root to its left into [+ATR]. The verb-final vowel is therefore the [+ATR] *-ó*. Examples are given of base verbs with [+ATR] roots, and with [−ATR] roots.

[+ATR] roots		[−ATR] roots	
ɓeló	'to be angry'	*ɓʊ́tá*	'to be hurting'
ɓelísó	'to make angry'	*ɓútísó*	'to hurt (somebody)'
ɓúngó	'to be lost'	*sʊ́mbá*	'to buy'
ɓúngísó	'to lose'	*súmbísó*	'to sell'
simó	'to go down'	*ɛ́'ná*	'to see'
simísó	'to put down'	*e'nísó*	'to show'
sùsùkó	'to get up'	*ɛ́'lɔ́ká*	'to be healed, saved'
sùsùkísó	'to lift, wake'	*e'lókísó*	'to heal, save (something)'
túmó	'to be filled'	*kákálá*	'to dry, intr.'
túmísó	'to fill'	*kákálísó*	'to dry (something)'
ɛ́'ná	*mɛ̄'ni ' tíko*	'I see the field'	
e'nísó	*mɛ̄'nisí ' tíko*	'I have shown the field'	

4.3.2 Reciprocal derivation

The reciprocal derivation takes the extension *-án-*, or *-ón-* in the [+ATR] environment. The use of the reciprocal extension implies that at least two people are involved in a reciprocal action: talking, agreeing, fighting, following, embracing. Some of these verbs can exclusively take a plural subject prefix. In some cases, there is a base verb and a derived verb; when the semantics require it, no base verb may exist for some meanings, since the action inherently requires more than one person.

tɔmbyá	'to follow'
tɔmbyáná	'to follow each other'
tùngó	'to embrace'
tùngónó	'to embrace each other'
ɛ́ˈká	'to hear'
ɛ́ˈkáná	'to agree'
dɔngà	'to disturb (somebody)'
dɔngáná	'to fight (only with plural subject)'

4.3.3 Applicative derivation

The semi-vowel -y- or the extension -ɪly-/-ɛly- following the verb root may be the remnant of an applicative derivation. This extension can hardly be called productive, since there are very few pairs of verbs without and with the extension. The meanings of the verbs which have no underived counterpart are such that it is plausible that they take a benefactive or locative complement or that such a complement is implied.

mɛm-á	'to ask, beg, pray' + D.O.
mɛm-íly-á	'to ask, beg, pray' + I.O.
mmemí eɓókò	'I asked (for) a banana'
mimemíli ˈnámá ámɪ	'I prayed for my brothers'
pèɗ-á	'to take'
pèɗ-y-á	'to work'
dŭá	'to leave'
dŭ-ély-á	'to leave behind'

Other verbs, without underived counterpart, which may be interpreted as original applicatives:

ɓésyá	'to accept'
ɓɪlyá	'to follow'
kɛɓyá	'to send'
ngʊɗyá	'to tell, explain'

4.3.4 Passive derivation

Two pairs of active/passive verbs have been found. The passive meaning is expressed by a non-productive combination of an -ɪk- + -an- extension and some morphophonological changes, resulting in the following forms:

ɓétá	'to beat'
ɓétíkáná	'to be beaten'
ɓɔkɔtá	'to give birth'
ɓɔkɔcháná	'to be born'

4.3.5 Object animacy and plurality

Bila has an unusual verbal derivational category for a Bantu language, namely infinitives which mark whether the object is animate or inanimate, and if animate, whether it is singular or plural. This process is quite productive, and there are a lot of verbs which have two or even three different forms.

The prefixes used are:

é-/é- for the inanimate object
mʊ- for the animate object, sg.
ɓʊ́- for the animate object, pl.

Morphophonological changes between the prefix and the verb-initial vowel surface as follows:

$$\varepsilon + \varepsilon \; > \; \varepsilon \qquad\quad e + e \; > \; e \qquad\quad \varepsilon + a \; > \; \varepsilon$$
$$mʊ + \varepsilon \; > \; mɔ \qquad mʊ + e \; > \; mo \qquad mʊ + a \; > \; mwa$$
$$ɓʊ + \varepsilon \; > \; ɓɔ \qquad ɓʊ + e \; > \; ɓo \qquad ɓʊ + a \; > \; ɓwa$$

The following are examples of verbs which have three separate infinitives:

é'ná	'to see' (inanimate object)	mě'ní ꞌ ɓúku	'I see the notebook'
mɔná	'to see' (animate object, sg.)	mimoní ꞌ kɔkɔ́	'I see the chicken, sg.'
ɓɔ́'ná	'to see' (animate object, pl.)	mě'ɓóní ɓakɔkɔ́	'I see the chicken, pl.'

épìlyò	mĕpìlĭ ꞌ ngɔmbé ꞌ l-ámɔ	'I know my clothes'
mópìlyó	mimɔ̃pìlí ɓʊte lí mamɔ	'I know my cow'
ɓópìlyó	mě'ɓópìli ɓaɓʊte lí ɓámɔ	'I know my cows'

ékìsò	mĕkìsĭ kìndo	'I have washed the corpse'
mõkìsó	mimõkìsí ꞌ míkí	'I have washed the child'
ɓókìsó	mě'ɓókìsí ɓamíkí	'I have washed the children'

Other sets are the following:

ɛndá	'to look at' (inanimate object)
mʊndá	'to look at' (animate object, sg.)
ɓʊndá	'to look at' (animate object, pl.)
é'ká	'to hear' (inanimate object)
mɔká	'to hear' (animate object, sg.)
ɓɔ́'ká	'to hear' (animate object, pl.)

5 SUMMARY

This chapter has given an initial view of phonological and some morphological and syntactic structures of Bila. The language appears to be of interest, especially because of a number of features which are unusual for a Bantu language: nine vowels, ATR vowel harmony, three tones and downstep, lack of a series of voiced stops, verbal tense/aspect forms marked by suffixes, and a verbal derivational category implying singular and plural animate objects.

Work is still in progress. Further studies will need to concentrate on the presence of downstep in morphological and syntactic environments, more details of inflectional paradigms, and the complexity of morphophonological changes in the combinations of subject and object prefixes in the various tense/aspect paradigms.

ACKNOWLEDGMENT

I would like to thank D. W. Boone, T. R. Raymond, and J. P. Thomas for their willingness to read through the draft of this chapter and provide helpful comments against the background of their experience with closely related languages and survey done in the area.

NOTES

1 This is the only language which is spoken not only in Congo (in the northern foothills of the Ruwenzori mountains), but also across the border in Uganda.
2 This language called Kango is spoken by a group of pygmies, and links the Bali and Komo areas (J. Paul Thomas pc).
3 Our reason for including Ndaka and Mbo in this group is based on lexical data and personal reporting from speakers; phonological and morphological information is not yet available.
4 The collaboration with Telamboli Ngbami on detailed checking of the vowels and tones deserves a special word of appreciation.
5 Special thanks to my colleagues J. Paul Thomas and Timothy R. Raymond for providing the Komo and Bhele data respectively.
6 This also holds true for the other languages of this subgroup of Bantu languages of the northern Bantu borderland: Amba, Bira, Bhele, and Komo.
7 Note that Bila does not use the general Bantu root ^{N}tu for the word 'person'. However, it does use this root in a system of productive compound constructions which are the equivalent of agentive nouns:

   tu á ¹ *támbá*   'traveller' (person of travelling), pl. *ɓatu á* ¹ *támbá*
   tu é kǔɓo   'thief' (person of stealing), pl. *ɓatu é kǔɓo*

   The neighboring language Kaiku, however, does use *nto/ɓato* for 'person/people'.
8 Upon checking these inalienable possessive constructions with Poyo Ngbami (in 2001), it appears that the different lexically determined sets are probably only used by the older generation. The younger generation still recognizes these forms, but they are simplifying the system into only using the first paradigm, *ámi, ákɔ, ákɛ*, etc. for all inalienable possessive constructions.

REFERENCES

Boone 1993; Guthrie 1970; Kutsch Lojenga 1994, 1995; Kutsch Lojenga and Raymond 1985; Wit 1994; Wit-Hasselaar 1995; Vorbichler 1966.

CHAPTER TWENTY-FOUR

KILIMANJARO BANTU (E60 AND E74)

Gérard Philippson and Marie-Laure Montlahuc

1 GENERAL

1.1 Introduction

The name 'Kilimanjaro Bantu' (henceforth KB) is here used as a cover term for the languages known as Chaga and Taita, spoken in Tanzania and Kenya respectively. Ethnic labels as well as Guthrie's classification are particularly misleading here: the numerous tongues (the term is used here purposefully) spoken on Mt Kilimanjaro by the Chaga people form a close linguistic unit with Rwa (known in Tanzania as 'Meru') spoken on Mt Meru to the west, as well as Gweno, spoken in the Pare Mountains to the east – speakers of Gweno being subsumed under the ethnic label 'Pare' together with their more numerous Asu-speaking neighbors (G22). It should thus be clear from the outset that there is no single 'Chaga' language: diversity is greater than for example among the E50 (Central Kenya) languages, in spite of the fact that each of these languages is known under a different ethnic label – Kikuyu, Kamba, Embu, etc. A glance at Nurse (1979b:393) or Philippson (1982) will discover the massive phonological discrepancies among 'Chaga dialects' which prevent intercomprehension.

As for Taita, it covers two sharply differing languages: Dawida [D.] (E74a) and Saghala [Sa.] (E74b). In spite of the proximity implied by Guthrie's numbering, D. and Sa. are by no means closely related to each other – only the former is part of 'Kilimanjaro Bantu' in any meaningful sense, and Sa. will be left out of the following discussion.

There are about 1,000,000 speakers for Chaga proper (Grimes 2000), with about 300,000 for D. and 90,000 for Rwa (= 'Meru'). The number of Gweno speakers is indeterminate but is likely to be rather small.

None of the Kilimanjaro Bantu languages enjoy official status, although several of them have been used for missionary purposes (mostly Rwa, Mashami, Mochi and D.) and parts of the Bible are available for some of them.

1.2 Classification

Guthrie's subclassification of his E60 group, following administrative boundaries, is of little value. As argued and defined in Nurse (1979b) and Philippson (1984), a more realistic classification is as follows (Guthrie's numbers indicated in parentheses):

- West Kilimanjaro [W.K.]: Siha [S.], Rwa [Rw.] (E61), Mashami [M.] (E62a), Kiwoso [K.]
- Central Kilimanjaro [C.K.]: Uru [Ur.], Mochi [Mo.] (E62a), Wunjo [W.] (E62b), Kahe [Ka.] (E64)

- Rombo [R.] (E62c): South-Rombo [S.R.], North-Rombo [N.R.], with the Mashati [Ma.] and Useri [U.] varieties
- Gweno [G.] (E65)

Following Winter (1980), Okuma (Guthrie's 'Rusha' E63) should probably be added to C.K., since it appears quite close to Ka.

1.3 Literature

Chaga was among the first languages in East Africa to receive extensive coverage, mostly from missionaries, during the German colonial period. The Mo. dialect has been particularly well studied. A complete list of earlier references can be found in the bibliography of Moore and Puritt (1977). Particularly noteworthy is Raum (1909), a remarkable achievement, still quite useful today (although tones are not recorded). Müller (1947), the only dictionary for a KB dialect, though late in publication, also belongs to that period. Apart from Sharp (1954), it would seem that nothing more was published on the language during the thirty-odd years following the Second World War. A renewal of interest took place in the 1970s and 1980s with Nurse and Philippson (1977), Nurse (1979b) and Philippson (1982, 1984). J. W. G. Möhlig and J. C. Winter undertook, at about the same time, an ambitious Linguistic Atlas of Kilimanjaro, which seems never to have seen the light of day, although part of the findings are reported in Winter (1980). More synchronic studies have dealt almost exclusively with the W. dialect and include McHugh's (1990) path-breaking studies of the tonal system and several syntactic articles (Dalgish 1979, Bresnan and Moshi 1993, Moshi 1994, 1998). There is only one substantial descriptive article on G. by Philippson and Nurse (in Kahigi *et al.* 2000). Practically nothing has ever been published on several dialects (including Rw., K., U. and the whole of R. – as well as D. if one excepts Woodward 1913–14, and Ryabova 1984, 1987, in Russian). G. being covered in a substantial sketch will not be treated in detail here.

1.4 Own names

The term Chaga is of doubtful origin (the best guess might be a form of the name given by the G. to the Chaga language: *ky≠àyá*, the people themselves being *mw≠àyá* (sg.)/*ß(à)≠àyá* (pl.)); the Chaga did not traditionally have a general name for themselves, but used chiefdom or clan names instead, or referred to themselves as (Mo.) *wà≠ndù wà* *ḿ≠ndèɲì* 'people in the banana gardens'. Nowadays, the Swahili loan *ßa≠tʃaka* or *ßa≠ʃaka* is generally accepted (tones not marked since they appear to vary from dialect to dialect). The G. call themselves *ßà≠yònù*; the D. call themselves *ßà≠dàßìdà* (and are called *ßà≠ràßìrà* by the G.), whereas they seem to have called the Chaga *ßà≠kìrìmà*.

2 SEGMENTAL PHONOLOGY[1]

2.1 Vowels

All K.B. languages have a balanced five-vowel system /a, e, i, o, u/ with some contextual effects on realization, e.g. in many dialects /a/ preceded by /u/ is noticeably backed and rounded; indeed in most C.K. dialects /ua/ has merged with /(u)o/:

(1)   M., S.R., G., D. *mbùà* 'nose' vs. Mo. *mbùò* 'id.'

---

[1] In this section tones, when given, are underlying.

The passive ending /u/ surprisingly has the same effect in some dialects that otherwise do not experience the merger, so:

(2) G. ≠káβwà, S.R., D. ≠káƃwà 'be hit' vs. M. ≠kápò 'id.'

In most C.K. dialects and D. /ue/ merges with /o/:

(3) M., S.R., G. ì≠wè 'stone' vs. Mo. ì≠hò, D. ì≠γò 'id.'

The question of length is complicated and cannot be dealt with in detail here. First of all, the occurrence of identical vowel sequences in the penultimate and the final is not relevant, since those sequences always straddle two syllables, as can be shown in verbal derivation:

(4) Mo. ≠láà 'lie down'>≠lá-i-à 'appl.', ≠lá-ɾ-à 'caus;' cf. D. ≠lál-à

Such processes do not apply to noun stems, but there is no reason not to analyze them in a similar fashion, especially since interdialectal comparison often testifies to the former presence of a consonant:

(5) M., Mo. ì≠βéè 'breast' vs. S.R., G. ì≠βélè 'id.'

(6) M. taa 'heifer' vs. W. tá(γ)ó

In other stem positions, some dialects (particularly Mo., G. and D.) do not exhibit any length contrasts, although this might well be a recent development in Mo. since Raum (1909) indicates length in his transcriptions. Other dialects have long vowels contrasting in three cases (although genuine pairs are hard to come by):

- unpredictably at the junction between prefix and stem: W. mííβì</m(ù)≠íβì/ 'thief', pl. βééβì</βà≠íβì/; but W. mánà</m(ù)≠ánà/ 'child', M. múʁò</m(ù)≠úʁò/ 'fire', W. móɹò</m(ù)≠óɹò/ 'id.', M. moʁe</m(a)≠uʁe/ 'boils, swellings', W. mooɹe</m(a)≠oɹe/ 'id.'; in W. length is particularly frequent when this context combines with the following.
- often when preceding a nasal cluster: M., W. ki≠maande 'red (earth)'; M. mundi</m(u)≠undi/ 'feeding-tray' vs. W. moondi</m(u)≠ondi/ 'id.'; M. mwàndú 'dispute, case' vs. W. mòòndú</m(ù)≠àndú/ 'id.'; M. mwàŋgò 'door' vs. W. mòòŋgò</m(ù)≠àŋgò/ 'id.'
- in the first stem syllable of a number of (mostly non-Bantu) lexical items, although there are often differences among dialects in this respect:

(7) S., Rw., M. ki≠ɗeeβa 'wooden plate'

(8) Rw., M., W. ≠kóòyà 'find, meet' vs. R. ≠kolya 'id.'

(9) M. ≠booka 'be thin', W. ≠póòkà 'id.'

2.2 Consonants (table 24.1)

Comments

- Where W. has /p/ along with C.K. and partly Rw./M., most other dialects have /b/ instead; only G. and D. have both; indeed D. also contrasts /ƃ/ and /b/, the only K.B. language to do so;
- /pf/ is present only in C.K. and G.; it has merged with /f/ elsewhere (but apparently /p/ in Ka.);
- /mv/ is found only in C.K. and G.; it is rare even there (one notes occasionally a realization [mpf], e.g. Mo. [mvuo ~ mpfuo] 'rain');

TABLE 24.1: CONSONANT CHART FOR KB LANGUAGES

	labial	cor [+ant]	cor [−ant]	back
[−cont] [−voi]	p	t		k
[−cont] [+voi]	b	d	dʒ	g
implos.	ɓ	ɗ		
affricate	pf	ts	tʃ	
prenasalized [+cont]	mv	ndz	ndʒ	
prenasalized [−cont]	mb	nd		ŋg
[+cont] [+voi]	β		ɹ	ɣ
[+str]	v	z		
[+cont] [−voi]	f	s	ʃ	h
liquid		l / r /ɾ		
nasal	m	n	ɲ	ŋ
glide	w		y	

- pre-nasalized stops are denasalized in S. apart from /ŋg/; W.K. also has /n[d]r/ contrasting with /nd/;
- /β/ is realized [β] in all dialects when followed by the front vowels /i/ and /e/; it is barely audible before /u/; before /a/ and /o/, it is [w] in C.K. and K., [β] elsewhere;
- /v/ has distinctive value only in D.; it is sometimes found as a realization of /β/ e.g. in R;
- the situation is complicated as regards the [+ant] coronal stops: all dialects have /t/, usually articulated quite forward ('dental' /t/, to be sharply differentiated from the (laminal?) interdental /t̪/ present in G. and from the [−ant] /ʈ/ found in N.R.); some dialects also differentiate between an explosive /d/ (usually dental) and the more or less retroflex implosive /ɗ/ (e.g. parts of M., S.R., D.), others have only /d/ (W.) – the situation is not clear for all dialects;
- /ts/ and /ndz/ are only found in C.K.; in G. they are replaced by interdental /t̪/ and /nd̪/ respectively; elsewhere the plain affricate is replaced by either /t/ or /s/, the prenasalized one mostly by /n[d]r/ (W.K.) and /s/ or /nd/ (R., D.);
- /z/ is only found in D. (it will be noted that D., alone in KB, has a contrast between [+voi] and [−voi] continuants, i.e. /v/ and /z/ have not merged with their voiceless counterparts);
- /s/ is realized [θ] in G.;
- /r/ in M. alone is realized as a uvular approximant [ʁ] (sometimes velar [ɣ ~ x]), even when prenasalized; elsewhere it is a strongly vibrated trill, sharply differentiated (except in G. and D. where /r/ is not found) from the lateral flap /ɾ/ (realized [r] in M.). In northern dialects of D. /ɾ/ is realized as a voiced lateral fricative [ɮ];

NB. Although Davey *et al.* (1982) show the /ɾ/ segment to be a post-alveolar lateral flap, we choose to transcribe it with a rhotic symbol, since it is 'felt' by the speakers to be a sort of 'r' and transcribed by them as such, and because it is either replaced by the trill, as in M. or is not distinct from it, as in D. and G. (according to Ladefoged and Maddieson 1996: 243, '[...] rhotics and laterals [...] have a member in common – the lateral flap');

- /dʒ/ is only found in D. and G. (it is quite rare in the latter); northern D speakers replace it with the fricative [ʒ];
- /tʃ/ is found in C.K., G., K., S.R. and D.; it is not distinct from [ʃ] elsewhere; /ndʒ/ is found in C.K., G. and parts of N.R.; it has merged with /tʃ/ in K. and D.; it is /ʃ/ everywhere else, except that some (younger?) speakers of N.R. have /ɲʃ/ – a most infrequent combination in Bantu languages overall, and particularly in Chaga, which has no voiceless pre-nasals otherwise…;
- /ɻ/ (a retroflex approximant similar to British English /r/) is only present in W. where it corresponds variously to /ɗ/ (Mo., K., D.), /h/ (S.), retroflex /ʈ/ (N.R.), and either /ɗ/ (before [+high] vowels) or /tʃ/ (before [−high]) in S.R.; in Rw., M. and G. it is not distinct from trilled /r/;
- /g/ only occurs in D. and G. where it is rather rare and in S.R. where it has been noted in two words only /–gwa/ 'to fall' and /gwe/ 'above';
- /ɣ/ occurs in the speech of a number of W. speakers and in G. and D.; in Mo. it has merged with /h/; elsewhere it is replaced by glides according to the phonetic environment.

[NB. In order better to preserve the variety in realizations among dialects, transcriptions in the rest of this chapter are rather of a (broad) phonetic nature than strictly phonemic.]

3 TONE

3.1 Introduction

The tone systems of several KB dialects rank among the most intricate to be found among Bantu languages. Apart from four brief articles (Sharp (1954) on M., Nurse and Philippson (1977), Saloné (1980) and Winter (1987) on Mo.), the only detailed description of any KB tone system is McHugh (1990) on W.

Apart from D., whose system is of a different type (for which see below), and from G. (described in Philippson and Nurse (2000)), KB languages are characterized both by 'tone shift' – where the tone underlyingly associated with one syllable is realized on the syllable immediately to the right, and by the presence of a three-way tonal contrast at utterance-level (Super-High (SH), High (H) and Low (L), plus Rising and Falling tones), although lexically syllables can be defined as simply H vs. L (or toneless).

Tonal data are not of equal quality for all dialects (and some of those are completely unknown tonally), but at least M., Mo., W. and S.R., while in no way identical, definitely exhibit both features mentioned above, and S., Rw. and K. probably do so. On the other hand, research by Montlahuc on R. dialects has shown that the Ma. variety of N.R. does not have tone shift, although the three-way tonal contrast is very much in evidence. Thus (abstracting away from some end-of-utterance intonational effects) we have the realizations in table 24.2 before pause.

TABLE 24.2: MA. AND W. LEXICAL TONE

	Mashati	Wunjo (McHugh 1990)
goat (HL)	mbúrù	… mbùrû
chicken (HH)	ŋgúkú	… ŋgùkú
house (LH)	m̀mbá	… nùmbǎ
meat (LL)	ɲàmà	…ɲámâ

(NB. W. forms are quoted as when preceded by a word underlyingly ending in a L tone (e.g. *ŋgíléúrà* 'I bought'), since, due to tone-shift, any tone realized on their initial syllable must have its source one syllable to the left; on the other hand, the – underlyingly all L, or toneless – word *ɲama* 'meat' appears in this position with an HF contour due to a rule assigning H tone (and accent, in McHugh's analysis) to toneless nouns which are final in their phonological phrase; see McHugh 1990).

3.2 SH tones

The arising of SH tones can be seen most clearly in Ma., since it is not obscured there by tone shift. SH are found:

- on the prefix syllable of many declarative affirmative verb forms, where there is evidence in at least part of the paradigm of the presence of the focus marker *ɲ(í)* (see below). This is one of the surest clues in distinguishing positive from negative verb forms:

(10) *ŋgí≠kúndí m̀≠t̰î ú ù≠t̰ǎ fó, ŋgî≠kúndí wǒ ù≠t̰wé*
      /1sg≠want cl3≠tree DEMcl3 cl3≠small NEG, (FOC)1sg≠want DEMcl3 cl3-big/
      'I don't want the small tree, I want the big one.'

- on many lexical items, when final in their p-group, but not utterance-final. This is seen clearly on nominals in certain syntactic positions, most often when followed by a demonstrative, whether they be subject or object. Taking as reference the nominals given in table 24.2, one would have (table 24.3):

TABLE 24.3: MA. CLASS 9 NOMINALS IN ISOLATION AND IN CONTEXT

	Isolation	N + DEM
HL	*mbúrù*	*mbǔrǔ î*
HH	*ŋgúkú*	*ŋgúkǔ î*
LH	*m̀mbá*	*m̀mbǎ î*
LL	*ɲàmà*	*ɲǎmǎ î*

NB. The rising tone on the first syllable of *mburu* rises from L to SH. What happens can be seen more clearly if we select noun stems preceded by a syllabic prefix (table 24.4)

What seems to happen is that a SH tone associates leftwards up to – and including – the first H syllable that it meets; if there is no such syllable it keeps on spreading leftwards and would in fact spread through the L syllables of a preceding word, e.g.:

(11) *...î-m̀≠lólyǎ m̀≠ndǔ só... (≠lòlyà)*
      /cl5-Objcl1≠see cl1≠person DEMcl1/
      '...to see that person...'

TABLE 24.4: MA. NOMINAL STEMS WITH SYLLABIC PREFIX

	Isolation	N + DEM
'women (HL)'	*và≠félè*	*và≠fělě vǎ*
'legs (HH)'	*mà≠t̰éndé*	*mà≠t̰éndě ǎ*
'men (LH)'	*và≠sèró*	*và≠sèrǒ vǎ*
'beds (LL)'	*fì≠t̰àrà*	*fî≠t̰ǎrǎ fî*

(12)   *n-ɻw-ěɟè≠ǎnîkǎ ŋgǔŏ sŏ...* (*≠ánikà*)
       /FOC-1pl-FUT≠spread cl10clothes DEMcl10/
       'We'll put the clothes out to dry'

In spite of the absence of tone shift, the system appears similar to, although not identical with, the W. system as described in McHugh (1990), to which the reader is referred.

3.3 Tone dissimilation

Although tone assimilation is much in evidence in Chaga, tone dissimilation does seem to play a role, although apparently not in W. In the closely related Mo. dialect however, a dissimilatory process, akin to 'Meeussen's Rule' (cf. Kisseberth and Odden this volume, Philippson 1998) can be seen to operate. Data from speakers of both the Mbokomu and Mowo varieties show that an H tone always dissimilates a following H at the junction between two morphemes, both within and across words; this process does not operate within stems, however:

(13)   *...mbùrú ndʒì≠ìwû* 'black goat(s)' vs. *...ŋgùkú ndʒí≠ìwû* 'black chicken(s)'
       (contrast is maintained between *mbúrù* and *ŋgúkù*)

But:

(14)   *ndʒî-lè≠húrà mbùrû* (*≠hùrà*)
       /(FOC)1sg-PAST≠buy cl9goat/
       'I bought a goat'

vs.

       (14 bis) *ndʒî-lè≠wónà mbùrû* (*≠wónà*)
       /(FOC)1sg-PAST≠see cl9goat/
       'I saw a goat'

Taking into account the effect of tone shift, we see that an H originates on the PAST marker *-le-* and associates to the verb radical; however, the second stem syllable is L in both cases, although we would expect an H in the case of *≠wona* 'see'. That this is in no way an effect linked to this tense in general is shown when we insert another morpheme, the Object Prefix, between the tense marker and the radical:

(15)   *ndʒî-lè-kú≠wònâ*
       /(FOC)1sg-PAST-2sg≠see/
       'I saw you'

The H originating on the tense marker associates to the next syllable, which is now the (L) OP; as the verb radical is not immediately preceded by an underlying H it is not subject to dissimilation and associates as expected to the final stem syllable.

Several other morphemes are affected by this dissimilation process, which does not exist in W. (according to McHugh's data). Its extent in other dialects is not known.

3.4 Dawida

D. tones work along different principles. D. does have tone-shift but it is mostly characterized by a regressive dissimilation principle ('anti-Meeussen'), whereby only the last of a series of H surfaces – on the next syllable; e.g. (Josa dialect):

(16)   *mw≠àná kù-nì≠βòɲèrèɣè nì ḿ≠kòŋgò < kù-ni-βóɲéréɣé ni...*
       /cl1≠child 2nd sg-1st sg≠see +CAUS+Rec.Past COP cl1≠sick/
       'the child you showed me is sick'

This process is also active within stems, so there is no contrast in D. between HH and LH stems. To a large extent (although this might vary among dialects and even speakers) there is no contrast with LL as well: most disyllabic stems realized LL in isolation tend to take an H on the initial syllable of the following word; in many cases this will be attributable to the fact of the LL stem being followed underlyingly by a floating H (i.e. stems etymologically LH/HH) due to the effect of tone shift, but the same initial H appears when preceded by a word whose underlying pattern is undoubtedly LL; this is fairly easy to evidence for those stems whose semantics makes them compatible with a locative suffix: this has the shape -*iɲi*, and although its initial vowel coalesces with the final vowel of the stem to which it is suffixed, it still acts as if disyllabic. Now when it is suffixed to an underlying LL (etymologically *LL) stem no H will appear; on the other hand an H (mostly realized as rising before pause), will appear if the previous stem is underlyingly followed by a floating H (*LH and *(H)H stems); e.g. (Josa dialect):

(17)   *tʃìà* 'path' (underlying LL)>*tʃìèɲì* 'in the path, on the way', as in:

(18)   *ʃìmbà y-á≠sìmámá tʃìèɲì* 'the lion is standing in the path'

(19)   *ɲùmbà* 'house' (underlying LH)>*ɲùmbĕɲì* 'in the house, at home' as in:

(20)   *àbà w-á≠sìndáyá ɲùmbĕɲì* 'father usually spends the day at home'

Although the distinction seems consistently maintained with the locative suffix, it is less significant in other contexts. For instance, while the forms *tʃìà yàpò* 'my path' vs. *ɲùmbà yápò* 'my house', do show the expected distinction, it is also possible to find *tʃìà yápò* and *ɲùmbà yàpò* with the same meanings. In most noun phrases, the presence or absence of an H on the initial syllable of a determiner does not seem to be attributable to the lexical tone of the noun any more but to play pragmatic functions which still await detailed description. As far as is known this is not the case with verbs, where the presence of a floating H is a characteristic of some tenses/aspects. In both following examples, the tone on the first syllable of the complement is not subject to variation:

(21)   *gùà má≠rùɣù* 'buy bananas!'

(22)   *dʼì-kà≠gùà mà≠rùɣù* '(and) we bought bananas'

4 NOUN MORPHOLOGY

4.1 Independent nominal prefixes (table 24.5)

The class system of K.B. does not exhibit any strong deviation from the ordinary pattern found in eastern Bantu. A few points are nevertheless worthy of mention.

4.1.1

In all W.K. dialects, the independent prefixes (IP) of classes 1 and 3 are realized as a syllabic nasal homorganic to the first stem consonant; in M. this assimilation process extends to denasalization before /-l-/, e.g. (M.):

(23)   *ǹ≠ndù<m̀≠ndù* 'person'   *ŋ̀≠ʁìmâ<m̀≠ʁìmâ* 'soul'
       m̀≠fòŋgó 'irrigation channel'   *ŋ̀≠kǎ<m̀≠kǎ* 'wife'
       ǹ≠tùʁû<m̀-tùʁû 'forest'   *l≠lò<m̀≠lò* 'digging-stick'

If the stem is vowel-initial, W.K. and R. realize the prefixes as [mw-] (but [m-] in front of /-u-/ and /-o-/. In Mo. and W. however the prefixes are always [m-] with various degrees of coalescence with the next vowel (table 24.6).

The underlying form of the prefix could thus be posited as /mu-/ which would explain the forms found in W. where /u+a/ and /u+e/ both >[o]. But the Mo. form for 'moon' is not so easily explained and 'child' would be an exception in both dialects.

4.1.2

In D., a rather large number of nouns (mostly, but not exclusively animates), take in the sg. a variety of IPs including zero; in the pl. the IP does not change but an extra-'prefix' /βeke-/ is added; a large subgroup has in the sg. another extra- 'prefix' /mwá-/, in the pl. they add /βeke-/ in front of this; in all cases the concords are those of cl. 1/2 respectively; e.g. (tones not indicated):

(24) *aba/βeke-aba*   'father(s)'
      kifondo/βeke-kifondo   'one-eyed person(s)'
      kaŋgulume/βeke-kaŋgulume   'banana cultivar(s)'

(25) *mwa-mwadú/βeke-mwa-mwadú* 'bee-keeper(s)' $<mw \neq àdù$ 'beehive'
      mwa-tʃwalɛni/βeke-mwa-tʃwalɛni 'klipspringer(s)' $<lw \neq àlà/tʃw \neq àlà$ 'flat rock' +loc. /-iɲi/
      mwa-pea/βeke-mwa-pea   'Catholic priest(s)' (<French 'mon père')

These could be called cl. 1a/2a.

TABLE 24.5: INDEPENDENT NOMINAL PREFIXES

	S.	M.	Mo.	S.R.	N.R.	D.
1	m-	m-	m-	m-	m-	m-
2	βa-	βa-	wa-	βa-	βa-	βa-
3	m-	m-	m-	m-	m-	m-
4	mi-	mi-	m-	m-	m-	mi-
5	i-	i-	i-	i-	i-	i-
6	ma-	ma-	ma-	ma-	ma-	ma-
7	ki-	ki-	ki-	ki-	ki-	ki-
8	ʃi-	ʃi-	ʃi-	ʃi-	ʃi-	vi-
9	N-	N-	N-	N-	N-	N-
10	N-	N-	N-	N-	N-	N-
10a	ŋgyo-	ŋgyu-	ndʒo-	–	–	tʃu-
11	(o-)	u-	o-	u-	u-	lu-
12	?	ka-	ka-	ka-	ka-	ka-
13	?	ru-	–	–	ʈu-	ɗu-
14	βu-	βu-	wu-	βu-	βu-	βu-
15	(ku-)	–	ku-	–	ku-	ku-
16	a-	a-	ha-	ha-	ha-	a-
17	ku-	ku-	ku-	?	ku-	–

TABLE 24.6: CLASSES 1 AND 3 IPs IN KB

Gloss	Mashami	Mochi	Wunjo
'child' (cl. 1)	mw≠ànâ	m≠ànâ	m≠ànâ
'fire' (cl. 3)	mùʁô	m≠òɗô	m≠òɗô
'moon' (cl. 3)	mw≠ìʁî	m≠èrî	mòrî
'girl' (cl. 1)	mw≠àlĭ	m≠àlĭ	mòlĭ

4.1.3

Cl. 3 and 4 IPs are identical in C.K. and R.; only their concords differentiate them (for which see §4.2).

4.1.4

The cl. 5 IP appears occasionally as /Ø-/ (mostly in C.K.), e.g.:

(26) (Mo.) ì≠rùhŭ ~ rùhŭ 'banana'; ì≠pfùmû ~ pfùmû 'spear'
(W.) ì≠ʌìmâ ~ ʌìmâ 'liver'; ì≠fùmvú ~ fùmvú 'mountain'

This, however, does not apply across the board. On the other hand, some C.K. items seem never to take /i-/, e.g.:

(27) W. rìsô 'eye' vs. M. ì≠ʙìsô

4.1.5

In accordance with the canonical Bantu pattern, cl. 9 and 10 have as their IPs a nasal, generally realized as homorganic to the first stem consonant (details are too varied to be presented here); only the concords allow sg. and pl. to be disambiguated.

4.1.6

Cl. 10a is found in most dialects (but apparently not in R.). It takes exactly the same concords as cl. 10 (the only difference being thus in the IP) and forms the plural of many (but not all) cl. 11 nouns, e.g. (D.):

(28) lùmí/tʃùmí 'tongue(s)'   lùmbó/tʃùmbó 'song(s)'
lù≠ßìyà/tʃù≠ßìyà 'vessel(s)'   lù≠ßìyí / tʃù≠ßìyí 'goshawk(s)'
lw≠àká/tʃw≠àká 'voice(s)'   lw≠àlà/tʃw≠àlà 'flat rock(s)'

Note however:

(29) lw≠èmbè/mbèmbè 'horn(s)'   lù≠kàŋgè/ŋgàŋgè 'bead(s)'
lù≠ßàrù/mbàrù 'rib(s)'

The situation is much the same in other dialects. In R., however, cl. 11 forms its plural either in ordinary cl. 10, or (increasingly?), by keeping the cl. 11 prefix (but still using cl. 10 concords), e.g. (Ma.):

(30) ù≠límí w≠ààʃá 'long tongue'   ù≠límí ~ ndímí ŋg≠ààʃá 'long tongues'

4.1.7

Cl. 11: although a number of nominals appear in S. with an IP /o-/, they take the cl. 5 concords, and should be numbered as 5a and not 11, e.g. (tones not known):

(31) ili ni o≠rika lakwa 'this is my country', cf. ili ni i≠ebe lakwa 'this is my hoe'

4.1.8

Cl. 12/13 are the classes of diminutives, sg. and pl. respectively; their IPs are generally added to and do not replace the IP of the original class of the noun concerned; in the plural two strategies are found, exemplified below:

(32) (N.R.) kà-mw≠ánà 'small child', pl. ʈù-mw≠ánà

(33)   (D.) *kà-mw≠àná* 'id.', pl. *d̠ù-ß(à)≠àná*

In the first case, the original cl. 1 IP is retained even in the plural; in the second the original pl. cl. 2 IP vacuously replaces the cl. 1 IP (note that in both cases, the concords will only be those of cl. 12 and 13; the original prefixes do not fulfil any function any more).

In C.K. dialects cl. 13 has entirely disappeared, and 12 does not act as a diminutive class (its role has been taken over by cl. 7). There remain however a very few words in cl. 12 (e.g. in Mo. *kà≠ndò* 'food').

4.1.9

Apart from D., cl. 15 is found with three stems only, namely those for 'ear', 'leg' and 'arm'. (In all KB languages, minus D., verbo-nominal forms – infinitives – do not belong to this class, but to cl. 5.) Probably due to this low functional load, cl. 15 has partially or totally disappeared from several dialects:

(a)   only W., N.R. and G. have kept all three original stems in cl. 15, with a plural in 6, e.g. (Ma.):

(34)   *kù≠ṭú/mà≠ṭú* 'ear(s)'; *kù≠ßókò/mà≠ßókò* 'arm(s)'; *kù≠ṭéndé/mà≠ṭéndé* 'leg(s)'

The same applies to D., save that the word for 'leg' is *kù≠yù* (it has disappeared from the southern dialects altogether and been replaced by a cl. 3 item: *mw≠indì*).

(b)   the W.K. dialects have put 'leg' and 'arm' into cl. 11, with a change of IP (in S., as indicated above, cl. 11 is not distinct from 5 as far as concords are concerned); for 'ear' however, the situation varies: Rw. would seem to have retained a cl. 15 for this one word (?), S. and K. have put the word in 7 (K. has strangely altered the IP in /ka-/), while M. has it in 5 (with change of IP). In all those cases, the plurals are invariably in 6., e.g. (M.):

(35)   *yàà꞊wĭ/màà꞊wĭ* 'ear(s)'; *w≠òkô/mààkô* 'arm(s)'; *ù≠ʁèndé/mà≠ʁèndé* 'leg(s)'

Mo. vacillates between the W. and W.K. patterns: *ò≠wòkô ~ kù≠wòkô* 'arm', etc.

(c)   S.R. has put the three stems in 7, which is understandable in view of the fact that all S.R. varieties have a phonetic process of syncopation: all high vowels fall between /k/ and another obstruent, like in [kʃŭ]<*kì≠ʃŭ* 'knife' or [ìksárà]<*ì-kú≠sàrà* 'think'; so that there could not be any difference in realization between /ku-/ and /ki-/, e.g.

(36)   *k≠d̠ŭ/mà≠d̠ŭ* 'ear(s)'; *kòkô/mà≠wòkô* 'arm(s)'; *k≠tʃèndè/mà≠tʃèndè* 'leg(s)'

4.1.10

Cl. 16 and 17 only contain one item each (the stem being the same in both classes, both meaning 'place'), i.e. *(h)à≠ndù ~ (h)à≠ndò* and *kù≠ndù ~ kù≠ndò*, respectively. A tendency is sometimes noticeable (e.g. in R.) to treat cl. 17 as the pl. of 16.

4.2 Concords

KB languages differentiate between two types of dependent prefixes (DP): one for adjectives (DP I) and one for other determiners (DP II) to which should be added verbal subject (SP) and object prefixes (OP).

4.2.1

As regards DP I, those of cl. 1, 2, 5, 6, 7, 8 and, where present, 12 to 17 are everywhere identical to the respective IP, except that a tendency appears in W.K., and D. for using the cl. 17 concords even with the cl. 16 noun (*h*)*àndù*/(*h*)*àndò*.

Differences are seen in the following cases:

4.2.1.1

Cl. 9 and 10 have the same form (an homorganic nasal) for DP I as for IP in D. only; W. dialects have /ʃi-/, C. dialects and R. have /ŋgi-/ (/ndʒi-/ in Mo/), e.g.:

(37)   (D.) *ɲùmbà ndátʃà<N≠làtʃà* 'tall house(s)'

(38)   (M.) *m̀mbà ʃàáʃǎ<ʃi≠àʃǎ* 'id.'

(39)   (W.) *mbùrú ŋgì≠nòrǔ* 'fat goat(s)'

4.2.1.2

Cl. 14 in D. has the same series of concords (including DP I) as cl. 3; this is also found at least optionally in S.R. (this is also the Swahili pattern, and language contact might be at work here; furthermore in S.R. cl. 11 and 14 have collapsed into one class, just as in Swahili); in N.R., it is rather cl. 3 which tends to take the cl. 14 prefix, e.g.:

(40)   (D.) *ßù≠lì m̀≠làtʃà* 'long bed', cf. *mù≠dʔì m̀≠látʃà* 'tall tree'

(41)   (Ma.) *ù≠lìlì ù≠àʃá* 'long bed', cf. *m̀≠ʈí ù≠àʃá* 'tall tree'

Similarly cl. 4 in N.R. tends to take cl. 10 concords (the normal pl. for cl. 11); the same is true to some extent of C.K. dialects.

4.2.1.3

Finally there is a tendency to use DP II concords instead of DP I, especially for those classes where the DP I series does not differentiate between sg. and pl. (mostly 9/10, and in C.K. 3/4); in that case DP II concords are underlyingly low-toned, e.g. (Mo.):

(42)   *m̀≠dʔò m̀≠lèʃì ~ fú≠lèʃì* 'long head'

(43)   *m̀mbà ndʒí≠tùtǔ ~ tsí≠tùtǔ* 'small houses'

4.3 DP II (table 24.7)

DP II are used with various qualifiers: demonstratives, connectives, possessives, 'other', 'all' (in M. 'all' takes DP I, although a younger informant did use DP II in most cases, possibly under Swahili influence; how far this applies to other W.K. dialects is not known – limited evidence for Rw. seems to indicate DP II are used) and 'which' (for numerals see below). The underlying tones, when known, as in Mo., are H for all classes, except 1, 4 and 9.

4.3.1

'Other' is /-ìŋgí/, in all dialects save D., with the first stem vowel assimilating to the prefix vowel (a+i>e, u+i>u) with no lengthening, even in those dialects which generally lengthen (including Mo. in Raum's description); this is in contrast with the

TABLE 24.7: DEPENDENT PREFIXES

	S.	M.	Mo.	S.R.	N.R.	D.
1	u-	u-	ù-	u-	u-	u-
2	ßa-	ßa-	wá-	ßa-	ßa-	ßa-
3	u-	u-	fú-	u-	u-	ɣu-
4	i-	i-	ì	i-	(si-)	i-
5	li-	li-	lí-	li-	li-	dʒi-
6	a-	a-	há-	a-	a-	ɣa-
7	ki-	ki-	ki-	ki-	ki-	tʃi-
8	ʃi-	ʃi	ʃi-	ʃi-	ʃi-	vi-
9	i-	i-	ì-	i-	i-	i-
10	ti-	ti-	tsí-	si-	si-	ri-
11		lu-	lú-	u-		lu-
12		ka-	ká-	ka-	ka-	ka-
13		ru-			ʈu-	ɗu-
14	u- /lu-	u- /lu-	ú-	u-	u-	ɣu-
15		ku-	kú-		ku-	ku-
16	a-	a-	há-	ha-	ha-	a-
17	ku-	ku-	kú-	ku-	ku-	ku-

adjectival stem /-í(:)ŋgì/, whose vowel coalesces in the same way, but where length is always retained (in the dialects concerned), e.g.:

(44)   (M.) *fì≠ndò fìŋgí* 'other things' *fì≠ndò fì:ŋgî* 'many things'

Ma. is apparently an exception to this statement since it lengthens the coalesced prefixes in both cases, with only the tones being different (recall that Ma. is the only KB dialect not to have tone shift), e.g.:

(45)   (Ma.) *fì≠ndò fí:≠ŋgí* 'other things' *fì≠ndò fí:ŋgì* 'many things'

In D., *-ŋgì* (with no trace of an initial vowel) means 'whatever', and takes DP II; 'other' is rendered by *-mù* (etymologically 'one') taking DP II as well, or else by the adjective *-zìmà* (with DP I).

4.3.2

'All' is *-ó(:)sè* in most dialects (*-óʃè* in G., in R. also *-ó(:)sà*); the first vowel coalesces and then normally lengthens in dialects with phonemic length. In several (all?) dialects, the stem is also used with 1st and 2nd person plural *verbal* prefixes, with the meaning 'we all', 'you all'.

4.3.3

'Which (of several)' is in most dialects a stem *-ŋga-*, with the class concord appearing both as a prefix and a suffix (in G. only as a prefix), e.g. (S.R., tones not known):

(46)   *mw≠ana u≠ŋga≠u* 'which child?'   pl. *ßana ßa≠ŋga≠ßa*
       mmba i≠ŋga≠i 'which house?'   pl. *mmba si≠ŋga≠si*

In C.K. the stem is *-há* (in Raum 1909, the Mo. form is given as *-hya*; no palatal is audible with contemporary Mo. speakers):

(47)   (Mo.) *mw≠àná ù≠hă* 'which child ?'   pl. *wàná wà≠há*

In D. the stem is *-ao* (tones doubtful), which takes *verbal* concords (for which see below).

4.3.4 Demonstratives

There are three degrees of demonstratives in K.B.: 'Near', 'Far' and 'Referential'.

4.3.4.1

The simplest is the 'Far' demonstrative which is everywhere expressed by a stem /-lyá/ (-la [tone?] in Rw. and S., -dʒà ~ -dʒè in D., mostly -yá in G.), preceded by a concord belonging to the DP II series presented above (in D. if the concord begins with a conso-nant it is itself preceded by a vowel identical to that of the concord), e.g.:

(48)   (Mo.) m̀≠ndù ù≠lyǎ 'that person', kì≠ndò kì≠lyá 'that thing'

(49)   (D.) ì-dʒà ndáɣà 'that knife', but pl. ì-rì-dʒá ndáɣà 'those knives'

4.3.4.2

The 'Near' demonstrative consists of the class concord itself, which may be (according to dialect and/or context) preceded by a vowel; furthermore, the concords for cl. 1 and 4 are sometimes different from those in the general DP II series, as a few examples will illustrate:

- In M. the concords are always preceded by (y)e-: (1) (y)e-u; (2) (y)e-ßa; (3) (y)e-u; (4) (y)e-i; etc. the concord being in all cases identical to the DP II series (NB. cl. 6 and 16: yaa<ye-a), e.g.:

(50)   (M.) n̂≠ndù yèú 'this person'; ßà≠ndù yèßá 'these people'; à≠ndù yàá 'this place'

- In Mo. the concords are preceded by i- when the demonstrative is used pronominally; otherwise the concords are just cliticized to the noun; the cl. 1 concord is tʃu, otherwise the others are from the DP II series. When clitic, cl. 16 and 17 concords appear as /-ha/ and /-ku/ respectively, as expected, but the pronominal form for cl. 16 is /aa/ rather than /iha/, and for cl. 17 the expected /*iku/ is replaced by /kunu/:

(51)   (Mo.) m̀≠sòrò-tʃû 'this man'   wà≠sòrò-wâ 'these men'

(52)   ì-tʃŭɲì m̀≠sòrŏ 'this is a man'   ì-wǎɲì wá≠sòrŏ 'these are men'

- In S.R. the situation is basically the same as in Mo. (the concords for both cl. 1 and 3 being -ʃu) but one frequently finds a (non-clitic) reduplicated form of the demonstra-tive, with -a- acting as link vowel: (1) -ʃu ~ ʃwaaʃu (<ʃu-a-ʃu); (2) -ßa ~ ßa-a-ßa; (9) -i ~ yaayi (<i-a-i); (10) -si ~ saasi; etc.

4.3.4.3

The 'Referential' demonstrative is the same as the 'Near' demonstrative, but suffixes -o to the concord, e.g.:

(53)   (M.) ßà≠ndù è-wó (<-e-wa-o) 'those people' – already referred to; n̂≠ndù è-tó (< e-tu-o, but *etu is not otherwise attested) 'that person'

(54)   (Mo.) m̀≠sòrò-tʃô (< -tʃu-o), pl. wà≠sòrò-wô 'that man/those men', etc.

(55)   (S.R.) 1. -ʃo ~ ʃwaaʃo, 2. -ßo ~ ßaaßo, etc.

4.3.5 Connective and possessives

The connective (or 'genitive particle', or 'extra-dependent prefix' for Guthrie) consists in all KB dialects of a vowel /-a/ preceded by the same concords as used for the 'Near' demonstrative. The syllable thus formed serves as prefix for the possessive, the basic shapes of which are indicated in table 24.8 for cl. 1 and 2.

In N.R. the human pl. possessors are based on a form with a /mu-/ prefix (*moʈu* is presumably from /mu-eʈu/, although the /ue>o/ assimilation, common in other dialects is normally unattested in N.R.); this is reminiscent of a cl. 18 locative concord, otherwise unknown in KB, so that those forms would mean literally: 'of at our/your/their place' (?).

For the other classes, the original system had as possessors the 'referential' demonstratives, so for instance (N.R.):

(56)   *mà≠ʈéndě ákwé* 'his legs' (cl. 1 poss.); *mà≠ʈéndě ákyó* 'its legs' (cl. 7 poss.); *mà≠ʈéndě áyó* 'its legs' (cl. 9 poss.), etc.

Nowadays there is a tendency to use the cl. 1 possessor for all non-human classes, after the Swahili fashion. In D. the only universal (non-human) possessor stem is the cl. 10 possessor form *-aro*.

4.3.6 Numerals (and 'how many')

Some numeral qualifiers are nouns with their own IP and never enter into agreement. Other numerals take as prefix the concord agreeing with the class of the head noun. Table 24.9 presents the basic shapes of numerals for '1' to '6', plus the stem for 'how many' which behaves like the variable numerals (where given, tones are underlying).

Several points deserve mention here:

4.3.6.1

The concords used with these stems are similar to the DP II series, with the exception of cl. 10, the concord of which is /í-/ in most dialects (but Mo. has /tsi-/, with /í-/ as variant before 'four' only); furthermore, several numeral stems have rather different shapes when they take the cl. 10 concord:

TABLE 24.8: POSSESSIVE STEMS

Possessor	S.	M.	Mo.	S.R.	N.R.	D.
1st sg.	-akwa	-akwa	-ako	-akwa	-akwa	-apo
2nd sg.	-afo	-afo	-apfo	-afo	-afo	-ako
cl. 1	-amwi	-akwe	-ake	-ake	-akwe	-akwe
1st pl.	-ehu	-eru	-edu	-edu	-a moʈu	-edu
2nd pl.	-anu	-aɲ	-anu	-enu	-a mwanu	-eɲu
cl. 2	-aβo	-aβo	-awo	-aβo	-a mwao	-aβo

TABLE 24.9: NUMERAL STEMS

	M.	Mo.	S.R.	N.R.	D.
'one'	≠mwí	≠mú	≠mu	≠mu~-mi	≠mwèrì
'two'	≠βìi	≠βí	≠βili	≠βili	≠βí
'three'	≠ʁáʁù	≠rárù	≠radu	≠ʈaʈu	≠dǎdù
'four'	≠:nà	≠:nà	≠:na	≠:na	≠nà
'five'	≠ʁá:nù	≠tánù	≠ʈanu	≠ʈanu	≠sánù
'six'	≠ʁindaʁu	≠randaru			≠randadù
'how many'	≠ìŋgá	≠ìŋgá	≠(i)ŋga	≠lìŋgá	≠lìŋgá

(57)   (M.) /≠ʁáʁù / 'three', cl. 10 /í≠sáʁù/; /≠ʁá:nù/ 'five', cl. 10 /í≠sá:nù/;
/≠ʁindaʁu/ 'six', cl. 10 /í≠sasaʁu/

This pattern seems widespread in W.K. and in G. The R. dialects have /-sáɗù/ and
/-sáʈù/ in S.R. and N.R. respectively, for 'three' in cl. 10; they also have, like C.K. and D.,
/í≠:ɲà/ for /≠:nà/ in cl. 10. Furthermore in D. the cl. 2 concord is /ɓá-/ before /-≠:nà/.

4.3.6.2

The length sign in front of the stem for 'four' indicates a lengthening of the prefix vowel in
those dialects having a length contrast. However, even in Mo. where such contrasts are not
synchronically present this 'lengthening' has an effect on the prefix H which does *not* shift
to the stem; e.g. (the downstep indicated by the raised exclamation mark is due to the final
L of the previous stem, which is prevented from shifting by the H blocked on the prefix):

(58)   (Mo.) *wàná ʹwánà* 'four children' (</wà≠ánà wá≠:nà/)

4.3.6.3

Although a stem /-ṭanu/ is present in R. for 'five', it is most likely a loan (as suggested
by the dental ṭ); the original word is the one for 'hand': *kòkô* (S.R.) and *kù(w)ókò* (Ma.);
similarly 'six' is 'hand+1', 'seven' is 'hand+2' and so on up to ten which is an independent nominal /ì≠kúmì/.

4.3.6.4

The other dialects have independent nominals for the numbers from 7 to 10, given in
table 24.10 (tones underlying).

TABLE 24.10: NOMINAL STEMS FOR NUMERALS 7 TO 10

	M.	Mo.	D.
'seven'	*ḿ≠fúŋgàʁé*	*ḿ≠fúŋgàré*	*ḿ≠fúŋgàré*
'eight'	*ɲáɲá*	*ɲáɲá*	*ɓù≠ɲàɲá*
'nine'	*kè:ndá*	*kèndá*	*ì≠kèndá*
'ten'	*ì≠kúmì*	*ì≠kúmi*	*ì≠kúmì*

5 VERB MORPHOLOGY

As in most Bantu languages (cf. Nurse this volume), the structure of verb forms in KB
comprises a number of slots corresponding to various morpheme paradigms. In KB, the
canonical form can be represented thus:

(59)   cop-sp- Neg-tam-op-Base-Suffix

Not all those slots need be filled in any one form and some items are mutually exclusive. Abbreviations will be explained as we deal with each position in turn.

5.1 Copula (COP)

In all KB dialects apart from D., the COP /ɲí/ can be prefixed to certain affirmative main
verb forms, the effect being one of focusing the verb phrase as a whole, as in

(60)   (Mo.) *ɲálèwónà m̀sòrŏ*   <   /ɲí-à-lé≠wón-à/
       'he saw a man (that's what he did)'   /cop-sp-Past2-Base-Suf/

as opposed to:

(61)   (Mo.) *ɲì m̀sòrò áléwónà*   'it's a man he saw (not a woman)'

As can be seen, the COP stands directly before the focused element. When proclitic to the verb, the COP appears under various allomorphs: most of the time [ɲ-] before vowels, and either a nasal or zero before consonants (the details are too intricate to be presented here). The tone of the SP will in all cases indicate whether the COP is present or not (cf. Ma., in (10)).

Even in those dialects that use it most, some verb forms do not normally take the COP; in C.K. this is the case with the P1 perfect in declarative sentences:

(62)   (Mo.) *àmě≠hùrà màrùhǔ* 'he has bought bananas'
       /á-à-mè≠hùr-à/
       /SP-Past1-Perf-Base-Suf/

but:

(63)   (Mo.) *ɲǎmè≠hùrà márùhǔ?* 'has he bought bananas?'

An entirely satisfactory account of the uses of the COP in this focalizing function hasn't yet been presented for any dialect (in spite of some attempts in Raum 1909, which do not seem to account well for contemporary Mo.; see, however, Dalgish 1979 and Moshi 1988 for W.).

In G. the COP appears in one tense only (cf. Philippson and Nurse 2000); in D. it doesn't exist and verb focus is expressed in different ways.

5.2 Subject Prefixes (SP) (table 24.11)

The most striking difference here is between D. and all the other dialects. As the table shows, D. has substituted /i/ for /a/ in all its SP (note particularly cl. 7 *tʃi-* and 12 *ki- !*). Cl. 1 /u-/ is not rare in neighboring Bantu languages but is unknown in the rest of K.B. Note also once again that the concords of cl. 16 and 17 have partially collapsed in D.

In the consecutive tense whose formative is /-ka-/, the prefixes in some dialects are slightly different, e.g. in Mo. 1st sg. is *ŋga-* instead of the expected **ndʒi-ka-*, 2nd sg. is *ko-* for **u-ka-* and cl. 1 *ka-* for **a-ka*. Other prefixes are unaffected.

In Mo. 2nd sg. is nowadays *o-* (Mowo variety) or *u-* (Mbokom variety), but *ku-* is found in some dependent forms.

For SP in negative forms, cf. below.

5.3 Neg.

Neg. refers here to the secondary negative prefix, for which see the special section on Negatives below.

5.4 TAM

TAM refers to the Tense–Aspect markers which are rather diverse in the various dialects and will be treated in the section on the Tense–Aspect (TA) system below.

5.5 OP

Object Prefixes (OP) are identical to SP, except for the following cases:

• The 2nd sg. OP is /-kù-/ even in those dialects with a different SP.

TABLE 24.11: KB SUBJECT PREFIXES

	M.	Mo.	S.R.	N.R.	D.
1st sg.	ʃì-	ndʒi-	ŋgi-	ŋgi-	ni-
2nd sg.	ku-	o-/u-	u-	u-	ku-
1st pl.	lu-	lu-	dú-	ʈu-	dì-
2nd pl.	mu-	mu-	mu-	mu-	mu-
cl. 1	a-	a-	a-	a-	u-
cl. 2	ßa-	wa-	ßa-	ßa-	ßi-
cl. 3	u-	fu-	u-	u-	ɣu-
cl. 4	i-	i-	i-/si-	(si-)	i-
cl. 5	li-	li-	li-	li-	dʒi-
cl. 6	a-	ha-	a-	a-	ɣi-
cl. 7	ki-	ki-	ki-	ki-	tʃi-
cl. 8	ʃi-	ʃi-	ʃi-	ʃi-	vi-
cl. 9	i-	i-	i-	i-	i-
cl. 10	ti-	tsi-	si-	si-	ri-
cl. 11	lu-	lu-	u-	–	lu-
cl. 12	ka-	ka-	ka-	ka-	ki-
cl. 13	ʁu-	–	–	ʈu-	dú-
cl. 14	u-	u-	u-	u-	ɣu-
cl. 15	–	ku-	–	ku-	ku-
cl. 16	a-	ha-	ha-	ha-	ku-
cl. 17	ku-	ku-	ku-	ku-	ku-

Note: Tones vary according to the particular tense.

- The 2nd pl. OP in R. is not attested; speakers of both S.R. and N.R. use the Swahili pattern i.e. 2nd sg. OP /-kù-/ plus a suffix /-èní/ added to the verb base, thus:

(64)   (Mo.) lòmẽmùwónà</lú-àmè-mú≠wón-à/ 'we have seen you'

(65)   (Ma.) ʈú-mé-kù≠lòly-èní 'we have seen you'

- The cl. 1 OP is /-mù-/ everywhere; it is mostly realized as a syllabic nasal, and in W.K. it assimilates to the following consonant in the same way as the IP for cl. 1 and 3 (see §4.1.1).

One should add to the list of OP the reflexive /-kú-/ tonally distinct from 2nd sg., e.g.:

(66)   (Mo.) ŋgĩ-lè-kú≠wòn-â 'I saw you'   ŋgĩ-lè-kú≠wón-à 'I saw myself.'

Many KB dialects (not D.) permit several OP to be present simultaneously; the case of W. is well documented by Moshi (1998).

For comparison, the independent personal pronouns are given in table 24.12.

5.6 Base

By base is meant any combination of radical (RAD) and extensions (EXT).

5.6.1

RAD are of various segmental shapes, as in most eastern Bantu languages. Whatever their syllabic make-up, they can only be H or L, e.g.:

TABLE 24.12: INDEPENDENT PERSONAL PRONOUNS

	M.	Mo.	S.R.	N.R.	D.
I, me	(y)ɛ́ɲì	íní	íní	íní	íní
you sg.	(y)éwè	íyò	íßè	ífè	óhò
cl. 1	wé	ó	ßé	fé	ómòni
we, us	(y)ésè	só	só	ṭó, ṭwé	ísì
you pl.	(y)éɲì	ɲó	ɲó	ɲó, ɲwé	íɲù
cl. 2	wó	wó	ßó	ßó	áßò

+C(G)-

(67) (Ma.)≠f-' 'die'   ≠v-' 'be'
     ≠w-' 'fall'   ≠ʃ-' 'come'
     ≠ly-' 'eat'   ≠ṭw-' 'go up'

+CV(C)-

(68) (Ma.)≠lì- 'cry'   ≠bó- 'be rotten'
     ≠fú- 'shout'   ≠hó- 'get well'
     ≠vés- 'ask'   ≠tém- 'play'
     ≠ʃìk- 'arrive'   ≠sèk- 'laugh'

+CVCV(C)-

(69) (Ma.)≠ṭáhik- 'vomit'   ≠kàmaṭ- 'bring, take'
     ≠húṭaɲ- 'listen'   ≠hóŋgo- 'rebuke'

5.6.2 EXT

For a survey of EXT in Bantu as a whole, see Schadeberg (this volume). EXT in KB are by and large the same as in other eastern Bantu languages. However, the (dissymetrical) vowel harmony discussed by Hyman (this volume) appears in KB in a rather restricted form.

- The situation is at its clearest with the stative /-ik-/: apart from G. and D., this extension does not harmonize in any KB dialect; in G. and D., on the other hand vowel harmony applies, so /-ik-/>/-ek-/ after mid-vowels, e.g.:

(70) (D.)≠ßàr- 'break, split'   stat.≠ßàr-ik-
     ≠vís- 'hide'   stat.≠vís-ik-
     ≠kúnd- 'want, love'   stat.≠kúnd-ik-

Harmonizing:
     ≠ßón- 'see'   stat.≠ßón-ek-
     ≠d'ék- 'cook'   stat.≠d'ék-ek-   vs.

(71) (M.)≠ón- 'see'   stat.≠ón-ik-
     ≠téreß- 'pray'   stat.≠téreß-ik-

- Things are much the same with the stative-reversive /-uk-/; it normally harmonizes to /-ok-/ after /-o-/ in G. and D. but not in the other dialects.
- Not so with the causative. This EXT is often realized as a modification of the final stem consonant with no vowel appearing; the question of harmony thus does not

arise, e.g.:

(72)   (D.) ≠*dʒòk-* 'go up'   caus. ≠*dʒòs-*
       yènd- 'go'   caus. ≠*yèndʒ-* 'bring'

etc.

The most frequent consonant alternation is /k/ > /ts/ (CK) ~ /t/ (WK) ~ /ṭ/ (G.) and /s/ (elsewhere). Also, with vowel-final bases, the causative is mostly formed by inserting /r/ (M., G. and D. /r/).

Otherwise, the most frequent allomorph of the causative extension is /-is-/ which doesn't seem to harmonize (but D. has /-iʃ-/ which does harmonize – this might be due to the influence of Swahili or other harmonizing languages).

- There exists another EXT whose relation to the causative is not too clear (it might appear as being a causative of the applicative ...) and which often has an intensive meaning. Its most basic shape is /-ir-/ and in Mo. at least, it does harmonize, e.g.:

(73)   (Mo.) ≠*pfúŋg-a* 'tie'   ≠*pfúŋg-ir-i-* 'arrest s.o.'
       ≠*d̵ɛ̵ts-* 'lose'   ≠*d̵ɛ̵ts-er-i-* 'erase'

- Most revealing is the case of the applicative. In all KB languages, this appears as /-i-/ (in R. and G. /-li-/ after a vowel-final base) and it never harmonizes, with the notable exception of the Useri sub-dialect of N.R., e.g.:

(74)   (D.) ≠*yènd-* 'go'   appl. ≠*-yènd-i-*
       ≠*yòr-* 'say'   appl. ≠*yòr-i-*

(75)   (Mo.) ≠*βéd̵-* 'wait'   appl. ≠*βéd̵-i-*
       ≠*olok-* 'fall'   appl. ≠*olok-i-*

but

(76)   (U.) ≠*nò-* 'sharpen'   appl. ≠*nò-le-*
       ≠*βéṭ-* 'wait'   appl. ≠*βéṭ-e-*

In D., however, when this extension is followed by the passive /-w-/, it appears as /-ilw-/ (/-l-/ is diachronically part of the extension but is manifested in that context only) which does harmonize:

(77)   (D.) ≠*ràm-i-* 'jump (appl.)'   pass. ≠*ràm-il-w-*
       ≠*ór-i-* 'appease spirits'   pass. ≠*ór-el-w-*

There are thus enough cases of harmony, closely paralleling what is found in other Bantu languages, to lead to the conclusion that this phenomenon was once prevalent also in KB. The source of the 'de-harmonizing' innovation is probably to be sought in W.K., since the clearest evidence for harmony still appears in the eastern part of KB.

- The other extensions found in KB are: /-w-/ (passive) (NB. In some dialects, e.g. M., passive /-w-/ irregularly coalesces with the default suffix /-a/ to give /-o/; in other dialects, this coalescence is regular, cf. 2.1), /-an-/ (reciprocal), and attested in D. only /-aɲ-/ (comitative), as in:

(78)   (D.) ≠*sàriɣ-* 'play'   comit. ≠*sàriɣ-aɲ-* 'play with s.o.'
       ≠*gál-* 'return'   comit. ≠*gál-aɲ-* 'return with s.o.'

5.7 Suffixes

These are five in KB and are found in combination with pre-Stem TAM markers. They are: /-a/ the default suffix, /-a(ɣ)a/, /-ie/, /-e/, and the somewhat marginal /-i/. Found only in D. is the curious /-ieɣe/ suffix, which would appear to be a combination of /-aɣa/ and /-ie/.

- /-a/ is by far the most frequent cross-dialectally and is found with a variety of TAM.
- /-e/ is universally found but normally only with a few subordinate forms in each dialect (especially the subjunctive or general dependent form).
- /-ie/ has either a past or anterior meaning (or both) according to the dialect and the particular TAM preceding it.
- /-aɣa/ seems to exist only in WK, G. and D.; it generally carries some sort of imperfective meaning.
- /-i/ appears in many dialects, but generally with a very few verbs, mostly those without an aspectual contrast between perfective and imperfective. The best example is with the verb 'see'. In practically all KB dialects, this verb takes an /-i/ suffix when a present punctual meaning has to be expressed (as against /-a/ for most other verbs). Thus:

(79)   (Mo.) *ndʒíꞌwóní* 'I see'   vs. *ndʒírùndâ* 'I am working'

Although there would seem to be some overlapping with /-ie/ (in M. in particular, /-i/ is an allomorph, sometimes in free variation, of /-ie/ for those verbs whose base ends in a nasal), the relationship between the two is by no means clear and this is an area where more research is needed.

5.8 Tense (T) and aspect (A)

We shall take Nurse's recent survey (Nurse forthcoming) as our guideline. Basing himself on Moshi's analysis of TA in W., Nurse proposes for KB as a whole (although he does not deal with D.) a system of five basic aspects: Simple, Progressive, Habitual, Retrospective and Perfect (which we prefer to call Anterior), intersecting with five basic tenses: Past 2, Past 1, Present, Future 1 and Future 2. Not all aspects are to be found with all tenses, however. (NB We omit G, for which see Philippson and Nurse 2000; D. being quite different from the rest, we will deal with it in a separate section.)

There is a major dividing line cutting across KB between WK and the rest: WK has an imperfective suffix *-aa* (Common Bantu *-aga*) marking Habitual and Future, e.g. in M. (perhaps also Progressive in K.); CK and R. have no such forms. Furthermore, although all use some form of the copula as formative for the Progressive, WK uses *-kee-* (probably originally a Retrospective form of *-kaa* 'dwell, remain'), whereas the latter two groups have different forms. Finally W.K. has three degrees of Past, whereas the rest have only two.

On the other hand, all groups have *-le-* for Before-Today Past, some form of *-(a)me-* for Anterior and a suffix *-ie* for Retrospective.

We will sketch the complete T/A of one representative WK dialect, namely M.; for an example of the system found in other dialects, the reader is referred to Moshi (1994).

5.8.1   The T/A system of M.

M. has three degrees of Past in the Simple Aspect, namely Past 3 (Remote) /-è- -à/, Past 2 (Intermediate) /-lé- -à/, Past 1 (Today) /-à- -à/. However, in the other aspects, only one

Past form is attested, the marker being normally /-è-/, thus Retrospective /-ø- -íè/, (Past) /-è- -íè/; Progressive /-kéè- -à/, (Past) /-èkéè- -à/; Habitual /-ø- -áá/, (Past) /-è- -àà/; an exception is apparently to be found in the Anterior, where the unmarked (Present) form is /-àmè- -à/ and where both Intermediate /-lémè- -à/ and Remote /-èmè- -à/ are attested.

The labels Progressive and Habitual are transparent enough not to need any detailed discussion. The difference between Retrospective and Anterior is that the former refers to a state entered upon at some indeterminate previous period, the process having led to it being considered as unimportant. With the Anterior, the process is of the essence: attention is directed to a change. Thus *păpă ≠ pfíé* means 'he is dead, i.e. he was alive formerly, but is nowadays dead', whereas *àmě ≠ pfă* means 'he has died (recently), he contracted some disease, etc., and so is now dead'.

In the Future M. appears to have only two forms, a Near Future /-àà/ (differing minimally in tone from the unmarked Habitual) and a Far Future /-ʃè- -àà/.

5.8.2 Negatives in main clauses

Contrary to the situation in many Bantu languages, KB (D. not included) does not have specific negative pre-stem markers; generally positive and negative verb forms are identical, with the exception of the focus marker being absent, and the underlying tone of the Subject prefix being H in the negative (however in M. – perhaps also in K. – the focus marker seems to be present, although without its accompanying SH tone !); cf.:

(80)   (M.) *ɲ-ʃí-ø-kù ≠ kàb-áá* 'I shall hit you' vs. *ɲ-ʃì-kú-ø ≠ kàb-áá fŏ* 'neg.'

The negative forms are always followed by a postposed end of phrase clitic, generally /pfó/ in CK and /fó/ elsewhere, but there are exceptions, e.g. Rw. /ndi/ and S.R. /ku/; /ɲí/ also occasionally appears in CK. The situation is made clearer by G. (for which see Philippson and Nurse 2000, where it is shown that the clitic in fact varies according to the class or person of the subject; other dialects – at least those with /(p)fó/ – have reduced the original system).

There exist however two dialects which seem to exhibit pre-stem negative markers. In S. a morpheme /-ta-/ found immediately after the Subject Prefix, as in (tones unknown):

(81)   (S.) *ti-li ≠ ua ma ≠ kudu* 'we are buying bananas' vs. neg. *ti-ta-li ≠ ua ma ≠ kudu (fo)*

As seen below (§5.8.3) this morpheme is the one used in several dialects (including S.) for dependent negatives.

In the U. variety of N.R. on the other hand, the morpheme /ʈe-/ precedes the prefix, as in:

(82)   (U.) *ʈé-lì-lé- ≠ ìdím-à ì ≠ àmbà...* 'it (the hyena) couldn't say...'

The closely related Ma. variety has an independent element /kwéʈé/ which optionally occurs before the verb, the clitic /fó/ being present in all cases:

(83)   (Ma.) *(kwěʈě) ŋgí-lìì ≠ ʈémá m̀ ≠ ʈěmě ŏ wákwá fŏ ...* 'I'm not cultivating my field...'

(This word resembles the stem / ≠ éʈè/ 'have', but the relationship is not clear.) It might well be that the U. form results from cliticization of the last syllable of /kwéʈé/ to give the negative marker seen above. This is only a hypothesis however.

5.8.3

Besides the main forms mentioned above, all KB dialects have several forms found only in subordinate contexts. A detailed analysis cannot be given here; we will just mention a few of the most common:

- /-ø- -è/: usually called 'Subjunctive' by Bantuists. It is found in commands and as a complement to verbs such as 'want', 'tell', etc.
- /-kà- -à/: the 'Consecutive' or 'Narrative'. It is the form most commonly found in a narrative or when a succession of actions is reported; it also serves as a potential.
- /-eki- -a/ (tones unknown). This form is usually found in 'when' clauses in the past.
- Relative constructions in KB are generally simple: there is no overt morphology on the verb in positive forms and the focus marker is never found immediately before the verb; in negative forms on the other hand, a pre-stem marker (/-lá-/ in M., K. and CK, /-ʈa- ~ -tʃa-/ in N.R. and S.R. respectively, and /-ta-/ in Rw. and S.) is inserted, and the phrasal clitic (/pfó/, etc.) is not found; e.g. (Mo.):

(84) *ɲ̀ kyókì ŏ≠húrǎ* (<u-a≠) [Today Past]? 'What is it you have bought?'

(85) *mbŏɗé m̀mbè ì-lé≠ʃáà* [Far Past] *mà≠hàtʃé hà≠βî* 'I have a cow that gave birth to two calves'

(86) *m̀mbà í ĩ-ø≠ìtʃûò wá≠ndù wà≠fóy ndʒí-là-wá≠kúndǐ* [Retrospective] 'This house is full of people I don't like'

This same negative is used in dependent verb forms, e.g. negative subjunctive.

5.8.4 The T/A system of Dawida

In this section, for the sake of simplicity, only H tones are indicated.

As mentioned in 5.7, D. has 5 suffixes. Leaving aside *-e* (Subjunctive), the other suffixes combine with a variety of pre-stem markers (including -ø-). It would be tempting to consider the suffixes as primarily aspectual and the pre-stem markers as temporal, but this is not entirely true. Grouping the various forms by suffix, we encounter the following:

5.8.4.1 -ieγe

This has the general meaning of Simple Past. Since D. recognizes three degrees of Past, the suffix will have to combine with specific tense markers to express these distinctions: *-ere- -ieγe* means Remote Past, *-e- -ieγe*, Intermediate and *-a- -ieγe*, Recent (whereas the first two forms can be used in both main and relative clauses, this is not the case for the last one, which has a special relative form *-ø- -ieγé*, with final H which shifts to the next syllable, cf. §3.4.), e.g.:

- *-ere- ieγe*
(87) *m≠yeɲi ore≠ser-ieγe* [<- u+ere-] *itʃí kí≠fumbi mw≠áká yu-ø≠sir-ie?* 'Did the guest sit on this chair last year?'

- *-e- -ieγe*
(88) *mw≠aná ko-ni≠βoɲér-éγe iguo ni m̀≠kóŋgo* 'The child you showed me yesterday is sick'

- *-a- -ieye*

(89) *n-a-ku≠ßon-iéye ku-ki≠dek-á má≠ruyu* 'I saw you cooking bananas (today)'

- *-ø- -ieyé*

(90) *ßa≠ndu ßi-ø≠bar-ieye ɲúŋgu rá ma≠tʃi ni ßéke aní?* 'Who are the people who broke the water-jars (today)?' (lit. the people who broke ... it is who?)

It should be borne in mind that those temporal distinctions overlap to a certain extent (cf. Ch 6).

5.8.4.2 -aya

This is clearly Imperfective (i.e. both Habitual and Progressive). It combines with both *-ere-* and *-e-* to yield more or less the expected meanings. However in combination with *-a-*, its meaning is Present Habitual (and not 'Immediate Past Imperfective', which would be rather meaningless anyway; note that the meaning Present Habitual is as frequently rendered by another form, mentioned below); similarly, the form *-ø- -aya* is not specifically relative, but is rather a general Present Imperfective as well as Near Future, e.g.:

- *-ere- -aya*

(91) *kíla ŋgéló ore≠yendʒ-aya ma≠dʒala kí≠dʒáleɲi* 'she used always to bring rubbish to the rubbish-pit'

- *-e- -aya*

(92) *...idʒi e≠ßiŋg-aya [<i-e-] aßadʒá ßaná ...* '... as it [the dog] was chasing those children...'

(NB. Examples in our data base are either relative or have a hypothetical meaning. This is a case where the 'Intermediate Past' meaning is difficult to exemplify.)

- *-a- -aya*

(93) *aba w-á≠sind-áyá ɲumbéɲi* 'Father spends the day at home'

(NB. We have no relative uses of this form, which might be an accidental gap.)

- *-ø- -aya*

In main clauses, the Near Future meaning is almost the only one attested:

(94) *dʼi-ø≠dʼum-áyá mw≠aná sókoɲi* 'We'll send the child to the market'

In relative clauses however, the Present meaning is frequent (here too, the suffix has a final H, realized on the next syllable); e.g.:

(95) *oho ní kazí kí i-ø-ku≠boi-aya kú≠ßoɲá?* 'Which work do *you* like doing?' (lit. you, it is which work which pleases you to do?)

5.8.4.3

-ie is Retrospective, but is found in only two forms *-a- -ie* in main clauses and *-ø- -ié* in relatives (note the tone again!). It does not seem to have any temporal meaning but derives it from the context, e.g.:

- *-a- -ie*

(96) *ma≠embe yá≠ßo-r-ie* 'the mangoes are rotten'

- *-ø- -ié*

(97) *u-ka≠dʼwa kí≠kápu tʃi-ø≠tʃú-e [<-tʃu-ie] má≠tʃúŋgwa* 'he picked up a basket (which was/is...) filled with oranges'

5.8.4.4

From the large number of forms with -*a*, we present just a few here:

- -*tʃa*- -*a* is Remote Future (from tomorrow onwards), e.g.:

  (98) *ßi-ká≠boɲ-á ßúdʒa ßi-tʃá≠pat-a sare i≠bo-ie* 'if they do thus, they will get a good name'

- -*aße*- is Present Progressive, e.g.:

  (99) *ßa≠limi ßaßé≠vimb-a ɲumba ráßo*: 'the farmers are thatching their houses'

- -*aɗa*- is Present Habitual, e.g.:

  (100) *ŋgelo ra súmésu m≠ruke ɣw-aɗa≠tʃu-a na i≠rußá dʒáɗa≠kal-á* [<dʒi-a] 'during the hot season, heat increases and the sun gets fierce'

The difference in meaning between this and the -*a*- -*aya* tense is at present not clear to us. For instance, the following sentence was produced by the same informant as an equivalent of example (93):

(101) *aba w-aɗá≠sind-á ɲumbéɲi* 'Father spends the day at home'

- -*a*- -*a*: this is Anterior and also Immediate Past; it differs from the Retrospective in that a process is involved; it can be found in both main and relative clauses – in the latter case the suffix has a H tone, e.g.:

(102) *ma≠tʃi ɣ-a≠ho-á* 'the water has cooled down'

(103) *ŋgelo w-a≠méri-a kú-ßi≠néká ma≠lemba ...* 'when he had finished giving them grass ...'

In combination with the Remote Past of -*koye* 'be', it has Remote Past Anterior meaning:

(104) *ore≠koye w-a-ßi≠zer-á ß≠aná ßáke áŋgú...* 'he had told his children that ...' (lit. he was he has told ...)

5.8.4.5

In addition to all the Past forms described above, there exists in D. a General Past: -(*e*)*ɗe*- -*a* (there does not seem to be any difference in meaning between -*eɗe*- and -*ɗe*-; our main informant used the latter much more often). Since there exists such a wealth of Past forms with various shades of temporal and aspectual meanings, it appears strange at first glance to encounter a form which is neuter in relationship to all the rest. Although we are not absolutely clear about the uses of this form, there is a strong presumption that it puts the verb under the dependence of some other element in the sentence, whether it be a circumstancial clause, an adverb, a locative, etc. The verb appears somehow out of focus – it is probably significant that this form never appears in the negative, nor in relative clauses, e.g.:

- locative

(105) *mae u-ɗé≠ßik-à kí≠kutʃu mézéɲi* '(their) mother put the bag on the table'

- temporal

(106) *imbiri ya m≠ka u-se≠mér-ié kú≠deká, ßi-ɗé≠vík-a* 'before the woman had finished cooking, they arrived'

- instrument

(107) *mw≠aná u-ré≠ßar-a ɲuŋgu ná i≠ɣo* 'the child broke the pot with a stone'

- various circumstances
- (108) *ß-eɗé≠ɓoɲ-á húßú eri aßadʒá ß≠aná ßi-se≠non-e* [Subjunctive] *ví≠lámbo*
  'they used to do this so that the children do not spoil things'
- (109) *aŋgú o≠zo-éɣé ku≠ɣosia m≠yoŋgo ɣw≠ake yoɗé≠yoyom-ék-a* [<ɣu-eɗe]
  'because he started to get old his back had become bent'

5.8.4.6

Main clause negatives are different in D. from the other KB languages, and more reminiscent of other languages, particularly Central Kenya Bantu. A negative marker *nde-* is put before the Subject Prefix for all person and classes except 1st sg. where expected **nde-ni-* is replaced by *si-*. Otherwise the range of meaning covered by each negative form is roughly similar to the respective affirmative.

Subordinate negatives insert a Pre-stem marker *-se-* after the *affirmative* Subject Prefix (see (108)).

5.8.4.7

Subordinate verb forms are at least as numerous as in other KB languages (cf. §5.8.3.). We cannot deal with them here (G. Philippson is preparing a complete survey of the D. verbal system).

6 CONCLUSION

As is often the case with Bantu languages, it is hard to find characteristics defining KB as a whole vs. its neighbors. Most diagnostic, since it includes D., is probably the restricted working of the harmony process in extensions (§5.6. above). The other characteristics all exclude D.:

- devoicing of most obstruents
- negative clitics
- infinitives in cl. 5 (of which some traces do appear even in D.)

Other criteria are less diagnostic but are shared mostly with Central Kenya (E50) languages, such as the intricate relationship of tone and syntax (not present in G. or D.) and the widespread use of the copula in main verb forms (again largely absent from G. and D.).

Also, KB (including D.) has a very distinctive vocabulary, much of it borrowed from non-Bantu sources (see Nurse 1979b and Philippson 1984).

REFERENCES

Bresnan and Moshi 1993; Dalgish 1979; Davey *et al*. 1982; Grimes 2000; Hyman, this volume; Ladefoged and Maddieson 1996; McHugh 1990; Moore and Puritt 1977; Moshi 1988, 1994, 1998; Müller 1947; Nurse 1979b, this volume, forthcoming; Nurse and Philippson 1977; Odden and Kisseberth, this volume; Philippson 1982, 1984, 1998; Philippson and Nurse 2000; Raum 1909; Ryabova 1984, 1987; Saloné 1980; Sharp 1954; Winter 1980, 1987; Woodward 1913–14.

CHAPTER TWENTY-FIVE

THE INTERLACUSTRINE ZONE (ZONE J)

Yvonne Bastin

CONVENTIONS

Examples are written in the spelling of the authors except for the notation of the seven standardized vowels /i e ɛ a ɔ o u/. Also, in the examples, high and low tones are marked in order to avoid any confusion due to the absence of tonal notation.

°aaa   regional protoform or form not allowed
*aaa   Proto-Bantu reconstruction

N   nasal
C   consonant
S   semi-vowel
V   vowel
-    morpheme boundary
P   prefix (NP: nominal prefix, VP: verbal prefix, OP: object prefix, PP: pronominal prefix, LP: locative prefix)
[ ]   phonetic notation

Documented sources (monographs and regional studies) for the languages involved are:

Gungu   Schoenbrun 1990; SIL (not consulted).
Bwari   Ankei 1979.
JD40   Bbemo Musubaho 1982; Black 1995; Hyman and Valinande 1985; Kahindo 1984; Mutaka 1994; Tucker 1960; Valinande 1984.
JD50   Aramazani 1985; Jouannet 1984; Kaji 1985, 1992, 1996; Mateene 1963, 1992; Nkiko 1977; Polak-Bynon 1980a; Shamavu 1982.
JD60   Coupez 1960; Gerdts and Whaley 1991; Kimenyi 1980; Meeussen 1959; Nakagawa 1992; Rodegem 1967; Van Sambeek n.d.
JE10   Chanda 1975; Cullen 1999 (not consulted); Maddox 1938; Musamba 1975; Paluku 1996; Taylor 1985; Wung'a Lomami 1973.
JE20   Bickmore 1991; Byarushengo *et al.* 1977; Hermann 1904; Hurel 1909; Muzale (forthcoming); Rascher 1958.
JE15   Ashton *et al.* 1954; Chesswas 1963; Huntingford 1965; Hyman and Katamba 1990, 1991, 1993; Mchombo 1993; Rodgers 1962; Walusimbi 1976, 1996.
JE25   Botne 1989; Downing 1996a,b; Sillery 1932.
JE30   Angogo 1983; Appleby 1961; Austen n.d.; Brown 1972; Chagas 1976; de Blois 1970, 1975; Goldsmith 1991; Morris 1963; Sample 1976; Schadeberg 1989; Leung 1991.

JE40   Cammenga 1994; Whiteley 1956, 1960.
JE   Mould 1976, 1981; Hinnebusch *et al.* 1981.

1 INTRODUCTION

The Interlacustrine zone lies at the sources of the White Nile and includes many of the languages classified in Zones D and E by Guthrie, combined as Zone J by Meeussen. To clarify the connection between these two classifications, they are here labelled JD and JE.

The map below offers a global view of the languages in this region, but does not always differentiate language and dialectal variety since dialects have generally been omitted. The languages of Rwanda and Burundi belong exclusively to the zone, which occupies the southern region of Uganda, the northwest fringes of Tanzania, and the southwest fringes of Kenya. In the Democratic Republic of Congo (DRC), some languages, several of which are spoken in more than one country, form the western boundary in contact with Zone D languages. In the south, adjacent languages belong to Zone F. An arc is formed from the northwest to the southeast by the Nilo-Saharan languages which, at their western end, split the northeast Bantu area, barring direct contact between languages in Zone E and those in the Interlacustrine zone.

Because of its geographic location, the Interlacustrine zone is characterized by mutual influence between Bantu and Nilo-Saharan languages or, to a smaller extent, Cushitic (Afro-Asiatic) languages, whose impact is mediated indirectly through other Bantu languages. The influences are usually noticed in borrowings, but can also induce language change. Thus, one group of Hima speaks Lendu (Nilo-Saharan, Sudanese), one group speaks a Bantu language, Hima-Nkore, in Uganda, and another group speaks a clearly distinct variety, Hema, in the DRC. The impact of borders, both natural and political, on linguistic differentiation is predictable since borders limit contact between speakers of the same language. This is evident in the differences that separate Talinga (JE102) from its dialectal variety Bwisi or from other JD40 languages, spoken on both sides of the border between the DRC and Uganda. 'Innovations' and loanwords, such as *sagame* 'blood' (Möhlig 1974), have an interesting distribution skirting around JD60, so that this group appears more conservative and, relatively speaking, less susceptible to external influences, something already observed by A. E. Meeussen, who considered Zone J, on the basis of JD60, 'archaic'. The same observation can be made about Jita-Kwaya-Ruri-Regi (JE25), which, in all of the Interlacustrine area east of the line of lakes, is the only group to have kept *-*dómè* 1/2 'man'.

In Bantu, lateral influence and diachronic inheritance overlap. This explains the difficulty of identifying specific, exclusive features that can distinguish the languages of one zone from the rest of Bantu. This is also true of Interlacustrine. However, the isogloss bundle that outlines this grouping is more compact than any interior bundle. What follows highlights some characteristic elements within the zone without covering it entirely. We deal fairly fully with augmentatives and diminutives formed by a change of prefix, which, however, is not limited to Zone J.

The synthesis of classification studies – which do not involve the same languages or include all speakers – suggests the following schematic representation.

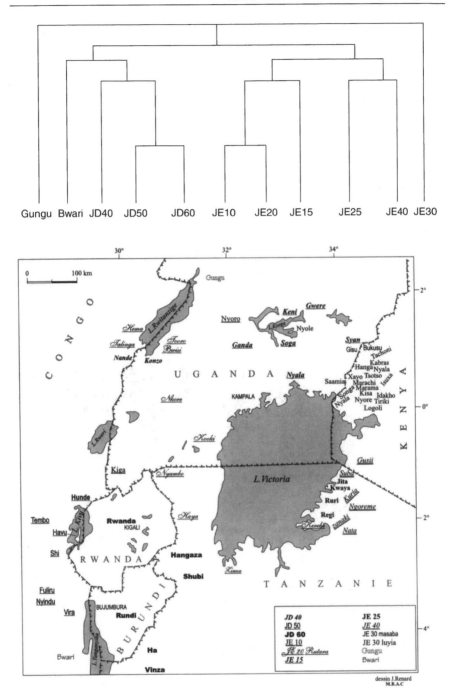

MAP 25.1 THE INTERLACUSTRINE LANGUAGES

For the nomenclature of languages from each group, refer to map 25.1. Bwari, for which there is little documentation, is included in J by Schoenbrun (1990), but a possible association with Zone D has not yet been completely discounted. Schoenbrun also suggests Gungu as an isolated branch; its geographic location at the northeastern end of Lake Rwitanzige suggests that differences are at least partly due to influences outside Bantu. The data collected by SIL on this language, not used here, support this hypothesis. The belated reclassification of Luhya (JE30) with J might also reflect external influences rather than its true genealogical position. Furthermore, it is with Guthrie's Group E40 and particularly with Kuria, that JE25 shows the most affinity, which suggests the inclusion of these languages (JE40) in the Interlacustrine area, with the exception of E46 Sonjo, which Nurse and Rottland (1991–2) have shown to belong to E50. We will not therefore claim that these branchings reflect historical affiliations. We attach no time scale to them.

The characteristics shared with Bantu are dealt with in the general chapters of this book and are only discussed briefly here. In what follows, we will concentrate on:

- specific shared features of part or all of the Interlacustrine zone, which does not exclude their presence elsewhere in Bantu;
- the facts we found interesting due to the originality of some of their developments.

2 PHONOLOGY

2.1 Vowels

Most Interlacustrine languages have five phonological vowels /i e a o u/, with exceptions in the northeastern extremities (Talinga-Bwisi, Nande-Konzo) and in the southeast, where some speakers of Luhya (Idakho, Isuxa, Tiriki, Logooli) have, as in JE40, seven vowels, for which we have adopted a unique transcription /i e ɛ a ɔ o u/. Gungu, according to SIL documents, has five, seven, or even nine vowels depending on regional or idiolectal variants. In addition to systematic lengthening before NC or after CS (except word-finally), Interlacustrine languages contrast long and short vowels, which occur in lexemes or are linked with rules of contact between vowels of different morphemes:

(1) Fuliiru *kúháànà*   'to give'   *kúhánà* 'to punish'
     Rundi   *kùbáànà (kù-bá-ànà)* 'to be together'

This is not the case in:

- Talinga, Nande-Konzo, and Hunde, where length is limited to the penultimate vowel at the end of an utterance or elicitation forms:

(2) Hunde *ìbàlé…*; ≠*ibă:lè*≠ 'stone'

- Nande-Konzo, Hunde and Tembo, where two identical vowels can follow one another, but do not create a long vowel:

(3) Nande *èrèhékà*   'to carry'
            hèkàà   'carry!' (imperative) cf. Shi *súníkàgá* 'push twice!'
     Hunde *bánà (bà-ánà)* 'children'
            ndàànò   'promise' cf. Shi *ééndágáánó*
            mbàèndà   'I will leave one day' cf. *ngèndé* 'that I leave'

Word-finally, only Shi and, to some extent, Logooli allow long vowels. These are usually underlying, at least in Ganda:

(4)   Ganda   *yàlyáá=kô*   'he ate a little'
              yàlyá kyô   'he ate it' (class 7) cf. *kúlábà=kô* 'to see a little'
      Shi   *óókúbáá*   'to be, exist, live' cf. Rundi *kùbá* (*kù-bá-à*)

Expressive lengthening, especially in interjections or demonstratives, is frequent:

(5)   Ganda   *kìzító*   'heavy'
              kìzítóóò   'very heavy'

Only open vowels (e/ɛ, o/ɔ, a) can occur word-initially except in two areas formed by JD60 and JD50 Hunde and part of JE40/JE30. In the second group, the distribution is surprising because if the southern JE30 varieties adjoin JE40, certain varieties of northern Masaaba form an isolate. This can be explained with examples from JD60 Fuliiru that differentiate between spontaneous and more fixed speech:

(6)   Haya   *òmútì* 'tree'   Rundi   *ìgìtì* 'tree', *ùmútì* 'medicine'
      Saamia   *omundu*   Logooli   *omondo* 'person'
      Bukusu   *òmù:ndù*   Masaaba Lusoba   *umundu*
      Fuliiru *ó-mú-hìndùùkò* 'circle'

               ú-mú-ndù àtàʃàgwá àyìʃágá yénènè
               'one doesn't respect a man, he respects himself'

Vowel height is not absolute. Exceptions can be either grammatically determined or connected with the ancient alternation *i/e*, which explains why class 5 is often involved.

In JE40, vowel height in prefixes is determined by the thematic vowel:

(7)   Gusii   *oko-goro*   'leg'
              ɔkɔ-bɔkɔ   'arm'

2.1.1 Semi-vowels (S)

The semi-vowels *w* and *y* are attested everywhere in the sequences (C)/(NC)SV. Three facts in particular should be mentioned:

- Talinga and Nande-Konzo distinguish two degrees of height for both semi-vowels, which is evident in the application of vowel assimilation rules:

  (8)   Talinga   *kùβyáálà*   'to give birth' cf. *kùsìmbà* 'to raise' *kòsèmbà* 'to dig'
        Nande   *ɔmúsyàkólò*   'old person'   *ɔmósyá*   'plain'

- In Rwanda-Rundi (JD60), semi-vowels often induce a co-articulated consonant so that $b+w \rightarrow bg$ and $p+w \rightarrow pk$, something official orthography does not reflect:

  (9)   Rwanda   *ùbùshì* [ùʋùʃkwì] 'summit'   *syà* [skyà]   'grind!'
                 ùbwâ:tò (ù-bù-átò) *amâ:tò* (à-mà-átò) [ùbgâ:tò àmâ:tò] 'boat'

- The opposition between ny and /ɲ/ is highlighted by linguists as occurring in a continuous area formed by Talinga, Nande-Konzo, Hunde, Fuliiru, and Rwanda-Rundi with a continuation in Nyankore-Kiga where the sequence nyV: seems to be limited to a few words:

  (10) Rundi   *yàrámènyè* [yàrámèɲè]   'he knew'
                yàrámènnyè [yàrámènìyè] 'he broke'

Fuliiru   *kụnimúlà*   'to hunt me'
          kúnyóólà   'wring (clothes)'

The rules that govern vowel contact and those of progressive or regressive vowel assimilation are low-level and widespread. The assimilation processes always involve affixes.

2.1.2 Consonants

Consonant systems are diversified and partially related to the five- or seven-vowel system. Palatalization of stops, often pronounced, before front vowels is frequent:

(11)   Kisa   *-kendo* 11/10 [oluče:ndo, tsi:nje:ndo] 'journey'
       Tembo   *-sìnd-* 'to finish'   *kú-sìnd-ír-á kúsìnjírá* 'to finish, limit to'
       Rwanda   *-ké* 'little'   [gʸíkʸé] 7

Outside JD60 (see §2.1.1), only Talinga has the co-articulated stops *gb* and *kp*:

(12)   Talinga   *gbàtèsà* 'to enlarge'

An isogloss distinguishes *vu/(fu)* and *ju/(zu)*, clearly isolating the Rutara (JE20, JE11–14) group, which lacks labiodental fricatives:

(13)   Nyankore   *enjura*
       Haya   *enjûla*; cf. Saamia *efula*; Fuliiru *mvùlá* 'rain'

JE25, 30 and 40 are characterized by the absence of voiced fricatives word-initially and intervocalically (with the exception of *ß*). Two languages of group JD50, Tembo and Hunde, should also be included. They are situated in the D43 Nyanga extension.

2.2 Facts of interest

The following are chosen for their originality or particular development in the Interlacustrine zone.

2.2.1 Syllabic consonants and long consonants

Syllabic nasals are often word-initial in Bantu, usually as predicative morphemes or as realizations of the prefix *mu-*. However, the syllabic consonants in Logooli are isolated:

(14)   Logooli   *ri-dɔ̌ši ḍdɔši* 5   'mud, earth'
                 ri-rahe ḷlahe 5   'pretty'   cf. *kerahe* 7, *rikudu* 5 'turtle'

Kisa has a similar reduction, which produces a [VC] syllable. Sample (1976) shows how this phenomenon is linked to the presence of an initial vowel:

(15)   Kisa   *eli-loka elloka* 5   'canine tooth'   cf. *elixutu* 'tortoise'

The reduction of *ru/ro* to *w* before *rV* (*o-ro-ritɔ uwrítɔ* class 11 'heavy') in Kuria reflects the same tendency even though the process is different.

Ganda has isolated occurrences of long consonants corresponding to Meinhof's Law (see below) or to the deletion of a close front vowel preceded by another vowel – as long as it derives historically from *(high) i:

(16) Ganda *ettabi, amatabi* 'branch'
     olukko, enziko 'long valley'
but *ekijiiko* 'spoon'

This process combines with the gemination or strengthening of consonants or semi-vowels:

(17) *eddume, amalume* 'male', *ejjiba amayiba* 'dove', *eggwanga, amawanga* 'nation'

When *pyV* is not preceded by a nasal, it is realized *ggyV* (*amaggya* 6, *empya* 9 'new').

2.2.2 The ŋ/ŋg opposition

/ŋg/ is attested throughout Interlacustrine, and the occurrence of a velar nasal is limited to the pre-consonantal context in Rutara, JD40, and JD50. Other groups attest ŋ/ŋg, but with variable status:

- In groups JE15, 30, and 40 the velar nasal often results from the application of Meinhof's Law (see below), but also appears in other contexts:

(18) Ganda *ku-ŋoola* 'despise, sneer at' *èŋŋo* 'banana bud'
     Kisa *oluŋala, tse:ŋala* 'leech'
     Idakho *loŋalɔ* 'frog'
     Syan *ekiŋàs* 'ground hornbill'
     Bukusu *ŋálí* 'truly'
     Kuria *okoŋáta* 'to be about to'

- The following examples show the relationship between *p/mp* and the velar nasal:

(19) Nyole *-ŋuliira* 'hear' *puliira* (*n–ŋ* → *p*) 'I hear'
     cf. Nande *èré-hòlèkèrérà* 'listen attentively'
     Gusii *ŋa* 'give me' *eŋiti* 'hyena'
     cf. Rundi *ìmpà*, Logooli *embiti* (*m–p* → *mb*)

- In Jita [ŋ] is a free variant of /ŋk/:

(20) Jita *ì:ŋkòkórà/ì:ŋòkórà* 'knee'

- In JD60 [ŋ] is related to the following (semi-) vowel, which appears in several JE30 varieties:

(21) Rwanda *-nywà* [-ŋwà]
     Idakho *xoŋwa*
     cf. Bukusu *xû:ɲwà* 'to drink'
     Logooli *omŋwaami o-mo-ami*, Rundi *ùmwă:mì* [ùmŋă:mì]
     cf. Saamia *umwaami* 'leader'
     Logooli *omŋwaana o-mo-ana*, Rundi *ùmwâ:nà* [ùmŋâ:nà] 'child'

This relationship with a back vowel manifests itself differently in Masaaba and Luhugu. Brown (1972) claims that, in Luhugu, [ɲ] is an allophone of [ŋ] before a front vowel when the palatal nasal is not subject to Meinhof's Law:

(22)   Luhugu   *ku-ɲila* [kuɲila]   'to wince' cf. *ßu-ŋoolo* [ßuŋoːlo]   'frogspawn'

Despite some realizations that highlight phonetic tendencies, the isogloss [ŋ, ŋg/ng] clearly separates JE15, 30 and 40 from the rest of Interlacustrine, although Ganda patterns with the western areas in other cases.

2.2.3 *Dentals and alveolars, trills and taps*

The relationship between dental/alveolar stops and trill/tap approximants is complex. Complementary distribution plays a role but is not without exceptions. Preceding nasals, Dahl's Law, and dialect interference are all involved. Some distributions can be explained diachronically; others appear to be random. Thus, the voiceless stop /t/ is attested everywhere and is aspirated in Rwanda-Rundi and Shi /tʰ/. Note:

- Nande contrasts a dental stop and a voiceless apico-alveolar stop, the former resulting at least partially from loanwords:

(23)   Nande   *àkàtèrà*   'striped rat, edible'
          àkáṭèndè   'small bottle'

- In JD50 the stop /t/ has a reduced function:

In Havu, /t/ only occurs in some loanwords, as in Shi, which contrasts *tu* and *rhu*, depending on whether *u* derives from **u* or **o*. In Shi, therefore, /t/ generally corresponds to a fricative and, more rarely, to an affricate, in the other five-vowel languages:

(24)   Shi   *íitúù*   'spear'   *óókúrhúmà*   'to send'
          Haya   *èicûmù*   'spear'   *òkùtûmà*   'to send'

In Shi and Havu, /rh/ (voiceless trill) generally corresponds to /t/, but in Tembo, only [ta] is attested, and [ts] is heard before a back vowel, [c] before a front vowel.

The /t/ of Logooli, Nyole, Luhugu, and some Masaaba varieties corresponds to /r/ in most Luhya varieties, including other Masaaba dialects and Lusoba:

(25)

	Nyole	Logooli	Kisa	Luhugu	Lusoba	Bukusu
to kill		*yita*	*oxwiːra*	*kukwiːta*	*xuxwiːra*	*xúxwìːrà*
NP13	*otù-*	*to-*	*oru-*			
ear	*oxùtwì*			*kukutu*	*xuxuru*	*lîːrù*

The voiceless stop is attested beside /r/, but corresponds to /d/. The appearance of stops is predictable when they result from the application of Dahl's Law or in postnasal position, but a certain number of unconditioned occurrences are observable, at least synchronically. The alternations *r/t/d* are similar enough to *ß/p/b* so that we will not deal with these here.

(26)

	Nyole	Luhugu	Lusoba	Bukusu	Kisa
fingernail		*cidete*	*çitere*		*lîːtèrè*
three	*-datu*	*-tàrù*			
draw (water)	*oxudaŋa*			*xûːtàà*	*oxutaha*
beer		*indali*	*indali*		
small beer		*kadali*	*xatali*		

As in JE30, occurrences of /d/ – common in Talinga, Shi, Havu, Fuliiru, partial in Nande and Ganda, marginal in Nyambo and Jita – do not occur within the contexts of Dahl's Law or of NC.

(27) Fuliiru *kúdòbà* 'to mix' *kúlòbà* 'to fish'
      Ganda *kùdálìzá* 'embroider' *kùdómòlá* 'dash to the ground'

In some cases, the explanation is historical. Thus, in Shi, *du* is the reflex of **du*, whereas in Havu and Fuliiru, *du* and *vu* are attested as being in free variation or lexically determined:

(28) Shi *oókúdúgá* 'stir flour when cooking'
      Fuliiru *kúdùgà* 'cook porridge'
      Havu *-dùg-/-vùg-* 'prepare porridge'
      Shi *óókúlúgà* 'be numerous'
      Fuliiru *kúlùgà* 'abound'

However, outside this context, except in certain long vowel stems such as *-dó:m-/-vó:m-* 'draw water' (°-*dùɔm-*) in Havu, numerous *l* or *r/d* alternations do not correspond to any known condition, diachronic or synchronic, even if the relationship between *l/r* and *d* is only visible through their production after a nasal.

This brings us to the *l/r* alternation. Lateral /l/ is attested in most JE30 varieties (except Nyole) and Haya (JE20). It corresponds to /r/ in Gusii and Kuria in the southeast and in Nyambo and Nyankore-Kiga in the northwest. Talinga, Ziba and Kerebe *l/r* are described as 'free variants'.

In other languages, *l/r* are at least partially in complementary distribution. In Jita, use seems to be linked to position in the word: *l* in prelexical morphemes and word-initially, otherwise *r*, whereas in Logooli *r→l* in the context *rV-r*. In JE10 (Hema, Nyoro), 15, 35, JD40, 50 and 60, occurrences are largely conditioned: *l* after *a, o, u* and initially; *r* after a front vowel. Furthermore, a following front (semi-)vowel can change its articulation, often to a lateral retroflex. This double conditioning disrupts the system, as elsewhere, causing the loss of alternations following the substitution of prefixes for which the criteria are based on statistical frequency and not on absolute conditioning.

(29) Nande *èrèkálà* ... 'smoke meat' but also *èrèkárà* .... 'to force'
            ɛre-cl.5 *-er*-applicative suffix *ɔlo*-cl. 11
      Fuliiru *iróngè* 'den, lair'
            múlózì 'sorcerer'
            kíḷígò 'well' but also *kílúlù* 'bitter'
            kíkáràzà 'chest'

Ganda patterns with the western group in terms of conditioned segments, which makes the distribution interesting even if based on somewhat superficial phenomena like the impact of vowels on the articulation of certain consonants. The same consonants (*l/r/t/d*) reflect quite different systems, Shi and Havu being the only ones to contrast voiced/voiceless trills.

2.2.4 NC sequences

Ignoring the application of Meinhof's Law and the common phenomenon of movement towards a homorganic nasal or a stop, where *r, l → d, h → p, ß → b*, and present everywhere as the deletion of a nasal in front of another nasal, realizations of NC fall into three main groups:

- Voiced/voiceless stops and fricatives are attested without restriction after a nasal in JE10, 15, 20, 25, JD60, and Shi and Havu (JD50). JE40 (Gusii, Kuria) may figure in this group, but with the total absence of voiced fricatives intervocalically, word-initially, and after a nasal.

In JE15 (Ganda, Soga, Syan), JE20 (Nyambo, Haya, Kerebe), and, it seems, only in Nyankore of group JE10, the apical feature persists when adjacent to labiodental *f* (*nf*):

(30)   Nyankore   *enfu*   'large mud-fish'   but,
        Nyoro   *emfubaso*   'bead necklace'

In Shi and Nyankore, there is a slight connection with JD50 Hunde/Tembo in the following:

(31)   Shi   [ẽ:fî] [ẽ:mfî]   'fishes'
        Nyankore   *énfu, éfu*   'large mud-fish'

In Jita, *ŋk* may be realized as *ŋ*, and we also find *Vmp/Vns* and *V:p/V:s*, similar to the realizations in Luhya varieties. All across Interlacustrine, however, *n-t* realizations are identical to those of the stem derived from *-*ntò* 1/2 'person', except all JE25 where all varieties attest *omu-nu*. This offers a possible direction for research on JE25, a relative isolate in the middle of Interlacustrine.

- In Fuliiru and Nande, only nasal-voiced consonant clusters are attested (although *nt* occurs in some Nande loanwords), which implies the voicing of voiceless consonants after a nasal.

- Tembo and Hunde show a partial connection with the preceding group because their stops produced through contact with a nasal are always voiced. Like Nande, these two languages have no intervocalic voiced fricatives (except bilabials), but in Hunde, contact with a nasal produces either a single fricative or a nasal-voiceless fricative sequence. In Tembo, the split is different; some fricatives act as stops and become voiced, whereas nasals delete in front of other nasals.

(32)   Hunde/Tembo   *ndúmwà/ńdzùmwà* 9   'messenger'
                          -túm-/-tsùm-   'to send'
                          ncìrà 9/njírá 9,   'path'
                          kácírá 12   'dim. path'
        Hunde   *xúkì* 9   'fly'
        Tembo   *éfì* 9   'fish'
                          éhònyí 9   'shame'

- Luhya varieties are more distinct and progressively different from north to south. Nyole and Luhugu Masaaba have kept nasals before voiced consonants, but deleted them before voiceless consonants, with compensatory lengthening of the preceding vowel at least in Masaaba. In the south, we observe increased voicing of voiceless stops. For instance, in Kisa *n-č* and *n-ts* → *nj* and *nz*. However, the nasal deletes before other voiceless consonants; in Logooli, *n-s* → *s*, but *n-ʃ* → *nʃ*, keeping the nasal, a feature which connects the language with JE40.

These different realizations are standard, the remarkable feature here being the disparity which has persisted in JD50 and JE30 varieties.

2.2.5 The Ganda Law or Meinhof's Law

Most Interlacustrine languages are not distinct from the rest of Bantu where different nouns of variable number are subject to Meinhof's Law. Their distribution often occupies a compact area, and numerous alternants *ŋ/nz*, *nj* in class 9/10 can be explained by Meinhof's Law.

(33)   Hunde   *lùbáncà, máncà* 11/10   'discussion'
       cf. Haya   *eibanja* 5   'debt'
       Rwanda/Rundi   *ùrùbàánzá, ìmàánzà* 11/10   'debt, lawsuit'

The rule is most productive in Ganda where it stops at the stage of double assimilation, maintaining a sequence of two nasals:

(34)   Ganda   *kùbûmbá*   'mould'   *`mûmbá*   'I mould'
               èŋŋómá   'drum'   cf. *èŋgábó*   'shield'

It is equally productive in Havu and Shi, though *ŋg* is retained. The rule applies systematically to *N-b/d/j* in front of *N-voiced C*. Before a simple nasal, the rule seems to be limited to *N-j*.

(35)   Havu   *ólúbándá, émándá* 11/10 'valley' *ényúmá*   'behind'
              cf. *njovu*   'elephant'
       Shi   *óólúbáànjà, éémáànjà, .m̀màànjà* 11/6 or 10   'court case'
              óókúlóónzáá 'look for'   *lóónzàà!*   'look for!'
              ńnóónzàà! 'look for me!'

In Shi, there is a word-initial occurrence of a two-nasal sequence where the first nasal is syllabic.

In the east, in Luhya varieties, the productivity of Meinhof's Law seems to diminish progressively towards the south. Common in Nyole, the rule has only occasional applications in Logooli.

(36)   Nyole   *nanga*   'I call'   *olanga*   'you call'
               olubanga, (e)manga   'rock'

A characteristic of the Luhya varieties is linked to the combination of two phenomena, the 'Luhya Rule' (Mould 1976) and the voicing of consonants after a nasal. This creates a phonological system where the application of Meinhof's Law only corresponds very slightly to the environment. The rule does not apply when a voiced consonant is the result of the voicing of a voiceless consonant after a nasal, or when it corresponds to a voiceless consonant in other varieties. This is seen by comparing the internal variation between two Masaaba varieties:

(37)   Lusoba   Lufumbu
       xutamba, indamba   *kudamba, indamba*   'to lack, I lack'
       xuwamba, imbamba   *xuhamba, impamba*   'to hold, I hold'
but   *xuβona, imona*   *kuβona, imona*   'to see, I see'

This situation supports Sample's (1976) claim that Meinhof's Law applies to the sequence *n-l* and optionally to *n-(z)*.

(38) Kisa *oxutema* 'try' *e:ndema* 'I try' (without Meinhof's Law)

　　　　　oxulima 'cultivate' *e:nima* 'I cultivate'

　　　　　oxwi:mba 'to sing' *e:nzi:mba/e:ɲi:mba* 'I sing'

Velar consonants are more complex. Historically **g* went to *k*, except in some peripheral varieties like Logooli. /g/ is not part of the phonological system of Luhya varieties except in a few cases produced by Dahl's Law, which we discuss later, and in the *ŋg* sequence *ŋg* (*n-k→ŋg*). In the following examples, the non-application of Meinhof's Law might also be supported by the fact that *ŋg* and *nj* are linked to the voicing of a voiceless consonant after a nasal.

(39) Bukusu *è:ŋgà:ŋgà -kà:ŋgà* 9 'profit'

Nevertheless, in most Luhya varieties, realizations follow Meinhof's Law:

(40) Bukusu *è:ŋòmà* 'drum', cf. Haya *eŋgoma*
　　　　Saamia *eŋoombe* 'cow'

The stems attesting velar nasals in class 9/10 as the result of the application of Meinhof's Law are often part of the Proto-Bantu stock and occur among the stems where this rule is widely attested, for instance Gusii *eŋɔɔmbɛ* 'cow' and Kuria *ɛɛŋɔina* 'crocodile', where the application of the rule is erratic. These frozen examples explain the difference in treatment, confirmed by diminutives where the velar nasal is maintained, whereas normally prefixes are replaced:

(41) Kisa *ŋomo* 9 'drum' *kaŋomo* 12 'small drum'
　　　 cf. *kuβona* 'see' *imoni* 9 'eye'
　　　　　kaβoni 12 'small eye'

It is therefore difficult to understand the realizations without resorting to historical explanations. The split distribution of the area of productive application is surprising. Indeed, if JE30 is contiguous with JE15, Havu and Shi (JD50) must be isolated from both JE15 and the interior of their group. Outside Interlacustrine only Gikuyu (E51), isolated by the Nilo-Saharan languages, is known for its regular application of Meinhof's Law.

2.2.6 Dahl's Law

This consonant dissimilation rule has diverse manifestations across parts of eastern Bantu. In the Interlacustrine zone, from a comparative standpoint, manifestations occur initially or, more rarely, within nominal or verbal stems. Their frequency diminishes progressively towards the boundaries of the phenomenon, which occur in northern Ganda and correspond to the boundaries of Zone J in the west. The stems affected by the process, as with Meinhof's Law, usually have a compact regional distribution in a variable area.

(42) Nande *èryɔgútà*
　　　　Jita *òkwì:gútá*
　　　　Shi *óókúyíigúrhá*
　 cf. Ganda *kú-kkùtá* **-jíkot-* 'be full, satiated'

Synchronically, Dahl's Law applies in JD60, Havu (JD50) and JE40. This distribution is unusual even though the details of the consonants and morphemes involved differ somewhat. As such, the rule applies to all cases of *t* and *k* in pre-root morphemes in Rwanda-Rundi, while in Gusii the negative morpheme *ti-* is not affected. It is induced by /*h*/ in Rundi, but not in Kuria.

(43) Gusii   *ege-tunwa*   'hill'   cf.   *eke-rongo* 'stool'

           tigekari aaria 'it is not over there'   *tikeri*   'it is not here'

     Rundi   *túdàsèkà* (*-tà-* negative morpheme) 'without our laughing'

     Rwanda   *dùhètà*   'we fold'   *tùgìhètà* 'we fold it'

     Rundi   *nìbó bàdàhá bà-tà-há-à*   'those who do not give'

     Kuria   *oyokáma*   'to milk'   *okohá*   'to give'

Rundi-Rwanda also exhibits the consonant alternations *t/d* and *k/g* at the end of certain verbal roots in relation to the voiceless or voiced feature of the suffix:

(44) Rundi   *-bád-ìk-*   'to transplant'   *-bád-ùk-*   'grow well'

          -bát-ùr-   'uproot'

          -shyíg-ìk-ìr-   'hold up'   *-shyìk-àm-*   'hold firm'

          -zìr-ìk-   'tie'   *-zìt-ùr-*   'untie'

The last example attests /*r*/ instead of the /*d*/ expected by Dahl's Law.

In Havu, /*rh*/ voices prefixes, but does not itself change in contexts where the rule applies:

(45) Havu   *égírhàkámwá*   'unmilkable animal',   *ógúrhwí* 'ear'

           égírhàkòlwá/éjírhàkòlwá 'that which cannot be done'

When not in stem initial position, this consonant is affected, as the following examples show:

(46) *ómúdó:rhó* 'young man' (reduplicated stem)   cf. *ékídàkàmwá* 'bracelet, sp.'

These examples demonstrate that the rule applies from right to left. We can therefore deduce that it will achieve its maximum development in Havu, where the preceding word can be affected:

(47)   *égí rhwá shóndó*   'what we are looking for'   cf. *ékí*

     ngá kúnŏ rhúdèrhéré 'as we just said'   cf. *nká*

In Shi, next to Havu, movement from *k* to *g* and from *c* to *j* is not observed in deliberate speech, but is clearly heard in spontaneous language. Anomalies in JE30 correspondences reflect Dahl's Law, as consonants do not reflect the expected voicing criteria, but must be explained historically.

(48) Nyole   *embeŋo*   'cold' (*m-ŋ → p*)

     cf. Ganda   *èmpéwò*   'draught, cold, wind'

            -daŋa   'draw water'

     cf. Shi   *oókúdáhá*   'dip into grain'   *lsuxa -taha*

           engoxo   (*n-x → k*   *kuba*   'I beat', *-xuba* 'beat')

     Kisa   *axakoxo*   'little chicken'   *i:ŋgoxo*   'chicken'

It is difficult to treat the applications of this rule only synchronically because the diachronic change from voiceless to voiced sometimes disrupts its application. From another viewpoint, based on the behavior of nasal clusters and using JE50 as an example, distributional analyzes show that, in the stem, certain consonants such as /*d*/ in

Nyindu (but excepting /du/ in Havu and Shi) require a following voiceless consonant. Conversely, in these same languages, /p/ or /h/ frequently occur before voiceless consonants, which suggests that they are less affected by the dissimilation.

Ha, located at the southwest border of the eastern region where Dahl's Law applies, has two dialects, Giha and Kiha, which are distinguishable by whether or not the NP is subject to the rule.

2.3 Tonality

Tonality in Interlacustrine languages has been the subject of an in-depth study so we will limit our discussion here to a few typological observations that exclude undocumented languages. Most of the languages contrast H and L. Where these come together on a (long) vowel, they create a contour tone, although these are rare or nonexistent in some languages:

(49)   Ganda *òmùsâ:jjà nóómwâ:ná*   'the man and the child'
    but   Hunde *á-mù-ánà → ámwánà...*   'the child ...'
                                       cf. *ámùlúmè ...*   'the male ...'

Some JE10 languages (Nyoro, Tooro ...) and Kuria have an accent system that corresponds to the syllable structure:

(50)   Kuria   *umurími* 'farmer'   *iyiçánérɔ* 'comb'

Kuria has a lowering rule that also occurs in Ganda, Shi, Havu, Gusii and Logooli, although the contexts that induce the lowering differ:

(51)   Logooli   *kórómà gáráhà*   'to bite slowly'
       Kuria   *uwiis'áá ́βá*   'to wash oneself'

Limited to the four classic types of canonical nouns with -CVCV stems, as in Talinga: (1) *àmà-ɣòlò* 'legs'; (2) *ɔkò-βɔkɔ* 'arm'; (3) *ɔmù-kálí* 'woman'; (4) *àmà-pàpá* 'wings', Nande-Konzo and Tembo have similar distinctions, although their tonal patterns do not necessarily correspond. Shi, Havu, and Fuliiru also differentiate all four, but the contexts in which types 2 and 3 contrast are rare because these languages are linked with those of the north–south axis, which don't distinguish these types. JD60 (Rwanda-Rundi) combines types 3 and 4. In the east, accentual languages are more evident; thus Bukusu contrasts type 1 with the other three, while Gusii seems to join 1/4 and 2/3. These 'two type' languages form a transition towards Kuria where all four are non-distinct.

Comparing the realizations of type 1 (*àmà-ɣòlò*), we observe a tone pattern that is entirely low, at least in certain contexts, except in Tembo, Shi, Havu, and Fuliiru (JD50):

(52) Nyankore   *òkùgùrù*   'leg'
      Hunde   *kìùlù/kùùlù, bìùlù≠*   'back foot'
      Ganda   *òkùgúlú≠ kùgúlú≠, òkùgùlù* ... (subject),   'leg'
                 òkùgúlú kwêndìgá   'leg of a sheep'
      but Tembo *kúúlú, máúlú*   'leg'

Identical contextual realizations may exist in languages of different groups. Consider the following elicitation form:

(53) Nande   *ɔkɔgòlò èkɔ kɥènè*
              ≠kògólò≠, ≠màgólò≠ [kògó:lò]   'the leg alone'
              ɔkɔgòló kɥènè   'the leg itself'
              and in   Fuliiru   *kúgúlú kúlà ≠kùgúlù≠,   ≠màgúlù≠*

Some languages tend to anticipate a tone (Nande, Hunde, Rwanda-Rundi), others to postpose (Jita) or spread a tone. This last phenomenon, especially when it is not limited to the word, induces diverse realizations. For example:

(54) Bukusu ≠kùmùlìlò≠   'fire'
             kúmùlílò níkwò kúnò   'the fire which …, this fire'
             kúmúlíló kúmùßò:fú   'the (big) fire'
             nè:kùmúlíló kúmùßò:fú 'with the big fire'

The syntactic impact of tonal realizations varies from language to language, but is practically nonexistent in JD60.

2.4 Syllable structure

The syllable structure of Interlacustrine languages is -CV- (-SV-, -CSV-, -NC(S)V-), and vowels occur short and long in the majority of languages. -V- occurs word-initially, but, in other positions, syllables without onsets are less frequent, except in some languages of JD40 and JD50 (see §2.1). Syan, marked by non-Bantu influences, only attests syllables of the form -CVC-. The problem of diphthongs or heavy syllables other than CSV remains since few linguists have explicitly distinguished sequences of two (or more) different vowels or diphthongs.

Kisa (JE32) also attests a few syllabic consonants and syllables of the type #V1 (see §2.2.1).

3 MORPHOLOGY

3.1 Class markers and class systems

For the 15 non-locative classes, the class and gender system is quite typical. Class 13 (NP *tò-) is not found in two small areas, one formed by Syan/Masaaba, including Bukusu, the other by Gusii/Kuria. In Bantu languages, nominal stems in 12/13 are rare since this gender occurs mainly in the formation of diminutives – discussed below – but class 12 (NP *kà-) is attested everywhere.

The class 19 prefix in JD40 and 50 languages forms part of the eastern border of the area in which the prefix is well attested. The other part of the southeast border is separated by JD60, found in Zone F and in Kuria (JE40). Again, the attested facts from both sides of JD60 are similar.

3.1.1 Augments and nominal prefixes

Structure

Augments can occur before nominal or pronominal prefixes but are excluded, by definition, before verbal prefixes. Structurally, joining the augment and NP in classes 5 and 10 creates particular problems, which are discussed later. Excluding these two classes, the augment consists of a long vowel in Shi (JD50), and a short vowel elsewhere (cf. §2.1), with the exception of Masaaba (JE31). In Masaaba varieties, augments have the structure CV- except in classes 1 and 9, and, alone in Bantu, a NP consonant may delete when identical to that of the augment:

(55) Bukusu kùmùlìlò 3 'fire' 1   ì:kòsì, kàmàkòsì 5/6 'neck'
             lù:kànò 11 'tall' (but) lùlw:à:ndà -ándà 11 'rock'

Augments take the unique form *á-* (similar to that of Nyanga (D43)) in Hunde (*ámùlúmè* 'the male', *mùlúmè* 'male'), and *é-* in the Bunyakiri dialect of Tembo (*émwànà ébànà* 'child, children').

Function

As the preceding examples demonstrate, definiteness – for which the range is language-specific – is marked by an augment before a noun in part of JD50 (Hunde, Tembo, Fuliiru), in Talinga, and perhaps in some southern Luhya varieties like Logooli. Elsewhere, situations vary, and augments mostly appear as relatively fixed morphemes before nouns (or adjectives). Certain conditionings widespread in Bantu operate, such as the absence of an augment after a negative verb. Generally, the contrast between definite and indefinite relates to the presence or absence of an augment, but the definite form (with augment) tends to become non-marked whereas that of the indefinite occurs in restricted contexts and varies to some extent with the language:

(56) Haya   *òmùsháíj' ómùtò yáíjà*   'the/a tall young man came'
        ómwáánà wàŋgè/mwáánà wàŋgè   'my child/it's my child'
   Ganda *báálàbà èbítábó byé twááwà àbáàná*
        'they see the books that we are giving the children'
        tèbáálàbà bìtábó byé twááwà báàná
        'they did not see the books that we are giving the children'
   but   *tèyàlàbà mwáàná ngà àgúlá èbítábó*
   litt.   'he didn't see the child as he was buying the books'
        ńjágálá ólúgânda   'I like the Ganda language'
   Rundi *àbàdntù*   'people'
        àbàdntù báàndì/àbáàndì bàdntù   'other people'

Particular cases: augments and NPs in classes 5 and 9/10. In class 5, there is a split between two language groups:

- Those which attest the alternation V(V)-/V(V)CV- according to whether the stem initial is a consonant or vowel:

(57) Nyankore *eihuri, amahuri* 'egg'   *eriino*   'tooth'
   Shi   *íísháká'*   'bush' *ééliínó, áámíínó* 'tooth'

The initial vowel alternates with ø in some languages and has the status of an augment:

(58) Talinga *èßèà, àmàßèà* 'shoulder(s)' *ɛlĭnɔ, àmănɔ* 'tooth/teeth'
        pàpá   'wing'   *lĭnɔ*   'tooth'

In Hunde and Nande, the process is different. The augment *á-/e-* is always followed by *le-/ri-* before a consonant, and *i-* therefore has the status of NP:

(59) Hunde *isìndà, màsìndà/álèsìndà*   'grave'
        línò, mínò mà-ínò/álínò   'tooth'
   Nande *èhándà/èrèhándà*   'to plant'
        línɔ, ménɔ 'a tooth' */èrínɔ, àménɔ* 'the tooth'

- Those which only attest (V)CV-: these occupy a compact area in the east: JE25, JE40, and JE30 (except Nyole (JE35) and Saamia (JE34) in Mould, 1976):

(60) Logooli *elidakɔ* 'buttock'
        eliinu   'tooth'

Context also plays a role in most of these languages, but variably:

(61) Jita   *lìnàjì, àmànàjì*   'coconut palm'   *èlí:sò* 'eye'
       Bukusu   *li:kósí, kámákósí*   'neck'
              lílì:nó, kámè:nó   'tooth'

The distribution clearly splits east and west; JE25 patterns with the eastern group whereas Nyole (JE35) rejoins the western group. The split, however, is partial because the realizations pattern together in specific 'definite' forms or where the stem has a vocalic initial.

In classes 9 and 10, prefixed elements are diverse in form and cannot always be related to NC contact (see §2.2.4) or to a specific realization *ɲ-* or *ny-* of class markers of type N before V-. Class 10 frequently attests a CV- structure. Based on this, typological classification permits the identification of two groups – taking the form with an augment where it is not fixed.

• First, there is perfect similarity between classes 9/10, whether class 10 is the plural of 9 or 11 (JE10/20, JE15, JD50 – except Hunde – and JD60):

(62) Nyankore   *embwa* 9/10   'dog'
                 orurimi, endimi 11/10   'tongue'

• Second, class 9 is *(e)N-* and class 10 *CV(-)N-* (JE25, JE30, JE40 and JD42 Nande which joins with JD50 Hunde):

(63) Bukusu   *é:ŋgúbó/cì:ŋgúbó* 9/10   'clothing'
             lú:béká/cí:mbéká 11/10   'side'

Some languages attest a split in one or both classes where, for instance, independently from specific realizations of N-C in which a nasal is deleted, they may possess a class 9a:

(64) Rwanda *ìhèné* 9a/10a 'goat', but *ìrùhú, ìmpú* 11/10 'skin'
       cf. Rundi *ìmpěnè/ìhénè*
       Rundi   *isúkà, àmàsúkà* 9a/6   'hoe'
            cf. *ìnsà:mìrìzì* 9/10   'resonance'
            isà:mìrizò, àmàsà:mìrizò 5/6   'leading drum'

Class 9 concords determine its membership, but the prefixed element is identical to that of class 5, and pairing with class 6 is quite frequent. Moreover, certain nouns reflect both class concords:

(65) Rundi   *ìsŭmbì ryó mù kwâhà*   'swelling of the armpit' (5 concord)
            ìsŭmbì yà gútwì   'shameless' (lit. swelling of the ear) (9 concord)

Kuria (JE43) is different because the absence of a nasal rather suggests its loan status, which does not necessarily exclude a relationship with class 5:

(66) Kuria   *eβata, içiβata* 9a/10a   'ducks'
       cf.   *eembéyo, içiimbéyo* 9/10   'seed(s)'
                irisána, amasána 5/6   'cave'

In Nande, the situation is somewhat similar, but more complex, since the variations are of three types, similar to those of the augment:

Type 1:   *ḿbènè* 9/10 'a goat(s)'   *èmbènè/èsyómbènè* 9/10 'the goat(s)'

This construction is canonical, also occurring in Konzo class 10, a free variation similar to Hunde:

(67)   Konzo   *èndâ* 9   'the belly'   *èsyɔ:ndâ, èsyà:ndâ* 10
      Hunde   *ángókó* ...   'the hen'   *ásàngókò≠*10

Type 2: *vɔhà/èvɔhá ngálè* 9   'dog(s)/the mean wild dog'

(68)   *èké:ngâ≠/èsyɔké:ŋgâ≠* 9/10   'the bicycle(s)'

Loanwords often integrate into this subgroup, which is comparable to 9a/10a in Kuria.

Type 3:   *èséndà* 9/10 'grave (s)   *ɛyéséndà/èsèséndà* 9/10 'the grave(s)'

(69)   *èsó:kè≠/èsésó:kè≠* 9/10   'the fly/the flies'
    cf.   *éyèndè nzérà* 9   'the other path'
        ésèndé ngɔkɔ 10   'the other hens'

Definite nouns act as pronouns, and, curiously, the majority of their stems have an initial fricative *s*. For indefinite forms, the prefixed element is identical to NP 5, as in JD60, but the similarity between singular and plural does not permit such a clear picture of interference between classes. Some of the stems in this series, however, e.g. *ísúkà* 'hoe', are found in class 9a/6 in Rwanda or Rundi or in 5/6, cf. *-sìndà* 5/6 'grave' in Hunde.

The three series of class 10 realizations also occur in 11/10:

(70)   *lòkémbà, ngémbà* 'clothing'   *lóbòèlè, bòèlè* 'change'   *lósákò, ísákɔ* 'tatoo'

In Tembo, the plural of class 11 is distinguished, with a few exceptions, from the plural of class 9:

(71)   *mbóó* 9,10 'buffalo'   *lúkúndá, nyíkúndá* 11,10   'cave'

This split is similar to class 10b of Chaga (E60) or Dawida (E74a), but also to Zone B. In Nande, the same alternation *n-/nye-* is used as a variant in order to avoid a consonant change after a nasal or its deletion in adjective concord prefixes, the differentiation here affecting grammatical category:

(72)   Nande   *sɔrɔ nyévè/mbí*   'a bad leopard'
        ısúkà nyékùhì/ngùhì   'a small hoe'
        mbùlà nyénéné/nénè   'a big rain'

In Konzo, the process extends to -CV type adjectives in class 9, which are generalized in class 10:

(73)   Konzo   *ènzèrá nyê:bé/ngù:hì/mbó:yà*   'bad/short/nice path'
        èsyànzèrá nyê:bé/nyékù:hì/nyébó:yà   'bad/short/nice paths'

In Ganda, *nnyi-* results from Meinhof's Law and therefore does not reflect the same process:

(74)   *nnyongera*   'I add to'   *-ongera*   cf. *ngaba*   'I divide'
    olunnyo ennyinyo 11/10   'stretcher'   cf. *oluzzi enzizi*   'well'

3.1.2 Augmentatives and diminutives

Throughout the Interlacustrine area, augmentatives and diminutives are formed by the substitution of prefixes. This creates problems for homophonous stems and for those that have already integrated into the classes concerned, which explains the existence of several autonomous classes.

• Augmentatives. Examples from Nande (JD40) are representative:

(75) Nande *mu-hámba* 3/4   'knife'
             ki-hámba   'big knife'   7/8 aug. derogatory
             ki-sándo 7/8   'foot'
             musándo   'long or big foot' 3/4 aug. pejorative
             lusándo   'big foot'   11/pl. 4 or 8 aug. derogatory
             mú-kalį 1/2   'woman'
             i-kalį   'big woman'   5/pl. 4 or 8 aug. pejorative

In the plural, pairings are irregular with a double choice that reflects the classes that might be considered most primary in the formation of augmentatives. Moreover, 7/8 is the most attested gender with this function in all of Bantu.

Apart from the constraints linked with primary noun classes, the choice might be based on the distinction between 'large' and 'long', or may approach a system of derivation involving class switching to reflect pejorative or laudative nuances:

(76) Nyankore *omushaija* 1/2   'man'
                ekishaija 7/8   'huge man'
                orushaija 11   'very tall man'
                eishaija 5   'aggressive attitude'

The Nande example manifests all the augmentative classes attested in the Interlacustrine area with the exception of class 20, which only occurs in the compact area of the eastern region from Ganda-Soga to Kuria, passing through Luhya varieties, but nevertheless excluding Gusii (JE40).

This class prefix (de Blois: 3a) is identical to the PP 3 and pairs with *mi-* NP 4 in the plural. It coincides with *ma-* NP 6 in Kuria, *ma-/ga-* in Ganda, and *ga-* in Soga. Its use, optional or not in a form similar to PP 6, shows the same interference between the two categories of prefixes in the singular and plural. These class 6 plurals coincide with the presence of a second augmentative 5/6 in these languages, which, although expressed differently, is reminiscent of the double plural of Nande, suggesting that 5/6 is more archaic in these languages:

(77) Ganda *mùsâjjá* 1   'man'
             ògùsâjjá, àgàsâjjá 20/6   'giant'
             `ssâjjá, gàsâjjá/màsâjjá 5/6   'big, hefty or fat man'
      Kuria *iriβéyo* 5/6   'large seed'
             oyosááŋga 20/4 or 6   'large bead'

This is a real gender since it triggers specific adjectival concord, as this Kisa example shows:

(78) Kisa *okuho:ⁿdo okuči:ši kuno kwa:ⁿje*   'this huge unripe pumpkin of mine'
            emiho:ⁿdo emiči:ši čino čya:ⁿje   'these huge unripe pumpkins of mine'

• Diminutives. Gender 12/13, the most attested Bantu diminutive, is present in JE25, JE30, JD60, and JD50. In this last group, however, the situation is complex and clearly demonstrates the disparity that exists.

• Besides 19/13 in Nyindu, Tembo and Shi, this last language also attests a diminutive 7/8.

- Nyindu and Hunde attest both pre-prefixation and substitution for 12/13 in partially distinct uses.
- In Nyindu, the pre-prefixation seems to associate diminutive and pejorative meanings:

(79) Nyindu *ká-lú-kòbà, tú-má-kòbà* 'small rope' (not solid)
       cf.   *hy-á:nà, tw-á:nà*   'very small child'
                ká-kìrà, tú-kìrà   'small tail'

- In Hunde, the distinction is more original – and also exists for augmentative 7/8 – although in a relatively unstable manner:

  – Pre-prefixation (inserting an augment before the second prefix) marks only the diminutive/augmentative:

(80) Hunde *kámbénè, twámbénè* 'small goat' *kyámbénè, byámbénè* 'big goat'

- Prefix substitution can play the same role, or can designate 'small' in classes 12/13. Classes 7/8 can mark the augmentative of a diminutive or convey pejorative meaning.

(81) Hunde *kàhénè* 'kid'   *kàtwi* 'tiny ear'
                kìhénè 'large kid' *kìtwi* 'deafness'

The class 19 prefix can also occupy these two positions and signifies 'a little bit of' or a plural with a pejorative nuance:

(82) Hunde *hyùndù*   'a bit of porridge' *hìkátsì* 'frail females'
                hyábánà 'thin children'

This plural use of class 19 is found in Nande, in variation with 13 for some nouns that belong primarily to classes 12/13 or 12/19, and in Kuria, where class 19 (beside 8 and 14) can be used as the plural for the diminutive classes 12, 7 and 11.

(83) *ihiβéyo* 'small seeds' *ayaanto* 'small person, small thing'

The use of class 11 to mark diminutives appears isolated, but, phonetically, class 11 of Kuria *oro-* is identical in Luhya varieties to class 13, which is absent in Kuria.

Examples in Hunde parallel the uses observed for class 13, which most often marks the plural of 12 but whose use is limited to 'a little bit of' in some languages, where the plural of the class 12 diminutive is therefore class 14. This situation exists in Rutara, in JE15 and Nyole, which is geographically close to Ganda. The specification 'a little bit of' sometimes appears in class 13 without class 12, attesting a double pairing:

(84) Nyindu *híbè:mbà* 'small peanut'   *túbè:mbà*   'a few peanuts'
       Ganda   *otuzzi*   'drop of water'   *otuzigo*   'a speck of
                                                                        butter'
       Haya   *otujuta*   'a little fat'   *aka:na/obwana*   'little child/
                                                                        children'
       Kerebe   *tu-zuta*   'a little butter'   *ka-bale/bu-bale*   'little stone(s)'
       Nyole   *otuŋande* 'a few groundnuts'   *axagingi/obugingi* 'little hill(s)'

In JD40, only 12/14 is attested for Nande, while in Konzo, 12/14 and 12/13 coexist without apparent semantic difference. Havu (JD50) has 12/13 and 19/14 and is therefore the only language in group JD50 to use the NP 14 in its formation of the diminutive. Recall that Havu is the only language in group JD50 where Meinhof's Law functions as in Ganda. Also interesting is the use of this class 14 in the eastern extremity of the area, in Kuria where Cammenga (1994) notes the possibilities 7, 12, 11/14, 19 or 8 without specifying the criteria which determine the choice of one class or other. We also note a curious distribution in which Kuria is isolated, showing a phenomenon that brackets JE25, wedged between Kerebe, Kuria and JD60.

Class 8 is paired with *ka-* 12 in Bukusu and in Gusii, which does not attest class 13. In Kwaya (JE25), the normal plural of 12 is 8, but 13 is equally used:

(85) Gusii   *akagena, ebigena*   'small stones'
      Kwaya *akamula, otumula* 'small boy(s)'

3.1.3 Locative classes

The three locative morphemes **pa- *ku- *mu-* occur in pre-prefix position, only rarely occurring in prefix position (locative nouns), all across Interlacustrine. Yet there are important geographical differences. In J10/J20, e.g. the locative prefix (LP) 17 is rare if not nonexistent:

(86) Haya *àhàkyààlò* 'in the village' *òmùkyààlò* 'in the village'

There is also a tendency to reduce concords. Class 16 agreement tends to replace those of classes 17 and 18 in JD60 and in Rutara, and the prefix involved may be repeated as a suffix:

(87) Rwanda   *kùmùgóròòbà hàràkóònjà*   'at night, it is cold'
      Nyankore *omunju egyo harimu abantu*   'in this house, there are people'
      Haya   *òmùkyààlò hákàbá hàlì hàlúngì* 'in the village was good'

The choice of concord is determined either by the category of the dependent word or by syntactic and semantic criteria:

(88) Haya *òmùkyààló kyàngè*   'in my village'
          òmùlùbàjù lw'ènjù   'beside the house'
          òmùkyààlò mwàngè 'in my village is mine'

The previous example demonstrates that concord 18 is attested in Haya alongside concord 16. The principal characteristic of Zone J is the LP 25, best developed in the western groups JD40, 50 and 60. Its use is limited to proper nouns of place and to 'restrictive locatives':

(89) Ganda *elugala*   'at Lugala'
      Luhya *emusanda*   'at Musanda'
      Shi   *éébúshí í èèlùg à ééntóòndò* 'in Bushi, there are many mountains'

This LP, which occurs in northwest Bantu and Zone S, isolates Interlacustrine from Zones D and E, but spills over into Zone F, where it is present in Sumbwa. Sumbwa shares several features with Zone J that are absent from other F languages, which suggests the effects of contact [Sumbwa is most likely an original member of J: editors]. It is therefore the absence of LP 25 in JE25 and 40 that prevents it from being considered a characteristic element of the Interlacustrine area.

The semantics and syntax of locatives are complex. Semantic variations associated with the applicative suffix offer valuable indications as to their function and status:

(90) Rwanda *ibùyè rìgù:yè mù:nzìrà*   'the stone fell on the path'
              ùmùgàbò yàgwìrìyè mù:nzìrà 'the man fell on his way'
      Haya   *ŋkàbónà kàt'ómúnjù*   'I saw Kato (while he was) in the house'
             ŋkàbónèlà kàt'ómúnjù 'I saw Kato (while I was) in the house'

3.2 The verbal system

3.2.1 Survey of conjugations

The verbal systems of Interlacustrine languages are rich and complex. Exhaustive descriptions being rare, comparison is often random insofar as the criteria for divisions in moods and tenses differ in the literature. As such, in Rundi, Meeussen distinguishes adhortative and optative moods which other linguists do not distinguish or join as 'subjunctive'. The structure of conjugated forms is 'typically' Bantu for most moods, tenses and aspects. Possible constituent morphemes are ordered: pre-initial (negative morpheme, focus marker), initial (VP), post-initial (negative), formatives (tense, aspect), infix(es), root, suffix(es), pre-final, final (tense, aspect), post-final. The following example includes most of these morphemes:

(91)   Rundi   *ntì-bà-zóò-tù-hít-ìr-à-mwó*   'they won't choose for us in that'
        not-they-future-us-choose-for-future affirmative-substitutive locative
        cl.18

The pre-initial and post-initial are defined in relation to the VP considered as an initial morpheme and do not designate the OP or tense/aspect morphemes which can also occur after the VP. The negative can occur in either position depending on mood or tense, which explains why these positions are rarely jointly occupied:

(92)   Rundi   optative
                ntìmúkàbùrè ìbìbòòndò   'may you not lack in offspring'
                immediate conjunctive imperfective
                ... *tútàrùkúbùùrà* ...   '... without us sewing it ...'

The following examples demonstrate the affirmative, particularly for finals:

(93)   Shi: indicative absolute narrative   *áábálúmé bá-à-bòn-à*   'the men saw'
                far past perfect   *n-á-súnís-ìrè (-súnìk-)*   'I pushed'
        Rundi: subjunctive   *tùbàrîìrè*   'let us sew'
                                                tù-zì-bàrîìrè   'let us sew
                                                                        them'
        subsecutive, conjoint   ... *tùkàbàrììrà ìmpùúzù*   '(and) we sewed the clothes'
        Hunde: conditional, irrealis; conditional, simple resultative
        tw-à-ngà-tèngùh-ìré ngé   *tù-tà-l-ìré kwèbùndù ùkù*
        'if we had disobeyed, then we wouldn't eat this gruel'

The condition, as the action which depends on it, is classified in the conditional mood in Hunde.

Relatives are characterized by prefixes that are identical to those of pronouns and which differ, at least partially, from absolute VPs. Furthermore, in the relative subjunctive, class 1/2 concord often occurs after a participant antecedent:

(94)   Shi   *óómúkàzì wáshákwììrè*   'the woman who pounded' (relative, remote
                                        past)
        cf.   *óómúkází ááshákwììrè*   'the woman pounded'
        Kisa   *ifwe aβarula kakamega*   'we who come from Kakamega' (*aβa*–cl. 2)

Relatives allow augments, like infinitives, which simultaneously carry verbal and nominal features, specifically at the syntactic level:

(95)   Nande   *òmòndò ɔ̀yólóérè*   'the man who is sick'
                cf. *òmòndó àlóérè*   'the man is sick'
                òmòndó ólóérè   'a man who is sick'

Rundi *àbàbáriìrà*   'those who sew'
       (ù)kùbàriìrà   'to sew'
       (ù)kùtábàriìrà 'to not sew'

Across Interlacustrine, the class 15 NP characterizes the infinitive except in Nande (JD40) and Hunde (JD50) which have NP 5, likening them to the northwest where this class is more frequent. The significance of this isogloss must be kept in proportion since several languages attest class 5 forms, which Meeussen (1959) defines as verbal nouns in Rundi, beside the class 15 infinitive:

(96)   ... *yàzíbòònyè* *itúrùkà* ...   '... who saw them going out ...'

In the literature, only Rwanda and Rundi are described as contrasting conjunctive and disjunctive:

(97)   Rundi *tùràbàriìrà*   'we will sew' (disjunctive, immediate)
              tùbàriìrà impùúzù 'we are sewing clothing' (conjunctive, immediate)

For details of conjugation, refer to Ch. 6. Here, we look at the details of certain morphemes.

3.2.2 Conjugational morphemes

VPS

The second person singular and plural VPS, *u-/o-* and *mu-*, have a wide distribution. However, in the first person plural, VP °*tu-*, frequent in Bantu, is replaced by *xu-/ku-* in JE30:

(98)   Tsotso: *xwaluma* 'we bit'

JE25 (Kwaya, Jita, Ruri) is alone in having the first person plural VP *ki-/ci-*:

(99)   Kwaya: *kikole* 'that we do'

As across Bantu, in the first person singular, besides contextual variations already mentioned for NP 9, most languages attest specific forms whose occurrences are contextually unpredictable:

(100) Kwaya *ni-li-kola*   'I did (a long time ago)' *n-da-kole*   'I will do'
       Luhya *nd-a-khola*   'I have done'   cf. *mw-a-khola* 'you (pl.) have done'

              ndi-li-khola 'I will do'   cf. *mu-li-khola* 'you (pl.) will do' (far future)

The VP *en-/in-* is curious. In the present progressive, the initial vowel is limited to the first person singular in JE30, whereas in JE25, all VPS throughout the paradigm have it – with the exception of class 1 where the VP *ka-*, to be discussed later, is replaced by the canonical VP *a-*:

(101) Kisa   *e:ⁿde:ma*   'I try'
       Luhya   *endeema*   'I am trying' cf. *muteema* 'you are trying'
       Masaaba Lusoba *i:tsowa*   'I pound'
       Lufumbu   *indzowa*
       Luhugu   *inzowa*

Kwaya   *enikola/ekikola/oukola/omukola/kakola/abakola*
'I am doing/we are doing/you are doing/he is doing/they are doing'
Ruri   *ènìmúsàkírà bwaǹgù*   'I helped him quickly'
kà:ßàlísòròtòrĕrâ   'he is pulling it out for them'
àßàlísòrótŏrâ   'they are pulling it out'
but,   *nìàßìrím-ìrê*   'I ran (long ago)'

The initial vowel is reminiscent of the augment whose use may characterize the relative – notably when the antecedent is defined or not expressed:

(102)   Nyankore   *abantu abakora*   'the men who work'
cf. *abantu bakora*   'the men work'
Haya   *àbájùnà*   'those who help'
Kisa   *omu:ndu u-rul-a ešisumo...*   'a person who comes from Kisumu...'
omu:ndu o-u-rul-a ešisumo...   'the person who comes from Kisumu...'

This similarity suggests that relatives express the present continuous in JE25, which may be accounted for semantically as the result of focusing. However, the presence of the VP *ka-*, since the relative generally attests the PP *u-* in class 1, casts doubt on this hypothesis. The presence of VP participants is less pertinent since it often occurs in the relative.

The variation *y(a)-/y-* unites the entire Interlacustrine area with the exception of the western (JD40, Talinga, JD50) and southeastern borders (JE25, JE40). It is attested for the class 1 VP and conditioned by the presence of a formative *-a-* (or of a following vocalic morpheme?), and, in certain languages by an OP of the shape *n-* in the first person singular:

(103)   Ganda   *y-a-lab-a* 'he saw'   cf. *a-lab-ye* 'he has seen'
Nyankore   *kagoro ya:gur embuzi*   'Kagoro bought his goats (today)'
cf. *katare aje:nda aba:na bage:nde*   'Katare wants the children to leave'
Haya   *ènyàm' éyó kàtó y-à-shál-à*   'the meat that Kato has cut'
cf. *òmùkàzy' à-kà-cùmb' ébìtòòkè*   'the woman cooked the bananas'
Tsotso   *yalasa* 'he stung'   cf. *xwaluma* 'we bit'
yaandamaanga (a-n-ram-ang-a)   'he defeats me'
Kisa   *ya:xupa (a-n-xupa)*   'he beats me' cf. *axupa* 'he beats'
afɲile   'he blew his nose'
Rundi   *yààbíímbwììyè (à-àà-bì-m-bwîr-yè)*   'he told me it'
Bukusu   *kăːßùkúl' ó:mwàn' ó:k:ù:ndì*   'and he took another child'
cf. *àmálìlé..*   'she had survived...'

However, with formative *-a-*:

(104)   Shi   *áásúnîrè/rhwáásúnísìrè*   'he/we pushed'
Jita   *à:cìlò:térè*   'he dreamed of us'
cà:ßàtògérè (ci- 'we')   'we named them'

Bukusu attests *ka-*, as in the 'present continuous' in JE25. Yet, *k* and *g* in JE25 correspond to *x,k* in JE30, and notably in Bukusu:

(105)   Jita   *òmù-gù:mbà* 'barren woman'   *òkùgùrà* 'to buy'   *ka-*   VP cl.1
Bukusu   *òmù-kù:mbà*   *xù:kùlà*   *ka-*

This intriguing similarity reflects the impact of language contact.

The attested VP variations share the intrusion of a segment, which doesn't occur in the western area or JE40. The very particular facts attested in JE25 also turn up in JE30 and illustrate the processes of diffusion in both directions.

Formatives

The most widespread formatives in the Interlacustrine area, *-a-, -ki-, -ka-, -da-/-daa- (da-a?)*, *-na-*, are common throughout Bantu. Several may follow one another in a single structure or demonstrate different tonalities, which alters their semantic value (tense and/or aspect).

The formative *-ma-*, on the other hand, is less common and especially characterizes the northwest. Its presence in Nande, Konzo, Hunde, Shi and Havu is situated in the extension of the area of distribution. This formative is also present in Jita and Ruri (JE25), isolated in the east. It is remarkable that *-ma-* is associated with the classic formative *-a-* on both sides of the area to mark the past, although it marks the immediate past on one side, the recent past on the other:

(106)	Konzo	*námàgú:là*≠	'I have just bought'	cf. *mwàkólâ* '... you did'
	Hunde	*ámùkàtsì àmèbútìrà ámwàmi*		'the woman just bore a child for the king'
		tù-à-mé-kìng-ùl-à lùtsì		'we just opened a door'
		-me- possibly *-ma-i/e-*;		cf. *tù-à-nè-fúl-ùk-à/tù-kà-ná-*
		'(today) we will return anyway'		*fúl-ùk-à*
	Ruri	*nì-àmà-à-sùmík-à*		'I tied' (intermediate past)
		nì-à-sùmík-à		'I tied' (near past)

However, *-ma-* also occurs further east, e.g. in Chaga (E60), which changes the problem: most Interlacustrine varieties lack a morphological feature present on the east and west and beyond.

Suffixes, extensions and prefinals

For extensions see Chapter 5 in this book. All are present in Interlacustrine languages, but *-al-*, *-am-* and especially *-at-* are not very productive. Unlike *-ik-* 'neuter', *-ik-* 'impositive, transitive' is not attested as an extension, but can be recognized in some verbal stems.

Reduplicated extensions are accompanied by either semantic change or additional meaning (*-il-* 'applicative', *-ilil-* 'intensive' or 'applicative intensive'; *-ul-* 'reversive', *-ulul-* 'repetitive reversive' in Tembo). The reduction of certain sequences such as *-ul-il-* to *-wil-* or *-il-il-* to *-iil-* is well known. However, the contrast between the extensions -VC-, -VVC- and -VCVC-, attested in Rwanda and Rundi (JD60), and Havu and Shi (JD50), appears to be an isolated process. These extensions are not in free variation even though it is difficult to suggest a semantic and/or syntactic value to explain the choice of one over the other:

(107)	Shi	*óókúyóók-éér-á*	'to set fire to the bush'
		óókúyóók-ér-á	'to grill for'
		óókúlól-éér-er-á	'to look at something too much'
		óókúlólá	'to look at'
		óókúsímík-irír-á	'to persevere'
		óókúsímíká	'to endeavour'

The prefinal *-ag-* replaces *-ang-* in some parts of JE30. The prefinal is incompatible with the perfect final [except in Luhya: editors] and marks habitual except in Tembo and Hunde where it is associated with an 'aspect momentané terminatif'. Furthermore, these two languages, as well as Talinga and Nande, contrast suffixal *-ang-* with prefinal *-ag-*. This suffix is defined as 'durative' in Talinga and Tembo, 'iterative and frequentative' in Nande and Hunde:

(108)   Talinga   *kùlúmàngà*   'to be biting;   *kùlúmà*   'to bite'
               βìló βyônà àɣèndáá mwèhìɣà 'every day, he went hunting' (far past imperfective habitual)

       Nande   *-lóm-àŋg-*   'nibble at'   *-lóm-*   'to bite'
       Hunde   *ì-ʃákà*   'tattoo'   *ì-ʃák-àng-à* 'tattoo a lot'
               tw-à-nà-híng-ìr-à̰-á mùndù
               'nevertheless we cultivated for someone' (hesternal concessive)
       Tembo   *nátèmà̰à̰* 'I have just cleared'   *nàtèmá̰à̰* 'I had cleared'

This situation suggests interference between two morphemes of different status, *-ag-* and *-ang-*, and can be related to the presence of a suffix of type *-agud-* 'repetitive' in JD60, and in Shi and Havu. It is, moreover, remarkable that in Haya, *-angan-/-an-* are mentioned as reciprocal suffixes: *-angan-* is the current form, *-an-* is associated with the final *-ile*. This distribution may be explained either in reference to syllabic structure, or in a more comparative manner by linking it to the incompatibility between the perfect prefinal and final.

Finals: *-a*, *-e*, and *-ile*

These finals carry different tones depending on the TAM category where they occur. The final *-e* characterizes the subjunctive and the imperative as an infix, with the exceptions of the presence of an OP in the first person singular, and occasionally in the future:

(109)   Hunde   *tùtèmùlé ncìrà*   'that we follow a path'
       Rundi   *bàrììrà̰*   'sew' *mbàrììrìrà̰* 'sew for me' *m-* OP 1sg.
               mùbàrììrìrḛ̀   'sew for him' *mù* OP cl. 1
       Ganda   *kì-wê*   'give it'   '*m-pâ* 'give me'
       but
       Bukusu   *mbḛ̀ βyáxúlyà*   'give me food'

The final *-a*, which may be considered unmarked, is also associated with the imperfective, whereas *-ide*, *-ire*, *-ye* characterize the perfect:

(110)   Hunde   *tùhìmbirè hǎlè* 'we built far away'

When combined with suffixes, this final is realized with imbrication:

(111)   Kisa   *oxumaɲixa* 'to become known'   *amaɲi:ʃe x → ʃ/−e* 'he became known'
               oxukulila   'to buy for'   *akuli:le*   'he bought for'

Apart from modifications linked to imbrication, verbal finals are of the type *-VCV*, except in Rwanda, Rundi, and Ha (JD60) where the final is *-ye* and where *Vr-ye → V:ye:*. As shown in the examples, the semi-vowel is absorbed by certain fricativized consonants:

(112)   Rundi   *dùkùbùùyè ùrùgó*   'we just swept the yard'
       cf.   *dùkùbùùrà ùrùgó*   'we are sweeping the yard'
               àràdúùzè à-rà-dúùd-yè 'he swept'

This same final is attested in Talinga, although we are not sure it is the only one. It alternates with *-ile, -ire* in Ganda (JE15), in Kwaya, Jita, Ruri (J E25), and in Kuria (JE40):

(113) Talinga *tátwáendié*   'we did not leave'
       Ganda   *twalimye*   'we cultivated'
                tubadde (tu-ba-ide) tukola   'we have been working'
                -gend- 'to go' *-genze*   *-buulira* 'to tell' *-buulidde*

In Ganda, *-ye* occurs after a root *-CVC-*. However, in the south *-ye* occurs after a root of type *CV-* and in realizations which imply a suffix of type *-Vl-/-Vr-*:

(114) Jita   *à:lùβìrè*   'he has already followed'
              à:làmù:yè (-làm-ùr-)   'he has already decided'
              à:lí:yè   'he has already eaten'
                                            cf. *à:màlyâ* 'he ate'
       Ruri   *nì:sùrùmùúyè -surumur-*   'I untied it'
              nì:sùmìkǐrê   -sumik-   'I tied'
       Kuria *m-ba-karaángéeye*   'I have fried for them'
              n-ga-tɛrɛkére   'I have brewed'

The similarity of the realizations of finals occurring after a root shape *-CV-* and in contact with the applicative is frequent in Bantu, whatever the form of the final. This is also the case in JE15, 25 and 40. The final *-ye* has a fragmented geographical distribution and a range of phonetic contexts. Note the following Kisa example, associated with a monosyllabic causative extension:

(115) Kisa   *-sumya*   'to extinguish'   *-sumi:ye*
              alo:ⁿjele (oxulo:ⁿga)   'he created'
              -fwa   'to die'   *-fwi:le*

The final *-ete* is only frequent in Gusii, connecting it with Zone E where it is better represented. However, it is attested as a specific final for certain verbs in many J (and other) languages:

(116)   *àbáánà mbááncɛ̀tɛ̀ ébìnt(ò) ébìyìà* 'children like new things'

Another feature that isolates Gusii from other Interlacustrine languages is the presence of a specific final *-i* in certain negative forms:

(117)   *tìtómànyètì às(è) áményètè* 'we do not know where he lives'

4 CONCLUSIONS

Despite its limited scope, this chapter outlines succinctly some details of Interlacustrine phonology and morphology. However, it does not deal with important domains like those of pronouns, syntax or the lexicon. Also, the data for certain languages are lacking or fragmentary.

Overall, Interlacustrine languages are typically Bantu and their essential features are described in the general chapters. The general impression is one of unity even if this is not transparent in this chapter since we have chosen to address the details, sometimes unique and for which the distribution only rarely coincides with that of another or several other groups. The restricted distribution of certain facts is intriguing (cf. §3.2.3: the VP first person plural °*ku-* or the verbal formative *-ma-*). We also observe that seven vowel languages are situated at the northwest and southeast fringes, where they only occupy a part of the perimeter. This suggests that the central languages spread by absorbing certain varieties or by pushing them towards the east. If the distribution of the final -*ye* turns out to be relevant, we can suppose that JE15 and JD60 were in contact before being separated by JE10/20, which indirectly confirms certain shared features by Ganda and all or part of JD50, moreover quite similar to JD60.

The boundary of Zone J is clear to the west even if the fringe languages of Zone D have a definite impact on JD50. To the southeast, the boundary is less clear since Gusii is often isolated. Furthermore, despite certain affinities with Kuria, JE25 varieties have intriguing similarities with languages in Zone G (notably G10), so that the VP *ki-* (first person plural) reflects *ci-* in Gogo and Kaguru where $k \rightarrow c/-i$, (cf. *ki-* in Zigula (G31)), and the class 1 VP *ka-* is also attested in Gogo. This very partial study leaves open numerous questions which deserve further study.

REFERENCES

Angogo 1983; Ankei 1979; Appleby 1961; Aramazani 1985; Ashton, Mulira, Ndawula, and Tucker 1954; Austen n.d.; Bastin 1978, 1983a; Bbemo Musubaho 1982; Bennett 1967; Bickmore 1991; Black 1995; Botne 1989; Brown 1972; Byarushengo, Duranti, and Hyman 1977; Cammenga 1994; Chanda 1975; Chagas 1976; Chesswas 1963; Confemen 1986; Coupez 1960, 1983; Cullen 1999 (not consulted); Davy and Nurse 1982; De Blois 1970, 1975; Downing 1996a, 1996b; Forges 1983; Gerdts and Whaley 1991; Goldsmith 1991; Greenberg 1977; Grégoire 1975, 1998; Guthrie 1967–71; Hadermann 1999; Herbert 1975, 1995; Hermann 1904; Hinnebusch, Nurse, and Mould 1981; Huntingford 1965; Hurel 1909; Hyman 1997a, 1997b; Hyman and Katamba 1990, 1991, 1993; Hyman and Valinande 1985; Janssens 1983; Jouannet 1984; Kadima 1969; Kahindo 1984; Kaji 1985, 1992, 1996; Kamba 1981; Katamba and Hyman 1991; Kerremans 1980; Kimenyi 1980; Ladefoged *et al.* 1972; Leung 1991; Maddox 1938; Mateene 1963, 1992; Mchombo 1993a; Meeussen 1953, 1959, 1962a, 1967; Möhlig 1974; Morris 1963; Mould 1976, 1981; Musamba 1975; Mutaka 1994; Muzale (forth.); Nakagawa 1992; Nkiko 1977, 1981; Nsuka Nkutsi 1982; Nurse 1999; Nurse and Muzale 1999; Nurse and Rottland 1991–2; Paluku 1996; Philippson 1991; Polak-Bynon 1975, 1980; Polomé and Hill 1980; Rascher 1958; Rodegem 1967; Rodgers 1962; Roehl 1918; Sample 1976; Schadeberg 1989, 1994; Schoenbrun 1990; Shamavu 1982; Sillery 1932; Taylor 1985; Tucker 1960; Valinande 1984; Van Sambeek n.d.b; Walusimbi 1976, 1996; Whiteley 1956, 1960, 1974; Wung'a Lomami 1973.

CHAPTER TWENTY-SIX

RUFIJI-RUVUMA (N10, P10–20)

David Odden

1 INTRODUCTION

This chapter presents structural basics of the languages of zones P10–20. With Ndendeuli, Ngoni, Matengo and Mpoto (N10), the P10–20 languages comprise the Rufiji-Ruaha group of Nurse (1999). Proceeding southwards in Tanzania from Dar-es-Salaam, Rufiji (P10) is composed of Ndengereko (110,000 speakers, according to Grimes 2000), Rufiji (200,000), Matuumbi (72,000) south of the Rufiji river, and Ngindo (220,000) around Liwale. Spoken inland around Ifakara, Mbunga (29,000) is also assigned to P10 by Guthrie. Nurse (1988:36–40) discusses the hypothesis that Mbunga was historically a P language much influenced by G50, or the opposite, and concludes that it probably started life as a P language. P20 is composed of Mwera (400,000) in Lindi region south of Ngindo, Machinga (36,000), Yao (1,597,000) spoken from the Makonde Plateau to Tunduru and south into Malawi and northwestern Mozambique, and Makonde (1,260,000) in the southeast corner of Tanzania and northeastern Mozambique. Yao and Mwera are very closely related, and might be treated as dialects: their similarity is comparable to that of the Makonde dialects. Makonde is no closer to Yao and Mwera than P10.

This chapter focuses on Matuumbi as a representative of P10, Yao (primarily the Tunduru dialect and Mozambican Yao from Ngunga 1997), and Makonde, focusing on the Shimakoonde dialect of Mozambique (Mak.), with additional data from Chimaraba (Mar.) and Chimahuta (Mah.) of Tanzania. Additional information will be added from Mwera, Ngindo and Ndengereko based on my own field notes, and Ngonyani (1999) on Ndendeuli (apparently a Rufiji language). Sources of futher information on these languages are as follows. Kimatuumbi: Odden 1996; Mwera: Harries 1950; Yao: Ngunga 1997, Sanderson 1922, Whiteley 1966; Makonde: Guerreiro 1963, Liphola 2001, Odden 1990a, 1990b, Yukawa 1986b.

2 PHONOLOGY

2.1 Vowels

The Rufiji languages maintain seven vowels [i̧, e, a, o, u, u̧], but P20 has [i, e, a, o, u], cf. Matuumbi *i̧imb-a* 'swell', *mu̧li̧k-a* 'burn', *biing-a* 'chase', *lum-a* 'bite', *belek-a* 'give birth', *lol-a* 'look at', *baamb-a* 'stretch'; Yao *iimb-a*, *mulik-a*, *viing-a*, *lum-a*, *velek-a*, *lool-a*, *vaamb-a*; Makonde *viimb-a*, *muliik-a*, *viing-a*, *luum-a*, *veleek-a*, *lool-a*, *vaamb-a*. Vowel length is preserved in Rufiji (except Ndendeuli) and Yao-Mwera, but is lost in Makonde, where length is reintroduced by penultimate lengthening and fusion of V–V sequences: word-penult vowels would be short phrase-medially in the Makonde examples.

(1) Matuumbi   Yao   Makonde

    ti̧il-a   *tiil-a*   *tiil-a*   'flee'

    i̧n-a   *vin-a*   *viin-a*   'dance'

529

puut-a	*puuta*	*puut-a*	'beat'
bulag-a	*ulag-a*		'kill'
biik-a	*viik-a*	*viik-a*	'put'
lim-a	*lim-a*	*liim-a*	'cultivate'
tuul-a	*tuul-a*	*tuul-a*	'unload'
kul-a	*kul-a*	*kul-umuuk-a*	'grow'
peet-a	*peet-a*	*peet-a*	'sift'
kem-a	*chem-a*	*seem-a*	'call'
loot-a	*loot-a*	*lot-aang-a*	'dream'
bon-a	*won-a*	*oon-a*	'see'
kaan-a	*kaan-a*	*kaan-a*	'refuse'
lam-a	*lam-a*	*naam-a*	'survive'

Ndengereko, Ngindo and Ndendeuli have nasal vowels, cf. Ndengereko *ba-tě#ŭbuk-y-a* 'they came out for me', *ba-té#úbuk-a* 'they came out'; Ngindo *ĩk-ílé* 'I came', *a#ĩk-ílé* 'he came'; Ndendeuli *māhā* 'well'. Nasalization arises by prefixing the 1s prefix to vowel-initial verbs in Ndengereko, by progressive nasalization (skipping *h*) in Ndendeuli (*ba-ki-ŋ#hĩh-ã* ← *ba-ki-mu-hih-a* 'they hid him') which persists even if the nasal deletes before *h* (*hãbi* 'witch' ← *mu-habi*, *ba-ki-hĩh-ã* ← *ba-k i-N-hih-a* 'they hid me'), and in Ngindo also by vocalization of /mu/ before /h/ (*ũ#heémb-e* 'you should dig', cf. *n#cheéng-e* 'you should build').

All languages have vowel height harmony, where /u/→[o] after *o* and /i/→[e] after *e,o*. Yao examples with the applied suffix are *lim-il-a* 'cultivate for', *wut-ila* 'pull for', *pat-ila* 'get for', *pet-el-a* 'ornament for', *soom-ela* 'read'. Makonde examples are *pit-iil-a* 'pass through for', *put-iil-a* 'wash for', *pat-iil-a* 'get for', *pet-eel-a* 'separate for', *pot-eel-a* 'twist for'. Matuumbi also harmonizes high and super-high vowels, so /i,u/→[į,ų] after *į ų*, and stem-medial *i* and *u* appear only after *i,u*. Thus see the alternations in the passive *įn-įlw-a* 'be danced', *kún-įlw-a* 'be grated', *twíik-ilw-a* 'be lifted', *úug-ilw-a* 'be bathed', *léet-elw-a* 'be brought', *bóol-elw-a* 'be de-barked', *pát-įlwa* 'be obtained'. Parallel harmony affects *ų*, seen in the vocalization of *w*, with the restriction that after *e* one finds *ų* and not *o*, cf. *líbu-lw-a* 'be ground', *yúpų-lw-a* 'be served', *tíiku-lw-a* 'be broken', *chéku-lw-a* 'be shaved', *bómo-lw-a* 'be destroyed', *kamų-lw-a* 'be grabbed'. The vowel of perfective *-ile ~ įte* does not harmonize, cf. Yao *-pet-ile* 'ornament', *-soom-ile* 'read'; Makonde *-tot-iile* 'sew', *-pet-iile* 'separate'; Matuumbi *-leet-įte* 'bring', *-lol-įte* 'look at'.

Unusual in Bantu, Makonde optionally reduces unstressed (pre-penult) mid vowels to *a*, resulting in alternations such as *kú#tétékéé-la ~ kú#tátákéél-a* 'to give up', *va-nda#tót-eél-a ~ va-nda#tát-eél-a* 'they will sew for'.

Vowel sequences are avoided to varying degrees. Matuumbi has the greatest tolerance for vowel hiatus. High vowels desyllabify prevocalically; *my#oótó* ← *mi#ótó* 'fires' (*ma#otó* 'large fires'), *ky#uúlá* ← *ki#úlá* 'frog' (*ka#úlá* 'small frog'), *lw#aaté* ← *lu#até* 'banana hand' (*até* 'banana hands'). Glide Formation lengthens the following vowel: initial length is contrastive, so see also *mw#eéla* ← *mu#eéla* 'in money' (*eéla* 'money'), *ly#éeke* ← *li#éeke* 'storage structure' (*ma#éeke* 'storage structures'), with an invariant long vowel. Combinations of *a* plus a high prefixal vowel optionally coalesce, thus *a-į#télíįke ~ ee#télíįke* 'he cooked them', *paú#kaát-įté ~ poó#kaát-įté* 'when you cut', *nau#chaápu ~ noo#chaápu* 'with dirt', but not between prefix and stem vowel, cf. *a#įnįte* (**eénįte*) 'he danced', except in a very few lexically marked nouns and adjectives (*móolį* ← *ma#óolį* 'tears' (*ly#óolį* 'tear'), *b#eepeésį ~ ba#epeésį* 'light (class 2)'). There is fusion of *a + a* when the first *a* is in the subject prefix (*áandįįke* ← *a#áandįįke* 'he wrote (recent)') but not in an object prefix (*nị-ga#áandịike* 'I wrote them (recent)'). Vowel sequences are tolerated (though not common) within stems, though the super-high vowels never stand before another vowel – see *kị#báo* 'stool', *lụ#báụ* 'rib', *maáu* 'mother', *kíndaáị* 'morning', *kị#télei* 'kitchen', *kị#yéụlị* 'stubbornness', *lị#bígiị* 'brewery', *ma#ñéeị* 'grass'.

In Makonde, hiatus is eliminated within the word and phrasally. High vowels become glides before another vowel (which lengthens), cf. *my#áaka* ← *mí#áaka* 'years', *kw#áádúúla* ← *kú#ádúúl-a* 'to destroy', *ly#éeve* ← *lí#éeve* 'fruit', *kw#óólóóta* ← *kú#ólóót-a* 'to point'. The vowel *a* merges with a following vowel, giving a long mid vowel as in *méembe* ← *ma#eémbe* 'mangos', *meéki* ← *ma#iíki* 'stumps', *moongaáno* ← *ma#ungaáno* 'unity'. Phrasally, non-low vowels undergo glide formation without compensatory lengthening, cf. *din#galóoshy ameéna* ← *din#galóoshi ameéna* 'cashews, eat them!', *lí#tátély eépa* ← *lí#tátééle eépa* 'cucumber, harvest it!'. Preceding *a* deletes, as in *li#mboónd ukaánga* ← *li#mboónda ukaánga* 'pumpkin, wash it!'. Some vowel hiatus remains in the Chimaraba and Shimakonde dialects, cf. *lu-m#baáu* 'rib', *si#leéu* 'beard', *si#pyaái* 'broom'. The consonant *h* found in Mahuta is deleted in Maraba and Shimakonde, creating new vowel hiatus. This hiatus remains if the result is a falling diphthong, as in (Mahuta) *ma#húuta*, (Shimakonde) *má#úúta* 'oil', (Mahuta) *li#káahi*, (Shimakonde) *lí#káai* 'bark', (Mahuta) *n'ááhu* (Shimakonde), *i#n'aáu* 'body dirt'. If the first vowel is high, glide formation applies too, as in (Mahuta) *lu#híimu*, (Shimakonde) *lw#íimu* 'song'; (Mahuta) *li#húúndi*, (Shimakonde) *ly#uúndi* 'cloud' (cf. *ma#uúndi* 'clouds').

Avoidance of hiatus is most strict in Yao (and Mwera), which have no V-V sequences within the word. Vowel fusion and glide formation are the rule within the word, with coalescence of /a + V/ giving a mid-vowel: cf. Yao *méésó* ← *ma#ísó* 'eyes' (*lííso* 'eye'); *moóngu* ← *ma#úngu* 'pumpkins' (*ly#uúngu* ← *li#úngu* 'pumpkin'), *my#éésí* ← *mi#ésí* 'moons', *mw#iisi* ← *mu#isi* 'pestle' (*miisi* 'pestles').

Matuumbi shortens vowels which are too far to the left in an utterance. At the word level, stem vowels are generally shortened before the antepenultimate mora, thus *áand-ịk-a* 'write', *ándịk-ịy-a* 'make write'; *tyátyaak-ịy-a* 'plaster', *tyátyak-ịy-ịlw-a* 'be plastered', *káat-a* 'cut', *kát-an-ịk-a* 'be cuttable'. With two long vowels, the first is shortened (*lóong-a* 'request', *lóng-eel-a* 'speak'; *tịịl-a* 'run', *tịl-aang-a* 'run (pl.)'; *tíikw-a* 'break off', *tíkw-aan-a* 'break pointlessly').

Similar word level shortening affects reduplicated stems. A long vowel in the penultimate syllable of a reduplicant (the second stem copy) is not shortened, cf. *káat-a* → *kát-a-kaat-a* 'cut'; *yúyuut-a* → *yúyut-a-yuyuut-a* 'whisper' (the first stem is shortened by positional limits on long vowels). A long vowel before the penult shortens, cf. *káat-an-a* → *kát-an-a-kat-an-a* 'cut each other'. At the phrasal level, long stem vowels are shortened in a word which is the syntactic head of the phrase, followed by a modifier in the phrase, cf. the alternations *kị#kóloombe* 'cleaning shell', *kị#kólombe ch#aángu* 'my cleaning shell'; *n-aa-n#kálaang-ịịle* 'I fried for him', *n-aa-n#kálang-ịle lị* 'I didn't fry for him'.

Mwera allows only a single long vowel in the stem, so when two long vowels would be present, only the rightmost remains long, thus *jw-aa-ngá#kaláang-a* 'he (jr.) didn't fry', *v-aangá#kaláng-áang-a* 'they didn't fry'; *n-aa#véleénj-e* 'I counted', *vaa#véleng-eénj-e* 'they counted'.

In Yao-Mwera, vowels are lengthened before NC sequences (Hyman and Ngunga 1997), within and between words, thus /ku-n#páta/ → *kuu-m#báta* 'to get me', /chiló m#bat-ílé/ → *chilóó m#bat-ílé* 'at night I got'. Yao and Mwera also have a contrastive syllabic nasal deriving from reduction of /mu/, which is phonetically tone-bearing, and which does not cause lengthening of a preceding vowel, as in /ku-mu#pát-á/ → [ku-m̩#pát-á] 'to get you pl.'. This nasal shortens a preceding long vowel, as in

/chí-á-mu#téléch-el-e/ → *ch-á-ǹ#téléch-el-e* 'he will cook for you' (cf. /chí-á-tu#téléchele/
→ *ch-áá-tu#téléch-el-e* 'he will cook for us' with lengthening of /a/ from glide formation).
In Mozambican Yao, there are a few non-syllabic, non-moraic nasals which cause no
lengthening but are otherwise identical to the nasal which triggers lengthening, viz.
ku#njándála 'to be tough'.

Makonde having lost vowel length, there is no lengthening before NC. Matuumbi lost
pre-NC lengthening, so there is no automatic lengthening there (cf. *kị#chénjele* 'cocks
comb', *lị#ngaánje* 'initiation rattle', *ámbatan-a* 'to agree on things', *n-tịndị* 'buttermilk',
pa#ndó 'where there is a bucket'). Within a morpheme, there are few short vowels before
NC clusters, cases like *áandịk-a* 'to write', *a#loóngo* 'family', *béend-a* 'to shout',
búundal-a 'to get blunt', *chéeng-a* 'to build' being more typical. Across morphemes, vowels do not lengthen, cf. *kụ-nị#páala* ~ *kụ-m#báala* 'to want me', *nga n#dịmịnị* 'it is a
warthog'.

2.2 Consonants

The consonants of the three main P zone languages are as follows; rare phonemes are
listed in parentheses:

(2)   Matuumbi   Yao   Makonde

   p t ch k (s)   *p t ch k s (f)*   *p t ch k s (sh)*
   b d j g   *b d j g*   *b d j g*
   m n ñ n'   *m n ny n'*   *m n ny n'*
   w l y   *v w l y*   *v w l y h*

where <ch> and <sh> are phonetic [č] and [š]; <n'> is phonetic [ŋ]; also, <v>
in Yao (and Mwera) is bilabial [β] but labiodental [v] in Makonde. The palatal nasal
is indicated as <ny> in most languages since it does not contrast with a sequence of *n*
+ *y*, but in Matuumbi the two do contrast so the palatal nasal is indicated as <ñ>.

The Mwera equivalent of Yao /č/ is [š], but [č] after nasals; in Makonde the phonetic
value of /č/ is [č] in Mahuta, Maraba but [š] ~ [s] in Shimakonde, except when preceded by
a nasal where it is [č]. In Matuumbi, [s] is a rare phoneme marginally contrasting with [č].
Ndengereko has [s] and [z] where Matuumbi has [č], [j]. Ngindo and Ndengereko also
have *h* (Ngindo *ku#hịn-a* 'to dance', Ndengereko *kụ#hák-a* 'to hunt'). Harries reports
'latent h' in Mwera careful speech, but speakers I worked with (two generations later)
have no trace of [h].

Voiced stops are generally found after nasals. In Matuumbi *b, g* are found everywhere,
and *j* is found root-initially before *ị*: [d] and [j] are otherwise rare. In Yao, independent
[b] and [d] not preceded by a nasal are rare, except Mozambican Yao changes /l/ into [d]
before [i]. Other than in postnasal position, the voiced stops in Mwera and all of Rufiji
are implosives.

Sequences of nasal plus consonant are modified, depending on the underlying nature
of the consonant and the nasal. Two kinds of nasals must be distinguished. One, the
N-type nasal, acts as a nonsyllabic consonant, and is represented by the verbal 1 sg subject and object prefixes and the class 9–10 noun prefix. The other is a syllabic consonant,
from reduction of /mu/ to [m̥], as represented by the noun prefixes for class 1, 3, locative
mu- (which sometimes does not reduce), and the verbal prefix for class 1 object and 2 pl.
subject and object. The treatment of postnasal voiced consonants is particularly complex
in this group.

Consonant changes in Matuumbi NC sequences follow.

(3)   p,t,ch,k   b,l,j,g   w,y   m,n,ñ,n'

  mu̧   *mp,nt,nch,nk*   *mm,nn,ññ,nn'*   *nn'w,ññ*   *mm,nn,ññ,nn'*
  N   *mb,nd,nj,ng*   *mb,nd,nj,ng*   *ngw,nj*   *m,n,ñ,n'*

Nasals agree in place of articulation with the following consonant, so orthographic
<nk> is [ŋk] and <nn'> is [ŋŋ].

Voiced consonants nasalize after the syllabic nasal (*n#nwáawá* ← *mu̧#lwáawá*
'woman', *m#maánda* ← *mu̧#baánda* 'slave', *n#n'wáachi̧* ← *mu̧#wáachi̧* 'thinker'), and
the nasal assimilates in place of articulation to following nasals and voiceless consonants
(*m#máti̧* ← *mu̧#máti̧* 'plasterer', *ku̧u̧-n#télek-y-a* ← *ku̧-mu̧#télek-y-a* 'to cook for him').
After nonsyllabic N, obstruents are voiced (*n#dilá* ← *N#dilá* 'road', *n#déli̧ike* ~
ni̧#téli̧ike 'I cooked (recent)', *m#baláai̧* ← *N#paláai̧* 'bald heads'), glides harden to
voiced stops (*n#jíma* ← *N#yima* 'poles') and nasals degeminate (*mamáandw-á* ←
N#mamáandw-á 'nailed up (class 9)').

The treatment of voiceless consonants after nasals is the same in Ngindo, Ndengereko
and Ndendeuli as in Matuumbi, but the languages differ in the treatment of postnasal
voiced consonants in verbs. In Ngindo, voiced consonants nasalize after both types of
nasal: *nyée-i̧té* ← *N#jée-i̧té* 'I went', *neét-i̧té* ← *n#leét-i̧té* 'I brought', *mutwi̧i̧ké* ←
N#butwi̧i̧ké 'I ran', *u̧u̧-nip-é* ← *u̧-N#lipe* 'you should pay me' = *u̧u̧#nip-é* ← *u̧-mu̧-lipé*
'you should pay him', *u̧u̧#maláang-e* 'you should count me~him'. However, there is no
nasalization in nouns after N-, cf. *m#búhi̧* 'goat' (PB *m#budi̧*), *n#góji̧* 'ropes' (*lu̧-góji̧*
'rope'). In Ndengereko, nasalization after /mu̧/ is optional (though most frequent) in
verbs, so one finds *ni̧i̧-n#gúndu̧mwi̧i̧ye* ~ *ni̧i̧#n'úndu̧mwi̧i̧ye* 'I scared him', *ni̧i̧-m#buli̧ge*
~ *ni̧i̧#muli̧ge* 'I killed him'. Ndengereko also has Ganda Law where /l/ is deleted in
the context N__VN, seen in the alternations *a-n#dalwi̧i̧ye* ← *a-N#lalwi̧i̧ye* 'he asked me',
a-n#de-i̧ ← *a-N#le-i̧* 'he left me'; *baa-m#búli̧i̧ge* ← *baa-N#búli̧i̧ge* 'they killed me',
~ *a#namwi̧i̧ye* ← *a-N#lamwi̧i̧ye* 'he greeted me'. In Ndendeuli voiced consonants
fuse with N into a nasal consonant (*a-ki̧-N#let-a* → *a-ki̧#net-a* 'she brought me', *a-ki̧-*
N#geg-a → *a-ki̧#ŋeg-a* 'she carried me'), but the nasal of *mu̧-* just assimilates to a
following voiced consonant (*a-ki̧-mu̧#bon-a* → *a-ki̧-m̧#bon-a* 'she saw him', *mu̧-lu̧ma* →
ņ-lu̧ma 'hunter').

The phonology of NC sequences in Yao is spelled out below.

(4)   p,t,ch,k   b,v,l,j,g   d   m,n,ny,n'

  N   *mb,nd,nj,ng*   *m(b),n(d),n(j),n(g)*   *n(d)*   *m,n,ny,n'*
  (9–10 noun N)   *mb,mb,nd,nj,ng*
  mu   *mp,nt,nch,nk*   *m̧b,m̧b,ņd,ņj,ņg*   *nn*   *m̧m,ņn,ņny,ņn'*

The reduced prefix /mu/ is realized on the surface as a syllabic nasal, and assimilates in
place of articulation to the following consonant, as in *chí-m̧#pat-e* 'you (pl.) will get',
chí-ņ#telech-e 'you (pl.) will cook'. Voiceless consonants become voiced after
N- (*chíí-n#delech-e* ← *chi-n#telech-e* 'I will cook', *n#gamílé* ← *n#kamile* 'I milked').

The disposition of voiced consonants after nasals is more complex. After N-, voiced
consonants generally nasalize and degeminate, so *N-v* → *m*, *N-l* → *n*, *N-g* → *n'*,
(*juu#máchiile* ← *ju-N#vakiile* 'she built for me', *ku#nápa* ← *ku-N#lapa* 'to curse me',
chíí#n'on-e ← *chi-N#gon-e* 'I will sleep'). In Mozambican Yao, /b/ nasalizes
(*juu#medudiile* ← *ju-N#bedudiile* 's/he broke off for me'), but [d] does not (*juu-n#déléele*
← *ju-N#deleele* 's/he underestimated me'). In other dialects, there is variation between
hardening and nasalization, so Sanderson reports *ti-n#dol-e* ← *ti-N#lol-e* 'I will look',

ti-n#gon-e ← *ti-n#gon-e* 'I will sleep', Whiteley reports free variation *n#dol-e* ~ *nol-e* ← *ti-N#lol-e* 'let me look' in Masasi, and the dialectal variants *chi#n'on-e* (Tunduru), *ti-n#gon-e* (Masasi) 'I will sleep'. I have found hardening of *l* in Tunduru *n#dim-íle* 'I cultivated', *chii-n#dy-e* 'I will eat', but nasalization of other voiced consonants (*maláás-ile* ← *N#valaas-ile* 'I counted', *nyigéele* ← *N#jigeele* 'I took', *n'uungwíile* ← *N#guungwíile* 'I harvested'); I also find the variation *n#dim-ílé* ~ *nim-ílé* (also *limílé*, with deletion) in Masasi. Nasalization is the most common pattern, and is the general rule in Mwera, viz. *nim-ílé* ← *n#lim-ile*, *shii#málaangany-e* ← *shi-N#valaangany-e* 'I will count', *n'w-iíle* ← *N#gwiile* 'I fell', though Harries gives *ku-m#bulag-a* ~ *ku#mulag-a* 'to kill me'.

Another rule involving NC in Mozambican Yao is Ganda Law, which deletes /d/ after a nasal when followed by an NC sequence, as in *n#aandawiile* ← *N-daandawiile* 'I lamented', *muu-n#iimbiile* ← *mu-N-diimbiile* 'you insisted on me'. The Yao version of Ganda Law specifically requires a following sequence NC, so a simple nasal does not trigger the rule (*n#dim-ílé* ← *N#dim-ílé* 'I cultivated'), which contrasts with Ganda Law in Ndengereko, where a simple nasal triggers the rule (cf. Ndengereko *aa#námuya* ← *aa-N#lámuya* 'he will greet me').

After /mu/, voiced consonants generally harden to stops in Yao, cf. *nga-ní-ń#joóg-a* 'you haven't bathed', *nga-ǹ#gon-á* 'you won't sleep', *chi-ǹ#dye* ← *chi-mu#lye* 'you will eat'. However, /v/ nasalizes, as in *nga-m̀#maláang-a* 'you won't count'. In Mozambican Yao, on the other hand, labials appear as stops (*tu-m̀#bátiiche* ← *tu-mu#bátiiche* 'we stuck on you', *tu-m̀#báchiile* ← *tu-mu#váchiile* 'we built for him') and *l* appears as a nasal (*ku-n#nápá* ← *ku-mu#lapa*) 'to curse (2pl.)'.

Nouns follow slightly different principles; voiced consonants after N- undergo hardening, not nasalization, thus *n#jété* 'salt' (*ka#jété* 'dim'.) *n#gono* 'sleep (pl.)' (*lu#gono* (sg.)). Most nouns appearing in class 9–10 which historically had an initial voiced consonant have been reanalysed as having an underlying voiceless consonant, viz. Proto-Bantu **m#budi* 'goat', Yao *m#búsí* which is synchronically analyzed as /N#púsí/, cf. diminutive *ka#púsí*.

Makonde also distinguishes the segmental effects of *N-* and *mu-*. Voiceless consonants are unaffected after /mu/ as in *kú-m̀#piíny-a* 'to pinch him', *kú-ń#talak-eél-a* 'to cook for him', save for affrication of /s/ to [ch] (*kú-ń#chom-eed-y-a* ← *kú-ń#som-eed-y-a* 'to read for him'); voiceless consonants nasalize after *N-* (*kú-m̀#miíny-a* 'to pinch me', *kú-ń#nalak-eél-a* 'to cook for me', *kú-ń#nyom-eed-y-a* 'to read for me'). After *N-*, voiced consonants harden (*kú-m̀#byaá-a* 'to kill me', *kú-m̀#balaáng-a* 'to count me', *kú-ń#doól-a* 'to look at me'). After /mu/, voiced continuants (/l,v/) nasalize (*kù-m̀#malaáng-a* ← *kú-m̀#valaáng-a* 'to count him', *kú-ń#noóla* ← *kú-ń#loóla* 'to look at him'), but voiced stops are unchanged (*kú-m̀#beéb-a* 'to hold him', *kú-ń#dadoól-a* 'to eat him').

2.3 Tone

All P-zone languages are tonal (though Ndengereko is losing distinctive prosody under Swahili influence). In terms of tonal inventory, all languages restrict contour tones to heavy syllables, long vowels, and VN sequences in Yao and Mwera. Makonde has the richest system of contours, allowing a 5-way contrast on the (automatically long) penult between LL (*nín'iindi* 'top'), HH (*lí#kaála* 'live coal'), HL (*lí#káana* 'wound'), LH (*li#poóndo* 'hole') and LHL (*li#vaâla* 'shoulder'); Matuumbi allows LL (*cháchaanduka* 'taste sour'), LH (*mboópo* 'machete') and HL (*íimba* 'swell'), but generally avoids HH. Tonal processes found in this area include Tone Doubling in Makonde (*va-ndi#tálák-an-iíl-a* ← *va-ndi#talak-an-iíl-a*) 'they cooked for e.o.' and Yao (*ku#pílíkan-il-a* ← *ku#pílikan-il-a* 'to listen'), but not in the Rufiji languages. Unbounded spreading is found in Makonde (*pá-tú-sí#tálák-án-ííl-a* ← *pá-tú-sí#talak-an-iíl-a* 'when we cooked for e.o'). There is attraction of final H to a long penult in Matuumbi (*m#boópo* ← *m#boopó* 'machete') and Yao (*n-aa#páámbukwiíle* ← *n-aa#páámbukwiilé* 'I uncovered'). Lastly, prepausal H is strongly avoided in Makonde, so only one tense (the subjunctive) allows a final H.

The most noteworthy feature of tone in zone P is the system of predictable verbal tones. Unlike most Bantu languages, there are no lexical contrasts in verb roots. Instead, surface tones are assigned to various positions, depending on tense-aspect. In Yao, H is assigned to V_1 in the infinitive and distal subjunctive (*ku#pílíkan-a* 'to listen', *tuka#pílíkan-e* 'let's go listen'), V_2 in the recent past, remote past negative and conditional (*tu#pilíkéene* 'we listened (recent)', *nga-ni-tu#pilíkán-a* 'we didn't listen (remote)', *tu-ka#pilíkán-ag-a* 'if we don't listen'), V_1 and V_2 in the suggestive negative (*nga-sí-tú#pílíkán-a* 'let's not listen'), and the final vowel in the remote past (*tw-aa#lim-ilé* 'we cultivated (remote)'). The stem is toneless in the future and subjunctive (*chi-tú#pilikan-e* 'we will listen', *tu#pilikan-e* 'we should listen').

In Matuumbi, H is assigned to V_1 in most main clause tenses, cf. *káat-a* 'to cut', *b-aa#télek-a* 'they will cook', *b-aa-ga#télíjke* 'they cooked them (class 6) (rem.)', *eend-a-nóo#télek-a* 'he is even *cooking*'. In some verb-focal tenses, H appears on the final vowel as in *nj-tj#balaang-á* 'I *counted* (rec)', *eend-á#kaat-á* 'he's *cutting*'. H appears in V_3 in the subjunctive (*ba#tem-é* 'they should chop', *n#telek-é* 'you (pl.) should cook', *u#lindiíl-e* 'you should guard', *j#n'alan'áat-e* 'it should shine', *u#buundáy-e* 'you should blunt', *u#keengéemb-e* 'you should dig'). When-clauses assign H to V_2, as in *pa-bá#kun-á-kun-a* 'when they grate', *pa-nj#kaát-a* 'when I cut', *pa-ú#lindiil-a* 'when you guard', *pa-á-kj#líndiil-a* 'when he guards it (class 7)'; in recent past when-clauses, H appears on V_2 and the final vowel (*pa-á#kaát-jté* 'when he cut', *pa-á#keéngjjmbé* 'when he dug up'), and in remote past when clauses, H is on the final vowel (*pa-n-áa#tem-jté* 'when I chopped').

Tense-determined tone assignment in Makonde verbs focuses on the type of tone on the penult (where nearly all words have H), so one finds rise in the recent past and future (*tu-ndi#táleék-a* 'we cooked', *tu-nda#taleék-a* 'we will cook'), level H with spreading from the stem initial in the infinitive (*kú#táléék-a* 'to cook'), rise-fall in the remote past and conditional (*tú-ndí#taleêk-a* 'we cooked (rem.)', *tu-ka#taleêk-a* 'if we cook'), level H in the negative past progressive (*a-tu-si#taléék-a* 'we weren't cooking').

3 MORPHOLOGY

3.1 Noun classes

The core Bantu noun classes are well represented in zone P, but the system of agreement has undergone restructuring. The class morphemes of Matuumbi are listed below. Distinctions are made between prefixes on nouns, nominally-inflected adjectives (adj(n)), quasi-verbally-inflected adjectives (adj(v)), the numeral '1', other agreeing numerals and determiners such as possessive pronouns and demonstratives.

(5) | Class | noun | adj(n) | adj(v) | obj | 1 | 2+ | det |
|---|---|---|---|---|---|---|---|
| 1 | *mu* | *mu* | *yu* | *mu* | *yu* | | *yu* |
| 2 | *(b)a* | *(b)a* | *ba* | *ba* | | *a* | *ba* |
| 3 | *mu* | *mu* | *u* | *u* | *gu* | | *gu* |

4	mị	mị	ị	ị		yi
5	lị	lị	lị	lị	lị	li
6	ma	ma	ga	ga		ga
7	kị	kị	kị	kị	chị	chi
8	ị	N	ị	ị		yi
9	N	N	ị	ị	yị	yi
11	lụ	lụ	lụ	lụ	lụ	lu
12	ka	ka	ka	ka	ka	ka
13	tụ	tụ	tụ	tụ		tu
14	(b)u	mụ	ụ	ụ	gụ	gu

There is a lexical split among adjectives where some stems (-kúlú 'big': mụụ#ndụụ n#kúlu≠ 'big person', ndó n#gulú 'big bucket') select adj(n) and some stems, especially deverbal ones (-naá#nog-á 'good' ← nóg-a 'be good': mụụ#ndụ yụ-naá#nog-á 'good person', ndó ị-naá#nogá 'good bucket') select adj(v), sometimes with the associative -a- following the agreement prefix as in ndó y-a-naanchímá 'many buckets'.

The class pairings in Matuumbi are typical of Bantu, viz. 1–2, 3–4, 5–6, 7–8. An innovation in Matuumbi is that most nouns in class 9 select a plural in class 6, viz. m#bwá 'dog', ma-pwá 'dogs'. Some class 9 nouns are invariant in the plural (ndo 'bucket(s)'), and could be assigned to 9–10, though there is no synchronic reason to distinguish historical classes 9 and 10. Exemplars of singular-plural pairings are as follows. 1–2 mw#aána ← mụ#ána, b#aána ← ba ána 'child'; 3–4 n#kún'ụụndo ← mụ#kún'ụụndo, mị#kún'ụụndo 'sieve'; 5–6 lị#kụn'ụúnda, ma#kụn'ụúnda 'filtered beer'; 7–8 kị#gómá, ị#gómá 'cassava'; 9–6 m#bwá, ma#pwá 'dog'; 11–9 lụ#gój, n#gój 'rope'; 12–13 ka#laáị, tụ#laáị 'bamboo (dim.)'; 14 bw-éembé 'flour'; 16, 17, 18 pa-kị#gómá, kụ-kị#gómá, mụ-kị#gómá 'at/to/in the cassava'.

The differences between noun prefixes and nominal adjective prefixes reduce to two complications in agreement pattern, that nouns in class 8 induce agreement in class 9 and nouns in class 14 agree in class 3. The difference between the verbal object prefix and adj(v) agreement is the class 1 form mụ for the OP and yụ for adjectives. Adj(v) prefixes also differ from subject marking on verbs only in the form of the class 1 prefix, a- for verbs, yụ- for adjectives. The difference between the determiner morphemes and most other forms of agreement lies in the height of non-low vowels: lower-high in determiners, super-high otherwise.

The stems for possessive and independent pronouns are seen in (6), using class 1 agreement for possessives.

(6) yw-aángu 'mine'   yw-aáko 'yours (sg.)'   yw-aáke 'his~her'
     yw-ịịtụ 'our'   yw-ịịnụ 'your (pl.)'   yw-aábe 'their'
     n-eénga 'I'   w-eénga 'you (sg.)'   yw-eémbe 'he~she'
     tw-eénga 'we'   mw-eénga 'you (pl.)'   b-eémbe 'they'

Certain animate nouns trigger class 1–2 agreement. In Matuumbi, class 1 agreement is used if the noun is singular, thus n'ombee n#kúlú 'large (class 1) cow (class 9)', n'oombé a#wịịle 'the cow (class 9) is dead (class 1)'. In the plural, grammatically based agreement is used, as in n'ombe n#gúlú n#gulú 'large (class 9) cows', n'oombé ị#w-ịịle 'the cows are dead (class 9)'. When an animate noun is in class 7–8, agreement in class 1 is optional in the singular (kị#ụụla kị#w-ịịle ~ kị-ụụla a#w-ịịle 'the frog is dead'), but not in the plural (y#ụụla ị#w-ịịle ~ *y#ụụla ba#w-ịịle 'the frogs are dead').

A special plural prefix *kị-* can be added to animate nouns, so alongside *n'oómbe* 'cows' and *naánkwakwa* 'lizards', one can have *kị#n'oómbe* 'cows' and *kị-naánkwakwa* 'lizards'. Such plurals always induce class 2 agreement, viz. *kị#n'ombe a#kúlu a#kúlú* 'large cows', *n-aa-ba#bwénị kị-naánkwakwa* 'I saw the lizards'. This same prefix is also added to personal names to indicate 'the family of so-and-so', i.e. *kị#Lịbụlụ́le* 'the Libulules'.

The class morphemes of Makonde are as follows: the rubric 'det' includes the agreement for possessive pronouns and the associative marker, demonstratives of various sorts, and long-form adjectives (-*ambone* 'good', vis *n#kóngwé w-ámboóne* 'good woman') which comprise the bulk of adjectives in the language (in contrast to short-form adjectives as in *n#kóngwé n#kúmeene* 'big woman' inflected with the 'adj' series of prefixes).

(7)	noun	adj	1	2,3	det	SP
1	*mu*	*mu*	*ju*		*u*	*a*
2	*va*	*va*		*va*	*va*	*va*
3	*mu*	*u*	*u*		*u*	*u*
4	*mi*	*vi~mi*		*mi*	*vi*	*vi*
5	*li*	*li*	*li*		*li*	*li*
6	*ma*	*ma*		*ma*	*a*	*a*
7	*shi*	*shi*	*shi*		*shi*	*shi*
8	*vi*	*vi*		*vi*	*vi*	*vi*
9	*(i)N*	*iN*	*i*		*i*	*i*
10	*diN*	*diN*		*N*	*di*	*di*
11	*lu*	*lu*	*lu*		*lu*	*lu*
12	*ka*	*ka*	*ka*		*ka*	*ka*
13	*tu*	*tu*		*tu*	*tu*	*tu*
14	*u*	*u*	*u*		*u*	*u*

Object prefixes other than class 1–2 *mu ~ va* do not exist in Mozambican Shimakonde; in Tanzanian dialects they have the same form as the determiner series. The class 6 determiner agreement is *la* in Chimahuta, *ya* in Chimaraba, and *a* in Shimakonde.

As in Matuumbi, animate nouns take their agreement in class 1–2 under certain circumstances. Animate nouns in class 9 without the prefix *i-* induce class 1 agreement (*n'úkú wa-ku#núúna* 'fat chicken'), but with the prefix *i-*, agreement is in class 9 (*i#n'úku yá-ku#núúna*). The plural in class 10 also conditions agreement in class 10 (*di#n'úkú dyá-kú#núúna* 'fat chickens'), but an alternative is to pluralize animate class 9 nouns in class 2 (*vá#n'úkú vá-kú#núúna*). In other classes, animate nouns optionally condition class 1 agreement in the singular but not in the plural (*li#túunu lii#mo ~ lí#túunu juu#mo* 'one hyena', *má#túunu ma#táátu* 'three hyenas'; *sh#úuni juu#mo ~ sh#úuni shi#mo* 'one bird'; *vy#úuni vi#táátu* 'three birds').

The class system of Yao is much simpler. There is one series of prefixes for nouns, and one set of morphemes for all agreement (with the sole exception that the class 1 subject prefix is *a-* and the object prefix is *-a-*: however, in Mozambican Yao, the subject prefix is *ju-*).

(8)	noun	agreement	noun	agreement
1–2	*mu*	*ju (a)*	*va*	*va*
3–4	*mu*	*u*	*mi*	*ji*
5–6	*li(i)*	*li*	*ma*	*ga*

7–8	*chi*	*chi*	*i*	*i*
9–10	*N*	*ji*	*N*	*si*
11–10	*lu*	*lu*	*N*	*si*
12–13	*ka*	*ka*	*tu*	*tu*
13	*u*	*u*		

All agreement is strictly according to formal class, thus *chi#juni chí#mo* 'one bird', *lii#jani límo* 'one baboon', *ma#jani gávili* 'two baboons', *n#gúkú j#aangu* 'my bird'.

The set of determiners is quite rich, maximally so in Kimatuumbi, which has numerous determiners involving morphological templates and modifications via lengthening and reduplication. There are four basic demonstratives, class 1 examples ordered in terms of proximity to speaker being *yu-no* 'this (nearest to speaker)', *a-yu* 'this (further from speaker)', *a-yw-o* 'that (even further from speaker)' and *yu-lu* 'that (furthest from speaker)'. There are phonological variants of this last series, involving the prefix -*a*- after the class agreement or *y* after *l*, viz. *ywalu ~ ywalyu ~ yulyu*. Reduplication of the agreement morpheme is also possible, giving *yuuyúno, ayuúyu, aywoóywo*, and *yuuyúlu* (*~ywaaywálu ~ ywaaywályu ~ yuuyúlyu*); iconic prosodic modifications indicating extreme distance are common viz. *yúúlyúú, yuúlúywa* 'that (quite distant)', *yúúlúywo* 'that (quite distant, pointing)'. A number of determiners translate as definite articles, such as *ywé, yweéne, ywa* 'the'. Finally, combinations of articles and demonstratives are frequent, such as *yulyu ywa, ywé ywa, yweéne ywa*, and *yweéne ywaywa*.

The Yao determiners are exemplified in class 1 by *a-ju* 'this', *a-jw-o* 'that (near)', *a-ju-no* 'that', *a-jul-a* 'that (remote)', *jw-e, jw-e-le* 'specific', and reduplicated variants *ajuju, jwejojo*. Liberal combinations of definitizers and demonstratives are allowed, such as *jw-ee ju-la* 'that', *jwele aju* 'this'. The Makonde demonstratives vary between dialects, and one can find (in class 1) *júu-no* 'this' in Maraba and Mahuta but not Shimakonde, *á-nee-ju* 'this' and *á-nee-jo* 'that remote' in Mahuta, *a-juu-lá* 'that further' in all dialects, *juu-ya* 'that' in Maraba and Mahuta, and *aa-jo* 'that (near listener)', *aa-ju* 'this' in all dialects.

3.2 Verb extensions

The productive extensions of Kimatuumbi are passive -(*il*)*w*- (*piim-ilw-a* 'be bought'), applied -*i*- (*píim-y-a* 'buy for'), reciprocal -*an*- (*píim-an-a* 'buy each other'), stative -*ik*- (*píim-ik-a* 'be buyable'), causative -*iy*- (*píim-iy-a* 'sell') and plural -*aang*- (*pím-aang-a* 'buy (pl.) objects'). Extensions are added in the order causative > applied > passive, reciprocal, plural, hence *piim-iy-an-a* 'sell e.o.', *piim-y-aan-a* 'buy for e.o.', *pím-iy-aang-a* 'cause pl. people to buy', *pím-ik-iy-ilw-a* 'be sold to', *pím-ik-iy-an-a* 'sell to e.o.'.

The causative suffix, which also has an intensive interpretation (*káatiya* 'cause to cut; cut intensively') has an allomorph where -*y*- replaces stem final *k, l*, as in *túúmbuk-a* 'fall', *túúmbu-y-a* 'cause to fall', *ból-a* 'be rotten' *bó-y-a* 'make rot'. It also combines with *y* to give -(*i*)*kiy*- as in root final *y* (*báy-a* 'say', *bá-kiy-a* 'make say'), applied *y* (*káat-y-a* 'cut for', *kát-ikiy-a* 'make cut for'), or when the causative affix combines with itself to yield a causative-intensive meaning as in *kún'uúnd-iy-a* 'be well filtered', *kún'und-ikiy-a* 'be really well filtered'.

Besides the usual reciprocal meaning, the reciprocal suffix has the meaning 'do pointlessly', as in *ttikw-a* 'break off', *tikw-aan-a* 'break off and discard'. The plural suffix generally refers to plural objects with transitive verbs (*búlag-a* 'kill', *búlag-aang-a* 'kill pl. things') and plural subjects with intransitive verbs (*tíil-a* 'run', *tíl-aang-a* 'run (pl. subj)').

The very complex grammar of extensions in Yao is studied in Ngunga (1997), who demonstrates the existence of 14 extensions including applied -*il*-, three causatives

-y-, -isy- and -aasy-, 'impositive' -ik-, intensive -isy-, passives -w- and -igw-, stative -ik-, reversives -ul- and -uk-, and reciprocals -an-, -aangan- and -agan-. Examples of the most productive extensions are applied telek-el-a 'cook for', iiv-il-a 'steal from', viinj-il-a 'chase toward', kaat-il-a 'cut with', gon-el-a 'sleep on'; intensive did-isy-a 'cry a lot', teend-esy-a 'do a lot'; passive suum-igw-a 'be bought'; causative suum-isy-a 'sell', viing-aasy-a 'make chase'; reciprocal puut-an-a 'beat e.o.'.

Extensions combine to give impressive morpheme combinations, for example jigal-a 'take' yields jigad-ich-is-y-aas-y-ana 'cause e.o. to make take for'. Extension combinations are subject to numerous rules. Combination of applied plus causative results in the replacement of the final consonant by ch (cf. the parallel replacement in Matuumbi) as shown by won-a 'see', won-esy-a 'make see', won-ech-esy-a 'make see for'; pol-a 'be cool', pol-aasy-a 'cool (tr.)', pol-aach-isy-a 'cool (tr.) for'. These examples also illustrate different orderings of causative and applied suffixes. The example pol-aach-isy-a from pol-aak-il-y-a also illustrates the common phenomenon in Bantu where the glide -y- of the causative may be separated from the rest of the causative by another suffix.

One of the morphotactic and syntactic restrictions in Yao extension combinations is that valence-decreasing affixes (reciprocal, stative or passive) cannot immediately follow valence-decreasing affixes, but two such suffixes are possible if a valence-increasing suffix such as the causative intervenes. Thus puut-a 'hit' forms puut-igw-a 'be hit', puut-igw-aasy-aan-a 'cause e.o. to be hit' but not *puut-igw-aan-a with adjacent passive and reciprocal; puut-ik-a 'be hittable' and puut-ik-aasy-aan-a 'cause e.o to be hittable' are possible, but *puut-ik-aan-a with adjacent stative and reciprocal is blocked. Phonotactic factors also affect morpheme combination, so chap-a 'wash' forms chap-isy-a 'wash well', chap-isy-aan-il-a 'wash well e.o. for', but *chap-isy-il-a which should mean 'wash well for' is blocked by a phonotactic constraint against *Cyi.

In Makonde, there are a few lexicalized passives such as lombw-a 'be married (of woman)' with -w-; otherwise, the productive passive suffix is -igw- (talak-eegw-a 'be cooked', lim-iigw-a 'be cultivated'). There are three causative suffixes with subtle semantic differences: -y- (liim-y-a 'make directly cultivate because of'), -iiy- (lim-iiy-a 'make directly cultivate') and the indirect causative -iidy- (lim-iidy-a 'make indirectly cultivate'); in addition, -iishy- forms an intensive causative (lim-iishy-a 'make cultivate intensively'). The language also has a productive pluractional suffix -aang-, which indicates either plural subjects acting, plural objects being acted on, or repeated or constant action, as in tukut-aang-a 'for many people to run, run many places, run repeatedly'; lim-aang-a 'for many people to cultivate, cultivate a lot of fields'. The applied suffix is -il-, cf. lim-iil-a 'cultivate for', and besides the benefactive meaning also indicates instrumental, comitative and locative objects (ly-el-a i#nyááma 'eat with meat', lim-il-a li#jéémbe 'cultivate with a hoe', lal-il-a li#káande 'sleep on the mat', tukutila m#méedi 'run into water'). The reciprocal is -an- (-put-aan-a 'beat each other'), which precedes the applied (-talak-an-iil-a 'cook for each other').

3.3 Verb inflection

The verbal subject and object prefixes for first and second person and class 1–2 in the three languages are listed in (9).

(9)	Matuumbi		Yao		Makonde		
	subject	object	subject	object	subject	object	
	nį	nį	n	n	ni/ngu	ngu	1s
	ų	kų	(u)/mu	mu	u	ku	2s

a	*mu̧*	*(v)a*	*(mu)/a*	*a*	*mu*	*Cl.1*
tu̧	*tu̧*	*tu*	*tu*	*tu*	*tu*	*1p*
mu̧	*mu̧*	*mu*	*mu*	*mu*	*mu*	*2p*
ba	*ba*	*(v)a*	*a*	*va*	*va*	*Cl.2*

Mwera distinguishes second and third person prefixes in terms of whether the referent is adult. The junior prefixes are *u-* (2 subject), *ku-* (2 object), *a-* (3 subject), *mu-* (3 object), and the adult prefixes are *mu-* (2 subject, object), *(v)a-* (3 subject), *a-* (3 object). The historical Bantu singular prefixes are used for junior referents and the original plural prefixes are used for adults. Plural subjects and objects are not distinguished by prefix, but rather by the plural suffix *-aang-*. Similarly, in Yao, the 2s subject prefix *u-* and the 3s object *-mu-* are used only refering to young children, and *u-* is used only rarely. Singular/plural distinctions are not generally made for second and third person, but in some dialects can be made by the verbal suffix *-aang-*. There does not appear to be any junior/adult distinction in the form of the second person object or the third person subject prefixes.

The form of the 1 sg. subject prefix in Makonde is determined by complex tense-dependent rules. In some tenses both *ngu* and *ni* are allowed, e.g. habitual (*ngú-ndá#taleêk-a* ~ *ní-ndá#taleêk-a* 'I cook'), future (*ngu-nda#taleék-a*, *ni-nda#taleék-a* 'I will cook'), negative habitual (*a-ngu-na#taléék-a* ~ *a-ni-na#taléék-a* 'I don't cook'). In some tenses, only *ni-* is possible, such as in the recent past (*ni-ndi#táleék#a* 'I cooked'), conditional (*ni-ka#taleêk-a* 'if I cook') and negative future (*a-ni#taleek-a* 'I won't cook'). In other tenses, such as the subjunctive (*ngu-taleék-e* 'I should cook'), recent past relative (*pá-ngú-táleek-e* 'when I cooked') and negative past (*a-ngu-táleék-e* 'I didn't cook'), only *ngu-* is possible.

Matuumbi has the simplest tense-aspect system. Except for two subordinate clause forms, there is no distinction between affirmative and negative verbs, negation being marked with the post-verbal particle *li̧~li̧ili̧*.There is a well-developed set of focal distinctions conveyed through verb tenses which marks neutral focus, focus on the postverbal word (generally a noun), or focus on the verb. Preceding the subject prefix may be either the relative clause head agreement, or a temporal prefix *pa-* or *ka-*. Following the SP, the main TA markers prefixes are *a* 'remote' and *ka* 'action away, conditional', with *nga* and *na* being used in the two negative inflections; verb-focus forms are marked with *-tj-*, *-eenda-*, and *-endee-*. The stem is generally inflected with the suffix *-a*, but certain past tenses use the perfective stem (described later in this section); the subjunctive selects the final vowel *e*, and the past progressive selects the clitic *-e* after *-a*. In this table, 'S' indicates 'stem', 'pfv' indicates the perfective stem, 'vf' indicates that the tense places focus on the verb, 'nf' indicates 'noun focus'.

(10)	tense	template	example	gloss
	infinitive	S + a	*líla*	'to cry'
	past	sp-S + pfv	*nilíli̧te*	'I just cried'
	past remote	sp-s-S + pfv	*naalíli̧te*	'I cried'
	fut remote	sp-a-S-a	*naalíla*	'I will cry'
	fut distal	sp-ka-S-a	*ni̧kalíla*	'I will go cry'
	pres prog nf	sp-S-a	*ni̧lila* ...	'I am crying (nf)'
	past prog nf	sp-S-a-e	*ni̧lilae* ...	'I was crying (nf)'
	past vf	sp-tj-S-a	*ni̧ti̧lilá*	'I just cried (vf)'
	past remote vf	sp-a-tj-S-a	*naatí̧lilá*	'I cried (vf)'
	pres prog vf	sp-endá-S-a	*neendálilá*	'I am crying (vf)'

past prog vf	sp-endeé-S-a	*neendeélilá*	'I was crying (vf)'
subjunctive	sp-S-e	*nįlilé*	'I should cry'
remote subjnct	sp-a-S-e	*naalilé*	'I should cry (rem)'
distal subjnct	sp-ka-S-e	*nįkalilé*	'I should go cry'
proximal subjnct	cha-sp-S-e	*chanįlilé*	'I should come cry'
subord neg	dem-nga-S-a	*wangalilá*	'without crying'
neg persistive	sp-ná-S-a	*nįnálila lį*	'I haven't yet cried'
past prog temp	ka-sp-S-a	*kanįlilá*	'when I was crying'
conditional	sp-ka-S-a	*nįkálilá*	'if I cry'

In addition, verb focus forms may include the prefix *-noo-* 'even', as in *nį-tį-nóo#líla* 'I even cried (vf)', *n-eenda-nóo#líla* 'I am even crying (vf)'.

Relative clause verbs have a demonstrative prefix agreeing with the head noun on an inflected verb, thus *yw-aá#lil-įté* 'who cried (recent)', *yw-áa#lilįté* 'who cried (remote)', *yw-aá#lilá* 'who is crying', *yw-aá#lil-įté* 'who was crying', *yw-áa#líla* 'who will cry' and *yw-aá#ka-líla* 'who will go cry'. Because of conflicting focus requirements, verb focus forms cannot be used in relative forms.

The tense-aspect systems of Ngindo and Ndengereko are similar to that of Matuumbi. In Ndengereko, the negative particle is *kwáaku* (*nį#lima kwáaku* 'I am not cultivating'), in Ngindo it is *ji* (*ba#lima jí* 'they are not cultivating') and in Ndendeuli it is *yi* (*akįtu yi kįhembe* 'he did not take a knife'). In Ndengereko, the nonprogressive verb-focus marker is *te* (*tų-té#líma* 'we *cultivated*') and the progressive marker is *-ndo-* in the present tense (*na-ndo#líma* 'I am cultivating'), *-ndagee-* in the past (*ba-nda-gée#lím-a* 'they were cultivating'). In Ngindo, the progressive is marked with *-teenda-* plus the infinitive (*tų-teenda ku-lím-a* 'we were cultivating'). The past clitic *-e* of Matuumbi appears as *-ge* in Ndengereko (*tų#lím-a-ge* 'we were cultivating') and in Ngindo where it marks habituals (*ba#lim-á-ge* 'they cultivate'). The form corresponding to the Matumbi conditional with the prefix *-ká-* functions as a persistive in Ndengereko (*a-ka-#téleka* 'he is still cooking'). The prefix *ka-* in Ngindo appears in negative imperatives (*ka-kema ji* 'don't yell'), and, combined with *-ge*, forms participials (*tų-ka#lím-a-ge* 'us cultivating').

Yao has a richer set of tense-aspect forms, since polarity (affirmative vs. negative clauses) are marked on the verb by distinct inflections. The main tenses of Yao are listed below:

(11)	future	chi-sp#S-e	*chítúlile*	'we will cry'
	future distal	chi-sp-ka#S-e	*chítúkalíle*	'we will go cry'
	neg future	nga-sp#S-a	*ngatulilá*	'we won't cry'
	future	ti-sp-chi#S-a	*tuuchílila*	'we will cry'
	present	sp-ku#S-a	*tukulíla*	'we cry'
	habitual	sp-ku#S-ag-a	*tukulílága*	'we usually cry'
	neg present	nga-sp-ku#S-a	*ngatukúlíla*	'we are not crying'
	habitual	sp-ku-saa#S-a	*túkúsaalilá*	'we usually cry'
	rec past	sp#S + pfv	*tulimíle*	'we cried (rec)'
	rem past	sp-a#S + pfv	*twaalílilé*	'we cried (rem)'
	past prog	sp-a#S-ag-a	*twaalílagá*	'we were crying'
	neg rec past	nga-ni-sp#S-a	*nganítúlilá*	'we didn't cry (rec)'
	neg rem past	nga-ni-sp#S-a	*nganitulilá*	'we didn't cry (rem)'
	neg particip	dem-ngá#S-a	*uungálilá*	'not crying'
	conditional	sp-ka#S-ag-a	*tukalilága*	'if we don't cry'

neg hortative	nga-si-sp#S-a	*ngasítúlílá*	'let's not cry'
subjunctive	sp#S-e	*tulile*	'we should cry'
subjunct neg	sp-ka#S-a	*tukalila*	'we shouldn't cry'
hort distal	sp-ka#S-e	*tukalíle*	'let's go cry'

Relative clause verbs are formed by prefixing demonstrative head agreement (without the associative -*a*-), as in *muundu jú-vá#wiíle* 'person who died'.

The tense-aspect categories of Makonde are listed in (12).

(12)

	affirmative	negative
rec. past	*tu-ndi#táleék-a*	*a-tu#táleeke*
rem. past	*tú-ndí#taleék-a*	*a-tu#taleéke*
pres prog	*tu-n-ku#táléék-a*	*a-tu-na#táléék-a*
hab pres	*tú-n(d)á#taleék-a*	
future	*tu-nda#taleék-a*	*a-tu#taleek-a*
past prog	*tú-si-nda#taleék-a*	*a-tu-si#táléék-a*
condit	*tu-ka#taleêk-a*	*tu-ka#taleek-e*
subjunct	*tu#taleék-e*	*a-tu-na#táléeke*
participial	*tú#táleek-a*	
suggestive	*tú-ká-ndí#taleêk-a*	*á-tú-ná#táléeke*
imprf	*pá-tú-sí#táléék-a*	*pá-tú-ká-si#tálééka*
past prog	*pá-tú-ná#táléék-a*	*pá-tú-ká-ná#tálééka*
rec past	*pá-tú#táleeke*	*pá-tú-ká#taleéke*
rem past	*pa-tu#taleéke*	*pá-tú-ká#taleéke*

The shape of the perfective stem in Matuumbi is determined primarily by prosodic properties of the basic stem. When the base is of the form CV(V)C, or if the last stem vowel is long, the suffix -*ite* (-*ike* in Ndengereko) is chosen, as in *nį#chól-įte* (*chól-a*) 'I drew', *nį#káat-įte* (*káat-a*) 'I cut', *nį#bálaang-įte* (*bálaang-a*) 'I counted'. When the final vowel of a polysyllabic stem is short, *į* is infixed, as in *ny#áandįįke* (*áandįk-a*) 'I wrote', *nį#bélįįke* (*bélek-a*) 'I gave birth', *nį#sábįįte* (*sábat-a*) 'I beat', *nį#búlwįįte* (*búlut-a*) 'I dragged'. Stems ending in a glide add -*įįle*, as in *nį#kúb-įįle* (*kúby-a*) 'I found', *nį#bóyw-įįle* (*bóyw-a*) 'I caught'. This is due to infixation of *į* into underlying stems /kubį/ and /boyų/ plus an independent rule of *l*- insertion. Monosyllabic stems select -*įįle* (cf. *nį#lįįle* (*lyá*) 'I ate'). A few lexically marked stems optionally or obligatorily select the reduced perfective, -*į*, along with vocalic irregularities, as in *į#-ból-įte* ~ *į-bó-į* 'it rotted', *nį#bwéen-į* (-*bon-a*) 'I saw', *nį#máañ-į* ~ *nį#máñ-įte* (-*mañ-a*) 'I knew', and a few stems have irregular consonant alternations, such as *nį#wéetį* (-*waal-a*) 'I dressed', *nį#téend-įte* ~ *nį#téeį* (-*teend-a*) 'I did', *nį#twéetį* ~ *nį#tóol-įte* (-*tool-a*) 'I took'.

Formation of the perfective stem in Yao is similar. With a CV(V)C stem the suffix -*ile* is added, as in *tu#tav-íle* (-*tav-a*) 'we built', *tu#suum-íle* (-*suum-a*) 'we bought'. Stems ending in -*y*- select -*iisye* as in *tu#kaaniisye* (-*kaany-a*) 'we prohibited', *tw#oosiisye* (-*oosya*) 'we gave a bath'; if the stem ends in surface *ch* (from /ky/), the affix has the shape -*iiche* (*tw#oochíiche* (-*ooch-a*) 'we roasted'). Monosyllabic stems select -*iile* or -*eele* (*tu#l-iile* (-*ly-a*) 'we ate', *tu#n'w-eéle* (-*n'w-a*) 'we drank', *tu#gw-iíle* (-*gw-a*) 'we fell'). Polysyllabic stems whose last vowel is short infix *i*, as in *tu#uléeje* (-*ulag-a*) 'we killed', *tu#piikéene* (-*piikan-a*) 'we heard', *tu#gaangáleeme* (-*gaangalam-a*) 'we are big', *tu#teléeche* (-*telek-a*) 'we cooked', *tu#chamwíil-e* (-*chamul-a*) 'we combed', *tu#lokwéet-e* (-*lokot-a*) 'we picked up'. If the final vowel is long, the suffix -*ile* is added, cf. *tu#kwalák-wáás-ile* (-*kwalakwaat-a*) 'we scraped', *tu#kaláánj-ile* (-*kalaang-a*) 'we fried'. There are a few lexically irregular perfective stems, such as *tu#weén-i* (*-won-a*) 'we saw', *tu#piit-e* (*-pit-a*) 'we passed', *tu#yiích-e* (*-yik-a*) 'we arrived'. Mwera differs from Yao in that infixation is found with all polysyllabic stems, even those with a final long vowel (*valaang-a* 'count', *méléenje* 'I counted'), it is unknown whether this extends to long vowels not followed by NC. When a stem ends in a series of [a]'s, each harmonizes to the following vowel (contrast Yao *tu#gaangáleeme* 'we are big').

In Makonde, CVC perfective stems select *-ite* ~ *-ile*. Generally the suffix *-ile* is used, e.g. *-vik-iile* 'put', *-pat-iile* 'get', *-lip-iile* 'pay', but some stems take *-ite* e.g. *-many-iite* 'know', *-uj-iite* 'return'. There is dialectal and speaker variation, so one may find *-div-iile* or *-div-iite* 'cover a hole': the choice of perfective forms requires deeper investigation. The suffix *-ile* causes final /l/ to become [d], cf. *-pad-iile* ← *pel-iile* 'finish'. CV stems all take *-ile* (*-ly-iile* 'eat', *-gw-iile* 'fall down'). If a CVC stem ends with a glide, the perfective affix is *-iidye*: *loody-a* → *lody-iidye* 'show', *tot-eey-a* → *tot-ey-iidye* 'make sew', *-uungw-a* → *ungw-iidye* 'hear'. Polysyllabic roots infix the vowel *i*, as in *tukuta* → *tukwiite* 'run', *taleka* → *taleeke* 'cook', *kalamola* → *kalamweele* 'cough', *valanga* → *valeenge* 'count'.

4 SYNTAX

Sentential word order is very free, especially in Matuumbi, and in that language all permutations of subject, object and verb are possible, viz. SVO *muu#ndú a#kat-íte kaámba* ('the person cut the rope') ~ OSV *kaámba muu#ndú a#káat-íte* ~ VSO *a#kat-íte muu#ndu kaámba* ~ VOS *a#kat-íte kaámba muú#ndu* ~ OVS *kaámba a#kat-íte muú#ndu*. While such variations in word order are frequent, the basic word order is SVO, found most often in pragmatically neutral contexts lacking specific emphasis on any word. An essential property governing word order is focus, expressed through the system of verbal inflection which distinguishes focally neutral tenses from tenses that require focus on the following element and tenses that require focus on the verb.

The present progressive of the form SP + stem is a noun-focusing tense. When followed by an NP, that NP receives focus, viz. *nj#kat-a kaámba* 'I'm cutting *rope* (not something else)'. Such verbs cannot stand at the end of the phrase, thus **nj#kaat-a*, since there is no following phrase which receives focus, and they cannot be followed by *tú* 'only' (**nj#kata tú*) which assign focus to the preceding word. Consequently, postposing of the subject NP becomes obligatory with intransitive verbs in this tense, e.g. **mwaána abutukae* → *abutukae mwaána* 'the child was running'. As a corollary, leftward preposing of an object, which is generally allowed regardless of tense (cf. *a#kat-íte kaámba* ~ *kaamba a#káat-íte* 'he cut the rope'), is blocked in a noun-focal tense when only a single object is present, viz. *a#kalang-a kj#njáambú* ↛ **kj#njáambú a#kalaang-a* 'he is frying cassava leaves'. Leftward preposing of the object is allowed if there is a second object which receives the focus (*a#kalang-y-a baa#ndu kj#njáambú* ~ *kj#njáambú a#kalaang-y-a baá-ndu* 'he's frying cassava leaves for the people'), or if the subject is postposed (*muu#ndú a#kalang-a kj#njáambú*→*kj#njáambú a#kalang-a muú#ndu* 'the person is frying cassava').

In contrast, the verb focus tenses disallow focused material after the verb, and prefer to be clause-final. Thus preposing of an object is preferred (*n-aa-tj#bulag-áa n#gúku* → *n#gukú n-aa-tj#bulag-á* 'I killed a chicken'), and postposing of the subject is impossible (*n#nwaáwa aa-tj#butuk-á* ↛ **aa-tj#butuk-áa n#nwaáwa* 'the woman ran'), since postposing the subject places focus on the subject. Verb-focus forms also cannot be followed by wh-phrases (*aa-tí-kụụ-m#mon-áa ñáị 'who did he see?', *b-eend-eé#cheeng-á ma-yụmba gá#liinga 'how many houses were they building'?), but can be followed by focus-assigning tụ́ 'only' (b-aa-tí#balaang-á tụ́ 'they were only counting').

Verbs may contain one OP, thus naa-ba-telekịịle 'I cooked for them', *naa-ba-kị#télekịịle, *naa-kị-ba#télekịịle ('I cooked it for them'). An OP can co-occur with a coreferential NP within the VP, indicating greater definiteness, thus nị-nolya baandụ yiímbe 'I'm sharpening knives for people', nị-ba#nólya baandụ yiímbe 'I'm sharpening knives for the people'. Unlike analogous structures in Chichewa, the coreferential object is fully integrated into the VP, so it can appear right after the verb, satisfies the focal requirement of noun-focal tenses, and phrases phonologically with the verb. The verb 'see' has the further syntactic requirement (shared with Makonde and Yao) that the verb must have an OP agreeing with the object, thus naa-m#mwénị mwaána ~ *naa#bwénị mwaána 'I saw the ~ a child'.

Relative clauses follow the nominal head, and are separated from the head by the determiner-series possessive prefix added to the verb, viz. mụụ#ndụ yw-áa-telịịke 'person who cooked', mụụ#ndụ ywa-náa#puutịte 'person who I beat'. The lower subject NP cannot intervene between the verb and the preceding clausal head, so in the lower clause, a full NP subject must be moved by passivization (ky#iimbé cha-kị́-tolịlwé na Lịbụlụ́le 'knife that was taken by Libulule'). Alternatively the subject may be directly demoted (ky#iimbé cha-kị́-twetị Lịbụlụ́le 'knife that Libulule took', literally 'knife that took Libulule'), in which case the subject marking of the relative clause verb agrees with the lower object 'knife'. Such structures are potentially ambiguous, so tend to be used only when subject and objects roles can be reasonably inferred from context.

As in many Bantu languages, if the NP immediately preceding the verb is a wh-phrase, the sentence is rendered as a relative clause with the head topicalized. Thus compare mw#aána aa#kém-ịte 'a child yelled' and mw#aaná yw#aaku yw-áa#kem-ịté 'which child yelled?', literally 'which child is it who yelled?'. This strategy holds for objects as well as subjects, cf. ky#iimbé ganị cha-báa#paál-a 'which knife do they want'. The wh-phrase must stand immediately before the verb in order to condition relativization (cf. ky#iimbé ganị baa#ndụ́ b-aa#twéetị 'which knife did the people take?').

The syntax of determiners in the P zone languages is different from that of typical Bantu language. Because of additional articles, a noun phrase can and frequently does contain multiple determiners, thus in Matuumbi kịtélekó cheéne chilu 'that pot'. The core determiners (chilu, chino, achi, acho) can also appear before the noun head, viz. achi kịtéleéko 'this pot'. In Yao and Mwera, demonstratives are usually placed before the head noun; quite frequently a noun phrase will contain both a pre-head and a post-head determiner.

5 SUMMARY

The Rufiji-Ruvuma languages present features of interest to the general linguist and the Bantuist alike. Noteworthy phonological features include the system of morphosyntactically predictable tone in verbs, limits on long vowels, and issues relating to nasality such as N + C alternations, the fact that two kinds of N must be distinguished segmentally and prosodically, plus emerging vowel nasalization. Noun class agreement is particularly complex, and the languages have a rich system of determiners. This study has only touched on the highlights: deeper investigation of these and other grammatical features in the languages of the area must await descriptive work of a number of still undescribed languages.

ACKNOWLEDGMENT

I would like to thank Marcelino Liphola for his extensive assistance in describing Makonde, Deo Ngonyani for providing information on Ndendeuli, and Larry Hyman for helping on Mozambican Yao. Research leading to this chapter was supported by NSF, the Fulbright Foundation, and NSF grant SBR-9421362.

REFERENCES

Harries 1950; Hyman and Ngunga 1997; Guerreiro 1963; Ngonyani 1999; Ngunga 1997; Nurse 1988; Liphola 2001; Odden 1990a, 1990b, 1996; Sanderson 1922; Whiteley 1966; Yukawa 1989b.

CHAPTER TWENTY-SEVEN

MAKHUWA (P30)

Charles Kisseberth

1 ZONE P30

Under Zone P30, Guthrie lists the following 'languages': Makhuwa, Lomwe, Ngulu, and Chuabo. This characterization of the zone is problematic in several ways.

Although speakers of some speech varieties may identify their language as 'Elomwe' and others may identify their language as 'Emakhuwa', we know of no evidence that this self-differentiation is linguistically based. The study of Makhuwa dialectology is not sufficiently advanced to determine whether a classification of dialects based on linguistic features would result in any bifurcation along a Makhuwa/Lomwe dimension. Specifically, it is unclear whether there are linguistic properties whose distribution coincides with either self-identifed Lomwe speech varieties or self-identified Makhuwa speech varieties. For example, in the (sparse) literature, it is said that Lomwe uses the affricates *c* [tʃ] and *ch* [tʃʰ] in place of the characteristic Makhuwa post-alveolar stops *tt* and *tth*. However, I have studied three dialects in Malawi (Emihavani, Emunyamwelo, and Ekokholani) whose speakers consider their language Lomwe but who use the stops *tt* and *tth* rather than the corresponding affricates. Given the uncertainty of a reliable Lomwe/Makhuwa distinction, I shall use the term 'Makhuwa' to include 'Lomwe' whenever the distinction between the two is not of immediate relevance.

Guthrie's reference to 'Ngulu' is also problematic. This term has been used in the non-linguistic literature to refer to Lomwe-speaking immigrants to Malawi, and it does occur among the list of terms speakers use to refer to different varieties of Lomwe in Malawi (which, besides the dialects already mentioned, includes also Emarenje, Emeetto, Emikukhu, Etakhwani, Emaratha among others). While we have not actually worked with anyone who identifies his speech as Ngulu, it is extremely doubtful that it represents a language distinct from Lomwe/Makhuwa.

I am not aware of any linguistically sophisticated work on the grammatical structure of Guthrie's last P30 language, Chuabo; however, there is a fairly substantial dictionary (Festi and Valler 1995). My brief exposure to the language and a cursory examination of written texts and the dictionary make it clear that this is a language distinct from Makhuwa. Spoken in and around the coastal city of Quelimane (in Zambezia province in Mozambique), Chuabo rests at the extreme southern edge of the Makhuwa-speaking territory. There is a strong possibility that Chuabo is not actually a 'sister' language to Makhuwa in the 'family-tree' model of language development, but rather a product of extensive language contact between a Makhuwa speech variety and some language of the central region of Mozambique such as Sena. Careful documentation of Chuabo remains a research desideratum. Of particular interest is the fact that initial work on the language suggests that there is a lexical tone contrast in verb stems, unlike Makhuwa and other Zone P languages, as well as in nominals.

Makhuwa has strong links to two languages not cited by Guthrie. Koti, spoken on the Mozambique coast in Angoche (Nampula province), clearly represents a 'mixed' language in that it has a largely Makhuwa morphology and tone structure and a Swahili-like lexicon. Koti has recently been the subject of linguistic research by Schadeberg, Odden, and myself, all in collaboration with Francisco Ussene Mucanheia, a bilingual Makhuwa/Koti speaker from Mulai in Angoche district. Sangaji (indigenous name: Enaatthempo), a coastal language spoken not far from Koti, shows a similar mixture of language elements. It has been reported to me that there is another mixed language, further to the south, based on Chuabo. If so, I know of no linguistic work that examines it.

In my view, then, Makhuwa(/Lomwe) is the only clearly 'unmixed' language in Zone P30 and it is the only language that I will discuss in this chapter. Throughout the chapter I rely principally on my own field research. The unpublished M.Phil. thesis written by Katupha at SOAS has, however, been very useful to me in gathering material on the verbal system. I have attempted to follow the orthography recommended by NELIMO (Núcleo de Estudo de Línguas Moçambicanas) in their publication *I Seminário sobre Padronização da Ortografia de Linguas Moçambicanas* (Maputo, 1989).

2 MAKHUWA: GEOGRAPHICAL DISTRIBUTION AND DIALECT DIFFERENTIATION

There are perhaps as many as 8 million speakers of Makhuwa, distributed principally in the north of Mozambique (Cabo Delgado, Nampula, Niassa, Zambézia provinces), in southern Tanzania (particularly in Masasi and Tunduru districts), and in Malawi (particularly in the Mulanje and Tyholo areas). There are additional communities further afield: e.g. in Madagascar (unpublished research conducted by Katupha), the Comoros Islands (though it is unknown whether the language has been maintained there), and the 'Zanzibaris' in Chatsworth outside Durban in South Africa (where the language has been maintained, though is increasingly threatened by English).

Some varieties of Makhuwa have labels that speakers use instead of (or in addition to) the more generic terms 'Makhuwa' or 'Lomwe'. Examples are: Ikorovere (Tunduru district in Tanzania), Imitthupi (Masasi district in Tanzania), Imeetto (Tanzania and Cabo Delgado and Niassa provinces in Mozambique), Enahara (Mozambique Isle and neighboring areas in Nampula province), Esaaka (coastal regions of Cabo Delgado and Nampula provinces), Eerati (coastal Nampula), Enlai (Angoche in Nampula), Ekokhola(ni) (in Malawi), Emihavani (in Malawi), etc. Speakers of other varieties failed to suggest any alternative to Makhuwa (e.g. speakers from Iapala, Nampula city, and Mogovolas).

Since there is no standard form of spoken (or written) Makhuwa, there is no extralinguistic motivation for using a particular dialect to serve as the basis for illustrating general points about the language. There are, however, numerous differences in pronunciation and morphology that make it impossible to give examples without reflecting some dialect. Given this dilemma, I have resolved the problem as follows. Whenever I am discussing some point that is not directly connected to dialectal differences, I cite data from the two dialects that I know best (Ikorovere and Imitthupi, both spoken north of the Ruvuma river in southern Tanzania) without further identification. I use a tonal transcription that removes the systematic phonetic tonal differences between these two dialects. When a form is not phonologically identical in both dialects, then I add a label [K] or [Mi] to identify the dialect. Whenever some point is being made that has to do with dialect differences, I shall explicitly indicate the source of the examples.

Makhuwa represents perhaps the least studied of the major Bantu languages. Most of the literature on the language falls into the category of 'missionary' linguistics. This missionary tradition has led to some notable contributions in the area of lexicon (see particularly

Prata 1973, 1990). In other areas of linguistic research, the results are much less sub-stantial (Prata 1960 delivers significantly less than its title promises, and in any case rep-resents a very 'traditional' account of the language that disregards critical aspects of the phonology and morphology). Besides the research that I have been involved with (large-ly unpublished as yet, but see Cassimjee and Kisseberth 1999a,b, Cheng and Kisseberth 1979, 1980, 1981), and Stucky (1979, 1980), the only work on Makhuwa in a modern linguistic framework is that of Katupha. While his Ph.D. thesis on verbal extensions has not been available to me, his M.Phil. (1983) thesis provides an excellent overview of the morphological structure of the Esaaka dialect.

3 MAKHUWA PHONOLOGY

3.1 Vowels

My initial research on Makhuwa (focusing on the 'Ruvuma' dialects, Ikorovere and Imitthupi), as well as the previous literature, indicated a typical Bantu five-vowel system, including monomoraic and bimoraic versions of each vowel: *i e a o u* and *ii ee aa oo uu*. The bimoraic vowels may be underlying, or derived as a result of the juxtaposition of vowels. Some examples are given in (1). Note that the acute mark over a vowel indicates high tone, while the absence of a mark indicates low tone. Underlined vowels are ones that are specified as H in the input to the phonology; H-toned vowels that are not under-lined receive their H tone by virtue of a rule referred to as High Tone Doubling.

(1)   *i*:   *u-líma* 'to cultivate', *mw-íri* 'tree', *u-vítha* 'to hide', *i-víli* 'puff adder'

   ii: *u-wíiha* 'to bring', *w-iítthána* 'to call', *n-thíkííla* 'ash used in making snuff'

   e: *u-pénya* 'to be clever', *n-létto* 'guest', *n-ráwe* 'cobra', *ki-tthawe* [K] 'that I run'

   ee: *u-ttéesa* [Mi] 'to lift', *u-véeha* 'to belittle', *i-théépéle* 'anthill', *u-hé-etta* 'to not walk'

   a: *u-mála* 'to finish', *ú-lya* 'to eat', *n-lápa* 'baobab tree', *i-khára* 'headpad'

   aa: *u-máala* 'to be quiet', *w-aápa* 'to whisper', *paákha* 'cat', *u-lwáa* 'to bewitch'

   o: *u-ttónya* 'to ooze, leak', *i-kóma* 'drum', *i-hópa* 'fish', *ni-pótto* 'supporting pole for roof'

   oo: *u-hóoxa* [K] 'annoy', *u-hóola* 'to precede', *i-poótiri* 'bottle', *ki-ho-ópa* 'I have beaten'

   u: *u-thúma* 'to buy', *u-lúlúma* 'to growl' (of stomach), *ni-híku* 'day', *i-kulúwe* 'pig'

   uu: *u-rúula* 'to take out of water', *u-hú-úpuwela* 'to not remember', *i-lúlu* 'ululation'

This vowel system is clearly correct for a range of other Makhuwa speech varieties: Imeetto, Esaaka, Enlai (to mention dialects I have studied in some detail). However, in the course of our work in Mozambique, Odden and I discovered that there are varieties of Makhuwa which have minimal pairs that establish seven rather than five vowels. It appears that where the aforementioned dialects have just two high vowels, *i* and *u*, some dialects distinguish between advanced and retracted tongue root varieties of these high vowels. I have observed the contrast in the Lomwe of Mucuba district in Zambézia province, as well as the Makhuwa of Nampula city, Mogovolas, and Iuluti in Nampula province. This aspect of Makhuwa phonology requires detailed study; the contrast is difficult to hear and easily missed. It is unclear as yet whether it is a pervasive feature of the lexicon or of more limited distribution.

3.2 Consonants

When one considers the consonant system of Makhuwa, there are three features that are quite striking. One is the absence, in many of the Mozambican dialects, of voiced prenasalized stops. Comparison of lexical items in Makhuwa with other languages immediately indicates that prenasalized voiced stops have been replaced by voiceless stops. For example, Swahili *nyumba* 'house' and *mbuzi* 'goat' correspond to Makhuwa *inúpa* and *ipúri*. The second feature is the absence of a contrast between voiced and voiceless stops, but the presence of a contrast between unaspirated and aspirated voiceless stops. The third feature is the existence of a contrast between dental (unaspirated and aspirated) stops and the corresponding (post-)alveolar stops.

In the discussion that follows, we set aside complexities associated with the fact that the replacement of prenasalized voiced stops is not fully carried out in all dialects: e.g. *e-hópa* 'fish' in Esaaka and many other dialects, but *e-hómba* in Malawi dialects; *ceémba* 'type of cricket' in [K] but *cempa* in [Mi]. We also set aside the expanded inventory that derives from the borrowing of words. We focus instead on the consonants that either occur uniformly throughout Makhuwa or show systematic cross-dialectal correspondences.

All Makhuwa varieties known to us contrast voiceless plain stops and voiceless aspirated stops. The most usual contrasts found are *p/ph*, *t/th*, *tt/tth*, and *k/kh* (where orthographic *tt* represents a post-alveolar, sometimes clearly retroflexed, in contrast to the dental *t*).

(2) *p: u-púha*   'to be happy'   *ph: u-phúka*   'to mix flour and water'
     t: u-téka   'to build'   *th: u-théka*   'millet beer'
     tt: u-ttápwa 'to be wet'   *tth: u-tthápa* 'to rejoice'
     k: u-kápa   'to thrive'   *kh: u-kháva*   'to skin'

However, in some Lomwe varieties, the stops *tt/tth* have been replaced by affricates, which we write as *c* and *ch*. Thus *i-mátta* 'field' corresponds to *e-máca* in these varieties of Lomwe.

TABLE 27.1: RUVUMA MAKHUWA CONSONANTS

	Labial	Dental	Alveolar	Alveo-palatal	Velar
Unaspirated plosive	*p*	*t*	*tt*	*c*	*k*
Aspirated plosive	*ph*	*th*	*tth*		*kh*
Prenasalized	*mb*		*nd*	*nj*	*ng*
Voiceless fricative			*s**	*x**	*h***
Voiced fricative	*v*				
Nasal	*m*		*n*	*ny*	*ŋ*
Glides				*y*	*w***

Notes: * 's' in Ikorovere is 'x' (i.e. [ʃ]) in Imitthupi; ** 'h' and 'w' both require a preceding moraic nasal to assimilate to a velar.

An affricate *c* does occur in varieties other than Lomwe, but with no corresponding aspirated sound. In the Ruvuma dialects we find examples like *u-kwéca* 'to sweep', *n-cúwa* 'sun', *i-páco* 'axe'. This affricate *c* corresponds to *s* in more central dialects in Nampula: *u-kwésa* 'to sweep', *n-súwa* 'sun', *e-pasó* 'axe'. In yet other dialects, we find either *dh*[= ð] or *z* corresponding to the Ruvuma *c*. For example 'axe' in Enlai is *epadhó* and among the 'Zanzibaris' in Durban is *e-pázo*.

The labial-dental fricative *v* and the glottal fricative *h* are attested across all Makhuwa varieties known to us; e.g. *u-váha* 'to give', *w-iíva* [Mi] 'to kill', *u-hóva* 'to try to do', *havára* 'leopard'. There is some complexity with respect to the sibilants *s* and *x* [ʃ]. We have already seen that there is the following sound correspondence *c/s/dh/z* across the Makhuwa dialect spectrum. Let us refer to this sound as the 'unstable coronal'. In Central Makhuwa, which uses *s* for the unstable coronal, we find many words containing the sound *x*. Let us call this the 'stable coronal' (although this term is a bit misleading). Among those dialects that do not use *s* for the unstable coronal, there is variation as to whether they use *s* or *x* for the stable coronal. Thus although the Ruvuma dialects are largely similar in their structure, Imitthupi uses *s* for the stable coronal whereas Ikorovere uses *x*: *i-sima* [Mi]/*i-xima* [K] 'stiff porridge', *ń-sépa* [Mi]/*n-xépa* [K] 'valley', *úsa* [Mi]/*ú-xa* [K] 'to dawn'. In Imeetto, one finds both *s*-subdialects and *x*-subdialects.

The remaining core sounds: *w*, *y*, *l*, *r*, *m*, *n*, *ny*, and *ŋ* require little discussion. The glides *w* and *y* sometimes derive from the adjustment of sequences of unlike vowels (see below). The velar nasal [ŋ] is fairly marginal in terms of its lexical dispersion.

(3) *w:* *u-wéha* 'to look at', *w-uúpúwéla* 'to remember', *i-wíri* 'stump of a hoe'
   y: *i-yaáwa* 'crook of the arm', *yéela* 'this', *u-yéva* 'to be small'
   l: *n-láko* 'door(way)', *u-lúma* 'to bite', *u-khwíila* 'to be red', *u-líva* 'to pay'
   r: *n-ráwe* 'cobra', *u-rópóttóla* 'to strangle', *va-raru* 'three times', *u-wúrya* 'to drink'
   m: *u-máala* 'to be quiet', *u-thúma* 'to buy', *m-eéle* 'millet', *u-kúmáána* 'to meet'
   n: *ni-hútte* 'cloud', *u-nánára* 'to be dirty', *i-níka* 'banana', *naphúlu* 'frog'
   ny: *u-pénya* 'to be clever', *u-nyáala* 'to shrink', *i-kónya* 'crocodile', *u-phwánya* 'to meet'
   ŋ: *i-ŋópe* 'cow', *i-ŋóotto* 'monitor lizard', *u-múŋúnya* [K] 'to crumble food'

Stems in Makhuwa display two significant limitations on the co-occurrence of consonants. Although the language contrasts aspirated and unaspirated voiceless stops, a stem may contain at most one aspirated stop (cf. Schadeberg 1999). Thus we may have stems with one or more unaspirated stops (*ma-vátta* 'twins', *u-kúkúttúwa* 'to be stunted', *n-táta* 'hand', *n-ttápwátta* 'rag'), or one aspirated stop and any number of unaspirated stops (*u-khúura* 'to chew', *u-tthúka* 'to tie', *i-phútta* 'zebra', *i-khorópa* 'snail'), but there are no stems with two aspirated stops (**u-khopha, *u-tthamakha,* etc.). As noted above, Makhuwa also contrasts dental and post-alveolar voiceless stops. However, within a stem, if there is more than one voiceless coronal stop, they must be either all dental or all post-alveolar. Thus we find stems like *n-táta* 'hand', *u-tóthóla* 'to hatch', *u-ttúttha* 'soften by oiling', *n-ttútto* 'ridge', etc., but not **u-tatta, *n-ttoti,* etc.

The preceding restrictions in stem shape do not lead to any morphophonemic alternation (since they function only as constraints on the shape of monomorphemic stems). Aspirated stops (at least in some dialects) seem to display a tendency to deaspirate in causative formations. Thus we find *u-thúma* 'to buy' but *u-túmíha* 'to sell'. However, this pattern is not uniformly imposed; we find, e.g. that *u-khǫtta* 'to refuse' retains its aspiration in *u-khǫttíha* 'to cause to refuse'.

The most important morphophonemic principle affecting consonants is nasal assimilation. In the Ruvuma dialects (as well as in Imeetto and some coastal Mozambican dialects), a prefix of the shape *mu* elides its vowel in front of a consonant. As a result of this elision, the *m* is juxtaposed to a consonant and it assimilates the point of articulation of that consonant (with *h* and *w* inducing a velar nasal in front of them). The noun class prefix *ni* (in all dialects) elides its vowel in front of coronal consonants, and the *n* will then assimilate to the following coronal. The so-called imbricated form of the perfect stem (see below) results in a pre-consonantal nasal, and this nasal also assimilates the point of articulation of a following consonant.

(4)   (a) /mu-píko/: *m-píko* 'pole for carrying load', /mu-ráma/: *n-ráma* [K] 'rice', /mu-thúpi/: *n-thúpi* [K] 'rooster', /mu-hálu/: *ŋ-hálu* 'sugar cane', /mu-kwáha/: *ŋ-kwáha* 'journey'

   (b) *ni-púhe* 'heap of grass', *ni-kóri* 'bracelet', *ni-húku* 'day', but: /ni-ráma/: *n-ráma* [K] 'cheek', /ni-ttáka/: *n-ttáka* 'bundle', /ni-tári/: *n-tári* 'baldness'

   (c) *kha-k-áá-ttupúlále* (non-imbricated) vs. *kha-k-áá-ttupúńle* (imbricated) 'I did not cut'
   kha-y-áá-pahále (non-imbricated) vs. *kha-y-áá-pańhe* '[cl. 2] didn't burn it'
   a-ki-rapále (non-imbricated) vs. *a-ki-rampe* (imbricated) 'I haven't bathed'

3.3 Syllable structure

Setting aside for the moment the matter of nasal consonants, Makhuwa syllables are generally of the shape C(G)V(V), where C stands for a consonant and G stands for the glides *y*, *w*. In the Ruvuma dialects, an additional syllable type occurs: CGGVV, though this shape is marginal (all examples being the consequence of glide formation triggered by an historical process of *k* deletion). Syllables with a VV nucleus generally involve identical vowels (i.e. a long vowel), although some dialects may marginally exhibit 'diphthong-like' structures in the formation of derived verbs. Vowel-initial syllables are restricted to (phrase-initial) word-initial position.

Some examples of the various syllable types (a period separates syllables) are given in (5).

(5)   V syllable (word-initial only)
   u.thé.la 'to marry (of a man)', *i.nú.pa* 'house', *a.ttha.we* [K] 'let [cl. 1] run!'

   CV syllable
   o.lú.ma 'to bite', *na.khǫ.pe* 'shoulderblade', *u.mę.nyé.kha* 'to be gluttonous'

   CVV syllable
   u.rée.ra 'to be good', *ee.ttétthe* 'that [cl. 1] thresh', *ni.wǫa* [Mi] 'a kind of water weed'

   CGVV syllable
   u.lwǫa 'to bewitch', *u.thyǫa* 'to laugh', *u.pó.twéé.la* 'to sink into'

   CGV(V) syllable
   u.lá.mwa 'to be tasteless', *ú.lya* 'to eat', *mweę.cána* 'last year', *myeę.ri* 'months'

CGGVV syllable

   u.khwyáa 'to put leaves in water to prevent spilling', *u.pí.lú.wyáa* 'able to be turned upside down'

In all dialects, moraic nasal consonants may occur. Moraic nasal consonants occur only in position before another consonant. In word-initial position, one might wish to consider them to be a syllabic nucleus. Their status in non-initial position is more complex. In the Ruvuma dialects it appears to be the case that non-initial moraic nasals form part of the preceding syllable. Evidence for this claim comes from the fact that (a) trimoraic syllables are not generally allowed and (b) an expected long vowel will shorten in front of a moraic nasal. This shortening is explicable if the nasal counts as part of the same syllable as the preceding vowel (i.e. vowel shortening is the consequence of the absence of trimoraic syllables).

(6)   word-initial moraic nasal: *ń-ríýa* [Mi] 'chameleon', *nlɛ́ma* 'fruit bat',
       ḿ-píla [Mi] 'sp. tree'
       word-medial moraic nasal: *nańrókottóle* 'quarrelsome person', *nańrúwa* 'kind of bean'
       shortening induced by medial moraic nasal: *a-nǫ́ǫ́-kí̲-ttérekhɛ́la* '[cl. 2] will cook for me' vs. *a-nǫ́-ń-ttérekhɛ́la* '[cl. 2] will cook for [cl. 1]'

There are a number of complexities regarding the moricity of pre-consonantal nasals (particularly in the Ruvuma dialects but also in the Mozambique dialects), but space does not permit detailed discussion.

Since medial vowel-initial syllables are disfavored and since VV syllables must involve two *identical* vowels, there are significant morphophonemic problems created by the juxtaposition of unlike vowels across morphemes and across word boundaries. Space does not permit detailed discussion of morpheme-specific complexities or of dialect variation. We will simply highlight some general patterns that hold in the Ruvuma dialects.

Inside words, the juxtaposition of two vowels results in a long vowel: e.g. /u-hí-apa/ 'to not whisper' yields [uháapa]. If the first vowel in the sequence is one of the following morphemes +*i*+, +*u*+, or +*mu*+, that vowel glides and compensatorily lengthens the following vowel: /u-ɛ́tta/ 'to walk' yields *w-eɛ́tta*. In all other cases, the first vowel assimilates the quality of the second vowel, but if the first vowel is non-high it will first induce a lowering of the second vowel. For example, in /ki-ho-íhána/ 'I have called', the *o* first lowers a following *i* to *e* and then assimilates to that *e*, yielding *ki-he-ɛ́hána*. In other dialects, the first vowel in a sequence simply assimilates the following vowel (without any lowering effect if it happens to be non-high).

If more than two vowels are juxtaposed across morpheme boundaries inside a word, they must be reduced to a single bimoraic syllable or organized into two separate syllables (each of which is maximally bimoraic). In the Ruvuma dialects, one can easily assemble sequences of three, four, even five moras in a row. Their resolution involves the same phenomena as mentioned in the discussion of two vowel sequences: the gliding of high vowels, lowering induced by a non-high vowel on a following high vowel, and the assimilation of a preceding vowel to a following vowel. In addition, the object prefix +*u*+; may induce lowering and assimilation on a preceding vowel, even if it itself glides.

(7) provides some examples. Note that the forms enclosed by slash marks assume that certain morpheme-specific adjustments have already been made, even if they happen to be historically connected to the issue at hand (specifically, adjustments in the shape of the subject marking prefix).

(7)   /y-á-hó-á-éttettha/: *y-á-h-é-éttettha* [K] '[cl. 2] beat [cl. 1]'
      /i-hi-ná-a-upuxe/: *i-hi-nó-ó-puxe* [K] '[cl. 2] does not have to remind [cl. 2]'
      /ŋká-Ø-aa-ópa/: *ŋk-ó-ópa* [Mi] 'and then [cl. 2] beat'
      /ŋka-Ø-aa-ú-ákhulá=ni/: *ŋk-óo-w-áákhulá=ni* [Mi] 'and then [cl. 1] answered
      you (respect)'

Across words, the juxtaposition of two vowels results in a single mora in the output. In Ruvuma dialects, the adjustments made are similar to those within words, except that gliding has a wider role. Without being exhaustive, we can simply note that word-final non-low vowels glide in front of a non-high vowel (e.g. *ŋtthú eeyíré* ... becomes *ŋtthw éeyíré* ... [Mi] 'the person who stole ...') and a final *a* elides but first lowers a following vowel (e.g. *ulímá imátta* 'to cultivate the field' yields *ulím émátta*).

3.4 Tone

Makhuwa dialects are very similar in the way that tone 'works'; they differ more substantially in the realization of the tones. We shall begin by describing the broad similarities and then provide some details in the way that the dialects vary.

There is no variety of Makhuwa known to us where there is anything resembling a fully articulated system of lexical tone contrasts. Verb stems exhibit no lexical contrasts whatsoever. High tone is assigned to a particular mora or moras in the stem on the basis of the morphology in which the stem is inserted. Assignment of H tone may be to the first, second, third, or last stem mora, and in some cases to both the first and the third. Complexities arise depending on whether there are sufficient moras in the stem to accommodate the H tone and whether or not there is an object prefix contained in the stem. In addition to the morphologically determined stem tone, some prefixes have a H tone associated with them in specific morphological constructions. Furthermore, the verbal enclitic element *ni* (signalling a second person respect form) requires the placement of a H tone on the mora in front of it.

Nominals (in non-focal contexts) must have at least one (underlying) H tone. In almost all dialects, this H tone must – at least in principle – be on one of the stem moras. Stems with two (underlying) H tones are restricted to stems with four or more moras. The location of a H tone in the stem is largely predictable on the basis of the noun class in which the stem appears. For example, in most dialects, trimoraic and longer nominal stems in Class 1a, like *havára* 'leopard' and *kharámu* 'lion', always have a H tone on their second mora; Class 5 and 6 nominal stems always have a H tone on the first stem mora (e.g. *n-lútto* 'knot' and *ni-váka* 'spear'). Marginal exceptions to such general principles do exist (e.g. in loanwords – cf. *ni-guruduumu* 'wheel').

One significant set of lexical contrasts is found in some central dialects (as well as in Lomwe) where bimoraic stems in class 7(9)/8(10) may have either a penultimate or an ultimate H tone. The following data from the Iapala region illustrate this:

(8)   *e-phocé* 'sp. rat'   *e-hopá* 'fish'   *e-phalá* 'sp. rat'
      vs.
      e-nári 'buffalo'   *e-tthépo* 'elephant'   *e-púri* 'goat'

Bimoraic stems in other noun classes do not seem to display this contrast. It should be noted that in the dialects that do not have the contrasts in (8) (e.g. the Ruvuma dialects, Imeetto, Esaaka, Eerati), the final H pattern is impossible due to a general ban on word-final (underlying) H tones.

The Imitthupi dialect has the most extensive set of contrasting patterns known to me; in this dialect, some – but not all – High tones appear one mora to the left of their location in other dialects. The underlining indicates a mora that bears an underlying H tone.

(9)   Imitthupi   Ikorovere
    má-aru   *ma-áru*   'ears'
    ń-khwíri   *n-khwíri*   'witch'
    i-wíri   *i-wíri*   'hoe stump'
    ń-thíyana *n-thíyána* 'woman'
    but:
    a-lómwe   *a-lómwe*   'the Alomwe people'
    i-hípa   *i-hípa*   'hoe'
    ni-híye   *ni-híye*   'grave'
    i-ttháya   *i-ttháya*   'earth'

We do not know the historical explanation for the Imitthupi contrast (though there appears to be a possible connection with lexical tone contrasts found in nominal and verbal forms in Chuabo).

High tones that are assigned to moras on the basis of either lexical or morphological considerations will be referred to as primary H tones (their status is indicated throughout by underlining). In the more 'central' varieties of Makhuwa (inland Nampula province) and in Lomwe varieties, primary High tones simply surface wherever they occur, without further ado. However, in many other dialects there is a systematic phenomenon of tone doubling.

(10)   *u-lípúla*   'to try s.t. new'   *u-cúkhúla*   'regurgitate'
    n-húkúlo   'sifting basket'   *ni-húláwe*   'anvil'
    k-aá-nó-lúpáttha 'I was hunting'   *y-aá-m-ó-ómoláníha* 'was chasing'
                                  '[cl. 2]'   '[cl. 1]'

Tone doubling, however, is typically blocked in certain environments. One of these environments is phrase-final position. Thus *u-hiyá* ... 'to leave (behind), stop' has a doubled H on the final vowel in medial position, but not phrase-finally: *u-híya*. A second environment where doubling fails to occur is on the second mora of a bimoraic syllable that is penult in the phrase. As a consequence of this restriction, we find alternations between (medial) *u-máála* ... 'to be quiet' and (phrase-final) *u-máala*. It should be noted that unlike many other languages, Makhuwa does not bar doubling onto a mora that is followed by a H tone. Thus in the infinitive, where the morphology requires a primary H tone both on the first mora and the third mora (if the stem is long enough), we get surface sequences of H tones like the following: *u-myááníháca* 'to chop into small pieces'.

Although doubling is entirely overt in Ikorovere, in other dialects there are complexities. In Imitthupi, e.g. the primary H tone is realized at a mid pitch when (a) its double follows, (b) there is no preceding H tone, and (c) it is not initial in a bimoraic syllable. In the examples in (11), the umlaut symbol indicates mid pitch. Furthermore, the doubled H has falling pitch when it is on a phrase-penult monomoraic syllable.

(11)   primary H tone realized as mid:
    ï-wíri .../ *ï-wîri*   'worn-out hoe'   *nañrûwa* 'sp. bean'
    ä-hâpa   'livers'   *ï-hîce* 'chair'

primary H tone alternating between mid and H due to presence or absence of a following double:

i-m*a*ttá ... vs. i-m*a*tta   'field'
ki-ho-*o*pá ... vs. ki-ho-*o*pa   'I have beaten'

primary H tone alternating between mid and H due to absence or presence of a preceding H tone:

ki-ho-k*a*víha ... 'I have helped' vs. k-*a*-hó-k*a*víha ... 'I helped'
hav*a*rá ... 'leopard ...' vs. *a*-háv*a*rá ... 'leopards ...'

primary H tone always retained on first mora of a bimoraic syllable:

u-m*á*ála .../ u-m*a*ala 'to be quiet'   u-h*ó*óla .../ u-h*o*ola 'to go in front'

In the Eerati dialect in Nampula, a primary High tone is fully low-pitched under exactly the same conditions as a primary H tone is mid-pitched in Imitthupi (and also exhibits the phenomenon where a phrase-penult double has a falling character). In Enlai (spoken near the city of Angoche in Nampula), the primary H tone is fully low as in Eerati. However, Enlai differs from most Makhuwa doubling dialects in that it doubles into phrase-final position and onto the second mora of a bimoraic phrase-penult syllable.

(12) other dialects Enlai   gloss
      u-m*á*na   o-man*á*   'to beat'
      u-k*i*-mána   o-k*i*-mána   'to beat me'
      u-m*a*ala   o-m*á*ála   'to be quiet'

In the Esaaka dialect, there is no *general* doubling, as in Ikorovere, Imitthupi, Eerati, and Enlai (thus we find ki-ho-l*o*vola ... 'I have transported ...' and not ki-ho-l*ó*vóla ... as in Ikorovere). However, doubling *does* affect the second mora of a bimoraic syllable (thereby avoiding a falling tone), provided that syllable is neither phrase-penult nor phrase-final: u-m*á*ála ... (but: u-m*a*ala phrase-finally), o-k*ú*-úpuw*é*la 'to remember me' and not *o-k*ú*-upuw*é*la. Doubling in Esaaka also affects a mora that is in turn followed by a H tone (thus avoiding a H0H sequence). We find examples like ki-ho-r*ú*kún*ú*sa ... 'I have turned over' rather than *ki-ho-r*ú*kun*ú*sa ..., *á*-háv*á*ra 'leopards' rather than *á*-hav*á*ra.

4 THE VERBAL SYSTEM

The verb system, as in most Bantu languages, is complex. We shall not dwell on matters that are characteristic of most Bantu languages. The core of the verbal word is the root, which is typically CVC in shape (e.g. /thum/ 'buy', /vah/ 'give') but may be VC (e.g. /ett/; 'go', /in/ 'dance'). A small number of 'consonantal' roots occur (e.g. /khw/ 'die', /ly/ 'eat', /w/ 'come', /ny/ 'defecate', /s/ or /x/ 'dawn'). While non-derived polysyllabic stems do occur (e.g. /lokotth/ 'pick up', /kurum/ 'rumble, make noise', /rakal/ 'be injured'), most longer stems involve the affixation of one or more verbal extensions. The following extensions occur in Makhuwa.

(13) applied: -el- (sometimes r occurs instead of l; this r appears to be partially conditioned by a preceding consonant and partially lexicalized); benefactive, instrumental, locational meanings

      u-kh*á*va 'to strip off bark' vs. u-kh*á*v-él-a 'to strip off bark for'
      u-h*á*ma 'to trim the hair' vs. u-h*á*m-él-a 'to use to cut the hair'

u-w̯iiha 'to bring' vs. *u-w̯iíh-ér-a* 'to bring to, for'
u-páttha 'to get' vs. *u-pátth-él-a* 'to get from, for'

causative: *-ih-*; besides causative-related interpretations, this extension conveys notion 'do very well'

u-lóka 'to be well-arranged, beautiful' vs. *u-lók-ih-a* 'to arrange s.t., beautify'
u-móra 'to fall, drop down' vs. *u-mór-ih-a* 'to drop s.t.'
u-háma 'to cut the hair' vs. *u-hám-iha* 'to cut the hair very well'
u-páttha 'to get' vs. *u-pátt-íh-a* [K] 'to cause to get, enable s.o. to get'

transitivizer: -Vx-/-Vs- according to dialect

u-láp-úx-a [K], *u-láp-ús-a* [Mi] 'to ferry, cause to cross' (cf. *u-láp-uw-a* 'to cross')
u-hihím-úx-a [K], *u-hihím-ús-a* [Mi] 'to bring back to life' (cf. *u-hihím̯m-w-a* 'to revive (intr.)'

transitivizer: -Vl- (sometimes -Vr-):

u-móny-ól-a 'to take a chip or lump out of s.t.'
u-hurúm-úl-a 'to cause to expand, be wide open'
u-ttém-úl-a 'to drill for water'
u-rém-úl-a 'to break off'

intransitivizer: -VØ- where Ø was historically *k* (which has elided in Makhuwa); in Ruvuma, a

preceding *o* glides while a preceding *u* triggers an epenthetic glide (however, an expected sequence *um-uw*-V surfaces as *umm-w*-V, where the first *m* is moraic)
u-láp-ú(w)-a 'to cross water'
u-móny-w-áa 'to come off in a lump'
u-hurúm̯m-w-a 'to expand (as of s.t. inflated), be wide open'
u-ttém̯m-w-a 'to have a hole, holes'
u-rém̯m-w-a 'to be broken off'

reciprocal: *-an-*

u-hám-án-a 'to trim one another's hair'
u-pátth-án-a 'to get one another'

plurality: *-ac-* (consonant varies across dialect as discussed above)

u-kháv-ác-a 'to strip off bark in several places'
u-hik-ác-a 'to smear'

habitual: *-ex-* (consonant varies with *s* across dialects)

u-mór-éx-a [K] 'to usually fall'
u-kháv-ís-a [Mi] 'to usually skin off'

passive: *-iy-* (some dialects: *-iw-*) but absent from the 'perfect' stem)

u-lúm-íy-a 'to be bitten'
u-w̯iíh-iy-a 'to be brought'

potential: *-e-* (which in some dialects glides to *y* and compensatorily lengthens following vowel, while in other dialects is separated from a following vowel by an epenthetic glide); the *-e-* developed historically from /ek/

hóm-y-áa 'able to be pierced' (cf. *u-hom-ey-a* in some dialects)
u-hám-y-áa 'to be capable of being trimmed' (cf. *u-ham-iy-a* in some dialects)

Some of these extensions may occur in bimoraic variants whose usage has not been explored.

(14) *u-kháv-éẹh-a* 'to skin off bark properly (cf. also with the same rough meaning: *u-kháv-íh-a*)'
    u-pátt-éẹh-a 'to get a lot of s.t.'

Examples of combinations of verbal extensions are given in (15).

(15) *u-hám-án-ẹl-a* 'to use s.t. to cut one another's hair'
    u-mór-ih-ẹl-a 'to pour a little at a time, drop s.t. at a certain point'
    u-láp-úw-ẹla 'to use for crossing, to cross over to (a place)'
    u-kháv-éx-ịh-a [K] 'to make sure s.t. is really skinned'
    u-wịíh-ẹr-án-a 'to bring to one another'

The combination *an-ih* is particularly extensive in its use:

(16) *-an-ih-*:
    u-hị́ y-án-ịh-a 'to cause to separate'
    u-họkól-y-ạ́án-ih-a [K], *u-họkól-y-aan-ịh-a* [Mi] 'to go and come back on the same day'
    u-khụ́p-án-ịh-a 'to heap up'
    u-lụ́m-án-ịh-a 'to clench the teeth'

Two other extensions are grammatical in nature rather than derivational: /ak/ and the 'perfect' stem-formative /al/ (in some dialects /il/) alternating with an infixed nasal element. The former does not exhibit much morphophonemic complexity, though it does alternate with /ek/ depending on the following vowel, e.g. *y-a-ki-thumel-ák-a* 'if [cl. 2] buys for me' but *n-kị-tthár-ek-e* 'follow me!' The perfect formative will be examined below.

It should be noted that there are hundreds of verbal stems that are systematically related to ideophones. A few examples follow.

(17) *u-cụcúmạ́la* 'to squat' (cf. *cucumá*)   *u-pụ́rúkụ̣ttúla* 'to chew s.t. hard' (cf. *purukuttú*)
    u-héḳa 'to slash' (cf. *héki*)   *u-pọ́céra* 'to receive (with the hands)' (cf. *pocee*)

So far we have confined our discussion to what may be referred to as the verb stem proper. In many Bantu languages, object prefixes cohere together with the verb stem to form what may be called a macrostem. This is the case in Makhuwa. One major argument for this position comes from tone assignment. For instance, infinitive verbs involve the assignment of a H tone to the first stem mora (*u-mạ́na* 'to beat', *u-kávíha* 'to help'); however, when an object prefix is included, it is the object prefix that takes the H tone (*u-kị́-mána* 'to beat me', *u-kị́-káviha* 'to help me'). A notable aspect of Makhuwa structure is that while there are object prefixes for first (*ki* sg., *hi* pl.) and second person (*u*, which by itself indicates the absence of 'respect' but in combination with an enclitic *ni* indicates respect), and reflexive (in Ikorovere: *i* before consonant-initial stems, but *ic* plus compensatory lengthening in front of vowel-initial stems; in Imitthupi: *i* before all stems) notions, the only noun classes that have a corresponding object prefix are Class 1 and 1a (*mu*) and Class 2 and 2a (*a*). A diminutive prefix *xi/si* occurs in the object prefix 'slot', but differs in that it co-occurs with an object prefix (while an object prefix may not co-occur with another object prefix). There is variation in the relative order of the diminutive prefix and the object prefix (e.g. *u-xị́-i-thumela* or *w-ịị-xi-thumela* 'to buy a little for oneself').

Turning to aspects of the tense/aspect/mood system, I shall confine my remarks to a few selected topics that are particularly characteristic of Makhuwa. Affirmative, finite, main-clause verb forms fall into two essential types in most varieties of Makhuwa: focal forms and non-focal forms. Focal forms require that the verb appear with a complement; further-more, the initial H tone specification of the complement is deleted. (In a doubling dialect, this means that neither the first primary H tone nor the double will appear.) In some dialects, if the result of deletion would be a toneless word, then the final vowel of the nominal may be raised in pitch. Here are some examples of focal vs. non-focal tenses:

(18)   non-focal present/future: *ki-nǫó-lǐm' é-mǎtta* 'I am cultivating/will cultivate the field'
   focal present: *ki-n-lǐm' é-matta* 'I am cultivating the field'

   non-focal perfect: *ki-ho-lǐm' é-mǎtta* 'I have cultivated the field'
   focal perfect: *ki-limalé̱ é-matta* 'I have cultivated the field'

   non-focal past: *k-ǎ̱-hó-lǐm' é-mǎtta* 'I cultivated the field'
   focal past: *k-aa-limǎ̱l' é-matta* 'I cultivated the field'

   non-focal past continuous: *k-a̱ǎ̱-nó-lǐm' é-mǎtta* 'I was cultivating the field'
   focal past continuous: *k-aa-lǐm' é-matta* 'I was cultivating the field'

If a verb with the same morphological structure as a focal verb form appears either without a complement or with a complement that has not undergone deletion of its initial primary H tone, then that verb will be interpreted as a non-main clause verb – specifically, a relative verb. For example, *ń-tthú aa-thumi̱lé m-u̱úttuka* is understood as 'the person who bought a car' whereas *ń-tthú aa-thumi̱lé m-uuttuka* is understood as 'the person bought a car'.

Another complexity involving the tense/aspect/mood system in Makhuwa is the exis-tence of two distinct negative formatives: *kha*, which is located initially in the verb before the subject prefix, and *hi*, which is located after the subject prefix. (19) gives examples of different verb tenses using these negative formatives. The list is not exhaustive.

(19)   *kha*   (main clauses)
   kha-n-ǎ̱ǎ̱-ttupúlále   'we did not cut'
   kha-n-a-rapá̱le   'we have not bathed'
   kha-ni-n(o)-lǐma   'we are not cultivating'
   kha-n-aa-tte̱rékha   'we were not cooking'

   hi   (subordinate clauses)
   u-hi̱-thúma   'to not buy'
   u-hi-tthuke   'that you (non-respect) should not tie'
   ki-(h)i̱-lókottanihacaka   'me not picking things up'
   k-a-ń-hi̱-lókottaniha=ru   'although I was not picking up pl.' (contracted form of *k-a̱ǎ̱-nó-hi̱-lókottaniha=ru*)
   ki-hi̱-límeke   'if I don't cultivate'
   a-hi̱-káa-ramu̱síle ··· 'if [cl. 2] had not greeted'
   ki-hi-na̱-púputthe   'even if I do not wash'
   ń-tthú hi-li̱íly=óoyo   'the person who hasn't eaten'

There are a number of verbal constructions that have little morphophonemic com-plexity (other than the usual ones resulting from the creation of potential sequences of vowels) and rather stable across all Makhuwa varieties. Some of these are listed in (20).

(20) infinitive (positive and negative): *u-líma* 'to cultivate', *u-hí-líma* 'to not cultivate'
subjunctive (positive and negative): *u-ttupúlánihe* 'you should cut to pieces',
n-hi-tthukule 'don't untie!'
participial (positive and negative): *ni-pupútthaka* 'we washing', *ki-(h)í-pángaka*
'me not working'
negative present: *kha-ni-n(o)-líma* 'we are not cultivating'
focal continuous: *k-aa-lúpáttha…* 'I was hunting'

Other morphological structures show considerable morphophonemic complexity as
well as cross-dialectal variation. An example of this is provided by the non-focal positive
perfect and non-focal positive past. In the Ruvuma dialects, these two tenses have the following canonical patterns: SP-*ho*-verb stem (perfect) and SP-*á-hó*-verb stem (past). The
latter structure has a tonal variant of the shape SP-*a-hǫ*-verb stem that we shall not discuss. In the Ruvuma dialects, while these transparent forms exist (e.g. *ki-ho-líma* 'I have
cultivated' and *k-á-hó-líma* 'I cultivated'), a 'contracted' form is available in many situations. The contracted form involves the elision of *h* from *ho* and adjustments to the
resulting vowel sequence.

Consider the perfect form first. The contracted form of *ki-ho-líma* is *ko-o-líma*. The *h*
elides and the vowel in the subject prefix assimilates to the following *o*. This elision of *h*
is not possible, however, when *ho* is followed by a vowel-initial element, whether the verb
stem or an object prefix (*h* cannot elide from *ki-he-ętta* 'I have walked' e.g. nor from
ki-ha-á-váha 'I have given [cl. 2] s.t.'). The *h* also may not elide if there is no overt
subject prefix (e.g. *ho-tthúka* '[cl. 1] has tied' cannot become *o-tthúka).

The *h* may also elide in the past tense form, but now the following *o* vowel assimilates to
the vowel to its left. Thus *k-á-hó-líma* contracts to *k-á-á-líma*. Elision continues to be impossible before a vowel-initial stem (*k-á-hé-ętta* 'I walked' has no form where the *h* is missing).

When we examine non-Ruvuma dialects, we find often that the complete set of full
and contracted forms are not available. As an example, consider the Makhuwa spoken in
Iapala in Nampula. The non-focal positive affirmative has the following shape when a
consonant-initial stem is used: *k-oo-tęexa* 'I lifted'. This form looks just like the contracted form of this tense in Ruvuma dialects. But in the Iapala dialect, there is no uncontracted form in use. However, when the stem is vowel-initial, we find examples like
ki-hi-ípa 'I sang', *ki-he-ętta* 'I walked', *ki-hu-úpuwęla* 'I remembered'; the *h* from original *ho* appears in this context and the vowel of *ho* assimilates completely to the following
vowel (as is the norm in this dialect).

In many non-Ruvuma dialects, a quite different non-focal positive past form has developed: namely, one where a bimoraic *aa* invariably appears followed by *hi* (which has a
primary H tone). Thus these dialects have past forms like *k-aa-hí-líma* 'I cultivated' (setting aside differences in tone realization). The historical explanation for the use of *hi* here
rather than *ho* is not clear.

Another area of morphophonemic complexity and dialectal differentiation involves the
non-focal positive non-past form of the verb. In the Ruvuma dialects, the non-focal non-
past form involves the bimoraic prefix *nǫo*. The shape *nǫo* is found in front of consonant-
initial stems. When the stem is vowel-initial, we find that the first mora of *nǫo* remains
intact, but the vowel occupying the second mora glides to *w* and there is an accompanying compensatory lengthening of the stem-initial vowel.

(21) *ki-nǫó-ttípúra* 'I'll hoe deeply, I am hoeing deeply'
vs.
ki-nǫw-éęmésa 'I'll prop it up, I am propping it up'

In a number of other dialects, the prefix *naa* occurs in front of consonant-initial stems, whereas in front of vowel-initial stems we find *naw* plus compensatory lengthening of the following vowel. The following examples from Esaaka illustrate.

(22)   *ki-náa-lya*   'I am eating'
      ki-náá-lima   'I am cultivating, I will cultivate'
      ki-náá-lóvola   'I am transporting'

      vs.

      ki-náw-óóna   'I see'
      ki-náw-iípa   'I am singing'
      ki-náw-éétta   'I am walking, going'

It appears that the origin of the construction must have been a sequence of vowels *a+u* (the *u* possibly representing the infinitive). The usual assimilation pattern in Ruvuma dialects predicts that this sequence will surface as *oo* when no other vowel follows, but as *ow* plus compensatory lengthening when a vowel follows. In other dialects, however, what has happened is that the *u* assimilated to the preceding *a* when pre-consonantal; otherwise it glided and compensatorily lengthened the following vowel.

A final case of dialect variation in the verb morphology has to do with the 'perfect' stem (which is used in focal affirmative formations, negative formations, and relative formations). All dialects use a final *e* vowel in these structures. All dialects agree that a stem of the shape -C- or -CC- must have an 'uncontracted' pre-final suffix, either /al/ (most common) or /il/. Stems that contain at least one vowel may, at least in some dialects, have both an uncontracted and a contracted pre-final suffix. The contracted suffix appears as a homorganic, moraic nasal located in front of the last consonant of the stem. Thus a stem like /rap/ 'bathe' will have either an uncontracted form *-rapíle/-rapále* or a contracted form *-rampe*. Some dialects may avoid the contracted form altogether, but in my experience a contracted form is usually available (but with certain stem-final consonants favoring it more than others). Detailed research is required.

5 THE NOMINAL SYSTEM

The inventory of noun classes in Makhuwa is considerably reduced in comparison to most Bantu languages. Specifically, original class 7 and class 9 have fallen together, as have original classes 8 and 10. In addition, class 11 and the diminutive classes 12 and 13 are entirely absent. In (23) we give examples of each noun class (the assumed underlying representation of the prefix appears inside slant marks). The Proto-Bantu distinction between pre-prefix and prefix is entirely absent (at least synchronically speaking).

(23)   Class 1 /mu/: *n-thíyána* 'woman', *n-cáwa* 'a Yao person', *n-létto* 'guest', *mw-aána* 'child'
      Class 2 /a/: *a-thíyána* 'women', *a-cáwa* 'Yaos', *a-létto* 'guests',
      Class 1a /Ø/: *kharámu* [K] 'lion', *rétthe* 'elephant shrew', *nakhúwo* 'maize', *hápa* 'liver'
      Class 2a /á/: *á-khárámu* 'lions', *á-rétthe* 'elephant shrews', *á-hápa* 'livers'
      Class 3 /mu/: *n-héenya* [K] 'unripe maize cob', *m-oólóko* 'river', *mw-íri* 'tree'
      Class 4 /mi/: *mi-héenya* [K] 'unripe maize cobs', *my-oólóko* 'rivers', *m-íri* 'trees'
      Class 5 /ni/: *ni-kháta* [K] 'shoulder', *n-lúku* 'stone', *ni-váka* 'spear', *n-rápála* 'hide'
      Class 6 /ma/: *ma-kháta* [K] 'shoulders', *ma-lúku* 'stones', *ma-váka* 'spears', *ma-rápála* 'hides'

Class 7,9 /i/: *i-nútto* 'hammer', *i-phíro* 'road', *i-kónya* 'crocodile', *i-léma* 'deformity'
Class 8,10 /i/: *i-nútto* 'hammers', *i-phíro* 'roads', *i-kónya* 'crocodiles', *i-léma* 'deformities'
Class 14 /u/ (in the Ruvuma dialects and Imeetto): *u-théka* 'beer', *ú-lóko* [Mi] 'potting clay'
Class 15 /u/ (in the Ruvuma dialects and Imeetto): *u-váha* 'to give', *w-aápa* 'to whisper'
Class 16 /va/: *va-culu* 'at the top', *va-tetho* 'on the sides, margin'
Class 17 /u/: *u-culu* 'on top, the upper side, high up, upstream', *u-tetho* 'at the sides, margin'
Class 18 /mu/: *n-culu* 'in the top of s.t.', *n-tetho* 'on the edge'

All Makhuwa dialects exhibit the same basic nominal system, with only phonological differences. The /u/ prefix in class 14 and 15 is *o* in non-Ruvuma dialects. The class 7, 9 /i/ prefix is *e* in non-Ruvuma dialects. The class 8, 10 prefix is not uniform in the non-Ruvuma dialects. In some varieties it is also *e*; in other varieties it is *i*, thereby showing a contrast between singular and plural forms. As a result, *i-phíro* 'road' in some dialects is either singular or plural, in other dialects it does not exist, and in yet other dialects it is only plural. The form *e-phíro* does not exist in Ruvuma dialects, while in other dialects it may either be both singular and plural or only singular.

There are also some morphophonemic differences in the prefixes with *mu*. In many dialects, the *mu* prefixes retain their vowel in all preconsonantal environments except when a labial follows, whereas in other dialects the *u* elides pre-consonantally and the *m* assimilates the point of articulation of the following consonant (note that before *h* and *w* the nasal is velar, although we do not indicate this in our transcription). In all dialects, the class 5 prefix *ni* elides its vowel in front of a coronal consonant but not in other pre-consonantal positions (see (23) e.g.).

Some brief comments on the morphological structure of nominal stems are in order. Class 1a/2a nominals show indications of complex morphological origins in some cases. For instance, the following class 1a/2a formations seem to be built on a stem that (at least from an historical point of view) already contains a class prefix: specifically, /mu/, in one of its morphophonemic variants: *mpétta* (*á-mpétta*) 'bamboo flute', *nkúnya* (*á-nkúnya*) [K] 'European' (cf. *n-kúnya* (*a-kúnya* [Mi]), *nthúlu* (*á-nthúlu*) [Mi] 'banded mongoose (Mungos mungos)').

Class 1a/2a nominal stems show a recurring element *na* in initial position in the stem: *nacóro* 'Natal duiker (Cephalophus natalensis)', *naciini* [Imeetto] 'a kind of witch doctor' (derived ultimately from the Arabic *djinn*), *namáara* 'a kind of bean', *namáme* 'barn owl'. Sometimes this *na* is followed by the /mu/ element mentioned above: *nampááphi* 'leaves of a type of bean plant', *nanhákwa* 'simsim', *nanrúwa* 'a type of bean'.

The system of kinship terminology is fairly complex in its morphological patterning. It does, however, provide instances of other recurring morphological elements. Specifically, since a class 2/2a kinship term is used to indicate respect rather than plurality, a device is needed to yield the concept of plurality. This is achieved by attaching /manya/ either directly to the stem or to the class 2/2a prefixed form. Some examples from Imitthupi.

(24)   *n-háno* 'wife'   *á-háno* 'chief's wife'
                                          manyá-háno or *manyá-á-hano* 'chief's wives'

       nanku 'sponsor of an initiate'   *á-nanku*, the class 2a form
                                          manyá-nanku, plural form

á-tíįthi '(my) father' *manyá-tíithi* or *manyá-á-tiithi* 'father and his brothers'

In addition to /manya/ one also finds /anga/ forming plurals (examples again from Imitthupi): e.g. *á-táátha* 'maternal uncle', *manyá-á-taatha/manyá-táatha* '(my) maternal uncles', but also *ángá-a-táátha* (the tone shape here is irregular, but consistent across this particular construction); *á-máányi* '(my) mother', *manyá-máanyi/manyá-á-maanyi* 'my mother and her sisters, etc.', but also *ángá-a-máányi*.

There are several morphologically productive processes that create complex nominal stems. One of these involves the formation of diminutive nominals. A diminutive singular is formed by the morpheme sequence *mw-a-* being prefixed to a (singular) nominal. In most cases the nominal retains its original prefix if it has one; however, in classes 7 and 9 there is some variation as to whether the prefix is retained or not. The following data are from Imitthupi.

(25) nominal   diminutive form
  kapútthi 'gun'   *mw-á-káputthi*
  ń-tthávi 'net'   *mw-á-ń-tthavi*
  i-kárikho 'cooking pot'   *mw-á-kárikho*

The diminutive plural is formed by prefixing the morpheme sequence *a-sį-* (*a-xį-* in some dialects). The original class prefix is maintained, e.g. when the noun class prefix has an initial consonant. When the noun class prefix is *i*, it typically elides. When the nominal is originally class 2/2a, the inherent prefix regularly elides.

(26) nominal   diminutive form
  má-tthávi 'nets'   *a-sį-má-tthavi*
  mi-pápáttho 'tool for pounding floor' *a-sį-mi-papattho*
  i-níka 'bananas'   *a-sį-níka*
  i-káríkho 'cooking pots'   *a-sį-kárikho*
  á-kárįróóre 'mirrors'   *a-sį-káriroore*

The reader may observe from the examples in (25) and (26) that there are tonal alternations associated with these two formations. Discussion is beyond the scope of this chapter.

There are not many stems that belong inherently to the locative noun classes. However, the formation of derived locatives is productive. There are two aspects to the derivation of locatives: the prefixation of one of the three locative prefixes (*u*, *va*, *mu*) and the encliticization of *ni*. Some examples from Imitthupi:

(27) *ú-ráwo* 'honey'   *nakótto* 'bark cloth'
  w-uu-ráwó=ni 'to the honey'   *u-nakóttó=ni* 'to the bark cloth'
  vo-o-ráwó=ni 'by the honey'   *va-nakóttó=ni* 'near the bark cloth'
  mu-u-ráwó=ni 'in the honey'   *n-nakóttó=ni* 'in the bark cloth'

The tonal complexities found in locative formation are beyond the scope of this chapter.

There is one productive element that occurs encliticized to the nominal: *=ene*. The following examples are from Ikorovere (notice incidentally that in most cases there is no overt agreement between the noun stem and *=ene*).

(28) *n-thúpi* 'rooster'   *n-thúpy=éene* 'a fairly big rooster'
  mi-thúpi 'roosters'   *mi-thúpy=éene* 'fairly big roosters'
  mw-á-ń-thupi 'dim. rooster'   *mw-á-ń-thupy=eene* 'fairly big little rooster'
  a-xį-mí-thupi 'dim. roosters'   *a-xį-mi-thupi=c-ene* 'fairly big little roosters

Finally, I should note that lexically reduplicated stems occur (i.e. stems for which a corresponding non-reduplicated does not exist):

(29) *ni-mórómóro* 'a drop of s.t.'   *ma-lilólílo* 'any exudate'
      mi-hílíhíli [K] 'greedy behavior'   *n-córócoro* 'waterfall'

I have no data that suggests that there is productive reduplication of nominals (but I also have not explored the matter specifically).

Nominals control a system of agreement on other elements in the nominal phrase (e.g. demonstratives, possessive enclitics, adjectives, associative phrases) as well as on the verb. The following chart illustrates the agreement pattern. Space does not permit discussion of phonological differences across dialects. We should note that in the case of possessive and associative agreement, when I write the null symbol, I indicate that there is no overt agreement. There could be covert agreement, but if so, one would need to be able to argue that independently needed phonological rules would account for the absence of the agreement element. I have grouped the infinitives with class 17 since wherever pertinent (e.g. demonstratives), the infinitive aligns with it rather than with class 14.

(30)

Class	Subject prefix	Adjective agreement	Possessive agreement	Associative agreement	Demonstratives
1, 1a	Ø	*mu*	Ø	Ø	*úla, úyo, úle*
2, 2a	*a ~ i (y)*	*a*	Ø	Ø	*ála, áyo, ále*
3	*mu*	*mu*	Ø	*w*	*úla, úyo, úle*
4	*i*	*ci*	*c-*	*c*	*cii/cíla cíyo, cíle*
5	*ni*	*ni*	*n-*	*n*	*ńna, ńno, ńne*
6	*a*	*ma*	Ø	Ø	*ála, áyo, ále*
7,9	*i*	*i*	Ø	*y*	*íla, íyo, íle*
8,10	*ci*	*ci*	*c-*	*c*	*cii/cíla, cíyo, cíle*
14	*u*	*u*	Ø	*w-*	*úla, úyo, úle*
15,17	*u*	*u*	*w-*	*w-*	*wúu, wúle*
16	*va*	*va*	*v-*	*v-*	*váa, vále*
18	*mu*	*mu*	*mw-*	*mw-*	*múu, múle*

Some cross-dialectal comments about the above table are in order. Except for Ruvuma dialects and Imeetto, initial *i* and *u* are lowered to *e* and *o* respectively. The consonant in the *ci* prefix is one that varies considerably across dialects, appearing elsewhere as *s*, *dh*, or *z*. The class 4 and 8,10 demonstratives cited from above are from Imitthupi. In Ikorovere, they are *íyya, íyyo,* and *íyye*. I have written a geminate *y* here, but the sound appears to have some nasalization associated with it. Other dialects reflect this same phonetic phenomenon, and detailed phonetic research is required to understand properly what is going on. Finally, the demonstratives *úyo* and *áyo* have medial *w* in some dialects.

Space permits only brief remarks about the various elements that, together with the nominal itself, make up the noun phrase.

Demonstratives are prolific in the language (besides the basic ones cited in (30), there are more emphatic ones as well), in terms of both their number and their use. It is possible for the demonstrative to appear both in front of the nominal that it modifies and after it: *ńná ní-pótthe ńna* [Mi] 'this boil'. In prenominal position, the final vowel of the demonstrative will coalesce with a vowel-initial nominal. In post-nominal position, an initial vowel in a demonstrative will coalesce with the final vowel of the nominal. There is dialectal variation as to whether the combination of a nominal stem and an enclitic demonstrative yields a monomoraic or a bimoraic initial vowel. (The demonstrative elides its H tone when in enclitic position, depending on the tonal context.)

(31) *ál' á-míráw' ála* [Mi] 'these young men' (from: /álá a-míráwo ála/)
      úlá mw-aán' óola [K] 'this child' (from: /úlá mw-aáná ula/)

An interesting use of the demonstrative involves relative clause formation. A demonstrative (agreeing with the head) is encliticized to a relative verb when that verb is clause-final. Some examples:

(32) *a-n-ttípúra=ayo* [K] 'the [cl. 2] who is hoeing'
      mw-írí u-wuluwily=óole [K] 'the tree [cl. 3] that has fallen'
      i-lákhú y-aa-hitíyé=eyo [K] 'the chicken [cl. 9] that was slaughtered'

When another word follows the verb in the clause, the demonstrative occurs encliticized to the clause-final word and not the verb: *no-wá meélwá=ayo* [K] (from: /no-wá meéló=ayo/) 'the [cl. 1] who is coming tomorrow'.

The following possessive stems occurs in Makhuwa.

(33) *-áka* [1p.sg.]   *-ínyu* [2p. respect]   *-áa/áo* [2p. non-respect]
      -íhu [1p.pl.]   *-áya* [3p. respect]   *-áwe* [3p. non-respect]

Across all Makhuwa varieties known to me, the initial vowel of the possesssive stems surfaces as bimoraic when it is coalesces with a preceding vowel: *i-hípa* 'hoe', *i-hípááka* 'my hoe', *i-hípéényu* 'your hoe', etc.

The use of the possessive stems is not particularly remarkable except in one case. When the head of a relative verb (whether explicit or implicit) is not the subject of that verb, a possessive enclitic agreeing in person with the subject is encliticized to the verb. This results in a double marking of the subject on the verb if the verb's prefixal agreement is with the subject and not the head. (Recall that a demonstrative agreeing with the head of the relative is encliticized to a clause-final relative verb. When both the demonstrative and the possessive are encliticized to the relative verb, the order of elements is for the possessive to precede the demonstrative.)

(34) *k-aa-púpúttha=aka* 'when/where I was washing' (with a null head of the
      relative verb)
      n-khóyí k-aa-tthuńky=áakó=oyo [K] 'the rope that I tied'
      kapwítthí k-a-n-thúmály=aakó=oyo [K] 'the gun which I bought'
      mw-írí k-aa-wulúxály=aakó=oyo [K] 'the tree that I felled'

As in most Bantu languages, adjectival stems are not numerous, and there is nothing particularly remarkable about this structure in Makhuwa. The associative construction is a very significant aspect of the system, but also not strikingly different in any respect from other Bantu languages. Perhaps the most noticeable difference is in the phonology. Although the usual *a* associative particle is in evidence in a limited range of examples (e.g. *i-hípá y-a céé jóoni* 'John's hoe'), it usually appears as *o* in [Mi] and as *oo* in [K].

(35) *n-lúp' óo-tthépo* [K] 'an elephant hunter'
      m-míní w-oo-hípa [K] vs. *ḿ-mini w-o hípa* [Mi] 'handle of a hoe'
      n-ttúttó n-oo nákhúwo [K] 'a ridge, mound of maize'
      vs.
      n-xáátti n-o kháanga [Mi] 'a shirt made of the *khaanga* cloth'

6 SYNTAX

There is little published work available on Makhuwa syntax, and my own research has hardly touched on syntactic matters. Stucky (1980) demonstrates that while word order is relatively fixed inside the nominal phrase, there is considerable variation in word order with respect to the verb and its arguments. It is unknown whether the severely reduced set of object prefixes in the language has had a significant impact in the realms of argument structure or anaphora. The relative verb is complex in its morphological and syntactic structure. The tense system in relatives is dramatically different from the tense system in main verbs. Examination of the texts in Katupha (1983) reveals an extensive system of demonstratives with considerable complexity in their usage. Ideophones are a rich aspect of Makhuwa traditional discourse and merit careful study.

REFERENCES

Cassimjee and Kisseberth 1999a,b; Cheng and Kisseberth 1979, 1980, 1981; Festi and Valler 1995; Katupha 1983; NELIMO 1989; Prata 1960, 1973, 1990; Schadeberg 1999; Stucky 1979, 1980.

CHAPTER TWENTY-EIGHT

WESTERN SAVANNA (K, R)

Gabriele Sommer

1 DEMOGRAPHY AND CLASSIFICATION

According to Guthrie Western Savanna consists of eight groupings, namely Chokwe-Luchazi (K10, Zaire, Angola, Zambia), Lozi (K20, Zambia, Namibia), Luyana (K30, Angola, Zambia, Namibia, Botswana) and Subiya (K40, Zambia, Namibia, Botswana) on the one hand as well as UMbundu and Ndonga (R10, 20, Angola, Namibia), Herero and Yeyi (R30, 40, Namibia, Botswana) on the other. Languages considered here comprise UMbundu (R11, Schadeberg 1990), Ndonga (R22, Fivaz 1986) as one of several Wambo languages, and Yeyi (R41, Gowlett 1992, Sommer 1995; for Herero, R31, see Ch 29). Furthermore, data on Mbukushu (K43, Fisch 1977), Gciriku (K38b, Möhlig 1967), Kwangari (K33, Dammann 1957), Lucazi (K13, Fleisch 2000), Luyana (K31, Givón 1970b) and Luvale (K14, Horton 1949) are also taken into account.

As far as the genealogical subclassification of Western (R, K) Savanna is concerned, internal relationships within the Wambo cluster, among members of the complex Luyana group as well as the general position of Yeyi within the wider Southern Bantu context have been dealt with to some extent (Haacke and Elderkin 1997). But until now several languages of Southern Angola, Southwestern Zambia and a number of Caprivian languages still await adequate linguistic description. In general, there are a number of features currently characterizing Western Savanna languages which seem to be due to the effects of language contact and shift situations. Both phenomena must have had a considerable impact on lexical, phonological and grammatical structures and sometimes to such an extent that genealogical links are nearly obscured. This is particularly true for those languages whose current distribution seems to be the result of complex migrational histories and which can today be found in linguistically diverse regions such as the Namibian Caprivi and Kavango areas and in the northwestern part of Botswana (Ngamiland). Yeyi, for instance, has in the past been influenced not only by neighboring Bantu but also Khoisan languages (see §2). While its speakers in Ngamiland are currently undergoing language shift towards the national language Tswana (S31, Ch 31), Eastern Caprivi Yeyi are at least bilingual in their own language and Lozi, the major lingua franca of this area. Lozi, however, exhibits structural influences from zones K and S, and despite its Eastern Savanna affiliation it has often been classified as a member of the Western Savanna group. Similarly, Gciriku 'shows typological and genetic resemblances with the languages of Guthrie's zones R and K' (Möhlig 1967, English summary). Today the language is mutually intelligible with Shambyu, but only some decades ago Gciriku speakers still remembered words in their former language, Manyo, which had been abandoned when most Gciriku men were killed by Tswana warriors shortly after 1900 and relations with neighboring Kavango groups were later intensified.

TABLE 28.1: SOME DEMOGRAPHIC INFORMATION ON SELECTED WESTERN SAVANNA LANGUAGES

UMBundu (R11) *Úmbundù*	Dialects: ? Distribution: Bié, Huambo and Benguela provinces of Southern Angola Number of speakers: 2 million (Schadeberg 1990) Status: ?
NDOnga (R22) *Oshindonga*	Dialects: South-Eastern division of Wambo group (see Baucom 1972) Distribution: Northern Namibia Number of speakers: 280,000 (Fivaz 1986) Status: Namibian national language, like Kwanyama (R21) used in the media, administration and in education up to university level
Herero (R31) *Otjiherero*	Dialects: Central Herero, Kaokoland varieties, 'Hereroland West' Distribution: (1) Northern, Central Namibia, (2) Northwestern Botswana Number of speakers: (1) 113,000 (Maho 1998), (2) 15,000 (Vossen 1991–2) Status: Namibian national language, Central Herero is norm variety ('standard'), used in the media, administration and education
YEYi (R41) *Shiyeyi, Shidzo* (autonyms), *Makoba* (xenonym)	Dialects: Caprivi and Ngamiland varieties (see Donnelly 1990, Gowlett 1997, Sommer and Vossen 1995) Distribution: (1) Eastern Caprivi, Namibia, (2) Northwestern Botswana Number of speakers: (1) 5,200 (Maho 1998), (2) 20,000 (Vossen 1988) status: minority language in Botswana, no official use
Subiya (K42) *eCisubiya,* *Ikuhane* (autonym)	Dialects: ? Distribution: (1) Eastern Caprivi, Namibia, (2) Northwestern Botswana Number of speakers: (1) 24,500 (Maho 1998), (2) 3,500 (Vossen 1991–2) Status: Lingua franca in the Caprivi area (see Ohly 1994)
MBUkushu (K43) *Thimbukushu,* Gova (xenonym)	Dialects: Member of the Kavango group (Möhlig 1997) Distribution: (1) Southern Kavango, Namibia, (2) Northwestern Botswana Number of speakers: (1) 8,200 (Fisch 1977), (2) 14,000 (Vossen 1991–2) Status: Namibian national language, some use in the media, in administration and education
GCIriku (K38b) *Rugciriku,* Mbogedo (xenonym), Manyo (obsolete idiom)	Dialects: Member of the Kavango group, mutually intelligible with Shambyu Distribution: (1) Kavango area, Namibia, (2) Northwestern Botswana Number of speakers: (1) 29,400? (Maho 1998), (2) 3,500 (Vossen 1991–2) Status: Namibian national language (see Mbukushu)
KWAngari (K33) *Rukwangali,* Mbunza (obsolete?)	Dialects: Member of the Kavango group, for Mbunza see Dammann (1957) Distribution: Kavango area, Namibia Number of speakers: 77,000 (Maho 1998) Status: Namibian national language, also lingua franca in the Kavango area
LUYana (K31) *Siluyana, Aluyi*	Dialects: Related to Kwangwa, Kwandi and Mbowe Distribution: Western Province, Zambia Number of speakers: Only a few elder speakers (Givón 1970a) Status: Luyana was still used as a ritual language in the 1970s
LUVale (K14), also Lovale, Lwena (toponym)	Dialects: ? Distribution: Northeast Angola; Zambezi and Kabompo districts, Zambia Number of speakers: 500,000, see Horton (1949), 90,000 in Zambia according to Ohannessian and Kashoki (1978) Status: Official language in Zambia, also lingua franca

2 PHONOLOGY, MORPHOPHONOLOGY AND TONE

Most Western Savanna languages have a five-vowel system comprising the short vowels *i, e, a, o, u* which are realized as [ɪ, ε, a, ɔ, ʊ] in Gciriku and Kwangari, for instance. Reduced inventories of this kind are reconstructable for proto-stages of Wambo (Baucom 1972:48) and Yeyi (Gowlett 1997:242). Synchronically, only Luvale and possibly Mbukushu (Möhlig 1997:221) make an additional distinction between the mid vowel pairs /e/, /ε/ and /o/, /ɔ/, respectively. In Luyana, reflexes of Proto-Bantu super-closed vowels *i̧ and *u̧ are said to be still present in underlying phonemic forms (Givón 1970a:89). UMbundu also shows a set of nasalized vowels as do some Caprivi Yeyi varieties (Donnelly 1990:27). Vowel length does not seem to be a prominent feature in Western Savanna. While long vowels in Ndonga are interpreted as sequences of identical vowels, there is a general tendency towards shortening of VV sequences in Luyana (Givón 1970a:89f). Vowel length is not phonologically distinctive in Gciriku (Möhlig 1997:218) whereas it is in Luvale where minimal pairs like *mu-sóji* 'small mud-fish' and *mu-sóoji* 'gravy, soup' can be found (see Horton 1949:3, where length is symbolized by a macron above the vowel). In his reconstruction of proto-Yeyi phonology, Gowlett (1997:242) provides evidence for positing two phonemically long vowels, namely *ii* and *ee*, whereas Caprivi Yeyi today exhibits an extended set of four long vowels (*ii, ee, aa, uu*).

Consonant inventories excluding clicks in Western Savanna are outlined in table 28.2. The ad- or inter-dental voiceless plosive occurs in Mbukushu and Gciriku [t̪], the voiceless palatal [c] is only found in UMbundu, Yeyi and Luyana. The latter two languages have a voiced counterpart [ɟ], too. Ndonga, Yeyi, Luyana and Luvale exhibit full sets of corresponding voiced sounds, while Luyana also has an additional voiced retroflex [ɖ]. Palatal plosives in Yeyi and Luyana are represented as *c* and *j* in the primary sources

TABLE 28.2: CONSONANT INVENTORIES (EXCLUDING CLICK CONSONANTS)

	UMB	NDO	YEY	MBU	GCI	KWA	LUY	LUV
Plosive	p,t,c,k	p,t,k,ʔ	p,t,c,k	p,t̪,t,k	p,t̪,t,k	p,t,k	p,t,c,k	p,t,k
	(b,d,g)	b,bb,d,ɟ,g	b,d	b,d	b,d,g	(b),d,g	(b,d,ɖ,ɟ,g)	(b,d,g)
Fricative	f,s,h,	f,θ,s,ʃ,x,h	f,s,ʃ,h	f,θ,ʃ,h	f,ʃ,h	f,s,ʃ,h	f,s,ʃ	f,s,ʃ,h
	v	v,ð,z,(ʒ),ɣ	v,z,ʒ	v,ð,ɣ	β,v,ɣ	β,v	β,z	v,z,ʒ
Affricate		ts	(ts)	tʃ	tʃ	tʃ	tʃ	tʃ
			dz	dʒ	dʒ	dʒ		dʒ
Trill			r/ɾ	r	r	r		
Lateral	l	l	l**		l	l	l	l
Glide	w,y	w,y	w,y	w,y	w,y	w,y	w,y	w,y
Nasal	m,n,ɲ,ŋ	m,n,ɲ	m,n,ɲ,ŋ	m,ŋ,n,ɲ,ŋ	m,ŋ,n,ɲ	m,ŋ,n,ɲ	m,n,ɲ,ŋ	m,n,ɲ,ŋ
Nasal	+	+	(+)	+	+	+	?	+
Compounds*		(also			(also	(also		
		aspirated)			aspirated)	aspirated)		
Nasal.	h̃,ṽ,l̃,w̃,ỹ							
Aspirated		see above	+		see above	see above		
Ejectives			+					
Palatal.		+	+	+				+
Labial.		+	(+)	+				+

Notes: Except (*y* = [j]), phonemes are here represented in IPA symbols; for orthographic conventions followed in the primary sources see entries in italics in the text; * according to Möhlig (1997) MBU, GCI and KWA have prenasals rather than nasal compounds; ** the contrasts [b], [bb] and [l], [r] are not found in Ngamiland Yeyi where [r] further has the allophone [ɾ], see Sommer (1995:365). Abbreviations: Nasal. = nasalized; Palatal. = palatalized; Labial. = labialized.

considered here. In descriptions of Kavango languages, on the other hand, *c* is rather used for the representation of dental clicks [/].

Fricatives form the most varied and complex group of consonants in Western Savanna. Voiceless and voiced interdentals [θ, ð] occur in Ndonga and Mbukushu (*th, dh*). A voiceless (alveo)palatal fricative [ʃ] occurs in Ndonga, Yeyi and Luyana (all *sh*) as well as in Mbukushu, Gciriku (both ş) and in Luvale (*x*). Ndonga and Yeyi also have a voiced alveopalatal (*zh*), whereas the corresponding sound in Luvale (*j*) is described as a palato-alveolar fricative in Horton (1949:8). Ndonga has a pair of velar fricatives [x, ɣ] which are written as *h* and *g* (Fivaz 1986) whereas the velar plosive (also *g*) only occurs in nasal compounds. The voiced velar fricative is not only found in Ndonga, but also in Mbukushu and Gciriku (*gh*). Ndonga has a voiceless affricate (*ts*) while Yeyi exhibits a dentisibilant pair [ts, dz]. Kwangari, Gciriku and Luvale, however, have alveolar-palatal affricates [tʃ, dʒ] which are written as *tj, dj* and *c, ɟ*, respectively. Nearly all Western Savanna languages have a voiced lateral [l], while the opposition between lateral and trill [r] is phonologically distinctive in some Yeyi varieties and in two Kavango languages only. With the exception of Ndonga, Western Savanna finally distinguishes at least four nasal consonants. In Kavango, bilabial and labiodental places of articulation [m, ɱ] are distinguished, although both are orthographically represented as *m*. Most languages have a palatal nasal [ɲ] which is either written as *nh* in UMbundu or as *ny* elsewhere. UMbundu, Yeyi, Mbukushu, Luyana and Luvale have a velar nasal phoneme /ŋ/ represented orthographically as *ng'* in UMbundu and Yeyi, as *ng* in Luvale and as *ñ* in Mbukushu.

Kavango languages and Yeyi have incorporated a number of click consonants into their phoneme inventories. While influxes in the former group are restricted to the voiced and voiceless dental click (*c, gc*) which may occur with prenasalized and/or aspirated effluxes (Möhlig 1997), Ngamiland Yeyi exhibits a total of twenty-seven different click phonemes (Sommer and Vossen 1992). As illustrated in table 28.3, the dental, alveolar, palatal and lateral clicks in Yeyi may be combined with a number of effluxes which further elaborates the complex consonant system of this particular Western Savanna language.

Vowel assimilation is a common phenomenon in Western Savanna. In Ndonga, prefix vowels are assimilated when they occur before vowel commencing-stems like in *oshéélo* (class 7, < *o-shi-elo*) 'doorway' and in *okúúli* (class 12, < *o-ka-uli*) 'small pot'. Similar phenomena are to be found in Caprivi Yeyi. Gowlett (n.d.) observes that the high front vowel *i* of the class 7 prefix *shi*, for instance, is backed to *u* in certain environments, i.e. when preceding a segment which is [-obstruent], [+back]. This rule also applies to stem-internal contexts as in *rùyùmbó* 'song' (< *rù-yìmb-ó*, cf. *-yìmb-á* 'sing') where the first

TABLE 28.3: CLICK CONSONANTS IN NGAMILAND YEYI (R41)

	Dental	Alveolar	Palatal*	Lateral
Voiceless (vl.)	/	!	ǂ	
Voiced	g/	g!		g//
Nasal	n/		nǂ	
Nasal-emphatic	n/n	n!n	nǂn	n//n
Vl. uvular fricative	/x		ǂx	
Ejective-uvular	/x'		ǂx'	
Aspirated	/h	!h	ǂh	//h
Glottal	/'	!'	ǂ'	
Ejective-nasal	n/'	n!'	nǂ'	n//'

Note: * The symbol ǂ will here be used for the notation of palatal clicks.

stem vowel *i* is assimilated to the preceding vowel *u* of the class 11 prefix *ru*. Donnelly (1990:31f.) also mentions the assimilation of prefix or stem vowels in Caprivi Yeyi such as in class 7 *shùpúndì* 'brat' (< *shì-púndì*, < class 1 *mù-púndì* 'child') and class 9 *ìnjúnjò* 'grave' (< *ìn-jínjò*).

Grégoire (1979) has further analyzed final vowel alternations in verbal forms where the final vowel *-a* is assimilated to the vowel quality of the respective root vowel in underived verb forms. These vowel alternations widely occur in Western Savanna including languages such as Herero and Kwanyama (zone R) as well as Kwezo, Pende and Chokwe (zone K). Full vowel assimilation, often referred to as vowel harmony, can also be found in Ndonga where pre- and post-root assimilation processes occur such as in *otéendé* (< *o-ta-a#end-V*, cf. *-end-a* 'to go') and *otákóoló* (< *o-ta-ka#ol-V*, cf. *-ol-a* 'to become rotten'). The subject concord (SC) *ta-* and the tense morphemes *-a-* and *-ka-* are here assimilated completely to the immediately following root vowels *e* and *o*, respectively. In Luvale, alternations of the final vowel can be observed in the context of anterior verb forms which have the structure SC-na-VB-V (VB = verbal base). In this case the final vowel *-a* may change to *-e, -i, -o* or *-u* as in *tunēce* 'we have let go' (< *-ec-a*), *tunēmbi* 'we have sung' (< *-imb-a*), *tunōngo* 'we have lied' (< *-ong-a*) and *tunōmu* 'we have become dry' (< *-um-a*) (Horton 1949:120).

In UMbundu, Ndonga and probably also in Yeyi, Luyana and Luvale high and low tones are lexically and grammatically distinctive. UMbundu, has high and low tones, which can

TABLE 28.4: VOWEL ALTERNATIONS IN VERBAL CONTEXTS

Language	Tense, aspect, mood context	Example
Ndonga (R22)	Present progressive and habitual, far future, past imperfective (see table 28.12)	*o-tá-ndi-yi#hól-ó* AFF-PROG-SC-OC-thin out-V 'I am thinning it out' (*-hola* 'to thin out')
Yeyi (R41)	Factual mode, anterior	*Nd-à#mòn-ó* SC-PAST-see-V 'I have seen' (*-mwàná* 'to see')
Mbukushu (K43)	Immediate and far future, (today) past and historical past	*(ni-)na#ruk-u* (SC)-PAST-plait-V 'I plaited (today)' (*-ruka* 'to plait')
Gciriku (K38b)	Anterior (*heutiges Perfekt*), definite (yesterday) past	*tu-nà#píng-i* SC-PAST-inherit-V 'We inherited (today)' (*-pinga* 'to inherit')
Kwangari (K33)	General and habitual present, definite past (*determiniertes Präteritum*), habitual, progressive -	*a-ni#mon-o* HAB-SC-see-V 'I used to see' (*-mona* 'to see')
Luyana (K31)	Past and non-terminated past, progressive and habitual present in the negative (see table 28.12)	*(s)ì-ná#kél-e* SC-PAST-come to-V 'I have come to' (*-kéla* 'to come to')
Luvale (K14)	Obsolete present ?, anterior ('perfect')	*tù-na#líng-i* SC-PAST-do-V 'We have done' (*-línga* 'to do')

Abbreviations: AFF = positive predicator; PROG = progressive; SC = subject concord; OC = object concord; V = alternating final vowel; HAB = habitual.

occur either lexically associated or floating. Verb roots in UMbundu have their own tonal patterns (*-làndà* 'to buy', *-kwátà* 'to take'). These may change, e.g. in the imperative singular where the final vowel invariably carries a high tone (*làndá* 'buy!', *kwátá* 'take!'). On the other hand, the so-called augment marked on nominals by a prefix-initial vowel *o-* before consonants (see §3), may be either high or low depending on the syntactic function of the noun. It thus appears as *ó-njó* 'house', for instance, when it is the first object of an affirmative verb in a main clause, while it exhibits the form *ò-njó* with the same meaning in all other contexts. In Ndonga, a high or low tone on the past marker *-a-* in postinitial position distinguishes between the non-completive and completive meaning of a state or action encoded by the respective verbal root (cf. *o-nd-a≠lánd-elé* 'I finished buying and will not buy again' vs. *o-nd-á≠land-éle* 'I finished buying and may buy again'). Lexical tone has sometimes been mentioned in the context of Kavango languages such as Kwangari (*ndì* 'fly', *ndi* 'or') and Mbukushu (*dí-na* 'louse', *dì-na* 'name'). Others, however, opine that tone as such is not distinctive within the Kavango group. In Gciriku, for instance, tone intervals seem to interact with other prosodic features such as stress, accent and vowel length as in presentative constructions like *ṣì-dírà* 'it is a taboo' which contrasts with *ṣí-dîìrà* 'it is a bird'. While in the first case the descending interval spreads over two subsequent syllables and the high toned syllable bears an additional respiratory stress and has a short vowel, the second distinctive prosodeme is also marked by a descending interval; in this case it spreads over the first syllable only and is accompanied by lengthening of the respective vowel segment (Möhlig 1997:220).

3 MORPHOLOGY AND SYNTAX

Nominal prefixes and their allomorphs in Western Savanna are listed in table 28.5 (for pre-prefix forms see tinted entries and discussion below). Included in this overview are nominal prefixes of the locative classes 16 to 18, i.e. *pa/ba/ha, ku* and *vu/mu*. Locative prefixes in UMbundu, for instance, lose their own vowel when prefixed to the inherent nominal prefix of a noun such as in *púliví* 'on, at, near the trap' (< class 3 *úliví* 'trap'), *kólwí* 'at, to, from the river' (< class 11 *ólwí* 'river') and *vísò* 'in the eye' (< class 5 *ísò* 'eye') (Schadeberg 1990:11). In Yeyi, high-toned locative prefixes precede nominals as in *pú-lì-wé* 'on the stone' (< class 5 *lìwé* 'stone'), *kw-ín-k'àmù* 'to the right' (< class 9 *ìnk'àmù* 'right hand') and *mú-shi-g//ánà* 'in the well' (< class 7 *shìg//ánà* 'well').

However, locatives may also function as independent nouns and thus as sentential subjects or objects in which case they are marked with their own subject concords on the verb (Donnelly 1990:90ff.). In Luyana, locative prefixes do not themselves take an initial vowel and preclude the taking of the initial pre-prefix vowel by the original noun prefix. Furthermore, locatives never seem to control verbal subject concords of a predicate in surface forms, although they do control concords of relative modifiers, for example. When a sentence like *i-na-ku≠ingena* **mu-ndo** 'I got **into** the house' is used as a relative construction, agreement may either be marked by a class 9 concord element *iti* or the class 18 locative marker *umu* (cf. **mu-ndo** *iti i-na-ku≠ingena* [~ **umu** *i-na-ku≠ingena*] **ti**-*na-ku≠bya* 'The house which/[into which] I entered burned', Givón 1970a:22).

Pre-prefix forms in Western Savanna occur in UMbundu, Ndonga, Yeyi and Luyana while they are missing in the Kavango languages and in Luvale. As is already indicated in table 28.5, particular pre-prefix forms are wide-spread in languages of Guthrie's zone R. Among these languages are also Nyaneka (R13), Nkhumbi (R14), Kwanyama (R21), and Herero (R31) (de Blois 1970). Like UMbundu and Ndonga these languages exhibit an invariable vocalic pre-prefix *o-* before consonants. When the noun prefix consists of

TABLE 28.5: PRE-PREFIX AND NOMINAL PREFIX (NP) FORMS

Class	UMB	NDO	YEY*	MBU*	GCI*	KWA	LUY	LUV
1	o- u-, o- mu-	o- m-, o- mw-	u- mu-	mu-	mu-	m-, mu-	u- mu-	mu-
2	a-, o- va-, o- ma-	a- a-	a- ba-	ha-	βa-	va-	a- a-	va-
3	u-, o- w-, o- mu-	o- m-, o- mw-	u- mu-	mu-	mu-	m-, mu-	u- mu-	mu-
4	o- vi-	o- mi-, o- mw-	i- mi-	mi-	(di)mu-	nom-, nomu-	i- mi-	mi-
5	e-, Ø	e- Ø	i- ri-, li-	di-	li-	e-	i- li-	li-
6	a-, o- va-	o- ma-	a- ma-	ma-	ma-	ma-	a- ma-	ma-
7	o- ci-	o- shi-	i- ci-, shi-	thi-	ʂi-	si-	i- si-	ci-
8		i- i-	i- zi-	yi-	βi-	i-	i- N-	vi-
9	o- n-	o- N-	iN-	N-, Ø	N-	N-, Ø	i- N-	Ø
10	o- lon-	o- oN-	ziN-	N-, ma(N)-	N-	no-(N-)	i- (ti-), tiN-	ji-
11	o- lu-	o- lu-, o- lw-	u- ru-	ru-	ru-	ru-	u- lu-	lu-
12	o- ka-	o- ka-	a- ka-	ka-	ka-	tu-	a- ka-	ka-
13	o- tu-		u- tu-	tu-	tu-	ka-	u- tu-	tu-
14	u- u-	u-	u- wu-	ghu-	(gh)u-	u-	u- u-	u-
15	o- ku-	o- ku-	u- ku-	ku-	ku-	ku-	u- ku-	ku-
16	pa-	pu-	pu-	pa-	pa-	pa-	ba-	ha-
17	ku-	ku-	ku-	ku-	ku-	ku-	ku-	ku-
18	vu-	mu-	mu-	mu-	mu-	mu-	mu-	mu-

Note: * For Botswana Yeyi, Mbukushu and Gciriku see Sommer (1995:366), Vossen (1991–2).

a single vowel as in some classes in UMbundu, the pre-prefix may be represented by a floating tone only (Schadeberg 1990:12). In Yeyi (R41) and Luyana (K14), on the other hand, the pre-prefix is vocalic but not invariable since in these languages it takes the quality of the prefix vowels in the corresponding classes. The pre-prefix is thus realized as *i-* before prefixes of classes 4, (5), 7, 8, (9, 10), as *a-* in classes 2, 6, 12 and as *u-* in the remaining ones. The occurrence of pre-prefix vowels in Luyana is described as being optional (Givón 1970a:5). In Yeyi they are retained for a small number of nouns and in some classes only, e.g. 1/2 *ùmùtú, àbàtó* 'person', 3/4 *ùmùyá, ìmìyá* 'thorn', 5/6 *ìrìnó, àmènó* 'tooth', 7/8 *ìcìtó, ìzìtó* 'thing', 13 *ùtùró* 'sleep', 14/6 *ùwòtó, àmàtó* 'dugout', 3/15 *ùmwèzí, ùkwèzí* 'moon, month' (Gowlett 1992b).

As indicated in table 28.6, nouns in Western Savanna may be recategorized to other classes and such derivational processes are linked to particular meanings. UMbundu, for instance, lacks a distinct class 14 where mass and abstract nouns are typically assigned to. The replacive use of the class 3 prefix is thus employed to express qualitative meaning (*ú-somá* 'royalty' < *ó-somá* 'king', Schadeberg 1990:28). In Luyana, the class 11 prefix *lu-* may be used as replacive prefix with the meaning of thinness as in *lu-kondo* 'thin leg' (< *li-kondo* 'leg', Givón 1970a:80). Further common nominal derivations in Western Savanna comprise the augmentative function of classes 5/6, the pejorative meaning of classes 7/8 and the widespread use of classes 12/13 to express diminutive

TABLE 28.6: NOMINAL DERIVATION

	UMB	NDO	YEY	MBU	GCI	KWA	LUY	LUV
Noun-to-noun								
cl. 3	QUAL							
cl. 5/6		AUG PEJO	AUG	AUG	AUG	AUG		AUG
cl. 7/8	AUG cl. 7/4	PEJO	AUG- PEJO	PEJO	PEJO	PEJO	AUG- PEJO THIN	PEJO
cl. 11								
cl. 12/13	DIM	DIM cl. 12/14	DIM- (PEJO)	DIM	DIM	DIM cl. 13/12	DIM	DIM
Verb-to-noun								
-i	AGENT		AGENT	AGENT	AGENT	AGENT	AGENT	AGENT
-o	ACTION RESULT INSTR		+	ABSTR	+	+	ABSTR	+
ma- + -o			PLACE	PLACE	PLACE		PLACE	
-a	+		+	+	+			
-e	+				+			+

Abbreviations: QUAL = qualitative; AUG = augmentative; PEJO = pejorative; DIM = diminutive; THIN = thinness; AGENT = agent nouns; INSTR = instrumental nouns; ABSTR = abstract nouns; +: this derivation is present in the respective language but has no clearly defined or consistent meaning (see e.g. Schadeberg 1990:26).

meaning as in Mbukushu class 5 *di-yoka* 'big snake' (< *thi-yoka*), class 7 *thi-nhwere* 'cripple' and class 13 *tu-nhwe* 'a little bit of milk' (< *ma-nhwe*) (Fisch 1977:27ff.). Diminutive meaning may also be formed by suffixing the elements *-yona/yena* and *-ana* in Gciriku and Luyana, respectively. In Gciriku, the class 1/2 noun *mu-rúti-yona* (missionary-DIM) means 'curate' (Möhlig 1967:139f.). In Luyana, *ndyana* 'little fish' is derived from the class 9 noun *n-di* 'fish' (Givón 1970a:79). In the Kavango languages a suffixed stem *-kǎdi* 'female' may also be used as derivational element as in Gciriku *mu-yóli-kǎdi* 'first/main wife'.

All Western Savanna languages further exhibit deverbatives, i.e. nouns derived from verbal bases by adding a nominalizing suffix and/or a particular nominal prefix (see table 28.6). In UMbundu, agent nouns are derived by adding the suffix *-i* as in *ú-píp-i* (class 1/2) 'fisherman' (< *-pip-a* 'to fish', Schadeberg 1990:26). In Yeyi, Mbukushu, Gciriku and Luyana the combination of a class 6 prefix *ma-* and the suffix *-o* is employed to express 'place of action'. In Luyana this kind of nominalization is regularly derived from the applied form of the verb (Givón 1970b:74). Similarly, nominalized Yeyi forms such as *mà-tánd-ìr-ó* 'place to hunt' or *mà-/ímb-ìr-ó* 'slaughtering place' are derived from applied forms of the verbs *-tándà* 'to hunt' and *-/ímbà* 'to stab, pierce', respectively (see table 28.13 for verbal extensions).

Besides nominal prefixes (see table 28.5) and independent pronominal forms (see table 28.10), Western Savanna languages further exhibit different sets of concordial elements whose segmental structure is identical with or derived from pronominal prefix (PP) forms (e.g. see tables 28.7–8). In some classes these forms differ from nominal prefixes and they agree in class with the noun to which they refer or which they depend on. For UMbundu, for instance, Schadeberg (1990) differentiates between pronominal forms of numerals (see table 28.7), adjectives and determiners. Concordial elements like substitutives or personal pronouns, however, do not only exist for all classes but also for participants (see table 28.9).

TABLE 28.7: PRONOMINAL CONCORDS (NUMERALS, POSSESSIVES) IN THREE SAMPLE LANGUAGES

Class	UMB		YEY (Ngamiland)		LUY	
	NUM	POSS	NUM	POSS	NUM	POSS
	PP	PP-o	PP/NP	PP-o	PP	a-PP-o
1	u-	-ĥe	mu-	-ke	u-	-aye
2	va-	-vo	wa-	-wo	a-	-ao
3	u-	-wo	mu-	-wo	u-	-oo
4	vi-	-vyo	(y)i-	-yo	i-	-ayo/-ato
5	li-	-lyo	ri-	-rio	li-	-alyo
6	(y)a-	-o	a-	-wo	a-	-ao
7	ci-	-co	shi-	-sho	si-	-aso
8	–	–	zi-	-zo	i-	-ayo
9	(y)i-	-yo	i(N)-	-yo	ti-	-ato
10	–	–	zi(N)-	-zo	ti-	-ato
11	lu-	-lwo	ru-	-ro	lu-	-alo
12	ka-	-ko	ka-	-ko	ka-	-ako
13	tu-	-t(w)o	tu-	-t(w)o	tu-	-ato
14	–	–	(w)u-	-wo	u-	-ao
15	ku-	-k(w)o	ku-	-ko	ku-	-ako

TABLE 28.8: CONCORDIAL ELEMENTS ON DEMONSTRATIVES IN NGAMILAND YEYI AND IN LUYANA

Class	YEY			LUY			
	DEM 1 PP-ni'i	DEM 2 PP-o'o	DEM 3 PP-na'a	DEM 1 V-PP	DEM 2 V-PP-o	DEM 3 PP-no	DEM 4 PP-ya
1	yini'i	yo'o	yina'a	uyu	oyo	uno	uya
2	wani'i	wa'a	wana'a	aa	ao	ano	aya
3	wuni'i	wo'o	wuna'a	uu	oo	uno	uya
4	yini'i	yo'o	yina'a	ii	eyo	ino	iya
5	rini'i	rio'o	rina'a	ili	elyo	lino	liya
6	ngani'i	nga'a	ngana'a	aa	ao	ano	aya
7	cini'i	co'o	cina'a	isi	eso	sino	siya
8	zini'i	zo'o	zina'a	ii	eyo	ino	iya
9	yini'i	yo'o	yina'a	ii, iti	eto	tino	tiya
10	zini'i	zo'o	zina'a	iti	eto	tino	tiya
11	runi'i	ro'o	runa'a	ulu	olo	luno	luya
12	kani'i	ka'a	kana'a	aka	ako	kano	kaya
13	tuni'i	to'o	tina'a	utu	oto	tuno	tuya
14	wuni'i	wo'o	wuna'a	uu	oo	uno	uya
15	kuni'i	ko'o	kuna'a	uku	oko	kuno	kuya
16	(po)pani'i	pa'a	pana'a	aba	abo	bano	baya
17	kuni'i	ko'o	kuna'a	uku	oko	kuno	kuya
18	(i)moni'i	mo'o	(i)muna'a	umu	omo	muno	muya

Note: For different forms of demonstratives in Caprivi Yeyi see Baumbach (1997).

TABLE 28.9: SUBJECT (SC) AND OBJECT (OC) CONCORD ELEMENTS

	UMB		NDO		YEY		MBU		GCI		KWA		LUY		LUV	
	SC*	OC	SC	OC	SC	OC	SC	OC	SC	OC	SC	OC	SC	OC	SC	OC
sg. 1	ndì, n		ndi	ndje	ndi		ni		ni, n	N, Ø	ni	nge	(s)ì, nì, Ṅ	ni, N	ngu	
2	ò	ku	u	kú	u	kú	ghu	ku	yu, u, w	ku	o	ku	u	ku	u	ku
pl. 1	tù		tu		ti		tu		tu, tw		tu		tù		tu	
2	(v)ù	ku	mu		ni		mu		mu, mw		mu		mu	mi	mu	mi
cl. 1	ò	u	Ø	mú	mu		gha	mu	a	mu	a	mu, u	ú, á	mu	a, u	mu
2	và		a	yá	wa	wá	ha	wa	βa		va		á	a	va	
3	ú		gú		u	wú	ghu		u		gu		u		u	
4	ví		dhi		i	yí	dhi		di		di		(t)i		yi	
5	lí		lí		ri		di		li		li		li		li	
6	(y)á		gá		nga	ngá, á	gha		ya		ga		a		wa, a	
7	cí		shí		shi		thi		ṣi		si		si		ci	
8	–		yi		zi		yi		βi		(y)i		i		vi	
9	(y)í		yi		i		gha	mu	ji		zi		(t)i	ti	yi	
10	–		dhí		zi		dhi		di		di		ti		ji	
11	lú		lú		ru	ri	ru		ru		ru		lu		lu	
12	ká		ká		ka		ka		ka		tu		ka		ka	
13	tú		–		tu	ti	tu		tu		ka		tu		tu	
14	–		ú		wu		ghu		u		u		u		u	
15	kú		kú		ku		ku		ku		ku		ku		ci	

Note: * if not indicated otherwise SC/OC forms are segmentally identical; sg./pl. = singular/plural; cl. = class.

With the exception of Mbukushu, numerals in Western Savanna are generally marked by pronominal prefixes. Attributive adjectives, however, seldom take simple pronominal prefixes as they do in UMbundu. In Ndonga and Luyana they are marked by nominal prefixes. In the remaining languages concordial elements on adjectives typically consist of complex forms.

These concords are based on a combination of PP, or PP-derived, and NP forms. Examples of such complex concordial elements would be *mù-púndì yô-mù-ré* 'the tall child (class 1)' in Yeyi and *ma-remo go-ma-zera* 'white clouds (class 6)' in Kwangari. Pronominal and nominal possessives in Western Savanna are finally marked by pronominal prefix forms followed by a final -*o* and -*a* element, respectively (see table 28.7 e.g. of pronominal possessives). As far as nominal possessives or connective forms are concerned, the one exception from the typical PP-a structure in Western Savanna is Ngamiland Yeyi where connectives are formed by complex concords. Furthermore, the final vowel of the second element alternates according to the vowel quality of the prefix vowel of an immediately following nominal form as in class 5 *rùanga rùrù mùnyánà* vs. *rùangà rìrìá wànyánà* 'the spear of the man/men'.

With the exception of Ndonga and Yeyi, demonstratives in Western Savanna typically distinguish four grades and sometimes also have additional sets of emphatic forms. While

TABLE 28.10: INDEPENDENT PERSONAL PRONOUNS

		UMB	NDO	YEY	MBU	GCI	KWA	LUY	LUV
sg.	1	ámè	ngame	yèmé	(y)ame	amè	ame	mene	àmi
	2	óvè	ngoyé	yèwé	(y)owe	oβè	ove	wene	òve
	3	éye	yé	yèyé	aye	(ɣ)úje	age	toto	ìkíye
pl.	1	étù	tsé	yètsʰwé	(y)atwe	atwè	ose	aci	ètu
	2	énè	né	yènwé	(y)amwe	anwè	one	anyi	ènu
	3	-vó	yó	wáwò	awo	βaβo	awo	oo	vakivo

TABLE 28.11: CONSTITUENT ELEMENTS OF NON-COMPOUND INFLECTED VERB FORMS

Slots, morphemes and their functions: an example from UMbundu (Schadeberg 1990:29)

Preinitial	Initial	Postinitial	Preradical	Radical	Postradical	Final	Postfinal
Ka	*tw*	*á-ka*	*va-u*	*pandw*	*íl*	*il-Ø*	*-i-kó*
NEG	SC	TAM	OC	VB	EXT	TAM/FV	CL
	1pl	past, itive			applicative	past	locative

'We did not go there to thank them for you.'

Abbreviations: NEG = negative marker; SC = subject concord; TAM = tense, aspect, mood markers; OC = object concords; VB = verbal base; EXT = verbal extension; TAM/FV = TAM marker/final vowel; CL = (en)clitic = plural vocative marker, locative complement.

in Ngamiland Yeyi DEM 1 indicates 'here', DEM 2 refers to 'there' and DEM 3 to 'over there', DEM 1 in Luyana implies 'close to both hearer and speaker', DEM 2 is 'close to hearer' and DEM 3 is 'close to speaker', while DEM 4 indicates remoteness (Givón 1970a:18). Ndonga again only distinguishes three locational positions of simple demonstratives. Here these forms indicate (1) relative nearness to the speaker or a reference point in space/time, (2) relative distance from these and (3) remoteness from the reference point (Fivaz 1986:63). Shortest forms of the three positions only refer to referents which are visible if these are concrete nouns. In Gciriku, subject relatives are marked by the occurrence of a DEM 2 form while the predicate in the relative clause is further characterized by the occurrence of a morpheme *-o* in final position (Möhlig 1967:251). In UMbundu and Luvale, relative verb forms are not overtly marked but exhibit specific tonal characteristics.

However, demonstratives in Western Savanna have yet another function. In Ndonga, Mbukushu, Gciriku, Kwangari and Luyana 'relative embedding is marked by the replacement of the identical noun in the relative sentence by a demonstrative, the latter functioning as a kind of "relative pronoun"' (Fivaz 1986:125). In Ndonga, relative verb forms differ from main verbs in the omission of a so-called positive predicator *o-* which occurs in affirmative verb forms and preinitial position (see table 28.12).

In Luyana, all four demonstratives may be used in relative contexts whereby their use in some cases is optional: (1) *mu-nu ú-nákù#tènd-à* (1-man SC1-PAST-work-FV) 'The man worked', (2) *mu-nu [oyo] ù-nákù#tènd-à* (1-man [DEM 2] SC1-PAST-work-FV) 'The man [that] who worked' (Givón 1970a:52); when used in object relative contexts, their use is obligatory.

Tables 28.12 and 28.13 are meant to illustrate the degree of variation which exists between tense, aspect and mood systems in Western Savanna. Non-compound affirmative and negative indicative verb forms may be morphologically complex, but they minimally

TABLE 28.12: TENSE, ASPECT AND MOOD IN NDONGA (R22) AND LUYANA (K31)

Ndonga o-ku#lánd-a 'to buy' (Fivaz 1986)		Luyana ku#kél-a 'to come to' (Givón 1970a)	
PAST (affirmative and negative forms)			
1 Past, completed – o-SC-a-VB-ile/ o-SC-á-VB-ile ka-SC-Ø-VB-ile	o-nd-a#lánd-elé 'I finished buying' ka-ndi#lánd-elé	*1 Past, completed –* SC-a-VB-ile ka-SC-a-si-VB-a	n-á#kel-ile 'I have/had arrived' kà-n-à-sí# kel-ile
2 Past, imperfective o-SC-á-VB-V i-na-SC-Ø-VB-a	o-nd-á#land-á 'I bought (and may again)' i-na-ndi#lánd-a	*2 Past, non-terminated, lingering –* SC-na-VB-V ka-SC-a-si-VB-a	(s)ì-nà#kél-e 'I have come (and am possibly still here)' kà-n-á-sí#kel-a
3 Past, perfective o-SC-à-VB-a i-na-SC-Ø-VB-a	o-nd-a#lánd-a 'I bought (and will again)' i-na-ndi#lánd-a	*3 Past, weak-link, non-lingering –* SC-na-ka-VB-(V) ka-SC-a-si-VB-a	(s)ì-ná-kà#kél-e/a 'I came' kà-n-á-sí#kel-a
		4 Past, strong-link, non-lingering – SC-na-ku-VB-a ka-SC-a-si-VB-a	(s)ì-ná-kú#kél-a 'I came' kà-n-á-sí#kel-a
		5 Past, very recent – naa-SC-Ø-VB-a ka-SC-aa-VB-a	náá-nì#kél-a 'I have just arrived' kà-n-áá#kel-a
NON-PAST (affirmative and negative forms)			
		1 Present, completed – SC-Ø-VB-ile excluding 1sg: ka-SC-Ø-VB-ile	nì#kél-ílè 'I have/am arrived' sí-í#kel-ile (cf. 1pl: kà-tú#kel-ile)
		2 (Present) persistive SC-si-VB-a ka-SC-si-VB-a	nì-sí#kél-a 'I am still arriving' kà-nì-sí#kél-a
1 (Present) progressive o-ta-SC-Ø-VB-V i-ta-SC-Ø-VB-V	o-tá-ndi#lánd-a 'I am buying' i-ta-ndi#lánd-a	*3 (Present) progressive* SC-li-a-VB-a ka-SC-Ø-VB-V	nì-lì-á#kel-a 'I am arriving' kà-ní#kel-e
2 (Present) habitual o-ha-SC-Ø-VB-V i-ha-SC-Ø-VB-V	o-ha-ndí#land-a 'I am always buying' i-ha-ndí#lánd-a	*4 (Present) habitual (see also past forms)* SC-ku-VB-a excluding 1sg: ka-SC-ku-VB-V	nì-kú#kél-a 'I (always) arrive' (sì)-í-ku#-kél-e
1 Future o-ta-SC-ka-VB-a i-ta-SC-ka-VB-a	o-tá-ndi-ká#lánd-a 'I will buy' i-ta-ndí-ka#lánd-a	*1 Future, close – (= inceptive?, see past forms)* SC-ka-VB-a excluding 1sg: ka-SC-VB-a	i-ká#kél-a 'I will soon come' (sì)-ì-ká#kél-á
2 Future, far – o-na-SC-Ø-VB-V ka-SC-Ø-VB-V	see Fivaz (1986:97)	*2 Future, simple –* mba-SC-Ø-VB-á excluding 1sg: ka-SC-ka-VB-a	mbà-nì#kél-á 'I will come' (sì)-ì-ká#kél-á

TABLE 28.13: VERBAL EXTENSIONS

	UMB	NDO	YEY	MBU	GCI	KWA	LUY	LUV
APPL	-il-, -el-, -ĩl-, -ẽl-	-el-, -il- -en-, -in-	-ir-	-er-, -en-	-ir-, -er-, -in-, -en-	-ir-, -er-	-el-, -en-	-il-, -el-, -in-, -en-
CAUS	-is-	-ik-, -ek- -ith-, -th-	-is-	-ek-, -ith-	-ik-*,-ek-	-is-, -es-, -ik-, -ek-	-is-	-is-, -es-
NEUT	-ik-, -ek-, -iȟ-, -eȟ *	-ik-, -ek-	-ik-	-ok-, -uk- (stative)	-uk-, -ok-	-ik-, -ek-	-ik-,-ek-* (stative)	-ik-, -ek-, -uk-, -ok-
REV	-ul-, -ol-, -uĺ-, -oĺ-*	-ul-, -ol-, -un-, -on-	-ur-	-ur-, -un-, -on-	-or-, -ur-, -on-, -un-	-ur-, -or-	-ul-*	-ul-, -ol-, -un-, -on-
PASS	-iw-	-(i,e)w-	-w-	-iw-**	-w-**	-w-**	-w-	-iw-*
REC		-athan-	-an-		-an-*	-an-	-an-	-asan-
POS	-am-*		-am-	-am-, -an-	-am-*	-am-	*-am-	-am-
prefinal		-a(n)g-	-ung-	-ang-	-ang-			-ang-

Notes: * Extension is no longer productive/does not occur frequently; ** Used with some verbs/in relic forms.

consist of a subject concord, the verbal base and a final vowel. The verbal base in turn may be extended by one or more derivational elements. Among the most frequently occurring verbal extensions in Western Savanna are applicative (APPL, UMbundu, *ó-ku#lim-iĺ-a* 'to work for'), causative (CAUS, Ndonga, *o-ku#tsim-ik-a* 'to make whirl') and neuter forms (NEU, Yeyi, *kù#vúndj-ìk-á* 'to become broken') as well as the reversive (REV, Mbukushu, *-fik-a* 'to cover', *-fik-ur-a* 'to uncover'), reciprocal (REC, Gciriku, *-rw-à* 'to fight', *-rw-án-a* 'to fight each other') and positional extensions (POS, Kwangari, *-sik-a* 'to arrive', *-sik-am-a* 'to stand'). The widespread and productive passive extension *-w-* is no longer used in the Kavango languages and in Luvale (see tinted entries, table 28.13). But it regularly occurs in zone R languages and in Luyana where the verb *-ba* 'to give', for instance, may be extended to *-biwa* 'to be given'. In Gciriku, passive meanings are expressed by constructions like *ßa-nà-mù#óyona na-ṣi-tíki* (SC2-PAST-OC3sg-beat with-7-rhizome) 'He was beaten with a taproot' (Möhlig 1967:230).

The element *-ang-* in prefinal position can be found in Ndonga, Yeyi, Mbukushu, Gciriku and Luvale. While this form is used to express habitual or continuous meaning in Gciriku and Mbukushu (cf. Gciriku *-yámb-a* 'to speak', *-yámb-ang-a* 'to speak continuously', Möhlig 1967:223), it is employed aṣ a TAM morpheme in Luvale. Here it is used to denote recent past (three to four days ago) or, more generally, it implies 'a short lapse of time' as is illustrated in the following example: *vamusaulanga, kaha nafundu-muka* 'They insulted him, and he has gone off in a huff' (Horton 1949:124). In general, finite verb forms in Western Savanna comprise a wealth of tense, aspect and mood markers which occur in preinitial, postinitial and final position. In some contexts, the final vowel may alternate (see table 28.5). In other contexts, it changes from *-a* to *-e*. The latter applies, e.g. to negative optatives in UMbundu which have the structure ka-SC-ka-(OC)-VB-e (cf. *hú-ka#táng-e* 'don't read!', Schadeberg 1990:40).

The negative marker *ka-* and its free variant *ha-* precede the subject concord, whereby the sequence ka-SC- always has a low–high tone pattern and subject concords for participants and class 1 are shaped by special contractions (singular: (1) *sí-*, (2) *kú-* = *hú-*, (3) *ká-*; plural (1) *ka-tú-*, (2) *ka-ú*, (3) *ka-vá-*; cf. Luyana negatives, table 28.12). In UMbundu, the final vowel may also be replaced by a postfinal plural marker *-i* which is used in conjunction with a second person singular or plural subject or object concord to mark the addressee as plural (see table 28.11).

With the exception of Yeyi, where this form is no longer productive, all Western Savanna languages employ a final element *-ile* or *-ire* which together with the postinitial morpheme *-a-* is used to mark remote or indefinite past (Maho 1998:90ff.). In conjunction with the final vowel *-a*, however, the former morpheme expresses near past or anterior. UMbundu, for instances, has two past forms, namely *tw-a#land-élè* and *tw-a#land-á* 'we bought', whereby the former denotes remote and the latter near past (Schadeberg 1990:37). In Gciriku, postinitial *-à-* and final *-ire* (or *-ine* when preceded by a nasal) are employed to express indefinite past, e.g. *n-à#ṣ-ire* 'I washed (a long time ago)', while postinitial *-à-* plus final *-a* are used to denote indefinite past actions or events with present effects as in *n-à#ṣ-à* 'I have washed (sometime)' (Möhlig 1967:195, 191). In Ngamiland Yeyi, a similar distinction exists between verb forms expressing past and those with anterior meanings. Anterior verb forms in Yeyi have the structure SC-a-VB-V as in *t-à#mòn-ò ì-zì-tù* (SC1pl-PAST-see-FV AUG-8-thing) 'we have seen things', whereas past forms employ a postinitial marker *-ata-* and the invariable final vowel *-a*, as is illustrated in the following example: *ù-mù-tú y-ó'ò m-àtà#dzw-á k-ó'ò* (AUG-1-person 1-DEM 2 SC1-PAST-come from-FV 17-DEM 2) 'That man (as the story goes) came from there'. Past tense in the Kavango languages, on the other hand, is further marked by a preinitial element *ka-* which occurs in Gciriku and Kwangari. In Gciriku, preinitial *ká-* denotes definite past as in *ká-ni#ṣ-à* 'I washed (yesterday)' (ka-SC-Ø-VB-a, Möhlig 1967:193). In Kwangari, the same morpheme may be used to either express definite or indefinite past, depending on whether this marker is used together with an alternating final vowel (ka-SC-VB-V) or with the morpheme *-ire* (or *-ere, -ene*). Kwangari verb forms with preinitial *ka-* are used to denote actions or events that took place in the immediate past, e.g. *ka-tu#mon-o* 'we saw (during the same day)', while forms like *ka-tu-mwene* (ka-SC-VB-ile) 'we saw' refer to actions or events that took place sometime further in the past (Dammann 1957:57).

Excluding the Kavango language group, affixal negation marking prevails in Western Savanna. In Luyana, negation of finite verb forms in the indicative is indicated by two bound morphemes, namely *ka-* and *-si-* which appear in pre- and postinitial position, respectively (see table 28.12). In UMbundu, preinitial *ka-* is used to negate the imperative, optative as well as indicative verb forms in the present, past and future tenses (Schadeberg 1990:41ff.). Luvale indicative verb forms are negated by preinitial *ka-* and a verb-final enclitic *-ko* in present and past tenses such as in the immediate past *ka-tw-a-ci#ling-ang-a-ko* (NEG-SC1pl-PAST-OC7-do-PAST-FV-NEG) 'we did not do it' (Horton 1949:127). In Yeyi, different ways of marking sentential negation are employed, whereby only some of these comprise affixal negation strategies. In non-declarative sentences in Caprivi Yeyi and in non-indicative contexts in the Ngamiland Yeyi variety, negation is expressed by means of a periphrastic construction consisting of a finite form of the inherently negative verb *kù#sìy-à* 'to leave', which is followed by the lexical verb of the affirmative sentence in the infinitive as in *nì#sìy-é kw#ènd-á má-sùkú* (SC2pl-leave-FV 15-go-FV 6-night 'You (pl) should not go at night!'). In the indicative mood, sentential negation can be expressed by adding a sentence or verb form-initial negation word *yòmùà* (also *y[y]émwà* 'never, no') to the affirmative sentence as in *yòmùà nd-àtì#énd-à mà-wùrìsizó nàmúshì* (NEG SC1sg-FUT/PROG-go-FV 6-market ADVERB) 'I will not go/am not going to the market today'.

The preinitial marker *ka-*, however, may be used to mark negation in non-declarative and declarative sentences. It appears as a double prefix *kaka-*, for instance, in the imperative singular and as a discontinuous marker in pre- and postinitial position in the person-inflected plural, cf. *yá!* 'come (sg)!', *kàkà#yà!* 'don't come (sg)!'; *nì#y-é!* 'you (pl) should come!', *kà-nì-kà≠yá!* 'You (pl) shouldn't come = don't come (pl)!'. The bound negative morpheme *ka-* in preinitial position may further be affixed to a finite form of the inherently negative verb *kù≠ciré* 'not to be able to'. In this case, the finite verb is followed by the lexical verb of the affirmative sentence in the infinitive, and it exclusively occurs with anterior verb forms, e.g. *kà-ndì#cìré kù#rìm-á* (NEG-SC1sg-not be able to 15-cultivate) 'I have not cultivated (this morning)'. Ngamiland Yeyi again has a compound negative form. The first part of this negative construction consists of a subject concord, optionally a TAM-marker, a class 1 or 2 nominal prefix and an invariable click-containing negative element *-!hu* (< *kù-!hú* 'nothing'). This latter form is always followed by the lexical verb of the affirmative sentence in the infinitive, e.g. *'á,'à, ndì-mù-!hú kù#shàngán-á ná yùú-mwè* (NEG, SC1sg-1-nothing 15-meet with PP1-some) 'No, no, I did not see/meet with anyone (yesterday)'. In Mbukushu, Kwangari and Gciriku, non-indicative and indicative finite verb forms are negated by the additive use of negation words. In Mbukushu, finite verbs in the main clause exhibit a verb-initial form *mbadi, badi* or *kadi*, while the respective negation word is followed by the finite verb form of the affirmative sentence (Fisch 1977:130). In the remaining Kavango languages, sentential negation is expressed by the use of a verb form-initial negation word *kapí* as in Kwangari *kapi tu-na#mon-o* (NEG SC1pl-PAST-see-FV) 'we did not see' and *kapi nga-tu#mon-a* (NEG FUT-SC1pl-see-FV) 'we will not see' (Dammann 1957:67).

In Gciriku, an invariable negation word *kapí* is used to negate finite verbs, whereas the negation of copulas and infinitives is achieved by the use of an equally invariable form *kapìṣì* (including the defective verb *-ṣì* 'to say'). This negative marker precedes the element to be negated as in *amĕ kapíṣí ku#jǐmb-a* (AP1sg NEG 15-sing-FV) 'I am not a singer' (Möhlig 1967:216). In Kwangari, negation is expressed by double marking as in *no ku#yung-a si* 'not to speak'. Similarly, UMbundu marks the negative in sentences with non-verbal predication by a negative index *há-* which precedes the predicative noun while it is followed by an enclitic *-kó* (Schadeberg 1990:53f.). When the subject is a participant the nominal predicate in UMbundu is preceded by a negated verbal prefix and followed by the enclitic *-kó* as in *ha-tú-vi-mbandà-kó* (NEG-SC1pl-4-doctor-NEG) 'we are not doctors'. In Yeyi, negation in sentences with a non-verbal predicate is marked by the negation word *yemua* as in *zi-kayi ziza-po ri-iro ri-i-njuwo yemua inz-anga* (8-skin SREL8-LOC16 5-top CONN5-9-house NEG 8-POSS1sg) 'The skins which are (lying) on top of the house are not mine' (example adapted from Schapera and van der Merwe 1942:39).

REFERENCES

Baucom 1972; Baumbach 1997; de Blois 1970; Dammann 1957; Donnelly 1990; Fisch 1977; Fivaz 1986; Fleisch 2000; Givón 1970b; Gowlett n.d., 1992, 1997; Grégoire 1979; Haacke and Elderkin 1997; Horton 1949; Maho 1998; Möhlig 1967, 1997; Ohannessian and Kashoki 1978; Ohly 1994; Schadeberg 1990; Schapera and van der Merwe 1942; Sommer 1995; Sommer and Vossen 1992, 1995; Vossen 1988, 1991–2.

CHAPTER TWENTY-NINE

HERERO (R31)

Edward D. Elderkin

1 INTRODUCTION

Herero has come to be used as a cover term for a number of language varieties. It is not known if an adequate linguistic demarcation between Wambo languages (R20) and Herero languages (R30) is possible at all points of their border. Equally the northward extension of Herero languages into Angola is known, but little documented.

The Herero variety spoken in Namibia south of the Etosha Pan seems fairly uniform, though there is some geographical lexical variation. It is this variety which is standard Herero; in it *i̥ is realized as /e/ (except in some nasal environments) and *u̥ as /u/. There are two relevant traditional political alignments, the Herero and the Mbanderu; their language is one. Recent pressure to acknowledge a distinct Mbanderu language in education is based on no convincing linguistic evidence. The variety which Dempwolff (Kavari and Ohly n.d.) recorded in 1904–5 as Mbanderu is clearly merely a Herero with a marked Tswana-like phonology and should not be taken as representative of a Mbanderu dialect at any time in the past without weighty corroborative evidence.

I do not know to what extent the Herero-related varieties north of the Etosha Pan have been influenced by tonal systems similar to those of Ndonga (R22) and Kwanyama (R21), in which high tone seems to have moved to the right and a tonal accent system may be developing; the tonal system described here relates to the southern (standard) variety.

It seems possible that Nkumbi (R14), and language varieties closely related to it, the Wambo dialects (R20), and Herero (R31), all form a unit, both areal and genetic; the nearest language is UMbundu (R11); I keep an open mind on the position of Kwangali (K33), which some scholars place within this grouping.

Superficially, lexical influence from Khoekhoe, German and Afrikaans is evident. More basic influence of Khoisan, in stem formation strategies, has been suggested (Güldemann 1999c), and perhaps more will be uncovered by careful historical investigation. Such work is hindered by the extinction of descendants of probable donor languages.

The number of speakers of Herero is probably approaching a fifth of a million (extrapolating from Grimes 2000). Many seem not to value the language too highly, except in traditional contexts, believing in the educational and economic advantages of now English, but formerly Afrikaans; the ideal of initial primary education in the language is usually bypassed and only two secondary schools offer it as a full subject in the curriculum. No language other than English has any official status in the Namibian constitution.

1.1 Sources

The major sources consulted are Hahn (1857), Volschenk (1968), Booysen (1982), and for vocabulary, Viljoen and Kamupingene (1983), whose glosses I have sometimes used without checking. Much of my field work was done with the help of Ms Jejamaije Mujoro, whom I thank.

1.2 Terminology

A 'root' is a presumed morpheme which is not found used as a stem in its own right. So, despite the existence of *-sèkàm-* vst 'become standing' and *-sèká* nst 3 'height', there is no known verb stem *-sèk-*. A 'stem' may consist of one or more morphemes: thus in *òmùndù* 'person', *-ndù* is the stem; in *òmùvérándú*, *-vérándú* is the stem, which consists of three morphemes (*-vêr-* vst 'be ill', *-a* 'default vowel', and *-ndù*).

Prefixes showing class have been grouped into two systems, 'Nominal Prefixes' and 'General Prefixes'. A 'nominal' is a word which shows a class by using a nominal prefix. An 'adnominal' is a word which shows a class by using a general prefix.

1.3 Orthographies and representation

Two orthographies are in use, the official orthography, Orthography No. 3 (Departement van Nasionale Opvoeding 1983), sanctioned by the educational authorities and therefore imposed in schools, and the orthography used in the *New Era*, a government newspaper which appears twice a week; this latter orthography continues earlier traditions, not using the letter *w* and using *j* for *y*.

Orthography No. 3 is disjunctive, but inconsistently so, and is inconsistent in the spelling of some nominal prefixes. The *New Era* orthography however uses correct word division (derived from linguistic intuition), except in a few cases often related to an unwillingness to use capital letters within words: *o Namibia* becomes two orthographic words. For example, the *New Era* has:

(1)   *kumavevanga*
      'where they want'

The official orthography, in its eurocentric way, wishes this to be three words, *ku* (where), *mave* (they), *vanga* (want). (For analysis see (27).)

A majority of Herero speakers prefer a traditional (*New Era*) orthography to the official one; each orthography could be developed to form the basis of a coherent writing system.

The representation of Herero used here is neither of these orthographies, nor a phonological transcription (because it uses letters of an alphabet and not phonetic symbols used phonologically), although it is in a consistent relationship with a phonological transcription. The correlation between the letters and letter groups of the representation used here and their usual phonetic realization, in terms of IPA symbols, is set out in table 29.1.

TABLE 29.1: CORRELATION BETWEEN IPA LETTERS AND THE LETTER GROUPS OF THE REPRESENTATION OF HERERO USED HERE

IPA						This representation, based on Orthography No. 3				
[	θ				h		s			h
	p	t̪	t	ç	k		p	t̪	t	tj	k
	ᵐb	ⁿd̪	ⁿd	ⁿdʐ	ⁿg		mb	nd̪	nd	ndj	ng
	m	n̪	n	ɲ			m	n̪	n	ny	
	v	ð	ɾ				v	z	r		
	w		j		]		w		y		

In the north of the Herero-speaking area, the main realization of *tj* is [tɕ]; where, elsewhere, the realization of *tj* is now [ç], the realization of *ty* and *ndy* is likely to be [tɕ] and [ⁿdʑ] respectively. The vowels *e* and *o* are nearer to close-mid than to open-mid. In some speakers, the alveolar column seems to have a slightly retroflex articulation.

2 PHONOLOGY

2.1 Segmentals

Syllable structure is:
  $(C_1)(C_2)V$

TABLE 29.2: SYLLABLE STRUCTURE OF HERERO

			I	II	III	IV	V	VI	VII
C_1	voiceless	fricatives			s				h
		plosives	p	ṭ	t	tj	k		
	voiced	prenasalized plosives	mb	nḍ	nd	ndj	ng		
		nasals	m	ṇ	n	ny			
		fricatives/tap	v	z	r				
C_2		semi-vowels				y		w	
V		close				i		u	
		mid close				e		o	
		open					a		

2.1.1 Restrictions

y is only found after those C_1 in table 29.2, columns I, III and VII (but *sy*, [θj], occurs, so *s* is placed in column III above); however, the sequence *n + y* does not occur (*ny* is one unit). *w* does not follow those C_1 in column II (though this restriction is in the process of being broken down, partly because of *-w-* passive).

2.1.2 Elision

In normal use of the language, where one word ends in a vowel (as it must), and the following word begins with a vowel, the word final vowel is elided and only the vowel initial in the following word is heard.

  (2)   *tw-a-mun-u o-ngombo*
       twamunongombo
       'we saw a goat'

In this way, an utterance will have fewer syllables than the total of syllables in its component words in isolation.

Elided vowels are here written subscript.

  (3)   *twamun_u ongombo*

Although the vowel is elided, the tone of the elided vowel is retained wherever possible.

In the morphophonology, underlying *y* and *w* are frequently lost in the environment *a–a*, and always where the distinction between the presence and absence of *w* or *y* is not made phonologically (between vowels: for *w*, adjacent to a close back vowel, and for *y*, adjacent to a close front vowel).

(4)   *o-kà-àṭù* 12/14   'small bag'   Stem: *-yàṭù ò-n-djàṭù* 9/10 'bag'

2.2 Tone

There are two tonal values, High, ´, and Low, `. Each syllable is associated with either a H or a L, or a sequence of H and L; a syllable is never found associated with the sequence LH, although the sequence ^{2}H^{1}H (which gives a phonetically rising tone, as would LH) can be heard. (The prefixed superscript numbers relate to tone keys, described next.)

2.2.1 Tone keys (Elderkin 1999)

The tones of certain sequences of syllables are heard as realized either in a higher or a lower pitch range. Sequences of syllables in the higher pitch range are said to be in Key 1; parts of the utterance in the lower pitch range are in Key 2. The following example illustrates this. Superscript figures indicate the key of the following syllables.

(5)

^{2}*ò-mù-hóná* ^{1}*w-é-ndjì-mún-ú* ^{2}*ò-mù-hóná* ^{1}*w-è-ndjì-mún-à*
'the chief saw me'   'the chief saw me'

A low tone in Key 1 has the same phonetic pitch as a high tone in Key 2 when the former is between two highs in Key 1, or when it immediately follows a high in Key 2. Otherwise a low tone in Key 1 has the same pitch as a low tone in Key 2.

A sequence of syllables which is heard in Key 1 often corresponds to a word, plus the beginning of the following word. However, there are words in which the key changes.

(6) ^{1}*má-tú-*^{2}*mún-ú*
'we see'

When a word finishes in Key 1 and another word which 'should' be in Key 2 follows, there are two possibilities.

The first possibility is that there is a temporary maintenance of Key 1 at the beginning of the following word which manifests itself in the raising of one, or if high tone spread is allowed, two low tone syllables to the pitch level of Key 1 high, often with a pitch fall on the last of these.

(7)

^{1}*v-á-mún-*`$_u$ $^{1(<2)}$*o-zó-ngómbè*      $^1$*v-á-mún-*`$_u$ $^{1(<2)}$*o-ngómbè*
'they saw the cows'   'they saw the cow'

^{1}*v-à-mún-*`$_a$ $^{1(<2)}$*o-ndjárà*   *-ngòmbè* 9/10 cow
'they felt hunger'   *-ndjàrà* 9/10 hunger

The verb which causes this effect may be Ø segmentally, being merely a specification of a low tone in Key 1. The segmentally Ø verb is a present copula. This form is also used as the citation form for nominals.

(8)

$^{1\,'1(<2)}$*o-zó-ngómbè*
'it's cows'

The second possibility is that there is no such temporary maintenance of Key 1, but an immediate drop to Key 2.

(9)

^{1}*v-à-ṭ'-*$_a$↓^{2}*o-ndjàrà*
'they died of hunger'

Imperative verbs are subject to such an absence of key maintenance.

As has been illustrated, the verb of a main clause is heard in Key 1. Where the verb itself contains a change of key, and therefore does not finish in Key 1, key maintenance in the next constituent is not heard.

(10)

^{1}*má-vé-*^{2}*mún-*$_u'$ ^{2}*o-zò-ngòmbè*
'they see the cows'

2.2.2 Downstep

Within sequences, both in Key 1 and in Key 2, a H may appear downstepped.

(11)

^{1}*v-à-zé*$^!$*p-á* ^{1}*v-à-zé*$^!$*p-*$_a'$ $^{1(<2)}$*o-zó-ngómbè*
'they killed'   'they killed cows'

Key maintenance in the second example demonstrates that the $^!$*pá* cannot be analysed as ^{2}*pá*, that is, in Key 2.

2.2.3 Transposition

Where a verb finishing in Key 1 is transposed to Key 2, the phenomenon of key maintenance is retained in the transposition.

(12)

^{2}ò-và-ndù $^{2\,<\,1}$m-b-á-mún-$_u^{\backslash}$ ^{2}o-zó-ngómbè
'the people who saw cows'

^{2}ò-và-ndù $^{2\,<\,1}$m-b-â-zé$^|$p-$_a^{\prime}$ ^{2}o-zó-ngómbè
'the people who killed cows'

^{2}èṭè ^{2}m-b-ú$^{2\,<\,1}$má-tú-^{2} zèp-$_a^{\prime}$ ^{2}o-zò-ngòmbè
'we, the people who kill cows'

3 INFLECTIONAL MORPHOLOGY

Word categories are defined by the structure of Herero and not by reference to similarly named categories in other languages.

3.1 Proper nouns

Proper nouns consist of a stem only, which may be complex. A pluralizing morpheme, òò-, may precede the stem; the whole refers to a group of like individuals, of which the referent of the stem is one. It is the fact of the possibility of this òò- that allows the morphological categorization of proper nouns. (Agreement for proper nouns is identical to that for nouns of Gender 1/2, irrespective of human/non-human status, although there may be doubt in a speaker's mind where there is an incorporated nominal prefix and no animate reference, as with the second example in (13).)

(13)   òò-ìnà   'his/her mother and the others with her'
       kàrìónà   'little finger'

Place names are not proper nouns; they are nominals, and may have a plural form to indicate 'the general area of ...':

(14)   ò-vì-néné   'the general area of Otjinene'

3.2 Nominals

A nominal shows class by using a nominal prefix. The structure of a nominal is:

   (Initial Vowel) + Nominal Prefix + Nominal Stem

(15)   o-mu-tímá
       IV-3-heart
       'heart'

There are two possibilities for the initial vowel. In the first, and usual, it has the form *o*, except when the following nominal prefix is the Ø of class 5, when it is *e*.

The second possibility is that the initial vowel is *i-*. Where the initial vowel is *i-*, the nominal prefix for class 5 is *ri-*, but otherwise the nominal prefix has its basic form. Forms with *i-* as the initial vowel are used in exclamations, both as such and as questioning, but are less frequent than is implied by Hahn (1857); forms with *o-* seem to be replacing them.

(16) *í-ngéàmà*
      iv-lion
      'It's a lion!'

The initial vowel is usually present. It is absent in a locative nominal, that is a nominal which is the first word in the structure:

   Nominal Prefix (Locative) + NP

A nominal prefix (locative) is of class 16, 17 or 18, for example:

(17) *mòméá òmàkòtò*
      mu-o-ma-'yá
      18-iv-6-water iv-6-deep
      'in deep water'

Other places where an Initial Vowel is absent are detailed in §5.1.
   The basic forms of the nominal prefix are:

1	3	5	7	9	11	12	15	16	17	18
mu	*mu*	Ø	*tji*	*ɴ*	*ru*	*ka*	*ku*	*pa*	*ku*	*mu*

2	4	6	8	10	13	14
va	*mi*	*ma*	*vi*	*zoɴ*	*tu*	*u*

ɴ in Gender 9/10 is used as the representation for a nasal homorganic to a following consonant. (An underlying segment ɴ appears also in the demonstrative morpheme and in an allomorph of the general prefix (oblique), 1Sg (*-ndji-*), used in a pleading sense.) It is deleted before a following morpheme with an underlying initial voiceless fricative (i.e. *s* and *h*, not *tj*), an initial nasal, or an initial prenasalized plosive. In all other positions it appears as a short nasal segment, homorganic to the following consonant and together with it forming one phonological unit, (except ɴ + *w*, where *mbw* is two phonological units).

	voiceless	plosives	p	ṭ	t	tj	k	
	voiced	fricatives/tap/semivowels	v	z	r	y	|g|	w
give:	voiced	prenasalized plosives	mb	nḍ	nd	ndj	ng	mbw

(18) *òmbwá*
      ò-ɴ-wá -wá ᴀꜱᴛ
      'good (9)'

      òmbé
      ò-ɴ-pé -pé ᴀꜱᴛ
      'new (9)'

Nominal stems are of two types, noun stems and adjective stems.
   Noun stems are associated with an intrinsic gender, which determines the choice of nominal prefixes showing singular and plural. Genders are here referred to by the

numbers of the nominal prefixes, in the sequence singular/plural; (e.g. *-ndù* 1/2 'person'; *-tá* 14/14 'bow'). Some noun stems do not allow the singular/plural choice (e.g. *-'yá* /6 'water'). The following genders have been noted.

1/2, 3/4, 5/6, 7/8, 9/10, 11/10, 11/13, 12/14, 14/14, 15/6

The nominal prefix of the singular is sometimes found incorporated into the stem used in the plural (see §4.1.1).

Noun stems and proper nouns may be used as stems in non-intrinsic genders; in principle, the prefixes of the intrinsic gender are not used, and are replaced by the prefixes of the non-intrinsic gender. When so used, there is an additional element of meaning, which can be pejorative, as follows:

(19) 5/6   *è-ndù*   'large'
      7/8   *ò-tjì-ndù*   'large'
      12/14 *ò-kà-ndù*   'small'
      11/13 *ò-rù-ndù*   'thin and long'

Adjective stems are not associated with a gender, and may therefore in principle be found preceded by a Nominal prefix of any class.

(20) *òndè*
      ò-ɴ-dè
      'long (9)'

      ò-và-wá
      'good (1)'

Some nominal forms always occur without initial vowel; many of these have sentence functions which are not typically nominal: *mùvyú* 'nine', *rùkúrú* 'earlier', *tjìnéné* 'a lot'.

3.3 Adnominals

Adnominals use a general prefix to show class. The forms of the general prefix are:

	1	3	5	7	9	11	12	15	16	17	18
Basic	*gu*	*vu*	*ri*	*tji*	*yi*	*ru*	*ka*	*ku*	*pa*	*ku*	*mu*
Usual	*u*	*u*	*ri*	*tji*	*i*	*ru*	*ke*	*ku*	*pe*	*ku*	*mu*

	2	4	6	8	10	13	14
Basic	*va*	*vi*	*ga*	*vi*	*za*	*tu*	*vu*
Usual	*ve*	*vi*	*e*	*vi*	*ze*	*tu*	*u*

The basic forms are only found in demonstratives; elsewhere, general prefixes with *a* have instead *e*. Class 6 usually has *ye*, but forms with an initial *w* are found. (However, *-ne* 'four' takes *va-* and *ya-* in classes 2 and 6.) Verbs are not here classified as adnominals, but as a separate word category.

The overall structure for an adnominal is:

(Initial Vowel) + General Prefix + Adnominal Stem

3.3.1 Simple adnominal stems

Relatively few adnominal stems are of a single morpheme, e.g.: *-íní* 'self, owner'; *-íngí* 'many'; *-ɲé* 'who?, what?'; *-ngapi* 'how many?'. A nominal prefix is used instead of the general prefix, with *-íní* in classes 1 and 3, and with *-íngí* in class 6.

(21) *ò-zò-ngòmbè z-éngí*
'many cows'

ò-mà-mbò m-éngí
'many books'

ò-mù-tí ò-mw-íní
'the tree itself'

3.3.2 Numerals

Numerals have the following structure:

General Prefix + Numeral Stem

except that there is no general prefix in class 10, where the nominal prefix of class 9 is incorporated into the stem.

(22) *ò-và-hóná vé-várì*
'two chiefs'

ò-zò-ngòrá mbárì
'two whips'

Only the numbers one to five are morphologically numerals.

3.3.3. -hè 'all'

The stem *-hè* 'all' is used with an extra vowel, *à-*, before the general prefix. This is, however, not an initial vowel. With *-hè*, first and second person plural general prefix forms are available:

(23) *à-vé-hè*
'all of them (2)'

à-tú-hè
'all of us (1Pl)'

Also used with the extra vowel before the general prefix is the derived stem:

Low Tone + Numeral Stem

(24) *ò-và-ndù àvêvárì*
      à-vé-`-várì
      à-2-all-two
'both the people (2)'

àzêndátú
à-zé-`-
'all the three (10)'

The low tone in the stem could be taken as an allomorph of *-hè* 'all'.

3.3.4 Demonstratives

Demonstratives are characterized by the morpheme ǹ appearing immediately before the general prefix.

(Initial Vowel) + ǹ + General Prefix + Demonstrative Stem

Demonstrative stems are:

-í   'this'
-íná   'that'
-íní   'that there'
-ó   'the'

and the compound:

-ínó- -í   'this here now'

With demonstratives, the initial vowel is *i-*, which carries the high tone underlyingly associated with ꞥ. Demonstratives may appear seemingly cliticized to nominal and adnominal categories; in this use they do not have an initial vowel. When a monosyllabic demonstrative is so used, the high tone of the ꞥ is heard on the preceding syllable, and a low tone on this preceding syllable is reassociated to the previous syllable. (This does not apply to ꞥ used with relatives.)

The forms given for demonstrative stems are underlying forms and rules of a non-general nature apply to produce the surface forms; the same is true of forms with *-ú-* which appear with relatives (see §3.3.5).

It is only in demonstratives, after ꞥ, that the consonant in the general prefixes *gu, vu, ga* and *yi* is realized; otherwise it is zero.

(25)   *ò-mù-ndú-n-gw-í*
        ò-mù-ndù- ꞥ -gu-i
        'this person'

        íngwí
        IV -ꞥ-gu-í
        'this one (1)'

        àzêhéndá
        à-10(zé)-hè-ꞥ-10(zá)
        'all those (10)'

        mòméá   òmàkòtò   mwíná
                                ꞥ-18-íná
        'in the deep water there'

        mòméá   òmàkòtò   ngéná
                                      ꞥ-6(ga)-íná
        'in that deep water'

        ndínóndí
        ꞥ-5-ínó-ꞥ-5-í
        'today'

3.3.5 Relative words

The presence of ꞥ + general prefix shows that the relative word is morphologically a sub-class of the demonstrative. There are two possibilities.

Where a verb begins with a general prefix which agrees with the antecedent noun, the following formula constitutes a relative word:

ꞥ + Verb

For example,

(26)   *ngwéérè*   *wéérè*
      ɴ̀-gu-é-Ø-ér-è   's/he came'   Ø < -i- vst 'come'
      's/he who came'

The second possibility is:

     ɴ̀ + General Prefix + *ú* + Verb

(27)   *kúmávévángà*   *mávévángà*
      ɴ̀-ku-ú-má-vé-váng-à   'they(vé) want'
      'where they want'

As *ú* is followed by a clause, it looks like a complementizer; I find no other evidence for this interpretation. Other uses of this *ú* are the following structures, where the material after *ú* could be considered a reduced clause:

     ɴ̀ + General Prefix + *ú* + Preposition (nà´) + NP

(28)   *púnáyé*
      ɴ̀-pa-ú-nà´-yé
      'with her/him'

and

     ɴ̀ + General Prefix + *ú* + Pronoun

(29)   *púyé* 'than, at her/him'
      ɴ̀-pa-ú-yé

3.4 Pronouns

3.4.1 Free standing

A pronoun contains no other information except a class, or a person and number. Those containing only person and number information are monomorphemic. When, in predication, they are required to be prefixed by an initial vowel, *o-* is used.

	Sg.	Pl.
1Pers	*àmì*	*èṱè*
2Pers	*òvè*	*èṋè*

(30) ²*àmì* ¹*mé-ká-*²*ròr-à*   ¹*ó-*²*ámí*
      'I went and tried(-ròr-)'   'it's me'

Those containing information as to class have the structure:

     Initial Vowel + General Prefix + *ó*

In all classes the initial vowel is *o-* except in class 1 where it is *e-*; in class 1 also, the sequence General Prefix + *o* is realized as *yé*. When these pronouns follow a verb, they are enclitic, and do not take an initial vowel:

(31)   *éyé*
      's/he'

¹*w-á-térék-é-*²*r-ó*
1-TAM-cook-FV-11-ó
's/he cooked it'

3.4.2 Genitive

Where a pronoun constitutes the NP in a genitive construction (cf. §5.2), it is not a word, but is bound. Where the genitive preposition in the form *-á-* is not separately quoted in the tables following, it is one formative with the pronoun:

	Sg.	Pl.
1Pers	*-á-ndjè*	*-étù*
2Pers	*-óè*	*-éṇù*

Otherwise, the forms are the usual general prefix + *o*; the forms for class 1 and class 2 are:

	1	2
3Pers	*-é*	*-á-ò*

(32)   *è-ná r-é*
       'his/her name'

       ò-zò-ndjúó z-á-ò
       'their houses'

3.5 Verbs

The morphology of the verb is treated in three subsections. First, the segmental structure of the core of the affirmative indicative verb is described. Second, formatives within the verbal word but outside the core are treated. A third section deals cursorily with forms other than affirmative indicative. The derivational morphology of the verb stem is covered in §4.2.3.

3.5.1 The verb core

3.5.1.1 Segmental morphology

The verb core contains a verb stem and consists of maximally the following structure in terms of formative classes in sequence:

General Prefix (Subject)	Pre-stem TA Marker	*tjí*	*kà*	General Prefix (Oblique)	Verb Stem	Post-stem TA Marker	Passive	Final Vowel

In verbs, the general prefix series has the following forms for persons and gender 1/2:

	Subject		Oblique	
	Sg./1	Pl./2	Sg./1	Pl./2
1Pers	*-mbì-*	*-tù-*	*-ndji-*	*-tu-*
2Pers	*-ù-*	*-mù-*	*-ku-*	*-mu-*
3Pers	*-ú-*	*-vé-*	*-mu-*	*-ve-*

The general prefix (oblique) series has the extra member *-ri-*, reflexive.

-tji- indicates that referent of the verb happens before something else, *-kà-* that it happens after a move or an interval.

In order to keep the verb stem integral, passive (*-w-*) is best considered to be an inflectional category, and not an extension.

The TA markers contain data relevant to tense and aspect. As pre-stem TAM marker, *-á-* and *-à-* are found; there is only one post-stem TAM marker, and that is *-er-*: it occurs in the affirmative only if a pre-stem TAM marker is also present. The passive *-w-* appears between this *-er-* and the final vowel *-e*, which is determined by *-er-*. The basic segmental form of the post-stem TA marker is *-er-*. But where the immediately preceding vowel is *i* or *u*, this suffix has the vowel *i* and not *e*; where the immediately preceding consonant is a nasal, this suffix has the consonant *n* and not *r*.

(33) *twámúninè*
    tu-á-mún-er-e
    'we saw'

Only the verb stem is an obligatory constituent of a verb, but the final vowel is not required only in a small number of verbs, and that only in forms which seem, in analysis, as if they should have no suffix after the stem and are here referred to as bare forms. But only verb stems of the form -CV- actually have no suffix.

(34) *w-á-ꞌṱú*
    's/he died'

Many other verb stems suffix a vowel of the same quality as the last vowel in the stem, called here a harmonic vowel (hv).

(35) *¹mé-²tón-ó*
    'I hit'

Some harmonic vowels are exceptional, most frequently examples of *i* when *e* is the last vowel in the stem, or vice versa.

(36) *¹mb-é-mù-ṱík-è*
    'I accompanied her'

Most other verb stems are incapable of taking a harmonic vowel or of appearing without a final vowel; they therefore use the default vowel.

(37) *¹mé-²zúng-á*
    'I mix'

Where the last vowel in the stem is *-a-*, either *-à-* or *-â-*, tonal phenomena can be used to establish whether the following *-a* is the default vowel or the harmonic vowel; I did not find a way of making this distinction with stems with *-á-*.

The choices at final vowel for affirmative indicative verbs are

    -e   (demanded by the presence of the post-stem TA marker)
    -hv harmonic vowel (see above)
    -a   default vowel (dv)
    zero

(38) *mb-á-pàmúk-á*
    1Sg.-TAM-hatch-FV
    'I've hatched out'

w-à-kùp-ír-w-é
1-TAM-marry-TAM-passive-FV
'she was married (and is no longer married)'

3.5.1.2 Paradigms

The three following choices:

(i)   Post-stem TA marker: present   absent
(ii)   Pre-stem TA marker: present   absent
(iii) Pre-stem TA marker: high toned low toned
      and/or final vowel: bare form default vowel

determine the paradigmatic structure of verb morphology, illustrated below with the verb stem *-mún-* VST 'see', with 1Pl *tu-* as the general prefix (subject).

	No Post-stem TA marker		Post-stem TA marker	
	Pre-stem TA marker	No pre-stem TA marker	Pre-stem TA marker	No pre-stem TA marker
High-toned `à- &/or bare form	*twámunu*	*-tumunu*	*twámunine*	*-tumunine*
Low-toned -à- &/or default vowel	*twàmuna*	*tumuna*	*twàmunine*	*-tumunine*

The semantic correlations of the paradigms have not been adequately worked out. *-à-* seems to involve a more remote past, and can indicate both the initiation and the progress of the referent to an end, whereas *-á-* seems to be more related to a commencement, rather than a progression and an ending. It is not yet clear whether a full tonal analysis should prefer to take *-á-* as the underlying form of both *-á-* and *-à-*, the latter being the result of the association of an unassociated low tone, or if automatic generation of a H is required after an underlying L. The post-stem TA marker seems to relate to the fact that something is finished, with *-à-*, the whole event, beginning, middle and end, but with *-á-*, it seems to relate to the fact that the beginning of the event has finished.

(39)   *w-à-póṭúpár-ér-è*
      's/he was blind (but is now no longer blind)'

      w-á-pòṭúpár-ér-è
      's/he has become blind (but the degree of future permanency of this situation is not indicated)'

3.5.2 *Peripherals of the verb word*

The hyphen in front of three of the forms quoted in the table of verb paradigms above indicates that those forms cannot appear as words without additional matter (bound adverbials, negative), preceding the general prefix (subject). With the paradigm *-tumunu* several bound adverbials are possible:

má-   present
máà- probable future

àmá-	simultaneous
áà-	past, but applies no longer
à-	consecutive/narrative

With the first three, there is a transposition to Key 2 after the bound adverbial, (as in (6)); with the others, there is no such transposition.

(40)   [1]*à-vé-úndj-ù*
　　　 BAdv-2-wait-FV
　　　 'and they waited'

　　　 [1]*áàtúnyándá*
　　　 BAdv-2Pl-play-FV
　　　 'we played, (but don't now)'

Some pronominal and interrogative forms (e.g. *-pí* 'which?') which appear after the verb core are enclitic (see (31)).

3.5.3   Other forms

The general prefix (subject) series used in the subjunctive has an innovation for class 1, *ma-*. This is presumably by analogy and back formation from the bound adverbial used for the present, *má-*. Subjunctive forms have *-e* as final vowel, which is not compatible with either of the TA markers (see (77)).

The imperative has the default vowel in the singular, and in the plural *-é(y)é*; the negative imperative uses a bound adverbial (*á-*) and the bare form.

(41)   *tòn-á*
　　　 'hit!'

　　　 [1]*kámbúr-é²é*
　　　 'catch hold! (Pl.)'

　　　 [1]*ó-²tjít-í* (*ó < á + ù* 2Sg.)
　　　 'don't do' (colloquially: 'you don't say!')

The negative morpheme is *ka-*, initial in the verb, or *-ha-*, preceding the general prefix (oblique), if present, according to paradigm.

(42)   [1]*kà-máà-²tú-kà-nyánd-á*
　　　 NEG-BAdv-1P.-kà-play-FV
　　　 'we won't go and play'

　　　 [2]*n-gú-há-tjíw-á* [2]*è-ráká*
　　　 'who does not know (-hà-tjíw-) the language'

　　　 [1]*à-tú-há-púnd-ù*
　　　 BAdv-1Pl-NEG-dance-FV
　　　 'and we didn't dance'

Hortative type forms use an initial *nga-*.

(43)   *ngà-tú-hóng-è*
　　　 'let's teach'

The post-stem TA marker only appears without a pre-stem TA marker in negative forms; the two forms differ tonally. Space has not allowed any treatment of verbal tone here. However, it can be noted that under certain conditions, high tone spreads: the stem of the first example in (40) is -ùndj- VST 'wait' and of the third example in (42) is -pùnd- VST 'dance'.

The question of Herero verb forms has not yet been adequately handled. Different authorities give different inventories of forms, as noted in Fleisch (1995), and confusion is compounded when constructions with class 15 nominalizations of verb stems to the right of a finite verb, identified as an auxiliary, have been taken as tense/aspect/mood paradigms. The treatment of the verb core in §3.5.1 above is a minimal statement, the degree to which bound adverbials are integrated into a system will depend on the orientation and prejudices of the grammarian.

4 LEXICON

4.1 Simple stems

4.1.1 Noun stems

With nominal stems with two syllables, all sequences of H and L occur.

(44) -gómbó   'goat'
      -húndjù   'fish'
      -bùngú   'hyena'
      -ngòmbè   'cow'

But stems with HL (of which there are few), fall into two classes. In one, the L always remains L; in the other, the L may be raised to H, e.g. when H in Key 1 follows.

(45) ²ò-ndjékè ¹y-á-ték-á   'the jack is broken'   òndjékè   'jack'
      ²ò-mw-átjé ¹w-á-ì   'the child went'   òmwátjè   'child'

The majority of noun stems begin with a vowel or with an acceptable syllable initial consonant or consonant cluster. A few must be analyzed as beginning with a tonal specification followed by an acceptable syllable initial consonant or consonant cluster (no example of a tonal specification followed by a vowel has yet been found). A few noun stems have a non-predictable allomorphy for singular and plural forms.

(46) -hò -'hó   5/6 'eye'
      -átjè -nátjè   1/2 'child'

A few, including -'hó above, show -me- and not -ma- as the nominal prefix of class 6.

(47) -'yá   /6 'water' (òméá)

Noun stems used in an non intrinsic gender have prefixes other than those of the intrinsic gender of the noun stem.

(48) ò-n-dànà   ò-kà-tànà   'calf' (-tànà 9/10)
      ò-và-nátjè   ò-kà-nátjè   'child'

It happens that with some genders, the singular prefix of the intrinsic gender is incorporated into the stem of a noun in a non-intrinsic gender. Nouns intrinsically in gender

11/13 have in these forms a number-sensitive allomorphy in the stem, the prefix of class 11 is incorporated in the singular and that of class 13 in the plural.

(49) ò-kà-mùtímá   ò-ù-mùtímá   'small heart'   (-tímá 3/4)
      ò-tjì-rùtúó   ò-vì-tùtúó   'large spoon'   (-túó 11/13)

Nouns intrinsically in gender 9/10 also show uncertainty as to the form of the stem. Although the usual analysis, and the historically appropriate analysis, is to consider the prenasalization, ᴎ, (part of) the prefix, the falling together of voiceless prenasalized plosives and voiced prenasalized plosives has obliterated the knowledge of the voicing of the historically correct stem-initial consonant. As stems with initial underlying fricatives and nasals delete the underlying prefix, the tendency is to generalize a zero prefix and to consider that the stem begins with a prenasalized consonant. For example, if a class 12 non intrinsic form of òndùkwá 'churning calabash' is required, a speaker is likely to produce òkàzùkwá and then wonder if òkàndùkwá were more appropriate. The form *òkàtùkwá does not come to mind, although the historically underlying form is derived from -tùk- vst 'swing backwards and forwards'. Stem forms with an initial prenasalized consonant exist in other intrinsic genders; this reanalysis of the nasal in the prefix for class 9 and class 10 has produced many stems with an initial prenasalized consonant in the competence of many speakers. Usually only forms with the voiced non-prenasalized consonant or the voiced prenasalized consonant exist, but many nouns do retain the original situation, òkàtànà 'calf'; see (48).

(50) òndjàtù   'bag'   ò-kà-àtù or ò-kà-ndjàtù
      òmbwá   'dog'   ò-kà-wá or ò-kà-mbwá

The fact that zoᴎ- is used before adjective stems, which do not show incorporation of the nominal prefix into the stem, disallows the analysis of ᴎ as an incorporated prefix in adjective stems.

In the derivation of stems, an earlier situation, without incorporation of ᴎ, is occasionally noted.

(51) -ndúòmbè 9/10 'ox'   cf. -twézù AST 'male, big'   *-gòmbè 9/10 'cow'
                                                        now: -ngòmbè
      -kéàmà 9/10 'lion'   -ké AST 'what kind of'   *-yàmà 9/10 'animal'
                                                        now: -nyàmà 9/10 'meat'

4.1.2 Verb stems

With verb stems having one vowel and a final consonant, there are three underlying tonal possibilities.

(52) -tòn- vst 'hit'
      -mún- vst 'see'
      -vêr- vst 'be ill'

The diacritic ˆ indicates a high tone associated with the vowel, but which does not spread onto the following syllable. So the nominalizations of the above forms are: okutònà, okumúná and okuvérà. A similar distinction is found with longer verb stems.

Pronouns suffixed to verbs are best analyzed as clitics, i.e. they are part of the morphological word. However, they are phonologically the bearers of the maintained key.

(53)   ¹*mb-á-vátér-é²yé*   'I helped him'
       ¹*mb-á-vátér-éyé* ²*tjì-néné*   'I helped him a lot'
       (Key 1 has not been maintained on *tjìnéné*)

In some verbs, where the verb stem and the suffixed locative pronoun together can be considered to form one lexical item, there has been a reanalysis of the stem when the post-stem TA marker has to be added.

(54)   -*váz*-   'arrive'
       -*váz-mo*   'find'
       ¹*tw-é-tjì-váz-á-²mó*   'we've found it (7)'
       ¹*tw-è-tjí-vázám-én-é*   'we found it'
       tu-à-tjí-vázám₆-ér-e

4.2 Derivation

Many lexical items consist of stems with more than one morpheme, and some include word boundaries. Some methods of derivation listed below can be considered to be productive and not applicable to restricted instances only; not all the stem formations listed in Haacke (1985) are acceptable to all informants.

4.2.1 Proper nouns

No statement can be made about the form of proper noun stems, except that anything goes. In addition to surnames and Christian names, personal names can be sentences, e.g. ²*òmàhózè* ¹*yéámàié* ¹*kàénòmbátèrò* 'what's the use of tears, they don't help', and the owner may use one or other of the words or parts of words of a longer name as a shorter name. So *yeamaie* (*Jejamaije*) or, with the usual reanalysis by speakers of the preposition *nà*'- as a verb, giving the 'words' *kaena ombatero*, and then segmenting it after the *a* has been elided, *kaeno* (*Kaeno*). Common nouns without the initial vowel can be used as proper nouns, (e.g. *mítìrì* 'Teacher'; *kàvàndjé* 'Mr Jackal'). And there is a number of unanalysable stems, often address forms for relations, which belong to this category, e.g. *inà* 'his/her mother'.

4.2.2 Noun stems

A few monomorphemic stems might be considered historically to be derived by reanalysis. If the stem of *ombépó* 9/10 'wind' is considered to be derived by suffixation from the verb stem -*pép*- VST 'blow', then -*vépó* 3/4 'wind' is a back-formation. *òndjúpá*, which has a historical stem *-*cúpà*, similarly gives *òkàyúpá* 'pear'. In these examples, the synchronic analysis should give -*vépó* and -*yúpá* as the stems.

However, there are many ways of forming nominal stems, of which the more important are listed below.

    (a)   Without Verb Stem

    (i)   Adjective Stem + Noun Stem

(55)   *òtjìwáròngò* (place name)   -*wá* AST 'good'   -*ròngò* 7/8 'place'
       omuníngàndú 'lucky person'   -*níngà* AST 'lucky'   -*ndù* 1/2 'person'
       òmùkéndù 'what sort of person?' -*ké* AST 'what kind of' -*ndù* 1/2 'person'

    (ii)   Noun Stem + Noun Stem

(56)   *-t̜úkúhùkà* 5/6 'dawn'   *-t̜úkú* 14 'night'   *-húkà* 3/4 'morning'
       -kùvíkòzè 7/8 'eagle'   *-ngùví* 9/10 'vulture'   *-kózé* 11/13 'hawk'
       -ngàràngòmbè 9/10 'eland'   *-ngàrà* 9/10 'flower'   *-ngòmbè* 9/10 'cow'

    (iii)   Noun Stem + Noun

(57)   *-kéàmàmùndù* 7/8 'werlion'   *-kéàmà* 9/10 'lion'   *-ndù* 1/2 'person'

    (iv)   Preposition + NP

The preposition in *nà-*; it is not associated with a following high tone. No constituent of the NP has an initial vowel. The noun appears first.

(58)   *-nàmàsà àéhè* 1/2 'the Almighty'   *-sà* /6 'strength'   *-hè* AdnSt 'all'
       -nàmbàngòmbì AST 'malevolent'   *-mbàngò* 9/10 'desire'   *-ví* AST 'bad'
       -nàùví AST 'evil'   *-ví* AST 'bad'
       -nàvìkóróvíné AST 'square'   *-kóró* 5/6 'side'   *-né* Num 'four'
       -nàzònd̜érá AST 'nervous, timid'   *-nd̜érá* 9/10 'bird'

Negative forms have the same structure preceded by *hí-*:

(59)   *-hínàtjìpò* AST 'without defect'   *-pò* 7/8 'defect'

    (v)   Noun Stem + Genitive

Lexical items can have a genitive construction. Here a noun stem contains a word boundary and is number-sensitive.

(60)   *-só ròmút̜átì* 5/6 'tree snake'   *-só* 5/6 'leaf'   *-t̜átì* 3/4 'mopane sp.'

    (vi)   Noun Stem + suffix

The only suffix is the diminutive, *-ona*.

(61)   *-kázónà* 1/2 'girl'
       -húngùrívòná 12/14 'chick (of domestic hen)'
       -mbóná 9/10 'small dog, puppy'

There is also a feminine association with this suffix:

(62)   *-sáóná* AST 'female red'
       -sázú AST 'male red'

but there is no such parallel regularity in the use of *-zu*.

    (vii)   Unknown

There are doubtless noun stems of more than one morpheme whose components are unretrievable, and there are those which are only recognized by the linguist as such and not by the speaker. One such is:

(63)   *-syótì* 9/10 'kidney'

This form is partly explained by comparing cognate forms from the Wambo dialect, for example, *oshitishanathigo*. The expected form for 'kidney', *-syó*, is only found in *kòzòsyó* 'on all sides'.

(b)   Containing a Verb Stem

'Verb stem' here can include general prefix (oblique), and passive.

(i)   Verb Stem + *e*

(64)   *-kúrúpè* AST 'old'   *-kúrúp-* VST 'become old'
     -nyóné 1/2 'destroyer'   *-nyón-* VST 'waste, destroy'
     -ndjáhé 9/10 'wounded person'   *-jáh-* VST 'shoot'
     -hìngè 1/2 'driver'   *-hìng-* VST 'drive'

With incorporation of general prefix (oblique), giving:

(65)   *-ríkóhé* 7/8 'sponge, soap'   *-kóh-* VST 'wash'

Verb stem + *-i* seems to be an alloform of the preceding morph(s), usually after a dental nasal:

(66)   *-tòṇì* 14/ 'victory'   *-tòṇ-* VST 'be victorious'

Two suffixes are involved, and lexicalization and high tone spread have often obliterated the difference, but occasionally a distinction is kept:

(67)   *-ràmbùkè* AST 'becoming thin'
     -ràmbùké AST 'thin'

(ii)   Verb Stem + *o*

(68)   *-tjàngèrò* 7/8 'blackboard'   *-tjàng-* VST 'write'
     -rárò 7/8 'sleeping mat'   *-râr-* VST 'sleep'

With general prefix (oblique):

(69)   *-rívérèrò* /6 'self regret'   *-vèr-* 'punish'

(iii)   Verb Stem + *u*

There seems to be a form *-ú* suffixed to verb stems and roots; usually a stem form with the suffix *-ur-* or *-uk-* is also found. *-ú* forms a nominal stem. There are unresolved tonal problems with this suffix.

(70)   *-hèngú* 1/2 'critic'   *-hèngùr-* VST 'criticize, find fault'
     -hándú 5/ 'naughtiness'   *-hándúk-* VST 'be naughty'
     -nyèngú /6 'scorn'   *-nyèngùr-* VST 'underestimate'

The stem *-párw-* seems to derive from general prefix 16 *pa-* + *-rwè* 'in another place' but still allows a back formation,

(71)   *-pàrú* 5/ 'wild shooting'   *-párwís-* VST 'err, miss'

and the first syllable of the verb stem has been reinterpreted as a nominal prefix in:

(72)   *-kùtú* 12/14 'sweat'   *-rùkùtùr-* VST 'sweat'

(iv)   Verb Stem + *dv* (+N)

The unmarked nominalization of a verb stem is effected by this construction in class 15.

(73)   *-ndjòrà* 9 'laughter'   *-yòr-* VST 'laugh'
     -pérwà 7/8 'the luck of being given' *-p-* VST 'give'

-pàrwá 12/14 'match' ('vuurhout')	-pàr- vst 'scrape'	
-ríkútjírwà 7/8 'blanket'	-kútjír- vst 'cover'	

In verb stem + *dv* + N the interpreted relation of the N to the verb stem varies, subject, object or other oblique.

(74) Subject

-ryángàvá 3/4 'euclea divinorum'	-rí vst 'eat'	-ngàvá 9/10 'rhinos'

Object

-kóhátjìnyó 3/4 'bluebush'	-kóh- vst 'wash'	-nyó 7/8 'mouth'
-nwámàéré 12 'evening star'	-nú vst 'drink'	-érè /6 'sour milk'

Other

-pósándjòmbó 12/14 'large frog'		-pós- vst 'make a noise'
		-ndjòmbó 9/10 'well'
-t̠àhón̠í 12/14 'hedgehog'	-t̠ú vst 'die'	-hón̠í 9/ 'shyness'
-tárákòkùrè 7/8 'binoculars'	-tár- vst 'watch'	-rè Ast 'far'

Some nominal stems show verb stem + *dv* + noun stem; there may be a connection between the intrinsic gender of the noun stem and that of the whole derived noun stem.

(75)

-vérándù Ast 'ill'	-vér- vst 'be ill'	-ndù 1/2 'person'
-zèmbàtìmà 3/4 'forgetfulness'	-zèmb- vst 'forget'	-tímá 3/4 'heart'

há + verb stem + *dv* gives a negative adjectival stem:

(76)

-hámúníkà Ast 'invisible'	-mún- vst 'see'
-hávérúkà Ast 'incurable'	-vér- vst 'be ill'
-hányándà Ast 'serious'	-nyánd- vst 'play'

4.2.3 Verb stems

   (a) Extensions

Only three extensions are at all productive. They are:

   (i) *-er-* Applied

The underlying form of this extension is *-er-*; it submits to the same morphophonological rules as the post-stem TAM. The applied form is used mainly in two contexts: as a benefactive and where a locative follows (see (105)). The instrumental use is rare.

(77)   ... ²mérìtáréré
   má-rì-tár-ér-é
   1-reflexive-see-APPLIED-SUBJUNCTIVE
   '... so he may see for himself'

   ¹má-ká-²ènd-èr-à ²k-òtjìtí
   BAdv + 1-kà-go-APPLIED-dv 17-stick
   'he walks using a stick'

   (ii) *-is-* Causative

Use of the causative form does not necessarily imply that the subject of the equivalent non-causative sentence is the object of the causative form; the situation is complex.

(78)   -rí vst 'eat'   -rís- vst 'feed'
       -ùngur- vst 'work'   -ùnguris- vst 'use'

    (iii)   -asan-   Reciprocal

(79)   ¹má-vé-²mún-ásán-á
       BAdv-2-see-RECIPROCAL-dv
       'they see (-mún-) each other'

The reciprocal form is not restricted to a strictly reciprocal use. It also indicates simultaneity or togetherness.

Two others, which often form a pair, have sometimes been referred to as semi-productive; they are fairly common, but neither use nor form can be predicted. An *o* is found rather than a *u* where the last vowel of the stem is itself *o*.

    (iv)   -uk-   Stative

(80)   -sèrùk- vst 'become smoothed'
       -kòtòk- vst 'come back'
       -zèmbùrùk- vst 'remember' (cf -zèmb- 'forget')

    (v)   -ur-   Causative, often in relation to (iv)

(81)   -sèrùr- vst 'smooth out something'
       -kòtòr- vst 'bring back'
       -pèngùr- vst 'ignore' (no form in -uk-)

The same form often has separative meaning:

(82)   -tàtùr- vst 'peel off'

A large number of verbs can be interpreted as containing fossilized extensions, either by internal evidence, historical evidence or analogy from both of these. The three most frequent are:

    (vi)   -ar-

(83)   -òngàr- vst 'assemble'   -òng- vst 'collect, gather'
       -zúvàr- vst 'become known, heard'   -zúv-(-zúú) vst 'hear'

    (vii)   -am-

(84)   -hèndàm- vst 'lean, not to be straight'   òhèndí 'askew'
       -ṭútám- vst 'urinate'   -ṭútá /6 'urine'

    (viii)   -ek-

(85)   -pàndèk- vst 'tie, to put bonds on'   -pàndùk- vst 'give birth (humans)'
       -pórèk- vst 'calm s.o. down'   -pór- vst 'get cold'

-ek- seems to be causative. Some examples of -ik- also seem causative:

(86)   -túrík- vst 'load, hang up'   -túrùr- vst 'take down'

But other examples of -ik- seem stative.

(87)   -hàṇìk- vst 'be scattered, separate'   -hàṇ- vst 'divide, to differentiate'

(ix)   Some other fossilized extensions can be seen in:

(88)   *-ryàt-* vst 'step, tread'   *-ryò* 7/8 'leg, hoof, paw'
       -ryàng- vst 'walk about, visit'
       -hàhìz- vst 'lose interest'   *-hàh-* vst 'stop speaking to a person, to throw
                                                 something down'

The only stem with two vowels which has come to my attention and does not seem to
be historically polymorphemic is *-tjókótj-* vst 'bubble up (e.g. of boiling water)' which
might seem onomatopoeic.

   (b)   By derivation

   (i)   Adjective Stem + *-p-*

But few examples:

(89)   *-kúrúp-* vst 'become old'   *-kúrú* AST 'old'
       -rivérìp- vst 'give birth to a first child'   *-vèrì* 7/8 'firstborn'

   (ii)   Adjective Stem + *-par-*

(90)   *-ṇíngápàr-* vst 'become happy'   *-ṇíngàndú* 14/ 'happiness'
       -syónápàr- vst 'become poor'   *-syónà* AST 'poor'

5 PHRASES

5.1 Noun phrases

The preferred position of a noun in an NP is at the beginning. There is more freedom about
the sequence of other constituents; although nominals tend to precede adnominals,
demonstratives may follow either.

A nominal in an NP is used with an initial vowel in all but the following two
cases.

   (i)   When it is the first, or only, constituent in a vocative NP

(91)   [1]*vá-ndù* [2]*ò-và-wá*
       'good people!'

   (ii)   When it is the first constituent in a negated NP used predicatively

(92)   [1]*ká-*[2]*mbó*
       'it's not an ostrich'

       [1]*ó-*[2]*mbó*
       IV-ostrich
       'it's an ostrich'

(Also, within derivation of noun stems, an initial vowel is not used; see, (58).)
Adnominals will usually appear without an initial vowel when they follow a nominal,
or are used without a nominal:

(93)   [2]*z-á-ndjè*   [1]*z-á-pándjár-á*
       10-PREP-1Sg   10-TAM-be lost-FV
       'mine are lost'

However, a genitive may appear with an initial vowel following a nominal with a suffixed demonstrative.

(94)   ²ò-zò-ngòmbé-n-ḏ-á   ò-z-á-ndjè   ¹z-á-pándjár-á
'those cows of mine are lost'

or when a demonstrative is suffixed:

(95)   ²ò-z-â-ndjé-n-ḏá   ¹z-á-pándjár-á
'those of mine are lost'

Where an NP is used in affirmative predication after a segmentally zero verb, an initial vowel must be present. A constituent which is initial in such an NP and which does not already have an initial vowel therefore must prefix one.

(96)   ²à-vé-hè
'them all'

¹á-à-²vé-hè
'that's all of them'

The question of the status of initial vowels (see §3.2) with nominals is interesting. Although there seems to have been a normalization process by which educated speakers believe that the initial vowel should be present, occasional examples of its absence are heard. Too few examples have been recorded to allow any statement of distribution. (In the construction illustrated in (109), its presence is optional.)

5.2 Preposition phrases

A preposition phrase (PP) has the structure

Preposition + NP

Prepositions are proclitics in Herero, and form one word with the first word of the NP.
There are three prepositions in Herero: all need comment.
The genitive preposition, -á´-, only occurs in the genitive construction, which has the structure

General Prefix + Genitive Preposition + NP

that is

General Prefix + PP

The segmental part of genitive preposition is often elided, for example in yòngómbè in the following example, in which òngómbè yándjè is the NP within the PP.

(97)   ò-séngó   yòngómbè   y-á-ndjè
IV-neck   yi-à´-ò-ngòmbè   9-PREP-1Sg.
          9-PREP-IV-cow
          of cow
'my cow's neck'

For forms when the NP within the PP is pronominal, see §3.4.2.
As the general prefix is obligatory in this construction, the genitive preposition never occurs initially in a word.

nà´ 'with' is used as a preposition, and if the following NP is a pronoun, the pronoun has the structure general prefix + *ó*

(98)   *n-ò-ká-tì*
       'with a stick'

       nà-k-ó
       'with it (12)'

i seems to be copular in origin, and sometimes still in use; it shows the agent of a passive, although the agent can be expressed by a bare NP.

(99)   *¹v-à-tó¹n-w-á ¹í-²vàyá*
       'they were hit by Vaja'

       ¹à-vàrék-w—´ₐ   *²-o-và-nátj-´ₑ ²o-và-zàndú*
       BAdv-choose-passive-dv   children   boys
       'she was chosen (by) boys'

Prepositions all have similar tonal properties, exemplified here using the genitive preposition *-à´-*.

Where the syllable following the eliding vowel is associated with a low tone, that syllable will take the high.

(100) *ò-ngòmbè*   *yòmùhóná*
       cow (9)   *yi-à´-òmùhòná*
                    9-PREP-chief(1)
                    'the chief's cow'

Where the following syllable is high, or the first syllable of a proper noun (the tones on which may not perturbed), the preposition takes the high tone and, where possible, the low appears on the previous syllable.

(101) *ò-zò-ngómbò*   *závàyá*
                       ze-à´-Vaja
                       10-PREP-Vaja
                       'Vaja's goats'

In this construction, falling tones may not be produced, therefore the low tone is sometimes lost.

(102) *ò-mi-tí vy-á-vàyá*
       'Vaja's trees'

6 SENTENCES

6.1 Sequence

The basic sequence of constituents is subject verb oblique.

(103) *²tàté ¹w-é-ndjì-tón-ò ¹n-ó-ká-²tí*
       'my father hit me with a stick'

A relative clause is, in principle, introduced by the demonstrative morpheme ꞓ; as this morpheme is the first in a word (see §3.3.5) which includes the subject agreement, any overt NP which is the subject of the verb within the relative clause precedes the *n̂*, that is, the subject appears extraposed to the relative clause strictly defined, but maintaining SVO sequence.

(104)   *òkàtí*   *tàté*   *kéndjìtónò*   *nàkó*
        ò-kà-tí   *tàté*   *n̂-ká-ú-u-á-ndji-tòn-o* *nà'-ka-ó*
        IV-12-tree   my father   *n̂*-12-ú-1-TAM-1Sg.-hit-FV   PREP-12-ó
        'the stick father hit me with'

6.2 Grammatical relations

Subject is defined by agreement in a fixed position in the verb. Considering those NPS standing to the right of the verb, it is superficially not easy to define their grammatical relations: tests for object status for example do not yield unambiguous results.

For some speakers, locative NPS to the right of the verb demand a verb in the applied form. Such speakers consider that outside influence causes others to fail to use the applied form of the verb.

What are locative oblique NPS in a basic sentence pattern may appear as subjects in related sentences without any extra marking in the verb, but a passive is also possible.

(105)   *²m-ò-rù-tjándjá* *¹mw-à-nyándér-ˀₐ* *¹o-vá-nátjè*
        on the pitch   played   children
        'children were playing on the pitch'

        ²m-ò-rù-tjándjá *¹mw-à-nyándér-w-ˀₐ* *¹o-vá-nátjè*
        on the pitch   was played   children
        'children were playing on the pitch'

The general prefix (oblique) within the verb is not restricted to what might narrowly be defined as an object. For example, with the benefactive use of the applied form, it may agree with either the 'retained object' or with the new NP introduced by the applied form. However, if a general prefix (oblique) is present, the NP with which it agrees must be absent. Herero only allows one general prefix (oblique), (unlike Ndonga, which allows two).

6.3 Copular

According to their behavior in the present, three uses of copular sentences can be distinguished: description, possession and location. The copular verb is *-rí*, which cannot take a final vowel.

In descriptive use in the present, the segmental verb is deleted, leaving the specification of a high tone in Key 1, which is maintained at the beginning of the predication.

(106)   *¹ómú²hóná*
        'he's king'
        ¹áà²véhè
        'that's all of them'

A PP with the preposition *nà'* is used as complement in a copular sentence showing possession. Most educated speakers of the language believe that *nà'* is a verb and equivalent to 'to have'. There seems no evidence for this in Herero (unlike Ndonga and Kwanyama, where it has to be considered a defective verb and can be found with an applied extension). For the present reference, all that remains of the copular verb is the general prefix (subject) and the specification of Key 1 for it. This general prefix forms one morphological word with what is otherwise the first morphological word of the PP.

(107)   ¹*tjí-n-ò-mw-ánò*   ²*m-bú-tjí-hóng-w-à*
        tjí-nà´-òmwànò   RELATIVE CLAUSE
        7-PREP-method
        'it (Herero)'s got a method (by) which it is taught'

With a locative, with present reference, the verb has the form: General Prefix + *-ri*

(108)   ¹*tùri* ¹*m-ó-ú-²zèù*
        tù-rí
        2Pl.-be
        'we're in difficulty'

6.4 Negatives

As well as negatives with *ka-* or *-ha-*, (see §3.5.3), a common negative for the present uses a copular plus PP. Negative forms can also be used with assertive and exclamatory affirmative interpretation.

(109)   ¹*kà-tú-nà-kú-²tjíw-á*
        NEG-1Pl.-nà´-15-tjíw-FV
        'we don't know'

6.5 Questions

A general slight raising of pitch with a fall on the final syllable yields a question from a statement.

(110)   ¹*éé²ngwi*   ²*ngwârí* ²*nòmúpítô*
        ¹*éyé*   ²*n-gw-í*   ²*n-gw-â-rí²nà´-ò-mù-pító*
        PRONOUN   DEMONSTRATIVE   who-was with-diarrhoea
        'is he the one who had diarrhoea?'

Interrogative morphemes include *-pi* 'where', *-ví* 'how' and *-ne* 'who'.

(111)   ¹*í-n-gâ*   ¹*ké-²pí*
        DEMONSTRATIVE   12-*pí*
        'this one?   where is it?'

A favourite question formation is by focusing.

(112)   ¹*ó-ú-²né* ²*n-gú-má-kánd-ₐ o-ngòmbè*
        IV-1-né   RELATIVE CLAUSE
        'who is the one who's milking the cow?'

6.6 Focus

This last question device involves focus. In statements it is not always necessary that a relative verb should follow this focusing device. The morphemes *tjí*, which can also be equivalent to 'if, when', when introducing a subordinate clause, and *ku* class 17, are so used.

(113) ^{2}*è-ná r-é* ^{1}*òtjâ^{2}rí* ^{2}*kàtjòrúòrú*
      name her   *ò-tjí-(ú)-à-rí*   *Katjoruoru*
                      IV-tjí-1-TAM-be
      'her name, she was Katjoruoru'

REFERENCES

Booysen 1982; Departement van Nasionale Opvoeding 1983; Elderkin 1999; Fleisch 1995; Grimes 2000; Güldemann 1999c; Haacke 1985; Hahn 1857; Kavari and Ohly n.d.; Viljoen and Kamupingene 1983; Volschenk 1968.

CHAPTER THIRTY

ZONE S

Derek Gowlett

1 GEOLINGUISTIC SITUATION

Guthrie's Zone S languages are essentially those of Zimbabwe, Mozambique, Botswana, South Africa, Swaziland and Lesotho. To these we have added Lozi (K21), a Sotho-based language of Zambia and Namibia. For each language, or language cluster, we include its major geographical situation and an approximate number of speakers (based on the latest census figures, and those in *Ethnologue*).

S10   Shona Group: Zimbabwe (8,200,000); Mozambique (750,000?); Zambia
      S11   Korekore: Northern Zimbabwe; Southeastern Zambia; Mozambique
      S12   Zezuru: North-central Zimbabwe
      S13   Manyika: Northeastern Zimbabwe; East-central Mozambique
      S14   Karanga: Southern Zimbabwe
      S15   Ndau: North-central Mozambique; East-central Zimbabwe
      S16   Kalanga: Eastern Botswana; West-south-central Zimbabwe

Shona is an official language in Zimbabwe, with a standardized written form used in education and literature.

S20   Venda Group
      S21   Venda: South Africa (Northern Province); Southern Zimbabwe:
           (876,500)

Venda is an official language in South Africa, used in education, and with its own written literature.

S30   Sotho-Tswana Group
      S31a   Central Tswana (Rolong, Hurutshe): Botswana; South Africa
            (Northern Province, Gauteng, Free State, Northern Cape): 3,940,000
            (figures include speakers of 31b, c and d)
      S31b   Eastern Tswana (Kgatla, East Kwena): Botswana; South Africa
      S31c   Northern Tswana (Ngwato, Tawana): Botswana; Zimbabwe
      S31d   Qhalaxarzi: Central and southern Botswana
      S31e   Southern Tswana (Tlharo, Tlhaping): Southern Botswana; South
            Africa (Northern Cape)
      S32a   Northern Sotho: South Africa (Northern Province, Gauteng,
            Mpumalanga): 3,700,000
      S32b   Lovedu: South Africa (Northern province)
      S33   Southern Sotho: Lesotho; South Africa (mainly Free State and
            Gauteng): 4,600,000
      S302   Kutswe: South Africa (Mpumalanga); threatened
      S303   Pai: South Africa (Mpumalanga); possibly extinct

S304   Pulana: South Africa (Mpumalanga); threatened
K21   Lozi: Zambia (Western Province); Namibia (Caprivi): 1,200,000

Below, we use 'SOTHO' to refer to the Sotho-Tswana Group, while 'Sotho' refers specifically to Southern Sotho.

Tswana, an official language in Botswana and South Africa, is used in education in both countries, and has an established literature. The dialects with smaller numbers of speakers enjoy no particular status, and it is probable that they will be swamped by the more standard forms. For Northern Sotho, which is an official, educational and literary language in South Africa, it is the Pedi dialect that is generally used, and forms such as Lovedu are threatened. Lozi is recognized both in Namibia and Zambia, and is used for education and literature.

S40   Nguni Group
      Zunda varieties:
      S41   Xhosa: South Africa (Eastern Cape, Western Cape, Gauteng, Free State): 7,200,000
      S41a   Mpondo: South Africa (Eastern Cape)
      S41b   Xesibe: South Africa (Eastern Cape)
      S42   Zulu: South Africa (KwaZulu-Natal, Gauteng, Mpumalanga): 9,200,000
      S42a   Ngoni (a Zulu dialect): Malawi
      S44   Zimbabwean Ndebele: West-central Zimbabwe

      Tekela varieties:
      S43   Swati: Swaziland; South Africa (Mpumalanga): 1,670,000
      S407   Northern South African Ndebele/Sumayela Ndebele: South Africa (Northern Province): numbers unknown
      S408   Southern South African Ndebele: South Africa (Northern Province, Mpumalanga, Gauteng): 590,000
      S404   Phuthi (Nguni dialect with heavy Sotho influence): Mainly in southern Lesotho
      S406   Lala: South Africa (KwaZulu-Natal)

Swati is recognized as an official language, and language for education both in South Africa and Swaziland. Zulu and Xhosa (though not the Mpondo or Xesibe varieties) are official languages in South Africa, and are well catered for on radio, TV, in education and in literature. Zimbabwean Ndebele is recognized in Zimbabwe. Southern South African Ndebele is an official language, but in practice enjoys lesser status than Zulu or Xhosa. Sumayela Ndebele is not recognized as an official language, or for education. We have no information as to the status or health of Malawian Ngoni. Phuthi and Lala are highly threatened language varieties, and are already showing signs of 'disease'.

S50   Tshwa-Ronga Group
      S51   Tshwa: North-central Mozambique; Southeastern Zimbabwe: 750,000
      S52   Gwamba
      S53   Tsonga: South-central Mozambique; South Africa (Northern Province, Gauteng, Mpumalanga): 3,250,000
      S54   Ronga: Southern Mozambique: 1,000,000

> S541 Thonga (Ronga dialect – heavily influenced by Zulu – apparently
> spoken only by women): Border Mozambique – Northern
> KwaZulu-Natal

Tsonga is an official language in South Africa, and is used in education. In practice it enjoys a lesser status than Xhosa, Zulu and the major Sotho languages. None of the Mozambican African languages listed here enjoys official status in Mozambique. Copi and GiTonga appear to be more marginalized than the Tsonga-Ronga-Tshwa cluster. Thonga is a threatened speech variety, but the continued existence of the other languages (with the possible exception of Gwamba about which we have no information) seems not to be threatened.

> S60 Copi Group
> S61 Copi: Mozambique (small coastal area south of Inhambane): 470,000
> S62 GiTonga: Mozambique (Inhambane area): 320,000

2 ORTHOGRAPHY

In order to indicate the approximate pronunciation of examples we use a phonologized IPA spelling for the various languages. Thus in GiTonga, which has a phonemic flap [ɽ], we use the symbol "ɽ", even though "l" would do as well. On the other hand, we use "y" for both [ɣ] and [ʝ] since in GiTonga the latter is a conditioned allophone found before front vowels and /y/. For nine-vowel languages we use the symbols /i, ɪ, e, ɛ, a, ɔ, o, ʊ, u/. Exceptions to standard IPA use are "y" for [j], and we do not raise "h" and "l" for aspiration and lateral release. Tone is indicated where it is available to us.

3 PHONOLOGY

3.1 Vowels

Except for SOTHO (excluding Lozi), Phuthi and possibly South African Ndebele, Zone S languages have a five-vowel system, with the Nguni languages splitting /e/ into [ɛ ~ i] and /o/ into [ɔ ~ o]. The raised allophone in each case is determined mainly by a following close vowel. Southern and Northern Sotho and Tswana have nine distinctive vowels, /i, ɪ, e, ɛ, a, ɔ, o, ʊ, u/, with /ɪ/ and /ʊ/ having allophones [ɪ] and [ʊ], determined by a following superclose vowel or syllabic nasal. The two extra vowel phonemes, compared to Proto-Bantu (PB), have two initial historical sources:

(a) phonologization of raised allophones of *e and *o, due to loss of the conditioning high vowel (there has been some analogical extension, and influence by English and Afrikaans which have entrenched this phonologization):

(1) Sotho
    èts'-à 'do, make' < *gèd-i-a* 'try, measure'

(b) the merger of PB sequences *ai and *oi to produce /e/ and /**we**/:

(2) Sotho
    -lélélé 'long, tall' < *-dàí*
    kw'ènà 'crocodile' < *ngòìnà*

Traditionally, Sotho-Tswana vowels have been treated using a multivalued or graded height feature. The features [Tense] or [ATR] have been used to differentiate /ɛ/ and /ɔ/ from /e/ and /o/, and /ɪ/ and /ʊ/ from /i/ and /u/. Without experimental data to back up the choice of either [ATR] or [Tense], however, we believe that a graded height system is preferable, since height is in any case an articulatory fact.

Qhalaxarzi has seven phonemic vowels, /i, e, ɛ, a, ɔ, o, u/, with apparent dialectal substitution of [ɪ] / [ʊ] for [e] / [o]. Where the other Sotho languages have /ɪ/ and /ʊ/, Qhalaxarzi has /e/ and /o/.

3.2 Vowel juxtaposition

The Nguni languages have a phonotactic constraint against vowel juxtaposition, and there are various strategies for its avoidance. These include:

(a) Vowel deletion

(3) Zulu
     í//hèkù lákhàní? 'What is the old man building?' < *i//heku li-akh-a-ni*

(b) 'Coalescence' (alternatively: vowel assimilation + deletion)

(4) Zulu
     $a+i>e$ *n̠én̠z̠ù* 'and a house'   < *na-i-n-z̠u*
     $a+a>a$ *n̠àmán̠z̠à* 'and strength'   < *na-a-ma-n̠z̠a*
     $a+u>o$ *n̠òmúnt'ù* 'and a person' < *na-u-mu-nt'u*

(c) Consonantalization

(5) Zulu
     wènz̠àní? 'What are you doing?' < *u-enz̠-a-ni?*

3.3 Vowel harmony

Southern Sotho, Northern Sotho and Tswana have a right-to-left vowel harmony system whereby /ɛ/ and /ɔ/ do not co-occur with any higher vowel to their immediate right in a word stem. In such cases they are replaced by /e/ and /o/. (As already mentioned above, there is also vowel-raising, but at the allophonic level, when /ɪ/ and /ʊ/ are followed by a higher vowel, or by a syllabic nasal.)

(6) Sotho
     mù≠rék'-í   'buyer'   < *rék'-à* 'buy'
     hù-sì≠lèlék'-ì   'not to expel' < *hù ≠ lèlèk'-à* 'to expel'
     bóf-úw-á   'be tied'   < *bóf-à* 'tie'

There is also left-to-right harmony whereby /e/ in a verb root may not be followed by a suffix of the form -ɛ or -ɔ, these being replaced by -e and -o, respectively.

(7) Sotho
     i ≠ tʃw'éts'-è! 'Tell yourself!'   < *ì ≠ tʃw'éts'-à* 'tell oneself'
     cf. *ì ≠ tshép'-è!* 'Trust yourself!' < *ì ≠ tshép'-à* 'trust oneself'
     k'èts'-ò 'act, action'   < *èts'-à* 'do'
     cf. *k'èp'-ò* 'digging'   < *èp'-à* 'dig'

This left-to-right harmony does not apply in the case of back vowels, where it is the stem vowel that assimilates to the suffix, i.e. right-to-left:

(8) Sotho
     phɔs-ò 'mistake'   < *fòs-à*   'make a mistake'
     kxhóts'-ò 'peace, security' < *kxhóts'-à* 'take refuge'

Qhalaxarzi has regressive vowel height harmony whereby non-high vowels other than *a*, are raised one degree when followed by /i/ or /u/. This rule, in non-deliberate speech, spreads beyond the immediately preceding vowel, until there is some opaque element. An interesting difference in this system from that of the other Sotho languages is that the vowel-raising occurs only before /i/ and /u/, so that /ɛ/ and /ɔ/ are not raised before /e/ or /o/, as is the case in the three main languages.

(9)   Qhalaxarzi
       bà ≠ réq-í   'buyers'   < *réq-á* 'buy'
       bà ≠ bón-í   'seers'   < *bɔ́n-á* 'see'
       lí ≠ phúɲ-á   'He (5) stabs'
   cf. *lí ≠ róq-á*   'He (5) sews'
       xù ≠ phúɲ-á   'to stab'
   cf. *xò ≠ róq-á*   'to sew'

The Nguni language, Phuthi, has been heavily influenced by Southern Sotho and has borrowed the superclose vowels [i] and [u], and has developed two interesting vowel harmony innovations, one right-to-left and one left-to-right. Phuthi has the phonemic vowels listed in table 30.1.

'Edge-based mid-vowel harmony' has stems as its domain, and *some* prefixes (see after (c) below). There are three rules (Donnelly 1996):

(a) Mid vowels (Grade 3 and 4) at the right edge of a word are of Grade 4:

(10) Phuthi
       bá ≠ kháb̭-è̤   'They should go'
       bá ≠ bít'-è   'They should call'
       í ≠ yʊ̀ɲ-ɔ́   'harvest'
       la̤ ≠ yè   'and him'

(b) Mid vowels that are word-medial and in an uninterrupted sequence of mid vowels up to the right edge are also of Grade 4. In other words, the rule is regressive, being stopped only by any intervening non-mid vowel, /i, u, ɪ, ʊ, a/, i.e. superclose, high or low vowels can interrupt this sequence.

(11) Phuthi
       bá ≠ sél-è   'They should drink'
       bá ≠ sél-l-ɛ́   'They should drink for'
       bá ≠ bɔ́n-él-èn-è   'they saw for each other'
       í ≠ wɔ́t'élɔ́   'drowsiness'

(c) 'Word-medial low-mid vowels that are *not* in sequence with the right edge' are Grade 3:

(12) Phuthi
       k'ʊ́ ≠ bón-à   'to see'
       yè-ná   'him/her'

TABLE 30.1: PHUTHI

1	*i*			*u*
2		*ɪ*		*ʊ*
3		*e*		*o*
4		*ɛ*		*ɔ*
5			*a*	

> *k'ù≠sébét'-él-àn-à*   'to work for each other'
> *бá≠бón-él-àn-έ*   'They should see for each other'

'Root-based Grade 1 vowel harmony' states that high vowel suffixes have Grade 1 vowels with roots having Grade 1 vowels, and Grade 2 vowels with roots having vowels lower than Grade 1. It has as its domain: (a) noun stems + locative suffix; (b) verbal radicals + Causative/Intensive/Passive/Reversive extensions; (c) verbal radicals + Present negative suffix or Anterior suffix. We thus find the following alternations:

(13) Phuthi
      Locative suffix: *-ɪnɪ ~ -ini*
      Present neg. suffix: *-ɪ ~ -i*
      Anterior suffix: *-ɪye ~ -iye*
      Causative extension: *-ɪs- ~ -is-*
      Intensive extension: *-ɪsɪs- ~ -isis-*
      Passive extension: *-ʋw- ~ -uw-*
      Reversive extension: *-ʋḷ- ~ uḷ-*

(14)   *k'ú ≠ ɪ̀im-ɪs-à*   'to help cultivate'   < *k'ú ≠ lɪ̀m-à*   'to cultivate'
         k'ú ≠ бón-ɪs-á   'to show'   < *k'ú ≠ бón-à*   'to see'
         k'ú ≠ !há!h-ɪs-à   'to pull to pieces'   < *k'ú ≠ !hà!h-à*   'to pull apart'
    cf. *k'ú ≠ бít'ɪs-à*   'to help call'   < *k'ú ≠ бít'-à*   'to call'
         k'ú ≠ thúɲɪs-à   'to shoot'   < *k'ú ≠ thúɲ-à*   'to shoot'

3.4 Consonants

Zone S languages have large consonant inventories (Lozi with its Luyana-influenced phonology is an exception). Typically, there is a three-way distinction between stops and affricates: voiceless unaspirated (often ejective), voiceless aspirated and voiced. Voiced implosive stops occur in some languages. Lateral stops, affricates and fricatives, though not found in GiTonga or many dialects of Shona, are typical of Zone S languages. Qhalaxarzi has a phonemic distinction between velar and uvular voiceless stops. Heterorganic affricates are a feature of several languages in this Zone.

Breathy-voiced or murmured consonants are a feature of Copi, Tsonga and Nguni, and it is usually held that the murmur is also manifest on the following vowel. Instrumental phonetic research on the so-called breathy-voiced (oral) stops of Swati and Zulu, however, reveal that these are not murmured and are voiceless (Traill *et al.* 1987, Traill 1990). Murmured fricatives and nasals do exist, though in the case of Zulu murmured fricatives, the following vowel is not breathy. It is likely that the putative murmured non-click stops of Xhosa are also not murmured or even voiced.

All Zone S languages have a parallel set of 'labiovelarized' consonants though there are frequently co-occurrence restrictions. We use the term 'labiovelarized' in preference to the traditional 'labialized', since the *w* element carries both labialization in the form of lip-rounding, and velarization in the raising of the velum. It is the velar-raising that is responsible for the co-occurrence restrictions, usually on labials, though sometimes elsewhere. The velar element causes assimilation of various sorts in the 'host' consonant. This may take the form of complete assimilation whereby the host consonant becomes velar (e.g. [mw > ŋw]); partial assimilation in that the host is backed to some position closer to velar (e.g. [mw > ɲw]); or partial assimilation in that some intervening velar element comes between the host and *w*, e.g. [pw > pxw].

Exemplifying the richness of Zone S consonant systems, we give consonant charts of Copi and Xhosa, and partial charts for Tsonga, Venda and Zulu. They are assigned to columns on a phonological basis. Foreign sounds are given in parentheses. Peripheral sounds, such as those found only in a few interjections, or in one or two items, are excluded.

In addition to the consonants in table 30.2, Copi, like other Zone S languages, has a parallel set of labiovelarized consonants (though Nguni, Shona and SOTHO (with the exception of Lozi) do not permit labiovelarized bilabials, and in some cases labiovelarized dentilabials). Copi, atypically, also has a parallel set of palatalized consonants.

TABLE 30.2: COPI

	Bilabial	Labio-dental	Labio-sibilant	Alveolar	Alveo-lateral	Alveo-sibilant	Alveo-palatal	Velar	Alveo-velar click
Voiceless	p	pf	ps	t	(tl)	ts	tʃ	k	!
Aspirated	ph	pfh	psh	th	(tlh)	tsh	tʃh	kh	!h
Breathy-voiced	b̤	b̤v	b̤z̤	d̤	(d̤ɮ̤)	d̤z̤	d̤ʒ	g̤	g̤!
Vd implosive	ɓ			ɗ			f		
Fricative¹		f	s̃w	r̤	(ɬ)	s	(ʃ)	ɦ̤	
	w	ʋ		l			y		
	m			n			ɲ	ŋ	ŋ!
	(m̤)			(n̤)					
	mb	mbv	mbz	nd	(ndl)	nz	nd̤ʒ	ng	
	m̤b̤			n̤d̤	(nd̤ɮ̤)			ng	ŋg!

Note: 1 /r̤/ is a breathy-voiced trill, while /ɦ̤/ is a breathy-voiced glottal fricative.

TABLE 30.3: XHOSA

p'	t'		ts'	tʃ'		c'	k'	kx'	/	!	//
ph	th		tsh	tʃh		chy	kh	kxh	/h	!h	//h
b̤	d̤		d̤z̤	d̤ʒ		ɟ̈	g̤		g̤/	g̤!	g̤//
ɓ											
f		ɬ	s	ʃ			h	x			
ʋ̤		ɮ̤	z̤				ɦ̤	ɣ̈			
		l				y	w				
m	n					ɲ	ŋ		ŋ/	ŋ!	ŋ//
m̤	n̤					ɲ̈					
mp'	nt'	ntl'	nts'	ntʃ'		nc'	nk'		ŋ/'	ŋ!'	ŋ//'
m̤b̤	n̤d̤	nd̤ɮ̤	n̤d̤z̤	nd̤ʒ		n̤ɟ̈	ng		ŋ̤/	ŋ̤!	ŋ̤//
mpf'											
m̤b̤v̤											

TABLE 30.4: TSONGA

b	*bv*	*d*	*dl*	*dz̦*	*dʒ*	*g*
b̤	*b̤v̤*	*d̤*		*d̤z̦̤*	*d̤ʒ̤*	*g̤*
	v			*r*	*y*	*w*
	v̤			*r̤*	*y̤*	*w̤*
m		*n*			*ɲ*	*ŋ*
m̤		*n̤*				*ŋ̤*

TABLE 30.5: VENDA

p	*pf*	*t̪*	*t*
ph	*pfh*	*t̪h*	*th*
b	*bv*	*d̪*	*d*
ɸ	*f*		
β	*v*		
		l̪	*r*
m		*n̪*	*n*

TABLE 30.6: ZULU

p'	*t'*	*ts'*	*tʃ'*	*k'*	*kl'*
ph	*th*			*kh*	
p	*t*		*tʃ*	*k*	
ɓ				*g*	
mp'	*nt'*	*nts'*	*ɲtʃ'*	*ŋk'*	*ŋkl'*
mb	*nd*	*ndz*	*ɲdʒ*	*ŋg*	

As shown in the Tsonga partial chart (table 30.4), Tsonga has a phonological distinction between breathy and non-breathy stops and continuants.

The Venda partial chart (table 30.5) reveals that Venda regularly distinguishes bilabial from dentilabial positions, as well as dental from alveolar.

The stop series of Zulu (table 30.6) is most unusual in that the basic opposition is between three types of voiceless stop – radical, ejective, and aspirated – and prenasalized voiceless and voiced stops. The velar-lateral [kl'] occurs only as ejective and prenasalized ejective. In the bilabial and velar positions there is a further contrast with voiced stops. The bilabial one is usually said to be implosive, though there is evidence that some speakers use an egressive airstream instead.

3.4.1 Clicks

Ndebele, Zulu, Xhosa (see Xhosa chart (table 30.3)) and Phuthi have borrowed extensively from the Khoesan click system. Southern Sotho, Swati and Copi, which have only the alveolar click, have done so to a lesser extent, and some other languages, such as Tsonga, have very few words with clicks. The clicks found in Ndebele, Phuthi, Xhosa and Zulu are the dental [ǀ], the alveolar [ǃ]' and the alveolateral [ǁ] (written *c*, *q* and *x*), which may occur as voiceless, voiceless aspirated, breathy-voiced, nasalized, breathy-voiced nasalized and in Xhosa, also voiceless nasalized ejective.

3.5 Syllabic system

The canonical syllable structure of these languages is CV. Syllabic consonants have developed in several languages through vowel-deletion. For example, the Nguni C1.1 and 3 prefixes, *mu-*, have become *m̥-*, except that Zulu retains the vowel before monosyllabic stems. There is a drift whereby other instances of *mu* and also *mi* become *m̥*. In Xhosa the first person singular Absolute Pronoun is *m̥(ná)*, compared with the Zulu *mì(ná)*. In both Xhosa and Zulu final *mu* and *mi* are often *m̥*, even where witten *mu* or *mi*. One of the sources of syllabic nasals in SOTHO is the soundshift *$*NV > N$* provided that the vowel is a vowel of Degree 1. Southern Sotho and certain Tswana dialects reduce *lVl* to *ll*, with the first *l* being syllabic: *l̩là* 'cry' < *$*lìl-á$*, *bófúllà* 'untie' < *$*bófúlùl-à$*, *ráp'á.llà* 'lie down (when ill), slant down' < *$*rápálàl-à$*.

There also appears to be a drift for the vowel of the basic noun prefix to fall away in other classes as well. Thus, in Zulu, *úbù≠sûgù* 'night' and *úgù≠théŋ(g)à* 'to buy' are commonly heard as *úb↓sûgù* and *úg↓théŋ(g)á*. Likewise in Southern Sotho, one hears *sì≠fát'è* 'tree' and *lì≠łábáthì* 'sand' pronounced as *s↓fát'è* and *łábáthì*.

3.6 Accent/stress

With the exception of Lozi, Zone S languages have a penultimate length-stress feature which signals the end of a phrase or sentence in declarative sentences. This accent is not used in interrogative and exclamatory sentences.

3.7 Tone

Zone S languages have a two-tone system, or a system in which some syllables are accented (by a High tone) while other syllables are unaccented. High tones may spread rightwards to unaccented (Low-toned) syllables under certain circumstances.

In general each syllable carries only one tone (High or Low), but some syllables are bimoric – they bear High-High, Low-Low, Rising (Low-High) or Falling (High-Low) tones.

Probably all Zone S languages, with the exception of Lozi, have tonal downstep (indicated in examples by '↓') – an unpredictable, and thus tonemic, lowering of a High tone after a preceding High tone.

A feature of the Nguni tonal systems is the so-called depressor consonants. These are consonants that have the effect of lowering a following High tone. In Zulu, at least, this lowering effect lowers the onset of a High to a point lower than an ordinary Low tone, from which point there is a rapid rise. A depressor may also cause a High tone to 'jump' to the following syllable (with concomitant lengthening) as seen in (15) where the presence of the depressor *z̤* in the plural prefix results in a different tonal pattern.

(15) Zulu
    ìsíłàlò 'chair' > *íz̤íłâlò* 'chairs' LHLL > LLHLL

In Zulu, and possibly also in the other Nguni languages, there is no common feature to these consonants, which include breathy-voiced fricatives and breathy-voiced nasals, voiceless radical stops, and voiceless fricatives. Diachronically they may all have had the feature [murmur], but synchronically, it appears that they should be assigned an *ad hoc* feature [depressor].

In Copi, murmured consonants act as depressors, lowering the onset of a following High. Tsonga also has depressors but their nature and effects are in our view uncertain.

3.8 Functions of tone

Tone commonly has the following functions:
(a) marking lexical differences

(16)   Copi
    ndòngá   'tin'
    ndóngá   'stick'
    ɦàl-à   'boil'
    ɦàl-á   'peel'

(b) marking TAM differences

(17)   Sotho
    ... *bátshèhà*   'and laughed' (Past Narrative)
    ... *bátshéhà*   'laughing' (Present Simultaneous)

(c) marking different form classes

(18)   Sotho
    dʒwàŋ   'grass' (noun)
    dʒwáŋ?   'how?' (adverb)
    lík'áì?   'Where are they?' (locative base)
    lík'àì?   'How many are there?' (adjective base)
    dʒwàlá bòú   'this beer' (1st position demonstrative)
    dʒwàlá bóù   'that beer' (2nd position demonstrative)
    t'àbà éŋŋwì   'another matter' (adjective)
    t'àbà éŋŋwì   'one matter' (relative based on enumerative)
    hú mùrènà   'There is a chief' (identifying copulative)
    húmúrènà   'to the chief' (locative)

(d) distinguishing first and second person subjects from third person ones

(19)   GiTonga
    ùngùhóngòɽà   'You go'
    úngùhóngòɽà   'He goes'

(20)   Zulu
    sìyàʋùmà   'We agree'
    sìyáʋùmà   'She (7) agrees'

(e) marking phrase structure

(21)   Sotho

AdvP	+	AdvP		AdvP	
Adv		Adv		Adv	Adv
hàhúlù		*bùsìù*		*hàhúlú*	*bùsìù*
'a lot ... at night'			'especially at night'		

(f) marking questions

(22)   Zulu
    ŋ(g)ùyênà   'It is her'
    ŋ(g)ùyéná?   'Is it her?'

3.9 Word-structure constraint

Zone S languages in general have an apparent constraint on the occurrence of monosyllabic words other than as interjectives or ideophones. Where normal grammatical rules would result in monosyllabic words, an extra syllable, known as a 'stabilizer', is prefixed or suffixed in order to make the word well-formed. (In certain cases, which differ from language to language, this 'aversion' to monosyllabicity holds also for stems.) Examples include the following:

The SOTHO noun prefix of Cl. 9 is $\emptyset$- before polysyllabic stems, but *N*- (a syllabic nasal, before monosyllabic stems.)

(23) Sotho
    ŋ≠kxhɔ́   'water-pot'
    m̀≠phì   'army'
    ∅≠kxhúhù 'chicken'
    ∅≠phírì   'hyena'

In Copi, GiTonga, and Tsonga the noun prefix of Cl. 9 is $\emptyset$- before polysyllabic stems and *yi*- (*yi-N*- for Tsonga) before monosyllabic stems. Shona has the same distinction, but with *i*- in place of *yi*-:

(24) GiTonga
    yi≠tshwa   'kidney'
    ∅≠tshahe   'spark'

Note that in the locative of 'kidney', the prefix is deleted, since the locative suffix functions as a stabilizer:

(25) *yi≠tshwa* 'kidney' > *tshwa-ni* 'in the kidney'

Similarly in GiTonga, among older people, in Cl. 1 and 3 the prefix is $\emptyset$- before consonant-commencing polysyllabic stems, but *mu*- before monosyllabic ones (younger speakers tend to use *mu*- throughout):

(26) GiTonga
    mù≠thù   'person (1)'
    ∅≠Tonga 'Tonga person (1)'
    mu≠ro   'gravy (3)'
    ∅≠roto   'beak (3)'

Common to all Zone S languages in our data, with the exception of Lozi, is the use of a stabilizer in the imperative, positive, without object concord. The stabilizer does not occur when there is an object concord or negative prefix, since these prefixes have the additional function of providing a second syllable to the word. Though the pluralizing suffix also provides a second syllable to monosyllabic forms, it does not result in the deletion of the stabilizer.

(27)

		Basic form	Stabilized form
	GiTonga	*R-a*	*R-a-yi*
	Southern Sotho	*R-a*	*í-R-á ~ R-à-á*
	Zulu	*R-a*	*(y)í-R-á ~ R-á-nà*

4 NOUN CLASSES

The Zone S noun class system is outlined morphophonemically as follows (table 30.7):

4.1 Noun prefix structure

Zone S languages generally have a monomorphemic noun prefix with canonical CV shape, except for Cl. 10, which has the historical augment *li- (Shona excluded). Shona has a latent initial vowel that is manifest under certain conditions. Zunda Nguni languages have an initial vowel as augment except for the locative classes 16 and 17. The

TABLE 30.7: ZONE S NOUN CLASS SYSTEM

Noun class	Zunda Nguni	South Sotho	Shona	Venda	Tsonga-Ronga-Tshwa	Copi	GiTonga
1	um(u)-	mù-	mù-	mù-	mù-	ìn- [ĩ-]	mu-
2	aɓa-	ɓà-	và-	ßà-	và-	và-	ßa-
1a	uθ-	θ-	θ-	θ-	θ-	θ-	θ-
2a	–	–	vá-	–	vá-	vá-	ßa-
2b	oo-	bó-	–	ßó-	–	–	–
3	um(u)-	mù-	mù-	mù-	mù-	ìn-	mu-
4	imi-	mì-	mì-	mì-	mì-	mì-	mi-
5	i(li)-	lì-	θ-¹	(lì-)¹	rì-	dì-	ɽi-
6	ama-	mà-	mà-	mà-	mì-	mà-	ma-
7	isi-	sì-	tʃì-	tʃhì-	ʃì-	tʃì-	ɣi-
8	(²)	(³)	ẑwi-	ẑwi-	swì-	si-	si-
8x⁴	i(ʐ)i-	lì-	–	–	–	–	–
9	iN-	(Ǹ-)	N-	N-	N-	(N-)	θ-
10	i(ʐ)iN-	lì(N)-	(dzì)N-	dzìN-	tìN-	tì(N)-	dziθ-
11	u(lu)-	–⁵	rù-	rù-	rì-	lì-	–
12	(⁶)	(⁷)	kà-	–	–	–	–
13	(⁶)	(⁷)	tù-	–	–	–	–
14	uɓu-	ɓù-	(ɦ)ù-	ßù-	vù-	wù-	wu-
15	ugu-	hù-	kù-	ù-	kù-	kù-	ɣu-
16	(pha-)		pà-	ɸà-	hà-	hà-	ßa-
17	(gu-)	hù-	kù-	kù-	kù-	–	ku-
18	–	mù-	mù-	mù-	mù-	–	mu-
19	–	–	(sŵì-)⁸	–	–	–	–
20	–	–	(⁹)	kù-	–	–	–
21	–	–	zì-	ḍì-	dyì-	–	–

Notes:

1 The Cl. 5 'prefix' is generally manifest as a series of morphophonemic changes to the initial consonant of the stem. For examples, see below.

2 Malawian Ngoni only.

3 Lozi and Qhalaxarzi only in SOTHO.

4 Cl. 8x is an innovation found in Nguni (excluding Malawian Ngoni), and in SOTHO (excluding Pai and Qhalaxarzi). It is presumably formed by analogy with the Cl. 10 augment with which it is homophonous. The various forms of the Cl. 8x prefix are not reflexes of PB *bi-, but of *li-.

5 In SOTHO, Cl. 11 has all but disappeared, having merged with Cl. 5 in Southern and Northern Sotho, as well as Qhalaxarzi. It occurs in Lozi, probably as an adoption from Luyana. In Tswana it has completely disappeared from some dialects, and is obsolescent in others. GiTonga has also merged Cl. 11 with Cl. 5.

6 Found only in Malawian Ngoni.

7 In SOTHO, Cl. 12 and 13 are found only in Lozi, as an adoption from Luyana.

8 Found mainly in the Mhari dialect of Karanga.

9 Found in Kalanga only.

augment takes the form *a-*, *e-*, *o-*, depending upon the vowel of the prefix. Tekela Nguni is inconsistent with respect to the presence or absence of an augment:

(a) Phuthi has an initial vowel *e-* only for Cl. 2 and 6, i.e. where the basic noun prefix has the vowel *a*.
(b) Lala has a peculiar distribution of the augment in that it occurs in Cl. 1 and 3 with CV^{+} stems, in Cl. 2 with C-commencing stems, and with all stems in Cl. 9. There are a few nouns of Cl. 11 with an initial vowel *i-*, for which there is no apparent explanation.

(28)   Lala
    Cl. 1: *u≠fat'i*   'woman' (CVCV stem)
        mu≠nu   'person' (CV stem) cf.: *u≠nw.ana* 'child'
        m≠on-i   'sinner' (V-commencing stem)
    Cl. 2: *a-ɓa≠nu*   'people'
        a-ɓa≠fat'i   'women'
        ɓ≠on-i   'sinners'
    Cl. 9: *i-m≠but'i*   'goat'
        i≠fene   'baboon'

(c) S. Ndebele has no augment.
(d) Swati has an augment when the basic noun prefix begins with a nasal; *u-* in Cl. 1 and 3, *i-* in Cl. 4 and 9, and *e-* in Cl. 6. In Cl. 1a a few noun stems have an obligatory augment *u-*, while for the majority the augment is optional. In Cl. 2, the augment *e-* occurs optionally, but is not common. (Note the dissimilation in Cl. 2 and 6.)

(29)   Swati
    Cl. 1: *ú-m̀≠f-ánà*   'boy'
    Cl. 2: *(é-)ɓà≠f-ánà*   'boys'
    Cl. 1a: *ú-∅≠yiɬó*   'your father' (obligatory)
        (ú-)∅≠ɓàɓé   'my/our father'
    Cl. 4: *ì-mí≠fùlà*   'rivers'
    Cl. 6: *è-má≠sì*   'sour milk'
    Cl. 9: *í-n≠ɡ̊òʋ̥ù*   'elephant'

The occurrence of the augment in Nguni is determined by a fairly disparate variety of syntactic rules. Some, but not all of these, suggest that it has the significance of an article.

4.2 Class 5 morphophonemics

With the exception of Copi, Nguni and SOTHO (in Tswana only, there is an obsolescent remnant of this phenomenon), Zone S manifests a series of morphophonemic changes associated with the Cl. 5 noun prefix. We illustrate *some* of these below:

(30)   Zezuru (essentially a process of voicing)
    p >*ɓ* *ɓàdzá* 'hoe'   pl. *màpàdzá*
    t >*ɗ* *ɗámá* 'cheek'   *màtámá*
    pf >*bv* *bvèní* 'baboon'   *màpfèní*

(31)   Venda
    r > *ʃ* *ʃámbó* 'bone'   pl. *màrámbó*
    ɦ > *f* *fúyù* 'wild fig'   *màɦúyù*
    β > *v* *vóhó* 'animal's foreleg' *màβóhó*

The other changes involve voicing and/or plosivization:

l	> *dz*	*dzémbé*	'hoe'	pl.	*màrémbé*		
k	> *g*	*gòré*	'cloud'		*màkòré*		
tsh	> *dʒ*	*dʒílá*	'big tail'	cf.	*mùtʃhílá*	'tail'	
ʃ	> *dʒ*	*dʒáßérò*	'place of refuge'		<*ʃáßer-a*	'flee from'	

(32)   GiTonga

ø	> *t*	*ɽitiyo*	'country'	pl.	*maiyo*	
		ɽitundu	'leg'		*maundu*	

4.3 Pairings/genders

Zone S languages have the typical singular/plural pairings. In the few languages that have Cl. 21, the pairing is 21/6. Some exceptional pairings are:

1/6	Nguni, SOTHO, Shona
1/4	Zulu, SOTHO
9/6	Nguni, SOTHO
11/6	Shona
11/8	Lozi
12/14	Korekore

4.4 Concordance

The concordial system in Zone S is exemplified by Southern Sotho, GiTonga, Tsonga and Venda (tables 30.8, 30.9, 30.10, 30.11). For each language, there are three subject markers (SM). SM1 is the canonical, most widespread form; SM2 is found before certain TAM

TABLE 30.8: SOUTHERN SOTHO

	SM1	SM2	SM3	OM	Adj	Rel	Gen	Quant
1st p. sg.	*kì-*	*k-*	*n-*[1]	*Ń-*				
pl.	*rì-*	*r-*						
2nd p. sg.	*ò-*	*w-*						
pl.	*lì-*	*l-*						
3rd p. 1	*ú-*	*ø-*	*a-*	*mú-*	*é-mù-*	*yá↓á-*	*w-á-*	–
2	*bá-*	*b-*			*bá-bà-*	*bá↓á-*	*b-ó-*	*b-ó-*
3	*ú-*	*w-*			*ó-mù-*	*ó↓ó-*	*w-á-*	*w-ó-*
4	*ì-*	*y-*			*é-mì-*	*é↓é-*	*y-á-*	*y-ó-*
5	*lì-*	*l-*			*lé-lì-*	*lé↓é-*	*l-á-*	*l-ó-*
6	*á-*	*ø-*			*á-mà-*	*á↓á-*	*ø-á-*	*ø-ó-*
7	*sì-*	*s-*			*sé-sì-*	*sé↓é-*	*s-á-*	*s-ó-*
8x	*lí-*	*ts'-*			*ts'é-Ń-*	*ts'é↓é-*	*ts'-á-*	*ts'-ó-*
9	*ì-*	*y-*			*é-Ń-*	*é↓é-*	*y-á-*	*y-ó-*
10	*lí-*	*ts'-*			*ts'é-Ń-*	*ts'é↓é-*	*ts'-á-*	*ts'-ó-*
14	*bú-*	*b-*			*bó-bù-*	*bó↓ó-*	*b-á-*	*b-ó-*
15	*hú-*	*h(w)-*			*hó-hù-*	*hó↓ó-*	*h(w)-á-*	*h-ó-*
17	*hú-*	*h(w)-*			*hó-hù-*	*hó↓ó-*	*h-á-*	*h-ó-*

Note:
1 This prefix is found before the experiential auxiliary *k-a*, and the conditional prefixes *-ka-* and *-ke-*.

prefixes with shape V, including the Past Narrative prefix -*a*-; SM3 is generally found in negatives, in the Subjunctive and Conditional moods, and in the Simultaneous aspect. Nguni generally has a special SM that occurs in the Simultaneous aspect. Unless specifically listed, it can be assumed that SM3 is segmentally identical to SM1. Similarly, unless otherwise indicated, the object marker (OM) is segmentally identical to SM1.

TABLE 30.9: GITONGA

	SM1	SM2	SM3	OM	Adj	Gen	Quant
1st p. sg.	ɲi-	ɲ-					ɲ-e- ~ ɲ-o-
pl.	hi-	h-				ha-	h-e- ~ h-o-
2nd p. sg.	u-	w-		ɣu-			w-e- ~ w-o-
pl.	mu-	mw-				mw-a-	mw-e- ~ m-o-
3rd p. 1	u-	∅-	a-	mu-	M-	w-a-	y-e- ~ y-o-
2	ßa-	ß-			ßa-	ß-a-	ß-e- ~ ß-o-
3	(w)u-	∅-/w-	a-/u-	mu-/wu-	M-	w-a-	w-e- ~ w-o-
4	yi-	y-		mi-/yi-	mi-	y-a-	y-e- ~ y-o-
5	ɽi-	ɽ-			ɽi-	ɽ-a-	ɽ-e- ~ ɽ-o-
6	ma-	m-			ma-	y-a-	m-e- ~ m-o-
7	yi-	ɣy-			yi-	ɣy-a-	ɣy-e- ~ ɣy-o-
8	si-	s-			si-	s-a-	s-e- ~ s-o-
9	yi-	y-			yi-	y-a-	y-e- ~ y-o-
10	dzi-	dz-			dzi-	dz-a-	dz-e- ~ dz-o-
14	wu-	w-			wu-	w-a-	w-e- ~ -w-o-
15	ɣu-	ɣw-			ɣu-	ɣw-a-	ɣ-e- ~ -ɣ-o-
17	ɣu-	ɣw-			?		

TABLE 30.10: TSONGA

	SM1	SM2	SM3	OM	Adj	Gen	Quant
1st p. sg.	ndzǐ-	ndz-					ndz-e
pl.	ɦǐ-	ɦ-					ɦ-e-
2nd p. sg.	ǔ-	w-		-ku-			w-e-
pl.	mǐ-	m-					ŋw-e-
3rd p. 1	ǔ-	w-	a-	ŋwi-	N-	w-a-	y-e-
2	vá-	v-			va-	v-a-	v-o-
3	wú-	w-			wu-	w-a-	w-o-
4	yǐ-	y-			yi-	y-a-	y-o-
5	rǐ-	r-			ri-	r-a-	r-o-
6	má-	m-			ma-	y-a-	w-o-
7	ʃǐ-	ʃ-			ʃi-	ʃ-a-	ʃ-o-
8	s͡wǐ-	s͡w-			s͡wi-	s͡w-a-	s͡w-o-
9	yǐ-	y-			yi-	y-a-	y-o-
10	tǐ-	t-			ti-	t-a-	t-o-
11	rǐ-	r-			ri-	r-a-	r-o-
14	byǐ-	by-			byi-	by-a-	by-o-
15	kú-	k-			ku-	k-a-	k-o-
17	kú-	k-			?	k-a-	k-o-
21	dyǐ-	dy-			dyi-	dy-a-	dy-o-

TABLE 30.11: VENDA

	SM1	SM2	SM3 High	OM	Adj	Gen	Quant
1st p. sg.	*ndi̋-*	*nd-*	*-thí-*	*N-*			*nd-o-*
pl.	*ri-*	*r-*					*r-o-*
2nd p. sg.	*ù-*	*w-*					*w-o-*
pi.	*ni̋-*	*n-*					*n-o-*
3rd p. 1	*u-*	*∅-*	*á-*	*mu-*	*mu-*	*w-a-*	*∅-o- ~ ∅-e-*
2	*ßa-*	*ß-*			*ßa-*	*ß-a-*	*ß-o-*
3	*u-*	*w-*			*mu-*	*w-a-*	*w-o-*
4	*i-*	*y-*			*mi-*	*y-a-*	*y-o-*
5	*ḽi-*	*ḽ-*			*ḽi-*	*ḽ-a-*	*ḽ-o-*
6	*a-*	*∅-*			*ma-*	*∅-a-*	*∅-o-*
7	*tʃhi-*	*tʃh-*			*tʃhi-*	*tʃh-a-*	*tʃho-*
8	*z͡wi-*	*z͡w-*			*z͡wi-*	*z͡w-a-*	*z͡w-o-*
9	*i-*	*y-*			*N-*	*y-a-*	*y-o-*
10	*dzi-*	*dz-*			*dziN-*	*dz-a-*	*dz-o-*
11	*ɾu-*	*ɾw-*			*ɾu-*	*ɾw-a-*	*ɾw-o-*
14	*ßu-/ɦu-*	*ɦ-*		*ßu-*	*ßu-*	*ɦ-a-*	*ɦ-o-*
15	*ɦu-*	*ɦ-*			*ɦu-*	*ɦ-a-*	*ɦ-o-*
17	*ɦu-*	*ɦ-*			*ɦu-*	*ɦ-a-*	*ɦ-o-*
20	*ku-*	*kw-*			*ku-*	*kw-a-*	*kwo-*
21	Uses Cl. 5 SM2						

TABLE 30.12: ZULU AND TSWANA

	Zulu		Tswana	
	(A)	(B)	(A)	(B)
1	*w-á-*	*gá-*	*w-á-*	*w-á-χa-*
2	*ɓ-á-*	*ɓá-ga-*	*b-á-*	*b-á-χa-*
3	*w-á-*	*gá-*	*w-á-*	*w-á-χa-*
4	*y-á-*	*gá-*	*y-á-*	*y-á-χa-*
5	*l-á-*	*li-ga-*	*l-á-*	*l-á-χa-*
6	*∅-á-*	*gá-*	*∅-á-*	*∅-á-χa-*
7	*s-á-*	*si-ga-*	*s-á-*	*s-á-χa-*

A partial table of genitive concords for Zulu and Tswana is illustrated in table 30.12. The (A) columns are the normal forms, while the (B) columns are those used with bases of Cl. 1a.

4.5 Reflexive prefix

TABLE 30.13: REFLEXIVE PREFIXES

Zunda Nguni	SOTHO	Shona	Venda	Tsonga	GiTonga
z̤i-	*í-*	*z͡wi-*	*ḓi-*	*ti-*	*dzi-*

5 ASPECTS OF NOMINAL DERIVATION

5.1 Diminutives

The suffixes **-ana* and **-ɲana* are widely used in Zone S for the derivation of diminutives ('small', 'small quantity') of nouns and adjectives. The significance, depending upon context, may also be pejorative or may indicate endearment, and in the case of colour adjectives, the suffix **-ana*, though not **-ɲana*, denotes 'feminine'. These suffixes may co-occur with placement of the noun in a diminutive class in languages which have this feature.

(33) Copi
    tʃindóngáná   'small tree' < *ndóngá*
    tʃindzèvyáná 'small ear' < *ndzèvé*

(34) GiTonga
    ɲaryana   'small buffalo' < *ɲari*
    ɽiphuβwana 'a little air'   < *ɽiphuβo*

(35) Sotho
    kxhòmú étshèɫá   'a yellow head of cattle'
    kxhòmú étshèɫáná   'a yellow cow'
    kxhòmú étshèɫáɲánà 'a yellowish head of cattle'

5.2 Feminine/augmentative suffix

The suffix **-(k)ali* signifies either 'female' or 'augmentative' depending on the base noun and the context.

(36) Lala
    iyomat'i   'cow'   < *iyomo* 'head of cattle'
    imbwak'at'i 'bitch'   < *imbwa* 'dog'
    ufat'ikat'i 'colossal woman' < *ufat'i* 'woman'

5.3 Pronouns

The pronouns called absolute (or emphatic) have forms for 1st and 2nd persons as well as for all the classes. Frequently there are discrete possessive forms for the 1st and 2nd persons and Cl. 1. In table 30.14 (possessives are labelled gen).

TABLE 30.14: ABSOLUTE (OR EMPHATIC) PRONOUNS

	1st p. sg.		1st p. pl.		2nd p. sg.		2nd p. pl.		Cl. 1	
	base	gen	base	gen	base	gen	base	gen	base	gen
Copi	*àní*	*-ngù*	*athu*	*-thú*	*awe*	*-ko*	*anu*	*-nu*	*èné*	*-kwe*
N. Sotho	*ǹná*	*-k'à*	*rìná*	*rìná xèʃú*[1]	*wèná*	*-xáxù*	*lìná*	*lìná*	*yèná xènú*[1]	*-xáxwè*
Shona	*iní*	*-ngù*	*isú*	*-idʼù*	*iwé*	*-kò*	*imí*	*-iɲù*	*iyè*	*-ké*
GiTonga	*eni*	*-ngu*	*ethu*	*-thu*	*uwe*	*-yo*	*enu*	*-nu*	*uye*	*-ye*
Tshwa	*mìná*	*-ngu*[2]	*hìná*	*-iru*[2]	*wèná*	*-ko*[2]	*ŋwìná*	*-inu*[2]	*yèná*	*-kwé*[3]
Venda	*ǹné*	*-ngá*	*rìné*	*-ʃú*	*iwè*	*-ù*	*inwí*	*-ɲú*	*éɲè*	*-wé*
Zulu[4]	*mìná*	*-mì*	*thìná*	*-ìthù*	*wèná*	*-khò*	*nìná*	*-ìnù*	*yèná*	*-khè*

Notes:
1 These indicate ownership at the family level.
2 These forms are almost obsolete, being found only in folklore, and restricted phrases.
3 The form *yèná* occurs as an alternative with genitives.
4 The stabilizer *-na* is generally deleted when a prefix is added.

6 QUALIFICATIVES

6.1 Genitives

The genitive construction has a wide range of significances, of which we illustrate the main ones:

(37) Sotho
    (a) possession/ownership:
        mɪbót'ùk'árà yáháɪ   'her cars'
    (b) social relationship:
        ŋàk'à yák'à   'my doctor'
    (c) function/use/purpose:
        lɪbálà lámɪ́dʒàhɔ̀   'a racecourse (open area for races)'
        tʃhélèt'ɛ́ yábàɪsɪk'ɔ́p'ɔ̀   'money for the cinema'
        k'ámùrɛ́ yáhùdʒélà   'dining room' < *hùdʒá* 'to eat'
    (d) type or characteristic, including ethnicity and sex:
        ŋàk'à yábànà   'paediatrician (doctor of children)'
        k'ùbɔ̀ yáSɪsúthù   'a Sotho blanket'
        sɪphèhɪ̀ sámùsálɪ́   'a woman chef'
    (e) material constituency:
        ǹtl'ù yádjwàŋ   'a grass house'
        màláùsɪ àsílɪ̀k'à   'silk blouses'
    (f) contents:
        kxhàlásɪ yálɪ́bɪsɪ   'a glass of milk'
    (g) order (ordinal numbers):
        mùìthút'ì wáhù!álà   'the first student'
        mùɲàk'ɔ̀ wábùrárù   'the third door(way)'
    (h) fractions:
        bùrárù bátl'ɪ́lásɪ   'a third of the class'
    (i) placing of qualified item in time or space, including habitat (with locative bases):
        lɪ̀nòɲànà ts'ánùk'éŋ   'riverine birds'
        ǹmɪ́nɔ̀ wásɪdʒwálèdʒwálé/wásɪdʒwálédʒwàlè   'contemporary music'

Genitive constructions have the order *qualified–qualifier* almost always with a genitive marker (which agrees with the qualified) linking the two. As seen above, in Zone S this genitive marker normally has the shape **C-a-, where C is the typical prevocalic class consonant in the non-nasal classes, and a glide in the nasal classes, or Ø- in Cl. 6.

Nguni and Tswana have a different genitive marker that occurs before nouns of Cl. 1a. This has the form *SM-á-SM-χa-* in Tswana, *(SM-)k'a-* in Xhosa and *(SM-)ga-* in Zulu. The element SM does not occur with bases of the nasal classes (1, 3, 4, 6 and 9).

(38) Tswana
    lì≠p'ùlì ts'-á-χá-ǹrɛ́   'my father's goats'

(39) Zulu
    úɓù≠só ɓù-gá≠ɓàɓá   'my father's face'

Tswana has a discrete set of genitive concords of shape *SM-oo-* used to denote communal possession by a family or larger social unit:

(40) Tswana
ŋw≠àná wóó≠Thàbɔ 'child of Thabo's family'
lì≠fátshì lóó≠Tlhàp'ìŋ 'territory of the Tlhaping people'

GiTonga has two possible genitive constructions. The structure *qualified ɲa- qualifier*, is used only for so-called 'descriptive possessives', i.e. those with a descriptive, non-possessive, function.

(41) GiTonga
ɽidángaɽiɽa ɲaɣuβiɽi 'the second book'
siwindri ɲaβaβaci 'stones at the bottom'
pfhumu ɲanombo 'enemy chief'

As base to the *ɲa* constructions, nouns and pronouns often suffix *-i*, with the following changes: $a + i > e, o + i > we, u + i > wi$

(42) GiTonga
simbo ɲangokhwe 'coconut palm' < *ngokho*
ɲumba ɲaɣurarwi 'the third house' < *ɣuraru*

Infinitives suffix *-i*, and either lose the infinitive prefix, or some form of contraction occurs:

(43) GiTonga
βathu ɲayufe 'the dead' < *ɣufa* 'to die'
muthu ɲotshambiɽe 'worthy person' < *ɣutshambiɽe* 'to have become worthy'
muthu ɲambatshambe 'worthless person' < *ɣumbatshamba* 'not to be worthy'

6.2 Numerals and numeration

Numerals as qualifiers occur with various types of qualificative concord. The stem denoting 'one', **-*mòi* (only Venda does not make use of a reflex of this stem), shows considerable diversity in its behavior:

Shona has the stem -*mwé*, used with enumerative concords.

(44) Shona
mù≠nĥù mù≠mwé 'one person'

(45) Sotho
(There are two alternative ways to express 'one'.)
mù-thù yá↓á- mù- -ŋ 'one person'
　　　　　Rel　Enum one
mùthù á- lì mú- ŋ 'one person'
　　　SM-SIMUL copula-SIMUL 'be' Enum one
cf. mù-thù émù-ŋ 'some/another person' with Adj Conc émù-

GiTonga and Copi have the construction *Adj Conc-mo-2nd pos Dem Pron:*

(46) GiTonga
mu≠thu mo-yo < *m-mo-uyo* 'one person' (1)
ɽi≠tshiɣu ɽi≠mwe-do < *ɽi-mo-ido* 'one day' (5)

ɣi≠pande ɣi≠mwe-ɣyo	'one piece' (7)
wu≠ɾanga wu≠mo-wo	'one place' (14)

Tsonga has the stem *-ŋwe* used with the enumerative concord:

(47)   Tsonga
ʃ≠àndlà ʃì≠ŋwè 'one hand'

In Xhosa the stem *-ɲè* occurs with the Adjectival concord, and follows the qualified item:

(48)   Xhosa
í ≠ làngà é-lí ≠ ɲè 'one day' (5)
cf. élíɲé ìlàngà 'some day (Adj.)'

In Zulu *-ɲe* occurs with the enumerative concord:

(49)   Zulu
mù ≠ nt'ù mù ≠ ɲè 'one person'
cf. ó-mú ≠ ɲ ' ú-mú ≠ nt'ù 'some person (Adj.)'

The above form appears to be obsolescent, and the more common construction is:
Rel Conc-Quant Marker-twa

(50)   Zulu
ù-mú ≠ nt'ú ó-y-é ≠ twà 'one person' (1)
ìlí ≠ fù é-lì-l-ó ≠ twà 'one cloud' (5)

Venda uses the adjectival stem *-thìhí:*

(51)   Venda
mù ≠ tùkà mù ≠ thìhí 'one youth'

In all Zone S languages, the stems for 2 and 3, and except for the Mozambican languages, also 4 and 5, are adjectival (though 4 is adjectival in Gitonga):

(52)   GiTonga
ßa ≠ thu ßa ≠ ßiɾi 'two people'
dzi ≠ ɓuru dzi ≠ tharu 'three donkeys'
si ≠ rengo si ≠ na 'four animals'

Other stems may be relative or genitive.
    The stems for 1 to 5 (and in some languages 6), 10 and 100 are primitive stems. For 6–9, some languages have derivative stems: 6 = 'thumb', 'cross over'; 7 = 'point'; 8 = 'break two (fingers)', etc. In the Mozambican languages 6 to 9 assume the forms 5 and 1, 5 and 2, which is also what occurs in all languages for 11 to 19.

6.3 Ordinal numbers

In Nguni and Shona, ordinal numbers are in Cl. 7:

(53)   Shona
mù ≠ ʃá wé-ʃì ≠ tánhàtú 'the sixth village'

In South Ndebele ordinal numbers for 2–5 are in Cl. 14, the others are based on Cl. 15 or Cl. 5 nouns. In Copi, Ronga, Tsonga and the Sotho languages, they are in Cl. 14.

(54)   Tsonga
yìn ≠ dlù yá-vù ≠ nkómbó 'the seventh house'

In GiTonga they are in Cl. 15 or 17:

(55)   GiTonga
       ŗi ≠ dangaŗiŗa ŋa-ɣu ≠ βiŗi 'the second book'

6.4 Demonstratives

Zone S languages generally distinguish at least three of the typical Bantu demonstrative positions – those signifying 'relatively near the speaker', 'relatively near the addressee' and 'relatively distant from both speaker and addressee'. Shona has only two basic positions, while Venda has four, adding a set meaning 'very close to the speaker'. One or other of these positions are used for temporal reference or for previous referents. Examples of demonstratives for five classes in GiTonga, Tsonga and Venda are presented in table 30.15.

6.5 Presentative demonstratives

Presentative demonstratives are special copulative forms of demonstratives. SOTHO lacks this separate formal category, since the normal identifying copulative prefix occurs before demonstratives. Venda, Shona and the Nguni languages, however, have special forms distinct from other copulatives. The older Zulu forms (table 30.16) under (A)

TABLE 30.15: DEMONSTRATIVES

	GiTonga			Tsonga			Venda			
	1	2	4	1	2	4	1	2	3	4
1	*oyu*	*uyo*	*muŗe*	*loyi*	*loye*	*loya*	*ùyù*	*ùyò*	*ùnò*	*ùļà*
2	*aβa*	*aβo*	*βaŗe*	*lava*	*lavo*	*lavaya*	*àβà*	*àβò*	*βànò*	*βàļà*
4	*eyi*	*iyo*	*yiŗe*	*leyi*	*leyo*	*leyiya*	*ìyì*	*ìyò*	*ìnò*	*ìļà*
6	*aya*	*ayo*	*yaŗe*	*lawa*	*lawo*	*lawaya*	*àyà*	*àyò*	*ànò*	*àļà*
10	*edzi*	*idzo*	*dziŗe*	*leti*	*leto*	*letiya*	*ìdzì*	*ìdzò*	*dzìnò*	*dzìļà*

TABLE 30.16: ZULU[1]

	1st pos.		2nd pos.	3rd pos.
	(A)	(B)	(A)	(A)
1	*nângù*	*nângù*	*nâng(ó)ò*	*nângùyá*
2	*nâmpà*	*nàbà*	*nâmp(ó)ò*	*nâmpàyá*
3	*nânkù*	*nâwù*	*nânk(ó)ò*	*nânkùyá*
4	*nânsì*	*nàyì*	*nâns(ó)ò*	*nânsìyá*
5	*nântì*	*nâlì*	*nânt(ó)ò*	*nântìyá*
6	*nânkà*	*nâwà*	*nânk(ó)ò*	*nânkàyá*
7	*nâsì*	*nâsì*	*nâs(ó)ò*	*nâsìyá*
8	*nâẓì*	*nâẓì*	*nâẓ(ó)ò*	*nâẓìyá*
9	*nânsì*	*nàyì*	*nâns(ó)ò*	*nânsìyá*
10	*nâẓì*	*nâẓì*	*nâẓ(ó)ò*	*nâẓìyá*
11	*nântù*	*nâlù*	*nânt(ó)ò*	*nântùyá*
14	*nâmpù*	*nàbù*	*nâmp(ó)ò*	*nâmpùyá*
15	*nâk(h)ù*	*nâk(h)ù*	*nâk(h)(ó)ò*	*nâk(h)ùyá*
17	*nâk(h)ù*	*nâk(h)ù*	*nâk(h)(ó)ò*	*nâk(h)ùyá*

Note:
1 We give (B) forms only for 1st position.

below are morphologically opaque, and this may be the reason that younger speakers use the more readily analyzable forms under (B).

6.6 Locatives

Lozi and Shona make use of Cl. 16, 17 and 18 prefixes to denote location, as do Tswana and GiTonga, though in conjunction with a locative suffix. All languages make use of a locative prefix with nouns of Cl. 1a, 2a/2b, and depending upon the individual language and the semantics or syntax, also with personal nouns. Otherwise, use is made of a locative suffix with protoform *-ini. In Nguni and some Tsonga dialects there is concomitant use of a locative prefix **e-.

(56) Sotho
 mùrít'í-ŋ 'in, to, from the shade' <*mùrit'i*

(57) GiTonga
 hungo-ni 'in, on, to the head' < *hungo*
 ɲumba-ni 'to/from/in the house' < *ɲumba*

(58) Zulu
 émthùnzíni 'in, to, from the shade' < *úmthûnzi*

GiTonga also has a locative suffix *-tunu* with a more general significance 'at', 'in the vicinity of':

(59) GiTonga
 hungo-tunu 'around the head'
 ɲumba-tunu 'at the house'

7 VERBAL RADICAL STRUCTURE

7.1 Denominative and deideophonic derivation

All Zone S languages show denominative (including de-adjectival) derivations, using some reflex of the PB verbalizer *-p-*, and often including the stative extension *-ad-*.

(60) Sotho
 swéú-f-àl-à 'become white' < *-swèú* 'white'
 ǹ-thù-f-àl-à 'become personified' < *mù ≠ thù* 'person'

7.2 Diminutive

Southern Sotho has extended the use of the nominal diminutive suffix to verbs:

(61) Sotho
 k'ìàphìlàɲànà 'I am sort of OK'
 cf. *k'ìàphìlà* 'I am well'
 lìdʒɔ́ liábìlàɲànà 'The food is simmering'
 cf. *liábìlà* 'It is boiling'

7.3 Extensions

Zone S languages have a typical range of productive and non-productive extensions, with standard significances and syntactic functions. They all have the following as productive extensions: applicative, causative (with suffix **-*is*-), passive, neuter, reciprocal. The intensive (**-*isis*-) and perfective (**-*elel*-) are also productive in most of them. In addition SOTHO has the reversive, neuter reversive and extensive (-*ak*-) as productive elements.

8 VERBAL INFLECTION

8.1 TAM

8.1.1 Tense

Typically, Zone S makes a basic distinction in absolute tenses between past, present and future, with Nguni, GiTonga and Tsonga distinguishing a far past from a near past (in GiTonga the far past refers to actions that occurred prior to the day before yesterday). Shona has discrete hodiernal and general pasts in the positive, and Southern Sotho distinguishes far, near and general past, though specification of far or near past seems to depend more on the speaker and on style, than purely on normal tense considerations. Nguni and Southern Sotho distinguish near future from far future, albeit not rigorously. The anterior (generally called the perfect tense) is best treated as aspect (see below), but it sometimes seems to function as a tense, and one could consider it as a 'tensepect', a form having elements of both tense and aspect.

(62) Shona (Zezuru)
Non-Hodiernal Past: pos. SM^c-*a-ka-R-a*
Nd-à-ká ≠ *tèng-à* 'I bought'
Hodiernal Past: pos. SM^c-*a-R-a*
Nd-à ≠ *múk-à màngwánàní ánò* 'I got up this morning'

(63) Sotho
Near Past: SM-*sá-tsw'à* ≠ *R-a*
Lí-sá-tsw'à ≠ *fíłà* 'They (10) have just arrived'
Past: SM-*ìlé* SM^c-*a* ≠ *R-a*
Líìlé ts'áfíłà kxhwèlíŋ é↓éfît'íléŋ 'They arrived last month'
Far Past: SM-*nè* SM-R-*ı*
Línè lìfíłı kxhálè 'They arrived long ago'

Relative tenses have as their point of focus either some point of time in the past or in the future, which, according to language, may be either far or near, and the situation in question may be specified as anterior, co-extensive or posterior to that point.

(64) Zulu
The auxiliary *ɓè-* (generally reduced to a pre-prefix in past tenses) characterizes relative tenses, both future and recent past:
Past Present: *ɓèŋ(g)íŋ(g)àɓí* 'I wasn't eating'
Past Anterior: *ɓèŋ(g)íŋ(g)àɓílè* 'I had not had enough to eat'
Past Past: *ɓèŋ(g)íŋ(g)àɓáŋ(g)à* 'I hadn't eaten'

Past Near Future: *ɓèŋ(g)íŋ(g)èzùgúɓà/ɓèŋ(g)íŋ(g)èzúgùɓá* 'I wasn't about to eat'

Past Far Future: *ɓèŋ(g)íŋ(g)èyúgùɓá* 'I wasn't going to eat (at some fairly distant time)'

(65)   Zulu
We illustrate two far past relative tenses:
Far Past Present: *ŋ(g)ááŋ(g)íŋ(g)àɓí* 'I wasn't eating (long ago)'
Far Past Far Future: *ŋ(g)ááŋ(g)íŋ(g)èyúgùɓá* 'I was not (long ago) going (in the distant future) to eat'

(66)   Zulu
Some near future relative tenses:
Near Future Present: *ŋ(g)ìzòɓè ŋ(g)íŋ(g)àɓí* 'I shall not be eating'
Near Future Past: *ŋ(g)ìzòɓè ŋ(g)íŋ(g)àɓáŋ(g)à* 'I shall not have eaten'
Near Future Far Future: *ŋ(g)ì z̧òɓè ŋ(g)íŋ(g)èyúgùɓá* 'I shall not be going (in the remote future) to eat'

(67)   Zulu
A future relative tense may be situated within a past relative tense:
Far Past Near Future Present: *ŋ(g)ááŋ(g)ízòɓè ŋ(g)íɓá* 'I was (long ago) going to be eating/I would have been eating (not too long after that time)'
Near Past Near Future Near Future: *ɓèŋ(g)ízòɓè ŋ(g)ízòɓá* 'I was going to be going to eat/I would have been going to eat'
Far Past Far Future Past: *ŋ(g)ááŋ(g)ìyó(ò)ɓè ŋ(g)ìlàlílè* 'I was going to have had slept/I would have had slept'

8.1.2 Mood

The basic modal distinctions in Zone S are: infinitive; imperative; indicative; subjunctive; and conditional/potential.

The infinitive and imperative moods have their usual significances. Most languages have negative infinitives, and some permit inflection for tense, mood and aspect in the infinitive:

(68)   GiTonga

ɣu-mba ≠ dwana	'not to fight'
ɣu ≠ won-iɽe	'to have seen (Anterior)'
ɣu-ta ≠ thum-a	'to come and work (Venitive)'
ɣu-ya ≠ man-a	'to go and get (Andative)'

(69)   Tswana

χù-k'á ≠ rèk'-á	'to be able to buy (Potential mood)'
χù-sá ≠ rèk'-á	'to still buy (Progressive aspect)'
χù-sà ≠ bónà	'not to have bought (Anterior, neg.)'
χù-tl'à ≠ rék'-à	'to be going to buy (Future)'

In Zone S languages factivity, with various subdivisions, is a modal category.

FACTIVE: Indicative   Definite   Potential   Conditional   Approximate

The indicative mood expresses a situation that the speaker asserts as factual, including deliberate false assertion. It includes interrogatives, in which the speaker asks for information as to the factuality of a situation. The definite mood is a more emphatic statement of factuality. The potential mood indicates the speaker's belief that a certain situation might arise, or has the potentiality of arising. The conditional mood indicates the speaker's belief that a certain situation may obtain should certain conditions be fulfilled. The conditional mood includes instances of unfulfilled past condition – 'I would have gone out if it had not rained'. (Not all Zone S languages distinguish potential and conditional moods.) The approximate mood indicates the speaker's belief that a certain event nearly took place, or that a certain situation almost pertains.

Other types of factivity would include counter-intuitive or contradictive factivity.

(70)   Sotho
    Indicative: *hàátl'ɪ*   'She isn't coming'
    Definite: *úfèlà ásàtl'á*   'She has really not come'
    Potential: *àk'ásitl'ɪ*   'She might not come'
    Conditional: *àk'ábé ásàtl'ɪ, hódʒà làsɪk'é làmúfá tʃhélèt'è*   'She wouldn't be coming if you hadn't given her money'
    Approximate: *úbàtl'ílé ásàtl'ɪ*   'She almost didn't come'
                   sɪfàt'é sɪbàtl'à sɪʃwɪlé   'The tree is almost dead'
    Contradictive: *úák'ùlà; úmp'á áɪtl'à fèélá*   'She is sick; she is nevertheless coming'

An unusual distinction that should probably be considered modal, is that signifying an action that occurs opportunely.

(71)   Sotho
    úɲáfà áɪtl'à   'She is coming *at the right time*'
    úɲàfílé àsɪk'é àtl'à   'It's *just as well* she didn't come'

The following are also best considered modal.

(72)   Sotho
    úánèlà hùtl'à álɪ ts'ɪléŋ   'She *just manages* to come on the way'
    útsw'àtsw'ílé áɪtl'à   'She came *in vain*'
    lɪtsw'àtsw'à lɪkw'àt'á   'You're getting angry *for nothing*'

(73)   Lala
    na<u>phuta</u> kufika   'You *were dilatory* in coming'

(74)   Swati
    U<u>mane</u> alale   'He *simply* sleeps'
    U<u>mane</u> uyangiɫupha   'He is worrying me *for no reason*'

(75)   Sotho
    àk'átshùhà átl'à   'She might *unexpectedly* come'
    útshùhílé áílìbànà   'She *suddenly* fainted'
    ... k'àtshùhà sɪfùfáni sɪwá   '... and *suddenly* the plane crashed (I suddenly the plane crashed)'

(76)   Swati
    W<u>etuka</u> imluma   'It *suddenly* bit him (He suddenly it bit him)'

In the last two examples, there are different subjects to the auxiliary and its complement. The auxiliary is a grammaticalization of verbs meaning 'get a fright'.

Various grammars posit other moods, such as Participial/Situational and Temporal, but these are best treated as aspect.

8.1.3 Aspect

Aspect may be indicated: (a) by a special auxiliary verb; (b) by a post-subject-concord prefix; (c) more rarely, by suffix.

Zone S languages (Shona being an exception) generally distinguish anterior (distinct from any past tenses and from the present tense) and perfective aspects. The perfective aspect is the 'default' aspect, and is generally unmarked. The anterior aspect has a common form ****SM-R-ile*. The desinence **-ile* may take a variety of forms in the various languages. The Sotho languages, for example, display remnants of vowel harmony, and other complexities:

(77)   South Sotho

álím-á 'borrow'	>	alimme
hán-á 'refuse'	>	hanne
ŋàŋ-à 'sulk'	>	ŋaŋŋe
tshwár-à 'catch'	>	tshwerɪ
bófʊ̀ll-à 'untie'	>	bofʊlʊts'ɪ
bɔ́k'ɔ́ll-à 'scream'	>	bok'olets'ɪ
sɪ̀ɲ-à 'spoil'	>	sɪnts'e

(78)   Tswana

ʃ-á 'give'	>	file
dʒ-á 'eat'	>	dʒɪle
nw-á 'drink'	>	nʊle
ʃw-á 'die'	>	ʃule

Southern Sotho illustrates the rich variety of aspectual distinctions found in Zone S languages. Probably more than other languages though, it may combine several aspects in one verb phrase.

(79)   Sotho

Perfective: ʊ́ìlé àrɔ̀bàlà   'He slept'
   ʊ́ìlé àts'àmàyà   'He went (but may have returned meanwhile)'
Anterior: ʊ́ròbèts'ɪ   'He's asleep'
   ʊ́ts'àmàìlè   'He has gone (and is still away)'
Completive: ʊ́sè áìthút'à   'He is studying now/He is already studying'
   ʊ́sè àìthút'ílè   'He has already studied'
   ʊ́sè átl'áìthút'à   'He will soon study'
Simultaneous: ʊ́màmélá m̀mínó áìthút'à   'She listens to music while studying'
Continuative: ʊ́ń↓ts'é áìthút'à   'He continues to study'
Durative: ʊ́ńnè àìthút'ɪ   'He keeps on studying'
Consecutive (not to be confused with the narrative):
   Past: k'ɪ̀dʒɪlé kànt'ànɔ̃ ànɔ̃ìthút'à   'I ate and then studied'
   Fut: k'ɪtl'ʾàdʒá k'ínt'ànɔ̃ìthút'à   'I shall eat and then study'
Immediate: ʊ́tl'ǎfìlà áìthút'è   'She will study at once'
Interim: ʊ́tl'ǎtsw'à áìthút'à   'She will study in the meantime'
Persistive: ʊ́sàìthút'à   'He is still studying'
Permanent: ʊ́ɬòts'ɪ áròbéts'ɪ   'He has been asleep the whole time'

hàátl'őƚɔ́là ábùá   'He will never again speak'
Frequentative: *ʋát'ìsà hʋìthút'à*   'He often studies'
Occasional: *ʋ̀k'è àìthút'ì*   'He occasionally studies'
Habitual: *ʋ́yè àìthút'ì*   'He generally/habitually studies'
Iterative: *ʋ́tl'ắphìt'à àìthút'à*   'She will study again'
Experiential: *ʋ̀k'ìlé àìthút'à*   'She once studied'
Nocturnal: *ʋ́lálà àìthút'à*   'He spends the night studying'
Matinal: *ʋ́ts'ʋ́hà àìthút'à*   'She studies first thing in the morning'

(80) Sotho
Aspects and tense may be combined to yield sentences such as:

ʋ́-	*nè*	*á-*	*k'è*	*à-*		*lál-*	*-ì*	*á-*	*ìthút'*	*-à*
SM	Past	SM	OCC	SM-HAB		NOC	HAB	SM	study	TAM

'He used occasionally to spend the night studying'

ʋ́-	*tl'â-*	*bé*	*á-*		*ńnè*	*à-*		*àt'ìs*	*-ì*
SM	FUT	FUT-RE	SM-SIMUL		DUR	SM-HAB		FREQ	TAM

hʋ̀-	*lálà*	*á-*		*ìthút'-*	*-à*
INF	NOC	SM-SIMUL		study	TAM

'He will keep on frequently studying at night'

ʋ́-	*sà-*	*ǹts'ání*	*á-*		*ƚɔ́lá*	*á-*		*sà-*
SM	PERS	CONT	SM-SIMUL		PERM	SM-SIMUL		NEG-SIMUL

ìthút'	*-ì*
study	NEG

'He keeps on not studying'

(81) Sotho
Of interest is that many auxiliary verbs require complements in a particular mood or aspect. Thus in the above sentences we find the following:
ʋ́nè (+ SIMUL aspect) *ák'è* (+ Habitual aspect) *àlálì* (+ SIMUL aspect) *àìthút'à*
ʋ́tl'âbé (+ SIMUL aspect) *ánnè* (+ Habitual aspect) *ààt'ìsì* (+ Infinitive mood) *hʋ̀lálà* (+ SIMUL aspect) *àìthút'à*

8.1.4 Deixis: venitive and andative

Nguni, SOTHO and GiTonga have venitive and andative forms of the verb through grammaticalization of verbs meaning 'come' and 'go to'. Venitive and andative markers come before the radical, after any pre-radical TAM markers.

(82) Zulu
ŋ(g)ìzɔ́lìmà   'I am coming to cultivate'

(83) Sotho
k'ìyòlìmà   'I am going to cultivate'

Venitive and andative forms 'remember' that the historical complement to the verbs meaning 'come' and 'go to' was an infinitive with TAM suffix *-a*, and this suffix is retained even in constructions which would otherwise require some other suffix.

(84) Zulu
àgázɔ̱síz̲à   'He is not coming to help'
cf. *àgàsíz̲ì*   'He is not helping'

ŋ(g)ìfúná úgúthì áyǒ-ósízà 'I want him to go and help'
cf. ŋ(g)ìfúná úgúthì ásìzé 'I want him to help'

(85)   Sotho
úyè àtl'óthúsá 'She normally comes and helps'
cf. úyè àthúsì 'She normally helps'

8.1.5 Negation

Negation in Zone S takes two main forms: (a) the use of a preconcordial negative
marker, with or without simultaneous suffixal marking; (b) the use of a post-concordial
negative marker, with or without simultaneous suffixal marking. In both cases, there is
generally also a tonal change in the verb stem, and sometimes also in the subject
concords, particularly those of the first and second persons.

9 SYNTAX

The most basic syntactic patterns are the following:

(a) SVO
This order applies to words as such, but the SOV order holds for concordial elements
within the verb:

(86)   Shona
vàsíkáná   vá- nò ≠ tʃhér- á   mvúrá   'The girls draw water'
girls   SM-TAM-draw-   TAM   water
vàsíkáná   vá- nò- í ≠ tʃhér- á   'The girls draw it'
girls   SM-TAM-OM ≠ draw-   TAM

In Xhosa and Zulu the subject is postponed in questions:

(87)   Zulu
ɓàyákùlà àɓántw'ànà?   'Are the children sick?'
cf. àɓántw'ànà ɓàyákùlà   'The children are sick'

The standard grammars of Zulu and Xhosa give the impression that the basic word order
is SVO, yet sentences such as the following seem to be the norm, and it is clear that
further research is needed on the syntax of these languages:

(88)   Zulu
ɓà- yá- lú ≠ phúẓ -à   û ≠ ɓìsì à-ɓá ≠ ntw' -ànà
they-disjunctive-it (11)-drink   -TAM   (11)-milk   (2)-   person-   Dimin
'The children drink milk'

The object concord in most Zone S languages is used pronominally (i.e. in place of a
noun) or emphatically (i.e. together with a noun, in order to emphasize it):

(89)   Sotho
k'ì ≠ dʒá łàp'ì   'I eat fish/I am eating fish'
k'ì-à-ì ≠ dʒá   'I eat it/am eating it'
k'ì-à-ì ≠ dʒá łàp'ì   'As for fish, I eat it'

In Xhosa and Zulu however, the use of the object concord is different, in that it serves to distinguish present continuous from simple present:

(90) Xhosa
    Ndìc'á ìntl'ànẕì   'I am eating fish'
    Ndìyàyíc'à ìntl'ànẕì 'I eat fish'

Our evidence is that only Tswana permits two, or even three, OMs in the verb:

(91) Tswana
    K'ɨ-tl'à`-kw'ál-él-él-à   ŋw ≠ àná   bà ≠ ts'álí   lù ≠ kw'áló
    I- Fut≠write-Dative-Dative-TAM (1) ≠ child (2) ≠ parent (11) ≠ letter
    'I shall write a letter to the parents for the child'
    K'ɨ-tl'à`-lù- bà- mù ≠ kw'ál-él- él- à
    I- Fut-OM(11)-OM(2)-OM(1) ≠ write-Dative-Dative-TAM
      'I shall write it to them for him'

(b) Qualified–qualifier
The above order holds in almost every instance. Exceptions include:

(92) Zulu (Quantitatives with stem *-nk'è* usually precede any noun qualified.
       Adjectives with stem *-ɲé* 'some, other' normally precede a noun
       qualified.)
    ɓónk'[↓]úɓùsîgà   'the whole winter'
    ámáɲ' àmátòtà   'some men'

(c) Verb–modifier
Though time and place adverbs may occur sentence-initially for focus, manner adverbs follow the verb.

(d) Noun–pronoun/pronoun–noun
Nguni and Sotho languages generally have the order noun–pronoun in subjectival position and the order pronoun–noun is obligatory in objectival position:

(93) Zulu
    àɓántw'ànà ɓòná ɓàɓángà ùḿsìndò 'As for the children, they are
    making a noise'
    àŋ(g)ìthándì ɓòná àɓántw'ànà 'I don't like *children*'

Louwrens (1991) states that in Northern Sotho the different orders in subject position have different significances: pronoun–noun particularizes the subject, while noun–pronoun contrasts the subject.

(94) N. Sotho
    yòná kw'ènà ḭát'ḭʃà xùβúláyà βàthù 'Particularly the crocodile is
    increasingly killing people'
    βàsálí βàk'ásḭbé xɔ̀nà, fḛlá βàńnà βòná βátl'ók'ɔpànà mó 'The women will
    not be present, but *the men, by contrast*, will meet here'

REFERENCES

Bailey 1976; Donnelly 1996; Louwrens 1991; Traill 1990; Traill *et al.* 1987.

FURTHER READING

Baumbach 1987; Cole 1955; Creissels 1996, 1998, 1999a,b; Dickens 1986; Doke 1954; Doke and Mofokeng 1957; Dos Santos 1941; Fortune 1995; Miti 1996; Persson 1932; Poulos 1985, 1990; Poulos and Louwrens 1994; Poulos and Msimang 1998; Van Dyk 1960; Ziervogel 1959; Ziervogel and Mabuza 1976.

CHAPTER THIRTY-ONE

A CLASSIFICATION OF THE BANTU LANGUAGES: AN UPDATE OF GUTHRIE'S REFERENTIAL SYSTEM

Jouni Maho

1 INTRODUCTION: WHAT, WHY AND HOW

This is an update of Malcolm Guthrie's classification of the Bantu languages, the latest version of which can be found in the second volume of his *Comparative Bantu* (Guthrie 1971). Guthrie's list of languages and the code numbers that he has assigned them are well-known and widely used in academic literature. The main aim here is to keep Guthrie's original list as it is, and add missing languages to that. This also means that the present update is referential, not genetic. There are good reasons for this choice. For better or for worse, Guthrie's reference numbers have stuck, while the renumberings aimed at being genetically more valid have not, mainly because these latter offerings tend to be revised with new insights. Add to this the fact that individual researchers are likely to reclassify specific languages or language groups as they see fit. Besides, our current state of knowledge about the internal subgrouping of the Bantu language group is still rather fragmentary. Thus any proposed genetic classification is likely to be subject to more dramatic future revisions than would a referential one, since there are (at least ideally) fewer problems involved in establishing a referential classification.

The starting point, then, has been Guthrie's 'Inventory of Bantu languages' (1971:28–64). To this, some 200 new languages/dialects have been added. Adding new languages to Guthrie's list means that they have to be assigned codes compatible with his original coding system. However, it should be clear from the codes themselves that they are not originally Guthrie's, but additions made by someone else. For this purpose, the principles adopted here for creating new codes are essentially identical to those used by Lowe and Schadeberg (1997) in their *Bantu MapMaker* program. Briefly, all new codes are distinguished from Guthrie's original codes by containing either three digits (as in A801, C161, K333, etc.) or two digits followed by an upper-case letter (e.g. A32C, S31E, etc.). The general rule has been to classify any new language/dialect within the group where it lies, or at least within any immediately adjacent group. (Groups are the ones with codes ending in zeroes, e.g. A10, A20, etc.) A new language code has then been created in accordance with one of the following four principles:

Principle 1: A third digit is added to an already existing language code, if the new language/dialect is closely affiliated to one of the languages already classified by Guthrie within the group. For instance, Ngoro and Bima have been coded A111 and A112, respectively, since they are closest to Londo (A11) within the A10 group. Note thus that A11, A111 and A112 refer to coordinate entities. A111 and A112 are not sub-entities of A11.

Principle 2: A third digit is added to the group code, if the closest affinity within the group is uncertain or impossible to decide. Thus Phalaborwa, Kutswe, Pai and Pulana have been coded S301, S302, S303 and S304, respectively, since they cannot be (safely) linked to any single language of those already classified/coded in the S30 group.

Principle 3: An upper-case letter is added to an already existing language code, if the addition can be considered to be a sub-entity of the latter or when the addition completes a series of languages/dialects already letter-coded by Guthrie. Thus the E72-dialects Jibana, Kambe and Ribe have been added as E72F, E72G and E72H, respectively, so as to complete Guthrie's incomplete list of E72 dialects.

Principle 4: Add an upper-case letter to the group code, if the new language is a pidgin, creole or mixed language. (These are listed separately at the end of the updated list.) The group code is chosen so as to be suggestive of the typological (and genetic?) affiliation of the language in question. Thus Kituba has been coded H10A, Mono kutuba H10B, and so on. (Note that this last principle is not used in the *Bantu MapMaker* program.)

Some codes in zones D and E have been amended with the letter J, in parentheses, as a recognition of the so-called J-zone established by the Tervuren scholars (see Bastin, this volume). Unfortunately, the J codes used in the literature vary to some extent. The main source used for the J codes here derive from the most recent lexicostatistical study by Bastin *et al.* (1999). Their list of languages is not complete, however, so any lacunas have been filled with information derived mainly from the *Ethnologue* (Grimes 2000), or else via personal contacts with other scholars (see below).

Guthrie's original spellings have not always been retained. For instance, obsolete and idiosyncratic spellings have been avoided as far as possible. Thus 'Kgalagadi' is used here instead of Guthrie's 'Kxhalaxadi'. Moreover, all symbols unique to particular transcription systems as well as all diacritics have been either changed or omitted. The characters used here are the ones included in the so-called ASCII set. Thus all name forms have been adapted for use in computerized information storage and retrieval systems.

Most lines below contain more than one name. Often they are simply variant spellings of the same name, both or all of which are commonly used in the literature (e.g. Cuka, Chuka). Some languages are commonly referred to with different names in different countries (e.g. Bomwali, Sanghasangha), in which case both/all names are listed. Sometimes a single code has been used to designate several (very) closely related varieties (see, for instance, the G40 group). The name forms adopted here are generally without prefixes; cf. Bailey (1995:34–5) for good arguments why prefixless names are to be preferred. Occassionally, however, a prefixed name has been added for clarifying purposes. It is worth emphasizing that it is not the purpose of the present enterprise to prescribe the use of any particular name, form or spelling. The ones given here are the ones commonly found in the (English) literature. However, clearly incorrect, derogative and obsolete names have been either omitted or marked as such.

There would seem to be no end to adding missing names to Guthrie's original list. Instead, the difficulty has been to decide which ones not to add. Even though the main aim has been to list languages, not dialects, it has not been possible to adhere to any consistent policy in this respect, partly because in many cases it has simply not been possibly to decide safely what to regard as languages or dialects, but also because Guthrie's original list is itself unsystematic on this issue. Where Guthrie lists dialects, these have been kept. Occasionally additions have been made. One unavoidable consequence of this has been that some groups contain more details than do others. Nonetheless, the general policy adopted here is a restrictive one. Doubtless many more names could have been added, but available data are still too scanty for many parts of the Bantu area. The list should therefore not be seen as the final version, but more like an interim report to which future additions are likely to be made.

Information about which languages to add or not to add, how to classify them and what to call them derive mainly from printed sources (see References section at the end). Where these have been non-informative, incoherent or generally inconsistent with each other (or themselves!), I have sought help (largely via email) from various scholars, especially the editors, Derek Nurse and Gérard Philippson, as well as Douglas Boone, Robert Botne, Derek F. Gowlett, Tore Janson, Lynn Kisembe, Myles Leitch, Connie Kutsch Lojenga, Balla Masele, Thilo Schadeberg, Gabi Sommer and Paul Thomas. I have smoothed out inconsistencies as I have seen fit, often with the invaluable advice of the just-mentioned people. Where I have failed to follow their recommendations is where future revisions are likely to occur.

2 THE NEW UPDATED GUTHRIE LIST

A10	*Lundu-Balong Group*		*A30*	*Bube-Benga Group*
A11	Londo		A31	Bobe, Bubi, Ediya
A111	Ngoro		A31a	North Bobe
A112	Bima, Batanga		A31b	Southwest Bobe
A12	Barue, Lue, West Kundu		A31c	Southeast Bobe
A121	Mbonge, Ekombe		A32a	Banoo, Nohu, Noko
A122	Bakundu		A32b	Bapoko, Puku, Naka
A13	Balong		A32C	Batanga
A14	Bonkeng		A33a	Yasa
A141	Bafo, Lefo'		A33b	Kombe, Ngumbi
A15	Mbo, Manenguba		A34	Benga
A15A	Northeast Mbo			
A15B	Northwest Mbo (incl. Nswase, Mienge)		*A40*	*Basa Group*
			A41	Lombi, Rombi
A15C	Central Mbo (incl. Akoose, Bafun, Elung)		A42	Bankon, Abo
			A43a	Mbene, Basaá, Koko, Mvele
			A43b	North Kogo
A20	*Duala Group*		A43c	South Kogo
A21	Mboko, Bomboko		A44	Nen, Tunen, Banen
A22	Kpe, Bakwiri		A441	Aling'a
A221	Bubia		A45	Nyo'on, Nyokon
A23	Su, Isubu, Bimbia		A46	Mandi, Lemande, Numaand
A231	Kole		A461	Bonek, Ponek, Otomb
A24	Duala		A462	Yambeta
A241	Bodiman			
A25	Oli, Ewodi, Wuri		*A50*	*Bafia Group*
A26	Pongo		A51	Fa', Fak, Balom
A261	Mongo		A52	Kaalong, Mbong
A27	Limba, Mulimba, Malimba		A53	Kpa, Bafia
			A54	Ngayaba, Djanti, Tibea

A60	*Sanaga Group*		B11e	Nkomi
A61	Ngoro		B11F	Nenga
A62	Yambasa			
A63	Mangisa		*B20*	*Kele Group*
A64	Bacenga		B21	Seki(yani), Bulu, Sheke
A65	Bati		B22a	West Kele
A601	Ki, Tuki		B22b	Ngom
			B22c	Bubi
A70	*Yaunde-Fang Group*		B23	Mbangwe
A71	Eton		B24	Wumbvu
A72a	Ewondo, Yaunde		B25	Kota
A72b	Mvele		B251	Shake
A72c	Bakja, Badjia		B252	Mahongwe
A72d	Yangafek		B201	Ndasa
A73a	Bebele		B202	Sigu
A73b	Gbigbil, Bebil		B203	Sama, Osamayi
A74a	Bulu		B204	Ndambomo
A74b	Bene		B205	Metombola
A75	Fang, Pangwe			
			B30	*Tsogo Group*
A80	*Maka-Njem Group*		B31	Tsogo, Mitsogo
A81	Mvumbo, Kwasio, Ngumba		B32	Kande, Okande
A82	So		B301	Viya, Avias
A83	Makaa		B302	Himba(ka), Simba
A831	Byep, North Makaa		B303	Bongwe
A832	Bikele, Kol, Bekol		B304	Apindji, Pinzi
A84	Koonzime, Njem		B305	Vove, Pove
A841	Badwee, Bajue			
A85a	Nkonabeeb, Konabem		*B40*	*Shira Group*
A85b	Bekwel, Bakwele		B41	Sira, Shira
A86a	Mezime, Medjime		B42	Sangu, Shango
A86b	Mpompon, Bombo		B43	Punu
A86c	Mpiemo, Mbimu		B44	Lumbu
A87	Bomwali, Sanghasangha		B401	Bwisi
A801	Gyele, Bagyeli		B402	Varama
A802	Ukhwejo		B403	Vungu
			B404	Ngubi
A90	*Kaka Group*			
A91	Kwakum, Bakum		*B50*	*Njabi Group*
A92a	Pol		B51	Duma, Adouma
A92b	Pomo		B52	Nzebi, Njabi
A92C	Kweso		B53	Tsaangi, Tsengi
A93	Kako, Kaka, Yaka		B501	Wanzi
			B502	Mwele
B10	*Myene Group*		B503	Vili, Ibhili
B11	Myene cluster			
B11a	Mpongwe		*B60*	*Mbete Group*
B11b	Rongo, Orungu		B61	Mbete, Mbere
B11c	Galwa		B62	Mbaama, Mbamba
B11d	Dyumba, Adjumba			

B63	Nduumo, Mindumbu	C12b	Gongo, Bogongo
B601	Mpini	C13	Mbati
B602	Kaning'i	C14	Mbomitaba, Bomitaba
		C141	Enyele
B70	*Teke Group*	C142	Bondongo
B71	North Teke	C143	Mbonzo, Impfondo
B71a	Tege-Kali	C15	Bongili, Bongiri
B71b	Njining'i	C16	Lobala
B72	Northeast Teke	C161	Bomboli, Bombongo
B72a	Ngungwel, Ngungulu	C162	Bozaba
B72b	Mpumpu	C101	Babole
B73	West Teke	C102	Ngando
B73a	Tsaayi	C103	Kota
B73b	Laali	C104	Aka, Yaka
B73c	Yaa, Yaka		
B73d	Kwe	*C20*	*Mboshi Group*
B74	Central Teke	C21	Mboko
B74a	Ndzindziu	C22	Akwa
B74b	Boo, Boma	C23	Ngare
B75	Bali, Teke, Tio	C24	Koyo
B76	East Teke	C25	Mboshi
B76a	Mosieno	C26	Kwala
B76b	Ng'ee	C27	Kuba
B77	South Teke	C201	Bwenyi
B77a	Kukwa		
B77b	Fumu	*C30*	*Bangi-Ntumba Group*
B78	Wuumu, Wumbu	C31a	Loi
		C31b	Ngiri
B80	*Tende-Yanzi Group*	C31C	Nunu
B81	Tiene, Tende	C32	Bobangi
B82	Boma, Buma	C321	Binza, Libinza
B821	Mpe	C322	Zamba, Dzamba
B83	Mfinu, Funika, Mfununga	C33	Sengele
B84a	Mpuono	C34	Sakata cluster
B84b	Mpuun	C35a	Ntomba
B85	Yans, Yanzi	C35b	Bolia
B85a	Mbiem, West Yanzi	C36	Losengo cluster
B85b	East Yans	C36a	Poto, Pfoto
B85c	Yeei	C36b	Mpesa
B85d	Ntsuo	C36c	Mbudza
B85e	Mpur, Mput	C36d	Ngala, Lingala
B86	Di, Dinga, Dzing	C36e	Boloki
B861	Ngul, Ngwi	C36f	Kangana
B862	Lwel, Kelwer	C36g	Ndolo
B87	Mbuun, Mbunda	C37	Buja, Budza
		C371	Motembo
C10	*Ngundi Group*	C372	Kunda
C11	Ngondi	C373	Gbuta
C12a	Pande	C301	Doko

C40	Ngombe Group
C41	Ngombe
C411	Bomboma
C412	Bamwe
C413	Dzando
C42	Bwela, Lingi
C43	Bati, Benge
C44	Bwa
C441	Bango, Babango
C45	Ngelima, Angba, Beo, Buru, Tungu
C401	Pagibete, Apagibeti
C402	Yewu
C403	Kango

C50	Soko-Kele Group
C51	Mbesa
C52	So, Soko, Eso
C53	Pfoke, Topoke, Gesogo
C54	Lombo, Turumbu
C55	Kele, Lokele
C56	Foma

C60	Mongo-Nkundu Group
C61	Mongo-Nkundu
C62	Lalia
C63	Ngando

C70	Tetela Group
C71	Tetela, Hamba
C72	Kusu, Fuluka, Kongola
C73	Nkutu, Nkucu
C74	Yela
C75	Kela, Lemba
C76	Ombo

C80	Kuba Group
C81	Dengese, Nkutu
C82	Songomeno
C83	Bushoong, Kuba
C84	Lele
C85	Wongo, Tukungo

D10	Mbole-Ena Group
D11	Mbole
D12	Lengola
D13	Mituku, Metoko
D14	Enya, Ena, Genya

D20	Lega-Kalanga Group
D21	Baali (Southeast Bua)
D22	Amba, Rwamba, Kwamba
D23	Kumu, Komo
D24	Songola, North Binja
D25	Lega-Mwenga
D251	Lega-Malinga
D26	Zimba, Nyangwe, South Binja
D27	Bangubangu
D28a	West Holoholo, Guha, Kalanga (Congo-Kinshasa)
D28b	East Holoholo (Tanzania)
D201	Liko, Lika

D30	Bira-Huku Group
D31	Bhele, Peri, Pere
D311	Bila, Forest Bira
D312	Kaiku
D32	Bera, Plains Bira, Sese, Sumburu
D33	Nyali
D331	Bvanuma, South Nyali
D332	Bodo, Ebudu
D333	Ndaaka
D334	Mbo, Imbo
D335	Beeke, Ibeeke
D301	Kare
D302	Guru, Kogoro
D303	Ngbinda, Ngminda
D304	Homa (extinct)
D305 (J)	Nyanga-li
D306 (J)	Gbati-ri
D307 (J)	Mayeka

D40	Konjo Group
D41 (J)	Konzo, Konjo
D42 (J)	Yira, Ndandi, Nande
D43 (D)	Nyanga

D50	Bembe-Kabwari Group
D51 (J)	Hunde, Kobi
D52 (J)	Haavu
D53 (J)	Shi, Nyabungu
D531 (J)	Tembo
D54 (D)	Bembe
D55 (D)	Buyi
D56 (J)	Kabwari
D501 (J)	Nyindu
D502 (J)	Yaka

D60	*Ruanda-Rundi Group*		E34 (J)	Saamia
D61 (J)	Ruanda, Kinyarwanda		E341 (J)	Xaayo, Khayo
D62 (J)	Rundi, Kirundi		E342 (J)	Marachi
D63 (J)	Fuliiro		E343 (J)	Songa
D631 (J)	Vira, Joba		E35 (J)	Nyuli
D64 (J)	Shubi (Sinja = *incorrect*)			
D65 (J)	Hangaza		*E40*	*Ragoli-Kuria Group*
D66 (J)	Ha		E41 (J)	Logooli, Ragoli
D67 (J)	Vinza		E411 (J)	Idaxo, Itoxo
			E412 (J)	Isukha
E10	*Nyoro-Ganda Group*		E413 (J)	Tiriki
E11 (J)	Nyoro, Kyopi		E42 (J)	Gusii, Kisii
E12 (J)	Tooro		E43 (J)	Koria, Kuria
E13 (J)	Nyankole, Nkole		E44 (J)	Zanaki
E14 (J)	Ciga, Chiga, Kiga		E45 (J)	Ikoma, Nata
E15 (J)	Ganda		E46 (E)	Sonjo, Temi
E16 (J)	Soga		E401 (J)	Ngur(u)imi, Ngoreme
E17 (J)	Gwere		E402 (J)	Ikizu
E18 (J)	(West) Nyala		E403 (J)	Suba
E101 (J)	Gungu		E404 (J)	Shashi, Sizaki
E102 (J)	Bwisi, Talinga		E405 (J)	Kabwa
E20	*Haya-Jita Group*		*E50*	*Kikuyu-Kamba/Central*
E21 (J)	Nyambo, Karagwe			*Kenya Bantu/Thagicu Group*
E22 (J)	Haya		E51	Kikuyu
E23 (J)	Zinza, Dzindza, Jinja		E52	Embu
E24 (J)	Kerebe		E53	Meru
E25 (J)	Jita		E54	Tharaka
E251 (J)	Kwaya		E541	Cuka, Chuka
E252 (J)	Regi, Kara		E55	Kamba
E253 (J)	Ruri, Rori		E56	Daisu, Se(n)geju
E30	*Masaba-Luhya Group*		*E60*	*Chaga Group*
E31 (J)	Masaba		E61	Meru, Rwo
E31a (J)	Gisu		E62a	Hai, Macame
E31b (J)	Kisu		E62b	Wunjo, Marangu
E31c (J)	Bukusu		E62c	Rombo
E31D (J)	Syan		E63	Rusha, Kuma
E31E (J)	Tachon, Tatsoni		E64	Kahe
E31F (J)	Dadiri		E65	Gweno
E31G (J)	Buya			
E32 (J)	Luhya		*E70*	*Nyika-Taita Group*
E32a (J)	Hanga, Wanga		E71	Pokomo, Pfokomo
E32b (J)	Tsotso		E72	North Mijikenda, Nyika
E32C (J)	Marama		E72a	Giryama
E32D (J)	Kisa		E72b	Kauma
E32E (J)	Kabarasi, Kabras		E72c	Conyi
E32F (J)	(East) Nyala		E72d	Duruma
E33 (J)	Nyore		E72e	Rabai

E72F	Jibana
E72G	Kambe
E72H	Ribe
E73	Digo (South Mijikenda)
E74	Taita
E74a	Dabida
E74b	Sagala
E74C	Kasigau
E701	Elwana, Mala(n)kote

F10	*Tongwe Group*
F11	Tongwe
F12	Bende

F20	*Sukuma-Nyamwezi Group*
F21	Sukuma (Gwe = *incorrect*)
F22	Nyamwezi
F23	Sumbwa
F24	Kimbu
F25	Bungu

F30	*Ilamba-Irangi Group*
F31	Nilamba, Ilamba
F32	Rimi, Nyaturu
F33	Langi, Irangi
F34	Mbugwe, Buwe

G10	*Gogo Group*
G11	Gogo
G12	Kagulu, North Sagara

G20	*Shambala Group*
G21	Tubeta, Taveta
G22	Asu, Pare
G23	Shambala, Shambaa
G24	Bondei

G30	*Zigula-Zaramo Group*
G31	Zigula, Zigua
G32	Nghwele, Kwere
G33	Zaramo, Dzalamo
G34	Ngulu
G35	Ruguru, Luguru
G36	Kami
G37	Kutu
G38	Vidunda
G39	Sagala
G301	Doe

G40	*Swahili Group*
G41	Tikuu, Tikulu, Bajuni, Gunya
G411	Socotra Swahili
G412	Mwiini, Miini, Barawa, Mbalazi
G42a	Amu, Pate, Siu
G42b	Mvita, Changamwe, Jomvu, Kilindini, Ngare
G42c	Mrima, Lugha ya Zamani, Mtang'ata
G42d	Unguja
G42E	Malindi, Mambrui
G42F	Chifundi
G42G	Chwaka
G42H	Vumba
G42I	Nosse Be (Madagascar)
G43a	Phemba
G43b	Tumbatu
G43c	Makunduchi, Ka(l)e (Hadimu = *derogatory*)
G43D	Mafia, Mbwera
G44	Comorian
G44a	Ngazija
G44b	Njuani, Hinzua
G44C	Mwali
G44D	Maore
G401	Mgao
G402	Makwe
G403	Mwani

G50	*Pogolo/Kilombero Group*
G51	Pogolo, Pogoro
G52	Ndamba

G60	*Bena-Kinga Group*
G61	Sango, Rori
G62	Hehe
G63	Bena
G64	Pangwa
G65	Kinga
G66	Wanji
G67	Kisi

H10	*Ki Group*
H11	Bembe
H111	Hangala
H112	Kamba
H12	Vili, Civili
H13	Kunyi
H131	Sundi-Kifouma

H14	Ndingi, Ndinzi (Cabinda)		K322	Liyuwa
H15	Mboka (Cabinda)		K33	Kwangari cluster
H16	Kongo cluster		K33A	Kwangari
H16a	South Kongo		K33B	Mbundza
H16b	Central Kongo		K331	Shambyu
H16c	Yombe		K332	Gciriku, Dciriku, Mbogedo
H16d	West Kongo, Fiote, Kakongo		K333	Mbukushu
H16e	Bwende		K34	Mashi
H16f	Northeast Kongo, Laadi		K35	Simaa
H16g	East Kongo		K351	Mulonga
H16h	Southeast Kongo		K352	Mwenyi
			K353	Koma, Makoma
H20	*Kimbundu Group*		K354	Imilangu
H21	Mbundu cluster, Kimbundu		K36	Shanjo
H21a	Mbundu, Ngola		K37	Kwangwa
H21b	Mbamba, Njinga		K371	Kwandi
H22	Sama			
H23	Bolo, Haka		*K40*	*Subiya Group*
H24	Songo		K41	Totela
			K42	Ikuhane, Subia
H30	*Kiyaka Group*		K401	Mbalangwe
H31	Yaka		K402	Fwe, We
H32	Suku			
H33	Hungu, Holo		*L10*	*Pende Group*
H34	Mbangala		L11	Pende, Pheende
H35	Shinji, Yungo		L12a	Samba
			L12b	Holu
H40	*Kimbala Group*		L13	Kwezo, Kwese, Pindi
H41	Mbala		L101	Sonde
H42	Hunganna, Huana			
			L20	*Songe Group*
K10	*Chokwe-Luchazi Group*		L21	Kete
K11	Chokwe		L22	Binji, Mbagani
K12a	Luimbi		L221	Lwalu, Lwalwa
K12b	Ngangela, Nyemba		L23	Songe, Yembe
K13	Luchazi, Lujazi, Ponda		L24	Luna, Inkongo
K14	Luvale, Lwena		L201	Budya
K15	Mbuunda		L202	Yazi
K16	Nyengo			
K17	Mbwela		*L30*	*Luba Group*
K18	Nkangala		L31	Luba-Lulua
			L31a	Luba-Kasai, Tshiluba
K20	*Lozi Group*		L31b	Lulua, Luluwa, West Luba
K21	Lozi, Kololo		L32	Kanyoka
			L33	Luba-Katanga, Kiluba
K30	*Luyana Group*		L34	Hemba, East Luba
K31	Luyana, Luyi		L35	Sanga, Garenganze,
K32	Mbowe			South Luba
K321	Mbume		L301	Kebwe

L40	*Kaonde Group*		M521	Ambo
L41	Kaonde, Kahonde		M522	Luano
			M53	Swaka
L50	*Lunda Group*		M54	Lamba
L51	Salampasu		M541	Lima, Bulima
L52	Lunda		M542	Temba
L53	Ruund, Luwunda		M55	Seba, Shishi
L60	*Nkoya Group*		*M60*	*Lenje-Tonga Group*
L61	Mbwera, Mbwela		M61	Lenje, Ciina Mukuni
L62	Nkoya		M62	Soli
L601	Kolwe		M63	Ila
L602	Lushangi		M631	Sala
L603	Mashasha		M632	Lundwe
			M633	Twa (of Kafue)
M10	*Fipa-Mambwe Group*		M64	Tonga cluster
M11	Pimbwe			
M12	Rungwa		*N10*	*Manda Group*
M13	Fipa		N11	Manda
M13A	Fipa-Sukuma		N12	Ngoni (Tanzania)
M13B	South Fipa		N121	Ngoni (Malawi)
M14	Rungu, Lungu		N13	Matengo
M15	Mambwe		N14	Mpoto
			N15	Tonga, Siska
M20	*Nyika-Safwa Group*		N101	Ndendeule
M21	Wanda, Wandia		N102	Nindi
M22	Mwanga, Namwanga			
M23	Nyiha, Nyika		*N20*	*Tumbuka Group*
M24	Malila		N21	Tumbuka cluster
M25	Safwa		N21a	Tumbuka
M26	Iwa		N21b	Poka
M27	Tambo		N21c	Kamanga
M201	Lambya, Rambia		N21d	Senga
M202	Sukwa		N21e	Yombe
			N21f	Fungwe
M30	*Konde Group*		N21g	Wenya
M31	Nyekyosa, Konde, Kukwe, Sokili		N201	Mbamba Bay Mwera
M301	Ndali		*N30*	*Nyanja Group*
			N31	Nyanja-Cewa cluster
M40	*Bemba Group*		N31a	Nyanja
M41	Taabwa, Rungu		N31b	Cewa, Peta
M42	Bemba, Wemba		N31c	Manganja
M401	Bwile		N31D	Nyanja-Cewa (Mozambique, Tanzania)
M402	Aushi, Usi			
			N40	*Senga-Sena Group*
M50	*Bisa-Lamba Group*		N41	Nsenga
M51	Biisa, Wisa		N42	Kunda
M52	Lala			

N43	Nyungwe, Tete
N44	Sena
N45	Rue
N46	Podzo
P10	*Matumbi Group*
P11	Ndengereko
P12	Ruihi, Rufiji
P13	Matumbi
P14	Ngindo
P15	Mbunga
P20	*Yao Group*
P21	Yao
P22	Mwera
P23	Makonde
P24	Ndonde, Mawanda
P25	Mabiha, Mavia
P30	*Makhuwa Group*
P31	Makhuwa
P311	Koti, Ngoji
P312	Sangaji, Sakati
P32	Lomwe (West Makhuwa)
P33	Ngulu (West Makhuwa)
P34	Chwabo
R10	*Umbundu Group*
R11	Mbundu, Umbundu, Nano
R12	Ndombe
R13	Nyaneka
R14	Khumbi
R20	*Ambo/(Ndonga) Group*
R21	Kwanyama
R211	Kafima
R212	Evale
R213	Mbandja
R214	Mbalanhu
R215	Ndongwena
R216	Kwankwa
R217	Dombondola
R218	Esinga
R22	Ndonga
R23	Kwambi
R24	Ngandyera
R241	Kwaluudhi
R242	Kolonkadhi, Eunda

R30	*Herero Group*
R31	Herero
R311	Northwest Herero
R40	*Yeyi Group*
R41	Yeyi (Kuba = *derogatory*)
R41A	East Caprivi Yeyi
R41B	Ngamiland Yeyi
S10	*Shona Group*
S11	Korekore
S12	Zezuru
S13	Manyika cluster
S13a	Manyika
S13b	Tebe
S14	Karanga
S15	Ndau, Sofala
S16	Kalanga
S20	*Venda Group*
S21	Venda
S30	*Sotho-Tswana Group*
S31	Tswana
S31a	Central (incl. Rolong, Hurutshe)
S31b	Eastern (incl. Kgatla, Kgafela)
S31c	Northern (incl. Ngwato, Tawana)
S31d	Kgalagadi
S31E	Southern (incl. Thlaping, Tlharo)
S32	Northern Sotho, Sesotho sa Leboa
S32a	Pedi
S32b	Lobedu, Lovedu
S33	Southern Sotho, Sesotho
S301	Phalaborwa
S302	Kutswe
S303	Pai
S304	Pulana
S40	*Nguni Group*
S41	Xhosa (Kafir = *derogatory*)
S42	Zulu
S43	Swati, Swazi, Ngwane
S44	Ndebele (Zimbabwe)
S401	Old Mfengu

S402	Bhaca
S403	Hlubi
S404	Phuthi
S405	Nhlangwini
S406	Lala
S407	Ndebele (South Africa)
S408	Sumayela Ndebele (South Africa)
S50	*Tswa-Ronga Group*
S51	Tshwa
S511	Hlengwe
S52	Gwamba
S53	Tsonga, Changana
S54	Ronga
S60	*Inhambane Group*
S61	Copi
S611	Lenge
S62	Tonga, Shengwe

Pidgin, creole and/or mixed languages

A70A	Ewondo Populaire, Pidgin-A70
G20A	Ma'a, Mbugu
G40A	Asian Swahili (Kenya, Uganda)
G40B	Cutchi-Swahili (Kenya)
G40C	Kisetla (Kenya)
G40D	Engsh (Nairobi)
G40E	Sheng (Nairobi)
G40F	Shaba/Katanga/Lubumbashi Swahili
G40G	Ngwana, Kingwana
H10A	Kituba, Kileta, Kikongo ya Leta
H10B	Mono kutuba, Munukutuba
L30A	Pidgin Chiluba
M40A	Town Bemba (Zambia)
S40A	Fanagalo, Chikabanga (Zambia), Chilapalapa (Zimbabwe)
S40B	Iscamtho (South Africa)

NOTES TO THE LIST

C60 – Hulstaert (1993) provides an authoritative listing of Mongo-Nkundo languages/dialects. Guthrie has scattered these over several groups in zone C.

D30 – Guthrie (1971) gives Mbuba as a D33 language/dialect, but it has been omitted here since it is a Nilosaharan language.

D60 – Apparently 'Sinja', given by Guthrie (1971:44), cannot be used as a variant for Shubi (Balla Masele, pc).

E10 – Guthrie (1971:44) gives Gungu in parentheses as a E11 variant/variety. It has here been broken out and given a code of its own (E101). He also gives Hima as a variant or variety of E13. If anything, it is either a dialect of Nyankole or it 'may be a separate language' (Grimes 1996:427). Many names could probably have been added in the E10 group, most of which seem best treated as dialects of languages already listed. See, for instance, Ladefoged *et al.* (1972:68–74) for information on various Ganda dialects.

E40 – See Kihore (2000) for some data on various E40 languages/dialects.

E60 – The Chaga varieties listed by Guthrie (1971:46) show a very arbitrary choice of names. The only correcting exercise here is the omission of the name 'Moshi'. See Nurse (1979b) and Philippson and Montlahuc (this volume) for more details.

F20 – Guthrie (1971:48) gives the name 'Gwe' as a variant for Sukuma, but it cannot apparently be used as such (Balla Masele, pc), so it has been dropped.

G10 – Botne (1989/90) has suggested a J-coding for Gogo.

G40 – Guthrie's Swahili Group makes little sense from a geographical as well as genetic view-point (Derek Nurse, pc). Thus it has been difficult to update this group in order to arrive at a comfortable consistency (which is true for many sections in Guthrie's classification). As a slight compensation for Guthrie's botch, some of the already existing codes in the G42 series have been amended with a few new names. See Nurse and Hinnebusch (1993:5–15) for information on language varieties within the G40 group. On Soqotra Swahili, see Whiteley (1969:77).

N20 – The Tumbuka dialects have been coded following Guthrie (1948:81). Hence the lower-case letters.

P30 – On Koti, see Schadeberg and Mucanheia (2000).

R20 – On the classification of Ambo dialects/languages, see Baucom (1975). His northern cluster include R21 and the ones coded R211 through R218 here. The rest belong to his southern cluster.

S30 – The Tswana dialects originally listed by Guthrie (1971) are far from complete; see Cole (1975:xvi–xix) for a more detailed discussion on these. Guthrie's S31a, S31b and S31c correspond roughly to the Central (incl. Rolong), Eastern (incl. Kgatla) and Northern (incl. Ngwato) dialect clusters, respectively. Consequently, Guthrie's original codes have been adapted to accommodate this classification. To these, a Southern dialect cluster has been added as S31E. Guthrie's S31d Kgalagadi should really have been assigned a code of its own (Tore Janson, pc), but since it is there it has to remain. As for the S30X additions (Pai, Phalaborwa, etc.), see Doke (1954).

S40 – See Doke (1954) for details about the S40 additions (Old Mfengu, Bhaca, etc.).

S50 – It is worth noting that what Guthrie gives as S52 (Gwamba) is in reality a dialect of his S53 (Tsonga).

Pidgin, creole and/or mixed languages – Most of the languages listed here derive from Heine (1970) and Holm (1989); further references can be found in their bibliographies.

REFERENCES

Many valuable (though sometimes conflicting) data on the distribution and classification of the Bantu languages as well as data on individual languages/dialects have been published; see especially the contributions to this volume. The main sources consulted for this appendix include Bailey 1995; Bastin *et al.* 1983, 1999; Baucom 1975; Botne 1989/90; Cole 1975; Cope 1971; Dalby 2000; Doke 1945, 1954; Grimes 2000; Guthrie 1948, 1953, 1971; *Linguistic Survey of the Northern Bantu Borderland* 1956; Heine 1970; Holm 1989; Hulstaert 1993; Kahigi *et al.* 2000; Kihore 2000; Ladefoged *et al.* 1972; Lowe and Schadeberg 1997; Mould 1981; Nurse 1979b; Nurse and Hinnebusch 1993; Nurse and Philippson 1980; Ohannessian and Kashoki 1978; Piron 1997; Polomé and Hill 1980; Schadeberg and Mucanheia 2000; Whiteley 1969, 1974.

BIBLIOGRAPHY

ABBREVIATIONS

AAP	*Afrikanistische Arbeitspapiere*
AL	*Africana Linguistica*
ALS	*African Language Studies*
AS	*African Studies*
AU	*Afrika und Übersee*
BLS	Berkeley Linguistic Society
BSOAS	*Bulletin of the School of Oriental and African Studies*
CLS	Chicago Linguistic Society
CNRS	Centre National de la Recherche Scientifique
CNWS	Centre for non-Western Studies (Leiden)
CSLI	Center for the Study of Language and Information
CUP	Cambridge University Press
EALB	East African Literature Bureau
IAI	International African Institute (London)
IJAL	*International Journal of American Linguistics*
ILCAA	Institute for the Languages and Cultures of Asia and Africa
INALCO	Institut National des Langues et Civilisations Orientales
JAH	*Journal of African History*
JAL	*Journal of African Languages*
JALL	*Journal of African Languages and Linguistics*
JWAL	*Journal of West African Languages*
LA	*Linguistica Africana*
MIT	Massachusetts Institute of Technology
MRAC	Musée Royal de l'Afrique Centrale (Tervuren)
MSOS	*Mitteilungen des Seminars für Orientalische Sprachen*
OUP	Oxford University Press
SAJAL	*South African Journal of African Languages*
SAL	*Studies in African Linguistics*
SCOPIL	Southern California Occasional Papers in Linguistics
SELAF	Société d'Etudes Linguistiques et Anthropologiques de France
SIL	Summer Institute of Linguistics
SLS	*Studies in the Linguistic Sciences*
SUGIA	*Sprache und Geschichte in Afrika*
UCLA	University of California at Los Angeles
UCP	University of California Press
ZDMG	*Zeitschrift der Deutschen Morgenländischen Gesellschaft*

Abdulaziz, M. H. (1996) *Transitivity in Swahili*, Cologne: Rüdiger Köppe Verlag.
——and Osinde, K. (1997) Sheng and Engsh: development of mixed codes among the urban youth in Kenya, *International Journal of the Sociology of Language* 25: 43–63.
Abwa, D. (1995) The Banen and slavery, *Paideuma* 41: 107–25.

652

Afido, P., Firmino, G., Heins, J., Mbuub, S., and Trinta, M. (1989) *Relatório do I Seminário sobre a Padronização da Ortografia de Línguas Moçambicanas*, Maputo: Universidade Eduardo Mondlane.

Alexandre, P. (1967) *Langues et langage en Afrique Noire*, Paris: Payot.

Allen, G. and Hawkins, S. (1980) Phonological rhythm: definition and development, in G. H. Yeni-Komshian, J. F. Kavanagh and C. A. Ferguson (eds) *Child Phonology*, New York: Academic Press. 227–56.

Allen, S. (1996) *Aspects of argument structure acquisition in Inuktitut*, Amsterdam: Benjamins.

Amboulou, C. (1998) *Le mbochi: langue bantu du Congo-Brazzaville (Zone C, Groupe C20), Etude descriptive*. PhD thesis. Paris: INALCO.

Anderson, L. K. (1935) *The Bafia language. A preliminary statement*. PhD thesis, Princeton.

Anderson, S. C. (1979) Verb structure, in Hyman (ed.) (1979b) 73–136.

——(1980) The noun classes of Ngyemboon-Bamileke, in Hyman (ed.) (1980b) 37–56.

——(1981) An Autosegmental account of Bamileke-Dschang tonology (revised from 1978). MS. Yaoundé: SIL.

——(1982) From semi-vowels to aspiration to long consonants in Ngyemboon–Bamileke, *JWAL* 12: 56–68.

——(1983) *Tone and morpheme rules in Bamileke–Ngyemboon*. PhD thesis. University of California.

——(ed.) (1991) *Tone in five languages of Cameroon*, Dallas: SIL.

Anderson, S. C. and Comrie, B. (eds) (1991) *Tense and aspect in eight languages of Cameroon*, Dallas and Arlington: SIL and University of Texas at Arlington.

Angogo, K. R. (1983) *Unity in diversity: a linguistic survey of the Abaluhyia of Western Kenya*, Vienna. Beiträge zur Afrikanistik. No. 20.

Ankei, Y. (1979) Notes Bwari. MS.

Annett, M. (1983) L'expression de la localisation en langue mundani, *JWAL* 13.2: 115–32.

Appleby, L. L. (1961) *A first Luyia grammar with exercises*, Dar es Salaam–Nairobi–Kampala: EALB.

Aramazani, B. (1985) *Description de la langue havu (bantou J52)*, 3 vols. Thesis. Brussels: University of Brussels.

Archangeli, D. and Pulleyblank, D. (1995) *Grounded phonology*, Cambridge: MIT Press.

Aroga Bessong, D. P. (1982) La traduction des formes verbales du présent français en bafia, *Meta, Journal des Traducteurs (Montréal)* 27.3: 257–70.

Aroga Bessong, D. P. and Marchal, A. [n.d.] (ed.) *Les phonèmes du bafia, application des techniques de la phonétique expérimentale à l'étude de voyelles*, Cameroon and Montreal: Direction des services linguistiques, Présidence Unie du Cameroun and Univ. of Montréal, Département de Linguistique et de Philosophie.

Aroga Bessong D. P. and Mel'cuk, I. (1983) Un modèle formel de la conjugaison bafia (à l'indicatif), *BSOAS* 46.3: 477–528.

Asangama, N. (1983) *Le budu: langue bantu du nord-est du Zaïre. Esquisse phonologique et grammaticale*, 2 vols. PhD thesis. Paris: Université Sorbonne Nouvelle.

Ashton, E. O., Mulira, E. M. K., Ndawula, E. G. M., and Tucker, A. N. (1954) *A Luganda grammar*, London: Longmans Green and Co.

Asongwed, T. and Hyman, L. M. (1976) Morphotonology of the Ngamambo noun, in Hyman (ed.) (1976a) 23–56.

Asoyo, S. K. (1973) *Aspects de la grammaire générative et transformationnelle de la langue boa*. Mémoire, Lubumbashi: Université nationale du Zaïre.

Austen, C. L. (n.d.) *Anatomy of the tonal system of a Bantu language*, Indiana: Indiana University.

Bailey, R. A. (1976) *Copi phonology and morphotonology*. BA Hons thesis. Johannesburg: University of the Witwatersrand.

——(1995) The Bantu languages of South Africa: towards a sociohistorical perspective, in Mesthrie (ed.) 19–38.

Baker, M. (1988a) Theta theory and the syntax of applicatives in Chichewa, *Language and Linguistic Theory* 6: 353–89.

Baker, M. (1988b) The mirror principle and morphosyntactic explanation, *Linguistic Inquiry* 16: 373–415.

Bancel, P. (1991) The three-way vowel harmony in Nen (Bantu A.44, Cameroon), in Hubbard (ed.) 3–14.

Barreteau, D. (ed.) (1978) *Inventaire des études sur les pays d'Afrique Noire d'expression française et sur Madagascar*, Paris: Conseil International de la Langue Française.

Barreteau, D. and Hedinger, R. (eds) (1989) *Descriptions de langues camerounaises*, Paris: ORSTOM.

Barreteau, D., Ngangtchui, E., and Scruggs, T. (1993) *Bibliographie des langues camerounaises*, Paris: ORSTOM.

Bastin, Y. (1975) *Bibliographie bantoue sélective*, Tervuren: MRAC. Archives d'anthropologie 24.

——(1978) Les langues bantoues, in Barreteau (ed.) 123–85.

——(1979) Statistique grammaticale et classification des langues bantoues, *Linguistics in Belgium* 2: 17–37.

——(1983a) Essai de classification de quatre-vingt langues bantoues par la statistique grammaticale, *AL* 9: 9–108.

——(1983b) *La finale verbale -IDE et l'imbrication en Bantou*, Tervuren: MRAC.

——(1986) Les suffixes causatifs dans les langues bantoues, *AL* 10: 55–145.

——(1989) Les déverbatifs bantous en –E, *JALL* 11: 151–74.

——(1989a) El prefijo locativo de la clase 18 y la expresión del progresivo presente en Bantu (1), *Estudios Africanos* 4.6: 35–55. (A French version of this and the next is available from the author.)

——(1989b) El prefijo locativo de la clase 18 y la expresión del progresivo presente en Bantu (2), *Estudios Africanos* 4.7: 61–86.

Bastin, Y. and Piron, P. (1999) Classifications lexicostatistiques: bantou, bantou et bantoide. De l'intérêt des 'groupes flottants', in Hombert and Hyman (eds) 149–64.

Bastin, Y., Coupez, A. and de Halleux, B. (1983) Classification lexicostatistique des langues bantoues (214 relevés), *Bulletin des séances de l'Académie Royale des Sciences d'Outre-Mer*, 27(2): 173–99.

Bastin, Y., Coupez, A. and Mann, M. (1999) *Continuity and divergence in the Bantu languages: perspectives from a lexicostatistic study*, Tervuren: MRAC.

Batibo, H. (1985) *Le kesukuma, langue bantu de Tanzanie: phonologie, morphologie*, Paris: Editions recherche sur les civilisations.

——(1994) Does Kiswahili have diphthongs? Interpreting foreign sounds in African languages, *SAJAL* 14: 180–6.

Baucom, K. L. (1972) The Wambo languages of South West Africa and Angola, *JAL* 11.2: 45–73.

——(1975) The phonology of Proto-Wambo, *AS* 34: 165–84.

Baumbach, E. J. M. (1974) *Introduction to the speech sounds and speech sound changes of Tsonga*, Pretoria: J. L. Van Schaik.

——(1997a) *Analytical Tsonga grammar*, Pretoria: University of South Africa.

——(1997b) Bantu languages of the Eastern Caprivi, in Haacke and Elderkin (eds) 307–450.

Bbemo Musabaho, T. M. (1982) *Le Kinande, langue bantoue de l'est du Zaïre (D42), phonologie et morphologie*, Thesis. Paris: Université Paris III.

Bearth, T. (1995) Wortstellung, Topik und Fokus, in G. Miehe and W. J. G. Möhlig (eds) *Handbuch des Swahili*, Cologne: Rüdiger Köppe Verlag.

——(1999) The contribution of African linguistics towards a general theory of focus. Update and critical review, *JALL* 20.2: 121–56.

Beavon, K. H. (1991) Koozime verbal system, in Anderson and Comrie (eds) 47–104.

Beckett, H. W. (1951) *Handbook of Kiluba*, Mulongo: Garenganze Evangelical Mission.

Bendor-Samuel, J. (ed.) (1989) *The Niger-Congo languages*, Lanham: University Press of America.

Bennett, P. R. (1967) Dahl's law and Thagicu, *ALS* 8: 127–59.

Bennett, P. R. and Sterk, J. P. (1977) South Central Niger-Congo: a reclassification, *SAL* 8.3: 241–73.

Bernsten, J. (1998) Runyakitara: Uganda's 'new language', *Journal of Multilingual and Multicultural Development* 19(2): 93–107.

Besha, R. M. (1989) *A study of tense and aspect in Shambala*, Berlin: Dietrich Reimer.

Bickmore, L. S. (1991) *Kinyambo prosody*, Ann Arbor, MI: University Microfilms International.

Bird, S. (1996) *Dschang syllable structure and moraic aspiration*, University of Edinburgh, Centre for Cognitive Science. Research paper.

Bissila, S. (1991) *Description phonologique du ilaale (dialecte teke du Congo)*. Mémoire, Brazzaville: Université Marien Ngouabi.

Bitjaa Kody, Z. D. (1990) *Le systeme verbal du basaa*. PhD thesis. Yaoundé: Université de Yaoundé.

Biton, A. (1907) *Dictionnaire français-ndumu et ndumu-français, précédé d'éléments de grammaire*, Franceville.

Black, C. A. (1995) Boundary tones on word-internal domains in Kinande, *Phonology* 12.1: 1–38.

Bladon, A., Clark, C. and Mickey, K. (1987) Production and perception of sibilant fricatives: Shona data. *Journal of the International Phonetic Association* 17: 39–65.

Blake, B. (1990) *Relational grammar*, London: Routledge.

Blanchon, J. A. (1987a) Les voyelles finales des nominaux en I-nzèbi (B52), *Pholia* 2: 23–45.

—— (1987b) Les classes 9, 10 et 11 dans le groupe bantou (B40), *Pholia* 2: 5–22.

—— (1988a) Relèvements tonals en eshira et en massango: approche d'une tonologie comparée du groupe bantou B40, *Pholia* 3: 71–85.

—— (1988b) Tonalité des nominaux à thème dissyllabique dans le groupe bantou B20, *Pholia* 3: 37–51.

—— (1988c) Une langue mixte en voie de disparition: le geviya, *Pholia* 3: 53–69.

—— (1989) Le wumvu de Malinga (Gabon). Tonalité des nominaux, *Pholia* 4: 39–44.

—— (1990) The great *HL split in Bantu B40, *Pholia* 5: 17–29.

—— (1998) Semantic/pragmatic conditions on the tonology of the Kongo noun-phrase: a diachronic hypothesis, in Hyman and Kisseberth (eds) 1–32.

Blanchon, J. A. and Alihanga, M. (1992) Notes sur la morphologie du lempiini de Eyuga, *Pholia* 7: 23–40.

Blanchon, J. A. and Creissels, D. (eds) (1999) *Issues in Bantu Tonology*, Cologne: Rüdiger Köppe Verlag.

Blanchon, J. A. and Mouguiama, L. (1997) Les thèmes à initiale vocalique et la tonalité du verbe conjugué en Eshira de Manji (Gabon), *Linguistique Africaine* 18: 5–49.

Bleek, W. H. 1 (1856) *The languages of Mozambique*, London: Harrison and Sons.

—— (1862) *A comparative grammar of South African languages. Part 1: phonology*, Cape Town and London: J. C. Juta and Trübner & Co.

—— (1869) *A comparative grammar of South African languages. Part 2: the concord. section 1: The noun*, Cape Town and London: J. C. Juta and Trübner & Co.

Blench, R. M. (1998) Are the Pygmies an ethnographic fiction? In K. Biesbrouck, S. Elders and G. Rossel (eds), Central African hunter-gatherers in a multi-disciplinary perspective: challenging elusiveness. Leiden: CNWS. 41–60. *Journal of the Sociology of Language* 144: 119–36.

BLR2. See Coupez, Bastin and Mumba (1998).

Bodinga-bwa-Bodinga, S. and Van der Veen, L. J. (1995) *Les proverbes Evia et le monde animal, la communauté Evia à travers ses expressions proverbiales*, Paris: L'Harmattan.

Bogers, K., van der Hulst, H. and Mous, M. (eds) (1986) *The phonological representation of Suprasegmentals*, Dordrecht: Foris.

Bokamba, E. G. (1979) Inversion as grammatical relation changing rules in Bantu, *SLS* 9.2: 1–24.

—— (1985) Verbal agreement as a noncyclic rule in Bantu, in Goyvaerts (ed.) 9–54.

Bokula F.-X. (1966) *Eléments de grammaire et de vocabulaire de la langue bodo*. Mémoire. Kinshasa: Université Lovanium.

—— (1970) La langue bodo: formes nominales, *AL* 4: 63–83.

Bold, J. D. (1977) *Fanagalo – phrase book, grammar, and dictionary*, Johannesburg: Emest Stanton.

Bolingola, M. (1995) *Esquisse de description phonétique, phonologique et morphologique du Bali (D21)*. Mémoire, Brussels: Université libre de Bruxelles.

Boone, D. W. (1993) Bila survey report, in *Compendium of survey reports, vol. 1, Bira-Huku group of Bantu*, Bunia: SIL Eastern Zaire group.

Booysen, J. M. (1982) *Otjiherero 'n Volledige grammatika met oefeninge en sleutels in Afrikaans*, Windhoek: Gamsberg.

Bot Ba Njock, H.-M. (1964) Les tons en basaa, *JAL* 3: 252–9.

——(1970) *Nexus et nominaux en basaa*. PhD thesis. Université de Paris-Sorbonne.

Botne, R. (1989) Reconstruction of a grammaticalized auxiliary in Bantu, *SLS* 19.2: 169–86.

——(1989/90) The historical relation of Cigogo to Zone J languages, *SUGIA* 10/11: 187–222.

——(1990) The origins of the remote future formatives in Kinyarwanda, Kirundi, Giha (J61), *SAL* 21.2: 189–210.

——(1990/91) Verbal prosody in Ciruri, *JALL* 12.2: 107–42.

——(1993) Noun incorporation into verbs: the curious case of 'ground' in Bantu, *JALL* 14: 187–99.

——(1994) *A Lega and English Dictionary*, Cologne: Rüdiger Köppe Verlag.

——(1995) The pronominal origin of an evidential, *Diachronica* XI1: 201–21.

——(1997) Evidentiality and epistemic modality in Lega, *Studies in Language* 21: 509–32.

——(1998) The evolution of future tenses from serial 'say' constructions in Central Eastern Bantu, *Diachronica* 15: 2.

——(1999) Future and distal -ka-'s: Proto-Bantu or nascent form(s)?, in Hombert and Hyman (eds) 473–515.

Boum, M. A. (1980) Le groupe Menchum: morphologie nominale, in Hyman (ed.) (1980b) 73–82.

——(1983) L'expression de la localisation en basaa, *JWAL* 13: 23–32.

Bouquiaux, L. (ed.) (1980) *L'expansion bantoue*, vols. 2 and 3, Paris: SELAF.

Bouquiaux, L. and Thomas, J. M. C. (1994) Quelques problèmes comparatifs de langues bantoues C10 des confins oubanguiens: le cas du mbati, du ngando et de l'aka, in Geider and Kastenholz (eds) 87–107.

Bourquin, W. (1923) *Neue Ur-Bantu-Wortstämme nebst einem Beitrag zur Erforschung der Bantuwurzeln*, Berlin: Dietrich Reimer.

Bresnan, J. and Kanerva, J. M. (1989) Locative inversion in Chichewa: a case study of factorization in grammar, *Linguistic Inquiry* 20.1: 1–50.

Bresnan, J. and Mchombo, S. A. (1987) Topic, pronoun, and agreement in Chichewa, *Language* 63: 741–82.

Bresnan, J. and Moshi, L. (1990) Object asymmetries in comparative syntax, *Linguistic Inquiry* 21.2: 147–85.

——(1993) Object asymmetries in comparative Bantu syntax, in Mchombo (ed.) (1993a) 47–91.

Breton, R. J. L. and Fohtung, B. G. (1991) *Atlas administratif des langues nationales du Cameroun*, Yaoundé: CREA.

Bright, W. (ed.) (1992) *International encyclopedia of linguistics*, 4 vols., Oxford: Oxford University Press.

Brown, G. (1972) *Phonological rules and dialect variation. A study of the phonology of Lumasaaba*, Cambridge: Cambridge University Press.

Brown, R. (1973) *A first language: the early stages*, Cambridge, MA: Harvard University Press.

Bruens, A. (1942–5) The structure of Nkom and its relations to Bantu and Sudanic, *Anthropos* 37–40: 826–66.

Brumfit, A. (1980) The rise and development of a language policy in German East Africa, *SUGIA* 2: 219–332.

Brusciotto, G. (1882) Grammar of the Congo language (as spoken two hundred years ago). Trans. H. G. Guiness. London. (Brusciotto, Giacinto. *Regulae quaedam pro difficillimi congensium idiomatis faciliori captu ad grammaticae normam redactae*. Rome, 1659.)

Bryan, M. A. (1959) *The Bantu languages of Africa*, London: IAI.

Buckley, E. (1997) Bare root nodes in Basaa, *Penn Working papers in Linguistics* 2: 27–38.

Burke, E. I. (1940) *A small handbook of the Kilega language*, Pittsburgh: Pittsburgh Bible Institute Press.

——(1956) Proverbes lega, *Zaire* 10.7: 711–15.

Büttner, C. G. (1881) Kurze Anleitung für Forschungsreisende zum Studium der Bantusprachen, *Zeitschrift der Gesellschaft fur Erdkunde zu Berlin* 16: 1–26.

Byarushengo, E., Duranti, A. and Hyman L. M. (eds) (1977) *Haya grammatical structure*, Los Angeles: University of Southern California. SCOPIL 6.

Bybee, J., Perkins, R. and Pagliuca, W. (1994) *The evolution of grammar: tense, aspect, and modality in the languages of the world*, Chicago: University of Chicago Press.

Calloc'h, J. (1911) *Vocabulaire français-ifumu (Batéké), précédé d'éléments de grammaire.* Paris: P. Geuthner.

Cammenga, J. (1994) *Kuria phonology and morphology.* Proefschrift. Amsterdam: Free University.

Campbell, L. (1998) *Historical linguistics: an introduction*, Edinburgh: Edinburgh University Press.

Carleton, T. C. (1996) *Phonetics, phonology and rhetorical restructuring of Chichewa.* PhD thesis. Austin: University of Texas.

Carrington, J. F. (1943) The tonal structure of Kele (Lokele), *AS* 2.4: 193–209.

——(1947) Notes sur la langue olombo (Turumbu), *Aequatoria* 10: 102–13.

——(1972) *Esquisse d'une grammaire lokele*, Stanleyville. Duplicated.

——(1977) Esquisse morphologique de la langue likile (Haut Zaïre), *AL* 7: 65–88.

Carstens, V. and Parkinson, F. (eds) (2000) *Advances in African Linguistics* (Trends in African Linguistics 4), Trenton: Africa World Press.

Carter, H. (1962) *Notes on the tonal system of Northern Rhodesia Plateau Tonga*, London: Colonial Office.

——(1984) *Geminates, nasals and sequence structure in Kongo (Special Issue: Essays in Memory of Jan Voorhoeve), Oso* 3.1: 101–14.

Cassimjee, F. (1986) *An autosegmental analysis of Venda tonology.* PhD thesis. University of Illinois (available through Garland Press).

——(1998) *Isixhosa tonology: an optimal domains theory analysis*, Munich: Lincom Europa.

Cassimjee, F. and Kisseberth, C. W. (1998) Optimal domains theory and Bantu tonology, in Hyman and Kisseberth (eds) 33–132.

——(1999a) Tonal variation across Emakhuwa dialects, in Kaji (ed.) 261–87.

——(1999b) A conspiracy argument for optimality theory: Emakhuwa dialectology, *Proceedings of the 23rd Annual Penn Linguistics Colloquium* 6:1.

Chagas, J. (1976) The tonal structure of Olusamia, in Hyman (ed.) (1976a) 217–40.

Chanda Musanda Chibila (1975) *Eléments de grammaire générative et transformationnelle de la langue Nkore*, 2 vols. Lubumbashi: Université du Zaïre.

Chaudenson, R. (1992) *Des Iles, des hommes, des langues*, Paris: L'Harmattan.

Chelo, L. (1973) *Phonologie et morphologie de la langue olombo (turumbu)*, Mémoire. Lubumbashi: Université nationale du Zaïre.

Cheng, C. C. and Kisseberth, C. W. (1979) Ikorovere Makua tonology part 1, *SLS* 9.1: 31–63.

——(1980) Ikorovere Makua tonology part 2, *SLS* 10.1: 15–44.

——(1981) Ikorovere Makua tonology part 3, *SLS* 11.1: 181–202.

Chesswas, J. D. (1963) *The essentials of Luganda*, London: Oxford University Press.

Chia, E. N. (1983) The expression of location in Kom, *JWAL* 13.2: 71–90.

Chimombo, M. (1981) *Overgeneralization in negation: a comparison of first and second language acquisition.* EdD thesis. New York: Columbia University Teachers' College.

Chimombo, M. and Mtenje, A. (1989) Interaction of tone, syntax and semantics in the acquisition of Chichewa negation, *SAL* 20: 103–50.

Chomsky, N. (1982) *Lectures on government and binding: The Pisa Lectures*, Dordrecht: Foris.

Chumbow, B. and Nguendjio, E. G. (1991) Floating tones in Bangwa, *JWAL* 21: 3–14.

Clark, M. (1993) Representation of downstep in Dschang Bamileke, in van der Hulst and Snider (eds) 29–73.

Claudi, U. (1993) *Die Stellung von Verb und Objekt in Niger-Kongo-Sprachen: Ein Beitrag zur Rekonstruktion historischer Syntax*, Cologne: University of Cologne, Institut für Afrikanistik.

——(1997) Some thoughts on the origin of gender marking, in Herbert (1997). 63–74.

Clements, G. N. (1991) Vowel height assmilation in Bantu languages, BLS, Special Session on African Language Structures. 25–64.

Clements, G. N. and Ford, K. C. (1979) Kikuyu tone shift and its synchronic consequences, *Linguistic Inquiry* 10: 179–210.

Clements, G. N. and Goldsmith, J. (eds) (1984) *Autosegmental studies in Bantu tone*, Dordrecht: Foris Publications.

Clist, B. (1995) *100,000 ans d'histoire*, Libreville: Sepia.

Cloarec-Heiss, F. and Thomas, J. M. C. (1978) *L'aka, langue bantoue des Pygmées de Mongoumba (Centrafrique)*, Paris: SELAF.

Cole, D. T. (1955) *An introduction to Tswana grammar*, Cape Town: Longmans, Green.

——(1967) The prefix of Bantu noun class 10, *AS* 26.3: 119–37.

——(1975) *An introduction to Tswana grammar*, Cape Town: Longman Penguin Southern Africa. Second impression with a new preface.

Cole, J. and Kisseberth, C. W. (eds) (1994) *Perspectives in phonology*, Stanford: CSLI.

Comrie, B. (1976) *Aspect*, Cambridge: Cambridge University Press.

——(1985) *Tense*, Cambridge: Cambridge University Press.

——(1989) *Language universals and linguistic typology*, Oxford: Blackwell Publishers.

Connell, B. (2000) Mambila fricative vowels, in Carstens and Parkinson (eds) 233–49.

Connelly, M. (1984) *Basotho childrens' acquisition of noun morphology*. PhD thesis. Colchester: Essex University.

Contini-Morava, E. (1997) Noun classification in Swahili, in Herbert (1997) 599–628.

Cope, A. T. (1971) A consolidated classification of the Bantu languages, *AS* 30: 213–36.

Corbett, G. (1991) *Gender*, Cambridge: Cambridge University Press.

Coupez, A. (1955) *Esquisse de la langue Holoholo, vol. 12*, Tervuren: Annalen van het koninklijk museum van Belgisch-Kongo.

——(1960) Grammaire rwanda simplifée suivie de notes de phonologie Rwanda, IRSAC.

——(1983) La tonalité du protobantou, *Review of Applied Linguistics*: 143–58.

Coupez, A., Bastin, Y. and Mumba, E. (1998) Reconstruction lexicales bantoues 2/Bantu lexical reconstructions 2. [Computerized data base. Download from: http://www.linguistics.berkeley. edu/CBOLD.]

Crabb, D. W. (1965) *Ekoid Bantu languages of Ogoja*, Cambridge: Cambridge University Press.

Craig, C. G. (ed.) (1986) *Noun class and categorization, typological studies in language 7*, Amsterdam: John Benjamins.

Creider, C. A. (1975) The semantic system of noun classes in Proto-Bantu, *Anthropological Linguistics* 17: 127–38.

Creissels, D. (1992) La problématique des constructions dites 'impersonelles' et la description des langues négro-africaines, *Verbum* 4: 237–64.

——(1996) Conjunctive and disjunctive verb forms in Setswana, *South African Journal of African Languages* 16: 109–14.

——(1998) Expansion and retraction of high-tone domains in Setswana, in Hyman and Kisseberth (eds) 133–94.

——(1999a) The role of tone in the conjugation of Setswana (S 31), in Blanchon and Creissels (eds) 109–52.

——(1999b) Bimoraic syllables in a language without length contrast and without consonants in coda position: the case of Siswati (S 43), in Blanchon and Creissels (eds) 153–96.

——(1999c) Remarks on the sound correspondences between Proto-Bantu and Tswana (S.31), in Hombert and Hyman (eds) 297–334.

——(2000) Typology, in Heine and Nurse (eds) 231–58.

Cullen, W. A. (1999) *Tense and aspect in Lubwisi narrative discourse*. PhD thesis. Arlington: University of Texas.

Dahl, O. (1985) *Tense and aspect systems*, Oxford: Basil Blackwell.

Dalby, D. (1970) West African indigenous scripts, in D. Dalby (ed.) *Language and History in Africa*, London: Frank Cass and Company.

——(2000) Inner-Bantu (web-document), Linguasphere Observatory.

Dale, D. (1972) *Shona Companion*, Gweru: Mambo Press.

Dalgish, G. M. (1979) The syntax and semantics of the morpheme *ni-* in KiVunjo (Chaga), *SAL* 10: 47–63.

Dammann, E. (1954) Reziprok und Assoziativ in Bantusprachen, *ZDMG* 104 (NF 29): 163–74.

——(1957) *Studien zum Kwangali: Grammatik, Texte, Glossar*, Hamburg: Cram, De Gruyter and Co.

——(1958) Die sogenannten Kausativa auf –eka in Bantusprachen, *AU* 42: 173–8.

——(1959) Inversiva und Repetitiva in Bantusprachen, *AU* 43: 116–27.

——(1961) Das Applikativum in den Bantusprachen, *ZDMG* 111(NF 36): 160–9.

——(1962) Kontaktiva in Bantusprachen, *AU* 46: 118–26.

——(1971) Vom Satz zum Wort in Bantusprachen, *Folia Orientalia* 13: 33–49.

Davey, A., Moshi, L. and Maddieson, I. (1982) Liquids in Chaga, *UCLA Working Papers in Phonetics* 54: 93–108.

Davies, M. B. (1952) *A Lunyoro-Lunyankole-English and English-Lunyoro-Lunyankole Dictionary*, Kampala and London: MacMillan and Co.

Davis, L. K. (1992) *A segmental phonology of the Oku language*. MA Thesis. Arlington: University of Texas.

Davy, J. I. M. and Nurse, D. (1982) Synchronic versions of Dahl's Law: the multiple applications of a phonological dissimilation rule, *JALL* 4: 159–95.

De Blois, K. F. (1970) The augment in the Bantu languages, *AL* 4: 85–165.

——(1975) *Bukusu generative phonology and aspects of Bantu structure*, Tervuren: MRAC. Annales Sciences Humaines 85.

De Boeck, L. B. (1951a) Een greep uit de Mombesa-taal, *Aequatoria* 14: 136–43.

——(1951b) La tonologie des parlers bantous du nord-ouest du Congo belge, *Bulletin des Séances* 22. 4: 900–19.

De Maret, P. and Nsuka, F. N. (1977) History of Bantu metallurgy: some linguistic aspects, *History in Africa* 4: 43–65.

De Rop, A. J. (1958) *Grammaire du lomongo, morphologie et phonologie*, Léopoldville: Studia Universitatis 'Lovanium'.

——(1971) Esquisse de grammaire mbole, *Orbis* 20.1: 34–78.

Deen, K. U. (2002) The acquisition of Nairobi Swahili: The Morphosyntax of inflectional prefixes and subjects. PhD thesis. Los Angeles: UCLA.

Delhaise, le C. (1900) La vie intellectuelle: langage, in *Les Warega*, Brussels: Albert de Wit. 251–61.

Demolin, D. H. and Delvaux, V. (2001) Whispery voiced nasal stops in Rwanda. Paper presented at the 32nd Annual Conference on African Linguistics, University of California, Berkeley.

Demolin, D. H., Ngonga-Ke-Mbembe, H. and Soquet, A. (1999) Phonetic characteristics of an unexploded stop in Hendo, *Proceedings of the 14th International Congress of Phonetic Sciences* 2: 1047–57.

Demolin, D. H., Hombert, J.-M., Ondo, P. and Segebarth, C. (1992) Étude du système vocalique fang par résonance magnétique, *Pholia* 7: 41–59.

Demuth, K. (1984) *Aspects of Sesotho language acquisition*, Bloomington: Indiana University Linguistics Club.

——(1987a) Prompting routines in the language socialization of Basotho children, in B. Schieffelin and E. Ochs (eds) *Language Socialization Across Cultures, Social and Cultural Foundations of Language Series*, New York: Cambridge University Press. 80–96.

——(1987b) Discourse functions of word order in Sesotho acquisition, in R. Tomlin (ed.) *Coherence and Grounding in Discourse*, Amsterdam: John Benjamins. 91–108.

——(1988) Noun classes and agreement in Sesotho acquisition, in M. Barlow and C. A. Ferguson (eds) *Agreement in natural languages: approaches, theories and descriptions*, Stanford: CSLI. 305–21.

——(1989) Maturation, continuity and the acquisition of Sesotho passive, *Language* 65: 56–80.

——(1990) Subject, topic and the Sesotho passive, *Journal of Child Language* 17: 67–84.

——(1992a) Accessing functional categories in Sesotho: Interactions at the morpho-syntax interface. In J. Meisel (ed.) *The acquisition of verb placement: functional categories and V2 phenomena in language development*, Dordrecht: Kluwer Academic Publishers. 83–107.

Demuth, K. (1992b) Acquisition of Sesotho, in D. Slobin (ed.) *The crosslinguistic-study of language acquisition*, Hillsdale, NJ: Lawrence Erlbaum Associates 3: 557–638.

——(1993) Issues in the acquisition of the Sesotho tonal system, *Journal of Child Language* 20: 275–301.

——(1994) On the 'underspecification' of functional categories in early grammars, in B. Lust, M. Suner and J. Whitman (eds) *Syntactic theory and first language acquisition: cross-linguistic perspectives*, Hillsdale, NJ: Lawrence Erlbaum Associates. 119–34.

——(1995a) Problems in the acquisition of tonal systems, in J. Archibald (ed.) *The acquisition of non-linear phonology*, Hillsdale, NJ: Lawrence Erlbaum Associates. 111–34.

——(1995b) Questions, relatives and 'minimal projection', *Language Acquisition* 4: 49–71.

——(1996) The prosodic structure of early words, in J. Morgan and K. Demuth (eds) *Signal to syntax: bootstrapping from speech to grammar in early acquisition*, Mahwah, NJ: Lawrence Erlbaum Associates. 171–84.

——(1998) Argument Structure and the acquisition of Sesotho applicatives, *Linguistics* 36: 781–806.

——(2000) Bantu noun class systems: loan word and acquisition evidence of semantic productivity, in G. Senft (ed.) *Classification systems*, Cambridge: Cambridge University Press. 270–92.

Demuth, K. and Mmusi, S. (1997) Presentational focus and thematic structure in comparative Bantu, *JALL* 18: 1–19.

Demuth, K., Faraclas, N. and Marchese, L. (1986) Niger-Congo noun class and agreement systems in language acquisition and historical change, in Craig (ed.) 453–71.

Demuth, K., Machobane, M. and Moloi, F. (2000) Learning word order constraints under conditions of object ellipsis, *Linguistics* 38: 1–24.

—— (in press) Rules and construction effects in learning the argument structure of verbs. *Journal of Child Language.*

Denny, J. P. (1986) The semantic of noun classes in Proto-Bantu, in Craig (ed.) (Revised version of 1976).

Denny, J. P. and Creider, C. A. (1976) The semantics of noun classes in Proto-Bantu, *SAL* 7: 1–30.

Department van Nasionale Opvoeding (1983) *Herero Spelreels Nr.3*, Gamsberg: Windhoek.

Diamond, J. M. (1997) *Guns, Germs, and Steel*, New York: W.W. Norton and Company.

Dickens, P. (1984) Qhalaxarzi verb tone classes, *AS* 43.2: 109–18.

——(1986) *Qhalaxarzi Phonology*. MA thesis, Johannesburg: University of the Witwatersrand.

——(1987) Qhalaxarzi consonants, *AS* 46: 297–305.

Dieu, M. and Renaud, P. (1983) *Atlas Linguistique du Cameroun*, Paris: Agence de coopération culturelle et technique and Yaoundé: ACCT/CERDOTOLA/DGRST.

Dik, S. (1989) *The theory of functional grammar. Part 1: the structure of the clause*, Dordrecht: Foris. Functional Grammar Series 9.

Dimmendaal, G. J. (ed.) (1986) *Current approaches to African linguistics, vol. 3*, Dordrecht: Foris.

——(1988) *Aspects du basaá*, Paris: Peeters/SELAF [translated by L. Bouquiaux].

Dixon, R. M. W. (1982) *The Dyirbal language of North Queensland*, Cambridge: Cambridge University Press.

——(1997) *The rise and fall of languages*, Cambridge: Cambridge University Press.

Doke, C. M. (1926) *Zulu phonetics*, Johannesburg: University of the Witwatersrand Press.

——(1927a) *Text-book of Zulu grammar*, Cape Town: Longmans and Green.

——(1927b) The significance of class 1 Bantu nouns, in F. Boas (ed.) *Festschrift Meinhof*, Hamburg: Heinrich Augustin. 196–203.

——(1931a) *Report on the unification of the Shona dialects*, Hertford: Stephen Austen and Sons.

——(1931b) *A comprehensive study in Shona phonetics*, Johannesburg: University of Witwatersrand Press.

——(1935) Bantu linguistic terminology, London: Longmans, Green & Co.

——(1945) Bantu: modern grammatical, phonetical and lexicographical studies since 1860. London: Dawsons of Pall Mall. Reprinted 1967.

——(1954) *The Southern Bantu Languages*, London: Oxford University Press for the International African Institute.

Doke, C. M. (1960) Early Bantu literature: the age of Brusciotto, *AS* 18:49–67. Reprinted in R. K. Herbert (1993) (ed.) *Foundations of South African Linguistics*, Johannesburg: Witwatersrand University Press.

Doke, C. M. and Cole, D. T. (1961) *Contributions to the history of Bantu linguistics: papers contributed 1935–1960*, Johannesburg: Witwatersrand University Press.

Doke, C. M. and Mofokeng, S. M. (1957) *Textbook of Southern Sotho grammar*, Cape Town: Longmans, Green.

Donnelly, S. (1990) *Phonology and morphology of the noun in Yeeyi*. BA thesis. Cape Town: University of Cape Town.

Donnelly, S. (1996) Phuthi vowel harmonies: twin innovations in Zone S. Unpublished paper presented at the Round Table on Bantu Historical Linguistics, Lyon, Université Lumière Lyon II, 30 May–1 June.

Dos Santos, L. F. (1941) *Gramática da Lingua Chope*, Lourenco Marques: Imprensa Nacional de Mocambique.

Downing, L. J. (1990) *Problems in Jita tonology*. PhD thesis. University of Illinois.

——(1996a) The moraic representation of nasal-consonant clusters in Jita, *AAP* 25: 105–30.

——(1996b) *The tonal phonology of Jita*, Munich: Lincom Europa.

Drinka, B. and Nurse, D. (eds) (2001) *African language and culture in historical perspective: essays in memory of Edgar. C. Polomé*. Special edition of *General Linguistics* 38. 3 vols.

Dryer, M. S. (1983) Indirect objects in Kinyarwanda revisited, in D. M. Perlmutter (ed.) *Studies in Relational Grammar*, Chicago: University of Chicago Press. 129–40.

Dugast, I. (1955) Monographie de la tribu des Ndiki (Banen du Cameroun), vol. I: vie matérielle, *Travaux et Mémoires de l'Institut d'Ethnologie 58*, Paris: Musée de l'Homme.

——(1959) *Monographie de la tribu des Ndiki (Banen du Cameroun)*, vol. II: *Vie sociale et familiale*, Travaux et Mémoires de l'Institut d'Ethnologie 63, Paris: Musée de l'Homme.

——(1967) Lexique de la langue Tunen, parler des Banen du sud-ouest du Cameroun, *Langues et Littératures de l'Afrique Noire 2*, Paris: Klincksieck.

——(1971) Grammaire du Tunen, *Langues et Littératures de l'Afrique Noire 7*, Paris: Klincksieck.

——(1975) Contes, proverbes et devinettes des Banen, *Langues et Civilisations à Tradition Orale 12*, Paris: SELAF.

Dunstan, E. (1963) Conjugation in Ngwe, *Journal of African Linguistics* 2: 235–43.

——(1964) Towards a phonology of Ngwe, *JWAL* 1: 39–42.

——(1966a) *Tone and concord systems in Ngwe nominals*. Ph.D. thesis. London: London University.

——(1966b) Tone in disyllabic nouns in Ngwe, *JWAL* 3: 33–8.

Du Plessis, J. A. and Visser, M. (1992) *Xhosa syntax*, Pretoria: Via Afrika.

Duranti, A. (1979) Object clitic pronouns in Bantu and the topicality hierarchy, *SAL* 10.1: 31–45.

Durie, M. and Ross, M. (eds) (1996) *The comparative method reviewed*, Oxford: Oxford University Press.

Dz'Ba, D. S. (1972) *Esquisse grammaticale du bira*. Mémoire. Lubumbashi: Université Nationale du Zaïre.

Dzokanga, A. (1979) *Dictionnaire Lingala-Français, suivi d'une grammaire Lingala*, Leipzig: Verlag Encyclopaedie.

——(1992) *Grammaire pratique du Lingala*, Paris: INALCO. Mimeo.

Ebobisse, C. (1989) Dialectometrie lexicale des parlers Sawabantu, *JWAL* 19.2: 57–66.

Ehret, C. E. (1998) *An African classical age: Eastern and Southern Africa in world history, 1000 B.C. to A.D. 400*, Charlottesville: University Press of Virginia.

——(1999) Subclassifying Bantu: stem-morpheme innovations, in Hombert and Hyman (eds) 43–148.

——(2000) Language and history, in Heine and Nurse (eds) 272–97.

——(n.d.) Suggestions regarding a possible set of pronouns characterizing Bantu within Niger-Congo. MS.

Elderkin (1999) Word keys in Herero, *AAP* 17: 151–66.

Elias, P., Leroy, J. and Voorhoeve, J. (1984) Mbam-Nkam or Eastern Grassfields, *AU* 67: 31–107.
Emanatian, M. (1992) Chaga 'come' and 'go': metaphor and the development of tense-aspect, *Studies in Language* 16: 1–33.
Endemann, K. (1876) *Versuch einer Grammatik des Sotho*. [Reprint Gregg Press International, 1964.]
Engstrand, O. and Lodhi, A. Y. (1985) On aspiration in Swahili: hypotheses, field observations, and an instrumental analysis, *Phonetica* 42: 175–85.
Erasmus, J. S. and Baucom, K. L. (1976) *Fanakalo through the medium of English*, Johannesburg: Anglo-American Corporation.
Ernst, U. (1991) Temps et aspect, in Anderson and Comrie (eds) 17–46.
Fabian, J. (1986) *Language and colonial power: the appropriation of Swahili in the former Belgian Congo 1880–1938*, Cambridge: Cambridge University Press.
Fehderau, H. (1966) *The origin and development of Kituba*. PhD thesis. Ithaca: Cornell University.
Festi, L. and Valler, V. (n.d.) *Dicionário etxuwabo-português*, n. l.
Finlayson, R. and Slabbert, S. (1997) I'll meet you halfway with language – code-switching within a South African context, in M. Puetz (ed.) *Language choices: conditions, constraints and consequences*. Amsterdam: John Benjamins. 381–421.
——(2000) 'I'm a cleva': the linguistic make up of identity in a South African urban context. *Witswatersrand International Journal of the Sociology of Language* 144: 119–36.
Fiore, L. E. (1987) *A phonology of Limbum*. MA thesis. Arlington: University of Texas.
Fisch, M. (1977) *Einführung in die Sprache der Mbukushu, Ost-Kavango, Namibia*, Windhoek: S.W.A. Wissenschaftliche Gesellschaft, Windhoek. Translated as *Thimbukushu Grammar*. Windhoek: Out of Africa Publishers.
Fivaz, D. (1986) *A reference grammar of Oshindonga*, Windhoek: The Academy.
Fleisch, A. (1995) *Tempus, Aspekt und Modus im Herero auf der Grundlage von Dokumentar-und Erzähltexten*. MA thesis. Cologne: Institut für Afrikanistik.
——(2000) *Lucazi Grammar. A Morphosemantic Analysis*. Cologne: Rüdiger Köppe.
Foley, W. A. and van Valin, R. D. (1984) *Functional syntax and universal grammar*, Cambridge: Cambridge University Press.
Fontaney, L. (1980) Le verbe, in Nsuka Nkutsi (ed.) 51–114.
——(1988) Mboshi: Steps towards a grammar, *Pholia* 3: 87–167 part 1; *Pholia* 4: 71–131 Part 2.
Forges, G. (1977) *Le kela, langue bantoue du Zaïre (Zone C). Esquisse phonologique et morphologique*, Paris: SELAF.
——(1983) La classe de l'infinitif en bantou, *AL* 9: 257–63.
Fortune, G. (1955) *An analytical grammar of Shona*, London: Longmans, Green.
Fransen, M. A. E. (1995) *A grammar of Limbum: a Grassfields Bantu language spoken in North-West Province*. PhD Thesis. Amsterdam: Free University of Amsterdam.
Gardner, W. (1990) *Language use in the Epena district of Northern Congo*. MA thesis. Grand Forks: University of North Dakota.
Gazania, R. (1972) *Aspects phonologiques et morphologiques du koyo*. Mémoire. Université de Grenoble.
Geider, T. and Kastenholz, R. (eds) (1994) *Sprachen und Sprachzeugnisse in Afrika: Eine Sammlung philologischer Beiträge, Wilhelm J.G. Möhlig zum 60 Geburtstag zugeeignet*, Cologne: Rüdiger Köppe.
Geitlinger, K. (in press) Discourse pragmatic correlates of word order variation and intonation: Swahili versus English – a preliminary inquiry, *Journal of Pragmatics*.
Gensler, O. (1997) Grammaticalization, typology, and Niger-Congo word order: progress on a still unsolved problem, *JALL* 18: 57–93.
Gérard, R. P. (1924) *La langue lebeo, grammaire et vocabulaire*, Brussels: Bibliothèque Congo XIII, Vromant & CO.
Gerdts, D. and Whaley, L. (1991) Locatives vs. instrumentals in Kinyarwanda, in K. Hubbard (ed.) *Proceedings of the Seventeenth Annual Meeting of the BLS*. 87–98.
Giacalone Ramat, R. and Hopper, P. (eds) (1998) *The limits of grammaticalization*, Amsterdam: Benjamins.

Gilliard, L. (1928) *Grammaire pratique du lontomba*, Brussels: Editions l'Essorial.

Givón, T. (1969) Studies in Chibemba and Bantu grammar, *SAL Supplement* 3.

——(1970a) The resolution of gender conflicts in Bantu conjunctions: when syntax and semantics clash, *Papers from the Sixth Regional Meeting, CLS, April 16–18*, Chicago: CLS. 250–61.

——(1970b) *The Si-Luyana language – a preliminary description*, Lusaka: University of Zambia, Institute for Social Research.

——(1971) Historical syntax and synchronic morphology: an archaeologist's field trip, *CLS* 7: 394–415.

——(1974) Syntactic change in Lake-Bantu: a rejoinder, *SAL* 5.1: 117–39.

——(1975a) Focus and the scope of assertion: some Bantu evidence, *SAL* 6.2: 185–205.

——(1975b) Serial verbs and syntactic change; Niger-Congo, in Li (ed.) 47–112.

——(1976) Topic, pronoun and grammatical agreement, in C. Li (ed.) *Subject and Topic*, New York: Academic Press. 149–88.

——(1979a) *On understanding grammar*, New York: Academic Press.

——(1979b) Language typology in Africa: a critical review, *JALL* 1: 199–224.

——(1990) *Syntax. a functional-typological introduction, vol. 2*, Amsterdam: John Benjamins.

Goldsmith, J. A. (1976) *Autosegmental phonology*, Bloomington: Indiana University Linguistics Club.

——(1981) *Towards an autosegmental theory of accent: the case of Tonga*, Bloomington: Indiana University Linguistics Club.

——(1987) Stem tone patterns of the Lacustrine Bantu languages, in Odden (ed.) 167–77.

——(1991) Tone and accent in Llogori, *AAP* 25: 7–29.

Gowlett, D. F. (1989) The parentage and development of Lozi, *JALL* 11: 127–49.

——(ed.) (1992a) *African linguistic contributions (presented in Honour of Ernst Westphal)*, Pretoria: Via Afrika.

——(1992b) Yeyi reflexes of Proto-Bantu, in Gowlett (ed.).

——(1997) Aspects of Yeyi diachronic phonology, in Haacke and Elderkin (eds) 235–63.

——(n.d.) Vowel Harmony in Yeyi. MS.

Goyvaerts, D. L. (ed.) (1985) *African linguistics: essays in memory of M.W.K. Semikenke*, Amsterdam: John Benjamins.

Grebe, K. (1982) Nouns, noun classes and tone in Lam-Nso, Yaoundé: SIL. MS.

Grebe, K. and Grebe, W. (1975) Verb tone patterns in Lamsok, *Linguistics* 149: 5–23.

Greenberg, J. H. (1948) The tonal system of Proto-Bantu, *Word* 4: 196–208.

——(1951) Vowel and nasal harmony in Bantu languages, *Revue Congolaise/Zaire* 5: 813–20.

——(1955) *Studies in African linguistic classification*, New Haven: The Compass Publishing Company.

——(1963a) *The languages of Africa*, The Hague: Mouton. Reprinted 1966. (also IJAL 29.1, Publication 25 of the Indiana University Research Center in Anthropology, Folklore and Linguistics. Bloomington: Indiana University Press).

——(1963b) Some universals of grammar with particular reference to the order of meaningful elements, in J. H. Greenberg (ed.) *Universals of language*, 2nd edn, Cambridge, MA: MIT Press.

——(1966) *The Languages of Africa*, Bloomington, IN and The Hague: Mouton & Co.

——(1972) Linguistic evidence for Bantu origins, *JAH* 13: 189–216.

——(1974) Bantu and its nearest relatives, *SAL* Supplement 5: 115–19 and 122–4.

——(1977) Niger-Congo noun class markers: prefixes, suffixes, both or neither, *SAL supplement* 7: 94–104.

——(1978a) *Universals of Human Language*, Stanford: Stanford University Press.

——(1978b) How does a language acquire gender markers?, in Greenberg (ed.) (1978a) vol. 3: 47–82.

——(1980) Foreword, in Hyman and Voorhoeve (eds) 39–42.

Gregersen, E. A. (1977) *Language in Africa: an introductory survey*, New York: Gordon and Breach.

Grégoire, C. L. (1975) *Les locatifs en bantou*. Tervuren: MRAC. Annales Sciences humaines 83.

Grégoire, C. L. (1976) Le champ sémantique du theme bantou *-bánjá, *African Languages/ Langues africaines* 2: 1–13.

——(1979) Les voyelles finales alternantes dans la conjugaison affirmative des langues bantoues centrales, *JALL* 1.2: 141–72.

——(1983) Quelques hypothèses comparatives sur les locatifs dans les langues bantoues du Cameroun, *JWAL* 13.2: 139–64.

——(1994) A diachronic approach to classes 10 and 11 in Bantu with special reference to North-Western languages, *Proceedings of the Special Session "Historical Issues in African Language"*. Berkeley: BLS. 21–34.

——(1998) L'expression du lieu dans les langues africaines, in *Les Langues d'Afrique subsaharienne*. Special issue of *Faits de Langues*: 285–303.

Grégoire, C. L. and Janssens, B. (1999) L'augment en bantou du Nord-Ouest, in Hombert and Hyman (eds). 413–29.

Grégoire, C. L. and Rekanga, J. P. (1994) Nouvelles hypothèses diachroniques sur la classe 10b du myene nkomi (B11e). *AL* 9: 71–8.

Grice, H. P. (1975) Logic and conversation, in P. Cole and J. L. Morgan (eds) *Syntax and Semantics Vol 3. Speech Acts*, New York: Academic Press. 41–58.

Grimes, B. F. (ed.) (2000) *Languages of the world: ethnologue*, 13th edition, Dallas: SIL International.

Guarisma, G. (1973) *Le nom en bafia. Étude du syntagme nominal d'une langue bantoue du Cameroun*, Paris: SELAF.

——(1980) Les voyelles centrales en bafia et dans d'autres parlers du groupe A50, in Bouquiaux (ed.) 447–54.

——(1983) Pour un traitement synchronique de la faille tonale, in Kaye *et al.* (eds) 151–69.

——(1992) Structure syllabique, accent et faille tonale en Bafia, *Verbum* 4: 299–310.

——(1994) Le Bafia, une langue bantoue à prosodie riche, in Geider and Kastenholz (eds) 165–76.

——(2000) *Complexité morphologique – simplicité syntaxique, le cas du Bafia. Langue bantoue périphérique (A50) du Cameroun*, Paris: Peeters (Langues et cultures africaines, 24).

Guarisma, G. and Möhlig, W. J. G. (eds) (1986) *La méthode dialectométrique appliquée aux langues africaines*, Berlin: Dietrich Reimer.

Guarisma, G. and Paulian, C. (1986) Dialectométrie lexicale de quelques parlers bantous de la zone A, in Guarisma and Möhlig (eds) 93–176.

Guerreiro, N. (1963) *Rudimentos de Lingua Makonde*, Lourenco Marques: Instituto de Investigacasho Cientifica de Mocambique.

Güldemann, T. (1996) *Verbalmorphologie und Nebenprädikation im Bantu: Eine Studie zur funktional motivierten Genese eines konjugationalen Subsystems*, Bochum: Universitätsverlag Dr. N. Brockmeyer.

——(1998) The relation between imperfective and simultaneous taxis in Bantu: late stages of grammaticalization, in I. Fiedler, C. Griefenow-Mewis and B. Reineke (eds) *Afrikanische Sprachen im Brennpunkt der Forschung*, Cologne: Rüdiger Köppe Verlag. 157–77.

——(1999a) The genesis of verbal negation in Bantu and its dependency on functional features and clause types, in Hombert and Hyman (eds) 545–87.

——(1999b) Towards a grammaticalization and typological account of the ka-possessive in Zulu, *JALL* 20.2: 157–84.

——(1999c) Head-initial meets head-final: nominal suffixes in eastern and southern Bantu from a historical perspective, *SAL* 28: 49–91.

——(2000) When 'say' is not say: the functional versatility of the Bantu quotative *ti* with special reference to Shona, in T. Güldemann and M. von Ronacdor (eds) *Reported speech: a meeting ground for different linguistic domains*. Typological Studies in Language 52. Amsterdam: John Benjamins. 253–87.

——(forth) Present progressive vis-à-vis predication focus in Bantu: a verbal category between semantics and pragmatics. *Studies in Language*.

Guma, S. M. (1971) *An outline structure of Southern Sotho*, Pietermaritzburg: Shuter and Shooter.

Guthrie, M. (1948) *The classification of the Bantu languages*, London: International African Institute. Reprinted 1967.

—— (1953) *The Bantu languages of Western Equatorial Africa*, London: IAI.

—— (1967–71) *Comparative Bantu: an introduction to the comparative linguistics and prehistory of the Bantu languages*. Vols. 1–4. Farnborough: Gregg Press.

—— (1971) *Comparative Bantu*, Vol 2. Farnborough: Gregg Press.

Guthrie, M. and Carrington, J. F. (1988) *Lingala grammar and dictionary: English-Lingala, Lingala-English*, London: Baptist Missionary Society.

Haacke, W. H. G. (1985) Noun phrase accessibility to relativization in Herero and Nama, *SAJAL* 5: 43–8.

Haacke, W. H. G. and Elderkin, E. D. (eds) (1997) *Namibian languages: reports and papers*, Cologne: Rüdiger Köppe Verlag.

Hadermann, P. (1994a) Aspects morphologiques et syntaxiques de l'infinitif dans les langues bantoues. *AL* 9: 79–92.

—— (1994b) Les marques *-yo-* et *-to-* dans quelques langues bantoues de zone C, *AAP* 38: 163–80.

—— (1996) Formes verbales complexes et grammaticalisation de la structure Infinitif + Verbe conjugués dans quelques langues bantoues de zones B et H, *SAL* 25.2: 155–69.

—— (1999) Les formes nomino-verbales de classes 5 et 15 dans les langues bantoues du Nord-Quest, in Hombert and Hyman (eds) 431–71.

Hagendorens, J. (1943) *Dictionnaire français-otetela, suivi de quelques notions pratiques de la grammaire otetela*, Tshumbe Ste Marie: Imprimerie de la Mission catholique.

Hahn, C. H. (1857) *Grundzüge einer Grammatik des Herero (im westlichen Afrika) nebst einem Wörterbuche*, Wilhelm Hertz: Berlin.

Haiman, J. (1978) Conditional are topics, *Language* 54.3: 564–89.

Hardcastle, W. J. and Brasington, R. W. P. (1978) Experimental study of implosive and voiced egressive stops in Shona: an interim report, *Work in Progress (Phonetics Laboratory, University of Reading)* 2: 66–97.

Harries, L. (1950) *A grammar of Mwera*, Johannesburg: Witwatersrand University.

—— (1959) Nyali, a Bantoid language, *Kongo-Overzee* 25.5: 174–205.

Harro, G. (1989) Extensions verbales en yemba (dschang-bamileke), in Barreteau and Hedinger (eds) 179–238.

Haspelmath, M. (1989) From purposive to infinitive: a universal path of grammaticalization, *Folia Linguistica Historica* 10.1/2: 287–310.

—— (1992) Grammaticalization theory and heads in morphology, in M. Aronoff (ed.) *Morphology Now*, New York: State University of New York Press. 69–82.

Haynes, N. (1989) Esquisse phonologique du yemba, in Barreteau and Hedinger (eds) 179–238.

Hayward, K. M., Omar, Y. A. and Goesche, M. (1989) Dental and alveolar stops in Kimvita Swahili: an electropalatographic study, *African Languages and Cultures* 2: 51–72.

Heath, D. (1984) Relative clauses in Makaá, *JWAL* 14. 2: 43–60.

—— (1991a) Tone in the Makaa associative construction, in Anderson (ed.) 3–28.

—— (1991b) Tense and aspect in Makaa, in Anderson and Comrie (eds) 3–16.

Heath, D. and Heath, T. (1982) *A phonology of the Makaá language*, Yaoundé: SIL.

—— (1984) Relative clauses in Makaa, *JWAL* 142: 43–60.

Hedinger, R. (1980) The noun classes of Bakossi, in Hyman (ed.) (1980b) 1–26.

—— (1984) *A comparative study of the Manenguba languages (Bantu A. 15, Mbo cluster)*. PhD thesis. London: London University.

—— (1985) The verb in Akoose, *SAL* 16.1: 1–55.

—— (1993) Review of Miehe's 1991 'Nasal Prefixes in Benue-Congo and Kwa', *AU* 76: 5–7.

Heine, B. (1970) *Status and use of African lingua francas*, Munich: Weltforum Verlag.

—— (1973) Zur genetischen Gliederung der Bantu-Sprachen, *AU* 56: 164–85.

—— (1976) *A Typology of African languages based on the order of meaningful elements*, Berlin: Dietrich Reimer.

Heine, B. (1980) Language typology and linguistic reconstruction: the Niger-Congo case, *JALL* 2.2: 95–112.

—— (1982) African noun class systems, in H. Seiler and C. Lehmann (eds) *Apprehension: das sprachliche Erfassen von Gegenständen. Vol. 1.* Tübingen: Gunter Narr Verlag. 189–216.

——(1997) *Possession: cognitive sources, forces, and grammaticalization*, Cambridge: Cambridge University Press.

Heine, B. and Nurse, D. (eds) (2000) *African languages*, Cambridge: Cambridge University Press.

Heine, B. and Reh, M. (1984) *Grammaticalization and reanalysis in African languages*, Hamburg: Helmut Buske.

Heine, B. and Vossen, R. (1981) Sprachtypologie, in Heine, Schadeberg, and Wolff (eds) 407–44.

Heine, B., Claudi, U. and Hünnemeyer, F. (1991) *Grammaticalization: a conceptual framework*, Chicago: University of Chicago Press.

Heine, B., Schadeberg, T. C. and Wolff, E. (eds) (1981) *Die Sprachen Afrikas*, Hamburg: Helmut Buske.

Heine, B. *et al.* (1993) Conceptual shift, a lexicon of grammaticalization processes in African languages, *AAP* 34/5.

Hendrikse, A. P. and Poulos, G. (1992) A continuum interpretation of the Bantu noun class system, in Gowlett (ed.) 195–209.

Henrici, A. (1973) Numerical classification of Bantu languages, *ALS* 14: 82–104.

Herbert, R. K. (1975) Reanalyzing prenasalized consonants, *SAL* 6.2: 105–23.

——(1977a) Phonetic analysis in phonological description: prenasalized consonants and Meinhof's Rule, *Lingua* 43: 339–73.

——(1977b) The non-dissimilatory nature of nasal compound dissimilation in Bantu, in P. F. A. Kotey and H. Der-Houssikian (eds), *Language and linguistic problems in Africa*, Columbia SC: Hornbeam Press. 395–411.

——(1986) *Language universals, markedness theory, and natural phonetic processes*, Berlin: Mouton de Gruyter.

——(1995) Pre-nasalized consonants and Dahl's Law: questions of representations and subclass, in Traill *et al.* (eds) 217–36.

——(ed.) (1997) *African linguistics at the crossroads*, Cologne: Rüdiger Köppe Verlag.

Hermann, C. (1904) Lusiba, die Sprache der Länder Kisiba, Bugabu, Kjamtwara, Kjanja und Ihangiro, speziell der Dialekt der Bayossa, *MSOS* 7: 150–200.

Hewson, J. and Nurse, D. (2001) Chronogenetic Staging in the Swahili Verbal System, in Drinka and Nurse (eds), *General Linguistics* 38: 75–108.

Hewson, J., Nurse, D. and Muzale, H. R. T. (2000) Chronogenetic Staging of Tense in Ruhaya, *SAL.* 29.2: 33–56.

Himmelmann, N. (1992) *Grammaticalization and Grammar*, Cologne: Institut für Sprachwissenschaft.

——(1997) *Deiktikon, Artikel, Nominalphrase: Zur Emergenz syntaktischer Struktur*, Tübingen: Niemeyer.

Hinnebusch, T. J. (1974) Rule inversion and restructuring in Kamba, *SAL* Supp. 5: 149–67.

——(1981) Northeast Coast Bantu, in Hinnebusch *et al.* (eds) 21–126.

——(1989) Bantu, in Bendor-Samuel (ed.) 450–73.

——(1999) Contact and lexicostatistics in comparative Bantu studies, in Hombert and Hyman (eds) 173–205.

Hinnebusch, T. J., Nurse, D. and Mould, M. (1981) *Studies in the classification of Eastern Bantu languages, SUGIA Beiheft 3*, Hamburg: Helmut Buske Verlag.

Holm, J. (1989) *Pidgins and creoles*, 2 vols. Cambridge: Cambridge University Press.

Hombert, J.-M. (1976) Noun classes and tone in Ngie, in Hyman (ed.) (1976a) 3–22.

——(1977) Notes on Ngie phonology, Santa Barbara: University of California. MS.

——(1979) Bibliography of the Grassfields (Cameroon), Leiden: University of Leiden. MS.

——(1980) Le groupe noun, in Hyman and Voorhoeve (eds) 143–63.

——(1990) Réalisations tonales et contraintes segmentales en fang, *Pholia* 5: 105–11.

Hombert, J.-M. and Hyman, L. M. (eds) (1999) *Bantu historical linguistics: theoretical and empirical perspectives*, Stanford: CSLI.

Hopper, P. (1987) Emergent grammar, *Proceedings of the BLS* 13: 139–57.
——(1994) Phonogenesis, in Pagliuca (ed.) 29–45.
Hopper, P. and Traugott, E. (1993) *Grammaticalization*, Cambridge: Cambridge University Press.
Horton, A. E. (1949) *A grammar of Luvale*, Johannesburg: Witwatersrand University Press.
Hubbard, K. (ed.) (1991) *Proceedings of the Seventeenth Annual Meeting of the Berkeley Linguistics Society, February 15–18, 1991. Special Session on African Language Structures.* Berkeley: Berkeley Linguistics Society.
——(1994) *Duration in moraic theory.* PhD thesis. Berkeley: University of California.
——(1995) Toward a theory of phonological and phonetic timing: evidence from Bantu, in B. A. Connell and A. Arvaniti (eds) *Phonology and phonetic evidence: papers in laboratory phonology* 4: 168–87.
Huffman, M. K. and Hinnebusch, T. J. (1998) The phonetic nature of the "voiceless" nasals in Pokomo: implications for sound change, *JALL* 19: 1–19.
Hulstaert, G. (1938) *Praktische Grammatica van het Lonkundo (Belgische Congo)*, Antwerp: De Sikkel.
——(1941) Over het dialekt der Boyela, *Aequatoria*. 4.5: 95–8.
——(1948) Le dialecte des pygmoïdes Batswa de l'Equateur, *Africa* 18.1: 21–8.
——(1961) *Grammaire du Lomongo.* 2 vols. Tervuren: MRAC. Annales Sciences humaines 39 and 57.
——(1970) *Esquisse du parler des Nkengo*, Tervuren: MRAC. Annales Sciences humaines 66.
——(1974a) Sur les dialectes des Bakutu, *Revue zaïroise des Sciences de l'homme* 4: 3–46.
——(1974b) A propos des Bangala, *Zaïre-Afrique* 83: 173–85.
——(1978) Notes sur la langue des Bafoto, *Anthropos* 73: 1–2, 113–32.
——(1982) *Esquisse de la langue des Eleku (Rép. Zaïre)*, Bandundu: Publications CEEBA 3,7.
——(1987) Les parlers des Bongando méridionaux, *Annales Aequatoria* 8: 205–88.
——(1989) L'origine du Lingala, *AAP* 17: 81–114.
——(1993) Liste et carte des dialectes mongo, *Annales Aequatoria* 14: 401–6.
——(1999) Eléments de dialectologie mongo, *Annales Aequatoria* 20: 9–322.
Huntingford, G. W. B. (1965) The Orusyan language of Uganda, *JAL* 4.3: 145–69.
Hurel, E. (1909) La langue kikerewe, *MSOS* 12: 1–113.
Hyman, L. M. (1971) Consecutivization in Fe'fe', *JAL* 10: 29–43.
——(1972) *A phonological study of Fe?fe?-Bamileke*, *SAL*, vol. 3, Supplement 4.
——(1975) On the change from SOV to SVO: evidence from Niger-Congo, in Li (ed.) 113–47.
——(ed.) (1976a) *Studies in Bantu Tonology.* Los Angeles: University of Southern California. SCOPIL 3.
——(1976b) D'ou vient le ton haut du bamileke-fe'fe'?, *SAL*, Supplement 6: 123–34.
——(1979a) Phonology and noun structure, in Hyman (ed.) 1–72.
——(ed.) (1979b) *Aghem grammatical structure*, Los Angeles: University of Southern California. SCOPIL 7.
——(1979c) Tonology of the Babanki noun, *SAL* 10: 159–78.
——(1979d) A reanalysis of tonal downstep, *JALL* 1: 9–29.
——(1980a) Babanki and the Ring group, in Hyman and Voorhoeve (eds) 223–58.
——(ed.) (1980b) *Noun classes in the Grassfields Bantu borderland*, Los Angeles: University of Southern California. SCOPIL 8.
——(1980c) Reflections on the nasal classes in Bantu, in Hyman (ed.) 179–210.
——(1980d) Relative time reference in the Bamileke tense system, *SAL* 11: 227–37.
——(1981) *Noni grammatical structure*, Los Angeles: University of Southern California. SCOPIL 9.
——(1982) Globality and the accentual analysis of Luganda tone, *Journal of Linguistic Research* 2/3: 1–40.
——(1985) Word domains and downstep in Bamileke-Dschang, *Phonology Yearbook* 2: 47–83.
——(1986) The representation of multiple tone heights, in Bogers *et al.* (eds) 109–52.
——(1987) Downstep deletion in Aghem, in Odden (ed.) 209–22.
——(1990) Non-exhaustive syllabification: evidence from Nigeria and Cameroon. In M. Ziolowski, M. Noske and K. Deaton (eds) *CLS 26. Papers from the 26th Regional Meetings of the CLS, volume 2, The Parasession on the syllable in Phonetics and Phonology.* 175–96.

Hyman, L. M. (1993) Conceptual issues in the comparative study of the Bantu verb system, in Mufwene and Moshi (eds) 3–34.

——(1994) Cyclic phonology and morphology in Cibemba, in Cole and Kisseberth (eds) 81–112.

——(1995a) Minimality and the prosodic morphology of Cibemba imbrication, *JALL* 16: 3–39.

——(1995b) Nasal consonant harmony at a distance: the case of Yaka, *SAL* 24: 5–30.

——(1997a) *Discontinuous cyclicity in phonology*, Tervuren: MRAC. Document.

——(1997b) *La morphologie et la 'frication' diachronique en bantou*, Tervuren: MRAC. Document.

——(1999) The historical interpretation of vowel harmony in Bantu, in Hombert and Hyman (eds) 235–95.

——(2000) Cyclicity and templatic morphology in the Basaá verb stem. Paper presented at the Second Round Table in Phonology of the GDR 1954, Bordeaux, June 8, 2000.

Hyman, L. M. and Byarushengo, E. R. (1984) A model of Haya tonology, in Clements and Goldsmith (eds) 53–103.

Hyman, L. M. and Duranti, A. (1982) On the object relationship in Bantu, in P. J. Hopper and S.A. Thompson (eds) *Syntax and Semantics vol. 15, Studies in Transitivity*, New York: Academic Press. 217–39.

Hyman, L. M. and Katamba, F. X. (1990) Final vowel shortening in Luganda, *SAL* 21: 1–60.

——(1991) Augment in Luganda tonology, *JALL* 12.1: 1–46.

——(1993) The augment in Luganda: syntax or pragmatics?, in Mchombo (ed.) 209–56.

Hyman, L. M. and Kisseberth, C. W. (eds) (1998) *Theoretical aspects of Bantu tone*, Stanford: CSLI.

Hyman, L. M. and Mathangwane, M. (1998) Tonal domains and depressor consonants, in Hyman and Kisseberth (eds) 195–229.

Hyman, L. M. and Moxley, J. (1992) The morpheme in phonological change: velar palatalization in Bantu, *Diachronica* 13. 259–82.

Hyman, L. M. and Ngunga, A. (1997) Two kinds of moraic nasal in Ciyao, *SAL* 26: 131–63.

Hyman, L. M. and Tadadjeu, M. (1976) Floating tones in Mbam-Nkam, in Hyman (ed.) (1976a): 57–111.

Hyman, L. M. and Valinande, N. (1985) Globality in the Kinande tone system, in D. Goyvaerts (ed.) *African linguistics*, Amsterdam: John Benjamins. 239–59.

Hyman, L. M. and Voorhoeve, J. (eds) (1980) *Les classes nominales dans le bantou des Grassfields. L'expansion bantoue, vol. I.* Paris: SELAF.

Hyman, L. M. and Watters, J.R. (1984) Auxiliary focus, *SAL* 15: 233–73.

Hyman, L. M., Voeltz, E. F. K. and Tchokokam, G. (1970) Noun-class leveling in Bamileke, *SAL 1:* 185–209.

Idiata, D. F. (1998) *Some aspects of the childrens' acquisition of the Isangu language.* PhD thesis. Lyon: Université Lyon 2.

IPA (1999) *Handbook of the IPA*, Cambridge: Cambridge University Press.

Jacobs J. (1964) *Tetela-Grammatica (Kasayi, Kongo)*, Gent: Orientalia Gandensia.

Jacottet, E. (1896) *Grammaire Soubiya. Études sur les langues du Haut-Zambèze: textes originaux recueillis et traduits en français et précédés d'une esquisse grammaticale.* Ed. E. Jacottet. Paris: Leroux. Vol. 1. 1–79.

Jacquot, A. (1976) *Etude de phonologie et de morphologie myene*, Paris: SELAF, *Etudes bantoues* II: 13–78.

——(1978) Le Gabon, in Barreteau (ed.).

——(1983) *Les classes nominales dans les langues bantoues des groupes B.10, B.20, B.30 (Gabon-Congo)*, Travaux et documents de l'ORSTOM 157.

Jacquot, A. and Richardson, I. (1956) Report of the Western team: Atlantic coast to Oubangui, in *Linguistic Survey of the Northern Bantu Borderland* [supervisors Malcolm Guthrie and A. N. Tucker], Vol. 1: 9–62.

Janson, T. (1991–2) Southern Bantu and Makua, *SUGIA* 12/13: 63–106.

Janson, T. (1995) The status, history and future of Sekgalagadi, in Traill *et al.* (eds) 399–407.

Janssens, B. (1982) *Phonologie historique du basaá*, Mémoire Brussels: Université Libre de Bruxelles.

Janssens, B. (1983) Review of Hinnebusch, Nurse, and Mould. (1981) *JALL* 5.2: 207–12.
——(1986) Éléments de phonologie et de morphologie historique du basaá (bantou A43a), *AL* 10: 147–211.
——(1988) Ton et elision vocalique en nen, *Linguistique Africaine* 1: 61–94.
——(1991) Doubles réflexes apparents en ewondo, ou les chassés-croisés de la derivation, *Pholia* 6: 155–80.
——(1992–3) *Doubles réflexes consonantiques: quatre études sur le bantou de zone A (bubi, nen, bafia, ewondo)*. PhD thesis. Brussels: Université libre de Bruxelles.
Johnson, F. (1939) *A Standard English-Swahili dictionary*, Nairobi: Oxford University Press.
Johnson, M. R. (1980) A semantic description of temporal reference in the Kikuyu verb, *SAL* 11: 269–320.
Johnston, Harry. H. (1919–22) *A comparative study of the Bantu and Semi-Bantu languages*, Oxford: Clarendon Press. 2 vols.
Jouannet, F. (1983) Phonétique et phonologie: le système consonantique du kinyarwanda, in F. Jouannet (ed.) *Le Kinyarwanda: Études Linguistiques*, Paris: SELAF. 55–74.
——(1984) *Phonologie du Kifuliru (Rwanda)*, Paris: SELAF.
Jusczyk, P. (1997) *The Discovery of spoken language*, Cambridge, MA: MIT Press.
Kabuyaya, K. P. (n.d.) Esquisse de la langue pere, Tervuren: MRAC. MS.
Kadima, M. (1969) *Le système des classes d'accord en Bantu*, Leuven: Vander.
Kadima, K., Mutombo, H.-K. *et al.* (1983) *Situation linguistique de l'Afrique Centrale, inventaire préliminaire: le Zaire*, Agence de Coopération Culturelle et Technique, Centre de Recherche et de Documentation sur les Traditions Orales et pour le Développement des Langues Africaines.
Kageyama, T. (1977) Conjunction, in Byarushengo *et al.* (eds) 133–41.
Kahigi, K. K., Kihore, Y. M. and Mous, M. (eds) (2000). *Lugha za Tanzania/Languages of Tanzania: a study dedicated to the memory of the late Prof. C. Maganga*, Leiden: CNWS publications, no. 89, and Dar es Salaam: Mkuki na Nyota.
Kahindo, L. M. (1984) *Description Syntaxique du Nande*. Ph.D. thesis Paris: Université Descartes/ Paris V.
Kähler-Meyer, E. (1966) Die örtliche Funktion der Applikativendung in Bantusprachen, in Lukas (ed.) 126–36.
——(1971) Bantu class 19 *pi-* in Benue-Congo, *Actes du Huitième Congrès International de Linguistique Africaine, Abidjan 24–28 Mars 1969. Vol. 2*, Abidjan: Université d'Abidjan.
Kaji, S. (1980) *Lexique Tembo*, Tokyo: ILCAA. Duplicated.
——(1985) *Lexique Tembo I. Tembo-Swahili du Zaïre-Japonais-Français*, Tokyo: ILCAA, 16.
——(1992) Particularités phonologiques en Tembo, in Yukawa (ed.) (1992). 363–72.
——(1996) Tone reversal in Tembo (Bantu J57), *JALL* 17.1: 1–27.
——(ed.) (1999) *Proceedings of the Symposium on Cross-linguistic studies of tonal phenomena: tonogenesis, typology, and related topics*, Tokyo: ILCAA.
Kamanda Kola, R. (1991) *Eléments de description du zamba, langue bantoue (C31e) du Zaïre*. Mémoire. Brussels: Université libre de Bruxelles.
——(1993) A propos de la tonalité en zamba, *AAP* 33: 83–103.
Kamba Muzenga, J. G. (1981) *Les formes négatives dans les langues bantoues*, Tervuren: Koninklijk Musuem voor Midden-Africa.
Kamwangamalu, N. M. (1985) Passivization in Bantu languages. Implications for relational grammar, *SLS* 15.1: 109–33.
Kapanga, M. T. (1991) *Language variation and change: a case study of Shaba Swahili*. PhD thesis. Urbana: University of Illinois.
Kashoki, M. E. and Mann, M. (1978) The Bantu languages of Zambia, in Ohanessian and Kashoki (eds). 47–100.
Katamba, F. and Hyman, L. M. (1990) Final vowel shortening in Luganda, *SAL* 21: 1–60.
——(1991) Nasality and morpheme structure constraints in Luganda, *AAP* 25: 175–211.
Katupha, J. M. M. (1983) *A preliminary description of sentence structure in the Esaaka dialect of Emakhuwa*. MPhil thesis. London: London University.

Kavari, J. U. and Ohly, R. (n.d.) The question of Herero dialects. MS.

Kaye, J., Koopman, H., Sportiche D. and Dugas, A. (eds) (1983) *Current Approaches to African Linguistics, vol. 2*, Dordrecht: Foris.

Kerremans, R. (1980) Nasale suivie de consonne sourde en proto-bantou, *AL 8*: 59–198.

Khumalo, J. (1987) *An Autosegmental Account of Zulu Phonology*. PhD thesis: Johannesburg: University of the Witwatersrand.

Kihore, Yared M. (2000) Historical and linguistic aspects of Kihacha, in Kahigi *et al.* (2000) 67–80.

Kimenyi, A. (1980) *A relational grammar of Kinyarwanda*, Berkeley: University of California Press.

——(1988) Passives in Kinyarwanda, in M. Shibatani (ed.) *Passive and Voice*, Amsterdam: John Benjamins. 355–68.

Kingston, J. (1983) The expansion of the Gusii tense system, in Kaye *et al.* (eds) 31–56.

Kiptoo, F. M. (2000) *An emerging interdialectal variation: a comparative study of Kariokor, Jericho, and Kangemi Sheng varieties*. MA thesis. Catholic University of East Africa.

Kisseberth, C. W. (1992) Metrical structure in Zigula tonology, in Gowlett (ed.) 227–59.

——(1994) On domains, in Cole and Kisseberth (eds) 136–66.

Kisseberth, C. W. and Abasheikh, M. I. (1974) The perfect stem in Chi-Mwi:ni and global rules, *SAL* 6: 249–66.

Kliemann, K. (1997) *Peoples of the western equatorial rainforest: A history of society and economy, from ca. 3000 B.C. to 1890*. PhD thesis. Los Angeles: UCLA.

Knappert, Jan. (1979) The origin and development of Lingala, in I. Hancock (ed.) *Readings in Creole Studies*, Ghent: E. Story-Scientia P.V.B.A. 153–64.

Koopman, H. (1994) Introduction, in H. Koopman and M. Kural (eds) *Aspects of Nchufie Grammar*. Los Angeles: UCLA (Occasional Papers in Linguistics 14).

Krifka, M. (1983) *Zur semantischen und pragmatischen Motivation syntaktischer Regularitäten. Eine Studie zur Wortstellung und Wortstellungveränderung im Swahili* (Studien zur theoretischen Linguistik 5), Munich: W. Fink.

——(1995) Swahili, in J. Jacobs *et al.* (eds), *Syntax, ein internationales Handbuch zeitgenössischer Forschung*. Vol. 2, Berlin: de Gruyter. 1397–1418.

Kunene, E. (1979) *The acquisition of Siswati as a first language: a morphological study with special reference to noun prefixes, noun classes and some agreement markers*. PhD thesis. Los Angeles. UCLA.

Kuperus, J. (1985) *The Londo word: its phonological and morphological structure*, Tervuren: Koninklijk Museum voor Midden-Afrika.

Kutsch Lojenga, C. (1994a) Kibudu: a Bantu language with nine vowels, *AL 9*: 127–34.

——(1994b) *The vowel system of Bila, a Bantu language of the northern Bantu borderland in Zaire*. Paper presented at the 24th colloquium on African languages and Linguistics, Leiden.

——(1995) *From two to three tones in Bila*. Paper presented at the 25th colloquium on African languages and linguistics, Leiden.

——(1999) *The vowel system of Lika: first impressions*. Paper presented at the 29th colloquium on African languages and linguistics, Leiden.

——(2001) *The two v's of Giryama*. Paper presented at the 32nd annual conference on African Linguistics, University of California, Berkeley.

Kutsch Lojenga, C. and Raymond, T. R. (1985) A linguistic picture of northeastern Zaire: Bera – Bila – Bele – Komo MS.

Kwenzi, Mikala, J. (1980) Esquisse phonologique du punu, in Nsuka-Nkutsi (ed.) 7–18.

Labroussi, C. (1998) *Le couloir des lacs – contribution linguistique à l'histoire des populations du sud-ouest de la Tanzanie*. PhD thesis. Paris: INALCO.

——(1999) Vowel systems and spirantization in Southwest Tanzania, in Hombert and Hyman (eds) 335–77.

Ladefoged, P. (2000) *A course in phonetics*, 4th edition, New York: Harcourt Brace.

Ladefoged, P. and Maddieson, I. (1996) *The sounds of the world's languages*, Oxford: Blackwell Publishers.

Ladefoged, P., Glick, R. and Criper, C. (eds) (1971) *Language in Uganda*, London: Oxford University Press.

Lakoff, G. (1987) *Women, fire and dangerous things: what categories reveal about the mind*, Chicago: Chicago University Press.

Lanham, L. W. (1958) The tonemes of Xhosa, *AS* 40: 53–130.

Lehmann. C. (1995) *Thoughts on grammaticalization: a programmatic sketch*, Munich: Lincom Europa (originally 1982, Cologne, Linguistics Institute).

Langacker, R. (1987) *Foundations of cognitive grammar*, Palo Alto: Stanford University Press.

Leitch, M. (1989) Langue et dialecte au sud du districte d'Epena. Unpublished report on the Linguistic survey of Epena District south, Libreville: SIL.

——(1991) *Lexique babole-français*, Brazzaville: Université Marien Ngouabi.

——(1994a) Negation in Babole, in P. Kahrel and R. van den Berg (eds) *Negation in the world's languages*. Amsterdam: John Benjamins. 190–210.

——(1994b) The properties and distribution of Babole prenasalized segments, in S. A. Marlett and J. Meyer (eds) *University of North Dakota Working Papers in Linguistics* 38: 101–12.

——(1996) Evolution of Bantu C vowel harmony. Unpublished paper presented at the Round Table on Bantu Historical Linguistics, Lyon, Université Lumière Lyon II, 30 May–1 June.

——(1997) *Vowel Harmonies of the Congo Basin*. PhD thesis. Vancouver: University of British Columbia.

——(2000) *SHOEBOX Babole dictionary, Computerized Babole-French research dictionary*, Libreville: SIL.

——(forthcoming) Le systeme babole, in F. Idiata (ed.) *Les classes nominales et leur semantisme dans les langues bantoues du nord-ouest*, Munich: Lincom Europa.

Lemb, P. and de Gastines, F. (1973) *Dictionnaire basaa-francais*, Douala: College Libermann.

Leroy, J. (1977) *Morphologie et classes nominates en mankon*, Paris: SELAF.

——(1979) A la recherche des tons perdus: structure tonal du nom en ngemba, *JALL* 1: 55–71.

——(1980) The Ngemba Group, in Hyman and Voorhoeve (eds) 11–141.

——(1982) Extensions en mankon, in G. Guarisma, G. Nissim and J. Voorhoeve (eds) *Le verbe bantou*, Paris: SELAF. 125–37.

——(1983a) Système locatif mankon et classes locatives proto-bantoues, *JWAL* 13.2: 91–114.

——(1983b) Notes sur l'expression de la localisation en yamba, *JWAL* 13:2: 133–8.

Leung, W. Y. (1991) *The tonal phonology of Llogoori: a study of Llogoori verbs*, Working Papers of the Cornell Phonetics Laboratory 6.

Levinsohn, S. H. (ed.) (1991) *Discourse features of ten languages of West-Central Africa*, Dallas: SIL and the University of Texas at Arlington.

Lewis, P. W. (1994) *Aspects of the phonological acquisition of clicks in Xhosa*. MA thesis. Stellenbosch: Stellenbosch University.

——and Roux, J. C. (1996) A phonological process analysis of the acquisition and loss of clicks in Xhosa, *SAJAL* 16: 1–7.

Li, C. N. (ed.) (1975) *Word order and word order change*, Austin and London: University of Texas Press.

Liljencrants, J. and Lindblom, B. (1972) Numerical simulations of vowel quality systems: the role of perceptual contrast, *Language* 48: 839–62.

Linguistic Survey of the Northern Bantu Borderland (1956) [supervisors Malcolm Guthrie and A. N. Tucker], Vol 1. London: Oxford University Press for IAI.

Liphola, M. (2001) *Aspects of Phonology and Morphology of Shimakonde*. PhD thesis. Colombus, Ohio: Ohio State University.

Lisimba, M. (1982) *A Luyana dialectology*. PhD thesis. Madison: University of Wisconsin.

Louw, J. A. (1975) *Clicks as loans in Xhosa. Bushman and Hottentot linguistic studies*, Pretoria: University of South Africa.

Louwrens, L. J. (1991) *Aspects of Northern Sotho grammar*, Pretoria: Via Afrika.

Lowe, J. B. and Schadeberg, T. C. (1997) *Bantu Map Maker* 3.1. Berkeley and Leiden. http://www.linguistics.berkeley.edu

Lukas, J. (1942) Das afrikanische Verkeshrssprachenproblem, *Beiträge zur Kolonialforschung* 2: 15–24.

Lukas, J. (ed.) (1966) *Neue Afrikanistiche Studien*, Hamburg: Deutsches Institut für Afrika–Forschung.

Lungumbu, B. W. (1988) La conjugaison en lega, *Journal of Asian and African Studies* 35: 85–111.

Maddieson, I. (1990) Shona velarization: Complex consonants or complex onsets?, *UCLA Working Papers in Phonetics* 74: 16–34.

——(1991) Articulatory phonology and Sukuma 'aspirated nasals', *Proceedings of the 17th Annual Meeting of BLS, Special Session on African Language Structures*. 145–54.

——(1993) Splitting the mora, *UCLA Working Papers in Phonetics* 83: 9–18.

Maddieson, I. and Ladefoged, P. (1993) Phonetics of partially nasal consonants, in M. K. Huffman and R. A. Krakow (eds) *Nasals, nasalization and the velum*, San Diego: Academic Press. 251–301.

Maddieson, I., Ladefoged, P. and Sands, B. (1999) Clicks in East African languages, in R. Finlayson (ed.) *African Mosaic: Festschrift for J. A. Louw*, Pretoria: University of South Africa. 59–91.

Maddox, H. E. (1938) *An elementary Lunyoro grammar*, London: Society for Promoting Christian Knowledge.

Maganga, C. and Schadeberg, T. C. (1992) *Kinyamwezi; grammar, texts, vocabulary*, Cologne: Rüdiger Köppe Verlag.

Magba, E. A. (1995) *The INFL constituent in the Mundani Language*. PhD thesis. London University.

Maho, J. F. (1998) *Few people, many tongues. The languages of Namibia*, Windhoek: Gamsberg Macmillan.

——(1999) *A comparative study of Bantu noun classes*, Gothenburg: Acta Universitatis Gothoburgensis.

Malasi, N. M. (1988) Trois cents noms de personnes lega: au-dela des figures, *African Study Monographs* 9.1: 11–53.

Mamet, M. (1955) *La langue ntomba telle qu'elle est parlée au lac Tumba et dans la région avoisinante (Afrique centrale)*, Tervuren: MRAC. Annales Sciences Humaines 16.

——(1960) *Le langage des Bolia (Lac Léopold II)*, Tervuren: MRAC. Annales Sciences de l'Homme 33: 267.

Mann, M., Dalby, D. *et al.* (1987) *A thesaurus of African languages*, London: Hans Zell Publishers.

Manuel, S. (1990) The role of contrast in limiting vowel-to-vowel coarticulation in different languages, *Journal of the Acoustical Society of America* 88: 1286–98.

Marchal-Nasse, C. (1979) *Esquisse de la langue tsogo: phonologie et morphologie*. Mémoire. Université libre de Bruxelles.

——(1989) *De la phonologie à la morphologie du nzebi, langue bantoue (B 52) du Gabon*. PhD thesis. Brussels: Université Libre de Bruxelles.

Massamba, D. (1982) *Aspects of tone and accent in Ci-Ruri*. PhD thesis. Bloomingon: Indiana University.

Mateene, K. (1963) *Esquisse grammaticale de la langue Hunde (phonologie et morphologie)*. Mémoire. Léopoldville: Université Lovanium.

——(1992) *Essai de grammaire du Kihunde: syntaxe, morphologie et phonologie mélangées*, Münster and Hamburg: LIT Verlag. Hamburger Beiträge zur Afrikanistik 1.

Mathangwane, J. T. (1998) Aspirates: their development and depression in Ikalanga, *JALL* 19: 113–35.

——(1999) *Ikalanga phonetics and phonology; a synchronic and diachronic study*, Stanford: CSLI.

Maw, J. (1969) *Sentences in Swahili. A study of their internal relationships*, London: SOAS.

——(1994) Bantu languages, in R. E. Asher and J. M. Y. Simpson (eds) *The encyclopedia of language and linguistics* 1: 123–37.

Mazrui, A. M. (1995) Slang and code-switching: the case of Sheng in Kenya, *AAP* 42: 168–79.

Mba, G. (1996–7) Les extensions verbales en ghomala, *JWAL* 26: 77–101.

McCawley, J. (1970) Some tonal systems that come close to being pitch accent systems but don't quite make it, *CLS* 6: 526–32.

McHugh, B. D. (1990) *Cyclicity in the phrasal phonology of Kivunjo Chaga*. PhD thesis. Los Angeles: UCLA.

McWhorter, J. H. (1998) Identifying the creole prototype: vindicating a typological class, *Language* 74: 788–818.

Mchombo, S. A. (ed.) (1993a) *Theoretical aspects of Bantu grammar 1*. Stanford: CSLI.

——(1993b) A formal analysis of the stative construction in Bantu, *JALL* 14: 5–28.

——(1993c) On the binding of the reflexive and the reciprocal in Chichewa, in Mchombo (ed.) 181–207.

Medjo Mvé, P. (1997) *Essai sur la phonologie panchronique des parlers Fang du Gabon et ses implications historiques*. PhD thesis. Lyon: Université Lumière-Lyon 2.

Meeussen, A. E. (1952) *Esquisse de la langue ombo*, Tervuren: MRAC. Annales du Musée royal du Congo belge 4.

——(1953) De talen van Maniema, *Kongo-Overzee* 19.5: 385–90.

——(1954a) The tone of prefixes in common Bantu, *Africa* 24: 48–52.

——(1954b) Werwoordafleiding in Mongo en Oerbantoe, *Aequatoria* 17: 81–6.

——(1959) *Essai de Grammaire Rundi*, Tervuren: Annales du MRAC Serie 8, Sciences de l' Homme, Linguistique Vol. 24.

——(1961) Le ton des extensions verbales en bantou, *Orbis* 10: 424–7.

——(1962a) Lega-teksten, *AL* 1: 75–98.

——(1962b) Meinhof's rule in Bantu, *ALS* 3: 25–9.

——(1963) Morphotonology of the Tonga verb, *Journal of African Linguistics* 2.1: 72–92.

——(1966) Syntactic tones of nouns in Ganda: a preliminary synthesis, in Y. Lebrun (ed.) *Linguistic Research in Belgium*. 77–86.

——(1967) Bantu grammatical reconstructions, *AL* 3: 80–122.

——(1969) *Bantu lexical reconstructions*, Tervuren: MRAC [Reprinted in 1980].

——(1971) *Eléments de grammaire lega*, Tervuren: MRAC. Archives d'ethnographie 15.

——(1973) Test cases for method, *ALS* 14: 6–18.

——(1974) Reply to Prof. Greenberg, *SAL* Supplement 5: 119–21.

——(1977) Exposé sur l'expansion bantou, in Bouquiaux (ed.) 595–606.

——(1979) Vowel length in proto-Bantu, *JALL* 1: 1–8.

Meeuwis, M. (1998) *Lingala*, Munich: Lincom Europa.

Meinhof, C. (1899) *Grundriss einer Lautlehre der Bantusprachen*, Leipzig: F. A. Brockhaus. Revised edn. 1910, Berlin: Dietrich Reimer.

——(1903) Das Dahlsche Gesetz, *ZDMG* 57: 299–304.

——(1906) *Grundzüge einer vergleichenden Grammatik der Bantusprachen*, Berlin: Dietrich Reimer. Revised edn. 1948, Hamburg: von Eckardt and Messtorff.

Meinhof, C. and Van Warmelo, N. J. (1932) *Introduction to the phonology of the Bantu languages*, Berlin: Dietrich Reimer.

Mesthrie, R. (1989) The origins of Fanakalo, *Journal of Pidgin and Creole Languages* 4: 211–40.

——(1992) Fanakalo in colonial Natal, in R. K. Herbert (ed.) *Language and Society in South Africa*, Johannesburg: Witwatersrand University. 305–24.

——(ed.) (1995) *Language and social history: studies in South African sociolinguistics*, Cape Town and Johannesburg: David Philip Publishers.

Meyer, E. (1944) Das Problem der Verkehrssprachen von Tropisch-Afrika, insb. von Kamerun, *Mitt. Geogr. Ges. Hamburg* 48: 253–88.

Mfonyam, J. N. (1982) *Tone in the orthography of Bafut*. PhD thesis. University of Yaounde.

——(1991) Prominence in Bafut: syntactic and pragmatic devices, in Levinsohn (ed.) 191–210.

Mickala-Manfoumbi, R. (1988) *Eléments de description du duma, langue bantu du Gabon (B51)*. Mémoire. Brussels: Université libre de Bruxelles.

——(1994) *Description du pove B 22*. PhD thesis. Brussels: Université libre de Bruxelles.

Miehe, G. (1979) *Die Sprache der älteren Swahili-Dichtung*, Berlin: Dietrich Reimer.

——(1991) *Die Präfixnasale im Benue-Congo and im Kwa: Versuch einer Widerlegung der Hypothese von der Nasalinnovation des Bantu*, Berlin: Dietrich Reimer Verlag.

Miti, L. M. (1996) Subgrouping Ngoni varieties within Nguni: a lexicostatistical approach, *SAJAL* 16: 82–92.

Moga, J. and Fee, D. (2000) *Dictionary ya Sheng*, Nairobi: Ginseng Publishing.

Möhlig, W. J. G. (1967) *Die Sprache der Dciriku. Phonologie, Prosodologie und Morphologie*. PhD thesis, Cologne: University of Cologne.

——(1974) *Die Stellung der Bergdialekte im Osten des Mt. Kenya. Ein Beitrag zur Sprachgleiderung im Bantu*, Berlin: Dietrich Reimer.

——(1979) The Bantu nucleus: its conditional nature and its prehistorical significance, *SUGIA* 1: 109–41.

——(1981) Stratification in the history of the Bantu languages, *SUGIA* 3: 251–316.

——(1997) A dialectometrical analysis of the main Kavango languages, in Haacke and Elderkin (eds) 211–34.

Moore, S. F. and Puritt, P. (1977) *The Chagga and Meru of Tanzania*, London: IAI.

Morris, H. F. (1963) A note on Lunyole, *The Uganda Journal* 27.1: 127–34.

Moshi, L. (1988) A functional typology of "ni" in Kivunjo, *SLS* 18.1: 105–34.

——(1994) Time reference in KiVunjo-Chaga, *JALL* 15: 127–39.

——(1998) Word order in multiple object constructions in KiVunjo-Chaga, *JALL* 19: 137–52.

Motingea Mangulu, A. (1982) Inventaire des éléments vocaliques en lingombe (Zaïre), *Annales Aequatoria* 3: 147–59.

——(1990) Esquisse du parler des Ohendo (Z), *Annales Aequatoria* 11: 115–52.

——(1993) Parlers riverains de l'entre Ubangi-Zaïre. Eléments de structure grammaticale, *Etudes Aequatoria* 8: 283.

——(1994) Note sur le parler des Batswa de Bosabola (Maindombe-Z), *Annales Aequatoria* 14: 483–501.

——(1995) Note sur le parler des Babale de la Dua, *Annales Aequatoria* 15: 365–401.

——(1996) *Etude comparative des langues Ngiri de l'entre Ubangi-Zaire*, Leiden: CNWS.

Mouandza, J. D. (1991) *Esquisse phonologique du iyaa (parler bantu du Congo)*. Mémoire. Brazzaville. Université Marien Ngouabi.

Mould, M. (1976) *Comparative grammar reconstruction and language syllabification: the North Victorian Bantu languages*. PhD thesis. Los Angeles: UCLA.

——(1981) Greater Luyia, in Hinnebusch *et al.* (eds) 181–261.

Mous, M. (1986) Vowel harmony in Tunen, in Bogers *et al.* (eds) 281–95.

——(1997) The position of the object in Tunen, in R.-M. Déchaine and V. Manfredi (eds) *Object positions in Benue-Kwa: papers from a workshop at Leiden University, June 1994*, The Hague: Holland Academic Graphics. 123–37.

Mous, M. and Breedveld, A. (1986) A dialectometrical study of some Bantu languages (A40–A60) of Cameroon, in Guarisma and Möhlig (eds) 177–241.

Mowrer, D. E. and Burger, S. (1991) A comparative analysis of the phonological acquisition of consonants in the speech of 21/2–6-year-old Xhosa- and English-speaking children, *Clinical Linguistics and Phonetics* 3: 139–64.

Moxley, J. (1998) Semantic structure of Bantu noun classes, in I. Maddieson and T. J. Hinnebusch (eds) *Language history and linguistic description in Africa*, Trenton, NJ and Asmara: Africa World Press Inc.

Mpiranya, F. (1997) Spirantisation et fusion vocalique en Bantu, *Linguistique Africaine* 16: 51–77.

Mufwene, S. S. (1980) Bantu class prefixes: inflectional or derivational? *Papers from the Sixteenth Regional Meeting*. Chicago: CLS. 246–58.

——(1988) Formal evidence of pidginization/creolization in Kituba, *JALL* 10: 33–51.

——(1989) La créolisation en bantu: les cas du kituba, du lingala urbain, et du swahili du Shaba, *Etudes Créoles* 12: 74–106.

——(1990) Time reference in Kituba, in John V. Singler (ed.) *Pidgin and Creole Tense-Mood-Aspect Systems*, Amsterdam: John Benjamins. 97–117.

——(1994) Restructuring, feature selection, and markedness: from Kimanyanga to Kituba, in K. E. Moore, D. A. Peterson, and C. Wentum (eds) *Historical issues in African linguistics*, Berkeley: BLS. 67–90.

Mufwene, S. S. (1997a) Kituba, in Thomason (ed.) 173–208.

—— (1997b) Jargons, pidgins, creoles and koinés: what are they?, in A. K. Spears and D. Winford (eds) *The structure and status of pidgins and creoles*, Amsterdam: John Benjamins. 35–70.

—— (1998) What research on creole genesis can contribute to historical linguistics, in M. Schmid, J. Austin and D. Stein (eds) *Historical linguistics 1997*, Amsterdam: John Benjamins. 315–38.

—— (2001) *The ecology of language evolution*, Cambridge: Cambridge University Press.

Mufwene, S. S. and Moshi, L. (eds) (1993) *Topics in african linguistics*, Amsterdam: John Benjamins.

Mukarovsky, H. G. (1976–7) *A study of Western Nigritic*. 2 vols. Vienna: Afro-pub.

Müller, E. (1947) *Wörterbuch der Djaga-Sprache (Madjame-Mundart) gesprochen am Kilimandjaro in Ost-Afrika*, Hamburg: Verlag Von Eckardt & Messstorff.

Musamba, C. (1975) *Eléments de grammaire générative et transformationelle de la langue Nkore. Volume 1: Composante logico-sémantique*, Lubumbashi: Université Nationale du Zaïre. Mémoire.

Mutaka, N. M. (1994) *The lexical tonology of Kinande*, Munich and Newcastle: Lincom-Europa.

Mutaka, N. M. and Ebobissé, C. (1996–7) The formation of labial-velars in Sawabantu: evidence for feature geometry, *JWAL* 27: 3–14.

Muzale, H. R. T. (1998) *The phonological relationship between Ruhaya and Runyambo*, St. John's NF: Department of Linguistics. MS.

—— (forthcoming) *A reconstruction of the Proto-Rutara tense-aspect system*, Cologne: Rüdiger Köppe Verlag (1998 PhD thesis. St. John's: Memorial University of Newfoundland).

Myers, S. (1996) Boundary tones and the phonetic implementation of tone in Chichewa, *SAL* 25: 29–60.

—— (1999a) Downdrift and pitch range in Chichewa intonation, *Proceedings of the 14th International Congress of Phonetic Sciences*, vol. 3: 1981–4.

—— (1999b) Tone association and f0 timing in Chichewa, *SAL* 28: 215–39.

Myers, S. and Carleton, T. (1996) Tonal transfer in Chichewa, *Phonology* 13: 39–72.

Myers-Scotton, C. (1993) *Social motivations for codeswitching: evidence from Africa*, Oxford: Oxford University Press.

Nakagawa, H. (1992) *A classified vocabulary of the Ha language*, Tokyo: ILCAA. Bantu Vocabulary Series 9.

Nash, J. (1992) *Aspects of Ruwund grammar*. PhD thesis. University of Illinois at Urbana-Champaign.

Nchimbi, A. S. A. (1997) *Formant structure of Standard KiSwahili vowels*. Paper presented at the Second World Congress of African Linguistics, Leipzig.

NELIMO (1989): See Afido et al. (1989).

Newman, James L. (1995) *The peopling of Africa: a geographic interpretation*, New Haven, CT: Yale University Press.

Ngalasso, Mwatha M. (1984) Pidgins, creoles ou koinès?: à propos de quelques langues vehiculaires africaines, *Cahiers de l'Institut de Linguistique de Louvain* 9: 135–61.

—— (1991) Tons ou accents? Analyse des schèmes intonatifs du kikongo véhiculaire parlé dans la région de Bandundu (Zaire), *Etudes Créoles* 14: 147–62.

—— (1993) Les procédés répétifs en kikongo: le redoublement et la reduplication, in Mufwene and Moshi (eds) 45–66.

Nguendjio, E.-G. (1992) Temps et aspect de la langue bangwa, *JWAL* 22: 89–100.

Ngonyani, D. (1999) *A descriptive grammar of Kindendeuli*, Michigan: Michigan State University. MS.

Ngulinzira, B. (1977) *Esquisse phonologique et morphologique du tetela*. Mémoire. Brussels: Université libre de Bruxelles.

Ngunga, A. (1997) *Lexical phonology and morphology of the Ciyao verb stem*. PhD thesis. Berkeley: University of California.

—— (2000) *Lexical phonology and morphology of the Ciyao verb stem*, Stanford: CSLI.

Nicolaï, R. (1990) *Parentés linguistiques: à propos du Songhay*, Paris: CNRS.

Nichols, J. (1992) *Linguistic diversity in time and space*, Chicago and London: University of Chicago Press.

Nissim, G. (1980) Quelques parlers bamileke de l'est, in Hyman and Voorhoeve (eds) 79–109.
——(1981) *Le bamileke-ghomala' (parler de Bandjoun, Cameroun)*, Paris: SELAF.
Nkabuwakabili, A. (1986) *Esquisse de la langue boa*. Mémoire. Brussels: Université libre de Bruxelles.
Nkiko, M. R. (1977) *Esquisse grammaticale de la langue luba-Shaba*, Lubumbashi: CELTA.
Nkiko, M. R. (1980) *Les langues interlacustres. Classification généalogique d'un groupe de langues Bantu*. Thesis. Lubumbashi: Université Nationale du Zäire.
Nkiko, M. R. and Kemp, B. (1977) *Système verbal du tembo, classes des morphèmes verbaux et catégories verbales*, Lubumbashi: Université Nationale du Zäire. Duplicated.
Nkemnji, M. (1995) *Heavy pied piping in Nweh*. UCLA Dissertations in Linguistics No, 3.
Nsuka Nkutsi, F. (ed.) (1980) *Eléments de description du punu*, Lyon: Université Lyon II, Centre de Recherches Linguistiques et Sémiologiques.
——(1982) *Les structures fondamentales du relatif dans les langues bantoues*, Tervuren: MRAC. Annales Sciences Humaines 108.
——(1986) Formatifs et auxiliaires dans les langues bantoues: quelques critères de détermination, *AL* 10: 339–64.
Nsuka Nkutsi, F. and de Maret, P. (1980) Etude comparative de quelques termes métallurgiques dans les langues bantoues, in Bouquiaux (ed.) 731–42.
Nurse, D. (1979a) Descriptions of sample Bantu languages of Tanzania, *African Languages/ Langues africaines* 5.1: 1–150.
——(1979b) *Classification of the Chaga dialects: language and history on Kilimanjaro, the Taita Hills and the Pare Mountains*, Hamburg: Helmut Buske Verlag.
——(1982) Bantu expansion into East Africa: linguistic evidence, in C. Ehret and M. Posnansky (eds) *The archaeological and linguistic reconstruction of African history*, Berkeley: University of California Press. 199–222.
——(1988) The diachronic background to the language communities of southwestern Tanzania, *SUGIA* 9: 15–116.
——(1994–5) Historical classifications of the Bantu languages, *Azania* 29: 65–89.
——(1997a) Prior pidginization and creolization in Swahili? in Thomason (ed.) 271–94.
——(1997b) The contributions of linguistics to the study of history in Africa, *JAH* 38: 359–91.
——(1999) Towards a historical classification of East African Bantu languages, in Hombert and Hyman (eds) 1–41.
——(2000) *Inheritance, contact and change in two East African languages*, Cologne: Rüdiger Köppe Verlag.
——(forthcoming) Tense and aspect in Chaga, in *Festschrift for Prof. C. Winter*.
Nurse, D. and Hinnebusch, T. J. (1993). *Swahili and Sabaki: a linguistic history*, Berkeley: UCP.
Nurse, D. and Muzale, H. R. T. (1999) Tense and aspect in Great Lakes Bantu languages, in Hombert and Hyman (eds) 517–44.
Nurse, D. and Philippson, G. (1977) Tone in Old Moshi (Chaga), *SAL* 8.1: 49–80.
——(1980) Bantu languages of East Africa: a lexicostatistical survey, in Polomé and Hill (eds) 26–67.
Nurse, D. and Rottland, F. (1991–2) Sonjo: description, classification, history, *SUGIA* 12/13: 171–291.
Nurse, D. and Spear, T. (1985) *The Swahili: reconstructing the history and language of an African society, 800–1500*, Philadelphia: University of Pennsylvania Press.
Odden, D. (1981) *Problems in tone assignment in Shona*. PhD thesis. Illinois: University of Illinois.
——(ed.) (1987) *Current approaches to African linguistics, vol. 4*, Dordrecht: Foris.
——(1989) Predictable tone systems in Bantu, in H. van der Hulst and N. Smith (eds) *Autosegmental Studies on Pitch Accent Systems*, Dordrecht: Foris. 225–51.
——(1990a) Tone in the Makonde dialects: Chimaraba, *SAL* 21: 61–105.
——(1990b) Tone in the Makonde dialects: Chimahuta, *SAL* 21: 149–87.
——(1994) The origin of leftward tone shift in Masasi Chiyao, *BLS 20: Special Session on Historical Linguistics in African Languages*, Berkeley: BLS. 101–11.
——(1995a) Phonology at the phrasal level in Bantu, in F. Katamba (ed.) *Bantu phonology and morphology*, Munich: Lincom Europa. 40–68.
——(1995b) Tone: African languages, in J. Goldsmith (ed.) *The handbook of phonological theory*, Oxford: Blackwell. 444–75.

Odden, D. (1996) *The phonology and morphology of Kimatuumbi*, Oxford: Clarendon Press.
——(1999) Typological issues in tone and stress in Bantu, in Kaji (ed). pp. 187–215
——(2000) The phrasal tonology of Zinza, *JALL* 21: 45–75.
Ohly, R. (1994) The position of the Subiya language in Caprivi, *AU* 77: 105–27.
Ohannessian, S. and Kashoki, M. E. (eds) (1978) *Language in Zambia*, London: International African Institute.
Omatete, A.-D. (1982) *Description du verbe dans la morphologie de la langue tetela*. Mémoire. Brussels: Université libre de Bruxelles.
——(1985) *Description syntaxique de la langue tetela*. PhD thesis. Brussels: Université libre de Bruxelles.
Ondo-Mebiame, P. (1986) *Esquisse de description du sangu. Langue bantoue de la zone B de sigle B 42*. Mémoire. Brussels: Université libre de Bruxelles.
Osinde, K. N. (1986) *Sheng: an investigation into social and cultural aspects of an evolving language*. MA thesis. Nairobi: Nairobi University.
Othman, S. A., Omar. H. K. and Kombo, J. K. (1991) *Upepo wa mabadiliko*, Zanzibar: Taasisi ya Kiswahili na Lugha za Kigeni.
Owens, J. (1998) Representativeness in the data base: polemical update for the twenty-first century, *Language Sciences* 20: 113–35.
Pagliuca, W. (ed.) (1994) *Perspectives on grammaticalisation*, Amsterdam: John Benjamins.
Palmer, F. R. (1986) *Mood and modality*, Cambridge: Cambridge University Press.
——(1994) *Grammatical Roles and relations*, Cambridge: Cambridge University Press.
Paluku, M. (1996) *Description grammaticale du Kitalinga (Langue Bantu du Nord-Est Zaïre)*. Thesis, Berne.
Parker, E. (1981) *Some aspects of the phonology of Mundani*. MA thesis. University of Reading.
——(1989) Le nom et le syntagme nominal en mundani, in Barreteau and Hedinger (eds) 131–77.
——(1991a) Conditional in Mundani, in Anderson and Comrie (ed.) 165–87.
——(1991b) Complex sentences and subordination in Mundani, in Anderson and Comrie (eds) 189–210.
Paulian, C. (1994) Nasales et nasalisation en ŋgùŋgwèl, langue bantu du Congo, *LA* 13: 83–129.
Persson, J. A. (1932) *Outlines of Tswa grammar*, Cleveland: Central Mission Press.
Peters, A. (1983) *The units of language acquisition*, Cambridge: Cambridge University Press.
——(1987) Language typology, prosody, and the acquisition of grammatical morphemes, in D. I. Slobin (ed.) *The cross-linguistic Study of Language Acquisition* 5. Mahwah, NJ: Lawrence Erlbaum Associates. 35–97.
Philippson, G. (1982) Essai de phonologie comparée des dialectes chaga, in M.-F. Rombi (ed.) *Etudes de bantu oriental*, Paris: SELAF. 41–71.
——(1984) *"Gens des bananeraies": contribution linguistique à l'histoire culturelle des Chaga du Kilimanjaro*, Paris: Editions Recherche sur les Civilisations.
——(1991) *Tons et accent dans les langues bantu d'Afrique Orientale*, 2 vols. PhD thesis. (Doctorat d'Etat). Paris: Université Paris-5. (available on-line at http://www.ddl.ish-lyon.cnrs.fr/ Publications/index.html).
——(1998) Tone reduction vs. metrical attraction in the evolution of Eastern Bantu tone systems, in Hyman and Kisseberth (eds). 315–29.
——(1999) *HH and *HL in Bemba and the Bemba tone system, in Hombert and Hyman (eds) 395–411.
Philippson, G. and Nurse, D. (2000) Gweno, a little-known language of Northern Tanzania, in Kahigi *et al.* (eds). 233–84.
Philippson, G. and Puech, G. (n.d.) Tonal domains in Galwa (Bantu B11c). MS. (available on-line at http://www.ddl.ish-lyon.cnrs.fr/Publications/index.html).
Picabia, L. (1994) Le sujet en comorien, in L. Picabia (ed.) *Syntaxe des langues africaines*. Paris-8: Documents Langues et Grammaire. 45–64. Recherches linguistiques de Vincennes 23.
Picavet, R. (1947) Het dialekt der Batswa, *Aequatoria* 10: 137–41.
Pinker, S. *et al.* (1987) Productivity and constraints in the acquisition of grammar, *Cognition* 26: 195–267.

Piron, P. (1995) Identification lexicostatistique des groups bantoides stable, *JWAL* 25.2: 3–30.

——(1997) *Classification interne du group bantoïde*, Munich and Newcastle: Lincom Europa.

Polak-Bynon, L. (1975) *A Shi grammar: surface structures and generative phonology of a Bantu language*, Tervuren: MRAC. Annales Sciences Humaines 86.

——(1980) Le groupe J occidental (J50), in Bouquiaux (ed.) 409–13.

Poletto, R. (1998) *Topics in Runyankore phonology*. PhD thesis. Columbus: Ohio State University.

Polomé, E. C. (1968) Lubumbashi Swahili, *JAL* 7: 14–25.

——(1971) The Katanga (Lubumbashi) Swahili creole, in Dell Hymes (ed.) *Pidginization and Creolization of Languages*, London: Cambridge University Press. 57–60.

Polomé, E. C. and Hill, C. P. (1980) (eds) *Language in Tanzania*, London: Oxford University Press.

Pongweni, A. J. C. (1990) An acoustic study of the qualitative and pitch effects of breathy-voice on Shona vowels, *Journal of Phonetics* 11: 129–38.

Poulos, G. (1985) Typological trends in South-Eastern Bantu, *SAJAL* 5: 17–23.

——(1986) Instances of semantic bleaching in South-Eastern Bantu, in Dimmendaal (ed.) 281–96.

——(1990) *A linguistic analysis of Venda*, Pretoria: Via Afrika.

Poulos, G. and Louwrens, L. J. (1994) *A linguistic analysis of Northern Sotho*, Pretoria: Via Afrika.

——and Msimang, C. T. (1998) *A linguistic analysis of Zulu*, Cape Town: Via Afrika.

Prata, A. P. (1960) *Gramática da lingua Macua e seus dialectos*, Cucujaes: Sociedade Missionária Portuguesa.

——(1973) *Dicionário Portugues-Macua*, Cucujaes: Sociedade Missionária Portuguesa.

——(1990) *Dicionário Macua-Portugues*, Lisbon: Instituto de Investigacao Científica Tropical.

Price, E. W. (1944) The tonal structure of Ngombe, *AS* 3.1: 28–30.

——(1947) *Ngombe grammar*. London. Duplicated.

Prince, A. and Smolensky, P. (1995) *Optimality theory in generative grammar*, Cambridge, MA: MIT Press.

Puech, G. (1980) La tonalité des thèmes nominaux en punu, in Nsuka-Nkutsi (ed.) 19–32.

——(1987) Tons structurels et tons intonationnels en teke, *Pholia* 2: 163–73.

——(1988) Augment et préfixe nominal en ngubi, *Pholia* 3: 247–56.

Puech, G. and Aleko, H. (1988) Notes sur la langue ngové des Ngubi, *Pholia* 3: 257–69.

Pulleyblank, D. (1986) *Tone in lexical phonology*, Dordrecht: D. Reidel.

Pullum, G. K. and Wilson, D. (1977) Autonomous syntax and the analysis of auxiliaries, *Language* 53: 741–88.

Purvis, J. B. (1907) *A manual of Lumasaba grammar*, London: Society for the Propagation of Christian Knowledge.

Quilis, A., Amdabiang, T. and Marrero, V. (1990) Phonologie et phonétique du gunu (langue bantu du Cameroun), *Travaux de Linguistique et de Philologie* 28: 343–77.

Rapold, C. (1997) *The applicative construction in Lingala*. PhD thesis. Leiden.

Raponda-Walker, A. (1934) *Dictionnaire mpongwe-français suivi d'éléments de grammaire*, Libreville: Mission Catholique de Sainte-Marie.

——(1937) Initiation à l'Ebongwè, langage des Négrilles du Gabon, *Bulletin Société de Recherches Congolaises* 23: 129–55.

——(1950) *Essai de grammaire tsogo*, *Bulletin Institut Etudes Centrafricaines* 1, suppl.: 5–67.

——(1967) *Contes gabonais, revised and completed edition*, Paris: Présence Africaine.

——(n.d.) Dictionaire getsogo-français. MS.

Rascher, A. (1958) *Guide for learning the Ruhaya language*, The Bethel Mission. Duplicated.

Raum, J. (1909) *Versuch einer Grammatik der Dschagga-Sprache (Moschi-Dialekt)*, Berlin: Reimer.

Redden, J. E. (1979) A descriptive grammar of Ewondo, *Occasional Papers in Linguistics 4*. Carbondale: Southern Illinois University Dept. of Linguistics

Reichenbach, H. (1947) *Elements of symbolic logic*, New York: Harcourt, Collier-Macmillan.

Renaud, P. (1976) *Le Bajele, Vol 1: Phonologie*, Yaoundé: ONAREST. Les Dossiers de l'ALCAM 1.

Richardson, I. (1957) *Linguistic survey of the Northern Bantu Borderland*, Volume 2. Oxford: Oxford University Press.

——(1959) *The role of tone in the structure of Sukuma*, London: SOAS.

Richardson, I. (1967) Linguistic evolution and Bantu noun class systems, *La classification nominale dans les langues négro-africaines*, Paris: CNRS. 373–90.

Roberts, R. (1992) A non-metrical theory of Sukuma tone, *Ohio State University Working Papers in Linguistics* 41: 135–48.

Rodegem, F. M. (1967) *Précis de grammaire rundi*, Bruxelles: Story-Scientia. Editions Scientifiques.

Rodgers, J. (1962) *A transformational approach to the Luganda verb*. MA thesis. University of Texas.

Roehl, K. (1918) Das Dahlsche Gesetz und verwandte Erscheinungen in Ruanda-Rundi-Ha, *Zeitschrift für Kolonialsprachen* 8.3: 197–207.

Rosenhuber, S. (1908) Die Basa-Sprache, *MSOS* 11: 219–306.

Roux, J. C. (1995) On the perception and production of tone in Xhosa, *SAJAL* 15: 196–204.

Roux, J. C. and Holtzhausen, A. J. (1989) An acoustic and perceptual analysis of Xhosa vowels, *SAJAL* 9: 30–4.

Rugemalira, J. M. (1994) *Runyambo verb extensions and constraints on argument structure*. PhD thesis. Berkeley: University of California.

Ryabova, I. (1984) Skazki Dabida, in *Afrikanskaja skazka*, Moscow: Nauka.

——(1987) Imennye klassy v jazyke Dabida (dialekt Kimbololo), in *Imennye klassy v jazykax Afriki*, Moscow: Nauka.

Rycroft, D. K. (1980) *The depression feature in Nguni languages and its interaction with tone*. Grahamstown: Rhodes University, Department of African Languages. Communication No. 8.

——(1981) *Concise SiSwati dictionary*, Pretoria: van Schaik, J. L.

Sadembouo, E. and Chumbow, B. S. (1990) Standardisation et modernisation de la langue fe'efe'e, *JWAL* 22: 47–69.

Saloné, S. (1979) Typology of conditionals and conditionals in Haya, *SAL* 10.1: 65–80.

——(1980) Vowel coalescence and tonal merger in Chagga (Old Moshi): a natural generative approach, *SAL* 11.1: 75–100.

Samarin, W. J. (1982) Colonization and pidginization on the Ubangi River, *JALL* 4: 1–42.

——(1986) Protestant missions and the history of Lingala, *Journal of Religion in Africa* 16.2: 138–63.

——(1989) *The black man's burden: African colonial labor on the Congo and Ubangi Rivers, 1880–1900*, Boulder: Westview Press.

——(1990) The origins of Kituba and Lingala, *JALL* 23: 47–77.

Sample, W. A. (1976) *The application of rules in the phonology of Olukisa*. Indiana University, PhD thesis. Ann Arbor: University Microfilms International.

Samsom, R. and Schadeberg, T. C. (1994) Kiinimacho cha mahali: kiambishi tamati cha mahali -ni [The locative suffix in Swahili], *Swahili Forum 1 = AAP* 37: 127–38.

Sanderson, G. M. (1922) *A Yao grammar*, London: Macmillan.

Satre, S. (1997) *A phonology sketch of Ngomba*, research paper, Yaoundé: SIL.

——(1998) *Expose de l'alphabet et de l'orthographe du ngomba*, Yaoundé: SIL.

Schachter, P. (1973) Focus and relativization, *Language* 49: 19–46.

Schadeberg, T. C. (1973) Kinga: a restricted tone system, *SAL* 4: 23–47.

——(1977) Der Kohortativ 'Dual' und Plural in den Bantusprachen, in W. Voigt (ed.) *Deutscher Orientalistentag vom 28. September bis 4. Oktober 1975 in Freiburg im Breisgau: Vorträge*. Wiesbaden: *Zeitschrift der Deutschen Morgenländischen Gesellschaft* Supplementa. 1502–7.

——(1980) La morphologie verbale du bantu commun et les langues bantoues du Cameroun, in Bouquiaux (ed.) 503–9.

——(1981) Das Kordofanische, in Heine, Schadeberg, and Wolff (eds) 117–28.

——(1982a) Nasalization in Umbundu, *JALL* 4: 109–32.

——(1982b) Les suffixes verbaux séparatifs en bantou, *SUGIA* 4: 55–66.

——(1986) The lexicostatistic base of Bennett and Sterk's reclassification of Niger-Congo with particular reference to the cohesion of Bantu, *SAL* 17: 69–83.

——(1987) Silbenanlautgesetze im Bantu, *AU* 70: 1–17.

——(1989) The velar nasal in Nyole, *Annales Aequatoria* 10: 169–79.

Schadeberg, T. C. (1990) *A Sketch of Umbundu*, Cologne: Rüdiger Köppe Verlag.

——(1994) Die extensive extension im Bantu, in Geider and Kastenholz (eds) 357–66.

——(1994–5) Spirantization and the 7-to-5 vowel merger in Bantu, in M. Dominicy and D. Demolin (eds) Sound Change (*Belgian Journal of Linguistics* 9), Amsterdam: John Benjamins. 73–84.

——(1999) Katupha's Law in Makhuwa, in Hombert and Hyman (eds) 379–94.

Schadeberg, T. C. and Mucanheia, F. U. (2000) *EKoti: the Maka or Swahili language of Angoche*, Cologne: Rüdiger Köppe Verlag.

Schapera, I. and van der Merwe, D. F. (1942) *Notes on the noun-classes of some Bantu languages of Ngamiland: Yeei, Subia, Gova, and Gcereku*, Cape Town: University of Cape Town, School of African Studies.

Schaub, W. (1985) *Babungo*, London: Croom Helm.

Schladt, M. (1998) Reciprocals in Bantu languages, *AAP* 53: 5–25l.

Schmidt, D. (1994) Phantom consonants in Basaa, *Phonology* 11: 149–78.

Schoenbrun, D. L. (1990) *Early history in Eastern Africa's Great Lakes Region: linguistic, ecological and archeaological approaches*. PhD thesis. Los Angeles: UCLA.

——(1994) Great Lakes Bantu: classification and settlement chronology, *SUGIA* 15: 91–152.

——(1997) *The historical reconstruction of Great Lakes Bantu cultural vocabulary*, Cologne: Rüdiger Koppe Verlag.

Scholaster, H. (1914) Basa Bakoko-Sprache, *Anthropos* 9: 740–59.

Schurle, G. (1912) *Die Sprache der Basa in Kamerun: Grammatik und Wörterbuch*, Hamburg: Abhandlungen des Hamburgischen Kolonialinstituts.

Schwartz, J.-L., Boë, L.-J., Vallée, N. and Abry, C. (1997). The dispersion-focalization theory of vowel systems, *Journal of Phonetics* 25: 255–86.

Scruggs, T. R. (1980) *Segmental phonology of nouns in Yamba*. MA thesis: University of Calgary

Sebasoni, S. (1967) La préfinale du verbe bantou, *AL* 3: 123–35.

Shamavu, H. (1982) *Esquisse phonologique et morphologique du Tembo*, Bukavu: Institut Supérieur Pédagogique.

Sharp, A. E. (1954) A tonal analysis of the disyllabic noun in the Machame dialect of Chaga, *BSOAS* 16.1: 157–69.

Shepardson, K. N. (1982) Toward a structural definition of direct and indirect objects; support from Swahili, *Word* 32.2: 109–31.

Siertsema, B. (1981) *Masaba word list: English-Masaba, Masaba-English*, Tervuren: MRAC. Archives d'Anthropologie 28.

Sillery, A. (1932) A sketch of the Kikwaya language, *BS* 4: 273–307.

Slabbert, S. and Myers-Scotton, C. (1997) The structure of the Tsotsitaaal and Iscamtho: code-switching and in-group identity in South African townships, *Linguistics* 35.2: 317–42.

Slobin, D. I. (1985) Cross-linguistic evidence for the language-making capacity, in D. I. Slobin (ed.) *The cross-linguistic study of language acquisition 2*, Hillsdale, NJ: Lawrence Erlbaum Associates. 1157–256.

Snider, K. (1998) Phonetic realization of downstep in Bimoba, *Phonology* 15: 77–101.

——(1999) *The geometry and features of tone*, Dallas: SIL and the University of Texas at Arlington.

Snyder, L. S. (1984) Cognition and language development, in R. C. Naremore (ed.) *Language science: recent advances*, San Diego: College-Hill Press. 107–45.

Sommer, G. (1992) A summary of language death in Africa, in M. Brenzinger (ed.) *Language death: factual and theoretical explorations with special reference to East Africa*, Berlin: Mouton de Gruyter. 301–418.

——(1995) *Ethnographie des Sprachwechsels. Sozialer Wandel und Sprachverhalten bei den Yeyi (Botswana)*, Cologne: Rüdiger Köppe Verlag.

Sommer, G. and Vossen, R. (1992) Schnalzwörter im Yei (R.41), *AU* 7: 1–42.

——(1995) Linguistic variation in Yei (R.41), in Traill *et al.* (eds) 407–79.

Spa, J. (1973) *Traits et tons en enya. Phonologie générative d'une langue bantoue*, Tervuren: MRAC. Archives d'anthropologie 20.

——(1975) Vocabulaire enya, *AL* 6: 159–85.

Spaandonck, M van (1967) *Morfotonologische Analysis in Bantutalen*, Ghent: Academisch Proefschrift.

——(1973) Transformations of sentence initial */NI/ in Bantu languages and their influence on tonal syntax, in D. Ziervogel (ed.) *Papers of the African Languages Congress*, Pretoria: University of South Africa. 92–110.

Spitulnik, D. (1999) The language of the city: Town Bemba as urban hybridity, *Journal of Linguistic Anthropology* 8: 30–59.

Spreda, K. W. (1986) *Tonologie des Metta (Western Grassfields): Eine Autosegmentale Beschreibung des einfachen unabhangigen Satzes*. PhD thesis, University of Cologne. (See review in English by M. Fransen and P. van Reenen (1989) *JALL* 11: 201–4.)

——(1991) Notes on markers of parallelism in Meta, in Levinsohn (ed.) 223–30.

Spyropoulos, M. (1987) Sheng: some preliminary investigations into a recently emerged Nairobi street language, *Journal of the Anthropological Society of Oxford* 18: 125–36.

Stallcup, K. (1980a) La geographie linguistique des Grassfields, in Hyman and Voorhoeve (eds) 43–57.

——(1980b) The Momo languages, in Hyman and Voorhoeve (eds) 193–224.

Stanley, C. (1991) *Description phonologique et morpho-syntaxique de la langue Tikar (parlée au Cameroun)*, Paris: SIL.

Stappers, L. (1952) Het tshiluba als omgangstaal, of unificatie van de luba-dialekten?, *Kongo-Overzee* 18.1: 50–65.

——(1965) *Het hoofdtalwoord in de Bantoe-talen*, *AL 2*: 175–98.

——(1967) Het passief-suffix -u- in de Bantoe–talen, *AL 3*: 137–45.

——(1971) Esquisse de la langue lengola, *AL 5*: 255–307.

——(1973) *Esquisse de la langue mituku*, Tervuren: MRAC. Annales Sciences Humaines 80.

——(revised and edited by H.-I. Weier) (1986) *Substitutiv und Possessiv im Bantu*, Berlin: Dietrich Reimer.

Stevick, E. (1969a) Tone in Bantu, *IJAL* 35: 330–41.

——(1969b) Pitch and duration in Ganda, *JAL* 8: 1–28.

Stewart. J. M. (1973) The lenis stops of the Potou Lagoon languages and their significance for pre-Bantu reconstruction, in M. E. Kropp Dakubu (ed.) *Research Review, supp. 4, papers in Ghanian Linguistics*. Legon. Institute of African Studies. University of Ghana. 1–49.

——(1981) Key lowering (downstep/downglide) in Dschang, *JALL* 3: 113–38.

——(1983) The high unadvanced vowels of proto-Tano-Congo, *JWAL* 13: 19–36.

——(1989) Fortis/lenis and vowel length in Proto-Bantu, *JALL* 11: 45–88.

——(1993) Dschang and Ebrie as Akan-type total downstep languages, in van der Hulst and Snider (eds) 185–244.

——(1993) The second Tano consonant shift and its likeness to Grimm's Law, *JWAL* 23.1: 3–39.

——(1995) Implosives, homorganic nasals and nasalized vowels in Volta-Congo, in E. N. Emenanjo and O.-M. Ndimele (eds) *Issues in African languages and linguistics: essays in honour of Kay Williamson*, Aba: National Institute for Nigerian Languages. 162–70.

——(1999) Nasal vowel creation without nasal consonant deletion and the eventual loss of nasal vowels thus created, in Hombert and Hyman (eds) 207–33.

——(2000a) An explanation of Bantu vowel height harmony in terms of a Pre-Bantu nasalized vowel lowering, *JALL* 21: 161–78.

——(2000b) Symmetric vs asymmetric vowel height harmony and *e, *o, vs. *I, *u in Proto Bantu and Proto Savanna Bantu. Paper read at the 30th Colloquium on African Languages and Linguistics. Leiden.

——(2001a) The stem initial consonant system of Proto-Potou-Tano-Bantu: an update. Paper read at the 32nd Annual conference in African Linguistics. Berkeley.

——(2001b) South Volta-Congo (Benue-Kwa) subclassification: the position of Tano (Akanoid). Paper read at the 32nd Annual conference in African Linguistics. Berkeley.

Stewart, J. M. and Van Leynseele, H. (1979) Underlying cross-height vowel harmony in Nen (Bantu A.44), *JALL* 1: 31–54.

Stockler, J. (1992) *Mungaka (Bali) Dictionary (revised and translated)*, Cologne: Rüdiger Koppe Verlag.

Stoop, H. (1989) Les préfixes du sogo, *Annales Aequatoria* 10: 127–40.

Struck, B. (1910) Vokabularien der Bakondjo-, Baamba-, Bambuba-, Babira-, Balega-, Lendu-, und Banyarisprachen, *MSOS* 13.3: 133–65.

Stucky, S. U. (1979) The interaction of tone and focus in Makua, *JALL* 1.2: 189–98.

——(1980) *Order in Makua syntax*, PhD thesis. University of Illinois.

——(1985) *Order in Makua syntax*, New York and London: Garland Press.

Sure, K. (1992) The coming of Sheng, *English Today* 32: 26–8.

Suzman, S. (1980) Acquisition of the noun class system in Zulu, *Papers and Reports on Child Language Development* 19: 45–52. Stanford: Stanford University Press.

——(1982) Strategies for acquiring Zulu concord, *SAJAL* 2: 53–67.

——(1985) Learning the passive in Zulu, *Papers and Reports on Child Language Development* 24: 131–7, Stanford: Stanford University Press.

——(1987) Passives and prototypes in Zulu childrens' speech, *AS* 46: 241–54.

——(1991) *The Acquisition of Zulu*. PhD thesis. Johannesburg: Witwatersrand University.

——(1996) Acquisition of noun class systems in related Bantu languages, in C. Johnson and J. Gilbert (eds) *Childrens' Language* 9: 87–104.

Tadadjeu, M. (1974) Floating tones, shifting rules, and downstep in DschangBamileke, *SAL*, Supplement 5: 282–90.

——(1980) Le dschang, in Hyman and Voorhoeve (eds) 165–81.

Tak, J.-Y. and Botne, R. (1998) Asymetric coordination in Lega, *AAP* 54: 47–68.

Tassa, O. L. G. (1994) *Esquisse de description phonétique, phonologique et morphologique du tofoke (C53)*. Mémoire. Brussels: Université libre de Bruxelles.

Taylor, C. (1959) *A simplified Runyankore-Rukiga-English and English-Runyankore-Rukiga dictionary*, Kampala: The Eagle Press, EALB.

——(1966) *A linguistic study of the names of persons, places, flora and fauna in Nkore-Kiga*. PhD thesis. London: University of London.

——(1985) *Nkore-Kiga*, London: Croom Helm.

Teisseres, U. and Dubois, V. (1957) *Méthode pratique pour apprendre l'omyene*, Société des Missions Evangéliques de Paris.

Tessmann, G. (1934) *Die Bafia und die Kultur der Mittelkamerun-Bantu*, Stuttgart: Strecker und Schröder.

The Times Atlas of the World (1999) 10th edition, New York: Times Books.

Thomas, J. M. C. (1976) *Classes et genres nominaux en aka, langue bantoue des Pygmées de Mongoumba (RCA)*, Paris: Bibliothèque de la SELAF. 27–35.

Thomas, J. M. C. and Bahuchet, S. (eds) (1983) *Dictionnaire ethnographique aka-français*, Paris: SELAF. Langues et Civilisations à Tradition Orale 50.

Thomas, P. (1994) Bantu noun-class reflexes in Komo, *AL* 11: 177–96.

Thomas Vilakazi, K. (1999) *Coproduction and coarticulation in IsiZulu clicks*. PhD thesis. Los Angeles: UCLA.

——(2000) Coproduction and coarticulation in IsiZulu clicks: aerodynamic and electropalatographic evidence, in Carstens and Parkinson (eds) 265–80.

Thomason, S. G. (ed.) *Contact languages: a wider perspective*, Amsterdam: John Benjamins.

Thompson, S. A. and Longacre, R. E. (1994) Adverbial clauses, in T. Shopen (ed.) *Language Typology and Syntactic Description*, Cambridge: Cambridge University Press. 170–234.

Toronzoni, N.-N. (1985) *Description du bomboma, langue bantoue de zone C*. Mémoire. Brussels: Université libre de Bruxelles.

Torrend, J. (1887) *Outline of Xosa-Kafir grammar, with a few dialogues and a Kafir tale*, Grahamstown: T. and G. Sheffield.

——(1891) *A comparative grammar of the South African Bantu languages*, London: Kegan Paul.

Traill, A. (1990) Depression without depressors, *SAJAL* 10: 167–72.

Traill, A. and Jackson, M. (1988) Speaker variation and phonation type in Tsonga nasals, *Journal of Phonetics* 16: 385–400.

Traill, A., Khumalo, J. S. M. and Fridhon, P. (1987) Depressing facts about Zulu, *Journal of African Studies* 46: 255–74.

Traill, A., Vossen, R. and Biesele, M. (eds) (1995) *The complete linguist. Papers in memory of Patrick J. Dickens*, Cologne: Rüdiger Köppe Verlag.

Traugott, E. and Heine, B. (eds) (1991) *Approaches to grammaticalization*. 2 vols. Amsterdam: Benjamins.

Tsonope, J. (1987) *The acquisition of Setswana noun class and agreement morphology, with special reference to demonstratives and possessives*. PhD thesis. Buffalo: State University of New York.

Tucker, A. N. (1960) Notes on Konzo, *ALS* 1: 16–41.

Tunen Linguistic Committee (1980) *Lisez et écrivez la langue tunen*, Ndikinimeki: Mission catholique de Somo.

Twilingiyimana, C. (1984) *Eléments de description du doko*, Tervuren: MRAC Annales Sciences 116.

Valinande, N. K. (1984) *The Structure of Kinande*, Washington: Georgetown University.

Van der Hulst, H. and Snider, K. (eds) (1993) *The Phonology of Tone*, Berlin: Mouton de Gruyter.

Van der Veen, L. J. (1986) *Notes en vue d'une description phonologique et morphologique de la langue pouvi (Gabon)*. MA thesis. Lyon: Université Lumière-Lyon 2.

——(1987) *De l'espace vocalique et des tons en Pouvi: notes descriptives*. Mémoire DEA. Lyon: Université Lumière-Lyon 2.

——(1988) Caractéristiques principales du groupe B 30 (Gabon), *Pholia* 3: 271–90.

——(1991) Etude dialectométrique et lexicostatistique du groupe B 30 (Gabon), *Pholia* 6: 191–217.

——(1991a) Le système tonal du gevia (Gabon), *Pholia* 6: 219–257.

——(1991b) *Etude comparée des parlers du groupe okani, B30 (Gabon)*, PhD thesis. Université Lumière-Lyon 2.

——(1999a) *Les bantous eviya (Gabon-B30): langue et société traditionnelle*, Habilitation thesis. Lyon: Université Lumière-Lyon 2.

——(1999b) La propagation de tons et le statut des indices pronominaux précédant le verbe en geviya, in Blanchon and Creissels (eds) 15–36.

Van der Veen, L. J. and Bodinga-bwa-Bodinga, S. (2002) *Gedandedi sa geviya, dictionnaire geviya-français*, Paris: Peeters.

Van Dyk, P. R. (1960) *'n Studie van Lala (sy fonologie, morfologie en sintaksis)*. PhD thesis. University of Stellenbosch.

Vanhoudt, B. (1987) *Elements d'une description du leke, langue bantoue de la zone C*. Tervuren: MRAC. Annales Sciences Humaines 125.

——(1994) L'expression de 'un' dans la numération absolue et référentielle en protobantou, *AL* 11: 215–21.

Vanhoudt, B. and Soky Mantoley, J. (1998) Lexique leke (bomitaba)–français, *AAP* 5: 5–59.

——(1999) Lexique français-leke (bomitaba), *AAP* 57: 5–46.

Van Leynseele, H. (1977) *An Outline of Libinza gramma*. Mémoire. Leiden: Université de Leiden.

Van Leynseele, H. and Stewart, J. M. (1980) Harmonie consonantique en pré-nen, in Bouquiaux (ed.) 421–33.

Van Sambeek, J. (n.d.) Dictionary English–Kiha. MS.

——(n.d.) Petite grammaire kiha. MS.

Vansina, J. (1990) *Paths in the rainforest: toward a history of political tradition in Equatorial Africa*, Madison: University of Wisconsin Press.

——(1995) New linguistic evidence and 'the Bantu expansion', *JAH* 36: 173–95.

Viljoen, J. J. and Kamupingene, T. K. (1983) *Otjiherero woordeboek dictionary embo romambo*, Gamsberg: Windhoek.

Vitale, A. (1981) *Swahili syntax*, Dordrecht: Foris.

Voeltz, F. K. E. (1980) The etymology of the Bantu perfect, in Bouquiaux (ed.) 487–92.

Volschenk, P. A. (1968) *Herero a morphological survey*. MA thesis. Cape Town: University of Cape Town.

Voorhoeve, J. (1963) La classification nominale dans le bangangte, *JALL* 2: 206–9.

——(1965) The structure of the morpheme in Bamileke, *Lingua* 13: 319–34.

——(1967) Personal pronouns in Bamileke, *Lingua* 17: 421–30.

Voorhoeve, J. (1968) Noun classes in Bamileke, *Lingua* 21: 584–93.

—— (1971) Tonology of the Bamileleke noun, *JAL* 10: 44–53.

—— (1973) Safwa as a restricted tone language, *SAL* 4: 1–21.

—— (1974) Locatives in Bangangte-Bamileke, *SAL* 5: 205–21.

—— (1980a) Bantu et Bane, in Hyman and Voorhoeve (eds) 59–77.

—— (1980b) Limbum, in Hyman and Voorhoeve (eds) 183–91.

Voorhoeve, J. (1980c) Noun classes in Adere, in Hyman (ed.) 57–72.

—— (1980d) Le pronom logophorique et son importance pour la reconstruction du proto-bantou (PB), *SUGIA* 2: 173–87.

—— (1980e) La derivation verbale en basaa, in Bouquiaux (ed.) 493–501.

Vorbichler, A. (1966) Zur tonalen Struktur des Verbalsystems im Wald-Bira (Ost-Kongo), in *Festschrift Klingenheben, Neue Afrikanistische Studien*, 5: 256–64. Hamburg: J. Lukas.

Vossen, R. (1988) *Patterns of language knowledge and language use in Ngamiland (Botswana)*. Bayreuth: University of Bayreuth. Bayreuth African Studies Series 13.

—— (1991–2) Strukturveränderung als Folge von Mehrsprachigkeit? Die Nominalklassenpräfixe der Bantusprachen Ngamilands, *SUGIA* 12/13: 343–71.

—— (1997) What clicks got to do in Bantu, in B. Smiejaand and M. Tasch (eds) *Human contact through language and linguistics*. Frankfurt: Peter Lang. 353–66.

Wald, B. (1975) Animate concord in northeast coastal Bantu: its linguistic and social implications as a case of grammatical convergence, *SAL* 6.3: 267–314.

—— (1994) East Coast Bantu and the evolution of constraints on passivization, *SUGIA* 15: 211–315.

—— (1997) The 0 tense marker in the decline of the Swahili auxiliary focus system, *AAP* 51: 55–82.

Walusimbi, L. (1976) *Relativization and focusing in Luganda and Bantu*, Ann Arbor: University Microfilms International.

—— (1996) *Relative clauses in Luganda*. Cologne: Rüdiger Koppe Verlag. East African Languages and Dialects 6.

Wamenka, N. (1992) *Recits épiques des Lega du Zaire*, Tervuren: MRAC.

Ward, I. C. (1938) The phonetic structure of Bamun, *BSOAS* 9: 423–38.

Warnier, J.-P. (1976) *Pre-colonial Mankon: the development of a Cameroon chiefdom in its regional setting*. PhD thesis. Philadelphia: University of Pennsylvania.

Watkins, M. H. (1937) *A grammar of Chichewa*, Philadelphia: University of Pennsylvania. (Suppl. to *Language*, No. 24.)

Watters, J. R. (1979) Focus in Aghem. A study of its formal correlates and typology, in Hyman (ed.) (1979b) 137–98.

—— (1980) Notes on Ngie. UCLA and SIL. MS.

—— (1982) Review of Hyman and Voorhoeve (eds), *JALL* 4: 87–92.

—— (1989) Bantoid overview, in Bendor-Samuel (ed.) 400–20.

Watters, J. R. and Leroy, J. (1989) Southern Bantoid, in Bendor-Samuel (ed.) 430–49.

Welmers, W. E. (1958) *The Mande languages*, Georgetown University Monograph Series in Languages and Linguistics 11. Washington: Georgetown University Press. 9–42.

—— (1973) *African Language Structures*, Berkeley: UCP.

Westermann, D. and Bryan, M. A. (1952) *The languages of West Africa*, Handbook of African Languages, part 2. London: Oxford University Press.

Whitehead, J. (1899) *Grammar and dictionary of the Bobangi language, as spoken over a part of the Upper Congo (West Central Africa)*, London: Kegan P. and Trench, Trübner & Co.

Whiteley, W. H. (1956) *A practical introduction to Gusii*, Nairobi: EALB.

—— (1959) Kinship terminology and the initial vowel, *Africa* 29.3: 253–62.

—— (1960) *The tense system of Gusii*, Kampala: East Africa Institute of Social Research. East African Linguistics Studies 4.

—— (1966) *A study of Yao sentences*, Oxford: Oxford University Press.

—— (1969) *Swahili: the rise of a national language*, London: Methuen & Co.

—— (ed.) (1974) *Language in Kenya*, Nairobi & Dar es Salaam: Oxford University Press.

Wiesemann, U., Nseme, C. and Vallete, R. (1984) *Manuel d'analyse du discours*. Yaoundé: Université deYaounde. Collection Propelca No. 26.

Wilhelm, M. (1981) Le Mbam central, in C. Tardits (ed.) *Contribution de la recherche ethnographique à l'histoire des civilisations du Cameroun*, Paris: CNRS (Colloques Internationaux du CNRS, Sciences Humaines). 439–52.

Wilkinson, R. W. (1975) Tunen tone changes and derived phonological contrast, *Language* 51.3: 561–75.

Williams, M. J. (1975) *The origin of the English language*, New York: The Free Press.

Williamson, K. (1971) The Benue-Congo languages and Ijo, in T. Sebeok (ed.) *Current Trends in Linguistics* 7, The Hague: Mouton. 245–306.

——(1986) Niger-Congo: SVO or SOV? *JWAL* 16.1: 5–14.

——(1989) Niger-Congo overview, in Bendor-Samuel (ed.) 3–45.

Williamson, K. and Blench, R. M. (2000) Niger-Congo, in Heine and Nurse (eds) 1–41.

Winter, J. C. (1980) International classification of Kilimanjaro Bantu compared: towards an East African Dialectometry, in G. Guarisma and S. Platiel (eds) *Dialectologie et comparatisme en Afrique Noire*, Paris: SELAF.

——(1987) Zur Prosodologie des Mochi-Dialekts des Chagga, *AAP* 12: 5–15.

Wit, G. de (1994) Bira survey report, in *Compendium of survey reports, vol. 1, Bira-Huku group of Bantu*, Bunia: SIL Eastern Zaire group.

Wit-Hasselaar, A. de (1995) Bira-Huku wordlists, in *Compendium of survey reports, vol. 1, Bira-Huku group of Bantu*, Bunia: SIL Eastern Zaire group.

Wolff, E. (2000) Language and society, in Heine and Nurse (eds) 298–347.

Woodward, H. W. (1913–14) Kitaita or Kisighau, *Zeitschrift für Kolonialsprachen* 4: 91–117.

Wright, R. and Shryock, A. (1993) The effect of implosives on pitch in SiSwati, *Journal of the International Phonetic Association* 23: 16–23.

Wung'a, Lomani, O. (1973) *Aspects et Structures du Hem*, Lubumbashi: Université Nationale du Zaïre. Mémoire.

Yahya, A. S. and Mulwa, D. (1988) *Mkimbizi*, Nairobi: Longman.

Young, T. C. (1932) *Notes on the speech of the Tumbuka-Kamanga peoples in the Northern Province of Nyasaland*, London: The Religious Tract Society.

Yukawa, Y. (ed.) (1987a) *Studies in Zambian languages (Bantu Linguistics, vol. 1)*, Tokyo: ILCAA.

——(1987b) A tonological study of Luvale verbs, in Yukawa (ed.) (1987a) 1–33.

——(ed.) (1989a) *Studies in Tanzanian languages (vol. 2)*, Tokyo: ILCAA.

——(1989b) A tonological study of Makonde verbs, in Yukawa (ed.) (1989a) 519–60.

——(ed.) (1992) *Studies in Cameroonian and Zairean languages (vol. 3)*, Tokyo: ILCAA.

Ziervogel, D. (1959). *A grammar of Northern Transvaal Ndebele*, Pretoria: J. L. van Schaik.

——(1973) *Papers of the African Languages Congress*, Pretoria: University of South Africa.

Ziervogel, D. and Mabuza, E. J. (1976) *A grammar of the Swati language (siSwati)*, Pretoria: J. L. van Schalk.

Ziesler, Y. and Demuth, K. (1995) Noun class prefixes in Sesotho child-directed speech, in E. Clark (ed.) *Proceedings of the 26th Child Language Research Forum*, Stanford: CSLI. 137–46.

Ziervogel, D., Lombard, D. P. and Mokgokong, P. C. (1979) *Handbook of the Northern Sotho language*, Pretoria: J. L. van Schaik Ltd.

Zwicky, A. M. (1970) Auxiliary reduction in English, *Linguistic Inquiry* 1: 323–36.

LANGUAGE INDEX

This index lists all African languages mentioned in the text (languages of European origin are not indexed; neither is Arabic). For individual languages, language family is indicated in square brackets; in the case of Bantu languages the reference number to Guthrie's referential classification, as completed by Maho (see chapter above), is given. Synonyms are cross-referenced.

N.B. We have eliminated all class prefixes in Bantu language names, except for the rare cases where confusion might arise: so we distinguish Tonga (M64) and GiTonga (S62), and Mbundu (H21) and UMbundu (R11). We also retain the prefix in language names where there is no genuine correspondance with any ethnic groups, as Lingala (instead of *Ngala). Finally, where we are unsure of the exact value of the initial syllable, as is the case with many of the smaller Zone C languages, we follow the author's conventions.

SUBJECT INDEX

absorption (of glides) 57

accent 40, 59, 190, 307, 310, 315, 393, 514, 571, 581, 617; accentual 220, 311, 514; pitch 59, 92, 200, 205, 207

acoustic: analysis 16–17, 23, 411; data 32–3; pattern 39; plot 21–2; space 16

acquisition, language 11, 209–22, 377; second 201

actuation 182, 204

Adamawa-Ubangi 1–2, 5, 155

adjective 9, 81–5, 104, 149, 262, 268, 271, 302, 316, 417–18, 433–4, 462, 537, 563, 575, 577, 588

adjunct 9, 125, 137–9, 248, 250

adnominal 588–90, 603; concord 111

adstrate phenomena 369

adverb 250, 339, 343, 345–7, 366, 408, 448, 461, 579, 594–6, 637; clauses 186, 188, 251, 345–7; locatives 244; see also ideophone

aerodynamic data 33, 36

affirmation 92, 176–7, 186

affirmatives 94–5; tense 69, 152, 187, 254, 281–2, 294, 325, 329, 366, 406; verbs 69, 107–8, 151, 404, 410–12, 420, 442, 469, 480, 490, 500, 540–2, 558, 577, 592–3, 604

affix 8, 103, 252, 284, 310, 439, 506; negation 579–80; noun 106, 120, 177, 187, 239, 338–9; order 126–8; verbal 8, 133, 183, 234, 237, 246, 291, 440, 538–9, 555

affricate 8, 19–20, 24, 28, 33, 35–6, 42, 51–5, 57, 148, 220, 235, 259, 355, 362, 378–9, 426, 456, 478, 508, 546, 549–50, 566, 569, 614

affrication 8, 35–6, 51, 236, 395–6, 413, 534

agent 73, 75–6, 133, 217, 279, 290, 319, 329, 339, 343, 346, 437–8, 446; nouns 80–1, 86, 88, 303, 474, 573; passive 75–6, 140, 189, 279, 319, 331, 346, 438, 605

agentive 54, 103, 277, 382, 429

agglutinate 44, 190, 207, 363; verbs 8, 184, 363, 366

agglutination 199, 366

agreement: anaphoric 9, 122–4, 315; grammatical 9, 122–4, 128–9; see also concord

allomorph 72, 78, 176–7, 261, 274–6, 279, 383–4, 389, 491, 494–5, 538, 571, 587, 589

allomorphy 151, 177, 596–7

alveolar 55, 57, 219, 235, 289–90, 309, 336, 426, 563, 615–16; fricatives 27, 569; places 25, 456; release 25; stops 19, 456, 508

ambivalent derivation 84–5, 125

analogy 54, 57, 595, 602; reanalysis 382

analytic 96, 277

anaphoric 243, 245, 307, 314, 403; agreement 9, 122–4, 315; reference 106, 218, 341

animacy 108, 113, 127, 200, 216, 452, 472–3

animate nouns 113, 118, 124, 127, 129, 152, 214, 216, 243, 299, 304, 363, 434, 452, 458–9, 462–4, 471–3, 483, 536–7, 586

antepenult see penult

anterior aspect see perfect

anticipatory (assimilation) 47

aorist 96, 295–6

applicative(s) 54, 57, 74, 80, 137, 141, 222, 245, 252, 258, 394, 424, 471–2, 494, 509, 521, 527, 576; derivation 472; extensions 72, 74, 91, 126, 210, 216, 274, 276, 289–90, 319, 415, 437, 440, 494, 578, 631; suffix 43–4, 46–7, 261, 274, 279, 365, 509

archaeology 160, 172, 179

argument 9, 66, 118, 125–7, 133, 135, 137–40, 216–17, 278; markers 151; nominal phrases 122, 125–7, 129, 132, 269; and verbs 10, 73–4, 122–3, 125–7, 346, 408, 415, 438, 565